PRINCIPLES AND PRACTICES OF WINEMAKING

Roger B. Boulton
Vernon L. Singleton
Linda F. Bisson
Ralph E. Kunkee

all of University of California, Davis

CBS

CBS Publishers & Distributors Pvt. Ltd.

New Delhi • Bengaluru • Chennai • Kochi • Kolkata • Mumbai
Hyderabad • Uttarakhand • Nagpur • Patna • Pune • Jharkhand

CBS Pubs ISBN: 81-239-0522-X
Chapman ISBN: 0-412-06411-1

First Indian Edition: 1997
Reprint: 2004, 2005

This edition has been published in India by arrangement with Chapman & Hall Inc., New York.

Published by **Satish Kumar Jain** and produced by **Varun Jain** for
CBS Publishers & Distributors Pvt. Ltd.,
4819/XI Prahlad Street, 24 Ansari Road, Daryaganj, New Delhi - 110002
delhi@cbspd.com, cbspubs@airtelmail.in • www.cbspd.com
Ph.: 23289259, 23266861, 23266867 • Fax: 011-23243014

Corporate Office: 204 FIE, Industrial Area, Patparganj, Delhi - 110 092
Ph: 49344934 • Fax: 011-49344935
E-mail: publishing@cbspd.com • publicity@cbspd.com

Branches:
- ***Bengaluru:*** 2975, 17th Cross, K.R. Road, Bansankari 2nd Stage, Bengaluru - 70 • Ph: +91-80-26771678/79 • Fax: +91-80-26771680 E-mail: cbsbng@gmail.com, bangalore@cbspd.com
- ***Chennai:*** No. 7, Subbaraya Street, Shenoy Nagar, Chennai - 600030 Ph: +91-44-26681266, 26680620 • Fax: +91-44-42032115 E-mail: chennai@cbspd.com
- ***Kochi:*** Ashana House, 39/1904, A.M. Thomas Road, Valanjambalam, Ernakulum, Kochi • Ph: +91-484-4059061-65 Fax: +91-484-4059065 • E-mail: cochin@cbspd.com
- ***Kolkata:*** 6-B, Ground Floor, Rameshwar Shaw Road, Kolkata - 700014 Ph: +91-33-22891126/7/8 • E-mail: kolkata@cbspd.com
- ***Mumbai:*** 83-C, Dr. E. Moses Road, Worli, Mumbai - 400018 Ph: +91-9833017933, 022-24902340/41 • E-mail: mumbai@cbspd.com

Representatives:
- Hyderabad: 0-9885175004
- Patna: 0-9334159340
- Jharkhand: 0-9811541605
- Nagpur: 0-9021734563
- Pune: 0-9623451994
- Uttarakhand: 0-9716462459

Printed at:
India Binding House, Noida, UP (India)

TO Maynard A. Amerine. Mentor, leader, and bon vivant. Professor Amerine developed (especially variety suitability and sensory analysis), chronicled, and taught enology for the world. He kept us all reminded that wine is far more a commodity or just a food. It contributes to sophisticated dining, enhances and facilitates social interaction, challenges the senses and the intellect, and makes glad the heart of the moderate and well-balanced man or woman.

ACKNOWLEDGMENTS

This book contains reports of some research conducted by the authors and not previously published. Thanks are due and gladly offered to donors supporting our research, including the American Vineyard Foundation, the Wine Institute, and the California Wine Advisory Board. Our own research students and supporting members of the Californian wine industry are also thanked. We greatly appreciate typing of some of the drafts by Jill Frommelt and Susan Woody with final manuscript preparation by Diane Eschenbaum. David M. Coons is thanked for preparation of many of the figures for Chapters 4 and 6.

Contents

Preface

Historically, scientific and educational books can be classified into three categories: those providing concepts and principles, those offering gathered information, and those presenting opinion or perspective (which may or may not be instructive).

While there are many wine-related books of the third kind and some of the second, there are few of the first, and this book attempts to fill that void. Of course, some aspects of categories two and three inevitably remain.

Because our teaching program at Davis has always been based on the interdisciplinary approach to enology, we have pooled our experience to provide a volume that provides the benefits of such interaction and discussion rather than the more usual self-styled expert approach to such books.

Much of the material in this book is used in our university courses in enology. These have been developed as part of our personal teaching duties and generally include a mixture of scientific understanding and practical observation of the phenomena that occur during winemaking and in wines. The aim is to control these phenomena to produce the highest quality of wine for the style sought.

Although many of the date presented and examples used throughout have been drawn from studies within California, the concepts developed will be generally useful to enologists throughout the world.

Although this volume covers the basic practices and their rationale for successful wine production, wines and wine regions of the world and details of specialty wine production (such as vermouths, fruit wines, etc.) are omitted as separate topics, although incorporated as appropriate in general explanations. The emphasis upon commercial scale by no means precludes use of the material by small-volume winemakers, for whom the principles of winemaking are equally valid, although practices may need to be adjusted for the scale. *Commercial scale* implies the consideration of economics and sensible expenditure of effort and analyses to ensure that marketably good wine is produced. Winemakers have been consulted regarding various sections and practices considered commercially advantageous. We hope to have eliminated errors of omission or commission; any lapses remain ours and, if informed, we will clarify them in following publications.

Vigourously we intend, then, to meet the need for a universally useful, detailed, deep, and broad text in English on the science, technology, and practices of making wine.

Consideration will be given to the grapes to be used, fermentation, processing, maturation, stabilization, and preparation for distribution and sale. An emphasis on quantitative details, as well as qualitative, will be given where possible. Metric (USI) units will be used throughout. An appendix is given for conversion to English, European, and older U.S. units.

Consider that this text is designed to be useful section by section. Nevertheless, we highly recommend the reader begin with the introductory chapter, where the hazards, economic and otherwise, in commercial winemaking are outlined. This will give a realistic perspective to the joy and satisfaction that uniquely come from creation of this product of science and art—wine.

This book is the latest in a long and distinguished line of texts written by faculty at the University of California, beginning with Professor W. V. Cruess' *The Principles and Practice of Wine Making*, first published in 1934. Subsequent editions, under the title *The Technology of Winemaking*, were written by Professor Cruess (University of California at Berkeley) and Professors M. A. Amerine, H. W. Berg, R. E. Kunkee, C. S. Ough, V. L. Singleton, and A. D. Webb (University of California at Davis). The current volume is a completely new book, yet it continues, as did its predecessors, to embody our department's three-part mission of scientific research, teaching, and outreach to the public and industry. As the University of California moves into its 115th year of teaching and research in viticulture and enology, we salute the many who have advanced these areas before us.

Roger B. Boulton
Vernon L. Singleton
Linda F. Bisson
Ralph E. Kunkee

Department of Viticulture and Enology
University of California, Davis

CHAPTER 1

INTRODUCTION

This chapter's topics are diverse. They are grouped here to set the stage. We recommend reading this chapter first as you learn about and consider going into winemaking. An occasional rereading may be helpful to the practicing winemaker.

A. BASIC PHILOSOPHY OF THIS BOOK

It is our intent to describe winemaking and enology (old spelling *oenology*) in a fashion, and to a reasonable degree of completeness, appropriate for a university-level course and as a reference for practicing enologists, but also understandable to the educated adult. Winemaking is the series of operations from harvesting of grapes through providing bottled wine ready for the consumer. Enology is often defined as the science of winemaking, but in practice it combines the science, technology, and engineering of the process. It is the combination of interdisciplinary knowledge and principles (from chemistry, biochemistry, microbiology, chemical engineering, and nutrition) which we consider to be the essence of enology. For that reason, these are the principles that will be emphasized throughout this book. We wish to explain why various operations are made, rather than merely how to perform them. Some points are necessarily complex, but we hope to provide clear understanding.

Authors of books of this sort often veer to one extreme or the other, either making authoritative statements as fact without giving the information upon which their conclusions are based, or giving tedious citations and failing to arbitrate among contending viewpoints. We hope to steer a middle course holding citations to an essential minimum and presenting our synthesis regarding each topic. We emphasize that, although we have been studying, learning, and teaching about these subjects individually and collectively for many years, we owe much to those who have preceded, corroborated, or amplified our knowledge and understanding. We have made strenuous efforts to keep up with the literature, to travel and consult with winemakers and researchers worldwide. The task is formidable, especially since much of the information is in languages other than English, but it is eased by the fact that the climates of wine regions are pleasant and so are the people. Wine people are, we have verified, lovers of fine dining and good social interaction. We remain conscious of our many debts and regret that it is not possible to detail them here.

In this text, winemaking in the United States, and particularly in California, is inevitably emphasized, but considerable effort has also been made to make the discussions as universally applicable as possible, regardless of country, locality, or size of winery. A few recent books in English are worth consulting for viewpoints from Australia (Rankine 1989), Czechoslovakia (Farkas 1986), the Eastern United States (Jackisch 1985), France (Peynaud 1984), and New Zealand (Jackson and Schuster 1987). For an additional Californian viewpoint, see Ough (1992).

Making of commercial table wines from wine grapes is emphasized. Most of the special considerations are omitted for other fruits, including nonvinifera grapes, which habitually require amelioration (acid dilution, sugar addition). Making of dessert and fortified wines is deemphasized, partly because of their currently decreased quantitative role. Brandy making or distillation for wine spirits is largely omitted. Specialty products, such as sparkling wines, flavored wines, and coolers are not fully covered here, although pertinent comments affecting base wine production for them will be made. Alternative products from wineries, such as vinegar or concentrated juice, and byproducts, such as grape seed oil or cream of tartar, will receive minimal mention.

Where there are alternate methods, we have described them and discussed the consequences of each. In most instances, there are no right and wrong choices, but rather opportunities to vary wines so that diversity remains, as is desirable for perpetually interesting the consumer. To the extent these differences are recognizable in the finished wine, they contribute to style. Like quality and character, style is a perception of the mind with different meanings for different individuals. This book, like our approach to teaching, does not try to convey a special style or recipe, but rather seeks to present understanding of the "why" as well as the "how" of various alternatives.

You may want to make wines emphasizing one feature and your neighboring competitor may want to play down that feature. Hopefully, you will both develop loyal customers and the market as a whole will benefit. Perhaps the word *competitor* is poorly chosen. One of the pleasant features of agricultural production is that weather and market conditions tend to affect producers similarly and neighbors tend to be fellow sufferers or beneficiaries rather than competitors. They have common interests in maximizing quality, keeping defective or illegal wines off the market, and maintaining the health and good reputation of winemaking. They will, of course, compete on a style and quality basis and guard against loss of their market share, but usually they are friends with common goals more easily reached by cooperation than by cutthroat competition. For such reasons, winemakers have generally supported importation of distinctive wines from other countries with minimal restrictions, as long as traffic in the other direction is fair and dumping at uneconomic prices does not occur. Exposure of the consumer to the fun and satisfaction of the whole spectrum possible with wine benefits all. Furthermore, we firmly believe that the evidence strongly demonstrates that moderate consumption of wines with meals not only is beneficial in decreasing atherosclerosis and prolonging the average life span, but also is associated with making life more pleasant and socially successful. This subject we cannot enlarge upon here, but the pride of winemakers in their profession and product is vindicated by careful study of the evidence gathered over millennia in many societies.

B. PLANNING BEFORE BEGINNING WINEMAKING

Here, we want to warn the prospective winemaker of the potential obstacles of a financial and regulatory nature, which may be associated with new winemaking ventures. We are making a point to introduce this subject early in the book to emphasize its importance.

Detailed guidelines for the prospective winery owner may seem strange in a textbook on processes of winemaking; however, we speak from the experience of witnessing the heartbreak of financial failures of many new wineries. In the decade of the 1980s the number of wineries in California, and the rest of the United States, have increased about fourfold. Most of these new owners have not had the advantage of inheriting the wineries and the accompanying vineyards as have many European colleagues. In a few cases, the new owners have been in the enviable position of having enough capital to consider the new venture a hobby, with only the vaguest worry about the adventure becoming solvent in some distant future. For others, where the financial backing is limited, stringent attention to the precautions is required. Over the last century, the average annual increase in wine production in California wineries has been around 6%, but it has come in boom and bust phases with production sometimes exceeding demand. This is a worldwide phenomenon. The financial stress resulting from failure to face reality is especially disheartening when we see it in the wine aficionados whose burning desire is merely to make good wine; but we have also seen financial catastrophes in large-scale, and supposedly sophisticated, corporations.

If one is making a small amount of wine at home, for personal use only, a few concerns and restrictions apply, but as soon as winemaking becomes commercial, there are many. Planning must take all factors into account or a winemaker risks many unpleasant surprises. The following list attempts to group and outline most of the things to consider. Pondering them must be circular, since the choice of one often affects others. The best solution must be arrived at by iterative thinking and rethinking before and during operation of a winery, like any other commercial enterprise.

Over the years we have seen a number of wineries start up with blithe attitudes about "you can always buy grapes," "good wine will sell itself," or "we'll cross that bridge when the time comes." Frequently they fail at considerable cost to the investors; always they have problems that could have been avoided if foreseen. In the past 30 years, in California, it has been common for the first two owners of new wineries to fail or get financially overextended before perhaps the third owner begins to profit. Exceptions to this pattern have generally been those who planned more thoroughly and grew carefully with little borrowing. Also, successful winemakers tended to be initially modest-sized, but not too small, with some of their own vineyards.

1. Some Planning Considerations Before Making Wine

Business Structure and Finances.

1. Who is to own and control the operation? What type of company is it, sole ownership, corporation or partnership?
2. How much money can I risk? How much additional money will be needed?
3. How much sacrifice can I endure for how long?
4. What are projected start-up costs?
5. What are operating costs and their schedules?
6. What must be borrowed and repaid?
7. When can sales begin?
8. When is an operating profit likely?
9. When is a return on investment likely?
10. What are the liability risks and insurance costs?

Regulations.

1. What are the federal, state, and local licenses that must be obtained?

2. What are the Environmental Impact Statement requirements and considerations?
3. What are the federal, state, and local regulations that must be satisfied?
4. What are the differences and similarities for (1–3) comparing any business with a winery?
5. What are the general and special taxes that apply? Are they likely to change?

Grapes.

1. Who is to own and manage the vineyards?
2. Where are the vineyards (location, climate, weather, soil) and what are the special risks (i.e., frosts, rain, pests, diseases)?
3. What are the grape varieties and rootstocks to be used?
4. How are the vineyards to be arranged and managed (rootstock, trellis, irrigation, pest control, pruning, etc.)
5. What fruit composition is wanted at harvest?

Winery.

1. What kinds, styles of wines are to be made?
2. Can owning a winery be avoided or delayed by custom crushing (contractual winemaking in a winery with extra capacity)?
3. Where is the winery to be located (site, access, utilities, marketing considerations, zoning laws, neighbors, visitor facilities)?
4. What equipment and facilities should it have (kinds and sizes of equipment, bottling versus contract bottling, on-site versus external, barrel storage, case storage, etc.)?
5. How functional and efficient will it be (layout, size, maintenance, expansion options, waste disposal)?
6. How attractive will it be (tasting room, architecture, etc.)?

Marketing.

1. What kinds of wines will/should be made for sale (generic, varietal; white, red; etc.)?
2. What price category should be targeted (superpremium, fighting varietal, house blend, standard, loss leader)?
3. How can our wines be made to be good values at their price?
4. How will the wine be distributed and sold (wholesale, contract buyers, direct retail, restaurants, bulk, combinations)?
5. In what markets are wines to be offered (local, state, nation, export, specialty, certain cities, catalog, etc.)? What are the expenses associated with entering and competing in these markets?
6. What can/will be done if wines are judged to be lower in quality or are slower to sell than anticipated?
7. How will public relations be handled and good publicity be sought?

This list is undoubtedly not all-inclusive, but it illustrates the breadth and depth of thought and planning that should precede and accompany making any wine. Cooke et al. (1977) estimated that 24 governmental and related agencies can be involved when new wineries are constructed in California and the list has certainly not decreased. Peterson (1975) has discussed the planning and construction of a sizeable Californian table wine winery.

Winemaking is unusual among agricultural operations in that one operator often covers the whole operation from land to consumer. It is as if the shepherd grew the pasture and the sheep, processed the wool, wove the cloth, made the suit, and presented it for sale. Suppose you wanted to start from scratch and market the best Cabernet. Preparing the vineyard land, particularly if it involves removing old vines or fruit trees and minimizing pest or disease carryover, is likely to take at least two years. From planting to reasonable crop is likely to take four more years, and to desired yield levels and stable quality can take a few more. The wine is likely to require at least three years of maturation and aging before release and you will be lucky if it is all sold within a year. So, from acquiring land to first meaningful return may be about nine or more years. Capital costs for land terracing, planting, grafting, training, trellising, etc., can be huge (over $100,000 per hectare) and operating costs for wages, taxes, irrigation, pest control, pruning, etc., are sizeable and annual. Of course, grapes may be purchased from growers, but growers must meet similar costs to remain in business. If one pioneers an area where wines have not been grown, land costs can be considerably less, but the quality may not prove out and attracting customers may be difficult. It is usually easier to succeed as winery number 50 in a famed district than number one in an unknown area.

Price and cost information will largely be omitted because it varies dramatically from country to country, even locale to locale, and is continually changing. A few sources and examples may nevertheless be useful. Cooke et al. (1977) estimated the construction costs (not including any loan interest) for a small commercial winery producing 10,000 cases (1 case = 12 bottles @ 750 mL = 9L) of table wine annually in coastal districts of California at $1.37 million, up from $0.79 million estimated by Peterson (1975) in the Monterey area. If only direct sale at the winery was contemplated, extra concern for the winery's attractiveness to buyers raised the estimate to $1.7 million. The 1977 estimate of winery construction costs of $137/case dropped to $36 if the coastal winery was constructed for an annual production of 175,000 cases and at 2.5 million cases to $12 coastally or about $5/case in the San Joaquin Valley. These differences reflect economies of scale, but also differences in land costs and production practices. Allowance must be made for inflation of costs of about 4% per year in the United States recently. Prices of standard wines have often not kept pace with general inflation.

A number of viewpoints on all aspects of the economics of small wineries (Moulton 1981) include an estimate that a 25,000-case-capacity premium table wine winery required about $67/case investment costs with an annual cost of depreciation plus interest at 10% of $10.70/case. Cash operating costs per case were $35.75, with grapes at $900/Tm for a total of $46/case or $3.85/bottle. Moulton (1986) summarized reports from nine wineries with 7,000- to 800,000-case annual output, which showed a fourfold range of total costs from $17.75 to $68.43 per case. Production costs were 2.3 to 15.9% labor, 13.1 to 42.4% raw product (grapes) and subtotaled 45.5 to 81.0%. The rest of the costs were assigned to sales and overhead and were 19.0 to 54.5% of the total costs. As a very rough comparison, the retail price including excise but not sales taxes is estimated to have been about $2 per bottle of competitive varietal wines such as Chenin blanc or Riesling in 1975 and $3 in 1990. Recent tax increases have been rapidly adding to costs to the customer without additional return to the winemaker.

Folwell and Castaldi (1987) further investigated economics of scale under various assumptions for wineries with storage cooperage capacity in the 2,500- to 250,000-kL range. Total investment costs decreased from $62/case to $36/case as winery size increased. Total operating costs similarly decreased from $40 to $25/case with both variable costs and fixed costs showing this trend. Grapes, packaging, wine taxes, labor, utilities, marketing, and office costs were listed as variable costs and were 82 to 85% of the total costs. Fixed costs made up the remaining 15 to 18% and included insurance, loan repayment, property taxes, and maintenance. The total costs of establishing the larger winery were greater, of course, but the proportionate labor costs were lower. Smaller wineries are more labor-intensive; larger wineries can save labor by using more capital. Returns to smaller wineries were more sensitive to wine selling prices than to grape and input prices.

A few general comments seem appropriate here regarding regulations (see also Appendix B). The alcoholic beverage industry of the United States has been called a permissive industry, meaning, contrary to what might be inferred, that nothing is permitted until approved. This industry is the only one prohibited and then restarted by Constitutional amendment. Some holdovers persist from the days of prohibition. For example, prospective owners of wineries are investigated for good character and fingerprinted. Previous felony convictions are disqualifying. Although the supervision by the Treasury Department's Bureau of Alcohol, Tobacco, and Firearms (BATF) is much less adversarial than it once was, any hint of irregularity produces investigation and may draw fines. Twenty-five years ago, if you wanted to treat a white port with activated carbon, you had to submit before and after laboratory samples and obtain permission in advance for each commercial lot. Things are much less onerous today, but still not as free as most other production industries. It still pays to be sure you are square with the BATF and other regulatory agencies. After all, they help protect your winery and your customers from unfair practices by others.

C. GENERAL SEQUENCE OF OPERATIONS IN WINEMAKING

In later sections, specific operations will be discussed in detail, but it is essential for the inexperienced winemaker to refer continually to the overall scheme into which each operation fits. These operations interact and their nature, timing, and sequence are key in producing different wine types and styles. Furthermore, failure to apply each operation optimally increases costs, is likely to change quality, and can lead to failure. Wines differ so much that processing by rote is possible only for mass-produced, relatively nondescript wines. Such wines may be inexpensive and pleasant, but they are out of favor with consumers and are likely to become more so since interest has focused on premium types with diverse and specific characteristics. Of course, quality relative to others available is still vital among wines competing primarily on the basis of low price. The U.S. market, and increasingly others also, will not buy poor wine regardless of low price.

To some degree, the nature and sequence of winemaking operations are obvious. The grapes must be obtained and fermented. The young wine must be clarified, processed, and distributed to the consumer. The winemaker must consider that wine may be held a long time before actually being consumed. Some operations may not be necessary for all wines (sterile filtration of microbially stable dry wines, for example) and others are applicable only where a specific style is sought (carbonic maceration, sur lies, etc.). The number of times a process such as centrifugation, fining, or filtration may be applied affects costs and ultimate quality owing to the potential for loss of wine volume, loss of volatiles, exposure to air, etc. Often more experience and restraint can give better but less costly wine if the objective desired is kept firmly in mind. Some wines might be filtered half a dozen times and others not at all or once. The latter is frequently better and certainly cheaper, barring special considerations. It may be fatuous to advise the novice winemaker "don't just do something, sit there," but contemplation of the ramifications should precede action in the well-managed winery. Figure 1-1 attempts to amplify the general sequence of operations to cover the full panoply of winemaking practices. It is recommended that it be consulted each time a new wine type is considered.

D. SOME HAZARDS SPECIFIC TO WINEMAKING

Again, it is not appropriate here to detail all hazards that threaten winemakers or their employees. Many, such as risks from falling heavy objects, noise, electricity, boilers, slippery floors, rotating shafts, operating equipment or vehicles, are common to production industries and, in fact, modern life. A few are unique to the winery laboratory, but analysts know the risks around concentrated alkalis, acids, etc. With ordinary care and attention, wineries are relatively safe and pleasant places to work. There are a few considerations rather special to wine production which it seems appropriate to mention early, in case the prospective winemaker should be unaware. The relative dearth of specific information on winery risks undoubtedly reflects that such risks are small, if common sense is followed. The Wine Institute has from time to time formulated suggestions for winery safety programs, and many of the larger wineries have their own protocols, safety officers, and training programs. These are not, however, readily cited or generally available. The regulations of California (*Confined* 1990) and other states and countries (including the United States) are often voluminous but scattered. Wineries are seldom mentioned separately from other food production industries. Rankine (1989) has some details on this topic, and to a lesser degree so do several other general works on winemaking. For readers with a deeper interest, consultation of general regulatory, health, safety, chemical, physical, and actuarial data is recommended (see also Appendix E).

In terms of known deaths caused (nearly one per vintage 30 years ago in California), carbon dioxide is probably the greatest hazard in wineries. Currently, CO_2 sensors and constant attention have drastically reduced such accidents. Absent ignorance or foolhardiness, the risk is easily avoided. Deaths most commonly have been caused by entering fermentors or confined spaces containing (or recently drained of) active alcoholic yeast fermentations and not adequately ventilated. The entering person is asphyxiated (defined as killed or rendered unconscious through lack of oxygen or excess of carbon dioxide in the body).

CO_2 is not toxic, being naturally enhanced in exhaled breath and needed in small content to stimulate normal breathing. It is classed as a simple asphyxiant along with nitrogen or any other nontoxic gas or vapor that can dilute air below the minimum safe oxygen content. Normal dry air is 20.9% oxygen and the rest inert gases, mostly nitrogen with natural CO_2 content of about 0.03%. The minimum breathable level of oxygen even for short periods at low altitudes is about 18% by volume. California (*Confined* 1990) regulations specify 19.5% oxygen and less as oxygen-deficient and dangerous. One reason that extinguishing a flame is not a very suitable indicator of borderline unbreathable air is that flames may continue to burn below the level of oxygen necessary to maintain consciousness. Another is the fire hazard if alcohol vapor or other combustible is a diluent in the air. Since the introduction of electronic meters reading oxygen content in the air, asphyxiation deaths have nearly disappeared from the wine industry.

If CO_2 (or other inert diluent) exceeds about 10% of the air volume, the oxygen content is too low and unconsciousness occurs rapidly. Unless the person is removed and resuscitated or the atmosphere quickly improved, brain death follows in a few minutes, much as in drowning. On the other hand, with quick aid and perhaps oxygen administration, recovery is usually rapid and complete. Especially sad winery cases have occurred when a worker collapses and is followed by would-be rescuers who also succumb. The proper procedure is to use fans to ventilate actively containers and rooms having or potentially having appreciable CO_2 until they are shown to be safe before entering. If there is the slightest doubt and access cannot be delayed, a worker entering, for example, a fermentor must be harnessed by a rope and pulley to an external worker able to retrieve him in case of trouble. Unconsciousness occurs so quickly that little exertion on the part of the affected person can be expected. Preferably, workers and rescuers should bear a self-contained breathing apparatus having a compressed air tank.

CO_2 is a particular hazard in a winery (or brewery, distillery) because to ferment a liter of 20% sugar grape juice to wine, yeasts produce about 60 liters of CO_2 at low temperature, and the gas volume is proportionately larger at higher temperatures (see also Chapter 5). If not allowed to escape, this CO_2 will drastically increase the pressure and may rupture the container, but that is a separate hazard, notably with sparkling wine. CO_2 gas is about 1.5 times as heavy as an equal volume of air and thus displaces air in low spots as it is vented. Gases rapidly mix by diffusion even without agitation (fans). As a consequence, once the fermentation, leak, or other source of CO_2 or other O_2-displacing gas is stopped

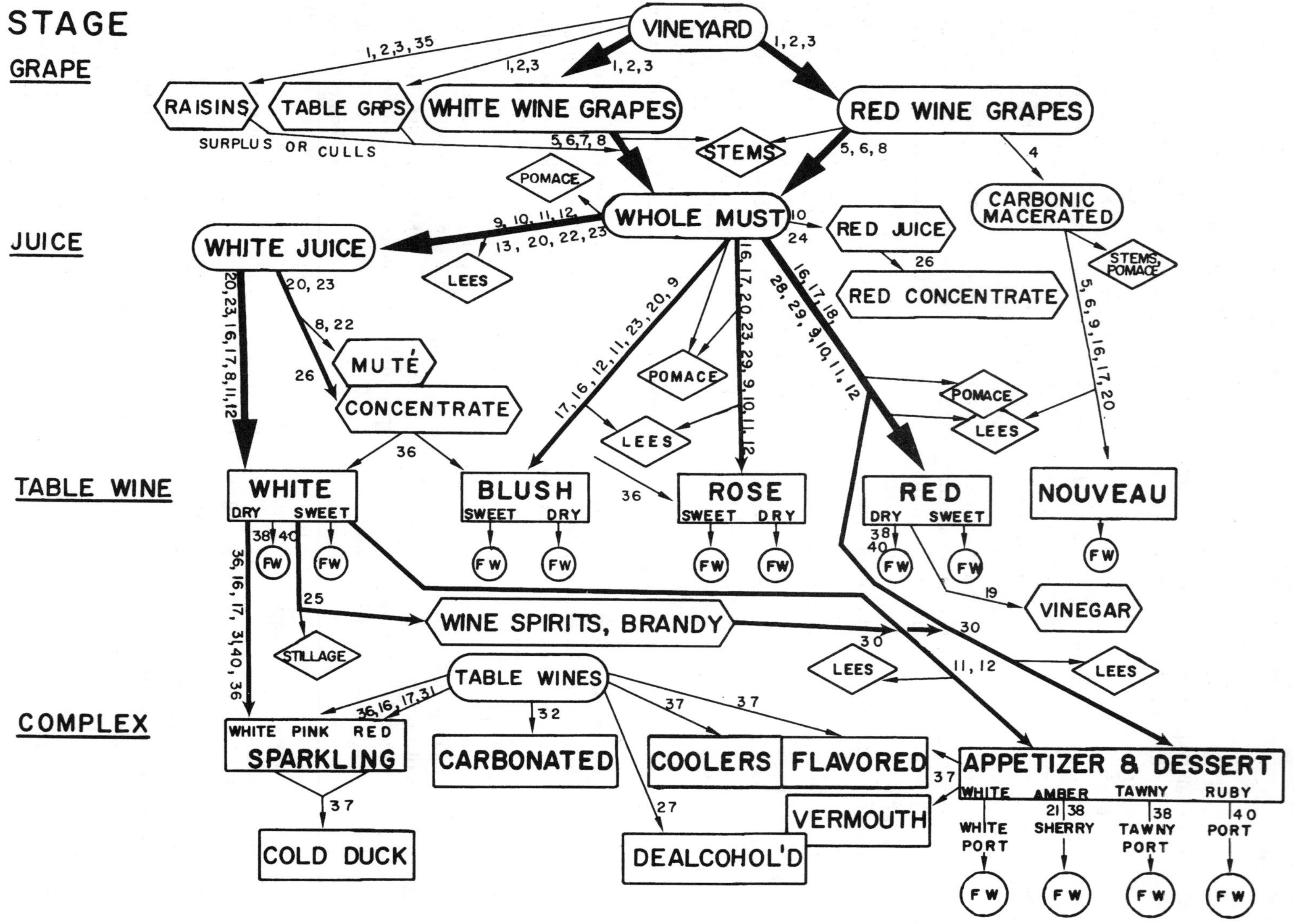
STAGE
GRAPE
JUICE
TABLE WINE
COMPLEX
VINEYARD
1,2,3
1,2,3,35
RAISINS
TABLE GRPS
WHITE WINE GRAPES
RED WINE GRAPES
SURPLUS OR CULLS
5,6,7,8
STEMS
5, 6, 8
4
POMACE
WHOLE MUST
CARBONIC MACERATED
STEMS, POMACE
9, 10, 11, 12,
13, 20, 22, 23
10
24
RED JUICE
26
RED CONCENTRATE
WHITE JUICE
LEES
20,23,16,17,8,11,12
20, 23
8, 22
26
MUTÉ
CONCENTRATE
17, 16, 12, 11, 23, 20, 9
16, 17, 20, 23, 29, 9, 10, 11, 12
16, 17, 18,
28, 29, 9, 10, 11, 12
5, 6, 9, 16, 17, 20.
36
WHITE
DRY SWEET
BLUSH
SWEET DRY
ROSE
SWEET DRY
RED
DRY SWEET
NOUVEAU
FW
38 40
19
VINEGAR
25
WINE SPIRITS, BRANDY
STILLAGE
30
11, 12
TABLE WINES
36, 16, 17, 31, 40, 36
36,16, 17,31
32
37
27
WHITE PINK RED
SPARKLING
CARBONATED
COOLERS
FLAVORED
VERMOUTH
DEALCOHOL'D
COLD DUCK
APPETIZER & DESSERT
WHITE AMBER TAWNY RUBY
21 38
WHITE PORT
SHERRY
TAWNY PORT
PORT

Ovals = Raw materials, sources
Rectangles = Wines
Hexagon = Alternate products (decreasing wine yield)
Diamond = Wastes

Footnotes:

A. To avoid some complexities, e.g., all the wine vinegar and all carbonic maceration are indicated as red. That is usual, but not necessarily true. Similarly, malolactic fermentation is desired in some white wines.

B. F.W. = Finished Wine and always involves clarification and stabilization such as 8, 11, 12, 13, 14 15, 33, 34, followed by 39, 41, 42. It may or may not include maturation (38) or bottle age (40) as indicated for usual styles.

C. Stillage and lees may be treated to recover potassium bitartrate as a by-product. Pomace may also yield red pigment, seed oil, seed tannin, and wine spirits as by-products.

D. Sweet wines are the result of either arresting fermentation at an incomplete stage (by fortification, refrigeration, or other means of yeast inactivation) or addition of juice or concentrate.

Operations / Actions

1. Analyze
2. Select
3. Harvest
4. Carbonic maceration
5. Destem
6. Crush
7. Pectinase treat
8. SO_2 addition
9. Drain
10. Press
11. Settle
12. Rack
13. Centrifuge
14. Filter
15. Microfilter (microbially stabilize)
16. Inoculate (yeast, lactic bacteria)
17. Alcoholic fermentation
18. Malolactic fermentation
19. Acetification
20. Protect from air
21. Aerate
22. Refrigerate
23. Temperature control (generally low)
24. Heat (pasteurize)
25. Distill
26. Concentrate (usually vacuum distill)
27. Alcohol removal (reverse osmosis, vacuum distill)
28. Cap management (punch down, pump over, irrigate)
29. Pomace contact
30. Fortify (wine spirits addition)
31. Champagnization, CO_2 retention
32. Carbonation
33. Fine, protein stabilize
34. Chemically stabilize (refrigerate, ion exchange)
35. Dehydrate
36. Sweeten
37. Blend
38. Bulk maturation (barrel, tank)
39. Bottle
40. Bottle age
41. Case
42. Market

Fig. 1. An amplified outline scheme of making various wines, alternate products, by-products, and associated wastes.

and access to even limited air circulation occurs, the hazard does not long remain. In submarines and similar confinement, CO_2 content in the atmosphere to 0.3% or perhaps 0.5% has not been a serious problem in moderately prolonged exposure.

Other gases that dilute the atmospheric oxygen content have similar effects, but may be more or less of a safety hazard than CO_2. Nitrogen (N_2) is purchased by winemakers to use as an oxygen (air) displacer from wine tanks, bottle headspace, etc. It is a safety consideration, but is less likely a risk because its density is that of air (78% nitrogen) and it does not collect in low places, as CO_2 does, unless much colder than the surrounding air. It is commonly sold in the usual steel cylinder for compressed gases. Such high-pressure cylinders pose an additional hazard that is not intuitively recognized by uninformed users. Just as a rubber balloon, inflated and released, will fly about, gas cylinders may do the same if the valve is broken off. A loose fallen tank can become a rocket which, as momentum builds, may ricochet about, smashing all in its path. Keep the protective shipping cap on such cylinders when they are not in use, treat them with care, and anchor them in place, valve end up, when not actually moving them.

It is helpful to remember that a gram-molecular weight (CO_2 = 44g, SO_2 = 64g, H_2S = 34g, N_2 = 28g, NH_3 = 17g) of any gas occupies 22.4 liters of space at 0°C (273 K) and one atmosphere pressure. Increased pressure diminishes the volume in proportion to the pressure (i.e., at 6 atmospheres the gas volume would occupy 1/6 of that at one atmosphere at constant temperature). Increased temperature increases gas volume in proportion to the absolute or Kelvin temperature (i.e., at 25°C or 298 K, the volume of an ideal gas at constant pressure would be 298/273 that at 0°C). One ppm in gases means 1 mL in a total volume of 1000 L or one cubic meter. For SO_2, for example, 1 mL of the gas constitutes only 2.86 mg (64 g ÷ 22,400 mL at standard conditions). In solution in wine or water 1 ppm = 1 mg/L, so it is important to keep these conventions in mind when comparing gas and solution concentrations. CO_2 concentration in air of 1000 ppm would be (without correcting for temperature and pressure) 1 mL/L of air or nearly 2 mg of CO_2 per liter of gas whereas 1000 ppm of CO_2 dissolved in water would be 1.0 g of CO_2 per liter of solution or 500 times as much CO_2.

Sulfur dioxide (SO_2) is widely used in wineries in one form or another and often is drawn from gas cylinders containing it in liquified form at about 2.5 atmospheres at 25°C. The gas is quite soluble in water to make an acidic solution and is very irritating to the eyes, nose and lungs. The safe threshold limit recommended for the gas in air for human exposure is 2 ppm (which can be detected by most people by smell) with a 10 ppm ceiling over 15 minutes (Appendix E). The eyes will smart and lungs be affected by 8 to 12 ppm; 150 ppm can be endured for only a few minutes; 500 ppm for 30 minutes or more is highly dangerous; and 1000 ppm (1 mL/L of air) or more may be fatal if exposure continues. With this and other gases, unusually sensitive persons with breathing difficulties (asthmatics) should be especially careful to avoid exposure. A very few individuals lack the enzyme sulfite oxidase and should avoid all exposure to SO_2, because they are highly sensitive. Because of extreme sensitivity to SO_2 by rare individuals, wine is required to be labeled "contains sulfites" if it has over 10 ppm and nearly all do by yeast action if not by addition.

SO_2 gas is heavy, 2.3 times dry air, and like CO_2 will temporarily collect in low places. It should be respected and handled very carefully, especially in concentrated aqueous solution or even more so in liquid form. Splashes in eyes or on skin can cause very serious damage. It is, however, so irritating and unpleasant that workers readily avoid it and treat it with respect. Serious accident incidence has been low. In dilute solution it is not dangerous and may be safely consumed in wine at low levels as demonstrated by centuries of use.

Bisulfite salts liberate SO_2 in acidic solution (wine, grape juice) and may be convenient to use with less worker risk. Many wineries meter SO_2 gas into the crusher's must pump. Improperly done, this can deliver SO_2 to the atmosphere and reduce the effective SO_2 concentration in the juice.

Ammonia (NH_3) gas is lighter than air and is only a concern if the winery has ammonia-charged refrigeration that might leak. It is highly odorous and caustic to the eyes so that leakage is quickly detected. Over 2000 ppm there is no permissible exposure and effects are quickly very serious. Infrequent exposure for under one hour at 400 to 700 ppm produces eye, nose and throat irritation but ordinarily no serious lasting effect. At the point of odor recognition by most persons, about 50 ppm, prolonged and repeated exposure produces no injury and 25 ppm is considered the maximum allowable concentration for an eight-hour working day producing no adverse effects for average persons (Appendix E). In high (and unlikely) concentrations between about 15 and 29% in air, ammonia is flammable.

Freon and related halogenated refrigerants are not flammable, but can be asphyxiants. Although proven safe and satisfactory as used in refrigerant systems, concerns about global destruction of atmospheric ozone are mandating the application of alternatives.

Hydrogen sulfide (H_2S) gas is liberated in relatively small amounts from fermentations lacking certain nutrients or containing dusting sulfur. The sulfur is used in the vineyard to prevent powdery mildew and if used excessively or too near harvest it may yield H_2S, the rotten-egg smelling gas, during normal fermentation. Many famous health spas have this gas in the bathing and drinking water, not to mention the whole atmosphere of the area. We know of no cases of serious injury to winery workers from this cause. Under good vineyard and winery practices, it is absent or minimal since we never want this off-flavor in wine. Its obnoxious odor and human's high sensitivity to it (threshold in air about 0.005 ppm) help prevent appreciable exposure. Nevertheless, repeated exposure may be debilitating and there is an insidious loss of detectable odor accompanying exposure to toxic levels.

Hydrogen sulfide's gas density is only slightly greater than dry air (1.2 vs. 1.0). Over 300 ppm for an hour is considered dangerous to life and health, but 150 ppm only gives slight symptoms after one to several hours; 10 ppm is considered the allowable maximum for continuous exposure (Appendix E). Any dangerous level is unlikely in a winery, but it is good to improve ventilation or leave the area, if it is smelled. If you must work in its high presence, use a self-contained breathing apparatus and even at low levels take frequent breaks in the open air to ensure odor fatigue has not set in. This is good advice also for other odorous gases including ammonia and SO_2.

There are a number of good general references to toxic hazards of these and other compounds. Owing to current interest in this area they are frequently updated. Among several consulted in preparing these comments we found particularly useful those by Sax and Lewis (1987, 1989) and Weiss (1986).

The final hazard to be mentioned is almost nonexistent as a special hazard in a table wine winery, but can be appreciable in a distillery—that of fire. Ethanol (ethyl alcohol), the significant component of alcoholic beverages, is flammable, of course (see Appendix E). The explosive limits for ethanol vapor are 3.3 to 19% in air at 60°C and one atmosphere of pressure according to standard handbooks, although such data vary somewhat depending on the method of measurement. Below 3.3% the mixture is too lean to burn and above 19% there is insufficient air to support combustion. Ethanol vapor is 1.6 times heavier than air and therefore lies on top of an aqueous alcohol solution as it is generated and could flow to lower places as it escapes. The minimum flash point has been calculated to be 13°C for pure ethanol (Appendix E), which should mean that below that temperature vapor content becomes too lean to support combustion. This would be even more so for dilute aqueous solutions of ethanol such as wine. Table wine itself is certainly not flammable and has been used, in the absence of water, to put out fires associated with wineries.

If wine is heated, however, the alcohol in the vapor above it is enriched and if boiled the ethanol must be below about 0.3% in the liquid for the vapor to stay too lean to burn. Ethanol boils at 78.3°C and with water forms an azeotrope 95.97% ethanol by weight boiling at 78.1°C. At any temperature approaching boiling, the ethanol content is so enriched in the vapor above aqueous solutions that it is likely to exceed the flammability limit on the too rich side at least within its container. As it escapes into open air it could be ignited by an open flame. The flash point above wine is of the order of 45°C (Appendix E). The autoignition point of ethanol vapor is, however, fairly high, of the order of 265°C.

Only at elevated wine temperatures need one be concerned with fire hazard associated with its alcohol content. At normal cellaring and handling temperatures and conditions risk is absent or essentially so even for fortified wines. The only instance brought to our attention in over 40 years involved baking some California sherry (probably 20% alcohol, 55°C). The worker lowered an electric light bulb into the tank to check the level, broke the bulb on the tank wall, and the tank top was blown through the roof of the building. The worker was injured, but not fatally, and the fire did not propagate. The window of hazardous conditions is small, but should be understood and explained to workers.

Fire insurance rates are about the same for wineries as for other food production plants, illustrating that the hazard is not significant under usual and sensible conditions.

E. REFERENCES

Confined Spaces. 1990. Title 8, Article 109, General Industry Safety Orders, State of California Division of Industrial Safety (Reprinted 4-1-1990).

COOKE, G. M., A. D. REED, and R. L. KEITH. 1977. *Sample Costs for Construction of Table Wine Wineries in California*. Leaflet 2972, Berkeley, CA: Division of Agricultural Sciences.

FARKAS, J. 1986. *Technology and Biochemistry of Wine*, Vols. 1 and 2. Montreux, Switzerland: Gordon and Breach Science Publishers.

FOLWELL, R. J., and M. A. CASTALDI. 1987. "Economies of size in wineries and impacts of pricing and product mix decisions." *Agribusiness* 3(3):281–292.

JACKISCH, P. 1985. *Modern Winemaking*. Ithaca, NY: Cornell University Press.

JACKSON, D., and D. SCHUSTER. 1987. *The Production of Grapes and Wines in Cool Climates*. Wellington, New Zealand: Butterworths of New Zealand.

MOULTON, K. S. (Ed.) 1981. *The Economics of Small Wineries*. Berkeley, CA: Cooperative Extension, University of California.

MOULTON, K. S. 1986. "Wine production costs and some strategy considerations." Paper read at Seminar on Winery Economics, May 9, 1986, Napa, CA.

OUGH, C. S. 1992. *Winemaking Basics*. Binghamton, NY: Food Products Press (Haworth).

PETERSON, R. G. 1975. "An expert plans the premium winery." *Wines and Vines* 56(10):40B–42; (11):35, 36, 38; (12):32–35.

PEYNAUD, E. 1984. *Knowing and Making Wine*. New York: John Wiley & Sons.

RANKINE, B. 1989. *Making Good Wine, A Manual of Winemaking Practice for Australia and New Zealand*. Melbourne: MacMillan Co. of Australia.

SAX, N. I., and R. J. LEWIS, SR. (Eds.). 1987. *Hazardous Chemicals, Desk Reference*. New York: Van Nostrand, Reinhold.

SAX, N. I., and R. J. LEWIS, SR. (Eds.). 1989. *Dangerous Properties of Industrial Materials*, 7th ed., 3 Vols. New York: Van Nostrand, Reinhold.

WEISS, G. (Ed.). 1986. *Hazardous Chemicals Data Book*. Park Ridge, NJ: Noyes Data Corp.

CHAPTER 2

Viticulture for Winemakers

INTRODUCTION

Viticulture is a science and technology separate from enology and winemaking per se. It has its own extensive literature. References that give more detail than possible here as well as additional perspectives include fairly recent examples in English from several different countries (Coombe and Dry 1988; Jackson and Schuster 1987; Pongrácz 1978; Wagner 1976; Weaver 1976; Winkler et al. 1974). Examples in other languages from major wine-producing countries can also be useful (Champagnol 1984; Galet 1988; Huglin 1986; Reynier 1989; Altman 1987; Currle et al. 1983; Kadisch 1986; Ferraro-Olmos 1983; Larrea-Redondo 1981; Fregoni 1985; Saracco 1984). Although winemakers should know as much as possible about viticulture, the professions are so demanding that it is difficult to be fully expert in both.

Suitable grapes are the first indispensable key to success in making wine and especially distinctive, high-quality table wine. It has become fashionable to intone "great wines are made in the vineyard." As with all cliches there is some truth in the statement, but the implication that the winemaker is just an impediment to the grape grower is just as wrong as the reverse opinion. It is regrettable that in some economic situations antagonism may exist between the grower and the winemaker. A grower may feel the grape price should be higher and restrictions on yield or composition less stringent. A winemaker may believe that high grape prices force penny-pinching in other areas and that some growers want to produce high tonnage not necessarily great wine. Wineries controlled by grape-producer cooperatives have seldom made highly or widely esteemed wine. Neither have wineries that purchase all their grapes without regard to the economic health of their grape suppliers, at least on a sustained basis.

It is clearly better for both and for commercial winemaking as a whole if empathy and cooperation prevail between the grape growers and the winemakers. The long-term best interests of both groups and their customers demand such understanding. Often the most successful and stable wineries own at least some of their own vineyards. Through means such as long-term contracts and close liaison the best winemakers cultivate good relationships with their growers.

Not all concerns of viticulturists need be of much direct concern to winemakers. For example, the winemaker wants undamaged grapes, but seldom needs to be directly concerned with particular pests and how to control them as long as approved practices are followed. We will focus on the viticultural aspects that are of most importance for the winemaker to understand.

If the owner of the winery is also to own the vineyards, initial decisions of vineyard location, rootstock planted, scion variety grafted, and trellising erected may have to be lived with for the winemaker's whole career. At best, such factors are costly to change. It is important that the best available choices be made with as much foresight as possible. If the grapes are to be purchased, freedom may be greater and the winery's investment much less, but alternatives will be limited and compromises inevitable. If better wine is to be made, the winemaker must identify and successfully bid for the better grapes. For economic and other reasons the vineyards should not be too far from the winery. The selected growers must be encouraged in practices leading to the best wines and the optimum returns to both the winery and the growers.

Starting with nothing in hand but money, initiating a winery involves circular decision processes. Probably the usual first choice is the country, state, region, or county in which to operate. Specific general and local choices of vineyard site and associated climatic influences may cause reconsideration of which grape varieties are suitable and which wine types and styles are to be made. Accessibility to appropriate markets and the fashions and attitudes of available consumers may further modify choices and require rethinking of the best approach in a given situation. The money available is never sufficient to allow all decisions to be made for the winemaker's ideal wine regardless of cost, at least if the fledgling winery is soon to be economically viable and more than a rich person's toy. These interactions should be remembered as plans proceed on the grapes to be vinified and their desired composition.

A. SPECIES OF GRAPES FOR WINE

Wild grapevines usually grow into tops of trees and have small, dark red, seedy berries. Birds are the natural feeders upon grapes and propagate them by scattering the seeds. Wild grapes are fundamentally dioecious having separate male (pollen-bearing, fruitless) and female (fruit-bearing) vines. Perhaps more than most plants the grapevine has been greatly modified by mankind in the course of adaptation to agriculture. Furthermore, grapes are botanically isolated and therefore often very different in their characteristics compared to other important crop plants.

Grapes are, of course, dicotyledonous angiosperms. Perennial vines, deciduous in temperate climates, they have porous weak wood, insufficiently strong to support themselves alone. One wild vine cut in Indiana showed 126 annual rings by hand lens. It had been growing in a second-growth forest on trees half its age or less. It had fallen and rerooted upon contact with the earth, presumably as its original support trees had died or were cut. Larger and older vines occur wild in older forests and as they reroot and regenerate seem to have a limitless lifespan.

Grapes belong to the genus *Vitis*, one of 11 genera in the family Vitaceae. The Vitaceae, Leeaceae, and the Rhamnaceae families make up the order Rhamnales. *Vitis* is divided into the two subgenera *Euvitis*, the true grapes, and the *Muscadinia*. *Muscadinia* (or *Vitis*) *rotundifolia* and a few relatives have 20 chromosomes and only cross with difficulty and special techniques with the 19-chromosome *Euvitis*. The different *Euvitis* species readily cross when pollen of one species reaches the pistil of another before that of its own species. In fact, hermaphroditic vines (nearly all commercial varieties) are usually self-fertile. *Vitis* encompasses nearly 60 wild species that have been described, essentially confined to the north temperate zone. The wine industry of the world, however, is built upon the one species *Vitis vinifera* L., which is native to areas of Asia Minor near the Black and Caspian seas and is, nevertheless, generally termed the European grape.

Other grape species have been used to make wine or to produce hybrids by crossbreeding with *V. vinifera*, but in spite of local interest or necessity, the famous wines have come from *V. vinifera*. Progeny involving other grape species often require special considerations in the vineyard and winery. This being true, unless specific note is made to the contrary, all reference will be to the so-called European wine grape, *Vitis vinifera*. Culture of this species of grape started very early. Arguably viticulture was a cause, not just a result, of the earliest civilization in the Persian, Mesopotamian, Caucasian, and Mediterranean areas from whence occidental civilization springs.

If *V. vinifera* is so important, why do we need to even take note of other species of *Vitis*? The native grapes of North America are especially diverse and numerous. Associated with some of them in some areas are native pests, diseases, and conditions, to which, over the ages, the wild grapes of that area became tolerant or immune. Among these are powdery mildew (caused by *Uncinula necator*, once called Oidium), downy mildew caused by *Plasmopara viticola* (once called Peronospora), phylloxera insects, nematodes, winter cold, and summer humidity. When the early transatlantic explorers and colonists transferred grape vines between the Old and New Worlds, *V. vinifera* became exposed to accompanying new pests and diseases to which it was not resistant. With the spread of these agents, European vineyards died or became unproductive. The New World's grapes could be grown and could be extended into areas with pests and climate unsuitable for *V. vinifera*.

However, the grapevines from wild North American sources, although resistant to specific conditions and pests, usually had other problems not found with healthy *V. vinifera*. Certain (but not all) of the North American species were resistant to phylloxera root lice and harmful nematodes. Therefore, growing rootstock vines, then grafting to them scions from *V. vinifera* varieties enabled tolerance to these pests and production of *V. vinifera* fruit. The rooting portion of the vine is the vine's feeder for water and inorganic nutrients. The same scion variety grown on different rootstocks in different soils will have more or less vigor, yield, and fruit quality even though the fruit remains that of the scion variety. Complete incompatibility of grafts, failure to unite and develop, is much rarer among *Vitis* species than among certain fruit trees. Nevertheless, the best combinations between rootstock, scion, and region are not static and well codified. A new strain of *Phylloxera* has recently invaded Californian areas planted on AxR#1 rootstocks and replanting with improved rootstocks is again required.

Rootstocks and grafting cause extra costs and do not transfer resistance to aboveground conditions. Pesticide applications are costly and have other disadvantages. The flavors of the wines produced from nonvinifera species are often strong and different from each other and from traditional *V. vinifera* wines. Two examples are the "foxy" varieties such as Concord, derived from *Vitis labrusca*, and the Muscadines with their potent and soon overpowering Scuppernong-like flavor. An obvious course to attack these problems is to crossbreed among different *Vitis* species with the ideal being a direct-producing, own-rooted vine resistant to both root and aboveground deleterious conditions, but with fruit composition like *V. vinifera*. This has been partially successful and might ultimately be completely so, but it is a monumental task if all the diversity of vinifera varieties is to be combined with all potential resistances. So far, varieties with vinifera and nonvinifera parentage (usually incorrectly lumped as French hybrids in the U.S. and American hybrids in Europe regardless of origin) are limited in plantings. In Europe, with lessening demand for ordinary wine, the plantings of hybrids are in fact decreasing. They have never been extensive in the United States, although locally important in some Eastern states. Some historical niches probably will survive indefinitely, such as Concord types for juice and jelly in the Northern United States and parts of Canada, and Isabella or other hybrids for fungal resistance in humid subtropical areas. It seems unlikely that presently available hybrid varieties will displace *V. vinifera* scions, although sufficient effort coupled with newer genetic engineering techniques still could revolutionize the grape variety picture. For now *V. vinifera*, grafted when necessary to nonvinifera rootstocks, remains the premier source for premium wines.

The depictions of *Vitis vinifera* grapevines from as early as at least 3000 B.C. do not illustrate any of the male vines one would expect in high percentage if the vineyards had come from wild seed. Self-fertile hermaphrodite vines were apparently selected and propagated so effectively they had already replaced the wild types. Early harvesters and the earliest farmers were quick to note unusual vines with more, bigger, earlier, redder, white, or more flavorful fruit. To retain such specific characteristics, the vine must be moved or multiplied by vegetative propagation. The parent vine must be transplanted or a piece of it rerooted or grafted onto another vine. If seeds from the desirable vine are planted, each seed produces a different type of vine. These heterogeneous seed progeny would nearly all be without the desirable characteristic.

Near the beginning of the Christian era with already thousands of years of viticulture, Pliny the Elder described in considerable detail about 90 varieties of grapes in use by the Romans. Perhaps 5000 or more varieties of *V. vinifera* and nearly as many hybrids with other *Vitis* species have now been named. With continued clonal selection and crossbreeding, the list can continue to grow without limit.

Differences among grape varieties make up the largest and most simply recognized and controlled differences affecting wine composition and quality. Essentially all the great table and dessert wines of the world, whether varietally labeled or not, owe their important characteristics in large part to a significant one or a small group of grape varieties. It is no accident that in the United States, Alsace, Australia, South Africa, and increasingly elsewhere the grape varieties are designated on the labels of premium wines. Such designation is useful to knowledgeable consumers in repeat buying of wines they like. In the United States, if a variety is named ordinarily 75% or more of the wine must come from that grape; 51% prior to 1983. In Bordeaux, Burgundy, Champagne, and other areas famous for wine, the vineyards are limited by appellation laws to a certain few designated varieties in order to maintain the characteristics that made their wines famous. Nuances that make the wines vary by vineyard, climate, and vintage are important, but they tend to be small compared to differences possible among different grape varieties. Clearly the choice of varieties is a crucial one.

B. THE GRAPE VARIETY, CLONES, AND VIRUSES

After one settles on a given variety, complications remain. The cuttings to propagate must be obtained from parent vines. Since annually only about 50 to 100 buds can be obtained from any one donor vine, a large number of new vines requires a sizeable number of parent vines. If the mother vines were themselves cuttings from a single vine the variability would be low, but that is rarely the case. Typically, with our classic varieties that have been propagated for hundreds if not thousands of years, each vine in an authentically monovarietal vineyard block may have somewhat different characteristics. This variation results from slow somatic mutation or genetic drift during the huge number of cellular generations involved. This divergence is more pronounced among older or more separate populations. So, for example, all Chardonnay vines from Napa County, California, may resemble each other more than those from Burgundy. Of course, this would depend upon the number, similarity, and recentness of introductions from elsewhere.

Another problem is that introductions, particularly in earlier days, of essentially the same variety from different sources may carry different names. The detailed description and identification of different grape varieties, ampelography, is an esoteric science and art in itself. Complicated measurements and fine details of leaf shape, seed appearance, berry characteristics, cluster habit, etc., are invoked. Seldom is much note reported of flavor or composition data on either the fruit or its wine, partly because such details are more variable and more difficult to measure. Ampelographers sometimes disagree whether or not two vines are the same variety. The population considered typical for a given variety in one place may differ from the populations of that variety elsewhere.

New plants propagated from cuttings of another single vine are clones of that vine. Selection of clones has been practiced to some degree since time immemorial in order to maintain the varietal identity and maintain or improve characteristics such as yield. The best and most characteristic vines are observed and marked in the vineyard to supply the cuttings for new or replacement plantings. More systematically in recent times, good clones have been experimentally compared and the better ones chosen for further propagation.

A confusion factor has been the discovery (beginning about 1935) of viruses that reside in the vine. They can cause specific diseases and are carried along in the cuttings or introduced through the rootstock or by certain insect or nematode vectors. Some of the earlier clonal selections may have only reflected accidental escapes from viral infection or relative weakness of the virus therein and not necessarily a genetically superior clone of a given variety. Some of the presumed clonal differences among vines of the same variety have disappeared or diminished when the vines are heat-treated or otherwise freed of viruses. Under circumstances of excessive vine vigor, for example, vines could give better wine when carrying mild viruses than when freed of them. Although there are some who argue this point (Pongrácz 1978), the best approach appears to be to propagate only scions and rootstocks freed of known viruses. Control of excessive vigor or other problems by other appropriate management is clearly preferable to unknown levels of virus sicknesses in the vines. Californian plantings with vines freed of known viruses have remained true to type in varietal characteristics and generally give at least as good and often better wine and in larger yield. This is partly a general impression, but the spread of the best clones of virus-free Chardonnay, for example, can be documented to have increased tons per hectare along with increasing reputation and acceptance of the wines (Singleton 1990).

C. VARIETY SELECTION

1. General

Given the importance already outlined of the grape variety and some of the problems indicated in selecting the best example of that variety to propagate, it seems a daunting task to select the few varieties one should grow from among the thousands possible. There appear to be four kinds of reasons to select a certain grape variety: tractability, distinctive flavor, other special characteristics, and economics-sales. These are not necessarily mutually exclusive and compromises may be required. The ultimate in tractability are those grapevines that are relatively easy to grow and very productive. Unfortunately they usually yield pleasant but unexciting wines that gain no great reputation even when widely planted. Airen, a white variety almost unknown outside of Spain, is planted on about 30% of the total vineyard area of that country. It is probably the most widely planted grape variety in the world (Robinson 1986), but its wines have no exceptional reputation. Among the top 20 of the most widely planted grape varieties (all vinifera) as shown in Table 2-1, probably Rkatsiteli, Trebbiano, Carignane, Mission/Criolla/Pais, and several more should be primarily in this category. From that listing[1], the varieties noted for making wines with desirably distinctive flavors include Grenache, Cabernet Sauvignon, Muscats as a group, Merlot, Sémillon, and Riesling. A modest number could be added including famous but lesser total area varieties such as Chardonnay, Gewürztraminer, and Pinot noir. Distinctive and desirably flavored varieties is the group from which further but lesser known varieties are sought by winemakers wanting a new flavorful wine to distinguish their listings from others in the marketplace.

Reasons of this latter kind are in the economics-sales category. A variety that has problems, occasionally poor berry count per cluster by Merlot for example, may still be a suitable choice for marketing reasons. Consideration must be given to the existence, accessibility, size, and price characteristics of the market whether you are a grape grower or a winemaker. The specific weighing of factors may be quite different for the grower compared to the vintner.

Other special characteristics important to selection of which varieties to grow include such factors as length of ripening and usual harvest date, retention of acidity at harvest, or tendency regarding certain processing problems as wines are made. With modern enology most of the processing problems can be overcome. Some will be the subject of specific comments elsewhere in this book.

From the vintner's viewpoint, and assuming the economic and growing conditions are acceptable, the flavor characteristics of the wine produced are probably the most crucial factor in variety selection. Two additional concepts in this regard appear useful for further comment: aroma families and intense versus subtle flavors. Many grape varieties may be placed in one of a relative few characteristic aroma families. A few appear unique and other background flavor or color factors distinguish the individual varieties classifiable into different aroma families. The "foxy" family derived from *Vitis labrusca* and epitomized by Concord and Niagara is in part due to the unique intensity of methyl anthranilate in these grapes. The Scuppernong-Muscadine aroma has not been chemically pinpointed but is also so strong and recognizable that it is easy to distinguish from *V. vinifera* varieties. Within the pure *V. vinifera* varieties the most intense and easily recognized aroma is that of the Muscat group involving monoterpene odorants such as geraniol. The pyrazine family has herbaceous, bell pepper aromas originating with 2-methoxy-3-isobutyl pyrazine. These aromas are characteristic in the Cabernet family both white and red (Sauvignon blanc, Sémillon, Ruby Cabernet, Cabernet Sauvignon, Cabernet franc, and others).

An aroma family characterized as berry-fruity and tending to resemble esters such as ethyl caproate is more heterogeneous and would include Zinfandel, Californian Petite Sirah, and probably Grenache, Shiraz, Chenin blanc, plus others not as individually distinctive but still fruity. Grenache can have a relatively unique fruitiness sometimes described as raspberry hard candy.

This concept of aroma families among grape varieties needs to be fleshed out with more research. Is the spicy character sometimes found in wines from Gamay, Merlot, and

[1]Any listing such as Table 2-1 is subject to a number of caveats. It depends on world statistical summaries which are of variable accuracy and several varieties and clones may be grouped under one name. The more expertise possessed by the variety identifier the less willing they are to express unequivocal sameness among selections of a variety grown in various countries. Contrary to recent practice, we believe laymen and others are generally best served if the valid varietal name current in a given country is accepted, e.g., California's Petite Sirah is not French Syrah or Australian Shiraz, nor is it, by recent findings, Durif. A range of different varieties are cultivated in France under the name Sirah.

Table 2-1. The top twenty winegrape varieties in the world based on area planted.

Variety[1]	Area (in thousands of ha)	Countries with the largest plantings (percent of global area)
Airén (W)	476	Spain (100)
Grenache (R)	331	Spain (72), France (23), United States (2)
Rkatsiteli (W)	267	Soviet Union (93)
Trebbiano[2] (W)	262	Italy (49), France (49)
Carignane (R)	221	France (94), United States (4)
Mission/Criolla/Pais[3] (R)	145	Argentina (72), Chile (27), United States (1)
Cabernet Sauvignon (R)	135	Chile (19), France (17), Soviet Union (16), United States (7)
Muscat[4] (W)	122	Argentina (20), Spain (19), Soviet Union (16), United States (9)
Mataro/Monastrel (R)	113	Spain (90)
Barbera (R)	102	Italy (90), United States (7)
Bobal (R)	95	Spain (100)
Merlot (R)	90	France (42), Italy (17), United States (1)
Sémillon (W)	75	Chile (47), France (31), United States (3)
Riesling (W)	66	Soviet Union (38), Germany (29), United States (8)
Verdicchio (W)	65	Italy (100)
Walschriesling (W)	64	Yugoslavia (33), Hungary (30)
Macabeo (W)	58	Spain (88)
Malbec (R)	43	Argentina (70), Chile (19)
Xarel-lo (W)	43	Spain (100)
Grenache blanc (W)	41	Spain (61), France (39)

[1]Letters in brackets denote color of the variety: W = white, R = red.

[2]Also called St. Émilion and Ugni blanc.

[3]A family of varieties including some white.

[4]Includes Muscat Alexandria, M. blanc, etc.

Source: Adapted from Robinson (1986). Vineyard area, owing to low productivity, overweights some countries. Soviet Union and Yugoslavia values do not reflect partition.

Gewürztraminer another flavor family? Do the black pepper and smoky odors from some Syrah/Shiraz wines form another? What are the ultimate categories possible in the overall genetic capabilities of *Vitis*? Some of the most interesting varieties such as Riesling and Gewürztraminer seem to combine the terpene flavors somewhat like Muscats with other fruity and spicy characteristics and represent more than one aroma family. When Cabernet types lack the bell pepper aroma they often are high in cassis-cherry odors. The aroma of violets is noted in Nebbiolo and sometimes other wines. Not to overwork this idea, it appears useful to think of these varietal families of grape aromas as the top notes of young wines and perhaps the "primary colors" useful in exciting new blended combinations.

It has been noted that wines made exclusively from Concord or Scuppernong grapes are usually too intensely flavored. Conversely, among distinctively flavored vinifera varieties more intensity is usually desired with the possible exception of the Muscat group and the Cabernet (pyrazine) group. Too intense and obvious flavors deprive the taster of the pleasure of searching out and contemplating subtle variations. Also intense flavors soon overwhelm the flavors of accompanying food and become satiating, cloying, and tiresome. Table wine is designed to be consumed as a complement to food in reasonably sizable, thirst-quenching amounts.

Vinifera wines are seldom obvious as to the grape variety even when 100% from that variety and tasted by experienced tasters, especially if from different vineyard areas. Table 2-2 (Singleton 1990; Winton et al. 1975) shows some examples. Muscat was most distinctive, being correctly named after blind tasting in

Table 2-2. Sensory panel designation of young wines as an indicator of relative distinctiveness of varietal wine flavor.

	Proportion named (%)						
Variety, white	Chardonnay	Chenin blanc	Gewürztraminer	Muscat	Sauvignon blanc	Thompson Seedless	White Riesling
Chardonnay	20	17	3	0	12	7	9
Chenin blanc	4	15	2	0	12	6	12
Gewürztraminer	12	6	28	0	6	0	15
Muscat	0	0	0	67	0	8	14
Sauvignon blanc	12	20	0	0	20	4	7
Thompson Seedless	4	11	2	0	8	27	14
White Riesling	7	6	4	8	7	4	38
Variety, red	Cabernet Sauvignon	Ruby Cabernet	Carignane	Petite Sirah	Pinot noir	Zinfandel	
Cabernet Sauvignon	36	10	0	10	16	9	
Ruby Cabernet	22	21	0	36	6	1	
Carignane	13	0	26	8	15	4	
Petite Sirah	26	0	4	49	0	5	
Pinot noir	20	0	2	4	39	13	
Zinfandel	29	0	3	7	8	40	

Source: Singleton 1990; adapted from Winton, Ough and Singleton 1975.

two-thirds of the cases when naming *any* white wine was possible. If it was confused, it was most often with Riesling. Thompson Seedless (Sultanina) made nondescript wines and their very lack of specific character made them somewhat recognizable. Poorly recognizable wines were produced in some instances by reputed varieties. Before criticizing either the tasting panel or the varieties, note that this panel was accustomed to tasting wines from a very wide range of varieties (therefore the possible choices were large), and the grapes came from vineyard areas not all suited to making good wines of the type. The results are nevertheless illustrative of the points made.

2. Recommended Varieties

What variety should be planted in a specific new vineyard depends on many factors of biology, climatology, and economics. No single variety can be recommended universally, nor should it be, remembering the value of diversity among wines to maintain consumer interest. Important considerations are the interests of the owners and the desire to have something special versus the desire to capitalize on an area's reputation with a certain variety.

The most exemplary early experimental study of variety-location suitability for wine of which we are aware is that of Amerine and Winkler (1944; 1963a, 1963b). A large number of varieties were studied by growing them in several areas of California. Wines were made and evaluated both by chemical composition and sensory characteristics, usually for several vintages. Further description and recommendations for Californian areas are the subject of other reports (Ough et al. 1973; Kasimatis et al. 1977, 1980; Kissler et al. 1973). Useful data for New Zealand and other cool areas are reported by Jackson and Schuster (1987), for Australia by Coombe and Dry (1988), for South Africa by Orffer (1979), for Washington by Nagel et al. (1972), and for Canada and Eastern United States by Bowen et al. (1972), Crowther and Bradt (1970), and Einsett and Kimball (1971). Varietal comparison is a never-ending task as new varieties are bred or imported and conditions change. For example, Ruby Cabernet, when introduced by Dr.

Harold P. Olmo, was very unpopular with pickers because the tough stems slowed the picking rate. With mechanical harvesting, this objection became unimportant and berry removal was actually facilitated.

Most general viticulture references (including those cited earlier) include descriptions and evaluations of grape varieties for winemaking. Color and other factors of interest to winemakers are mentioned such as early or late ripening, suitability for mechanical harvesting, and general repute for one or more wine types. Owing to interactions with climate, marketing, etc., it is very difficult to make unequivocal recommendations for varieties. The number of varieties that are world-famous for distinctive noble wines are relatively few and even fewer are suited to a given vineyard/winery situation.

For dry white table wines Chardonnay, Sauvignon blanc, Sémillon, genuine Riesling, and Gewürztraminer certainly must be mentioned. Highly distinctive and especially suited for sweet table, sparkling, and fortified white wines is Muscat blanc and its cousins. Another group less widely reputed for distinctive white table wines could include Aligoté, Chenin blanc, Colombard, Melon, Müller-Thurgau, Pinot blanc, Pinot gris, and Sylvaner. Bland, seldom recognizable by wine flavor are such varieties as Burger, Sultanina (Thompson Seedless), and Trebbiano (Saint Émilion). Champagnes are traditionally largely from Chardonnay and Pinot noir. Since the processing and not the grape (except for sparkling Muscats) gives much of the character, sparkling wines from less traditional areas are often from blends such as Chenin blanc and Colombard. A clean, tart, generally light white base wine is desired. For sherries Palomino is traditional, but specific varietal flavors are unimportant in these wines. Varietal flavors are seldom emphasized for white ports, although varieties such as Grillo and Verdelho can make attractively distinctive wines of this class without becoming muscatel-like. For all fortified dessert wines a well-ripened grape without too low an acidity is desired. Unless such flavors are desired for the particular type and style (perhaps Malaga, Marsala) raisining is to be avoided.

For dry red table wines the world-famous distinctive varieties include Cabernet Sauvignon, Merlot, Gamay, Grenache, Pinot noir, and Syrah/Shiraz. Perhaps a lesser and certainly more locally restricted distinctive tier could include Barbera, Grignolino, Nebbiolo, Ruby Cabernet, Sangiovese, and Zinfandel. Most of these red grapes are or can be suitable for rosé and faintly pink blush wines also. These pink wines are often slightly to moderately sweet, notably the recently popular "white" Zinfandel types. Occasionally fully red sweet table wines such as late-harvest types appear, but they have not developed a sustained following nor a specific varietal pattern. Port-type wines, on the other hand, can be quite special and distinctive from such varieties as Souzão, Tinta Cão, Tinta Madeira, Tinta Roriz, Touriga Franceso, Touriga Nacional, and Trousseau. Muscat Hamburg and perhaps Aleatico are made into "black" or red muscatels. Red and pink sparkling wines, except for the late unlamented Cold Duck types which usually had a Concord portion, have rarely emphasized flavors of specific grape varieties.

Suitability and specific characteristics of individual grape varieties will draw comments under other topics in this and later chapters. However, it is informative to consider the total (bearing and not yet bearing) plantings in California over the last few decades (Table 2-3). Keep in mind that a newly planted vineyard only bears some fruit after three years and a full crop after about five years. It should be commercially productive for at least 25 years and can have a much longer life. Obviously, massive statewide changes will be slow. An existing vineyard can be grafted over to another variety. This speeds change by only losing about $1\frac{1}{3}$ year's crop and by causing a drop in hectarage of the old variety equal to the rise in that of the new scion variety.

Several factors have had major influences on the wine growers of California since World

Table 2-3. California grape hectarage by years, classes, and varieties.

	1960	1970	1980	1985	1990
Total grapes	186,930	193,830	276,810	294,710	280,710
Raisin varieties	100,300	100,790	110,520	117,830	112,060
Muscat Alexandria	9230	5010	4310	3680	2320
Thompson Seedless (Sultanina)	89,550	93,050	105,020	112,780	108,160
Table varieties	35,430	29,300	29,580	37,680	34,530
Flame Tokay	9300	8320	7370	7510	5540
Concord (+ Niabell, etc.)	110	100	60	70	50
White wine varieties	9460	17,460	55,930	79,020	72,660
Burger	1200	890	730	930	930
Chardonnay	—	1110	6890	11,100	21,110
Chenin blanc	—	2140	13,063	16,780	13,340
Colombard	920	5520	17,910	29,640	23,830
Emerald Riesling	—	320	1150	1180	530
Feher Szagos	370	210	120	50	20
Gewürztraminer	—	260	1475	1610	750
Gray Riesling	—	330	980	990	200
Malvasia bianca	—	150	340	750	860
Muscat blanc (+Orange M.)	—	150	570	670	570
Palomino (Golden Chasselas)	3700	2590	1520	1090	600
Pinot blanc	370	290	780	920	740
Riesling (White)	—	650	4120	4070	2020
Sauvignon blanc	830	550	2940	6230	5440
Sémillon	510	500	1150	1230	900
St. Emilion (Trebbiano)	—	260	470	470	310
Sylvaner	530	460	570	500	80
Other white	2090	1070	1160	810	460
Red Wine Varieties	41,740	44,470	80,390	59,810	61,030
Alicante Bouschet	4150	2660	2000	1300	850
Barbera	—	1340	7810	6000	4320
Cabernet Franc	—	60	60	260	660
Cabernet Sauvignon	290	2460	9230	9150	13440
Carignane	10,100	10,550	10,240	6610	4470
Carnelian	—	—	1110	640	510
Centurion	—	—	420	240	230
Gamay (Napa)	320	580	1920	990	620
Gamay Beaujolais (Pinot noir)	—	630	1620	1020	580
Grenache	5020	5130	7110	6350	5520
Malvoisie	430	330	210	100	40
Mataro	1240	750	380	200	110
Merlot	—	110	1080	1010	3010
Mission	3700	2620	1490	940	470
Petite Sirah (Durif)	1900	1650	4550	2070	1240
Pinot noir	280	1280	3800	3160	3864
Rubired and Royalty	—	1730	5220	3740	3240
Ruby Cabernet	—	1120	6850	4280	2800
Salvador	890	670	1040	510	300
Syrah/Sirah/Shiraz	—	—	30	40	140
Tinta Madeira	—	230	270	70	20
Valdepeñas	380	780	760	390	220
Zinfandel	10,150	8210	11,800	10,270	13,830
Other Red	2870	1570	1370	450	610

Source: Adapted from annual reports by California Crop and Livestock Reporting Service.

War II. There has been a shift from about 80% fortified wine to 80% table wine or more. This accounts for much of the decrease in plantings of Palomino (sherry), Mission, and Tinta Madeira (port). This is not clear from Table 2-3, but formerly a considerable part of the Thompson Seedless and Flame Tokay went to wineries to be used for sherry, white port, fortifying spirits, or brandy. Such use is much reduced in recent times. Thompson Seedless is now seldom used for wine (although a considerable amount is still crushed for juice and concentrate). Thompson Seedless was rapidly replaced for wine usage in the 1980s by Colombard (which retains acid well in warm areas) and Chenin blanc (which generally makes more flavorful wine). Barbera (also a retainer of acidity in warm areas) followed a similar trend and often makes a better red table wine from hot vineyards than most other varieties. All three of these varieties were evidently considered somewhat overplanted in California since they have decreased slightly recently.

The great increase in Chardonnay and Cabernet Sauvignon is the result of the increased demand both for premium table wines in general and these in particular. Similarly, although less in total magnitude, the increases of Merlot, Cabernet franc, Pinot noir, and Sauvignon blanc may be laid to this cause and the fact that, with Chardonnay and Cabernet Sauvignon so omnipresent, consumers seek additional premium labels. Rhone varieties such as Viognier and Syrah are widely predicted to be the next such fashion. Riesling and Gewürztraminer have gone out of fashion with consumers, but are expected to return, since fine dry and slightly sweet table wines can be made from them. Related, perhaps, is the continuing increase of Muscat blanc and Malvasia bianca (also muscat flavored in California). These varieties produce aromatic table or sparkling wines in their own right and can be useful for blending. Similarly, Muscat Alexandria, although listed as a raisin grape, often is also used by wineries. With the decline in seeded or deseeded raisins and of muscatel, this variety has declined, but not as much as it might have without some use in table winemaking. Concord and its relatives are mentioned only to show they are vanishingly small in California.

Most red grapes have anthocyanins only in the skins of their berries. Exceptions having also red pulp and juice are the dyers (*tienturiers* from French), Alicante Bouschet, Salvador, Rubired, and Royalty. These have some nonvinifera (*V. rupestris*) parentage and make wines mainly useful for blending because of their high red color. Rubired and Royalty (produced by Professor H. P. Olmo of the University of California, Davis) were released in 1958. They are replacing the other two dyers just mentioned. Rubired now has eightfold more hectares than Royalty. Other varieties bred, tested, and introduced by Professor Olmo include pure viniferas: Emerald Riesling and Ruby Cabernet released in 1948, Carnelian in 1973, Centurion in 1975, and Carmine in 1977. They appear to follow a rather typical course with early plantings exceeding what may become the permanent level. There can be several reasons for this pattern. Among them, the grapes or wines may need special management not initially understood, or consumer awareness and demand may not develop as rapidly as hoped. In fact, the lag between planting vineyards and having wine to market plus the disruptions inherent in a large and somewhat volatile industry has historically led to considerable boom-bust fluctuation in general and with individual varieties or areas in particular.

Another major trend in the period shown in Table 2-3 is the shift of consumer demand from red to white table wine. In 1960 the hectarage of white wine grapes was less than one-fourth of that of the red wine grapes. While red wine grape planted area doubled by 1980, and was still $1\frac{1}{2}$ times as large in 1990 as in 1960, white wine grape plantings increased eightfold by 1985 and were 1.3 times as large as red in that year.

Owing to good yield and versatility, some varieties such as Grenache and Zinfandel have deservedly remained widely planted over the whole period. Burger and Mission are examples of varieties that have decreased but perhaps not as much as would be expected, considering their rather ordinary table wines. A few of the older varieties, Feher Szagos for example, are slow to completely disappear in spite of major difficulties (susceptibility to berry cracking and rot in this instance) and strong recommendations against them (Amerine and Winkler 1944).

Additional factors of great importance, not illustrated by total hectarage, include typical yield and price. To illustrate how large these factors can be, Burger averaged nearly 30 metric tons/hectare in California in 1990, whereas Pinot noir averaged about 7 Tm/ha. In the highest premium wine area, growers received, in 1992, about $410/Tm for Burger, $985/Tm for Pinot noir, $1805/Tm for Cabernet Sauvignon, and $1580/Tm for Chardonnay. Growing area makes a great difference as well. Chenin blanc from the highest premium county brought $525/Tm and from the lowest priced area $210/Tm in California in 1992.

Similar statistical data may be derived from other states and countries. Each would likely show considerable differences with special varieties and different climatic and economic conditions. Conservative owners of small vineyards are well advised to plant the varieties which the wineries of their area want to buy, keeping an eye on prospects for change and probable dollars per hectare.

D. EFFECTS OF VINEYARD LOCATION

1. General

Climate is inextricably tied to the location of the vineyard as is, of course, the topography and physicochemical nature of the soil. Before considering these in more detail, a few general comments are in order. The effects of weather as it relates to vintage differences and of climate as it relates to regional differences can be great. Although we will consider the typical effects on grapes in general, interaction with variety can be great. For example, Ruby Cabernet often yields a higher-quality wine than Cabernet Sauvignon in hot areas of central California. The reverse is usual in cooler coastal areas.

It is useful to consider climate at four levels from global to local. Commercial winegrowing is largely confined to the North and South temperate regions of the earth. Although special techniques can extend the limits, lack of dormancy and problems with disease restrict viticulture on the equatorial sides and so does cold on the polar sides of these belts. Eliminating deserts, marshes, higher altitudes, too-rocky areas, and prevailing conditions unsuitable for viticulture leaves large areas possibly available for viticulture. Study of climatic variables can help decide where to locate a new vineyard, for example, in one state versus another.

Regional climate, that of the district, county, or section of the state will help delineate the best vineyard areas from a more local perspective. Next the mesoclimate must be considered. This refers to the particular vineyard relative to its neighbors or even sections of the same vineyard. For example, a vineyard up a slope may be less subject to spring frosts than the one at the bottom of the valley, since cold air is more dense and can slide down the slope. Air drainage, wind exposure, and sun aspect are important parts of mesoclimate. Microclimate, as presently defined, means the immediate environmental influences (airflow, sunlight, humidity, etc.) around and within the canopies of particular vines.

Microclimates are most easily modified by vineyard management. Mesoclimate is largely a result of vineyard site selection influenced sometimes by layout (east-west versus north-south rows, for example). Climate on a larger scale is largely beyond control once a vineyard site is selected, but the incidence, timing, and severity of storms remains a concern. Continental climates have wider variations and annual vintages differ more than in coastal climates or others moderated at least in temperature by the nearness of a large body of water. Often the best guide to new vineyard siting is the existence and reputation of nearby vineyards and the interest of winemakers in your prospective crop. If more grapes of a certain type are needed, winemakers will encourage plantings; however, excess supply or lower quality will certainly lower prices.

2. Land for Vineyards

Famous, high-quality wines often come from vineyards with relatively low fertility. In fact, owing to such factors as excessively vigorous vine growth as opposed to fruit production, highly fertile soils are considered undesirable for wine vineyards. The healthy grapevine is a good feeder with its deep, perennial root system which becomes relatively large compared to the severely pruned aboveground vine.

European vintners have tended to emphasize the importance of the specific vineyard location and ascribe the major effects to the soil itself. New World specialists have tended to emphasize climatic effects and consider the soil per se relatively unimportant. Extreme emphasis on the one and denigration of the other is probably wrong in both cases. However, the almost mystical attribution of unique greatness to a particular patch of soil for growing grapes is certainly untenable. It stems in part from efforts, conscious or not, to cripple competition. An advantage is gained if the consumer can be convinced that no one could possibly make an equally good wine without owing a particular piece of real estate. By detailed analysis of a wide range of soil-derived mineral elements, it can be possible to distinguish wines from one area from those from another, especially if rootstock and variety are the same. There is no evidence that a specific constellation of unessential trace minerals has bearing on wine quality. Seguin (1986) found that the great Bordeaux vineyards differed from poorer ones mainly in their ability to moderate the effects of extreme vintage conditions such as long drought or heavy rainfall, and still produce a relatively constant level of alcohol and acid in the wines.

The chemical composition of the soil is important, but generally it is either not limiting or correctable. There are a number of potential deficiencies, excesses, and imbalances in the minerals of the soil and irrigation water from the viticultural viewpoint. For example, boron can be deficient, normal, or present at toxic levels in the soil or irrigation water. Winemakers should be alert for such problems and work with growers to avoid or solve them, but usually the details require the attention of viticultural specialists.

Two exceptions which may cause trouble with winemaking before the grower is aware of vineyard problems are musts with low nitrogen and those with excessive potassium. Lack of enough usable nitrogen for complete yeast fermentation leads to stuck fermentations. The problem is often alleviated by adding ammonium phosphate to the must rather than by improving nitrogen fertility in the vineyard. Since nitrogen fertilization seldom pays off in increased grape yield unless the vineyard is appreciably depleted, not enough usable nitrogen for the yeasts tends to show up in musts from older, nutrient-depleted, unfertilized vineyards, which otherwise may be well managed. The problem can be more severe with some varieties than with others. For example, varieties high in proline can appear adequate from analyses for total nitrogen but not be so because proline nitrogen is not used by yeasts during wine fermentation. Excessive nitrogen fertilization causes other problems related to excessive vine vigor and excessive must arginine. High arginine can lead to increased ethyl carbamate in wines.

The second problem, excess must potassium, can result in wines too high in pH although high in titratable acid. This problem tends to surface in areas planted with grapes for the first time. Since appreciable potassium is removed with the harvested crop, it decreases with time and the problem corrects itself.

Soil factors, besides chemical composition, are of more widespread impact on grape growing. Mostly these relate to water supply for the vine. Shallow soils overlying impenetrable hardpan tend to waterlog owing to poor drainage or dry out too easily because of low capacity. Soil depth of at least 1.5 m is desired. If the impenetrable layer can be broken up by subsoil ripping so that roots and water may penetrate the hardpan layer, the land may be made useful, but the procedures are costly. If the shallow soil is over impermeable rock without usable subsoil, little can be done. Soils good for vineyards should be well drained without a high or fluctuating water table. Unless dormant, grapes do not tolerate "wet feet" and roots soon die without oxygen in waterlogged soil. Sand, gravel, or even coarse rocky material with little visible soil are well drained down to the water table and are often good for vineyards. Poor water retention by such soils may require frequent irrigation. In contrast, heavy, high-sodium clay soils which have a high water capacity, but swell when wet and obstruct further water penetration are a problem for vineyards. Some clay soils may be too dense for root penetration. But, within rather extreme limits, excellent vineyards exist on soils with a wide range of properties and parent materials.

The best soils for growing grapes for premium wines should, then, be well drained, reasonably deep, but not overly fertile. Some organic matter for tilth, friability, and penetrability is generally desirable. Provided that good-quality water (low content of undesirable salts, especially boron and sodium) is available, irrigation can be very useful, if vineyard layout and costs allow and soil infiltration and drainage are good.

It is not clear from these comments that growing grapes in large vineyards under apparently optimum conditions on uniform, alluvial, deep, well-drained soils does not usually lead to the most esteemed premium wines. There are a number of reasons for this. To some extent snobbishness and economics play a role. Large well-managed vineyards in areas propitious for grapes produce relatively high yields and large volumes of wine. Plentiful products seldom command premium prices. If costs of grape production and crop failures are relatively low, winegrowers are willing to compete by lowering prices. With lower prices, income can be maintained only by raising yield or eliminating some costs. Mass-processing and mass-marketing tend to lead to fault-free, more uniform, but sometimes less exciting wines.

Dividing up a large relatively uniform area into small vineyards, each managed by different growers, and the grapes processed by different winemakers, could increase the diversity among wines and interest in them at the expense of economics of scale. Owing to a few inept, small producers, some wines would be bad. This tended to be the situation some years ago in countries where a large amount of inexpensive wines were produced and consumed. Modernization has led to consolidation of growers and wineries in such conditions.

Contrarily, if the vineyards are small for reasons such as hilly terrain with suitable sites interspersed by unsuitable ones, costs tend to remain higher and wines more variable, regardless of expert technology. Increased quality, interest, and diversity can be produced because the grapes are not all the same. The winemaker can produce better wines by blending products from several different vineyards or, if one vineyard does exceptionally well, making its grapes into an extra premium bottling. A large producer tends to find a small amount of exceptional wine a nuisance to keep separate and incorporates it into the general product to raise the average quality. If it changes the average characteristics too much it disorients consumers expecting uniformity and it may be sold to a smaller winery that can make use of its special nature. The producer of premium wine, however, need not be small in total, but needs to keep more lots separate. By vineyard selection and delayed blending, a diverse range of premium-priced products can be produced. The two extremes of plentiful and inexpensive wines versus rarer premium-priced ones are not at odds but rather can be helpful to each other. As viticulture and enology improves, the average quality of standard wines has improved greatly, but the zenith and frequency of exciting premium wines has risen also. A wine-producing country needs for long-term health both good standard and exceptional premium wines as well as interested clientele that enjoy them both.

3. The Growing Season and Environmental Conditions

Grapevines normally are deciduous, dropping their leaves to go dormant in the winter. Their fruiting in the following season is much more tolerant of the lack of a dormant period than that of temperate fruit trees such as peaches. In subtropical and tropical areas with insufficient winter cold to induce dormancy in grapes, withholding of water, severe pruning, and/or leaf removal can synchronize and stimulate budbreak for the next crop. Otherwise fruiting remains sporadic and limited in tropical areas. The buds containing the primordial new clusters are formed the year before they produce their crop. During the time the current crop is growing, fruiting buds for the following year's crop are also being developed.

Starting with a mature, leafless, dormant vine, the buds for this year's crop sprout in early spring already bearing cluster primordia generated the previous summer. Several more or less obvious stages follow: budburst (the first visible green of the new shoot), full bloom (more than 50% of flower caps detached), berry set (stamens falling and enlargement beginning), onset of ripening (veraison), berries ripe (commercial harvest), cane maturation, leaf fall, and renewed dormancy. Probably the best brief recent summary of these changes is by Coombe (1988). Figure 2-1 adapted from his article illustrates this seasonal cycle.

Budburst in 11 varieties over a five-year period varied in date from one to six weeks with a two-week difference being most common. Varieties bursting early are thought to be those with a low temperature threshold. Both a warming trend prolonged for a few weeks as winter departs and higher daily maxima in the later days precede budburst. The most statistical variance in date of budbreak was accounted for among several districts and varieties by mean temperatures after February 1 (August 1 in the Southern Hemisphere) and, to a lesser extent, maximum temperatures during the last 10 days. Since budburst is apparently controlled by spring warming, different grape varieties are relatively similar. Budburst tends to occur in mid-to-late March (mid-to-late September in the Southern Hemisphere). It is obviously desirable, but not always the case, that buds do not begin to open before frost danger is past. That budbreak requires both a fairly prolonged warming trend and, in the later stages, increased temperature maxima indicates nature's adaptation to avoid frost risk and await true spring.

Flowering is even more heavily influenced by weather than is budburst. It is relatively uniform among varieties within a region, although it varies among regions and years. This is attributed to the unifying effect of the onset of spring heat in each region each year. Flowering occurs as mean daily temperature (mean of maximum and minimum) reaches about 18°C. Flowering is usually six to nine weeks (about eight average) after budburst. The flowers of a single cluster ordinarily open in one to three days, but over the whole vine a week or more may be required. Warmer temperatures increase the rate of flowering, but high temperatures, 35°C or more, retard without preventing eventual flowering. Averaged maximum daily temperature, particularly in the period after March 1 (September 1 in the Southern Hemisphere) accounted for more of the variation in flowering date than did the mean, the minimum, or the range in temperature. The flowering date varied only about one week among varieties in any one district and season, but as much as six weeks between districts (Coombe 1988).

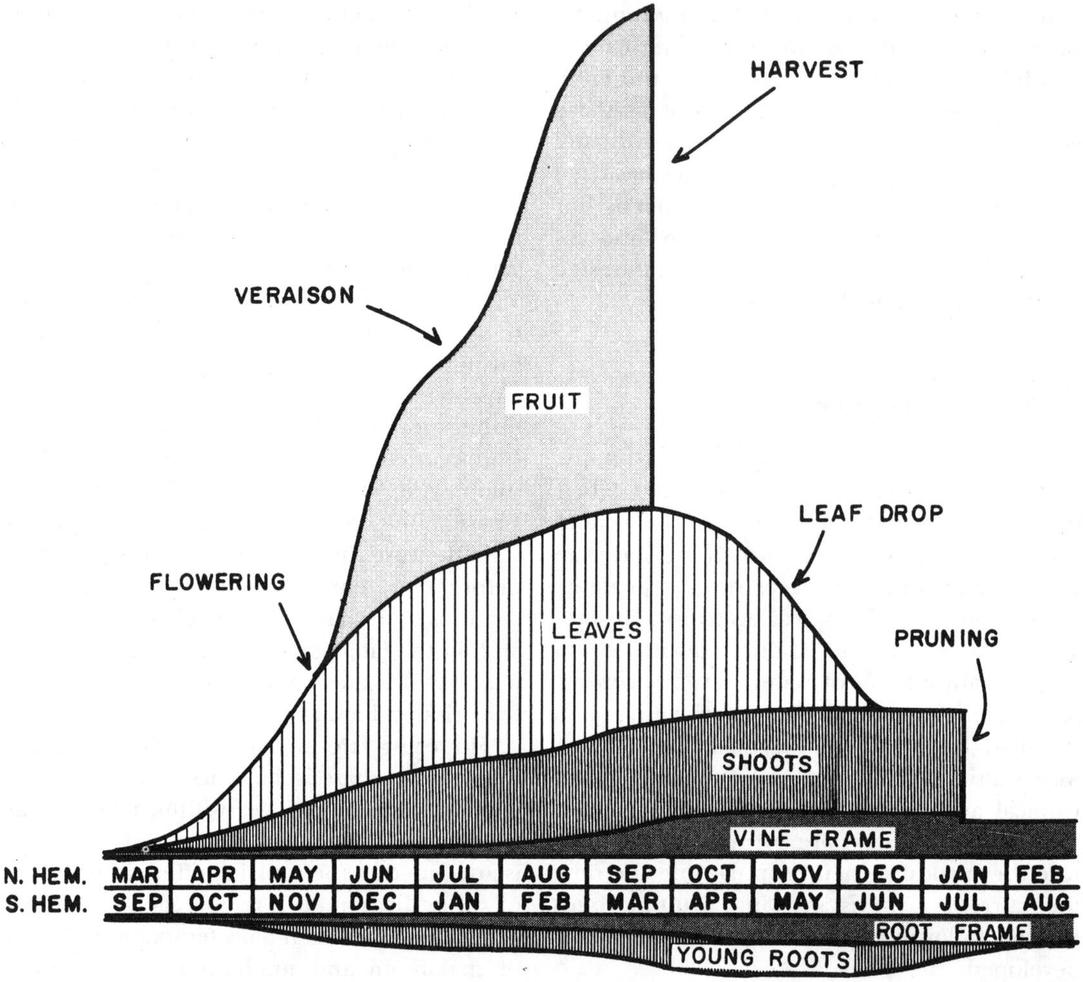

Fig. 2-1. Approximate scheme of annual accumulation and loss of fresh weight of a mature grape vine.

Fruit set is the result of successful pollination. Although insects and wind may have some small role, direct self-pollination appears the rule with modern varieties (Winkler et al. 1974). Actual events following pollination depend on varietal characteristics such as seedlessness, but need not concern us. If an individual flower is not properly pollinated it usually drops away in a week or so. If it persists or if nutritional deficiencies (particularly zinc or boron) prevail, it may remain to become a small, seedless "shot" berry that ripens differently. Some ripen early and some stay hard and green. The latter are useless to the winemaker. The percentage of potential berries that actually set and develop normally is obviously important. Only about one-fifth to one-half of the flower count appears as berries per ripe cluster. Set is considerably influenced by the grape variety involved. Poorer set than normal for the variety or berry drop may be associated with high temperature, especially night temperatures of 33°C or so (Winkler et al. 1974). Water stress, high winds, and cold cloudy conditions also reduce fruit set and retention (Champagnol 1984).

The length of the period between flowering and harvesting of ripe grapes varies considerably among varieties. It may be from 70 to 170 days (Coombe 1988), but 125 days may be considered typical for commercially important wine varieties in typical areas. Nevertheless the weather, particularly the temperature, considerably affects the harvest date for ripe grapes (warmer = earlier) of either a given variety or a group of varieties. As a rule, different varieties tend to maintain their relative progression compared to each other as weather varies from place to place and year to year, but the actual dates of veraison and harvest can vary considerably. However, varieties do respond to environmental regimes somewhat differently, so the relative order of ripening may be reversed in different districts. For examples, in one Australian district Chardonnay and Pinot noir were ripe for harvest on, February 10 and 13 (August 10 and 13, Northern Hemisphere), respectively, with a standard error of only two to three days over seven to ten years (Coombe 1988). Riesling ripened earlier than Shiraz in warm regions but in reverse order in cool regions.

Leaf fall and entrance into dormancy, like flowering, is more set by the general environment as winter arrives and varieties again behave more uniformly. The vine stores more reserves for the next season between harvest and leaf fall. The canes and their buds mature and "harden" so they can better withstand winter cold.

Depending on timing and severity, storms and unseasonal episodes can have great effects. Late spring frosts decrease this year's crop because the fruit-bearing structures are present on the shoots as they emerge. Early fall freezes while the vine is still green kill leaves and immature canes, decrease reserves, and weaken the vines. High-humidity weather during the growing season promotes fungal diseases. Wind can break shoots and scar berries. Rain on nearly ripe berries can cause splitting, as can improperly managed irrigation. Hail at any time outside dormancy can be devastating. Unusually prolonged or severe cold below about -18°C can kill dormant vinifera grapevines. Cold tolerance varies greatly by variety, level of hardening, and vineyard conditions. Viticulture is not recommended if the mean temperature of the coldest month is below -1°C or a freeze of -20°C occurs more than once per 20 years (Jackson and Cherry 1988). This enforces polar limits for commercial growing of vinifera and is affected by altitude above sea level as well as maritime proximity. Viticulture with *V. vinifera* is most successful in areas with moderate temperate climates and predictably uniform seasonal progression as free as possible from severe and untimely storms.

Although temperature is the major and most easily measured factor influencing grapevine seasonal development, other factors can be important, such as length of growing season, sunlight, daylength, and water flux. Slight water stress can hasten fruit development. The lower the stress the longer the cycle in a given variety from budburst to harvest. Plentiful water throughout the season is generally detrimental to wine quality and increases the risk of fall frost damage by keeping the vine green. Daylength and radiation intensity are important and, of course, interact with temperature. High light favors high cluster numbers per vine, high content of anthocyanins and other skin phenols relative to a given sugar content, and decreased shoot elongation. Direct sun combined with temperatures above about 40°C leads to sunburn of exposed berries. If this happens early in the summer, the affected berries remain small and hard; yield is decreased but wine quality should not be lowered. Late in the season the berries are already developed and vineyard yield may not be much affected, but wine quality will be lowered if appreciable sunburn or scald occurs. In addition to possible sunburn, excessively high temperatures can close stomates and inhibit photosynthesis. Other effects related to ripening will be covered later in this chapter.

4. Classification of Regions and Heat Summation

The temperature is so important to grape development that it can be used to predict seasonal and regional differences in grape characteristics. Additional factors such as hours of cloudless sun are related to temperature. In the absence of more complete data, temperature can be useful as a catchall indicator. For example, cloudy weather ordinarily lowers temperature, may raise humidity and certainly lowers insolation. Other influences should not be ignored, however, as improved understanding is sought about location-weather effects on wine grapes in specific areas.

Amerine and Winkler (1944; 1963a, 1963b) divided California into Climatic Regions I through V based upon degree-days above 10°C summed between April 1 and November 1 (October 1 to May 1, Southern Hemisphere). The temperature of 10°C was chosen as that below which grapes are too cold to be significantly active. The typical seasonal degree-day heat summations are calculated from climatic records in the particular area preferably covering at least 10 years. Ordinarily the mean daily temperature is calculated from the maximum and minimum for each day. For example, a five-day period with the daily maximum of 30°C and a minimum of 15°C would contribute $[(30 + 15) \div 2] - 10 = 12.5$°C for each day or a total of 62.5°C degree-days or heat summation units (HSU) toward the seasonal total. These Climatic or Heat Summation Regions are designated as follows: I—below 1390, cool; II—1391 to 1670, moderately cool; III—1671 to 1940, moderately warm; IV—1941 to 2220, warm; V—2221 or more, hot. These numbers are actually conversions from 50°F base HSU of Region I less than 2500, II = 2501 to 3000, III = 3001 to 3500, IV = 3501 to 4000, V = greater than 4000.

It is easily seen that these Climatic Region designations are only a rough approximation and may not extrapolate well outside California. For example, hot vineyards are usually well irrigated in California, but may not be elsewhere. These Climatic Regions are more useful the more uniform the weather year to year. The growing season heat summation calculated this way may be the same, yet the effects on grapevines quite different for an area (or year) that has a short hot season compared to another that has a longer cooler one. The 10°C minimum temperature may not be the best base for all comparisons. An integrated value of hours of warmth per day should be better than the simple maximum temperature for that day (or worse yet, longer periods) in measuring effects on grapevine physiology. No allowance is made for excessive heat. This subject is long overdue for further intensive study.

Nevertheless, these Climatic Regions have been very useful in California for generally characterizing existing and potential new vineyards and recommending varieties for them. Table 2-4 gives some instructive examples (Amerine and Winkler 1963b). Regions I and II are recommended for table wines, IV and V for dessert wines. Region V is not recommended for table wine varieties, but if you must make table wines in Regions IV and V, Colombard and Emerald Riesling may be useful for white and Barbera or Ruby Cabernet for red. This is partly because they retain their acid relatively well in hot weather. Note that early-ripening varieties are particularly to be avoided for hot vineyards unless they retain acid well. Late varieties may ripen in hot vineyards after fall cooling begins. Slowly ripening varieties may not necessarily be excluded from the coolest regions of California, but sufficient total heat summation to produce acceptable ripeness is required. Slow ripening during prolonged, cool autumns often is favorable to wine quality. The coolest commercially successful vineyards in France and Germany, about 940 HSU or degree-days, use only relatively early varieties. On the hot end of this scale, temperate zone areas above about 2500 HSU (10°C basis) have extra problems of sunburning, raisining, acid loss, etc., and are not recommended for wine grapes. They may be suitable for early table grapes.

A number of studies have compared other techniques to improve upon the Region I to V

Table 2-4. Grape varieties for white, red or pink table, and dessert wines with recommended regions for their production. (E = early; M = mid-season; L = late; N = neutral; S = slightly distinctive; D = distinctive; HR = highly recommended; R = recommended; Q = qualified recommendation; blank = not recommended; (w) = white.)

Variety	Production (metric tons/hectare)	Ripens	Flavor	Region				
				I	II	III	IV	V
			WHITE TABLE WINES					
Chardonnay	9–13	E	D.	HR	R			
Chenin blanc	13–22	M-	N +	R	Q	Q		
Colombard	13–22	E +	D-	Q	Q	R	R	Q
Emerald Riesling	13–26	M-	D-			Q	R	Q
Gewürztraminer	9–13	E	D	R	Q			
Muscat blanc	9–13	E	D	Q	R	R		
Pinot blanc	9–13	M-	D-	R	Q	Q		
Sauvignon blanc	9–15	M	D	HR	R	R		
Sémillon	9–13	M	D-	Q	R	R	Q	
Slyvaner	9–13	E	S	Q	R	Q		
White Riesling	9–13	M-	D-	HR	R			
			RED AND PINK TABLE WINES					
Barbera	11–18	E	S		Q	R	R	Q
Cabernet Sauvignon	9–13	L	D	HR	R	Q		
Carignane	18–26	L	S		Q	R	Q	Q
Gamay (Napa)	13–20	L	N +	Q	Q			
Grenache	13 ±	M	N +	Q	R	Q		
Petite Sirah (Durif)	9–18	M	S	Q	R	Q		
Pinot noir	7–9	E	D	R	Q			
Ruby Cabernet	13–18	M	D		Q	R	R	Q
Zinfandel	9–13	M	D	R	Q	Q		
			DESSERT WINE					
Carignane	18–26	L	S-			R	R	R
Grenache	13–26	M	S-			Q	R	R
Grillo (w)	13–22	M-	N			Q	R	R
Malvasia bianca (w)	9–15	M	D			Q	R	R
Mission (pink)	13–26	L	N				Q	R
Muscat of Alexandria(w)	9–22	L	D			Q	Q	R
Orange Muscat (w)	9–20	M	D			Q	R	R
Palomino (w)	13–22	L	N				Q	R
Rubired	13–20	M	S			Q	Q	R
Souzão	9–18	M	S			Q	R	HR
Tinta Madeira	9–18	M-	D-		Q	Q	R	HR
Verdelho (w)	9–13	M-	N +			Q	R	HR

Source: Amerine and Winkler (1963b).

system. Data were tabulated from one warm vineyard over 114 varieties for seven years (McIntyre et al. 1982). Cumulative maximum daily air temperature was the best prediction of the days from budbreak to bloom. Cumulative daily air temperature range (maximum minus minimum) was the best prediction of the bloom to maturity time, and cumulative sunlight irradiation was best for timing of days from budbreak to maturity. Jackson and Cherry (1988) (see also Coombe and Dry (1988), Jackson and Schuster (1987)) reviewed the literature and compared 14 different measures including degree-days calculated from different base temperatures. Daily degree-day summations gave better correlations than monthly with an area's ability to ripen a certain variety of grapes. Base temperature of 10°C distinguished among areas growing cool-climate grape varieties but lower base temperatures were better for warmer areas. A number of the indices were either inadequate or unnecessarily complicated. Degree-days (base 10°C) were improved and then separated more clearly which groups of varieties were more suitable for an area if they were modified by latitude (Northern or Southern) according to the formula DD (60-latitude)/10 = LDD. The LDD (latitude-modified degree-days) was little or no improvement and more cumbersome than LTI (latitude temperature index) calculated from the mean temperature of the warmest month times (60 − latitude) in predicting a district's grape-ripening capacity and suitability for different varieties.

Such calculations are of most help in grasping the typical relationships among widely scattered vineyards and the varieties to be grown. Clearly, more complicated formulas taking into account further factors such as altitude and maritime versus continental variations could be developed. In siting most new vineyards, and particularly one within a reasonable distance from a given winery, latitude will not vary much and mesoclimate factors become more important. They are less subject to calculation, but can be estimated reasonably well by considering the factors indicated and comparing existing vineyards in the vicinity. In certain areas of Europe, the Chasselas variety has been used as a reference against which other varieties are compared and upon which regional differences are based. Similar comparisons using other varieties more appropriate depending on the country are certainly helpful.

E. VINEYARD MANAGEMENT

1. General

Vineyard management is still important after the site is chosen and planted with a given rootstock/scion varietal combination. Of course, distances between vines interact with farming practices and a myriad of details can be important from the training and trellising system through fertilization, irrigation, pest control, cultivation, and pruning. Again, full details cannot be given here and viticultural references should be consulted for additional information. A few aspects, however, seem important to orient prospective winemakers.

2. Overcropping

The dormant vine habitually is pruned to remove canes past production, those poorly placed, and a good portion of next year's potential producers. The manner of pruning can range from meticulous hand-pruning adjusted for each vine according to its age and size to mass hedging and pruning completely by machine. The latter, of course, is much faster and less labor-intensive. There are advocates for both extremes and intermediate combinations in various situations. A major purpose of such pruning is to help control the size of next year's crop. Pruning down to four two-bud spurs per vine might be normal to low; 18 four-bud spurs per vine have been seen after pruning in foreign vineyards noted for overcropping. In a very few varieties (mostly raisin or table grapes) the basal buds are not fruitful and longer canes must be left.

If too many fruitful buds are left, the vine's photosynthetic capacity will be inadequate to ripen all the clusters. This situation is termed *overcropping*. If vines are overcropped, the berries fail to develop normal sugar content by normal harvest dates. Harvest is either significantly delayed, compared to adjacent normally cropped vineyards of the same variety, or the grapes never reach desired sugar levels. Since sugar is the direct product of photosynthesis by the leaves and ripe grapes contain about 200 g/kg, low sugar is the primary signal for overcropping. Other components are affected as well, however, and genuinely overcropped vines produce poor wine not only because the alcohol will be low. Delayed harvest in hot weather leads to flat wines with inadequate acidity. In cool weather retained acid may be adequate, but the wine remains unbalanced. Grape aroma and other constituents appearing late in ripening are likely to be deficient.

Theoretically it should be simple to determine and specify the square centimeters of leaf surface necessary to mature one berry and extrapolate that to larger scale. Although studies to that end have been informative, a number of practical problems complicate the picture. Young leaves can be net consumers of photosynthate, not exporters. Position of a leaf relative to its nearest cluster is a factor. Exposure to sunlight is very important. Freeing vines from viruses and other deleterious factors, improving canopy and fruit exposure to sunlight via better trellises, and control of vine vigor have all contributed to raising the size of crop that can be matured to give excellent wine. Yields per hectare, especially in the best vineyards, have risen in recent decades concomitant with increased average quality of table wines produced.

When true overcropping exists, decreased wine quality results, but it does not follow that lowering the crop below some optimum level further increases quality, although this is sometimes assumed. Agreement and research conclusions upon this point are rather equivocal, but no one, grower, winemaker, or consumer, is well served if crop yield is lowered more than absolutely necessary for high-quality wine (Singleton 1990). It is clear that high-quality wine can be made from relatively high yielding vineyards (allowing for variety, soil, and weather conditions) if that crop is produced on vines which are healthy and appropriately managed. Winemakers should monitor development and ripening and be alert for early indications that optimum cropping is being exceeded. They should also be wary of trying to lower yield below the level giving high-quality wine. Unfortunately, the maximum yield for fully acceptable quality is not a constant, nor perhaps an entirely definable point.

Overcropping occurs at widely different Tm/ha depending upon variety, weather, area, and traditional practices (vines/ha, trellis and training form, etc.). It is therefore not possible to specify yields beyond which overcropping will be the case. Penning-Rowsell (1985) describes the minimum alcohol content and maximum crops permitted for various Bordeaux *appellations contrôlées*. There is a basic maximum but it may be raised in "exceptional years when quality and quantity coincide." All those Bordeaux subregions producing dry table wines, white or red, had a *basic* permitted maximum wine yield up to 1983 of 4.0 to 5.0 kL/ha with a minimum alcohol 10 to 13% depending on subregion. In 1983, a large vintage, the annual permitted maxima were all above the basic level, mostly 5.8 to 6.0 kL/ha. In 1983 the permitted basic maximum was raised substantially, typically 1.5 kL/ha for dry white wines and 0.5 kL/ha for reds. The *basic* maximum in the Haut Medoc, one of the most prestigious red wine areas, was 4.3 kL/ha before 1983 and 4.8 kL/ha in 1983 and after. These figures translate to about 5.8 and 6.5 Tm/ha for Cabernet Sauvignon and related red varieties under Bordeaux conditions. Similar calculations from Bordeaux indicate *basic* permitted maxima from 1983 for *appellation contrôlée* Sauvignon blanc or Sémillon of about 8.8 Tm/ha.

Crop levels can be regulated by means other than cane pruning. Spurs or canes can be pruned long and then a portion of the clusters may be removed after berry set and early development is past. Clipping off whole clusters (cluster thinning) or parts of clusters (berry thinning) are, of course, labor-costly operations and subject to some of the same uncertainties as cane pruning. Clearly it must be done as early as possible to minimize overloading stress on the vine. Special management such as early water stress may keep berry size small and thus lower crop size. This is very difficult to accomplish except on shallow or fast-draining sandy soils in hot areas. At least for red wines, smaller berries give redder and generally better wines (Singleton 1972).

3. Vigor Level

That a robust vine apparently bursting with healthy shoot growth is not desirable for the production of wine grapes is not intuitively obvious. High vegetative growth is counterproductive to desirable fruit production. Excessively fertile soils, excessive fertilization especially with nitrogen fertilizers, strong-feeding and vigor-promoting rootstocks, and the particular scion variety all can contribute to excessive vine vigor. Excessive vigor results in decreased yield and decreased wine quality. This is one reason to be skeptical that the minimum crop gives the best wine as crop load is reduced.

Excessive vigor has become more obvious a problem as viruses and other pests and diseases are eliminated or successfully controlled. Excess vigor is, for this reason and others, more often a problem in newer viticultural areas with modern farming than in old, depleted, and traditionally managed vineyards. Devigorating rootstocks are being sought and other techniques such as topping or green pruning are being used or developed to cope with excessive vigor in specific situations. Control of water and nitrogen can help avoid the problem, and the trellising arrangement is an important factor.

4. Canopy Management

Interacting with both overcropping and vigor management is the arrangement of the leaf canopy of the vines. The training of the vines and the trellising system upon which they are trained can be very important in two major regards: the leaves' exposure to sunlight and the fruits' exposure to light and air. Leaves, as far as possible, should each be directly exposed to the sun and not shaded by each other or other vine or trellis parts. New shoot production as the crop is maturing is undesirable. The concept is fairly obvious as light enables photosynthetic production of sugar, but its full implementation in commercial vineyards is not. Various systems of training and trellising have been developed and improvements are still being made. Training each vine up a stake and heading it at the top has been largely replaced by training cordon arms along support wires. The number and arrangement of further foliage wires has followed many patterns having common objectives of displaying the leaves and fruit as optimally as possible in a given situation.

It is important for the fruit to be exposed to light and air. Direct overhead sunlight is not desirable because it risks sunburning, but fruit buried within the canopy often fails to develop properly, particularly with regard to color. Full fruit exposure by positioning of clusters and basal leaf removal increases the sugar near maturity by nearly 1 Brix (Kliewer and Smart 1988). The acidity may also be reduced proportionally to the additional ripening. Anthocyanin may be doubled comparing full leaf shading to full exposure of the fruit. Far-red light penetrates the canopy better than shorter-wavelength red light and western exposure increased the Brix more than eastern (Reynolds et al. 1986). Berry temperature also can be a factor. Western exposed white grapes were 3 to 5°C warmer every hour of the 24 compared to shaded berries at the end of July in New York. Red grapes are ordinarily warmer than white under the same exposure.

Air circulation is important to minimize fungal attack on the shoots and berries and to facilitate rapid drying if they receive rain. An additional factor in the case of pyrazine family varietal flavors (Cabernet, Sauvignon blanc, et al.) is that the methoxypyrazines are unstable to light evidently even within the fruit (Heymann et al. 1986; Pszczolkowski et al. 1985). Exposure of the fruit to light lowers or removes these herbaceous components of varietal flavors and shading retains them.

5. Application of Sulfur and Other Pesticides

Elemental sulfur as a dust or spray of the wettable powder is frequently applied to grapevines at risk for powdery mildew. Early applications, depending on conditions, sublime away and do not affect harvested fruit. If applied too near harvest, sulfur can appear in the must and then will be converted by yeast fermentation to hydrogen sulfide in the wine. Settling of white musts before fermentation will remove the sulfur in the lees, but the problem is more difficult with red wines. In any case the prevention of the problem is the better goal and is achievable by controlling the applications of dusting sulfur. Downy mildew is unknown or seldom a problem in areas like California with rainless summers, but its control can pose special problems. It has been controlled by use of Bordeaux mixture and other copper-containing materials. We are told that in certain old European vineyards, copper has accumulated to the point of decreasing vine health and yield. Copper salts on the fruit can cause copper-catalyzed oxidation and haze formation in the wine. Control of other diseases and pests is generally quite specific to the area and pest involved and, again, falls beyond the scope of this book.

Other fungicides carried into the fermentation might inhibit yeasts, but with approved applications this does not happen. Everyone is concerned that usage and residues of pesticides are minimal and safe. In this country, as in most others, all pesticides must be specifically approved after extensive evaluation before they may be used legally on wine grapes. Approval for a different crop does not carry over to wine grapes. The timing, level, and manner of application are usually specified as well. It behooves the winemaker to be sure that these laws have been followed. Since laws differ, practices cannot be transferred at will from country to country, a fact of special interest to wine exporters and importers.

F. BERRY COMPOSITION, RIPENING, AND SEASONAL VARIATION

1. Berry Development and Ripening

The winemaker is directly concerned with the ripening of the berries, particularly in the late stages. The period from berry set to veraison (onset of ripening) is less subject to problems such as overcropping, because the tiny berries, although numerous, are less total consumers of photosynthate than they become as ripening and rapid sugar accumulation begins. Nevertheless, considerable growth takes place during this early period. Berry size increases but pulp composition remains relatively constant especially in terms of high acid and low sugar concentration. Initial berry size increase is mostly from cell multiplication followed soon by both cell enlargement and cell multiplication. In the final stages berry enlargement is exclusively from cell enlargement (Staudt et al. 1986).

Two methods are commonly used to estimate the relative contribution of cell division versus cell enlargement: mitosis occurrence and cell volume measurement. Mitotic cells become vanishingly small early in the development of most fruits. The grape is no exception, although it may have a less abrupt and early transition from division to enlargement than some other fruits. Cessation of cell division in the epidermis is probably not as early as in the pulp of the berry. Epidermal cells per berry only increased about 10% in the last 50 days of ripening (Staudt et al. 1986). Cell division and enlargement cease earliest in the seeds, being complete well before veraison. For these reasons the relative proportion of the berry tissues changes. At veraison, and when ripe, representative proportions would be pulp 74, 88%; skins 13, 8%; seeds 13, 4% by fresh weight.

The pericarp tissue (berry pulp between the outer vascular layer by the skin and the seed locules) accounts for a large part of ripe berry volume. The total number of pericarp cells became constant (i.e., multiplication ceased) in Thompson seedless about 25 days after flowering (Harris et al. 1968). The average volume per cell, however, gives a double sigmoid curve as does berry volume or berry weight. Figure 2-2 shows a typical example of this curve. These data are from Tokay, a larger-berry, lower-sugar, table grape, but are

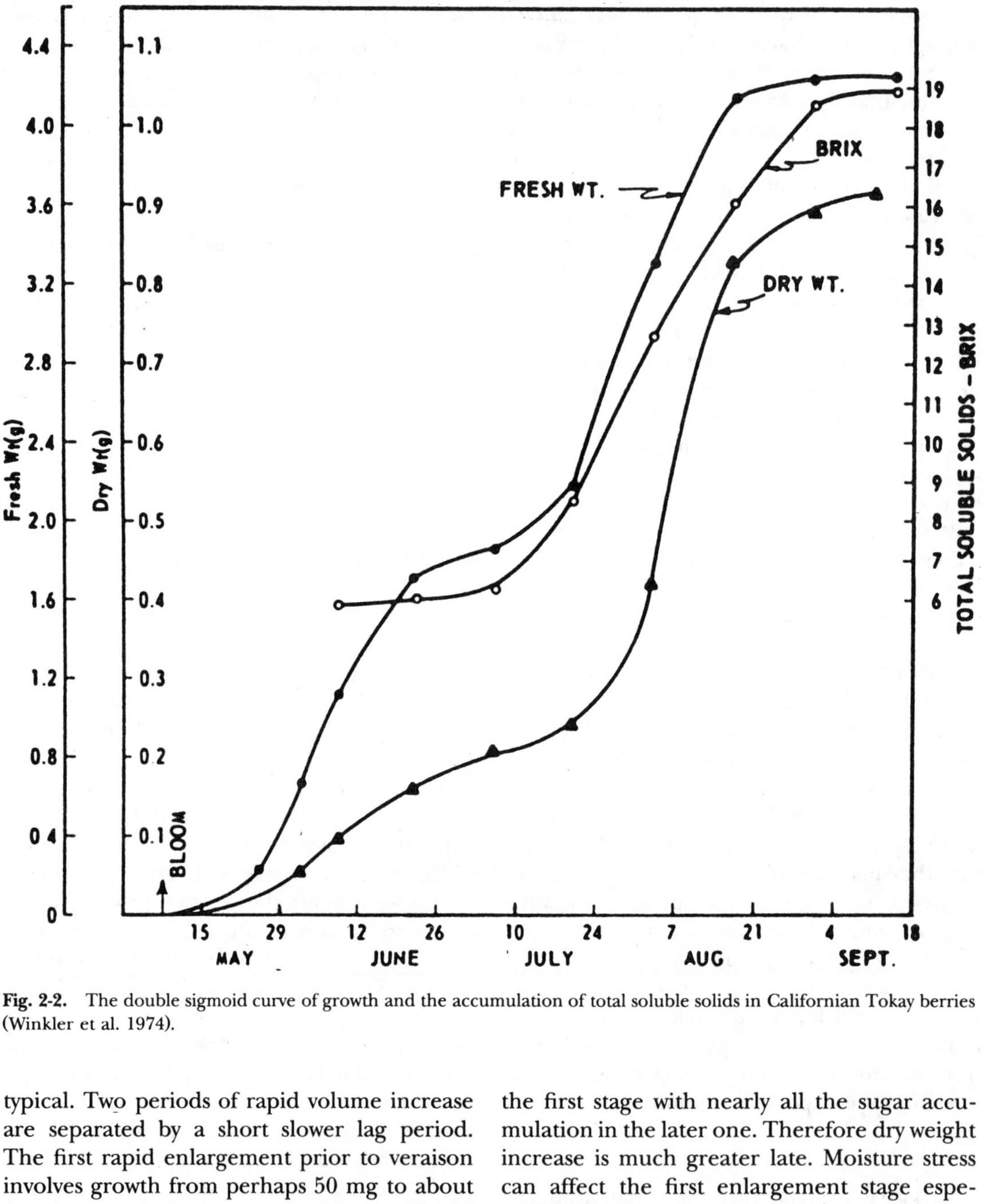

Fig. 2-2. The double sigmoid curve of growth and the accumulation of total soluble solids in Californian Tokay berries (Winkler et al. 1974).

typical. Two periods of rapid volume increase are separated by a short slower lag period. The first rapid enlargement prior to veraison involves growth from perhaps 50 mg to about 1 g for a typical wine grape giving a 20-fold increase. The second rapid growth period produced only another doubling or so, but the amount of increased fresh weight is equivalent to or greater than the whole previous period. Furthermore the moisture content is higher in the first stage with nearly all the sugar accumulation in the later one. Therefore dry weight increase is much greater late. Moisture stress can affect the first enlargement stage especially strongly.

The intermediate lag period marks the transition from growing to ripening (Figure 2-2). Veraison, the onset of ripening, marks the resumption of rapid enlargement and coincides with the beginning of color changes (loss of chlorophyll and production of anthocyanins in red varieties) and sugar accumulation. Veraison is an abrupt change in a berry, but varies a little within a cluster and increasingly over the vine, the vineyard, and the area. Veraison is considered to follow the completion of development of viable seeds. With seed maturity presumably assured (but at a similar stage for seedless varieties), the vine is free to make the berry as attractive as possible for birds and other potential seed dispersers. Desirable ripeness is the culmination of the production of more attractive odors and flavors begun at veraison. High sugar, lower acid, rich color, and full varietal fruitiness are criteria for harvesting the ripe fruit.

At normal fruit maturity, enlargement ceases and physiological accumulation of sugar ceases at about 25 Brix (Singleton et al. 1966a) in wine grapes. Further increase in the Brix of the juice is the result of water loss which decreases berry volume and turgor, eventually leading to raisining. Shriveling of the berries is ordinarily undesirable especially for table wines, since loss or modification of flavor and color are likely. In overcropped berries with inadequate sugar, concentration will occur, but this is a poor way to compensate for overcropping.

A few specialty late-harvested table wines, notably Sauternes from France and Trockenbeerenauslesen from Germany, make use of shriveling to get must sugar content so high that the wines remain sweet after fermentation. In these cases, infection by the so called noble mold, *Botrytis cinerea*, is a required, desirable factor. An appropriate weather cycle of sufficient humidity for infection followed by drying conditions is needed. The *Botrytis* infection makes the berry skin permeable to rapid water loss and dehydration concentrates the sugar to 30% or more. Owing to red color loss via oxidation by the mold's enzyme laccase, the process is not suitable for red wines. Botrytization is a serious problem even at low percentage for red table wines and for any grape if continued high humidity leads to bunch rots of other types rather than dehydration. In the special instances that botrytization is favorable, new and concentrated flavors develop, in addition to increased sugar. Since the mold metabolizes some of the acid, excessive acidity in the wine is prevented and the acidity does not rise as fast as the sugar during the evaporative concentration. One indicator that *Botrytis* has been involved is the production of gluconic acid, which can be found in the must or wine.

2. Climatic Variation

Regional and seasonal climate affect the rate and timing of berry development and ripening in each variety. The same variety grown in a warm vineyard, as compared to a cooler one, is expected to ripen earlier, accumulate more sugar by a given date, have less acid, and have less red color at a given sugar content. Table 2-5 shows data drawn from five vintages of one specific red variety grown in several plots in

Table 2-5. Average composition over five vintages by Climatic Region in California of Petite Sirah grapes and wines.

Climatic harvest		Must			Wine				
Region	Date	Brix	Acid (g/L)	pH	Alcohol (%)	Acid (g/L)	Extract (g/L)	Tannin (mg/L)	Color (arbitrary units)
I	October 7	21.9	7.3	3.35	12.6	6.3	22	2500	679
II	October 3	22.5	6.6	3.41	13.0	5.5	29	2080	697
III	September 21	23.3	6.5	3.48	12.4	5.6	30	2000	645
IV	September 25	23.9	6.2	3.62	12.3	4.6	31	1980	487
V	September 2	22.7	5.7	3.65	11.7	4.8	27	1920	358

Source: Calculated from Amerine and Winkler (1944).

each of the five DD or HSU 10°C Climatic Regions of California. The wines were made and they and the musts were analyzed in one experimental winery by constant techniques thereby minimizing extraneous variability. Nevertheless, vintages did differ considerably, especially in total phenol and color as shown in Table 2-6. In fact these vintage differences statewide were as large or larger than the average HSU 10°C Climatic Region differences. How much of this vintage variation could be related to heat summation for the year falling outside the historical classification for the areas is unclear. The topography and soils did, of course, remain constant. The vintage compositions over all five HSU 10°C Climatic Regions were generally consistent with higher Brix coinciding with lower must acid and higher pH, as expected.

The decrease in total fixed acids during ripening, and especially in hot areas/vintages, is partly the result of respiratory catabolism of these acids by the grape being enhanced by the warmer temperature. L(+)-tartaric acid, the major grape acid, is resistant to such catabolism, whereas the second-most predominant acid, L(−)-malic, is not. Therefore, the ratio of tartaric acid to malic acid of a given variety of grape is increased as ripeness nears in the warmer districts. However, if the harvest is made very early in a warm region or normally in a cool one this difference may not exist. Vintages may differ from expectations in this regard if no hot period occurs during ripening in a normally warm vineyard or such a hot period does occur in a cool region.

Another, and often the more consistent reason for decreased acid concentration during ripening, is enlargement. Total acid by titration is usually about 30 g/kg in the green berries before veraison. If the weight per berry doubled without introduction of more acid, the concentration would fall to 15 g/kg. In fact, in a series of eight varieties, the titratable acid calculated as tartaric was only 3.7 to 7.7 g/ kg fresh weight when considered fully ripe (Kliewer 1965a). The tartrate/malate ratio generally favors tartaric acid early, falls as malic acid rises during the onset and early stages of ripening, and then the ratio rises again in the final stages of ripening. Varieties differ considerably within this general pattern. Acid-retaining varieties doing relatively well in hot climates may lose nearly all their malic acid while retaining tartaric (e.g., Emerald Riesling) or may retain them both in nearly equal proportions (e.g., Colombard) (Kliewer 1965a). Varieties high in malic acid, e.g., Trebbiano or Malbec, are especially likely to go flat in hot vineyards. Such relationships are important to winemakers because of the interactions with malolactic fermentation and tartrate stabilization (Chapters 6 and 8). Several other acids are present, including citric and ascorbic, but only in relatively small portions of the total acidity, generally totaling less than 10%.

A third reason titratable acidity falls during ripening is that grape roots draw in against a

Table 2-6. Variation by vintage in Petite Sirah over all five Climatic Regions (same data as Table 2-5).

	Must			Wine	
Vintage	Brix	Acid (g/L)	pH	Tannin (mg/L)	Color (arb. units)
1936	25.2	5.6	3.95	2800	1281
1937	23.3	6.4	3.54	2260	443
1938	21.0	6.1	3.44	2360	435
1939	23.0	6.7	3.28	1440	417
1940	21.8	7.5	3.37	1620	307
High/low x 100	120%	134%	120%	194%	417%

Source: Calculated from Amerine and Winkler (1944).

gradient certain cations, notably potassium. The roots and plant cells generally excrete protons by an energy-requiring membrane transfer to take these cations into the cells. The pH rises inside the root or cell concerned as does ash (mineral) content and alkalinity of this ash along with the potassium during berry ripening. Part of the tartaric and other acids is thus neutralized, and a larger part as ripening proceeds. Like many other fruits, grapes and wine are relatively low in sodium and high in potassium. Low solubility of potassium bitartrate in wine requires chemical stabilization for permanently precipitate-free wine (see Chapter 8).

Glucose and fructose make up a very high percentage of the total soluble carbohydrates in grape berries. In *Vitis vinifera* sucrose is very low, and seldom is over 10% of the total sugars in other *Vitis* species. Although the total level of sugar is the major criterion for ripeness, all three of these sugars are easily fermented by yeast and the winemaker has little reason to be concerned with their relative content in grapes. The rapid increase of sugar concentration during ripening in spite of further rapid enlargement shows that a great deal of the leaves' photosynthate is being accumulated in the berry. At veraison, glucose is usually higher than fructose. Most varieties have a glucose/fructose ratio near 1.0 at ripeness but lower (more fructose) when overripe (Kliewer 1965a, 1965b).

The prevailing weather affects sugar accumulation, acid loss, and directly or indirectly all other constituents important to eventual wine quality. Selecting the optimum harvesting point can, if harvest season weather permits, do much to compensate for variety-region-weather differences. At proper harvest maturity the desired composition is relatively constant for good wines of a given type and style.

3. Berry Composition

The winemaker obviously is concerned with the composition of the berry at harvest and the variations near harvest that can affect the wine's composition and, therefore, quality. Classes of grape berry components in roughly decreasing order are water and other inorganic substances, carbohydrates, acids, phenols of all types, nitrogen compounds, terpenoids, fats and lipoids, volatile odorants, or other flavorous compounds. In each of these categories and among others not so easily categorized, there usually are very many individual substances. Analytical methods have been improved in many cases and could be in others to the point of detection and quantitation of parts per billion (ppb) or less. One p.p.b. is equivalent to 1 mg per kL or in more readily comprehended terms about 4 cm in the distance from San Francisco to New York, or 3 cm out of the London to Moscow distance or one heartbeat in the life of a 25-year-old person. Obviously, at some minimum the presence of a component or a contaminant becomes unimportant.

New compounds in grapes continue to be reported and added to the several hundred already identified. Again, grapes often differ by variety and source. Therefore, it does not appear particularly useful to attempt to tabulate in detail all the known components of a typical grape or wine. Rough estimates of general analyses by classes are given in Table 2-7. Some possible components can be important in trace amounts for particular reasons or under peculiar circumstances (biotin as a yeast growth factor or pesticide residues for regulation, for example).

Another problem is the distribution of particular components within the grape. Even major components are not uniformly distributed. For example, the most easily expressed juice usually comes from the outer flesh or mesocarp. It is usually nearly 1 Brix higher in sugar and often half the acidity compared to the juice from nearer the seeds produced by firmer but still moderate pressure. Grinding or hard pressing yields higher pH, higher potassium, higher nitrogen, and, unless some shriveled or raisined berries are present, lower sugar compared to the more easily expressed juice. Some

Table 2-7. Rough estimates of the typical percentages by weight of components of wine grapes at harvest, in juice and in wines.

Class of compound	Berries	Juice	Dry Table Wines	
			From juice	Pomace fermented
Water	74	76	86	85
Inorganic salts	0.5	0.4	0.2	0.2
Carbohydrates	24	23	3	4
Alcohols	0	0	10	10
Acids	0.6	0.7	0.7	0.6
Phenols	0.2	0.01	0.01	0.1
Nitrogenous compounds	0.2	0.1	0.1	0.05
Lipids	0.2	0.01	0.01	0.02
Terpenoids	0.02	0.01	0.01	0.015
Other volatiles	0.01	0.01	0.1	0.1
Miscellaneous	0.1	0.01	0.5	0.1
Total	100	100	100	100

components are confined to or much enhanced in seeds, skins, or stems and are particularly variable in must or wine, depending on the sampling and processing involved. Grape skins, for example, are ordinarily the sole source of anthocyanins. Pressure alone at a commercially practical level does not release much red color from fresh skins, but after heating to about 70°C or greater or with alcohol as in fermentation the anthocyanins readily leach into the pressable fluid.

Ignoring the possibility of leaves or other contaminants in commercially harvested grapes, the fresh weight of typical wine grape clusters are made up of about 3% (2 to 8%) stems, 15% (5 to 20%) skins, 4% (0 to 6%) seeds, with the flesh/pulp/juice accounting for the remaining 78% (74 to 90%). Small-berried varieties have proportionately less flesh and more skins. Berry size increases with seeds per berry (minimum zero, maximum four) considerably more than just the added weight of each seed within a specific varietal harvest. Of course, varieties and harvests having small berries and average seed numbers approaching four have the highest percentage of fresh weight as seed. These figures become important to wines made by fermenting, and thereby extracting, these relatively solid tissues along with the juice. For example, only about 10% of the total phenols of the berry are present in the juice whereas about 30% is in the skins and 60% in the seeds of seeded varieties. About half of the total extractable phenol of the berries appears in red wines.

a. *Water and Minerals*

Traces of almost any leachable component of the soil can be found in grapes, but not in the same ratios—some are favored and some are excluded by grape roots. Grapes require the same minerals all plants need. Potassium is by far the major cation taken up followed by magnesium and calcium. Major inorganic anions are nitrate and phosphate. These plus sulfur, iron, and certain trace minerals are all needed in varying amounts as vine nutrients. Total ash content of ripe juice is of the order of 2 to 6 g/kg.

The mature grape vine via its very deep root system is reasonably tolerant of dry conditions. Mild water stress as harvest approaches speeds sugar accumulation by slowing vine growth, and is generally considered good for quality. Nevertheless, the vine's capacity to minimize water needs by restricting berry size, etc., is limited, and the water content of an unshriveled ripe berry is high and relatively constant.

b. *Carbohydrates*

Berries contain in their vascular and other tougher tissues some cellulosic polymers. These are insoluble and do not appear in juice or wine. Pectins are sizable polymers of galacturonic acid and its methyl ester with a small proportion of other sugar units. Total pectin per berry approximately doubled after veraison but, since berry enlargement was greater, dropped in concentration (Silacci and Morrison 1990). A majority of the pectin is bound to the cell wall, presumably via calcium linkages since it can be freed by a chelator. Water-soluble free pectin increased during ripening and was higher in a warmer climate vineyard. The total of pectic polysaccharides at ripeness was about 0.75% of the fresh weight of Cabernet Sauvignon berries and those that were water-soluble made up a little less than one-tenth of that concentration.

Glucose plus fructose are by far the greatest portion of total soluble solids in the grape or its juice. Sucrose is low in grapes, especially *Vitis vinifera*, and is readily hydrolyzed to glucose plus fructose. As a consequence, Brix (by definition g of sucrose/100 g solution), properly determined in juice by densitometry or refractometry, is often considered a sugar concentration measure. It is important to remember that other sugars, acids, and other soluble solids are present and may contribute to mouth feel, but the unfermented, nonvolatile extract in dry wines is only of the order of 2 Brix when the must Brix was 22 Brix. One would expect about 100 g/kg (110 g/L) each of glucose and fructose in that must.

Fructose especially and glucose as well are sweet and contribute this feature to juice and, if still present, to wine. Several other sugars have been identified from grapes and/or are known to be present owing to biosynthetic considerations. Arabinose, rhamnose, ribose, xylose, fucose, maltose, mannose, melibiose, raffinose, and stachyose may be mentioned. Yeast may modify these or contribute others to wine. Some carbohydrate derivatives are produced by molds (such as gluconic and glucuronic acids) or by pectinases (such as galacturonic acid). These are also carboxy acids, of course, and thus confuse classification. Similarly anthocyanins and certain other phenols and terpenes occur in grapes as glycosides, malvidin-3-glucoside for example, and also muddle easy categorization. For the most part the winemaker can focus on glucose and fructose and ignore other carbohydrates as such except in special cases such as pentoses, unfermentable by yeasts, or anthocyanin-3,5-diglucosides as indicators of nonvinifera parentage.

c. Alcohols

Ethanol is nearly absent in musts prior to fermentation unless carbonic maceration of the grapes has been practiced (see Chapter 5). This is true of most other alcohols. Traces of inositol or glycerol are present in grapes. Methanol in parts per million is found in musts or wine from hydrolysis of pectin methyl galacturonate.

d. Acids

Free acids and the resultant low (3.1 to 3.5) pH are the causes of tart flavor; and also help keep the microbiological and chemical reactions properly controlled. Small amounts of many acids occur in grapes or their products. Many, such as amino acids or fatty acids, are considered in other categories and contribute little to the total titration value of wines. In addition to the major acids mentioned earlier (tartaric and malic) small amounts of citric, isocitric, aconitic, glutaric, fumaric, pyrrolidone carboxylic, 2-ketoglutaric, and shikimic acids may also be found in musts. Caftaric (caffeoyl tartaric) acid and its relatives are the major phenols of fresh juice. Additional acids, notably lactic and succinic, are found in wine. Acetic acid is high in wines turning to vinegar, and propionic or butyric acids may also be found in spoiled grapes or wines.

e. Phenols

Phenolic substances are very important to grape and wine characteristics and quality. Collectively they include the red pigments, the brown-forming substrates, the astringent flavors, and the known bitter substances of grapes and wine. Some of them are easily oxidized and participate in further reactions. At least three entire books have been written about this important, diverse, and complicated group of compounds from grapes (Durmishidze 1955; Singleton and Esau 1969; Paronetto 1977). The qualitative mixture of particular phenols is genetically controlled and grape varieties differ both qualitatively and quantitatively over a considerable range. Vintage differences or location differences with a specific variety also can be quantitatively large.

To simplify considerably, the major groups of phenols the winemaker need be particularly concerned about in the grape are the phenolic acids, the flavonoids, and the tannin polymers. Beware that in older or less critical literature they may be all lumped as tannins. Each group differs in berry location and sensory or reactivity contributions.

The two major subgroups of the phenolic acids are the hydroxycinnamates and the hydroxybenzoates. The important hydroxycinnamates in grapes are derivatives of caffeic, *p*-coumaric, and ferulic acids. They occur primarily in the easily expressed juice and are about the same (within varietal variation) in red or white wines. Their actual form in the grape is as esters on tartaric acid—caftaric, coutaric, and fertaric acids (Figure 2-3). Although subject to considerable varietal variation, the typical juice content in *Vitis vinifera*, if all oxidative and hydrolytic losses are prevented, is respectively about 150, 20, and 1 mg/L (Singleton et al. 1986a). About 20% of its total is usually in the *cis* form for coutaric and only about 2% for caftaric acid.

Postharvest hydrolysis, especially by pectin esterase, frees at least part of the hydroxycinnamates of grapes from their tartrate portion. Thus, the three original compounds with their respective hydrolysis products and *cis*-trans iso-

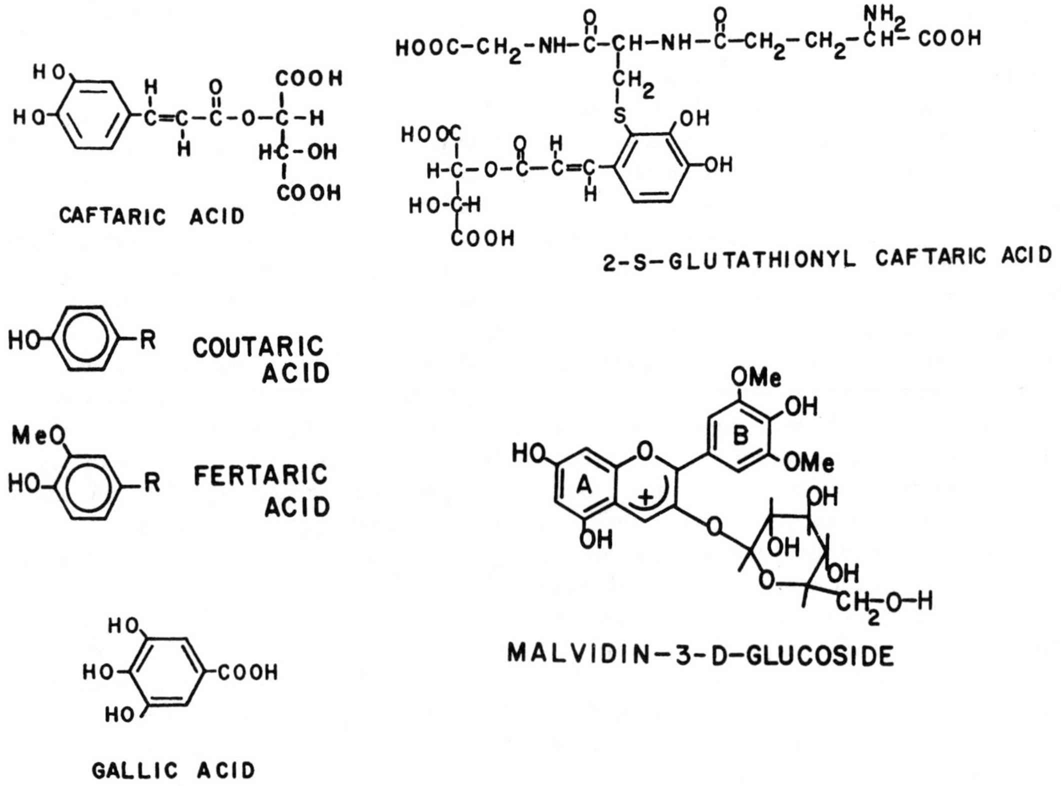

Fig. 2-3. Structures of representative phenols of grapes.

mers total 12 phenolic substances capable of giving different HPLC (high performance liquid chromatography) peaks. There are additional bound forms of these acids in grapes, for example *p*-coumarate and caffeate acyl groups on anthocyanin sugars. Caftaric and coutaric acids give the same quinone when oxidized by polyphenoloxidase (PPO). This and other quinones from the vicinal diphenols of grapes react rapidly with sulfhydryl derivatives. In grapes the first product is ordinarily 2-S-glutathionyl caftaric acid (Figure 2-3). While this product does not occur in undamaged grapes, its formation is so rapid that extreme care must be taken in preparing samples to be sure they reflect the grape's original content. Losses, reactions, and color changes (golden through amber) in musts and wines depend upon original caftaric-coutaric acid content, exposure to air, PPO content and activity, other phenolic substrates, pH, and glutathione (or other reactant) content.

Individual *V. vinifera* varietal samples vary in all these components. Caftaric acid ranged from 16 mg/L in Calmeria to 435 mg/L in Carnelian; coutaric from a trace in Calmeria and 4 mg/L in Gewürztraminer and Thompson Seedless to 53 mg/L in Emerald Riesling (Singleton et al. 1986a). Other *Vitis* species varied even more widely with *V. rotundifolia* lacking these specific compounds, commercial varieties derived from *V. labrusca* averaging about 100 mg/L higher than *V. vinifera*, and *V. aestivalis* the highest at 1350 mg/L caftaric and 340 mg/L total coutaric acid. Within a given variety these compounds increase over the ripening period on a per berry basis showing net biosynthesis (Singleton et al. 1986b). This synthesis is usually adequate to maintain the concentration nearly constant if all oxidation is prevented in sampling (Table 2-8). In the typical commercial situation with pH increase, etc., the residual must sample concentration decreases with ripening.

The hydroxycinnamates are important to the winemaker as the essentially irreducible minimum phenols of all musts and wines and as a preferred PPO substrate leading at least initially to desirable golden colors for white wines. They are in most wines, at least those not subjected to appreciable barrel extraction, the major phenols that are not flavonoids. The hydroxybenzoic acids and other smaller phenols are primarily degradation products and most only appear, then in small amounts, with mold action or wine aging. The most important is gallic acid (Figure 2-3). Ordinarily low in fresh juice (1–2 mg/L) gallic acid increases with pomace contact yet was very low in grape skins of four white varieties over two seasons (Singleton and Trousdale 1983). These and other data indicate that hydrolysis of (-)-epi-

Table 2-8. Colombard grapes, caftaric and coutaric acid content as affected by ripeness

		Caftaric Acid			Coutaric Acid		
		μg/ml			μg/ml		
Juice Brix	Berry weight g	trans	cis	μg/berry trans	trans	cis	μg/berry trans
12.8	1.60	95	Trace	141	13	2.8	19
13.4	1.57	98	Trace	143	12	2.4	18
14.2	1.64	94	1.1	142	11	2.2	17
15.4	1.68	96	1.4	148	13	2.7	21
16.2	1.64	94	0.9	141	12	2.4	19
17.2	1.63	95	1.3	142	13	2.5	19
18.3	1.79	93	1.6	152	13	3.5	21
19.0	1.77	97	2.2	156	14	4.3	23
19.8	1.79	97	2.5	157	15	4.1	24

Source: Singleton et al. (1986b).

catechin gallate is probably a major source of gallic acid. This gallate ester is found in seeds and decreases as grapes ripen (Singleton et al. 1966b; Su and Singleton 1969).

The flavonoids make up a very large fraction, 85% or so, of the total phenols of the usual seeded grape berry. As a group they are very low in juice, quite high in seeds, and generally high in skins but variable by variety. The skins have, except for red juice varieties, all the anthocyanins of the grape. They have some but variable portions of the flavan-3-ols (catechins) and most if not all of the small amount of flavonol and flavanonol glycosides. The seeds have the rest of the monomeric catechins and a large portion of the berry's dimeric and larger catechin polymers. The latter are the condensed or nonhydrolyzable tannins of the grape. Gallates esterified to (-)-epicatechin, (-)-gallocatechin, their polymers and possibly other units in that series might be confused with gallotannins or ellagitannins, but these latter truly hydrolyzable tannins are believed absent in *V. vinifera* grapes. They are found in aged wine from barrel extracts.

The anthocyanins of vinifera varieties are found as 3-glucosides of all nature's most common anthocyanidins except pelargonidin, i.e., cyanidin, peonidin, delphinidin, petunidin, and malvidin. Malvidin-3-glucoside, at least in most of the dark red wine varieties, is the major anthocyanin representing usually 40% or more and it apparently makes up a majority of those red pigments that are acylated. The acylated pigments of the grape have acetate, *p*-coumarate, caffeate, and perhaps other acids esterified to carbon six of the sugar. In most nonvinifera varieties anthocyanin-3,5-diglucosides also occur. Most redjuice dyer (see Glossary) varieties including Rubired and Alicante Bouschet have *Vitis rupestris* parentage and 3,5-diglucoside pigments. Some countries, notably Germany, do not allow growing of fruiting varieties with nonvinifera parentage and exclude wine importations having this feature. There is nothing wrong with such grapes or wines, but they have been proscribed in connection with local control of the insect pest phylloxera. The thinking appears to be since our growers are forbidden to grow nonvinifera varieties, we will not permit importation of wines from such varieties. Presence of 3,5-diglucoside anthocyanins is the identifier used for red non-vinifera.

Red grape varieties can generally be distinguished from one another or at least divided into groups by their specific ratios of the different anthocyanins. The chemistry of these compounds is complex with the pH of the medium having a great effect on the color intensity displayed. Copigmentation (color effects related to concentration and association with other noncolored phenols and other substances), reactivity, and polymerization affect analyses and apparent content. For our purposes here it is most useful to consider anthocyanins as a group. Calculated as malvidin-3-glucoside (Figure 2-3), the total amount of pigment in berries of a dark red wine variety such as Cabernet Sauvignon is of the order of 1000 mg/kg fresh weight. It may be as high as 5000 mg/kg for a dyer (red juice variety) like Alicante Bouschet. Lighter varieties, especially if a hot growing season prevails, have a fraction of Cabernet's value down to perhaps 10 mg/kg for pink varieties and, of course, zero for white.

Veraison, the onset of ripening, is easiest to note in red varieties as the point at which anthocyanin accumulation begins in each berry. Seed flavonoids are high early and generally do not change greatly in total amount during ripening. The other flavonoids of skins, anthocyanins, and along with them the berry's total phenol content increase on a per berry basis until the sugar content is fairly well developed (Singleton 1966). In the last month or so of ripening the total per berry tends to be fairly constant and then may fall with high ripeness. On the other hand, since the seeds are high in phenol and mature early, the juice is low and fairly constant in content, and berry enlargement great, the concentration of total extractable phenol as a portion of the fresh weight in a typical variety falls from perhaps 5 g/kg or so at veraison to 3 to 4 g/kg calculated as gallic acid when fully ripe.

The flavan-3-ols (catechins) are the most important monomeric flavonoids and by far the most prevalent of this group are (+)-catechin and (-)-epicatechin (Figure 2-3). Although high in the seeds and usually in roughly equal amounts, they are also found in the skins but in varietally variable amounts (Singleton and Esau 1969; Singleton and Trousdale 1983). Total content in the berry of ripe, seeded *V. vinifera* wine varieties is of the order of 500 mg/kg fresh weight for each of these two catechins with much smaller amounts of gallocatechins and epicatechin gallates. The flavan-3-ols are not found as glycosides, methoxylated derivatives, or, except for gallates, acylated forms. They occur free (or as dimers and polymers which we will consider as tannins).

Catechins contain two chiral centers or asymmetrically substituted carbon atoms and therefore can have four isomers for each group (catechins or gallocatechins, Figure 2-4). The asymmetric carbon two is set by biosynthetic considerations in the Rectus form, whereas both carbon three isomers, R and S, exist in grapes giving (+)-catechin and (-)-epicatechin (and not all catechin or ± catechin as is sometimes erroneously stated). The same con-

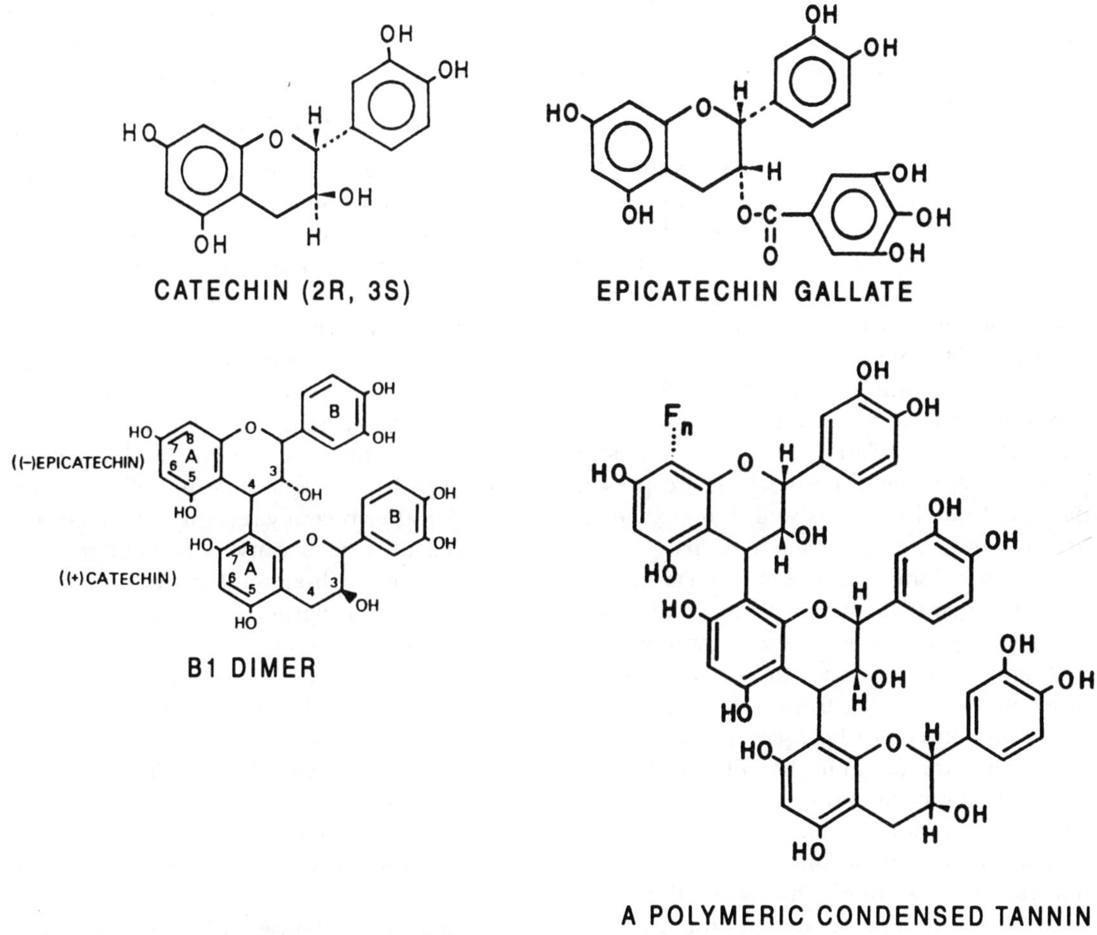

Fig. 2-4. Structures of representative flavan-3-ols of grapes.

dition prevails in the gallocatechin series. This is true in tea and plants in general although isomerization at both centers is possible. Any one isomer can give all four, if fully isomerized. This does not seem to occur with wines under usual processing or aging. (+)-Catechin and (-)-epicatechin have different rates of reactivity in certain situations and therefore should not be considered equivalent.

The catechins are dimerized in the grape and all four possible isomers four-six linked between catechin and epicatechin occur (Lea et al. 1979). In the sense that these dimers easily precipitate with added gelatin and the monomers do not, they are tannins. The formation of trimers, tetramers, and larger tannins apparently proceeds similarly in grape seeds producing all possible isomers but not necessarily in equal proportions. Consider that the four-eight carbon linkage produces a new chiral center at carbon four and thus doubles the possible isomers. That, plus other linkages such as four-six and different order and proportions of catechin, epicatechin, and some gallocatechins and gallates make the polymeric group potentially very diverse. They all are astringent, bitter, and precipitate with proteins. The molecular weight of these tannins appears to be about 4000 and less or roughly decameric maximum. They are called procyanidins because when appropriately treated with acid and oxidation they yield cyanidin. To the extent that gallocatechins are present they yield delphinidin as well, but that seems usually very small with grape tannins.

Because of their important effects in wine and on its characteristics the winemaker should be very concerned with these tannins. The total amount in seeded wine grapes is of the order of 1000 mg/kg fresh weight. Seeds are the main source of these compounds in the berry. They are absent in the juice of commercial vinifera varieties and variably low in skins. Stems contain tannins, but tend to be difficult to control in winemaking and to yield off-flavors. From a viticultural view the winemaker's concerns center mostly on the varietal differences, but there are considerable differences by region and year. In general, providing the grapes get ripe, cooler conditions give more tannins as well as more anthocyanins. Too little red color in grapes from hot climate vineyards is compounded in the wines by too little tannin (Singleton and Trousdale 1992).

If one tabulates all the individual phenols which have been identified in grapes it is a substantial list. Compounded by changes wrought during must preparation, fermentation, processing, and aging, several hundred different specific phenolic substances may be present in aged red wines. Their characteristics, reactivity, and sensory contributions vary tremendously by class and even individually. Owing to their rather high amount and wide range of properties, they are considered the most important compounds in differentiating grapes and wines of different types.

f. Nitrogenous Substances

Ammonium salts, amino acids and peptides, proteins, and nucleic acid derivatives are the major nitrogen-containing components of grapes. Minor amounts of others may be present and important in some contexts, e.g., pyrazines in Cabernet or Sauvignon blanc aromas. From the winemaker's viewpoint the grape's nitrogen compounds are important as nutrients for the yeast's fermentation, as enzymes such as phenolase (PPO), and as factors involved in haze formation especially in white wines. Another recently recognized concern is with urea in wine because with heat or time urea combines with ethanol to yield urethane. While this is primarily a wine fermentation and processing matter (because urea is not present in grapes), the amount produced during fermentation depends partly upon the arginine content of the must. Arginine is higher if grapes have plentiful nitrogen and this is also true of other free amino acids. Arginine can be the highest amino acid in must and usually is in other vine parts (Kliewer 1967).

Peynaud and Maurié (1953) showed that the total nitrogen content increased during ripening in Bordeaux during August 25 to October 8 from 1.00 mg/berry to 1.27 mg/berry for Cabernet Sauvignon, 1.07 to 1.51 for Merlot, 0.95 to 1.93 for Sauvignon blanc, and 0.97 to 1.59 mg/berry for Sémillon. During the same period the berry weight increased, respectively, 216, 182, 184, and 193%, and thus the concentration of total nitrogen per kg fresh weight decreased in all but the Sauvignon blanc. The total nitrogen per berry in the seeds was relatively high with a slight intermediate maximum, whereas that in skins and pulp or juice increased during this ripening period. Table 2-9 gives the relative distribution of the total nitrogen on October 1 which had the highest sugars. The relatively high percentage of the total nitrogen in the skins and seeds is probably a reason pomace-fermented wines more rarely stick for lack of yeast nutrients than do juice wines. Some of this nitrogen is usable by the yeast, but a relatively large proportion, compared to juice, must be in polymeric and less soluble forms including proteins and nucleic acids. Much of this material is not extracted or precipitates and is carried away in discarded pomace and lees rather than appearing in the wine.

Juice contains from 0 to 150 mg/L of nitrogen as ammonium salts (Cordonnier 1966). Ammonium content depends upon nitrogen availability to the vine and is rapidly used by yeast. The majority of the proteins that can cause haze in white wines come from the grapes and at least part survives fermentation. The usual wine yeasts are not very good at hydrolyzing and using polypeptides or proteins. Most of the nucleic acid fragments found in wine apparently arise not from the grapes but from the yeasts. About 23 mg/L of one wine's nitrogen was from nucleic acid fragments (Tercelj 1965) and the content is typically low. Using the usual conversion factor, if 1 g N/kg fresh weight were all protein (of course it is not) the maximum total protein would be 6.25 g/kg fresh weight. Murphey et al. (1989) found 70 to 120 mg/L of protein in juice of Gewürztraminer and Riesling increasing with increasing pH in the 2.9 to 3.6 range. No soluble protein was detected in juice before veraison, but it accumulated afterward in parallel with sugar.

Table 2-10 (from data of Peynaud and Maurié 1953) indicates about 300 mg/L of total nitrogen in juice. Other studies report 200 to 2000 mg/L or so in all forms in musts (Ough 1968). Protein at about 280 mg/L is indicated in Table 2-10. About 100 mg N/L as polypeptides should mean about 625 mg/L of the peptides themselves and one would expect total amino acids to be of the same order of magnitude. Cantagrel et al. (1982) report values for mg of amino acids/L of must to cover a two- to sixfold range in any one variety and average from 400 mg/L for Grenache to 2.15 g/L for Pinot noir. In view of such variation one must beware of generalizations.

A large fraction of the amino acids of juice ordinarily is proline. Ough (1968); and Ough and Stashak (1974) reported proline was appreciable in all cluster tissues, although low in stems. Of the whole cluster's proline 52 to 76% was in the juice from five varieties. Proline nitrogen accounted for 8 to 30% of the

Table 2-9. Distribution of total nitrogen in ripe berries of four varieties (Peynaud and Maurié 1953).

Variety	Sugar %	Total N mg/kg fresh weight	% of Total N		
			Seeds	Skins	Pulp
Cabernet Sauvignon	21.2	977	42	43	16
Merlot	22.4	981	49	33	18
Sauvignon blanc	22.2	1291	25	54	22
Sémillon	18.0	849	26	51	23

Table 2-10. Distribution of total nitrogen in ripe juice of four varieties (Peynaud and Maurié 1953).

Variety	Total N (mg/L)	% of Total N			
		NH_4	Amino N	Polypeptide	Protein
Cabernet Sauvignon	257	19	31	37	13
Merlot	285	28	29	28	15
Sauvignon blanc	460	17	39	37	8
Sémillon	282	24	39	19	18

total juice nitrogen and the percentage increased during ripening while ammonium salts fell. The range of proline content was 304 to 4850 mg/L of juice and the mean was 742 mg/L for 78 samples involving several varieties. A Malbec sample was the highest in total nitrogen (2160 mg/L) and proline (1660 mg/L) but Ruby Cabernet was highest in the percentage of nitrogen in the proline fraction and second highest in proline, 1190 mg/L. Chardonnay and Cabernet Sauvignon average high in proline while Riesling and Sauvignon blanc are low. Among 20 amino acids usually found in musts, proline was almost always the highest one and frequently half of the total (Huang and Ough 1989; Usseglio-Tomasett and Bosia 1990). Only 10% or so of the proline was in peptides. Some other amino acids, e.g., glutamic acid, had a larger portion in the peptides. The second most abundant amino acid was present usually of the order of one-fourth of the proline content. It varied by grape variety and was arginine with Cabernet Sauvignon, Barbera and Riesling, serine derivatives with Cortese, and alanine with Nebbiolo. The amount and distribution of the various amino acids were considerably affected by variety, vineyard, and rootstock (Huang and Ough 1989).

Most of these amino acids are readily utilized by yeasts and their content drops or disappears with fermentation. Proline is an exception (Ingledew et al. 1987). Under usual wine fermentation conditions—anaerobic, high initial sugar—yeasts do not use proline and may excrete some so that the content in the wine is not much lower or even higher than in the juice. Of course, extraction from skins or seeds may raise the value if pomace is fermented with the juice.

g. Lipids and Related Compounds

The extractable fat content in grape seeds is about 10% as an average but can range from about 1 to 20% (Kinsella 1974). Grape seed oil can be a useful byproduct, but has no known direct effect in winemaking. About 90% of the fatty extract is triglycerides with about 75% linoleic and 10% oleic acid. It is a good semidrying, edible oil and has a relatively high vitamin E content.

There is lipoidal material extractable from other berry parts including glycolipids, phospholipids, perhaps free fatty acids, bloom wax on the skin, etc. Gallander and Peng (1980) reported 1.5 to 2.4 g/kg of fresh weight in the flesh and skins. Polar lipids made up more than half of this total with *V. vinifera* and the reverse for *V. labrusca* varieties tested. In the neutral fraction the major fatty acids were palmitic, stearic, arachidic, and behenic acids for all varieties. In the polar fraction, linoleic and linolenic were major contributors for *V. vinifera* and palmitic acid for *V. labrusca*. The total fatty acids released by saponification from flesh and skins was rather similar, 403 to 519 mg/kg berries for one white and three red vinifera varieties (Roufet et al. 1987). The content in the skins was one and one-half to three times that in the seed-free pulp. Although generally reaching maximum content during the final stages, the lipid content was quite variable over the last month of ripening (Barron et al. 1989). The variability did not appear to be random or experimental, but related to an alternating sequence.

Also extracted by lipophilic solvents along with true lipids would be small amounts of carotenes, chlorophylls, and sterols. Fatty acids and sterols can have a role in yeast multiplication. Lipoxygenase action on unsaturated fatty acids produces hexenal and derivatives contributing to grassy odors sometimes noted. Barron and Santa-Maria (1990) have suggested a role for triglycerides as a ripening indicator based on their postulated status as an energy reserve.

h. Terpenoids

Terpenes are metabolites of mevalonic acid characterized by multiples of branched five-carbon units resembling isoprene. Carotenes and sterols have already been mentioned under lipids because they are extractable with fats by solvents such as ether. The group of primary interest to grape growers and winemakers is the monoterpenes and their derivatives.

Monoterpenes are 10-carbon compounds many of which are volatile and odorous. Some such as pinene in turpentine have solvent-like, resinous odors, are hydrocarbons, are not very stable and not always pleasant. Many, such as geraniol and linalool (Figure 2-5), have pleasant floral odors. This group is the important factor in the aroma of the Muscat family of aromatic grapes (Strauss et al. 1986; Rapp 1988).

Renewed studies in recent years have shown the great complexity possible among the terpenoid odorants of grapes. It has also been found that a considerable portion of these compounds occurs in bound forms, particularly glycosides. These bound forms are too large and water soluble to have odors and they do not seem to contribute appreciably to bitterness, but when they are hydrolyzed the odor is released. Furthermore, others including 24 different C_{13} norisoprenoids have been found in varieties outside the Muscat group, Chardonnay for example (Sefton et al. 1989). Examples include vitispirane, 1,2,6-trimethyl-1,2-dihydronaphthalene (TDN), and damascenone (Figure 2-5). These three are present in juice of mainly Riesling largely as precursors that convert to these compounds upon heating (or aging) at up to about 150, 100, 70 μg/L, respectively (Strauss et al. 1987).

In Muscat Alexandria the free and especially the bound terpenes increased about threefold during ripening reaching a total of about 2000 μg/kg fresh weight (Park et al. 1991). This was distributed about 48% in the flesh, 42% in the skins in bound forms, and 6% in the flesh, 4% in the skins in free forms. Although the total amount and distribution of individual terpenes varies, these relationships appear typical.

The distribution and amount of monoterpenes appeared to fluctuate in response to temperature (Park et al. 1991). The bound forms increased even in overripening but the free forms decreased suggesting loss by volatilization. In Gewürztraminer in distinction from Muscat, linalool is low relative to geraniol, nerol, and citronellol (Marais 1987). The total of free monoterpenes in free-run juice was the order of 730 μg/L for Muscat Alexandria, 25 μg/L for Riesling, and 35 μg/L for Bukettraube (Marais 1986; Marais and Van Wyk 1986). Gewürztraminer berries exposed to light had more bound monoterpenes than those partially shaded and they had more than fully shaded ones (Reynolds and Wardle 1989). The total free monoterpenes were relatively constant about 1200 μg/L in their rather cool (British Columbia, Canada) vineyard.

The glycosidically bound forms can be converted to the free odorous form by time, heat, or hydrolysis with glycosidases. Adaptation of this knowledge to winemaking is being extensively studied. The empirical treatments practiced years ago by muscatel makers involving heating of muscat musts with their skins to increase aroma are now seen to have had a sound basis.

i. Volatile Aroma Compounds

In addition to monoterpenes, there are many odorous compounds and their precursors present in grapes. Relatively large amounts of

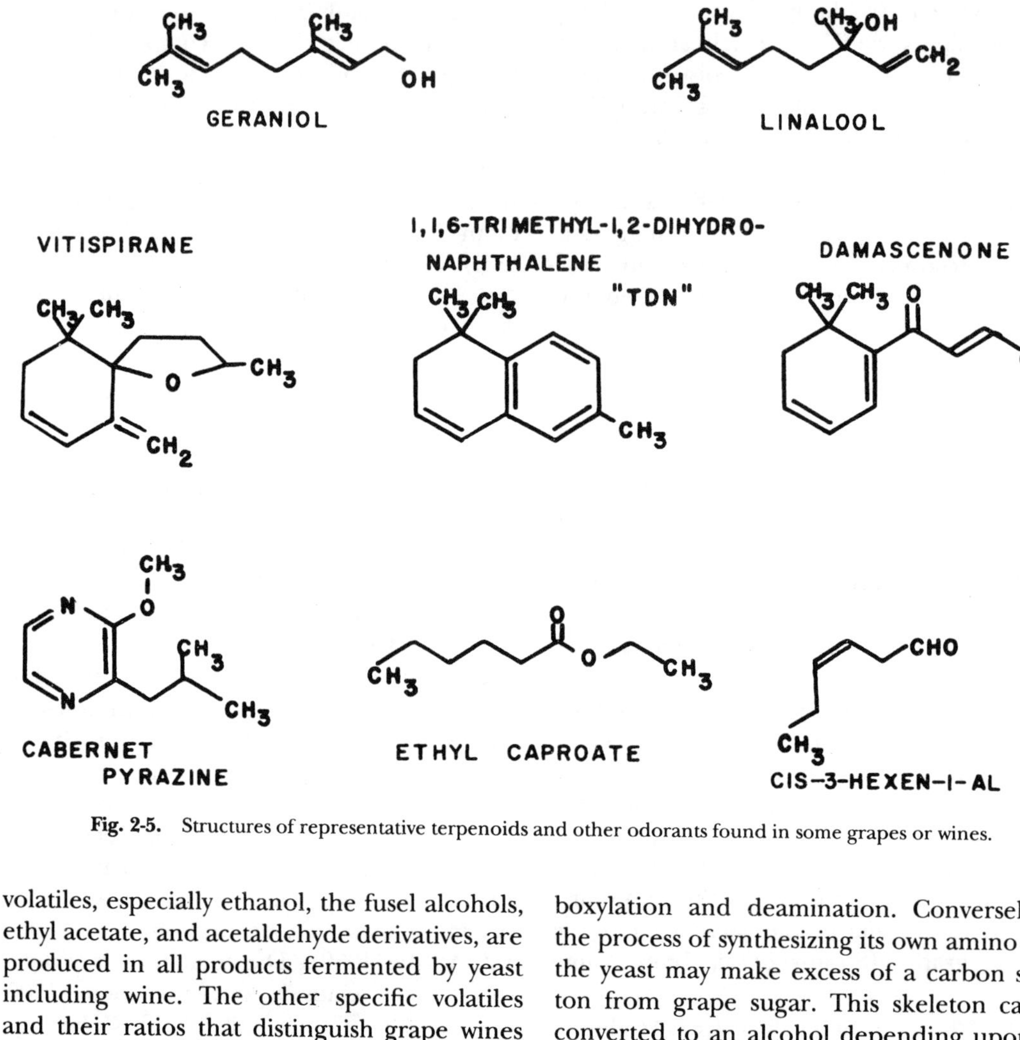

Fig. 2-5. Structures of representative terpenoids and other odorants found in some grapes or wines.

volatiles, especially ethanol, the fusel alcohols, ethyl acetate, and acetaldehyde derivatives, are produced in all products fermented by yeast including wine. The other specific volatiles and their ratios that distinguish grape wines from other beverages and varietal wines from each other obviously depend on grape constituents. The lists of such compounds are very long (Nykänen and Suomalainen 1983).

As far as sinks for photosynthetic carbon, the specific grape aroma compounds are not very significant since their amounts individually and collectively are small. Nevertheless they can be crucial to varietal distinctiveness and wine quality. Even some of the fermentation products can reflect grape composition indirectly. For example, fusel alcohols can be affected by the nitrogen nutrient status. Excess of an amino acid results in its conversion to the fusel-type alcohol resulting from decarboxylation and deamination. Conversely, in the process of synthesizing its own amino acids the yeast may make excess of a carbon skeleton from grape sugar. This skeleton can be converted to an alcohol depending upon the yeast's nitrogen nutrient status, oxidation-reduction conditions, and other factors.

Biosynthesis of these aroma compounds is ordinarily fairly late in ripening. Although new enzymes may be required, some of the aroma compounds appear to be degradation products. They generally reach maximum as sugar accumulation slows and before senescence sets in (Deibner, Mourgues, and Cabibel-Hughes 1965). This is the basis of the known high attractiveness of fruit fully ripened on the vine. Birds recognize it as well as we do and sometimes appear to descend en masse on the vineyard just as we are preparing to harvest. It seems nature's way of encouraging seed dispersal. Since these products are volatile and can be smelled around the ripe fruit, they are being lost. This is thought to be one reason varietal aromas tend to be stronger in fruit ripened in a cooler area.

Not all the odorants are highest at the ripest stage. The clearest example is the pyrazine family. They are ordinarily maximum at veraison, decreasing both in concentration and amount per berry from perhaps 30 to 1 ng/L or less in warmer vineyards in unshaded fruit (Lacey et al. 1991). Destruction of the odorant forms by light is a factor. This particular flavor can be too strong, but some is a part of distinguishable varietal character. The sensory thresholds are of the order of 2 ng/L. A small portion of a Cabernet or Sauvignon blanc vineyard could be managed to give shaded fruit while the majority was exposed to light. The wines made separately would allow the winemaker to adjust the final style by judicious blending. From the above data, inclusion of late-ripening second-crop fruit could affect this herbaceous character greatly in the wine.

The aroma compounds and their ratios are so varied and present in such small amounts that further useful generalizations are difficult. One approach has been to determine the total volatile material. Egorov et al. (1978) found the total volatile oils including alcohols, esters, and terpenes increased in the last month of ripening from 44 mg/kg to 70 mg/kg for Riesling and from 59 to 117 mg/kg for Cabernet. Ester increases were, respectively, 18 to 22, and 27 to 62 mg/kg. The designation volatile and potential contributions to odor in this work might be questioned since, for example, ethyllinoleate was included, but the trend and amounts are illustrative.

j. Miscellaneous Compounds, Vitamins

The study of grapes and wine in a practical way goes back at least 5000 years and a great deal of know-how developed even if the know-why was weak. In the development of modern-type scientific research by Pasteur and others before and after 1856, wine, grapes, and fermentation were foremost among organic, biochemical, and microbiological systems studied. One might incorrectly assume that following this early and intense research, everything is known about grape composition and how it is modified in winemaking. There is great variability among varieties and large differences wrought by development and vineyard conditions as we have pointed out. However, one can be confident that no major portion of the substance of grapes or wine is unknown. Nevertheless important new facts are regularly brought to light.

In order to establish a rational base and contribute most usefully to winemakers, we have done our best to categorize and systematize the topic rather than clutter it up with excessive detail. Discovery continues of further new compounds in the categories discussed above and of new compounds not easily fitting these categories. The ones of most interest are those found to have some specific function or role and not just one more identified compound. Some compounds, even those present in small amount, can prove to have vital actions once they are discovered.

Glutathione, a tripeptide with unusual linkage, is the major soluble compound of grape juice bearing a free sulfhydryl group. Since glutathione occurs in most living things, it was to be expected in grapes, but it was not identified until shown to be part of an oxidation product in musts (Singleton et al. 1985). Other sulfhydryl compounds, including cysteine and even hydrogen sulfide, also react with quinones to form thio ethers and regenerate the colorless *ortho*-dihydroxyphenol (Singleton 1987). Glutathione has important roles in other biochemical systems and should be important in grapes in addition to must-browning inhibition. The amount present in grape leaves is considerably higher than in fruit (Adams and Liyanage 1991). The level in berries was somewhat variable by variety, 17 to 114 mg/kg with an average of 44 mg/kg in 34 varieties (Cheynier et al. 1989).

Another cogent example is the discovery that putresine rises 20-fold or more in grape leaves, whereas spermidine does not rise when potassium is deficient (Adams et al. 1990). The levels are small, about 40 mg/kg for putresine and 90 mg/kg for spermidine in leaves with normal potassium and about half that in ripe fruit flesh. Further research with these polyamines and similar work with other trace components should lead to deeper understanding of grape biochemistry and metabolism, which, in turn, should enable improved farming and winemaking.

Vitamins are biochemically important compounds over and above their role in human nutrition. Fat-soluble vitamins and their precursors, with the exception of E in grape seed oil, are low to absent in grapes or wines. The water-soluble B vitamins generally occur but not at levels sufficient to make these sources especially attractive nutritionally in the human diet. Thiamine is low in stored or SO_2-treated juices or wine.

Ascorbic acid, vitamin C, is typically present at about 100 mg/kg in fresh grapes. This level is about 1/10 that of citrus fruit, but can be important in processing. More may be added to wine later, but for antioxidant not nutritional reasons. In the course of normal processing of grapes, especially if phenolase (PPO) has not been inhibited by sulfur dioxide, most of the ascorbic acid is likely to have been removed by oxidation. As long as it is present in excess, oxidative browning is minimized or prevented.

G. SELECTION OF STATE OF RIPENESS FOR HARVEST AND HARVESTING

1. General

The culmination of the vintage is sealed at the moment of harvest, at least so far as viticulture is concerned. Harvesting is the irrevocable step linking enology and viticulture. The winemaker and the grapegrowers must closely cooperate in selecting the time to harvest each variety in each vineyard as near as possible to its optimum stage under the prevailing circumstances. Another good recent reference to this topic is by Hamilton and Coombe (1992).

In commercial-scale operations the decision to harvest is not only affected by the grape composition that is expected to give maximum wine quality. In most wineries the vintage period is rather hectic. Logistics and capacities may force compromises. A large uniform vineyard cannot be harvested instantaneously and depending on crew size or the machinery available may take several days. Transport and reception equipment may be limited. Vineyards expected to ripen differently may be ready simultaneously. If the weather is hot, it is important to harvest promptly before acid is too low or shriveling becomes a problem. If weather promises to be sunny and cool, waiting can be tolerated; if rainstorms or heavy frosts loom, under-ripeness may be chosen. If grapes or wines are accepted that have a compositional deficiency the harvest of other vineyards may be adjusted so that blending may compensate.

There are two extremes of fruit sampling techniques that it may be useful to outline. They may be termed *general* versus *intensive* or *commercial* versus *research*. The general or commercial would be those tests intended to select the moment to start full harvest in a given vineyard. They would be the minimum effective procedure; the pressures of the season mitigate against tedious, detailed testing. Nevertheless, if they are inadequate or slapdash, wine quality will likely suffer. At the other extreme, very detailed and more carefully controlled sampling during the latter stages of ripening plus more detailed analyses can be applied. The work involved may make the value retrospective, i.e., the optimum harvest may be past in the vineyard sampled before the results are available. These research-type analyses are the basis of much of the data already cited upon the detailed changes of grape components during ripening. As new relationships are investigated, such studies must continue. They can be very useful to commercial wineries and vineyards to determine details of ripening with their clones in their locations. The results can be guides for future harvests and, as specific tests are found to be important and simplified they may become useful as harvesting criteria in current vintage seasons. Requirements for adequate sampling can be rather different if small research plots are being tested compared to whole vineyards for harvesting decisions, see further discussion under sampling grapes.

2. Criteria for the Time to Harvest

a. *Date*

The date of previous harvests can be some guide to when the grapes should be ready to pick. If data are available for each variety in each vineyard and the weather of the area is relatively uniform year to year, the estimate will be closer. However, such dates alone should never be relied upon exclusively. Field sampling should begin about four weeks before the probable date of harvest to obtain compositional data so that the final changes can be monitored and harvesting date adjusted for the current season. Sampling should continue about every five to seven days, more often if the weather is hot, so that the rates of change and optima can be followed. Mean Brix rise of 0.5 to 1.0 Brix per week (more in hot sunny weather) is fairly typical in California.

It is assumed that for most wine grape vineyards there will be a single harvest. This is mandatory for mechanical harvesting and less costly for manual harvesting. Selective harvesting by passing over the same vines more than once is not usually practiced, although selectively leaving unharvested second crop or damaged clusters often is. The focus here is to choose the timing of the single harvest to the best advantage. For specific, high-cost wines, Sauternes for example, there may be several pickings in the same vineyard to get the desired effect, botrytization and shriveling in this example. More commonly, it is possible to pick portions of the same monovarietal vineyard differently for different product objectives such as sparkling wine base, dry table, sweet table, and fortified dessert wines.

b. *Sugar*

Sugar is by far the greatest part of the carbon substance and dry weight of ripening grapes. Ripening is fundamentally defined as the accumulation of sugar. A juice at 22 Brix is considered to be from riper grapes than one at 20 Brix. Sugar accumulation in *V. vinifera* grapes levels off and appears to cease at about 25 to 26 Brix (Singleton et al. 1966a). Sugar per berry does not rise further but sugar per kg fresh weight will if berries shrivel. It follows that sugar content and its change must be considered when deciding to harvest grapes. It is a convenient measure because dissolved solids (sugars being predominant) can be readily estimated by hydrometry (with minimum juice sample volumes of the order of 100 ml) or refractometry (even one berry). Unlike some other criteria such as anthocyanins, sugar is easily evaluated in the juice. Sugar alone, however, is not a fully adequate criterion for harvesting wine grapes. The acceptable sugar level will vary with the wine type to be made and the immediate prospects for further changes. In a hot, early-ripening season harvesting should start at the lower end of the Brix range in order to preserve desirable acid. In cool, late-ripening years it may be desirable to wait for the higher end of the preferred Brix range in order that acidity will drop as much as possible. The latter situation predominates in Northern Europe and the former in much of California, Southeastern Australia, South Africa, and Southern Europe. Table 2-11 gives some approximate ranges recommended for harvesting grapes for different wines.

c. *Acidity*

Also in Table 2-11 are given general approximations for titratable acidity and pH. Remember that low must pH and high acidity would be associated with a higher proportion of malic acid. After a malolactic fermentation, wine from a high malic acid must drops most in

Table 2-11. General recommendations for must composition at harvest for various wine types.

Type of wine	Brix	Titratable acidity (g tartaric/L)	pH
Sparkling base	18.0–20.0	7.0–9.0	2.8–3.2
White table	19.5–23.0	7.0–8.0	3.0–3.3
Red table	20.5–23.5	6.5–7.5	3.2–3.4
Sweet table	22.0–25.0	6.5–8.0	3.2–3.4
Dessert	23.0–26.0	5.0–7.5	3.3–3.7

acidity and rises most in pH. Precipitation of potassium bitartrate lowers titratable acid. Unusually high-potassium musts can have both high titratable acid and high pH.

Acidity tends to move oppositely, going down (pH rising) as sugar rises. For this reason and because of acidity's effects on flavor and processing, it is considered the essential minimum to combine some measure of acidity with sugar content when deciding whether it is time to harvest a given group of vines for wine.

d. Weight

Although seldom included in picking estimates, the average berry volume or weight can be a useful criterion and one that is not difficult to obtain or to understand. Berry weight increases during ripening but levels off at maturation and with dehydration (termed *overmaturation* by some) will decrease. If a sequence of representative samples is taken, full maturation by size, the initiation and extent of shriveling, and the effects of ill-timed rain or irrigation can be noted. Furthermore, if berry size is typical for the variety but Brix low, overcropping is doubly indicated (Singleton et al. 1973).

e. Other Criteria for Ripeness to Harvest

Anthocyanin content and total phenol content are of interest, but require more equipment and laboratory expertise to analyze than may be quickly available during vintage. Furthermore, inadequate color or tannin is not readily improved by a small shift in the harvest date. Similarly, varietal aroma and general fruitiness can be very important, but difficult to measure and tend to be lost rather than improved by overmaturation. Volatile and bound terpenes in Muscat grapes may prove to be an exception, but more detailed analyses have not been very useful for timing commercial harvesting. Berry tasting can substitute to a degree for volatile flavor analysis by physicochemical means.

In a review of data on the optimum grape maturity in relation to wine quality Du Plessis (1984) considered aroma compounds, polysaccharides, pH, potassium, phenolics, nitrogenous compounds, turbidity and insoluble solids, other physical aspects, and *Botrytis cinerea*, as well as sugar and acidity. Picking at the proper maturity was often as important to quality or more so than climate, soil, viticultural practices, and winemaking methods. Short of more research involving more parameters studied at once and correlated statistically, no obvious improvement over proper sugar-acid measurements was apparent. Sugar-acid relationships have been used with a good deal of success, especially in warmer areas.

Barron and Santa-Maria (1990) were able to explain 87% of the variance over all samples during the latter stages of ripening of a white and a red variety via factor analyses with the first three factors. Factor I was considered an energy reserve factor and correlated with total lipid content and the major triglycerides. Factor II, considered a secondary metabolism factor, correlated with phenols, sugar × weight, tartaric/malic ratio, and triolein content. Factor III, considered the primary metabolism or physiological maturity indicator, had high correlations with sugar/acidity, glucose/fructose ratios and sugars × weight. These factors have not yet been reduced to easy application, but factors II and III encompass the usual ripeness indices used commercially.

Another factor that may need consideration is mold and bunch rot incidence and likely progression. The conditions leading to inclusion of more or less materials other than grapes (MOG) in a harvest are not usually but may be related to ripeness (leaf dryness, juice stickiness, etc.).

f. Ripeness Indices for Field Use

Various methods have been tried to combine measurements into a single index for timing the harvest to get the best quality of must (Du Plessis 1984). For simple commercial use one would recommend some combination of sugar and acidity measurement coupled with more subjective estimation of flavor, color, health, and general prognosis. In spite of myths to the contrary, no one can accurately estimate sugar and acidity of grapes by taste, but thoughtful examination and tasting preferably by a small panel including the winemaker and the grower can give some perspective on varietal aroma, color, balance, and potential good and bad features of a particular harvest. These will supplement normal sugar and acid analyses and perhaps alert one to the need for additional analyses in a given case if time and facilities permit. After several vintages from a given variety in a given area, experience will lend validity to the more subjective estimates, if they can be backed up with good harvest and wine quality data.

The range in Brix/acid ratio values reflects mainly the acidity, presuming sugars in the 18 to 26 Brix range but acids in the range of 4 to 9 g/L as tartaric acid, and therefore B/A 2.0 to 6.5 with perhaps 3.1 ideal. If blindly applied, this index can be met by deficient grapes. For example, an overcropped late harvest may be so deficient in sugar and acid that it has a proper ratio but cannot make acceptable wine. For such reasons it is recommended that the best combination of components be sought by the winemaker by considering each aspect rather than combining them into a single value. Nevertheless, such indices can provide perspective and furnish useful specifications for grapegrowers. Tabulation of ranges considered acceptable for 52 varieties and all regions for Brix and acidity established commercial grades for California wine grapes (Berg 1960).

For dry table wines Brix $\times$ pH^2 was better as a quality predictor at harvest than Brix/Acid, Brix $\times$ Acid, and Brix $\times$ pH (Coombe et al. 1980). The use of the pH value gives consideration to the high-potassium, high-pH, high-acid possibility. It also relates to the fact that pH has more influence than does titratable acid on fermentation and processing reactions. The range of Brix x pH^2 considered optimal was roughly 200 to 270 (35% range) when the same data gave a Brix/Acid of only 2.8 to 3.2 (14% range). Thus, Brix $\times$ pH^2 gave a relatively wider and more integral range for comparisons.

Van Rooyen et al. (1984) showed that Brix $\times$ pH was better than Brix alone or B/A in predicting grape maturity relationships to table wine quality in Pinotage or Cabernet Sauvignon. It gave a narrower optimum range and in contrast to the other two gave similar results with both cultivars. A value of about 85 to 95 was satisfactory for both. Principal component analysis showed in the same wines that aroma components separated by gas chromatography distinguished the two varieties from each other but gave inconclusive results within a variety in predicting wine quality. With Chenin blanc and Colombard it was not possible to select a specific index for optimum maturity to predict wine quality in all cases. Optimum values for each index including Brix $\times$ pH differed according to geographic locality (Ellis et al. 1985). Phenol analysis was shown to be unimportant to the quality of these white wines by principal component analysis.

3. Sampling Grapes

In the context being discussed, a sample of grapes is desired for analysis so that the progress of ripening can be evaluated and plans made to harvest the vineyard at the optimum stage. In this situation relatively few grapes must represent the whole vineyard. In research plots the problem may be simpler since the number of vines per plot is limited, the vines within a plot should be uniform, and the plots are replicated according to a statistically governed plan. The research sampling must include proportionately each replication plot of every treatment. Furthermore, the individual samples must be sufficiently large to provide the tissue needed and to allow for extraneous variation within plots not part of the experiment. The within-plot and between replicate plot extraneous variation and the variation caused by treatment may be different depending upon what is being measured. The sample size must be larger if the extraneous variation is larger and a given degree of treatment difference is sought with a high degree of confidence. In plot research, but ordinarily not in field sampling, you also may need to consider the depletion of fruit by sampling and the effect on following samples of removal of earlier ones.

To obtain a sample representing a vineyard population the whole vineyard must be sampled. End vines and, unless they make up a sizable portion of the whole, perimeter rows should be omitted as should vines adjacent to spots with missing vines or under trees, etc. If the vineyard is large or has topographically or otherwise distinctly different sections, appropriate subsections should be specifically sampled. Even if relatively uniform, a large vineyard being managed as a unit should be divided into approximately 2-ha portions for careful subsampling. This will provide additional replication and will indicate which portion should be harvested first.

A systematic method of ensuring full vineyard section coverage should be followed in selecting the grapes for the sample to be analyzed. A common and satisfactory method is to walk along alternate balks (spaces between vine rows) and take a grape sample every 10th (or other appropriate number) vine, alternating right or left. It is generally recommended that the fruit selected should be as random as possible, but from all areas such as high or low on the vine on its sunny and shady sides in approximate proportion to their yield. However, if sufficient numbers of vines are sampled, grab sampling may be as effective as randomized sampling for cluster weight, Brix, and acid (Rankine et al. 1962).

Comparing random selection of 100 to 200 berries from a large number of vines, random selection of 10 to 20 clusters from a smaller number of vines, and complete harvest of a few vines, Roessler and Amerine (1958) found the variance to be greatest among means of single vine samples, less among cluster samples, and least among the berry samples (Table 2-12.). From these data, 95% of the time you should miss the population mean not more than twice the standard deviation by using the sample means for the sampling indicated. For example, to come within 0.78 Brix of the population mean Brix, you would average two 100-berry samples, four 10-cluster samples, and 11 whole vine samples. Application of these sampling methods to 10 varieties again showed the lowest standard error for 100-berry compared to 10-cluster or single vine samples. In

Table 2-12. Approximate equivalent numbers of lots for equal reliability.

Standard Error of Means	Number of Lots of 100 Berries	10 Clusters	Vines
		Brix	
0.39	2	4	11
0.32	3	5	17
0.28	4	7	22
0.25	5	9	27
		Total Acid (g/L as tartaric)	
0.28	2	4	8
0.23	3	6	10
0.20	4	8	14
1.18	5	10	18
		pH	
0.028	2	2	8
0.023	3	3	10
0.020	4	4	14
0.018	5	5	18

Source of data: Roessler and Amerine (1958).

the seven cases where the whole winery harvest was compared, berry sample Brix agreed within 0.5, acid within 0.5 g/L, and pH within 0.17 of the winery value (Roessler and Amerine 1963).

The most effective sampling is to take a minimum amount of grapes from a large number of vines (Rankine et al. 1962). Irrigated vines were more variable than nonirrigated at least up to 20 Brix. Mean sugar content per vine was inversely proportional and acid content directly proportional to yield. With Concord grapes also (Wolpert et al. 1980), vines contributed an average of 60% of the variance in cluster weight, soluble solids, and acidity. Exposure and cluster position along the shoot together contributed most of the rest of the variance with only about 7% unexplained. Kasimatis and Vilas (1985) found berry samples did not as easily represent the true Brix of a population as did adequate cluster sampling, at least in part because outer exposed berries tended to be higher in Brix than the rest of the cluster. Particularly with tight clusters, inclusion of berries or cluster sections from all parts of the clusters in approximate proportions can be recommended. Sample variance in Brix measurement dropped rapidly as berries per sample increased to about 70 but little thereafter.

Another point that needs to be made is that the method of converting the fruit sample into the juice to be analyzed affects the results. In measuring ripeness to decide when to harvest, an objective is to predict the Brix and acid that the whole crushed harvest would have in the winery. If one is using a hand refractometer and squeezes each berry on the prism for measurement, two systematic errors are likely to be present. First, the outer berry which has been chosen is likely to be higher in Brix as just noted. Second, the first few drops of juice come from the softest pulp tissue highest in Brix. In our experience an average of such values is likely to be nearly 1 Brix higher than the whole harvest even on a small plot. Furthermore blending the whole tissue compared to expressed juice leads to 0.2 to 0.3 higher pH (Carter et al. 1972). The best approach seems to be processing the collected berry or destemmed cluster sample into juice via an auger or lever press in small amounts so that the pomace is free of releasable juice to about the same degree as the winery pomace. Since red wines are fermented on the pomace, juice from blender-processed berries gave pH and acidity more nearly corresponding to that of the fermented wines according to Carter et al. (1972). This may be illusory, however, because grinding the seeds and other tissues changes the acidity, pH, and buffer capacity in ways different from the mechanisms during fermentation (Ough and Amerine 1988).

4. Population Distribution Effects

The grapes of a monovarietal vineyard represent a population at any one instant up to and including harvest that contains a more or less wide range of any one characteristic. Obtaining a representative sample is truly successful only if the sample has the same variability and the same proportions of individual berries with different characteristics. We tend to assume that two vineyards or two vintages giving the same must analysis at harvest should give the same wine. This can be far from the truth even without differences arising from processing. The simplest example is that the weighted average Brix, that in the must tank, can remain the same with very different population distributions. If the winery must was 22.0 Brix, it might be composed of a narrow distribution with few berries at 20 Brix or below and few at 23 Brix or higher. It might be a wide distribution with berries below 18 and above 24 Brix, and it could be the result of two overlapping populations with their own means peaking at, perhaps, 18.0 and 24.0 Brix. Clearly the wines from these three situations would be unlikely to be similar in acidity or any other variable characteristic except for alcohol content.

Populations of grapes can be characterized by Brix without destruction by their distribution in a series of flotation baths of decreasing density (Singleton et al. 1966a, 1973). Since the ripening grape has no air space within its flesh and the seeds and skins are more dense than juice, the juice Brix of a grape is a little lower than that of a sugar solution in which it hovers without floating or sinking. Using flotation solutions 1 Brix apart and comparing the juice Brix with the mean of the two solutions in which it just sank or floated, the regression equation averaged for six white seeded varieties was: Juice Brix = 0.98 (flotation Brix minus 0.86). Perfect correlation would equal 1.0 rather than 0.98 and intercepts varied from -0.6 to -1.6 depending on variety. Berry weight and pH varied as expected with Brix over the ripening (increasing juice Brix) sequence.

This technique is a bit tedious for everyday use in monitoring ripening, but it deserves more use than it has had because it can provide three kinds of information not readily obtainable any other way. It can characterize a ripe harvest population for comparison with others. It can give a ripeness sequence free from weather influences. All Brix categories from 14 to 25 Brix or perhaps wider can be obtained at one sampling and these subsamples analyzed to determine trends in any other component related to that ripeness (Brix). For example this approach was very useful in monitoring caftaric acid changes during the last stages of ripening (Singleton, Zaya, and Trousdale 1986b). Third, such segregation of whole berries by Brix can provide a restricted Brix fraction that can be analyzed in detail to characterize vineyard or vintage differences freed of ripeness and population diversity differences. For *V. rotundifolia* berries that develop an abscission layer and are harvested as single berries, density segregation has been shown to have potential to remove under-ripe and lesser-quality grapes from commercial harvests (Lanier and Morris 1979). Finally, density segregation can be useful in demonstrating overcropping and the shift from physiological production to increase of sugar by shriveling.

If one determines the Brix of each berry in a fairly ripe cluster, berries are usually found covering nearly the whole range of ripeness. They are not very systematically arranged, with various degrees of ripeness distributed rather randomly over the cluster. This is one reason that picking one berry at random from each of 100 vines is so successful at estimating the population Brix mean for those vines. It is similar with berry weight, which, not counting shot berries, may range from about 0.5 to 2.5 g/berry in the same cluster depending on variety. One would expect that, as a normal ripeness progression, the increased Brix would be associated with increased berry weight.

If the berries all had the same number of seeds this should be true. However, berries without seeds are both a good deal smaller and earlier-ripening than those with one seed on the same vines. The differences between one-seeded berries and those with two, three, and finally four seeds are in the same direction; more seeds give a larger berry accumulating a given Brix more slowly and usually retaining acid longer. As an example, Peynaud (1984) lists a Malbec progression from one-seeded at 1.9 g/berry, 18.8 Brix, and 6.7 g/L acid to four-seeded at 3.2 g/berry, 14.5 Brix, and 8.0 g/L acid. In a density distribution, the highest Brix berries are either unseeded berries, shriveled ones, or a combination of the two. In both cases they are smaller in weight.

Part of the reason berries in the same cluster are not at the same ripeness could be their different time of blooming, and this difference would be larger between clusters and larger yet between vines. The number of seeds formed is seen to be another important variable and will spread the population further. The number of seeds per berry and the amount of flesh per seed varies by variety although the average seeds per berry is often between one and two for wine grapes, with four being maximum. Further data appears needed on the population distributions of these factors by variety and season correlated with wine quality.

5. Harvesting Practices

Once the time is chosen and assuming a single harvest there are two primary objectives: getting the grapes picked as completely and expeditiously as possible and getting them to the winery in as near perfect condition as possible. The main choice is between manual and machine harvesting. Manual harvesting *can* (but may not) be more selective and thorough, less damaging to the vineyard, and less damaging to the grapes. It is adaptable to vineyards too hilly or otherwise unsuitable for machine harvests. Machine harvesting is faster, more economical, less prone to error or skipping, and can more easily work at night giving the advantages of cooler grapes at the winery. Properly operated, modern machines give good recovery, sometimes better than harvesting by hand. The fraction of grapes for wine or juice harvested by machine has steadily grown since 1969 when an estimated 40% of New York's grapes and 10% of California's were so harvested. By 1980, California had reached an estimated 25% and currently it is probably 35% overall with as much as 75% in the areas producing grapes for less expensive wines. Although machine usage is more limited in areas noted for premium wines, it is still appreciable, probably 10 to 15% of the tonnage. The use for premium grapes is generally acceptable from a processing viewpoint but more restricted because of such factors as small plots and rough terrain.

Chardonnay harvested in a premium area by two types of machine harvesters and by hand gave no significant difference in the quantity of fruit delivered or the eventual wine quality (Clary et al. 1990). Although a taste panel could differentiate the manual harvest from the mechanical harvests (but not the two mechanical harvests from each other) there was no significant difference in preference. The must was 22.2 Brix from the machine and 22.6 Brix by hand because of a greater level of second crop in the mechanically harvested. For the same reason, the total acid and malic acid were higher in the machine-harvested must about 0.5 g/L each. In these valuable grapes ($1164/Tm), 6 to 8% juice loss by mechanical harvesting plus extra costs for repairing trellis and sprinkler damage made the return to the winery slightly greater for hand harvesting, even though the actual cost of hand harvesting was $121/Tm versus $55/Tm by machine.

In the same paper (Clary et al. 1990) the previous literature was outlined. The results of many studies on mechanical harvesting are rather consistent. Most of the grapes are removed as berries leaving the stem (rachis) on the vine. Raisined berries and those early sunburned are mostly left attached to the vines as are lightweight rotten clusters. Second crop and clusters still heavy but with bunch rot are usually harvested. Proper use of blowers removes leaves and light detritus from the grapes and they may be as clean or cleaner (less MOG) than piecework manual harvests. Since many cluster stems are left on the vine, the stem content was half or less of that from hand harvests and fewer bits got through the crusher. Typically, the machines miss or lose on the ground fewer berries than do hand harvesters, but lose more juice.

The key differences from mechanical harvesting relating to wine quality have to do with the handling and time between harvest and winery processing. With hand harvesting the desired standard has been getting the grapes to the winery with no berry breakage. Depending on the handling, the roughness of transport, the depth of the load, and the distance to the winery this may not be achieved even with manual harvesting. Depending on the strength of the berry attachment and the skin more or less damage will occur—variable by variety and conditions. With mechanical harvesting some damage is inevitable as the pedicel brush is jerked from most of the berries. A portion of the berry is exposed to oxidation and microbial attack. Various ways of minimizing detrimental effects have been applied, but if times and distances are short enough wine quality need not suffer.

Machine-harvested wine grapes in California almost invariably receive metabisulfite in the field. In some cases the mechanically harvested fruit is received directly into a mobile tank that has been precharged with sulfur dioxide or sulfite salts and with carbon dioxide to displace the air. The grapes may be passed through a destemmer-crusher mounted on this tank vehicle. The sulfur dioxide inhibits phenol oxidase and undesirable microbes and the air exclusion also helps prevent oxidation. Upon arrival at the winery the whole crushed grape mass may be pumped to further processing with perhaps even less exposure to deleterious effects than would have been the case from manual harvesting. The total time of maceration contact between the pomace and the juice would be the remaining consideration and this will be addressed in later sections.

H. REFERENCES

ADAMS, D. O., K. E. FRANKE, and L. P. CHRISTENSEN. 1990. "Elevated putrescine levels in grapevine leaves that display symptoms of potassium deficiency." *Am. J. Enol. Vitic.* 41:121–125.

ADAMS, D. O., and C. LIYANAGE. 1991. "Modification of an enzymatic glutathione assay for determination of total glutathione in grapevine tissues." *Am. J. Enol. Vitic.* 42:137–140.

ALTMAN, H. (Ed.). 1987. *Weinbau.* Vienna: Österreichischer Agrarverlag.

AMERINE, M. A., and A. J. WINKLER. 1944. "Composition and quality of musts and wines of California grapes." *Hilgardia* 15:493–676.

AMERINE, M. A., and A. J. WINKLER. 1963a. "California wine grapes: Composition and quality of their musts and wines." *Calif. Agric. Exp. Stn. Bull.* 794. Berkeley, CA: University of California, Division of Agricultural Sciences.

AMERINE, M. A., and A. J. WINKLER. 1963b. "Grape varieties for wine production." *Calif. Agric. Expt. Stn. Leaflet 154.* Berkeley, CA: University of California, Division of Agricultural Sciences.

BARRON, L. J. R., M. V. CELAA, and G. SANTA-MARIA. 1989. "Triacylglycerol changes in grapes in late stages of ripening." *Phytochemistry* 28:3301–3305.

BARRON, L. J. R., and G. SANTA-MARIA. 1990. "A relationship between triglycerides and grape-ripening indices." *Food Chem.* 37:37–45.

BERG, H. W. 1960. *Grade Classification by Total Soluble Solids and Total Acidity*, pp. 53. San Francisco, CA: Wine Institute.

BOWEN, J. F., D. R. MACGREGOR, and D. V. FISHER. 1972. "Wine grape varieties for British Columbia." *Can. Inst. Food Sci. Technol. J.* 5:44–49.

CANTAGREL, R., P. SYMONDS, and J. CARLES. 1982. "Composition on acides aminés du moût en fonction du cepage et de la technologie et son influence sur la qualité du vin." *Sci. Aliment* 2 (*Num. hors Ser.* 1):109–142.

CARTER, G. H., C. W. NAGEL, and W. J. CLORE. 1972. "Grape sample preparation methods representative of must and wine analysis." *Am. J. Enol. Vitic.* 23:10–13.

CHAMPAGNOL, F. 1984. *Elements de Physiologie de la Vigne et de Viticulture Generale.* Saint-Gely-du-Fesc, France: Francois Champagnol.

CHEYNIER, V., J. M. SOUQUET, and M. MOUTOUNET. 1989. "Glutathione content and glutathione to hydroxy-cinnamic acid ratio in *Vitis vinifera* grapes and musts." *Am. J. Enol. Vitic.* 40:320–324.

CLARY, C. D., R. E. STEINHAUER, J. E. FRISINGER, and T. E. PEFFER. 1990. "Evaluation of machine vs. hand-harvested Chardonnay." *Am. J. Enol Vitic.* 41:176–181.

COOMBE, B. G. 1988. "Grape phenology." In *Viticulture*, B. G. Coombe and P. R. Dry, Eds., pp. 139–153. Adelaide: Australian Industrial Publishers.

COOMBE, B. G., and P. R. DRY (Eds.). 1988. *Viticulture*, Vol. 1, Resources in Australia. Underdale, South Australia: Australian Industrial Publishers.

COOMBE, B. G., R. J. DUNDON, and A. W. S. SHORT. 1980. "Indices of sugar-acidity as ripeness criteria for winegrapes." *J. Sci. Food Agric.* 31:495–502.

CORDONNIER, R. 1966. "Étude des protéins et des substances azotées. Leur évolution au cours des traitements oenologiques. Conditions de la stabilité protéique des vins." *Bull. Off. Int. Vin* 39:1475–1489.

CROWTHER, R. F., and O. A. BRADT. 1970. "Evaluation of grape cultivars for production of wine." *Rept. Hort. Res. Inst. Ontario* 121–128. Toronto, Canada: Ontario Dept. of Agriculture and Food.

CURRLE, O., O. BAUER, W. HOFÄCKER, F. SCHUMANN, and W. FRISCH. 1983. *Biologie der Rebe*. Neustadt an der Weinstrasse, Germany: D. Meininger Verlag.

DEIBNER, L., J. MOURGUES, and M. CABIBEL-HUGHES. 1965. "Évolution de l'indice des substances aromatiques volatiles des raisins de deux cépages rouges au cours de leur maturation." *Ann. Technol. Agric.* 14:5–14.

DU PLESSIS, C. S. 1984. "Optimum maturity and quality parameters in grapes: A review." *S. Afr. J. Enol. Vitic.* 5:35–42.

DURMISHIDZE, S. V. 1955. *Dubil'nye Veshchestva i Antotsiany Vinogradnoi Lozi i Vina*, pp. 1–323. Moscow: Izda. Akad. Nauk. SSSR.

EGOROV, I. A., A. K. RODOPULO, A. A. BEZZUBOV, A. Y. SKRIPNIK, and L. N. NECHAEV. 1978. "Investigation of the volatile oils in several grape varieties during ripening (trans.)." *Prikl. Biokhim. Mikrobiol.* 14:135–139.

EINSETT, J., and K. H. KIMBALL. 1971. "1969–70 vineyard and cellar notes." *NY State Agric. Expt. Stn. Special Rept.* 4:1–27. Geneva, NY: NY State Agric. Expt. Stn.

ELLIS, L. P., P. C. VAN ROOYEN, and C. S. DU PLESSIS. 1985. "Interactions between grape maturity indices and the quality and composition of Chenin blanc and Colombar wines from different localities." *S. Afr. J. Enol. Vitic.* 6:45–50.

FERRARO-OLMOS, R. 1983. *Viticultura Moderna*. Montevideo, Uruguay: Hemisferio Sur.

FREGONI, M. 1985. *Viticoltura Generale*. Rome: Editoriale degli Agricolturi.

GALET, P. 1988. *Précis de Viticulture*, 5th ed. Montpelier, France: Déhan.

GALLANDER, J. F., and A. C. PENG. 1980. "Lipid and fatty acid compositions of different grape types." *Am. J. Enol. Vitic.* 31:24–27.

HAMILTON, R. P., and B. G. COOMBE. 1992. "Harvesting of winegrapes." In *Viticulture, Vol. 2 Practices*, B. G. Coombe and P. R. Day, Eds., pp. 302–327 Underdale, South Australia: Winetitles.

HARRIS, J. M., P. E. KRIEDEMANN, and J. V. POSSINGHAM. 1968. "Anatomical aspects of grape berry development." *Vitis* 7:106–119.

HEYMANN, H., A. C. NOBLE, and R. B. BOULTON. 1986. "Analysis of methoxypyrazines in wines. I. Development of a quantitative procedure." *J. Agric. Food Chem.* 34:268–271.

HUANG, Z., and C. S. OUGH. 1989. "Effect of vineyard locations, varieties and rootstocks on the juice amino acid composition of several cultivars." *Am. J. Enol. Vitic.* 40:135–139.

HUGLIN, P. 1986. *Biologie et Ecologie de la Vigne*. Lausanne: Editions Payot.

INGLEDEW, W. M., C. A. MAGNUS, and F. W. SOSULSKI. 1987. "Influence of oxygen on proline utilization during wine fermentation." *Am. J. Enol. Vitic.* 38:246–248.

JACKSON, D. I., and N. J. CHERRY. 1988. "Prediction of a district's grape-ripening capacity using a latitude-temperature index (LTI)." *Am. J. Enol. Vitic.* 39:19–28.

JACKSON, D., and D. SCHUSTER. 1987. *The Production of Grapes and Wine in Cool Climate*. Wellington: Butterworths of New Zealand.

KADISCH, E. 1986. *Weinbau*. Stuttgart: Verlag Eugen Ulmer.

KASIMATIS, A. N., B. E. BEARDEN, and K. BOWERS. 1977. "Wine grape varieties in the North Coast Counties of California." *Divn. Agric. Sci. Univ. Calif. Publication* 4069, 1–30. Berkeley, CA: University of California, Division of Agricultural Sciences.

KASIMATIS, A. N., L. P. CHRISTENSEN, D. A. LUVISI, and J. L. KISSLER. 1980. "Wine grape varieties in the San Joaquin Valley." *Division of Agric. Sci. Univ. Calif. Publication* 4009, 1–33. Berkeley, CA: University of California, Division of Agricultural Sciences.

KASIMATIS, A. N., and E. P. VILAS. 1985. "Sampling for degrees Brix in vineyard plots." *Am. J. Enol. Vitic.* 36:207–213.

KINSELLA, J. E. 1974. "Grapeseed oil. Rich source of linoleic acid." *Food Technol.* (Chicago) 28:58–60.

KISSLER, J. J., C. S. OUGH, and C. J. ALLEY. 1973. "Evaluations of wine grape varieties for Lodi." *Univ. Calif. Agric. Exp. Stn. Bull.* 865, 1–12. Berkeley, CA: University of California, Division of Agricultural Sciences.

KLIEWER, W. M. 1965a. "Changes in the concentrations of malates, tartrates, and total free acids in flowers and berries of *Vitis vinifera*." *Am. J. Enol. Vitic* 16:92–100.

KLIEWER, W. M. 1965b. "Changes in concentration of glucose, fructose, and total soluble solids in flowers and berries of *Vitis vinifera*." *Am. J. Enol. Vitic.* 16:101–110.

KLIEWER, W. M. 1967. "Annual cyclic changes in the concentration of free amino acids in grapevines." *Am. J. Enol. Vitic.* 18:126–137.

KLIEWER, W. M., and R. E. SMART. 1988. "Canopy manipulation for optimizing vine microclimate, crop yield and composition of grapes," In *Manipulation of Fruiting*, C. J. Wright, Ed, pp. 275–291. London: Butterworths Scientific Ltd.

LACEY, M. J., M. S. ALLEN, R. L. N. HARRIS, and W. V. BROWN. 1991. "Methoxypyrazines in Sauvignon blanc grapes and wines." *Am. J. Enol. Vitic.* 42:103–108.

LANIER, M. R., and J. R. MORRIS. 1979. "Evaluation of density separation for defining fruit maturities and maturation rates of once-over harvested Muscadine grapes." *J. Am. Hort. Soc.* 104:249–252.

LARREA-REDONDO, A. 1981. *Viticultura Basica*. Barcelona: Editorial Aedos.

LEA, A. G. H., P. BRIDLE, C. F. TIMBERLAKE, and V. L. SINGLETON. 1979. "The procyanidins of white grapes and wines." *Am. J. Enol. Vitic.* 30:289–300.

MARAIS, J. 1986. "A reproducible capillary gas chromatographic technique for the determination of specific terpenes in grape juice and wine." *S. African J. Enol. Vitic.* 7:21–25.

MARAIS, J. 1987. "Terpene concentrations and wine quality of *Vitis vinifera* L. cv. Gewürztraminer as affected by grape maturity and cellar practices." *Vitis* 26:231–245.

MARAIS, J., and C. J. VAN WYK. 1986. "Effect of grape maturity and juice treatments on terpene concentrations and wine quality of *Vitis vinifera* L. cv. Weisser Riesling and Bukettraube." *S. African J. Enol. Vitic.* 7:26–35.

MCINTYRE, G. N., L. A. LIDER, and N. L. FERRARI. 1982. "The Chronological classification of grapevine phenology." *Am. J. Enol. Vitic.* 33:80–85.

MURPHEY, J. M., S. E. SPAYD, and J. R. POWERS. 1989. "Effect of grape maturation on soluble protein characteristics of Gewürztraminer and White Riesling juice and wine." *Am. J. Enol. Vitic.* 40:199–207.

NAGEL, C. W., M. ATALLAH, G. H. CARTER, and W. J. CLORE. 1972. "Evaluation of wine grapes grown in Washington." *Am. J. Enol. Vitic.* 23:14–17.

NYKÄNEN, L., and H. SUOMALAINEN. 1983. *Aroma of Beer, Wine and Distilled Alcoholic Beverages*. Berlin: Akademie Verlag.

ORFFER, C. J. (Ed.) 1979. *Wine Grape Cultivars in South Africa*. Cape Town South Africa: Human and Rousseau.

OUGH, C. S. 1968. "Proline content of grapes and wines." *Vitis* 7:321–331.

OUGH, C. S., C. J. ALLEY, D. A. LUVISI, L. P. CHRISTENSEN, P. BARANEK, and F. L. JENSEN. 1973. "Evaluation of wine grape varieties for Madera, Fresno, Tulare, and Kern Counties." *Univ. Calif. Agric. Expt. Stn. Bull.* 863, 1–19. Berkeley, CA: University of California, Division of Agricultural Sciences.

OUGH, C. S., and M. A. AMERINE. 1988. *Methods for Analysis of Musts and Wines*. New York: John Wiley and Sons.

OUGH, C. S., and R. M. STASHAK. 1974. "Further studies on proline concentration in grapes and wines... *Am. J. Enol. Vitic.* 25:7–12.

PARK, S. K., J. C. MORRISON, D. O. ADAMS, and A. C. NOBLE. 1991. "Distribution of free and glycosidically bound monoterpenes in the skin and mesocarp of Muscat of Alexandria grapes during development." *J. Agric. Food Chem.* 39:514–518.

PARONETTO, L. 1977. *Polifenoli e Tecnica Enologica*. pp. 1–324. Milan: Editioni Agricole Edit. Selepress.

PENNING-ROWSELL, E. 1985. *The Wines of Bordeaux*, 5th ed., pp. 562–565. San Francisco, CA: Wine Appreciation Guild.

PEYNAUD, E. 1984. *Knowing and Making Wine*, pp. 60–61. New York: John Wiley and Sons.

PEYNAUD, E., and A. MAURIÉ. 1953. "Sur l' évolution de l'azote dans les différentes parties du raisin au cours de la maturation." *Ann. Technol. Agric.* 2:15–25.

PONGRÁCZ, D. P. 1978. *Practical Viticulture*. Cape Town, South Africa: David Philip.

PSZCZOLKOWSKI, P., M. I. QUIROZ, and A. M. SALVATIERRA. 1985. "Efecto de la epoca y numero de chapodas en parronales viniferos, sobre la luminosidad, productividad y calidad del mosto y vino. II. Temporada." *Cienc. Invest. Agrar.* 12:37–48.

RANKINE, B. C., K. M. CELLIER, and E. W. BOEHM. 1962. "Studies on grape variability and field sampling." *Am. J. Enol. Vitic.* 13:53–72.

RAPP, A. 1988. "Studies on terpene compounds in wines." *Dev. Food Sci.* 17:799–813.

REYNIER, A. 1989. *Manuel de Viticulture*, 5th ed. Paris: Lavoisier.

REYNOLDS, A. G., R. M. POOL, and L. R. MATTICK. 1986. "Influence of cluster exposure on fruit composition and wine quality of Seyval blanc grapes." *Vitis* 25:85–95.

REYNOLDS, A. G., and D. A. WARDLE. 1989. "Influence of fruit microclimate on monoterpene levels of Gewürztraminer." *Am. J. Enol. Vitic.* 40:149–154.

ROBINSON, J. 1986. *Vines, Grapes and Wines*. New York: Alfred A. Knopf.

ROESSLER, E. B., and M. A. AMERINE. 1958. "Studies on grape sampling." *Am. J. Enol.* 9:139–145.

ROESSLER, E. B., and M. A. AMERINE. 1963. "Further studies on grape sampling." *Am. J. Enol. Vitic.* 14:144–147.

ROUFET, M., C. L. BAYONOVE, and R. E. CORDONNIER. 1987. "Étude de la composition lipidique du raisin, *Vitis vinifera* L.: Evolution au cours de la maturation et localisation dans le baie." *Vitis* 26:85–97.

SARACCO, C. 1984. *Guida Practica del Viticolture*, 2nd ed. Bologna, Italy: Edagricole.

SEFTON, M. A., G. K. SKOUROUMOUNIS, R. A. MASSY-WESTROPP, and P. J. WILLIAMS. 1989. "Norisoprenoids in *Vitis vinifera* white wine grapes and the identification of a precursor of damascenone in these fruits." *Aust. J. Chem.* 42:2071–2084.

SEGUIN, G. 1986. 'Terroirs' and pedology of vine growing. *Experientia* 42:861–873.

SILACCI, M. W., and J. C. MORRISON. 1990. "Changes in pectin content of Cabernet Sauvignon grape berries during maturation." *Am. J. Enol. Vitic.* 41:111–115.

SINGLETON, V. L. 1966. "The total phenolic content of grape berries during the maturation of several varieties." *Am. J. Enol. Vitic.* 17:126–134.

SINGLETON, V. L. 1972. "Effects on red wine quality of removing juice before fermentation to stimulate variation in berry size." *Am. J. Enol. Vitic.* 23:106–113.

SINGLETON, V. L. 1987. "Oxygen with phenols and related reactions in musts, wines, and model systems: Observations and practical implications." *Am. J. Enol. Vitic.* 38:69–77.

SINGLETON, V. L. 1990. "An overview of the integration of grape, fermentation, and ageing flavours in wines." *Proc. 7th Wine Industry Tech. Conf.*, pp. 96–106. Adelaide, So. Australia, 13–17 Aug., 1989.

SINGLETON, V. L., P. DE WET, and C. S. DU PLESSIS. 1973. "Characterization of populations of grapes harvested for wine and compensation for population differences." *Agroplantae* 5:1–12.

SINGLETON, V. L., D. E. DRAPER, and J. A. ROSSI, JR. 1966b. "Paper chromatography of phenolic compounds from grapes, particularly seeds, and some variety-ripeness relationships." *Am. J. Enol. Vitic.* 17:206–217.

SINGLETON, V. L., and P. ESAU. 1969. "Phenolic substances in grapes and wine and their significance." *Adv. Food Res.* Suppl. 1:1–282.

SINGLETON, V. L., C. S. OUGH, and K. E. NELSON. 1966a. "Density separations of wine grape berries and ripeness distribution." *Am. J. Enol. Vitic.* 17:95–105.

SINGLETON, V. L., M. SALGUES, J. ZAYA, and E. TROUSDALE. 1985. "Caftaric acid disappearance and conversion to products of enzymic oxidation in grape must and wine." *Am. J. Enol. Vitic.* 36:50–56.

SINGLETON, V. L., and E. TROUSDALE. 1983. "White wine phenolics: Varietal and processing differences as shown by HPLC." *Am. J. Enol. Vitic.* 34:27–34.

SINGLETON, V. L., and E. K. TROUSDALE. 1992. "Anthocyanin-tannin interactions explaining differences in polymeric phenols between white and red wines." *Am. J. Enol. Vitic.* 43:63–70.

SINGLETON, V. L., J. ZAYA, and E. TROUSDALE. 1986a. "Caftaric and coutaric acids in fruit of *Vitis*." *Phytochem.* 25:2127–2133.

SINGLETON, V. L., J. ZAYA, and E. TROUSDALE. 1986b. "Compositional changes in ripening grapes: Caftaric and coutaric acids.,, *Vitis* 25:107–117.

STAUDT, G., W. SCHNEIDER, and J. LEIDEL. 1986. "Phases of berry growth in *Vitis vinifera*." *Ann. Botany* 58:789–800.

STRAUSS, C. R., B. WILSON, R. ANDERSON, and P. J. WILLIAMS. 1987. "Development of precursors of C_{13} nor-isoprenoid flavorants in Riesling grapes.;; *Am. J. Enol. Vitic.* 38:23–27.

STRAUSS, C. R., B. WILSON, P. R. GOOLEY, and P. J. WILLIAMS. 1986. "Role of monoterpenes in grape and wine flavor." *ACS Symp. Ser.* 317:222–242.

SU, C. T., and V. L. SINGLETON. 1969. "Identification of three flavan-3-ols from grapes." *Phytochemistry* 8:1553–1558.

TERCELJ, D. 1965. "Étude des composés azotés du vin." *Ann. Technol. Agric.* 14:307–319.

USSEGLIO-TOMASETT, L., and P. D. BOSIA. 1990. "Évolution des acides aminés et des oligopeptides du moût au vin." *Bull. Off. Int. Vin* 63:21–46.

VAN ROOYEN, P. C., L. P. ELLIS, and C. S. DU PLESSIS. 1984. "Interactions between grape maturity indices and quality for Pinotage and Cabernet Sauvignon wines from four localities." *S. Afr. J. Enol. Vitic.* 5:29–34.

WAGNER, P. M. 1976. *Grapes into Wine: A Guide to Winemaking in America*. New York: Knopf.

WEAVER, R. J. 1976. *Grape Growing*. New York: Wiley-Interscience.

WINKLER, A. J., J. A. COOK, W. M. KLIEWER, and L. A. LIDER. 1974. *General Viticulture*. 2nd ed. Berkeley, CA: University of California Press.

WINTON, W., C. S. OUGH, and V. L. SINGLETON. 1975. "Relative distinctiveness of varietal wines estimated by the ability of trained panelists to name the grape variety correctly." *Am. J. Enol. Vitic.* 26:5–11.

WOLPERT, J. A., G. S. HOWELL, and C. E. CRESS. 1980. "Sampling strategies for estimates of cluster weight, soluble solids, and acidity of 'Concord' grapes." *J. Am. Soc. Hort. Sci.* 105:434–438.

CHAPTER 3

PREPARATION OF MUSTS AND JUICE

The natural variation in almost every aspect of grape composition is a major feature of wines and is the cause of the seasonal, varietal, and regional differences that they display. The application of scientific understanding to the production of the best possible wines requires that we take steps to protect the most desirable components of the juice, sometimes by intervening with natural reactions and sometimes to overcome natural deficiencies or imbalances that exist by nutrient additions and physical treatments.

One of the main purposes of juice preparation will be the prevention of undesirable reactions in juices (and subsequent defects in wines) and the following section aims to provide the basis for the many options that exist with respect to juice preparation. The addresses of equipment companies mentioned in this chapter can be found in Appendix I.

A. CRUSHING AND DESTEMMING

1. The Role of Crushing

Crushing is employed to cause berry breakage and juice release from the grapes, and ordinarily 100% of the berries will be broken. It is the beginning of the juice, skin, pulp, and seed contact that will influence the extent of extraction from these grape components. A secondary aspect of the crushing process is the elimination of the stems from the juice and skins and the isolation and collection of them for disposal. Stems are often shredded and dispersed throughout the vineyard, dumped as solid waste, or incinerated. Under some conditions, to be discussed later, partial stem removal or addition of some stems back to the must is practiced. However complete removal is generally sought.

2. Crushing and Destemming Equipment

Crushing equipment can be classified according to which action takes place first. There are destemmer crushers in which the clusters are broken apart as the grape berries are torn from the stems. The berries fall through the cage and are then crushed by rollers before falling into the must pan of the crusher. The advantages of this sequence are thought to be that some whole berries can be left and that the stems are not in contact with the must, thus preventing extraction of undesirable stemmy components. There are no convincing experimental verifications of extraction from stems during this process and the likely contact time between stems and juice within the crusher is of the order of seconds, far too short for significant extraction.

Crusher destemmers break the berries while they are attached to the stems and the destemming action is to remove the berry skins rather than whole berries. As a result, these stems are generally covered in juice and are a bigger potential source of microbial contamination and odor than those from a destemmer crusher.

a. *Crusher Capacities*

Crushers are available with capacities of 5 to 10 Tm/hr up to 50 to Tm/hr. The capacity is primarily determined by the diameter of the destemming cage and secondarily by the rotational speed of the axle carrying the destemming blades or fingers relative to the cage. The ratio of the motor gear to that of the axle and the power of the motor will determine the rotational speed. If the axle is rotating too quickly, insufficient wall impacts and contact time within the cage will cause some berries to be ejected with the stems, leading to a loss in juice recovery. Excessive speed can also lead to more extensive shredding and attrition which results in higher levels of fine suspended solids that will have to be removed later during clarification of white juices.

b. *Grape Delivery and Must Transfer*

Grapes or musts are usually delivered to the winery in grape bins (gondolas) that are 0.5, 1, 2, or 5 Tm in capacity. The grapes are typically dumped into a receiving hopper and the crusher is commonly fed by a screw conveyor. The must (juice and skins), is generally pumped to either a drainer or a tank by a positive displacement pump. The nature of this pump, the flow rate generated, the diameter and length of the must line, and the way in which the must is delivered into the tank all influence the level of suspended solids in the resultant juices and wines. The use of progressive cavity pumps is preferred for must transfer due to the smooth surfaces and fluid path. These pumps are discussed in more detail in Chapter 13. Small diameter lines, long distances, and many bends are to be avoided as they provide the conditions for the further generation of solids through impacts and shear stress. The generation of solids is a major concern in the production of unaged, varietal white wines and will be further addressed in later sections (see Chapter 5).

c. *Field Crushing*

Several wineries have moved toward the crushing of grapes in vineyards in conjunction with machine harvesting so that the stems are dumped directly into the vineyard. This is commonly done where there is a considerable distance to the winery and where the stems pose a disposal problem at the winery. Further advantages to field crushing are that cooling of the must is easier to perform and antioxidant additions are more effective than the same treatments with whole clusters. Some wineries have taken this to its logical extension with the field pressing for white grapes, returning the white pomace to the vineyard, and transporting only turbid juice to the winery. This increases the effectiveness of any added sulfur dioxide in preventing the onset of fermentation by natural yeast. The musts and juices generally are transported in closed vessels to prevent enzymatic oxidation, spillage of the contents, and the loss of volatile components during the transfer.

d. *Manufacturers of Crushers*

The two main manufacturers of crushers in this country are the Healdsburg Machine Co. and formerly, the Valley Foundry Co. The majority of those crushers installed in coastal wineries are produced by the former, while most of those installed in the Central Valley have been made by the latter. There are a number of European models in use and these include Vaslin, Demoisy, and Amos units. A typical grape crusher is shown in Figure 3-1.

(a)

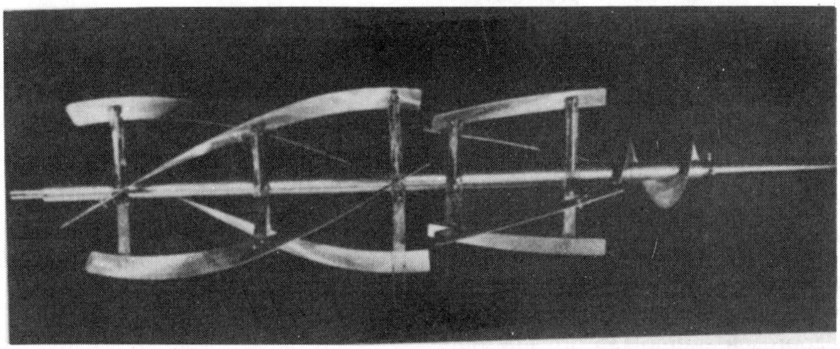

(b)

Fig. 3-1. A typical grape crusher.

e. *Crusher Location and Stem Removal*

The crusher is preferably located outside of the main winery building so that the stems can be collected and removed at this point rather than from within the building. This is usually most convenient for truck deliveries in open bins. The stem removal system can range from simply forking them into a bin, to belt or screw conveyors, or to a pneumatic conveying system with a cyclone separator discharging the solids into a bin. Many wineries shred or chop the stems prior to dispersal in the vineyards to reduce their bulk volume and to permit more uniform spreading and integration into the soil. Another alternative would be the collection of stems from many wineries in a district and the use of them as a fuel supplement at a cogeneration facility.

3. Special Conditions of Crushing

There are several alternative ways in which grapes can be prepared for fermentation and there are certain conditions under which the crushing can be modified. These include:

1. The production of a wine using the carbonic maceration approach. In this procedure some extent of internal cellular fermentation takes place and whole berries are essential for this activity (refer to Section 5). Following this cellular activity, the clusters are sometimes

transferred directly to the press, bypassing the crushing step entirely, or crushed and fermented by a yeast culture.

2. The fruit is in a late harvest condition or is infected by either *Botrytis cinerea* or other molds. Under these conditions grape yields are low and berries are very high in sugar content. With mold infections, the grape skin is generally frail and easily torn and the removal of shriveled berries from the stems is less successful, often leading to significant loss of berries with the stems if crushing and destemming is attempted. This type of fruit is also much more difficult to press due to the deterioration of the cell wall and the slimy nature of the corresponding pulp. Instead, whole clusters are usually pressed directly (and the stems or an inert plant fiber such as rice hulls, are often included as a press aid) to provide a more open press cake and more complete juice recovery. This practice can also be employed for the slip-skin cultivars (most of the native American and some hybrid cultivars) and often with the pulpy Muscat cultivars and Sultanina (Thompson Seedless).

3. Red wine styles in which partial crushing and some whole berries are desired in the skin cap. This approach attempts to provide some berry aromas or carbonic maceration character to the wine by having them released at the point of pressing. Levels of between 10 to 30% whole berries are typical in such applications.
4. Red wine styles in which partial or complete stem addition to the fermentation is considered desirable. Such styles involve adding back dry stems at levels of 20 to 50% to provide some woody herbaceous aromas and additional tannin to the wines.
5. Whole cluster pressing procedures such as those often employed in the production of sparkling wines. This provides the minimum time between berry breakage and juice separation or removal and can provide juices with much lower flavonoid extraction and sometimes with lower levels of suspended solids. The use of whole cluster handling approaches for direct pressing is more common in the production of white juices from Pinot noir and Meunier for sparkling wines and sometimes for the blush white wines from red cultivars such as Zinfandel and Grenache. It also provides juices from berries that have not been exposed to the normal contact surfaces of must pump and the transfer line.

In all other cases, the vast majority of grape loads will be crushed as completely as possible in order to enhance juice release and will be destemmed as completely as possible by the crushing equipment.

B. MUST HANDLING

A number of the defects and undesirable features of young wines such as low titratable acidity, high pH, the formation of significant hydrogen sulfide or volatile acidity, the incidence of incomplete fermentation, and low intensity of fruit aromas can often be attributed to inadequate or inappropriate treatment of the original must.

The first opportunity for the manipulation of juice composition is with the freshly crushed grapes. A number of important wine components have been shown to display different concentrations between the central juice and pulp and the skin. The most obvious of these are the anthocyanins, tannins, potassium and other minerals in the skin, the flavonoid and procyanidin phenols in the skins and seeds, a number of the terpene fractions (Wilson et al. 1986; Marais 1987) and other volatiles related to varietal character of the Sauvignon family—Sauvignon blanc, Sémillon, Cabernet Sauvignon, Cabernet franc, and Merlot—(Bayonove et al. 1975; Augustyn et al. 1982; Heymann et al. 1986; Lacy et al. 1991). The desire to promote the extraction of these and other flavorants has led to the practices of skin contact, which involves the use of pectic and various hydrolytic enzymes and to the widespread introduction of membrane presses that favor juice release with a minimum of skin tearing.

1. Skin (or Pomace) Contact

The purpose of deliberate contact between skins and juice of white grapes is to provide the time and conditions for an extraction that cannot be duplicated by extraction during fermentation, or other skin treatments. The extraction is primarily of the flavonoid phenols associated with the skins and seeds as well as other less well-defined flavorants. (Ramey et al. 1986). This is preferably done at intermediate temperatures of 15 to 20°C (59–68°F) in order to minimize the onset of fermentation by native organisms. These manipulations can vary from those without control of temperature, without mixing or juice pumping and imprecise times between 12 and 24 hours, to cooled must, often blanketed with an inert gas, together with pump-over operations and contact times so that a predefined degree of extraction is obtained, generally measured as a spectrophotometric assay of the phenolic content. Depending on the winery facilities, in particular the ability to drain juices quickly, some skin contact will become inevitable and this should be recognized.

a. *White Musts*

In general, the best white table wines of the young varietal style are obtained primarily from free-run juices and low phenolic press fractions. The greatest potential for the manipulation of juice flavor lies in the treatment of the terpene-based cultivars by heat, pH, and commercial enzyme preparations. The commercial availability of glycosidases of microbial origin permits the option of skin and juice treatment of Riesling, Muscat, and Gewürztraminer cultivars for the release of free terpenes from their more common nonvolatile glycosides (Williams et al. 1980). Studies of the influence of temperature on the rates of the enzyme-based hydrolysis in juices are not presently available nor are studies of the desirability of a selective treatment of the skins rather than the juice itself.

In the past, the use of screw presses, which result in more skin tearing, provided desirable skin components but with an unacceptable level of tannins. Much of the extraction that would naturally occur for cultivars such as Chardonnay and Sauvignon blanc can now be recovered in the fractions from membrane presses without their corresponding tannins. Although these press fractions can often provide many of the components that would normally result from skin contact, they cannot replace the long-term diffusional extraction and chemical reactions that may occur during the skin contact period, especially when enzyme-mediated reactions, with cultivars such as Gewürztraminer, Riesling, and the Muscats are concerned.

b. *Red Musts*

With red musts, the time available and the solvent conditions for selective extraction of flavorants are much greater. The application of skin contact for color and flavor extraction prior to fermentation has recently received renewed interest. The extraction and retention of the anthocyanin pigments during the fermentation is still not completely understood. Particular interest lies in obtaining earlier anthocyanin extraction together with alternative tannin extraction patterns, but almost all of this is obtained by way of a conventional warm fermentation.

There is limited interest in thermal extraction conditions such as those generated by the process referred to as thermovinification, in which juices are heated to temperatures of between 50°C and 60°C (122°F and 140°F) and mixed with the skins to provide a rapid, short term extraction condition. Of more interest, especially with hybrid grapes, is the use of must warming to promote the activity of added pectic enzymes and to facilitate pressing of the skins. Red juices prepared in this way for either fermentation or concentration have the advantage of having kept the skins out of the fermentor, but the extraction conditions result in the production of wines different to those made in the conventional manner.

2. Must Cooling or Heating Requirements

The use of must cooling will be dependent on the temperature of the grapes when delivered and for white must, the desired temperature for skin contact (if it is to be used) and the time delay associated with the draining operation before juice cooling can take place. One disadvantage with must cooling is the slowing of the activity of any added enzymes such as pectic or other hydrolytic enzymes. The concern with a warm must lies in the accelerated enzyme reactions resulting in both more extensive browning and oxygen consumption and faster growth of native organisms. The ability to cool the juice and the addition of sulfur dioxide are often deferred until after skin separation has taken place so that a significant amount of the refrigeration energy is not wasted by cooling the skins. A more complete discussion of the heat transfer calculations associated with juice cooling can be found in Chapter 14.

3. Inert Gas Blanketing

The juice released from the grapes at crushing will initially be saturated with oxygen from the air. The mixing of oxidases and their substrates in the juice will generally result in the complete consumption of this dissolved oxygen in a matter of minutes under natural conditions. The pickup of oxygen from the air during the harvesting, transport, crushing, draining, and pressing operations can be minimized by the use of inert gas blanketing.

Carbon dioxide is the gas of choice because it is heavier than air and will fall and displace the air from the must or juice surface in a partially filled container. Applications vary from the use of solid CO_2 blocks and chips in harvesting bins and crusher and press sumps, to the in-line sparging of musts with liquid CO_2 and gas dispersal over the must surface with gas from storage cylinders. Although it is seldom practiced, fermentation gases can be recovered from fermentors and used during juice transfers and wine storage for potential savings, especially in larger facilities. The use of solid and liquid CO_2 have the additional advantages of providing must cooling by direct heat transfer as they sublime or evaporate to form the inert gas blanket (Chapter 14), however, this process is relatively expensive when compared to conventional refrigeration.

The use of nitrogen, argon or other inert gases offers no advantage at this point in winemaking, although the solubility of the gas becomes a factor during the use of inert gas in procedures close to bottling (Chapter 11). Nitrogen gases will not have the denser-than-air blanketing effect of CO_2 and being closer in molecular weight to oxygen, the diffusivity of O_2 in it will be greater. This will generally require volumetric displacement in order to completely remove oxygen.

The use of inert gases to exclude oxygen from juices as well as the opposite approach of hyperoxidation (that is, not slowing oxidative enzyme activity by cooling or sulfur dioxide additions and the deliberate introduction of air) can lead to juices that are depleted of dissolved oxygen prior to fermentation. While the inert gas case is a desirable storage condition for juice, it is a precursor for poor cell viability in the latter stages of the alcoholic fermentation (Andreasen and Strier 1953, 1954). Aeration of the juice to provide between 4 and 8 mg/L of dissolved oxygen at the time of inoculation is recommended to avoid this situation. In situations where natural flora are to be used to conduct the fermentation, there will always be a competition for oxygen between the oxidases and the yeast, in which the oxidases would appear to always have the advantage. The problem is enhanced by the presence of significant levels of suspended solids, which contain additional oxidase activity, in white juices and incomplete fermentation caused by this continues to be a problem in certain countries (Ribéreau-Gayon 1985).

4. Metering and Measurement of Musts and Juices

The most common procedure for the measurement the quantity of grapes in a load is by weight determinations. This can be done by weighing either individual delivery bins (or gondolas) or entire truckloads, first when full, then again when emptied, with the weight of the load determined by the difference.

The bin-weighing approach uses a scale attached to the beam which picks up the bin and can make both the full and empty determinations as part of the dumping cycle. The major operating difficulty lies in the swinging motion of the bin since this needs to be stopped before an accurate reading can be made. Some systems dispense with the second determination and use a predetermined value for the empty bin weight.

The truck-weighing approach is the more common one in the United States and below-ground scales are used to weigh the truck prior to and after delivery. The scales are generally located at the grape load inspection or sampling station and the returning of trucks to this location for the second weighing can result in delays in the delivery of incoming trucks.

The alternative approach is to perform must measurements of the rate of delivery by in-line procedures (such as mass flow or volumetric flow rates) that when integrated provide the same information. This method can also be used for the control of metered additions of sulfite, nutrients, yeast, and sometimes, malolactic bacteria.

Such instrumentation can be installed with both must and wine applications in mind. The meters could be installed in a removable section of line and be used for flow measurements and in-line additions of fining agents or blending of wines at later stages of production.

a. *The Quantity of Must*

Metering of the quantity of must can best be done volumetrically by using a positive displacement pump such as a rotary vane or progressive cavity pump (Chapter 13). These can be calibrated in terms of rotational speed and throughput. If the pump is used with a variable speed control, the speed can be monitored by a counting sensor and a sensing mark located on the pump axle. Such a volumetric metering system can then be used for the accurate control of in-line additions of any concentrated enzyme, sulfite, or nutrient solutions prior to the must entering the drainer, fermentor, or press. In the case of constant operating speed for the pump, other in-line dosing pumps can be set at a desired capacity and the entire system controlled for intermittent operation based on the availability of must to the inlet of the must pump.

There are a number of mass flowmeters, generally based on magnetic sensing or Coriolis principles that could be used for measuring must additions. This approach has the advantage of being able to allow for variations in the pumping rate and for gas entrainment within the must line (by comparison, a volumetric meter would presume that only must had been delivered). These meters would be particularly suited to the determination of the mass of a load by an in-line procedure as an alternative to the present double-weighing procedure that often impedes the rapid delivery and handling of loads.

b. *In-Line Additions to Musts*

The nature of the addition will influence whether the must is the appropriate point for it to be made. For example, with pectic enzyme additions to release more free-run juice, the principal substrates will be in the skins and the juice merely acts as the delivering agent. The activity will be best at warmer temperatures and adequate time should be allowed for the hydrolysis reaction to proceed prior to pressing. In the case of sulfite, there will be activities of oxidative enzymes both in the juice and associated with the pulp, and the presence of natural microorganisms both in the juice and on the skins. There will also be considerable loss of added material to the skins and suspended pulp. In the case of nutrient additions, there will also be a loss of added material associated with the removal of skins for pressing of white cultivars. As a result, some wineries have opted to make the additions of sulfur dioxide, nutrients, and yeast only to clarified juices for white wine production.

The use of different levels of addition to white and red musts can be easily handled by the use of a programmable controller on the addition pump that would only need to know the type of must, or by the use of separate crushing units or must lines for the two must types.

Whatever the choice, the result of in-line rather than batch addition will be a more uniform mixing of the addition in the must during transport to the fermentor, resulting in a more uniform distribution of the addition throughout the entire load. The must will also be in a more protected state should production difficulties arise which might delay the timing of the yeast inoculation.

c. *Juice Properties*

The use of in-line refractometers for the determination of must density (and hence the sugar content of the load) is popular in parts of Europe. The refractive index value of the load is taken as the average value recorded during the transfer period. There are a number of meters for solution density which are based on the vibrational frequency of an internal oscillating element, the difficulties lie in the separation of clear juice from the skins in a proportionate manner and the disadvantage is that a juice-only measure is obtained.

The juice-only value can be quite different from that of the skins of certain cultivars and especially for partially dehydrated berries, where it can be higher by as much as 10% of the density or sugar value. The higher sugar in the skins is usually only apparent during skin contact, pressing, or fermentation and can pose later difficulties with grape payment, incomplete fermentation due to the higher ethanol levels, or the taxation or classification of wines based on their ethanol content.

An in-line monitoring system for sugar content would be a desirable alternative to the present manual sampling procedure (of a predetermined number of tube samples from a preselected number of delivery bins). The decision to reject a load based on the juice density could, however, only be made after the grapes are crushed and transported into a holding tank, rather than before, as the present scheme allows. Many wineries have grape buying contracts that have bonus functions for certain sugar contents so that the accurate determination of the sugar level can be of significant financial importance. From a fermentation point of view, the juice density at the time of inoculation is more important than that at delivery. Some cultivars and maturity conditions have shown a tendency to release additional sugar from more concentrated layers of the pulp and skins after the initial juice release. This can result in a rise in the sugar content when associated with skin contact and press fractions and higher than expected ethanol yields from the measured sugar content. If raisined berries are present, the discrepancy is even larger.

d. *Other Measurements of Composition*

There are now several commercial spectrophotometers that can measure in the near-infrared (NIR) region of the electromagnetic spectrum. These can be used for the accurate determination of sugar content, either by an in-line or sampled measurement. The main advantage is that the actual sugar content as glucose and fructose would be measured rather than a solution property such as density or refractive index. A second advantage is that the solution properties are temperature dependant while the spectrophotometric determination is not. The solution property approach requires that the sample temperature be recorded and for corrections to be made. (The same spectrophotometers have the capability of determining ethanol content and the extraction of phenolics and could be used as general analytical sensors for fermentation monitoring and wines rather than sugar instruments alone). Some of these units use optical fiber probes that would be particularly useful in the process analysis of juice and wine composition. There do not appear to be any of these units presently in a production-scale application in the U.S. wine industry.

5. Must Lines and Tank Filling

Must lines provide the most common means by which must is directed to selected drainers or fermentors. They should be made from stainless steel, 102 to 153 mm in diameter, sloping for self-draining and able to be isolated and rinsed easily or taken apart in sections for cleaning. They should be free of small-radius right-angle bends, with a minimum of vertical rises and overall distance. Drainers should be located adjacent to or as close as possible to the crusher (and the must pump) to minimize the formation of fine solids associated with the shearing and tearing of pulp during the transfer operation.

Drainers and tanks should be filled from the base, to avoid solids generation by skins falling from the top of the tanks to the surface and through a ball valve, to avoid obstructions and to permit the line to completely close in the presence of solids. The flow resistance experienced by the must pump, due to the must line and all of its fittings will be least at the beginning and increasing throughout the filling, but always less than that required to raise the must to the level that would be used if it was to be filled from the top of the tank.

In cases where in-line must cooling is desired, the heat exchanger should be located so as to minimize the downstream length of the must line. This is because the must being transported is under conditions of relatively high surface area per unit volume and a significant heat load can be gained from warm ambient air. The alternative is to provide thermal insulation for the must line from this point to the tank so as to minimize the pickup of heat from the surrounding air.

C. JUICE AND SKIN SEPARATION FOR WHITE WINES

The juice to be prepared for white table wine will generally be removed from its skins for two main reasons. The first is the skins represent a major source of natural microflora and the second is the desire to minimize the extent of phenol extraction from the skins.

1. Natural Settling for Skin Separation

The use of gravity settling for the separation of skins from the juice in vertical tanks continues to be a fairly common practice. The time required will be determined by the rate at which the skin cap rises in relation to the height of the tank. The rate of rise of the skin cap is influenced by the extent of gas inclusions in the cap. The rate is fastest at the beginning and then declines, taking progressively longer times for the successive improvements in separation. The practice of introducing an inert gas at the base of the tank to assist in the rise of the cap is not widely practiced.

2. Static Drainers

A drainer is a specially designed piece of equipment that makes use of some kind of screen for the separation of free-run juice from the associated skins. This separation is essential for the production of distinctive varietal white wines, and may take place either immediately after crushing or after a period of juice and skin contact. Drainers can also be used in some production of blanc-de-noir, blush, and rosé style wines, port-style wines, and early-press red table wines.

In a general sense, many wineries use the cylindrical fermentation tanks as drainers, by transporting the must into the tank, allowing a skin cap to rise, and then drawing off the juice from a point near the base of the tank in an operation referred to as *racking*. The suspended solids in the racked juice are then allowed to settle further under the action of gravity before being removed by another racking step prior to fermentation. The problem with this method is that the suspended solids content of the resulting juice is generally unacceptably high at best and the juice will almost always require further clarification prior to fermentation.

Most draining equipment uses some type of screen (made of wire bars or sheet material with slotted or circular holes) to obtain the separation. There are drainers in which the skins are not moving with respect to the screen while juice is removed (static drainers) and those in which the skins move across the screen by sliding over the surface (such as the Dutch State Mines, DSM screens) or by an advancing helical screw during juice removal (continuous drainers).

a. *Early Types of Static Drainers*

The earliest developments in static drainers appear to be those in Australia, South Africa, and Germany where the importance of low solids juices in the production of varietal white wines was first recognized. Static drainers built by (and referred to as) the Mackenzie, Potter, Miller, and Willmes drainers were introduced in those countries in the late 1960s. The first two mentioned were upright cylinders which were mounted over a hopper. The Mackenzie unit had an inverted conical screen at the base and another screen at the wall. The bottom door was opened after drainage to allow for the skins to be removed. The Potter tank was an upright cylinder with a conical base section. The screen was a central cylinder which was drawn out through the top door of the unit in order to permit skin discharge from the base of the cone. The first commercial drainers to be used in California appear to be the Potter Drainer and the Winery Systems unit that was tested during the 1973–74 seasons (Zepponi and Cottrell 1975). The latter was similar to the Potter tank except that the central screen did not have to be completely withdrawn from the unit to allow skin removal and discharge was through a front door. The limitations of these units were caused by slotted screen employed and difficulty of skin removal following the draining operation. The screen type had a direct bearing on the filtration effectiveness and the ease of cleaning.

b. *Contemporary Drainers*

The drainer design most widely used in California today is an upright cylinder with a tapered conical section offset at the base (Figure 3-2). This is a shape that was in use in several European countries in the mid 1970s, but the important improvement lies in the introduction of bar screens that provide superior retention of grape pulp during the draining operation, when compared to slotted screens, and easier cleaning. Screens of this type are manufactured in the United States by the Wedge Wire and Johnson companies and a typical cross section is shown in Figure 3-3.

The skins are removed by a gravity generally into either a hopper or directly into a batch press. This is the most successful drainer yet designed and the drained juice is generally less than 1% vol/vol solids and can be fermented directly without the need for further clarification. Almost all of the earlier designs required either additional clarification equip-

Fig. 3-2. A juice drainer.

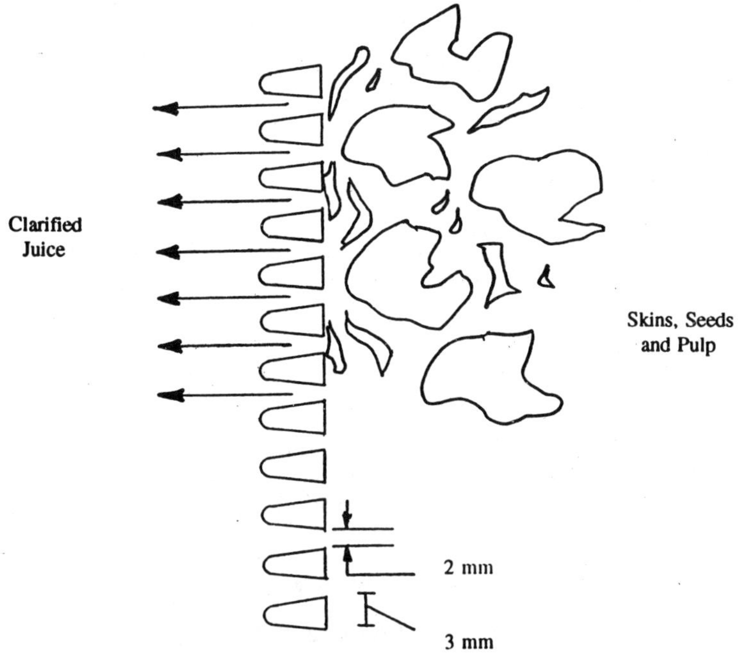

Fig. 3-3. Cross-section of the bar screen used in the juice drainers.

ment or further settling time and a racking operation before inoculation could proceed.

At present, 10-, 20-, and 40-Tm capacity units are being used in California. These generally have a single semicircular screen, although some units have two screens. The screen area per unit volume determines the rate at which the screen fouls and in larger units the screen area needs to be increased in order to maintain this ratio. Manufacturers in the United States include Santa Rosa Stainless Steel (bar screen type), and the Paul Mueller Company (slotted screen type). Present installations in California have all been set up to discharge directly into batch presses. This eliminates the need for screw or belt conveyors for the transfer of skins.

Some units have been fitted with cooling jackets, but this is of limited effectiveness due to the stationary must at the inside wall and the poor heat transfer coefficient in such a static arrangement. The poor thermal conductivity of a skin cap ensures that while cooling is applied to the outer layers of the must, only slow and limited heat conduction from the center of the drainer occurs.

3. Continuous Dejuicers

The alternative type of dejuicer that was used in the past was the continuous inclined dejuicer. This consisted of an inclined hopper in which the base section was replaced by a slotted screen to allow the juice to be removed as the skins were swept over it by a helical screw. While these units do provide considerable juice recovery prior to pressing, the suspended solids content is usually increased significantly and requires further clarification, commonly by centrifuges or settling, prior to fermentation. Typical suspended solids levels and juice composition from such dejuicers have been reported to be approximately 4% vol/vol by Maurer and Meidinger (1976).

D. JUICE CLARIFICATION FOR WHITE WINES

White juices can be clarified by several alternative methods. The reduction of suspended grape solids to levels of 1 to 2% by volume prior to fermentation is now a common practice and is supported by sensory evaluations (Singleton et al. 1975; Van Wyk 1978; Houtman and Du Plessis 1981; Williams et al. 1978) which show the preferences for such juices in the production of fruit-style white table wine.

There are several reasons for the clarification of white juices prior to fermentation or storage. These include: (1) A major proportion of the oxidative enzyme activity is associated with the pulp and skin fragments, (2) the incidence of mold and wild flora is highest on the skin fragments; (3) the laccase from botrytis or other molds will be present in both pulp and skin tissue; (4) elemental sulfur and other vineyard residues will be more associated with the skin and pulp; and (5) there is some evidence of an esterase activity within the grape tissue which reduces the accumulation of esters produced by the yeast during fermentation. For most purposes an opalescent juice is adequate, water-clear juice is not necessary and is more likely to lead to fermentation difficulties when juices have a low nutrient status.

The higher oxidase or laccase activity is associated with a more rapid natural oxygen uptake rate by the juice, leading to an increased possibility of an oxygen-depleted condition at the point of inoculation. The presence of high residues of elemental sulfur is a major source of the formation of hydrogen sulfide by yeast during fermentation. One of the main differences between the traditional and New World approaches to white table wine production has been the desire to produce fruitier and varietally distinctive white wines by more extensive juice clarification.

The extent to which grape pulp particles are present in the free-run and press juices will depend not only on the cultivar and the physical condition of the fruit at harvest, but also on the methods and equipment used for harvesting, grape delivery, crushing, must transfer, and juice and skin separation. The crushing conditions, the type of must pump; the diameter, length, and bends in must transfer lines and mode of delivery into the drainer; tank; or press can all influence the quantity and size of suspended pulp present in the juice.

The properties and the size distribution of these suspended solids need to be further quantified before a more complete evaluation of the separation alternatives can be made. These particles, together with compositional aspects of the juice such as polysaccharides, proteins, phenolics, and pH, will often determine the ability of these fine suspended solids to be removed by alternative separation methods due to hindered settling and the role of charged particle interactions which will impede the clarification by natural settling.

1. Natural Settling

The natural settling of fine suspended matter by gravity is governed in part by the density difference between the suspended pulp and the juice. Other factors include the size of the particle, the attachment of bubbles, juice viscosity and fluid currents within the tank caused by thermal convection or rising gas bubbles. Typical particle sizes in the range 20 to 100 μm and settling times of the order of 10 to 20 hours indicate that the density difference between the pulp and the juice is of the order of 0.03 to 0.05 g/mL.

At certain concentrations, the mass of the particle can become secondary to the electrostatic repulsions of surface charges between similar nearby particles and settling is prevented. The role of colloids in the juice, the pH and temperature of the juice then have a major influence on the rate of settling under these conditions. It is at this level that the clarifying effect of added pectic enzyme preparations becomes most apparent.

The rate at which various levels of the tank can clear will usually be influenced by what is referred to as hindered settling. At the base of the tank, especially, the solids will settle more slowly as they encounter increasing solids concentrations and particle-particle interactions limit the rate and extent of settling. The extent to which they will compact depends on many of the factors mentioned above. The position and sharpness of the clear juice/solids interface is dependent on the juice and its handling history. There is a widespread variation in the settling and compaction of such lees. The use of a racking arm (Figure 3-4) and a sight glass fitting in conjunction with the racking valve will greatly enhance the recovery of clear juice fractions in the presence of such variations in settling. In California, the racking arms are made by York Machine Works.

The effect of circulation patterns within the tank caused by either thermal convection or the onset of fermentation, can easily prevent normal settling from taking place. The benefits of juice cooling in order to promote rapid settling is well recognized and this is due to the minimization of natural convection patterns and microbial activity rather than other explanations. Similarly, tall, small-diameter tanks will generally minimize the role of natural convection patterns and provide more ideal settling conditions even though the settling path is longer. As a result, the ability to clarify juices by this method depends on the ability to cool juices and to prevent spontaneous fermentations.

2. Clarification by Disc or Desludging Centrifuges

One alternative to natural settling which provides higher handling rates and a more extensive and predictable clarification is the use of the centrifugal separators known as centrifuges. The rapid clarification of juice and wine during the harvest permits better use of other equipment, but at considerably higher capital costs. There is a more extensive removal of larger grape pulp particles than by natural settling (Maurer 1978), and the hindered setting is practically eliminated.

The disc (or desludging) centrifuges have been used in winemaking throughout the world for more than 25 years. They have been used for the clarification of settled white juices and press fractions as well as for wines after fermentation and fining additions. They are mostly used in the two latter applications today, primarily because of the introduction and advantages of the decanting centrifuge for juice applications (see Chapter 7 for a more complete description of these machines and their operation).

The desludging centrifuges are best used to clarify juices of solids from typically less than 4% by volume (vol/vol) down to 1% or less.

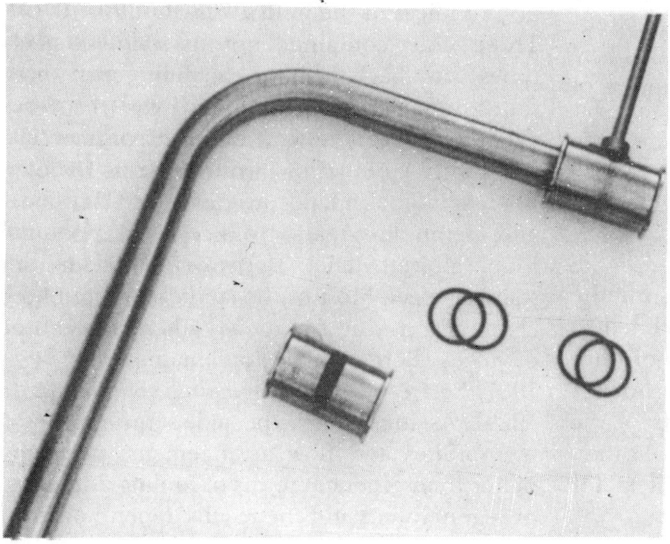

Fig. 3-4. A typical racking arm.

The flow is semicontinuous, being interrupted for the solids removal operation that is referred to as desludging. The frequency of desludging is proportional to the quantity of solids being removed and the juice throughput is reduced accordingly. This operating characteristic provides higher-capacity clarification only in juices with lower solids contents and their usefulness is limited with juices that are high in solids. It has the attractive feature of rapidly clarifying juices and yet allowing a small but predetermined quantity of natural solids to remain in the juice.

3. Clarification by Scroll or Decanting Centrifuges

The decanting centrifuges are more suitable for handling juices with higher solids contents than the desludging units, and they provide continual rather than intermittent solids discharge. The solids are discharged at one end as a relatively dry paste while the clarified juice leaves at the other end. The decanters develop much lower separating forces, have longer residence times for the juice, and are more suited to heavy lees clarification, primarily on juices rather than wines. Their capacity is not greatly affected by a high level of solids in the feed material. They also have operating advantages over the alternative diatomaceous earth lees filters and can also produce extensively, but not completely, clarified juices (see Chapter 7 for a more complete description of these machines and their operation).

4. Clarification by Filtration

a. *Diatomaceous Earth Filtration*

The use of diatomaceous earth filters for the general clarification of juices has declined in recent years. The most common type of filter employed for this task is the rotary drum vacuum filter which is still used in parts of the world for this purpose. The other application is the use of plate-and-frame lees filters for juice recovery from settled lees.

Specially designed lees filters which can operate at pressure differences of above 6 bar (90 psi) are generally used either with or without the use of a filter aid. Rotary vacuum filters are sometimes preferred due to the ease of removal of the filter cake compared to those developed in pressure- leaf and plate-and-frame filters. While there is evidence of the adsorption of amino acids by diatomaceous earth (Tercelj 1965), this is not a major effect during normal filtrations. The first juice to contact the earth cake may be significantly depleted of these components, but once the precoat becomes saturated, it cannot adsorb further. The fraction of the juice which is depleted in this way is usually insignificant in most juice filtrations.

b. *Cross-Flow Filtration*

The present interest in cross-flow filtration is that it provides a continuous filtration alternative without the need for diatomaceous earth. The most important features of a cross-flow filter for this application are its ability to perform under a wide range of suspended solids contents and to be periodically cleared by a back-flushing operation. (A more complete discussion of the principles of cross-flow can be found in Chapter 7).

Microfilters with nominal pore sizes of 0.2 and 0.5 μm were first tested for the clarification of juices in the mid 1970s (Boulton 1976). These units contained porous stainless steel tubes with back-flushing capability and were tested in juice clarification and yeast recovery studies. There is now a range of commercial units with various flow arrangements (hollow-fiber, spiral-bound, porous tube, and flat plate) and membranes made from ceramics, polysulfone, polyethylene, polyvinyl chloride, or stainless steel. Most of the studies to date have centered on wine filtrations rather than those of juices (Berger 1985; Ludemann 1987; Peri 1987; Peri et al. 1988; Descout 1989; Gaillard 1989). As might be expected, some of these membranes and flow arrangements perform better than others in terms of fouling and ease of regeneration and the results depend on the particular juices (or wines) tested. The more chemically inert surfaces of stainless steel and ceramic materials seem to have less colloidal adsorption effects than most of the polymer materials and can be cleaned by stronger methods if fouled. The volume of the grape solids, which increases during batch operation, becomes a significant operating problem in some arrangements and there are obvious effects due to the colloid content of the juice. Further studies of the nature of the colloidal materials that cause the rapid initial decline in flux and the development of strategies to minimize these effects in grape juices are needed.

As with most cross-flow units there is a need for cooling of the recirculating retentate juice stream. Much larger areas than those normally used for conventional perpendicular-flow filters are required because of the relatively low flux rates. At present there are very few installations for juice clarification in wineries although there are a number of commercial installations for cranberry and apple juice products in the United States.

Cross-flow microfiltration provides an alternative to diatomaceous earth filtration for the production of very clear, nominally sterile juice. It is be best used in conjunction with other equipment that can provide partially clarified juices (such as a centrifuge) rather than for use with turbid juices directly. It will be discussed in Chapter 7 with regard to wine clarification applications.

5. Flotation Methods

The application of flotation principles to the separation and collection of grape solids has received attention from time to time. In this approach, fine gas bubbles, usually nitrogen, are introduced into a static or slowly moving juice. Much of the suspended pulp becomes attached to the bubbles due to the surface tension and then floats upwards toward the surface where it can be collected. The main feature of the flotation vessel is a minimum of turbulence and mixing. All have a method for the selective removal of the clarified juice and/or the floating foam containing the solids. Both batch and continuous approaches are possible. One of the earliest trials of this approach (Boulton and Green 1977) involved two long horizontal tanks, the first for bubble introduction and the second for separation and removal of the phases. The tanks were partially filled with juice, and headspace nitrogen was re-introduced into the juice by ejectors. The separation in the second stage was achieved by an overflow weir. Juices containing 6 to 12% by volume solids could be clarified into a stream with typically 2% solids with a recovery of 85%, while the solids stream contained between 30 and 36% solids. The heavy solids fraction contained significant juice and further treatment of it was required. There were factors within the juices which affected the stability of the bubbles and the foam phase and this was even more so when pectic enzymes were used. The process has potential as a continuous, relatively fast, low-energy process for the clarification of more than 80% of white juices and has recently received renewed interest in Europe (Ferrarini et al. 1992; Davin and Sahraoui 1993).

E. JUICE AND MUST TREATMENTS

The materials that are permitted to be added to juices (and wines) are described in the winemaking regulations issued by the Bureau of Alcohol, Tobacco, and Firearms (BATF) (see Appendix B). These regulations also control the limits of addition for certain materials while others are referred to as GRAS (Generally Recognized As Safe) materials that can be used without limit. The procedure by which processes, treatments, and materials are approved for winemaking involves the development of a proposed rule or action, public comment, and the rendering of a decision by the BATF. As a result there is somewhat of an evolution in winemaking regulations with periodic updates of the general regulations. There is also an option for winemakers to request a conditional use permit for small-scale trials with new materials, specific preparations or new processes.

The treatment of musts and clarified juices prior to fermentation will often include one or more of the following actions:

1. Nutrient addition
2. Sulfur dioxide addition
3. Acidity adjustment
4. Juice oxidation
5. Thermal treatment
6. Enzyme addition
7. Addition of inert solids.

Some of these treatments are often essential for making sound wines while others are more appropriately termed *stylistic* treatments where the value is more a matter of wine style or individual opinion. The extent to which some of these treatments is necessary or desirable can vary quite widely depending on the cultivars involved and the wine style that is sought. There are often quite different approaches between regions and even countries. Within the stylistic treatments, there is usually a spectrum of opinions ranging from minimizing the effect to maximizing it, with many levels of acceptance in between.

1. Nutrient Additions

The rate-limiting aspect of microbial cell growth or fermentation is generally thought to be the rate of transport of nutrients into cells by membrane-bound enzyme systems, or carriers. The response of the activity of organism to the concentration of a rate-limiting nutrient is usually one, in which there is a linear response at low levels but a move toward a saturation condition, which shows little further enhancement, at higher concentrations. When a nutrient becomes growth-limiting, small additions will generally result in more rapid growth, while additions to levels above that required, lead to little if any further enhancement. One of the dilemmas that winemakers face is that there will generally be a positive response to the addition in a deficient juice, but usually no effect will be seen for the same action in nutritionally adequate juices. Nutrients of importance to the growth of yeast and bacteria in juices include nitrogen sources (both ammonia and free amino acids) and the vitamins (biotin, thiamin, pantothenic acid, and inositol). The problem is compounded since it is not easy or practical to assay juices for all growth-limiting nutrients in advance.

The nutrient status of the juice is particularly important for clarified white juices. This is because red musts are in contact with their skins and grape pulp during most of the fermentation. White juices which have been settled to moderate solids levels of 3 to 4% vol/vol will rarely show signs of nutritional deficiencies. However, juices which are clarified extensively, typically to 1% vol/vol or less by settling, centrifugation, or filtration, will display a higher incidence of nutritional deficiencies. The results can range from slower than usual fermentation rates (Schanderl 1959), and even incomplete fermentation, to the production of unusually high levels of such byproducts as acetic acid, pyruvic acid, and hydrogen sulfide. The extent to which these abnormalities is observed is higher among small fermentation volumes in which grape loads from individual vineyards are fermented separately. These effects are encountered far less in wineries where different loads of grapes or loads of different cultivars are fermented together, primarily due to some loads with lower than usual levels being compensated for by other loads with higher than usual levels of a limiting component.

a. *Ammonium Salts*

Ammonium salt additions have been known to stimulate the rate of fermentation of certain musts for more than 30 years. There are early examples of ammonium additions to juices since the early 1900s (Archer and Castor 1956). Since that time, ammonium salt additions have been used in winemaking regions throughout the world, although the response to such additions will often vary from vineyard to vineyard and from season to season. Studies in California have often shown little if any effect of such additions (Archer and Castor 1956), while others in regions of South Africa and Australia (Agenbach 1977; Monk 1986) have resulted in significant effects indicating inadequate levels of assimilable nitrogen or phosphorus.

The unique feature of ammonium salts is that they were found to be more stimulatory than an equivalent amount of any corresponding amino acid in beer worts. This is now thought to be due to different transport systems for the ammonium ions and amino acids, and a more responsive system for the ammonium ion. The amino acids are mostly transported into the yeast cell by a general amino acid carrier, while the ammonium ion is transported by an entirely different carrier (see also Chapter 4). The form of nitrogen added by most investigators is generally the monohydrogen phosphate salt, although other forms have been used. The additions are commonly reported in terms of the quantity of elemental nitrogen rather than the quantity of the salt. There are, however, few studies in which other phosphate additions have been made to help in determining whether the effect is due to the ammonium, the phosphate, or the combination of the two (Archer and Castor 1956). Some phosphate is required for yeast growth and other salts (chloride, sulfate, nitrate) are less attractive.

Some wineries perform routine analyses of the must ammonium content as a basis for the addition of ammonium salt supplements. The specific ion electrode procedure with a known addition (McWilliam and Ough 1974) is usually employed and corrections are made to levels in the range 100 to 120 mg/L of ammonia (82.5–98.8 mg N/L). Other approaches include the determination of the free amino nitrogen (FAN) content by a spectrophotometric assay (Mandl et al. 1971; Lie 1972) and a routine addition to all juices, without any attempt to determine the levels of assimilable nitrogen present.

b. Amino Acids

The amino acid content of juice can be shown to depend on a number of factors such as cultivar, rootstock, and vineyard location (Huang and Ough 1989), as well as cultural conditions. With mold-infected clusters, there should be concern regarding the depletion of some of the amino acids and most of the significant vitamins due to growth of the mold organisms. Examples of the general depletion of amino acids due to botrytis infection and the corresponding fermentation problems have been reported (Kielhofer and Wurdig 1960, Dittrich and Sponholz 1975).

The assimilable nitrogen content of a juice is generally agreed to be confined to the free alpha-amino acids plus ammonia since proline and hydroxyproline are not used by *Saccharomyces cerevisiae* under anaerobic conditions. The free alpha-amino acid content can be determined by one of two colormetric methods based on the ninhydrin (Lie 1972) or trinitrobenzenesulfonic acid (TNBS) derivatives (Mandl et al. 1971). The differences in the values obtained by these methods are due to the inclusion of the ammonium content in the ninhydrin procedure, its absence from the TNBS method, the inclusion of some peptide materials in the TNBS method (Mandl et al. 1971), and the partial color yield of certain amino acids by each assay.

The only amino acid presently permitted in the United States as an additive to juices is glycine, perhaps because permission has not been sought for any others. There are, however, several yeast hydrolysate and proprietary preparations that are approved for this, purpose although few of these contain a full compliment of vitamins.

c. Vitamins

The vitamin pool, in particular biotin, pantothenate, and thiamin, is usually at the tens to hundreds of micrograms per liter. Due to the trace levels of these compounds, the percentage reductions of their concentrations would be greater as a result of mold growth.

Early studies of the role of vitamins in byproduct formation on 23 strains of five yeast species showed that in many vitamin-deficient juices, the fermentations can be completed

(Ribéreau-Gayon et al. 1954). The levels of nicotinic acid and aminobenzoic acid had no effect of byproduct formation. Juices with pantothenic acid deficiencies produced higher acetic acid and more glycerol, while those with thiamin deficiencies decreased the levels of 2,3-butanediol formation. The effect of low levels of biotin, pyridoxine, or inositol was found to result in elevated formations of succinic acid. Similar studies of byproduct formation of the widely used commercial strains in use today, need to be done.

Perhaps the best examples of such effects are the elevated levels of bound sulfur dioxide in finished wines made from mold-infected fruit (Kielhofer and Wurdig 1960). Pyruvic acid is one of the major byproducts that would be expected to accumulate due to a thiamin deficiency and it is responsible for much of the nonacetaldehyde sulfite binding pool (Dittrich and Sponholz 1975).

The biotin requirements for maximal growth and fermentation of several widely used wine yeast strains has been determined to be between 0.7 and 1.3 $\mu g/L$ (Davenport 1985). The minimum levels of pantothenic acid required are approximately 50 $\mu g/L$ (Ough et al. 1989). The corresponding thiamin requirements are not readily available for the common wine yeast strains, but it is present in most yeast food preparations.

2. Sulfur Dioxide Additions

The use of sulfur dioxide to restrict the extent of juice browning and to inhibit or kill most of the natural microflora in the juice has been practiced for many decades. The minimum levels of addition required to obtain a particular effect, such as 90% inhibition of the phenol oxidase or a 90% reduction in the natural viable cell count, are dependent on many factors, and are considered in more detail in Chapter 12.

a. *Inhibition of Oxidative Enzymes*

Levels of 25 to 75 mg/L of sulfur dioxide in clarified juices led to inhibitions of 75 and 97% of phenol oxidase activity (Dubernet and Ribéreau-Gayon 1973; Amano et al. 1979). The level required for a 50% inhibition under these conditions is approximately 15 mg/L of added sulfur dioxide. The results from these two independent studies show a common inhibition curve with sulfite concentration (Fig. 3-5).

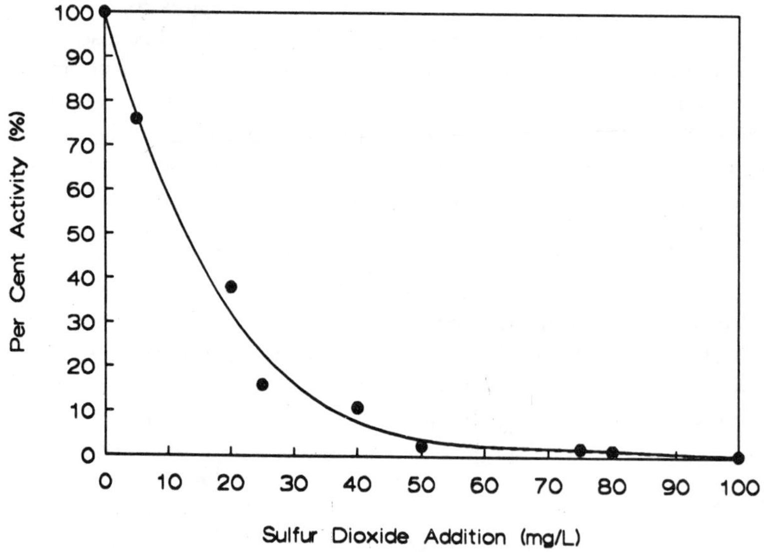

Fig. 3-5. Effect of sulfur dioxide on grape phenol oxidase activity.

Since the levels of enzyme activity in these studies were not necessarily the same, one could conclude that the inhibition is more likely to be of a competitive type, that is, between the sulfite and the oxygen for the oxygen binding site of the enzyme. There is recent evidence that the binding of one form of sulfur dioxide is also irreversible (Sayavedra and Montgomery 1986). A more complete discussion of the nature of this inhibition can be found in Chapter 12.

Differences in natural enzyme activity between white grape cultivars can vary by up to an order of magnitude (Traverso-Rueda and Singleton 1973; Hooper et al. 1985). With such a wide variation in natural activity it would seem that a similar variation in the minimum free sulfur dioxide level for similar inactivation or inhibition would be needed. The situation is further complicated due to the enzyme activity associated with the suspended solids from the berry. The binding of sulfur dioxide by grape solids plays a major role in the effectiveness of any addition and the activity observed can be due primarily to the enzyme activity associated with the pulp, (Amano et al. 1979). As a result, much higher levels of addition are often required to prevent browning in turbid juices. Actual practice varies from relatively high additions of 75 to 100 mg/L to must, of 30 to 50 mg/L to clarified juices, and in some cases no addition at all until after the fermentation.

The reaction of sulfite ions with oxygen as a competing chemical reaction is very slow at juice pH and the enzyme reaction dominates. The rate of oxygen uptake is further influenced by the variation in the enzyme activity, the temperature, the concentration of the major phenols in the juice, the substrate preference of the enzyme, and the competition between substrates for binding and reaction. This results in considerable variation in the uptake rates even for juice of the same cultivar as observed by White and Ough (1973).

The extent to which this oxygen uptake results in browning depends on the formation of a colorless reaction product between oxidized caftaric acid and the peptide glutathione (Singleton et al. 1984). There is considerable variation in the caftaric acid and glutathione contents of cultivars and consequently in browning potential due to enzyme-mediated oxidation.

The nature of the inactivation (or inhibition) of laccase as a function of sulfite level has been less extensively investigated; however, even at a sulfur dioxide level 150 mg/L free, an unacceptably high level for the production of wines, only 20% inhibition was observed, (Dubernet and Ribéreau-Gayon 1973). Since there will generally be residual laccase activity in finished wines from botrytis-infected grapes, sulfur dioxide does not provide an acceptable treatment for its inhibition. The higher activity and wider range of substrates of laccase (Table 3-1) make it especially troublesome in both red and white wines.

Ascorbic acid can be used as an antioxidant either alone or in conjunction with sulfur dioxide. It affects the enzyme activity only by its competition for and depletion of the available oxygen. It can reverse the first step of phenol oxidation, that is, converting the quinone back to its corresponding phenol. This leads to a delay in the onset of browning. It does not provide any demonstrated enzyme inhibition or antimicrobial activity and can decrease the free sulfur dioxide level by way of

Table 3-1. The relative activity of laccase on substrates in juices and wines.

Substrate	Relative activity (%)
4-methylcatechol	100
Catechol	104
Protocatechuic acid	119
Caffeic acid	132
(+) Catechin	100
Gallic acid	109
Phloroglucinol	143
p-Coumaric acid	90
Ferulic acid	109
Ascorbic acid	95
Anthocyanins	97
Leucoanthocyanins	84

Source of Data: Dubernet et al. (1977).

peroxide formation associated with its reaction with oxygen in wines.

It is important to realize that ascorbic acid is a substrate for the laccase enzyme (Dubernet et al. 1977) and is expected to behave as such in juice and wine conditions. While its consumption by either route leads to oxygen consumption and eventual brown pigment formation, the enzyme reaction does not lead to peroxide formation.

Levels of ascorbic acid addition range between 50 mg/L and 200 mg/L, depending on pH since the activity is due to the ascorbate ion rather than the undissociated form. The primary oxidation product, dehydroascorbic acid, is a potential binding agent for bisulfite ions and a precursor of nonoxidative browning reactions in finished wines. Unused ascorbate in finished wines can react in a manner similar to certain phenolic compounds and lead to the production of acetaldehyde in the presence of oxygen (Wildenradt and Singleton 1974).

b. The Inhibition and Killing of Natural Yeast and Bacteria

The second aspect of the application of sulfur dioxide to juices is the rapid killing of natural bacteria and yeast that have been present on the grape skins. While a number of studies have isolated and characterized the major strains of yeast found on grapes, there are few studies of their sensitivity to sulfur dioxide or the rate at which they are killed by it under juice conditions.

With wine yeast, the sensitivity to sulfur dioxide varies throughout the growth phase, with better survival capability as the stationary phase is approached. Studies of the killing power of sulfur dioxide in model wines (10% ethanol) indicate that levels of the order of 0.875 mg/L of the molecular form are quite capable of reducing the viable cell population by several decades in a day or so (Beech et al. 1979). In the absence of corresponding studies of the killing power of sulfur dioxide in juices, a more specific recommendation cannot be made at this time. It is generally assumed that the levels required for enzyme inhibition are adequate to provide a significant reduction in the level of viable microflora or alternatively, inhibition of their growth. The alternative approach in which no juice addition of sulfur dioxide is made then relies on the overpowering nature of the added inoculum and the developing ethanol to eliminate natural flora. While this strategy is often successful with respect to ethanol-sensitive strains, it can lead to undesired levels of natural flora which are ethanol-tolerant. This approach is favored if concurrent alcoholic and malolactic fermentations are to be encouraged.

3. Acidity Adjustment

In the cooler climates of the world such as Northern Europe, Eastern United States, and Canada, *acidity adjustment* generally means a reduction in titratable acidity so that the resulting wine will be acceptable. In the warmer climates, in regions of Southern Europe, California, Australia, and South Africa, it generally means increasing the titratable acidity, or the more critical situation of lowering the pH. A more complete discussion of acidity and pH in juices and wines can be found in Chapter 15.

It is generally accepted that a juice (or must) treatment is preferred to a wine treatment and this is especially so for the carbonate deacidifications or unless concurrent alcoholic and malolactic fermentations are desired. The adjustments will generally be based on target values for titratable acidity and pH rather than by sensory evaluation, due to the overwhelming influence of sugar levels in the juice. While these target values are usually based on previous experience with the extent of malic acid modification by yeast and the precipitation of potassium bitartrate during fermentation, typical ranges for titratable acidity in juices are 7 to 9 g/L as tartaric acid and pH 3.1 to 3.4.

The ability to obtain the desired level of acidity adjustment is very much influenced by the natural variation in the buffer capacity of various juices. The buffer capacity is primarily proportional to the concentrations of tartaric and malic acids and will decrease with reductions in their levels. It also depends on pH and has secondary contributions from most of the amino acids in juices and from the acids lactic, succinic, and proline in wines.

Acidity adjustments can be made by at least three alternative methods. These are the addition of an approved acid, the chemical deacidification with approved salts, and the use of ion exchange, either cation, anion, or both. The range of alternative methods approved by governments for the adjustment of acidity varies considerably, with perhaps most disagreement related to the use of ion exchange as a treatment for acidity adjustment.

a. *Acid Additions*

The addition of tartaric acid to juice can be used to increase the titratable acidity and reduce the pH. The extent of these changes depends on the amount of precipitation of potassium bitartrate and the buffer capacity of the juice. Tartaric is the acid of choice since it is not used by organisms at wine pH while both malic and citric acids are substrates for a number of lactic acid bacteria. It is also capable of precipitation as the potassium salt from most wines and in so doing can lower the pH provided it is the major acid present and the initial pH is below 4.0. The net effect of a tartaric acid addition is the release of protons due to its dissociation and the displacement of potassium ions from the buffer. The actual increase in titratable acidity will be the difference between the magnitude of the addition and the extent of the bitartrate precipitation. Such a precipitation can be viewed as simply the reversal action of the ATPase enzyme that is thought to control the accumulation of potassium in the vine and its fruit (Boulton 1980). The corresponding pH change will also depend on the strength of the buffer to resist the change, that is, its buffer capacity. The factors affecting the buffer capacity and changes in pH due to precipitation are discussed in more detail in Chapter 15.

b. *Acidity Reduction*

The reduction of titratable acidity (and the accompanying rise in pH) by the addition of carbonate salts has been most extensively studied in Germany. Calcium carbonate ($CaCO_3$) can be used to neutralize the titratable acidity and to precipitate calcium tartrate, or mixtures of calcium tartrate and calcium malate. The removal of the acid anions from the solution as salt causes further acid dissociation of the corresponding acid and a compensating drop in pH to partially offset the pH rise associated with the carbonate neutralization (Boulton 1984).

The calcium carbonate application can be addressed in one of two ways. The first, a direct addition to the juice, is not recommended as it results in wines which are clearly unstable with respect to calcium tartrate, a difficult stability to resolve. The second is to treat only a portion of the juice with all of the carbonate, adding the juice in increments over a 20- to 30-minute period. This process causes the pH to rise up as high as 6.5 initially before falling back to 4 or 4.5 at the end of the addition. The calcium concentration is several times that which would result from direct addition and the tartaric and malic acids are primarily in the tartrate and malate ion forms. As a result, the precipitation of their calcium salts is favored and this lowers the calcium concentration as well as that of the organic acids in conjunction with the neutralization. This method, often referred to as the *double-salt* or Acidex procedure was developed in the mid 1960s (Munz 1960, 1961; Kielhofer and Wurdig 1963) and has undergone a number of secondary modifications since then (Wurdig 1988). The precipitation is primarily that of calcium tartrate (and under certain circumstances, the coprecipitation of calcium malate). After a period of approximately 60 minutes, the treated volume is filtered to remove both the precipitates and any unused carbonate, and then blended back with the untreated portion.

This method is commonly referred to as the double-salt procedure since earlier investigations concluded that a special combined crystal form of Ca_2TaMa, with the appearance of a *sea urchin* shape, was produced under these conditions. Several investigations in other locations (Nagel et al. 1975; Munyon and Nagel 1977; Steele and Kunkee 1978, 1979) found far less malate removal than expected and it has been shown that the one-to-one removal of the acids only occurs when the initial malic acid level is approximately twice the tartaric level (Murtaugh 1990). The double salt is thought to form in the pH range 4.5 to 5.5, although the evidence of this is weak.

The fraction of the juice to be treated is given by:

$$f = -\frac{\Delta \text{TiA}}{(\text{TiA}_0 - \text{TiA}_{\text{corr}})}$$

where TiA_0 is the initial acidity and TiA_{corr} is a correction term that has a value of 2 g/L for juices and 3 g/L for wines (Troost 1980). The magnitude of this term influences the extent of neutralization and the final pH of the treated volume. If too little juice is treated, not all of the carbonate will be dissolved, while if too much juice is used the calcium concentrations will be lower and the desired pH ranges will not be obtained. If too much juice is treated, the initial pH rise will not be satisfactory and the calcium concentration will be lower, resulting in a less complete precipitation of the salts. These correction terms are expected to need refinement for juices from other regions. The quantity of calcium carbonate required is:

$$M = \Delta \text{TiA}\, 0.667\, V$$

where V is the total juice volume. It is the mass of the acidity change (as tartaric, MW = 150) scaled by that of calcium carbonate (MW = 100) to give the carbonate equivalent.

c. *Ion Exchange Treatments*

The application of ion exchange treatments to juices (and wines) has been proposed and evaluated for many years (Austerweil 1954, 1955; Hennig 1955; Peterson and Fujii 1969; Rankine et al. 1977).

Ion exchange, either cation exchange (H^+ for K^+) alone or as a combination of anion (OH^- for various anions) and cation exchange, can be employed to provide almost any specified acidity changes.

The present BATF regulations permit cation exchange and anion exchange provided that inorganic anions are not added to the wine. Hence, OH^- exchanging for organic ions is acceptable as would be the use of $CO_3^=$ for deacidification applications.

Today, the most common use of ion exchange is with cation resins in the H^+ form, for increasing titratable acidity and removing K^+ from either juice (or wine). There is some use of the combined cation and anion (OH^- form) treatments for pH reduction with essentially constant titratable acidity (Peterson and Fujii 1969). This procedure enables the organic anion concentration to be lowered under conditions in which the treatment pH is kept low, avoiding the undesirable changes that would occur if the pH was even temporarily allowed to rise to 6.0 or higher.

Most cation exchange resins deplete a wide range of nitrogenous compounds from juice in addition to the potassium ions and secondary metal cations such as calcium and magnesium. Most of the amino acids and several vitamins are cationic at juice pH. This can lead to induced nutrient deficiencies in the juices which will not be adequately addressed by ammonium salt additions alone, and generally thiamin and biotin will be required as well.

The styrene-divinyl benzene polymer that forms the supporting matrix of most commercial ion exchange resin beads can also be involved in reactions with nonionic components (Peterson and Caputi 1967). While they are not usually large from a sensory point of view they are considerable in the lifetime of the resin that will eventually require replacement. Un-ionized phenolic components are often adsorbed and as an anion resin is regenerated in the OH^- form, these phenols will oxidize and blind and discolor the resin. For this reason, regenerated resins more or less gradually deteriorate due to the inability of the regeneration to remove all adsorbed materials.

The exchangers are typically arranged as upright cylindrical columns containing a bed of resin. They are operated in a cyclic mode so that when the exchanging ions has been exhausted from the resin, a regeneration cycle is initiated. The regenerating stream is usually a strong mineral acid for the cation resins (and a strong alkali for the anion resins). The exchange resins can experience considerable fouling by proteins and gums with juices, and additional cleaning is generally required.

The number of bed volumes of juice that need to be treated in order to obtain a certain increase in titratable acidity can be calculated from the specific exchange capacity of the resin beads and the bed volume.

An emerging problem associated with the use of the conventional ion exchange applications is the handling of the waste streams from the regeneration cycles. These streams are relatively high in inorganic ions such as chloride, sulfate, sodium, or potassium, depending on the regenerant used. A number of regional authorities are becoming more concerned with the salinity and ionic strength of wastewater discharges and salt recovery, and water recycling options may need to be developed.

4. Juice Aeration (Air, Oxygen)

One approach to handling the control of oxidation at the juice level has been to deliberately aerate the juice of white grapes prior to fermentation in a process sometimes referred to as *hyperoxidation*. The aim of this approach is to oxidize many of the phenolic components which would normally be the substrates for chemical oxidation (and browning) in the subsequent wine. The brown pigments formed by this action will generally be adsorbed to solids and be removed by precipitation during fermentation, leaving only the light golden, straw-colored pigments in the wine (Cheynier et al. 1990).

The difficulty in obtaining consistent results associated with this treatment lies in the failure to realize how much oxygen is needed to deplete the phenol substrates, the wide natural variations in the enzyme activity, and the proportions of the phenolic components that are substrates for the enzyme. As previously mentioned, the natural levels of polyphenol oxidase can show an order of magnitude variation between cultivars and vineyards (Traverso-Rueda and Singleton 1973; Hooper et al. 1985).

Studies of the oxidative capacity measured by successive saturations of the juice show that one Muller-Thurgau juice could provide as many as 40 saturations before any appreciable decrease in the rate occurs (Perscheid and Zurn 1977), while others seem to show a decline in rate from the outset (Amano et al. 1979). This latter study was able to demonstrate that the depletion of the phenolic substrates was the reason for the decline by the recovery of the oxygen consumption activity when fresh substrate was added.

The browning effect of one or more oxygen saturations will be dramatically different depending not only on the level of enzyme activity and phenolic composition, but also on the proportion of caffeic acid and the tripeptide, glutathione (Singleton et al. 1984; Cheynier et al. 1986), or other phenol-generating reactions of the quinones (Singleton 1987).

It is our general experience (White and Ough 1973) that the majority of juices have sufficient activity to consume the initial oxygen saturation associated with the crushing stage within a matter of minutes, so that purely anaerobic handling is practically impossible. The extent to which further oxidations are beneficial is variable and quite subjective. In our experience, hyperoxidation diminishes varietal character and is undesirable in wines that emphasize the contributions of the grape.

The residual oxygen content at the time of yeast inoculation is a major influence on the viability of the cells at the end of cell division and their death rate in the remainder of the fermentation (Andreasen and Strier 1953, 1954; Ribéreau-Gayon 1985).

The solubility of oxygen from air in juice and wine is approximately 8 to 9 mg/L at 20°C due to the partial pressure of oxygen being approximately 20% that of the air. By comparison, if a pure oxygen headspace is used, the oxygen solubility rises to about 40 mg/L. The affinity of the enzyme for oxygen does not appear to have been reliably determined; however, a saturation constant estimated from unpublished phenol oxidase experiments would indicate that it is above 10 mg/L oxygen, and that the enzyme is always less than saturated with oxygen under winemaking conditions. If consistent and extensive oxidation of the phenol pool is to be obtained, a high level of purified enzyme should be added to override the variation in natural levels.

Finally, there is an assumption in this approach that the phenols involved in the oxidation and browning of wine are substrates for the enzyme activity. Many of the flavonoids are not good substrates for the enzyme, their nonoxidative browning and their ability to be regenerated during coupled oxidation (Singleton 1987) will be major factors in final wine color. As a result, the rote application of juice aeration and enzymatic oxidation approach will not be a consistent or reliable treatment for the minimization of eventual wine browning capacity.

5. Thermal Treatments of Juices and Musts

I. HTST Treatment of Juices. Juices from mold-infected grapes can be exposed to high-temperature short-time treatments (HTST) to kill fungi and/or to denature laccase, a potent oxidative enzyme commonly found in grapes infected with *Botrytis cinerea*. Effective HTST treatment requires rapid heating to 80° or 90°C, usually by heat transfer from steam, holding at that temperature for a number of seconds, and then subsequent rapid cooling with a refrigerant, in a plate heat exchanger. The HTST treatment can also be used to inactivate the phenol oxidase activity of juices (Jankov 1962; Demeaux and Bidan 1967).

Based on the studies of Dubernet and Ribéreau-Gayon (1973), the holding times required for the destruction of 95% of the activity at various temperatures is presented in Figure 3-6. This action can also denature a major proportion of the phenol oxidase, grape proteins, and virtually eliminates the need for bentonite additions after fermentation. The denatured juice can sometimes be difficult to clarify by natural means due to protective colloid formation in some instances. It has been used in various parts of the world for a number of years, but is in limited use due to the lack of the plate heat exchanger necessary for the treatment.

II. Thermovinification. Juices of red must can be heated to temperatures of approximately 50°C and contacted with the skins for a period of 10 to 30 minutes, to promote color extraction in a process called *thermovinification*. The juice is then separated and cooled prior to fermentation. The process is often employed with grapes that are poor in pigmentation, caused by either very warm or very cool climatic conditions.

6. Enzyme Additions

A number of enzyme preparations have been proposed for applications in juices and wines. These are necessarily hydrolyzing enzymes such as the pectic enzymes, proteases, cellulases, glucosidases, glucanases, and ureases. Their application has almost always been by direct addition rather than immobilized contacting. Juices and wines pose some unusual environmental conditions for enzyme activity due to the pH, ion strength and their sulfur dioxide, ethanol and phenol contents. The desirable temperature ranges for the treatment of wines often keep activities low and the use of enzymes in solution causes low concentrations and longer treatment times to be necessary.

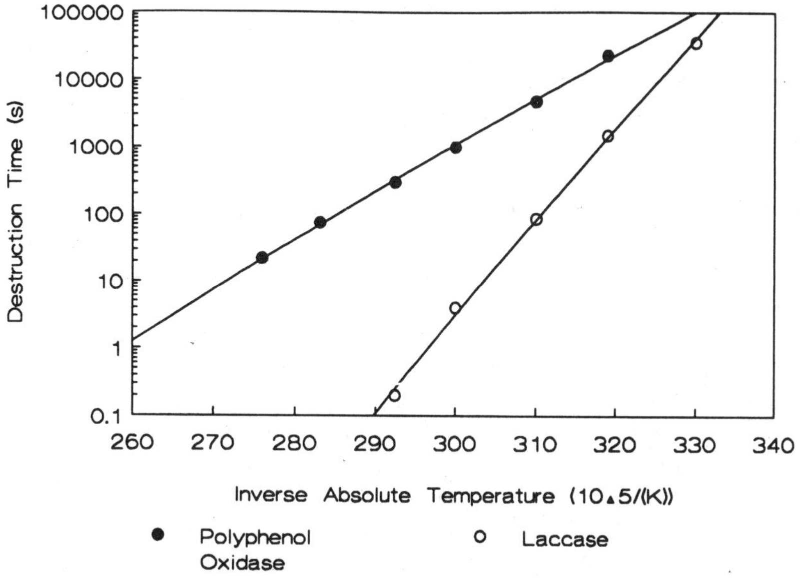

Fig. 3-6. Temperatures and times for the thermal destruction of oxidative enzymes.

I. Pectic Enzymes. The addition of a pectic enzyme preparation to white musts is generally made to enhance the fraction of juice released during draining, reducing the fraction that is released during pressing. They have also been used in the enhancement of natural clarification of wines (Hickenbotham and Williams 1940, Besone and Cruess 1941). The effectiveness of such an addition depends on the levels and previous action of natural enzymes in the grapes, and the temperature and holding time prior to the separation of the skins from the juice. One early report indicated that holding times of the order of 24 hours were required for complete reaction at the 120-mg/L addition level (Berg 1959). Today there are several commercial preparations for either ambient or elevated temperature (60°C) treatments and addition levels are generally at the 240- to 480-mg/L level for ambient conditions.

Variations in the performance of added enzymes in certain juices is sometimes attributed to the natural protease activities of musts. These have been found to vary both within and between the cultivars, and with the extent of mold infections.

Pectic enzymes are used to assist the hydrolysis of pectin, a cell wall constituent in most fleshy fruits. In vinifera grapes, the pectin content ranges between 0.6 and 2.6 g/L (Amerine and Joslyn 1951) and depends on the cultivar. Levels in native American grapes are considerably higher (Rice 1974), and the growing region and the extent to which natural pectic enzymes have been active during maturation also affect the levels found. Grape pectin includes polymeric galacturonic acid in which approximately two-thirds of the carboxyl groups have been esterified into methoxy rather than the free acid forms. A useful method of analysis of pectin fractions has been developed by Robertson (1987).

Commercial pectic enzymes are generally a mixture of at least two particular enzymes, pectin methyl esterase (PME) (EC 3.1.1.11) and polygalacturonase (PG) (EC 3.2.1.15). The PME hydrolyzes the methoxy ester part of the polymer, allowing the PG to break the interlinking bonds (Fig. 3-6). Small amounts of methanol result from this action and most of it is removed with the carbon dioxide during fermentation. Both *exo-* and *endo-* forms of PG are commonly used. The *exo-* form cleaves galacturonic acid from the terminal of the polymer, while the *endo-* form cleaves randomly within the polymer. At juice pH and normal temperatures these enzymes perform well below their maximum activities, typically at 40 to 60% in the pH range 3.0 to 3.5 at 25°C. They can be used in juices either with or without sulfur dioxide since they are not inhibited by it at levels below 400 mg/L.

Many commercial preparations also contain other hydrolytic activities such as pectate lyase (EC 4.2.2.2,6,9) and cellulases in an attempt to enhance cell wall breakage. Others can have appreciable levels of β-glucosidase activity and this has been used with limited success for the release of volatile terpenes and anthocyanins from their glucoside forms in juice and wines.

Pectic enzymes are often assayed using an apple juice pectin (or a similar pectin extract from another fruit) as the substrate and activities are commonly reported in apple juice depectinizing units (AJDU), apple pomace units (APU), or citrus pomace units (CPU).

The addition of pectic enzymes usually results in improved clarification by natural settling, but there are other polysaccharides which may be the cause of poor settling characteristics which would not be addressed by these enzymes.

Although the use of pectic enzymes helps to prevent the development of pectin hazes in wines, the addition is usually made to enhance free-run yield in draining and pressing operations. The hydrolysis of pectin in the cell wall leads to earlier juice release, and in some cases, total juice yields (free-run plus press fractions) are increased (Ough and Berg 1974, Ough and Crowell 1979). They generally contribute to more rapid and extensive natural settling of juices and in some cases improved filterability of the juice.

II. Glucosidases. The two most important groups of wine components that are found in juices partly in the form of β-glucosides are the terpenes of the Muscats, Riesling, and Gewürztraminer and the anthocyanin pigments of most red grapes.

The glucosidase is at almost full activity in the pH range 3.0 to 4.0, but its activity is severely inhibited by glucose in the juice. The presence of ethanol at wine levels also inhibits the activity to about 30% of the maximum, although the effect of glucose inhibition has been eliminated in dry red wines. The activity increases threefold over the range 10°C to 20°C, but it is severely inhibited by even 20 mg/L free sulfur dioxide. There appears to be some benefit of making the addition midway through the fermentation to minimize the combination of these effects.

The desire to enhance varietal character in the terpene-rich cultivars has lead to studies of native and commercially available glucosidases to hydrolyze the glucosidic bond of the terpene, allowing it to become volatile and to contribute to the aroma. Two studies that have demonstrated the effectiveness of this treatment are those by Aryan et al. (1987) and Park et al. (1991).

The glucoside of the anthocyanins make them more stable against color loss and oxidation and it is more soluble than the free anthocyanidin aglycone. One approach to the removal of color from rosé or blush juices has been to perform this enzyme treatment followed by oxidation and or clarification with filtration, bentonite, or carbon treatments. It is rarely used for this purpose in current commercial practice.

III. Glucanases. Glucans are glucose polymers with an unusual ß 1-3 linkage. They are produced primarily in fruits by the action of *Botrytis cinerea* (Dubourdieu et al. 1981) and can lead to the rapid fouling of tight pad and membrane filters. They are not adsorbed by the common fining agents but show a strong affinity to the pad and membrane filters that often only becomes apparent shortly before or during bottling.

This colloid can be hydrolyzed slowly by a glucanase (EC 3.2.1.91) which only has about 50% of its activity at wine pH and only 10 to 15% of this activity at cellar temperatures (*e.g.*, 10°C). It is not very sensitive to SO_2, but its activity is further halved at wine ethanol concentrations. Cellar trials with the effectiveness of the treatment on the filterability of wine have been reported (Villettaz et al. 1984; Wucherpfennig and Dietrich 1982).

7. Addition of Inert Solids

Many insoluble particles that are added to a juice will have some capacity for the adsorption of solutes to their surface. This adsorption of solutes to a particle surface is the basis for most fining treatments, wherein the agent is to be removed together with solutes that are adsorbed to its surface.

There are many small-scale fermentation studies that have reported effects of suspended solids on the fermentation rate, completion, or byproduct formation, but these effects are rarely observed at the commercial scale. The most common practice of such an addition is that of bentonite in white juices and fermenting in its presence. This is not a widespread practice today as it adds to the lees volume and has shown little of the benefits attributed to it from small-scale trials. (A more detailed review of these studies and a discussion of the role of suspended solids can be found in Chapter 5.)

F. PRESSING

1. The Role of Pressing

The purpose of pressing is to recover the juice (or wine) associated with the pulp and skin section of the grapes that are not readily released by natural draining.

Presses can be classified into batch and continuous types and there are several types of batch presses. The composition of the press fractions has long been known to be different from that of the free-run fraction. These differences can be positive in terms of varietal character and flavor attributes (for example the terpenes, Wilson et al. (1986), and Park et al. (1991)) and for the precursors of certain aging components, but are often negative in terms of lower acidity and higher pH, excessive tannin, and gum content. The extent of these differences is determined by the condition of the fruit, the way in which pressure is applied, the nature of the screen employed, and the movement of the skins with respect to the screen. In this regard the batch presses are generally less prone to skin tearing (and subsequent phenol and tannin extraction) than are the continuous presses.

The generation of suspended solids is a concern because it leads to the need for further clarification of the press fractions. Studies of solids levels and composition in press fractions of batch (including membrane or tank presses) and continuous presses have been reported by Maurer and Meidinger (1976), Meidinger (1978), and Lemperle (1978). There are similar concerns for higher tannin levels and high pH conditions. These fractions generally require special attention such as fining and acidity adjustment that the free-run fractions do not. The higher gum content would be expected to contribute to poorer settling and enhanced filter fouling in the latter stages of winemaking.

It was not until the introduction of the larger membrane presses in the mid 1970s that acceptable press fractions could be produced at rates comparable to those provided by the screw presses, and the screw presses have now almost been completely replaced by recent generations of membrane presses.

2. Batch Presses

Batch presses operate in a cycle in which they are filled, pressurized, rotated, and sometimes held at, pressure depressurized, and emptied. The filling time is determined by the capacity of the must pump or conveyors and size of the press. The pressure is generally increased to a maximum pressure of 4 to 6 atm (bars) in stages over a period of between 1 and 2 hours. Most batch presses (excepting basket presses) are rotated while the pressure is being applied so that a regular-shaped cake is developed. Although older and smaller models were often manually operated, most of these presses today have extensive programming capability and the pressures and holding times of the press cycles can be preprogrammed.

a. Basket Presses

Basket presses range from simple presses in which a wooden basket with vertical slats provides the restraining surface and a capstan is used to apply the pressure to horizontal versions that have become known as moving head presses. The use of vertical basket presses is now limited almost exclusively to home winemakers. Reasons for this include their small volume, difficulties in applying uniform pressure to all parts of the cake, the tendency to squirt juice at high pressures and the labor-intensive operations of loading and unloading these presses.

b. Moving Head Presses

The mechanical modifications of the basket press have been to mount the screen on its side and to provide a motor drive of an axial screw to move the pressing head. Such presses are generally referred to as *moving head presses*. The moving head presses range from those with only one moving head (Howard) to those in which a head advances from each end (Vaslin). Some have an internal threaded axle (Howard and Vaslin) while others have it external of the pressing cage (Willmes). There are even hydraulically displaced rams (Bucher and Diemme). Most of the moving head presses also have internal hoops connected by chains which are used to help in the breakup of the cake between successive pressings as the head is retracted.

c. Bladder Presses

The major limitation of the basket and moving head presses is that juice channels in the cake are quickly closed off as pressure is applied. This results in a dry outer section of the cake with a wet core. The hoop and chain arrangement attempts to overcome this but is of limited success. An alternative design was to mount a long cylindrical rubber tube (or bladder) down the center of the screen cage so that the cake would become an annulus rather than a cylinder. These presses (most commonly made by Willmes) were also rotated as the pressure is increased so as to develop a uniformly thick cake of skins. The pressure is supplied by an external compressed air supply.

d. Membrane Presses

The other type of press which is pressurized by air is the tank (or membrane) press. The membrane is generally mounted on opposite sides of a cylindrical tank diametrically across the ends. When evacuated, the membrane is drawn back against one-half of the circumference while the skins enter either through doors in the side walls or axially at one end. Drain screens are mounted along the length and the membrane is inflated like a balloon by an onboard air compressor. The main producers of membrane presses are Bucher (now incorporating Vaslin), Willmes, and Diemme. Two examples of the membrane press are shown in Figure 3-7.

Membrane presses have gained widespread acceptance due to the preferred composition of their press fractions. In these presses the pressure is applied with a minimum of skin movement across the screen surface, and this leads to much less tearing and grinding of skins and seeds. As a result the tannin released and fine solids generated due to this action is greatly reduced and the press fractions are lower in both suspended solids and condensed phenols (Table 3-2). These presses are available in capacities from 4 Tm (approximately 2.5 kL of lightly drained must in volumetric terms) to 40 and 50 Tm. It is common for manufacturers to use the approximate hectoliter (hL) capacity in the model name e.g., RPM 100 or RPZ 150.

3. Continuous Pressing

a. Screw Presses

The alternative arrangement for developing pressure is to feed the skins into a cylinder in which a large helical screw is used to force the

(b)

Fig. 3-7. Two examples of a membrane press.

Table 3-2. White juice composition from a membrane press.

	Free run	During filling	Press fraction 1	3	6	9	Last
Juice density (°Brix)	17.7	18.0	17.9	17.9	17.8	17.7	17.7
pH	3.07	3.1	3.2	3.29	3.36	3.35	3.35
Titratable acidity (g/L)	10.7	10.0	9.35	9.25	9.15	9.1	9.1
Tartaric acid (g/L)	3.2	3.85	2.55	2.55	2.65	2.4	2.4
Phenol content (mg/L)	357	433	486	439	403	440	473
Condensed phenols (mg/L)	133	188	263	68	123	100	145
Brown color (absorbance units @ 420 nm)	0.175	0.076	0.663	0.553	0.697	0.603	0.566
Solids (g/L)	39.1	27.0	19.1	15.4	5.2	9.2	9.8

Source of Data: Maurer and Meidinger (1976) with corrections.

skins into a plug against a restriction at the far end. The restriction is usually a door which is held partially closed by hydraulic pressure. The screw presses provide a continuous operation that is not possible in the batch presses and most units have throughputs of between 50 and 100 Tm/hr. The throughput is determined by the diameter of the screw and its rotational speed. Makers of screw presses have included Coq, Marzola, Mabille, Diemme, Pera, and Blachere. The models are generally classified by the diameter (in mm) of the screw, i.e., the COQ 1000, has a 1-m-diameter screw. Screw presses have been generally replaced by membrane presses in modern wineries. There are however still some in use throughout the world.

Screw presses had two disadvantages. The first was that the movement across the cylindrical screen caused considerable tearing and grinding of the outer skin tissue, leading to press fractions which are considerably higher in mineral content, tannin, and gums. The second was that their press juices were also high in suspended solids content, typically above 4 vol/vol (Table 3-3). This is an unacceptable level of suspended solids for white juices and further equipment will be needed to address a problem that has been generated by the choice of a seven press.

b. *Impulse Presses*

A modification of the screw press to make it more like a batch press with respect to skin tearing led to the *impulse press*. In this press, the screw could be moved horizontally by hydraulic pressure for a distance of up to 1 m. The screw was drawn back at the beginning of the cycle and the press volume was filled by the screw rotating like an auger. Once a cake had developed at the far end of the press, the screw was forced horizontally like a ram, producing an effect similar to the moving head presses. The result was an intermittent operation in which the skin tearing was reduced, leading to more acceptable press fractions but at the expense of throughput. There are very few of these presses in service today.

c. *Belt Presses*

There have been a number of belt presses developed for juice recovery from grapes and other fruits. These date back to the Mackenzie press, which used a series of air-inflated pads to provide pressure to the pomace that was supported by a belt made of metal mesh. The belt was advanced so several meters of fresh pomace was spread out over a horizontal section of the press. The air pressure was applied, held and then released, and the belt advanced again, dumping the pressed material and providing fresh pomace for the next pressing.

Contemporary belt presses have a continuous perforated belt that moves over several sets of rollers that apply the pressure to the grape skins. The juice extracted falls through the screen and is collected in one or more pans. These units have been used extensively for the production of whole cluster processing for sparkling wine production and can have

Table 3-3. White juice composition from a screw press.

			Press section		
	Drained	Feed	1	2	3
Juice Density (°Brix)	n/a	17.2	17.5	17.5	17.5
pH	3.1	3.1	3.2	3.4	3.5
Titratable acidity (g/L)	8.9	9.9	9.1	8.8	9.1
Tartaric acid (g/L)	4.5	4.1	3.3	3.1	3.1
Phenol content (mg/L)	306	472	607	1142	1988
Condensed tannin (mg/L)	65	176	211	738	2045
Brown color (AU @ 420 nm)	0.149	0.249	0.412	0.730	0.965
Solids (g/L)	46.2	42	16.8	27.9	23.7

Source of data: Maurer and Meidinger (1976).

very high capacities. They have not gained widespread acceptance for table wine production due to concerns of high solids in the juice, juice aeration, and the difficulty of cleaning.

4. Compositional Changes

The juice that is expressed from the skins can be significantly different from that which is not in several respects. These include the desirable aspects of different flavor components (Wilson et al. 1986). The undesirable aspects are higher levels of suspended solids, higher phenol and tannin concentrations, lower acidity, higher pH, and a higher concentration of polysaccharides and gums. The press juices appear to have higher levels of oxidative enzymes, due to the solids content, and they can brown more readily due to the higher concentration of the phenol substrates.

The extent to which these differences are found depends primarily on the type and operation of the press and secondarily on the condition of the grapes. Tables 3-2 and 3-3 show the differences in several aspects of juice composition from a screw press and a membrane press (Maurer and Meidinger 1976) with Riesling grapes. Similar results have been reported by Lemperle (1978) with three white cultivars (Muller-Thurgau, Rulander, and Gutedal) over two seasons with a bladder, a moving head, a membrane, and two screw presses. Meidinger (1978) describes a comparison of several press types (bladder, moving head, membrane, and screw) with Muller-Thurgau grapes from one season. A more recent press comparison (Weik 1992) provides compositional data for Muller-Thurgau, Bacchus, and Kerner grapes with a membrane and impulse presses. The differences in the total and condensed phenol values are particularly important in the coarseness and browning potential of white juices, and the level of solids generated is directly related to the need for additional clarification.

Of particular concern today are the changes in polysaccharide and gum content since they affect settling and filter fouling, especially with membrane filters and cross-flow filters. There are a number of recent studies (Wucherpfennig and Dietrich 1989; Bellville et al. 1991) of the behavior of these components in finished wines, but few have covered the effect of pressing or other handling on their release from grape tissue.

5. Pomace Handling

The wet pomace will need to be transferred to the press and the pressed pomace will need to be removed and taken from the winery. The most common means by which this is done is the use of belt or screw conveyors. These are often fixed in place, but in smaller wineries can be portable and moved into place as needed. In larger wineries, it is more usual to transfer the pomace by a series of interconnecting screw conveyors that feed a group of presses and have a common dumping system.

In some locations where small presses are in use, the presses have been placed on rails and moved to the front of a fermentor (or drainer) and the press is filled directly. It is then moved to a central location for pressing and dry pomace removal. Other approaches include a hybrid system for white and red pomace handling. This makes use of gravity to discharge the pomace from elevated drainers and conveyors to move the pomace from red fermentors. The application of pneumatic conveyors for pomace movement has received only little attention.

G. JUICE STORAGE ALTERNATIVES

Juices are often stored to be used as a sweetening component or to extend the fermentation period. They can be prepared in one of the following ways.

1. Sulfiting

This approach involves the addition of high levels of sulfite (typically 1000 mg/L) to clarified (and sometimes cation exchanged) juice, followed by ambient temperature storage of the juice for several months, and then sulfite stripping with direct steam prior to fermentation. The sulfite that is removed in the vapor is then trapped in a lime ($CaOH_2$) solution and the hot juice is cooled down to ambient temperature. The principal difficulties have been in the loss of thiamin by sulfite cleavage during long-term storage and the stripping of most amino acids during the cation exchange treatment. These limitations may be further amplified by a low level of dissolved oxygen in the stripped juice and the lack of suspended solids in the juice for fermentation. This has led to sluggish and incomplete fermentations in deficient juices unless a nutrient mixture is added prior to yeast inoculation. The elevated sulfite levels are also more hazardous generally, and more corrosive, requiring type-316 stainless steel storage tanks rather than the more common 308 steel used in the United States.

2. Refrigeration

One alternative storage option is to clarify the juice by one of several means and then to filter it to a level approaching sterility, usually by a rotary vacuum or pressure leaf filter with fine grades of diatomaceous earth, then chilling to a temperature between -2°C and 0°C for storage in well-insulated tanks. The disadvantages of this option are the energy load to maintain the temperature and the loss of potassium bitartrate deposition during storage. The clear juice is then warmed and fortified with nutrients prior to fermentation. The loss of thiamin can also occur over a period of months if even low levels of sulfur dioxide are present.

3. Cross-Flow Microfiltration

The application of cross-flow microfiltration offers the potential for the generation of a nominally sterile juice to be prepared in a single step from a clarified juice. The principle of cross-flow filtration is discussed earlier (in section 3.4) and in more detail in Chapter 7.

Unlike perpendicular-flow membrane filtration in which absolute retention of microorganisms is possible, the nominal pore size rating of the cross-flow filters is only approximate, usually being based on average flows or pore intrusion estimates. While some filters rated at 0.2 μm will not be able to perform a sterile filtration, they are able to move close to it even in the presence of significant suspended solids contents, and do so without the use of diatomaceous earth.

The main factor associated with the fouling of cross-flow membranes is the colloidal polysaccharide content of juices (and wines). There are several studies indicating a reduction in fouling with the addition of various hydrolytic enzyme preparations and enhancements in the flux rate by heating the juice to 40°C or 50°C. These results are similar to those obtained with a number of other fruit juices, especially apple juices.

4. Evaporative Concentration of Juices

High-sugar solutions (60 + Brix) are relatively stable with respect to yeast and bacterial growth and, therefore, one alternative for juice storage, especially with juices to be transported long distances, is to concentrate juice to 65 to 68 Brix. This is usually chosen as the concentration limit because it is close to the solubility limit of glucose and fructose at ambient temperatures.

The most widely practiced operation for the production of juice for storage at moderate temperatures is evaporative concentration. There are a number of evaporator designs in use and these include the vacuum evaporative pan, falling film and climbing film designs in both tubular and plate configurations, as well as other evaporator designs. These units are generally connected in series for reasons of energy efficiency in what are referred to as multiple-effect evaporators. Steam is applied indirectly to the first unit (or effect) and provides the latent heat for the evaporation of water vapor under vacuum conditions. This vapor is then used as the heating medium in the second effect, and the vapor from the second effect is used as the heating medium in the third effect, in what is referred to as a feed-forward flow arrangement. The more efficient multiple-stage evaporators are not generally employed for grape juice due to concerns about product deterioration at these temperatures with longer residence times. There has only been limited introduction of the rising and falling plate configurations even though they provide greatly reduced contact times, generally one-half to one-third those of the tubular designs, with the shortest times being possible with the falling film plate alternative. There has also been limited introduction of thermal vapor recompression and mechanical vapor recompression between stages of multistage units. The recompression of water vapor from one stage gives it a higher condensing temperature in the next stage and thereby a higher transfer rate in that stage.

The vacuum maintained in each effect (often as low as 100 or 120 mm Hg) as well as the sugar concentration determine the boiling point within the evaporator. There is an elevation of the boiling point of approximately 4°C (8°F) as the sugar content rises from 22 to 68 Brix. The evaporation rate is generally controlled by the vacuum pumps employed and this in turn determines the residence time in each effect. The residence time of several minutes and the temperatures of 50°C to 95°C (150–202°F) play a major role in the extent of juice browning by Maillard reactions and the formation of hydroxy-methyl furfural. The browning of concentrates during storage continues to be a problem that needs to be further investigated.

During the process of concentration from 22 Brix to 66 Brix, 700 mL water/L of juice is removed at a theoretical evaporative energy requirement of 2326 kJ/L (8350 BTU/gal) of juice. Actual energy inputs are usually significantly higher due to juice preheating, and thermal losses. It is common for significant potassium bitartrate precipitation to occur within the concentrator, as well as afterward while in storage.

There are concerns with respect to low nitrogen and vitamin content and lower than usual titratable acidity when the concentrate is reconstituted (Amano and Kagami 1977). Potassium bitartrate lost during the concentration step will need to be added back for acceptable wine acidity. The reconstituted must is also clear and the role of suspended solids on the fermentation rate can be an important factor (see Chapter 5 for a more complete discussion of this point).

5. Nonevaporative Concentration of Juices

The direct concentration of juice or wine by reverse osmosis membranes has received only limited attention in winemaking to date. Sugar content in the range of 200 to 250 g/L provides an osmotic pressure that is close to the operating limit of most commercial systems, with increasingly reduced flux rates as 275 g/L as approached.

There are two alternative approaches using membranes that are capable of producing sugar concentrations equivalent to those of the evaporative methods. The first approach uses a two-stage system that produces an intermediate stream of 40 to 45 Brix with transmembrane pressures of approximately 10.5 MPa. A less retentive membrane in the second stage and a transmembrane pressure of 13 MPa provides sugar strengths of above 60 Brix. This process was developed by Du Pont and FMC and this system is used for the production of apple juice concentrate in the United States. The second approach uses a concentrated salt (or sugar solution) to increase the osmotic pressure gradient across the membrane, thereby requiring lower transmembrane pressure differences. This system has been used for the production of varietal grape juice in Australia (Thompson 1991; Ray 1991) and the membranes are manufactured by Hoechst Celanese in the United States. The process is sometimes referred to as *osmotic distillation* although osmotic concentration might be a more suitable description. Juice concentrates of 68 Brix can be produced in this way without the thermal effects usually associated with the evaporative concentrates. There is a need for the salt stream to be reconcentrated and recycled with a corresponding evaporative energy requirement. There are questions concerning the fouling of the membranes by colloidal components such as polysaccharides and proteins and few operating data are available. A more detailed description of reverse osmosis and its application to juices and wines can be found in Chapter 7.

H. REFERENCES

AGENBACH, W. A. 1977. "A study of must nitrogen content in relation to incomplete fermentation, yeast production and fermentation activity." *Proc. S. Afr. Soc. Enol. Vitic.* 66–87.

AMANO, Y., and M. KAGAMI. 1977. "Winemaking from foreign-made concentrated grape must." *Hakkokogaku Kaishi* 55:330–336.

AMANO, Y., M. KUBOTA, and M. KAGAMI. 1979. "Oxygen uptake of Koshu grape must and its control." *Hokkokogaku Kaishi* 57:92–101.

AMERINE, M. A. and M. A. JOSLYN. 1951. *Table Wines. The Technology of Their Production in California*. Berkeley, CA: University of California Press.

ANDREASEN, A. A. and T. J. B. STRIER. 1953. "Hanaerobic nutrition of *Saccharomyces Cerevisiae*. 1. Ergosterol requirement for growth in a defined medium." *J. Cell. Comp. Physiol.* 41:23–36.

ANDREASEN, A. A. and T. J. B. STRIER. 1954. "*Anaerobic nutrition of Saccharomyces Cerevisiae*. 2. Unsaturated fatty acid requirement for growth in a defined medium." *J. Cell. Comp. Physiol.* 42:271–281.

ARCHER, T. E., and J. G. B. CASTOR. 1956. "Phosphate changes in fermenting must in relation to yeast growth and ethanol production." *Am. J. Enol.* 7:45–52.

ARYAN, A. P., B. WILSON, C. R. STRAUSS, and P. J. WILLIAMS. 1987. "The properties of glycosidases of *Vitis vinifera* and a comparison of their beta-glucosidase activity with that of exogenous enzymes. An assessment of possible application in enology." *Am. J. Enol. Vitic.* 38:182–188.

AUGUSTYN, O. P. H., A. RAPP, and C. J. S. VAN WYK. 1982. "Some volatile aroma components of *Vitis vinifera* L. cv. Sauvignon blanc." *S. Afr. J. Enol. Vitic.* 3:53–60.

AUSTERWEIL, G. V. 1954. "Einige anwendungsverfahren von ionaustauschern in der oenologie." *Weinburg und Keller* 1:195–198.

AUSTERWEIL, G. V. 1955. "Ion exchange and its applications." *Soc. Chem. Ind.* 141–145.

BAYONOVE, C., R. A. CORDONNIER and P. DUBOIS. 1975. "Etude d'une fraction caracteristique de l'aroma du raisin de la variete *Cabernet Sauvignon*; mise en evidence de la 2-methoxy-3-isobutylpyrazine." *C. R. Acad. Sci. Paris* Ser. D 281:75–78.

BEECH, F. W., L. F. BURROUGHS, C. F. TIMBERLAKE, and G. C. WHITING. 1979. "Progres recent sur l'aspect chimique et l'action antimicrobienne de l'anhydride sulfureux (SO2)." *Bull. O.I.V.* 586:1001–1022.

BELLVILLE, M.-P., J.-M. BRILLOUET, B. TARODO DE LA FUENTE, L. SAULINIER and M. MOUTOUNET. 1991. "Differential roles of red wine colloids in the fouling of a cross-flow microfiltration alumina membrane." *Mitt. Klost.* 46:100–107.

BERG, H. W. 1959. "The effects of several fungal pectic enzyme preparations on grape musts and wine." *Am. J. Enol. Vitic.* 10:130–134.

BERGER, J. L. 1985. "Etude de la microfiltration tangentielle sur des Beaujolais." *Rev. d'Oenol.* 36:17–21.

BESONE J. and W. V. CRUESS. 1941. "Observations on the use of pectic enzymes in winemaking." *Fruit Prod. J.* 20:365–367.

BOULTON, R. 1980. "A hypothesis for the presence and activity and role of potassium/hydrogen, adenosine triphosphatases in grapevines." *Am. J. Enol. Vitic.* 31:283–287.

BOULTON, R. 1984. "Acidity modification and stabilization," *Proc.* 1st Intl. Symp. Cool Climate Vitic. & Enol., pp. 482–495. Corvallis, OR.

BOULTON, R. and G. GREEN. 1977. "Field testing of the Wemco juice clarifier." *Proc. Wine Ind. Tech. Sem.* Monterey, CA.

CHEYNIER, V., J. RIGAUD, J. M. SOUQUET, F. DUPRAT, and M. MOUTOUNET. 1990. "Must browning in relation to the behavior of phenolic compounds during oxidation." *Am. J. Enol. Vitic.* 41:346–349.

CHEYNIER, V. F., E. K. TROUSDALE, V. L. SINGLETON, M. SALGUES, and R. WYLDE. 1986. "Characterization of 2-S-glutathionylcaftaric acid and its hydrolysis in relation to grape wines." *J. Agric. Food. Chem.* 34:217–221.

DAVENPORT, M. 1985. The effects of vitamins and growth factors on growth and fermentation rates of three active dry wine yeast strains. M.S. thesis, Davis, CA: University of California.

DAVIN, A., and A. SAHRAOUI. 1993. "Debourbage rapide des mouts de raisin par flottation a l'aide de bulles generees au sein du liquide par depressurisation." *Rev. Fr. Oenol.* 140:53–64.

DEMEAUX, M., and P. BIDAN. 1967. "Etude de l'inactivation par la chaleurde la polyphenoloxydase du jus de raisin." *Technol. Agric.* 16:75–79.

DESCOUT, J. L. 1989. "Utilisation des metaux frittes dans la filtration des vins." *Rev. d'Oenol.* 51:11–17.

DITTRICH, H. H. and W.-R. SPONHOLZ. 1975. "Die aminosaureabnahme in *Botrytis*-infizierten Traubenbeeren und die Bilund hoherer Alkohole in deisen Mosten bei ihrer Vergarung." *Wein-Wissen.* 30:188–210.

DUBERNET, M. and P. RIBÉREAU-GAYON. 1973. "Presence et significance dans les mouts et les vins de la tyrosinase du raisin." *Conn. Vigne Vin* 7:283–302.

DUBERNET, M., P. RIBÉREAU-GAYON, H. R. LERNER, E. HAREL, and A. M. MAYER. 1977. "Purification and properties of laccase from *Botrytis cinerea.*" *Phytochem.* 16:191–193.

DUBOURDIEU, D., J. C. VILLETTAZ, C. DESPLANQUES, and P. RIBÉREAU-GAYON. 1981. "Degradation enzymatique du glucane de Botrytis cinerea." *Conn. Vigne Vin* 15:161–177.

FERRARINI, R., R. ZIRONI, E. CELOTTI and S. BUIATTI. 1992. "Premiers resultats de l'application de la flottation dans la clarification des mouts de raisin." *Rev. Fr. Oenol.* 138:29–42.

GAILLARD, M. 1989. "Essais de microfiltration tangentielle de vins avec le filtre Memcor." *Rev.d'Oenol.* 51:65–68.

HENNIG, K. 1955. "Behandlung ser Weine mit Kationen- und Anionen-Austauschern." *Deu. Weinbau* 5:126–128.

HEYMANN, H., A. C. NOBLE and R. B. BOULTON. 1986. "Analysis of methoxypyrazines in wines: 1. Development of a quantitative procedure." *J. Agric. Food Chem.* 34:269–271.

HICKENBOTHAM, A. R., and J. L. WILLIAMS. 1940. "The application of enzymatic clarification to winemaking." *J. Agric. South Australia.* 43:491–495; 596–602.

HOOPER, R. L., G. G. COLLINS, and B. C. RANKINE. 1985. "Catecholase activity in Australian white grape varieties." *Am. J. Enol. Vitic.* 36:203–206.

HOUTMAN, A. C., and C. S. DU PLESSIS. 1981. "The effect of juice clarity and several conditions promoting yeast growth or fermentation rate, the production of aroma components and wine quality." *S. Afr. J. Enol. Vitic.* 2:71–81.

HUANG, Z., and C. S. OUGH. 1989. "Effect of vineyard locations, varieties and rootstocks on the juice amino acid content of several cultivars." *Am. J. Enol. Vitic.* 40:135–139.

INGLEDEW, W. M., and R. E. KUNKEE. 1985. "Factors influencing sluggish fermentations of grape juice." *Am. J. Enol. Vitic.* 36:65–76.

JANKOV, S. I. 1962. "Hitze-inaktivierung der Polyphenoloxydasen in einigen Fruchtsaften." *Fruchtsaft-Ind. Confructa* 7:13–32.

KIELHOFER, E., and G. WURDIG. 1960. "Die an unbekannte Weinbestandteile gebund ene Schweflige Saure (rest SO_2) und ihre Bedeutung fur den Wein." *Weinberg Keller* 7:313–328.

KIELHOFER, E., and G. WURDIG. 1963. "Die Entsauerung sehr sauer Traubenmoste durch Ausfallung der Weinsaure und Apfelsaure als Kalkdoppelsalz." *Deut. Wein-Ztg.* 99:1022, 1024, 1026, 1028.

LACY, M. J., M. S. ALLEN, R. L. N. HARRIS, and W. V. BROWN. 1991. "Methoxypyrazines in Sauvignon blanc grapes and wines." *Am. J. Enol. Vitic.* 42:103–108.

LEMPERLE, E. 1978. "Untersuchungen zur Qualitatsbeeinflussung der Moste durch unterschiedliche Traubenpressen." *Die Weinwirt.* 31:861–870.

LIE, S. 1972. "Die EBC-Ninhydrin-Methode zur bestimmung des freien alpha-aminostickstoffs: Mitteilung im auftrag des EBC-Analysesnkomitees." *Brauwissen.* 25:250–253.

LUDEMANN, A. 1987, "Wine clarification with a cross-flow microfiltration system." *Am. J. Enol. Vitic.* 38:228–235.

MANDL, B., F. WULLINGER, D. WAGNER, and A. PIENDL. 1971. "Zur einfachen bestimmung des alpha-Aminostickstoffs von Malz, Wurze und Bier mittels der TNBS Methode." *Brauwissen.* 24:227–230.

MARAIS, J. 1987. "Terpene concentrations and wine quality of *Vitis vinifera* L. cv. Gewürztraminer as affected by grape maturity and cellar practices." *Vitis* 26:231–245.

MAURER, R. 1978. "Neue Gesichtspunkte bei der Weinklarung durch Sedimentation. Schonung und Separierung." *Deu. Weinbau* 33(13):496–502.

MAURER, R., and F. MEIDINGER. 1976. "Einfluss von Schnecken- and Tankpressen auf die Mostzusammensetzung." *Deu. Weinbau* 31(11):372–377.

MCWILLIAM, D. J., and C. S. OUGH. 1974. "Measurement of ammonia in musts and wines using a selective electrode." *Am. J. Enol. Vitic.* 25:67–72.

MEIDINGER, F. 1978. "Die Entwicklung der Pressemtechnik bis zur pneumatischen Grossraumpresse mit Ergebnissen und Auswertungen vom Herbst 1977." *Deu. Weinbau* 33(27):1228–1232.

MONK, P. R. 1986. "Formation, utilization and excretion of hydrogen sulphide by wine yeast." *Aust. N.Z. Wine Ind. J.* 1(3):10–16.

MUNYON, J. R., and C. W. NAGEL. 1977. "Comparison of methods of deacidification of musts and wines." *Am. J. Enol. Vitic.* 28:79–87.

MUNZ, TH. 1960. "Die Bindung des Ca-Doppelsalzes der Wein- und Apfelsaure, die Moglichkeiten seiner Fallung durch $CaCO_3$ im Most." *Weinberg und Keller.* 7:239–247.

MUNZ, TH. 1961. "Methoden zur prakischen Falung der Wein- und Apfelsaure als Ca-Doppelsalzes." *Weinberg und Keller.* 8:155–158.

MURTAUGH, M. 1990. Calcium salt precipitation of malate and tartrate from model solutions, wines and juices. M.S. thesis, CA: University of California Davis.

NAGEL, C. W., T. L. JOHNSON, and G. H. CARTER. 1975. "Investigation of the methods of adjusting the acidity of wines." *Am. J. Enol. Vitic.* 26:12–17.

OUGH, C. S., and H. W. BERG. 1974. "The effect of two commercial pectic enzymes on grape musts and wines." *Am. J. Enol. Vitic.* 25:208–211.

OUGH, C. S. and E. A. CROWELL. 1979. "Pectic enzyme treatment of white grapes: Temperature, variety and skin contact factors." *Am. J. Enol. Vitic.* 30:22–27.

OUGH, C. S., M. DAVENPORT, and K. JOSEPH. 1989. "Effects of certain vitamins on growth and fermentation rate of active dry wine yeasts." *Am. J. Enol. Vitic.* 40:208–213.

PARK, S. K., J. C. MORRISON, D. O. ADAMS, and A. C. NOBLE. 1991. "Distribution of free and glycosidically bound monoterpenes in the skin and mesocarp of Muscat of Alexandria grapes during development." *J. Agric. Food Chem.* 39:514–518.

PERI, C. 1987. "Les techniques de filtration tangentielle des mouts et des vins." *Bull. O.I.V.* 60:789–800.

PERI, C., M. RIVA, and P. DECIO. 1988. "Cross-flow membrane filtration of wines: Comparison of performance of ultrafiltration, microfiltration and intermediate cut-off membranes." *Am. J. Enol. Vitic.* 39:162–168.

PERSCHEID, M., and F. ZURN. 1977. "Der einfluss von Oxydationsvorgangen auf die Weinqualitat." *Weinwirt.* 113:10–12.

PETERSON, R. G., and A. CAPUTI, JR. 1967. "The browning problem in wines. II. Ion exchange effects." *Am. J. Enol. Vitic.* 18:105–112.

PETERSON, R. G., and G. R. FUJII. 1969. "Two stage sequential ion exchange treatment." U.S. Patent 3,437,491.

RAMEY, D. D., A. BERTRAND, C. S. OUGH, V. L. SINGLETON, and E. SANDERS. 1986. "Effects of skin contact temperature on Chardonnay must and wine composition." *Am. J. Enol. Vitic.* 37:99–106.

RANKINE, B. C., K. E. POCOCK, W. D. HARDY, J. C. KILGOUR, A. W. HOEY, and C. WEEKS. 1977. "Acidification of wine by ion exchange." *Aust. Wine Brew. Spirit Rev.* 96(10):42–46

RAY, M. A. 1991. "The use of grape derived concentrate and aroma in winemaking." *Aust. & N. Z. Wine Ind. J.* 6:272–274.

RIBÉREAU-GAYON, P. 1985. "New developments in wine microbiology." *Am. J. Enol. Vitic.* 36:1–10.

RIBÉREAU-GAYON, J., E. PEYNAUD, and M. LAFON. 1954. "Growth factors and secondary products of alcoholic fermentation." *Comp. Rend.* 239:1549–1951.

RICE, A. 1974. "Chemistry of winemaking from native American grapes varieties." In: *The Chemistry of Winemaking*. Am. Chem. Soc. Symposium Series. No. 137. Chapter 4, A. D. Webb, Ed., 88–116. Washington, DC: Am. Chem. Soc.

ROBERTSON, G. L. 1987. "The fractional extraction and quantitative determination of pectic substances in grapes and musts." *Am. J. Enol. Vitic.* 30:182–186.

SAYAVEDRA, L. A., and M. W. MONTGOMERY. 1986. "Inhibition of polyphenoloxidase by sulfite." *J. Food. Sci.* 51:1531–1536.

SCHANDERL. H. 1959. Die Mikrobiologie des Mostes and Weines, Stuttgart, Germany; Eugen Ulmer.

SINGLETON, V. L. 1987. "Oxygen with phenols and related reactions in musts, wines and model systems: Observations and practical implications." *Am. J. Enol. Vitic.* 38:69–77.

SINGLETON, V. L., H. A. SIEBERHAGEN, P. DE WET, and C. J. VAN WYK. 1975. "Composition and sensory qualities of wines prepared from white grapes by fermentation with and without grape solids." *Am. J. Enol. Vitic.* 26:62–69.

SINGLETON, V. L., J. ZAYA, E. TROUSDALE and M. SALGUES. 1984. "Caftaric acid in grapes and conversion to a reaction product during processing." *Vitis* 23:113–120.

STEELE, J. T., and R. E. KUNKEE. 1978. "Deacidification of musts from the western United States by the calcium double-salt precipitation process." *Am. J. Enol. Vitic.* 29:153–160.

STEELE, J. T., and R. E. KUNKEE. 1979. "Deacidification of high acid California wines by calcium double-salt precipitation." *Am. J. Enol. Vitic.* 30:227–231.

TERCELJ, D. 1965. "Etude des composes azotes du vin." *Ann. Technol. Agric.* 14:307–319.

THOMPSON, D. 1991. "The application of osmotic distillation for the wine industry." *Aust. Grapegrower & Winemaker.* 328:11, 13–14.

TRAVERSO-RUEDA, S., and V. L. SINGLETON. 1973. "Catecholase activity in grape juice and its implications in winemaking." *Am. J. Enol. Vitic.* 24:103–109.

TROOST, G. 1980. *Technologie des Weines*, 5th ed. Stuttgart Germany: Ulmer.

VAN WYK, C.J. 1978. "The influence of juice clarification on composition and quality of wines," *Proc. 5th Intl. Oenol. Symp.*, pp. 33–45. Auckland, New Zealand.

VILLETTAZ, J.C., D. STEINER, and H. TROGUS. 1984. "The use of a beta-glucanase as an enzyme in wine clarification and filtration." *Am. J. Enol. Vitic.* 35:253–256.

WEIK, B. 1992. "Schubkolbenpresse contra Tankpresse." *Weinwirt. Technik.* 7:16–19.

WHITE, B. B. and C. S. OUGH. 1973. "Oxygen uptake studies on grape juice." *Am. J. Enol. Vitic.* 24:148–152.

WILDENRADT, H. L. and V. L. SINGLETON. 1974. "The production of aldehydes as a result of polyphenolic compounds and its relation to wine aging." *Am. J. Enol. Vitic.* 25:119–126.

WILLIAMS, J. T., C. S. OUGH, and H. W. BERG. 1978. "White wine composition and quality as influenced by methods of must clarification." *Am. J. Enol. Vitic.* 29:92–96.

WILLIAMS, P. J., C. R. STRAUSS, and B. WILSON. 1980. "Hydroxylated linalool derivatives as precursors of volatile monoterpenes of Muscat grapes." *J. Agric. Food Chem.* 28:766–771.

WILSON, B., C. R. STRAUSS, and P. J. WILLIAMS. 1986. "The distribution of free and glycosidically-bound monoterpenes among skin, juice and pulp fractions of some white grape varieties." *Am. J. Enol. Vitic.* 37:107–111.

WUCHERPFENNIG, K. and H. DIETRICH. 1982. "Verbesserung der Filtrierfahigkeit von Weinen durch enzymatischen abbau von kohlenhydrathaltigen Kolloiden." *Weinwirt.* 23:598–603.

WUCHERPFENNIG, K. and H. DIETRICH. 1989. "Die Bedeutung der Kolloide fur die Klarung von Most und Wein." *Mitt. Klost.* 44:1–12.

WURDIG, G. 1988. "Doppelsalzent sauerung Hinweise zur Anwendung." *Weinwirt. Technik* 124(2):6–11.

ZEPPONI, G. and T. COTTRELL. 1975. "White juice separation system." *Am. J. Enol. Vitic.* 26:154–157.

CHAPTER 4

YEAST AND BIOCHEMISTRY OF ETHANOL FERMENTATION

The transformation of grape juice into wine is essentially a microbial process. As such, it is important for the enologist to have an understanding of yeast and fermentation biochemistry as the fundamental basis of the winemaking profession. The alcoholic fermentation, the conversion of the principal grape sugars glucose and fructose to ethanol and carbon dioxide, is conducted by yeasts of the genus *Saccharomyces*, generally by *S. cerevisiae* and *S. bayanus*. The current use of the old term *bayanus* for the yeast closely related to *S. cerevisiae* is controversial (see Section A3c); but we expect *bayanus* to become once more an accepted appellation (Vaughn-Martini and Kurtzman 1985).

A. DEFINITION, ORIGINS, AND IDENTIFICATION OF WINE-RELATED YEASTS

1. Definition of Wine-Related Yeasts

By wine-related we mean those yeasts which have been found on grapes or in vineyards; in wines, table or dessert, sound or spoiled; or associated with wineries or winery equipment. Comprehensive listings of these organisms have been published (Amerine and Kunkee 1968; Kunkee and Amerine 1970; Kunkee and Bisson 1993). The taxonomies of the wine-related yeast genera given in this section are based on these listings, and include some 18 genera—the more obscure and rare being omitted.

Wild yeasts are those non-*Saccharomyces* fermentative yeasts found on grapes, which may take part, if not hindered, in wine fermentations, at least at the outset, and include *Kloeckera*, *Hanseniaspora*, *Debaryomyces*, *Hansenula*, and *Metschnikowia*. Wine yeasts then are the many strains of *Saccharomyces*, which not only can carry out a complete fermentation of grape juice, or other high sugar-containing medium, but also provide the fermented product with pleasant, winelike flavors and odors. Species of *Schizosaccharomyces* can also completely ferment grape juice, and in special cases they have been suggested as wine yeast substitutes for *Saccharomyces*; however, more often than not, the fermentations produced by *Schizosaccharomyces* are unappealing. Using the above subjective definition for wine yeast, several other genera could also be included: *Brettanomyces*, *Dekkera*, and *Zygosaccharomyces*.

We make these distinctions between wild yeasts and wine yeasts for convenience; it would be just as sensible to call "wild yeasts" those yeasts which have never been isolated and grown in vitro and placed in laboratory storage conditions, and wine yeasts could mean all wine-related yeasts. Furthermore, we are not using the term *wild yeasts*, in the genetically correct way to indicate the parent strain from which various mutant strains have been derived.

2. Origins of Wine-Related Yeast

The presence of many yeast genera on grapes in the vineyard at ripeness has long been established (Amerine and Kunkee 1968; Kunkee and Amerine 1970). Indeed electron scan microphotographs of the surface of grape skins showing distinct and intact bipolar budding yeast have been made (Belin 1972; Belin and Henry 1972). The presence of multilateral budding wine yeasts also on grapes has been supposed for as long. There are many reports of the presence of strains of *S. cerevisiae* on grape skins, but generally these have either been vague as to actual numbers or have been the result of enrichment culturing. For enrichment culturing, whole berries, or skin washings, are used to inoculate a selective nutrient broth. The presence of wine yeast in the incubated medium indicates that at least one viable yeast cell was initially present. These reasonable assumptions have lead to extensive written and oral speculations, anecdotally based, on the importance of both wild yeasts and wine yeasts found on the grapes with respect to subsequent natural fermentations. It has been advocated by others that the distinct characteristics of wines from various long-established, and often famous, wineries come from the yeast in residence in the vineyards associated with wineries. The wild yeasts are thought to provide their own special flavor nuances before being overwhelmed by the wine yeasts, and the wine yeasts add their own distinctive flavor notes. Both of these postures are now generally discredited, with some possible exceptions (Bisson and Kunkee 1991).

Alternatively there has been a renewal of the suggestion that perhaps there are no wine yeasts on the grapes at all (Martini and Martini 1990), and that the inoculations in a natural fermentation come from yeast indigenous in the winery (see below). It is true that most of the evidence for wine yeast actually present on the skins of ripe berries comes from enrichment culture studies. Furthermore, we have demonstrated long delays in commencement of fermentations of juice from grapes prepared outside the winery, whereas when the juices from the same grapes were prepared (stemmed and crushed) in the winery, there was little delay in the start of the fermentation. The question arises, how does the yeast become resident in the winery? The answer is essentially the same as for the infections of wineries by spoilage yeast and bacteria (Chapter 9); but it is based on the simple idea that whenever there is an environment favorable enough for the survival or growth of a microorganism, given enough time, the population will become established.

We have demonstrated the presence of strains of *S. cerevisiae* on skins of ripe grapes without resorting to enrichment culturing. The main difficulty with this kind of demonstration is that the number of wine yeasts cells is so low that the grape skins must themselves be applied directly to the solid nutrient medium; or a minimal volume of liquid must be used to wash the surface of the grapes, and then plated, that is, spread directly onto solid medium. The problem comes from the great susceptibility of the plating method to contamination by molds, which are fast growing. The growth of a single mold cell on a plate can overrun any other colonies within a day or two. For the demonstration of the presence of wild yeast, such as *Kloeckera* or *Hansenula*, which are there in much higher numbers, samples from the grapes can be greatly diluted so that the chance of getting even a single mold cell on a plate is substantially diminished. Chemicals such as biphenyl and thymol have been touted as useful for prevention on mold growth under these conditions, but we have not found them to be effective. Rather, we have developed a selective medium, containing sorbate and ethanol (Appendix F), which, when incubated mildly anaerobically, will (after some two weeks' delay) allow the formation of wine yeast colonies. Further identification needs to be made because this method could also allow for the growth of *Brettanomyces* (and presumably *Dekkera*), *Schizosaccharomyces*, and *Zygosaccharomyces*.

3. Identification of Wine-Related Yeasts

It is important to be able to identify the genus and species of wine-related yeasts in order to compare them and their contribution to a given wine or winery, to assess problems arising during fermentation and microbial spoilage, and to evaluate different yeasts as inocula.

a. *The Taxonomy of the Wine-Related Yeasts*

The key to the identification of wine-related yeast genera used below is derived from *Yeast —A Taxonomy* (Kreger-van Rij 1984). Both this edition and the previous editions (Lodder and Kreger-van Rij 1952; Lodder 1970) rely almost exclusively on morphological and physiological tests for assignment of the various characteristics to the genera, making it relatively easy to carry out the identification in a microbiologically equipped winery laboratory. The taxonomy of the earlier editions is often obsolete, but contains a lot of important historical and descriptive material not compiled elsewhere.

The wine-related yeasts are included in the *Ascomycetes* and the *Deuteromycetes* yeast classes, but not in the *Basidiomycetes*. The former two classes either produce sexual spores and have sexual forms of reproduction, or lack both of these features. None of the *Basidiomycetes*, having sexual reproduction without sexual spores, is included in this special grouping of wine-related yeasts (with the possible exception of an unusual species of *Cryptococcus*, *C. laurentii*) (Kurtzman 1973).

The yeasts are not grouped together as a taxon, but generally are defined as unicellular fungi (Hawksworth et al. 1983). The fungi are distinguished from the other eucaryote (nucleated) microorganisms, protozoa, and algae, by having rigid cell walls and no photosynthetic pigments, and from bacteria by having a membrane-bound nucleus. Without being stained, the yeast nucleus cannot be seen in the light microscope. However, the distinction between wine-related yeast and bacteria comes easily with experience since in most cases yeasts are much larger.

A dichotomous key for organism identification is based upon the deceptively simple concept of answering a series of questions regarding the traits or characteristics of the organism under study. The answers to these questions are mutually exclusive, that is, the organism either will or will not possess a given trait. Some traits carry more weight than others in taxonomy, depending upon the number and different kinds of genes predicted to be required for the given characteristic. For example, spore shape and type is under the control of many genes and is, therefore, a primary distinguishing taxonomic character. In contrast, the ability to utilize a particular carbon source may reflect a difference in a single gene. The questions posed of the key must be asked in proper sequence in order to reach the appropriate identification.

In the scheme presented here for yeast genus identification, the first tests, that is the first key questions, have to do with cellular morphology, followed immediately by the question of sexual spore-forming capability. Important distinction is made by taxonomists between the yeasts which form sexual spores (the perfect, that is, complete yeast), as compared to those which do not (the imperfect, or incomplete). The main problem is the establishment that no spores are apparent. Yeast taxonomists are loath to assign imperfect status unless fully convinced that all efforts to find spores have been made. A pragmatic trick is to examine the description of the suspected genus in one of the taxonomy texts given above to discover what might be the corresponding perfect genus of the yeast in question, if known (some information in Table 4-1 may be helpful). The investigator should then be satisfied that spore formation tests were carried out as has been described successfully for the perfect form. Many other structural, but nonsexual, spores can be important for the genus identification, but they do not have the primary importance of the sexual spores. In all tests, it is imperative that both positive and negative controls be conducted. Poorly made media or inaccurate incubation conditions may yield false results. The accuracy of the test is readily known if well-characterized yeasts are run simultaneously and yield the predicted results.

b. Genus Identification of the Wine-Related Yeasts

Our key (Table 4-2) for identification of the genera of the wine-related yeast is an abridgment from the definitive yeast taxonomy edited by Kreger-van Rij (1984), and gives unambiguous identifications. However, some of the morphological tests, such as those indicating the nominal life cycles as being either diploid or haploid, and whether conjugation takes place immediately preceding ascus formation (or not), are rather demanding and may be difficult to interpret for workers without experience. This is especially true for distinguishing between the genera *Torulaspora*, *Debaryomyces*, *Pichia*, *Zygosaccharomyces*, and *Saccharomyces*. We have provided an additional key (Table 4-3), which relies on further physiological tests and removes these difficulties. The reader is admonished to bear in mind that the keys presented here are appropriate only for wine-related yeast genera; and the key in Table 4-3 is applicable only to those genera which have not been eliminated in application of the tests given in Table 4-2—to that point in the key, namely, "asci persistent."

As with any microbiological identification efforts, it is imperative that the organism to be identified is a pure culture and is free from contaminating organisms. Procedures for isolation and purification of cultures are given in Chapter 9.

Table 4-4 gives various yeast genera which can be used as controls. For example, to determine whether a subject yeast will form a pellicle or not, besides testing the unknown yeast, a genus known to produce a pellicle, such as *Pichia*, should be used as a positive control. Also, one known not to produce a pellicle, such as *Saccharomyces*, should be used as a negative control. For our key, unless otherwise indicated, *spores* refer to sexual spores (ascospores). Once an identification is made, a standard taxonomic description of the genus should be consulted for confirmation.

*I. **Type of Cell Division.*** The first identification tests are morphological, the determination of the type of vegetative cell division (nonsexual division). This gives rise to a three-way split in this otherwise dichotomous key. For these tests the cultures must be in a growing phase and sometimes need to be examined microscopically within a day after inoculation on solid medium. The type of cell division is given as either fission, bipolar budding, or multilateral budding (see Figure 4-1), and are described below.

Colonial morphology should also be noted. The color may be an important characteristic to be used later in the key, and the size and shape of the colonies can be important confirmatory characteristics.

Fission yeast divide in the same manner as most bacteria, at the position of a newly formed perpendicular septum, giving rise to two new individuals. For identification purposes, the yeast fission process is different from that in the bacteria. The progress of the division can be readily noted using light microscopy, the two progeny cells giving a zipper-like separation (see Fig. 4-1a). Fission yeast can be classi-

Table 4-1. Species of wine-related yeasts.[1]

Species in Genus	Genus	Wine-related Species	Corresponding Perfect Species
4	*Schizosaccharomyces*	*japonicus*	
		var. *japonicus*	
		var. *varsatilis*	
6	*Kloeckera*	*apiculata*	
		corticis	
		japonica	*Hansenaspora uvarum*
			H. osmophila
			H. valbyensis
1	*Saccharomycodes*	*ludwigii*	
6	*Hanseniaspora*	*osmophila*	
		uvarum	
		valbyensis	
2	*Dekkera*	*bruxellensis*	
		intermedia	
9	*Brettanomyces*	*anomalus*	
		bruxellensis	*D. bruxellensis*
		claussenii	
		custersianus	
		custersii	
		intermedius	*D. intermedia*
		lambicus	
30	*Hansenula*	*anomala*	
		fabrianii	
		jadinii	
		subpelliculosa	
6	*Metschnikowia*	*pulcherrima*	
51	*Pichia*	*delftensis*	
		fermentans	
		kluyveri	
		membranaefaciens	
11	*Kluyveromyces*	*marxianus*	
		var. *bulgaricus*	
		var. *vanudenii*	
		var. *wikenii*	
		termotolerans	
3	*Torulaspora*	*delbrueckii*	
9	*Debaryomyces*	*hansenii*	
8	*Zygosaccharomyces*	*bailii*	
		bisporus	
		cidri	
		florentinus	
		microellipsoideus	
		rouxii	

Table 4-1. (Continued)

Species in Genus	Genus	Wine-related Species	Corresponding Perfect Species
7	*Saccharomyces*	*cerevisiae*	
		[baynanus][2]	
		17 races[2]	
19	*Cryptococcus*	*laurentii*	
8	*Rhodotorula*	None[3]	
196	*Candida*	*apicola*	
		beechii	
		boidinii	
		cantrellii	
		colliculosa	*T. delbrueckii*
		dattila	*K. termotolerans*
		diversa	
		hellenica	
		humilis	
		incummunis	
		intermedia	
		kefyer	
		krusei	
		lambica	*P. fermentans*
		mesenterica	
		mogii	*Z. rouxii*
		pelliculosa	*Hansenula jadinii*
		pulcherrima	*M. pulcherrima*
		sake	
		sorboxylosa	
		spandovensis	
		stellata	
		utilis	*Hansenula jadinii*
		valida	*P. membranaefaciens*
		vanderwaltii	
		vartiovaarai	
		veronae	
		vinaria	
		vini	

[1]As defined, but also includes species found within other (nonmilk) fermented beverages, such as beer and its production equipment—but not barley itself.

[2]*S. bayanus* is not currently a bona fide species designation, but is expected to become one with the next edition of the *Yeast—A Taxonomy*. In the meantime, it is given as a race *S. cerevisiae*.

[3]Species of *Rhodotorula* are not actual wine-related yeasts but are often found as a wine microbiological laboratory contaminants.

fied automatically as *Schizosaccharomyces*, as this is the only genus of wine-related yeast with this mode of division. The microscopic appearance of these yeasts is usually enough for classification, since they have a characteristic rectangular appearance. This is the only genus of the wine-related yeasts that will produce a true mycelium (see below), with straight perpendicular septa. The rectangular appearance is not easily confused with the kind of rectangular appearance sometimes found in a small portion of *Brettanomyces* and *Dekkera* yeast (see below). Furthermore, *Schizosaccharomyces* are always rather large, and not easily confused

Table 4-2. Key to the wine-related yeast genera.

I. Fission: *Schizosaccharomyces*
II. Bipolar budding (on broad base)
    A. No spores: *Kloeckera*
    B. With spores
        1. Spores spherical and smooth (conjugation in ascus): *Saccharomycodes*
        2. Spores hat-or helmet-shaped (no conjugation in ascus): *Hanseniaspora*
III. Multilateral budding
    A. Strong acetic acid from glucose, resistant to cycloheximide, some cells ogival, pungent odor on old plates, colonies clear $CaCO_3$
        1. Spores found: *Dekkera*
        2. Spores not found: *Brettanomyces* (may form nonseptate mycelia)
    B. Not A
        1. Spores found
            a. Nitrate assimilated: *Hansenula*
            b. Nitrate not assimilated
                i. Spores needle-shaped: *Metschnikowia*
                ii. Spores hat- or saturn-shaped: *Pichia*
                iii. Spores reni- or crescentiform: *Kluyveromyces*
                iv. Spores spherical or ellipsoidal
                    (1) Asci dehiscent: *Kluyveromyces* or *Pichia* (fermentation: vigorous weak or absent-see p. 114)
                    (2) Asci persistent
                        (a) Conjugation immediately preceding ascus formation[1]: *Torulaspora, Debaryomyces, Pichia, Zygosaccharomyces*
                        (b) Conjugation after ascus formation[1]: *Saccharomyces*
        2. No spores found
            a. Colonies pink or red
                i. Inositol assimilated: *Cryptococcus*
                ii. Inositol not assimilated: *Rhodotorula*
            b. Colonies not pink or red
                i. No arthrospores; inositol assimilated: (no pseudomycelium): *Cryptococcus*
                ii. Not i: *Candida*

[1]See Table 4-3.

Table 4-3. A taxonomic key to wine-related asci-persistent yeast genera.

This table draws distinctions between the several asci-persistent genera: *Torulaspora, Debaryomyces, Pichia, Zygosaccharomyces*, and *Saccharomyces*.

	Pellicle formation	Fermentation	Assimilation of		
			Cadaverine	Lysine	Sucrose
Pichia	+	weak			
Debaryomyces	-	weak			
Zygosaccharomyces	-	strong	+	+	
Sacch. kluyveri	-	strong	+	+	+
Sacch. unisporus	-	strong	+	+	-
Torulaspora	-	strong	-	+	
Other *Saccharomyces*	-	strong	-	-	

Table 4-4. Yeast taxonomic identification examples.

Mycelium development	
mycelium:	*Schizosaccharomyces japonicus*
pseudomycelium:	*Candida vini*
loose budding cells:	*Saccharomyces cerevisiae*
nonseptate mycelium:	*Brettanomyces* spp.
Pellicle development	
positive: film in five days:	*Pichia fermentans*
negative:	*Saccharomyces cerevisiae*
Morphology	
cell shape:	oval—*Saccharomyces cerevisiae*
	apiculate—*Kloeckera apiculata*
	ogive—*Dekkera intermedia*
colored colony:	red—*Rhodotorula rubra*
	pink—*Sporobolomyces salmonicolor*
division:	multilateral budding—*Saccharomyces cerevisiae*
	bipolar budding—Saccharomycodes ludwigii
	Kloechera apiculata
	fission—*Schizosaccharomyces pombe*
Ascospore formation: Persistent:	*Saccharomyces* spp.;
Dehiscent:	*Pichia* spp.
On wort or Gorodkowa:	*Saccharomycodes ludwigii*, *Pichia fermentans*
On Gorodkowa:	*Hanseniaspora valbyensia*
On V-8:	*Hansenula anomala*, *Pichia fermentans*
On acetate:	*Saccharomyces cerevisiae*
On wort:	*Saccharomyces cerevisiae*
Ballistospore formation	
On wort:	*Sporobolomyces salmonicolor*
Ploidy	
Conjugation immediately precedes ascospore formation:	*Torulaspora pretoriensis*
Conjugation does not immediately precede ascospore formation:	*Saccharomyces cerevisiae*
Fermentation	
glucose positive:	*Saccharomyces* spp.
glucose negative:	*Rhodotorula rubra*
Nitrate assimilation	
positive:	*Hansenula* spp.
negative:	*Saccharomyces* spp.
Cycloheximide ("Actidione") sensitivity (100 mg/L)	
sensitive:	*Saccharomyces cerevisiae*
resistant:	*Dekkera intermedia*
Lysine assimilation	
positive:	*Zygosaccharomyces bailii*
negative:	*Saccharomyces cerevisiae*

with bacteria, even with the latter's fission mode of division.

Vegetative cell division of budding yeast can also be observed with the light microscope. The newly forming progeny cell has the appearance of an extrusion of the parent cell, becoming larger and larger until it is of nearly the same size and is excised. In contrast with the fission process, the budding division does not give rise to two new individuals, but rather one parent and one progeny cell. With an electron-scanning microscopy, one can detect the circular ridges of chitinous material indicating bud scars and birth scars. Budding may be either bipolar or multilateral.

Bipolar budding cells have a distinctive apiculate, or lemon-shaped appearance, and it seems natural for the budding to take place at one end of the cell or the other (Figure 4-1b). The multilaterally budding cells are often somewhat ellipsoidal and when both ends have become the seats of the budding process, the next buds will form randomly on the surface (Figure 4-1c), not at the ends as with bipolar budding. Bipolar budding is on a broad base, the diameter of the progeny bud approaching that of the parent very early. Multilateral budding is on a narrow base which appears as a restriction nearly from the outset until the end of the budding cycle. For the wine-related taxonomy, bipolar budding yeasts can automatically be classified either as *Kloeckera*, *Hanseniaspora*, or *Saccharomycodes*, depending upon their spore-forming abilities.

The use of electron scan microscopy also reveals an important difference between these two kinds of budding. The bud scars from bipolar budding are formed concentrically, as compared to the broadcast positions of those of the multilaterally budding yeast. The notion that the death of the parent cell takes place when, and as a result of, the utilization of all the surface area as fresh budding sites has been discredited (Jazwinski 1993).

As mentioned above, a portion of cells of *Brettanomyces* or *Dekkera* genera sometimes appear as rather large rectangles, compared to the other cells (Figure 4-1d). These cells usually form buds, maybe more than one at a time, at the end of the rectangle. Thus, the descriptions of budding patterns as given above may sometimes seem to be imprecise. However, the great majority of the budding cells in these cases show rather typical multilateral budding and any ambiguity is easily resolved.

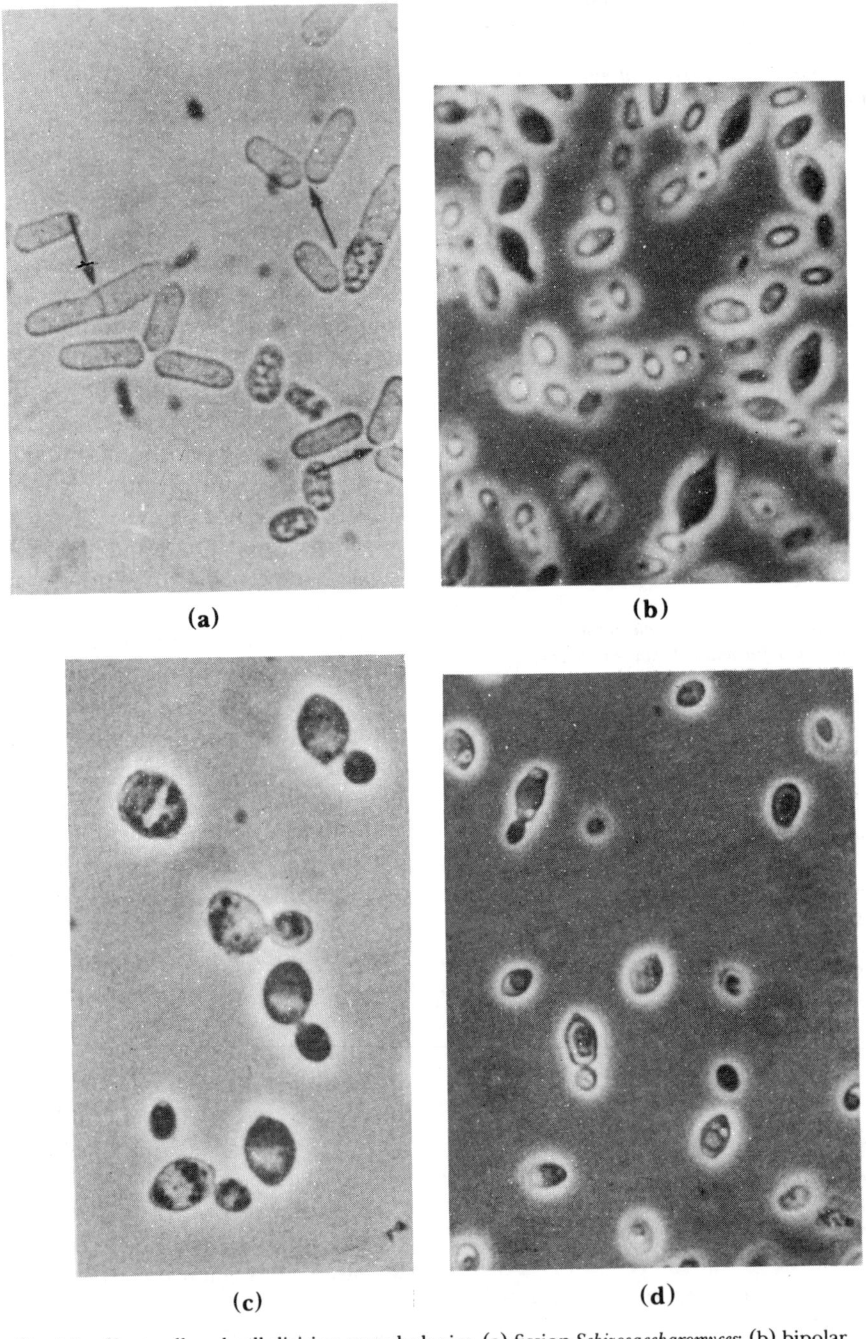

Fig. 4-1. Yeast cell and cell division morphologies. (a) fission-*Schizosaccharomyces*; (b) bipolar budding-*Kloeckera*; (c) multilateral budding-*Saccharomyces*; (d) multilateral budding-*Brettanomyces* (rectangular and ogive shapes); (e) *Zygosaccharomyces* conjugation ("dumbbell" shape). (Fig. 4-1a reprinted by permission of the publishers of *The Life of Yeasts*: *Their Nature, Activity, Ecology and Relation to Mankind* by H. J. Phaff, M. W. Miller and E. M. Mrak, Cambridge, Mass.: Harvard University Press, Copyright © 1966, 1978 by the President and Fellows of Harvard College.)

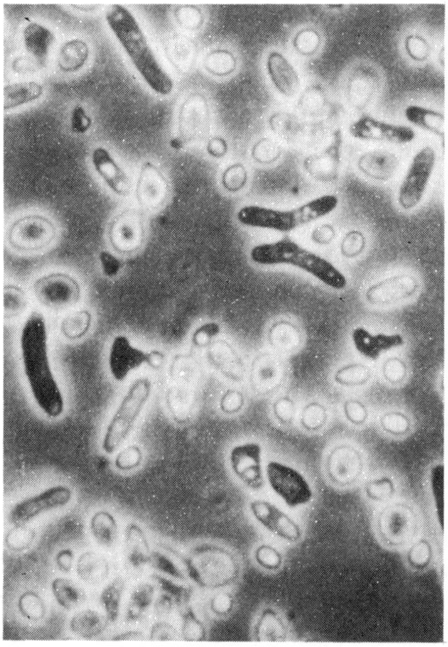

(e)

Fig. 4-1. (*Continued*).

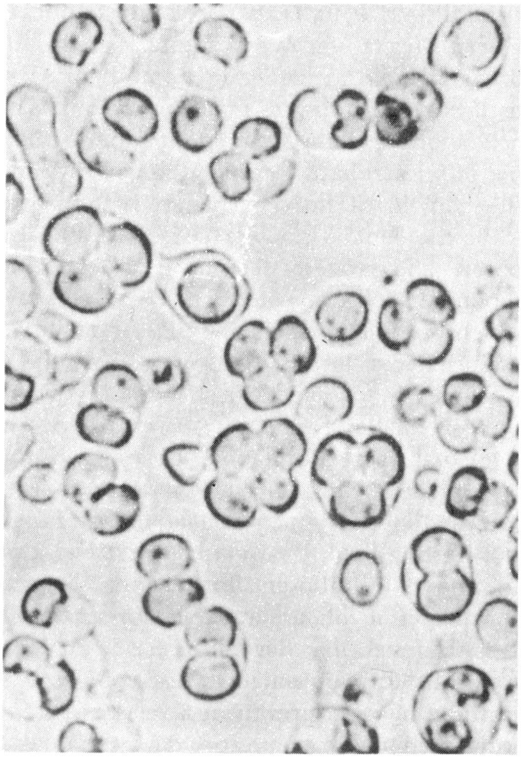

Fig. 4-2. *Saccharomyces* Spores (Reprinted by permission of the publishers of *The Life of Yeasts: Their Nature, Activity, Ecology and Relation to Mankind* by H. J. Phaff, M. W. Miller and E. M. Mrak, Cambridge, Mass.: Harvard University Press, Copyright © 1966, 1978 by the President and Fellows of Harvard College.)

II. Sporulation. The cells of wine strains of *Saccharomyces* are generally diploid during the vegetative cycle; that is, they have two sets of each of their 16 chromosomes. The chromosomes are invisible under the light microscope and are located in a transparent nucleus. However, the sporulation process is quite visible in the light microscope, especially with the use of phase-contrast optics (Figure 4-2). The following description of the sporulation process oversimplifies the far greater understanding which modern yeast physiologists and geneticists enjoy (Esposito and Klapholz 1981), but is suitable for our purposes.

The sexual cell cycle is a reductive, meiotic division—one partner of each chromosome pair going to each new primeval spore—followed by a mitotic division. This results in four new haploid entities—now called *ascospores*—all contained within the original cell wall. The cell wall has undergone a change, seeming to lose some of its rigidity and more or less circumscribing the four new ascospores. The ascus wall becomes weaker, and eventually breaks open, or dehisces, releasing the ascospores. This can be seen with the light microscope. The four spores are of two sexual types, called *a* and α. After some time, and after certain defined and well-studied conditions, these haploid cells of the two opposite mating types may conjugate (mate) and become a single, new diploid cell, continuing its life cycle in the vegetative, budding mode. There are many variations on this theme, some of which are important for our taxonomic decision-making, and are discussed appropriately below. At this stage, it is important to note that the formation of the ascospore is relatively easy to observe with the light microscope. Spore stains are available (Bartholomew and Mittwer 1950), but phase-contrast optics is more than a satisfactory substitute. Wine strains of *S. cerevisiae* are generally homothallic. For us *homothallic* indicates that the haploid yeast cell/spore resulting from sporulation is capable of self-fertilization. Following cell division, the haploid parent cell changes mating type while the haploid progeny cell does not. The parent and progeny cells mate and become diploid. In contrast, a heterothallic yeast is one which cannot switch mating type and will remain haploid during vegetative growth unless it comes in contact with a haploid of the opposite mating type.

Sexual spore formation, at least in the wine-related yeasts, is usually induced by first growing the cells on a rich medium, and then transferring them to a poorer one, or at least to one of a different formulation. Several sporulation media are available (Appendix F). It is suggested that they all be used. We have found it most convenient to use solid media, starting the yeast growth on a yeast mold (or wort) medium for one or two days, then transferring the culture to a sporulation medium. Rather unusual materials have also been used for sporulation, such as vegetable slices or gypsum blocks. We have generally not needed to resort to these for sporulation of wine-related yeasts.

Cells on sporulation media should be examined at least daily for the presence of spores. If microscopic examinations are made too infrequently, the cells may go through the sporulation process and return to the vegetative mode without notice. Alternatively, inoculations can be made on a daily basis and microscopic examination of the spores made at one sitting. In addition to noting the formation of spores, the shapes of the spores also need to be recorded. The following descriptive shapes and textures are important in the identification procedures used here: spherical, hat-shaped, helmet-shaped, Saturn-shaped, needle-shaped, reniform (kidney-shaped), crescent-shaped, or ellipsoidal; and whether smooth, warty, or with ridges (Figure 4-3). While these names seem whimsical, they are not only rather accurate descriptions of the varieties of spore shapes that can be found, but are operative in our taxonomic identification (see Table 4-2). The number of spores, the timing of spore development, and the induction medium used may be helpful confirmatory information.

Bipolar genera are distinguished by their ability to form sexual spores, and by the shapes of the spores formed (Table 4-2). *Kloeckera* are nonspore formers; *Saccharomycodes* form spherical and smooth spores; and *Hanseniaspora* form hat- or helmet-shaped spores. The remaining wine-related genera show multilateral budding.

III. Multilateral-Budding Acetic Acid Producers. The next two genera in the scheme (Table 4-2), *Dekkera* and *Brettanomyces*, are distinguished from the other genera by their formations of obvious amounts of acetic acid. The

Fig. 4-3. Shapes of yeats spores: Left to right: spheroidal, ovoidal, kidney- or bean-shaped, crescent- or sickle-shaped, hat-shaped, helmet-shaped, spheroidal with warty surface, walnut-shaped, Saturn-shaped, spheroidal with spiny surface, arcuate, needle-shaped with appendage (Reprinted by permission of the publishers of *The Life of Yeasts: Their Nature, Activity, Ecology and Relation to Mankind* by H. J. Phaff, M. W. Miller and E. M. Mrak, Cambridge, Mass.: Harvard University Press, Copyright © 1966, 1978 by the President and Fellows of Harvard College.)

amounts formed are large enough to bring about lethal conditions for the yeast when this end product is locally concentrated (as when colonies are grown on a solid medium). A diagnostic test for this characteristic employs malt agar containing calcium carbonate. The carbonate suspended in the medium is dissolved by the formation of the acetic acid. An easily observed translucent ring forms around the yeast colony. Other acids may also be formed, some more typically associated with spoilage odors from these yeast, such as butyric acid. The use of calcium carbonate serves an additional purpose besides the diagnostic one—it protects the yeast colony from the lethally acid milieu. Strains of these two genera are routinely maintained on calcium carbonate-containing media for storage in culture collections.

While the above methodology is diagnostically accurate, another screening method is more commonly used for *Brettanomyces* and *Dekkera*. Both genera are resistant to the fungicide cycloheximide. Colonial growth on solid medium in the presence of 3 to 25 mg/L of cycloheximide can be considered presumptive evidence of these genera. However, since species of other genera are also resistant to cycloheximide, confirmatory evidence is needed. The use of 100 mg/L is a better diagnostic test, but here the colonial growth may take some 10 to 14 days, as compared to two or three days with the lower concentrations. For screening, especially for *Brettanomyces* as a spoilage yeast, sometimes both calcium carbonate and the lower concentrations of cycloheximide are used, giving good diagnosis and maintenance.

In addition to the above diagnoses, two confirmatory morphological tests are also often used for *Brettanomyces* and *Dekkera*. A substantial number of the cells of these genera have a characteristic ogive shape at one end of the cell, giving an outline suggesting a gothic arch (Figure 4-1d). Electron scan photomicrographs show these pointed ends apparently result from distal, but adjacent bud scars (Ilagan 1979). Confirmatory evidence for *Brettanomyces*, but apparently not *Dekkera*, is the formation of nonseptate mycelia in the mycelium test (see below).

Ability to form sexual spores differentiates *Brettanomyces* and *Dekkera*. The detection of spore formers, here, is more difficult than as described above for *Saccharomyces*. In fact, the recognition of *Dekkera* as a sporulating form of *Brettanomyces* came about only relatively recently. The spores do not appear as a quadruplet package as described above, but rather as two hat-shaped cells attached to a structure having the superficial appearance of an eyeball (Ilagan 1979). This is especially notable after the ascus has begun to dehisce and the coupled spores are partly or completely extruded, best seen with electron scan optics. Spore formation for *Dekkera* is favored under aerobic, high-temperature conditions (Ilagan 1979), and would not be expected to take place in wine. Although *Dekkera* have been isolated from wine, it is not clear whether this genus, in addition to *Brettanomyces*, should be considered a serious wine spoilage organism (Chapter 9).

IV. Multilateral Budding Sporulating Nitrate-Positive Assimilators. The remainder of our key divides itself into large sections concerned with yeasts which form spores and those which do not. The next test is a physiological one showing whether the yeast can assimilate, that is, grow on nitrate. For some steps in other yeast taxonomy keys, it is important to determine if various other nitrogenous forms, such as amino acids, simple peptides, or proteins, can also be assimilated. For those kinds of determinations, an auxanogram (Kreger-van Rij 1984) can be used. A simpler test, solely for nitrate assimilation is used here. A liquid medium, with nitrate as the only nitrogen source is prepared. The medium is inoculated, under rigidly standardized conditions, with a loop of a diluted suspension of the yeast in question. One looks for turbidity in the medium after several days. A negative control medium, having no nitrogen source, and a positive one, having ammonium as the nitrogen source, are also employed. All yeasts will assimilate the latter. In some cases, the negative control will register turbidity, the yeast apparently obtaining assimilable nitrogen from the inoculum. In these cases, a second tube of each of the nitrogen sources—nitrate, ammonium, and no nitrogen—needs to be inoculated from the corresponding initial tube and checked for growth after several days.

The inexperienced taxonomist is warned again that it is imperative to follow the key (Table 4-2) step by step, until a dead end indicates the genus has been identified. That is to say, nitrate assimilation itself does not automatically indicate the presence of *Hansenula*; some species of the genera listed above and below this part of the key are also nitrate positive.

V. Multilateral Budding Sporulating Nitrate-Negative Assimilators. At this stage (Table 4-2), the shapes of the spores of the nitrate-negative assimilating yeast become important. If needle-shaped, the genus is *Metschnikowia*; if hat- or Saturn-shaped, the genus is *Pichia*; and if reniform or crescent-shaped, the genus is *Kluyveromyces*. Note the key is redundant at this point and the latter two genera may be encountered again below.

If the spores are spherical or ellipsoidal, whether the ascus is dehiscent or persistent is important. These are relative terms, since even the persistent yeast will eventually dehisce their contents—of ascospores. By dehiscent we mean that the ascus wall becomes very friable and tends to release the newly formed ascospores quickly. In this case it is difficult to find intact asci with its four or so ascospores as described above. Instead, one finds under the light microscope the released ascospores, either as single cells, or in some cases as conjugating pairs, and the empty ghosts of the former asci. With the persistent situation, the ascus wall is less likely to fragment early, and the microscopic appearance shows a high proportion of the asci with the spores still intact. Again timing is important; and the sporulation media need to be examined frequently.

In the case of dehiscent yeast, the next test is to determine if the yeast is capable of fermentation. If it can ferment at all, it will ferment glucose. The distinction between fermenting yeast and respiring yeast is not exact and often it is a question of the conditions. Many of the wine-related yeasts are facultative. Lagunas (1979) showed that even under strict respiratory conditions, with low concentrations of glucose so that the Crabtree effect is not in place, some of the sugar is catabolized by the fermentation pathway—incomplete oxidation to ethanol rather than to carbon dioxide and water. An operating definition of fermentation here is the anaerobic formation of gas. This test is simply an inoculation of glucose medium containing an inverted (Durham) tube. The inverted Durham tube floating on the medium will be submerged after the medium has been autoclaved. Any gases trapped in the tube after inoculation will necessarily have been produced from yeast at the bottom of the tube, that is, anaerobically. In the glucose fermentation test, *Kluyveromyces* will give rapid fermentation, filling the inverted tube with gas within several days, whereas *Pichia* will give hardly any gas formation. The assignment should be made using proper control examples, of course. It must be noted that the glucose fermentation test is not a test of assimilation; growth, as indicated by turbidity, will most certainly be noted—it is the formation of gas, carbon dioxide, that is operative.

In the case of the asci-persistent yeast, a further difficult point in relying on morphological traits is reached in this taxonomic scheme (Table 4-2), where conjugation "immediately preceding ascus formation" or "after ascus formation" must be noted. Four genera of wine-related yeasts, *Torulaspora*, *Debaryomyces*, *Pichia*, and *Zygosaccharomyces* fall into the first category, and *Saccharomyces* falls into the second. Fortunately, physiological tests are available (Table 4-3), the application of which overrides the need for the difficult determination of the conjugation schedule. These physiological tests are not to be applied for identification for all yeast with persistent asci, but only those for which the other genera have been eliminated; that is, they only include the multilateral budding, non-nitrate assimilating yeasts which form spherical or ellipsoidal spores. An important physiological test here is to determine whether the yeasts form a pellicle or not, which can be determined in conjunction with the glucose fermentation test. The pellicle is the formation of an obvious surface film of yeast, which can actually become quite thick after several days of incubation. This indicates that the yeasts are using aerobic metabolism, and in this case *Pichia* are distinguished from the rest in the group (Table 4-3). The qualification of several days is important since many fermentative yeasts will form a thin surface film after several weeks. The next distinguishing feature is the vigor of glucose fermentation, already discussed. A weak fermentation segregates *Debaryomyces* from the remainder.

Assimilation tests are then used to identify the last three genera of this grouping. We have mentioned the assimilation of nitrate as a sole nitrogen source. For the tests here, the assimilation of cadaverine and lysine are tested in the place of nitrate, and with the same admonitions concerning the use of proper controls. *Zygosaccharomyces* assimilates (grows on) both cadaverine and lysine, *Torulaspora* assimilates lysine, and most species of *Saccharomyces* assimilate neither. Two species of *Saccharomyces* will assimilate both of these nitrogen sources, *S. kluyveri* and *S. unisporus*, but these would rarely be encountered. The separation of these two species from *Zygosaccharomyces* can be made by use of a half dozen additional physiological tests involving assimilation of sugars, growth on various concentrations of cycloheximide, and growth at high temperature (Kreger-van Rij 1984). However, a morphological test can be used instead. Strains of *Zygosaccharomyces* grown on malt agar so readily conjugate before ascus formation, that microscopic examination typically shows the conjugated forms, resembling dumbbells (Figure 4-1e). This feature can be used to distinguish them from all *Saccharomyces* species. A selective medium containing 1% acetic acid, used for cultivation of spoilage yeast, allows the growth of most strains of wine-related *Zygosaccharomyces* but not *Saccharomyces*.

VI. Multilateral Budding Nonspore Formers. Genus assignment in this last category is relatively easy. If the colors of the colonies are pink or red, as compared to the usual cream color, an assimilation (growth) test for inositol is made (Table 4-2). In this case, inositol is supplied as the sole carbon source. Inositol positive genera are *Cryptococcus*, and the negative genera are *Rhodotorula*. The latter genus is not properly classified as a wine-related yeast; but since it occurs as a very common microbiological laboratory contaminant, we have included it here. It is conspicuous by its bright red colonies. Cream- or light-yellow-colored colonies can be either *Cryptococcus*, again, or members of the rather large and diverse genus *Candida*. In the latter are many imperfect forms of wine-related genera, including *Hansenula*, *Pichia*, and *Torulaspora* (see Table 4-1). The cryptococci assimilate inositol, but do not form arthrospores (see below), which are often found in conjunction with mycelial formation (Table 4-2). The test for mycelium formation is tedious, but not complicated. It involves inoculation of the yeast on a thin layer of agar so later growth can be examined microscopically, in place, directly on the agar. The agar is inoculated with a streak of the subject yeast. Along the edge of the streak of growth, *Saccharomyces* and many other genera will typically give the appearance of loose budding cells. However, *Schizosaccharomyces* and other fission yeast will show mycelial growth, where the cells remain connected to one another in long lines, the cells separated by septa running perpendicular to the cell length Figure 4-4a. Often in this case, at the end of the mycelial row, the last several cells will have separated from each other, and appear as isolated rectangles (Figure 4-4a). These latter are called arthrospores. Sometimes long nonseptated mycelia are formed (see *Brettanomyces* above)

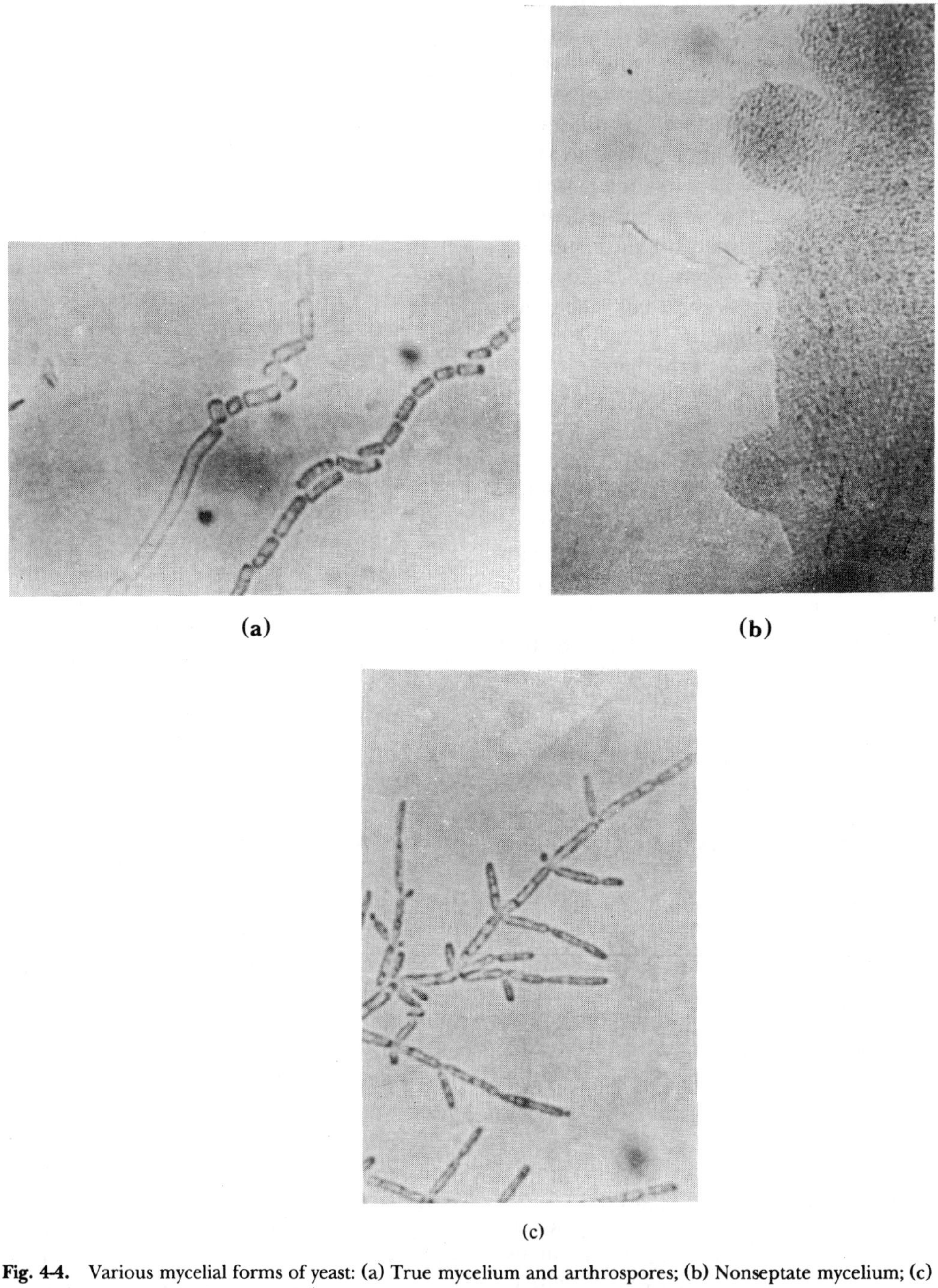

(a) (b)

(c)

Fig. 4-4. Various mycelial forms of yeast: (a) True mycelium and arthrospores; (b) Nonseptate mycelium; (c) Pseudomycelium with blastospores. (Fig. 4-4a reprinted by permission of the publishers of *The Life of Yeasts: Their Nature, Activity, Ecology and Relation to Mankind* by H. J. Phaff, M. W. Miller and E. M. Mrak, Cambridge, Mass.: Harvard University Press, Copyright © 1966, 1978 by the President and Fellows of Harvard College.)

(Figure 4-4b). Another kind of development is the pseudomycelium (Figure 4-4c). Here the cells are still in line, but with the appearance of the budding progeny cells, which remain attached together, and with no distinct perpendicular septa. Often there is a proliferation of additional cells at the junctions, and these are called blastospores. Back to our last stage in the genus taxonomy of wine-related yeasts, if the nonpigmented yeast assimilate inositol, but do not form arthrospores (and no pseudomycelium), they are *Cryptococcus*, otherwise they are *Candida*.

c. Species and Race Identification of the Wine-Related Yeasts

Species identifications rely heavily on additional physiological tests and some morphological tests, all similar to those encountered in genus identification. The additional physiological tests utilize a much broader range of carbon and nitrogen sources, as well as tests for growth in the presence of and at specified concentrations of various compounds, such as cycloheximide. Morphological tests include determination of spore shape, number of spores, presence of nonseptate mycelia, and colony color. Each of these tests has been mentioned above.

Additional physiological tests also might include the determination of growth at increased temperatures (34°C and 37°C); and the fermentation of sugars other than glucose. The latter fermentation tests are performed as before, but other sugars, monohexoses, dihexoses, and trihexoses, are substituted for glucose. Again, turbidity formation indicates the growth of the yeast, not fermentation. Only the formation of gas in the Durham tubes gives the indication of fermentation. Conversely, a positive fermentation test with a certain sugar does indicate that the yeast will assimilate that sugar. Another physiological test of importance for some species is growth of the culture on a vitamin-free medium. This test is as simple as indicated; however, it often may take numerous generations (40 or more) to reveal a vitamin deficiency. Vitamin-free media are commercially available.

The classifications of the seven species of *Saccharomyces* (Kreger-van Rij 1984) requires the determination of the assimilation of sucrose and maltose as carbon sources, and of cadaverine and lysine as nitrogen sources; the growth in various concentrations (0, 100, or 100 mg/L) of cycloheximide; and two morphological tests: whether the spores are smooth or rough and whether the cells are small or large, in this case, whether they are 2.5 to 5.5 x 3.7 to 7.0 μm or larger. The latter two tests are not difficult to determine with the light microscope. For the size measurements, the microscope should be equipped in one eyepiece with a reticle, which can easily be calibrated with the use of the precisely etched grid of a yeast counting chamber as a specimen (the smallest distance between the lines of the grid in a Levy-Hausser chamber being 50 μm). A key which defines *S. cerevisiae* using these tests, and which indicates the other six species of *Saccharomyces*, is given in Table 4-5.

In Table 4-1 are listed the most likely species to be encountered by the wine microbiologist and it includes the total number of species in each genus. For the imperfect yeast, with no sexual spores or sexual cycles, the corresponding perfect species, when known, are also listed. The genera are listed in the order given in Table 4-2, but the species within each genus are listed alphabetically.

It is beyond the scope of this text to show which actual tests are used for the identification of each species, those are found in Kreger-van Rij (1984); but it is within the scope to assure the would-be taxonomist that these tests can be readily applied. In many cases, perusal of our parent taxonomy (Kreger-van Rij 1984) at the species level shows additional and more complicated tests than are indicated here. However, these tests are needed for species not given in Table 4-1, and can safely be ignored. The one exception might be with speciation of *Metschnikowia*, but since only one species, *M. pulcherrima*, has been found on grapes, this problem is avoided. See Chapter 9

Table 4-5. The definitions of the species of *Saccharomyces*

Saccharomyces cerevisiae defined as follows:		
Cells large (3–10) × (4.5–21) μm: (maltose may be assimilated)		
Cadaverine not assimilated:	if yes and sucrose +	*S. Kluyveri*
	if yes and sucrose −	*S. unisporus*
No growth on 100 mg/L cycloheximide:	if yes and sucrose +	*S. exiguus*
	if yes and sucrose −	
	Growth on 1000 mg/L cycloheximide	*S. servazii*
	No growth on 1000 mg/L cycloheximide	*S. dairensis*
Ascospores smooth:	if rough	*S. telluris*

for further discussions of species of *Zygosaccharomyces*, *Brettanomyces*, and *Dekkera*.

In many cases varieties or subspecies are shown arising when the differences between strains are too small to consider each of them a bona fide species, but too large to lump them together. Sometimes the difference between the subspecies seems far too large, as with two varieties of *K. marxianus*, where the subdivision is based on the shapes of the ascospores, a difference which is large enough to assign genus status in other cases (Table 4-2).

An especially difficult situation comes up with the naming of some closely related strains, which in earlier taxonomies had been classified as several species of *Saccharomyces*. These strains are separated from one another only by the results of their sugar fermentation tests. One strain gives a positive fermentation test with a monosaccharide other than glucose, namely, galactose. Others have the enzymes for the hydrolysis of disaccharides, such as maltose, lactose, sucrose or melibiose, or the trisaccharide raffinose—that is to say, these enzymes are induced in certain strains in the presence of the sugars. These strains are so similar, perhaps having only one gene difference between them, that each strain has now been named a race of the species *S. cerevisiae*, rather than a species in its own right (Kreger-van Rij 1984). There are 17 of these races. Essentially all of the *Saccharomyces* strains important in industrial fermentations fall into this grouping. While the clumping of these organisms into one species solved a difficult situation for the taxonomists, it brought up a cumbersome one for enologists. Races of *S. cerevisiae* of the most importance to wine microbiologists are probably, in addition to race *cerevisiae*: *bayanus*, *capensis*, *chevalieri*, *steineri*, and *uvarum*. Part of the rationale for this subdivision of *S. cerevisiae* as races rather than as species comes from some instability of the distinguishing characteristics, the absence of consistent isolations, and the high degree of DNA homology between them (Kreger-van Rij 1984).

The situation with respect to the races *cerevisiae* and *bayanus* is special. These races differ in their fermentations of galactose—*S. cerevisiae* race *cerevisiae* being positive—and this trait has long been used to distinguish the two. Vaughn-Martini and Kurtzman (1985) have made important contributions to resolve this troublesome question by showing that these two races should be returned to species status, along with another close relation, *S. pastorianus*. This will be acceptable to enologists, who have long recognized the differences between *S. cerevisiae* and *S. bayanus*, in that essentially all of the strains useful in sparkling wine production are of the latter.

In earlier taxonomies, strains of flor yeast, for production of film sherry, were named *S. chevalieri*, along with other species, *S. cheriensis* and *S. beticus*. But these are not closely related to race *S. cerevisiae* race *chevalieri*. Instead, most of the flor strains have been placed in the genus and species *Torulaspora delbrueckii* (or the imperfect form *Candida colliculosa*).

Before leaving the subject of sugar fermentations, it should be noted that for a positive fermentation test, not only must the strain have the needed enzyme to hydrolyze the polysaccharide, but it also must have the capability to ferment at least one of the hexoses released. For example, breaking of the bond between galactose and sucrose moieties of the raffinose molecule would result in a fermentation-negative test if the yeast was not able to ferment either galactose or not able to hydrolyze sucrose to its fermentable moieties, glucose and fructose.

Two rules often mentioned by yeast taxonomists are that if a yeast ferments glucose, it will also ferment fructose; and if it ferments maltose, it will not ferment lactose. The former is always true. However, this second rule will not do for us, since at least one species of *Brettanomyces* ferments both maltose and lactose.

From Table 4-1 we see that *Candida*, with 196 species, is an oversized genus. Indeed, it is a collection of convenience and the species therein show a wide spectrum of characteristics. It has been divided into 10 groups. The yeasts in group I are separated from the rest by their ability to be stained by the dye, Diazonium Blue B, but none of the individuals in group I is wine related. The rest of the groups are separated by the ability to assimilate various compounds. Within each group, the various physiological and morphological tests already discussed are employed. Running these tests may be tedious, but they are straightforward, and so is the assignment of the results. In addition, taxonomists also use the "coenzyme Q system" developed by Yamada and co-workers (Kreger-van Rij 1984), where the number of isoprene units per ubiquinone molecules are determined. The resulting Co-Q number ranges between 6 and 10 and is useful in confirming species of *Candida*, and indeed species of other genera, as well as some genera, themselves.

d. Strain Identification of the Wine-Related Yeasts

There are a number of reasons it may be necessary to verify the identity of a particular strain: to be certain that a proposed inoculum is the same or different from another; to prove that an added strain is in fact surviving and is present at the end of fermentation; or to determine which strain is actually conducting the fermentation; or to know if an unwanted strain has become established in the winery.

I. ***Physiological Tests.*** The acquisition of yes or no answers, which make dichotomous keys so convenient, comes to an end with the species classifications. For yeast strain identification, until very recent times, definitive strain classifications were virtually impossible, relying on difficult physiological characterization. However, new karyogamic technology now available allows fingerprinting of the nuclear material and for decisive assignment of strains, and is described in the next section.

Growth and fermentation performances and viabilities were used in the past to differentiate strains. These traits can be measured under many sets of circumstances—environmental manipulations—and some sort of numerical values can be attached to the performances. These kinds of tests must be made under scrupulously standardized conditions, and that the finding of identical values for various yeast strains is no proof of the identity of the strains. However, lack of identical values should indicate that the strains are not identical. Thus, this kind of methodology, although difficult and often not very helpful, has provided answers to demanding questions. Some of the measurements which have been used in this way are duration of the growth lag period and growth rate constants under standard conditions. The use of various concentrations of several vitamins to obtain what were called BIOS numbers turned out to be less satisfactory, but other nutrients might be more effective (Kunkee and Bisson 1993). During standard fermentation trials, the fermentation lag period, the maximum fermentation rate, and the overall duration (to some final Brix reading) have been used with some success in this context.

There is vast literature on the effect of yeast strains on the formation of various end products during the fermentation. Within each experiment, reliable differences in the performances are obvious, but there is no justification for extrapolation of these results willy-nilly to other experiments. Of course, if a yeast strain (such as UCD Enology #694, a leucine-less mutant of Montrachet) really does produce lower concentrations of isoamyl alcohol, then this trait ought to show up during essentially all fermentation tests, and it does (Section H.2).

Sensitivities to inhibitory agents, such as sulfur dioxide, ethanol, and sugars (at high concentrations) have been used to distinguish yeast strains. The sensitivities sometimes have been measured by the effect on growth rates or on viability, but generally not on fermentation performance per se. More sophisticated tests have involved the electrophoresis pattern of various enzymes of a cell-free preparation; the measurement of alcohol dehydrogenase, in this regard, has been somewhat successful (Singh and Kunkee 1977).

In some cases, strains are naturally rather specifically labeled, and appraisal of that can be used, again not to identify but to exclude. For example, California Champagne (UCD Enology #505) is extremely flocculent, and can almost be identified by this behavior. Month-old colonies of the flor strain of *Torulaspora delbrueckii* (UCD Enology #519) give a characteristic crinkled appearance. Typing of various killer-factor phenomena (Section K.1) —killer production, killer sensitivity, and killer neutrality — could be used, again to show exclusion, not identity.

Fermentation efficiencies, measured as the rate of carbon dioxide production per unit dry weight, have been used to proof yeast strains used for other fermentation industries and seem to be useful in categorizing some strains of yeasts (Thorne 1958). This has not been very successful with wine yeasts. And neither has another kind of fermentation efficiency, the ethanol production for units of sugar fermented; or for the more common measurement, the ethanol produced in relation to starting Brix (a measurement which includes other soluble solids besides sugar) (Chapter 3).

Some other strain identification techniques have shown some limited success, but have a disadvantage in that the results are dependent upon the different physiological states of the cell. One of these is the study of the profiles of the volatile fatty acids (Cottrell et al. 1986). This has been used especially to identify wine spoilage yeasts (Malfeito-Ferreira et al. 1989), but also to try to characterize various wine yeast strains (Tredoux et al. 1987; Augustyn and Kock 1989; Kunkee 1990). Another has been electrophoretic examination of proteins: extracellular (Molan et al. 1982; Bouix and Leveau 1983) and intracellular (van Vuuren and van der Meer 1987).

Even less successful has been the attempt to relate the effect of the yeast strain used for the alcoholic fermentation on any subsequent malolactic fermentation. Undoubtedly there is an effect, but it would seem to be overwhelmed by other factors.

Most unsuccessful of all is the attempt to relate the wine yeast strain with the flavor of the end product (Bisson and Kunkee 1991; Kunkee and Bisson 1993; Kunkee and Vilas 1994).

II. Karyotype Analyses. The most useful methods for strain identification involve analysis of nuclear material. Since they are so closely related, the various strains show extensive DNA homology and identical GC (guanine cytosine) content, thus, methods, based on these measurements are of little use in differentiating strains. However, two other kinds of methods are successfully used, which are based upon detecting the frequency of base pair differences of the DNA or of rearrangements of the genome or both. These procedures are summarized as follows.

Restriction enzymes are proteins that recognize a specific sequence of double-stranded DNA, cleaving the DNA at or near that sequence. Single base pair changes of the DNA can alter the sequence so that it is no longer a substrate site for the restriction enzyme. The more distantly related two strains are, the greater the frequency of differences in both the location and number of restriction sites in the DNA. Restriction enzyme treatment or digestion of DNA results in the generation of specific DNA fragments or restriction fragments, that will differ more in pattern the more distantly related the strains are. If the fragments are low enough in number, they can be separated electrophoretically in a gel matrix and then visualized with ethidium bromide, a fluorescent dye that binds to DNA. Restriction enzyme digestion of total genomic DNA often results in the generation of too many fragments to allow resolution of discrete bands on a standard electrophoretic analysis. It is then necessary to develop a strategy for examining only a subset of the restriction fragments. This is accomplished by using repetitive DNA elements as probes that will reveal or light up a subset of the restriction fragments. Repetitive DNA elements are sequences that are found multiple times dispersed throughout the genome. For *Saccharomyces*, the virus-like Ty elements can be used to probe the restriction digest. The "probe" is labeled or tagged in some way as to make the restriction fragments that it recognizes visible. The probe DNA can be radiolabeled with ^{32}P, for example, and the location of the ^{32}P bands in the gel determined for comparison to other strains. The probe reacts with or hybridizes to homologous sequences. This methodology has been applied to identification of wine yeast strains (Degré et al. 1989).

An alternative method for examining the relatedness of strains of *Saccharomyces* is to do a restriction digest and comparison of the mitochondrial DNA. The mitochondria are DNA-containing eucaryotic organelles. The mitochondrial genome is much smaller than the nuclear genome. Restriction digestion of the mitochondrial DNA often yields a discrete banding pattern. This procedure also has been applied to identification of wine yeast strains (Dubourdieu et al. 1987; Hallet et al. 1988; Vezinhet et al. 1990a).

Strains can often be distinguished from one another on the basis of genome rearrangements. Genome rearrangements will also lead to changes in the pattern of restriction fragments. This analysis is called restriction fragment length polymorphisms (RFLP).

Saccharomyces has 16 distinct chromosomes. Over time, there is exchange of nonhomologous material between chromosomes, altering their length. Intact chromosomes can also be separated electrophoretically, revealing a distinct karyotype, or chromosome pattern (Skinner et al. 1991). Care must be taken not to damage or break the chromosomes during karyotyping. For successful karyotyping a pulsed current is used, often involving an alternating change in the direction or orientation of the electric field, providing a tortuous path for the chromosomes to traverse. Smaller molecules have an easier time shifting direction in response to a change in current than do larger ones. These various techniques have given rise to now very familiar acronyms: FIGE (field inversion gel electrophoresis) (Carle et al. 1986); OFAGE (orthoganal field alternating gel electrophoresis) (Carle et al. 1986); CHEF (contour-clamped homogeneous electric field) (Chu et al. 1986); and TAFE (traverse alternating field electrophoresis) (Gardiner and Patterson 1988; Stewart et al. 1988). These techniques are somewhat cumbersome and expensive, but are now being used not only in research, including enological research (Blondin and Vezinhet 1988; Vezinhet et al. 1990a), but also by culture collection curators and yeast production laboratories (Degré et al. 1989). We and others (Section C.1) have used these analyses to document that a wine strain used as inoculum indeed dominates and completes a vinification fermentation.

A newer technology, polymerase chain reaction (PCR), which amplifies discrete DNA fragments via de novo synthesis starting with known DNA primers, is also being applied to strain analysis and identification (Ness et al. 1993).

B. NATURAL GRAPE AND WINERY FLORA

Although *Saccharomyces* species are not normally found to any large extent on grapes in the natural environment, grapes, as delivered to the winery, host a variety of other microbial organisms (Section A.3). However, *Saccharomyces* is so well adapted to grape juice as a growth medium, that these yeasts readily dominate grape juice fermentations, making up essentially a pure culture by the end of fermentation.

The grape microbial flora is dependent upon many factors, such as rainfall, humidity, vineyard spray regimes, vineyard altitude, insect vectors, nitrogen fertilization regime, and winery waste disposal practices. In general terms, the population of molds is usually quite high. The principal genera found are: *Aspergillus*, *Penicillium*, *Rhizopus*, and *Mucor* (Amerine et al. 1980). Under certain conditions, detailed below, members of the genus *Botrytis* can be found on grapes. Infection of grapes with *Botrytis* can produce wines of a very characteristic composition and flavor, highly desirable in certain white wine styles (Chapter 2). If there is significant berry damage and mold growth, the molds present may deplete essential vitamins and minerals, reducing the nutrient content of the juice sufficiently such that the yeast will have a difficult time completing the grape juice fermentation (Chapter 9).

The population of aerobic and facultative anaerobic bacteria may also be high on damaged grapes at harvest. The principal prokaryotic genera present are the bacilli, lactic, and acetic acid bacteria, and they are found in much lower numbers on healthy fruit than are the eucaryotic wild yeasts. The wild yeasts present are principally of the genera *Kloeckera*, *Metschnikowia*, *Hansenula*, *Candida*, and *Hanseniaspora*. *Saccharomyces* can also be occasionally found in vineyards where it is common practice to dispose of winery waste—pomace and yeast lees—in the vineyard as fertilizer. In the absence of this practice, *Saccharomyces* species are very difficult to isolate from surfaces of grapes from the vineyard (Section A.3). *Kloeckera apiculata* seems to be the dominating yeast species on grapes in cooler growing regions, whereas *Hanseniaspora uvarum* is more prevalent in warmer regions (Castelli 1957; Adams 1960).

The molds and aerobic bacteria fail to grow under the anaerobic conditions of the alcoholic fermentation, and do not persist in grape juice fermentations. An exception is when red wine fermentation and CO_2 production are delayed during which a cap of grape skins forms on the surface of the must that provides an environment suitable to the growth of some of these organisms, particularly *Acetobacter*. Regular pumping over of the fermentation to bathe and submerge the cap will eliminate this problem. The wild yeasts, on the other hand, are capable of anaerobic as well as aerobic growth, and may persist during the fermentation. These yeasts will compete with *Saccharomyces* for nutrients and may produce fatty acid esters and other compounds affecting the fermentation bouquet of the wine. Very few of these other yeasts are as ethanol-tolerant as *Saccharomyces*, and, therefore, are generally undetectable by the end of fermentation. The persistence of these non-*Saccharomyces*, or wild yeasts during a fermentation depends upon many factors, such as the temperature of fermentation, nutrient availability, inoculum strength of *Saccharomyces*, use and levels of sulfur dioxide, and the numbers and kinds of organisms present on the grapes in the first place. Spoilage yeast, such as *Brettanomyces*, often find their way into the winery with the reception of the grapes, and although originally in small numbers, establish residence within the winery (Chapter 9). While *Saccharomyces* species are not prevalent on grapes, they are common flora of winery equipment and facilities. Even when well cleaned, winery equipment is not sterile unless very unusual measures are taken.

The lactic acid bacteria are an especially important class of microorganisms found in wines. They are responsible for the "malolactic" fermentation, which is the conversion of malic acid to lactic acid. These microorganisms and this fermentation are described in detail in Chapter 6.

C. FERMENTATION INOCULATION PRACTICES

Grape juice fermentation may be either natural, conducted by the flora present on the grapes and in the winery, or inoculated, conducted by the addition of a known strain of *Saccharomyces*. This latter practice minimizes the influence of wild yeasts on wine quality. Fermentations may be inoculated with a rehydrated commercial preparation of a suitable wine yeast strain or with a portion of actively fermenting wine. A good wine yeast strain for table wine production should:

- Conduct a vigorous fermentation.
- Conduct fermentation to dryness (low to no residual fermentable sugar).
- Possess reproducible fermentation characteristics and behave predictably.
- Possess good ethanol tolerance.
- Possess good temperature tolerance.
- Produce no off-flavors or aromas.
- Be SO_2 tolerant.
- Flocculate so as to be easy to remove (particularly for secondary fermentation in sparkling wine production).

1. Starter Cultures

The identification of a good wine strain having the above characteristics supposes that a conscious selection of a certain wine yeast strain as a starter culture has been made. If so, the strain may be commercially available in a dried form; or it may be from a culture collection, and a liquid inoculum needs to be prepared. Whichever type of starter culture is used, the amount should be large enough to assure the winemaker that the fermentation is made and completed by the inoculated strain. Until recently, this assurance was not easily demonstrated. However, with the available new biotechnologies, the identity of the dominant yeast strain at the end of a fermentation can be determined. Recent research employing genetic markings and karyogamic typing (Section A.3d) confirms that under normal conditions, the inoculated strain commands the fermentation and constitutes most of the total yeast population at the finish (Delteil and Aizac 1989; Vezinhet et al. 1990b; Petering et al. 1991).

a. *Active Dry Wine Yeast*

The commercial availability of wine yeast in the active dried form is rather recent, but its use has received dramatic acceptance in the newer wine regions, especially in the United States (Reed and Nagodawithana 1988; Kunkee and Bisson 1993). Currently there are at least nine companies worldwide producing some three dozen strains of wine yeast—although probably less than six strains are the most popular. The wine yeasts are produced, as are Baker's yeast, under highly aerobic conditions on media with abundant nutrients but having very low concentrations of glucose (Kraus et al. 1983, 1984). Often diluted molasses is used. These conditions encourage formation of biomass, with a minimum formation of ethanol. The high concentration of oxygen induces the formation of survival factors, unsaturated fatty acids, and sterols in the cell membranes which are needed for the cells' high tolerance to ethanol during wine production (Sections K.1b and L). The low concentration of glucose and aerobic conditions generate cells with active mitochondria, which also have survival factors in their membranes. Thus, during the vinification fermentation, these commercially prepared yeasts are endowed with enough survival factors to avoid sluggish fermentations (Section K1) under normal conditions.

Although these yeasts are called active dry, they contain up to 9% moisture. They are usually marketed hermetically sealed under nitrogen. When stored in the cold, they maintain viability for at least one year. During most of the drying processes, the cellular membranes of the yeast tend to lose their permeability barrier function. Thus, it is important to reestablish this barrier function, which is a metabolic process and is optimally done by adding the yeast to a small volume of warm water (40°C) for 20 minutes before adding the yeast to the must. The recommended dosage of about 0.1 to 0.2 g dry yeast per L of must should give an initial concentration of about 10^6 cells/mL. Higher and lower amounts can be used; the lower amounts are less costly, but this increases the risk of not providing enough survival factors for a complete fermentation. Inoculation at the ultimate population level (10^8 cells/mL) minimizes yeast multiplication, raises ethanol yield slightly, and can give a decided yeast note to the finished wine.

Although the starter cultures for the commercial preparations are pure, and efforts are made to maintain aseptic production facilities, the product itself is not completely free from contamination; some bacteria and other yeast are usually found.

b. Liquid Inocula

Starter cultures can be prepared in the winery laboratory from stored cultures. This has the dubious advantage of providing a starter culture of some special strain that is not commercially available but is labor-intensive and needs to be done carefully by microbiologically trained personnel. Again, it is expected that the culture in the collection is a pure one. The first few stages of the expansion of the culture should be done aseptically. A loop of yeast from slant culture might be transferred to 5 mL of autoclaved grape juice. After one or two days, active growth is evident and the culture can be conveniently transferred into 50-fold volume (250 mL) of autoclaved juice. Such serial transfers can be made perhaps one or two more times, but then the volumes become too large for convenient aseptic transfer. Since wine yeast grow very rapidly and since grape juice is an ideal medium for these organisms (its nutrients and pH allowing expansion of the culture but discouraging growth of most extraneous organisms), large inocula (2%) and judicious amounts of added sulfur dioxide essentially maintain asepsis.

2. Natural Fermentations

The conditions of inoculation depend to a certain extent upon regional practices and experiences. A natural fermentation is one in which no yeast starter is intentionally added. We say intentionally because in most cases where a winemaker may be expecting to bring about a natural fermentation, yeasts are actually being introduced during winery operations. Natural fermentations in the absence of sulfur dioxide may allow the wild yeast flora to persist and possibly make a contribution to the overall sensory character of the wine. This may be a good idea, adding to wine complexity, or a serious mistake, detracting from wine quality, depending upon the grape variety, the wine style, and the actual flora present during the fermentation. Certainly, the impact of a natural fermentation on wine flavor and aroma is not predictable. Some particularly nasty off-flavors and aromas can be produced by wild yeasts and bacteria that are difficult if not impossible to diminish in the finished wine. Another disadvantage of natural fermentations is their unpredictability in terms of fermentation onset and duration. Use of a starter culture ensures a more rapid takeover by *Saccharomyces*. There is generally a lag period or time of adaptation required before cell growth and fermentation even if a commercial preparation is used, since the commercial yeasts are grown under strictly aerobic and low substrate conditions. These growth conditions of high oxygen exposure also ensure that the starter yeast contains an ample supply of survival factors, sterols, and unsaturated fatty acids necessary for ethanol tolerance. Given what we now know about wine yeasts, it is fair to conclude that so-called natural or wild yeast fermentations are always conducted by wine strains of *Saccharomyces*. It is significant that inoculation with selected strains is growing as a practice worldwide.

The practice of using juice from one tank in midfermentation to inoculate the next, results in a rapid fermentation initiation as the yeasts are preadapted to the grape juice; however, it has the disadvantage of introducing a nutrient-depleted inoculum if the first juice itself is nutritionally deficient. It also depletes the cells of survival factors, and can foster the spread of spoilage organisms if they become established in the juice utilized for inoculation. Generally, a 2 to 5% (v/v) inoculum is used from a fermenting juice at 12 to 15 Brix. *Saccharomyces* species readily dominate grape juice fermentations, even when greatly outnumbered in the initial stages of fermentation.

3. Dominance by Saccharomyces

Many physiological parameters allow *Saccharomyces* to dominate grape juice fermentations. Rapid high-level production of a toxic end product is one strategy to ensure dominance in the fermenting medium. Tolerance to high concentrations of ethanol is the principal feature of this yeast allowing survival in the fermenting medium. *Saccharomyces* produces ethanol as the major end product of the fermentation of grape sugars. The non-*Saccharomyces* wild yeasts and other grape flora are not nearly as ethanol tolerant as *Saccharomyces*, although some are capable of ethanol production themselves. Common spoilage yeasts of wine, *Brettanomyces* and *Zygosaccharomyces*, are as tolerant of ethanol as the *Saccharomyces* species.

A second parameter that may also give *Saccharomyces* species a competitive advantage is tolerance to higher temperatures than many other yeasts. Anaerobic fermentation is somewhat inefficient, generating waste energy in the form of heat. During vinifications, wine strains of *Saccharomyces* can maintain viability and continue to ferment at temperatures approaching 38°C, while most of the wild flora are inhibited at temperatures in excess of 25°C. Production of heat as an end product and ability to survive warmer temperatures may have selected traits in *Saccharomyces* contributing to dominance of fermentations.

Successful competition for limiting nutrients is also a factor contributing to the dominance of one species or genus over another in a mixed microbial fermentation (Bisson and Kunkee 1991). Much study has been made on nutrient utilization and uptake in *Saccharomyces* species, but very little comparative analysis with other flora has been undertaken. Juice nutrient content can vary widely as a function of numerous variables such as grape variety, growing region and climatic effects, nutritional richness of the soil, and vineyard fertilization practices. In general, juices produced in the older grape growing regions of Europe appear to be more nutritionally deficient than those of relatively newer growing regions such as California. The nutritional content of a juice impacts the number and kinds of organisms that can multiply. In general, California experience has been that natural (uninoculated) fermentations are risky in that off-characters are often produced by the wild yeasts and can persist in the finished wine, detracting from wine quality. This does not appear to be the experience in older growing regions where natural fermentations have been routine, producing wines with distinctive regional character. The distinctive regional character is more likely associated with viticultural and climatic considerations than with the dominant yeast strain, which is probably resident in the winery rather than associated with the vineyard in any case (Müller-Thurgau 1889; Kunkee 1984). The relative nutritional weaknesses of the juices may play an important role in limiting the contribution or impact of the wild flora on wine flavor and aroma. It also may be that more blending of the finished wines limits the obtrusiveness of the occasional off-lot. A poor quality or non-vintage year in a European growing region may be an indicator of poor grape quality for that season, but may also reflect microbial activity detracting from varietal flavor and aroma. It is also important to remember that in many regions in Europe, winery waste, pomace and yeast lees, are used to fertilize the vineyard post fermentation. After several years of such disposal, this treatment may constitute an inoculation of the vineyard with winery yeast, which impact the flora on the fruit at subsequent harvest.

D. YEAST MORPHOLOGY AND CELLULAR ORGANIZATION

Saccharomyces is a eucaryotic microorganism that reproduces by budding (Figure 4-1). These cells are surrounded by a rigid cell wall comprised of glucan, mannan, and protein, allowing the cells to withstand dramatic changes in osmotic pressure. Beneath the cell wall is a periplasmic space, the site of localization of secreted proteins. Intact cells of *Saccharomyces* do not secrete proteins into the surrounding medium. Instead, extracellular enzymes are confined to the exterior of the cell by the cell wall. Other yeasts do secrete enzymes into the surrounding medium. The yeast cell cytoplasm is surrounded by a plasma membrane which serves as the principal permeability barrier.

Saccharomyces also displays subcellular organelles characteristic of higher eucaryotic organisms. A membrane-bound nucleus is present as well as endoplasmic reticulum, golgi bodies, and secretory vesicles. Mitochondria are also found. Because of their fermentative nature, *Saccharomyces* strains can exist without mitochondria, the so-called petite or respiratory-deficient mutants. Petite strains are incapable of growth on nonfermentative substrates such as ethanol, pyruvate, and lactate, but can grow fermentatively on sugars. During anaerobic fermentation, mitochondrial activity is suppressed and the enzymes of the electron transport chain are not synthesized. In addition to respiration, many oxidative reactions are confined to the mitochondrion and hence are not functional during fermentation. These include the reactions of the tricarboxylic acid (TCA) cycle, proline oxidation, and fatty acid biosynthesis. Due to their extensive membranous nature, mitochondria also serve as a reserve of lipid material which can be cannibalized and used for plasma membrane biosynthesis during anaerobic growth.

Yeasts also possess vacuoles analogous to the plant cell vacuoles which serves as the site of hydrolysis of macromolecules; storage of amino acids, some high-energy compounds such as *ortho* phosphate, and other cellular components, and is involved in maintaining turgor pressure and ion balances (Section I-1).

E. YEAST NUTRITION AND GROWTH CHARACTERISTICS

1. Carbon Metabolism

When compared to many microorganisms, *Saccharomyces* species are fairly limited in the compounds that can be utilized as carbon and energy sources. The monosaccharides glucose, fructose, mannose, and galactose can support growth and metabolism of this yeast. The disaccharides sucrose, maltose, and melibiose can be utilized by most wine strains of *Saccharomyces*, but not by all, depending upon the genetic background of the strain, usually involving the formation of the appropriate enzymes in response to the respective sugar substrates. The trisaccharide raffinose can also serve as a substrate. Pentoses are not utilized by *Saccharomyces* wine strains. Substrates supporting oxidative or respiratory growth are also limited: pyruvate, lactate, ethanol, acetate, and glycerol. However, glycerol supports growth poorly as the sole carbon and energy source in minimal, defined medium (Wills 1990). Other organic acids cannot be utilized by *Saccharomyces* as carbon or energy sources, although some, such as malic acid, can be metabolized to other compounds by some strains.

The major routes of carbon metabolism in *Saccharomyces* are depicted in Figure 4-5. Which pathways are operational depends upon the substrate available and growth conditions. Availability of oxygen plays a critical role in metabolism as molecular oxygen is required as the terminal electron acceptor during respiration, but it has a different role during high-sugar, relatively anaerobic fermentations.

The major pathway for glucose (fructose, mannose) catabolism is glycolysis. Many of the pathways presented in Figure 4-5 are not operational during fermentation, but are briefly discussed to place the biochemistry of fermentation within the greater context of cellular biochemistry. The earliest studies that led to the development of microbiology, biochemistry, and stereochemistry were accomplished by scientists studying wine and yeast fermentations. Indeed, enzyme means "in yeast." Enology can be considered the parent of these discipline-based sciences.

The glycolytic pathway, conversion of glucose to pyruvate, is a virtually universal pathway for glucose catabolism found throughout the eucaryotic kingdom and in many procaryotes. The pathway is operational under both fermentative and respiratory modes of metabolism. In fermentation, a carbon compound serves as terminal acceptor of the electrons that are generated in the pathway in the course of converting the sugar metabolites to energy in the form of ATP (adenosine triphosphate). In *Saccharomyces*, pyruvate is converted to acetaldehyde, which serves as terminal electron acceptor generating ethanol. Other organisms utilize other electron acceptors during fermentation producing reduced acids such as the lactic acid bacteria, which utilize pyruvate itself as hydrogen acceptor in being reduced to lactic acid. In muscle, pyruvate also serves as terminal electron acceptor generating lactic acid.

During respiration, which may be important in the earliest phases of vinification fermentation and in all phases of commercial yeast production, more of the energy of the catabolism of carbon compounds is captured in the form of ATP. This is a consequence of the action of two metabolic pathways—the tricarboxylic acid (TCA) cycle and the electron transport chain (Figures 4-6 and 4-7).

In the TCA cycle, pyruvate is decarboxylated and reacts with Coenzyme A to yield acetyl-CoA. The enzyme catalyzing this reaction is pyruvate dehydrogenase. Acetyl-CoA condenses with the four-carbon acid, oxalacetate, to produce citrate, a six-carbon acid, and, subsequently, several other organic acid intermediates are formed. One turn of the cycle generates two molecules of CO_2 and regenerates oxalacetate. Also generated are three molecules of reduced nicotinamide adenine dinucleotide (NADH), and one of flavine adenine dinucleotide ($FADH_2$). Respiratory-chain-linked phosphorylation during the oxidation of NADH yields three molecules of ATP and two for $FADH_2$, for a total of 14 molecules of ATP for each pyruvate metabolized. The generation of ATP during respiration is called *oxidative phosphorylation*; that resulting from glycolysis is called *substrate level phosphorylation*.

The reactions that generate NADH and $FADH_2$ are listed in Table 4-6. An additional substrate-level phosphorylation occurs at the succinyl CoA synthase reaction. Therefore, a single pyruvate molecule traversing the TCA cycle generates 15 molecules of ATP. Two molecules of pyruvate (equivalent of one glucose) generate 30 molecules of ATP. There are two molecules of ATP produced during glycolysis for a total of 32. If the pyruvate is being completely oxidized to CO_2, then the two NADH molecules produced during glycolysis may also be a source of ATP. These NADH molecules are cytoplasmic and not mitochondrial, and in order to generate ATP the elec-

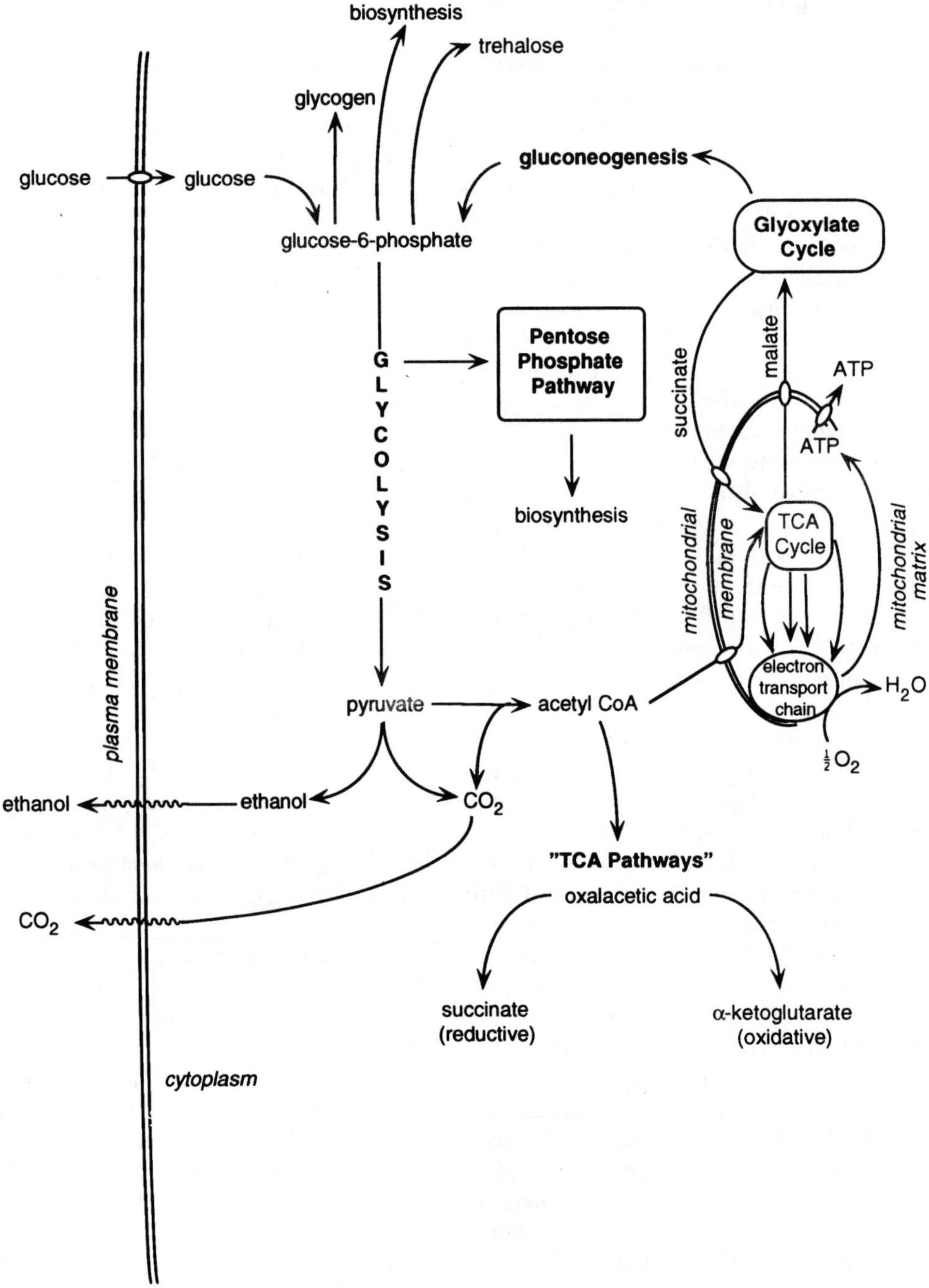

Fig. 4-5. Major pathways of carbon metabolizing *Saccharomyces*.

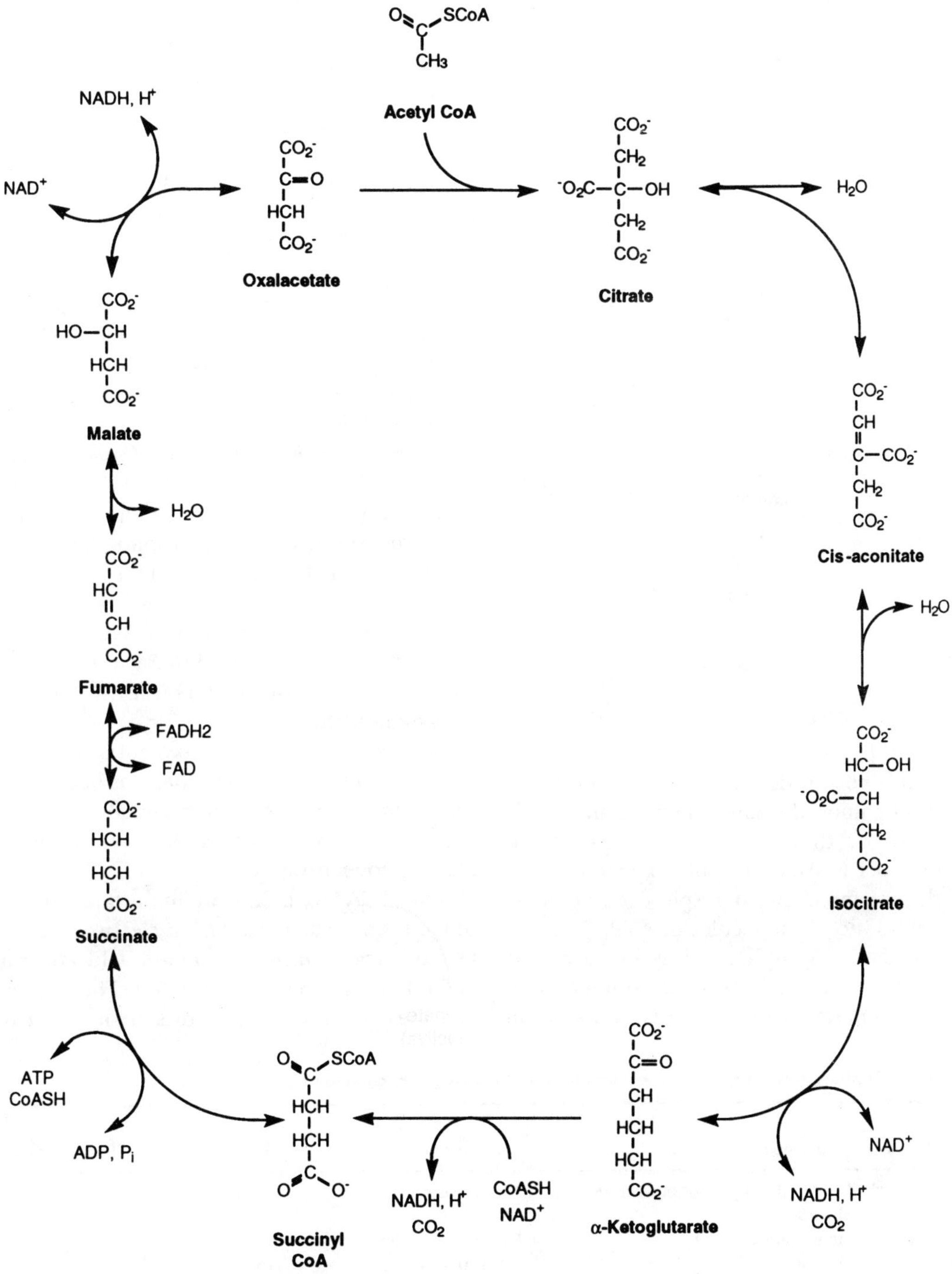

Fig. 4-6. Enzymatic steps of the citric acid (TCA) cycle.

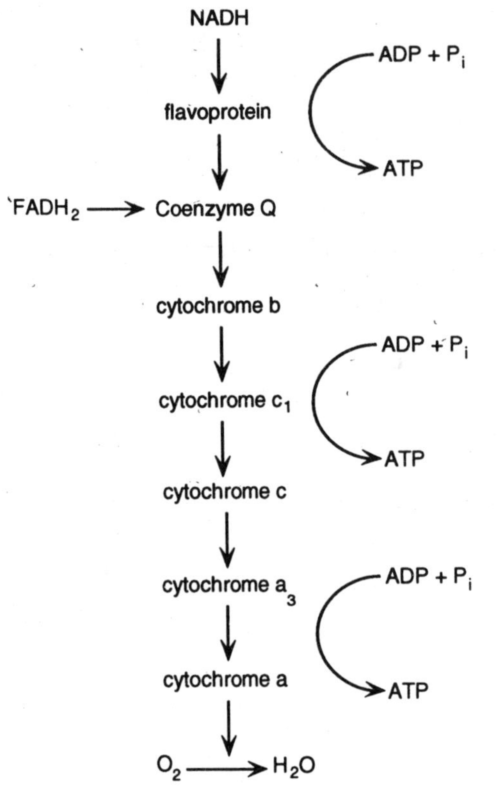

Fig. 4-7. Steps of the electron transport chain.

trons must be shuttled into the mitochondria. Depending upon the shuttling mechanism utilized, two or three ATP molecules may be obtained per NADH molecule oxidized. A single glucose molecule, if respired completely, will yield 36 to 38 molecules of ATP, 33 to 35 from oxidative phosphorylation and a net of three from substrate-level phosphorylation. Thus, the energy yielded by yeast metabolism is 15 fold higher for aerobic as compared to anaerobic sugar catabolism.

Enzymes of the TCA cycle and electron transport chain are localized in a subcellular organelle, the mitochondrion. Since respiration is ultimately dependent upon oxygen, these enzymes are not synthesized constitutively, but only when required for metabolism. In yeast, expression of the genes encoding these enzymes is controlled by the concentration of glucose or other fermentable sugar in the medium. The genes are repressed by high glucose concentration, meaning that mRNA is not made; there is no transcription. This regulatory phenomenon is variously called *glucose repression*, *glucose catabolite repression*, *carbon catabolite repression*, or the *Crabtree effect* (Crabtree 1929; De Deken 1966). When substrate is not limiting, yeasts rely upon fermentation or substrate-level phosphorylation exclusively for ATP production. Thus, fermentation is the preferred mode of metabolism even when molecular oxygen is available. As sugar concentration becomes limiting, yeast must switch to respiratory metabolism in order to generate sufficient ATP for growth and metabolism. Of course, if oxygen is not available this metabolic switch does not occur. It is not surprising that oxygen availability is also a regulator of gene expression in addition to glucose concentration.

The TCA cycle has an important role in biosynthetic reactions. The cycle provides intermediates required for amino acid and nucleotide biosynthesis (Figure 4-8). The enzyme activities generating these precursors must be

Table 4-6. Enzyme reactions generating coenzymes for oxidative phosphorylation.

Enzyme reaction	Location	Coenzyme	ATP Produced
Glyceraldehyde-3-Pi → 1,3 diphosphoglycerate	Cytoplasm	NADH	2–3
Pyruvate → Acetyl-CoA	Mitochondrion	NADH	3
Isocitrate → α-Keto-glutarate + CO_2	Mitochondrion	NADH	3
Isocitrate → α-Keto-glutarate	Cytoplasm	NADPH	0
α-Ketoglutarate → Succinyl CoA + CO_2	Mitochondrion	NADH	3
Succinate → Fumarate	Mitochondrion	$FADH_2$	2
Malate → Oxalacetic acid	Mitochondrion	NADH	3

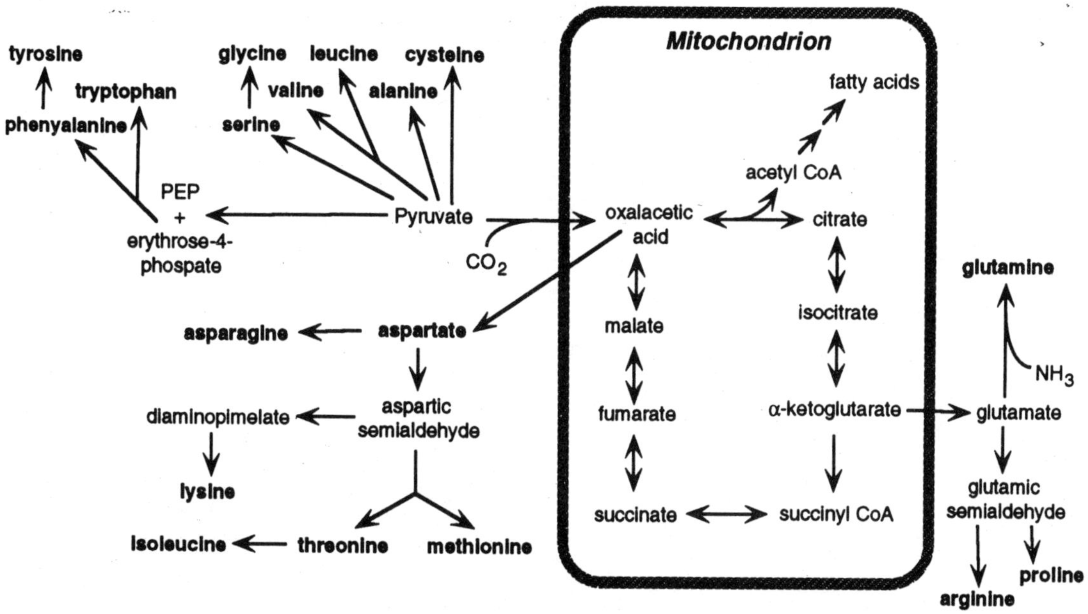

Fig. 4-8. Role of TCA cycle organic acids in amino acid biosynthesis.

present even under anaerobic conditions in *Saccharomyces*. Under anaerobic conditions, mature, fully functional mitochondria are not present in *Saccharomyces*. TCA cycle enzymes required for biosynthesis are not localized to the mitochondria as they are during respiratory metabolism, but are found instead in the cytoplasm. Although this has not yet been rigorously proven, the mitochondrial and cytoplasmic forms may be isozymes, that is, the products of separate genes. The TCA cycle does not exist as a complete cycle in the cytoplasm, but serves to form biosynthetic intermediates or end products of amino acid metabolism. Reverse flow of the pathway consumes acetyl-CoA and is involved in acetate ester formation. We refer to all these enzymatic reactions as the TCA pathway.

If regeneration of NAD^+ from NADH via conversion of acetaldehyde to ethanol is restricted, the reductive arm of the TCA pathway can be used to regenerate NAD^+ with the production of malate and succinate, acids which can be produced by yeast during wine fermentation. Alternatively, if reducing power (NADH) is needed, it can be generated via the oxidative arm of the TCA pathway.

Saccharomyces also possess the glyoxylate cycle (Figure 4-9). This cycle generates from two-carbon substrates the net production of TCA cycle intermediates required for macromolecular synthesis. Since the TCA cycle gives no net accumulation of intermediates, the yeasts can use the glyoxylate shunt for their net synthesis. Thus, yeast can use the glyoxylate cycle to synthesize sugars needed for cell wall structural components, glucan and mannan, from growth substrates such as ethanol and acetate. This pathway, obviously, only needs to operate when cells are growing in the absence of sugar. The glyoxylate cycle enzymes are also subject to glucose repression.

Another important pathway for the production of biosynthetic precursors is the pentose phosphate shunt (Figure 4-10). In some microbes, such as the heterolactic malolactic bacteria, this pathway is used to metabolize pentoses, allowing those organisms to use five-carbon sugars as carbon and energy source. Such is not the case in *Saccharomyces*. *Saccha-*

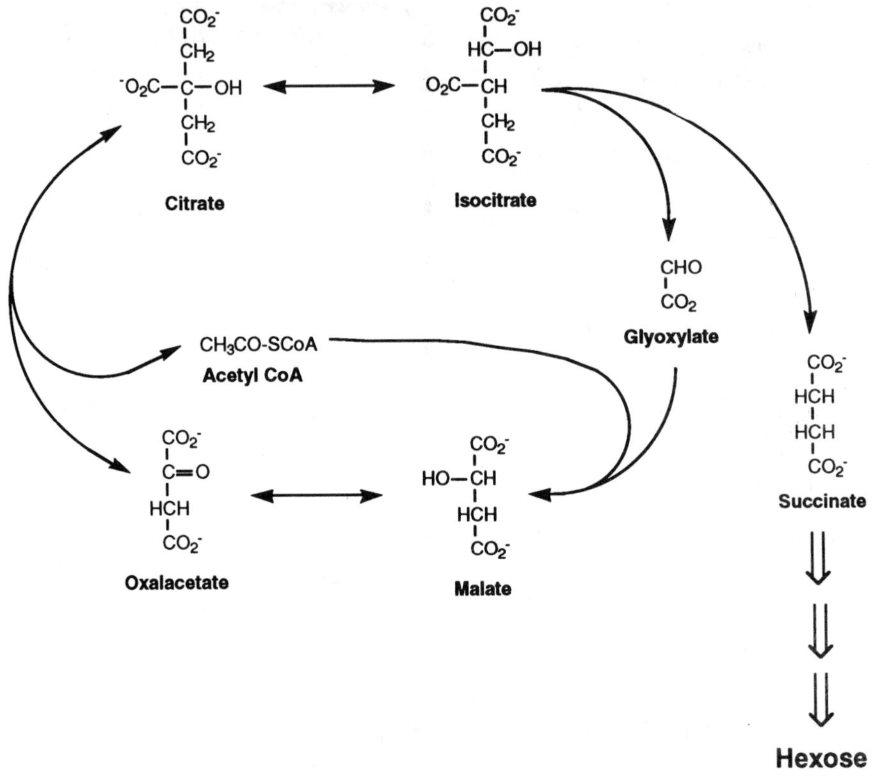

Fig. 4-9. Enzymatic steps of the glyoxylate cycle.

romyces requires this pathway for the generation of ribose-5-phosphate, a precursor for nucleotide biosynthesis. *Saccharomyces* also uses this pathway to make erythrose-4-phosphate required for the initial step of the shikimic acid pathway, for the synthesis of the aromatic amino acids. This pathway also generates NADPH, which is also required for biosynthesis. Thus, the pentose phosphate pathway is operational during both fermentative and respiratory growth.

It is important to note that fermentation and respiration are not mutually exclusive modes of metabolism. *Saccharomyces* increases reliance on respiration for ATP production as fermentation becomes incapable of supplying needed ATP levels, provided oxygen is available and glucose concentrations are low. There is not an abrupt switch from fermentation to respiration, or from respiration to fermentation. This is one reason yeasts require a period of adaptation to different growth conditions. Fermentative growth can be influenced by respiration capacity, depending upon growth conditions and the cellular demand for ATP.

2. Noncarbon Nutrition

Ammonium ion and most amino acids can serve as nitrogen sources for *Saccharomyces*. Lysine, histidine, and glycine are not well-utilized by *Saccharomyces*. Urea, γ-aminobutryic acid, short peptides, and purine and pyrimidine bases (except thymine) can be degraded by *Saccharomyces*. Nitrate, nitrite and most other organic amines cannot be used. The ability to utilize a particular nitrogen-containing compound as a nitrogen source is dependent upon several factors. For example, degradation of the amino acid proline requires molecular

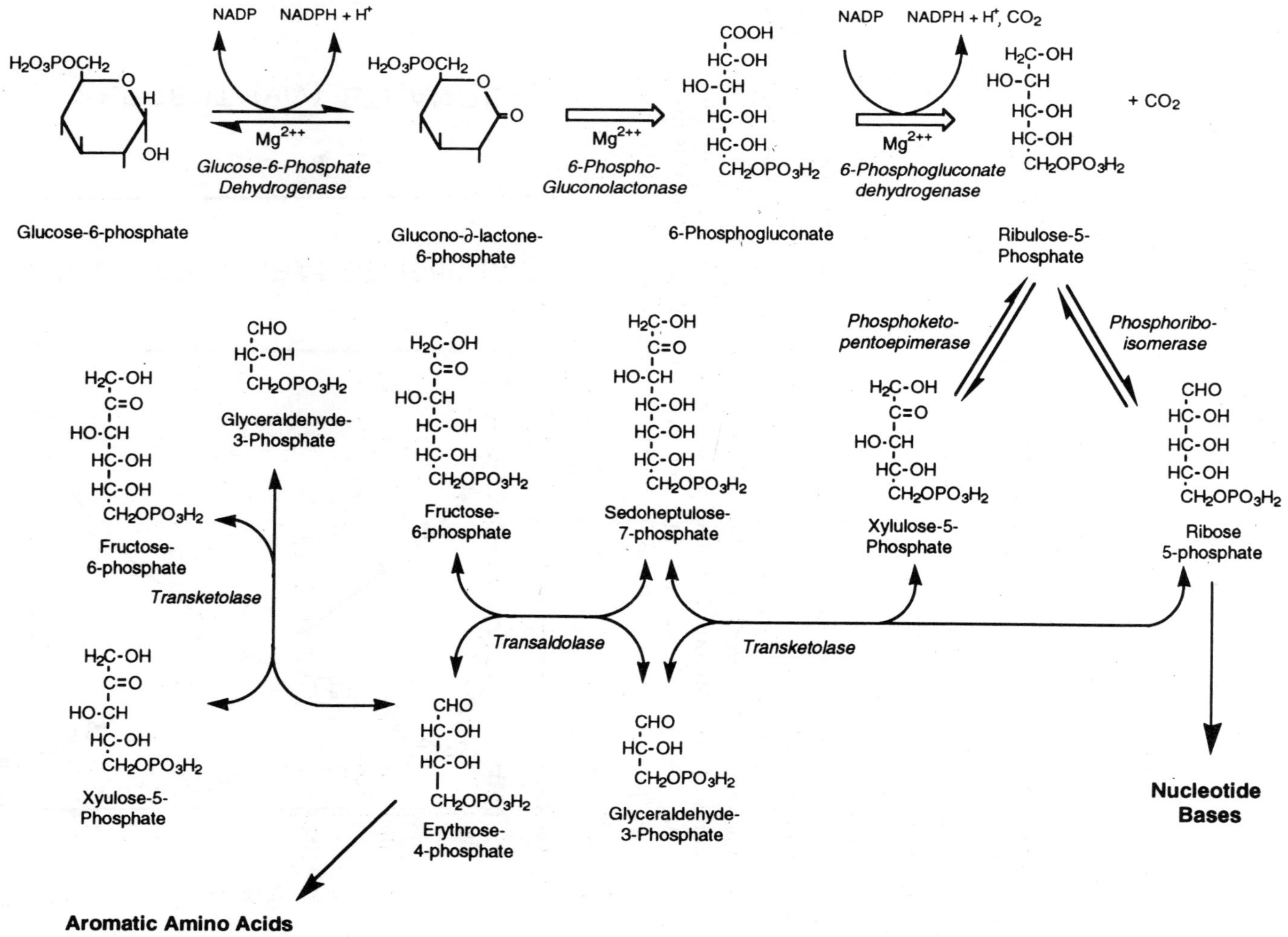

Fig. 4-10. Enzymatic steps of the pentose phosphate pathway.

oxygen. Proline cannot be used as nitrogen source in the absence of oxygen.

As a phosphate source, yeasts prefer inorganic phosphate, but can use phosphate esters. An acid phosphatase is secreted by *Saccharomyces* catalyzing the hydrolysis of these esters outside of the cell proper in the periplasmic space. Sulfate, sulfite, and thiosulfate can be utilized as sulfur sources, as can the sulfur-containing amino acids, cysteine and methionine, and homocysteine and S-adenosyl-methionine (Thomas et al. 1992). A recent report suggests that glutathione can also be used as a source of sulfur for *Saccharomyces* (Elskens et al. 1991).

Typically, the only vitamin required by *Saccharomyces* is biotin, but other vitamins may be very stimulatory to growth (Castor and Archer 1956). *Saccharomyces* readily depletes the medium of vitamins. Minerals are also needed, particularly Fe, Mg, Mn, Cu, Ca, K, and Zn. Sodium is relatively toxic to *Saccharomyces*, as it is in many plants, probably as an evolutionary consequence of the fact that it is not a prevalent ion in grape juice or other yeast-natural media.

Nutrient limitations may result in a sluggish or incomplete fermentation, depending upon the extent of the limitation. Lack of nutrients may also result in the formation of undesirable end products of metabolism such as hydrogen sulfide and acetic acid. Nutrient supplementation with diammonium phosphate (DAP) is legally permitted up to a limit of 0.96 g/L, and DAP addition is utilized by a number of wineries.

Saccharomyces displays typical exponential growth kinetics in grape juice (Figure 4-11). If the inoculum has not been preadapted to growth in grape juice, there is an initial lag phase followed by exponential growth to a maximal cell density of around 2×10^8 cells/mL. The reasons for this approximate maximum cell population are not clear, but it

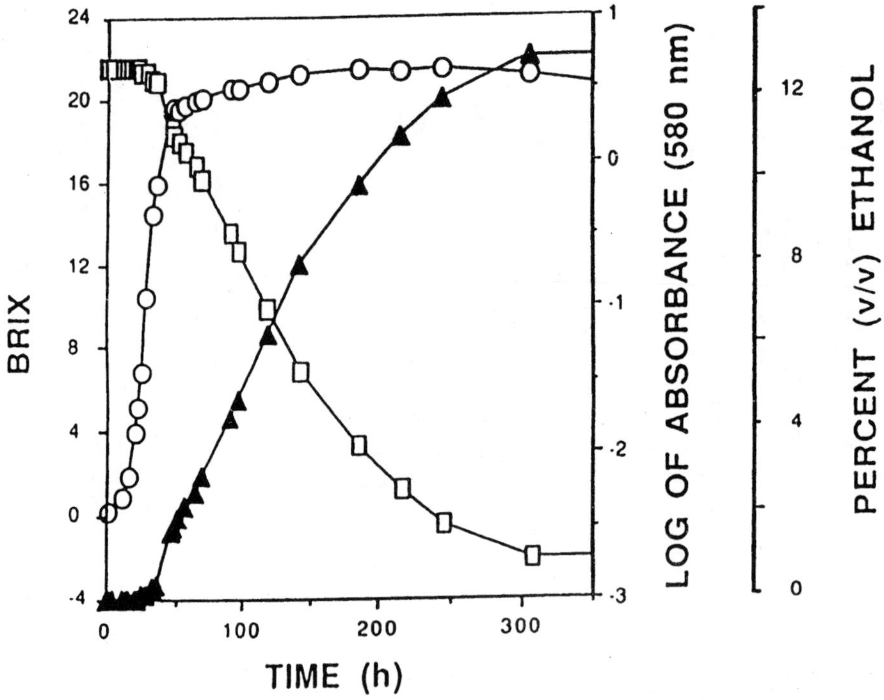

Fig. 4-11. Fermentation profile of grape juice. Absorbance (0); ethanol (▲); Brix (□).

is true whether yeast growth or excessive inoculation has led to the population number. It should be noted that the growth rate in grape juice, even with a high concentration of nutrients, is slower than would be expected because of the inhibitory effect of the sugar. In grape juice, approximately 50% of the total available sugar may be fermented during the growth phase and the remainder during stationary phase. Although net growth has ceased, the cells are still metabolically quite active at this stage. The death or decline in viable cell numbers will occur generally once the sugars have been depleted from the medium. The death phase is accelerated under conditions of low concentrations of Mg and Ca and under conditions that result in low levels of sterols and fatty acids required for the production of an ethanol-tolerant plasma membrane. Release of small molecules may also occur. The release of hydrolytic enzymes from the vacuole is responsible for the autodigestion, leakiness, and subsequent rupture of the yeast cells, termed *autolysis*. But this occurs under winemaking conditions only several months after the end of the alcoholic fermentation. The release of small molecules can occur in fully viable cells and does during sur lies aging and should not be confused with autolysis. Cells that are autolyzing are no longer viable. Yeast autolysis is important to the production of sparkling wines in the *méthode champenoise* style.

F. FERMENTATION BIOCHEMISTRY

Saccharomyces metabolizes glucose and fructose to pyruvate via the glycolytic pathway. Primarily in order to recycle cofactors, pyruvate is decarboxylated to acetaldehyde, which is then reduced to ethanol. One molecule of glucose (or fructose) yields two molecules each of ethanol and carbon dioxide. In a model fermentation starting with about 22 to 24% sugar (22 to 24 Brix), 95% of the sugar is converted into ethanol and carbon dioxide, 1% is converted into cellular material, and the remaining 4% is converted to other end products. Fermentation in terms of end products formed is inefficient as a significant amount of energy is lost as heat. In general, there is a 1.3°C rise in temperature for each Brix consumed per liter if heat is not removed by loss or cooling. A typical plot of consumption of sugar, production of ethanol and biomass versus time is presented in Figure 4-11. Approximately 50% of the sugar in a typical wine fermentation is consumed by cells during the stationary phase, although this percentage may vary depending upon inoculum size, fermentation temperature, and nutrient availability (Kunkee and Bisson 1993). With a typical inoculum of $1x10^6$ cells/mL, as many as five to seven generations will occur to reach a final cell density of 1 to $2x10^8$ cells/mL.

1. Glycolysis

a. *Glycolytic Pathway*

Glucose and fructose are converted to pyruvate via the glycolytic pathway (Figure 4-12). In fact, the glycolytic pathway, universal among the eucaryotes, was first delineated in yeast. The first cytoplasmic reaction is the phosphorylation of glucose to glucose-6-phosphate, catalyzed by one of three enzymes: hexokinase PI (A), hexokinase PII (B), or glucokinase. ATP serves as the phosphate donor in this reaction. All three enzymes also catalyze the phosphorylation of mannose, but only the hexokinases catalyze the phosphorylation of fructose. Hexokinase PII is the major species present initially in grape juice fermentations, with hexokinase PI being expressed as the culture enters the stationary phase of growth and fermentation. Expression of glucokinase has not been extensively studied under these conditions.

The next step in the pathway is the conversion of glucose-6-phosphate to fructose-6-phosphate. This reaction is catalyzed by the enzyme phosphoglucose isomerase. Mutant strains of *Saccharomyces* have been isolated lacking phosphoglucose isomerase activity. These mutants are unable to grow on glucose, meaning that glycolysis is the sole pathway in this organism for glucose catabolism. The pen-

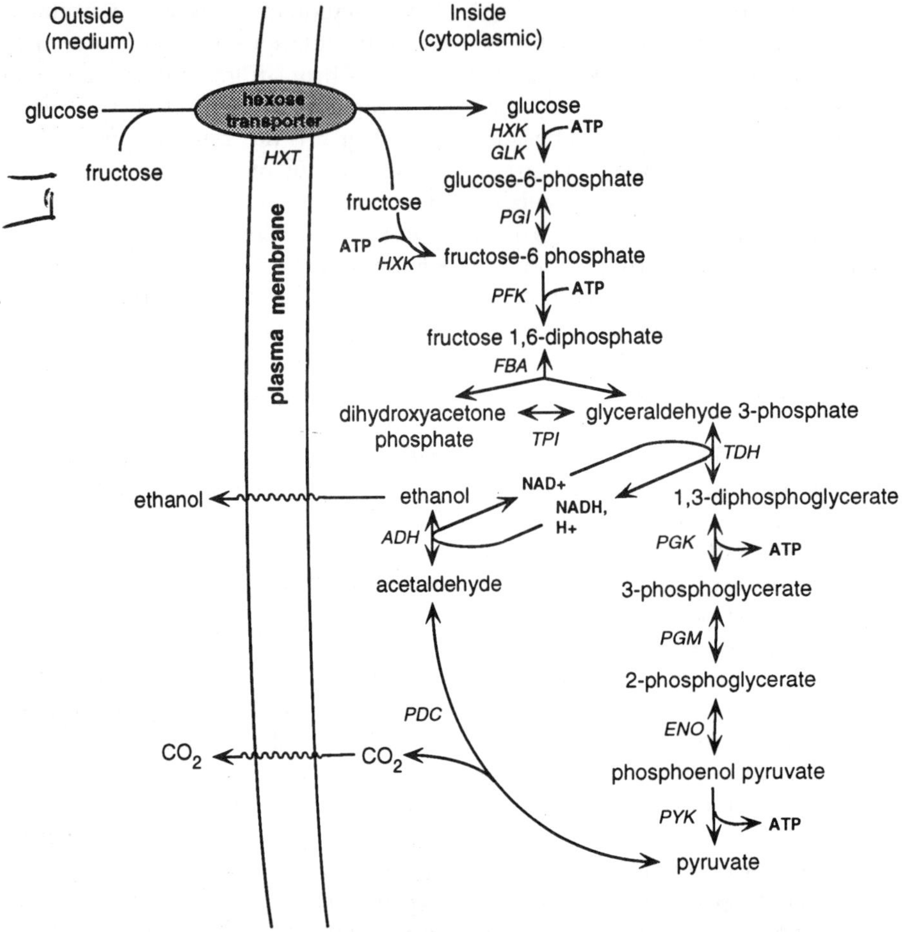

Fig. 4-12. Enzymatic steps of the glycolytic pathway HXT (hexose transporter), HXK (hexokinase) GLK (glucokinase), PGI (phosphoglucose isomerase), PFK (phosphofructokinase), FBA (aldolase), TPI (triosephosphate isomerase), TDH (glyceraldehyde-3-phosphate dehydrogenase), PGK (phosphoglycerate kinase), PGM (phosphoglycerate mutase), ENO (enolase), PYK (pyruvate kinase), PDC (pyruvate decarboxylase), ADH (alcohol dehydrogenase).

tose phosphate pathway, which in other organisms can serve as a route of glucose catabolism appears to be involved only in the production of pentose phosphates as precursors of nucleic acid bases, and in the generation of the reduced cofactor, NADPH, which is required for a variety of anabolic reactions in *Saccharomyces*.

Fructose-6-phosphate undergoes a second phosphorylation to fructose-1,6-bisphosphate, catalyzed by the enzyme phosphofructokinase. Again, ATP serves as the phosphate donor in this reaction. Phosphofructokinase is an allosteric enzyme, and its activity is modulated by a wide variety of effectors: ATP, ADP, AMP, citrate, Mg, fructose 2,6-bisphosphate, to name a few. This step in the pathway is a key site of regulation of overall metabolic flux, or flow of carbon through the pathway.

The next enzyme, aldolase, catalyze's the hydrolysis of fructose 1,6-bisphosphate to dihydroxyacetone phosphate and glyceraldehyde-3-phosphate. Glyceraldehyde-3-phosphate is the molecule ultimately converted to pyruvate, and the enzyme triosephosphate isomerase will interconvert dihydroxyacetone phosphate and glyceraldehyde-3-phosphate.

Glyceraldehyde-3-phosphate is converted to 1,3-diphosphoglycerate by the enzyme glyceraldehyde-3-phosphate dehydrogenase. Inorganic phosphate serves as the phosphate donor in this reaction. Since this reaction is an oxidation, the cofactor NAD^+ is required which is reduced to NADH.

To this point, two molecules of ATP have been consumed, and two molecules of NADH generated. No net energy has been produced. The next step, the conversion of 1,3-diphosphoglycerate to 3-phosphoglycerate results in the generation of one molecule of ATP. At this point, two molecules of ATP have been consumed and two produced (one for each three-carbon unit), so the net energy balance is zero.

The next three steps of glycolysis result in the generation of a high-energy phosphate bond which can be used to synthesize a second molecule of ATP. Phosphoglycerate mutase catalyzes the formation of 2-phosphoglycerate from 3-phosphoglycerate. Enolase generates phosphoenolpyruvate from 2-phosphoglycerate. Pyruvate kinase catalyzes ATP production from ADP and phosphoenolpyruvate, generating pyruvate as an end product. At this point, assuming all carbon has gone through glycolysis, two molecules of ATP have been consumed early in the pathway, but four molecules generated subsequently for a net production of two molecules of ATP for each glucose or fructose molecule metabolized. However, a reduced cofactor, NADH, has been generated which must be recycled in order for fermentation to continue.

b. *Ethanol Yield*

Various organisms have evolved different strategies for the regeneration of NAD^+ from NADH. In *Saccharomyces*, acetaldehyde serves as the ultimate electron acceptor, being reduced to ethanol. Pyruvate is first decarboxylated by pyruvate decarboxylase to yield carbon dioxide and acetaldehyde. This enzymatic step requires thiamine pyrophosphate as a cofactor. Acetaldehyde is reduced to ethanol by alcohol dehydrogenase, regenerating NAD^+. There are four species or isozymes of alcohol dehydrogenase in *Saccharomyces*, designated ADHI, II, III, and IV. ADHI is the species present for alcoholic fermentation, responsible for the conversion of acetaldehyde to ethanol. It is constitutive, but the concentration or activity is dependent upon the growth phase, stage of fermentation temperature, and yeast strain (Kunkee 1990). ADHII and III are glucose repressed, meaning they are not found during fermentative growth on high sugar concentrations, but are expressed instead during aerobic growth with ethanol as a carbon and energy source. ADHIII is localized to the mitochondrion, while ADHII is cytoplasmic. ADHII can compensate for loss of ADHI at very low concentrations of glucose and permit fermentative growth, ADHIII cannot. ADHIV is present in the cell at a very low activity level. Its metabolic function is uncertain. Alcohol dehydrogenase requires Zn.

The amount of ethanol produced per unit of sugar during the wine fermentation is of considerable commercial importance. The theoretical conversion of 180 g of sugar into 88 g of CO_2 and 92 g of ethanol (or 51.1% on a weight basis) could only be expected in the absence of any yeast growth and loss of ethanol as vapor. Pasteur's original experiments indicated that he observed an ethanol yield of 48.5% w/w, with 46.7% as carbon dioxide and the balance of 4.8% w/w going to glycerol, succinate and other products, including yeast cell mass. One early figure used in U.S. tabulations for the estimation of potential ethanol was the empirical value of 47.0% w/w presented by Bioletti (Marsh 1958).

Alternatively, a number of studies have tried to determine empirical conversion factors that go directly from the Brix value to the final ethanol content on a volume basis:

$$[\text{EtOH}]\ \%\text{v/v} = a + b * \text{Brix}$$

where values of the factor b range from 0.55 to 0.63 depending on the growing region (perhaps more due to the cultivars within the region) and the season. Ough and Amerine (1963) calculated such a factor for several years and for wines from various locations in California. They reported factors ranging between 0.55 and 0.61 %v/v per Brix with the higher values being from grapes grown in cooler coastal regions. A more recent investigation of the same factor by Jones and Ough (1985) found values of 0.575 to 0.605, again with grapes grown in the coastal regions providing the higher conversions. There were differences due to cultivars (0.580 for Colombard and 0.603 for Zinfandel) and slight seasonal variation between the two years considered.

The reasons for the variations reported can be explained in part by a consideration of the nature of the nonsugar components. The quantity of these materials will vary from season to season, and from region to region, and so will their contribution to carbon of the cell mass that would otherwise come from sugar (and therefore not appear as ethanol) (see also Chapter 5).

The other contributing factor to the variation in conversion factor is the variation in the sugar determination. The extraction of fermentable sugar from the skins during the first days of fermentation is a major cause of elevated conversion factors since the ethanol formed comes from sugar which does not appear in the initial sugar determination. This is especially true of certain red cultivars such as Pinot noir and Zinfandel, that show a tendency to dehydrate under dry conditions.

c. *Extract in Wines*

The concentration of the components other than sugar and ethanol in wines has been given considerable attention by regulating bodies, especially in Europe. The adulteration of wines with water or dissolved materials at the gram per liter level is often detected by the determination of the sugar-free extract. This is especially true in small districts in which there is little variation in the cultivars that are grown and similar winemaking practices are employed. The largest variation is attributed to seasonal effects, but when all of the wines of one season are compared, those with unusually low or high extracts will be obvious. The application of these empirical values to wines today or to wines from different countries is far less valid. The use of heat treatments, yeast strain, and even hydrolytic enzymes can lead to variations that are comparable in magnitude to those that might be expected by illegal additions. The extract value is still an interesting measure of solute concentrations in berries and the extent to which they have been extracted (and perhaps precipitated) during the fermentation and is sometimes used within wine companies for comparative purposes.

The major components in the extract of dry wines are glycerol and the organic acids. The quantity of glycerol produced can range from 5 to 8 g/L depending on the initial sugar content, fermentation temperature, yeast strain, and pantothenic acid levels. The tartaric acid content can change from that in the juice due to precipitation as potassium bitartrate during fermentation. This is greatly affected by the fermentation temperature, the surface roughness of the fermentor, and the interference of crystallization due to polysaccharides and other colloidal components. The malic acid is partially consumed by the yeast and there are pH, strain, and temperature effects on the extent to which this occurs (Rankine 1966; Radler and Fuck 1970). Some of the malate will appear as ethanol but much of it is converted into succinic acid at levels between 0.8 and 1.5 g/L. The levels of acetic and lactic acid are of the order of 0.3 to 0.5 g/L each and a similar amount of the 2,3 butanediols are found (Winger 1982).

The amount of cell mass generated is strongly correlated with the initial amount of nonproline amino nitrogen content, and higher yeast populations will result in more carbon being converted into the nonsoluble cell mass. Typical final cell masses of 6 to 8 g/L can be found in white wine fermentations, again with variations due to the yeast strain and the level of other nutrients.

Fermentation temperature also influences the evaporative loss of ethanol which can be as much as 1 g/L (which will not appear in the extract determination in any case) and the precipitation of potassium bitartrate can lead to a loss of perhaps 1 g/L from the extract balance. Wet extract values (determined by measuring the density of a wine after the evaporation of ethanol and the return to its initial volume with water) have been found to average approximately 22 g/L for dry white wines (Winger 1982), with the biggest effects due to yeast strain and fermentation temperature. While the use of a nonsugar extract value of 30 g/L would seem high if applied to wines from California, any value in the range of 18 to 26 g/L would be within one standard deviation of the mean. This extract value corresponds to an ethanol equivalent of 10.5 g/L, or approximately 1.35% v/v if it was all fermentable sugars and completely fermented.

In wines with residual sugar, the extract will include the unfermented sugars and have slightly less of the glycerol. Some groups analyze for the residual sugar content and then calculate the nonreducing sugar extract in order to compare it to that for dry wines. A nomogram for the estimation of this extract in terms of the ethanol content and the density of the wines has been developed by Vahl (1979). It is reproduced in Figure 4-13.

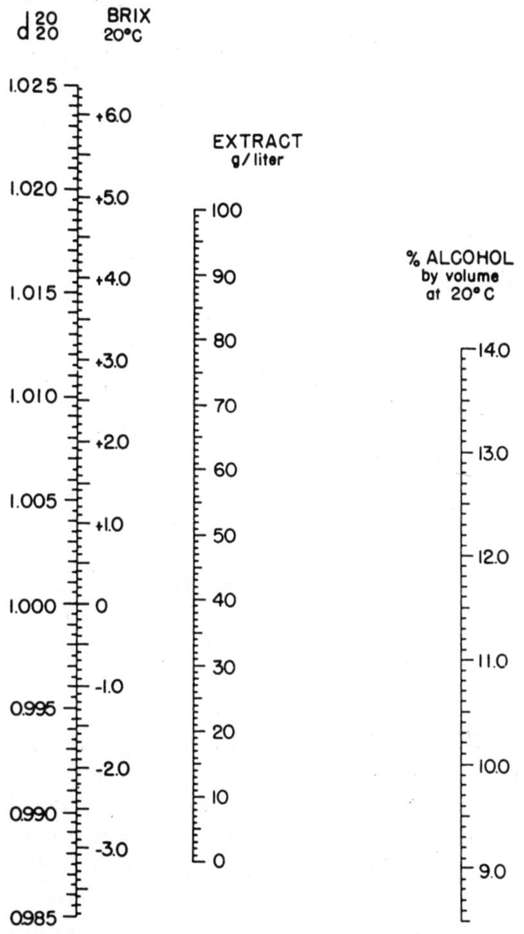

Fig. 4-13. The ethanol-density-extract nomograph for table wines.

d. Regulation of Glycolysis

Three enzymatic steps of the glycolytic pathway (glucose to pyruvate) are irreversible: hexokinase (glucokinase), phosphofructokinase, and pyruvate kinase. The remainder of the enzymes function in gluconeogenesis (the production of glucose or glucose-6-phosphate from respiratory substrates such as pyruvate) as well as glycolysis. In the anabolic direction, fructose bisphosphatase catalyzes the conversion of fructose 1-6,diphosphate to fructose-6-phosphate, and PEP carboxykinase replaces pyruvate kinase, generating phosphoenolpyruvate from oxalacetic acid and ATP. The irreversible steps are important sites of control of flux through their respective pathways of glycolysis or gluconeogenesis. Inhibition of phosphofructokinase activity by ATP and citric acid has been postulated as being largely responsible for the decline in fermentation rate of glucose, and an important operative switch in the so-called Pasteur effect. However, control of carbon flux through glycolysis is probably not mediated by a single rate-limiting step. Multiple points of control serve to coordinate upper glycolysis (or energy consumption) with lower glycolysis (net energy production).

The major site of control of the rate of anaerobic glycolysis is the step of entry of the sugar into the cell, or sugar transport. Sugar transport in *Saccharomyces* is a kinetically complex process in that there appear to be several glucose transporters of differing affinities and times of expression. Many factors affect both the number and kinds of transporters present in the plasma membrane: sugar concentration, stage of growth, presence or absence of molecular oxygen, growth rate, rate of flux through glycolysis, and nutrient availability (particularly of nitrogen). In this sense, glucose uptake is not rate-limiting in glycolysis, but rather the principal site of rate control, any alteration in rate of flux being translated into a compensating alteration in rate of uptake of substrate. These factors ensure that the rate of glucose uptake will equal that of metabolism and will adapt quickly to any changes in metabolism. The reason that control of entry is important lies in the fact that ATP is consumed early in glycolysis but generated late in the pathway. Any block in metabolism would or could result in the conversion of total cellular ATP to ADP in the production of glucose-6-phosphate, leaving insufficient ATP to complete metabolism via the pathway. ATP depletion occurs rapidly with the substrate 2-deoxyglucose which can be phosphorylated but not metabolized further. Control at the site of entry allows the cell to assess its metabolic state at time of crisis to avoid a costly error in energy consumption. Under aerobic growth conditions, control at the site of transport is not as tight as it is under anaerobic conditions, perhaps reflecting the fact that respiration yields much more ATP per glucose molecule than does fermentation.

At increasing concentrations of sugar, sugar uptake and, therefore, sugar consumption, is inhibited. This phenomenon is termed *substrate inhibition*. Winemakers are aware that at extremely high concentrations of sugar, as found in grape juice concentrates and in honey—having approximately 70 Brix—*Saccharomyces* fermentations are completely inhibited. However, the substrate inhibition we are discussing here is noticeable at very low concentrations of sugar (> 8.0 g/L glucose)—although this concentration might seem extremely high to yeast researchers not accustomed to thinking in enological terms. Mechanistically, substrate inhibition is thought to reflect more than one point of attachment of the substrate to its respective transporter. At high substrate concentrations, more than one molecule may attempt to bind simultaneously, thereby inhibiting overall binding and uptake. Growth conditions seem to influence whether or not glucose-mediated substrate inhibition of uptake occurs. This observation may indicate that substrate inhibition is not a common trait of all sugar transporters. Thus, under some conditions of growth a transporter with more than one point of attachment for substrate may be expressed. Jamming of transport by a sudden high concentration of substrate may reflect an important site of metabolic control, limiting flux of substrate until cellular metabolism can adapt to the change.

In fermentations of mixtures of glucose and fructose, glucose can be seen to disappear more quickly than fructose, leading to the description of strains as "glucophilic." We have seen reports of "fructophilic" *Saccharomyces*, but have not been able to reproduce these observations in our own laboratories, although strains of *Zygosaccharomyces* are often fructophilic. The historical reports of fructophilic *Saccharomyces* are likely erroneous due to the polarographic analyses utilized. The difference in rates of disappearance of glucose and fructose is most likely due to the differences in kinetic properties of the sugar transporters for these two substrates. The differences become especially important to the winemaker toward the end of grape juice fermentation, when glucose is completely fermented but the other sweeter sugar, fructose, is still present.

The mode of metabolism of sugars in *Saccharomyces* is largely dictated by the concentration of sugars in the medium. At sugar concentration of greater than 2 g/L, fermentation is the preferred mode of metabolism, whereas respiration is utilized at lower sugar concentrations. This is achieved by two regulatory phenomena: glucose repression and glucose inactivation. Glucose repression has been discussed previously.

Glucose inactivation refers to the inhibition of activity and subsequent proteolytic destruction of many of the same proteins that are regulated by glucose repression and is also catalyzed by high sugar concentration. In the cases where it has been best examined, this process appears to involve protein phosphorylation as an initial step with subsequent degradation occurring by the yeast proteases present in the vacuole. The initial phosphorylation event is reversible, allowing the cells a window of time to determine if there is indeed sufficient sugar present to commit to fermentation. As yet, unknown mechanisms are responsible for the delivery of the proteins to the vacuole for degradation.

Why would cells evolve preferring to ferment even in the presence of oxygen when more ATP can be produced during respiration per glucose molecule consumed? Respiration is an expensive process, requiring more in the way of enzymatic machinery and mitochondria which can be dispensed with during fermentation. Thus, while respiration produces more energy, more energy is consumed in maintaining respiratory capacity. If sugar is not limiting, fermentation allows a fast growth rate and the same total amount of ATP can be produced. In grape juice, sugar is never the limiting nutrient, meaning that carbon and energy are plentiful.

A related regulatory phenomenon is referred to as the Pasteur effect. This effect is the inhibition of fermentation by oxygen. Oxygen availability will foster respiration over fermentation as an energy-generating pathway only if glucose (or fructose) concentrations are low and if some other nutrient, such as nitrogen, is limiting. Aeration of grape juice fermentations will not result in a respiratory mode of metabolism as sugar concentrations are simply too high, even in stationary phase when nitrogen is low. Aeration of grape juice will stimulate yeast growth, but this is not due to respiration (see p. 139).

In addition, ethanol is disruptive of lipid bilayers and toxic to most microorganisms at the concentrations produced by *Saccharomyces*. Rapid fermentation producing a toxic end product confers a competitive advantage to an ethanol-tolerant organism such as *Saccharomyces*. *Saccharomyces* can utilize ethanol as a carbon and energy source aerobically, and this is seen in the production of flor sherry by surface yeast in dry wines. If oxygen becomes available and glucose concentration is low, *Saccharomyces* can readily utilize ethanol as a carbon and energy source. Many organisms, including humans, metabolize ethanol for energy.

G. FERMENTATION KINETICS

Grape juices have the highest sugar concentration among the many substrates used for the production of ethanol by fermentation. As a result, the level of ethanol is among the highest seen and the importance of substrate and ethanol inhibition of growth, cell viability, and maintenance activity is far greater than those in brewing or other fermented beverages.

The wine fermentation is a good example of a fermentation in which there are major contributions due to both cell growth and the resting phase maintenance activity. In many white wine fermentations the growth of cell mass has essentially ceased at a point at which one-half to one-third of the sugar remains (Castor and Archer 1956). The remainder of the fermentation is conducted by the maintenance or turnover activity of nongrowing but viable and fermenting cells.

Any description of the kinetics of wine fermentations must therefore include both of these activities. Unfortunately the study of fermentation conditions generally places an inordinate amount of attention of factors influencing growth, with far less study directed to the conditions that influence the resting behavior and viability of the cells.

There are several reasons for the development of a suitable mathematical description of the fermentation process. These include the ability to interpret fermentation measurements with a view to the early detection of poor fermentation performance, the ability to predict future fermentation behavior, and the application to the design and advanced control of fermentations and the optimization of their refrigeration systems.

1. The Rate of Cell Growth

The rate of cell growth can be expressed in terms of the specific growth rate, μ and the viable cell mass, X_v.

$$dX/dt = \mu[X_v]$$

Several studies with yeast have suggested that the specific growth rate is determined by the rate of transport into the cells of the growth-limiting substrate (van Uden 1971). In adequate media this is simply the rate of uptake of the sugars, glucose and fructose, but in deficient media it will be determined by the rate of transport of other nutrients such as amino acids, ammonia, or of any growth-limiting nutrient such as the vitamins.

The general expression for the specific growth rate in terms of a single uninhibited substrate [S] concentration (Monod 1949) is:

$$\mu = \mu_m[S]/[K_m + [S]]$$

where μ is the specific growth rate at a concentration of substrate $[S]$ that is limiting; μ_m is the maximum specific growth rate which would occur at saturating concentrations of substrate; K_m is a constant numerically equal to the substrate concentration at which $\mu = \mu_m/2$. In grape juices, the two hexose sugars inhibit each other's uptake in a competitive way (van Uden 1971) and the ethanol produced does so in a noncompetitive manner (Aiba and Shoda 1969). This results in a more complex expression for rate of substrate transport and therefore growth:

$$\mu_s = \frac{\mu_m[S]}{[K_m(1 + [I]/K_i) + [S]]\big[1 + [P]/K_p\big]}$$

where I is the competitive inhibitor concentration (glucose for the growth on fructose and vice versa) and K_i is the corresponding substrate inhibition constant. Noncompetitive inhibition by the product P (ethanol) is scaled by a corresponding product inhibition constant, K_p.

2. Cell Growth and Substrate Preference

The rate of consumption of each sugar due to the growth activity can be expressed in terms of the growth rate and cell yield for that sugar together with its consumption by the maintenance activity.

The maximum specific growth rate μ_m, the concentration of the sugar (e.g., glucose, G) being transported and the inhibitory influence of the competing sugar (e.g., fructose, F) and the inhibiting product ethanol, E:

$$\mu_g = \mu_m[G]/\big[K_m(1 + [F]/K_f) + [G]\big]/ \\ [1 + [E]/K_e]$$

where K_f is the competitive inhibition constant for fructose, and K_e is the noncompetitive inhibition constant for ethanol.

A similar expression can be written for the rate of utilization of fructose:

$$\mu_f = \mu_m[F]/\big[K_m(H[G]/K_g) + [F]\big]/ \\ [1 + [E]/K_e]$$

The relative values of the constants K_g and K_f are related to the substrate preference of the yeast strain and they have been estimated for a number of wine yeast strains (Johnston 1983). All of the yeasts considered are glucophilic and consume glucose more rapidly than fructose (Figure 4-14). For some yeasts, the rates of utilization are similar, but for others the glucose is almost completely consumed before the fructose begins to be utilized.

3. Sugar Consumption by Cell Maintenance

The consumption of a sugar (and the production of ethanol) due to the maintenance activ-

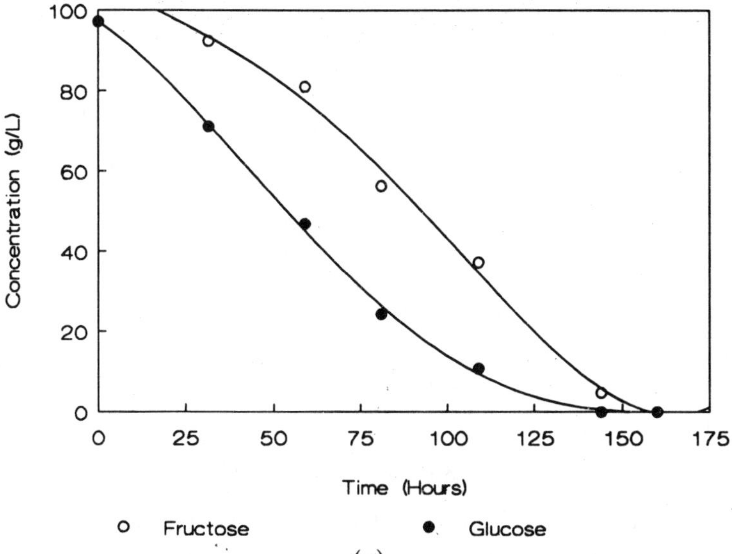

(a)

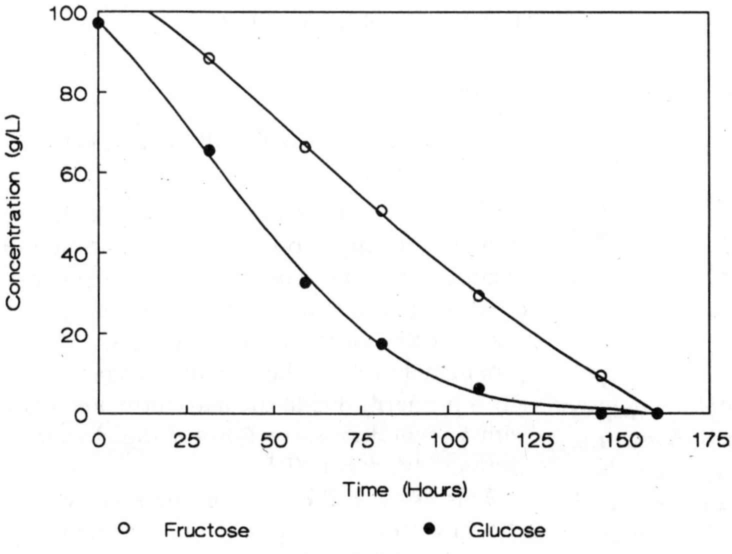

(b)

Fig. 4-14. Selective hexose utilization by wine yeast. (a) Montrachet UCD #522; and (b) Champagne UCD #595.

ity is generally expressed in terms of the viable cell mass and the specific maintenance rate, m:

$$dS/dt = m[X_v]$$

The maintenance activity is generally considered to be the turnover energy of the non-growing cell as it degrades and rebuild enzymes and maintains the concentration gradients across its membrane.

4. Rate of Sugar Consumption

The combined rate of glucose consumption due to the growth and maintenance activities can be written:

$$dG/dt = -\frac{\mu_g[X]}{Y} - m_g[X_v]$$

where m_g is the specific maintenance rate for glucose, multiplied by the total number of viable cells and Y is the cell yield, that is the mass ratio of the cells produced and to mass of substrate used for growth. (This is a special definition of yield coefficient necessary in the special case when the substrate in question is also an energy source.) X is cell mass and μ_g the maximum specific growth rate for glucose, as defined above. With a corresponding form for fructose:

$$dF/dt = -\frac{\mu_f[X]}{Y} - m_f[X_v]$$

where m_g and m_f are the maintenance rates based on each sugar. These maintenance rates are considered to be the same in the absence of any data indicating otherwise. There is a need for more detailed studies of the influence of juice nutrients and cell age effects on the maintenance activity of wine yeast.

Total sugar utilization is simply the sum of these rates:

$$dS/dt = dG/dt + dF/dt$$

and this rate can be expressed in other measures of sugar concentration such as Brix, Baume, or Oechsle that are more familiar to winemakers.

5. Rates of Cell Death

The fermentation activities are deliberately expressed in terms of the viable cell mass, since, in wine fermentations the viability is not always 100% and there is a significant decline in viability in the later stages of the fermentation. Unfortunately, there are very few studies of the rate of death of cells due to the ethanol concentration and even fewer mathematical descriptions of it. A first attempt has been to assume that cell viability declines in a manner related to both fermentation time and ethanol content:

$$[X_v] = [X][1 - [E] * t/K_v]$$

where the viability constant K_v is related to strain and medium conditions such as the initial oxygen content, nutrition, and temperature. There is a need for studies to further quantify these effects and to improve the mathematical descriptions of cell viability.

6. Rate of Formation of Ethanol

The rate of formation of ethanol is directly related to the utilization of the sugar and the conversion yield, typically reported to be approximately 95%.

$$dE/dt = 0.95 * 92/180 * dS/dt$$

7. Rate of Change in Density

The rate of change in solution properties such as Brix or other density measures can also be predicted from the rates of change in mass and volume of the medium:

$$dB/dt = d(M/V)/dt$$
$$= [dM/dt * V - dV/dt * M]/V^2$$

The first term represents the rate of change in mass and the second represents the rate of change in volume. The overall volume change dV during fermentation is approximately 5% and half that of the change in mass, dM (approximately 10%). The rate of change in density is primarily due to the mass term, $dm/dt/V$ with a secondary correction for the change in volume, $dV/dt * M/V^2$.

This is why the use of mass or weight changes (which are independent of temperature) correlate well with the density changes (El Haliou et al. 1987). The use of weight loss as a measure of fermentation progress was used as early as the mid 1950s (Schanderl 1959). Weight changes can be used in process monitoring (see Chapter 5 for examples of this) rather than the more usual density measures (which are temperature dependent). It also shows why the rate of CO_2 evolution, which is proportional to the mass term dm/dt, can be used as an alternative for process measurements.

8. Temperature Effects

Any comprehensive description of the fermentation should include the effects of temperature on the various activities and properties of the yeast. The temperature effect on cell growth rate is well described by the summation of an exponential growth term and a concurrent death term:

$$\mu_m = \mu_g \exp(E_{actg}/RT) - \mu_d \exp(E_{actd}/RT)$$

and estimates of the activation energies, E_{actg} and E_{actd}, are 60,668 and 506,264 kJ/mole, respectively (Boulton 1980). R is the gas constant and T is temperature, in K. The effect of temperature on the growth rate of a brewing yeast together with the temperature expression shown here can be found in Figure 4-15.

Corresponding activation energies for the maintenance term have not been determined for wine yeast and are assumed to be 37,656 kJ/mole based on other organisms (Boulton 1980). There is a need for continuous culture studies of the grape juice fermentation to determine a number of these constants for wine yeasts under wine-like conditions.

There is new information indicating an effect of ethanol concentration (van Uden and Cruz Duarte 1981) on the rate of the concurrent death term in the above expression and this can be included in future developments of this fermentation model. These authors also showed that the maximum growth temperature was affected by the ethanol concentration, falling from 41°C in the absence of ethanol to 30°C at 10% ethanol.

9. Rates of Heat Release

Of more importance than the quantity of heat released is the rate at which it is released or escapes from the fermentor. The rate of release is determined by the rate of fermentation and this is in itself a function of the must temperature. The rate of accumulation of energy in the form of a rise in temperature is the difference between the rates of generation by fermentation and of removal by various cooling mechanisms. The main cooling contribution will be from heat transfer in equipment such as jackets, coils, or external exchangers. Other components will be the removal of energy in the form of water and ethanol vapors in the exit gas and the exchange by convective and radiative heat transfer to (and from) the ambient air and surroundings. The cooling effect due to the evaporation of water and ethanol increases as the temperature increases and is of the order of 10% of the heat gener-

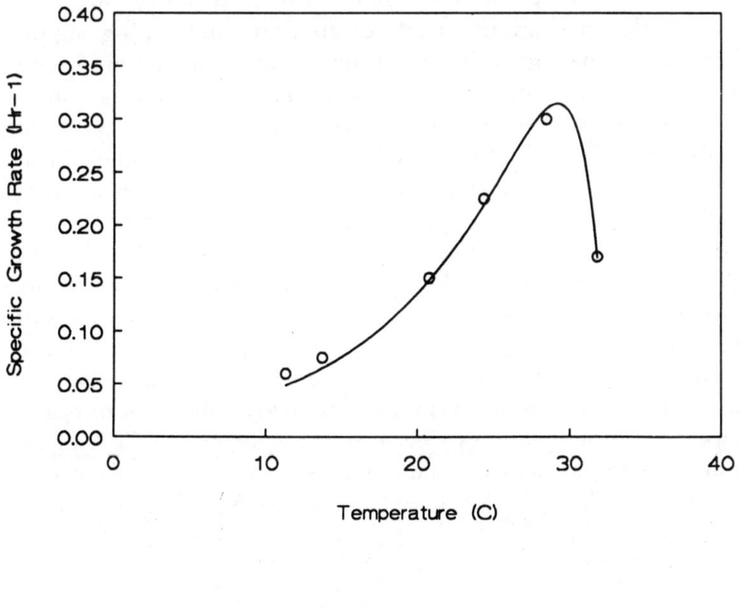

Fig. 4-15. Effect of temperature on the growth rate of yeast.

ated. The interchange with the surroundings can vary from a loss of between 5 and 10% of the fermentation release to gains of up to twice that if the fermenting juice is cold with respect to the ambient or when a significant gain due to solar radiation contribution occurs.

One of the most important calculations that can be made is that of the instantaneous rate of heat release from each fermentor in order the predict the dynamic values of the cooling requirement for any number of fermentors with differing starting times and temperatures of fermentation. The development of this fermentation model and its application to such calculations was first demonstrated a number of years ago (Boulton 1979, 1980). A more extensive treatment of fermentation cooling requirements can be found in Chapter 5.

H. END PRODUCTS OF YEAST METABOLISM

One of the principal end products of sugar metabolism by *Saccharomyces cerevisiae* and its closely related species is, of course, ethanol, giving some 92 to 95% conversion of the sugar. Carbon dioxide is also formed, in equal molar amounts to ethanol, but most of the CO_2 escapes into the atmosphere during and after the fermentation. Even so, it should be noted that carbon dioxide is very highly soluble in wine, especially in comparison with other atmospheric gases, nitrogen and oxygen. At high pressures, yeast fermentation is slowed and eventually stopped, presumably by CO_2 toxicity.

Other major end products including glycerol and various volatile and nonvolatile organic acids are discussed directly below; the higher (fusel) alcohols are discussed in Sections H.2 and I.7. The volatile esters, produced in small amounts but having great impact on the quality of the final product, are discussed at the end of this chapter (Section M), while the often unpleasant odorous sulfur-containing compounds are discussed in the section on sulfur metabolism (Section J). Spoilage end products, coming from non-*Saccharomyces* sources, are discussed in Chapter 9.

Diacetyl, which has a sweet butter-like off-aroma, can make an important contribution to the flavor profile of a wine. While it and its close relatives, acetoin and butane-2,3-diol, are formed by yeasts, their presence in wine more generally comes from lactic acid bacteria (Chapter 6). The pathway of formation diacetyl in yeasts involves a decarboxylation of α-keto-acetolactate, which is an intermediate in the pathway of formation of valine from pyruvate. The two other compounds, generally considered flavorless, are either reduction products of diacetyl or come directly from α-keto-acetolactate. The formation of diacetyl by yeast is of far greater consequence in brewing than in winemaking—the formation is stimulated by aeration of the yeast, which more commonly occurs in brewing—probably because its flavor threshold in beer would be lower.

1. Glycerol, Volatile, and Nonvolatile Organic Acids

Except for acetic acid, a volatile acid, the other organic acids, such as pyruvate and the acids of the TCA cycle, are not of much consequence as wine flavor components. The organic acids may derive from either sugar or amino acid catabolism, depending upon growth conditions and available nitrogen sources. Acetic acid may also arise as a consequence of fatty acid metabolism. Enzymes of the tricarboxylic acid (TCA) cycle and electron transport chain are required for respiration, the complete oxidation of the six carbon atoms of glucose to six molecules of CO_2. In addition to a role in energy metabolism, the tricarboxylic acid cycle serves to equilibrate pools of organic acids utilized for biosynthesis of the precursors of macromolecules, particularly of amino acids. Amino acids utilized as nitrogen sources yield organic acids of the TCA cycle. Thus, while the TCA cycle per se is not essential for energy production during anaerobic fermentation, the organic acids produced by some of the enzymatic reactions of the cycle are still needed for biosynthesis.

Under anaerobic conditions, cytoplasmic forms of all of the enzymes of the TCA cycle are synthesized with the exception of α-keto-glutarate dehydrogenase and succinyl-CoA synthase (Polakis and Bartley 1965; Polakis et al. 1965; Beck and von Meyenburg 1968; Chapman and Bartley 1968; Duntze et al. 1969). These enzymatic characterizations were extensive. However, Radler recently reported observations of these activities in fermentative yeasts (Radler 1992). This discrepancy may be explained by strain differences as a single mutational event can alter the pattern of expression of these enzymes. There are two paths of metabolism from pyruvate (Figure 4-16), a reductive pathway producing malate, fumarate, and succinate, and an oxidative pathway to α-keto-glutarate, which is an important nitrogen acceptor for biosynthesis of nitrogen-containing compounds. Entry of pyruvate into the TCA cycle or its cytoplasmic equivalent is via oxalacetic acid. Oxalacetic acid is formed from pyruvate and CO_2 via pyruvate carboxylase, an enzyme requiring biotin as cofactor. As biotin is the only essential vitamin required by *Saccharomyces* species, a rare biotin-deficient grape juice may have a striking impact on yeast metabolism and end products.

When grape must or juice is inoculated with aerobically grown *Saccharomyces*, as is the case with an active dry starter, ethanol is not immediately produced (Pena et al. 1972; Whiting 1976). In respiring cells, pyruvate decarboxylase and alcohol dehydrogenase (ADHI) activities are low. Both of these enzymes are induced by the presence of glucose (Denis et al. 1983; Rieger et al. 1983; Schmitt et al. 1983; Sharma and Tauro 1986). As a consequence, compounds other than ethanol are initially produced at the beginning of fermentation of grape juice. Glycerol, pyruvate, and succinate are formed at this time, as are other organic acids (Ribéreau-Gayon et al. 1956a, 1956b). Glycerol derives from sugar and is formed from dihydroxyacetone phosphate, one product of the aldolase reaction, via two enzymatic reactions (Figure 4-17). Dihydroxyacetone phosphate is reduced to glycerol phosphate by dihydroxyacetone phosphate reductase, converting one molecule of NADH to NAD^+. Glycerol phosphate is then dephosphorylated by glycerol phosphate phosphatase yielding glycerol. A ratio between pyruvate and glycerol seems to be maintained as these components are found in equimolar concentration in the medium. Both may be reconsumed later in fermentation. Overproduction of glycerol occurs in the presence of high SO_2 (Neuberg 1946). SO_2 forms a complex with acetaldehyde, thus making this compound unavailable for reduction and regeneration of NAD^+ from NADH. SO_2 will also form a complex with thiamine preventing synthesis of thiamine pyrophosphate, a cofactor for pyruvate decarboxylase, the enzyme generating acetaldehyde. Glycerol formation may serve as a route for regeneration of NAD^+ from NADH. However, in this process no net ATP can be produced if all triose units are shunted to glycerol and it is therefore energetically unfavorable and biologically unfeasible for excessive glycerol production to be an end product of glycolysis. Some winemakers believe that increased glyc-

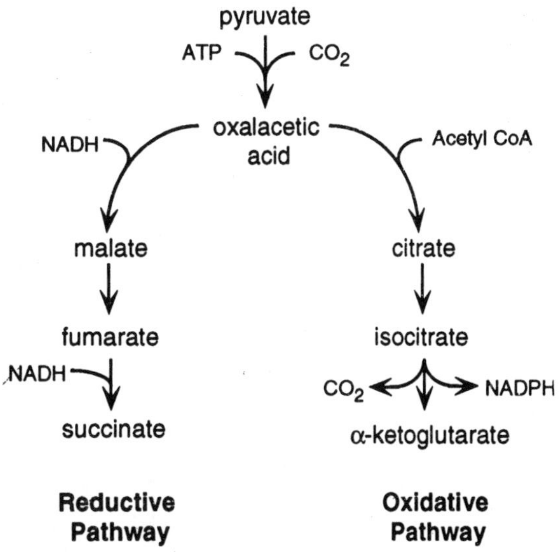

Fig. 4-16. Anaerobic cytoplasmic TCA pathways.

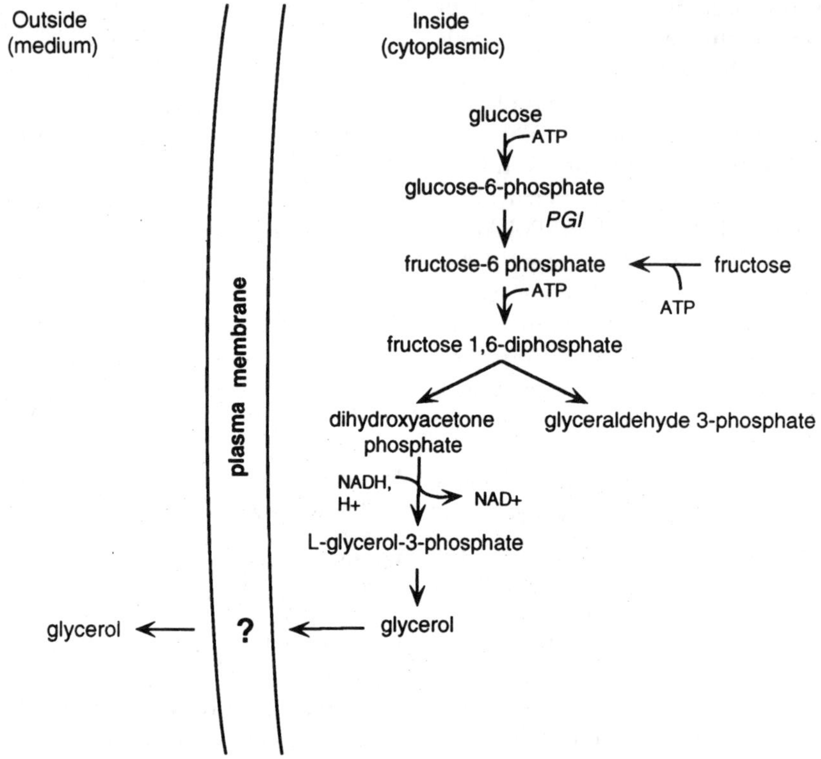

Fig. 4-17. Enzymatic steps leading to glycerol formation.

erol production will improve wine quality, leading to better mouth feel and enhanced complexity; glycerol at high levels tastes sweet and increases viscosity, but levels higher than the differences found among wines appears to be required (Noble and Bursick 1984; Yunome et al. 1981). Glycerol is commercially produced by utilization of this fermentation pathway, but requires very high concentrations of SO_2 and very high pH (pH > 9) (Neuberg 1946), conditions completely unacceptable to winemaking.

The major factor directing the formation of other end products of sugar metabolism is the enzymatic machinery of the yeast cells at the time of inoculation into grape juice. Pyruvate carboxylase, which catalyzes the conversion of pyruvate to oxalacetic acid, is thought to compete with pyruvate decarboxylase for substrate (Van Urk et al. 1988; Whiting 1976). Under conditions of limited pyruvate decarboxylase activity, pyruvate carboxylase has the kinetic advantage, directing carbon into the TCA cycle (Van Urk et al. 1988). This comes about by a lowering of the glycolytic flux. The resulting low concentrations of pyruvate shunts pyruvate into the TCA cycle because of the relative affinities (K_m's) of pyruvate decarboxylase (high K_m) and pyruvate carboxylase (low K_m) to pyruvate (Holzer 1961). The switching of pyruvate pathways, depending on the concentration of pyruvate and relative K_m's for the two enzymes, plays a major role in the Pasteur effect—the theoretical change over from fermentation to respiration.

When the TCA cycle is operational, a third enzyme for pyruvate metabolism, pyruvate dehydrogenase, catalyzes the conversion of pyruvate to acetyl CoA, which condenses with oxalacetic acid to produce citrate. This pathway is not active fermentatively. The organic acids produced during adaptation to glucose are those found as intermediates in the TCA cycle (Suomalainen and Keranen 1967; Van Urk et al. 1988). Succinic acid is found in levels of 0.5 to 2 g/L, pyruvate at 0 to 0.5 g/L, citrate at 0 to 0.5 g/L, and α-keto-glutarate at 0 to 0.2 g/L (Radler 1992). Production of oxalacetic acid from pyruvate is energy-consuming; pyruvate carboxylase requires ATP. For each pyruvate entering the TCA cycle via pyruvate carboxylase, one ATP would be consumed. Net ATP would have to come from the limited respiration still occurring under these conditions. Indeed, glycerol and succinate formation do seem to be stimulated by aeration (Ribéreau-Gayon et al. 1956a, 1956b). However, grape juice fermentations rapidly become anaerobic, and nitrogen gas flushed grape juice can be fermented starting with aerobically grown yeast.

The main volatile acid in fermented beverages is acetic acid. Because of the negative sensory attributes of high concentrations of this acid and its association with *Acetobacter* spoilage, its appreciable production during grape juice fermentation is highly undesirable. Acetic acid appears to be formed early in the fermentation (Whiting 1976), coming from acetic acid or lactic acid bacterial infections. However, *Saccharomyces* and other yeasts can produce acetic acid. It is usually produced at levels in the range 100 to 200 mg/L by *Saccharomyces* and is influenced by yeast strain (Shimazu and Watanabe 1981), fermentation temperature and juice composition. The production of acetic acid as a trace byproduct during fermentation is a poorly understood aspect of the wine fermentations. The legal limit for acetic acid in U.S. table wines is 1.2 g/L for white and 1.4 g/L for red. Even though *Saccharomyces* can produce some acetic acid, it does not produce it at levels in excess of the legal limit. There are a number of explanations for its excessive formation ranging from a nutrient deficiency or a nutrient imbalance in the juice to similar effects produced by the competition between coexisting yeasts and bacterial populations during concurrent malolactic fermentations. The aerobic conversion of ethanol to acetic acid such as that which occurs during a vinegar fermentation by *Acetobacter* is not expected due to absence of oxygen after the onset of fermentation.

There have been many suggestions of possible enzyme reactions in yeast that could lead to acetic acid formation (Jost and Piendl 1975). These include: (1) Reversible formation from acetyl Co-A and acetyl adenylate through acetyl Co-A synthetase; (2) cleavage of citrate by citrate lyase; (3) production from pyruvate by pyruvate dehydrogenase; (4) reversible formation from acetyl-phosphate by acetyl kinase; and (5) oxidation of acetaldehyde by aldehyde dehydrogenase. There do not appear to have been labeled studies of acetic acid pathways with wine yeast under juice conditions.

One study of the contribution of various nutrients to the formation of acetic acid during beer fermentations (Jost and Piendl 1975) reported effects due to absorbed isoleucine, tryptophan, and arginine and lower fermentation temperatures. Earlier studies with various wine yeast reported a doubling of acetic acid production when pantothenate was absent from the medium and that its formation was inhibited by biotin, thiamin, or inositol (Ribéreau-Gayon et al. 1954).

In comparing anaerobic growth of two strains of *Saccharomyces*, Verduyn et al. (1990) found a striking strain difference in acetate production. The strain not excreting acetate was found to possess higher levels of acetyl-CoA synthetase activity, in agreement with earlier observations (Postma et al. 1989). Fatty acid biosynthesis utilizes acetyl-CoA as 2-carbon donor. Fatty acid production is stimulated by molecular oxygen. Cultures exposed to oxygen, actively synthesizing fatty acids for growth, may produce acetic acid upon entry into anaerobic conditions as a mechanism for the regeneration of free Coenzyme A to be utilized for other biosynthetic activities. Other, less well-characterized factors also seem to influence acetate production (Shimazu and Watanabe 1981). Investigation of the production of acetic acid is complicated by the fact that other organisms such as acetic acid and lactic acid bacteria and the yeast *Brettanomyces* may be present during must fermentation. These organisms are capable of producing this compound in high concentration under the appropriate conditions (Chapter 9). It is important to note that the presence of other microorganisms and the resulting competition with *Saccharomyces* may impact the metabolic activities of the yeast and thus affect the end products produced (Drysdale and Fleet 1989).

The actual spectrum of end products of carbon metabolism found in a finished wine depends upon a variety of factors. The growth conditions of the inoculum dictate the initial enzymatic composition of the cell. Availability of and need to regenerate cofactors also affects the cell's ability to conduct certain types of reactions. The presence of SO_2 also plays a role in directing early carbon flux. SO_2 can complex important cofactors such as thiamin required for decarboxylation reactions such as that catalyzed by pyruvate decarboxylase. It can also bind to acetaldehyde, preventing regeneration of NAD^+ from NADH through the reduction of acetaldehyde to ethanol. The presence of other microorganisms complicates the situation in that they also will be contributing end products of their own and may impact *Saccharomyces* metabolic activities.

2. Higher (Fusel) Alcohols

During all yeast fermentations, small amounts of higher alcohols, the *higher* molecular-weight analogs of ethanol, with *higher* boiling points, are formed, which include, in order of the amounts produced: 3-methyl butanol (isoamyl alcohol), 2-methyl butanol (active amyl alcohol), 2-methyl propanol (isobutyl alcohol), and 1-propanol (*n*-propyl alcohol) (Figure 4-18). The biochemical pathways for the formation of these alcohols, except for the very last steps, are identical with those for the formation of the similarly structured amino acids, leucine, isoleucine, valine, and threonine, respectively. The higher alcohols are formed either anabolically from sugars, utilizing these pathways, or as the transamination products of these amino acids. The formation of the higher alcohols from the respective amino acids is discussed further below, in the section on nitrogen metabolism (Section I.5).

The physical properties of the higher alcohols and their metabolism have been reviewed by Webb and Ingraham (1963). They pointed out that fusel oil formation seems to be a common characteristic of all yeasts, including nonfermenting yeasts such as some species of *Pichia*, but the amounts formed are, in fact, genus-, species- and strain-dependent. Webb and Ingraham (1963) point out that the components of fusel oil are not necessarily limited to the four alcohols mentioned above, but more than 100 other components have also been identified in the fraction. Many of the supernumerary compounds are the ethyl, isoamyl, and active amyl esters of various organic acids. Even though the higher alcohols are constituents of these volatile esters, some of which are very highly and pleasantly aromatic, there seems to be no direct quantification between the amounts of the alcohol formed and the corresponding ester. One of the alcohols, phenethyl alcohol, is not generally classified in with the higher alcohols, but perhaps ought to be. It is found in very low concentrations, but it is highly aromatic; it is an important component in the fragrance of roses. Other discussions of higher alcohol formation by yeasts are given by Watson (1976), Ingledew (1993) and Hammond (1993). The formation of higher alcohols from their analogous amino acids is given in Section I.5.

The higher alcohols themselves have little impact on the sensory properties of wine, but they can be of major importance in wine distillates, in which they are much more concentrated. Indeed, their early recognition, if not their discovery, came from the immiscible layer noticed in distillation products of yeast fermentations whenever most of the ethanol had been removed. This oily layer has a bad, *fousel* (foul) smell, and was early on named *fusel oil* (Webb and Ingraham 1963). Subsequently, the fusel fraction was found to be made up mainly

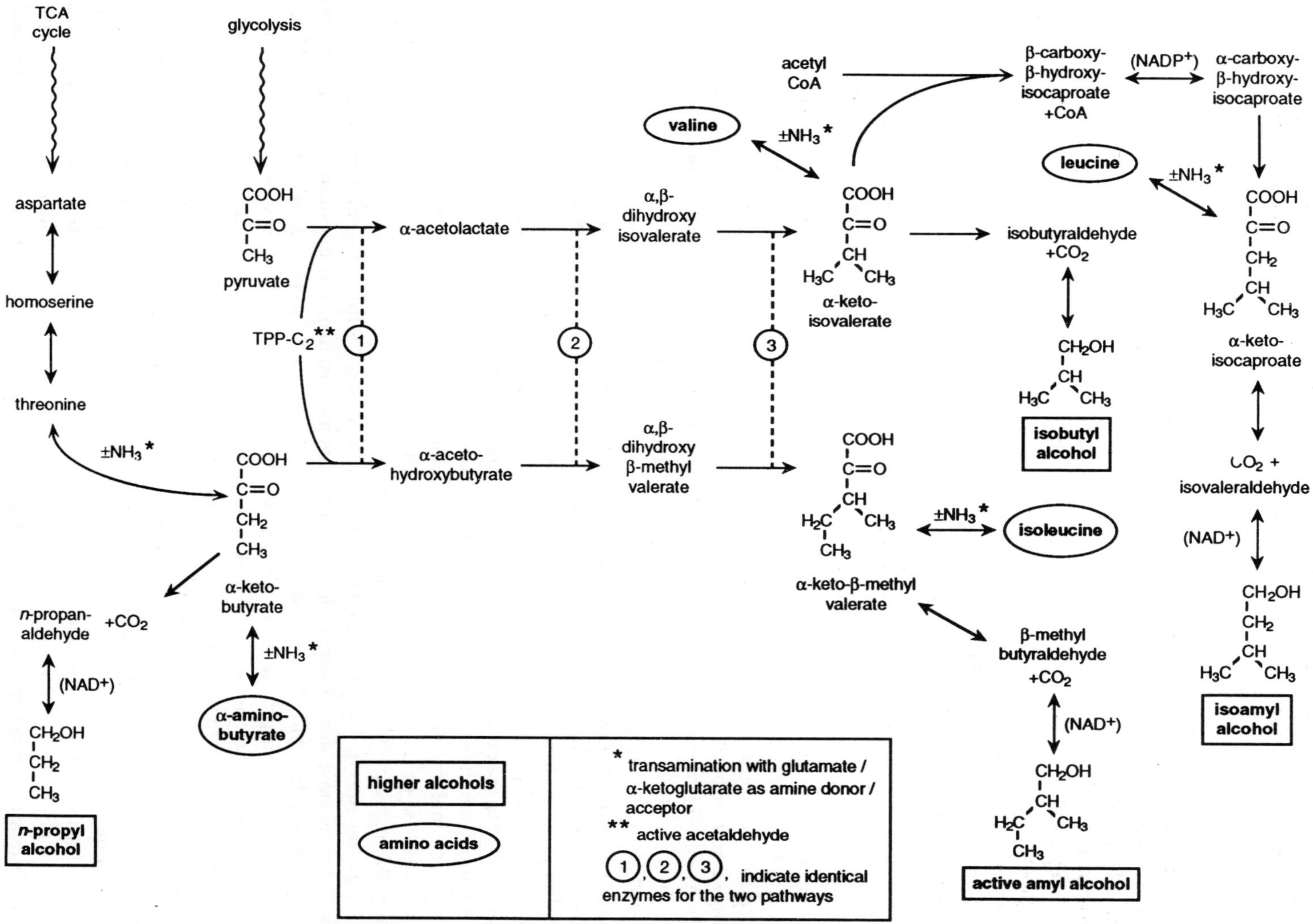

Fig. 4-18. Pathway for formation of higher alcohols from glucose.

of the four components already mentioned. The concentrations of the total higher alcohols in 120 California white wines has been found to range from 162 to 266 mg/L and from 140 to 417 mg/L in 130 reds wines (Guymon and Heitz 1952). Similar ranges have been reported in 172 Italian wines by Usseglio-Tomasset (1975). The level of isoamyl alcohol, the major component, has been reported to be in the range 90 to 292 mg/L (Usseglio-Tomasset 1975).

Because it is the major component, isoamyl alcohol is the predominant odorous component of fusel oil. The impression, especially with dessert wines, is that while high fusel content is not desired, too low is associated with less full, thin, or simple wines. Reed and Nagodawithana (1991) have compiled data from several reports from more than two decades ago, giving a wide scatter of results but showing that the threshold values for isobutyl alcohol were always somewhat higher than for isoamyl alcohol. In one of these reports, Rankine (1967) showed that the sensory thresholds were generally higher than the amounts normally found in wine. Active amyl alcohol was not tested because of the difficulty in obtaining sufficient quantities in pure form for sensory analysis. Active amyl alcohol is so named because of its optical activity; that is, it causes the rotation of the plane of polarized light, as measured by polarimetry (Dubos 1988). Active amyl and isoamyl alcohols are structurally similar and thus are difficult to separate. It is not surprising to enologists to learn that Pasteur was the first to discover the optical activity of active amyl alcohol, after separation of it from isoamyl alcohol by fractional crystallization of the barium salts of the sulfuric acid esters (Pasteur 1855). Enologists are also quick to proclaim that this discovery of optical activity in yeast fermentation distillates—and not found in unfermented material—led Pasteur to the ingenious conclusion that the fermentation was a result of a biological process (Dubos 1988), and laid the foundation for the science of microbiology—and hopefully for better control over the vinification processes. Coincidentally, Pasteur's separation of optical isomers of tartaric acid isolated from grapes and wine led to stereochemistry in organic chemistry.

As we have said, the higher alcohols (including phenethyl alcohol, ß-hydroxy phenethyl alcohol, and tyrosol) can be byproducts of amino acid catabolism. However, the higher alcohols are also formed from sugars, utilizing part of the enzymatic pathways needed for formation of the corresponding amino acids, as shown in Figure 4-18. This formation is found in the absence of added amino acids (Thoukis 1958; Ingraham and Guymon 1960). The last two steps of the pathway, the decarboxylation of the α-keto acid and the reduction of the subsequent aldehyde by alcohol dehydrogenase, with NADH as the electron donor, apparently involves the same enzymes as those needed for conversion of pyruvate (an α-keto acid) to ethyl alcohol (SentheShanmuganathan 1960a, 1960b; Webb and Ingraham 1963; Kunkee et al. 1966 and 1972; Singh and Kunkee 1977). Other workers (Dickinson and Dawes 1992) have found a branched-chain dehydrogenase system in *Saccharomyces* mitochondria, similar to that found in mammalian cells, by which the branched-chain α-keto acids are oxidatively decarboxylated to give a CoA derivative, in much the same way that pyruvic acid is respired via the TCA cycle. While this pathway might be real, its importance is in question, especially under vinification conditions where it would be restrained by the presence of high concentrations of glucose and by the anaerobic conditions.

The winemaker has some possibilities for control over the formation of higher alcohols. Foremost in importance is the content of the nitrogenous components. This is discussed in detail in the next section (Section H.2), but suffice it to say here that deficiencies in ammonia or free amino nitrogen sets the yeast cell in need to scavenge nitrogen from available amino acids, leaving the transaminated moiety, a higher alcohol, behind; contrariwise, excess nitrogenous components brings about a decrease in formation of fusel alcohols. The yeast employed is also of importance. Our experience has been the same as that given by Guymon et al. (1961), where a yeast such as *Hansenula anomala*, which may carry out only a limited fermentation of grape juice, produces high concentrations of fusel alcohols, especially where aerated; whereas strains of *Schizosaccharomyces pombe*, which happen to be much better fermenters, produce very low amounts. What is more to the point for the winemaker is the effect of wine yeast strain used for the vinification. We have confirmed the early observations (Rankine 1967) that the concentration of higher alcohols formed, under standardized conditions, is dependent upon yeast strain used. Claims of this sort are sometimes made for various yeast strains by their commercial producers. While these claims can be documented, the variations are generally so small that the differences are essentially sensorially undetectable. More importantly might be the effects of aeration, temperature and pH, the increase of each of these tending to increase the formation of higher alcohols (Webb and Ingraham 1963; Rankine 1967). However, it is an unlikely winemaking situation where the fermentation would be manipulated by any of these possibilities, since the amounts of higher alcohol in table wine are either so low as to be unnoticed, or if high enough to be noticed, would not be desired. The situation for beverage brandy, the distillation product of wine, where the volatile flavor compounds are concentrated, may be different. Where a fine and long-aged product is to be made, the presence of increased amounts of congeners, including some of the higher alcohols, can be desirable. However, where a fresher and less expensive product is being made, fermentation of distilling material with minimal fusel oil is preferred. For the latter type of vinification, a new wine yeast strain was especially constructed which produced very low concentrations of isoamyl alcohol (Rous et al. 1983). The use of this strain for distilled beverage production has met with some success (Kunkee and Bisson 1993). This is the first and one of the few practical examples of the use of molecular genetics and biotechnology for improvement of a wine yeast strain, or indeed the manipulation of any yeast strain for a commercial fermentation.

I. NITROGEN METABOLISM DURING FERMENTATION

The major nitrogen species in the average grape juice are: proline, arginine, alanine, glutamate, glutamine, serine, and threonine. Ammonium ion levels may also be high, depending upon the variety and time of harvest. Of the amino acids, proline and arginine are the major species. Proline accumulation at high levels appears to be associated with grapevine stress, particularly low moisture. Another nitrogen compound, γ-aminobutyrate, may also be present in high concentration in grape juice. Some studies indicate that this compound may form in the fruit postharvest and prior to processing of the grapes.

Nitrogen-containing compounds in grape must might meet one of three fates: (1) Utilized as that compound directly in biosynthesis; (2) converted to a related compound and utilized in biosynthesis; or (3) degraded releasing nitrogen either as free ammonium ion or as bound nitrogen via a transamination reaction. In case 3, the carbon skeleton of the nitrogen-containing compound would be a waste product.

1. Uptake and Transport

In a typical grape juice fermentation, nitrogen-containing compounds present in low concentration are taken up very quickly, within the first two Brix drop or prior to the start of growth. Biosynthetic pools of amino acids are filled first, before degradation of compounds as nitrogen sources occurs. Metabolizable nitrogen compounds present in excess do not disappear as quickly from the medium. However, they are also taken up at this time. Once pools have been filled and growth commences, nitrogen compounds will be taken up and degraded in a specific order of preference. The timing of utilization of a nitrogen compound is dependent upon two factors, the need for that compound directly in biosynthesis with respect to its starting concentration and the preference for that compound as a nitrogen source once cellular pools have been filled. Thus, one cannot directly equate time of disappearance of a compound with preference as a nitrogen source unless it is clear that the compound is present in excess.

An overall scheme of nitrogen metabolism is given in Figure 4-19. Ammonium ion and glutamate are generally the two most preferred nitrogen sources as these two compounds are the species utilized directly for biosynthesis. Glutamine, since it can generate ammonium ion and glutamate is also a preferred nitrogen source. In general, most yeast species will deplete the medium of these three nitrogen compounds first, before attacking other sources of nitrogen. The next group of nitrogen compounds in terms of preference includes alanine, serine, threonine, aspartate, asparagine, urea, and arginine. Proline is a relatively good source of nitrogen only under aerobic conditions as the first enzymatic step in the catabolic pathway catalyzed by proline oxidase requires molecular oxygen and is confined to the mitochondria. Glycine, lysine, histidine, and the pyrimidines, thymine and thymidine, cannot be utilized by most strains of *Saccharomyces* as sources of nitrogen, but they can be readily utilized directly as biosynthetic precursors. Metabolism of the aromatic amino acids is complex, with some reactions requiring oxygen or cofactors that may be limiting during fermentation.

The order of preference of utilization of nitrogen-containing compounds may change, depending upon environmental, physiological, and strain-specific factors. Generally speaking, a preferred yeast nitrogen source is one that is most readily converted into a biosynthetically useful nitrogen compound, ammonia or glutamate, or one that requires the least in terms of energy input or cofactors which may be in limiting supply for mobilization of the nitrogen moiety. Furthermore, from the winemaker's perspective, it should not, when in excess, lead to undesirable residues. Table 4-7 displays how the various nitrogen-containing compounds generate ammonium ion or glutamate, and shows the organic acids generated from the carbon skeletons of the nitrogen compounds following deamination (see also Table 4-11).

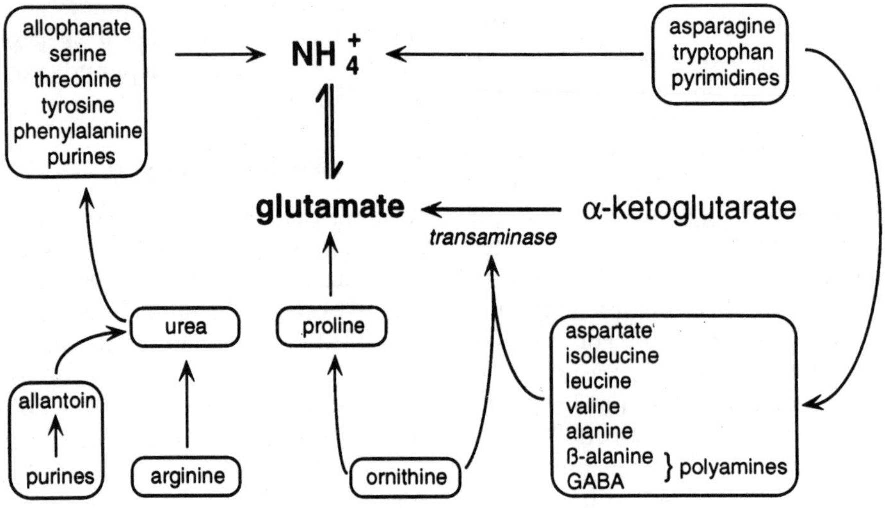

Fig. 4-19. Figure 4-19. Products of amino acid degradation.

Table 4-7. Anaerobic amino acid metabolism in *Saccharomyces*.

Amino acid	Metabolism	End products N-compound	End products C-compound
Aliphatic amino acids			
Alanine	transamination	glutamate	pyruvate
Glycine	not metabolizable as N source	—	—
Valine	transamination subsequent metabolism	glutamate	isobutyryl SCoA succinyl SCoA
Leucine subsequent metabolism	transamination	glutamate acetyl SCoA	isovaleryl SCoA acetoacetyl SCoA
Isoleucine subsequent metabolism	transamination	glutamate acetyl SCoA	methylbutryl SCoA succinyl SCoA
Hydroxyamino acids			
Serine	deamination	NH_4^+	pyruvate
Threonine	deamination	NH_4^+	propionyl SCoA
Acidic amino acids and Amines			
Aspartate	transamination	glutamate	oxalacetic acid
Asparagine	deamination	NH^+ + aspartate	
subsequent metabolism	glutamate	oxalacetic acid	
Glutamate	deamination	NH_4^+	α-ketoglutarate
Glutamine	deamination	NH_4^+, glutamate	—
	subsequent metabolism	NH_4^+	α-ketoglutarate
Basic amino acids			
Lysine	not metabolizable as N source	—	—
Histidine	not metabolizable as N source	—	—
Arginine	anaerobic products	2 NH_4^+ proline glutamate	CO_2
Aromatic amino acids			
Tryptophan	metabolism requires O_2	—	—
Phenylalanine	deamination subsequent metabolism requires O_2	NH_4^+	phenylpyruvate
Tyrosine	deamination subsequent metabolism requires O_2	NH_4^+	hydroxyphenyl-pyruvate
Sulfur-containing amino Acids			
Cysteine	Not metabolizable as N source	—	—
Methionine subsequent metabolism	transamination	glutamate succinyl SCoA	α-ketobutyric acid
Imino amino acid			
Proline	metabolism requires O_2		

A key step for the control of utilization of any metabolite is transport of the compound into the cell. There are basically three types of cellular transport of metabolites: simple diffusion, facilitated diffusion, and active transport (Figure 4-20). In simple diffusion, the compound must be able to pass through the plasma membrane lipid bilayer unassisted by any protein component. Facilitated diffusion is protein-mediated, but does not require the input of an energy source. Such transport systems can serve to equilibrate internal and external concentrations of substrate, but are not concentrative, meaning that a substrate cannot be accumulated inside of the cell against its concentration gradient via facilitated diffusion. Facilitated diffusion systems can function to excrete metabolites from the cell if the internal concentration becomes high relative to that outside of the cell. Active transport systems are protein-dependent and energy-requiring and can therefore be utilized to concentrate a compound against its concentration gradient. Most nitrogen-containing compounds are transported via active mechanisms since, in general, the cellular concentrations of each of these components will need to be higher than outside of the cell. An interesting exception is the urea-facilitated diffusion carrier (Cooper 1982b; Cooper and Sumrada 1975). Numerous amino acid transport systems have been described in *Saccharomyces*, and many remain to be elucidated (Horak 1986). Sugars are often transported via facilitated diffusion because they are rapidly metabolized once inside of the cell. As a consequence, there is always, in commercial fermentations, a high concentration of the substrate externally when compared to internal concentration. These compounds, therefore, are always being transported along a concentration gradient which is energetically favorable.

Amino acid active transport in yeast is typically coupled to the movement of ions (Cooper 1982b). Several transport systems have been described, some with very general substrate specificities and some transporting only a single or highly related cluster of amino acids (Cooper 1982b; Horak 1986). Many yeast amino acid transport systems are proton symports, coupling uptake of a substrate molecule to that of a hydrogen ion, an excellent metabolic strategy considering that the difference in grape juice pH relative to that of the yeast cytoplasm is typically at least three pH units. In this way a component running along a strong gradient (pH) is energetically linked to uptake of one that is running against

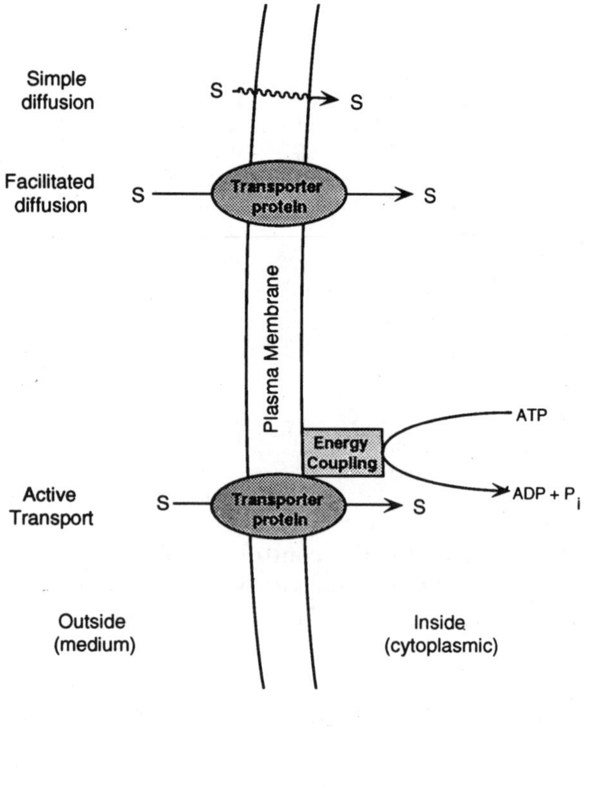

Fig. 4-20. Mechanisms of solute transport.

its gradient, such as an amino acid (Figure 4-21). The protons that enter the cell must be excreted to prevent acidification of the cytoplasm and cell death. Protons are excreted via the plasma membrane ATPase, a hydrogen ion pump, which uses energy from the hydrolysis of one ATP molecule for each hydrogen ion pumped out of the cell (Serrano 1978), thus explaining the energy requirement for the active transport process (Figure 4-20). The cell's ability to excrete protons is an important regulatory factor for amino acid uptake (Roon et al. 1975, 1977a, 1977b). Mutations of plasma membrane ATPase activity decrease permeability of amino acids and ammonium ion (McCusker et al. 1987; Vallejo and Serrano 1989), and render the cells sensitive to inhibition of growth at low pH. Thus, in the presence of acids which will enter the cell in the undissociated form, a proton is generated once the acids in the cytoplasm (McCusker et al. 1987; Vallejo and Serrano 1989). Amino acid transport is strongly inhibited by ethanol

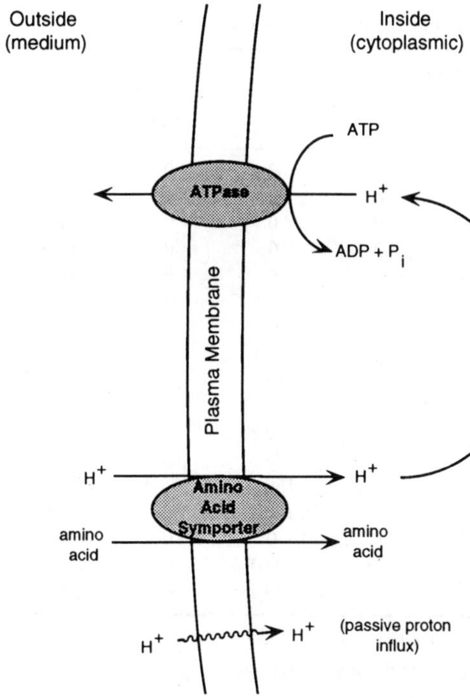

Fig. 4-21. Amino acid transport.

(Ferreras et al. 1989; Leão and van Uden 1984a). Ethanol increases the rate of passive proton influx into the yeast cells, making the cells leakier to hydrogen ions from the medium (Leão and van Uden 1984b; Cartwright et al. 1986) (Figure 4-22), which is at least one of the mechanisms of ethanol's toxicity to yeast (p. 170). The cell can eliminate the excess hydrogen ions via the ATPase, but may need to shut down hydrogen ion-coupled transporters to avoid overloading the capacity of the ATPase to remove excess cytoplasmic protons. These observations lead to a physiological model that is highly consistent with the pattern of uptake of amino acids that is observed during grape juice fermentation (Monk et al. 1986; Monteiro and Bisson 1991a). As shown in Table 4-8, most amino acids are consumed early in the fermentation prior to the appearance of significant amounts of ethanol in the medium. This, in turn, explains why much of the ethanol is secreted after growth ceases. Adenine is also consumed at this time (Monteiro and Bisson 1992c). The yeast is able to store amino acids in the vacuole, and thus can keep cytoplasmic pools of amino acids low for metabolic regulatory purposes while total cellular levels are in great excess over what is needed to produce a new cell (Cooper 1982a; Kitamoto et al. 1988; Messenguy 1987). The yeast strategy that appears to have evolved during grape juice fermentation is to transport the amino acids while energy is available, but ethanol is low, store the amino acids in the vacuole to use at leisure when needed for biosynthesis. As more and more energy must be consumed to deal with the increase in hydrogen ions due to increased passive flux into the cells as a consequence of ethanol production, the nitrogen has long since been depleted from the medium and the proton-coupled transport systems are not necessary. This strategy explains why late additions of nitrogen to correct a nitrogen deficiency of a juice may have little to no impact on yeast metabolism simply because the cells are unable to transport the added compounds. Some amino acid transporters

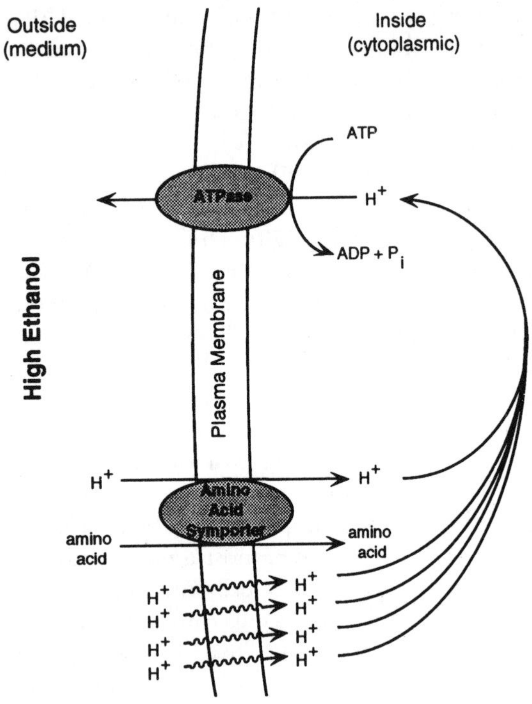

Fig. 4-22. Effect of ethanol on passive proton flux.

may function as potassium symporters following a similar logic if potassium ions have a high external as compared to internal cellular concentration (Horak 1986).

Amino acid transport shows the phenomenon of transinhibition in which amino acids that do not appear to share the same transporter essentially compete with each other for uptake (Cooper 1982b). This competition is thought to reflect a limitation of some common component, perhaps the ability to extrude the protons (Roon et al. 1977), but may also serve to guarantee that a mixture of amino acids will be taken up if such a mixture is present in the medium.

The major sugars in grape juice are glucose and fructose which are transported via facilitated diffusion, not requiring any energy input. In contrast, the disaccharide maltose is transported via a proton symport system (Figure 4-23). Amino acid utilization is influenced by the available sugar in beer or other starch-hydrolysate fermentations, because maltose

Table 4-8. Amino acid levels (μM) during fermentation of Sauvignon blanc juice[a] by Montrachet.

	Brix fermented								
Amino Acid	0	0.2	0.8	2.2	3.4	11.7	16.2	17.8	18.2[d]
ASP	426.2	249.9	139.0	0[b]	0	0	0	0	16.9
THR	629.8	349.0	265.8	9.8	0	0	0	0	0
SER	541.5	334.0	383.4	15.3	0	0	0	0	0
GLU	700.6	505.0	323.6	0	0	0	0	0	11.3
GLN	146.1	—[c]	149.6	22.4	0	0	0	0	10.1
GLY	0	43.1	60.8	74.0	0	0	0	0	0
ALA	1290.9	820.1	1089.1	314.2	0	0	0	0	13.4
VAL	184.7	119.8	158.7	50.8	0	0	14.8	0	0
ILE	255.9	60.4	68.3	0	9.5	0	12.3	0	11.8
LEU	438.3	107.2	82.1	0	12.5	0	0	0	11.3
TYR	968.8	406.5	338.3	22.4	0	0	122.3	0	8.0
PHE	294.3	336.4	218.0	0	0	0	63.5	0	71.4
GABA	668.1	519.1	572.4	644.3	381.3	232.0	156.0	375.9	234.3
NH_3	934.0	871.2	524.5	73.0	0	0	121.9	0	14.9
HIS	216.8	31.1	115.3	24.8	0	0	0	0	0
LYS	259.8	0	124.2	0	0	0	37.1	0	0
ARG	1473.3	932.1	1091.0	1370.1	17.4	0	44.1	0	25.1

[a]Juice did not contain any detectable methionine, cysteine, asparagine, or citrulline.

[b]0 = not detected, less than 1–10 μmole/L, depending upon the amino acid and sample dilution.

[c]— = peak not well resolved, concentration could not be accurately determined.

[d]The dry sample, 18.2 Brix fermented was taken nine days after inoculation.

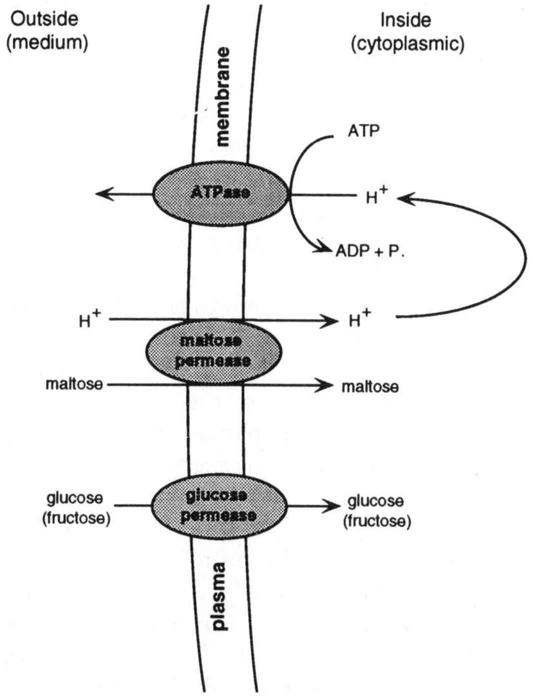

Fig. 4-23. Mechanisms of sugar transport.

also is competing for the capacity to extrude protons (Egbosimba and Slaughter 1987; Egbosimba et al. 1988) while glucose (and fructose) do not compete for that capacity.

2. Utilization Preferences

The extensive work of Jones and Pierce (1964) and Pierce (1982) on the consumption of amino acids in wort revealed that these compounds could be broken down into four classes, based upon the time of disappearance from the medium. Class A amino acids were consumed first. Class B amino acids started to be consumed prior to depletion of the class A compounds. Class C amino acids were not taken up until the medium was depleted of the class A compounds. Class D amino acids did not appear to be consumed under the growth conditions used. The classes are presented in Table 4-9. Ammonium ion, generally a preferred yeast nitrogen source, is in class C, not consumed early as would be predicted.

Table 4-9. Classification of amino acids by time of consumption from wort.

Class A	Class B	Class C	Class D
Aspartate	Histidine	Alanine	Proline
Asparagine	Isoleucine	Ammonium	
Arginine	Leucine	Glycine	
Glutamate	Methionine	Phenylalanine	
Glutamine	Valine	Tryptophan	
Lysine		Tyrosine	
Serine			
Threonine			

Ammonium ion is the species that is transported (Dubois and Grenson 1979; Roon et al. 1975a) (Figure 4-24), which decreases the plasma membrane potential, necessitating the extrusion of protons. In this case the cell obtains a single nitrogen for a single proton, but each disaccharide molecule is also bringing in a proton. Metabolizable nitrogen sources such as arginine which bring in four nitrogen atoms per proton would be preferable to take up

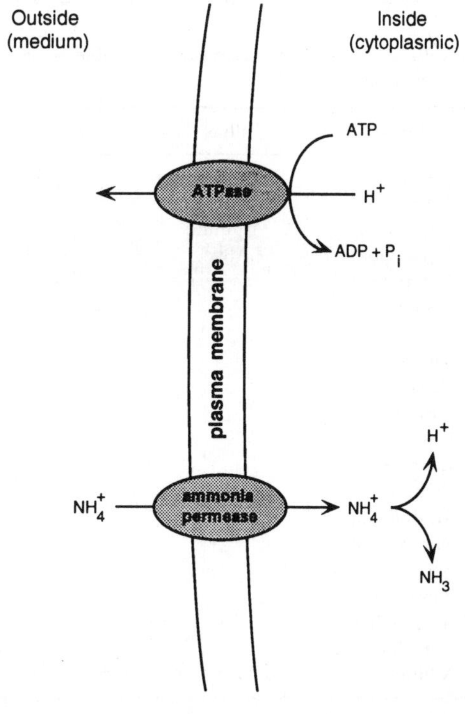

Fig. 4-24. Ammonium ion uptake.

under these conditions, which is exactly what is seen in wort. In grape juice, however, ammonia is readily utilized as a nitrogen source, being a preferred nitrogen source in this environment. Since glucose and fructose, the two main sugars of grape juice, are transported via facilitated diffusion (Cirillo 1968; Kotyk 1967), not involving movement of ions, there is no interference between nitrogen and carbon uptake systems due to the limitations of the hydrogen ion pumping ATPase. The overall pattern of utilization of amino acids in grape juice fermentation is given in Table 4-10. Early in the fermentation, at times prior to the onset of growth phase, all amino acids appear to be transportable, although the relative fraction consumed of the major amino acid species is small at this time. As the amino acids originally present in low concentration are consumed, those present in excess are then taken up in a pattern consistent with work on laboratory strains concerning yeast preference for amino acids as nitrogen sources (Cooper 1982a). Proline does not appear to be taken up from grape juice significantly under anaerobic fermentative conditions. The proline content of wine is not less than must and may, in fact, be higher under some conditions.

Table 4-10. Pattern of consumption of amino acids from grape juice.

Phase I	Phase II	Phase III
Alanine	Ammonium	Proline
Ammonium	Alanine	
Arginine	Arginine	
Asparagine	GABA[1]	
Aspartate		
Cysteine		
Glutamate		
Glutamine		
Glycine		
Histidine		
Isoleucine		
Leucine		
Lysine		
Methionine		
Phenylalanine		
Serine		
Threonine		
Tryptophan		
Tyrosine		
Valine		

[1]GABA = γ-Aminobutyrate

The rate of uptake of a compound depends upon the activity and number of permeases in the membrane for that compound. Factors other than permease activity seem to become important later in fermentation (Cartwright et al. 1986), as cells removed from fermenting media and assayed for amino acid uptake display higher rates of uptake in the assay than is observed in the medium itself. The most likely cause of the decreased rate of uptake is ethanol, and the dissipation of the proton motive force as previously suggested.

Yeasts contain a general amino acid permease, which serves to transport several amino acids (Garrett 1989; Grenson et al. 1966; Horak 1986). This transport system is expressed under conditions of nitrogen limitation (Woodward and Cirillo 1977), and would be predicted to be functional during grape juice fermentation. Several specific anabolic amino acid permeases also exist with very high affinity that function in the uptake of minor amino acids when such amino active transport systems also exist for the nucleoside bases. Adenine, guanine, hypoxanthine, and cytosine share an active, proton symport permease of high substrate affinity (Parlebas and Chevallier 1977; Reichert and Foret 1977). Uracil is transported via two different permeases, of differing affinities (Grenson 1969). There is also a specific uridine permease (Grenson 1969; Parlebas and Chevallier 1977). Thymine and thymidine are not taken up by *Saccharomyces* (Bisson and Thorner 1982; Brendel et al., 1975). In wild-type strains, transport of phosphorylated nucleotides is not observed; however, *tup* mutations confer permeability to dTMP, which appears to be mediated by a phosphate, not a nitrogen-compound permease (Bisson and Thorner 1982).

3. Intracellular Pools

In contrast to bacteria, *Saccharomyces* can accumulate large intracellular pools of amino acids.

Amino acid concentrations in the yeast cell range from 10^{-4} M for tryptophan to 10^{-2} M for glutamate (Messenguy 1987). The basic and neutral amino acids are largely found in the vacuole while the acidic amino acids, aspartate and glutamate, are found in the cytoplasm. This subcellular compartmentalization serves to separate the enzymes of metabolism from their substrates, thus allowing better coordination of amino acid metabolism. Vacuolar sequestration allows the cells to rapidly consume all available nitrogen, store the nitrogen in the vacuole, then utilize compounds as they are needed by regulating the release of amino acids from the vacuole to the cytoplasm. This metabolic strategy is in contrast to that of many microorganisms which regulate cellular pool levels by regulating net uptake into the cell. The yeast strategy appears to be a sound one considering their environment, the need to guard against excessive proton influx as ethanol accumulates in the medium, and the competitive edge obtained by the rapid depletion of available nitrogen compounds from the medium against other organisms unable to accumulate and store amino acids in this manner. As would be predicted, the composition of the amino acid pool in yeast is dictated by the available nitrogen source or sources (Watson 1976). In general, the available amino acids and closely related derivatives are the ones seen to accumulate inside of the yeast cell (Watson 1976).

4. Utilization Pathways

There have been many recent studies on the pattern of nitrogen compound utilization during grape juice fermentation (Monteiro and Bisson 1991a, 1991b, 1992a, 1992b, 1992c; Jiranek et al. 1991). Many factors complicate the interpretation of these results. Both the total amount of nitrogen and the kinds of nitrogen-containing compounds are important. A given amino acid may display different patterns of utilization depending upon its concentration relative to cellular needs for biosynthesis and to total nitrogen availability. If present at a concentration near or below the level needed for biosynthesis, the amino acid species will be depleted from the medium rapidly. If present in excess of the concentration needed for biosynthesis, the amino acid species may persist in the medium.

Another important factor in these types of studies is the choice of medium to use for the investigation. A defined or synthetic juice medium allows the experimenter complete control over the composition. Definitive experiments can be undertaken, and general rules or principles can be determined. However, to be certain these rules or principles accurately reflect the situation in grape juice, the work should be repeated using grape juice itself. Grape juice is not a defined medium, containing unknown substances and unknown concentrations of known substances. If the pattern observed in juice-like medium is repeatable in grape juice, then the unknowns do not affect the phenomenon under investigation. If dissimilar findings are obtained, then it becomes necessary to analyze other components not previously thought to play an important role. The ultimate goal of such studies is to accurately reproduce the grape juice phenomenon in a synthetic, defined medium.

Strain differences may also play a very important role. In comparison of the effect of nitrogen content of grape juice on fermentation parameters distinct strain differences were observed (Monteiro and Bisson 1991a). Fermentation rate in Montrachet was more strongly correlated with nitrogen content than in the Prise de Mousse strain. It would be unwise to generalize an observation made on a single yeast strain to all strains. Direct comparison of different strains in different juices is the worst possible scenario. Different strains must be compared in the same medium.

Nitrogen can be incorporated into a receptor molecule via direct amination using ammonia or via a transamination reaction in which a second nitrogen-containing compound serves as the nitrogen donor. Glutamate serves most often as nitrogen donor in biosynthetic transamination reactions. Thus, the cell needs to maintain a proper balance of these two nitrogen compounds which are central to the coordinated biosynthesis of all biologically active nitrogen-containing components (Figure 4-19). Two enzymatic reactions serve to equilibrate levels of these compounds and to couple nitrogen and carbon metabolism. NAD^+-dependent glutamate dehydrogenase and NADP-dependent glutamate dehydrogenase (GDH) are catabolic and anabolic reactions, respectively (Cooper 1982a; Middlehoven et al. 1978). In general, either NAD^+- or NADP-dependent glutamate dehydrogenase is expressed depending upon the available nitrogen source, rarely are they expressed equally (Cooper 1982a). Maximal levels of NADP-GDH are observed when ammonium ion is the sole nitrogen source in the medium or is the major nitrogen form produced intracellularly from the degradation of the available nitrogen sources (Cooper 1982a). This enzyme thus performs primarily an anabolic role in the synthesis of glutamate from ammonium ion and α-ketoglutarate. In contrast, the maximal levels of NAD^+-GDH are observed when glutamate, aspartate, or alanine are provided as sole nitrogen source, compounds which generate high glutamate levels. Thus, this enzyme is involved in the catabolism of glutamate to yield ammonium ion for biosynthesis. Loss of NAD^+-dependent glutamate dehydrogenase necessitates provision of ammonia or a nitrogen source generating ammonia. Similarly, loss of NADP-dependent glutamate dehydrogenase requires provision of glutamate or a nitrogen source generating glutamate (Middlehoven et al. 1978). Amino acids lysine, histidine, cysteine (cystine), and glycine are good nitrogen sources for many yeasts, however, none of these compounds is utilized efficiently by *Saccharomyces* as a nitrogen source (Cooper 1982a; Large 1986). In fact, there are many nitrogen-containing compounds which serve as good nitrogen sources for many other yeasts which are not catabolized by *Saccharomyces* (Large 1986).

a. *Arginine and Proline Metabolism*

Arginine and proline represent the major amino acids found in grape juice. The proline metabolic pathway is given in Figure 4-25. Molecular oxygen is required as hydrogen acceptor for the first step in proline degradation, proline oxidase, which occurs in the mitochondrion (Tomenchok and Brandriss 1987). Under anaerobic fermentation conditions, proline cannot be utilized as a nitrogen source due to lack of oxygen which is needed stoichiometrically, not catalytically, for the degradation of proline. The proline permease also requires O_2 for expression, thus, this amino acid will not be taken up by the cells in the absence of O_2. In wines, the proline content is generally as high or even higher than that in the must.

Arginine degradation is first catalyzed by arginase (Figure 4-26) yielding ornithine and urea (Middlehoven 1964). Urea is further degraded by a bifunctional enzyme urea amidolyase (Sumrada and Cooper 1982; Whitney and Cooper 1972). Urea amidolyase comprises two activities: urea carboxylase, yielding allophanate, and allophanate hydrolase, producing two molecules each of ammonia and carbon dioxide. Many other organisms possess ureases, which degrade urea directly to two molecules of ammonia and one of carbon dioxide (Large 1986). *Saccharomyces* does not possess a urease activity (Cooper 1982a; Large 1986). The question arises as to the physiological reason for the evolution of a two-step degradation pathway for urea. This pathway consumes energy in the urea carboxylase reaction, as well as requiring an essential vitamin, biotin, for the degradation of urea. Thus, urea will not be degraded by *Saccharomyces*, if energy or vitamins are insufficient. This strategy may serve to release excess nitrogen in the form of urea, which is relatively nontoxic, via the urea-facilitated diffusion permease rather than produce ammonium ions, the latter being more toxic and not as readily excreted since a facilitated diffusion system has not been described for ammonium ion. As men-

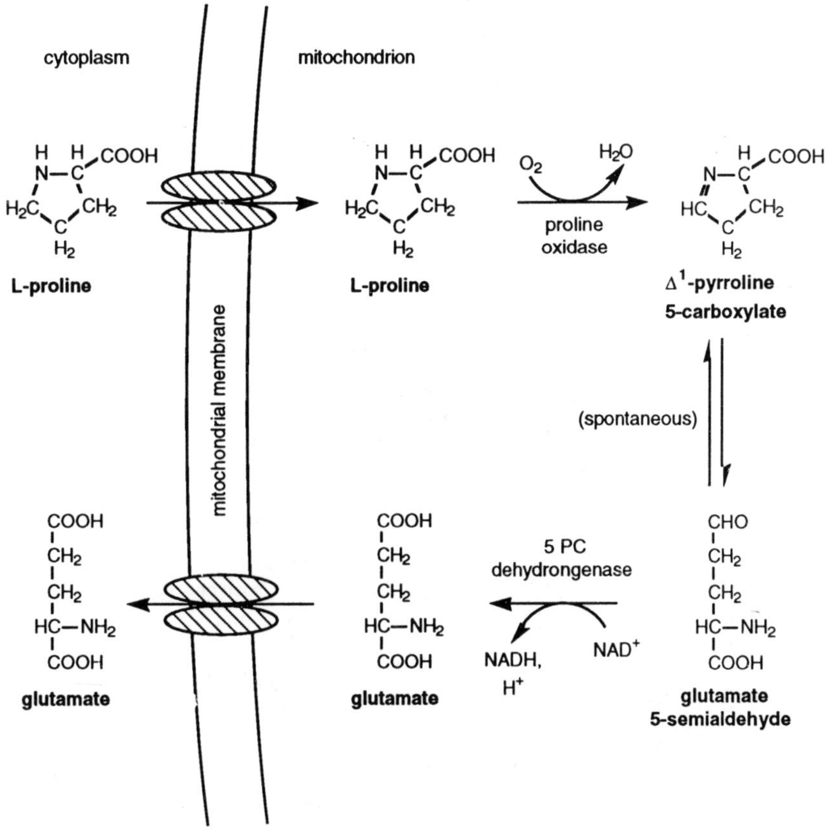

Fig. 4-25. Pathway of proline degradation.

tioned above, *Saccharomyces* tends to deplete the medium rapidly of available nitrogen-containing compounds, and may on occasion wind up with an excessive internal concentration of nitrogen-containing compounds. The ability to release urea would allow the cell to adjust internal total metabolite pools of nitrogen compounds by producing a nitrogen compound of low toxicity that can be readily taken back up when physiological or environmental conditions warrant it. It is interesting that urea is taken up via two distinct transport mechanisms: an active, high-affinity transport system coupled to ion movements as are the amino acid permeases; and a low-affinity facilitated diffusion system, independent of ion movements (Cooper 1982b; Cooper and Sumrada 1975).

Ornithine, the other end product of the arginase reaction, can be further degraded via glutamate semialdehyde to proline or can be converted to polyamines. The genetic analysis of proline degradation revealed that ornithine degradation proceeds via proline as intermediate (Cooper 1982b). Proline is formed from ornithine in the cytoplasm, transported into the mitochondrion as proline, then converted to glutamate, as shown in Figure 4-25. Since proline cannot be metabolized under anaerobic fermentation conditions, ornithine cannot serve to form glutamate in the absence of oxygen. This is why, considering the usually high arginine content of musts, wines can contain more proline than musts. However, ornithine is also the precursor of polyamines spermine, spermidine, and putrescine (Tabor

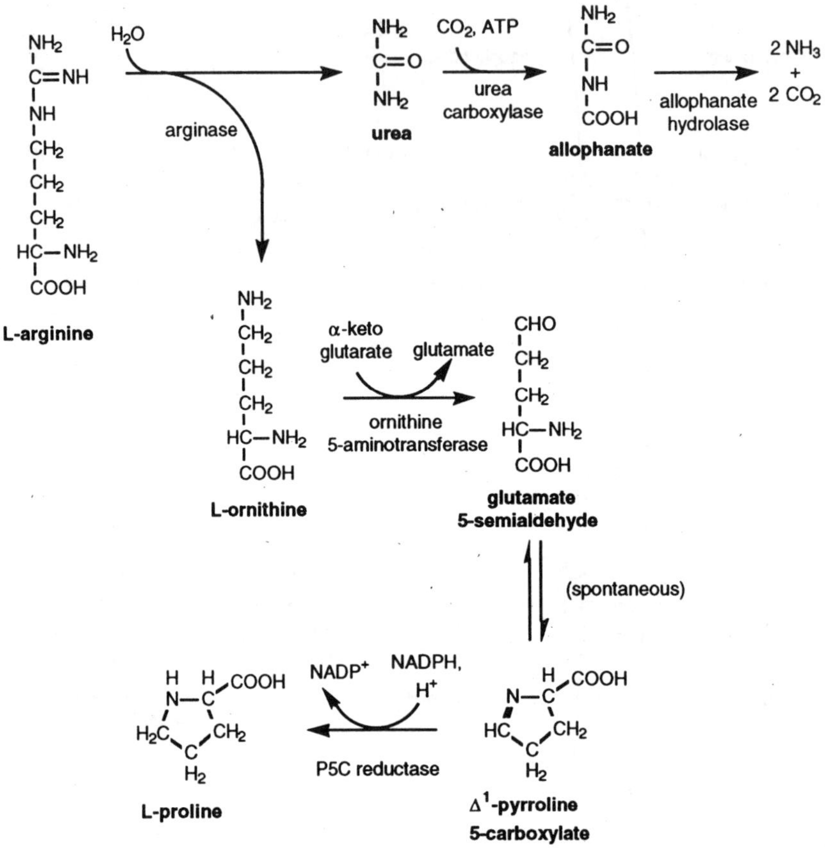

Fig. 4-26. Pathway of arginine degradation.

et al. 1983) (Figure 4-27). Polyamines are required in high concentration during growth, although the exact physiological function of the polyamines remains obscure.

5. Important End Products of Nitrogen Metabolism

a. *Branch-Chain Amino Acids and Higher Alcohols*

The metabolism of nitrogen-containing compounds yields end products of sensory importance in perceived wine quality. Amino acids that are deaminated catabolically in order to release their nitrogen components leave behind carbon skeletons which will generally represent a waste product from the yeast's viewpoint. Deamination of amino acids can result in the formation of the α-keto acids or of higher (fusel) alcohols via the metabolic mechanism shown in Figure 4-28. In addition to being produced due to deamination, decarboxylation and reduction of nitrogen-source amino acids, higher alcohols can also be produced during the biosynthesis of amino acids from the excess of their corresponding keto acids, which has been best characterized in resting cells (Nykanen 1986; Webb and Ingraham 1963). This formation from glucose has already been discussed above (Section H.2). Another paradox is that the formation of fusel alcohols also occurs late in fermentation, also after the period of rapid consumption of amino acids (Webb and Ingraham 1963). Labeling studies using radioactively labeled precursors demonstrated that fusel oil could be

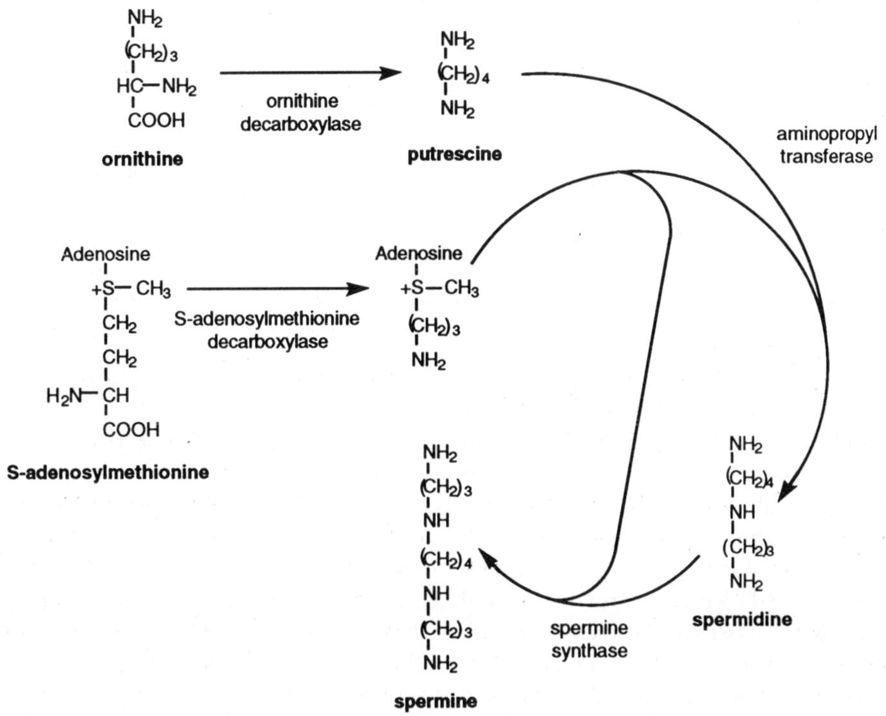

Fig. 4-27. Pathway of polyamine biosynthesis.

formed from carbon substrates, the so-called Ehrlich reaction (Nykanen 1986; Webb and Ingraham 1963). This work was also confirmed by the investigation of fusel oil formation during resting cell fermentations using mutations of specific steps in amino acid biosynthesis (Webb and Ingraham 1963). These auxotrophic mutants were supplied with the required amino acids needed for growth, yet no corresponding higher alcohols were observed, which would have been expected if degradation were the main route to fusel oil formation under these conditions. In these mutants, different higher alcohols were produced, with the final total concentration of higher alcohols being similar. The principal higher alcohols and their precursors are shown in Table 4-11. The experimental evidence for this pathway has been verified in the induction and isolation of a leucine-less homothallic mutant of Montrachet wine yeast strain, which does not produce isoamyl alcohol from glucose (Rous et al. 1983; Kunkee et al. 1983). The addition of the amino acids valine, leucine, and isoleucine can enhance the formation of the corresponding higher alcohol (isobutanol, isoamyl alcohol, and active amyl alcohol, respectively) but not proportionately so (Guymon

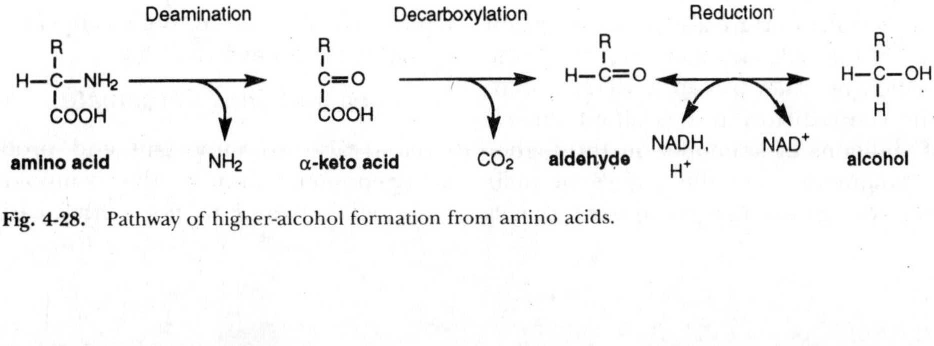

Fig. 4-28. Pathway of higher-alcohol formation from amino acids.

Table 4-11. Derivatives of amino acid metabolism.

Amino Acid	α-Keto Acid	Higher alcohol
Leucine	α-Isocaproate	3-Methylbutanol
Isoleucine	α-Keto-β-methyl valerate	2-Methylbutanol
Valine	α-Ketoisovalerate	Isobutanol
Threonine	α-Ketobutyrate	Propanol
Tyrosine	3-(4-Hydroxyphenyl)-2-ketopropionate	Tyrosol
Phenylalanine	3-Phenyl-2-ketopropionate	Phenethyl alcohol
Tryptophan	—	Tryptophol

1972). Their formation is tied to the production of ethanol (from sugar) rather than the uptake of amino acids during yeast growth and they are produced at levels above that expected from the utilization of the corresponding amino acid. The one exception to this appears to be the formation of *n*-propanol (Guymon et al. 1961) which seems to be tied to yeast growth (Usseglio-Tomasset 1975). Other studies investigating the role of threonine and isoleucine (Reazin et al. 1973) found that in *S. cerevisiae*, isoleucine is converted to only active amyl alcohol as a product while threonine produces *n*-propanol, active amyl alcohol, and isoamyl alcohol. One of the few reports in which the amino acid content of 70 juices (from six cultivars) was correlated with the formation of the corresponding higher alcohol (Cantagrel et al. 1982) found only phenethyl alcohol to be enhanced at low phenylalanine concentrations. Dickinson and Norte (1993) have studied a transaminase system in *Saccharomyces cerevisiae* specific for branched-chain amino acids, which they claim obviates the Ehrlich pathway, or at least the first part of it. However, it is doubtful that their system is operative during fermentation conditions. In any case, the Ehrlich pathway, and the transaminase portion thereof, has been firmly established (see above).

The higher alcohols are also produced when ammonia is the sole nitrogen source in the fermentation medium (Äyräpää 1973). There are some contradictory results about the effects of additions of ammonia on the higher alcohol production, but the nature of their formation with most nitrogen sources, that is increasing with increasing nitrogen concentration up to a point and then decreasing at higher nitrogen concentrations (Äyräpää 1973), may explain much of the variation in the results. The peak production appears at approximately 120 mg/L assimilable nitrogen (with ammonia) and 200 mg/L in amino acid mixtures. At levels above 400 mg/L nitrogen there is essentially no concentration effect (Äyräpää 1973, Rapp 1975). The general exception to this pattern is the production of *n*-propanol, which usually increases with increasing nitrogen concentration up to the 400 mg/L level (Äyräpää 1973; Vos et al. 1978; Ough and Bell 1980; Cantagrel et al. 1982).

The exact function of fusel oil formation is not known. Fusel oil formation may simply serve to detoxify any aldehydes that are produced during amino acid catabolism. Another speculatory role for fusel oils might be in regulation of amino acid anabolism. Accumulation of fusel alcohols may indicate a block of or lack of available nitrogen for amino acid biosynthesis and these compounds may somehow mediate the starvation signal, serving to modulate nitrogen metabolism as opposed to being simple waste carbon. The formation does not seem to be important as a means for reoxidation of NADH, which occurs during the reduction of the higher aldehyde to the higher alcohol, since there appears to be enough acetaldehyde for this.

b. Urea and Ethyl Carbamate

Urea is also an important end product of nitrogen metabolism as this compound can react with ethanol to form ethyl carbamate

(Monteiro et al. 1989; Ough et al. 1988a; Ough et al. 1988b), a suspected carcinogen (Pound 1967; Mirvish 1968; McCann et al. 1975). It is highly desirable therefore, to eliminate or reduce as much as possible the appearance of urea in the fermentation medium. Striking strain and temperature effects have been observed which affect final juice urea levels (Famuyiwa and Ough 1991). Urea levels are also strongly correlated with juice arginine content, not surprisingly considering urea is an intermediate of arginine breakdown. Urea in wine can be eliminated by enzymatic treatment with urease (Famuyiwa and Ough 1991) and minimized by fermentation and fortification timing.

Amino acids appear in the wine postfermentation (Monteiro and Bisson 1991a, 1992b; Ough et al. 1990, 1991). Release of amino acids at the end of wort fermentation has also been reported (Lewis and Phaff 1964). The distribution of the amino acids at the end of fermentation is not well-correlated with the starting composition of the juice (Monteiro and Bisson 1992b), most likely reflecting the optimal yeast cellular pool levels for these compounds. These compounds may be released as a function of yeast autolysis; however, we have observed this release when greater than 90% of the cells present in the wine are still viable, suggesting that the release may serve some metabolic or physiological role for the yeast, perhaps in enhanced survival.

6. Nitrogen Metabolism and Effect on Glycolytic Flux

Nitrogen affects fermentation rate directly by controlling availability of amino acid precursors for the biosynthesis of proteins of glycolysis and yeast cell biomass, as well as affecting flux through the glycolytic pathway. Two mechanisms explaining the effect of nitrogen on fermentation rate have been proposed. Ammonium ion serves as an allosteric effector in regulation of phosphofructokinase activity and there is as yet an ill-defined effect of nitrogen compounds on glucose (fructose) transporter activity (Busturia and Lagunas 1986; Lagunas et al. 1982; Pena et al. 1987). Nitrogen limitation results in the accelerated turnover of glucose permeases, thus reducing fermentative capacity (Lagunas et al. 1982; Salmon 1989). This reduction in sugar permease activity subsequently slows rate of fermentation, resulting in a sluggish or incomplete fermentation, another reason nitrogen deficiency correlates with the incidence of high residual sugar.

J. SULFUR METABOLISM DURING FERMENTATION

Saccharomyces can utilize sulfate, sulfite, sulfide, or thiosulfate as a source of sulfur for biosynthesis (Thomas et al. 1992). Thiosulfate is first cleaved to sulfite and sulfide prior to utilization and, therefore, both sulfur atoms can be used (Thomas et al. 1992). Utilization of sulfite is limited by the toxicity of this compound (Stratford and Rose 1985). Organic compounds, cysteine, methionine, homocysteine, and S-adenosylmethionine can also serve as sulfur sources (Thomas et al. 1992).

The assimilation of sulfate requires five enzymatic reactions (Figure 4-29). Sulfate reduction proceeds via formation of phosphosulfate intermediates. ATP sulfurylase catalyzes the formation of adenosine 5′-phosphosulfate (APS) from ATP and sulfate. APS kinase catalyzes the formation of 3′-phosphoadenosine 5′-phosphosulfate (PAPS). PAPS reductase is responsible for the formation of sulfite. Sulfite reductase catalyzes the six-electron reduction of sulfite to sulfide and is a complex enzyme. There appear to be two distinct sulfite reductases in *Saccharomyces*, one that utilizes carrier-bound sulfite and the other free sulfite (Umbarger 1978). Mutations of five different genes affect sulfite reductase activity and either encode subunits of the enzyme or are involved in the generation of siroheme required for sulfite reductase activity (Thomas et al. 1992; Cherest and Surdin-Kerjan 1992). In *Saccharomyces*, sulfide is then transferred to O-

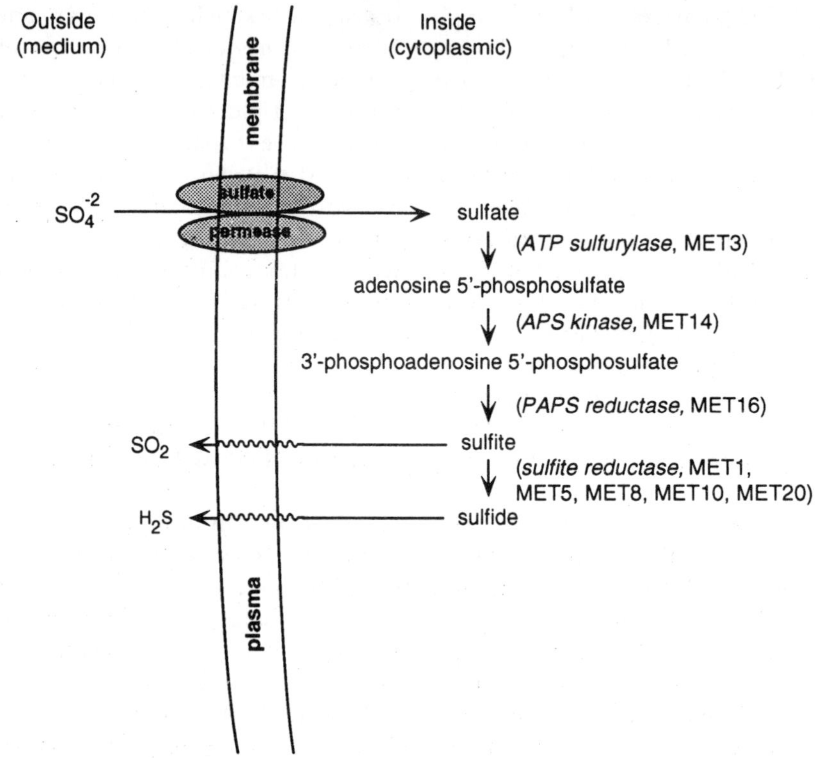

Fig. 4-29. Pathway for sulfate reduction.

acetylhomoserine generating homocysteine (Cherest and Surdin-Kerjan 1992). Sulfide does not appear to be incorporated directly into O-acetylserine in *Saccharomyces* in contrast to other microorganisms (Cherest and Surdin-Kerjan 1992). Therefore, cysteine is not produced directly from sulfation of serine. Homocysteine (4C) and cysteine (3C) are interconverted by the C3 to C4 and C4 to C3 *trans* sulfuration pathways (Figure 4-30). Interestingly, the zero-valent (elemental) form of sulfur is not observed in any of the enzymatic pathways of the reduction of sulfate or sulfite to sulfide.

Organic sulfur sources can also be interconverted using the *trans*-sulfuration pathways. The genetics of sulfate reduction, assimilation, and utilization are complex and several genes involved in sulfur assimilation have as yet unidentified functions (Thomas et al. 1992; Cherest and Surdin-Kerjan 1992).

The sulfur source utilized during fermentation depends upon the compounds available. Methionine represses synthesis of the sulfate permease and of the enzymes involved in sulfate reduction. Sulfite competes with sulfate for uptake, but there are reports of transport of sulfite in the absence of sulfate uptake ability (Stratford and Rose 1985). Sulfite uptake did not require an energy source, and may occur by simple diffusion (Stratford and Rose 1986).

K. PROBLEM FERMENTATIONS

1. Stuck or Sluggish Fermentations

There are two general classes of problems for the winemaker that can arise during the alcoholic fermentation: sluggish or stuck fermentations and off-flavor production. In some in-

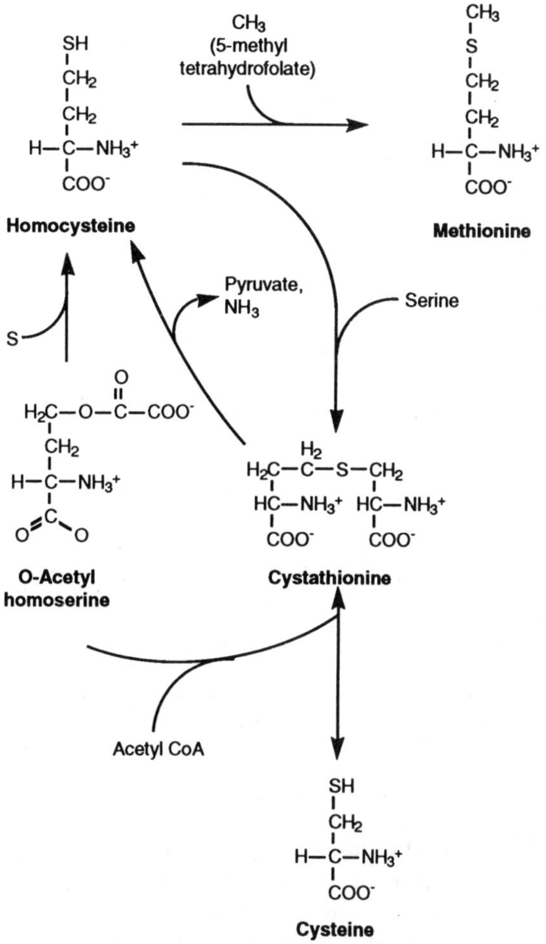

Fig. 4-30. Pathways of sulfur assimilation.

stances these problems are easily treated, while in others they present a serious challenge to the production of a sound wine. Causes of sluggish or stuck fermentations are given in Table 4-12. The effect of excessive sugar content on yeast growth and fermentation has been discussed (Section E). The production of excessive amounts of ethanol, coming from harvest of over-ripe grapes can play a role. However, contrary to what might be expected, the intracellular concentrations of ethanol nominally produced do not seem to exhibit any toxic effects specifically associated with sluggish fermentations (see below).

a. *Nutrient Deficiency*

A sluggish fermentation is one in which the rate of fermentation of sugar slows dramatically, leaving a high (greater than 0.2% v/v) sugar concentration in the finished wine, or where the end of the fermentation is so protracted, even if dryness eventually arrives, much extra care and attention must be given to the wine so as to make the economics of its production of special concern (Kunkee 1991). Sluggish fermentations are often caused by nutrient limitation. Deficiencies in nitrogen or phosphate are most frequently responsible for a stuck fermentation. Agenbach (1977) reported that 0.5 g/L of usable nitrogen was necessary for maximal yeast biomass production and rapid fermentation rates. Approximately 0.2 g/L of nitrogen is needed for fermentations to go completely to dryness. Phosphate may also be limiting in grape juice. Occasionally, both nitrogen and phosphate may be limiting. It is common industry practice to supplement with diammonium phosphate, thereby providing both nutrients simultaneously.

As mentioned earlier, yeast strains display different sensitivities to nitrogen limitation. Some strains maintain fermentation rates at nitrogen concentrations that are deficient for other strains.

Grape juice generally contains sufficient micronutrients, vitamins and minerals, to support yeast growth. In contrast to macronutrients, micronutrients such as vitamins are not used stoichiometrically, but can be utilized repeatedly. Thus, numerous generations may be required before a micronutrient deficiency becomes apparent, while the impact of a macronutrient deficiency will be almost immediate. Two situations may generate a micronutrient deficiency. Extensive mold infestation of the grape berries may deplete the juice of nutrients or introduce inhibitors leading to a stuck fermentation. Second, if the winery practice is to inoculate from one tank to another, the yeast population may be prestarved for a limiting nutrient.

Table 4-12. Causes of stuck or sluggish fermentations.

Nutrient limitation:	Macronutrient:	Nitrogen Phosphate
	Micronutrient:	Vitamins Minerals
	Improperly grown inoculum	
Substrate inhibition:	Excess of sugars, glucose and fructose (high Brix)	
Ethanol toxicity:	Deficiency of survival factors:	Sterols, unsaturated fatty acids
	Deficiency of oxygen	
	Improperly grown inoculum	
Toxic substances:	Organic acids:	Acetate Propionate Butyrate Pentainoate
	Fatty acids:	*cis* rather than *trans* medium chain (C_6–C_{10})
	Fungicide residues	
	Pesticide residues	
	Microbial toxins:	Yeast killer factors Mycotoxins
	Excess SO_2	
Temperature shock:	Supercooling of fermentation	
	Overheating due to release of heat from yeast metabolism	

Addition of the nutrients that are deficient in the grape juice in some cases may allow the fermentation to complete. However, if the fermentation has been arrested for too long or the limitation has resulted in loss of yeast cell viability, simple nutrient addition will probably not resolve the problem. Reinoculation with a healthy yeast culture is often required. In all cases, the best procedure is to begin with a new starter culture, in fresh medium, and to which is added, stepwise, equal volumes of the stuck fermentations. The additions of the stuck material are made only to the new starter after vigorous fermentation is evident, that is when the new culture has shown adaptation to the problem medium. It is important that sluggish fermentations be recognized and properly diagnosed early, prior to full arrest of the culture. Computer-assisted fermentation monitoring at very early stages in the fermentation should allow later detection of problem fermentations so that corrective steps can be taken.

b. Ethanol Toxicity

While several conditions can ultimately result in a sluggish or stuck fermentation of grape juice, the underlying cause must always be attributed to the toxic effect of the high concentration of ethanol produced. Interestingly, with the advent of higher gravity wort fermentations, the modern brewing industry also has problems with sluggish fermentations (Casey et al. 1984).

The inhibitory effect of ethanol ought to be seen early in the fermentation, since yeast growth rates are more sensitive to ethanol inhibition than are the fermentation rates (Leão and van Uden 1985; Navarro and Durand 1978). The inhibitory effect of ethanol on the specific growth rates of yeasts has been measured (Aiba et al. 1968; Thomas and Rose 1979; Beavan et al. 1982), and mathematical models have been derived to show the relationship between yeast growth and ethanol concentration (Boulton 1980; Pamment 1989).

Furthermore, ethanol is known to inhibit the uptake of sugars and amino acids (Kunkee and Bisson 1993), which should also contribute to the inhibitory effect on growth. However, in a grape juice fermentation, the concentration of ethanol needed to show an effect on growth rate does not come, in fact, until the yeasts are nearing the stationary phase of growth (Boulton 1980; Pamment 1989). The noticeably slower growth rate of yeasts in grape juice, as compared to that in laboratory medium, is an effect of sugar inhibition—glucose repression (Section E)—and not of ethanol toxicity.

In this regard, it is well to point out here that the inhibitory effects of high concentrations of sugar in grape juice on the fermentation are often not appreciated. Under certain conditions, where the sugar concentrations are intentionally kept low, as in the syruped fermentations, the ethanol production will far exceed that of the accepted cutoff point of 14% (v/v). In fact, saké fermentations normally result in a product of 20 to 21% (v/v) ethanol! The latter fermentation (Kodama 1993) takes place in the continual presence of very low concentrations of glucose, coming from the balance between the hydrolysis of rice (starch) by the koji mold (*Aspergillus*) and fermentation by yeast (*Saccharomyces*). Thus glucose repression factors are avoided.

The inhibitory effect on yeast activity, obvious at the end of grape juice fermentations, does come from ethanol toxicity. The toxic effects of ethanol seem to be several, and the yeasts' responses to ethanol challenge seem also to be several (Section L); but the chief impact of ethanol is its effect on the yeast plasma membrane and on the membrane's permeability. This has been demonstrated in two important kinds of experiments. In the first, increased formation of ethanol, which inhibits yeast fermentation, also led to a loss in cellular constituents, especially in the metal ion components, primarily magnesium and calcium. Replacement of these components reversed the inhibition (Dombeck and Ingram 1986; Nabais et al. 1988). Interestingly enough, the effective supplemental concentrations of these ions were about that found naturally in grape juices (Kunkee and Bisson 1993). The other evidence for increased permeability is the increased passive diffusion of protons, resulting in an acidification or a deacidification of the medium, depending upon the initial pH, as ethanol is produced (Leão and van Uden 1984b; Jiménez and van Uden 1985; Cartwright et al. 1986; Juroszek et al. 1987; Delfini and Pravex 1989; Malfeito-Ferreira et al. 1990).

The mechanisms of the increased permeability of the plasma membrane due to ethanol challenge are not well understood, but they seem to have to do both with the effect on the activity of membrane ATPase and on the fluidity of the membrane. The increased passive diffusion of protons mentioned above indicates a greater expenditure of ATP needed by the cell to maintain the desired internal pH, in confrontation to the high concentration of external protons. That is to say, the dissipation of the proton gradient induced by ethanol could be explained both by the effect on the permeability and on the membrane ATPase activity. These two effects are summarized here (Kunkee and Bisson 1993).

The effect on changes in permeability of the membrane brought about by ethanol are associated with fluidity changes of the membrane, which has been shown to occur in many cellular membranes exposed to ethanol (Kunkee and Bisson 1993; Sun and Sun 1985; Goldstein 1987). The membrane's permeability and fluidity have to do with the complement in the membrane of certain sterols and long chain fatty acids, especially unsaturated ones. These components, the so-called survival factors, are produced by the yeast only under aerobic conditions. Molecular oxygen is required as the hydrogen acceptor in the first reaction of sterol biosynthesis, the folding of the precursor compound into the sterol form, catalyzed by squalene oxidase (Henry 1982); and molecular oxygen is also required as the hydrogen acceptor during the introduction of double bonds in the generation of unsaturated fatty acids, by the enzyme desaturase (Kirsop

1982). Neither of these activities is subject to glucose repression. The survival factors—these unsaturated long-chain fatty acid and sterols, the latter often also having unsaturated side chains—are so named because their effects are especially demonstrable in yeast in overcoming the toxicity of high concentrations of ethanol. That is, their presence gives an increased concentration of viable cells at the end of vinification fermentations (Lafon-Lafourcade et al. 1979; Traverso-Rueda and Kunkee 1982). These compounds are also undoubtedly needed at very low concentrations as "growth factors," but this need can be demonstrated only under rigorously anaerobic conditions (Macy and Miller 1983; Lagunas 1981). Further discussion of the survival factors, and their role in response to ethanol challenge, is given in the section below on ethanol tolerance (Section L).

The other effect of the increased passive diffusion of protons is a greater expenditure of ATP needed by the cell to maintain the desired internal pH (Figure 4-22). The dissipation of the proton gradient induced by ethanol can be explained by the increased permeability and by the inhibition of membrane ATPase activity (Cartwright et al. 1987). It could also be explained by an activation of ATPase activity (Rosa and Sá-Correia 1991) — for reestablishment of the disturbed intracellular pH (Kunkee and Bisson 1993).

Ethanol toxicity in yeast is complex and apparently multivalent. A single mechanism of toxicity would seem to invite a genotypic response. However, all kinds of exposures of yeasts to ethanol, even haploid heterothallic strains, has never resulted in the selection of a mutant with obviously increased ethanol tolerance.

One early attempt to explain the toxicity was the obvious one that there is a buildup on the internal concentration of ethanol, resulting in denaturation of key enzymes (see Kunkee and Bisson (1993) for further details and references for the work summarized here). The experiments made to measure the intracellular ethanol concentration have generated a lot of controversy. The best efforts (Rose et al. 1982) indicate that the internal concentration of ethanol does build up, to be at least the same, or slightly higher, as that on the outside, which is considerable in a vinification fermentation. Nevertheless, studies of the effect of ethanol on enzyme activities did not substantiate this role in the toxicity (Kunkee and Bisson 1993).

The inhibitory effect of ethanol seen at the end of a wine fermentation, especially in sluggish fermentations, may be a result from the effect on the fermentation capacity of the cell or from the effect on the viability. Important as this consideration is, the assessment of viability versus fermentative capacity is difficult. Viability as measured by plating of the culture on an enriched medium is not necessarily the same as that obtained by measurement with methylene blue stain (Pierce 1970). It is also difficult to assess the correct proportion of the total yeast biomass, much of which has settled with the gross lees, contributing either to the viable count or to the fermentation capacity. Sá-Correia and van Uden (1986) found an exponential relationship between ethanol and the specific death rate of yeast. Kalmokoff and Ingledew (1985) showed that cell growth was already inhibited when significant losses in viability were first noticeable. Brown et al. (1981) also found that the loss of cell viability was the most important effect.

Further insight into the effects of ethanol can be obtained from reviews by Ingram and Buttke (1984), van Uden (1989), and by the examination of the *responses* of yeast to the toxicity, given in the section on ethanol tolerance (Section L).

c. *Toxins*

If a stuck fermentation is a consequence of the presence of toxic substances on the fruit, reinoculation and fermentation to dryness might be unsuccessful. Ethanol decreases plasma membrane impermeability to many small ions in addition to H^+. The simultaneous presence of ethanol plus a toxic ion such as F^- found in some pesticides, for example, may more strongly inhibit yeast growth and fermentation than either substance alone.

Toxins might also arise as a consequence of microbial activity. *Saccharomyces* will be inhibited by many organic acids, medium-length fatty acids, and *cis* fatty acids. These compounds are not normally present in grape juice, but can be synthesized by microorganisms found in the fruit or juice, or can derive from grape components depending upon must treatment. Organic acid inhibition of growth is thought to be due to the reduction of cytoplasmic pH caused by uptake of these compounds (Cardoso and Leão 1992). Medium-chain-length fatty acids such as decanoic acid, are produced by yeast and are also inhibitory to cell metabolism (Rosi and Bertuccioli 1984). However, under vinification conditions, these acids seem either to be adsorbed by the yeast or metabolized by them midway through the fermentation and exhibit no inhibitory effect (Lee and Kunkee 1988). Certain strains of *Saccharomyces* produce a small peptide known as killer factor that inhibits the growth of other killer-sensitive strains of *Saccharomyces*. There are three major different classes of killer factor, known as K1, K2, and K3 (Young 1987; van Vuuren and Jacobs 1992). The K2 toxin has been shown to be active in grape juice. If the yeast conducting the fermentation is sensitive to this toxin and it is produced by a wild strain of *Saccharomyces*, stuck fermentation may result. Reinoculation with a killer factor resistant strain will overcome this problem. The trichothecene mycotoxin, T2, produced by *Fusarium*, *Mycothecium*, *Trichothecium*, *Cephalosporium*, and *Stachybotrys* species inhibits *Saccharomyces* (Koshinsky et al. 1992). These mold genera are less commonly found on fruit and more commonly found in grains and cereals, but are fairly widespread in nature. An inhibitory product, botrycin, has been invoked but not entirely justified in sluggish fermentations of botrytized musts.

d. *Temperature Effects*

Extremes of temperature, either too warm due to the heat given off during fermentation combined with little to no heat exchange capability of the fermentor, or too cool due to supercooling of the fermentation, will impact yeast growth and metabolism. However, once stuck, fermentations do not easily restart by simple adjustment of the temperature, even if that was the original problem. Temperature also affects plasma membrane fluidity. The combination of ethanol and extremes of temperature is particularly challenging to a microbial cell in terms of maintenance of plasma membrane function and integrity.

2. Production of Off-Characters

The second class of fermentation problems, besides stuck fermentations, concerns the production of off-characters, off-flavors, or aroma compounds detracting from overall wine quality. Acetic acid has already been discussed, in this regard, as have the higher (fusel) alcohols (Section H). *Saccharomyces* strains have also been implicated in the production of certain volatile phenols in wine (Chatonnet et al. 1993). The yeast enzymatically produce vinyl phenols from plant phenolic precursors. These compounds may have a decided medicinal or phenolic aroma.

a.. *Sulfur-Containing Volatiles*

An important class of spoilage compounds are the sulfur-containing volatiles. The formation of trace levels of volatile sulfur compounds during fermentation continues to be a significant problem. This group includes compounds which are very volatile and have unpleasant odors generally described in terms of rotten eggs, skunk aroma, garlic, or onion. Although they are produced at only tens to hundreds of micrograms per liter levels, and represent only a trace abnormality in fermentation biochemistry, their sensory impact is obvious and damaging. The formation of the thiols, ethane thiol, and methane thiol, during wine fermentations by yeast has recently been investigated with the aid of gas chromatography using capillary columns and sulfur-specific detectors. The formation of other sulfur compounds such as carbonyl sulfide, carbon disulfide, and dimethyl disulfide has also only recently been investigated (De Mora et al. 1986; Eschenbruch et al. 1986). The factors influencing their formation are not well understood at this time.

Foremost among the sulfur-containing volatiles is hydrogen sulfide (H_2S), or the rotten egg character. Many factors may drive or contribute to H_2S production. Hydrogen sulfide can be produced by yeast during fermentation due to the presence of elemental sulfur on grape skins (Rankine 1963; Acree et al. 1972; Schütz and Kunkee 1977; Wenzel and Dittrich 1978; Thomas et al. 1993b); inadequate levels, or mixtures of free α-amino nitrogen (FAN) in the must (Vos and Gray 1979; Monk 1986; Henschke and Jiranek 1991; Jiranek and Henschke 1991), a deficiency of pantothenic acid (Tokuyama et al. 1973) or pyridoxine (Wainwright 1971) or higher than usual levels of cysteine (Eschenbruch and Bonish 1976) in the juice; and yeast strains (Rankine 1964; Acree et al. 1972; Thomas et al. 1993b). A role of added sulfite has also been suggested (Müller-Späth et al. 1978; Wenzel and Dittrich 1978; Jiranek and Henschke 1991) and there are opinions that the formation can be prevented by yeast selection (Rankine 1963; Zambonelli et al. 1984).

Hydrogen sulfide may arise as an offshoot of sulfate reduction for biosynthesis. Sulfate uptake and reduction is regulated by methionine levels, not by the levels of reduced sulfur within the cell. Thus, a block in metabolism or biosynthesis of the sulfur-containing amino acids may result in the formation of excess reduced sulfur, which is then released from the cells to the medium. Pantothenic acid deficiency, which would block methionine biosynthesis, can lead to H_2S formation. Nitrogen deficiency would also block amino acid biosynthesis and lead to H_2S formation. High concentrations of metal ions may also lead to H_2S production. Yeast biomass, postfermentation in a medium high in copper, appears black due to the formation of cupric sulfide. Resistance to metal ions is in part due to the generation of metal ion-sulfide complexes that are deposited and effectively removed from the medium.

There are clearly yeast strain factors that are important in hydrogen sulfide formation but many trials throughout the world have failed to come up with a consistently better yeast strain in terms of sulfide production. There continue to be strain effects in many of the possibilities that have been proposed and it is not clear which of these results is specific and which are general. Similarly, medium supplements that have been found to be useful in certain regions have sometimes shown to be inconsistent when applied to juices in other places. This is generally due to investigators focusing more on what their treatments are rather than the juices to which they are applied. Even today it is usually not easy to conclude why a certain fermentation produces sulfides without sufficient chemical analysis of the initial juice. The analysis of the vitamin pool in juices remains difficult and is generally not attempted even though pantothenate deficiency is known to be a possible cause of this problem.

b. *Elemental Sulfur*

The linkage of the presence of elemental sulfur during fermentation with hydrogen sulfide production is well known (Rankine 1963). In a later studies, Acree et al. (1972), Schütz and Kunkee (1977), Wenzel and Dittrich (1978) showed similar results using different measurement methods ranging from the methylene blue assay to a sulfide-specific ion electrode. These early works bought about fuller attention to the importance of better vineyard management in the use of dusting sulfur for the control of mildew; and led to the current recommendations of no applications of sulfur within six weeks of harvest, and preferably none after veraison.

It was not until recently that the actual levels of sulfur residues were measured and found to be in the range 1 to 5 mg/L for a number of field trials (Thomas et al. 1993a). Fermentations with additions at the 2- and

4-mg/L level were shown to exhibit more variation in sulfide production due to yeast strain and medium (model vs reconstituted juice) than that due the presence of the elemental sulfur (Thomas et al. 1993b). It is clear, looking back, that the earlier laboratory studies showing the formation of hydrogen sulfide from elemental sulfur had used levels of sulfur that are rarely found if recommended practices (Gubler 1992) are followed. Nevertheless, it is still not uncommon to find intentional violation of these practices, especially in regions of high mildew susceptibility, often with the expected bad results of hydrogen sulfide production. In white wine production, the problems coming from the presence of dusting sulfur in the juice are greater lessened, in fact avoided, by conscientious settling and racking of the juice before fermentation.

c. *Amino Nitrogen*

The first studies to suggest a role of the nitrogen level (in particular the free α-amino nitrogen or FAN) of the juice in the formation of hydrogen sulfide was that by Vos and Gray (1979). Using primarily juices of one cultivar from one growing region, they found a general reduction in the levels of H_2S formed from around 100 μg/L at 100 mg/L FAN to essentially zero at 300 to 400 mg/L FAN. These authors proposed that sulfide formation was caused by hydrolysis of juice proteins by extracellular proteases produced by the yeast when the available amino nitrogen pool was low. The release of sulfide from the scavenged amino acids from the hydrolyzed protein would explain their results, even though no extracellular proteases have even been demonstrated in *Saccharomyces*. The authors were able to show that a bentonite addition and removal prior to fermentation lowered the amount of sulfide formed, but it also caused drawn out and incomplete fermentations (see Chapter 5 for additional discussion of the role of suspended solids and fining materials on fermentation). Additions of diammonium phosphate at levels of 160 mg N/L and 250 mg N/L were found also found to lower the sulfide formation in certain juices but these led to available nitrogen concentrations well above the 140 to 160 mg N/L generally considered adequate for normal fermentations. In the overall correlations presented, even at levels of 200 mg/L FAN, there is very large scatter among the data, with sulfide production ranging between 50 and 900 μg/L.

It is clear from this study that the FAN concentration alone is not the only factor responsible for the sulfide production, but rather there are secondary effects that vary widely in many juices. Other possible interpretations of these findings are that many of the juices used were deficient in pantothenic acid or pyridoxine, or that it is the proportions of certain amino acids within the FAN pool that are important in sulfide production.

d. *Presence of Sulfite and Strain Effects*

Recently there have been studies of the medium conditions that cause sulfide formation particularly in defined model juices (Eschenbruch 1978; Jiranek and Henschke 1991; Hewitson 1993; Giudici and Kunkee 1994). The first study suggested that hydrogen sulfide was produced when ammonia was depleted from the medium and bisulfite was present; however, this is not in line with most commercial fermentations in which ammonia is depleted within the first third of the fermentation and there is little if any bisulfite remaining either from addition or natural production. The second study found strain differences in the influence of bisulfite on the hydrogen sulfide production, even with yeast strains that were considered to be unable to produce hydrogen sulfide. The third and fourth studies showed formation of H_2S in nitrogen-deficient medium from the reduction of sulfate in the absence of sulfite.

e. *Vitamin Deficiencies*

The role of the vitamins, pantothenate, and pyridoxine, as requirements for the production of the coenzymes essential to methionine and cysteine synthesis was investigated by

Wainwright (1970, 1971). He classified several yeast strains according to whether they had an absolute requirement for pantothenate or whether they could synthesize it. The need for pantothenate has been determined for some common wine strains (Ough et al. 1989) but there are others in general use whose requirements for either pantothenate or pyridoxine are not known.

There continues to be a possible role of pantothenate deficiency in many commercial fermentations and experimental studies of hydrogen sulfide production. The addition of levels of pantothenate in the range 50 to 75 $\mu g/L$ to all experimental juices is recommended to eliminate any contributions of this kind.

f. Other Factors

There have also been a number of statistical studies of the amino acid composition of juices that have produced sulfides during fermentation, but there is no obvious correlation with individual or groups of amino acids. The effects of added threonine and methionine on hydrogen sulfide production found by Wainwright (1971) have not been seen in these correlations with problem juices over several seasons.

One major component which has received little attention is the peptide pool, in particular the tripeptide glutathione. Recent work in which glutathione was added to model juices (Park 1993) suggests a role of glutathione suppression of sulfide formation under certain conditions.

Another driving force for H_2S production may be the need to regenerate oxidized cofactors, NAD^+ or NADP. Sulfate can serve as a terminal electron acceptor in many organisms. Initially, high levels of SO_2 may lead to H_2S production because of the inhibition of acetaldehyde reduction. Amino acid, vitamin, metal ion content and SO_2 utilization are all factors which contribute to H_2S production. Sulfur dioxide can convert H_2S to S, which may precipitate out of the wine, only later to reform H_2S when conditions become favorable for reduction, unless the precipitate is removed. A very important determinant of H_2S production is the yeast strain itself. Some wine yeasts seem to be high H_2S producers depending upon sulfur source, for as yet undetermined reasons. Often the fastest fermenters produce more H_2S.

Complex sulfur-containing compounds such as dimethyl sulfide, methanethiol (methane thiol), ethanethiol (ethane thiol), dimethyldisulfide, and diethyl disulfide can also be produced as a consequence of yeast metabolism (Table 4-13). While the factors leading to the production of these components have not been thoroughly elucidated, metabolism of sulfur-containing amino acids has been implicated in their synthesis. If metal ions are present in high enough concentrations, under the appropriate conditions synthesis of the sulfur-containing components may occur chemically within the wine as opposed to biochemically within the cells. The reactions involving hydrogen sulfide and the thiols after they have been produced is discussed in more detail in Chapter 8.

L. ETHANOL TOLERANCE

We have mentioned that genetics of ethanol toxicity must be polyvalent, since, of the many research efforts to develop some sort of genotypic resistant strain, none has met with real success. Aquilera and Benitez (1985) have suggested that some 250 genes might be involved

Table 4-13. Sulfur and thiol compounds commonly found in defective wine.

Compound	Threshold of detection in wine ($\mu g/L$)
Hydrogen sulfide	< 1
Dimethyl sulfide	25
Dimethyl disulfide	29
Diethyl sulfide	0.92
Ethyl mercaptan	1.1

Source: From Goniak and Noble (1987); hydrogen sulfide value from MacRostie (1974).

in the control of ethanol tolerance in yeast. Nevertheless, yeasts do show some adaptive responses to the challenge of ethanol toxicity.

The most important response is that to the major toxic effect, the disruption in the membrane permeability and change in fluidity. The membrane integrity depends upon the complement of the survival factors, the sterols, and long-chain unsaturated fatty acids, which are formed only in the presence of molecular oxygen. Thus, yeast cells with high concentrations of these factors have greater ability to finish a wine fermentation rapidly and with completeness. That is part of the great success in the use of commercial available active dry wine yeasts as inocula, since they are grown under highly aerobic conditions and in low concentrations of glucose. That is, these cells have high concentrations of the survival factors, which can be distributed to the progeny formed during the six or seven generations of growth in a typical vinification (Section 6.1a). Survival factor formation is not subject to glucose inhibition, but the absence of glucose during the aerobic growth of the commercial cultures provides formation of other membraniac organelles in the cell, especially the mitochondria, which are also survival-factor-rich, and the factors therein can also be distributed to progeny after the switch to the fermentative anaerobic conditions. The ability for the survival factors to be formed in presence of glucose helps explain the standard procedures used in natural fermentations, at least in Europe, of rousing the grape juice several times a day immediately after the crushing and before the fermentation is evident. This stirring (aeration) provides the very much needed survival factors for the yeasts, which in these uninoculated fermentations must go though some 20 generations before full growth is obtained.

Many yeast workers have shown an increased incorporation of the survival factors, including saturated fatty acids of increased chain length, in the cell membranes in response to ethanol challenge (Beavan et al. 1982; Lafon-Lafourcade et al. 1977; Traverso-Rueda and Kunkee 1982). This increased complement of survival factors somehow overcomes the disruptive effect of the ethanol, tending to return the membranes to their original permeability and fluidity. Most of these experiments were done in rather low concentrations of ethanol, but Beavan et al. (1982) and Kunkee (1990) also found the response under winemaking conditions. Kunkee (1990) also found that wine yeast strains normally had higher complements of survival factors, as compared to nonwine strains; and that strains in both groups responded to the ethanol challenge, but that the response was greatest in the wine strains.

We have been careful to mention the *change* in fluidity, which accompanies the change in permeability, without identifying whether the fluidity is increased or decreased. The kind of fluidity change is somewhat controversial, and probably dependent upon the method of measurement. (See Kunkee and Bisson (1993) for selected references for the following technologies.) Magnetic resonance and fluorescence polarization have both been used to measure fluidity, defined as the restriction of the free lateral diffusion of membrane proteins in the fluid-mosaic bilayer of the membrane. Differential scanning calorimetry has also been used, with increased fluidity defined in relation to the disorder in the membrane. Further discussion on fluidity, with relation to the permeability in the membrane is given by Kunkee and Bisson (1993), who also pointed out that the response of mammalian cells to the disordering or fluidizing effects of ethanol may not be appropriate when applied to microorganisms.

Another mechanism implicated in ethanol tolerance is the cellular alcohol dehydrogenase (ADH) activity. In model wine fermentations, the highest ADH activities were found in those yeast strains which showed the fastest fermentation rates during the end phases of fermentation; that is, in those strains which were the most ethanol tolerant (Chin 1989; Kunkee 1990). Furthermore, the fermentation rates of the final phases of fermentation, over a spectrum of temperatures, showed a correlation between the temperatures of the fermentation and the specific activities of ADH measured at a fixed temperature (Massantini and Kunkee 1989). This again shows a difference between wine yeast strains and other yeast strains, and also a difference in their relative adaptive behaviors. The increased ADH activity at the end of the fermentation reflects some sort of increased metabolism, and may be related to the removal of acetaldehyde, itself a toxic product.

The adaptive behavior of yeast to ethanol response is also found in the relative resistance of the cells to ethanol *formed* during fermentation, in contrast to the high sensitivity of cells to ethanol *supplementation*. For example, in dessert wine production, the ethanol addition necessary to arrest the fermentation is less than that which brings about a natural arrest (Kunkee and Amerine 1968). Other workers, however, have found an opposite effect. Nagodawithana and Steinkraus (1976) and Novak et al. (1981) measured short-term metabolic rates of yeast and found them to be especially sensitive to ethanol produced by the yeast, as compared to the same amount of ethanol added. A resolution to this controversy is difficult because of the presence of fermentable sugars, which are also inhibitory, in the former example—and in every consideration of ethanol toxicity and tolerance under winemaking conditions. Moreover, the experimental time frame of the latter works may have been insufficient to allow for yeast adaptation.

M. FERMENTATION BOUQUET AND OTHER VOLATILE ESTERS

In general, yeast contribution to the overall flavor and aroma profile of a table wine is minimal or at least universal during fermentation. It is most important that the yeast strain conduct a clean fermentation, that is, not produce any negative characters detracting from wine quality. However, if white or pink juice is clarified and fermented by ordinary wine yeasts at low temperature and closely protected from air contact, a special fruity aroma reminiscent of Juicy Fruit chewing gum is found in the young wine. This is called fermentation bouquet (Singleton et al. 1975). This is a very attractive odor in young wines and could be quite salable in wines kept cold and purveyed to consumers directly at the winery or in nearby or closely supervised outlets. It is, however, very unstable and disappears rapidly at room temperature (Ramey and Ough 1980). This instability arises because the flavor is caused by volatile esters and the equilibria at the conditions and concentrations in wine favors hydrolysis. Our best evidence indicates that the special fruity odor is primarily due to a mixture of hexyl acetate, ethyl caproate, and isoamyl acetate in the ratio of about three to two to one (Fischer 1973). Odorwise, the hexyl acetate appears the most important, and isoamyl acetate the least imortant to the special fermentation bouquet. There is no apparent way, other than low temperature, to stabilize these esters in the wines. As little as a week at room temperature destroys fermentation bouquet. Therefore, interesting though it is, the procedure has limited practical value as a way of making especially attractive wines. Nevertheless, wines that have had fermentation bouquet remain, unless otherwise abused, as good as or better than their companion lots that never had fermentation bouquet, in our experience.

There is a grape component to the production of fermentation bouquet, since model systems and other media do not produce the same odor even if fermented identically. This is believed, at least in part, to be due to the production of hexyl aldehydes probably by lipoxidase as the grapes are crushed. This is a known reaction producing grassy or newly mown hay odors in crushed vegetable matter. This is further substantiated by the fact that the same type of odor and similar intensities are produced in all white juice musts tested regardless of grape variety. The yeasts reduce hexyl aldehyde to hexanol and then convert this alcohol to hexyl acetate. Hexanols are not normal products of yeast's fermentation of sugars.

Lower fermentation temperature, to about 15°C, encourages production of volatile esters by yeasts, but further lowering does not continue the trend (Killian and Ough 1979). This is thought to be predominantly a shift in the biosynthesis pattern by the yeasts, but prevention of hydrolysis is probably also a factor. Several widely employed wine-yeast strains have given similar qualities and intensities of fermentation bouquet in direct comparison, but differences among yeasts in ester synthesis are to be expected and are well known among various yeast genera. On the basis of adding back heat-treated grape solids to clarified must compared to nonclarified portions of the same must, the presence of grape solids appears to prevent accumulation of fermentation bouquet by hydrolyzing the esters as they form via esterase activity in the fine grape solids. The presence of air is known to inhibit ester production by yeasts.

The acetate esters of ethanol and the higher alcohols are often the volatiles providing the major aroma impact of freshly fermented white wines. The formation of the fermentation bouquet is little influenced by the cultivar involved or the yeast strain conducting the fermentation (Houtman et al. 1980; Houtman and Du Plessis 1981). There are, however, some strains that can produce significantly higher concentrations of the individual esters (Soles et al. 1982), although very high levels of some of these may not be desirable. Almost all of these esters are produced at levels well above their equilibrium levels that would be expected from the acetic acid and alcohol concentrations of the wine.

Whether or not these esters will be present in the wine at the time of consumption depends upon the level produced, the length and temperature of aging pre- and postbottling, and other factors affecting ester stability. Since acetate and ethanol are present in the highest concentrations during fermentation, esters of ethanol and acetate predominate, with ethyl acetate being the major species.

Esters can arise from different sources during yeast metabolism (Nordstrom 1962, 1963, 1965). Esters can be produced from the alcoholysis of acyl-CoA compounds (Figure 4-31), which may occur if fatty acid biosynthesis or degradation is interrupted in the cell and regeneration of free Coenzyme A is needed. Oxidative decarboxylations involving Coenzyme A can also lead to ester formation (Figure 4-31). Esters can be formed from the carbon skeletons of amino acids. Isoamyl acetate and ethyl 3-methylbutyrate can be formed from leucine following the scheme presented in Figure 4-31. Leucine is first deaminated and decarboxylated yielding an aldehyde. The aldehyde can be either reduced to an alcohol and react with acetyl-CoA to yield isoamyl acetate or be oxidized to a monocarboxylic acid, activated and bound to Coenzyme A in an ATP-requiring step, and then react with ethanol to form ethyl 3-methylbutyrate. In a general sense, acetyl-CoA can react with higher alcohols to yield the acetate esters and acyl-CoA compounds can react with ethanol to yield the ethanol esters. Small acyl chain esters are typically fruity or floral while longer acyl chain

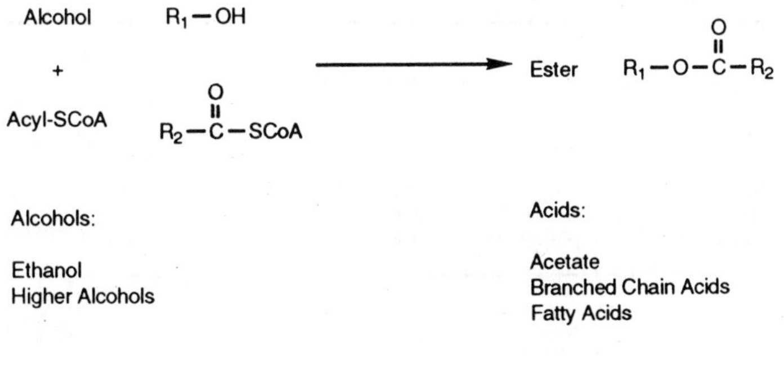

Fig. 4-31. Pathway of ester formation from amino acids.

esters are more sweaty or soap-like. If larger than a total carbon number of about 12, they are too low in volatility to have much odor effect.

The formation of the esters is influenced primarily by temperature as discussed above (Killian and Ough 1979), the amino nitrogen content (Vos et al. 1978; Bell et al. 1979; Ough and Lee 1981) of the juice, and the yeast strain employed (Soles et al. 1982). There is presumably a secondary effect due to a requirement of pantothenate as it affects the formation of acetyl Co-A, the acetate donor for the esterification. The early studies of Nordstrom (1962, 1963) proposed the pathway for the acetate ester formation in yeast and later studies of the reverse TCA pathway (Oura 1973) explained the link of the amino acids via alpha-keto glutarate and how acetyl Co-A would be produced (rather than consumed in the TCA cycle) under anaerobic fermentations conditions. The correlation of ester formation with amino nitrogen is probably a general result when a more specific one relating the concentrations of those amino acids which are catabolized through the reverse TCA pathway (that is arginine, glutamate, and glutamine). The sum of these acids usually forms the largest fraction of the amino acids consumed by yeast during fermentation and that is perhaps why the correlations exist.

Generally, total ester production is similar for strains of *Saccharomyces*, but the spectrum of esters produced can vary dramatically. Non-*Saccharomyces* or wild yeasts can produce significantly greater amounts of esters than does *Saccharomyces*. This is one explanation that is often given but not substantiated as to why natural fermentations might yield wines of greater complexity than inoculated ferments. Growth conditions also affect ester formation. Molecular oxygen is inhibitory to ester formation. The decreased ester production reported to occur at higher fermentation temperatures may not actually reflect decreased production but rather increased hydrolysis or loss of esters formed during fermentation (Table 4-14). Grape juice nutrient content may also impact ester levels. Ester formation is decreased in juices of very low nitrogen content, not surprising since amino acid carbon skeletons serve as precursors of esters. Conditions inhibiting fatty acid synthesis also limit ester production, confirming the central role of acyl-CoA in ester formation. The presence of unsaturated fatty acids in the grape juice can suppress ester synthesis, so grape juice composition is likewise an important factor. Some of the longer acyl chain esters are only found upon yeast cell autolysis, and may be important flavor contributors in sparkling wine production. This may also be important in wines with extended yeast lees contact (sur lies) (Chapter 6).

The physiological driving force for ester production remains obscure. These components could simply be end products of various metabolic pathways. They could be synthesized primarily as a means of regeneration of Coenzyme A or for cofactor, NADP, balancing. Since these esters serve as insect and animal attractants, the evolutionary selection for their production may have been dispersal of the yeast species.

Table 4-14. The first order hydrolysis rates of acetate esters in wine.

Ester	Pre-exponential factor (1/s)	Activation energy (kJ/mol)	Temperature coefficient %/C)
Isobutyl acetate	3530	62.0	9.0
Isoamyl acetate	61000	69.1	9.6
Hexyl acetate	4380	62.0	9.0
2-Phenethyl acetate	37.3	50.2	7.0

Source of data: Ramey and Ough (1980).

Yeasts are important in the overall vinous flavor of wines, although their contribution to all wines is grossly similar. That is, they confer the same spectrum and type of compounds to all wines. Early chromatographers showed that volative yeast products, in addition to ethanol, were major components of all fermented beverages.

While there certainly are variations in flavor components produced by yeast, we have not directly addressed in this section the role, if any, of specific yeast strains in the sensory character of the wines they produce. On the one hand, it has been said that any such effects are subliminal and/or short-lived — that there is no published hard evidence to show any real effect of yeast strain (Kunkee and Bisson 1993). On the other hand, there is anecdotal evidence aplenty for cellar workers, and others, that the yeast strain is important in this regard. Some research with Sauvignon blanc grapes indicates that transformation of materials in the grape juice by the yeast enzymes produce new and highly flavored materials, such as terpenes (Dubourdieu et al. 1988) or mercaptans (Dubourdieu et al. 1989, Dubourdieu et al. 1993); and that these enzymatic activities are yeast strain dependent. Furthermore, the nutritional complement of the juice is suggested to play a role; those juices with nutritional deficiencies may place the yeast under some sort of stress conditions known to effect the formation of end products —and the effect could well be yeast strain related. It was indicated above that there is a great variation in the amount of nutritional components in grape musts in California as compared to those in Europe. Thus, the discrepancies in the results on the effect of yeast strain may arise from the kinds of substrates, grape variety, and region, which have been used for these investigations (Kunkee and Vilas 1994). Nevertheless, until published evidence is presented involving verified replicate fermentations and stringent sensory analyses, any effect of wine yeast strain on flavor is disputable. Also, single mutational events or changes in gene dosage could affect the enzyme composition of the cells and impact the profile of compounds produced. Caution must be taken in extrapolation of data obtained with one strain in a particular juice.

N. REFERENCES

ACREE, T. E., E. P. SONOFF, and D. F. SPLITTSTOESSER. 1972. "Effect of yeast strain and type of sulfur compound on hydrogen sulfide production." *Am. J. Enol. Vitic.* 23:6–9.

ADAMS, A. M. 1960. "Yeasts in horticultural soils." In *1959-60 Report of the Horticultural Experiment Station and Products Laboratory*, pp. 79–82. Toronto. Ontario Department of Agriculture.

AGENBACH, W. A. 1977. "A study of must nitrogen content in relation to incomplete fermentations, yeast production and fermentation." *Proc. S. Afric. Soc. Enol. Vitic.* 66–87.

AIBA, S., and M. SHODA. 1969. "Reassessment of the product inhibition in alcoholic fermentation." *J. Ferm. Technol.* 47:790–794.

AIBA, S., M. SHODA, and M. NAGATANI. 1968. "Kinetics of product inhibition in alcohol fermentation." *Biotech. Bioeng.* 10:845–864.

AMERINE, M. A., H. W. BERG, R. E. KUNKEE, C. S. OUGH, V. L. SINGLETON, and A. D. WEBB. 1980. In *Technology of Winemaking*, 4th ed., Westport, CT, Avi Publishing Co.

AMERINE, M. A., and R. E. KUNKEE. 1968. "Microbiology of winemaking." *Ann. Rev. Microbiol.* 22:323–353.

AQUILERA, A., and T. BENITEZ. 1985. "Role of mitochondria in ethanol tolerance of *Saccharomyces cerevisiae*." *Arch. Microbiol.* 142:389–392.

AUGUSTYN, O. P. H., and J. L. F. KOCK. 1989. "Differentiation of yeast species, and strains within a species, by cellular fatty acid analysis. 1. Application of an adapted technique to differentiate between strains of *Saccharomyces cerevisiae*." *J. Microbiol. Meth.* 10:9–23.

ÄYRÄPÄÄ, T. 1973. "Studies on the formation of higher alcohols and esters by brewers' yeast." In, *Proceedings of the Third International Specialized Symposium on Yeasts*, H. Suomaleinen, Ed., pp. 31–45, Otaniemi/Helsinki.

BARTHOLOMEW, J. E., and T. MITTWER. 1950. "A simplified bacterial spore stain." *Stain Technol.* 25:153–156.

BEAVAN, M. J., C. CHARPENTIER, and A. H. ROSE. 1982. "Production and tolerance of ethanol in relation to phospholipid fatty-acyl composition of *Saccharomyces cerevisiae* NCYC 431." *J. Gen. Microbiol.* 128:1447–1455.

BECK, C., and H. K. VON MEYENBURG. 1968. "Enzyme pattern and aerobic growth of *Saccharomyces cerevisiae* under various degrees of glucose limitation." *J. Bacteriol.* 96:479–486.

BELIN, J.-M. 1972. "Recherches sur la répartition des levures à surface de la grappe de raisin." *Vitis* 11:135–145.

BELIN, J.-M., and P. HENRY. 1972. "Contribution à l'étude écologique des levures dans le vignoble. Répartition des levures à la surface du pédicelle et de la baie de raisin." *C. R. Acad. Sci.* Paris 274D:2318–2320.

BELL, A. A., C. S. OUGH, and W. M. KLIEWER. 1979. "Effects on must and wine composition, rates of fermentation and wine quality of nitrogen fertilization of *Vitis vinifera* var. Thompson Seedless grapevines." *Am. J. Enol. Vitic.* 30:124–129.

BISSON, L. F., and R. E. KUNKEE. 1991. "Microbial interactions during wine production." In *Mixed cultures in Biotechnology*, J. G. Zeikus and E. A. Johnson, Eds., pp. 37–68. New York: McGraw-Hill.

BISSON, L. F., and J. THORNER. 1982. "Mutations in the *PH080* gene confer permeability to 5'-mononucleotides in *Saccharomyces cerevisiae*." *Genetics* 102:341–359.

BLONDIN, B., and F. VEZINHET. 1988. "Identification de souches de levures oenologiques par leurs caryotypes obtenus en électrophorèse en champs plusès." *Rev. Fr. Oenol.* 28(115):7–11.

BOUIX, M., and J. Y. LEVEAU. 1983. "Electrophoretic study of the macromolecular compounds excreted by yeasts: Application to differentiation between strains of the same species." *Biotech. Bioeng.* 25:133–142.

BOULTON, R. 1979. "A kinetic model for the control of wine fermentations." *Biotech. Bioeng. Symp. Series*, No.9:167–177.

BOULTON, R. 1980. "Prediction of fermentation behavior by a kinetic model." *Am. J. Enol. Vitic.* 31:40–45.

BRENDEL, M., W. W. FATH, and W. LASKOWSKI. 1975. "Isolation and characterization of mutants of *Saccharomyces cerevisiae* able to grow after inhibition of DTMP synthesis." *Meth. Cell Biol.* 11:287–294.

BROWN, S. W., S. G. OLIVER, D. E. F. HARRISON, and R. C. RIGHELATO. 1981. "Ethanol inhibition of yeast growth and fermentation: differences in the magnitude and complexity of the effect." *Appl. Microbiol. Biotech.* 11:151–155.

BUSTURIA, A., and R. LAGUNAS. 1986. "Catabolite inactivation of the glucose transport system in *Saccharomyces cerevisiae*." *J. Gen. Micro.* 132:379–385.

CANTAGREL, R., P. SYMONDS, and J. CARLES. 1982. "Composition on acides amines du mout en fonction du cepage et de la technologie et son influence sur la quality du vin." *Sci. Aliment.* 2:109–142.

CARDOSO, H., and C. LEÃO. 1992. "Mechanisms underlying the low and high euthalpy death induced by short-chair monocarboxylic acids and ethanol in *Saccharomyces cerevisiae*." *Micro. Biotech.* 38:388–392.

CARLE, G. F., M. FRANK, and M. V. OLSON. 1986. "Electrophoretic separation of large DNA molecules by periodic inversion of the electric field." *Science* 232:65–68.

CARTWRIGHT, C. P., J.-R. JUROSZEK, M. J. BEAVAN, F. M. S. RUBY, S. M. F. DEMORIAS, and A. H. ROSE. 1986. "Ethanol dissipates the proton-motive force across the plasma membrane of *Saccharomyces cerevisiae*." *J. Gen. Micro.* 132:369–377.

CARTWRIGHT, C. P., F. J. VEAZEY, and A. H. ROSE. 1987. "Effect of ethanol on activity of the plasma membrane ATPase in and accumulation of glycine by *Saccharomyces cerevisiae*." *J. Gen. Microbiol.* 133:857–865.

CASEY, G. P., C. A. MAGNUS, and W. M. INGLEDEW. 1984. "High-gravity brewing: effects of nutrition on yeast composition fermentative ability and alcohol production." *Appl. Env. Micrbiol* 48:639–646.

CASTELLI, T. 1957. "Climate and agents of wine fermentation." *Am. J. Enol.* 8:149–156.

CASTOR, J. G. B., and T. E. ARCHER. 1956. "Amino acids in must and wines, proline, serine and threonine." *Am. J. Enol.* 7:19–25.

CHAPMAN, C., and W. BARTLEY. 1968. "The kinetics of enzyme changes in yeast under conditions that cause the loss of mitochondria." *Biochem. J.* 107:455–465.

CHATONNET, P., D. DUBOURDIEU, J.-N. BOIDRON, and V. LAVIGNE. 1993. "Synthesis of volatile phenols by *Saccharomyces cerevisiae* in wines." *J. Sci. Food Agric.* 62:191–202.

CHEREST, H., and Y. SURDIN-KERJAN. 1992. "Genetic analysis of a new mutation conferring cysteine anxotrophy in *Saccharomyces cerevisiae*: Updating of the sulfure metabolism pathway." *Genetics* 130:51–58.

CHIN, H.-W. 1989. "Relationship between the fermentation performances of various yeast strains and their alcohol dehydrogensase activities." M.S. thesis, Davis, CA: University of California.

CHU, G., D. VOLLRATH, and R. W. DAVIS. 1986. "Separation of large DNA molecules by contour-clamped homogeneous electric fields." *Science* 234:1582–1585.

CIRILLO, V. P. 1968. "Relationship between sugar structure and competition for the sugar transport system in baker's yeast." *J. Bacteriol.* 95:603–611.

COOPER, T. G. 1982a. "Nitrogen metabolism in *Saccharomyces cerevisiae*." In *The Molecular Biology of the Yeast Saccharomyces: Metabolism and Gene Expression*, J. N. Strathern, E. W. Jones, and J. R. Broach, Eds., pp. 39–100. Cold Spring Harbor, New York: Cold Spring Harbor Laboratory.

COOPER, T. G. 1982b. "Transport in *Saccharomyces cerevisiae*." In *The Molecular Biology of the Yeast Saccharomyces: Metabolism and Gene Expression*, J. N. Strathern, E. W. Jones, and J. R. Broach, Eds., pp. 399–462. Cold Spring Harbor, New York: Cold Spring Harbor Laboratory.

COOPER, T. G., and R. SUMRADA. 1975. "Urea transport in *Saccharomyces cerevisiae*." *J. Bacteriol.* 121:571–576.

COTTRELL, M., B. C. VILJOEN, J. L. F. KOCK, and P. M. LATEGAN. 1986. "The long-chain fatty acid compositions of species representing the genera *Saccharomyces*, *Schwanniomyces*, and *Lipomyces*." *J. Gen. Microbiol.* 132:2401–2403.

CRABTREE, H. G. 1929. "Observations on carbohydrate metabolism of tumors." *Biochem. J.* 23:536–545.

DE DEKEN, R. H. 1966. "The Crabtree effect: a regulatory system in yeast." *J. Gen. Microbiol.* 44:129–156.

DE MORA, S. J., R. ESCHENBRUCH, S. J. KNOWLES, and D. J. SPEDDING. 1986. "The formation of dimethyl sulfide during fermentation using a wine yeast." *Food Microbiol.* 3:27–32.

DEGRÉ, R., D. Y. THOMAS, J. ASH, K. MAILHIOT, A. MORIN, and C. DUBORD. 1989. "Wine yeast strains identification." *Am. J. Enol. Vitic.* 40:309–315.

DELFINI, D., and C. PARVEX. 1989. "Study on pH and total acidity variations during alcoholic fermentation. Importance of the ammoniacal salt added." *Riv. Vitic. Enol.* 42:43–56.

DELTEIL, D., and T. AIZAC. 1989. "Yeast inoculation techniques with a 'marked' yeast strain." *Pract. Winery Vineyard*, May/June:43–47.

DENIS, C. L., M. CIRIACY, and E. T. YOUNG. 1983. "MRNA levels for the fermentative alcohol dehydrogenase of *Saccharomyces cerevisiae* decrease upon growth on a non-fermentable carbon source." *J. Biol. Chem.* 258:1165–1171.

DICKINSON, J. R., and I. W. DAWES. 1992. "The catabolism of branch-chain amino acids occurs via 2-oxoacid dehydrogenase in *Saccharomyces cerevisiae*." *J. Gen. Microbiol.* 138:2029–2033.

DICKINSON, J. R., and V. NORTE. 1993. "A study of branched-chain amino acid aminotransferase and isolation of mutations affecting the catabolism of branched-chain amino acid in *Saccharomyces cerevisiae*." *FEBS* 326:29–32.

DOMBECK, K. M., and L. O. INGRAM. 1986. "Magnesium limitation and its role in apparent toxicity of ethanol during yeast fermentation." *Appl. Environ. Microbiol.* 52:975–981.

DRYSDALE, G. S., and G. H. FLEET. 1989. "The effect of acetic acid bacteria upon the growth and metabolism of yeasts during the fermentation of grape juice." *J. App. Bacteriol.* 67:471–481.

DUBOIS, E., and M. GRENSON. 1979. "Methylamine/ammonia uptake systems in *Saccharomyces cerevisiae*: Multiplicity and regulation." *Molec. Gen. Genetics* 175:67–76.

DUBOS, R. 1988. *Pasteur and Modern Science*. Madison, WI: Science Tech Publishers.

DUBOURDIEU, D., P. DARRIET, and P. CHATONNET. 1989. "Intervention of enzymatic systems of *Saccharomyces cerevisiae* on some precursors of grape aroma." Paper presented at XIIth International Symposium Specialized on Yeast, September 18–22 1989 at Université Catholique de Louvain, Belgium.

DUBOURDIEU, D., P. DARRIET, and V. LAVIGNE. 1993. "Investigations on the varietal aroma of Sauvignon wines." *10th International Oenological Symposium*, Montreux, May 3–5 1993, pp. 258–267. Breisach: Internationale Interessengemeinschaft für Kellertechnik u. Betriebsführung.

DUBOURDIEU, D., P. DARRIET, C. OLLIVIER, J.-N. BOIDRON, and P. RIBÉREAU-GAYON. 1988. "Rôle de la levure Saccharomyces cerevisiae dans l'hyrolyse enzymatique des hétérosides terpéniques du jus de raisin." *C. R. Acad. Sci.* Paris Ser III 306:489–493.

DUBOURDIEU, D., A. SOKOL, J. ZUCCA, P. THALOUARN, A. DATTEE, and M. AIGLE. 1987. "Identification des souches de levures isolées de vins par analyse de leur ADN mitochondrial." *Conn. Vigne Vin* 21:267–278.

DUNTZE, W., D. NEUMANN, J. M. GANCEDO, W. ATZPODIEN, and H. HOLZER. 1969. "Studies on the regulation and localization of the glyoxylate cycle enzymes in *Saccharomyces cerevisiae.*" *Eur. J. Biochem.* 10:83–89.

EGBOSIMBA, E. E., E. LINUS, C. OKAFOR, and J. C. SLAUGHTER. 1988. "Control of ammonia uptake from malt extract medium by *Saccharomyces cerevisiae.*" *J. Inst. Brewing* 94:249–252.

EGBOSIMBA, E. E., and J. C. SLAUGHTER. 1987. "The influence of ammonium permease activity and carbon source on the uptake of ammonium from simple defined media by *Saccharomyces cerevisiae.*" *J. Gen. Micro.* 133:375–379.

EL HALIOU, N., D. PICQUE, and G. CORRIEU. 1987. "Mesures physiques permettant le suivi biologique de la fermentation alcoolique en oenologie." *Sci. Alim.* 7:241–265.

ELSKENS, M. T., C. J. JASPERS, and M. J. PENNINCKX. 1991. "Glutathione as an endogenous sulphur source in the yeast *Saccharomyces cerevisiae.*" *J. Gen. Micro.* 137:637–644.

ESCHENBRUCH, R. 1978. "Sulphide formation by wine yeasts." *Proc. 5th Intl. Oenol. Symp*, pp. 267–273. Auckland, New Zealand.

ESCHENBRUCH, R., and P. BONISH. 1976. "Production of sulphite and sulphide by low- and high-sulphite forming yeasts." *Arch. Microbiol.* 107:299–302.

ESCHENBRUCH, R., S. J. DE MORA, S. J. KNOWLES, W. K. LEONARD, T. FORRESTER, AND D. J. SPEDDING. 1986. "The formation of volatile sulphur compounds in unclarified grape juice." *Vitis* 25:53–57.

ESPOSITO, R. E., and S. KLAPHOLZ. 1981. "Meiosis and ascospore development." In *The Molecular Biology of the Yeast Saccharomyces, Life Cycle and Inheritance*, J. N. Strathern, E. W. Jones, J. R. Broach, Eds., pp. 211–287. Cold Spring Harbor, New York: Cold Spring Harbor Laboratory.

FAMUYIWA, O. O., and C. S. OUGH. 1991. "Modification of acid urease activity by fluoride ions and malic acid in wines." *Am. J. Enol. Vitic.* 42:79–80.

FERRERAS, J. M., R. IGLESIAS, and T. GIRBES. 1989. "Effect of the chronic ethanol action on the activity on the general amino-acid permease from *Saccharomyces cerevisiae* var. *ellipsoideus.*" *Biochimica et Biophysica Acta* 979:375–377.

FISCHER, G. 1973. "Studies on fermentation bouquet in white table wines." M.S. thesis, Davis, CA: University of California.

GARDINER, K., and D. PATTERSON. 1988. "Transverse alternating electrophoresis." *Nature* 331: 371–372.

GARRETT, J. M. 1989. "Characterization of *AAT1*: A gene involved in the regulation of amino acid transport in *Saccharomyces cerevisiae.*" *J. Gen. Micro.* 135:2429–2437.

GIUDICI, P., and R. E. KUNKEE. 1994. "The effect of nitrogen deficiency and sulfur-containing amino acids on the reduction of sulfate to hydrogen sulfide by wine yeast." *Am. J. Enol. Vitic.* 45:107–112.

GOLDSTEIN, D. 1987. "Ethanol-induced adaptation in biological membranes." *Ann. N. Y. Acad. Sci.* 492:103:111.

GONIAK, O. J., and A. C. NOBLE. 1987. "Sensory study of selected volatile sulfur compounds in white wine." *Am. J. Enol. Vitic.* 38:223–227.

GRENSON, M. 1969. "The utilization of exogenous pyrimidines and the recycling of uridine-5'-phosphate derivatives in *Saccharomyces cerevisiae,* as studied by means of mutants affected in pyrimidine uptake and metabolism." *Euro. J. Biochem.* 11:249–260.

GRENSON, M., M. MOUSSET, J. M. WIAME, and J. BECHET. 1966. "Multiplicity of the amino acid permeases in *Saccharomyces cerevisiae.* I. Evidence for a specific arginine-transporting system." *Biochimica et Biophysica Acta* 127:325–338.

GUBLER, W. D. 1992. "Grape powdery mildew." *Practical Winery and Vineyard.* Jan/Feb:12–16.

GUYMON, J. F. 1972. "Higher alcohols in beverage brandy: Feasibility of control of levels." *Wines and Vines* 53:37–40.

GUYMON, J. F., and J. E. HEITZ. 1952. "The fusel oil content of California wines." *Food Technol.* 6:359–362.

GUYMON, J. F., J. L. INGRAHAM, and E. A. CROWELL. 1961. "The formation of *n*-propyl alcohol by

Saccharomyces cerevisiae." *Arch. Biochem. Biophys.* 95:163–168.

HALLET, J. N., B. CRANEGUY, J. ZUCCA, and A. POULARD. 1988. "Caracterisation de differentes souches industrielles de levures oenologiques par les profils de restriction de leur ADN mitochondrial." *Prog. Agric. Vitic.* 105:328–333.

HAMMOND, J. R. M. 1993. "Brewer's yeasts." In *The Yeasts*, 2nd ed., Vol. 5, A. H. Rose and J. S. Harrison, Eds., pp. 7–67. London: Academic Press.

HAWKSWORTH, D. L., B. C. SUTTON, and G. C. AINSWORTH. 1983. *Ainsworth & Bisby's Dictionary of the Fungi (Including the Lichens)*, 7th ed. Kew, Surrey:Commonwealth Mycological Institute.

HENRY, S. A. 1982. "The membrane lipids of yeast: biochemical and genetic studies." In *The Molecular Biology of the Yeast Saccharomyces: Metabolism and Gene Expression*, J. N. Stratern, E. N. Jones, and J. R. Broach, eds., pp. 101–158. Cold Spring Harbor, New York: Cold Spring Harbor Laboratory.

HENSCHKE P. A., and V. JIRANEK. 1991. "Hydrogen sulfide formation during fermentation: Effects of nitrogen composition in model grape musts." In *International Nitrogen Symposium on Grapes and Wine*, J. M. Rantz, ed. Davis, CA: American Society for Enology and Viticulture.

HEWITSON, D. 1993. "Relationships between ammonium ion availability and hydrogen sulfide formation by Saccharomyces cerevisiae." M.S. thesis, Davis, CA: University of California.

HOLZER, H. 1961. "Regulation of carbohydrate metabolism by enzyme competition." *Cold Spring Harbor Sym. Quan. Biol.* 26:277–288.

HORAK, J. 1986. "Amino acid transport in eucaryotic microorganisms." *Biochimica et Biophysica Acta* 864:223–256.

HOUTMAN, A. C., and C. S. DU PLESSIS. 1981. "The effect of juice clarity and several conditions promoting yeast growth or fermentation rate, the production of aroma components and wine quality." *S. Afric. J. Enol. Vitic.* 2:71–81.

HOUTMAN, A. C., J. MARAIS, and C. S. DU PLESSIS. 1980. "The possibilities of applying present-day knowledge of wine aroma components: Influence of several juice factors on fermentation rate and ester production during fermentation." *S. Afric. J. Enol. Vitic.* 1:27–33.

ILAGAN, R. D. 1979. "Studies on the Sporulation of *Dekkera.*" M.S. thesis, Davis, CA: University of California.

INGLEDEW, W. M. 1993. "Yeasts for production of fuel ethanol." In, *The Yeasts*, 2nd ed., vol. 5, A. H. Rose and J. S. Harrison, Eds. pp. 245–291. London: Academic Press.

INGRAHAM, J. L., and J. F. GUYMON. 1960. "The formation of higher aliphatic alcohols by mutant strains of *Saccharomyces cerevisiae.*" *Archives Biochem. and Biophys.* 88:157–166.

INGRAM, L. O., and T. M. BUTTKE. 1984. "Effects of alcohol on microorganisms." *Adv. Microbial Physiol.* 25:253–300.

JAZWINSKI, S. M. 1993. "Genes of youth: Genetics of aging in baker's yeast." *ASM News* 59:172–178.

JIMÉNEZ, J., and N. VAN UDEN. 1985. "Use of extracellular acidification for the rapid testing of alcohol tolerance in yeast." *Biotech. Bioeng.* 27:1596–1598.

JIRANEK V., and P. A. HENSCHKE. 1991. "Assimilable nitrogen: Regulator of hydrogen sulfide production during fermentation." *Aust. Grape. & Wine* (325):27–30.

JIRANEK, V., P. LANGRIDGE, and P. A. HENSCHKE. 1991. "Yeast nitrogen demand: Selection criterion for wine yeasts for fermenting low nitrogen musts." pp. 266–269. In *Proceedings of the International Symposium on Nitrogen in Grapes and Wine*, Davis, CA: American Society for Enology and Viticulture.

JOHNSTON, J. 1983. "Substrate Preference in Wine Yeast." M.S. thesis, Davis, CA: University of California.

JONES, M., and J. S. PIERCE. 1964. "Adsorption of amino acids from wort by yeasts." *J. Inst. Brewing* 70:307–315.

JONES, R. S., and C. S. OUGH. 1985. "Variations in the percent ethanol V/V per °Brix conversions of wines from different climatic regions." *Am. J. Enol. Vitic.* 36:268–270.

JOST, P., and A. PIENDL. 1975. "Technological influences on the formation of acetate during fermentation." *J. Am. Soc. Brew. Chem.* 34:31–37.

JUROSZEK, J. R., O. RAIMBAULT, M. FEUILLAT, and C. CHARPENTIER. 1987. "A new method for determination of ethanol tolerance in vinification yeast: Measurement of glucose-induced proton movements." *Am. J. Enol. Vitic.* 38:336–341.

KALMOKOFF, M. L., and W. M. INGLEDEW. 1985. "Evaluation of ethanol tolerance in selected *Saccharomyces* strains." *J. Am. Soc. Brew. Chem.* 43:189–196.

KILLIAN E., and C. S. OUGH. 1979. "Fermentation esters—Formation and retention as affected by fermentation temperature." *Am. J. Enol. Vitic.* 30:301–305.

KIRSOP, B. H. 1982. "Developments in beer fermentation." *Top. Enzyme. Ferment. Biotechnol.* 6:79–131.

KITAMOTO, K., K. YOSHIZAWA, Y. OHSUMI, and Y. ANRAKU. 1988. "Dynamic aspects of vacuolar and cytosolic amino acid pools of *Saccharomyces cerevisiae.*" *J. Bacteriol.* 170:2683–2686.

KODAMA, K. 1993. "Saké-brewing yeasts." In *The Yeasts*, 2nd ed., Vol. 5, A. H. Rose and J. S. Harrison, Eds., pp. 129–168. London: Academic Press.

KOSHINSKY, H. A., R. H. COSBY, and G. G. KHACHATOURIANS. 1992. "Effects of T-2 toxin on ethanol production by *Saccharomyces cerevisiae.*" *Biotech. App. Biochem.* 16:275–286.

KOTYK, A. 1967. "Properties of the sugar carrier in baker's yeast. II. Specificity of transport." *Folia Microbiologia* 12:121–31.

KRAUS, J. K., G. REED, and J. C. VILLETTAZ. 1983. "Levures sèches actives de vinification 1re partie: fabrication et caractéristiques." *Conn. Vigne Vin.* 17:93–103.

KRAUS, J. K., G. REED, and J. C. VILLETTAZ. 1984. "Levures sèches actives de vinification 2e partie et fin: utilisation et évaluation." *Conn. Vigne Vin.* 18:1–26.

KREGER-VAN RIJ, N. J. W. 1984. *The Yeasts, A Taxonomic Study*. Amsterdam: Elsevier Science Publishers.

KUNKEE, R. E. 1984. "Selection and modification of yeasts and lactic acid bacteria for wine fermentation." *Food Microbiol.* 1:315–332.

KUNKEE, R. E. 1990. "Some relationships between the strain of wine yeast and its tolerance to ethanol or to other products of alcoholic fermentation." In *Actualities OEnologiques 89*, P. Ribéreau-Gayon and A. Lonvaud, Eds., pp. 238–242. Paris: Dunod.

KUNKEE, R. E. 1991. "Relationship between nitrogen content of must and sluggish fermentation." In *International Nitrogen Symposium on Grapes and Wine*, J. M. Rantz, Ed., pp. 148–155. Davis, CA: American Society for Enology and Viticulture.

KUNKEE, R. E., and M. A. AMERINE. 1968. "Sugar and alcohol stabilization of yeast in sweet wine." *Appl. Micro.* 16:1067–1075.

KUNKEE, R. E., and M. A. AMERINE. 1970. "Yeasts in wine-making." In *The Yeasts*, Vol. 3, A. H. Rose, and J. S. Harrison, Eds., pp. 50–71. London: Academic Press.

KUNKEE, R. E., and L. F. BISSON. 1993. "Wine-making yeasts." In *The Yeasts*, 2nd ed., Vol. 5, A. H. Rose and J. S. Harrison, Eds., pp. 69–127. London: Academic Press.

KUNKEE, R. E., J. F. GUYMON, and E. A. CROWELL. 1966. "Formation of n-propyl alcohol by cell-free extracts of *Saccharomyces cerevisiae.*" *J. Inst. Brew.* 72:530–536.

KUNKEE, R. E., J. F. GUYMON, and E. A. CROWELL. 1972. "Studies on control of higher alcohol formation by yeasts through metabolic inhibition." *1st Specialized International Symposium on Yeasts*, A. Kockova-Kratochivilova and E. Minarik. Eds., Bratislava, Slovakia: Publishing House of the Slovak Academy of Sciences.

KUNKEE, R. E., S. R. SNOW, and C. ROUS. 1983. "Method for reducing fusel oil in alcoholic beverages and yeast strain useful in that method." U.S. Patent 4,374,859.

KUNKEE, R. E., and M. R. VILAS. 1994. "Toward a better understanding of the relationship between yeast strain and flavor production during vinifications: Flavor effects in vinifications of a nondistinct variety of grapes by several strains of wine yeast." *Vitic. Enol. Sci.* 49:46–50.

KURTZMAN, C. P. 1973. "Formation of hyphae and chlamydospores by *Cryptococcus laurentii.*" *Mycologia* 65:388–395.

LAFON-LAFOURCADE, S., F. LARUE, P. BRÉCHOT, and P. RIBÉREAU-GAYON. 1977. "Steroids survival factors of yeasts during the process of alcoholic fermentation of grape must." *Compt. Rend. Acad. Sci.* 284D, 1939–1942.

LAFON-LAFOURCADE, S., F. LARUE, and P. RIBÉREAU-GAYON. 1979. "Evidence for the existence of survival factors as an explanation for some peculiarities of yeast growth especially in grape must of high sugar concentration." *Appl. Environ. Microbiol.* 38:1069–1073.

LAGUNAS, R. 1979. "Energetic irrelevance of aerobiosis for *S. cerevisiae* growing on sugars." *Mol. Cell. Biochem.* 27, 139–148.

LAGUNAS, R. 1981. "Is *Saccharomyces cerevisiae* a typical facultative 'anaerobe?'" *Trends Biochem. Sci* (Pers. Ed) 6:201–203.

LAGUNAS, R., C. DOMINGUEZ, A. BUSTURIA, and M. J. SAEZ. 1982. "Mechanisms of appearance of the Pasteur effect in *Saccharomyces cerevisiae*. Inactivation of the sugar transport systems." *J. Bacteriol.* 152:19–25.

LARGE, P. J. 1986. "Degradation of organic nitrogen compounds by yeasts." *Yeast* 2:1–34.

LEÃO, C., and N. VAN UDEN. 1984a. "Effect of ethanol and other alkanols on the general amino acid permease of *Saccharomyces cerevisiae*." *Biotech. Bioeng*. 26:403–405.

LEÃO, C., and N. VAN UDEN. 1984b. "Effects of ethanol and other alakanols on passive proton influx in the yeast *Saccharomyces cerevisiae*." *Biochim. Biophys. Acta* 774:43–48.

LEÃO, C., and N. VAN UDEN. 1985. "Effects of ethanol and other alkanols on the temperature relations of glucose transport and fermentation in *Saccharomyces cerevisiae*." *App. Microbiol. Biotechnol.* 22:359–363.

LEE. S. O., and R. E. KUNKEE. 1988. "Relationship between yeast strain and production or uptake of medium chain fatty acids during fermentation." *1988 Technical Abstracts*, p. 10. Annual Meeting, American Society for Enology and Viticulture, June 22–24 1988, Reno, Nevada.

LEWIS, M. J., and H. J. PHAFF. 1964. "Release of nitrogenous substances by brewer's yeast. III. Shock excretion of amino acids." *J. Bacteriol.* 87:1390–1396.

LODDER, J. 1970. *The Yeasts, A Taxonomic Study*. Amsterdam: North-Holland Publishing Company.

LODDER, J., and N. J. W. KREGER-VAN RIJ. 1952. *The Yeasts A Taxonomic Study*. Amsterdam: North-Holland Publishing Company.

MACROSTIE, S. W. 1974. "Electrode measurement of hydrogen sulfide in wine." M.S. thesis, Davis, CA: University of California.

MACY, J., and M. W. MILLER. 1983. "Anaerobic growth of *Saccharomyces cerevisiae* in the absence of oleic acid and ergosterol?" *Arch. Microbiol.* 134:64–67.

MALFEITO-FERREIRA, M., J. P. MILLER-GUERRA, and V. LOUREIRO. 1990. "Proton extrusion as an indicator of the adaptive state of yeast starters for the continuous production of sparkling wines." *Am. J. Enol. Vitic.* 41:219–222.

MALFEITO-FERREIRA, M., A. ST. AUBYN, and V. LOUREIRO. 1989. "Rapid testing to differentiate between fermenting and spoilage yeasts in wine." *Yeast* 5 (Spec. Issue), S47-S51.

MARSH, G. L. 1958. "Alcohol yield: Factors and methods." *Am. J. Enol.* 9:53–58.

MARTINI, A., and A. V. MARTINI. 1990. "Grape must fermentation—past and present." In *Yeast Technology*, J. F. T. Spencer and D. M. Spencer, Eds., pp. 105–123. Berlin: Springer-Verlag.

MASSANTINI, R., and R. E. KUNKEE. 1989. "Influence of temperature on alcohol dehydrogenase in yeast during vinification." *Yeasts* 5:S201–S205.

MCCANN, J., E. CHOI, E. YAMASAKI, and B. N. AMES. 1975. "Detection of carcinogens as mutagens in the Salmonella/microsome test: assay of 300 chemicals." *Proc. Nat. Acad. Sci. USA.* 72:5135–5139.

MCCUSKER, J. H., D. S. PERLIN, and J. E. HABER. 1987. "Pleiotropic plasma membrane ATPase mutations of *Saccharomyces cerevisiae*." *Molec. Cell. Biol.* 7:4082–4088.

MESSENGUY, F. 1987. "Multiplicity of regulatory mechanisms controlling amino acid biosynthesis in *Saccharomyces cerevisiae*." *Microbiol. Sciences* 4:150–153.

MIDDLEHOVEN, W. J. 1964. "The pathway of arginine breakdown in *Saccharomyces cerevisiae*." *Biochim. Biophys. Acta* 93:650–652.

MIDDLEHOVEN, W. J., J. VAN EUK, R. VAN RENESSE, and J. M. BLIJHAM. 1978. "A mutant of *Saccharomyces cerevisiae* lacking catabolic NAD^+-specific glutamate dehydrogenase." *Antonie van Leeuwen.* 44:311–320.

MIRVISH, S. S. 1968. "The carcinogenic action and metabolism of urethan and N-hydroxyurethan." *Adv. Cancer Res.* 11:1–42.

MOLAN, P. S., M. EDWARDS, and R. ESCHENBRUCH. 1982. "Foaming in wine making. II: Separation and partial characterization of foam inducing proteins excreted by pure culture wine yeasts." *Eur. J. Appl. Microbiol. Biotechnol.* 16:110–113.

MONK, P. R. 1986. "Formation, utilization and excretion of hydrogen sulphide by wine yeast." *Aust. N.Z. Wine Ind. J.* 1:10–16.

MONK, P. R., D. HOOK, and B. M. FREEMAN. 1986. "Amino acid metabolism by yeasts." *Proceedings of the Sixth Australian Wine Industry Technical Conference*, pp. 129–133.

MONOD, J. 1949. "The growth of bacterial cultures." *Ann. Rev. Microbiol.* 3: 371–394.

MONTEIRO, F. F., and L. F. BISSON. 1991a. "Amino acid utilization and urea formation during vinification." *Am. J. Enol. Vitic.* 42:199–208.

MONTEIRO, F. F., and L. F. BISSON. 1991b. "Biological assay of nitrogen content of grape juice and prediction of sluggish fermentations." *Am. J. Enol. Vitic.* 42:47–57.

MONTEIRO, F. F., and L. F. BISSON. 1992a. "Nitrogen supplementation of grape juice. I. Effect on amino acid utilization during fermentation." *Am. J. Enol. Vitic.* 43:1–10.

MONTEIRO, F. F., and L. F. BISSON. 1992b. "Nitrogen supplementation of grape juice. II. Effect on amino acid and urea release following fermentation." *Am. J. Enol. Vitic.* 43:11–17.

MONTEIRO, F. F., and L. F. BISSON. 1992c. "Utilization of adenine by yeast during grape juice fermentation and investigation of the possible role of adenine as a precursor of urea." *Am. J. Enol. Vitic.* 43:18–22.

MONTEIRO, F. F., E. K. TROUSDALE, and L. F. BISSON. 1989. "Ethyl carbamate formation in wine: Use of radioactively labeled precursors to demonstrate the involvement of urea." *Am. J. Enol. Vitic.* 40:1–8.

MÜLLER-SPÄTH, V. H., N. MOSCHTERT, and G. SCHÄFER. 1978. "Beobachtungen bei der weinbereitung." *Die Weinwirt.* 114:1084–1089.

MÜLLER-THURGAU, H. 1889. "Ueber die Vergährung des traubenmostes durch zugesetzte Hefe." *Weinbau Weinhandel* 7:477–478.

NABAIS, R. C., I. SÁ-CORREIA, C. A. VIEGAS, and J. M. NOVAIS. 1988. "Influence of calcium ion on ethanol fermentation by yeasts." *Appl. Environ. Microbiol.* 54:2439–2446.

NAGODAWITHANA, T. W., and K. H. STEINKRAUS. 1976. "Influence of the rate of ethanol production and accumulation on the viability of *Saccharomyces cerevisiae* in rapid fermentation." *Appl. Envir. Microbiol.* 31:158–162.

NAVARRO, J. M., and G. DURAND. 1978. "Alcoholic fermentation: Effect of temperature on ethanol accumulation in yeast cells." *Ann. Microbiol.* 129B:215–224.

NESS, F., F. LAVALLEÉ, D. DUBOURDIEU, M. AIGLE, and L. DULAU. 1993. "Identification of yeast strains using the polymerase chain reaction." *J. Sci. Food Agric.* 62:89–94.

NEUBERG, C. 1946. "The biochemistry of yeast." *Ann. Rev. Biochem.* 15:435–474.

NOBLE, A. C., and G. F. BURSICK. 1984. "The contribution of glycerol to perceived viscosity and sweetness in white wine." *Am. J. Enol. Vitic.* 35:110–112.

NORDSTROM, K. 1962. "Formation of ethyl acetate in fermentation with brewer's yeast. III. Participation of coenzyme A." *J. Inst. Brew.* 68:398–407.

NORDSTROM, K. 1963. "Formation of ethyl acetate in fermentation with brewer's yeast. IV. Metabolism of acetyl-coenzyme A." *J. Inst. Brew.* 69:142–153.

NORDSTROM, K. 1965. "Possible control of volatile ester formation in brewing." *Proc. Euro. Brew. Conv.* 10th Congress, Stockholm, Sweden, pp. 195–208.

NOVAK, M., P. STREHAIANO, M. MORENO, and G. GOMA. 1981. "Alcoholic fermentation: On the inhibitory effect of ethanol." *Biotech. Bioeng.* 23:201–211.

NYKANEN, L. 1986. "Formation and occurrence of flavor compounds in wine and distilled alcoholic beverages." *Am. J. Enol. Vitic.* 37:86–96.

OUGH, C. S., and M. A. AMERINE. 1963. "Regional, varietal and type influences on the degree Brix and alcohol relationship of grapes musts and wines." *Hilgardia* 34:585–599.

OUGH, C. S., and A. A. BELL. 1980. "Effects of nitrogen fertilization of grapevines on amino acid metabolism and higher-alcohol formation during grape juice fermentation." *Am. J. Enol. Vitic.* 31:12–123.

OUGH, C. S., E. A. CROWELL, and R. B. GUTLOVE. 1988a. "Carbamyl compounds reactions with ethanol." *Am. J. Enol. Vitic.* 39:239–242.

OUGH, C. S., E. A. CROWELL, and L. A. MOONEY. 1988b. "Formation of ethyl carbamate precursors during grape juice (Chardonnay) fermentation. I. Effects of fortification on intracellular and extracellular precursors." *Am. J. Enol. Vitic.* 39:243–249.

OUGH, C. S., M. DAVENPORT, and K. JOSEPH. 1989. "Effects of certain vitamins on growth and fermentation rate of several commercial active dry wine yeasts." *Am. J. Enol. Vitic.* 40:208–213.

OUGH, C. S., Z. HUANG, D. AN, and D. STEVENS. 1991. "Amino acid uptake by four commercial yeasts at two different temperatures of growth and fermentation: Effects on urea excretion and reabsorption." *Am. J. Enol. Vitic.* 42:26–40.

OUGH, C. S., and T. H. LEE. 1981. "Effect of vineyard nitrogen fertilization level on the formation of some fermentation esters." *Am. J. Enol. Vitic.* 32:125–127.

OUGH, C. S., D. STEVENS, T. SENDOVSKI, Z. HUANG, and D. AN. 1990. "Factors contributing to urea formation in commercially fermented wines." *Am. J. Enol. Vitic.* 41:68–73.

OURA, E. 1973. "Some aspects of the growth of baker's yeast." *Proc. 3rd Intl. Spec. Symp. on Yeast.* Helsinki, Finland, Part II, p. 215–230.

PAMMENT, N. B. 1989. "Overall kinetics and mathematical modeling of ethanol inhibition in yeasts." In, *Alcohol Toxicity in Yeast and Bacteria*, N. van Uden, Ed., pp. 1-75. Boca Raton, FL: CRC Press.

PARK, S. K. 1993. "Factors affecting formation of volatile sulfur compounds in wine." PhD thesis, Davis, CA: University of California.

PARLEBAS, N., and M. R. CHEVALLIER. 1977. "Genetic studies of the pyrimidine permeases from *Saccharomyces cerevisiae*: Lack of intragenic complementation." *Molec. Gen. Genetics* 154:199–202.

PASTEUR, L. 1855. "Mémoire sur l'alcool amylique." *Compt. Rend.* 41:296–300.

PENA, A., G. CINCO, A. GOMEZ-PUYON, and M. TUENA. 1972. "Effect of the pH of the incubation medium on glycolysis and respiration in *Saccharomyces cerevisiae*." *Arch. Biochem. Biophys.* 153:413–425.

PENA, A., J. P. PARDO, and J. RAMIREZ. 1987. "Early metabolic effects and mechanism of ammonium ion transport in yeast." *Arch. Biochem. Biophys.* 253:431–438.

PETERING, J. E., P. A. HENSCHKE, and P. LANGRIDGE. 1991. "The *Escherichia coli* ß-glucuronidase gene as a marker for *Saccharomyces* yeast strain identification." *Am. J. Enol. Vitic.* 42:6–12.

PHAFF, H. J., M. N. MILLER, and E. M. MRAK. 1978. *The Life of Yeasts*, 2nd ed. Cambridge, MA: Harvard University Press.

PIERCE, J. S. 1970. "Institute of brewing: Analysis committee measurement of yeast viability." *Inst. Brew J. London.* 76:442–443.

PIERCE, J. S. 1982. "The Margaret Jones Memorial Lecture: Amino acids in malting and brewing." *J. Inst. Brewing* 88:228–233.

POLAKIS, E. S., and W. BARTLEY. 1965. "Changes in the enzyme activities of *Saccharomyces cerevisiae* during aerobic growth on different carbon sources." *Biochem. J.* 97:284–297.

POLAKIS, E. S., W. BARTLEY, and G. A. MEEK. 1965. "Changes in the respiratory enzymes during the aerobic growth of yeast on different carbon sources." *Biochem J.* 97:298–302.

POSTMA, E., C. VERDUYN, W. A. SCHEFFERS, and J. P. VAN DIJKEN. 1989. "Enzymatic analysis of the Crabtree effect in glucose-limited chemostat cultures of *Saccharomyces cerevisiae*." *App. Environ. Micro.* 55:468–477.

POUND, A. W. 1967. "Initiation of skin tumors in mice by homologs and N-substituted derivatives of ethyl carbamate." *Aust. J. Exp. Bio. Med. Sci.* 45:507–516.

RADLER, F. 1992. "Yeasts—Metabolism of organic acids." In *Wine Microbiology and Biotechnology*, G. H. Fleet, Ed., pp. 165–182. Camberwell, Victoria, Australia: Harwood Academic Publishers.

RADLER, F., and E. FUCK. 1970. "Conversion of L-malic acid during Saccharomyces cerevisiae fermentation." *Experientia* 26:731.

RAMEY, D. D., and C. S. OUGH. 1980. "Volatile ester hydrolysis on formation during storage of model solutions and wines." *J. Agric. Food Chem.* 28:928–934.

RANKINE, B. C. 1963. "Nature, origin and prevention of hydrogen sulphide aroma in wines." *J. Sci. Food Agric.* 14:79–91.

RANKINE, B. C. 1964. "Hydrogen sulphide production by yeasts." *J. Sci. Food Agric.* 15:872–877.

RANKINE, B. C. 1966. "Decomposition of L-malic acid by wine yeasts." *J. Sci. Food Agric.* 17:312–316.

RANKINE, B. C. 1967. "Formation of higher alcohols by wine yeasts, and relationship to taste thresholds." *J. Sci. Food Agric.* 18:584–589.

RAPP, G. 1975. "Studies on the biosynthesis of fermentation amyl alcohol." *Proc. 4th Intl. Oenol. Symp.*, Valencia, Spain, pp. 394–411.

REAZIN, G., H. SCALES, and A. ANDREASEN. 1973. "Production of higher alcohols from threonine and esoleucine in alcoholic fermentation of different types of grain mash. *J. Agric. Food Chem.* 21:50–54.

Reed, G., and T. W. Nagodawithana. 1988. "Technology of yeast usage in winemaking." *Am. J. Enol. Vitic.* 39:83–90.

Reed, G., and T. W. Nagodawithana. 1991. *Yeast Technology*, 2nd ed. New York: Van Nostrand Reinhold.

Reichert, U., and M. Foret. 1977. "Energy coupling in hypoxanthine transport of yeast." *FEBS Letts.* 83:325–328.

Ribéreau-Gayon, J., E. Peynaud, and M. Lafon. 1954. "Growth factors and secondary products of alcoholic fermentation." *Comp. Rend.* 239: 1549–1951.

Ribéreau-Gayon, J., E. Peynaud, and M. Lafon. 1956a. "Investigations on the origin of secondary products of alcoholic fermentation, Part I." *Am. J. Enol.* 7:53–61.

Ribéreau-Gayon, J., E. Peynaud, and M. Lafon. 1956b. "Investigations on the origin of secondary products of alcoholic fermentation, Part II." *Am. J. Enol.* 7:112–118.

Rieger, M., O. Kapelli, and A. Fiechter. 1983. "The role of limited respiration in the incomplete oxidation of glucose by *Saccharomyces cerevisiae*." *J. Gen. Micro.* 129:653–661.

Roon, R. J., H. L. Even, P. Dunlop, and F. Larimore. 1975a. "Methylamine and ammonia transport in *Saccharomyces cerevisiae*." *J. Bacteriol.* 122:502–509.

Roon, R. J., F. Larimore, and J. S. Levy. 1975b. "Inhibition of amino acid transport by ammonium ion in *Saccharomyces cerevisiae*." *J. Bacteriol.* 124:325–331.

Roon, R. J., J. S. Levy, and F. Larimore. 1977a. "Negative interactions between amino acid and methyl amine/ammonia transport systems of *Saccharomyces cerevisiae*." *J. Biol. Chem.* 252:3599–3604.

Roon, R. J., G. M. Meyer, and F. S. Larimore. 1977b. "Evidence for a common component in kinetically distinct transport systems of *Saccharomyces cerevisiae*." *Molec. Gen. Genetics* 158:185–191.

Rosa, M. F., and I. Sá-Correia. 1991. "In vivo activation by ethanol of plasma membrane ATPase of *Saccharomyces cerevisiae*." *Appl. Envir. Microbiol.* 57:830:835.

Rose, A. H., M. J. Beavan, and C. Charpentier. 1982. "Physiological basis for enhanced ethanol production by *Saccharomyces cerevisiae*." In, *Overproduction of Microbiol Products*, FEMS Symp. No. 13, V. Krumphanzyl, B. Sikyta, and Z. Vanek, Eds., pp. 211.219. New York: Academic Press.

Rosi, J., and M. Bertuccioli. 1984. "Effect of lipids on yeast growth and metabolism under simulated vinification conditions." *1984 Technical Abstracts*, p. 20, Annual Meeting, American Society for Enology and Viticulture, June 21–23 1984, San Diego, California.

Rous, C. V., R. Snow, and R. E. Kunkee. 1983. "Reduction of higher alcohols by fermentation with a leucine-auxotrophic mutant of wine yeast." *J. Inst. Brew.* 89:274–278.

Sá-Correia, I., and N. van Uden. 1986. "Ethanol-induced death of *Saccharomyces cerevisiae* at low and intermediate growth temperatures." *Biotech. Bioeng.* 28:301:303.

Salmon, J. M. 1989. "Effect of sugar transport inactivation in *Saccharomyces cerevisiae* on sluggish and stuck enological fermentations." *App. Environ. Micro.* 55:9535–9538.

Schanderl, H. 1959. *Mikrobiologie des Mostes und Weines*. Stuttgart, Germany, Ulmer.

Schmitt, H. D., M. Ciriacy, and F. K. Zimmermann. 1983. "The synthesis of yeast pyruvate decarboxylase is regulated by large variations in the messenger RNA level." *Molec. Gen. Genetics* 192:247–252.

Schütz, M., and R. E. Kunkee. 1977. "Formation of hydrogen sulfide from elemental sulfur during fermentation by wine yeast." *Am. J. Enol. Vitic.* 28:137–144.

SentheShanmuganathan, S. 1960a. "The mechanism of the formation of higher alcohol from amino acids by *Saccharomyces cerevisiae*." *Biochem. J.* 74:568–576.

SentheShanmuganathan, S. 1960b. "The purification and properties of the tyrosine-2-oxoglutarate transaminase of *Saccharomyces cerevisiae*." *Biochem. J.* 77:619–625.

Serrano, R. 1978. "Characterization of the plasma membrane ATPase of *Saccharomyces cerevisiae*." *Molec. Cell. Biochem.* 22:51–63.

Sharma, S., and P. Tauro. 1986. "Control of ethanol production by yeast: Role of pyruvate decarboxylase and alcohol dehydrogenase." *Biotech. Letters* 8:735–738.

Shimazu, Y., and M. Watanabe. 1981. "Effects of yeast strains and environmental conditions on formation of organic acids in must fermentation." *J. Fermen. Tech.* 59:27–32.

SINGH, R., and R. E. KUNKEE. 1977. "Multiplicity and control of alcohol dehydrogenase isoenzymes in various strains of wine yeasts." *Arch. Microbiol.* 114:255–259.

SINGLETON, V. L., H. A. SIEBERHAGEN, P. DE WET, and C. J. VAN WYK. 1975. "Composition and sensory qualities of wines prepared from white grapes by fermentation with and without grape solids." *Am. J. Enol. Vitic.* 26:62–69.

SKINNER, D. Z., A. D. BUDDE, and S. A. LEONG. 1991. "Molecular karyotype analysis of fungi." In, *More Gene Manipulations in Fungi*, pp. 86–103. New York: Academic Press.

SOLES, R. M., C. S. OUGH, and R. E. KUNKEE. 1982. "Ester concentration differences in wine fermented by various species and strains of yeasts." *Am. J. Enol. Vitic*, 33:94–98.

STEWART, G., A. FURST, and N. AVDALOVIC. 1988. "Transverse alternating field electrophoresis (TAFE)." *Biotech.* 6:68–73.

STRATFORD, M., and A. H. ROSE. 1985. "Hydrogen sulphide production from sulphite by *Saccharomyces cerevisiae*." *J. Gen. Micro.* 131:1427–1424.

STRATFORD, M., and A. H. ROSE. 1986. "Transport of sulphur dioxide by *Saccharomyces cerevisiae*." *J. Gen. Micro.* 132:1–6.

SUMRADA, R., and T. G. COOPER. 1982. "Urea carboxylase and allophanate hydrolase are components of multifunctional protein in yeast." *J. Biol. Chem.* 257:9119–9127.

SUN, G. Y., and A. Y. SUN. 1985. "Ethanol and membrane lipids." *Alcohol. Clin. Exp. Res.* 9:164–180.

SUOMALAINEN, H., and A. J. A. KERANEN. 1967. "Keto acids formed by baker's yeast." *J. Inst. Brewing* 73:477–484.

TABOR, H., C. W. TABOR, and M. S. COHN. 1983. "Mass screening for mutants in the polyamine biosynthetic pathway in *Saccharomyces cerevisiae*." *Meth. Enzymol.* 94:104–108.

THOMAS, C. S., R. B. BOULTON, M. W. SILACCI, and W. D. GUBLER. 1993a. "The effect of elemental sulfur, yeast strain and fermentation medium on hydrogen sulfide production during fermentation." *Am. J. Enol. Vitic.* 44:211–216.

THOMAS, C. S., W. D. GUBLER, M. W. SILACCI, and R. MILLER. 1993b. "Changes in elemental sulfur residues on Pinot noir and Cabernet sauvignon berries during the growing season." *Am. J. Enol. Vitic.* 44:205–210.

THOMAS, D., R. BARBEY, D. HENRY, and Y. SARDIN-KERJAN. 1992. "Physiological analysis of mutants of *Saccharomyces cerevisiae* impaired in sulphate assimilation." *J. Gen. Micro.* 138:2021–2028.

THOMAS D. S., and A. H. ROSE. 1979. "Inhibitory effect of ethanol on growth and solute accumulation by *Saccharomyces cerevisiae* as affected by plasma-membrane lipid compositions." *Arch. Microbiol.* 122:49–55.

THORNE, R. S. W. 1958. "Statistical survey of the fermentation efficiencies of a large number of strains of brewery yeasts and a consideration of the utility of these efficiencies in classification." *J. Inst. Brew.* 64:411–421.

THOUKIS, G. 1958. "The mechanism of isoamyl alcohol formation using tracer techniques." *Am. J. Enol.* 9:161–167.

TOKUYAMA, T., H. KURAISHI, K. AIDA, and T. UEMURA. 1973. "Hydrogen sulfide evolution due to pantothenic acid deficiency in yeast requiring this vitamin, with special reference to the effect of adenosine triphosphate on yeast cysteine desulfhydrase." *J. Gen. Appl. Microbiol.* 19:439–466.

TOMENCHOK, D. M., and M. C. BRANDRISS. 1987. "Gene-enzyme relationships in the proline biosynthetic pathway of *Saccharomyces cerevisiae*." *J. Bacteriol.* 169:5364–5372.

TRAVERSO-RUEDA, S., and R. E. KUNKEE. 1982. "The role of sterols on growth and fermentation on wine yeasts under vinification conditions." *Developments in Industrial Microbiology* 23:131–143.

TREDOUX, H. G., J. L. F. KOCK, P. M. LATEGAN, and H. B. MULLER. 1987. "A rapid identification technique to differentiate between *Saccharomyces cerevisiae* strains and other yeast species in the wine industry." *Am. J. Enol. Vitic.* 38:161–164.

UMBARGER, H. E. 1978. "Amino acid biosynthesis and its regulation." *Ann. Rev. Biochem.* 47:533–606.

USSEGLIO-TOMASSET, L. 1975. "Volatiles of wine dependant on yeast metabolism." *Proc. 4th Intl. Oenol. Symp.* Valencia, Spain, p. 346–370.

VAHL, J. M. 1979. "A relative density-extract-alcohol nomograph for table wines." *Am. J. Enol. Vitic.* 30:262–263.

VALLEJO, C. G., and R. SERRANO. 1989. "Physiology of mutants with reduced expression of plasma membrane H + -ATPase." *Yeast* 5:307–319.

VAN UDEN, N. 1971. "Kinetics and energetics of yeast growth." In: *The Yeasts*, Vol.II, A. H. Rose and J. S. Harrison, Eds., New York, Academic Press.

VAN UDEN, N. 1989. *Alcohol Toxicity in Yeast and Bacteria*. Boca Raton, FL: CRC Press.

VAN UDEN, N., and H. DA CRUZ DUARTE. 1981. "Effects of ethanol on the temperature profile of *Saccharomyces cerevisiae*." *Zeit. Allg. Mikrobiol.* 21:743–750.

VAN URK, H., P. R. MAK, W. A. SCHEFFERS, and J. P. VAN DIJKEN. 1988. "Metabolic responses of *Saccharomyces cerevisiae* CBS 8066 and *Candida utilis* CBS 621 upon transition from glucose limitation to glucose excess." *Yeast* 4:283–292.

VAN VUUREN, H. J. J., and C. J. JACOBS. 1992. "Killer yeasts in the wine industry: A review." *Am. J. Enol. Vitic.* 43:119–128.

VAN VUUREN, H. J. J., and L. VAN DER MEER. 1987. "Fingerprinting of yeasts by protein electrophoresis." *Am. J. Enol. Vitic.* 38:49–53.

VAUGHN-MARTINI, A., and C. P. KURTZMAN. 1985. "Deoxyribonucleic acid relatedness among species of the genus *Saccharomyces sensu stricto*." *Int. J. Syst. Bacteriol.* 35:508–511.

VERDUYN, C., E. POSTMA, W. A. SCHEFFERS, and J. P. VAN DIJKEN. 1990. "Physiology of *Saccharomyces cerevisiae* in anaerobic glucose-limited chemostat cultures." *J. Gen. Micro.* 136:359–403.

VEZINHET, F., B. BLONDIN, and J-N. HALLET. 1990a. "Chromosomal DNA patterns and mitochondrial polymorphism as tools for identification of enological strains of *Saccharomyces cerevisiae*." *Appl. Microbiol. Biotechnol.* 32:568–571.

VEZINHET, F., D. DELTEIL, and M. VALADE. 1990b. "Les apports du marquage génétique de souches de levures oenologiques pour le suivi des populations levuriennes en oenologie." In *Actualities OEnologiques 89*, P. Ribéreau-Gayon and A. Lonvaud, Eds., pp. 233–237. Paris: Dunod.

VOS, P. J. A., and R. S. GRAY. 1979. "The origin and control of hydrogen sulfide during fermentation of grape must." *Am. J. Enol. Vitic.* 30:187–197.

VOS, P. J. A., W. ZEEMAN, and H. HEYMANN. 1978. "The effect on wine quality of diammonium phosphate additions to musts." *Proc. S. Afric. Soc. Enol. Vitic.* Stellenbosch, South Africa:87–104.

WAINWRIGHT, T. 1970. "Hydrogen sulfide production by yeast under conditions of methionine, pantothenate or vitamin B_6 deficiency." *J. Gen. Microbiol.* 61:107–119.

WAINWRIGHT, T. 1971. "Production of H_2S by wine yeast: Role of nutrients." *J. Appl. Bacteriol.* 34:161–171.

WATSON, T. G. 1976. "Amino-acid pool composition of *Saccharomyces cerevisiae* as a function of growth rate and amino acid nitrogen source." *J. Gen. Micro.* 96:263–268.

WEBB, A. D., and J. L. INGRAHAM. 1963. "Fusel oil." *Adv. App. Micro.* 5:317–353.

WENZEL, K., and H. H. DITTRICH. 1978. "Zur beeinflussung der schwefelwasserstoff-bildung der hefe durch trub, stickstoffgehalt, molecularen schwefel und kupfer bei der vergarung von traubenmost." *Wein Wissen.* 33:200–214.

WHITING, G. C. 1976. "Organic acid metabolism of yeasts during fermentation of alcoholic beverages: A review." *J. Inst. Brewing* 82:84–92.

WHITNEY, P. A., and T. G. COOPER. 1972. "Urea carboxylase and allophanate hydrolase: Two components of adenosine triphosphate: Urea amido-lyase in *Saccharomyces cerevisiae*." *J. Biol. Chem.* 247:1349–1353.

WILLS, C. 1990. "Regulation of sugar and ethanol metabolism in *Saccharomyces*." *Crit. Rev. Biochem. Molec. Biol.* 25:245–280.

WINGER, C. M. 1982. "Effect of fermentation temperature and yeast strain on residual compounds in wine." MS thesis, Davis, CA: University of California.

WOODWARD, J. R., and V. P. CIRILLO. 1977. "Amino acid transport and metabolism in nitrogen-starved cells of *Saccharomyces cerevisiae*." *J. Bacteriol.* 130:714–723.

YOUNG, T. W. 1987. "Killer yeasts." In *The Yeasts*, Vol. 2, 2nd ed., A. H. Rose and J. S. Harrison, Eds., New York: Academic Press.

YUNOME, H., Y. ZENIBAYASHI, and M. DATE. 1981. "Characteristic components of botrytised wine-sugar, alcohols, organic acids and other factors." *Hakkokogaku* 59:169–175.

ZAMBONELLI, C., M. G. SOLI, and D. GUERRA. 1984. "A study of H_2S non-producing strains of wine yeasts." *Arch. Microbiol.* 34:7–15.

CHAPTER 5

Red and White Table Wines

A. ASPECTS OF WINE FERMENTATIONS

There are several aspects of wine fermentations that are of general interest and these will be considered in detail before consideration is given to the major wine types. The addresses of equipment companies mentioned in this chapter can be found in Appendix I.

1. Measures of Sugar Content and Extent of Fermentation

There are a number of ways in which the sugar content of juice and the progress of an ethanol fermentation can be monitored. These methods can be classified as the actual concentration of sugar (or ethanol), those involving intrinsic fluid properties, such as the density, refractive index, or osmotic pressure, and those related to aggregate properties of the entire volume such as the weight loss, carbon dioxide volume evolved, or the heat released. The most common method in use today is measurement of the solution density in a manually drawn sample, even though there are several limitations to this procedure due to localized sampling and the effects of suspended solids (Cooke 1964).

a. *Density Scales*

There have been a number of density scales developed for sugar determination and these have generally been applied to the extent of fermentations. These are generally amplifications of the changes in the density or specific gravity of solutions when compared to that of water. The specific gravity (s. g.) is the ratio of the density of a solution to that of water, usually at 4°C or 20°C. The practice of calibrating hydrometers on the basis of weight percent was developed in the late 1700s by Antoine Baume. At one point there were at least four such scales (Balling, Klosternerburg, Wagner, and Oechsle) in use in Germany and Austria (Von der Lippe 1894). Scales of this kind are now widely used in the measurements of sugar and ethanol solutions, acid and salt solutions, and even petroleum products.

The scales most commonly used today in winemaking are Brix (used in the United States and South Africa), Baume (France, Italy, Spain, Portugal, Australia, and New Zealand), and the Oechsle scale (Germany, Switzerland, and Austria). The Klosternerburg scale, originally developed by Babo in Austria to facilitate the estimation of wine ethanol content, was not widely adopted. Von der Lippe (1894) describes three unique hydrometers that were in use at the time. The first, the Guyot hydrometer, had two sugar scales (Wagner or Baume units and percent sugar) and another a third scale with the potential ethanol content. The second, the Barth hydrometer, used in Alsace, measured Oechsle and had two different sugar scales, one for red grapes and the other for white grapes, each with a different correction for the nonsugar extract. The third, the Schmidt-Artersche hydrometer, used in the Pfalz region, measured Oechsle and contained the temperature corrections to be applied within the spindle. The scales usually differed in terms of the reference temperature (12.5, 15.6, and 17.5°C). The Wagner scale was similar to the Baume scale but calibrated at 15.5°C, while the Baume, Balling, and Oechsle scales were based on 17.5°C. The Plato and Brix scales are generally used in the brewing industries throughout the world.

The use of hydrometers calibrated for sugar solutions is favored over those in degrees proof or percent by volume ethanol, or those using percent by weight such as the Richter, Cartier, Sikes, or Tralles scales, due to the need for analysis in both grapes and wines. These scales have traditionally been used on distillates of wines, beers, and other preparations to determine the ethanol content.

I. The Baume Scale. Antoine Baume developed the earliest density scale based on the concentration of salt solutions in 1768. Each degree of the scale corresponds to 1% by weight of salt at 12.5°C and it originally ranged from 0 (water) to 15 with each degree being of equal length on the hydrometer stem (Baume 1797). It has since been widely used for the measurement of sugar solutions and the scale used today has been recalibrated to 20°C and is characterized by the modulus 145 (Bates et al. 1942). One degree on the Baume scale is approximately 1.8 degrees of the Brix scale.

$$(20^\circ\text{C})\ \text{Baume} = 145.0 - \frac{145.0}{\text{s.g.}(20/20^\circ\text{C})}$$
$$= 0.0181 + 0.5532 * \text{Brix}\ (@\ 20^\circ\text{C}).$$

The Baume scale is approximately related to potential ethanol in percent by volume (0.553 versus 0.595), but only if the nonsugar extract is ignored. In Europe, the earlier scale, calibrated at 15.5°C, can still be found in older texts and is characterized by a modulus of 144.32:

$$(15.5^\circ\text{C})\ \text{Baume} = 144.32 - \frac{144.32}{\text{s.g.}(15.5/15.5^\circ\text{C})}$$

II. The Balling Scale. This scale was named after its developer, Karl Balling, who calibrated it against the concentration of sucrose solutions at (17.5°C). It is no longer used since the Brix scale has been adopted with a 20°C reference temperature as the standard scale for sugar analysis in the United States.

$$\text{Balling} = \text{weight percent sucrose at } 17.5^\circ\text{C}.$$

III. The Brix Scale. This scale was developed in the mid 1800s when Antoine Brix recalculated Balling's scale to the reference temperature of 15.5°C. Today the Brix scale has been recalculated again to a reference temperature of 20°C and national standards in several countries have been adopted for this scale. The scale can be characterized with a modulus of 261.3 based on nonlinear regression of published tables:

$$\text{Brix} = 261.3 - \frac{261.3}{\text{s.g.}(20/20^\circ\text{C})}$$
$$= \text{weight percent sucrose at } 20^\circ\text{C}.$$

IV. The Oechsle Scale. This scale, like the Plato scale, simply amplifies the density contributions of the solute over that of water, by a factor of 1000. It was originally calibrated at 15.5°C but today the temperature of 20°C, is used. The Oechsle of a sugar solution is a good estimate of the potential ethanol (in g/L) if the fermentation goes to dryness (Jakob 1984). This is a fortunate circumstance of canceling effects since there is no correction for the nonsugar extract.

$$\text{Oechsle} = [\text{s.g.}\ (20/20°\text{C}) - 1.000] * 1000$$

*V. **The Plato Scale.*** This scale was based on Plato's original density measurements (Bates et al. 1942) in which the density was scaled by that of water at 4°C and which has been recalculated to 17.5 °C. It is otherwise similar to the Brix scale, but instead with a modulus of 260.0 (De Clerke 1958). It is still widely used within the brewing industry.

$$\text{Plato} = 260.0 - \frac{260.0}{\text{s.g.}(17.5/17.5°\text{C})}$$

*VI. **The Klosternerburg Scale.*** This scale was a modification of the Balling scale that attempted to estimate the actual sugar content of grape juices by factoring out 2 to 4% w/w as nonsugar components. It shows the early recognition of these effects and an attempt to correct for them. The one degree on the Baume or Wagner scales was approximately 1.5 degrees on the Klosternerburg scale. The level of nonsugar solutes is not proportional to the sugar content and this correction overestimates the sugar content at high values (greater than 20°) and underestimates it at lower values (Marsh 1958). It has been superceded by the Brix and Baume scales.

b. *Temperature Corrections*

Since the specific gravity of a solution is temperature dependent, these measurements should be either performed at the reference temperature of the hydrometer scale or the measurement temperature recorded and a correction applied. For the Brix scale at 25 Brix, the corrections are approximately -0.06 Brix per °C below 20 and +0.07 Brix per °C above. A more complete table of corrections can be found in the National Bureau of Standards Circular 440 (Bates et al. 1942), Ough and Amerine (1988), or other wine analysis texts.

2. Potential Ethanol Content

Of more significance than the initial sugar level is the estimation of the final ethanol concentration. There are a number of formulas that have been proposed for the estimation of this in wines. These generally include a correction to the sugar content to allow for the nonsugar content before applying a fermentation yield factor. In this way the effects of the nonsugar extract of the grapes are not confused with those due to the fermentation conditions.

One formula widely used in Europe is that proposed by Dubrunfaut and used with the Dujion-Saleron hydrometers (Benvegnin et al. 1951). This formula estimates the potential ethanol by using early assumptions of 30 g/L of nonsugar extract and a conversion factor from 0.059 from percent sugar to percent by volume ethanol:

$$\text{Potential ethanol (v/v\%)} = 0.059 * [2.66 * \text{Oe} - 30]$$

where Oe is the Oechsle of the juice. The factor 0.059 is the actual yield of mL of ethanol per 100 mL from one gram per L of sugar. The theoretical yield would be 0.064 and Pasteur's value was 0.061 (Marsh 1958).

If this approach is applied to the data of the Dujardin Company, presented by Dubet (1913), for juice density and potential ethanol, the formula becomes:

$$\text{Potential ethanol (v/v\%)} = 0.0595 * [2.66 * \text{Oe} - 31.8]$$

but this is based on a limited range of sugar contents (130 to 148 g/L). One approximation proposed by Benvegnin et al. (1951) for the Oechsle scale is:

$$\text{Potential ethanol (v/v\%)} = \frac{\text{Oe} - 15}{6} = \frac{\text{Oe}}{6} - 2.5$$

Another variation of this formula, using a more recent expression for ethanol yield based on the reducing sugar content (Ribéreau-Gayon et al. 1975), is:

$$\text{Potential ethanol (v/v\%)} = 0.0595 * [2560 * \text{s.g.}(20/20°\text{C}) - 1.000 - 22.2]$$

and this corresponds to an ethanol conversion factor of 0.0573 and a nonsugar extract of 21.4 g/L. When expressed in the early form it becomes:

$$\text{Potential ethanol (v/v\%)} = 0.0573 * [2.66 * \text{Oe} - 23.1]$$

Based on Californian data, Bioletti (Marsh 1958) proposed the formula based on the Brix of the juice:

$$\text{Potential ethanol (g/100mL)} = 0.47 * [(\text{sugar w/w\%}) - 3.0]$$

where the 0.47 factor is 92% of the theoretical conversion of 1 g of sugar to 0.51 g of ethanol and it is 97% of Pasteur's conversion value. The nonsugar extract was taken to be 3.0% by weight (i.e., 30.3 g/L). This, when divided by 0.794 (the density of ethanol) to bring the units to a volume basis becomes:

$$\text{Potential ethanol (v/v\%)} = 0.592 * [(\text{sugar w/w\%}) - 3.0]$$

In an attempt to develop a simpler form using a direct conversion factor, Ough and Amerine (1963) and Jones and Ough (1985) have analyzed hundreds of wines from several years in all growing regions of California. They cast their results in the form:

$$\text{Potential ethanol (v/v\%)} = a + b * \text{Brix}$$

where the conversion factor b has been found to vary by year, cultivar, and the growing region and a was given less attention. They found that the conversion factor had values in the range 0.51 (dry red wines, region IV) to 0.66 (dry white wines, region I). The annual conversion factors varied considerably more, ranging from 0.49 (dry red wine, region IV, 1961) to 0.79 (dry white wine, region I, 1959).

The value of a was found to vary between -4.92 and $+4.37$. The negative values of a are to be expected and correspond to non-sugar extract included in the Brix reading. These authors assumed the non-sugar extract to be 2.5% for white juices in both regions, 3.0% for the red musts from region I, and 3.5% for those from region IV.

The positive values of a imply that additional ethanol was formed from solutes other than those measured as Brix, and this is presumably due to additional sugar release from the skins during the fermentations as noted. The conversion factor b is consequently distorted upward under these conditions.

If the data for 18 cultivars (nine red and nine white) is averaged over nine years (Ough and Amerine 1963) and cast in the Dubrunfaut form using a nonsugar extract of 3 g/100 g, the ethanol yield factors for the two regions can be calculated as seen in Table 5-1a. Alternatively, by assuming the ethanol conversions to be those used by earlier authors, the non-sugar content can be estimated from the same

Table 5-1a. The ethanol yield factor for grapes from two regions based on 3 g / 100 g of non-sugar content.

Region	White wines (nine-year mean)	Red wines (nine-year mean)
I	0.665	0.635
IV	0.655	0.588

[1]Based on nine cultivars.

[2] Data from Ough and Amerine (1963).

Table 5-1b. The non-sugar content of grapes from two regions based on a conversion factor of 0.595.

Region	White wines (nine-year mean)	Red wines (nine-year mean)
I	0.673	1.86
IV	1.08	3.25

[1]Based on nine cultivars.

[2]*Source of data:* Ough and Amerine (1963).

data. This leads to nonsugar contents much lower than the 3 g/100 g value in the grapes considered (Table 5-1b).

The practice has developed in some quarters of simply dividing the ethanol obtained by the initial Brix to estimate the ethanol conversion. This is an inappropriate use of the conversion formulas and it ignores the effect and variation of the nonsugar content. As can be seen from Tables 5-1a and 5-1b, the difference of 1 g/100 g of nonsugar extract can result in a variation in the apparent yield of approximately 0.03 v/v% per Brix. The major physiological factor related to the extract value would seem to be berry size but this has not been taken into account in these studies. There are also potential errors in the initial Brix content due to slightly dehydrated berries, and this tends to underestimate the sugar available and to overestimate the ethanol yield. The formation of different levels of cell mass during fermentation (Jones and Ough 1985) due to differences in the amino acid content, may, together with differences in malate content contribute to the yield factor, but this has yet to be demonstrated in defined media.

The early formulas were based primarily on wines made by natural yeast fermentations with little control of fermentation temperature and not necessarily dry by today's standards. There is a need for further study of the factors influencing the nonsugar extract of different cultivars grown in different regions.

3. Yeast Inoculation

The usual practice for many years has been the use of a single strain inoculum for the initiation of wine fermentations. The early development of yeast preparations (Castor 1953; Thoukis et al. 1963) was quickly adopted in California in the 1960s and is now a widespread practice throughout the world (Kraus et al. 1983). The main advantages of this practice are the rapid initiation and predictable nature of the fermentations and the ability to eliminate undesirable byproduct formation by natural flora. It also permits the rapid development of inocula when compared to the use of yeast propagation tanks and is more convenient for small wineries.

a. *Inoculum Levels*

The standard level of inoculation involves the addition of yeast cells at levels which correspond to between 1 and 2% of the typical final populations. This is equivalent to approximately three million to six million cells/mL and obtained by the addition of 120 to 240 mg/L of active dry yeast. The use of larger inoculations by some wineries, such as twice or three times the standard, while costing proportionately more, can have important advantages in the certainty and speed of fermentation, the insensitivity of the fermentation to the nutritional status of the juice, and perhaps the extent of accumulation of certain byproducts related to the growth phase. There are, however, few studies of the influence of the initial cell population level on the formation of such components as the acetate esters, higher alcohols, acetic acid, urea, sulfite, or hydrogen sulfide, even though these effects might be expected.

The effect of a larger initial yeast population is to deplete most of the nutrients more quickly, often leading to only two or three doublings rather than the more usual four to five. One important result of this practice is the generation of a population which is more similar in age (and perhaps other factors, such as cell viability). Another is the reduction in the fraction of the fermentation which occurs by growth and cell division. A third is the more rapid onset of active fermentation and the point at which the beginning of fermentation is detected.

While at least one study has attributed poorer fermentation performance to very large inoculation (up to 20%) and postulated an inhibitor associated with the inoculum, (Strehaiano et al. 1983), an alternative explanation is that the effect observed was more likely due to the significant dilution of the nutrient concentration in the fermentation medium, of the order of 15 to 20%, with the volume of an inoculation medium that had been depleted of most nutrients during culture.

4. Gas Evolution During Fermentation

The volume of carbon dioxide and the rate at which it is released are important features of the fermentation. This gas evolution poses a significant working hazard within buildings unless it is removed by either ducting or by the inflow of outside air. The volume of carbon dioxide evolved is one possible means of measuring the progress of the fermentation and its rate of evolution is essentially proportional to the rate of fermentation. Both of these quantities are of importance to the design of gas venting and air intake systems in wineries.

a. *Volume of Carbon Dioxide*

The total volume of carbon dioxide produced by a grape juice fermentation is of the order of 56 L/L of must for the complete fermentation of a sugar content of 210 g/L (approximately 24 Brix as juice) at 20°C. The volume is influenced by the gas temperature (Tg) and this effect is accounted for by the ratio of absolute temperatures:

$$\text{Volume of } CO_2 = \underset{\text{per mole } CO_2}{\text{gas volume}} * \underset{\text{per Litre}}{\text{moles } CO_2} * \underset{\text{term}}{\text{temperature}}$$

$$= \left[\frac{22.4\ \text{L}}{\text{mol } CO_2}\right] * \left[\frac{210\ \text{g}}{\text{L}} * \frac{1\ \text{mole sugar}}{180\ \text{g}} * \frac{2\ \text{moles } CO_2}{1\ \text{mole sugar}}\right] * \left[\frac{(273.2 + T_g)}{273.2}\right]$$

$$= 56.0\ \text{L } CO_2 \text{ per L of juice at } 20°\text{C}.$$

The actual values for typical fermentation temperatures range from 55.0 L/L at 15°C to 57.9 L/L at 30°C without the volumetric corrections for the presence of water vapor.

b. *Rate of Carbon Dioxide Release*

The daily or hourly rate of gas release can be obtained by scaling this volume by the fraction of sugar consumed (in g/L) in the period of interest. For example, 10,000 L of a white juice fermenting at a rate of 1 Brix per day (approximately 11 g/L/day) at 15°C, would produce carbon dioxide at a rate of:

$$dV_{CO_2}/dt = 55.0\ \text{L } CO_2/\text{L juice} * 11/210 \times * 10{,}000\ \text{L juice}$$

$$\text{or } 28.8 \times 10^3\ \text{L of } CO_2 \text{ per day.}$$

c. *Gas Release from Barrel Fermentations*

The maximum rates of gas evolution can be used to calculate the air replacement rate to maintain safe carbon dioxide and oxygen levels in the fermentation room, and this is especially important for barrel fermentations, which are often conducted by the hundreds in poorly ventilated tunnels or rooms.

It is not generally appreciated that the introduction of large volumes of outside air poses a very large additional load on any air conditioning system that attempts to regulate the cellar temperature. In one particular installation, a large barrel storage building was to be used for barrel fermentations. The air conditioning load was doubled by the heat released during the fermentations, but the introduction of outside air required a further sixfold increase in cooling capacity.

Assuming that the juice occupies two-thirds of the barrel volume, the total gas release figures become 9537 L/barrel at 15°C and 9702 L/barrel at 20°C.

d. Safe Working Conditions

The federal safety regulations in the United States related to workplace conditions have an upper limit of 0.5% (5000 ppm, or 9000 mg/M^3) for the carbon dioxide concentration (Crowl and Louvar 1991). The quantity of outside air that needs to be introduced in order to maintain this level in the presence of a fermentation can be calculated to be 24.75 times the carbon dioxide evolved (assuming that the outside air has 600 ppm of carbon dioxide to begin with). This amounts to approximately 1423 L air/L must during the course of a typical fermentation.

The specific rate of air intake (that is L per L of fermenting juice) on a daily or hourly basis is then this value scaled by the fraction of the total sugar that is fermented in the period. For the example considered above, of the 10,000 L of white juice fermenting at 1 Brix per day, the required air intake is:

$$dV_{air}/dt = 24.75 * 55.0 * 11/210$$
$$= 71.3 \text{ L air per L of juice per day}$$

e. Fermentation Gas Removal

One approach is not to conduct the fermentations inside closed buildings using either outside fermentation pads that are covered or protected from the weather. The alternative approach, which is used by a limited number of wineries, is to remove the carbon dioxide from each fermentor through a ducting system to the outside of the building. This can be done by either using the headspace pressure of each active fermentor, or by venting with a fan or blower. The headspace venting approach would need additional fittings to isolate fermentors that are not in use from the duct.

This venting approach has the advantage of then requiring an air intake to the building that is only once or twice the volume of carbon dioxide removed. This also permits a far more energy-efficient operation since a much smaller volume of outside air needs to be cooled in order to maintain the cellar at a chosen temperature. A third consideration for the future is the ability to collect the fermentation gases for further treatment or component recovery. While it is presently not considered to be financially advantageous to recover the CO_2 or to attempt to recover fermentation volatiles, future interests in these options might make the installation gas collection and temporary on-site processing systems more common.

The production of industrial and scientific grades of carbon dioxide can be produced from air by either cryogenic distillation and membrane separation processes; starting with a 98% CO_2 gas phase would seem to have dramatic advantages over the use of air as a starting material.

The practical implications of the venting approach are related to the potential for microbial contamination within the ducts and the ease with which they can be cleaned, the need for enclosed fermentors, and some kind of individual or group collection manifolds for barrel fermentation areas.

The removal of ethanol vapor from exit gases on the suggestion that it was a potential precursor of atmospheric ozone formation has been under serious consideration for several years in California. The scientific evidence to date is that ethanol does not contribute significantly to ozone formation. It has been grouped with a number of other compounds based on its initial reactivity under radiation conditions, but there is no evidence that it continues to react in the same way based on final ozone yield. While there has been an interest in the commercial recovery of the ethanol from the vapors of alcoholic fermentations for decades, the changing economic and environmental considerations continue to make this of interest.

Whether because of a safer working environment or energy efficiency considerations in cellars, increases in the commodity values of carbon dioxide or ethanol, a significant decrease in the expense of separation technologies, or the introduction of such regulations, the installation of such gas collection systems may well become an essential part of winery buildings in the future.

5. Heat Release During Fermentation

The conversion of the grape sugars to ethanol by yeast under anaerobic conditions is a considerably exothermic series of reactions. The generally accepted value for the energy release of this fermentation is 101.2 kJ/mole. A critical review of this value and the related studies has been prepared by Williams (1982). The quantity of energy released is such that if it was all transformed into an adiabatic temperature rise in the juice, increases of the order of 26°C would occur for a juice of 210 g/L (24 Brix as juice). This is equivalent to a rise of 0.125°C per g/L fermented, or 1.37°C rise per Brix fermented.

a. *The Need for Temperature Control*

The rate of heat release is directly proportional to the rate of fermentation, but these rates increase exponentially with increasing temperature. If the temperature cannot be controlled by heat removal, the temperature will begin to rise and the rate of heat release will continue to grow in a runaway situation.

The existence of elevated temperatures during fermentation can lead to the death of the added yeast and the allowance of the more thermally tolerant strains and species to complete the fermentation. Many wine yeast strains are killed rapidly at temperatures of 40 to 42°C (Jacob et al. 1964; van Uden et al. 1968). The maximum growth temperature of wine yeast decreases with the formation of ethanol, from 40°C in the absence of ethanol to 30°C at 10% ethanol (Loureiro and van Uden 1982). Thermal death of the desired yeast simply permits the possibility of dominance by other microorganisms and the formation of undesirable byproducts. For this reason the temperature of red wine fermentations is generally not permitted to rise to above 30°C. Prior to the introduction of refrigeration, incomplete fermentations due to this were quite common (Bioletti 1906). The widespread use of refrigeration or other cooling methods to control the fermentation temperature makes this a rare situation today.

b. *Potential Temperature Rise*

In practice, the temperature rise will always be less than the theoretically expected value due to the energy converted into the latent heat of evaporation of the water and ethanol, which are at saturation levels in the exiting carbon dioxide. The calculated energy release corrected for this is shown in Figure 5-1. This corresponds to about 7 to 10% of the heat release for red wines and typically 5% for white wines. Some of the energy released is also lost as enthalpy of warm carbon dioxide in the exit gas of red fermentors, by the conductive and convective transfer to the ambient air, and by radiation with the surroundings. The contributions to the gas enthalpy and the transfer to (or from) the surroundings will obviously vary according to the fermentation temperature of either white juices or red musts, the geometry, size, and insulation of the fermentor and the extent to which solar and internal radiation contributions are present.

The formula proposed by Bioletti (1906) for the degrees of cooling required during fermentation is:

$$\text{Degrees of cooling (°F)} = 1.17 * \text{Brix} - T_{juice} + T_{max},$$

where T_{juice} and T_{max} are the initial juice and maximum fermentation temperatures. In the absence of cooling, the temperature rise due to fermentation becomes:

$$\Delta T\ (°F) = 1.17 * \text{Brix}$$

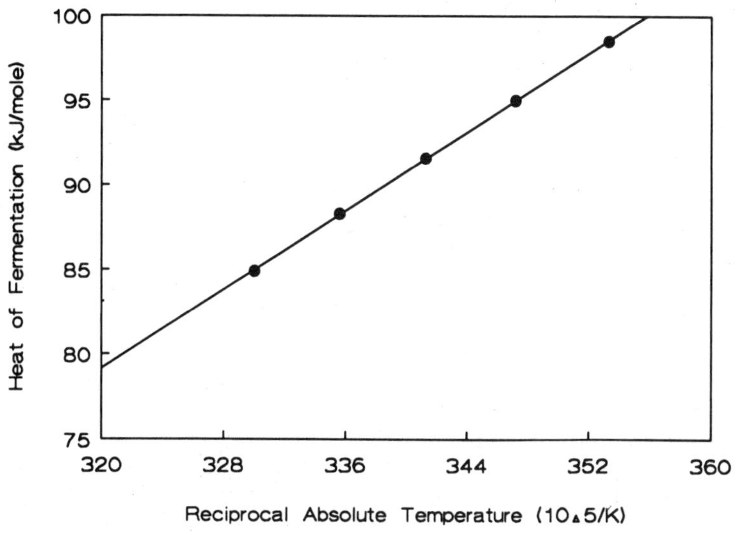

Fig. 5-1. Fermentaton heat release as a function of temperature.

or

$$\Delta T\ (°C) = 0.65 * \text{Brix}$$

and appears to be based on an assumption of 40% of the heat being lost in the exiting gas and to the surroundings. This may have been developed for very warm fermentation temperatures and wooden fermentors that have limited application today. The actual temperature rise will depend on several factors and these include the cellar temperature, the surface area to volume ratio, and the thermal conductivity of the fermentor wall. At cellar temperatures of 15°C to 20°C, barrel fermentations display temperature rises that suggest that the temperature factor should be 0.25°C rather than the 0.65°C per Brix that was probably derived from much larger wooden fermentors.

c. *Rates of Heat Release*

For isothermal conditions, the rates of heat removal by refrigeration and ambient means must equal the rate of generation. The rate of heat generation for a juice fermenting at a rate of 11 g/L/day (approximately 1 Brix/day) can be calculated to be 77.5 x 10^{-3} W/L. For red wine fermentations at 25°C and 30°C, with peak rates of 44 to 66 g/L/day (4 to 6 B/day), this corresponds to maximum rates of approximately 310 to 465 x 10^{-3} W/L, respectively. For white wines at 15°C and 20°C, with peak rates of 22 and 33 g/L/day (2 to 3 B/day), the values are 155 and 233 x 10^{-3} W/L. These are theoretical values without taking into account the 5 to 10% of the heat generated that is lost in the enthalpy of the fermentation gas.

These peak rates provide the minimum design criterion for the cooling demand of the fermentor and when summed for all fermentors, the total fermentation cooling demand at any time. The daily loads can be found by using the fraction of the heat released during each 24-hour period, assuming a normal distribution in time in which the standard deviation is one-sixth of the fermentation period and the mean is three standard deviations in magnitude.

Given the different fermentation temperatures for red and white wines this may lead to different choices of a cooling medium when in all other respects the fermentor could be used for both situations. The fermentors need to be specially fabricated if direct expansion of a refrigerant is to be used in the jackets. This is because the refrigerant will be under much higher pressure in the jacket than for glycol or chilled water and the design will need to satisfy the safety codes for pressure vessels.

Although the jackets have relatively poor heat transfer coefficients, they are commonly employed because of their ease of use. The coolant flow to the jacket is controlled by a solenoid valve on the coolant line to or from the jacket.

The use of an external heat exchanger is somewhat more laborious in that hose connections need to be made and broken each time cooling is needed. This can be easily achieved if the cooling can be scheduled to coincide with the pump-over operation.

The rate of heat transfer required to maintain a constant temperature is highest for red wines because they ferment faster at the higher temperatures employed. As a result, it is these conditions that should be used for the proper design of the cooling arrangement for the fermentor.

d. Jacketed Fermentors

For small and medium-sized, upright, cylindrical fermentors, it is common for a cooling jacket to be mounted on the outside of the tank wall. The ratio of wall area to volume is inversely proportional to the fermentor diameter so that a fermentor with twice the volume will have only half of the wall area per unit volume for cooling. Conversely, smaller fermentors will have a larger wall area per unit volume. This translates into a practical upper limit for the size of a fermentor that can be economically managed by jacket cooling.

A fermentation model was used to estimate any particular combination of fermentation temperature and volume, the available heat transfer area, exchanger type, and the required coolant temperature to be evaluated for either design or process control applications. Typical examples are the need for a 10°C (50°F) coolant to control a 30,000-L (120,000-gal.) wine fermentation at 25°C (77°F) if 50% of the tank wall area was jacketed or 17.5°C coolant if the entire wall was jacketed, (Boulton 1979).

While the rate of heat removal depends on both the overall coefficient and the coolant temperature, colder coolants can be used to compensate for poor coefficients but only with decreasing refrigeration efficiency and additional energy expense. The extent of the ambient loss term depends on both the ambient temperature and the overall heat transfer coefficient (U) of the surface which in turn depends on factors such as solar radiation and thermal insulation on the tank.

e. External Heat Exchangers

The way in which external cooling is performed can have a significant effect on the time required to obtain a particular degree of cooling. It is shown in Chapter 12 that batch cooling of an unagitated tank is more effective than a batch which is being mixed as the cooled juice is being returned. This happens to be the common practice in wineries since the fermentors are not well mixed and the returning juice is generally returned to either the top (over the skins of a red fermentation) or to the base of a white fermentor. The reason for the faster cooling of the nonmixed arrangement is that the effective temperature difference between the juice and the coolant is larger throughout the cooling cycle than when continual mixing occurs. The mixing causes the juice temperature to approach that of the coolant, decreasing the temperature driving force and, therefore, the rate of heat transfer throughout the cooling cycle.

f. Barrel Fermentations

For barrel fermentations, the absence of refrigeration and the poor heat transfer coefficient of the wooden staves requires cooler ambient temperatures if the fermentation temperature rise is to be limited. In practice, it is common for such fermentations to be allowed to experience temperature rises of between 5°C to 10°C. The early measurements of Müller-Thurgau (Schanderl 1959) show that the relationship between the temperature rise during fermentation is proportional to the cube root of the volume (Figure 5-2). It can be shown that larger barrels with the same juice and in the same ambient temperature will experience larger fermentation temperature

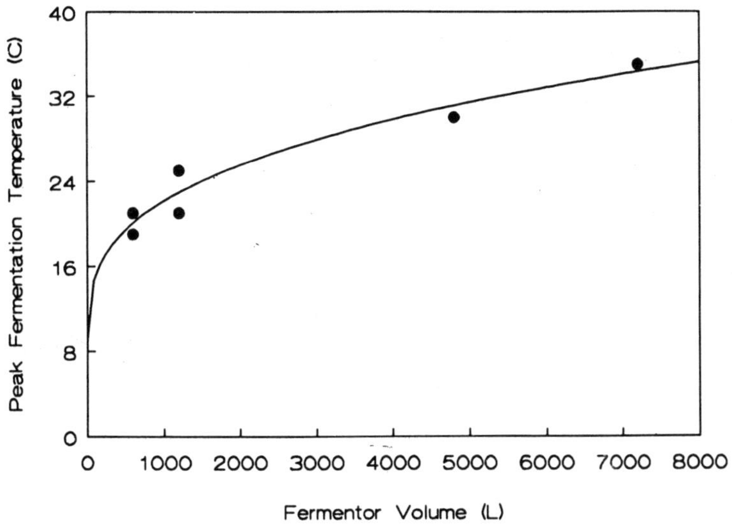

Fig. 5-2. Effect of fermentor size on peak fermentation temperature.

rises than smaller ones due to the ratio of surface area of the container to the fermenting volume. This ratio has the dimensions of length and that is why the temperature rise varies with the cube root of the volume (Boulton 1979). The rate of temperature change is related to the difference of the rates of formation and removal:

$$dT/dt = \Delta H dS/dt/\rho C - [T_w - T_a] U A/V \rho C$$

where ΔH is the heat of fermentation (101.2 kJ/mole of sugar); ρ and C are the density and heat capacity of the wine; and the subscripts w and a refer to the temperature of the wine and ambient air, respectively.

At the peak temperature, the rate of heat removal is exactly equal to the rate of heat generation, that is $dT/dt = 0$, and the maximum temperature can be estimated:

$$T_{max} = T_a + [\Delta H dS/dt]V/(UA).$$

The peak temperature achieved in the fermentation can be shown to depend on the ambient or cellar temperature T_a, the overall heat transfer coefficient U, and the ratio of surface area to fermenting volume (Boulton 1979). The temperature rise above ambient is then:

$$\Delta T = T_{max} - T_a = [\Delta H dS/dt]V/(U/A).$$

For 250 L-barrel sizes, the overall heat transfer coefficient has been estimated to be approximately 24 x 10^{-4} W/m^2/°C, and a typical barrel fermentation, (150 L at 20°C), would result in a temperature rise of:

$$\Delta T = \left[\frac{101.2 * 1000}{\text{J/mole}}\right] \times * \left[\frac{44\ \text{g/L/day} * 150\ \text{L}}{180\ \text{g/mole}\ 1000\ \text{L/m}^3}\right] \times * \left[\frac{10^4}{24}\right] * \left[\frac{1}{1.9\ \text{m}^2/\text{m}^3}\right]\left[\frac{1}{24 * 3600\text{s/day}}\right]$$

$$= 9.4°\text{C at 4 Brix/ day}$$

$$(4.7°\text{C at 2 Brix/ day}).$$

An example of such a temperature rise can be seen for a typical barrel fermentation in a cellar at 18°C (Figure 5-3).

6. Volume Changes

The most significant physical change that occurs during the fermentation is a shrinkage due to the change in the specific volumes of the major solutes. The volume occupied by

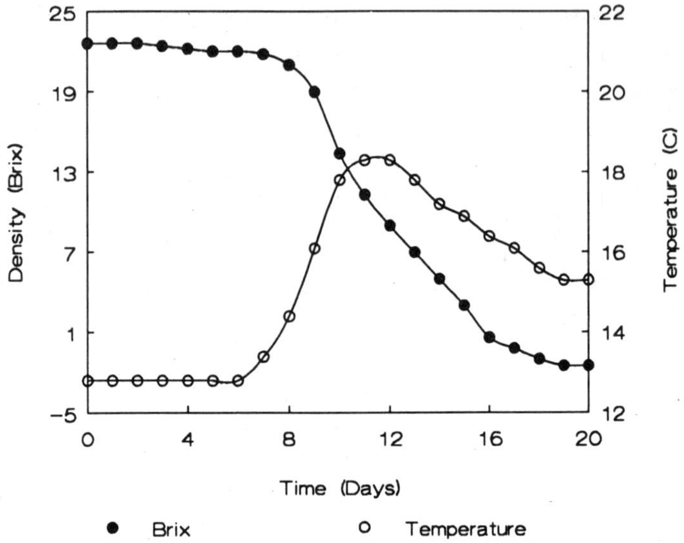

Fig. 5-3. Temperature rise during a barrel fermentation.

sugar in a 22 Brix solution is 164 mL/L, while that due to ethanol in a 12% v/v solution is 114 mL/L. A further 6 mL/L is due to glycerol formation. This 44 mL/L (or 4.4%) loss in volume at 20°C is due to the change in solute volume during fermentation. The specific volumes of glucose and ethanol are influenced slightly by temperature. The evaporative losses of water and ethanol during fermentation at 20°C are approximately 1200 and 600 mg/L (or 1.2 and 0.75 mL), respectively, and this accounts for only 0.2% as a volume contraction.

7. Dissolved Carbon Dioxide

During fermentation, juices will contain carbon dioxide concentration well above the saturation concentration. This is because the rate of bubble formation and gas evolution is usually slower than the rate of generation by fermentation. For this reason there is little possibility of oxygen pickup during pump-over operations due to the denser-than-air property of carbon dioxide. The promotion of bubble formation (and gas release) is enhanced during pump-over operations due to the turbulence generated during swirling and mixing. However, this enhanced release does not occur for white wines since they are not usually mixed or circulated during fermentation. At the end of fermentation, young wines will hold considerable quantities of dissolved carbon dioxide, usually two or more times the saturation concentrations, and this will be released during transfers and barrel storage in the following months.

The quantities of dissolved carbon dioxide for saturated conditions are almost 1.8 g/L (or 920 mL of CO_2/L wine) at a storage temperature 10°C. This would be expected for white wines normally held under a complete carbon dioxide headspace at one atmosphere pressure. The solubility is quite sensitive to temperature and if the wine temperature is to rise to 15°C (where the solubility has fallen to about 1.6 g/L), there will be the potential for approximately 100 mL of CO_2 to be evolved for each liter of wine, or approximately 22 L of CO_2 per barrel.

During processing, it will be desirable to utilize the denser-than-air properties of CO_2 for blanketing wines during tank transfers, but it will be important to remove the majority of this dissolved gas and to convert to nitrogen as the wines move closer to bottling.

8. Evaporative Ethanol Losses

The headspace above a fermenting juice or wine will generally be saturated in both water

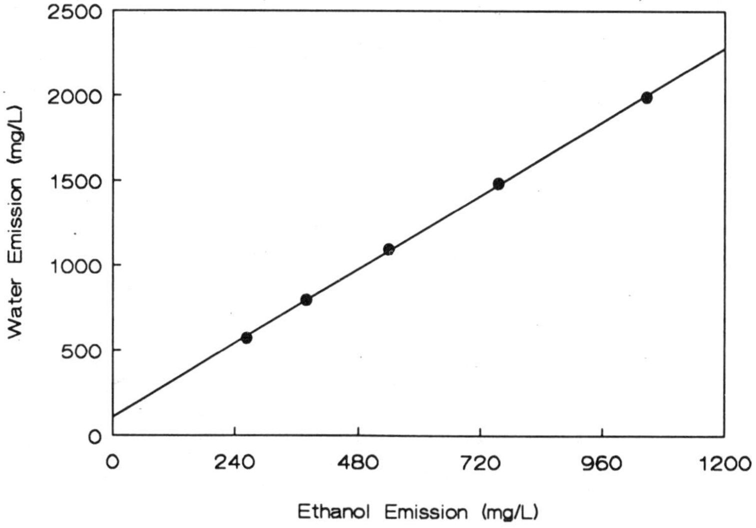

Fig. 5-4. Comparison of ethanol and water emissions during fermentation.

vapor and ethanol vapor. During the alcoholic fermentation, the release of large volumes of carbon dioxide sweeps with it these saturated vapors, leading to a small but significant ethanol loss from the wine. The values of water vapor and ethanol vapor contents are shown in Figure 5-4 for temperatures between 10°C and 30°C. The main concern with this evaporation is that it is a volatile emission that has been considered by some groups to be a precursor of photochemical smog. As a result there have been proposals to strip the ethanol vapor from fermentation gases prior to release to the atmosphere. These proposed processes range from condensation, adsorption on carbon, and catalytic combustion. There are several difficulties with each of these. The condensation temperature of the ethanol at the concentrations seen in these vapors is approximately -10°C, and the water vapor will have condensed (and frozen onto the condenser surface) before this can occur quite apart from other design difficulties. The catalytic combustion is complicated by the absence of oxygen in the gas, which then requires the introduction of approximately twice the volume of air to that of the fermentation gas for complete combustion of the ethanol present.

The loss of ethanol is insignificant with respect to the final ethanol content of the wine, and is estimated to be 1060 mg/L (8.8 lb/kgal) for red wines (30°C), and 400 mg/L (3.2 lb/kgal) for white wines at 15°C (Williams and Boulton, 1983). There have been many proposals for the recovery of the ethanol for other reasons, typically as a byproduct for sale, as an essence for adding back to wines, and as a means of purifying the carbon dioxide prior to its recovery for reuse or sale. As might be expected, a number of other trace volatile components are also at saturation levels in the headspace. These include esters, aldehydes, sulfur dioxide, terpenes, and sulfides, but their recovery by condensation or membrane methods is not commercially feasible at present since they are in extremely low vapor concentrations and the treatment volumes are large and seasonal.

The evaporative loss is strongly dependent of the juice and skin cap temperature, since this influences both the vapor pressure and the liquid phase activity coefficient of the ethanol. The total amount of the emission also increases with the square of the sugar content, assuming complete fermentation. The peak emission rate is somewhat delayed from the maximum fermentation rate due the effect of increasing ethanol content with fermentation progress.

The total ethanol emission for particular sugar content and fermentation temperature can be determined from generalized relationships shown in Figure 5-5 (Williams and Boulton 1983).

9. On-Line Fermentation Measurements

The traditional method by which fermentation progress and extent have been measured is by drawing samples from the fermentor one or two times each day. The density values are usually tabulated and in some cases graphed, but that is usually the extent to which they are analyzed. The main limitation of this approach is that the sample drawn is generally very small in comparison to the volume being fermented and often is not a good indication of the entire volume. A second limitation is the time required for sample collection when many fermentors are involved.

a. *Direct Measurements of Fermentation Rate and Extent*

There have been a number of attempts to automate the measurement of fermentation progress and these can be classified as those based on point sampling and those based on aggregate or overall properties of the fermenting volume.

I. ***Point Sampling Approaches.*** The traditional use of solution density is favored over other solution properties such as refractive index partly due to the instruments available and partly due to sensitivity. Of all the solution properties, the osmotic pressure shows the largest change from juices to wine, but the lack of commercially available osmometers has prevented this measure from being adopted.

Advances in the autosampling of small volumes has not been successfully adopted for several reasons. These include the need for a central instrument and a network of sampling lines with one to each fermentor. The blocking of the line by solids and yeast, fermentation within the line and degassing of the sample are complicating factors that exist in wine applications. The sample that needs to be drawn is often not that required by the instrument, but instead the volume required to dis-

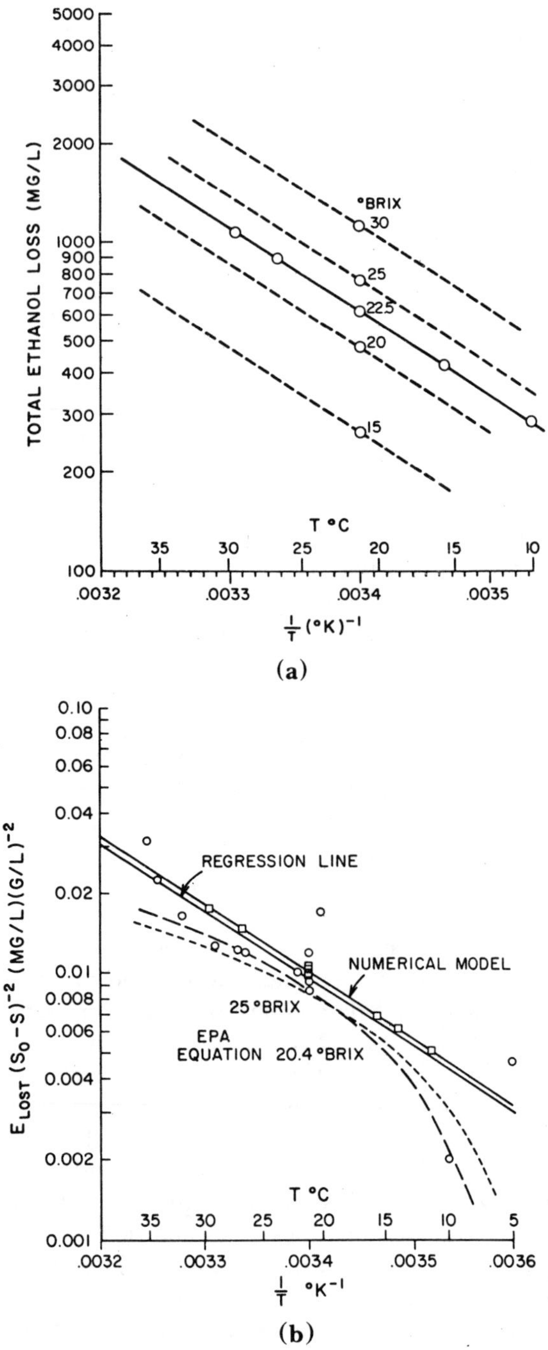

Fig. 5-5. a) Effect of temperature and sugar concentration on ethanol emissions. b) General relationship for the ethanol emission as a function of sugar level and temperature.

place the contents of the line before a sample of the fermentor juice reaches the instrument.

All of the solution approaches need temperature corrections to be applied, but this is usually a simple matter. The main limitation continues to be the concentration gradients within unstirred fermentors and the accuracy of the sample as it reflects the contents of the fermentor.

II. Aggregate Fermentation Approaches. The alternative to drawing samples for analysis is to measure features of the fermentation such as the volume of carbon dioxide evolved, the amount of heat released, or the change in juice or must weight. These features and their rates of change are closer reflections of the properties of the entire volume, are not intrusive, and avoid losses of juice.

The heat evolution approach has been attempted with beer fermentations (Ruocco et al. 1980) and is based on the measurement of flow rate and temperature rise of the coolant. The secondary contributions are significant both as losses of heat in released carbon dioxide and the radiant interchange of energy with the surroundings.

The gas evolution approach requires the measurement of gas flow and its integration over time. There are corrections for water and ethanol vapor pressures, but like the heat release approach, the measurements cannot be interrupted due to opening the fermentor for pump-overs or for the addition of juice. The accurate measurement of gas rates usually involves more than one meter since the flow rate varies from low rates at first to a peak value several times the earlier rates before it subsides again to low values. Examples of this approach are the studies by Shibata (1979) and El Haloui et al. (1988).

Both the heat release and gas evolution approaches require extensive instrumentation on each tank and uninterrupted measurements with no opportunity for shared sensors.

The measurement of weight loss by a shared pressure transducer has all of the desirable features of the aggregate measures but several advantages over the previously mentioned methods. The weight (and changes in it) is independent of temperature and it does not need to be read continuously. Rather, reading the weight of the juice in a fermentor need only be performed every four to six hours at most, and a central transducer can be shared among many fermentors by using a gas bubbling and switching valve. The weight loss can be related to the change in density (and therefore values such as Brix, Baume, or Oechsle) given the initial weight and its density by an external analysis.

The presence of skins and grape solids represent a constant background contribution to the weight that can be accounted for in the density estimation. The measurement is unlikely to be affected by pump-overs unless they are in progress during a reading and values on either side of this can be used for detecting such a situation and correcting for it. The addition of juice to a tank can be corrected for if the composition of the juice being added is determined or, alternatively, if the tank is mixed and a new starting density is determined. The weight loss associated with the pressing of red skins can also be accounted for from readings before and after the event.

Such a system for the direct measurement of wine fermentations has been developed and tested (Wheat 1991). The full-scale testing of this system was performed during the 1991 harvest at a major winery in the Napa Valley. The automated and manual sampling measurements for a 60,000-L fermentation are shown in Figure 5-6a. The fermentation had begun before the system was installed and the regions without measurements are due to power fluctuations external of the measurement system. This represents the first direct fermentation measurements at the commercial scale.

b. The Real-Time Interpretation of Fermentation Behavior

The direct fermentation measurements described previously enable the interpretation of

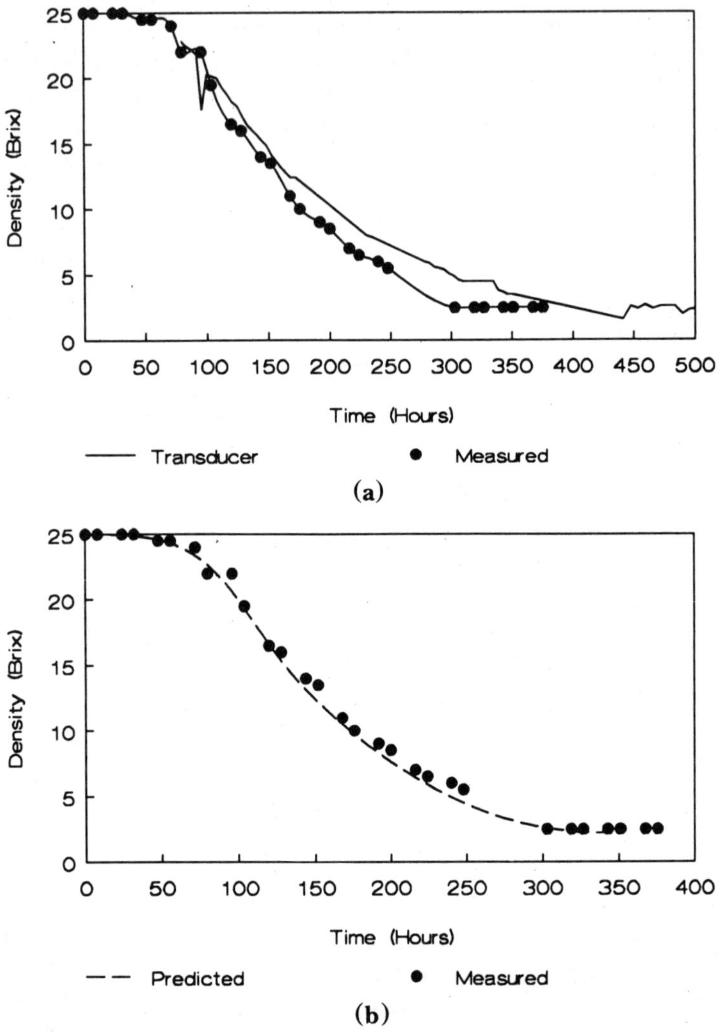

Fig. 5-6. a) A comparison of on-line and manual fermentation measurements. b) A comparison of model prediction and fermentation measurements.

the fermentation curves as they are developing. The interest in this is the accurate determination of the lag phase, the estimating of nutrient status early in the growth phase, the estimation of the maintenance activity of the yeast, and the prediction of heat release and expected completion times.

These features can be estimated for each individual fermentation by the application of previously developed fermentation models (Boulton 1980) in what is referred to as parameter estimation. In this approach the model equations are integrated using initial guesses of the lag time, specific growth rate, and maintenance rate of the yeast (the parameters in this case) and the numerical solution of the model is compared to the fermentation measurements. The estimation algorithm then makes refined estimates of the parameters until good agreement is obtained. This is usually done in a matter of minutes on a typical computer and it can be done without interrupting the measurement program. The values can then be used to interpret the nutritional status of the juice and the fermenting performance of the yeast population. The model prediction is compared to the measurements of the 60,000 L fermentation in Figure 5-6b.

10. Fermentor and Tank Designs

Fermentors usually differ from general storage tanks in several ways. There are particular aspects which relate to the filling with must, handling of skins, and temperature control that make the requirements of red fermentors somewhat different from those of white fermentors. Ideally, fermentors should be designed and selected so that they are general-purpose units and can handle both red and white musts. The design requirements will be set by the need to handle skins and the rates of heat and CO_2 release of the red fermentations.

a. *Filling and Emptying*

For red wine fermentations, smaller fermentors can be filled from the base, through a ball valve, rather than from the roof so as to minimize the extent of solids generation. Larger fermentors, with larger valve ports, will usually be filled from the top from an overhead must line. The ball or guillotine valve to be used for musts should have a diameter of approximately twice that of the corresponding valve for juice alone. Similarly, if this valve is to be used for emptying the skins by sluicing the skins out of the fermentor into a juice sump, or a pomace pump, it should be at the lowest point of the base, and this is usually near the front door, especially for tanks with sloping floors.

White musts can also be introduced through the red must valve (using a reducing fitting) or through the racking valve. The racking valve should be positioned at approximately 10% of the fermentor height from the base. This valve will usually be smaller in diameter since it will be used for liquids with some suspended pulp only. It is often offset to one side of the front of the tank and will sometimes be aligned so that it is tangential to the tank wall rather than radially in toward the center to promote swirling or vortex motion during mixing. Other designs have used an inlet inclined to the horizontal in order to develop a helical flow pattern to provide some vertical mixing.

The racking valve will be used for wine removal from the tank and is located above the base so as to minimize the solids drawn from the lees layer at the base of the fermentor. In the case of the red fermentor, the racking valve will be used to draw juice/wine for the pump-over operations as well as the racking of the wine at the end of the fermentation. As the wine is drawn off, the skin cap will move down the tank until no more wine can be racked. Small and medium-sized red fermentors will usually have a second door, (outward opening) located at about the same height as the racking valve which will then be opened to assist the removal of the skins by manual means. In larger fermentors this is often replaced by a screw conveyor in the base of the tank to remove the skins.

b. *Gas Venting*

It is not uncommon in large fermentors for the gas to be released suddenly, often during some agitation such as a pump-over operation, in what are referred to as *foam-overs*, where a liquid foam is actually blown out of the gas vents or roof door. One design rule is to size the gas vent system for 50% above the maximum expected gas release rate. Today, many of the vapor vents used are bidirectional in that they will not only permit gas venting during fermentation, but also allow air to enter as the tank is being emptied to prevent the development of a vacuum that could collapse or damage the tank by implosion.

c. *Expansion and Contraction*

Wine undergoes thermal expansions (and contractions) of approximately 0.2% per 10°C (18°F) at 20°C. While this might seem small, it is significant, (2 per 1,000, 20 per 10,000, and 200 per 100,000 volumes). Expansion risers and appropriate placement of the top access hole can account for this. They should be placed at the highest point of the tank so that headspace is not trapped inside the tank when it is completely full. If no expansion volume is provided and no appreciable headspace exists, the pressure of the expansion will easily exceed that needed to rupture the tank or cask. There are now several inert gas systems for maintaining headspace pressures that permit gas to leave the tank during liquid expansion and to enter during periods of contraction.

With barrels, the expansion at the rate of 0.1% for a 5°C change corresponds to an expansion (or contraction) of approximately 240 mL per barrel. Good temperature control during the storage of wine is not only of importance to the chemical stability of the wine but also to the physical integrity of the storage container and the minimization of barrel leaking associated with this.

d. Headspace and Ullage

The headspace in partially filled tanks is referred to as *ullage* and is of concern in terms of both surface deterioration where oxygen is present and the pitting of the steel by condensed droplets of wine vapor rich in sulfur dioxide. While one approach has been the development of the variable-volume tanks in which the roof is lowered to the wine surface, the more usual practice is to completely fill the tank whenever possible and to employ the expansion risers mentioned above.

The use of inert gas in a partially filled tank certainly addresses the problem of oxidation, but it does not prevent the condensation of moisture on the walls. The headspace above a wine will reach saturation with respect to ethanol, water, and other volatiles shortly after filling. Even small changes in the ambient wall temperature either due to wine cooling or a fall in the ambient temperature will result in condensation. Wine with a free sulfur dioxide level will provide a vapor phase concentration of sulfur dioxide that causes the pH of the condensate to become acidic since it is only weakly buffered. This can result in attack of the oxide layer of the stainless steel, and point corrosion and pitting can occur at the headspace wall.

e. Cleaning

Almost all fermentors used in the U.S. wine industry are stainless steel (generally Type 308 rather than 316, see Appendix C for a more detailed discussion of stainless steels) and the reason for this is the ease of cleaning this surface. The walls will often be coated with pigments, colloidal deposits, and tartrates after wine fermentations. This is especially true in the region of the cooling jacket and on the floor of the tank. Most wineries will employ one of several kinds of high-pressure spray cleaners to clean the fermentors and storage tanks. These spray units can be mounted on a tripod or stand that sits on the tank floor, and others have been suspended from the roof door in smaller tanks. Generally, cleaning begins with a hot-water cycle followed by sanitation with a 200-mg/L hypochlorite solution, and this is generally completed with a citric acid rinse solution.

f. Fermentor Shapes

The vast majority of fermentors are upright cylinders which are at least two diameters in height. Some have geometries of three to five diameters in height and this is usually due to floor space considerations. There are also many examples of square tanks and horizontal cylindrical tanks being used for fermentation. There is a variety of stands and support arrangements for smaller tanks. Most fermentors have an inclined floor sloping toward the front, while others have hemispherical or domed bases. The use of conical-based fermentors has not been generally accepted despite some advantages in pomace discharge for red wines. The outlet pipe in the floor of the tank should be located at the lowest point so that any liquid (wine or rinsing solutions) will be free to drain without leaving a residual pool that could become a source of contamination or corrosion associated with the salt content and pH of the residue.

One recent review of alternative fermentor designs with an emphasis in automated control has been made by Peyron and Feuillat (1985).

g. Circulation Patterns

Although it would be more predictable and reliable to have fermentations that are uniform in concentration, it is not a common practice to provide any mixing or stirring to fermenting wines. The only circumstance under which this might arise is as a result of circulation through an external heat exchanger.

As a result, most fermentors are mixed only by the natural convection circulations that will arise due to the momentum imparted by rising gas bubbles, and to a lesser extent, by the buoyancy effects of thermal convection currents. The thermal currents are generated by a warm, rising central core and cooler, descending layers adjacent to the outside wall. These outer, down-flowing layers are accelerated by the presence of a cooling jacket at the wall. The result is a toroid of fluid rotating by an upflow at the center and by a downflow at its outer circumference.

The extent of the circulation is controlled by the size and geometry of the fermentor and the rate of fermentation. The most favored shape for this pattern is a cylinder which has a diameter twice its height. The resistance to the circulation comes from the viscous effects associated with the velocity gradients near the walls, and as the fermentor becomes taller than its diameter a much more restricted circulation results. Fermentors which are several diameters tall, typically two to four diameters high, will have essentially no natural circulation pattern, and mixing will be limited to the motion caused by the ascending bubbles. Under these conditions the settling of yeast and suspended matter will be more extensive and the development of vertical concentration gradients enhanced. They are usually chosen for reasons of floor space utilization.

B. WHITE TABLE WINES

1. Styles of White Table Wines

White wine styles range from the aromatic fruit styles typified by most Riesling, Gewürztraminer, and Muscat wines to the barrel-aged, yeasty, and malolactic emphasis in many Chardonnays. These represent the extremes of wines dominated by cultivar attributes and grape composition and those whose main features come from winemaking treatments and nongrape materials. There are many white wine styles that fall between the extremes, some will be made to show fruit characteristics and others will be made to emphasize treatment effects, while still others will be made to show distinctive character only after some period of bottle aging.

Another important aspect of the style for white wines is whether there is to be significant residual sugar in the wine. The fermentation can be arrested with some level of sugar remaining by one of several ways and these include quickly lowering the wine temperature to 5°C or below, centrifuging, or a course and sterile filtration combination. The presence of residual sugar has an immediate bearing on the approach to clarification following fermentation, the maintenance of adequate free sulfur dioxide levels, and the extent to which the malolactic fermentation is discouraged. While some wines have significant residual sugar when bottled, they are often made as dry wines with a small juice addition just prior to bottling. This greatly reduces the chance of microbial growth during aging and storage so that the time between the juice addition and membrane filtration is as short as possible.

The complications and differences of opinion begin to arise when traditional European cultivars are grown in regions throughout the world and produce different degrees of varietal intensity, sometimes with more distinctive character than that normally seen in their traditional settings. The widespread practice of making and marketing varietal wines has posed dilemmas for many winemakers as to the extent to which fruit character should compete with winemaking treatments in the structure of a varietal wine. As a result there are many varietal wines which are made in the wine treatment style, and the importance of cultivar, appellation, and vintage are more related to birthright and marketing considerations than flavor attributes of the bottled wine. This is no better illustrated than by the common styles of California Chardonnay and the extent to which it can easily be mimicked in almost any part of the world using present winemaking techniques. The pursuit of such styles, while popular among some groups, has little, if anything, to gain from viticultural or enological techniques that enhance or capture fruit characteristics and has little relationship to the appellation or vintage.

The style in which some wines are made in New World countries today is considerably influenced by the opinions or personal preferences of some wine writers rather than by any regard to traditional styles or varietal characteristics. The emphasis in the following sections is on describing the basis for the many alternative treatments available to winemakers to pursue whatever style they please.

2. The Effect of Skin Contact

The effects of skin and seed extraction on the coarseness and astringency of white wines has long been understood. This was especially obvious in the press fractions from presses whose design permitted skin tearing and the excessive browning of the corresponding wines. The move toward fruitier white wines in the mid 1970s led to the development of highly clarified juices that experienced little skin contact and were essentially free of grape pulp during the fermentation (Singleton et al. 1975). In white wines containing sugar, this is preferable, since sugar, acidity, and grape flavors form the main components of the mouth feel and the wines are generally not aged further in wooden cooperage. In wines that are to be aged, there is a need for somewhat higher phenolic content, and this led to the introduction of controlled conditions of skin contact prior to fermentation.

The importance of the press fractions to the development of mouth feel and aging potential is well recognized in the production of sparkling wines and this is discussed further in Section D of this chapter.

The main interest in the use of skin contact was to generate the phenolics responsible for the development of aged character without the additional tannin and astringency associated with the press fractions. The fresh must would be transferred into a fermentor and allowed to undergo natural extraction for periods ranging from six to 24 hours. The juice is then drawn off, settled if necessary, and fermented in the usual ways. Studies of the changes in a number of aroma and phenolic components have shown that significant changes in composition occur during this time (Ramey et al. 1986). The actual practice gave rise to considerable variation in the effects obtained since few wineries took steps to control the contacting temperature and the importance of contact time was generally emphasized.

The widespread adoption of machine harvesting of grapes in the late 1970s provided conditions in which some skin contact was usually unavoidable and the extent of the practice at the winery was reduced accordingly. The introduction and adoption of the membrane presses in which skin tearing and seed attrition were essentially eliminated enabled the more desirable press fractions to be obtained without the usual tannin concentrations. These press fractions were very similar to the juices produced by skin contact and much easier to produce and control. As a result, the practice of deliberate, extended skin contact is rarely used anymore.

Under certain conditions, the extraction from skins cannot be well controlled, and the interest in lowering the astringency and browning potential of the finished wine gave rise to the deliberate oxidation of the juice, sometimes referred to as *hyperoxidation*. In this treatment, the natural grape phenoloxidase is used to promote the oxidation and polymerization of juice phenolics prior to fermentation. This is said to reduce the astringency and browning of the finished wine since a significant fraction of the juice phenols can be oxidized and their products will precipitate during the ethanol fermentation. The resulting wines are usually higher in straw and golden colors (Cheynier et al. 1990). The extent to which this objective can be achieved is dependent on the natural enzyme activity and the concentrations of the substrates that it prefers. A more detailed discussion of this treatment can be found in Section 3d of Chapter 3. There are few sensory studies of the effect on varietal character and the practice is rarely used in California.

The effects of fermentation and other winemaking actions on the levels of terpene volatiles have been studied in both Muscat (Gunata et al. 1986) and Gewürztraminer (Marais 1987), even though these components are generally present at concentrations well above threshold levels.

3. Role of Suspended Solids

The presence of the grape pulp that remains in a white juice after clarification is usually significant for a number of reasons. There are concerns about the further extraction of astringency during fermentation, the presence of significant oxidative enzyme activity in the pulp, the interference in the formation of fermentation bouquet, and the effects that this pulp can have on the rate and extent of the ethanol fermentation (Singleton et al. 1975; Tromp 1984).

The concentration of grape solids in many settled juices and most drained juices is of the order of 1 to 2% by volume. At this level there is unlikely to be significant extraction compared to that obtained by prior skin contact and the press fractions. The ability of the enzyme to contribute to oxidation ceases as soon as the dissolved oxygen is depleted. Most juices will consume at least one saturation of oxygen in handling, but unless the juice is deliberately aerated, further oxygen dissolution is limited. The other important aspect involves the role of these (and other) solids on the rate of fermentation.

In the mid 1970s winemakers began to prepare cleaner juices in order to emphasize the varietal character and a higher incidence of sluggish and incomplete fermentations began to appear (Wucherpfennig and Bretthauer 1970). Early studies in Germany, Schanderl (1959), had shown that in some juices the removal of suspended pulp by fining with gelatin or filtering caused much slower fermentation rates, but that by adding diatomaceous earth it fermented even faster than the original juice.

One common explanation of these findings was that the pulp was a source of additional yeast or yeast nutrients, and that clarification led to lower cell counts or poorer nutrient levels in some juices (Houtman and Du Plessis 1986). However, this could not explain the enhancement in rate that was observed by the addition of the diatomaceous earth (Schanderl 1959), bentonite (Groat and Ough 1978), yeast hulls (Geniex et al. 1983) or cellulose (Larue et al. 1985; Minarik et al. 1992). Another explanation was that the solids were providing nucleation sites for the development of carbon dioxide bubbles, carrying with them clumps of yeast in a rafting action. A correlation between the suspended viable yeast count and the fermentation rate was considered to be the cause of the faster fermentations (Groat and Ough 1978), although others consider it to be an effect. Others suggested that the supersaturated solution of carbon dioxide was inhibitory to yeast growth (Siebert et al. 1986), and that the presence of suspended solids helped to remove the level of supersaturation, thereby enabling faster fermentations. However, the effect of supersaturation levels of carbon dioxide on fermentation rate at normal pressures is slight, if at all, until pressures of several atmospheres are reached (Chen and Gutamis 1976), well above that which could exist during wine fermentations. Perhaps the two most important features of all of these studies are that they were all performed on a small scale (of different volumes and geometries) and generally unagitated, other than by the natural convection currents created by bubble evolution.

There is generally a poor correspondence between the small-scale fermentation rates of white juices and those at the commercial scale, even with the same juice. This paradox is added to by the conflicting results that were reported by various researchers on the extent to which clarification can affect fermentation rates and the response due to the levels of natural grape pulp (Ribéreau-Gayon 1953; Williams et al. 1978) or the addition of such solids as bentonite (Ough and Amerine 1965; Groat and Ough 1978), diatomaceous earth (Schanderl 1959; Thornton and Rodriguez 1986), activated carbon (Siebert et al. 1986), yeast hulls (Lafon-Lafourcade et al. 1985; Sponholz et al. 1990; Minarik et al. 1992), and colloidal or crystalline polysaccharides (Van Wyk 1978; Larue et al. 1985; Lonvaud-Funel et al. 1985; Thornton and Rodriguez 1986; Axcell et al. 1988; Minarik et al. 1992).

The role of the suspended solids grew more complicated as investigations began to study the formation of acetate esters, higher alcohols, and other fermentation byproducts (Crowell and Guymon 1963; Wucherpfennig and Bretthauer 1969; Ribéreau-Gayon et al. 1975; Fetteroll and Wurdig 1977; Williams et al. 1978; Groat and Ough 1978; Van Wyk 1978; Marino et al. 1983; Ribéreau-Gayon 1985; Amati 1986) whose formation is generally considered to be altered by the level of amino nitrogen, specific amino acids, and vitamins present in the juice.

An alternative and more general explanation of these results is that the solids are acting as adsorbers to which a range of juice components are attracted and held at concentrated levels. If a juice was deficient in one of the adsorbed nutrients, a stimulation in growth rate and/or byproduct formation could be expected if a significant number of yeasts grew in the presence of the solid surface. If, however, the juice has adequate concentrations of all nutrients, no growth rate enhancement would be expected although small changes in byproduct formation might be expected due to compositional changes near the solid surface. The adsorption of other components such as the fatty acid by various solids is to be expected and has been shown for the yeast hulls (Ribéreau-Gayon 1985), but this should occur in all juices and is probably not the reason for the observed effects in certain juices. Bentonite is known to be a weak cation exchanger with some preference for cationic solutes such as amino acids, and perhaps for thiamin and biotin. One study of the adsorption of amino acids from a juice by diatomaceous earth (Tercelj 1965) showed successive reductions in most amino acids with additional filtrations even if under exaggerated proportion of the earth to the juice.

If this adsorption picture is further tested, the removal of the solids should lead to a weak but significant depletion in the levels of the adsorbed components. This would be expected to amplify a nutritional deficiency when one exists and to have little if any effect in adequate juices. There are some anecdotal examples of this occurring and at least two studies have shown much poorer fermentation completion due to bentonite additions to juices (Bach and Hoffmann 1979; Vos and Gray 1979), and these support the view that nutrient depletion had actually occurred. These effects would also be juice dependent and this is probably why there are conflicting conclusions in different studies. The adsorption picture would also predict that at higher additions of the solids, the concentrations at the solid surface would be lower and the effects would be less. This has been reported for the formation of fatty acid esters in the presence of grape solids (Houtman and Du Plessis 1981, 1986) and for the same group in the presence of yeast hulls (Ribéreau-Gayon 1985).

Four features of this explanation which are well supported by general experience are: (1) not all juices benefit from the additions; (2) there is often an increase in cell populations associated with the addition; (3) there are several studies which show clear modifications in the pattern of trace byproduct formation in the presence of the solids; and (4) the effects do not continue as higher concentrations of the solid are used. The enhancement of fermentation can only occur in juices in which a growth limitation exists, and it is not surprising that some authors have not been able to reproduce the findings of others since they have been using different juices.

The enhancement of fermentation rates and extent of completion in some juices have often been attributed to a number of factors, but the general feature of nutrient adsorption has not been among them.

The effects that have been demonstrated have only been seen in unstirred, bench-scale fermentations and there are apparently no reports of such effects in commercial fermentors. One of the differences in small-scale, unstirred fermentations is the significant role of gravity in the settling of added yeast within the first 8 to 10 hours. This usually results in a far higher concentration of yeast in the lower fraction of the juice, often two or more times the usual concentration. When yeast growth begins there is a good possibility of local nutrient deletion and quite different growth history to that found in either moderately stirred or commercial-scale fermentors. The role of suspended solids seems to be an influence on the extent of this yeast settling effect.

Recent studies in juices (Guell and Boulton 1994) have shown that the effects of suspended solids (bentonite, diatomaceous earth, colloidal polysaccharide, carbon and cellulose acetate) on the rate of fermentation are only significant when the juice is not stirred and that the fastest rates were always obtained when concentration gradients were eliminated and the yeasts were kept in uniform suspension.

4. The Effect of Fermentation Temperature

The contribution of the fermentation temperature to white wine aroma is directly related to the retention of grape-based aromas and formation of the group of volatile byproducts referred to as *fermentation bouquet* (see Chapter 4 for a more detailed discussion of the compounds concerned). The second group of components is formed in clarified juices by most strains of *Saccharomyces cerevisiae* provided the temperature is controlled at 20°C or below. This is generally desirable in young, fruit-style wines, but the esters produced will hydrolyze within a matter of months unless the wine is stored at low temperatures.

The fermentation temperature for most white wines is in the range of 18°C to 24°C and there is little interest in fermenting at higher temperatures due to the progressive loss of volatiles under these conditions. In barrel fermentations beginning at 18°C, the temperature will usually rise to a peak of 22°C in midfermentation (Figure 5-2) before returning to the cellar temperature. The fermentation of white wines in larger wooden cooperage leads to higher peak temperatures as described in Section A.5 above, and is not widely practiced.

While there are additional effects of fermentation temperature on the formation of glycerol (Ough and Amerine 1965) and the higher alcohols (Ough et al. 1966), these are generally at less than threshold levels and the effects are insignificant from a sensory point of view. The formation of higher alcohols is of interest in the production of base wines for distillation and this is discussed in further detail in Section E.

5. The Malolactic Fermentation

The practice of conducting the malolactic fermentation in white wines is based on its traditional occurrence in wines during barrel aging in some regions for reasons of acidity adjustment. In other regions, it is discouraged and considered undesirable when fruit character is a major attribute of the wine style.

Within contemporary Chardonnay styles, there is a variation in which the malolactic fermentation is sought for reasons of flavor and mouth feel rather than for reasons of deacidification. The alternative of having concurrent malolactic fermentations is now common, in part to minimize the random variations of these contributions to the sensory aspects of the wine. The ability to ensure concurrent malolactic fermentation has been greatly increased with the advances in the commercial availability of bacterial starter cultures.

Generally this fermentation is not encouraged in other white wines such as varietal Sauvignon blanc, Chenin blanc, and the terpene cultivars Riesling, Gewürztraminer, and the Muscats. It is prevented by immediate clarification following the ethanol fermentation and the addition of sulfur dioxide to protective levels. The microbiology of the fermentation is discussed in more detail in Chapter 6.

6. Postfermentation Handling

At the end of the ethanol fermentation, the wine treatments will depend considerably on the extent to which further microbial activity is to be discouraged, the desire for *sur lies* contact, the aging pattern to be followed, and the level of residual sugar in the wine. Wine for sur lies contact will be transferred to a barrel with yeast lees, while those fermented in the barrel will be topped on the existing lees.

In many cases there will be adjustment of the sulfur dioxide levels to prevent further microbial activity such as additional bacterial action or the development of spoilage yeast. The sulfur dioxide will play a secondary role in the quenching of hydrogen peroxide that will be produced as a byproduct of certain oxidation reactions, even though its ability to compete for oxygen is practically nonexistent.

7. Aging and Sur Lies

The aging options range from placing clean wines into barrels, to placing wines with their yeast and some grape solids into the barrels (sur lies), to placing wines into larger cooperage and stainless steel tanks. There is often a hybrid of treatments with different wines that will form the basis of a blend or some distribution between the options with the same wine.

The sur lies approach provides the conditions, primarily several months of yeast contact, for many components within the yeast to leak into the wine. This is usually not actual autolysis in which the cell membrane is ruptured and the entire cellular contents are released (Feuillat and Charpentier 1982). The time required for autolysis is generally considered to be close to a year rather than the sur lies contact of three to six months. The resultant wines have a distinctive aroma that is usually recognizable and it has become another variation of contemporary Chardonnay styles. There are examples of the addition of fresh yeast and of periodic stirring of the lees, but there appear to be no reports indicating significant effects due to these treatments.

White wines will be much more sensitive to oxygen exposure than will red wines and there is a need for more careful handling during the aging period (Singleton 1987; Cilliers and Singleton 1990). The use of ascorbic acid as an oxygen-consuming additive has particular concerns in the barrel aging of white wines due to the possibility of acetaldehyde production (Wildenradt and Singleton 1974). This reaction is discussed in more detail in Chapter 10.

Following the aging or storage period the wines will generally be tested for several physical instabilities and treated as needed to ensure that these do not occur following bottling.

8. Continuous and Batch-Fed Fermentations

One example of special fermentation conditions that is interesting to consider is the case of the so-called syruped fermentations. These are produced by making several successive additions of fresh juice during the actual fermentation. The additions can be of the order of 10 to 25% by volume and several are made during the course of the fermentation. The result is the production of wines of much higher alcohol (typically 16 to 18% v/v) by fermentation rather than by fortification. This would enable more distinctive fortified wines of higher extract (in particular glycerol) to be made since all of the ethanol would be produced by fermentation.

The fermentations also pose some challenging questions to some common beliefs concerning the ability of yeast to remain viable and to ferment at these higher ethanol levels. While the term *ethanol tolerance* is often mentioned in regard to yeast strains and problem fermentations, it has been demonstrated that common wine yeast can complete fermentations at 18% v/v ethanol under the syruped conditions (Hohl and Cruess 1936; Hohl 1938). The syruped fermentation is somewhat akin to the fermentation producing sake in which the starch and protein of the rice mash are being hydrolyzed by enzymes from one particular yeast while a *Saccharomyces* strain is fermenting the glucose produced into ethanol. There is an ongoing release of amino acids as the rice protein is hydrolyzed, and this permits continued yeast growth throughout most of the fermentation. The same effect occurs in the juice additions of a syruped fermentation, but there is an additional effect due to the dilution of ethanol by the fresh juice volume.

The effect of making a juice addition to a fermentation can be analyzed by considering a starting sugar concentration of 210 g/L. When the fermentation has reached 140 g/L (and is approximately 33 g/L in ethanol), less than 20% of the original assimilable amino acid content will be remaining and the yeasts are approaching the transition phase. An addition of 20% of the same juice causes the sugar concentration to increase by $[S_j * 0.2 + S_w * 0.8]$ to 154 g/L. In the process, the ethanol is diluted by $[E * 0.8]$ to 26.5 g/L and the amino acid (and other nutrient) pool is increased by $[AA_j * 0.2 + AA_w * 0.8]$ to 36% of the initial value. The effect on the nutrient concentrations is the most pronounced on a percentage basis and a higher and younger yeast population is encouraged under slightly lower inhibition of ethanol but with almost twice the nutrient concentrations. As a result, more of the fermentation occurs by the growth activity and less by the maintenance activity, without relying on the viability of a smaller, stationary-phase cell population for the completion of the fermentation.

The production of fortified wines in this way would still require a spirit addition to achieve a desired level of 21% ethanol by volume. The quantity of spirit would be much less, the dilution of flavor components would be proportionately lower, and the rise in pH would be less than that under the usual fortification scheme.

C. LATE-HARVEST WINES

The term *late harvest* is used in the context of grapes whose harvesting has been delayed to allow or encourage the growth of molds such as *Botrytis cinerea*. Such grapes undergo a number of compositional changes ranging from simple concentration due to dehydration, microbial modification of tartaric acid and some phenolic, the production of several unusual keto acids (Wurdig and Schlotter 1969), enzymes such as laccase (Dubernet et al. 1977), and polysaccharides such as the β 1-3 glucan (Dubourdieu et al. 1981). Recently, an enzyme-linked assay for the detection of *Botrytis cinerea* has been developed (Ricker et al. 1991) which may aid in the quantification of the level of infection in future fermentation studies.

The sugar content of juices for botryized grapes is much higher than that normally obtained by sugar accumulation. They are often in the 250 to 300 g/L level, and these provide unusual conditions for yeast growth and fermentation. The resulting wines have aroma attributes that are very characteristic and sought after. In addition, the breaking of the berry skin leads to significant reductions in the levels of most amino acids and vitamins by the mold and other organisms.

1. Laccase Activity

The laccase enzyme is a more general and active enzyme than phenoloxidase and is unusual in that it is not inhibited by sulfur dioxide at the levels used in winemaking. The enzyme can use anthocyanins and some procyanidins as substrates and its activity, although reduced, continues in the wine after fermentation. While there have been a number of methods proposed for the measurement of the laccase activity, the simplest procedure is the measurement of oxygen consumption by the juice in the presence of 50 to 75 mg/L sulfur dioxide. The sulfur dioxide will almost completely inhibit the phenoloxidase activity but will have little effect on the laccase activity.

The important fermentation consideration of laccase activity in these juices is that because of its ability to consume dissolved oxygen it poses a special challenge in the supply of adequate oxygen for the yeast inoculum. The most effective means of controlling its activity is the lowering of juice temperature to 10°C to 12°C and juice aeration should be delayed until this has occurred.

The wine will also need to be held at lower than usual temperatures (5°C to 10°C) and handled with inert gas during storage to minimize the enzyme activity until the point of bottling.

2. Nutrient Status

The growth of the mold will consume some amino acids and a significant portion of the vitamin pool as it develops its colony on the berries. The depletion of the vitamins is usually larger on a percentage basis since these are generally at the tens and hundreds of micrograms per liter rather than the tens and hundreds of milligram per liter of most amino acids. This, together with the enhanced formation of sulfite-binding products, such as pyruvic and α-keto-glutaric acids, means that a more complete supplement of nutrients will be required for a satisfactory fermentation. The addition of thiamin, biotin and pantothenic acid, and nitrogen sources to juices is discussed in Section E.1 of Chapter 3.

3. Fermentation Temperature

As previously mentioned, the usual practice will be to ferment these juices at colder temperatures, in part to minimize the effects of laccase activity on the initial oxygen concentration, also for the retention of the aroma of the distinctive constituents in these juices.

The fermentations of late-harvest juices are generally slower than expected due to the slowing of the rate of yeast growth by substrate inhibition. The yeast fermentation is fastest at glucose or fructose contents of 60 g/L and below (Hopkins and Roberts 1935a, 1935b). At the concentrations typically found in late-harvest juices (250 to 300 g/L), the fermentation rate would be expected to be at least 20% slower due to the sugar concentration alone. This will be in addition to the effects of colder fermentation temperatures and the probability of being deficient in one or more nutrients.

As a result, it is common for these fermentations to continue for six to eight weeks before fermentation ceases. The cessation of the fermentation will occur when there are no viable yeast remaining. This point is reached shortly after the rate of cell death exceeds the rate of cell growth and the viable population has fallen to zero. The death rate is influenced by the ethanol concentration and temperature, while the growth rate is controlled by inhibitions due to the prevailing sugar and ethanol concentration and the availability if nutrients, typically assimilable nitrogen. As a result, there is considerable variation in the final sugar and ethanol concentrations in wines of this kind.

4. Postfermentation Handling

The possibility of significant laccase activity after fermentation requires that these wines be handled in a strictly anaerobic manner. They will usually be stored in stainless steel rather than small wooden cooperage and held at low storage temperatures with an inert gas headspace.

The wines from such mold-infected grapes are also higher than usual in polysaccharide content due to more extensive cell wall degradation. The implications for wine treatments involve the more difficult filtration of these wines especially with nominallysterile pads and membranes. The application of the glucanase enzymes to enhance such filtration has been demonstrated (Wucherpfennig and Dietrich 1982; Villettaz et al. 1984), and this is discussed in more detail in Section E.3.f of Chapter 3.

D. PREPARING BASE WINES FOR SPARKLING WINE

The preparation of base wines for the production of sparkling wine has several unique features that differ from those of white table wines. There will be some variations in style within this group due to the exclusion or otherwise of the malolactic fermentation and the extent of aging some components in wooden cooperage. The following section will be restricted to the juice preparation and fermentation conditions rather than all aspects of the production of sparkling wines.

1. Direct Pressing

The juices for sparkling wines are typically generated without crushing and the grape clusters or partially broken fruit and juice are conveyed directly into the press. This is true for both white and colored grapes and they will be handled in the same manner from this point on. The distinction between free-run and the press fractions is less obvious under these conditions since much of the berry breakage only begins after the press cycle has begun. There is considerable importance given to the press cuts that are taken and these are often clarified and fermented separately. The phenolic content and aging potential of the second cut is often given more importance than the first cut in such wines.

The juices are usually clarified by centrifuging or filtration and cooled prior to fermentation. The quantity of sulfur dioxide employed at the juice stage ranges from none at all to 50 mg/L and the low pH of these juices (2.8 to 3.0) favors the molecular form and the use of lower sulfur dioxide levels for antibacterial action. There are variations in the extent to which juice aeration and must oxidation are practiced as style factors, but the general approach is one of juice protection for multiple oxygen saturations.

2. Primary Fermentation

Most base wines are fermented at temperatures in the range of 18°C to 22°C in order to have swift fermentations without the obvious formation of fermentation bouquet, yet warm enough to retain most of the grape volatiles. It is not traditional to have concurrent malolactic fermentations in these wines, it is usually encouraged in the wines after fermentation when desired.

The yeasts employed are selected to favor neutral characteristics since much of the components of the traditional style will come from treatments to the young wines and the yeast contact of the second fermentation. Yeast selection has generally been based on the minimization of esters and of sulfite and sulfide formation.

3. Secondary Fermentation

The base wine will often be stabilized and a sugar and nutrient mix with an inoculum will be added to initiate the second fermentation in the bottle (for the *méthode Champenoise* and transfer method). The yeast growth will be limited to usually one division before it is inhibited by ethanol and carbon dioxide pressure, while the remainder of the sugar is fermented by yeast in the stationary phase. For this reason more attention has been directed toward the fermentation condition of the yeast inoculum in these wines (Monk and Storer 1986; Malfeito-Ferreira et al. 1990). The effect of pressure is primarily on the growth rate of the yeasts rather than on their fermentation rate. The fermentation rate is unaffected by pressure up to approximately five atmospheres (Chen and Gutamis 1976).

The laborious process of riddling in which the yeast sediment is edged down toward the neck of the bottle has been circumvented by the introduction of immobilized yeast in alginate beads (Bidan et al. 1978) and on solid supports (Müller-Spath 1982; Coulon et al. 1983). While early practical difficulties associated with this approach involved the uniform inoculation of bottles, the process has been adopted to some degree by a number of companies.

A related development for the production of large volumes of sparkling wines has been the application of two to three fermentors in which the yeast are immobilized onto a bed of wood chips. The base wines are passed through the fermentors in a continuous manner while under pressure and bottled soon after.

E. PREPARING WINES TO BE DISTILLED

Wines to be distilled have special requirements that differ significantly from those to be prepared as table wines. The main aim is to minimize the concentration of acetaldehyde that will carry over in the first vapors to become a defect in the new distillate. A second aim is to discourage the formation of acetate esters, and a third is to prevent the malolactic fermentation in the young wine. Some of these requirements have led to the development of viticultural conditions that favor the preparation of low-pH, low-ethanol, neutral young wines. The use of primarily one cultivar (Ugni blanc) in most of the Cognac region and the heavy cropping of these vines have led to juices that only reach moderate sugar levels and are low in potassium and, therefore, pH.

1. Juice Preparation

The juices are not treated with sulfur dioxide since it will increase the quantity of acetaldehyde retained in the young wine. There is little concern for juice oxidation, even the solids content of the juice is quite high by wine standards, and the phenoloxidase would be expected to be quite active. In the absence of sulfur dioxide additions, even to the newly fermented wines, the discouragement of bacterial activity in young wines that are held on the lees prior to distillation is left to the naturally low pH and wine storage temperature.

The juices are prepared by direct pressing of the clusters and all of the press fractions are combined and fermented. The relatively high solids content and somewhat aerobic juice handling have been shown to lead to higher levels of the fusel oils during fermentation (Crowell and Guymon 1963), and this a desirable feature of these wines.

2. Fermentation Temperature

The juices are fermented at temperatures in the range of 20°C to 25°C and in the presence of grape solids to provide a swift fermentation and yet to avoid the formation of significant acetate ester character. The final ethanol content will usually be in the range of 7 to 9% by volume. The fermentations are generally spontaneous in Cognac but the use of selected, low-sulfite strains would seem to provide advantages in more rapid and complete fermentations and lower final aldehyde levels. The wines will be distilled shortly after the fermentation has been completed or as the stills become available.

3. Retention of Yeast Lees

The wines are not racked and the wine lees are mixed and transferred into the stills for distillation. There will be a range of fatty acid esters that are released from the yeast during distillation and these have positive sensory attributes in the new distillates and the aged spirits. The discouragement of the malolactic fermentation seems to be to minimize the formation of diacetyl and ethyl acetate and their presence in the young distillate. The wine lees would also contain the spent bacterial culture and this is likely to release additional quantities of these components during distillation.

F. RED TABLE WINES

The composition of a wine is predetermined by the initial composition of the grapes and subsequently determined by the particular treatments that it undergoes during the winemaking sequence. The combination of the effects of grape cultivar and maturity, must handling, fermentation conditions, microbial control, aging, and other treatments constitute the style in which the wine is made.

1. Styles of Red Table Wines

Red wine styles can range from those which reflect the composition of the grape to those which reflect the winemaking treatments that it will receive following the fermentation. The factors influencing composition such as the cultivar, the location, and manipulation of the vineyard and the growing season are of utmost importance in the first style while the postfermentation handling, age and type of cooperage, and length of the aging period are of utmost importance in the second style. The winemaking options which can contribute to both styles involve the management of the fermentation and extraction flavor and phenolics by the choice of temperature, juice and skin contact, and the timing of pressing.

The variations in winemaking approaches to juice and skin contact involve the partial crushing of clusters, destemming, and the transfer of some whole berries into the fermentor along with the must and the less common practice of retaining part or all of the stems in the must. The extent to which whole berries are included can vary from 10 to 50%, but typically is in the region of 15 to 20%. The practice of stem retention varies with the condition of the stems, which can show wide seasonal variation, and is generally less than 50% when used. The stems can cause significant color loss due to anthocyanin adsorption, but they also contribute to the tannin extraction and provide a different phenol pattern than that generally contributed by the skins and seeds. The dry woody stems of some cultivars can contribute herbaceous aromas to the wine, but, in general, the stems are considered to be of little value or a negative influence.

A contrasting approach is the use of carbonic maceration in which crushing is minimized or avoided entirely. Instead, the clusters are placed inside the fermentor either stacked in trays or dumped in with a minimum of breakage. This approach is considered in more detail in Section 9 of this chapter. The resulting wine is lighter in color and phenolic extraction than those made in the traditional, crushed-berry contacting method, and it possesses characteristic aromas due to the treatment. The method requires hand-picked fruit, free of mold, and the ability to hold the grapes at temperatures of 20°C to 25°C for several days.

2. Juice, Skin, and Seed Contacting

Of the phenols that are found in the seed and skins of grapes, less than half them will be available for extraction into the wine. The proportion of the anthocyanins and total phenols that were extracted into the wine varied between 20 to 30% depending on the cultivar and vineyard location. In one study, Cabernet Sauvignon grapes were found to contain 1.4 mg of phenols, 4.3 mg of anthocyanin per g of fresh berries, yet only 27 and 28% of these are extracted into the resultant wines (Van Balen 1984). Similar variations have also been reported with Pinot noir (Siegrist 1985).

The contacting method employed will have a significant effect on the rate and a lesser effect on the extent of extraction, and a winemaker may adopt a particular contacting approach based on previous experience with the grapes to be used. Within each of the following contacting approaches there are nuances that can be introduced in an attempt to either enhance or diminish the natural variations in composition between the cultivars, but the composition is generally not known before the extraction occurs.

One additional consideration is the presence of elemental sulfur residues on red grape skins and the contribution that this might have to the production of hydrogen sulfide during fermentation. Early studies that showed this relationship (Rankine 1963; Acree et al. 1972; Schütz and Kunkee 1977; Wenzel et al. 1980) was generally conducted with residue levels much higher than the 1 to 2 ug/L usually found on grapes (Wenzel et al. 1980; Thomas et al. 1993b). Recent studies have shown that hydrogen sulfide formation cannot be correlated with the sulfur residue levels when they are less than 2 ug/L (Thomas et al. 1993a).

a. Maceration Prior to Fermentation

In this approach, the skins and seeds are permitted to soak for a period of one to two days prior to the initiation of the fermentation in an attempt to get a more aqueous extraction without the effects of ethanol on the grape cells. The must is generally cooled to between 15°C and 20°C to slow the onset of a natural fermentation and is usually pumped over once or twice each day to enhance the extraction. A heavily colored juice is obtained within 24 hours but the skins are retained and the mixture is inoculated. The fermentation usually proceeds slowly at first until the temperature rises to 25°C or higher within two days. While this approach is practiced by a number of wineries, there are few analytical studies comparing either young or aged wines obtained by the method to those made by conventional contacting. This approach is alternatively referred to as *cold maceration* or *cold soaking*. The influence of this extraction approach on the color retention during subsequent aging needs to be investigated.

b. Conventional Maceration

The conventional approach to must contacting is to transfer the new must into a fermentor, to inoculate with yeast (and if desired, malolactic bacteria) and to control the temperature in the range of 25°C to 30°C. Within the first day of active fermentation the skins will rise to the top of the juice and form a skin cap that usually occupies about one-third of the fermenting volume. Throughout the fermentation period, usually twice each day, juice will be drawn from the fermentor and pumped up to the top of the fermentor and distributed over the cap. This pump-over operation usually provides a predetermined juice volume to the cap that will permeate the cap, displacing interstitial juice, and partly lowering the cap temperature. The setup used for the pump-over operation varies from simple discharge of a transfer hose into the headspace to rotating irrigators suspended from the door in the roof. In California, the cap irrigators are made by Westec Winery Equipment and York Machine Works.

The most common practice uses one juice volume during each pump-over operation and two such operations per day. Some wineries use two volumes per pump over while others vary the volume and frequency, often beginning with larger volumes or more frequent pump overs in the early stages of fermentation and then reducing this toward the point of pressing. In larger fermentors, the cooling of the juice by external heat exchangers is generally incorporated into the pump-over operation.

c. Maceration after the Fermentation

The practice of additional maceration following the completion of the fermentation has traditionally been used in various parts of Europe. The approach is claimed to provide additional extraction from the skins which modifies the mouth feel of the young wine. Once the fermentation is over, the fermentor is closed and left alone for between one and three weeks. When the gas bubbles which provide the buoyancy have left the skin cap, it typically submerges and the skins fall to the base of the fermentor.

Studies of component extraction in red wine indicate that the peak in color occurs within the second day of fermentation and those of skin tannins and flavonoids (or total phenols) usually show complete extraction by the end of the fermentation (Ribéreau-Gayon 1974; Somers and Evans 1979; Van Balen 1984). It is doubtful that further extraction from the skins can take place if effective contacting was provided during the fermentation. The more likely event is the continued extraction from the seeds which have usually only provided about 70 to 80% of their possible extract by the end of a five- or six-day fermentation. Studies of the extended maceration practice at wineries in California, primarily with Cabernet Sauvignon and Merlot grapes, have generally shown insignificant differences in composition, polymerization rates, or sensory differences due to this treatment and only slight effects have been noted when an effect was seen.

Table 5-2. Pigment distribution in a young Cabernet Sauvignon wine.

Anthocyanin	Concentration (mg/L)	Percentage of total
Delphinidin glucoside	49.4	12.9
Cyanidin glucoside	2.8	0.7
Petunidin glucoside	30.5	8.0
Peonidin glucoside	12.9	3.4
Malvidin glucoside	144.8	37.9
Malvidin glucoside acetate	77.0	20.2
Malvidin glucoside p-coumerate	15.8	4.1
Other acetates	41.4	10.8
Other cinnamates	7.5	2.0
Total	382.1	100

Data of Nagel and Wulf (1979).

d. Component Extraction from Skins and Seeds

I. Anthocyanins. The extraction of the flavonoids, anthocyanins, and tannins from the seeds and skins during red wine fermentations show patterns that depend on the group involved. It is important to understand these patterns when attempting to manipulate the extent and proportions of extraction by alternative contacting approaches.

The chemical components responsible for the red and purple colors of red wines are the anthocyanins and these are found only in the outer layers of the skin of red wine grapes. In *V. vinifera* cultivars these include malvidin, peonidin, petunidin, and cyanidin, primarily as the free form and secondarily as their β-3-glucosides. The glucosides often have a smaller fraction acylated with acetic acid or one of the cinnamic acids. Table 5-2 shows the distribution within the pigments of a young Cabernet Sauvignon wine (Nagel and Wulf 1979). One notable exception to the presence of acylated pigments in *V. vinifera* grapes is the cultivar Pinot noir (Rankine and Webb 1958). The anthocyanin patterns of other cultivars have been determined in Syrah (Roggero et al. 1984), in several Port wine cultivars (Bakker and Timberlake 1985), in Tempranillo (Herbrero et al. 1988) and several others (Lay and Dreager 1991).

The monomeric anthocyanins are involved in two equilibria which influence the observed color of the wine. The first is a pH-dependent ionization in which the colored flavylium ion (a red cation form at low pH) is in equilibrium with a colorless pseudobase. At a pH of 3.0, approximately 50% of malvidin-3-glucoside is in the colored form. The second is the binding equilibrium with bisulfite ions to form a colorless sulfonic acid. The contribution of the monomeric forms to red wine color depend on the pH and the free SO_2 level in the wine and the age of the wine.

II. Procyanidins and Tannins. The procyanidins are polymers of the flavan-3-ols that are between two and eight units in size. They represent the major fraction within the polymeric phenols and their special status is due to their role in the polymerization of the anthocyanins during the first years in the life of a red wine.

In the past 10 years there have been a number of important studies that have quantified the dimer, and more recently, trimer procyanidin fractions of several red wine cultivars (Ricardo da Silva 1990). The four main dimers, generally referred to as B1, B2, B3, and B4, have been quantified by HPLC for Cabernet

Sauvignon, Merlot, and Malbec (Salagoity-Auguste and Bertrand 1984) and for Carignan and Mourvedre (Ricardo da Silva et al. 1992). Other studies have analyzed their levels in wines from different cultivars and regions (Etievant et al. 1988), their extraction from seeds during fermentation (Oszmianski and Sapis 1989), and their source in grape skins, seeds, and stems (Ricardo da Silva et al. 1991a, 1992). Recent studies have addressed their interaction with various proteins used in the fining of wines (Ricardo da Silva et al. 1991b), but the roles that these components play on sensory and long-term color stability are not yet fully understood. The tannins are generally defined as polymeric phenols capable of binding with proteins and they include the procyanidins as well as the nonflavonoid polymers.

III. Pigment-Tannin Complexes. As indicated earlier, there is now good evidence (Kantz and Singleton 1990; Singleton and Trousdale 1992) that the anthocyanins and tannins are involved in the formation of complexes that help to keep both the anthocyanins and the tannins in solution. This feature is particularly important in retaining and stabilizing the pigments so that they are available to partake in the polymerization that occurs during aging, especially during the first year, when most of it takes place. It has now been established that the procyanidins are found in the grape skins of most red cultivars and they are extracted during the fermentation. One important exception to this pattern is with grapes of Pinot noir which lack the procyanidins in its skins (Thorngate 1992). As a result Pinot noir grapes seem to be unable to form the anthocyanin-tannin complexes and this probably accounts for the less intense color and unusual color stability of wines from this cultivar.

e. *Rates of Component Extraction During Conventional Contacting*

There are several alternative descriptions of the extraction of components from the skins and seeds during fermentation. These range from dissolving of components from a porous matrix until it is exhausted, a release that is controlled by cell leakage and a combination of extraction with diffusional control and the establishment of certain equilibria between some of the components.

One of the few studies to analyze the extraction of the flavonoids from skins during fermentation found little difference between the extraction rates of anthocyanins, their glucosides, and their acylated forms, but their extraction was significantly different from that of catechin and epicatechin (Nagel and Wulf 1979).

The slower extraction of polymeric materials cannot be explained simply by their lower diffusivity and there appear to be different factors controlling their release and extraction.

The extraction curve for anthocyanins rises steeply at first then slows as it approaches a maximum by day two or three and then declines slightly during the remainder of the fermentation as shown in Figure 5-7. Several studies (Ribéreau-Gayon 1974; Somers and Evans 1979; Nagel and Wulf 1979) have shown this general pattern while the extraction of other components (flavonoids and tannins) shows increasing concentration with contact time (see Fig. 5-8 [Van Balen 1984]). If the extraction is simply based on the diffusion of pigments from the grape skin into the juice, an exponential approach to the final level would be expected and the extraction could be accelerated by increasing the mixing of the juice and skins. This is not observed however and other descriptions of the color extraction are required.

One possible explanation is that the rate of development of cell leakage is controlling the release of pigments but this does not account for the subsequent decline in concentration in the second phase of the fermentation. Another is that a rapid extraction takes place followed by a slower complexing or binding that causes the decline in concentration. The establishment of a secondary equilibrium in-

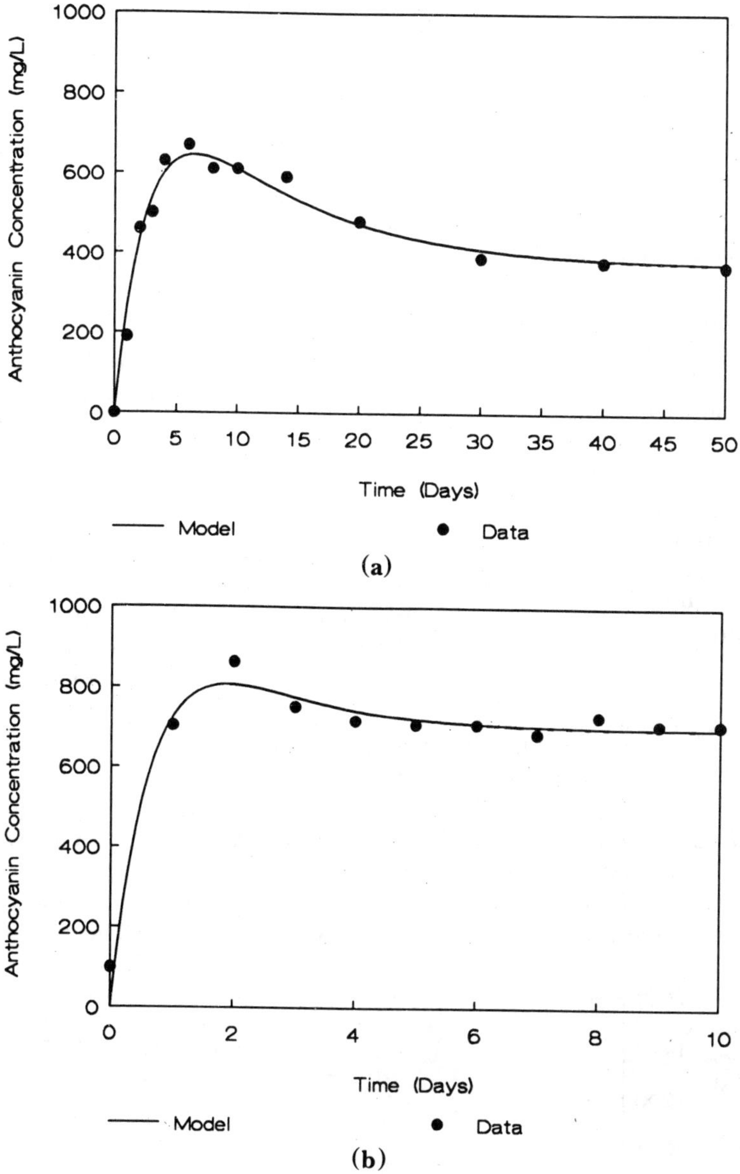

Fig. 5-7. The extraction of anthocyanins during fermentation. a. Bordeaux red wine (data of Ribéreau-Gayon 1964). b. A Shiraz wine (data of Somers and Evans 1979).

volving the pigments has been thought to occur for some time. Possibilities would be self-associations of the pigments and/or coupling with groups such as the tannins (Singleton and Trousdale 1992) which follow a slower, two-stage, extraction pattern coming from both the seeds and the skins. Our present understanding of the extraction of the anthocyanins compared to other flavonoids favors the interpretation in which the extracted anthocyanins quickly form a stable coupling with the extracted tannins (Singleton and Trousdale 1992).

The extraction of flavonoids from the skins follows a typical first-order rate equation:

$$d[F]/dt = k * [F_e - F], \qquad (5.1)$$

in which the rate of extraction is proportional to the current and final concentrations. F_e is the final concentration and k is the rate constant. When integrated, this leads to an exponential approach to a limiting concentration at long times:

$$[F]_t = F_0 + F_e[1 - \exp(-k * t)], \quad (5.2)$$

where F_t is the flavonoid content at time t and the initial flavonoid concentration; F_0 is usually not zero. Measurements of the flavonoid extraction (Van Balen 1984) confirm this description, showing that half of the final concentration is achieved by the end of the second day of fermentation (Figure 5-8).

The pigment extraction patterns reported in the literature are well described by a two-term extraction model in which the initial faster extraction is followed by a second but slower depletion to a lower final value. In this situation the rate of extraction can be described by:

$$d[A]/dt = k_1 * [A_1 - A] - k_2 * [A - A_2], \quad (5.3)$$

where $[A]$ is the anthocyanin concentration and A_1 and A_2 are the equilibrium values for the first and second equilibria. The constants k_1 and k_2 are the first-order rate constants for the irreversible extraction and second equilibrium.

The concentration of anthocyanins in the juice at any time during fermentation is then described by the following relationship:

$$[A]_t = A_1 * (1 - \exp(-k_1 * t)) - A_2 * (1 - \exp(-k_2 * t)), \quad (5.4)$$

where the constants k_1, k_2, A_1, and A_2 are the same as in Equation (5.3). The data of Riberean-Gayon 1964 and Somers and Evans (1979) are shown in Figure 5-7 together with the best fit of the proposed model for the extraction. The rate constants and anthocyanin values for this model are summarized in Table 5-3, together with the corresponding values determined for other studies of this kind. The large variations in the rate constants suggest that the factors responsible for the rates are not the same for all fermentations and there is a need to further identify the species involved and mechanism of this extraction process with different grapes.

This model describes the actual changes in the anthocyanin concentration and not those of observed color. The dynamics of the observed color are more complicated, being a result of at least two main effects. The first is

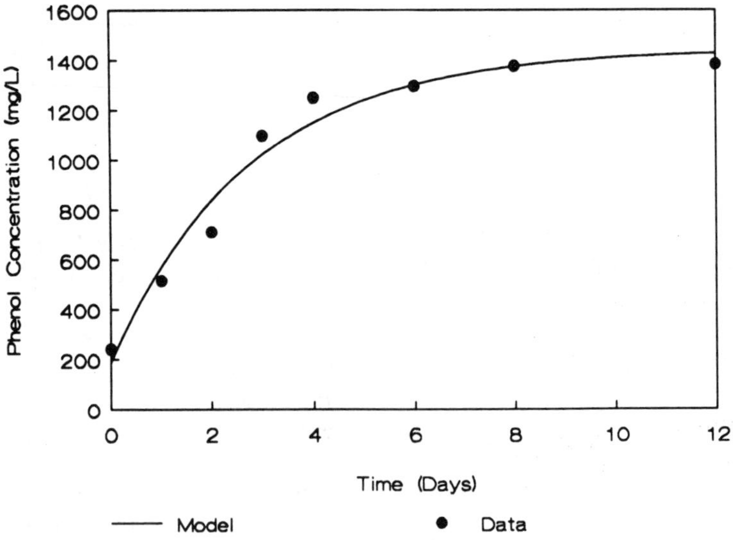

Fig. 5-8. The extraction of flavonoids during fermentation.

Table 5-3. Model constants for the extraction of anthocyanins into wines.

Author(s)	Temperature (C) cultivar	Rate constant $k1$ (1/day)	Rate constant $k2$ (1/day)	Concentration A_1 (mg/L)	Concentration (A_2 (mg/L)
Ribéreau-Gayon (1974)	Unknown Unknown Total anthocyanin	0.319	0.098	1200	842
Somers and Evans (1979)	Unknown Shiraz (Syrah) Total anthocyanin	1.39	0.690	1500	802
Nagel and Wulf (1979)	20–22°C Cabernet Sauvignon Malvidin-3-glucoside	1.42	0.196	189	69.7
Nagel and Wulf (1979)	20–22°C Cabernet Sauvignon Total anthocyanin	1.62	0.175	572	327
Van Balen (1984)	20-23°C Ruby Cabernet Total anthocyanin	0.657	0.221	992	625
Van Balen (1984)	20-23°C Cabernet Sauvignon Total anthocyanin	0.405	0.114	882	482

an association between anthocyanin molecules at concentrations above 50 mg/L and this has been demonstrated to provide almost double the color expected from the anthocyanins at normal wine concentrations of 300 to 500 mg/L (Somers and Verette 1988). The second is the color loss during fermentation due to the solvent effect of the increasing ethanol concentration during the fermentation (Somers and Evans 1979).

The extraction of tannins during fermentation lags behind that of the anthocyanins, displaying a two-term extraction model with first- and zero-order terms. This is in contrast to the exponential rise to a final value of the flavonoids or the rise to a maximum followed by a depletion to a final level of the anthocyanins.

One description of the rate of tannin extraction suggests that there is a diffusion term that depends on the wine concentration and a leakage (or dissolution) term that is independent of the wine concentration. The rate equation takes the form:

$$d[T]/dt = k_3 * [T1 - T] + k_4 \qquad (5.5)$$

where $[T]$ is the tannin concentration; k_3 and k_4 are the first- and zero-order rate constants and $T1$ is the equilibrium tannin concentration of the diffusional extraction. This might be interpreted as an equilibrium extraction from the skins and a parallel dissolution/extraction of tannin from the seeds.

The extraction of tannin during fermentation would then be described by the integrated form of (5.5):

$$[T]_t = T_1(1 - *\exp(-k_3 * t)) + k_4 * t \qquad (5.6)$$

The tannin extraction pattern during one example of fermentation and extended maceration (Ribéreau-Gayon 1974) is shown in Figure 5-9. The pattern for tannin extraction from seeds alone (Singleton and Draper 1964), in water and model wine, is shown in Figures

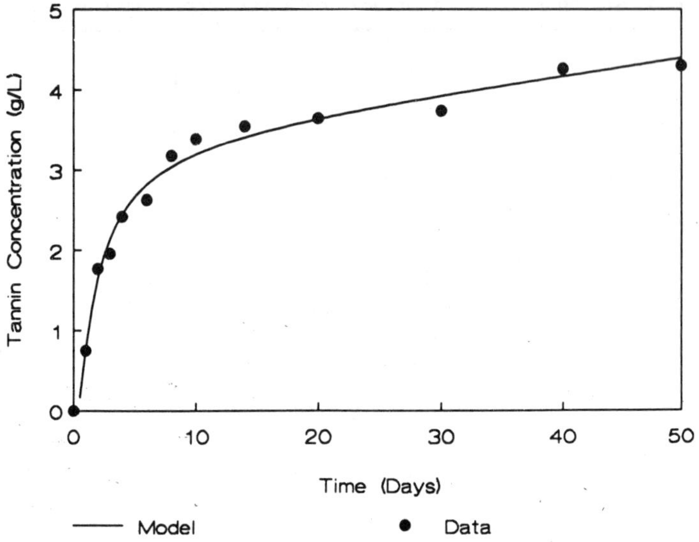

Fig. 5-9. The extraction of tannin during fermentation (data of Ribéreau-Gayon 1964).

5-10a and 5-10b. The corresponding rate constants are summarized in Table 5-4. The first-order constant is quite sensitive to temperature in the absence of ethanol but less so at wine concentrations. The larger constant observed in the wine extraction is probably due to this analysis showing tannin from the skins as well as from the seeds. The zero-order constant shows the same temperature characteristic as the first-order constant, decreasing at higher temperatures. The equilibrium tannin concentration increases with both temperature and ethanol content. The effect of the 20°C increase is to increase tannin concentration by 80 to 90%, and that of 14% v/v ethanol is to increase it by 50 to 60%. The tannin extraction into wine differs in terms of the presence of other tannin sources and the use of another concentration measure. However the slower constant for long-term component may be due to the adsorption of other material onto the seeds or more stratified conditions within a fermentor. It appears from the similarity of the extraction kinetics that much of the tannin extraction that occurs during extended maceration may be coming from the seeds rather than the skins, as is generally believed, and this may have sensory implications (Rossi and Singleton 1966).

3. Fermentation Temperature

The fermentation temperature influences the rate of yeast growth and thereby the time course of ethanol formation. There are increasing rates of extraction of all phenolic components at higher temperatures, but as discussed previously, this does not usually increase the solubility of the anthocyanins that are extracted and often there is little enhancement in color. The higher rate of heat release can lead to increasing temperature when inadequate cooling is available, and this in turn can lead to the enhanced formation of undesirable byproducts if a nutrient limitation exists. Examples of such components are hydrogen sulphide and acetic acid. The cessation of yeast fermentation due to temperatures rising above 35°C are rare today due to better cooling capability.

The influence of fermentation temperature on the retention of varietal character appear to be secondary to that caused by the stripping associated with the volumes of carbon dioxide evolved. The existence of any varietal aromas in wines is due to the fact that these components have very low volatility, and as a result are not readily depleted by entrainment in the carbon dioxide evolution. They do however

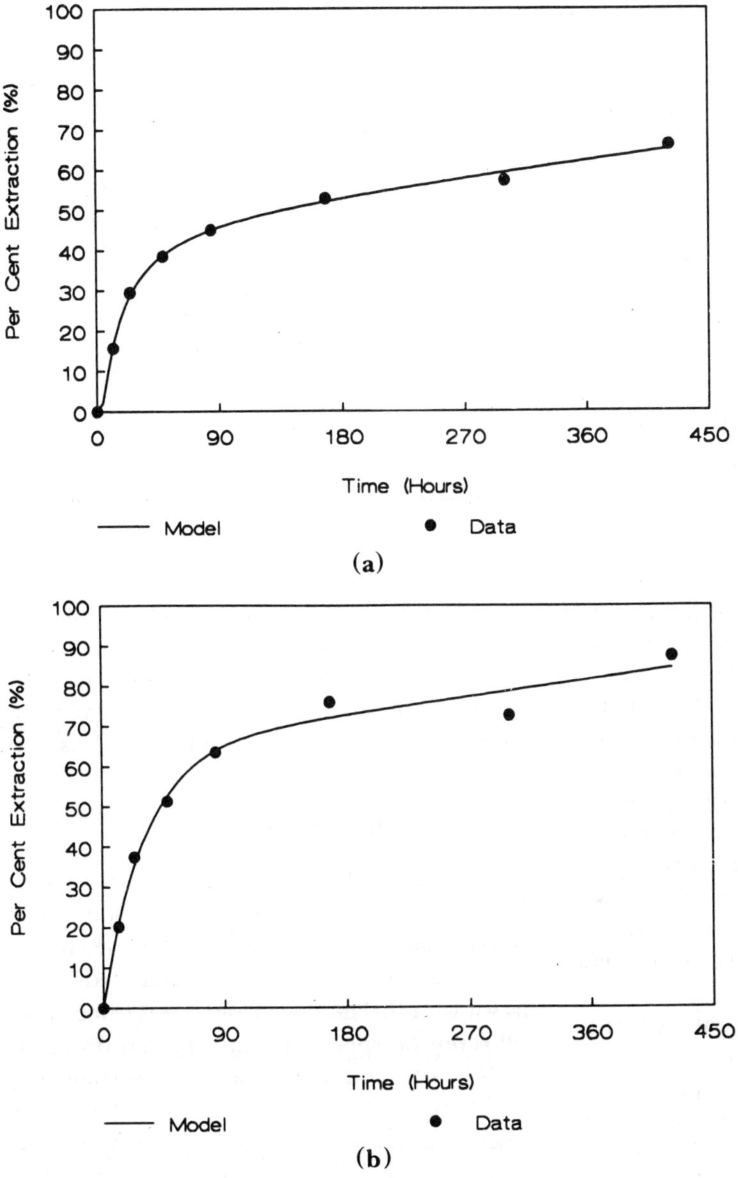

Fig. 5-10. The extraction of tannin from grape seeds (data from Singleton and Draper 1964). a) Water at 20°C b) Model wine at 20°C.

have sensory thresholds that are at very low concentrations. The major effect due to fermentation temperature appears to be due to the extraction of phenolic components other than the anthocyanins.

4. The Pump-Over Operation

During red wine fermentations, typically once or twice a day, one to two volumes of juice or wine will need to be drawn from the base of the fermentor and pumped to the top and sprayed or trickled onto the skin cap in what is referred to as the pump-over operation. The reasons for the pump-over operation are to provide the liquid below better access to the skins in the cap in order to promote extraction of color and flavor constituents and to cool the skin cap rather than to break the cap

Table 5-4. Rate constants and equilibrium tannin concentrations.

Author	Medium	First-order constant (1/h)	zero-order constant (mg/L/h)	Equilibrium concentration (%, g/L)
Singleton and Draper (1964)	seeds 0% EtOH, 11°C	0.100	0.094	25.0
Singleton and Draper (1964)	seeds 0% EtOH, 20°C	0.041	0.055	42.4
Singleton and Draper (1964)	seeds 0% EtOH, 30°C	0.066	0.061	48.2
Singleton and Draper (1964)	seeds 14% EtOH, 11°C	0.038	0.076	41.2
Singleton and Draper (1964)	seeds 14% EtOH, 20°C	0.032	0.048	64.3
Singleton and Draper (1964)	seeds 14% EtOH, 30°C	0.038	0.078	75.3
Ribéreau-Gayon (1974)	wine	0.013	0.009	3.22

up by a high pressure stream of juice. Some wineries schedule the pump-over operation with that for fermentation cooling by passing the wine through an external heat exchanger at the same time. This requires an arrangement in which the cooling can be controlled as the time required for each operation will vary throughout the fermentation. There are some instances in which the pump-over operation is varied as the fermentation progresses, even though the relative rates of extraction of the various components will be continually changing.

One good example of pigment extraction can be found in the production of red port wine, where there is considerable pumping of the juice over the skins during the first two to three days of fermentation only. The extraction is primarily due to enhanced contact of warm juice with the ethanol playing only a minor, if significant, role.

The temperature and contacting methods employed in the production of red table wines range from the cold (or warm) juice and skin contact to the other extreme. There is the practice of extended maceration in which the skins (and more importantly the seeds) are allowed to remain in contact with the wine for several days or weeks after the end of the fermentation, with or without further pumping over. There are also many situations in which the skins (and seeds) are removed during the fermentation, at anywhere from 12 to 0 Brix, depending on the cultivar and its maturity.

a. *Pump-Over Arrangements*

The racking valve will generally be used to draw the juice to be used for the pump-over rather than the bottom filling valve which would allow much of the yeast and seeds to be drawn with it. The juice from the racking valve will often be splashed over a screen (to catch seeds, skins, and stems) and into a sump before passing though the pump and transfer hose. It is then transferred, often by a centrifugal pump, to the top of the tank by either a long flexible hose or a fixed stainless line with short flexible hose connected from the pump to the bottom end and a second flexible hose connected from the top across to the manhole. The outlet of the hose is introduced into the tank through a door in the roof which is generally accessed from an elevated walkway. The liquid is often sprayed through a nozzle fitting to make a high-velocity jet. This will usually be moved around during the pump over and spraying on the skin cap is generally controlled by a winery worker.

Several designs of automatic pump-over sprinklers ranging from spinning discs to rotating channels, have been used with various degrees of success (see also section 26). There are also vertical draft tube units which are suspended from the roof of the fermentor to the top surface of the skin cap and which penetrate the cap into the juice below. These have a propeller mounted at the juice end and the motor is mounted at the headspace end. When the motor is switched on, the juice is drawn up and sprayed out over the cap by the protective scroll at the motor end. The units are difficult to move and remain suspended free of the skin cap when the tank is drained. There is a concern about the generation of suspended solids and the extraction of components that lead to poor settling due to the action of the propeller.

Other designs range from the Algerian gas buildup/flooding system (Troost 1980) to mechanical punching-down plate devices and wood or steel grids for submerged cap arrangements. Those that rely on the buildup of fermentation gases cannot provide early extraction very well since they provide pumping over in proportion to the rate of fermentation. They should provide close to a pump-over value of 60 volumes of liquid (equivalent to the volumes of CO_2 evolved) during the fermentation, this will actually be slightly less due to some gas evolution from the wine in the pump-over reservoir before it flows over the skin cap. Even so, this is considerably more than the 10 to 24 volumes commonly used in a twice per day pump-over regime.

b. Extraction Considerations

One of the poorly understood aspects of extraction during red wine fermentations is that associated with the seeds as discussed previously. The seeds are initially distributed between those caught in the skins in the cap and those that have fallen to the floor of the fermentor. As the pump-over operations progress, some of those in the cap will be released and will collect at the base of the fermentor. The extraction from components at the base will be controlled almost entirely by diffusion through a stagnant liquid rather than the more active and displacing nature of the extraction obtained by the seeping of wine through the skin cap. The seeds at the base will be passed over during each pump-over operation since the wine is commonly drawn from a point above the base. The extraction will consequently be in favor of that from the skins rather than the seeds. From the earlier discussion, it seems that the major effect of prolonged skin contact would seem to be the ongoing extraction from seeds rather than the further extraction of skin tissue.

c. Time of Pressing

Perhaps as significant as the temperature of extraction and the contacting method is the timing of the separation of the skins and seeds from the liquid. While the anthocyanin extraction will have approached its limit by the third day, the tannin extraction from skins and seeds can continue beyond the end of the fermentation or until separation takes place. The timing of the separation can be used to influence the relative proportions of color and tannin in the young wine however desirable, or target analytical values for these components are still unknown. They are complicated by the anthocyanin-anthocyanin association and anthocyanin-tannin couplings discussed previously.

The most obvious criteria for the separation are then color, tannin content, taste, sugar content, and contact time. The ideal situation would be to get maximal color and an acceptable tannin level at the same time. There are still questions as to the ideal level of tannin since the levels for good taste may not coincide with those for good color stability. Further, the kinetics of these extractions outlined above and the variations that exist between grape loads would suggest that such a coincidence is likely to occur only by chance. Following the extraction during a particular fermentation poses a dilemma in that while there are good analytical measures for anthocyanin (and tannin) there is not a good relationship between tannin level (or total phenol content) and the astringency of the finished wine, as indicated by tasting. Tasting for astringency during the fermentation is not productive due to the effect of unfermented sugars. Since the relative proportions of color and tannin will be quite variable between and within loads of any cultivar, most winemakers continue to base the timing of the separation and pressing on the sugar content or juice density. This is only a first approximation to the level of extraction, perhaps better than contact time alone and the actual astringency will be modified by blending or fining with one of the protein fining agents during the months following the fermentation. Winemakers typically choose densities in the range of 5 to 0 Brix to draw the liquid off and to press the skins with the conventional maceration. The timing of the draw when prefermentation contact has been employed can be earlier, but is usually similar due to the enhanced tannin extraction associated with the formation of ethanol.

Today, the press fractions are generally added back to the wine to complete the fermentation, unlike older practices of keeping them separate. The widespread application of membrane presses has essentially eliminated the extensive skin tearing and unacceptable composition associated with the fractions obtained from the continuous screw and moving head presses.

5. Malolactic Fermentation

The trend in the past decade has been for winemakers to also inoculate red musts with a prepared culture of malolactic bacteria rather than to inoculate the wine after the completion of the ethanol fermentation. The purpose is to have this fermentation completed more rapidly, consistently, and with less undesirable byproduct formation than occurs in the young wine. The wide variation in the initiation and completion of the fermentation in young red wines, even when prepared cultures are used, continues to be a scientific and winemaking concern, especially in regions where the ethanol contents are typically 12 and 13% by volume. While the existence of nutrient deficiencies in musts (and the addition of supplements) is now generally accepted for the yeast fermentation, the corresponding acceptance of nutritional deficiencies as a cause of poor bacterial growth and byproduct formation in wines has yet to be adopted.

Inoculation of the must with malolactic bacteria avoids the inhibition due to ethanol and possibly other yeast byproducts. The complex nutrient requirements of these organisms is well established (Chapter 6) and the must provides a much more complete nutrient medium than does the finished wine.

6. Postfermentation Handling

Red wines will generally be clarified by racking, centrifuging, or filtration immediately after fermentation and usually transferred into wooden cooperage for an aging period. In wines that have not completed the malolactic fermentation concurrently, this transformation will generally occur in the following months either by a bacterial inoculation or resident microflora in the cooperage. The practice of loose bunging during this time is to allow for carbon dioxide from the primary and malolactic fermentations that will continue to be slowly released.

One approach to handling young wines is the practice of inoculating the malolactic fermentation concurrently with the yeast fermentation, adjusting the sulfur dioxide level from microbial protection, clarifying the wine so that the lees are insignificant, and tight bunging and rolling the barrels so that they can be stored undisturbed during the aging period. This is the nontraditional, low-input, nonmicrobial approach favored in the production of varietal wine styles.

Another approach is the racking of some wine lees into the barrel, conducting the malolactic fermentation in the barrel, racking after its completion, fining in the barrel, and storing the barrels in the upright position with loose bunging and periodic topping. The latter is the traditional approach which encourages unreliable microbial contributions and considerably more time involvement without any demonstrated benefits.

The aging pattern and the cooperage available will determine the period of time for which the wines are held in barrels. This will also depend on the style being sought and attitudes regarding clarification, topping, and fining during this time. While there are some strongly held opinions with regard to the importance of some of these practices, there is little if any evidence that they are of sensory significance in the bottled wine.

7. Aging and Fining

When polymeric color is produced by linking of a pigment monomer with another flavonoid, the resulting flavine is more likely to be colored and is likely not to be influenced by pH or SO_2. This permits polymeric color to be distinguished from monomeric color and is the basis of spectrophotometric methods for the estimation of pigment quantities (Somers and Evans 1977).

The changes in anthocyanin content of a young red wine are well illustrated by the Cabernet Sauvignon and Merlot wines analyzed by Nagel and Wulf (1979). The decline in the anthocyanin content during the first eight months of age is shown in Figure 5-11 for the Cabernet Sauvignon and Merlot. Note that the total color content is measured at a pH of 1 at 520 nm, and falls from a level of 16 absorbance units at the end of fermentation to approximately 5 units at 8 months. Figure 5-12a shows the rise in the polymeric pigment (nonbleachable red color at 520 nm) and Figure 5-12b, shows the increase in the percentage of the total color due to the anthocyanin during this period. The polymeric color, measured as the nonbleachable color at 520 nm has risen from zero to about two absorbance units in this time and it accounts for approximately 68% of the total color at this time.

The formation of the polymer follows a sigmoid-shaped curve, beginning slowly then accelerating and then slowing down again at longer times. This suggests that the monomers are involved in at least one intermediate form before they behave as polymers in this context. Their decline is exponential, indicating a first-order rate of disappearance in which most of it has been consumed within the first year (Figure 5-11). The red polymer formation (Figure 5-12a,b) shows a kinetic pattern that would

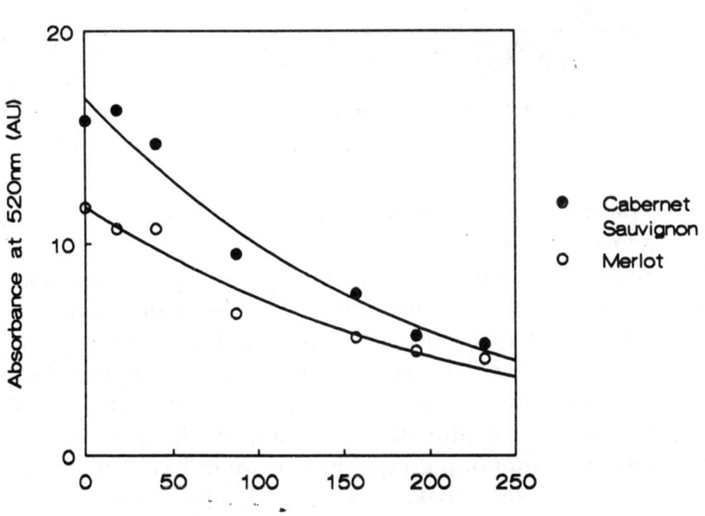

Fig. 5-11. The decline in total red color in Cabernet Sauvignon and Merlot during the first 200 days after fermentation (data from Nagel and Wulf 1979).

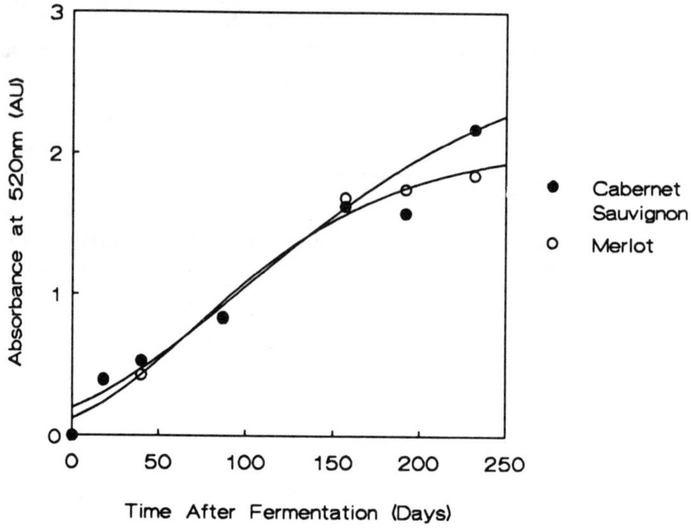

(a)

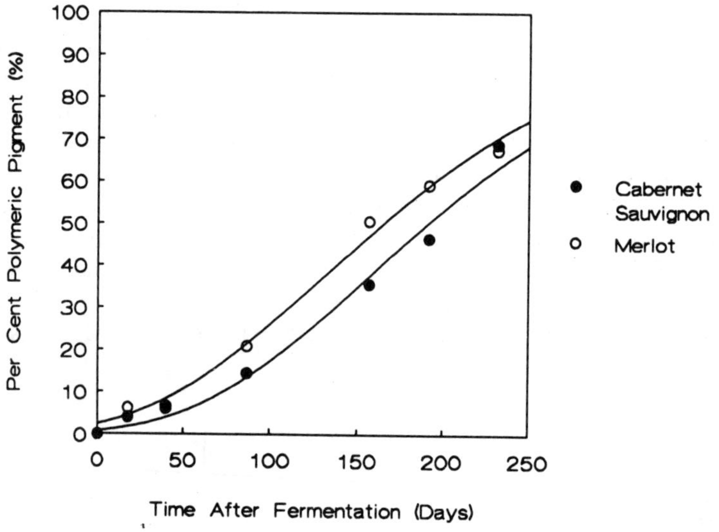

(b)

Fig. 5-12. a) The development of polymeric pigment in Cabernet Sauvignon and Merlot during the first 200 days after fermentation (data from Nagel and Wulf 1979). b) The development of the degree of polymerization in Cabernet Sauvignon and Merlot during the first 200 days after fermentation (data from Nagel and Wulf 1979).

be expected from an intermediate pool rather than the monomer itself. The slow beginning indicates that there is little of the intermediate form, the acceleration suggests that the intermediate concentration has increased, and the final slowing of the rate of polymer formation toward the end suggests that the intermediate pool is beginning to become depleted. By contrast, the formation of brown-colored polymer is essentially linear with time during the first eight months after fermentation (Figure 5-13), showing no tendency to run out of precursor material.

The role of oxygen in these polymerization reactions has been the subject of discussion for several years with somewhat conflicting evidence. The influence of acetaldehyde on the polymerization of the 3,5 diglucosides is clear and its involvement in the polymerization of pigments in Port wines has been established (Bakker et al. 1993), albeit under exaggerated concentrations. The involvement of

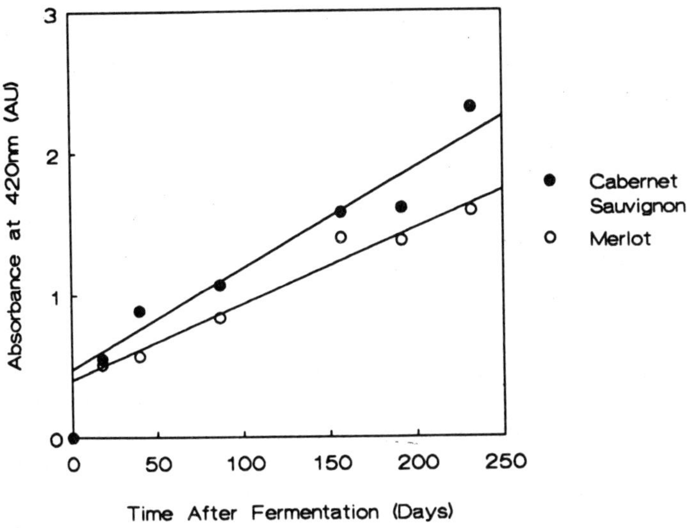

Fig. 5-13. The increase in brown color in Cabernet Sauvignon and Merlot during the first 200 days after fermentation (data from Nagel and Wulf 1979).

oxygen in the formation of acetaldyhde is well established (Wildenradt and Singleton 1974) but the role of acetaldehyde in accelerated polymerization in short-term studies with multiple oxygen saturations (Pontallier and Ribéreau-Gayon 1983) does not appear to be generally true. Other studies under essentially anaerobic conditions (Nagel and Wulf 1979; Somers and Evans 1986, Somers and Wescombe 1987; Somers and Pocock 1990) show that polymerization occurs even in the absence of oxygen, indicating that its involvement during the aging of table wines is secondary in this respect.

The polymer can be regarded as stable in color in that it is less prone to browning and independent of free SO_2 bleaching. The monomer, however, is a relatively unstable form in that it can be oxidized during aging to a brown polymeric form. The rate of condensation compared with that of oxidation determines the final color in the aged wine. The orange tinge in many rosé wines is a good example of a situation in which oxidation has developed more quickly than condensation, and where higher free SO_2 may have slowed the first and had less effect on the second. Some rosé wines are made by blending small amounts of older red wines with young white wines, providing stable red color which will not be bleached by SO_2 and will not be easily oxidized to give the orange condition.

The isolation of the intermediates and the further characterization of this reaction sequence would greatly enhance our ability to predict these changes from young wine composition. There may also be an effect on these reactions and the stability of the polymers due to presence of certain polysaccharide fractions that have been isolated from red wines (Brillouet et al. 1990) and the changes in others due to fermentation (Deitrich et al. 1992). Further studies in these areas would help to complete our understanding of the effects of grape maturation and red wine skin contacting on the color of both young and mature red wines.

a. *Fining Effects*

There is a common misconception that a more complete extraction produces a more flavorful wine. The potential for tannin extraction is difficult to estimate even during the fermentation itself. Some grapes will provide more color and flavor in proportion to the tannin and the only option is to try to obtain primarily early extraction which favors the monomeric phenols over the tannin by more extensive pump overs and early pressing. In wines which are too astringent, this can be modified by fining with any of the proteins. There will be some secondary color and possible flavor loss during this treatment but these changes are often insignificant.

During the first year, between 50 and 70% of the pigments will be incorporated into polymeric forms. Fining with proteins should be done early in the life of red wines so that the astringency can be reduced with the minimum of polymeric color removal. Fining with polyvinyl polypyrrolidone/(PVPP) or nylon (see Chapter 7) in order to reduce bitterness should be done in older wines when most of the pigment is in the polymeric form. Higher-pH wines tend to have slower polymerization of pigments when compared to oxidation and are therefore more prone to browning and eventual color decline due to precipitation.

8. Carbonic Maceration

The alternative contacting method in which the extraction for the grape is quite different from that of conventional contacting is carbonic maceration. In this approach, the intact berries are surrounded with a carbon dioxide atmosphere and allowed to respire and to have partial fermentation by the grapes' own glycolytic enzymes. Some winemakers add a small volume of fermenting juice to the fermentor to provide the carbon dioxide for the atmosphere. The onset of the transformation generally takes place after several days at a preferred temperature of 35°C and is usually detected by a bubbler when gas generation occurs within the fermentor. There is a vacuum developed initially, then gas evolution during the metabolic phase, and cessation of gas production when the fermentation has finished.

In the process, the cell walls in the skin become permeable allowing the pigments, many of the phenols, and other extractables to leak into the intracellular fluid. After eight to 10 days of berry fermentation, the enzymes lose their activity and the process ceases. The clusters are then transferred into a press and the berries are broken to yield their colored, partially fermented juice containing 1 to 1.5% ethanol by volume. This juice is then inoculated and fermented to completion at temperatures of 15°C to 20°C, without the skins.

The wines produced in this way are usually lower in tannin with a distinctive aroma contribution in addition to the fruit character. The main chemical changes are the degradation of almost half of the malic acid, consumption of ammonia, and the formation of the amide amino acids and succinic, fumaric, and shikimic acids. The aroma produced by this procedure is quite distinct and studies of the volatiles formed (Ducruet 1984) have shown significantly higher concentrations of benzaldehyde, ethyl salicylate, vinyl benzene, and ethyl-9-decanoate. A comprehensive monograph covering most of the current understanding of this process has recently been published (Flanzy et al. 1987).

While the traditional procedure employs carbon dioxide, the sugar conversion can be extended, almost to completion, by the use of nitrogen instead of carbon dioxide. It appears that it is the gas phase concentration of carbon dioxide that leads to a loss of enzyme activity. This would appear to provide possible variations from the traditional procedure that might be investigated further.

9. Thermovinification

In certain locations and in some seasons, the lack of color or the presence of mold requires that heat be used to enhance the extraction from skins and the inactivation of juice and mold-derived enzymes. This treatment, known as *thermovinification*, is applied to the skins prior to fermentation and the fermentation is conducted without the skins or seeds present (Martiniere 1981). In practice, the clusters are crushed and the must transferred to a tank from which a fraction of the juice is drawn, heated to a temperature of 45°C to 55°C and then pumped over the skin cap either continuously or periodically to obtain the extraction. The temperature employed, and the time and the skin-juice contact during the treatment, control the extent of extraction. Such juices are generally intensely colored but can be overextracted in tannin. They are usually fermented before the composition is modified by the adsorptive (fining) treatments. The use of temperatures above 60°C leads to a more complete but usually unacceptable level of phenol extraction.

G. FORTIFIED WINES

The production of fortified wines has traditionally followed winemaking patterns that have permitted significant phenolic extraction, which is important for a relatively long and oxidative aging process. This is true for both red and white fortified wines of the Port style compared with the relatively low-phenolic white wines that will form the base for the production of traditional Sherry. The use of natural flora is not an issue in a wine style which is primarily associated with fruit character, low to moderate aging, and spirit components.

1. Must Handling

The grapes will be crushed and transferred directly into the fermentors as would normally be done for a red table wine. The skin extraction is encouraged from an early stage in both red and white styles. This is achieved by early and extensive juice pump overs, even before the onset of fermentation, continuing until shortly before the juice is drawn off and subsequently fortified.

Traditionally, spontaneous fermentation is encouraged primarily due to economics and the shorter-than-usual fermentation period. The use of a selected yeast inoculation would ensure a more predictable onset and pattern of fermentation.

2. Fermentation Temperature

The fermentation temperature is generally chosen to ensure swift fermentation without encouraging the formation of fermentation esters. Temperatures in the range of 25°C to 30°C have traditionally been used, but this seems to be a practical choice rather than one based on optimized extraction rates of skin components or other considerations. Lower fermentation temperatures would seem to be desirable for wine to be made from the Muscat cultivars.

3. Timing of the Fortification

The timing of the fortification is determined by the ratio of ethanol to sugar desired in the young wine. The microbial stability of the fortified wine is greatly enhanced when the ethanol content is 20% or above. Many traditional Port wines are made in the 18 to 20% range. The factors to be considered are the quantity of spirit used to the quantity of fortified wine produced, and there is a range of points during the fermentation at which fortification can take place. As the fermentation advances, less spirit will be required and yet less sugar will be remaining.

The wine will be drawn off the skins when the juice density is between 16 to 12Brix and transferred to a measuring tank. The skins are then transferred to the press and the press fractions are usually added back to the corresponding juice and the fortification performed. In red fortified wines, the color extraction is of considerable importance due to the short contact time, and the press fractions are usually heavily colored.

4. Selection of Fortifying Spirit

The spirit options range from those produced by pot stills which are relatively high in fusel content and at 70 to 75% ethanol, to those produced from columns in which a lower fusel content is sought but at higher ethanol levels and often with significant acetaldehyde content.

The volume of spirit required can be estimated from the following equation in which the volumetric contractions have been ignored:

$$V_s = V_j * \frac{[x_f - x_j]}{[x_s - x_f]}$$

where V_s and V_j are the volumes of spirit and juice respectively, x is the ethanol concentration in volume percent; and the subscripts f, j, and s refer to the final wine, the juice being fortified, and the spirit being used, respectively.

The volumetric contraction associated with such fortifications can be estimated from the volumes of water and ethanol in various ethanol solutions and these can be found in references such as the U.S. Gauging Manual. A better approach is to perform the calculation on a weight basis, using the weight fraction of the desired mixture and estimating the spirit volume from the computed weight of spirit that is required.

5. Aging

The aging of fortified wines is based on the development of color, the extraction of small amounts of oak components, and the evaporative loss of volatile spirit components. This usually requires a minimum of two years of aging in older wooden cooperage to produce a wine that has significant fruit character, a low level of barrel extractives, and a relative absence of sharp and undesirable spirit components. The wines of this style are made to undergo a continued development of aged characteristics within the bottle.

Common faults in some young fortified wines are the dominance of new oak extractives caused by the use of relatively young cooperage and the presence of aldehydic components from an inappropriate spirit.

H. REFERENCES

ACREE, T. E., E. P. SONOFF, and D.F. SPLITSTOESSER. 1972. "Effect of yeast strain and type of sulfur compound on hydrogen sulfide production." *Am. J. Enol. Vitic.* 23:6–9.

AMATI, A. 1986. "L'impiego dei coadiuvanti nella fermentazione dei mosti." *Vini d'Italia.* 28:19–25.

AXCELL, B., L. KRUGER, and G. ALLAN. 1988. "Some investigative studies with yeast foods." *Proc. Inst. Brew. (Aust. N.Z.) 12th Conv.*:201–209.

BACH, H.-P., and P. HOFFMANN. 1979. "Versuche zur Frage der Bentonitzugabe zum Most." *Weinwirts.* 115:1119–1132.

BAKKER, J., A. PICINELLI, and P. BRIDLE. 1993. "Model wine solutions: Color and composition changes during ageing." *Vitis* 32:111–118.

BAKKER, J., and C. F. TIMBERLAKE. 1985. "The distribution and content of anthocyanins in young port wines as determined by high performance liquid chromatography." *J. Sci. Food Agric.* 36:1325–1333.

BATES, F. J., and ASSOCIATES. 1942. *Polarimetry, Saccharimetry and the Sugars.* Circular 440, NBS, Washington, DC: Department of Communications.

BAUME, A. 1797. *Elements de Pharmacie. Theorique et Practique.* Paris: Samson.

BENVEGNIN, L., E. CAPT, and G. PIGUET. 1951. *Traite de Vinification.* 2nd ed. Lausanne, Switzerland: Librairie Payot.

BIDAN, P., C. DIVIES, and P. DUPUY. 1978. "Procede perfectionne de preparation de vins mousseux." French Patent 7822131.

BIOLETTI, F. T. 1906. "A new wine-cooling machine." *Calif. Agric. Expt. Stn. Bull.* 174:1–27.

BOULTON, R. 1979. "The heat transfer characteristics of wine fermentors." *Am. J. Enol. Vitic.* 30:152–156.

BOULTON, R. 1980. "The prediction of fermentation behavior by a kinetic model." *Am. J. Enol. Vitic.* 31:40–45.

BRILLOUET, J. M., C. BOSSO, and M. MOUTOUNET. 1990. "Isolation, purification and characterization of an arabinogalactan from a red wine." *Am. J. Enol. Vitic.* 41:29–36.

CASTOR, J. G. B. 1953. "Experimental development of compressed yeast as fermentation starters." *Wines and Vines* 34(8):27 and (9):33.

CHEN, G. N., and F. GUTAMIS. 1976. "Carbon dioxide inhibition of yeast growth in biomass production." *Biotechnol. Bioeng.* 18:1455–1462.

CHEYNIER, V., J. RIGAUD, J. M. SOUQUET, F. DUPRAT, and M. MOUTOUNET. 1990. "Must browning in relation to the behavior of phenolic compounds during oxidation". *Am. J. Enol. Vitic.* 41:346–349.

CILLIERS, J. J. L., and V. L. SINGLETON. 1990. "Nonenzymic autoxidative reactions of caffeic acid in wine." *Am. J. Enol. Vitic.* 41:84–86.

COOKE, G. M. 1964. "Effect of grape pulp upon soluble solids determinations." *Am. J. Enol. Vitic.* 15:11–15.

COULON, P., B. DUTEURTRE, M. CHARPENTIER, A. PARENTHOEN, C. BADOUR AND J. P. MOULIN. 1983. "New prospects in the 'Methode Champenoise' utilization of enclosed yeasts during bottling." *Le Vigneron Champenois*. 104:516–532.

CROWELL, E. A., and J. F. GUYMON. 1963. "Influence of aeration and suspended material on higher alcohols, acetoin and diacetyl during fermentation." *Am. J. Enol. Vitic.* 14:214–222.

CROWL D. A., and J. F. LOUVAR. 1991. *Chemical Process Safety: Fundamentals with Applications*. Englewood Cliffs, NJ: Prentice Hall.

DE CLERKE, J. 1958. *A Textbook of Brewing*. Vol 2. London. Chapman & Hall.

DIETRICH, H., H. SCHMITT, and K. WUCHERPFENNIG. 1992. "The alteration of the colloids of must and wine during winemaking. II. Change of the charge and the molecular weight distribution of the polysaccharides." *Vitic. Enol. Sci.* 47:87–95.

DUBERNET, M., P. RIBÉREAU-GAYON, H. R. LERNER, E. HAREL, and A. M. MAYER. 1977. "Purification and properties of laccase from *Botrytis cinerea*." *Phytochemistry* 16:1.

DUBET. J. 1913. *Petite Traite de Vinification a l'usage des Vignerons*. Paris: Librairie des Sciences Agricoles.

DUBOURDIEU, D., J.-C. VILLETTAZ, C. DESPLANQUES AND P. RIBEREAU-GAYON. 1981. "Degradation enzymatique du glucan de Botrytis cinerea. Application a l'amelioration de la clarification des vins issus de raisins pourris." *Conn. Vigne Vin* 15:161–177.

DUCRUET, V. 1984. "Comparison of the headspace volatiles of carbonic maceration and traditional wine." *Lebensm. Wiss. Technol.* 17:217–221.

EL HALOUI, N., Y. CLERAN, J. M. SABLAYROLLES, P. GRENIER, P. BARRE, and G. CORRIEU. 1988. "Suivi et control de la fermentation alcoolique en oenologie." *Rev. Fr. Oenol.* 115:12–17.

ETIEVANT, P., P. SCHLICH, A. BERTRAND, P. SYMONDS, and J.-C. BOUVIER. 1988. "Varietal and geographic classification of French wines in terms of pigments and flavonoid compounds." *J. Sci. Food Agric.* 42:39–54.

FETTERROLL, B. M., and G. WURDIG. 1977. Die Vergrosserung der "inneren Oberflache" des Mostes und deren Wirkung auf sulfitbildende Hefen. *Wein Wissen*. 32:25–33.

FEUILLAT, M., and C. CHARPENTIER. 1982. "Autolysis of yeast in Champagne." *Am. J. Enol. Vitic.* 38:6–13.

FLANZY, C., M. FLANZY, and P. BERNARD. 1987. *La Vinification Par Maceration Carbonique*. Paris: INRA.

GENIEX, C., S. LAFON-LAFOURCADE, and P. RIBÉREAU-GAYON. 1983. "Les causes, la prevention et la traitment des arrets de la fermentation alcoolique." *Conn. Vigne Vin* 17:205–217.

GROAT, M., and C. S. OUGH. 1978. "Effects of soluble solids added to clarified musts on fermentation rate, wine composition and wine quality." *Am. J. Enol. Vitic.* 29:112–119.

GUELL C., and R. B. BOULTON. 1994. "The influence of suspended solids and stirring on the rate of small-scale fermentations," *Am. J. Enol. Vitic.* (Submitted).

GUNATA, Y. Z., C. L. BAYONOVE, R. L. BAUMES, and R. E. CORDONNIER. 1986. "Stability of free and bound fractions of some aroma compounds of grapes cv Muscat during the wine processing: Preliminary results." *Am. J. Enol. Vitic.* 37:112–114.

HERBRERO, E., C. SANTOS-BUEGLA, and J. C. RIVAS-GONZALO. 1988. "HPLC-Diode array spectroscopy identification of anthocyanins of *Vitis vinifera* variety *Tempranillo*." *Am. J. Enol. Vitic.* 39:227–233.

HOHL, L. 1938. "Further observations on production of alcohol by Saccharomyces ellipsoideus in syruped fermentations." *Food Res.* 3:453–465.

HOHL, L., and W. V. CRUESS. 1936. "Effect of temperature, variety of juice and method of increasing sugar content on maximum alcohol production by Saccharomyces ellipsoideus." *Food Res.* 1:405–411.

HOPKINS, R. H., and R. H. ROBERTS. 1935a. "The kinetics of alcoholic fermentation of by brewers yeast. 1. Effect of concentrations of yeast and sugar." *Biochem. J.* 29:919–930.

HOPKINS, R. H., and R. H. ROBERTS. 1935b. "The kinetics of alcoholic fermentation of by brewers yeast. 2. The relative rates of fermentation of glucose and fructose." *Biochem. J.* 29:931–936.

HOUTMAN, A. C., and C. S. DU PLESSIS. 1981. "The effect of juice clarity and several conditions promoting yeast growth or fermentation rate, the production of aroma components and wine quality." *S. Afric. J. Enol. Vitic.* 2:71–81.

HOUTMAN, A. C., and C. S. DU PLESSIS. 1986. "Nutritional deficiencies of clarified white grape juices and their correction in relation to fermentation." *S. Afric. J. Enol. Vitic.* 7:39–44.

JACOB, F. C., T. E. ARCHER, and J. G. B. CASTOR. 1964. "Thermal death time of yeast." *Am. J. Enol. Vitic.* 15:69–74.

JAKOB, L. 1984. *Taschenbuch der Kellerwirtschaft.* Weisbaden, Germany, Fachverlag Dr. Fraund.

JONES, R. S., and C. S. OUGH. 1985. "Variations in the percent ethanol v/v per Brix conversions of wines from different climatic regions." *Am. J. Enol. Vitic.* 36:268–270.

KANTZ, K., and V. L. SINGLETON. 1990. "Isolation and determination of polymeric polyphenols using Sephadex LH-20 and analysis of grape tissue extracts." *Am. J. Enol. Vitic.* 41:223–228.

KRAUS, J. K., G. REED, and J. C. VILLETTAZ. 1983. "Levures seches actives de vinification." *Conn. Vigne Vin* 17:93–103.

LAFON-LAFOURCADE, S., C. GENIEX, and P. RIBÉREAU-GAYON. 1985. "Les modalities de mise de oeuvre des ecore de levures en vinification." *Conn. Vigne Vin* 18:111–125.

LARUE, F., C. GENIEX, M.-K. PARK, Y. MURAKAMI, S. LAFON-LAFOURCADE, and P. RIBÉREAU-GAYON. 1985. "Incidence de certains polysaccharides insoluble sur la fermentation alcoolique." *Conn. Vigne Vin* 19:41–52.

LAY, H., and U. DRAEGER. 1991. "Profiles of pigments from different red wines." *Vitic. Enol. Sci.* 46:48–57.

LONVAUD-FUNEL, A., C. DESENS, and A. JOYEUX. 1985. "Stimulation de la fermentation malolactique par l'addition au vin d'enveloppes cellulaires de levure et differents adjuvants de nature polysaccharidique et azotee." *Conn. Vigne Vin* 19:229–240.

LOUREIRO, V., and N. VAN UDEN. 1982. "Effects of ethanol on the maximum temperature for growth of *Saccharomyces cerevisiae*: A model." *Biotechnol. Bioeng.* 24:1881–1884.

MALFEITO-FERREIRA, M., J. P. MILLER-GUERRA, and V. LOUREIRO. 1990. "Proton extrusion as an indicator of the adaptive state of yeast starters for the continuous production of sparkling wines." *Am. J. Enol. Vitic.* 41:219–222.

MARAIS, J. 1987. "Terpene concentrations and wine quality of *Vitis vinifera* L. cv. Gewürztraminer as affected by grape maturity and cellar practices." *Vitis* 26:231–245.

MARINO, M., J. I. MESSIAS IGLESIAS, F. HENAO DAVILA, R. ZAMORA CORCHERO, AND I. MARECA CORTES. 1983. "Presence et evolution des esters superieurs, en fonction desdifferents factuers, au cours dela fermentation alcoolique." *Rev. Fr. Oenol.* 90:41–48.

MARSH, G. L. 1958. "Alcohol yield: Factors and methods." *Am. J. Enol.* 9:53–58.

MARTINIERE, P. 1981. "Thermovinification et vinification par maceration carbonique dans le Bordelais." In: *Actualite Oenologies et Viticoles.* P. Ribéreau-Gayon and P. Sudraud, Eds., Paris: Dunod, 303–310.

MINARIK, E., O. JUNGOVA, R. KOLLAR, and E. STURDIK. 1992. "Wirkung verschiedener Hefezellwand- und Cellulose Praparate auf die alkoholische Garung des Mostes." *Mitt. Kloster.* 42:13–15.

MONK, P. R., and R. J. STORER. 1986. "The kinetics of yeast growth and sugar utilization in tirage. The influence of different methods of starter culture preparation and inoculum levels." *Am. J. Enol. Vitic.* 37:72–76.

MÜLLER-SPATH, H. 1982. "Elaboration de vins mousseux en continu." *Rev. Fr. Oenol.* 119:43–45.

NAGEL, C. W., and L. W. WULF. 1979. "Changes in the anthocyanins, flavonoids and hydroxycinnamate acid esters during the fermentation and aging of Merlot and Cabernet Sauvignon." *Am. J. Enol. Vitic.* 30:111–116.

OSZMIANSKI, J., and J. C. SAPIS. 1989. "Fractionation and identification of some low molecular weight grape seed phenolics." *J. Agric. Food Chem.* 37:1293–1297.

OUGH, C. S., and M. A. AMERINE. 1963. "Regional, varietal and type influences on the degree Brix and alcohol relationship of grape musts and wines." *Hilgardia.* 33: 585–599.

OUGH, C. S., and M. A. AMERINE. 1965. "Studies with controlled fermentations. 9. Bentonite treatment of grape juice prior to wine fermentation." *Am. J. Enol. Vitic.* 16:185–194.

OUGH, C. S., and M. A. AMERINE. 1988. *Methods of Analysis of Musts and Wines.* New York: John Wiley and Sons.

OUGH, C. S., J. F. GUYMON, and E. A. CROWELL. 1966. "Formation of higher alcohols during grape juice fermentations at various temperatures." *J. Food Sci.* 31:620–625.

PEYRON, D., and M. FEUILLAT. 1985. "Essais comparatifs de cuves d'automaceration en bourgogne." *Rev. d'Oenol.* 38:7–10.

PONTALLIER, P., and P. RIBÉREAU-GAYON. 1983. "Influence de l'aeration et du sulfitage sur l'evolution de la matiere colorante des vins rouges au cours de la phase d'elevage." *Conn. Vigne Vin* 17:105–120.

RAMEY, D. D., A. BERTRAND, C. S. OUGH, V. L. SINGLETON, and E. SANDERS. 1986. "Effects of skin contact temperature on Chardonnay must and wine composition." *Am. J. Enol. Vitic.* 37:99–106.

RANKINE, B. C. 1963. "Nature, origin and prevention of hydrogen sulphide aroma in wines." *J. Sci. Food Agric.* 14:79–91

RANKINE, B. C., and A. D. WEBB. 1958. "Comparison of anthocyanin pigments of *Vinifera* grapes." *Am. J. Enol.* 9:105–110.

RIBÉREAU-GAYON, J. 1953. "Etude experimentale de la vinification en blanc." Paper presented at *7th Cong. Intl. Vigne et Vin.* Rome.

RIBÉREAU-GAYON, P. 1974. "The chemistry of red wine color." In *The Chemistry of Winemaking*, 4th ed., A. D. Webb, Ed., *Am. Chem. Soc. Symposium* Series No. 137. Washington, DC: Am. Chem Soc.

RIBÉREAU-GAYON, P. 1985. "New developments in wine microbiology." *Am. J. Enol. Vitic.* 36:1–10.

RIBÉREAU-GAYON, J., E. PEYNAUD, P. RIBÉREAU-GAYON, and P. SUDRAUD. 1975. *Sciences et Techniques du Vin.* Paris: Dunod.

RICARDO DA SILVA, J. M. 1990. "Separation and quantitative determination of grape and wine procyanidins by high performance reversed phase liquid chromatography." *J. Sci. Food Agric.* 53:85–92.

RICARDO DA SILVA, J. M., M. BOURZIEX, V. CHEYNIER, and M. MOUTOUNET. 1991a. "Procyanidin composition of *Chardonnay*, *Mauzac* and *Grenache* blanc grapes." *Vitis* 30:245–252.

RICARDO DA SILVA, J. M., V. CHEYNIER, J-M. SOUQUET, and M. MOUTOUNET. 1991b. "Interaction of grape seed procyanidins with various proteins in relation to wine fining." *J. Sci. Food Agric.* 57:111–125.

RICARDO DA SILVA, J. M., J-P. ROSEC, M. BOURZIEX, J. MOURGUES, and M. MOUTOUNET. 1992. "Dimer and trimer procyanidins in *Carignan* and *Mourvedre* grapes and red wines." *Vitis* 31:55–63.

RICKER, R. W., J. J. MAROIS, J. W. DLOTT, R. M. BOSTOCK, and J. C. MORRISON. 1991. "Immunodetection and quantification of *Botrytis cinerea* on harvested wine grapes." *Phytopathology* 81:404–411.

ROGGERO, J. P., B. RAGONNET, and S. COEN. 1984. "Analyse fine des anthocyanes des vins et des pelliculules de raisin par l a technique HPLC." *Vigne Vins* 327:38–42.

ROSSI, J. A., and V. L. SINGLETON. 1966. "Flavor effects and adsorptive properties of purified fractions of grapeseed phenols." *Am. J. Enol. Vitic.* 17:240–246.

RUOCCO, J. J., R. W. COE, and C. W. HAHN. 1980. "Computer assisted exotherm measurement in full-scale brewery fermentations." *Mast. Brew. Assoc. Am. Tech. Quart.* 17:69–76.

SALAGOITY-AUGUSTE, M-H., and A. BERTRAND. 1984. "Wine phenolics-Analysis of low molecular weight components by high performance liquid chromatography." *J. Sci. Food Agric.* 35:1241–1247.

SCHANDERL, H. 1959. *Die Mikrobiologie des Mostes und Weines*. Stuttgart, Germany: Eugen Ulmer.

SCHÜTZ, M., and R. E. KUNKEE. 1977. "Formation of hydrogen sulfide from elemental sulfur during fermentation by wine yeast." *Am. J. Enol. Vitic.* 28:137–144.

SHIBATA, M. 1979. "Control of alcoholic fermentation by use of a gas meter." *Hakkogaku* 57:445–452.

SIEBERT, K. J., P. H. BLUM, T. J. WISK, L. E. STENROOS, and W. J. ANKLAM. 1986. "The effect of trub on fermentation." *Mast. Brew. Assoc. Amer. Techn. Quart.* 23:37–43.

SIEGRIST, J. 1985. "Les tannins et les anthocyanes du pinot et les phenomenes de maceration." *Rev. Oenol.* 38:11–13.

SINGLETON, V. L. 1987. "Oxygen with phenols and related reactions in musts, wines and model systems: Observations and practical implications." *Am. J. Enol. Vitic.* 38:69–77.

SINGLETON, V. L., and D. E. DRAPER. 1964. "The transfer of polyphenolic compounds from grape seeds into wines." *Am. J. Enol. Vitic.* 15:34–40.

SINGLETON, V. L., H. A. SIEBERHAGEN, P. DE WET, and C. J. VAN WYK. 1975. "Composition and sensory qualities of wines prepared from white grapes by fermentation with and without grape solids." *Am. J. Enol. Vitic.* 26:62–69.

SINGLETON, V. L., and E. K. TROUSDALE. 1992. "Anthocyanin-tannin interactions explaining differences in polymeric phenols between white and red wines." *Am. J. Enol. Vitic.* 43:63–70.

SOMERS, T. C., and M. E. EVANS. 1977. "Spectral evaluation of young red wines: Anthocyanin equilibria, total phenolics, free and molecular SO_2 and chemical age." *J. Sci. Food Agric.* 28:279–287.

SOMERS, T. C., and M. E. EVANS. 1979. "Grape pigment phenomena: Interpretation of major color loss during vinification." *J. Sci. Food Agric.* 30:623–633.

SOMERS, T. C., and M. E. EVANS. 1986. "Evolution of red wines. 1. Ambient influences on color composition during early maturation." *Vitis* 25:31–39.

SOMERS, T. C., and K. F. POCOCK. 1990. "Evolution of red wines. 3. Promotion of the maturation phase." *Vitis* 29:109–121.

SOMERS, T. C., and E. VERETTE. 1988. "Phenolic composition of natural wines." In, *Modern Methods of Plant Analysis*, New Series, Vol. 6, H. F. Linkens and J. F. Jackson, Eds., Berlin: Springer-Verlag.

SOMERS, T. C., and G. WESCOMBE. 1987. "Evolution of red wines. 2. An assessment of the role of acetaldehyde." *Vitis* 26:27–36.

SPONHOLZ, W. R., K. D. MILLIES, and A. AMBROSI. 1990. "Die Wirkung von Hefezellwanden auf die Vergarung." *Wein Wissen.* 45:50–57.

STREHAIANO, P., M. MOTA, and G. GOMA. 1983. "Effects of inoculum level on kinetics of alcoholic fermentation." *Biotechnol. Lett.* 5:135–140.

TERCELJ, D. 1965. "Etude des composes azotes du vin." *Ann. Technol. Agric.* 14:307–319.

THOMAS, C. S., R. B. BOULTON, M. W. SILACCI, and W. D. GUBLER. 1993a. "The effect of elemental sulfur, yeast strain and fermentation medium on the hydrogen sulfide production during fermentation." *Am. J. Enol. Vitic.* 44:211–216.

THOMAS, C. S., W. D. GUBLER, M. W. SILACCI, and R. MILLER. 1993b. "Changes in the elemental residues of Pinot noir and Cabernet Sauvignon grape berries during the growing season." *Am. J. Enol. Vitic.* 44:205–210.

THORNGATE, J. 1992. Flavan-3-ols and their polymers in grapes and wines: Chemical and sensory properties. PhD dissertation, Davis, CA: University of California.

THORNTON, R. J., and S. B. RODRIGUEZ. 1986. "Genetics of wine microorganisms: Potentials and problems." *Proc. 6th Aust. Wine Ind. Tech. Conf.* pp. 98–102.

THOUKIS, G., G. REED, and R. J. BOUTHILET. 1963. "Production and use of compressed yeast for winery fermentations." *Am. J. Enol. Vitic.* 14:148–154.

TROMP, A. 1984. "The effect of yeast strain, grape solids, nitrogen and temperature on fermentation rate and wine quality." *S. Afric. J. Enol. Vitic.* 5:1–6.

TROOST, G. 1980. *Technologie des Weines*. Stuttgart, Germany: Verlag Eugen Ulmer.

VAN BALEN, J. 1984. Recovery of anthocyanins and other phenols from converting grapes into wine. MS thesis, Davis, CA: University of California.

VAN UDEN, N., P. ABRANCHES, and C. CABECA-SILVA. 1968. "Temperature functions of thermal death in yeasts and their relation to the maximum temperature for growth." *Arch. Mikrobiol.* 61:381–393.

VAN WYK, C. J. 1978. "The influence of juice clarification on composition and quality of wines." *Proc. 5th Intl. Oenol. Symp.* Auckland, N.Z. pp. 33–45.

VILLETTAZ, J.-C., D. STEINER, and H. TROGUS. 1984. "The use of beta-glucanase as an enzyme in wine clarification and filtration." *Am. J. Enol. Vitic.* 35:253–256.

VON DER LIPPE, H. 1894. *Die Weinbereitung und die Kellerwirtschaft*. Weimar, Germany: B. F. Voigt.

VOS, P. J. A., and R. S. GRAY. 1979. "The origin and control of hydrogen sulfide during fermentation of grape must." *Am. J. Enol. Vitic.* 30:187–197.

WENZEL, K., H. H. DEITRICH, H. P. SEYFFARDT, and J. BOHNERT. 1980. "Schwefelruckstande auf Trauben und im Most und ihr Einfluss auf die H_2S Bildung." *Wein Wissen.* 35:414–420.

WHEAT, J. K. 1991. An automated fermentation monitoring system. MS thesis, Davis, CA: University of California.

WILDENRADT, H. L., and V. L. SINGLETON. 1974. "The production of aldehydes as a result of polyphenolic compounds and its relation to wine aging." *Am. J. Enol. Vitic.* 25:119–126.

WILLIAMS, J. T., C. S. OUGH, and H. W. BERG. 1978. "White wine composition and quality as influenced by methods of must clarification." *Am. J. Enol. Vitic.* 29:92–96.

WILLIAMS, L. A. 1982. "Heat release in alcoholic fermentation: A critical reappraisal." *Am. J. Enol. Vitic.* 33:149–153.

WILLIAMS, L. A., and R. B. BOULTON. 1983. "Modeling and prediction of evaporative ethanol loss during wine fermentations." *Am. J. Enol. Vitic.* 32:234–242.

WUCHERPFENNIG, K. AND G. BRETTHAUER. 1969. "Der Einfluss der Bentonitbehandlung des Mostes auf die Aromabildung wahrend der Garung." *Wein Wissen.* 24:443–451.

WUCHERPFENNIG, K. AND G. BRETTHAUER. 1970. "Uber die Bildung von fluchtigen Aromastoffen in Traubenwein in Abhangigkeit von der Mostvorbehandlung sowie von der verwendeten heferasse." *Mitt. Kloster.* 20:36–46.

WUCHERPFENNIG, K. AND H. DIETRICH. 1982. "Verbesserung der Filterierfahigkeit von Weinen durch enzymatischen Abbau von kohlenhydrathaltigen Kolloiden." *Weinwirt.* 118:598–603.

WURDIG, G. AND H. A. SCHLOTTER. 1969. "Untersuchungen zur Aufstellung einer SO_2-Bilanz im Wein." *Deu. Wein Ztg.* 105:34–42.

CHAPTER 6

MALOLACTIC FERMENTATION

INTRODUCTION

This chapter defines the malolactic fermentation and covers the practical aspects of the fermentation under winemaking conditions, including its control. The chapter also describes fundamental aspects, that is, the intermediary metabolism of the malolactic bacteria with respect to malic acid. For convenience, the taxonomy of the wine-related lactic acid bacteria, which embrace the malolactic bacteria, is also included here.

In addition to the alcoholic fermentation, other microbial activities, with positive and negative effects, are associated with winemaking. This includes the secondary fermentations of sparkling wine and flor sherry and various microbial spoilages. Of these secondary wine fermentations, those carried out by the malolactic bacteria, are probably the most intensively studied. The word *malolactic* comes from the conversion of L-malic acid to L-lactic acid, the operative activity of these bacteria. While regarded in some cases as a spoilage activity, under proper circumstances, the malolactic fermentation, either naturally expected or artificially encouraged, can be a normal part of good winemaking practice—something to be appreciated and desired. General review articles on malolactic fermentation spanning several decades include: Radler (1966), Kunkee (1967a, 1974, 1991), Beelman and Gallander (1979), Wibowo et al. (1985), Davis et al. (1986), and Edwards and Beelman (1989).

The bacterial causes of the malolactic fermentation were noted a century ago by early wine microbiologists, uncharacteristically not including Pasteur (Kunkee, 1968). However, the modern awareness of the significance of the fermentation in winemaking can be said to have two origins: from the realization of the absolute requirement for this fermentation in wines of Burgundy, with the practices employed to ensure its occurrence; and from the rather sudden awareness three decades ago in California of the coincidence of the occurrence of the malolactic fermentation in many of the wines from California with the perception that these same wines were those of generally higher quality (Ingraham and Cooke

1960). These two cases illustrate the most notable and positive effects brought about by the malolactic fermentation, namely, the deacidification, the bacteriological stabilization, and the increased flavor and aroma complexity. Currently the malolactic fermentation is recognized, and most often desired, in virtually every wine growing region of the world (Kunkee 1967a)—for one or more of the three properties just mentioned. Wherever tested, a large percentage of the premium red wines of the world have had malolactic fermentation, whether or not so recognized by the winemaker.

From a microbiologist's point of view, the time span of the malolactic fermentation begins at the introduction, purposely or accidentally, of viable bacteria into the wine or must, and ends when the bacteria have gone through the growth phase and have reentered their final resting or stationary phase. However, the winemaker is more likely to think of the fermentation as beginning when there is a noticeable drop in the concentration of malic acid, and as being completed when the malic acid has finally disappeared. Thus, the deacidification aspects of the malolactic fermentation have to do with this feature, and we employ the term *malolactic conversion* for the deacidification feature. We reserve the term *malolactic fermentation* to refer to the other aspects of the complete cycle, such as the stability brought about by uptake of micronutrients during growth and flavor changes brought about by formation of end products.

These three major effects of the malolactic fermentation in winemaking are discussed in the following sections.

A. DEACIDIFICATION BY MALOLACTIC CONVERSION

The operative activity of malolactic bacteria, and that uniquely found in this group of microorganisms, is the capacity to convert malic acid to lactic acid. This conversion is now established as being a direct decarboxylation, by a single enzyme, and essentially stoichiometric (Figure 6-1), but see Section I. Historical arguments leading to these conclusions are given by Kunkee (1967a, 1974, 1975). In addition to the decarboxylation of malic acid by these kinds of bacteria, they also have the capacity to metabolize citric acid (Vetsch and Lüthi 1964). Citric acid is present in only small amounts in grapes and in wine, unless added. The metabolism of citric acid is not always seen in commercial winemaking; however, this metabolism can have an important influence on the formation of diacetyl, and thus on the flavor of the wine (Section C.2).

The two aspects of *deacidification*, the decrease in titratable acidity and the increase in pH, have important, but nearly separate, consequences for the winemaker. On the one hand, the perception of sourness comes essentially from the titratable acidity (Amerine and Roessler 1983); thus wines too tart will benefit from having undergone malolactic conversion, but those already too flat will be further spoiled by this microbial activity. On the other hand, the microbial stability of the wine is primarily influenced by the pH. The winemaker needs

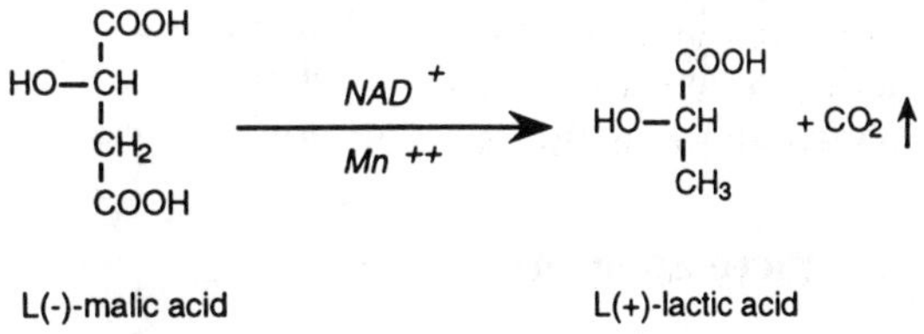

Fig. 6-1. Malolactic conversion. The conversion is a direct decarboxylation of L(-)-malic acid to L(+)-lactic acid. The released carboxyl group is represented as anhydrous carbon dioxide, but in fact has been shown to be released in the hydrated form (Pilone and Kunkee 1970). The acids are depicted as being completely undissassociated; however at wine pH, they are partly in the ionized form [in wine, the pKa_1 of malic acid is 3.45 and the pKa of lactic acid is 3.78 (Kunkee 1967a)]. Although NAD^+ is shown as a cofactor, not being consumed in the reaction, in fact a very small amount (> 0.2%) is reduced, giving the same small amounts of pyruvic acid and NADH as end products. Nevertheless, the "malolactic enzyme," malate carboxy lyase, is not to be confused with other malate decarboxylases, where pyruvic acid or oxaloacetic acid is the major end product.

to be alert to the increased susceptibility of wines to further microbial and chemical attack brought about by the elevation of pH resulting from the malolactic conversion (Chapter 9).

1. Decrease in Titratable Acidity

The stoichiometric loss of one carboxyl group per molecule of malic acid during malolactic conversion (Figure 6-1) should make the extent of the deacidification resulting from malolactic fermentation quantitatively predictable. That is, the titratable acidity should be reduced by one-half of that represented by malic acid (expressed as tartaric acid where this convention is used for expressing titratable acidity) found before the malolactic conversion. In practice, several other activities may upset this convenient relationship. For example, titratable acidity may be altered by additional formation of lactic acid from residual sugar—including pentoses, which the yeasts ignore—during malolactic fermentation, by catabolism of malic acid by wine yeasts themselves, or by loss of potassium bitartrate by precipitation if the wine is already saturated with this ion and if the pH before the malolactic conversion is below pH3.56. (The latter value is the midpoint pH between the two disassociation constants of tartaric acid and where potassium bitartrate ion is the prevalent ionic species.)

2. Increase in pH

The change in pH resulting from malolactic conversion is not so easily predicted. The increase in pH depends upon the buffering capacity of the medium (wine), and thus on the concentrations of the various weak acids before and after the decarboxylation, and also on the starting pH. Furthermore, lactic acid is a weaker acid than malic acid; the pKa of lactic acid is greater than the pKa_1 of malic acid (see Figure 6-1). Equations have been set up for prediction of the change in pH (Kunkee 1967b) supposing the conversion to take place completely after the alcoholic fermentation. For this, various assumptions were made including the constancy of concentrations of the total tartrate anions and of the major cations during the conversion, taking the change in concentration of ammonium ions to be negligible. The calculations showed that with nominal amounts of acidity, the greatest pH change, as much as 0.2 units, was found when the initial pH was around pH 3.4. When starting pHs were lower, where the change in pH coming from the deacidification is not so important from a bacteriological stabilization point, the theoretical increase in pH was only 0.1 unit or less. Ordinarily, however, the flavor effect of acidity decrease is most desired in high-acid, low-pH, sour-tasting wines.

3. Secondary Effects of Deacidification

Besides the effects on the sensory perception and on the biological stability of malolactically converted wine, a change in color also is found in red wine following the activity of these bacteria. A sizable loss in red color comes from equilibrium shifts in anthocyanin pigments' configurations resulting from the increase in pH. If the conversion brings about an unusually high pH, the quality of the color may also change, from a full red to bluish hue. In addition, Vetsch and Lüthi (1964) pointed out that a further potential loss of color could come from the bacterial catabolism of citric acid, the latter being a carbon source ultimately providing NADH for reduction somehow of anthocyanin. However, citric acid is generally not attacked until well after the malolactic conversion is finished, if at all, and seems to be dependent upon the strain of bacteria, the state of aerobiosis of the wine, and perhaps the presence of glucose. (Section C.2).

4. Adjustment of Acidity after Deacidification

Under situations of initially moderate or low acidities in grape musts or wines, the malolactic conversion may bring about the need for use of acidulating agents to bring the titratable acidity and pH back to acceptable values. For this, the use of neither malic acid nor citric acid is recommended. Unless the wine has been rendered completely free from malolactic bacteria, the addition of malic acid will bring about a continuation of bacterial activity, and considerable loss of the acid added. Metabolism of added citric acid, even if minimal, by residual leuconostocs will very likely result in production of objectionable amounts of diacetyl (Section C.2). This leaves tartaric acid as the acidulating agent of choice, in spite of its sometimes being the most expensive of these acids, and in spite of the foreknowledge that much of the acidulating power will be precipitated. A fourth possible acidulating agent is lactic acid, however, commercial preparations of this product are generally recovered from lactic acid bacterial fermentations and carry with them small amounts of impurities with high flavor profiles, especially reminiscent of spoilage malolactic fermentations. It should be noted that commercial preparations of malic acid are most often recovered from apple wastes, and if so, the product is the natural [L(-)] isomer. In some cases, the product has been produced by chemical processes and then is composed of both the L(-)- and the D(+)-isomers of malic acid. The D-isomer, which has been approved as an acidulating agent for wine in the United States, is not catabolized by lactic acid bacteria.

B. BACTERIOLOGICAL STABILITY FOLLOWING MALOLACTIC FERMENTATION

The most important consequence of the malolactic fermentation in warmer wine regions, where the decreased acidity is frequently a liability, is the effect of stabilization of the wine against further growth by any lactic acid bacteria. The malolactic bacteria are proverbially nutritionally fastidious; the accepted wisdom is that during their growth they bring about an uptake, and thus, a depletion of micronutrients, rendering the medium, especially nutritionally poor media such as wine, incapable of supporting any further growth of such fastidious microorganisms. For this reason, and for the concerns expressed in the next paragraph, it is important for the winemaker to supply a known and trustworthy malolactic strain when bacteriological stabilization is the objective.

Evidence from practical winemaking operations supports this viewpoint. Nevertheless, it has been suggested (Davis et al. 1986) that the increased pH resulting from one round of malolactic fermentation can allow for second or third growths of other resident strains of lactic acid bacteria, strains which themselves are not so nutritionally fastidious, but which are more sensitive to the initially low pH as compared to the first-round bacteria. Furthermore, in the cases where the malolactic fermentation is induced to occur along with the alcoholic fermentation, or when it occurs during storage of new wine on the yeast lees (as with the practice of sur lies in Burgundy), adequate nutrients would be present to support more than one bloom of lactic acid bacteria. Nonetheless, we accept the anecdotal evidence that in the commercial situation, wine is rendered malolactically stable by this treatment. Whenever we have seen microbiological activity in wine that has already undergone malolactic fermentation, the spoilage has always been from yeast, acetic acid bacteria, or bacilli. Blending of a malolactically stabilized wine with one not so stabilized is another source of refermentation.

With a few exceptions (Pilone and Kunkee 1965; Prahl et al. 1988; Edwards et al. 1993), wine strains of the genus *Lactobacillus* have made poorly defined contributions to wine complexity and quality. Actually, some California winemakers have recently become aware of wild strains of lactobacilli, which have appeared as potent wine spoilage agents having nothing to do with their malolactic capabilities. More concerning these organisms, and their control, is given in Chapter 9.

C. FLAVOR CHANGES FROM MALOLACTIC FERMENTATION

1. Strain Specificity

The difference in titratable acidity brought about by the malolactic conversion is usually the change most easily detected by the senses. Sometimes more noticeable than the change in acidity are the unfortunate, and hopefully rare, sensory changes brought about by infection of wines by spoilage strains of malolactic bacteria. We have been able to produce, consistently, experimental wines with the off-flavors reminiscent of damp, moldy wood by use of one strain of pediococci (UCD Enology C-5) to carry out the malolactic fermentation. This example serves to emphasize the importance of strain selection for malolactic fermentation, not only for deacidification, but with respect to flavors—contrasted to the situation for selection of wine yeast strains for the alcoholic fermentation (Chapter 4).

Alternatively, it is expected that desirable end products, specifically associated with various nonspoilage strains of malolactic bacteria, are also made. However, in red wine the flavor effect of most of these malic fermenters is subtile and generally not perceived except under rigid taste panel conditions—in which case, one bacterial strain might be said to produce a wine with more complexity of flavor than another (Pilone and Kunkee 1965). An exception is diacetyl, an end product with a low sensory threshold.

2. Diacetyl Formation

In the pure form, diacetyl (2,3-butane dione) is described as having various odors including those of butter, rancid butter, or butterscotch—probably depending upon concentration of the compound. An earlier judgment that the malolactic fermentation is a spoilage phenomenon comes from malolactic fermentations that brought about an excess formation (> 5 mg/L) of diacetyl (Rankine et al. 1969), which is easily detected by its odor, even in red wines (Kunkee et al. 1965). In white wine production, the flavorful end products of malolactic fermentation are more apparent and the fermentation makes a stronger contribution to the bouquet—and to the style of wine expected. The malolactic tone of some modern-day California Chardonnay wines, emulating Burgundian white wines, undoubtedly comes from a noticeable production of diacetyl. Bacterial formation of diacetyl arises mainly from catabolism of citric acid, which under winemaking conditions occurs generally after all of the malic acid has been converted. The metabolism of diacetyl from citric acid has been studied mostly in streptococci, that is, lactococci (Harvey and Collins 1963; Kümmel et al. 1975; Hugenholtz and Starrenburg 1992), but some studies have been made in leuconostocs (Collins 1972). There seem to be two pathways of catabolism of citric acid (Figure 6-2). In the more familiar pathway, found in yeast (Chapter 4) and most of the lactic acid bacteria, citric acid is split to oxaloacetic and acetic acids. The oxaloacetic acid is decarboxylated to give pyruvic acid. The catabolism of pyruvic acid is the same as that shown in yeast metabolism in the formation of valine and isobutyl alcohol (Figure 4-18). The decarboxylation of pyruvic acid, and the complexing with the coenzyme thiamine pyrophosphate, give a product called *active-acetaldehyde*. The latter further combines with another molecule of pyruvic acid to give α-acetolactic acid. Diacetyl then comes from an oxidative decarboxylation of α-acetolactic acid. However, in bacteria which cannot make valine, such as most of the wine leuconostocs (Weiller and Radler 1972; Benda 1982), α-acetolactic acid is not formed (Figures 4-18 and 6-2). In these bacteria, diacetyl apparently arises directly from the condensation of acetyl-CoA with active-acetaldehyde (Collins 1972), the acetyl-CoA coming from oxidative reaction of coenzyme-A with another active-acetaldehyde. In both pathways of diacetyl formation, an oxidation step is involved. In the second

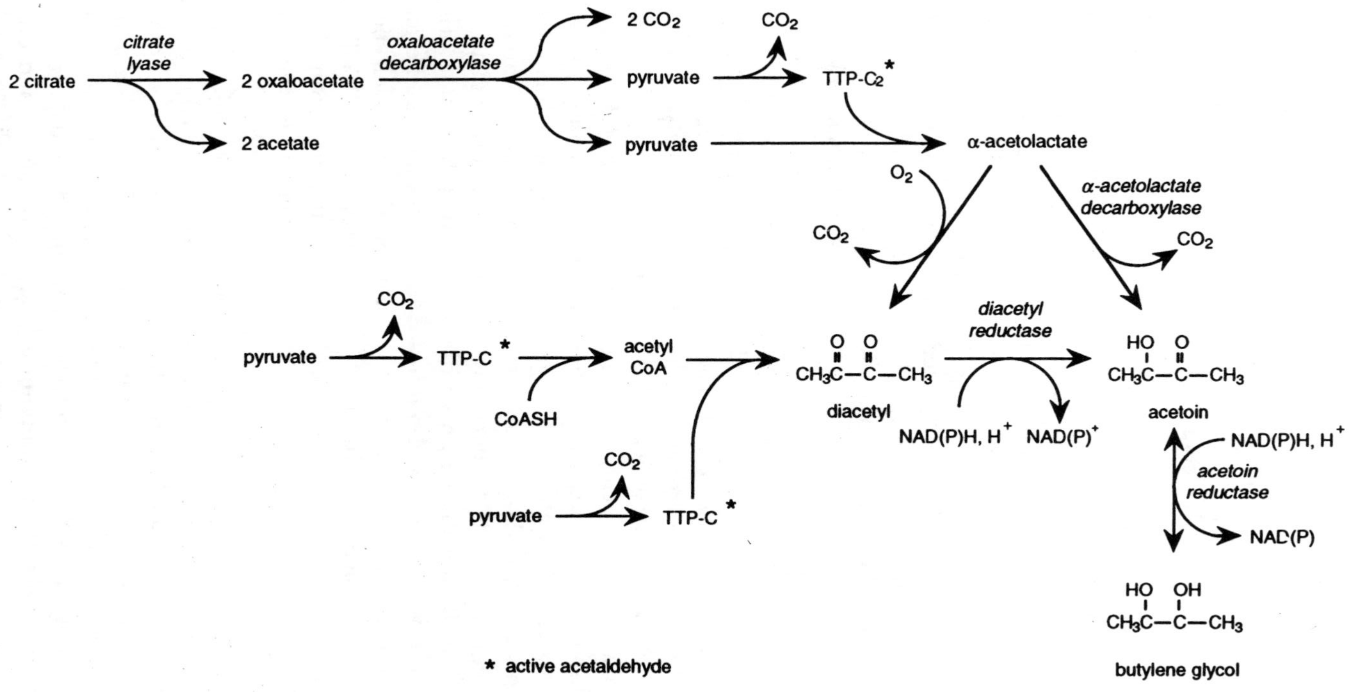

Fig. 6-2. Pathways of diacetyl formation.

pathway, one would think that the presence of pyruvic acid would be sufficient for formation of diacetyl without involving the utilization of citric acid. However, pyruvic acid is normally present only in small concentrations 10 to 50 mg/L (Rankine 1967). Even when it is externally supplied, only a comparatively small amount is degraded (Radler 1975). Pantothenic acid is a part of the coenzyme-A molecule and part of the pathway of its formation is identical to the pathways for valine/isoleucine. Thus, most of the wine leuconostocs also need an exogenous source of this vitamin. There are some indications that energy from citric acid metabolism is also coming from chemiosmotic uptake of citric acid (Hugenholtz et al. 1993), as has also been suggested for the uptake of malic acid (Section I). The presence of glucose may be required for citric acid uptake in some bacterial strains.

From the mechanisms involved, it is not surprising that diacetyl formation is dependent on the bacterial strain (Kunkee et al. 1965; Rankine et al. 1969), the oxygen concentration or the redox potential of the medium (Krieger et al. 1993; Bassit et al. 1993), and the catabolism of citric acid, after the malic acid has disappeared. Thus, the sur lies condition—with extended duration of storage, low concentration of sulfur dioxide, and imposed stirring regimes—tends to encourage diacetyl production. In the discussion of diacetyl production by yeast, which is also influenced by aeration (Chapter 4), it was pointed out that in wine, the diacetyl production by bacteria is far more important than the small amount which might be produced by yeast during vinification.

Two other end products, acetoin (3-hydroxy-2-butanone) and butylene glycol (2,3-butane diol), are closely related to diacetyl (2,3-butane dione), although neither of them has a significant impact on the sensory characteristics of wine (Figure 6-2). The relative amounts of each of these three compounds apparently depends upon the state of aerobiosis/anaerobiosis of the cell. Acetoin can be formed either by the decarboxylation (not oxidative) of α-acetolactic acid (by acetolactate decarboxylase), or the reduction of diacetyl (by diacetyl reductase), with NADH or NADPH as cofactor. Acetoin can itself be reduced, with the same cofactors, to butylene glycol (by acetoin reductase). The latter enzyme reaction is the only one of the group which is reversible.

3. Other End Products

Important as diacetyl is, there is evidence from early work of other flavor components brought about by the malolactic fermentation (Pilone and Kunkee 1965). Modern evidence for these components has been in the application of sniff gas chromatography (Acree et al. 1984) to wines with and without malolactic fermentation (Henick-Kling 1993), if not in the actual sensory examination of the wines themselves.

Histamine is not a flavor component of wines, but its formation is of concern since it is thought, apparently erroneously, to be the origin of physiological distress experienced by some individuals following ingestion of red wine (Ough et al. 1987). A wide range of concentrations of histamine have been reported in red wines, in which their presence seems to be of greater concern as compared to white wines, with an average of about 5 mg/L (Frohlich and Battaglia 1980). It has been supposed that histamine arises from enzymatic decarboxylation of the amino acid histidine, possibly during malolactic bacterial fermentation, even though Weiller and Radler (1976) showed that most wine lactic acid bacteria do not contain this enzyme. More recent research has substantiated this, that histamine is not produced by malolactic bacteria (Ough et al. 1987; Delfini 1989) in the presence or absence of histidine. However, other workers monitoring red wines during and after the alcoholic and malolactic fermentations, and during storage, found a small, but quite variable formation of histamine and other biogenic amines such as tyramine (Buteau et al. 1984; Vidal-Carou et al. 1990, Vidal-Carou et al. 1991).

D. MALOLACTIC FERMENTATION AND WINE STYLE

The various changes associated with malolactic fermentations (already discussed) provide winemakers with a range of options for affecting specific wine styles—traditional ones or those newly inspired. The employment of these changes is reviewed here. Procedures to induce or to prevent the changes are given in the next section.

1. Red Wines

Most of the red wines of the world, including a high proportion of the premium ones, undergo malolactic fermentation, the attributes of the fermentations to be exploited being greatly dictated by the climate. In cold regions where acid levels in grapes at harvest are high, the change in acidity is needed. Indeed, in some regions the initial acidity is too high for the wines to be palatable without the malolactic conversion. In warmer regions, the wines are already more or less deficient in acidity—here the fermentation is favored to provide for bacteriological stability. In the rare cases of premium red wines stored for delayed release, in which the malolactic fermentation has not occurred by bottling time, the winemaker usually assumes that the wine is not susceptible to the secondary fermentation and it is bottled without any special precautions. With red wines for early consumption, this assumption cannot be made if the malolactic fermentation has not yet occurred. Here the winemaker must take special measures (see below) to prevent the malolactic activity from taking place in the bottle. Of course, such fermentation in the bottle gives turbid and gassy wines, as found historically in the vinhos verdes (see below). In general, in the production of red wine, the effect of flavor enhancements coming from malolactic fermentation, except that from changes in acidity or those which should be classified as spoilages, the sensory effect is not the chief feature.

The special style of red wine production utilizing carbonic maceration, as currently practiced in Beaujolais (Flanzy 1972; Hiaring 1974; McCorkle 1974; Flanzy and André 1973) involves the malolactic fermentation in an unusual way. With carbonic maceration, the malolactic fermentation is essentially completed at about the same time as the alcoholic fermentation, and without deliberate addition of bacteria. The stimulation of the bacterial growth seems to arise from the conditions of the vinification during the first several days where the whole berries, as clusters, are immersed (the original sense of the word *macerate*) in carbon dioxide gas; ethanol is subsequently formed anaerobically by fermentation of the grape sugars *inside* the berry, by *berry enzymes*, and the ethanol remains inside the fruit until the berries are later pressed. Some juice is naturally expressed during the filling of the tanks and during subsequent storage. The special conditions of this juice make it well able to support the rapid growth of indigenous bacteria. These special conditions include the absence of ethanol, being retained in the berry; the high temperature of the operation, generally greater than 35°C; the absence of added sulfur dioxide; and the initially high concentration of micronutrients, not yet having been depleted by yeast. The anaerobic conditions prevent the analogous growth of acetic acid bacteria. After the grapes are pressed, the alcoholic fermentation continues and is quickly completed. The special conditions seem to allow adequate red pigments to be extracted during the pressing operation, but leave behind much of the astringent materials. Altogether this results in a product that is more or less stable by all standards, including microbiological, and one that is ready for immediate bottling and consumption. In France, these *vins nouveaux* can be marketed legally on the third Thursday of November as premeur wines, the first wines of the vintage. Some California winemakers have ventured to imitate this style of wine, calling them new wines or wines of the year—also aiming for the November date for release. Very often, strict *macération carbonique* is not employed; but other procedures, such as heavy fining and sterile filtration, are used to provide early stability and drinkability. Malolactic fermentations have not always been induced in these wines.

2. White Wines

Since the flavor and aroma inherently associated with white wines are less conspicuous as compared to those found in red wines, the presence of extra nongrape odors is generally intrusive in them. This explains why the malolactic fermentation is found in only a relatively small portion of the world's white wines; and in most white wine, steps are taken to prevent the malolactic fermentation. Indeed, until recently the malolactic fermentation was essentially avoided in the white wines of Germany, even though one would expect that those wines would especially profit from the accompanying deacidification. The delicate flavor characteristics of wine made from typical German white varieties may be easily overwhelmed by the lactic acid bacterial activity, although the notion of this negative effect undoubtedly comes from an uncontrolled use of indigenous, and improper, bacterial strains (Kunkee 1967a). It should be noted that there is now an increasing utilization of the malolactic conversion for deacidification in German wine regions, partly due to the increased production of red wines there, but also because of the ready availability of suitable cultures for inoculation (Kreiger et al. 1993).

As in red wines, the utilization of malolactic fermentation in white wine has, first of all, to do with the climate of the vineyards and the acidity of the wine. Notable examples are the wine regions of northern France, where the climate is generally so cool that not only is the fermentation required for deacidification, but the initial acidities are so high in the white wines as to all but prevent the growth of the operative bacteria. The Burgundian winemaker stores the wines on the yeast lees for several months after the alcoholic fermentation. This sur lies treatment provides for release from the lees of small-molecular-weight materials—amino acids and vitamins—from the settled yeast, which then serve as nutrients for the bacteria. This special use of the malolactic fermentation has provided a unique style of Chardonnay production that is often mimicked in other regions, including California. In California the sur lies procedure is employed not out of necessity for encouraging bacterial growth, but to provide the special changes thought to occur during this treatment and also thought by some winemakers to have a positive influence on the flavors of the wine. The treatment is sometimes applied to other white varieties also. It is clear that the malolactic fermentation can bring about important changes in flavor of white wines, largely dependent on the bacterial strain—the resulting formation of diacetyl tending to overwhelm the native floral and fruity tones. However, what is not clear is which style should be most favored.

The sur lies treatment can also be used in white wine production for the stimulation of the growth of the bacteria, as needed. Much of the white wine production in the cold regions of eastern Europe is produced by storing the wine over the winter in inert tanks in the naturally very cold cellars. The resulting wines have the needed deacidification, but still retain the intended varietal attributes. Nevertheless, there is no doubt of the importance of sur lies for its influence on style. In the Chablis region, where the fruity style of Chardonnay production has been classic, it is increasingly common to find sur lies treatment in oak barrels as compared to the established practice there of storage in stainless steel tanks. This is being done apparently to emulate the flavors of the wines from the neighboring Côte de Beaune—and perhaps also to emulate their rather higher retail prices. See LaFollette (1991) for a discussion of the considerable literature on sur lies treatment and of the controversies over its influence on malolactic fermentation and on flavor of Chardonnay wines.

The Champagne wine region of France is even colder than the other regions just mentioned. The grapes from this region are used, of course, especially for making the base wines used in the production of sparkling wines, the latter by the *méthode champenoise*, the traditional procedure of the region (de Rosa 1987; Amerine et al. 1980; Troost and Haushofer 1986). Because of the climate, the base wines are especially acidic, with pHs often of 3.0 or less, and the malolactic conversion is a very important part of the production. The required clarity of the final product demands that the malolactic fermentation take place before the secondary alcoholic fermentation, since it is impossible to remove the bacteria from the bottle during the riddling (*remuage*) operation, as is used for removing the yeast. Furthermore, the delicacy of flavors and the enhancement of aromas and bouquets by the effervescence of sparkling wines demand that the malolactic conversion occur without the addition of obvious bacterial flavor notes. The base wines are also stored in contact with yeast lees to encourage the bacterial growth; however, this is done in tanks, where the lees depth is high and surface low, as compared to such storage in smaller barrels. This seems to account for the minimal influence of the malolactic fermentation on the flavor of the wines of Champagne, except for the flavor change in acidity. It is remarkable that the base wines, with their initially very low pHs, support the bacterial growth at all. Apparently, the rather low concentrations of ethanol and the rather long, if cold, storage times overcome the inhibitory influences. Possibly the strains of bacteria employed, which are indigenous to the region and which have been selected over the years, are especially tolerant to these conditions. However, we are aware that bacterial strains that have been touted as being especially acid tolerant because they have been isolated from wines from cold regions, more often than not are successful strains for carrying out the malolactic fermentation in these regions because of the lower ethanol content of the wines rather the special acid tolerance of the bacteria. The employment of malolactic conversion in sparkling wine production seems to be unique to the Champagne regions. It is generally not found in other sparkling wine regions, with the possible exception of some from New York state.

Another interesting style of white wine production employing the use of malolactic bacteria is that of the Minho region of northern Portugal. Here the wines are traditionally very acidic, not from the influence of the climate, but rather from the viticultural practices. Customarily, the grapevines here have been planted next to poplar trees, these tall trees becoming the support for very lofty, and nearly impossible to train, grapevines. It is equally impossible to control the quantity and quality of the fruit. The berries, precariously hand-harvested from tall ladders, show the negative effects of the unavoidable overcropping. The resulting wines are thus named *vinhos verdes* (green wines), not from their color, but from the lack of ripeness in the harvested fruit. It is imperative that these wines undergo the malolactic deacidification. Years ago this conversion seemed to take place rather haphazardly, often by benign neglect after the wine had been bottled. The retention of the carbon dioxide in these wines gave then an added sensory dimension of effervescence and of consumer acceptance—and of the birth of a new style of wine. However, the turbidity in these wines, from the bacterial growth, was not so readily accepted; they generally became marketed in ceramic and then in opaque glass bottles to hide this defect. The haphazardness of the presence of the effervescence made the merchandising of these wines uncertain. Modern standards of quality control have now forced a change in procedure to induce the malolactic conversion prior to bottling and to substitute the bacterial effervescence with artificial carbonation. It is essentially impossible now to find any commercial example of an original-type *vinho verde* in the Minho.

E. CONTROLLING THE MALOLACTIC FERMENTATION

Over the last few decades, research efforts, both fundamental and applied, have provided winemakers with a number of tools to allow encouragement or discouragement of the malolactic fermentation.

1. Metabolic Interactions between Yeast and Malolactic Bacteria

One of the tools for controlling malolactic fermentation could be the employment of the natural metabolic interactions between the yeast strain, used for the alcoholic fermentation, and the subsequent malolactic bacteria. The competition for nutrients, the formation and binding of sulfur dioxide by the yeast, the formation of inhibitory medium-chain fatty acids by the yeast, the strain variation in release of intracellular materials from the yeast during sur lies aging are all important factors. With respect to the last, cell-wall polysaccharides and proteins liberated by wine yeast, probably strain-related, have been shown to have a stimulatory effect on malolactic bacteria (Guilloux-Benatier et al. 1993). However, Dick et al. (1992) isolated proteins from *Saccharomyces cerevisiae*, which inhibited malolactic bacteria.

The formation of the high concentrations of ethanol by the yeast would be expected to have an important influence on the secondary fermentation, depending on the strain of bacteria involved. While this effect has also been studied (Fornachon 1968), no definite or consistent correlation between yeast strain used for the alcoholic fermentation and its influence on various malolactic strains, or vice versa, has as yet been established. One study between Montrachet yeast strain and PSU-1 strain of *Leuconostoc oenos*, however, reveals some unexpected interactions (King and Beelman 1986). On the one hand, the yeast inhibited the early bacterial growth, but not because of ethanol formation. In fact, ethanol at low concentrations stimulated the growth of the bacteria. This effect has been confirmed (see below). On the other hand, the bacteria stimulated the death phase of the yeast. This was not the result of ornithine production by the bacteria, which had been indicated in earlier literature (Kuensch et al. 1974). The high concentration of sugars in grape juice was inhibitory to the growth of both the yeast (Chapter 4) and the bacteria; when the medium was diluted 1:1, the yeast and the bacteria reached their stationary phases simultaneously. The antagonism between yeast and malolactic fermentation has also been shown by Rynders (1993), where the effect on the yeast was generally alleviated by additions of riboflavin.

The interrelationships between the yeast and bacteria are extremely complex and they are further complicated by the relationships between the various environmental factors, having inhibitory and synergist effects. We have already mentioned the interplay between acidity (low pH) and ethanol concentration and bacterial growth. Another relationship between the effects of ethanol concentration and temperature has also been shown (Asmundson and Kelly 1990). The latter workers also found the slight stimulation of growth rate and biomass yield of malolactic bacteria at 2 to 4% ethanol, as compared to no ethanol or to higher concentrations.

2. Stimulation

The malolactic fermentation is stimulated either by making the conditions more favorable to the bacteria so as to speed up their growth rate or by supplying a high starting population of bacteria, or both.

a. *Stimulation of Bacterial Growth*

The conditions for stimulation of the growth rate are simply stated and generally not too difficult to implement (Kunkee 1967a, 1974, 1984, 1991).

I. Sulfur Dioxide. Nominal additions of sulfur dioxide inhibit bacterial growth and should be used as little as possible, or not at all, where the malolactic fermentation is desired. Additions of sulfur dioxide to the must can delay or prevent the onset of bacterial growth, even when the latter is expected or desired after the end of the alcoholic fermentation (Kunkee 1967a) when all of the sulfur dioxide is bound. Sulfur dioxide is largely bound as its addition product with acetaldehyde, and this addition product has been shown, itself, to be toxic to the bacteria—presumably by catabolism of the carbon moiety by the bacteria, thus freeing the toxic sulfur dioxide (Fornachon 1957).

II. Temperature. If the malolactic fermentation is to be encouraged, the temperature of the wine during storage is a major consideration; it ought to be maintained above 18°C—but not much higher because of potential damage to the wine. In some climates, this may mean an artificial increase in the ambient temperature of at least some isolated storage area, if not of the whole cellar.

III. Acidity. Acidity can be modified to stimulate the growth rate. Where pH needs to be raised, there should be, of course, no acid addition before malolactic conversion. Where the pH is so low as to prevent the onset of bacterial growth, for example in some parts of New York state, winemakers have used chemical deacidifications, such as additions of calcium carbonate, to raise the pH enough to allow bacterial growth.

IV. Ethanol. Stimulation of the bacterial growth by overcoming the inhibitory presence of ethanol is not easily accomplished—but the situation often takes care of itself. While some lactic acid bacteria can thrive at very high (> 20%) concentrations of ethanol, the malolactic bacteria are generally sensitive to the ethanol concentrations of table wine, and the inhibition becomes more and more evident as the ethanol reaches about 14% (vol/vol) (Kunkee 1967a). However, since wines of high ethanol concentration are generally those of higher pH—except where sugar amelioration is practiced—the inhibitory effect of ethanol is compensated for by the higher pH. As we have said, malolactic bacterial strains touted to have special resistance to the inhibitory effects of wines with low pH, very often, in fact, are merely benefiting from the low concentration of ethanol that is usually associated with these wines.

V. Macronutrients. In grape juice or laboratory media, the wine malolactic bacteria easily utilize glucose and fructose. In the absence of these sugars, as at the end of the alcoholic fermentation, it is not clear what the bacteria use as sources of energy. Malic acid has a dramatic stimulatory effect on the growth of these bacteria (Section I), but the bacteria cannot use it as a sole energy source. All of the malolactic bacteria can metabolize ribose, and some can metabolize other pentoses (Melamed 1962). These sugars are in low concentrations in wine, but sometimes might be high enough to provide sufficient energy for cell biomass to reach the limited amount typically found in wine. However, there may be a problem in induction of the permeases and enzymes for catabolism of these substrates, which are at such low concentrations (Rogosa and Sharpe 1959). Apparently some amino acids can be utilized as energy sources (Weiller and Radler 1976), although they too are at low concentrations at the very end of the alcoholic fermentation.

VI. Micronutrients. The micronutrient requirements for the lactic acid bacteria are extensive (Henick-Kling 1988), nutritionally fastidious being a common descriptor for them. They all require some amino acids and several vitamins. Indeed, growth of some of these bacteria has been used for bioassays of factors especially difficult to assay by other means. Lists of nutritional requirements for selected strains of malolactic bacteria can be found in the older literature (Lüthi and Vetsch 1960; Peynaud et al. 1965; Du Plessis 1963; Radler 1966; Kunkee 1967a; Weiller and Radler 1972, 1976), and also more recently (Tracey and Britz 1989b). Generally, strains of

Leuconostoc oenos are the most fastidious of all (Section H.2).

The use of information concerning micronutrient requirements as a means to control malolactic fermentation is complicated by several factors. The amino acid may be being used as an energy source, rather than a required nutrient. Furthermore, the availability of the amino acids is not necessarily growth stimulating. In order to involve micronutrients for control of malolactic fermentation, not only would it be necessary to know the micronutrient complement of the particular bacterial strain to be used, but also the extract micronutrient complement of the wine. Both of these requirements are difficult, if not impossible, to ascertain during practical winemaking operations. Moreover, the addition of specific nutrients usually requires government permission, not likely to be as quickly procured as needed.

One more complicating fact is that lactic acid bacteria have been shown to produce extracellular proteases, and the concentration of free amino acids has been observed to increase during growth of these bacteria (Henick-Kling 1988). Some bacteria of this group are stimulated by peptides more than by the constituent amino acids.

VII. Oxygen. The lactic acid bacteria are microaerophilic, indicating a love for small amounts of oxygen. Oxygen can be considered a nutrient. In the heterolactic bacteria (Section H), the presence of molecular oxygen ought to stimulate their growth by providing a direct means of reoxidation of NADPH. The latter is a required catalyst during the first steps in the heterolactic fermentation of hexoses—that is, in their oxidative decarboxylation. However, there is essentially no evidence to indicate that aerobic conditions are more favorable than anaerobic conditions with regard to malolactic bacterial growth under practical winemaking conditions (Kunkee 1991), and in some cases, the opposite has been indicated (Kelly et al. 1989). It is generally more useful for the winemaker to think of these bacteria as anaerobic, remembering the requirement is by no means as stringent as for strict anaerobes.

b. Increased Size of Bacterial Inocula

In the traditional management of malolactic fermentation, the inoculating bacteria are present as indigenous residents of the cellar, especially in used cooperage. It was pointed out in this section that the use of bacterial starter cultures to stimulate the fermentation is becoming more and more popular. Often the desired strains are purchased as liquid cultures or as frozen or freeze-dried cultures. About a dozen cultures are commercially available, most of them being strains of *Leuconostoc oenos* (Pompilio 1993), but strains of pediococui and lactobacilli are also distributed. The frozen or dried cultures ought to be rehydrated in sterile water or medium (Fugelsang and Zoecklein 1993) before being expanded. Ideally, the latter is done aseptically in a modified grape juice medium (Appendix F) to provide for an inoculum of 10^8 colony-forming units (cfu) per mL. One strain of lactobacillus (*L. plantarum*) is distributed commercially for use without being expanded. In this case, a large inoculum is added to the grape juice, where the malolactic deacidification is made by the nongrowing bacteria (in this case inhibited by the low pH of the grape juice) before the wine yeast inoculation is made.

Because of the relatively slow growth and low biomass formation of the malolactic bacteria, malolactic starter cultures are much more difficult to prepare, as compared to yeast starter cultures. For the preparation of the latter, asepsis is generally not necessary since the wine yeast, at any reasonable inoculation level, will outgrow any other organisms resident in the grape juice, or other medium, used for the starter. For bacteria expansion, autoclaved media can be used until the volumes become too unwieldy. After that, one relies on high inoculation concentrations. This means that the initial inoculations, whether at time of harvest, in the middle, or at the end of the alcoholic fermentation, must generally be small. Furthermore, there is often a dramatic loss of viability of these bacteria when they are transferred from one medium to another, especially when the latter is a less favorable one.

Two routines have been devised to help overcome the difficulties of malolactic starter preparation (Beelman and Kunkee 1987). To allow better bacterial growth, the grape juice to be used as starter is initially soaked on the grape skins overnight and then the pressed juice receives the following commercially acceptable manipulations: dilution 1:1 with water, adjustment of pH to pH 4.5 with calcium carbonate, and then addition of 0.1% yeast nutrient. To this is added a 1% starter of malolactic bacteria *and* a 0.1% inoculum of wine yeast. The latter is added to allow an alcoholic fermentation to occur following the full growth of the bacteria. The resulting ethanol helps protect the starter from unwanted invasive microorganisms. In about two weeks' time this starter can be used, at a concentration of 1%, for inoculation of freshly harvested musts.

However, once malolactic fermentation has commenced, or once the malolactic conversion is evident in this initial material, a method of rapid induction of malolactic fermentation becomes available. The wine which has just undergone malolactic conversion can now can be employed as a starter culture. While the final concentration of bacteria in this new starter material (wine) may be low, reaching a concentration of only 10^7 cfu/mL, as compared to 10^9 cfu/mL in laboratory cultures, the winemaker now has a large volume of it available and thus can use it at a high inoculation rate, say, 50%. Since a 50% inoculation rate in this case would give an initial bacterial concentration of about 5×10^6, and since there is essentially no loss of viability in transferring between such similar media, the consequent malolactic conversion rate is rapid, and may occur in a few days and furnish even more starter material. Although this method is somewhat labor-intensive, it provides a powerful tool for obtaining rapid malolactic fermentations under practical winemaking conditions.

3. Inhibition

Contrariwise, the malolactic fermentation is inhibited either by making the conditions less favorable to the bacteria so as to slow down their growth, or by assuring that there is a low initial concentration of bacteria, or both. Of course, for absolute prevention, viable malolactic bacteria must be completely eliminated.

a. *Repression of Bacterial Growth*

The conditions for inhibition are as simply stated as those for stimulation and are also generally not too difficult to implement (Kunkee 1974, 1984, 1991).

I. Sulfur Dioxide. Sulfur dioxide, of course, inhibits bacterial growth; however, its presence at the concentrations acceptable in good winemaking operations is not sufficient in itself to assure complete absence of bacterial activity. To control the malolactic fermentation, the oft-recommended concentration of 0.8 mg/L of molecular sulfur dioxide, which of course takes into account the pH of the wine, is advised; however, unless both the temperature and the concentration of bacteria are kept low, this concentration of sulfur dioxide ought to be considered as a delaying operation (Kunkee 1967a).

II. Temperature. To inhibit bacterial growth, the stored wine should be kept at normal cellar temperatures, at least below 18°C. Often temperatures as low as 13°C are used; the latter corresponding to temperatures often found in premium wine region cellars. Nevertheless, we have observed the occurrence of the malolactic fermentation even in white wines in some of the coldest wine growing regions, for example, in Chablis and in Brataslavia, where the inhibitory cold conditions were balanced by stimulation from increased nutrients coming from storage of the wine on the yeast lees.

III. Ethanol. We have mentioned the natural reciprocal conditions of high concentrations of ethanol and of high pH. Here, again, the inhibitory effect of high concentrations of ethanol cannot be counted on to prevent bacterial growth, since these wines do not usually have a pH low enough to be restrictive.

IV. Acidity. Since the bacterial growth is inhibited by low pH, acid additions, preferably tartaric acid, can be used to control the fermentations. As with low temperature, low pH is not in itself assurance of complete inhibition of bacterial growth. The base wines for sparkling wine production in the Champagne region are commonly pH 3.0, or less, and these wines generally can be and are handled in such a way as to bring about the malolactic fermentation.

A rule of thumb, at least under California winemaking conditions, has been given (Kunkee 1967a): when wine has a pH less than 3.3, stimulatory operations (see above) need to be employed in order to obtain the fermentation; if the pH is greater than 3.3, it will be difficult to prevent malolactic fermentation with the use of regular cellar operations (see above). In order to discourage the fermentation where it is not wanted, winemakers have been advised to remove the wine from the yeast lees and to make fining and filtration operations as early as possible, to store the wine at low temperature in noninfected (stainless steel) cooperage, and to maintain judicious concentrations of sulfur dioxide (Kunkee 1967a, 1991). However, absolute inhibition of malolactic fermentation is assured only by complete removal or destruction of the causative bacteria.

b. Elimination of Viable Malolactic Bacteria

The need to block malolactic fermentation is usually most important in bottled white wines which are considered at risk, but which have not as yet undergone fermentation. For example, this situation might arise from a blend of wines having and not having already undergone malolactic fermentation. With varietally distinct white wines, it is especially important to choose the method of elimination of bacteria which has minimal or no effect on sensory properties. With red wines, bottling is often long enough delayed that the wines have already been bacteriologically stabilized by malolactic fermentation; or if not by this time, it is reasonable to suppose that they do not support the growth of bacteria. With young pink and red wines, the methods and precautions are the same as with white ones.

Several methods are used for absolute inhibition of malolactic fermentation: sterile filtration, treatment with chemical inhibitors, and heating of the wine. The action of bacteriophage can have a dramatic inhibitory effect on malolactic bacteria and their fermentations; however, the use of bacteriophage is not an established winemaking control operation. Their activities, and associated problems, are discussed below.

I. Sterile bottling. Sterile filtration, followed by sterile bottling, is the method of choice for prevention of bacterial activity in bottled wine. When properly performed this operation assures complete removal of the microbes; and when it is properly done, it confers no perceptible sensory effect. The procedure is the same as that used for removal of yeast to stabilize semidry wine (Chapters 5 and 9), except the nominal porosity of the filter must be smaller, no larger than 0.45 μm. As with the yeast removal, the essential removal of microbes may be done with depth filters, but the final filtration ought to be made with a membrane filter, which allows integrity testing (bubble point) (Chapter 11). Again, the sterilization of the filter and housing, and all of the equipment downstream, including various parts of the filling equipment, can be safely and reliably achieved only by use of heat (hot water or steam). Quality control of the operation is the same as that used for yeast removal: removal of bottled wines from the production line, filtration of contents though a sterile membrane, incubation of the membrane on a nutrient medium, followed by visual inspection for colony development. These bacteria are both nutritionally fastidious and slow growers; for some the optimal temperature for growth in not much above room temperature. Thus, it is important for these bacteria to use a highly enriched medium, such as modified Rogosa (Appendix F), and to incubate the plates for at least 10 days and at a temperature of about 25°C.

II. Heat. Heating methods for prevention of yeast activity in bottled wine can also be used for elimination of malolactic bacteria. Flash pasteurization and high-temperature short-time heating procedures will effectively destroy the bacteria, with minimal effect on flavor, but the entire system downstream (lines, filling equipment, bottles, bottle closures) must also be rendered and maintained sterile. Hot bottling, where the wine is heated and allowed to cool after it has been bottled, has generally been considered unacceptable because of the accompanying deterioration of the wine flavor. However, some inventive research has shown that when this is done in small-sized bottles (375 mL volume) in a tunnel pasteurizer, there is no sensory deterioration of the product (Malletroit et al. 1991). This method would seem to be an attractive one for stabilization of wine in small-sized containers, where sterile filling is often troublesome, especially at high speed.

III. Chemical Inhibitors. There is increasing pressure to limit the use of sulfur dioxide in winemaking, including its use to control malolactic fermentation. This has renewed interest in the use of other chemical inhibitors.

Fumaric acid has been shown to be toxic to lactic acid bacteria at low pH (Cofran and Meyer 1970; Pilone 1975). It has been successfully used to inhibit malolactic fermentation under good winemaking conditions; that is, when the pH is less than 4, and when the concentration of bacteria is relatively low—such as would be obtained after a rough filtration. A disadvantage of this procedure is the relative insolubility of fumaric acid, especially in wine; but since only a low final concentration (0.5 g/L) is needed, winemakers have found that occasional stirring of the wine for a day or two after addition allows the material to become fully dissolved. This drawback makes the treatment impractical for use for very large-scale volumes of wine. Wine producers should be cautioned that even though fumaric acid is a widely used acidulating agent for the food and beverage industry and is a common component of human cell metabolism, its use in wine is restricted in many countries outside of the United States.

Dimethyl decarbonate (Velcorin®) is also approved for use in the United States. This chemical has been used mainly for control of yeast in wine (Chapter 7), but it has also been found to be an inhibitor of malolactic bacteria in the presence of SO_2 in wine, providing again, as with fumaric acid, that the pH is reasonably low (Ough et al. 1988). The use of this product in wine in Europe is awaiting approval.

Not yet reduced to practice in wine production is the use of nisins, small polypeptides produced by certain lactic acid bacteria inhibitory to other bacteria. Recent research has demonstrated the effectiveness of these, and also the possibilities of the development of resistance to them by the bacteria (Radler 1990a, 1990b; Daeschel et al. 1991).

Another natural product showing promise for inhibition of malolactic bacteria in wine is the enzyme lysozyme. Some problems with increased turbidity in white wines and color instability in red wines need to be overcome (Amati et al. 1993).

c. *Bacteriophage*

It is unlikely that winemakers would ever wish to employ the use of bacteriophages—bacterial viruses—to control (inhibit) malolactic fermentation; but it is in their best interest, and in the best interest of the producers of malolactic bacterial starter cultures, to understand how potentially dangerous these agents could be. Whereas bacteria grow at an exponential rate—a parent cell producing two progeny cells during each cell cycle, *each* parent bacteriophage commonly produces 100 to 200 progeny phages. As with other viruses, the phages cannot reproduce on their own, but after invasion into the host bacteria, they take over some of the reproductive apparatus of the cells to make copies of themselves. After a relatively short time, in about 20 minutes under defined conditions with some bacteria, the integrity of the host's cell wall is destroyed and lysis ensues. The newly formed phages are released to infect other host cells in the medium. One or two cycles of this can completely blight the culture. The use of bacteriophages in transduction or plasmid interactions, or in other genetic manipulations of the lactic acid bacteria is only beginning to be realized (Klaenhammer 1987). However, the commercial significance of the phages has long been known in the disastrous interruptions of acetone-butanol fermentations by infection of *Clostridium acetobutylicum*, and closer to our subject, in the disruptions of cheese manufactures by infections of *Lactococcus* spp. The discoveries of bacteriophage invasion of the malolactic bacteria in winemaking have not been so dramatic. However, the phage problem can be potentially as important for winemakers as more use is made of single-strain cultures for malolactic fermentation. The wine bacteriophages were first reported in Switzerland almost two decades ago (Sozzi et al. 1976), and 10 years later in Australian wines (Davis et al. 1985a; Henick-Kling 1986), with photographs of the phages, and of the plaques—the holes of lysed cells in a lawn background of the susceptible bacteria on nutrient agar plates. Initially, there seemed to be no compelling reason to think that phage infections would be important in commercial wine production, or could account for stuck malolactic fermentations; however, later research clearly showed the potential dangers of this infection (Henick-Kling et al. 1986). As yet there have been no known incidents involving bacteriophages in the California wine industry (Kunkee 1991), nor are we aware of any problems with them in the commercial production of malolactic bacterial starters. However, some assessments of the situation suggest that the potentialities of the problem are severe; many strains of *Leuconostoc oenos* are lysogenic and there can be a contamination on an industrial scale (Cavin et al. 1991). The range of sensitivities of the hosts for the phages seems to be narrow; thus, the protective measures would seem to be the same as those used in the dairy industry, to have other strains of starter cultures in reserve.

F. DETECTION OF MALOLACTIC CONVERSION

Changes in titratable acidity and pH characterize the malolactic conversion; however, these changes are variable in degree and may be masked by or arise from other reactions in wine. The measure of increase in lactic acid is also not sufficient evidence, since this acid might also be formed by yeast or by bacteria from other carbohydrate sources. Thus, the measurement of disappearance of malic acid is the accepted means for determining whether the malolactic conversion has occurred. Procedures for malic acid measurement are given below.

Visual inspection can provide some indications of malolactic activity: An increase in turbidity can be seen in relatively clear and light-colored wines coming from the increased concentration of bacteria; increased effervescence may be evident from the formation of carbon dioxide; and a loss in color may be seen from the change in pH and available hydrogens, the latter from NADH formed during the fermentation. The first two visual changes should not be considered definitive: they are either too subjective or too difficult to quantify because of their lack of specificity; however, the loss in color in red wine can often be measured spectrophotometrically. Some loss in color, due to the increased pH, is reversible and returns with adjustment of the wine to its original acidity. Another loss of color may come from reduction of anthocyanin pigments by net production of NADH by the bacteria, but this is not common (Section A.3).

1. Malic Acid Analyses

Among methods available, practically speaking, paper chromatography, enzymatic analyses, and liquid chromatography are used for determination of malic acid. The last method requires rather expensive equipment and is usually found only in consulting wine laboratories or very large wineries; however, the methodology for the first two procedures is readily available in most wineries.

a. *Enzymatic Procedures*

The enzymatic procedures utilize the reduction of NAD^+ (which can then be measured spectrophotometrically at 340 mμ) by L(-)-malic acid in the presence of the malic dehydrogenase, at pH 9.5. The equilibrium is in favor of the substrates. One procedure speeds up the reaction by removing the oxaloacetic acid produced by condensing it with hydrazine (Poux and Caillet 1969). Another procedure employs addition of L-glutamate and the removal of it, and oxaloacetic acid coming from L-malic, by a second enzyme, glutamate-oxaloacetate transaminase (McCloskey 1980). The enzymatic analysis materials are available in convenient kit forms from biochemical supply houses.

b. *Paper Chromatography*

The paper chromatographic procedure is described in detail here (Kunkee 1968, 1974). Chromatographic-grade filter paper rectangles of 20 cm × 30 cm (commercially available precut) are spotted with the must or wine for analysis along one of the longer edges, about 2.5 cm from the edge and about 2.5 cm between spots. Each spotting is made four times, to a diameter of about 1 cm (and the spot allowed to dry in between spottings) from 1.2- × 75 mm-sized micropipettes, giving a total volume of approximately 10 μL (the smaller the spots, the greater the resolution). The paper is then formed into a cylinder with the use of three staples along the short ends, care being taken not to contact or overlap the edges. Screw-lid commodity jars of approximately 4 L (of some 14 cm in diameter and 25 cm in height) serve well as chromatography jars. The solvent is prepared in a fume hood, or a well-ventilated, fire-free area, by shaking together in a separatory funnel 100 mL H_2O, 100 mL *n*-butanol, 10.7 mL concentrated formic acid, and 15 mL of a 10-g/L solution of bromocresol green (this dye is available in a water-soluble form). After several minutes the lower (aqueous) phase is drawn off and discarded. Seventy mL of the upper layer are placed in the jar, the chromatogram is inserted (the spotted edge down), the jar lid closed, and the jar stored at room temperature in a draft-free space. For best results the running time is about six hours; this may be safely extended to overnight, even if the solvent reaches the upper edge; or the chromatogram can be removed after about three hours (and a paper cylinder of only 10 cm height used). After the yellow chromatogram is removed, it should be stored in a well-ventilated area until dry and until the formic acid has volatilized, leaving a blue-green background with yellow spots of acids having the following approximate Rf (the ratio of spot movement to solvent front distance) values: tartaric acid 0.28, citric acid 0.45, malic acid 0.51, lactic and succinic acids 0.78, and fumaric acid 0.91. The Rf of the dye front is between 0.8 and 0.9. Standard solutions (2 g/L) of malic and lactic acids should also be run as controls. The solvent may be used repeatedly if care is taken to remove any aqueous layer which may have separated after each run.

For faster results, thin layer chromatography can be used, but we are not confident that the lower levels of malic acid (0.6 g/L) sometimes found in California wine before malolactic fermentation (Ingraham and Cooke 1960) are easily detected by this means. Where results are needed in less than three hours, the enzymatic procedures given above should be employed.

G. POSTMALOLACTIC FERMENTATION OPERATIONS

After the malolactic fermentation is finished, several winery operations are advised for good storage of the wine. As mentioned above, the fermentation is not complete until some few days after the malolactic *conversion* is finished —that is, not until several days after the malic acid has disappeared—since the bacteria usually need an additional growth cycle or two before they enter their resting phase. Sometimes the loss of malic acid is not complete, or at least the last traces are very slow to disappear. Practically, one can say that the malolactic conversion is finished when the malic acid concentration decreases to less than 0.2 g/L, or when the acid spot on the chromatogram is hardly visible.

For most individual wines, the malolactic fermentation readily goes to completion. Climate conditions may lower the storage temperatures so as to delay the finishing of the fermentation until warmer weather arrives. It is more difficult to explain the situation where a wine is said to have had a limited malolactic fermentation. This may reflect a micronutrient or energy source deficiency, either of which may be extremely difficult to determine. Bacteriophage infection is an unlikely cause, but cannot be completely ignored. After some months, the wine probably can be considered bacteriologically stable. The most critical thing to remember is that bacteriological stability is likely to be lost if this wine is then blended with any other. In fact, one worries that a wine with partial malolactic fermentation is a blend of one with and one without and a problem waiting to happen.

The postfermentation treatments usually mimic those specified for discouragement of the fermentation: transfer of the wine off of any lees and a rough filtration; adjustments of temperature and pH and addition of sulfur dioxide. Fining operations could also be employed at this time. The temperature should be adjusted to that used for cellar storage (13°C to 15°C). Acid adjustment can now be made (Section A.4) The sulfur dioxide additions should follow normal cellar guidelines, that is, 0.8 mg molecular-SO_2 per liter.

Sometimes a ventilation of the wine is helpful. This treatment serves to remove some unwanted volatile odors, such as traces of hydrogen sulfide, which can arise chemically during the reducing conditions of the fermentation, regardless of bacterial strain. This treatment is often accomplished merely by splashing the wine during a racking operation against the side of the air-filled container. The ventilation by this means includes, of course, a limited aeration, which may be beneficial for other reasons.

H. IDENTIFICATION AND CULTIVATION OF MALOLACTIC BACTERIA

1. Description of Malolactic Bacteria

The malolactic bacteria are those which have the capability of direct decarboxylation of malic acid to lactic acid—by the enzyme malate carboxy lyase. This enzymatic activity is unique in the biological world, being found only in several genera of lactic acid bacteria. The malolactic bacteria as a group are not a separate taxon—the strains belonging to this grouping cut across several genera of lactic acid bacteria. Here we are mainly interested in those malolactic bacteria that have high tolerance to acidity and ethanol, that is, those which will grow in wine, and thus are limited to certain species of three genera: *Lactobacillus*, *Pediococcus*, and *Leuconostoc*. However, malolactic bacteria are involved in other kinds of fermentations including pickle, sauerkraut, and soy sauce manufactures and in silage production. It has generally been expected that most lactic acid bacterial isolates from wine would have malolactic conversion capabilities, but that is not always the case (see below).

Some of the older literature incorrectly reports the isolations of strains of micrococci and streptococci from wine. However, many strains of *Lactococcus lactis*, the modern classification of several species of *Streptococcus*, do have malolactic capability. These bacteria, important in cheese manufacture, cannot grow in wine; but because they are relatively easy to cultivate they are being used by some workers as good substrate microorganisms for malolactic research. Since this enzymatic activity has no known or obvious value to bacteria growing in the absence of malic acid, either it would seem that this is a primitive activity, but was not lost when the lactococci adapted to animal substrates from plant substrates, or that we do not understand the definitive role of the enzyme.

Some recently described pediococci isolated from wine (Edwards and Jensen 1992) do not have the malolactic capability. It is not clear how important spoilage of wine by non-malolactic pediococci would be, either in bringing about microbiological stability or in production of unacceptable flavors and odors.

2. Cultivation of Wine-Related Lactic Acid Bacteria

Lactic acid bacteria, in culture, are generally grown in complex media, often containing peptone, tryptone, or yeast extract, at pH 5 to 6, and usually are stored in such media with agar, as stab cultures. The wine-related lactic acid bacteria will grow at much lower pH values, approaching 3.0; and low-pH media are sometimes used by wine microbiologists.

The cultivation of the wine leuconostocs is often especially difficult. While many of these strains will show better growth at the low pHs just mentioned than members of the other genera, they usually need special nutritional supplementation. A potent growth factor for these organisms has been isolated from tomato juice: 4'-*O*-(*β*-D-glucopyranosyl)-D-pantothenic acid (Figure 6-3) (Amachi et al. 1971; Amachi 1975; Yoshizumi 1975). This tomato juice factor seems also to be found in apple and grape juices, which are used as supplements in media for these organisms. A source of fatty acids

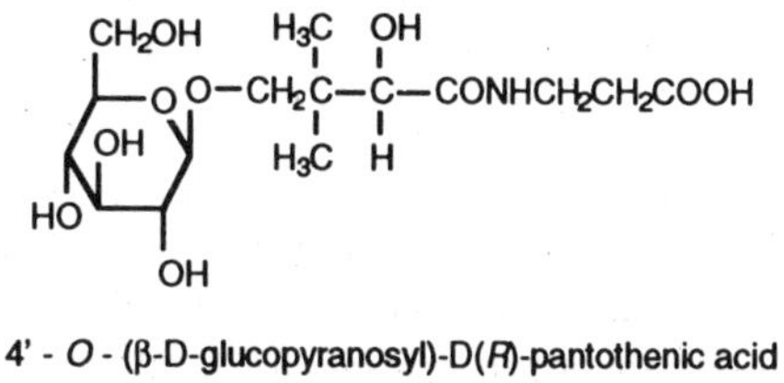

Fig. 6-3. Tomato juice factor.

is also helpful, the commercial mixture Tween 80 being commonly used.

For isolation of lactic acid bacteria from wine, or similar materials, a small volume (0.1 mL) is spread on solid medium of the type mentioned above, such as apple Rogosa medium (Appendix F). Because the starting materials often also contain yeast, which will overgrow the slow-growing lactic acid bacteria, a yeast inhibitor, such as cycloheximide, is employed. Isolation of lactic acid bacteria from wine is discussed further in Chapter 9.

3. Identification of Wine-Related Lactic Acid Bacteria

The criteria given here for identification of lactic acid bacteria are implicitly for the wine-related lactic acid bacteria; that is, those bacteria found in or isolated from grape juice, wine or its distillates, or winery equipment. The categorizations for genus and species are in agreement with those found in *Bergey's Manual of Systematic Bacteriology* (Sneath 1986), and Ninth Edition of *Bergey's Manual of Determinative Bacteriology* (Holt et al. 1993).

Preliminary tests for classification of the bacteria as lactic acid bacteria are prerequisite. The first assignment for classification as lactic acid bacteria is a negative catalase test (Appendix 6), which conveniently categorizes them as anaerobes. Many bacteriologists consider anaerobes to be inhibited, prevented from growth or killed, by oxygen. In fact, the lactic acid bacteria are microaerophilic—literally meaning they grow best in the presence of low amounts of oxygen—behaving nominally as facultative aerobes/anaerobes. They grow well as surface colonies in the presence of air and equally well as submerged stab cultures. (In stab cultures, the growth often appears to be somewhat heavier a few mm below the surface, as compared to that at the surface or further below, which probably has given them the microaerophilic description.) For definitive classification, the formation of lactic acid is tested after good growth of the organism on a nutrient medium containing a fermentable sugar but, of course, no malic acid. As mentioned above, it is often difficult to grow some of these organisms without supplements of apple or grape juices. However, these juices also contain malic acid. Thus, to determine the formation of lactic acid from sugar, supplementation with tomato juice, which has only a negligible concentration of malic acid, is indicated. An accepted procedure for assaying for lactic acid is paper chromatography (Section F1b), since the precise amount or indication of which optical isomer is formed is not required at this stage in the identification. The malolactic attribute is not a part of the taxonomic characterization; nevertheless, the presence of this trait is important for us. This can be determined by growth of the organism on a medium *with* malic acid, followed by paper chromatography to determine if the malic acid had been catabolized.

a. Genus Identification of the Wine-Related Lactic Acid Bacteria

Generic assessment of lactic acid bacteria is relatively easy. Two characteristics are used for this: cellular morphology and the determination of whether they are hetero- or homolactic fermenters. Bacteria found in wine, or grape juice, fitting the above tests as lactic acid bacteria and which are microscopically obvious rods, can directly be classified as lactobacilli (Figure 6-4). Those that are cocci, either perfect or elongated spheres, are then classified either as pediococci or leuconostocs (Figure 6-4). Fermentation tests are required to segregate further these latter genera, the pediococci being homolactics and the leuconostocs being heterolactic.

I. Homolactic versus heterolactic fermentation. The homolactic fermenters (Wood 1961), utilize the familiar Embden-Myerhof glycolytic pathway of fermentation (Figure 6-5), producing primarily a single product, lactic acid, from sugar. The heterolactic fermenters (Wood 1961), using the phosphoketolase pathway (Figure 6-5), give a mixture of products, roughly one-sixth as carbon dioxide, one-third as C_2-units such as ethanol, acetic acid, or acetaldehyde, and the remainder as lactic acid. The lactic acid produced may include either or both optical isomers. In practice, the distinction between hetero- and homolactic fermentation is not as clear-cut as indicated; strains producing 80% lactic acid can be homofermenters, and the heterofermenters may produce somewhat greater or less than 50% lactic acid. See Section I-2 on the biochemistry of the malolactic fermentation for further discussion of the fermentative pathways.

II. Coccal morphology. The precise spherical cell morphology of the pediococci make them easily identifiable as such. Furthermore they usually appear as two cells together (diplococci), helping to confirm the classification (Figure 6-6). However, with the leuconostocs, the assignment by cellular morphology can be more difficult. The wine leuconostocs, especially when growing on vegetable material, appear as elongated cocci rather than precisely spherical (Figure 6-7). We have empirically suggested that if the length-to-width ratio is > 2, the organisms should be designated as lactobacilli (Figure 6-8). The elongated cocci of width/length < 2 that are homolactic and produce only L-lactic acid from sugar are considered short-rodded lactobacilli. That leaves us with the heterolactic, D-lactic acid-producing, elongated cocci, which could be classified either as lactobacilli or leuconostocs. The assignment of genus to these confusing coccal forms is aided by the information that many strains of *L. oenos* are devoid of the enzymes to catabolize arginine (Garvie and Farrow 1980; Pilone and Liu 1992). This inability to produce ammonia from arginine can be used to verify

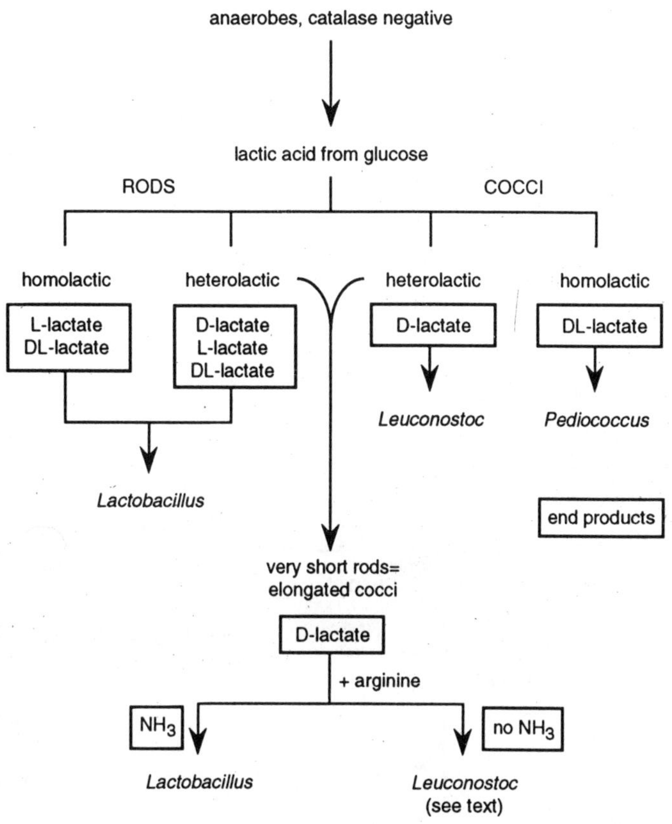

Fig. 6-4. Genera of wine-related lactic acid bacteria.

strains as *L. oenos*, rather than as short-rodded, heterolactic, D-lactic acid-producing lactobacilli. Two nonammonia-producing lactobacillus species, with apparently all of these other features, are *L. viridescens* and *L. confusus*. However, these two species are easily distinguished from *Leuconostoc oenos* in that the first one has always been isolated from animal sources, and the second one appears generally as single cells and rarely in chains (Sneath 1986). Pilone and Liu (1992) found under special conditions that some *L. oenos* do, indeed, produce ammonia from arginine. However, by use of the standard assay medium for this (Appendix F), with incubation at 20°C for two to three weeks, we usually have not had this experience.

Pilone and Liu (1992) have expressed their worry that malolactic bacteria with high capabilities of degrading arginine might under winemaking conditions—in the presence of high concentrations of arginine—excrete enough citrulline to give ethanolation of the latter at high temperature to produce the undesirable end product ethyl carbamate (urethane) (Chapter 4).

Garvie (1967) earlier made the very good suggestion, which has not been accepted, that these closely related short rodded or elongated coccal organisms be placed in the same genus, since they have many other important features in common, such as the characteristics of their lactic dehydrogenase enzymes.

b. Species Identification of the Wine-Related Lactic Acid Bacteria

I. Leuconostoc. The species identification for the wine leuconostocs is especially simple.

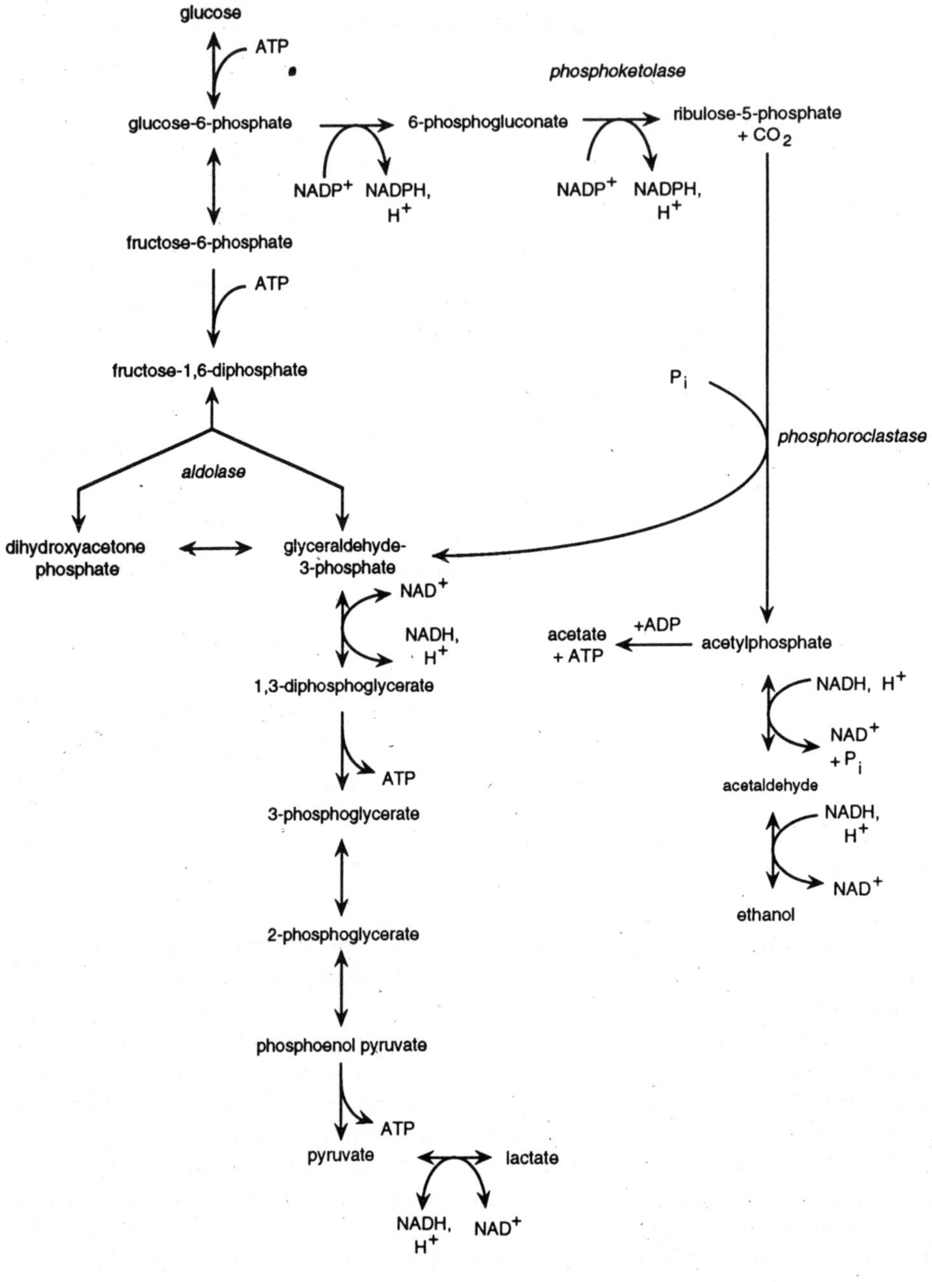

Fig. 6-5. Heterolactic and homolactic fermentations.

If the leuconostoc in question has been isolated from wine, then it is automatically classified as *L. oenos*; only strains of this species will grow in the presence of 10% ethanol at pH values less than pH 4.2 (Garvie 1967; Sneath 1986; Holt et al. 1993) (see Figure 6-7).

II. Pediococcus. Except for *Pediococcus urinaeequi*, the eight species of pediococcus are widely distributed in fermenting vegetable material (see Figure 6-6). Table 6-1 gives the distinguishing characteristics of the four species that will grow at pH 4.2 or below. The

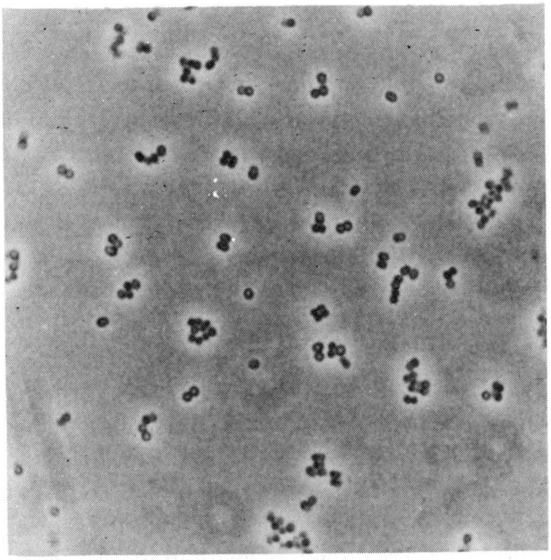

Fig. 6-6. *Pediococcus parvulus.*

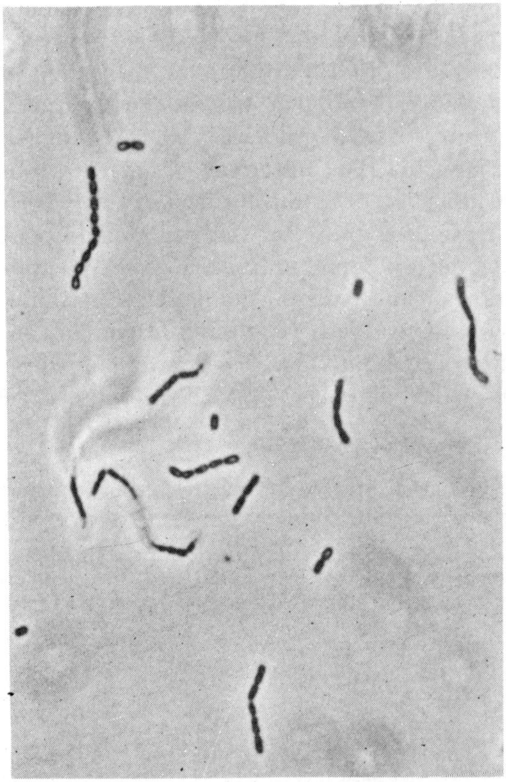

Fig. 6-7. *Leuconostoc oenos.*

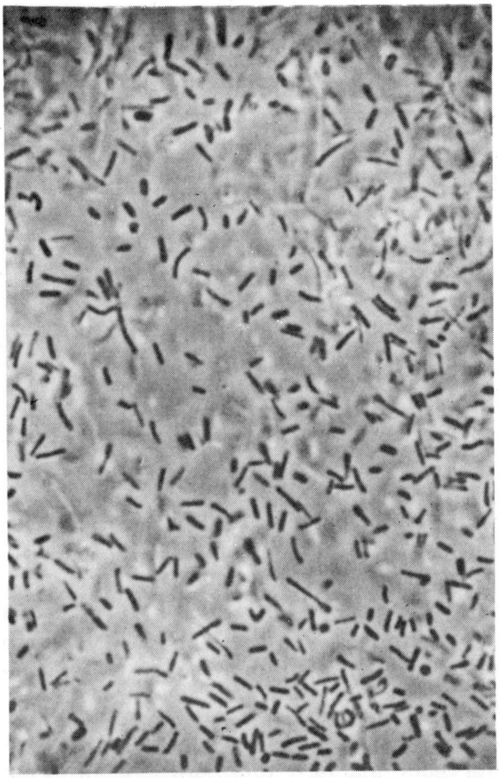

Fig. 6-8. *Lactobacillus buchneri.*

wine-related pediococci have earlier been classified *Pediococcus damnosus* (formerly *P. cerevisiae*), but *P. parvulus* and *P. pentoseus* have also been isolated from wine, the latter from thermovinifications, and will show growth at 40°C (Barre 1978). *P. acidilactici* is closely related. There is a general, and probably unfounded, abhorrence of pediococci by winemakers, possibly stemming from the close as-

Table 6-1. Wine-related *Pediococcus* species. The eight species of *Pediococcus* (except for *P. urinaeequi*) are widely distributed in fermenting vegetable material. Below is an abbreviated taxonomy (from Sneath 1986) of those species that will grow at pH 4.2 or below.

Growth at:	35°C	40°C	50°
P. damnosus	–		
P. parvulus	+	–	
P. pentosaceus	+	+	–
P. acidilactici	+	+	+

sociation of beer spoilages with one of these species having the unfortunate name of *P. damnosus*. Work by Edwards and Jensen (1992) indicates that the former designation of wine-related pediococci as *P. damnosus* is incorrect and they should be classified as *P. parvulus*.

Several strains of nonmalolactic pediococci have been recently isolated from wine (Edwards and Jensen 1992). We have noted above, it is not clear what role they might play either in providing bacteriological stability or being the source of spoilage end products.

III. Lactobacillus. In Table 6-2 are listed the distinguishing characteristics of species of lactobacilli which have been isolated from wine and from other plant materials (see Figure 6-8). Species classification of the wine-related lactobacilli has not commanded great attention of winemakers, since these organisms as a class show little resistance to the low pHs found in wine (Davis et al. 1988). However, during the last decade in California, some species have shown themselves as ferocious spoilers of wine. They manifest themselves by bringing about a rapid spoilage, especially of red wines, very early in the vinification, producing enough acetic acid in two to three days to bring about inhibition of the wine yeast metabolism. This dramatic spoilage, discussed further in Chapter 9, seems to be related to the initial high pH of some musts, along with a deficiency in nutrients in the must and with employment of improper winemaking techniques.

Of the lactobacilli, two species have been shown to be especially important in the spoilage of high-alcohol dessert wine *L. hilgardii* and *L. fructivorans* (Table 6-2) (Figure 6-9). Older winemakers may recognize the latter species by the former names of *L. fermenti*, or *L. trichodes* (Radler and Hartel 1984). Further discussion of this spoilage and its control is given in Chapter 9.

c. *Strain Identification of the Wine-Related Lactic Acid Bacteria*

So many of the attributes of malolactic bacteria which make them desirable candidates as starter cultures for winemaking are strain dependent, including behavioral performance during the malolactic fermentation—speed and reliability in initiation of the growth phase and completion of the deacidification; sensory characteristics of the fermented product; ease in growth of the bacteria for commercial distribution; and extent of recovery of viability after the cultures have been subjected to being frozen and dried. Furthermore, the extent of stimulation of initial growth rate by malic acid, a primary consideration, is also strain related (Section I-1). The historical attempts at strain identification of malolactic bacteria have been as tenuous as those for the wine-related yeast (Chapter 4). Some attempts at strain identification on the basis of fatty acid composition, as was shown with yeast strain identification, have given limited success (Tracey and Britz 1989a; Schmitt et al. 1989). Efforts to use some

Table 6-2a. Wine-related *Lactobacillus* species. Homolactic fermenters: aldolase present, phosphoketolase may be inducible.

Species	Type of lactice acid formed	Growth on			
		Mannitol	Melibiose	Galactose	Arabnose
L. bavaricus	L	−			−
L. casei subsp. *casei*	L	+			−
L. murinus *	L	+/−	+	+	+
L. homohiochii	DL	−	−	−	
L. curvatus	DL	−	−	+	
L. sake	DL	−	+	+	
L. plantarum	DL	+	+	+	

* Isolated from rodent gut, but has malolactic activity.

Table 6-2b. Heterolactic fementers: aldolase not present, phosphoketolase always inducible.

Species	Growth at 15°C	Growth on			Short rods?
		Melibiose	Melezitose	Xylose	
L. fermentum	−				
L. brevis	+	+	−		yes
L. buchneri	+	+	+		yes
L. fructivorans	+	−		−	
L. hilgardii	+	−		+	
L. kefir *	+	+			no

* *L. kefir*, from fermented milk, has also been isolated from beer; but it is genomically unrelated to the other heterolactics.

sort of karyogamic analysis, the hybridization with DNA probes, resulted in distinguishing lactic acid bacteria, but only at the species level (Lonvaud-Funel et al. 1991). However, the use of karyogamic typing holds promise. The initial works for the distinguishing *Leuconostoc oenos* strains by pulsed-field gel electrophoresis (PFGE) patterns of nuclear material after restriction enzyme treatment, which have been used for other lactic acid bacteria (LeBourgeois et al. 1989), are very encouraging (Kelly et al. 1993; Daniel et al. 1993). Undoubtedly this methodology will be further applied, although the technology is not readily available to winery laboratories at present.

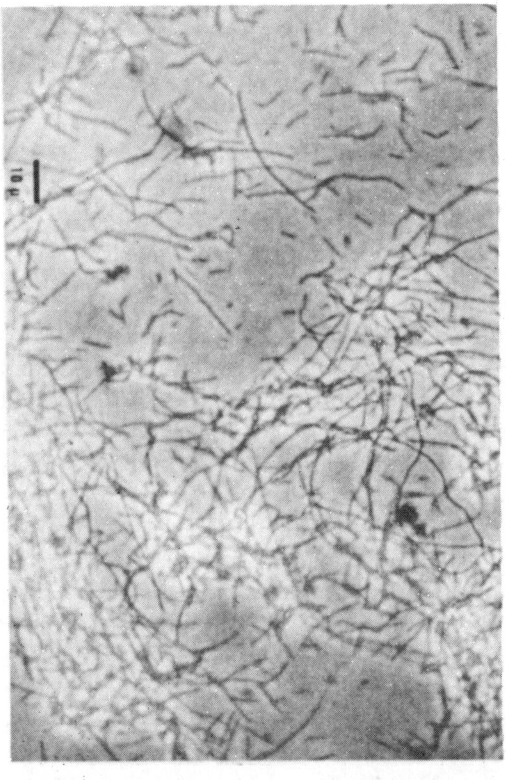

Fig. 6-9. *Lactobacillus fructivorans.*

I. INTERMEDIARY METABOLISM OF THE MALOLACTIC CONVERSION

Malate carboxy lyase (the malolactic enzyme) is the operative enzyme carrying out the malolactic conversion (Table 6-3). It is a direct decarboxylation of L(−)-malic acid to L(+)-lactic acid. The enzyme has not yet been crystallized; however, there has been an extensive study on the isolation and characterization of the enzyme(s) from various malolactic strains (Schütz and Radler 1973; Lonvaud et al. 1977; Caspritz and Radler 1983; Spettoli et al. 1984) and a summary by Kunkee (1991). It is interesting to note that although the substrate and the product are of the same enantiomophoric configurative, they rotate the planes of polarized light in opposite directions (Kunkee 1967a). The malolactic enzyme is inducible, and the activities found are dependent upon the strain and the cultural conditions of the bacteria. The presence of glucose, or at least a fermentable sugar, is necessary for induction of the malolactic enzyme (Nathan 1961).

Table 6-3. Malic acid enzymes.

malolactic enzyme	L-malate: NAD carboxy lyase	
	L-malate $\langle \xrightarrow[Mn^{++}]{NAD} \rangle$ L-lactate + CO_2	(1)
malic dehydrogenase	L-malate: NAD oxidoreductase EC 1.1.1.37	
	L-malate + NAD $\langle \xrightarrow{Mn^{++}} \rangle$ oxaloacetate + NADH	(2)
malate oxidase	L-malate: NAD oxidoreductase (decarboxylating) EC1.1.1.38 or .39	
	L-malate + NAD $\langle \xrightarrow{Mn^{++}} \rangle$ pyruvate + NADH + CO_2	(3)
	malate-lactate transhydrogenase	
	L-malate + pyruvate $\langle \xrightarrow{NAD} \rangle$ oxaloacetate + L-lactate	(4)

1. Stimulation of Initial Growth Rate by Malic Acid

Other enzymes which have malic acid as a substrate are given above in Table 6-3. Malic oxidase is an important enzyme found in many lactic acid bacteria. It also is induced by malic acid. One important distinction between it and the malolactic enzyme, however, is that the formation of malic oxidase is repressed by glucose. The presence of both enzymes in the same strain, depending upon the concentrations of glucose, has been reported (Schütz and Radler 1973). The malate-lactate transhydrogenase enzyme (Table 6-3) is not a decarboxylation (Allen and Patil 1972), but is included for completeness.

The thermodynamics of the malolactic conversion, and the relationship to the intermediary metabolism and cellular physiology of the malolactic bacteria have intrigued some enologists for several decades. For a more thorough exposition of the following discussion see: Schanderl (1959), Kunkee (1974), Pilone and Kunkee (1976), Kunkee (1991), and Zhuorong and Kunkee (1993). The decarboxylation of malic acid to lactic acid provides very little free energy ($\Delta G = -8.3$ kJ/mole), if the carbon dioxide is released in the hydrated form, which it is (Kunkee 1967a, Pilone and Kunkee 1970). Furthermore, if the reaction is stoichiometric, then there is no biochemical basis for capturing the small amount of free energy as biologically utilizable energy, either in formation of ATP or in reoxidation of reduced coenzymes. On the other hand, the presence of malic acid has a dramatic stimulatory effect on the initial growth rate on many strains of malolactic bacteria (Figure 6-10), which cannot be explained solely by the accompanying favorable pH change provided by the decarboxylation (Pilone and Kunkee 1976).

2. Spill Off of Intermediary Pyruvic Acid

One cause of the stimulation of the initial growth rate of the bacteria in the presence of malic acid has been given by showing in vitro that the reaction is not stoichiometric. A small spill off of the intermediate pyruvic acid and reduced NAD^+ occurs (Morenzoni 1973; Kunkee 1975). This spill off comes from less than 1 % of the substrate malic acid, but the small amount of NADH accompanying it can be detected by its fluorescence. Enzymatic studies indicated that pyruvic acid accompanied the NADH, rather than the nondecarboxylated intermediate, oxaloacetic acid. An enzymatic phosphoroclastic attack of the pyruvate results in the formation of acetyl phosphate. This is then available as a hydrogen acceptor, not only to reoxidize the NADH formed in the spill off, but of another NADH as well. This net formation of reoxidized coenzyme thus allows the stimulation of the growth of the bacteria out of the lag phase, where the NAD^+ moieties are generally in the reduced state.

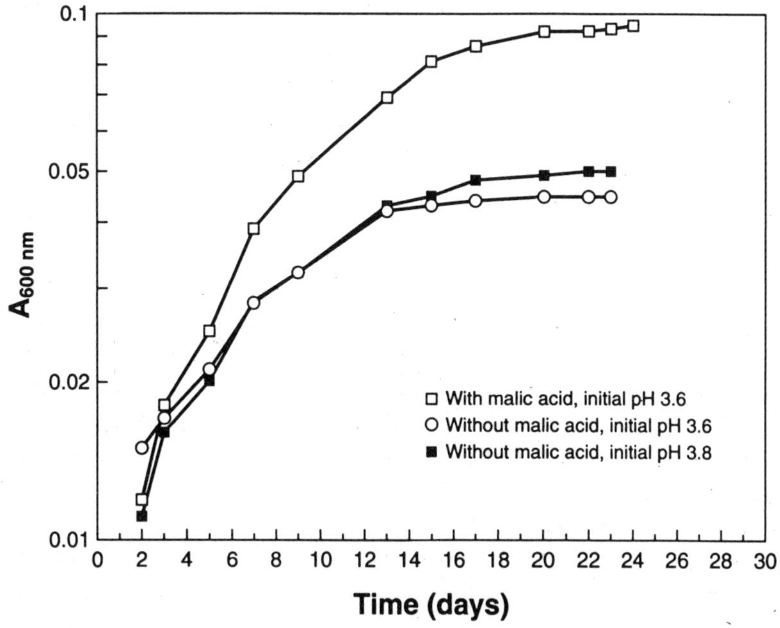

Fig. 6-10. Stimulation of initial growth rate of Leuconostec oenos MCW by malic acid.

Any acetyl phosphate formed from the spilloff could also result in the formation of ATP, which could have a positive effect either on the bacterial growth rate or the formation of bacterial biomass. However, increased ATP would serve as increase in substrate, rather than as increase in a catalyst, as with reoxidized NAD^+; and the small increase in ATP would seem to be insignificant and essentially unmeasurable.

Confirmatory evidence that the stimulatory effect on growth comes from the acetyl phosphate acting as a hydrogen acceptor is found in the fact that other hydrogen acceptors also induce the same effect. For example, fructose can be reduced to mannitol by heterolactic bacteria, and the presence of fructose brings about the same stimulation of initial growth rate of these bacteria (Kunkee 1974). Moreover, in malolactic fermentations of cider, it has been shown that the quinates (quinic, shikimic and dihydroshikimic acids) are easily reduced by malolactic bacteria, and their growth is stimulated thereby (Whiting and Coggins 1971; Whiting 1975) (Figure 6-11). Although these compounds are found in higher concentrations in apples, they are also found in crushed grapes (Flanzy et al. 1967); their effect as hydrogen acceptors helps confirm the mechanism of malic acid stimulation. Lee and Pack (1980) also found a stimulation in the presence of malic acid, in this case of D-lactate dehydrogenase. This, along with increased reoxidation of reduced NAD^+, serves to explain the increased formation of D-lactic acid also found during malolactic fermentation (Alizade and Simon 1973; Kunkee 1991). But the most striking confirmatory evidence comes from the results which showed that in the malolactic strains where the stimulation of the early growth rate by malic acid was found, and only in those, was the corresponding spilloff also found. That is, of the strains tested, the growth of 11 strains was stimulated in the presence of malic acid, and these 11 strains also gave the formation of NADH in cell-free

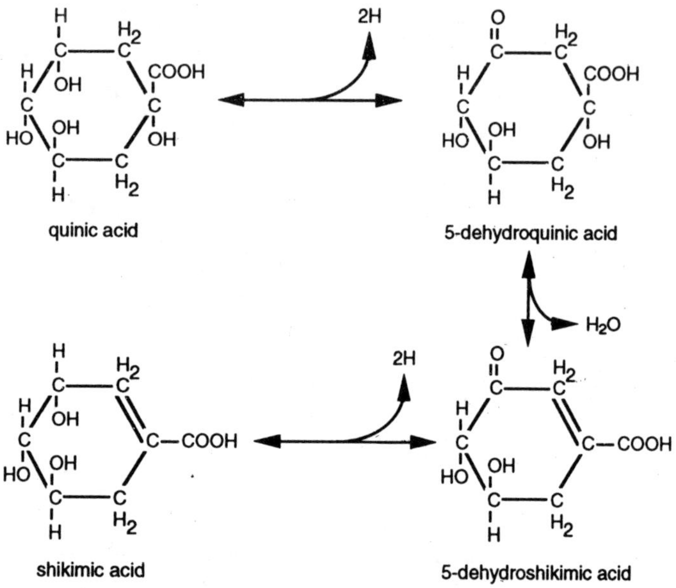

Fig. 6-11. Hydrogen acceptors for malolactic stimulation and for lactic acid oxidation.

extracts; the remaining four strains showed neither effect (Pukrushpan 1976; Zhuorong and Kunkee 1993).

3. Efflux of Lactic Acid

A cellular efflux of lactic acid arising from the malolactic conversion could also provide extra energy, in the same manor as it is generated by lactic acid coming from sugar fermentation. This involves membrane ATPase and reentry of the protons through a contiguous symport with the resulting formation of one ATP for every three protons (Michels et al. 1979; Otto et al. 1980). Renault et al. (1988) adapted the idea of this unexpected source of energy to help explain the effect of malic acid on malolactic bacterial energetics—however, using nonwine-related lactococcus. In fact, Cox and Henick-Kling (1989), using a very sensitive bioluminescence technique, showed an increased formation of ATP in malolactic cells in the presence of malic acid. However, increased ATP formation, if in the significant amounts suggested, would seem to have the greatest operative effect as a stimulation of formation of biomass toward the end of the growth cycle, precisely when the efflux effect would be minimal due to the increased extracellular concentrations of lactic acid.

Another source of energy could come, unexpectedly, from the metabolism of lactic acid, itself. In the reductive steps of the quinate, discussed above, it has been shown that either D- or L-lactic acids can serve as hydrogen donors. Even though lactic acid is considered to be an end product of anaerobic metabolism of the lactic acid bacteria, it is at least, theoretically, possible for these bacteria to produce an electron acceptor alternative to oxygen (London 1968) (Figure 6-11).

$$2 \text{ quinate} + \text{lactate} \rightarrow 2 \text{ dihydroshikimate} + \text{acetate} + CO_2 + H_2O$$

$$\text{quinate} + \text{lactate} \rightarrow 3,4 \text{ dihydroxycyclohexane-carboxylate} + \text{acetate} + CO_2 + H_2O$$

4. Significance of the Malic Acid Stimulation

In any case, it is certain that the malolactic conversion has a positive effect on bacterial growth in wine, at least by bringing about an increase in pH and helping to maintain the higher internal pH of the cells. The question as to additional mechanisms of stimulation by malic acid may seem moot to many winemakers, since malic acid will always be present whenever there is concern for induction of the malolactic fermentation. However, it is important to select strains in which the initial stimulation by malic acid has been shown. Moreover, additional information on the fundamental aspects of the malolactic metabolism can lead to improvements in the practical aspects, as has happened before. Modern winemakers may be pleased with the dramatic improvement made in the practical applications of the malolactic fermentation over the last three decades; however, intractable fermentations still occur, for which new stimulatory technology would be welcome.

J. REFERENCES

ACREE, T. E., J. BARNARD, AND D. G. CUNNINGHAM. 1984. "A procedure for the sensory analysis of gas chromatographic effluents." *Food. Chem* 14:273–286.

ALLEN, S. H. G., AND J. R. PATIL. 1972. "Studies on the structure and mechanism of action of malate-lactate transhydrogenase." *J. Biol. Chem.* 247:909–916.

ALIZADE, M. A., AND H. SIMON. 1973. "Zum Merchanismus und zur Kompartmentierung der L- und D-Lactatbildung aus L-Malat bzw. D-Glucose in *Leuconstoc mesenteroides*." *Z. Physiol. Chem.* 354:163–168.

AMACHI, T. 1975. "Chemical structure of a growth factor (TJF) and its physiological significance for malo-lactic bacteria." In *Lactic Acid Bacteria in Beverages and Food*, J. G. Carr, C. V. Cutting, and G. C. Whiting, Eds., pp. 103–118. London: Academic Press.

AMACHI, T., S. IMAMOTO, AND H. YOSHIZUMI. 1971. "A growth factor for malo-lactic fermentation bacteria. Part II. Structure and synthesis of a novel pantothenic acid derivative isolated from tomato juice." *Agric. Biol. Chem.* 35:1222–1230.

AMATI, A., G. ARFELLI, E. DELL'ACQUA, AND R. ZIRONI. 1993. "Lysozyme: A new product to control malolactic fermentation in enology. Its application and results." Paper presented at 44th Annual Meeting of the American Society for Enology and Viticulture, June 22–25 1993, at Sacramento Convention Center, Sacramento, California. 1993 Technical Abstracts, p.42.

AMERINE, M. A., H. W. BERG, R. E. KUNKEE, C. S. OUGH, V. L. SINGLETON, AND A. D. WEBB. 1980. *The Technology of Wine Making*, 4th ed. Westport, CT: Avi Publishing Co.

AMERINE, M. A., AND E. B. ROESSLER. 1983. *Wines Their Sensory Evaluation*, 2nd ed. San Francisco: W. H. Freeman and Company.

ASMUNDSON, R. V., AND W. J. KELLY. 1990. "Temperature and ethanol effects on growth of *Leuconostoc oenos*." In *Fermentation Technologies: Industrial Applications*, P.-K. Yu, Ed., pp. 128–131. International Biotechnology Conference, February 12–15 1990, Massey University, Palmerston North, New York: Elsevier Applied Science.

BARRE, P. 1978. "Identification of thermobacteria and homofermentative, thermophilic, pentose-utilizing lactobacilli from high temperature fermenting grape musts." *J. Appl. Bacteriol.* 44:125–129.

BASSIT, N., C.-Y. BOQUIEN, D. PICQUE, AND G. CORRIEU. 1993. "Effect of initial oxygen concentration on diacetyl and acetoin production by *Lactoccocus lactis* subsp. *lactis* biovar diacetylactis." *Appl. Environ. Microbiol.* 59:1893–1897.

BEELMAN, R. B., AND J. F. GALLANDER. 1979. "Wine deacidification." *Adv. Food. Res.* 25:1–53.

BEELMAN, R. B., AND R. E. KUNKEE. 1987. "Inducing simultaneous malolactic/alcoholic fermentations." *Pract. Winery Vyd.* July/Aug:44–56.

BENDA, I. 1982. "Wine and brandy." In, *Prescott and Dunn's Industrial Microbiology*, G. Reed, Ed., pp. 293–402. Westport, CT: AVI Publishing.

BUTEAU, C., C. L. DUITSCHAEVER, AND G. C. ASHTON 1984. "A STUDY OF THE BIOGENESIS OF AMINES IN A VILLARD NOIR WINE." *Am. J. Enol. Vitic.* 35:228–236.

CASPRITZ, G., AND F. RADLER. 1983. "Malolactic enzyme of *Lactobacillus plantarum*. Purification, properties, and distribution among bacteria." *J. Biol. Chem.* 258:4907–4910.

CAVIN, J. F., F. Z. DRICI, H. PRÉVOST, AND C. DIVIES. 1991. "Prophage curing in *Leuconostoc oenos* by Mitomycin C induction." *Am. J. Enol. Vitic.* 42:163–166.

COFRAN, D. R., AND J. MEYER. 1970. "The effect of fumaric acid on malo-lactic fermentation." *Am. J. Enol. Vitic.* 21:190–192.

COLLINS, E. B. 1972. "Biosynthesis of flavor compounds by microorganisms." *J. Dairy Sci.* 55:1022–1028.

COX, D. J., AND T. HENICK-KLING. 1989. "Chemosmotic energy from malolactic fermentation." *J. Bacteriol.* 170:5750–5752.

DAESCHEL, M. A., D.-S. JUNG, AND B. T. WATSON. 1991. "Controlling wine malolactic fermentation with nisin and nisin-resistant strains of *Leuconostoc oenos*." *Appl. Environ. Microbiol.* 57:601–603.

DANIEL, P., E. DE WAELE, AND J.-N. HALLET. 1993. "Optimization of transverse alternating field electrophoresis for strain identification of *Leuconostoc oenos*." *Appl. Microbiol. Biotechnol.* 38:638–641.

DAVIS, C., N. F. A. SILVEIRA, AND G. H. FLEET. 1985a. "Occurrence and properties of bacteriophages of *Leuconostoc oenos* in Australian wines." *Appl. Environ. Microbiol.* 50:872–876.

DAVIS, C. R., D. J. WIBOWO, R. ESCHENBRUCH, T. H. LEE, AND G. H. FLEET. 1985b. "Practical implications of malolactic fermentation: A review." *Am. J. Enol. Vitic.* 36:290–301.

DAVIS, C. R., D. WIBOWO, G. H. FLEET, AND T. H. LEE. 1988. "Properties of wine lactic acid bacteria: Their potential enological significance." *Am. J. Enol. Vitic.* 39:137–142.

DAVIS, C. R., D. J. WIBOWO, T. H. LEE, AND G. H. FLEET. 1986. "Growth and metabolism of lactic acid bacteria during and after malolactic fermentation of wines at different pH." *Appl. Environ. Microbiol.* 51:539–545.

DELFINI, C. 1989. "Ability of wine malolactic bacteria to produce histamine." *Sci. Aliments* 9:413–416.

DE ROSA, T. 1987. *Tecnologia dei Vini Spumanti*. Brescia, Italy: Edizioni AEB.

DICK, K. J., P. C. MOLAN, AND R. ESCHENBRUCH. 1992. "The isolation from *Saccharomyces cerevisiae* of two antibacterial cationic proteins that inhibit malolactic bacteria." *Vitis* 31:105–116.

DU PLESSIS, L. DE W. 1963. "The microbiology of South African winemaking. Part V. Vitamin and amino acid requirements of the lactic acid bacteria from dry wines." *S. African J. Agric. Sci.* 6:485–494.

EDWARDS, C. G., AND R. B. BEELMAN. 1989. "Inducing malolactic fermentation in wines." *Biotech. Adv.* 7:333–360.

EDWARDS, C. G., AND K. A. JENSEN. 1992. "Occurrence and characterization of lactic acid bacteria from Washington State wines: *Pediococcus* spp." *Am. J. Enol. Vitic.* 43:233–238.

EDWARDS, C. G., J. R. POWERS, K. A. JENSEN, K. M. WELLER, AND J. C. PETERSON. 1993. "*Lactobacillus* spp. from Washington State wines: isolation and characterization." *J. Food Sci.* 58:453–458.

FLANZY, C. 1972. "La vinification par macération carbonique." *Rev. Franc. Oenol.* 13 (45):42–50.

FLANZY, M., AND P. ANDRÉ. 1973. *La Vinification par Macération Carbonique*. Versailles, France: Ministère de l'Agriculture, Institut National de la Recherche Agronomique.

FLANZY, C., M. ANDRÉ, M. FLANZY, AND Y. CHAMBROY. 1967. "Variations quantitives des acides organiques stables, non cetoniques, non volatils, dans les baies de raisin placées en anaérobiose carbonique. II. Influence de la durée d'anaérobiose." *Ann. Technol. Agric.* 16:89–107.

FORNACHON, J. C. M. 1957. "The occurrence of malo-lactic fermentation in Australian wines." *Austral. J. Appl. Sci.* 8:120–129.

FORNACHON, J. C. M. 1968. "Influence of different yeasts on the growth of lactic acid bacteria in wine." *J. Sci. Food Agric.* 19:374–378.

FROHLICH, D., AND R. BATTAGLIA. 1980. "HPCL-Analyse von biogenen Aminien in Wein." *Mitt. Geb. Lebensmittelunters. Hyg.* 71:38–44.

FUGELSANG, K. C., AND B. W. ZOECKLEIN. 1993. "Exclusive PW MLF survey." *Pract. Winery Vyd.* May/June 12–18.

GARVIE, E. I. 1967. *Leuconostoc oenos* sp. nov. *J. Gen Microbiol.* 48:431–8.

GARVIE, E. I., AND J. A. FARROW. 1980. "The differentiation of *Leuconostoc oenos* from non-acidophilic species of leuconostoc, and the identification of five strains from the American Type Culture Collection." *Am. J. Enol. Vitic.* 31:154–157.

GUILLOUX-BENATIER, M., H. S. SON, S. BOUHIER, AND M. FEUILLAT. 1993. "Activités enzymatiques: Glycosidases et peptidase chez *Leuconostoc oenos* au cours de la croissance bactérienne. Influence des macromolécules de levures." *Vitis* 32:52–57.

HARVEY, R. J., AND E. B. COLLINS. 1963. "Roles of citrate and acetoin in the metabolism of *Streptococcus diacetilactis*." *J. Bacteriol.* 86:1301–1307.

HENICK-KLING, T. 1986. "Control of malolactic fermentation." In *Technical Review No. 41*, pp. 3–6. Adelaide: The Australian Wine Research Institute.

HENICK-KLING, T. 1988. "Yeast and bacterial control in winemaking." In *Wine Analysis*, H.F. Linskens, and J. F. Jackson, Eds., pp. 276–316. Berlin: Springer-Verlag.

HENICK-KLING, T. 1993. "Modification of wine flavour by malolactic fermentation." *10th International Oenological Symposium,* May 3–5, 1993, pp. 290–306. Breisach, Germany: International Association for Winery Technology and Management.

HENICK-KLING, T., T. H. LEE, AND D. J. D. NICHOLAS. 1986. "Inhibition of bacterial growth and malolactic fermentation in wine by bacteriophage." *J. Appl. Bacteriol.* 61:287–293.

HIARING, S. 1974. "Carbonic maceration as done in California." *Wines & Vines*. 55(4):65–66.

HOLT, J. G., N. R. KRIEG, P. H. A. SNEATH, J. T. STALEY, AND S. T. WILLIAMS. 1993. *Bergey's Manual of Determinative Bacteriology*, 9th ed. Baltimore: Williams & Wilkins.

HUGENHOLTZ, J., L. PERDON, AND T. ABEE. 1993. "Growth and energy generation by *Lactococcus-lactis* subsp. *lactis* biovar. *diacetylactis* during citrate metabolism." *Appl. Environ. Microbiol.* 59:4216–4222.

HUGENHOLTZ, J., AND M. J. C. STARRENBURG. 1992. "Diacetyl production by different strains of *Lactococcus lactic* subsp. *lactis* var. *diacetylactis* and *Leuconostoc* spp." *J. Dairy Res.* 55:17–22.

INGRAHAM, J. L., AND G. M. COOKE. 1960. "A survey of the incidence of malo-lactic fermentation in California table wines." *Am. J. Enol. Vitic.* 11:160–163.

KELLY, W. J., R. V. ASMUNDSON, AND D. H. HOPCROFT. 1989. "Growth of *Leuconostoc oenos* under anaerobic conditions." *Am. J. Enol. Vitic.* 40:277–282.

KELLY, W. J., C. M. HUANG, AND R. V. ASMUNDSON. 1993. "Comparison of *Leuconostoc oenos* strains by pulsed-field gel electrophoresis." *Appl. Environ. Microbiol.* 59:3969–3971.

KING, S. W., AND R. B. BEELMAN. 1986. "Metabolic interactions between *Saccharomyces cerevisiae* and *Leuconostoc oenos* in a model grape juice/wine system." *Am. J. Enol. Vitic.* 37:53–60.

KLAENHAMMER, T. R. 1987. "Plasmid-directed mechanisms for bacteriophage defense in lactic streptococci." *FEMS Microbiol. Rev.* 46:313–325.

KRIEGER, S. A., B. PFITZER, AND W. P. HAMMES. 1993. "Evaluation of lactic acid bacterial strains for diacetyl production." Poster presented at 44th Annual Meeting of the American Society for Enology and Viticulture, June 22–25 1993, at Sacramento Convention Center, Sacramento, California. 1993 Technical Abstracts, p. 64.

KUENSCH, W., A. TEMPERLI, AND K. MEYER. 1974. "Conversion of arginine to ornithine during malolactic fermentation in red Swiss wine." *Am. J. Enol. Vitic.* 25:191–193.

KÜMMEL, A., G. BEHRENS, AND G. GOTTSCHALK. 1975. "Citrate lyase from *Streptococcus diacetilactis*. Association with its acetylating enzyme." *Arch. Microbiol.* 102:111–116.

KUNKEE, R. E. 1967a. "Malolactic fermentation." *Adv. Appl. Microbiol.* 9:235–279.

KUNKEE, R. E. 1967b. "Theoretical changes in pH accompanying malolactic fermentation." Paper presented at 18th Annual Meeting of the American Society for Enology and Viticulture, June 22–24 1967, at Santa Barbara, California. 1967 Technical Abstracts, p. 10.

KUNKEE, R. E. 1968. "Simplified chromatographic procedure for detection of malo-lactic fermentation." *Wines & Vines* 49(3):23–24.

KUNKEE, R. E. 1974. "Malo-lactic fermentation and winemaking." In, *The Chemistry of Winemaking*, Adv. Chem. Ser. 137, A. D. Webb, Ed., pp. 151–170. Washington DC: American Chemical Society.

KUNKEE, R. E. 1975. "A second enzymatic activity for decomposition of malic acid by malo-lactic bacteria." In *Lactic Acid Bacteria in Beverages and Food*, J. G. Carr, C. V. Cutting, and G. C. Whiting, Eds., pp. 29–42. London: Academic Press.

KUNKEE, R. E. 1984. "Selection and modification of yeasts and lactic acid bacteria for wine fermentation." *Food. Microbiol.* 1:315–332.

KUNKEE, R. E. 1991. "Some roles of malic acid in the malolactic fermentation in wine making." *FEMS Microbiol. Rev.* 88:55–72.

KUNKEE, R. E., G. J. PILONE, AND R. E. COMBS. 1965. "The occurrence of malo-lactic fermentation in southern California wines." *Am. J. Enol. Vitic.* 16:219–223.

LaFollette, G. T. 1991. Chemical and Sensory Influences of sur Lies on Chardonnay Wines. MS thesis, Davis, CA: University of California.

LeBougeois, P., M. Mata, and P. Ritzenthaler. 1989. "Genome comparison of *Lactococcus* strains by pulsed-field gel electrophoresis." *FEMS Microbiol. Lett.* 59:65–70.

Lee, S. O., and M. Y. Pack. 1980. "Malate stimulation on growth rate of *Leuconostoc oenos*." *Korean J. Appl. Microbiol. Bioeng.* 8:221–227.

London, J. 1968. "Regulation and function of lactate oxidation in *Streptococcus faecium*." *J. Bacteriol.* 95:1380–1387.

Lonvaud, M., A. Lonvaud-Funel, and P. Ribéreau-Gayon. 1977. "Le mecanisme de la fermentation malolactiques des vins." *Connais. Vigne Vin* 11:73–91.

Lonvaud-Funel, A., C. Fremaux, N. Biteau, and A. Joyeux. 1991. "Speciation of lactic acid bacteria from wines by hybridization with DNA probes." *Food Microbiol.* 8:215–222.

Lüthi, H., and U. Vetsch. 1960. "Contributions to knowledge of the malolactic fermentation in wines and ciders. II. The growth promoting effect of yeast extract on lactic acid bacteria causing malolactic fermentation in wines." *J. Appl. Bacteriol.* 22:384–391.

Malletroit, V., J.-X. Guinard, R. E. Kunkee, and M. J. Lewis. 1991. "Effect of pasteurization on microbiological and sensory quality of white grape juice and wine." *J. Food Process. Preserv.* 15:19–29.

McCloskey, L. P. 1980. "Enzymatic assay for malic acid and malo-lactic fermentation." *Am. J. Enol. Vitic.* 31:212–215.

McCorkle, K. 1974. "Carbonic maceration...a beaujolais system for producing early-maturing red wine." *Wines & Vines.* 55(4):62–65.

Melamed, N. 1962. "Détermination des sucres résiduels des vins, leur relation avec la fermentation malolactique." *Ann. Techn, Agric.* 11:5–11,107–119.

Michels, P. A. M., J. P. J. Michels, J. Boonstra, and W. N. Konings. 1979. "Generation of an electrochemical proton gradient in bacteria by the excretion of metabolic end products." *FEMS Microbiol. Lett.* 5:357–364.

Morenzoni, R. A. 1973. A Second Enzymatic Malic Acid Decomposing Activity in Leuconostoc oenos. PhD thesis, Davis, CA: University of California.

Nathan, H. A. 1961. "Induction of malic enzyme and oxaloacetate decarboxylase in three lactic acid bacteria." *J. Gen. Microbiol.* 25:415–420.

Otto, R., J. Hugenholtz, W. N. Konings, and H. Veldkamp. 1980. "Increase of molar growth yield of *Streptococcus cremoris* for lactose as a consequence of lactate consumption by *Pseudomonas stutzeri* in mixed culture." *FEMC Microbiol. Lett.* 9:85–88.

Ough, C. S., E. A. Crowell, R. E. Kunkee, M. R. Vilas, and S. Lagier. 1987. "A study of histamine production by various wine bacteria in model solutions and in wine." *J. Food Proc. Pres.* 12:63–70.

Ough, C. S., R. E. Kunkee, M. R. Vilas, E. Bordeu, and M.-C. Huang. 1988. "The interaction of sulfur dioxide, pH, and dimethyl decarbonate on the growth of *Saccharomyces cerevisiae*, Montrachet and *Leuconostoc oenos* MCW." *Am. J. Enol. Vitic.* 38:279–282.

Peynaud, E., S. Lafon-Lafourcade, and S. Domercq. 1965. "Besoins nutritionnels de soixante-quarte souches de bactéries lactiques isolées de vins." *Bull. O.I.V.* 38:945–958.

Pilone, G. J. 1975. "Control of malo-lactic fermentation in table wines by addition of fumaric acid." In, *Lactic Acid Bacteria in Beverages and Food*, J. G. Carr, C. V. Cutting, and G. C. Whiting, Eds., pp. 121–138. London: Academic Press.

Pilone, G. J., and R. E. Kunkee. 1965. "Sensory characterization of wines fermented with several malo-lactic strains of bacteria." *Am. J. Enol. Vitic.* 16:224–230.

Pilone, G. J., and R. E. Kunkee. 1970. "Carbonic acid from decarboxylation by "malic" enzyme in lactic acid bacteria." *J. Bacteriol.* 103:404–409.

Pilone, G. J., and R. E. Kunkee. 1976. "Stimulatory effect of malolactic fermentation on the growth rate of *Leuconostoc oenos*." *Appl. Environ. Microbiol.* 32:405–408.

Pilone, G. J., and S.-Q. Liu. 1992. "Arginine metabolism by malolactic bacteria and its oenological implications." In, *Proceedings of the New Zealand Grape and Wine Symposium—Profit: In the Market, in the Winery, in the Vineyard*, D. J. Jordan, Ed., pp. 100–105. Auckland, New Zealand: New Zealand Society for Viticulture and Oenology.

POMPILIO, R. 1993. "Malolactic fermentation...Who's doing what—and why?" *Vyd. Winery Manag.* 19(6):44–47.

POUX, C., AND M. CAILLET. 1969. "Dosage enzymatique de l'acide L(-)malique." *Ann. Technol. Agric.* 18:359–366.

PRAHL, C., A. LONVAUD-FUNEL, S. KORSGAARD, E. MORRISON, AND A. JOYEUX. 1988. "Etude d'un procédé de déclenchement de la fermentation malolactique." *Conn. Vigne Vin* 22:197–207.

PUKRUSHPAN, L. 1976. The role of L-Malic acid in the metabolism of malo-lactic bacteria. PhD thesis, Davis, CA: University of California.

RADLER, F. 1966. "Die mikrobiologischen Grundlagen des Säureabbaus im Wein." *Zbl. Bakteriol. Parasitenkd. Infektionskr. Hyg. Abt. II*, 120:237–287.

RADLER, F. 1975. "The metabolism of organic acids by lactic acid bacteria." In *Lactic Acid Bacteria in Beverages and Food*, J. G. Carr, C. V. Cutting, and G. C. Whiting, Eds., pp. 17–27. London: Academic Press.

RADLER, F. 1990a. "Possible use of nisin in winemaking. I. Action of nisin against lactic acid bacteria and wine yeasts in solid and liquid media." *Am. J. Enol. Vitic.* 41:1–6.

RADLER, F. 1990b. "Possible use of nisin in winemaking. II. Experiments to control lactic acid bacteria in the production of wine." *Am. J. Enol. Vitic.* 41:7–11.

RADLER, F., AND S. HARTEL. 1984. *Lactobacillus trichodes*, ein Alkoholabhängiges Milchsäurebakterium. *Wein-Wiss.* 39:106–112.

RANKINE, B. C. 1967. "Influence of yeast strain and pH on pyruvic acid content of wines." *J. Sci. Food Agric.* 18:41–44.

RANKINE, B. C., J. C. M. FORNACHON, AND D. A. BRIDSON. 1969. "Diacetyl in Australian dry red table wines and its significance in wine quality." *Vitis* 8:129–134.

RENAULT, P. C. GAILLARDIN, AND H. HESLOT. 1988. "Role of malolactic fermentation in lactic acid bacteria." *Biochimie* 70:375–379.

ROGOSA, M., AND M. E. SHARPE. 1959. "An approach to classification of the lactobacilli." *J. Appl. Bacteriol.* 22:329–340.

RYNDERS, A. J. 1993. Effects of yeast strain, pH, and vitamin supplementation during vinification with simultaneous inoculation of saccharomyces cerevisiae and lactic acid bacteria. MS thesis, Davis, CA: University of California.

SCHANDERL, H. 1959. *Die Mikrobiologie des Mostes und Weines*, 2nd ed. Stuttgart: Verlag Eugen Ulmer.

SCHMITT, P., A. G. MATHOT, AND C. DIVIÈS. 1989. "Fatty acid composition of the genus Leuconostoc." *Milchwiss.* 44:556–559.

SCHÜTZ, M., AND F. RADLER. 1973. "Das 'Malatenzym' von *Lactobacillus plantarum* und *Leuconostoc mesenteroides*." *Arch. Mikrobiol.* 91:183–202.

SNEATH, P. H. A. 1986. *Bergey's Manual of Systematic Bacteriology*, 1st ed., Vol. 2. Baltimore: Williams and Wilkins.

SOZZI, T., R. MARET, AND J. M. POULIN. 1976. "Mis en evidence de bacteriophages dans le vin." *Experientia* 32:568–569.

SPETTOLI, P., M. P. NUTI, AND A. ZAMORANI. 1984. "Properties of malolactic activity purified from *Leuconostoc oenos* ML34 by affinity chromatography." *Appl. Environ. Microbiol.* 48:900–901.

TRACEY, R. P., AND T. J. BRITZ. 1989a. "Cellular fatty acid composition of *Leuconostoc oenos*." *J. Appl. Bacteriol.* 66:445–456.

TRACEY, R. P., AND T. J. BRITZ. 1989b. "The effect of amino acids on malolactic fermentation by *Leuconostoc oenos*." *J. Appl. Bacteriol.* 67:589–595.

TROOST, G., AND H. HAUSHOFER. 1986. *Perl- und Schaumwein*. Stuttgart, Germany: Eugen Ulmer.

VETSCH, U., AND H. LÜTHI. 1964. "Decolorisation of red wines during biological decomposition of acids." *Mitt. Geb. Lebensmittelunter. Hyg.* 55:93–98.

VIDAL-CAROU, M. C., A. AMBATLLE-ESPUNYES, M. C. ULLA-ULLA, AND A. MARINÉ-FONT. 1990. "Histamine and tyramine in Spanish wines: their formation during the winemaking process." *Am. J. Enol. Vitic.* 41:160–167.

VIDAL-CAROU, M. C., R. CODONY-SALCEDO, AND A. MARINÉ-FONT. 1991. "Changes in the concentration of histamine and tyramine during wine spoilage at various temperatures." *Am. J. Enol. Vitic.* 42:145–149.

WEILLER, H. G., AND F. RADLER. 1972. "Vitamin- und Aminosäurebedarf von Milchsaurebakterien aus Wein und von Rebenblättern." *Mitt. Klosterneuburg* 22:4–18.

WEILLER, H. G., AND F. RADLER. 1976. "Über den Aminosäurestoffwechsel von Milchsäurebakterien aus Wein." *Z. Lebensm. Unters. Forsch.* 161:259–266.

WHITING, G. C. 1975. "Some biochemical and flavour aspects of lactic acid bacteria in ciders and other alcoholic beverages." In, *Lactic Acid Bacteria in Beverages and Food*, J. G. Carr, C. V. Cutting, and G. C. Whiting, Eds., pp. 69–85. London: Academic Press.

WHITING, G. C., AND COGGINS, R. A. 1971. "The role of quinate and shikimate in the metabolism of lactobacilli." *Ant. Leeuwen.* 37:33–49.

WIBOWO, D., R. ESCHENBRUCH, C. R. DAVIS, G. H. FLEET, AND T. H. LEE. 1985. "Occurrence and growth of lactic acid bacteria in wine: a review." *Am. J. Enol. Vitic.* 36:302–313.

WOOD, W. A. 1961. "Fermentation of carbohydrates and related compounds." In *The Bacteria*, I. C. Gunsalus and R. Y. Stanier, Eds., Vol. 2, pp. 59–149. New York: Academic Press.

YOSHIZUMI H. 1975. "A malo-lactic bacterium and its growth factor." In *Lactic Acid Bacteria in Beverages and Food*, J. G. Carr, C. V. Cutting, and G. C. Whiting, Eds., pp. 87–102. London: Academic Press.

ZHUORONG, Y., AND R. E. KUNKEE. 1993. "Stimulation of growth rates of malolactic bacteria from incomplete conversion of L-malic acid to L-lactic acid." *FEMS Microbiol. Rev.* 12(1–3):50.

CHAPTER 7

THE FINING AND CLARIFICATION OF WINES

A. ASPECTS OF CLARIFICATION

The purposes of clarification and fining during wine processing include removal of excessive levels of certain wine components, achieving clarity, and making that clarity stable especially from a physicochemical viewpoint. The noun *fining* is used in winemaking to describe the deliberate addition of an adsorptive compound that is followed by the settling or precipitation of partially soluble components from the wine. The materials used for these reasons are collectively referred to as fining agents, even though the solutes that they address and the mechanism of their removal vary considerably. The need to employ such treatments is often determined not only by compositional aspects of the musts but also by the winemaking practices that have been employed.

Examples of such fining reactions are: (1) The removal of tannic and/or brown polymeric phenols by proteinaceous fining agents such as casein, isinglass, albumin, and gelatin; (2) the adsorption of wine proteins by exchanging clays such as the bentonites; (3) the depletion of monomeric and small polymeric phenols by polyamide materials such as polyvinylpolypyrrolidone (PVPP, trade name Polyclar AT) and nylon; (4) the elimination of unpleasant odors by copper sulfate or other procedures, and (5) the removal of fine colloidal particle and incipient precipitates by the sieving effect of other gelatinous materials.

In each case, the adsorbent (or fining agent) has several adsorption sites on each bead or molecule and a number of solute molecules are either adsorbed to its surface or exchanged into its interior. The mechanism is usually one of hydrogen bonding between exposed carbonyl groups at the surface of the adsorbent (the protein) and hydroxy groups of the phenol (or tannin). Several of the agents currently in use (such as the proteins and the gums) are colloidal in nature and as the adsorption occurs their solubility is reduced, resulting in precipitation of the solute/agent complex from the solution.

The amount of solute removed by a certain addition of an agent will depend on the solute/agent pair as well as the concentration of the solute in the wine and the quantity of the agent added. In special circumstances there is a direct relationship between the amount of agent added and the amount of the component removed, but in general, this will not be the case. The more usual condition will be one in which increasing levels of addition will result in further depletion of component concentrations, but with decreasing effectiveness. For this reason, it is necessary to understand the equilibrium that is established between the solute and the agent to understand the way in which the solute concentration is reduced as the agent addition is increased.

It is important to realize that the fining of wines by the addition of an adsorptive agent does not mean that the solute concentration is reduced to zero. The equilibrium nature of adsorption is such that as the component concentration is reduced, the tendency for further adsorption is also reduced and the agent becomes increasingly less effective. In most, if not all cases of fining, the solute concentration is merely lowered to a point at which it remains below a solubility condition (in a stability test) or a taste threshold (in a sensory test), and at such a concentration it is considered to be acceptable.

The addresses of equipment companies mentioned in this chapter can be found in Appendix I.

1. Characterization of Hazes

The need for fining and/or clarification will depend on the nature of the components that are responsible for the haze. Some haze particles can be insolubles such as fine dust, small fibers of grape pulp, and yeast or bacteria that remain in suspension due to very small settling velocities or charge repulsions that prevent more compact settling from occurring. Others can be partially soluble components that have precipitated from solution due to limited solubility at the ethanol content of wine and lower temperatures. Examples would be fine tartrate crystals and protein and polysaccharide hazes or finely dispersed precipitates of large-molecular-weight tannin materials that are often combined with some proteinaceous components. Clarification is generally considered to provide insignificant compositional changes compared with fining in which compositional changes are sought to prevent further precipitation. Fining can also be used to modify (improve) the sensory or stability attributes of wines even though existing clarity may not be an issue.

2. Adsorptive Phenomena

The adsorption equilibrium that is established in solution is a reversible distribution of the solute between the liquid and solid (or colloid) phases. The adsorption equilibrium relationship, often referred to as an adsorption isotherm, since the data is obtained at one temperature, can usually be quantified by one of the following equations, due to Langmuir and Freundlich:

$$\text{Langmuir: } \frac{x}{m} = (x/m)_{max} * \frac{[S]}{[K_L + [S]]}$$

$$\text{Freundlich: } \frac{x}{m} = K_F * [S]^{1/n}$$

where x is the mass of the solute (or adsorbate) on m mass of solid (or adsorbent); and S is the equilibrium solute concentration in the liquid after the equilibrium is established. It is this equilibrium level of the solute that is the concentration that will remain in the wine after fining. These relationships determine the way in which the solute concentration (S) determines the amount of material to be removed (x) for a given addition (m) of the fining agent.

The constants K_L and $(x/m)_{max}$ (or K_F and n) are properties of the adsorption pair, and can be determined by plotting double reciprocal plots (m/x) against ($1/S$) for the Langmuir equation, log-log plots of (x/m) against (S) for the Freundlich equation, or by using general nonlinear regression methods.

While a number of other relationships have been developed for the description of adsorption systems, most of the fining treatments used in winemaking can be described by one or the other of the simpler equations.

3. Agents that Obey Langmuir's Equation

The Langmuir relationship readily describes the nature of protein adsorption by clays such as bentonite, as well as that of ions by ion exchange resins. The adsorption curves for a standard protein with the sodium and calcium forms of bentonite are shown in Figure 7-1.

The adsorption is analogous to the binding and dissociation steps of the Michaelis-Menten rate equation for enzyme reactions, except that no reaction takes place. In these cases, there are a fixed number of adsorption sites and once these are filled (or saturated), the adsorption per unit of agent reaches its maximum value, $(x/m)_{max}$, and the adsorption becomes independent of the solute concentration. At low solute concentrations, the binding is proportional to the concentration but the adsorption (x/m) is small and much less than the maximum. By analogy, the Langmuir constant K_L, like the K_m of the enzyme relationship, is a measure of the affinity of the solute for the adsorbent, a measure of the ability to perform close to the saturation level at lower concentrations. Like the enzyme case, a larger K_L value means less affinity of the agent for the solute.

The K_L values for sodium and calcium bentonites with a standard protein (bovine serum albumin) have been determined to be 2.14 and 93.4 mg/L respectively (Blade and Boulton 1988).

4. Agents that Obey Fruendlich's Equation

The Freundlich relationship is entirely empirical but it effectively describes many of adsorption systems found in nature. It can be viewed as a form of a distribution equation in which the concentration on the solid phase (x/m), is related to the solution concentration (S) by a $(1/n)$th-order form and the distribution coefficient, K_F.

Combinations of agents and solutes which show this type of adsorption in wines are the phenolics in general (Singleton 1967) and the hydroxy-benzoic acids in particular (Mennett and Nakayama 1970a) with PVPP as well as several classes of phenolics with the proteinaceous agents (Wucherpfennig et al. 1975). The adsorption of wine color by activated carbon, although not usually considered to be a fining

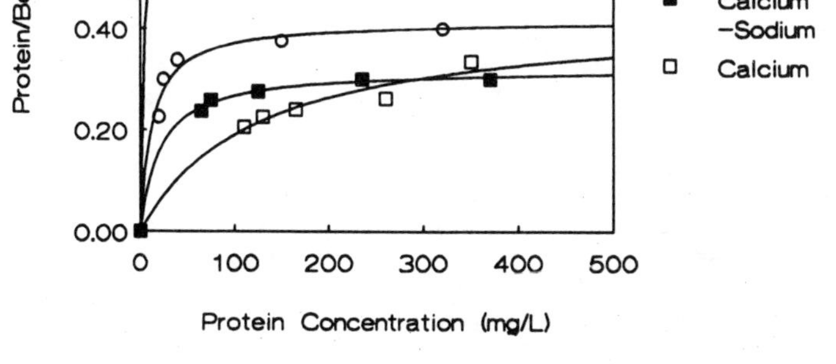

Fig. 7-1. The Langmuir adsorption isotherms for sodium and calcium bentonites.

treatment, also obeys the Fruendlich equation. The adsorption of a number of wine components by different fining agents obeys this relationship as is shown in Figure 7-2.

The adsorption equilibrium in solutions is not strongly sensitive to temperature and when well mixed, it is very rapidly established, typically of the order of seconds or minutes. Examples of such effects of temperature and time on the adsorption of pigments and nonpigment phenolics from a wine by PVPP have been determined (Mennett and Nakayama 1970b).

Data for the removal of phenolic dimers and polymers by the protein fining agents generally follow the Freundlich equation but can display deviations from it. In practice, the adsorbate is often a mixture, rather than a single component, and can exhibit differences in the functional groups and molecular sizes within a class of components, such as the phenolics. The adsorption from mixtures such as wines can therefore demonstrate curves which are a composite of the progressive depletion of components as the dosage of the agent is increased. In instances where tightly adsorbed components can freely displace less tightly held substances, the composition of individual wines, the level of agent used, and the manner in which the contacting is performed can greatly affect the outcome. Laboratory trials are always recommended to account for such variations.

B. THE FINING AGENTS

Fining agents can be classified into one of the following groups and their common dosage ranges are shown in Table 7-1. The groups include the proteins (casein, albumen, isinglass, and gelatin), the earths (bentonite forms and other clays), synthetic polymers with amide or pyrridone components (nylon and PVPP), and colloidal materials with limited soluble residues (natural polysaccharides and ferrocyanide preparations and their salts). The level that is suitable for any given wine can vary from none to those indicated. Some wines will have little, if any, need for such treatment while grape composition and winemaking practices will determine the need in others.

1. The Proteins

The purpose of adding a protein preparation to wine is to soften or reduce the wine's astringency or reduce its color by the adsorption and precipitation of polymeric phenols and tannins. Although it is rarely practiced today,

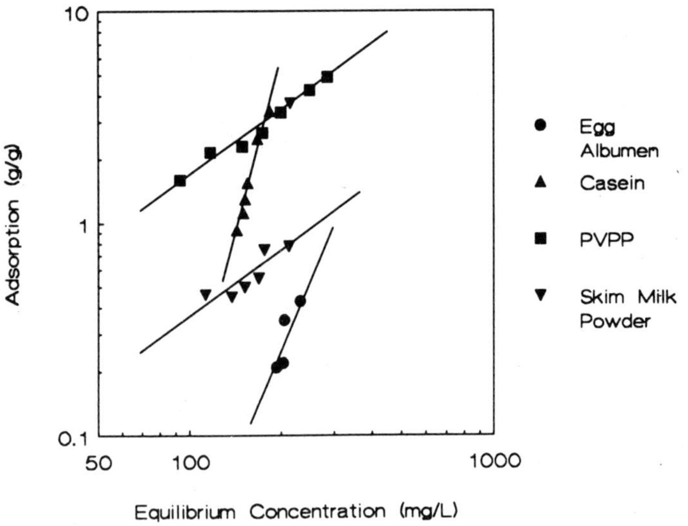

Fig. 7-2. The Freundlich adsorption isotherms of several fining agents.

Table 7-1. Typical ranges of application for fining agents.

Agent	Common Range of Application (mg/L) White Table Wines	Red Table Wines
Casein	60 to 120	60 to 240
Albumen	N/A	30 to 240
Isinglass	10 to 120	30 to 240
Gelatin	15 to 120	30 to 240
Bentonite (Na form)	120 to 720	N/A
Silica Sol	40 to 200	40 to 200
PVPP	120 to 240	120 to 480
Agar/Alginate	120 to 480	120 to 480
Activated Carbon	120 to 600	120 to 600

white wines can be clarified by adding a protein followed by a tannin due to the coprecipitation that occurs. All of these proteins come from natural sources, usually in a partially purified form. The four most commonly used proteins for wine applications are casein, gelatin, albumen, and isinglass. Their properties are summarized in Table 7-2.

Proteins have two aspects to their solubility in acid solutions, charge and hydration. All proteins have a pH at which they carry no net charge in solution, and this is known as the isoelectric point, pI. Although most proteins are least soluble at their isoelectric point, certain proteins such as gelatin and ovalbumin have significant concentrations in solution when brought to their isoelectric point. In contrast, other less soluble proteins such as casein readily precipitate and have essentially no residue when brought to their isoelectric point, or even in acidic conditions such as wine. Ovalbumin and gelatin form stable emulsions of neutral particles, while casein flocculates when its charge is neutralized.

Gelatin is a hydrolysis product of ligament, skin, or tendon tissue from animals. It is classified as a collagen derivative and can have a broad molecular weight range as a result of the source and method of preparation. Casein is a mixture of the major proteins precipitated by acid from milk, mostly the α form with half as much of the β form and lesser amounts of the ε and τ forms (Jenness 1970).

Albumen is an egg white mixture of the ovalbumin and conalbumin proteins. The ovalbumin accounts for 50% of the egg white proteins with the conalbumin making up a further 15%. Albumen is an albumin, a water-soluble class of proteins that includes bovine serum albumin (BSA). Isinglass is a collagen protein from the membranes of the swim bladder of sturgeon fish and is thought to have similar molecular weight and properties to gelatin. It is ordinarily more soluble in cold water than some of the gelatin preparations.

These agents are made up in solutions of 1 to 5% (depending on the agent) in water, and in certain cases, a salt solution (sodium or potassium chloride), or at alkaline pH (with ammonium hydroxide). Whipping is sometimes used to enhance the dissolution and, by physical denaturation, the effectiveness of these preparations.

Table 7-2. General properties of protein fining agents.

Protein	Source	MW range	pI	Major amino acids
Casein	milk	20, 30K	4.55	Glu, Pro, Leu, Lys
α Casein		30K	4.1	
ε Casein		20K	3.7	
β Casein		24K	4.5	
τ Casein		30K	5.8, 6.0	
Albumen	egg			
Ovalbumin		46K	4.55, 4.90	Glu, Leu, Asp, Val, Ser
Conalbumin		87K	6.8, 7.1	
Gelatin	animal tissue	60K	4.80, 4.85	Gly, Pro, Hyp, Glu, Arg
Isinglass	fish	Unknown	4.50, 4.80	Unknown

A common feature of all of these proteins is that they have isoelectric points close to but above the wine pH range (Table 7-2) (Haurowitz 1963). This ensures that they will have limited solubility in wines and their molecules carry an overall positive charge so that any excess of added protein can be removed by a subsequent bentonite fining. The isoelectric point of the protein also has important effects on the behavior of the corresponding protein-tannin complexes that it will form (Oh and Hoff 1987). The tannins efficiently form complexes at pH values up to the pI of the protein but far less effectively at higher pH values. One reason for this is the loss of hydrogen bonding if the phenols are in the phenolate ion form.

The principal differences among the proteins are in their molecular weights and their composition of amino acids. The amino acid composition, in particular the higher proportions of proline and hydroxyproline in gelatines, is related to the tendency of water exclusion and subsequent clumping behavior. There is presently no demonstrated relationship of preference between polymeric phenols and the more abundant amino acids found in the different protein fining agents. There are considerable differences in the interactions of phenolic monomers, dimers, and tannins with different molecular weight fractions of gelatin (Yokotsuka and Singleton 1987). There is little difference in the haze formation of fractions in the range 2,000 and 70,000 Daltons with tannin, but only the smaller 2,000 and 5,000 Dalton fractions formed significant haze with phenolic dimers and none formed hazes with the monomeric phenols.

While there is a common impression that all proteins are heat sensitive, it is important to note that gelatins (and perhaps isinglass) are thermally stable and residues of them will generally pass a heat stability test. A further important feature of gelatin is that it has essentially no response to the Coomassie Blue dye-binding reagent that is often used for the assaying of protein content. It is also important to note that if excessive gelatin remains after fining, haze may result in the bottle after further polymerization of the remaining phenols.

When corrected for moisture content, these proteins have similar adsorption capacities but with some differences in terms of their affinity for certain subgroups of phenolics. Gelatin, casein, and isinglass have capacities for tannin in the range 80 to 110 mg per 100 mg protein with no significant adsorption of catechin (Rossi and Singleton 1966).

2. The Earths

Bentonite is widely used for the adsorption of proteinaceous materials from wines. See also Chapter 8 for a more complete discussion of protein stability in white wines. Bentonite was originally introduced as a means of clarifying wines and vinegars (Saywell 1934a, b) and its application to inducing heat stability in white wines came several years later. Saywell attributed its action to removing the iron involved in metal protein hazes rather than the removal of protein fractions as such.

Bentonite is a natural clay that is classified as a montmorillonite, with a general composition of the form: Mg, Ca, Na, $Al_2O_3 \cdot 5\,SiO_2 \cdot n\,H_2O$ (Siddiqui 1968). A number of other clays that have the silica, alumina matrix with exchangeable cations have been considered as alternatives to bentonite and these include kaolin, Spanish earth. They generally have a lower adsorption capacity and therefore are not preferred in winemaking applications.

The source of the bentonite influences its properties slightly and the main differences lie in the proportions of Mg^{++}, Ca^{++}, and Na^{+} in the lattice. The bentonites from Germany and North Africa, generally used in Europe are predominately Ca^{++} forms which swell less in water and have lower protein exchange capacity per unit weight. Those from Wyoming, generally used in the United States, are Na^{+} forms and swell more and have approximately twice the protein exchange capacity of the Ca^{++} forms (Figure 7-1) (Blade and Boulton 1988). The calcium form has a basal spacing between silica layers of the order of ten Å and adsorbs proteins primarily on the external surfaces. The sodium form expands to give basal spacings of hundreds of angstroms and the protein adsorption is over the entire surface area (Rodriguez et al. 1977).

Bentonite has a structure which expands after contact with water and preparations have optimum adsorption after two days of soaking. The limited cation exchange capacity of bentonite poses particular problems with the removal of negatively charged and neutral protein fractions from wines. Bentonite is essentially inert with respect to the phenolic components in wine except for cationic anthocyanins. The sodium form has approximately twice the adsorption capacity of the calcium form for the proteins used as fining agents in wine (Sudraud and Caye 1985). There have been a number of comparative studies of the two forms (Rankine and Emerson 1963; Jakob 1965), but the adsorption per unit of flocculated sediment favors the sodium form. The preparation in wine provides slightly less capacity than the preparation in water (Jakob 1968) due to the salt strength reducing the swelling capacity (Siddiqui 1968). There is little effect of temperature on the adsorption (Jakob 1968; Blade and Boulton 1988). The adsorption was almost three times higher at pH 3.0 than at pH 4.5 (Jakob 1968), as might be expected from the ionization of the proteins involved.

The cation exchange mechanism requires that the sodium (or calcium) ions from the bentonite enter the wine as it takes up the proteins in the exchange process. The quantities of these cation increases can be shown to be of the order of 14 mg/L for sodium form, based on an addition of 0.960 g/L in a water solution, a relatively high treatment. The pickup associated with an equivalent adsorption capacity of a calcium form would be 24 mg/L of calcium. There will also be some pickup of other metal cations (such as potassium, magnesium, and trace levels of some transition metals) that are present within the clay matrix. Recent studies (Postel et al. 1986a, 1986b, 1987) of the secondary metal pickup from several calcium-based bentonite preparations noted an average increase of 30 $\mu g/L$ in the lead content of a treated wine when 4 g/L. While this level of bentonite addition is almost four times that considered high for the corresponding sodium preparation, the same study measured much higher increases in model solutions. There does not appear to be a corresponding survey of the trace metal content of commercial sodium bentonites.

Bentonites have also been used as settling aids to clarify juices and to lower the levels of components other than proteins (Mobius and Görtges 1976). They have significant adsorption capacity for amino acids and other components in juices and when added and removed from juice can lead to extended fermentations (Bach and Hoffman 1978).

Undesirable features of bentonite relate to dust generation during its handling as a powder, the poor compaction of its sediment, and the widespread use of diatomaceous earth filtration to clarify the wines after treatment. It also tends to seal percolation ponds that are sometimes used for water treatment and irrigation applications. The increasing trend toward minimization of solid waste should focus directly upon the development of alternatives for bentonite that are adsorptive agents capable of regeneration and suitable for bed-based contacting methods.

One such development relates to the preparation of a silica bead that contains an amount of bentonite internally (Welsh and Parent 1985; Parent and Welsh 1986). The calcium form has been used due to its limited swelling capacity and the resulting material can be used in an adsorption column. It could be regenerated with a calcium solution rather than being discarded, and there is no need for the filtration step and the subsequent waste disposal. As yet, there does not appear to be commercial adoption of this approach in winemaking. The limited swelling capacity is related to a lower internal surface area and therefore limited capacity for fining, but this would be compensated by the particle-bed application, elimination of fining lees, and the regeneration features.

Other approaches to the adsorption of proteins from wines center on the use of immobilized tannin or tannin fractions. The adsorption is then based primarily on a hydrogen bonding rather than charge attraction or ion exchange. It would seem to be a more general adsorption mechanism and a more desirable approach to addressing the more neutral and anionic protein fractions. The influence of phenol polymer size on the binding and precipitation of wine proteins has been studied for a limited range of conditions (Yokutsuka et al. 1983). One of the earliest such approaches was the use of immobilized tannin attached to activated cellulose for the adsorption of proteins from sake or rice wine (Watanbe et al. 1979; Chibata et al. 1982, 1986). Similar studies with grape seed tannin attached to glutaraldehyde (Weetall et al. 1984) have not been reproducible. Other encouraging applications are the immobilization of tannins on Sepharose (Oh et al. 1985) and agarose (Powers et al. 1988); however, a problem with such preparations has been that regeneration with alkaline solutions leads to phenol oxidation that, in turn, leads to loss of capacity.

There is considerable scope for the evaluation of either natural product based materials or new protein separation materials being used and developed for the isolation and recovery of proteins and enzymes from other fermentation and pharmaceutical media. A recent study evaluated a number of alternative exchanging clays and a synthetic weak cation exchanging matrix (trade name of Macroprep) that has an adsorption capacity that is about one-quarter of that of sodium bentonite and can be regenerated for multiple uses and column operations.

3. Synthetic Polymers

Materials such as polyglycine, polyamide (nylon), and polyvinyl-polypyrrolidone (PVPP) are synthetic products with available carbonyl oxygen atoms at the surface that act as adsorption sites. Nylon and PVPP are both insoluble white powders that have been used in wine. The more efficient adsorption of PVPP has led to its preferential use (Caputi and Peterson 1965; Rossi and Singleton 1966) over nylon (Fuller and Berg 1965). The agents are generally added in a batch treatment and commonly settled or filtered out of the wine and discarded after one use. There have been several trials with the use of PVPP in columns during the 1980s in California and more recently as part of a filter cake (Oechsle and Schneider 1992).

The developments in polymer technology since the introduction of PVPP and the spectrum of related heterocyclics that possess similar carbonyl components would suggest that there should be one or more alternatives to these agents and perhaps ones with improved selectivity or more easily regenerated surfaces. There are applications in other fields in which coatings of polymers like PVPP are placed onto beads for more desirable buoyancy and particle size features, but as yet these have not been applied to wine treatments.

The particular interest in these agents lies in their ability to adsorb monomeric phenols such as catechins (and other flavonoids) with a higher preference than the monomers and dimers (Rossi and Singleton 1966), over the polymeric compounds which are adsorbed more efficiently by the protein fining agents. The catechins are involved in the chemical browning of white wines and are thought to be particularly bitter in nature above their sensory threshold level of 20 mg/L (Singleton and Noble 1976).

4. The Colloids

a. Natural Polysaccharides

The polysaccharides, agar and acacia (gum arabic), both have protective colloid properties and can partially neutralize surface charges on other naturally dispersed colloids, thereby allowing them to either dissolve or to coagulate. In the United States the propriety preparation known as Sparkolloid (either in a hot-mix or cold-mix form) are alginate-based materials that can aid in the settling of finely suspended matter.

The polysaccharide agents of this kind are especially useful in neutralizing the charge of other haze components of what are generally referred to as protective colloids. In protective colloids, one polar or charged entity is adsorbed to the outer surface of another, causing the overall complex to repel like species and causing a suspension to occur.

In wines and juices natural polysaccharide contents are in the range 200 to 1000 mg/L (Usseglio-Tomasset 1976; Villettaz 1988; Feuillat 1987; Wucherpfennig and Dietrich 1989) and additional ones, principally mannans, are formed by yeast during fermentation (Llaubères et al. 1987; Feuillat et al. 1988) or certain bacterial activity (Llaubères 1990). Mannan has been shown to be a major constitutent of yeast cell walls (Bauer et al. 1972), and most of its production and release appears to occur during fermentation. These often form combined hazes and protective colloids with other wine constituents such as various protein and peptide fractions. The action of an added polysaccharide with limited solubility is to adsorb away some of these, in effect altering the charge neutrality and allowing either or both components to redissolve or to combine with like material and form a precipitate.

Unstable colloidal components also tend to adhere to suspended particles such as crystals of tartrate salts and tannin precipitates. Materials such as gum arabic and metatartaric acid have been used in some regions for the inhibition of the crystal growth of tartrates, thereby delaying the onset of precipitation in unstable wines. The problem with this approach is that the inhibition is temporary, often lasting only several months and other wine treatments such as cold storage and the use of charge-modified pad and membrane filters can alter the concentrations of these polymeric colloids and their stabilizing effects.

b. *Ferrocyanide Preparations*

The application of ferrocyanide salts for the removal of transition metal cations from wine has been widely practiced in Europe for more than 50 years. Sometimes referred to as *Moslinger* fining, after its inventor, the form used is potassium ferrocyanide, $K_4Fe(CN)_6$. The ferrocyanide salts of most metals are blue (hence the term *blue-fining*), sparingly soluble, and when used properly, the residue should be less than 0.02 mg/L (Würdig and Woller 1989). Table 7-3 provides the aqueous solubility products of several such salts (Dean 1987) and the expected concentration limits of several cations in the presence of 0.02 mg/L of the ferrocyanide ion. It can be seen that ferrocyanide is most effective against iron, less so with copper, and of no practical use for the removal of manganese, mercury, and lead. With silver, it leaves no significant residue (< 1 μg/L).

The use of potassium ferrocyanide in wine remains prohibited in the United States and instead colloidal forms of it which left lower residues were used for many years. The trade names of these preparations were Cufex and Metafine but they are no longer commercially

Table 7-3. Solubility products and residues for various ferrocyanide salts.

Salt	Solubility product	pK_{sp}	Residual (mg/L)
$Cu_2[Fe(CN)_6]$	1.3×10^{-16}	15.89	2.4
$Fe_4[Fe(CN)_6]_3$	3.3×10^{-41}	40.52	0.8
$Pb_2[Fe(CN)_6]$	3.5×10^{-15}	14.46	39.9
$Ag_4[Fe(CN)_6]$	1.6×10^{-41}	40.81	0.001
$Mn_2[Fe(CN)_6]$	8.0×10^{-13}	12.10	163

The relative concentration of each metal remaining in the presence of 0.02 mg/L of the $Fe(CN)_6^{=}$ ion, based on aqueous solubility constants.

available. The use of these colloidal forms is legally approved in the United States but it is not used in other wine producing countries. The use of potassium ferrocyanide in other wine producing countries, even under strict supervision, as is required in some cases, remains one of the major regulatory conflicts related to wine treatments at the international level. When used for metal-depleting applications, these materials were generally followed by a tight pad or membrane filtration for the collection of finely suspended residues. Wines treated in this way must be analyzed by the Hubach test (Ough and Amerine 1988) for the detection of any significant ferrocyanide residues.

5. Alternative Methods of Metal Depletion

Elevated metal content can arise from pesticide or copper spray residues (Lay and Lemperle 1981; Lay and Leib 1988; Lemperele 1989) or from additions of copper sulfate to remove hydrogen sulfide or mercaptans from wines. Typical levels of metals in Californian wines have been determined (Ough et al. 1982), and are presented in Table 8-9.

The removal of metals could be achieved by the use of immobilized forms of ferrocyanide or alternatively, other chelating materials. There are presently a number of chelating resins available commercially, but several of them have limited chelating functions at pH values less than 4.0. There have been evaluations of wine treatments using a 8-hydroxyquinoline ligand attached to styrene-divinylbenzene resin (Loubser and Sanderson 1986) that was capable of removing relatively high levels of iron and copper from several wines. The treatment also resulted in significant phenolic and amber color loss in a white wine, but the process warrants further development and attention. More recently, commercial resins with an imidodiacetate functional group linked to the same resin matrix have been tested for this application (Kern and Wucherpfennig 1991; Kern et al. 1992). The resin is commercially available as Lewatit TP 207 and BioRad Chelex 500 and has some difficulty in lowering the copper content to a 0.2 mg/L level under wine pH conditions. The pKa of acetic acid is 4.76 and at pH conditions below this the acetate is predominantly undissociated, losing its selectivity for the divalent cations. The possibility of alternative but stronger acidic groups in the chelating bridge may provide more useful materials for this application.

Alternative polymeric materials based on 1-vinylpyrrolidone and 1-vinylimidazole have also been suggested for the removal of metals from wine (Fussnegger et al. 1992). The polymer containing a ratio of the pyrrolidone to imidazole of 9:1 gave the best results, although a significant pH rise occurred at treatment levels that were required to lower the copper content to below 0.2 mg/L, the level generally considered to be acceptable.

6. Activated Carbon

The activated carbons have high and broad affinities particularly for benzenoid and nonpolar substances. They are used to remove color pigments and a wide range of phenolics but are rather nonselective in their adsorption (Singleton 1964). They do not adsorb substances such as sugars and amino acids which are highly water soluble. They are not generally used and offer no benefits to most wines. They adsorb a range of other trace constituents including some vitamins and this could have secondary effects on microbiological stability. The carbons are usually sold as either decolorizing or deodorizing forms. The treatment levels are determined by a dose-response trial on the wine in question with the specific carbon.

7. Silica Suspensions

Silica suspensions, or sols, are most often used in clarification and settling applications, particularly with apple and fruit wines. In such cases, the silica sol preparation is used in conjunction with gelatin in proportions which vary with the loading and wine concerned

(Wucherpfennig and Possmann 1972; Wucherpfennig et al. 1975). They have particular applications to peptide tannin hazes. The clearest explanation for the mechanism of action is that gelatin and tannin precipitate each other and silica prevents an excess of gelatin. The treatment limit in the United States is 2.4 g/L of a 30% by weight silica solution.

8. Copper Sulfate

Copper sulfate is used to remove H_2S and thiols from wines and the level of addition should be less than 0.5 mg/L. Traces of a brown/black precipitate of CuS can be formed, but is often not observed. The residual of copper should be less than 0.5 mg/L in the United States and 0.2 mg/L in most other countries. This removal of copper is due to the limited solubility of the CuS salt and not an adsorption mechanism. An excess of copper should be avoided to satisfy legal limits, to minimize catalysis of oxidation reactions and to avoid precipitation of complexes with proteins. Copper treatments such as this will not remove dimethyl sulfide (DMS) from wines.

Copper sulfate can be used in conjunction with a sulfite/ascorbate addition to remove disulfides from wines. The kinetics of this reaction have been studied recently (Bobet et al. 1990) and it is extremely slow under wine pH conditions, typically requiring months at 20°C rather than minutes or hours. The reaction is rapid enough (within two months) to be useful for a laboratory diagnosis. The role of the sulfite is to cleave the disulfide, forming a Bunte salt intermediate and eventually producing two thiols in the process. The role of the ascorbate seems to be that of trapping for oxygen thereby preventing the reoxidation of the thiol to the disulfide. The presence of copper ions at this time is to ensure the immediate precipitation of the thiol as it forms.

Copper sulfate is preferable to the silver salts, as used in parts of Europe, because it does not appear to form chloride and tartrate precipitates under wine conditions and is less toxic than silver residues. The solubility product for CuS is 4×10^{-36} at 25°C in water, while that for AgS is 6×10^{-50}, however, at wine pH only a trace of any hydrogen sulfide is in the sulfide ion form so that significant additions (> 0.1 mg/L) are needed to have an effect.

C. WINE CLARIFICATION

1. Natural Settling

The simplest form of clarification is the natural settling of suspended solids under the action of gravity. The time required to completely clarify a juice is the time taken for the smallest particles to fall through the height of the tank. In practice, there is a range of particle sizes and the extent and time of settling will depend on a number of other factors such as the interactions between particles as their concentration increases and the presence of any natural convection currents or bubbles rising from the onset of fermentation within the tank. Studies of suspended particles in beer indicate average particle diameters of 2 to 4 μm, with some as large as 16 and 20 μm (Morris 1984).

The rate at which particles that are denser than the juice (or wine) settle depends on the density difference between the particle and the fluid, $(\rho_p - \rho_f)$, the particle diameter, and the viscosity of the fluid. Particles will rapidly accelerate until they reach a steady falling speed known as the terminal velocity. The relationship between the terminal velocity and the fluid and particle properties for a sphere is given by Stokes' Law:

$$V_t = \frac{D_p^2(\rho_p - \rho_f)}{18\mu}$$

where D_p is the particle diameter; ρ_p and ρ_f are the density of the particle and fluid, respectively; and μ is the fluid viscosity. This assumes that there are laminar flow conditions, that is, the particle Reynold's number, $D_p V_t \rho_f/\mu$ is less than 0.1 and this is true for grape fragments smaller than 500 μm in size.

The particles of grape pulp which are generally the solids of interest in juices have densities close to that of the juice, making their terminal velocities relatively small and requiring considerable time to fall the height. As the fermentation proceeds, the juice density falls and the density difference increases significantly. Based on a density difference of 100 kg/m^3, typical of grape pulp in a juice, the settling times of particles of 20-, 50-, 100-μm diameters to fall through 1m are approximately 6 hours, 1 hour, and 14 minutes, respectively. The density difference for the same solids following fermentation is 110 kg/m^3 and the viscosity is less than one-half of that of the juice. The settling times for the corresponding particles to fall through 1m are then 4.2 hours, 40 minutes, and 10 minutes, respectively.

The estimation of the natural settling time for a medium like juice or wine is influenced by the size distribution of the particles and the existence of at least three different mechanisms of settling within the tank. These are the laminar settling of independent particles, the hindered settling within dense layers of particles and the compaction of heavy solids layers. The settling is also dramatically altered in the presence of bubble formation and thermal convection currents.

Perhaps the largest effect that influences natural settling is the interaction of particles as they come into closer proximity with others as they move toward the lower regions of the tank. This effect is referred to as hindered settling and is due to interferences in the fluid movement around them and the force of repulsion of particles of like charge can counterbalance the settling force due to gravity. This leads to a retardation of the settling velocity and results in a significant volume of unsettled juice. The solids layers that have collected at the base of the tank also undergo much slower compaction and this is influenced by the nature of the solids. A major influence on the magnitude of these interparticle forces is the presence of colloidal polymers such as polysaccharides and proteins which are carrying a slight positive charge at juice pH. This is the main reason for the wide variation in the settling ability of different juices and the reason that the application of hydrolytic enzymes can have a dramatic clarifying in some juices.

2. Settling Aids

The use of bentonite in juices as a settling aid, while still practiced in some areas, is not recommended since it will only benefit juices in which there is a significant interference due to proteinaceous colloids and in some cases it can actually cause the problem to be magnified. In the absence of colloidal effects, the mechanical effect of a more dense particle suspension falling about the pulp will generally promote the settling and provide a more compact lees volume although variation in the extent of this exists (Wagener 1970). The nature of bentonite in acidic pH solutions and the presence of a significant amount of very fine dust in most preparations generally leads to little enhancement in the density of the lees.

Alternative agents that has been used in many juices are preparations of silica suspensions commonly referred to as silica sols. These can be used alone or in conjunction with gelatin to promote the mechanical settling action by falling faster than many of the fine particles and dragging them along. However, the additional volume of lees often offsets the benefit. There are expected to be some adsorption and colloidal effects with this treatment but these have not been well characterized in grape juices (Wucherpfennig et al. 1975).

The most immediate alternative to natural settling is the use of centrifugal effects to increase the settling force from one to several hundred or a thousand times that of gravity. Such forces greatly increase the effective terminal velocity and decrease the separation time required. These forces also overwhelm the hindered settling effects observed that are so obvious under gravity settling conditions, providing a more consistent clarifying effect even when such particle interactions are present. Furthermore, the distance for the particles to travel is greatly reduced by the design of the equipment.

The most widely used form of clarification by centrifugal action are the desludging and decanting centrifuges. Another less common approach is the use of hydrocyclones for the partial removal of the larger suspended particles from juices and wines.

3. Desludging Centrifuges

The centrifuge consists of a stack of truncated cones which are mounted in the center on a spindle (Figure 7-3). The spindle is hollow and allows the feed stream to enter from the top and then to be distributed at the base of the centrifuge bowl. The entire bowl, outer wall, and disc stack are rotated at high speeds producing outward radial forces on particles of > 10,000 times that of gravity. The stream that is distributed at the base is then forced up between the discs leaving the unit at the top of the conical section. The particles are collected on the underside of each disc as they are spun out while the fluid moves between the discs. The particles then collect at the outer wall of the bowl and when the bowl becomes full the solids begin to appear in the outlet stream. The accumulated solids are removed in an operation known as desludging.

a. *Desludging Operations*

The desludging is usually triggered by an optical sensor in the outlet stream which detects the overflow of solids when the bowl is full. The inflow is stopped while the bowl continues to spin and the base section of the bowl chamber drops down, allowing a series of holes or ports in the circumference to open. The solids in the bowl (and the associated juice or wine) are then forced through these ports by the radial centrifugal reaction, being collected in an outer chamber. The base section is then repositioned so that the ports no longer have an open channel and the flow and operation are allowed to resume. Such an operation is referred to as a total desludge because the entire contents of the bowl are ejected. With the use of interval timers or manual operation, a more efficient desludging in which less juice (or wine) is lost can be performed. In this partial desludge operation the base section of the bowl is allowed to remain in the down position for a shorter time so that only about one-half of the bowl contents are ejected (typically most of the solids and little of the juice or wine).

b. *Solids Ejection Rates*

The rate at which the desludging centrifuge can eject the solids is determined by the number and size of the desludging ports and the frequency of desludging. The frequency of desludging is determined by the flow rate at which the solids are entering the unit. This is equal to the volumetric flow rate times the fraction of the feed which is due to solids (% v/v). The throughput of the centrifuge is dependent on the liquid fraction of the feed stream times the flow rate and the fraction of the time which the unit is not desludging. The largest commercial centrifuge of this type (the Westphalia SA160) has a solids ejection capacity of 4500 L of solids per hour and a liquid throughput of approximately 120,000 L/hr. The throughput of these centrifuges is reduced inversely as the solids content of the feed stream is increased and the performance of these units is not favored at high (> 4 to 5% v/v) solids contents. This is why they are seldom used for the clarification of juices prior to fermentation.

c. *Residence Times*

The residence time during which the particles are under the influence of the super gravity force is of the order of seconds. This is determined by the bowl volume divided by the volumetric flow rate. A typical value would be 25 L divided by 60,000 L/hr, giving an average residence time of 1.5 seconds.

d. *Manufacturers*

The two main manufacturers of desludging centrifuges for the wine industry at present

(a)

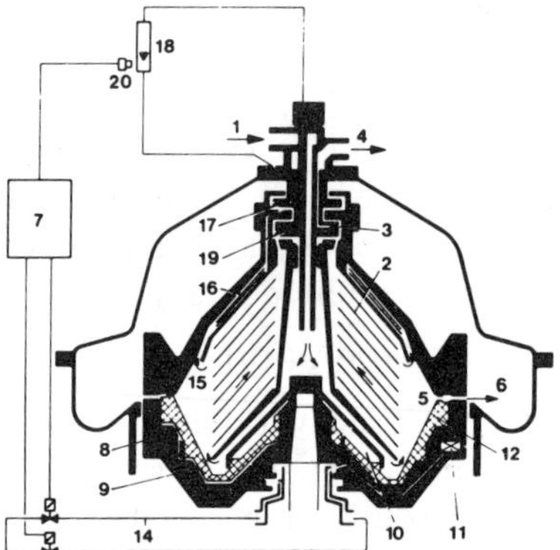

1 Feed	11 Bowl valve
2 Discs	12 Piston
3 Centripetal pump	13 Opening water
4 Discharge	14 Closing water
5 Sediment holding space	15 Sensing zone disc
6 Sediment ejection ports	16 Sensing liquid clarifying discs
7 Timing unit	17 Sensing liquid pump
8 Outer closing chamber	18 Flowmeter
9 Inner closing chamber	19 Sensing liquid pump
10 Opening chamber	20 Switch

(b)

Fig. 7-3. A disc centrifuge.

are Westphalia and Alfa-Laval. The vast majority of installed systems in the United States are Westphalia centrifuges. This company has several sizes of centrifuges which are generally designated by the initials SA or SB and a bowl diameter in centimeters, such as SB 80 or SA 160. Typical capacities for these units for juice and wines are presented in Table 7-4.

4. Decanting Centrifuges

Decanting centrifuges are a relatively recent (within the last 15 years) introduction to winemaking. They have been successfully applied to the clarification of juices prior to fermentation because their capacity (unlike that of the desludging machines) is essentially independent of the suspended solids content in the inlet stream.

The decanting centrifuge has a cylindrical shell with a long conical end which contains a similarly shaped large-pitch screw (or auger) (Figure 7-4). The separating force is generated by both of these rotating about a horizontal axis, in the same direction, at several hundred revolutions per minute, producing a radial force which is a few hundred times that of gravity. The feed stream is introduced through the hollow center of the screw and enters the middle of the cylindrical section. Both the liquid and the solids are spun to the wall with the solids lining the wall. The screw is rotating at a few revolutions per minute faster than the wall, and thereby produces a scraping action on the solids, conveying them into the liquid layer and are discharged continuously as a soft paste. The clarified liquid leaves continuously through ports in the other end. The control of the solids removal rate is performed by changing the differential rotational speed of the screw with respect to the outer wall. As a result, the liquid throughput is essentially independent of the level of solids in the feed and the capacity is only slightly affected by solids contents as high as 12 to 20% v/v. The liquid discharge stream may be further clarified since typical solids contents of this stream can be above that desired for white wine fermentations.

Table 7-4. Typical capacities for desludging centrifuges.

Juice (feed 3 to 10% v/v, discharge 0.8 to 2% v/v)	
SA 160	65,000
SA 80/SB 80	25,000
SA 60/SB 60	19,000
SA 45	14,000
Racked wine (feed 1% v/v, discharge 0.01% v/v)	
SA 160	115,000
SA 80/SB 80	45,000
SA 60/SB 60	31,000
SA 45	22,000
Clarified wine (feed 0.15 to 0.2 % v/v, discharge < 0.002%	
SA 160	55,000
SA 80/SB 80	22,000
SA 60/SB 60	15,000
SA 45	11,000

a. *Residence Times*

The liquid residence times in these units, that is the annular liquid volume divided by the volumetric flow rate, can be of the order of 10 to 15 seconds, much longer than for the desludging centrifuges.

b. *Manufacturers*

The major supplier of decanting centrifuges to the wine industry at present is Westphalia although Alfa-Laval, DDS, Dorr-Oliver, and Bird Machine Company have also tested units for juice and wine applications. The performance of some of the Westphalia decanters (feed 25% v/v, discharge 2 to 5% v/v) is given in Table 7-5.

D. WINE FILTRATION

Filtration as applied to winemaking is a very general operation which encompasses a wide range of conditions from the partial removal of large suspended solids (approximately 50 to 200 μm in diameter, grape pulp, bitartrate crystals, or some of the yeast) by various grades of diatomaceous earth or filter sheets to the complete retention of microbes (approximately 0.5- to 1.5-μm diameter) by perpendicular flow polymeric membranes. The terms

(a)

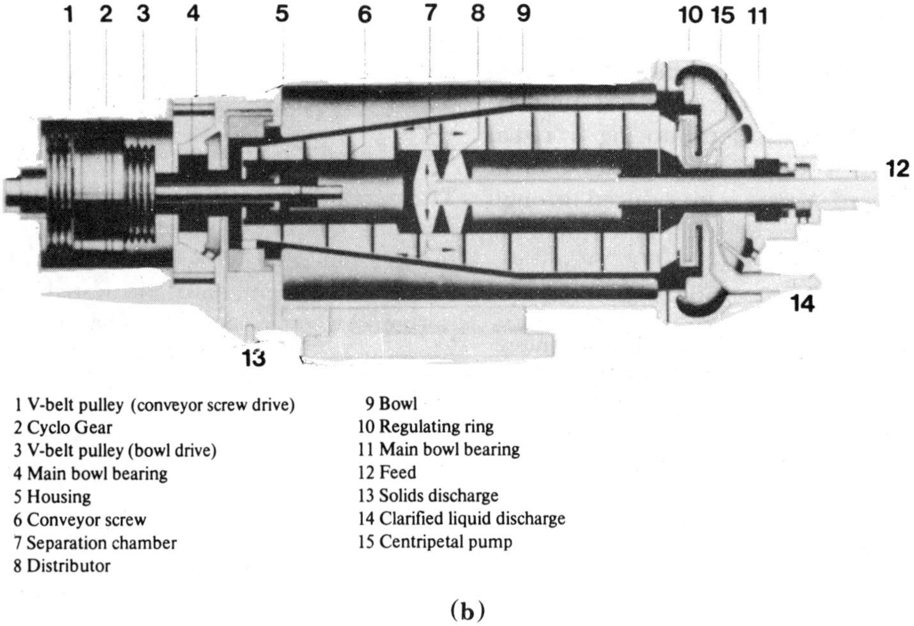

1 V-belt pulley (conveyor screw drive)
2 Cyclo Gear
3 V-belt pulley (bowl drive)
4 Main bowl bearing
5 Housing
6 Conveyor screw
7 Separation chamber
8 Distributor
9 Bowl
10 Regulating ring
11 Main bowl bearing
12 Feed
13 Solids discharge
14 Clarified liquid discharge
15 Centripetal pump

(b)

Fig. 7-4. A scroll centrifuge.

rough, *polish*, *tight*, or *sterile* will often be used to distinguish the openness (or the porosity) of the filter medium. This openness determines the minimum size of the solids that are collected from the juice or wine and it also affects the resistance to flow and therefore the throughput of a filter unit.

The following sections will deal with perpendicular flow arrangements which are in common use in the wine industry. With per-

Table 7-5. Performance of Westphalia decanters.

Model/type	Maximum capacity (L/hr)
CA 220	2000
CA 225	2800
CA 360	5000
CA 365	7000
CA 650	20,000
CA 655	25,000

pendicular flow there is ordinarily a point at which fine particles blind the filter and pressure increases while the flow rate falls. An objective of cross-flow is to sweep the surface clean of such blinding solids. It is easy to see why perpendicular filtration must be done in stages so that the coarser solids are removed first so that the finer filters are not overloaded. Section 4 of this chapter will address the application of cross-flow filters which range from the sterile filtration of juices and wines to the removal of solutes such as proteins (in ultrafiltration or UF) or the modification of composition such as ethanol removal (in reverse osmosis or RO).

Filters can be classified according to their porosity, the nature of the filter medium, the method of housing the filter medium or the arrangement of the fluid flow path. Examples would be rough versus sterile, pad versus diatomaceous earth, plate and frame versus pressure leaf, and perpendicular flow versus cross-flow. In this section, the emphasis will be on the nature of the equipment and its operation and therefore filters will be divided into plate and frame, pressure leaf, cartridge, and traditional membrane (meaning perpendicular flow, synthetic polymer membranes).

While the principal means of particle collections will be the size of the pores or flow channels through which the wine travels, there are secondary effects due to a charge-based collection mechanism due to the zeta potential. The zeta potential is caused by the unequal distribution of charges on the surface of certain particles and fibers when a fluid flows around them. During flow past such materials, a potential gradient develops between the boundary layers of the fluid and parts of the solids surface. Small, charged, solid, or colloidal particles will be attracted and usually captured as the fluid passes over the surface, and a more extensive clarification will be achieved than that due to the pore size alone.

In the past, the use of asbestos as a component in filter sheets provided this effect, but today a number of cellulose-based fibers which have similar properties are used in filter pads, cartridges, and precoat preparations. The important features of the zeta-potential mechanism are that it is finite, consumable, and flow-rate-dependent. This means that as the charged particles are collected, they progressively neutralize the potential; and if the flow rate falls or drops to zero, some of the captured material will be released into the surrounding fluid. This is especially true if the flow is stopped then restarted, and is most troublesome during filtrations that are upstream of a membrane filter or bottling line. This is also one of the reasons that recommended flow rates are given by manufacturers of pad filters.

The zeta-potential is also pH-dependent as shown in Figure 7-5, and thus the practice of rinsing pads with hot water provides the conditions under which the fibers release captured particles due to this mechanism. The potential is always positive under wine conditions and the attraction is greatest for anionic colloidal particles, such as some fractions of proteins and polysaccharides and their complexes. This action is not always desirable since physical stabilities associated with protective colloids and haze-protecting factors (Waters et al. 1993) may be disturbed by such filtrations. In contrast, the zeta potential of diatomaceous earth is always negative under wine conditions (Figure 7-5), and this is why it (and pads containing it) exhibit quite different interactions with such colloids.

1. Diatomaceous Earth Filters

Diatomaceous earth (or Kieselgur) (brand names eg. Celite, Diatomite, and Dicalite) is

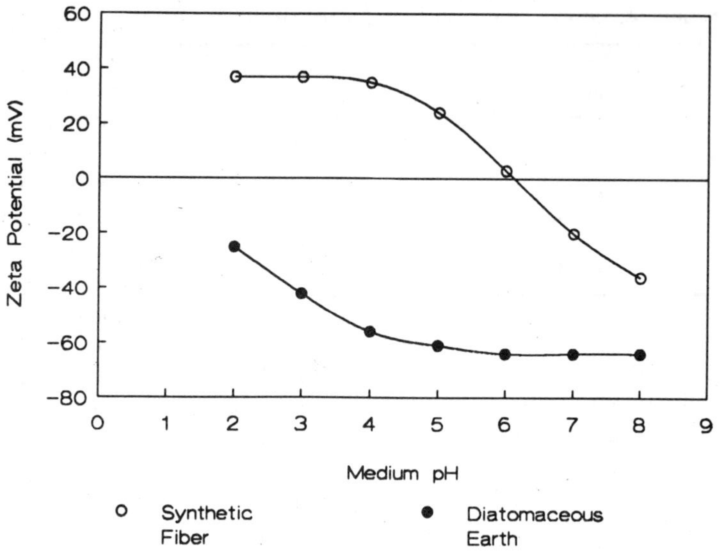

Fig. 7-5. The effect of pH on the zeta-potential of filter media.

used to provide structural support in a developing filter cake so that compressible solids do not form a tight film across the filter surface, thereby reducing the filtration rate eventually to zero. The continual addition of diatomaceous earth during the filtration, referred to as body feed, continues to build a porous cake as the filtration progresses. Even with the use of filter aids, most filters will eventually plug due to the collection of fine particles within the filter cake or their blinding of the supporting precoat, paper, or septum.

The quantity and the particle size of the filter aid should be related to the size and quantity of the solids being removed. The use of too fine of a grade of diatomaceous earth provides little additional clarity but rather more cake resistance and a lower flow rate. The commercial grades of diatomaceous earth used for wine filtrations have median particle sizes between 14.0 μm in Celite 500 and 36.2 μm in Celite 545. The first of these powders can be used in place of tight pads prior to a membrane filtration while the second would be a coarse filtration of juice or following fermentation. Further variations involve the acid calcining (pink) fine grades or the coarser alkaline (white) grades.

It is particle size distribution rather than the median size of the powder that has most to do with the capturing capability and flow resistance of the cake. The cumulative size distributions for the more commonly used grades of diatomaceous earth are shown in Figure 7-6. The appearance of several grades of filter aids is shown in Figure 7-7. The relationship between the median pore size and permeability of various grades of the Celite filter aids is shown in Figure 7-8.

At wine and juice pH values, diatomaceous earth has a relatively large negative surface charge (Figure 7-5). As a result, nitrogenous compounds such as ammonia and cationic amino acids and proteins might be expected to be partially adsorbed to the surface, and this has been shown experimentally (Tercelj 1965). Diatomaceous earth is a very weak adsorbent and these results were obtained in laboratory conditions with unusually high quantities of filter aid in proportion to wine. In practice, the precoat and cake will be quickly saturated by contact with the first volumes of wine through the filter. Once saturated, they are unable to contribute to further adsorption of wine components. The proportion of diatomaceous earth that a wine is con-

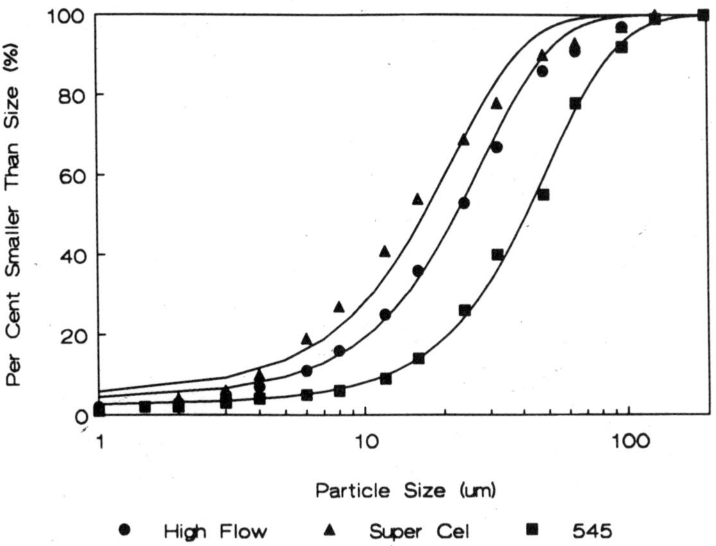

Fig. 7-6. The cumulative size distribution of three filter aids.

tacted with will be influenced by the solids loading and the number of filtrations performed. In order to eliminate any undesirable filter aid flavors, the filter is usually rinsed with an acidic solution and/or a small portion of the wine, which is then discarded.

a. *Pressure Leaf Filters*

Pressure leaf filters use a screen to provide the support of the diatomaceous earth cake during the filtration. The leaf is the supporting element which holds the screen and provides the path for the filtrate into the outlet manifold (Figure 7-9). The leaves are generally square in shape, although circular units are also made. The leaves are completely immersed and surrounded by the juice or wine that is being filtered. They can be placed vertically in upright cylinders, vertically in longitudinal cylinders, or horizontally in vertical cylinders. The difference is due to manufacturer's preference rather than superior filtration performance.

Pressure leaf filtration can be used from the rough filtration of tank settlings through to the prefiltration of wines for membrane filtration. This is achieved by the use of successively finer grades of diatomaceous earth and it is practiced by several large and medium-size wineries.

b. *Precoating*

The screens of a pressure leaf unit are usually precoated prior to the introduction of the juice or wine. This is done to provide clarity in the first filtrate, to protect the screen or septum, and to facilitate the removal of the spent cake. This is done by filtering a volume of slurry containing the 0.5 to 1.0 kg diatomaceous earth per square meter, to provide the desired thickness of precoat (typically 1 to 2 mm), on the screens. The concentration of the slurry should be at least 3 kg/L and up to 6 kg/L. The application flow rate should be controlled so as to provide a flux of 2500 to 5000 $L/m^2/h$. This will often result in a pressure drop across the filter of approximately 15 kPa.

The precoat grade is usually a finer grade than that to be used for the body feed during the filtration. The exception to this is for the use of coarse grades when the same grade is often used for precoat and body feed. The trend has been to use cellulose fiber preparations (Berg et al. 1986) in 0.5:1 proportions fiber to diatomaceous earth in the precoat

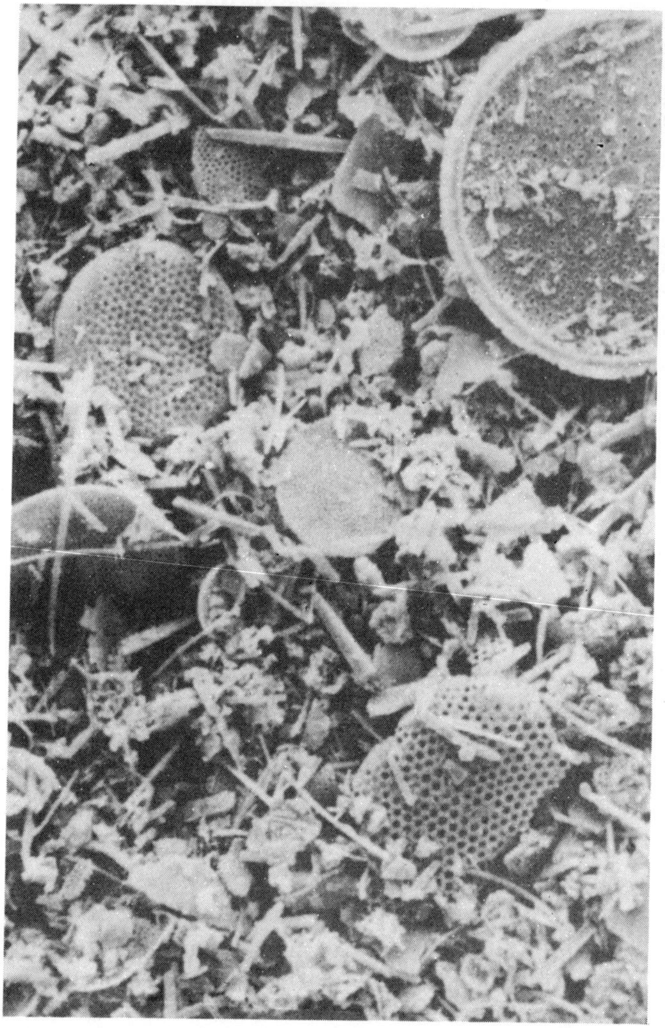

Fig. 7-7. Scanning electron micrographs of several grades of diatomaceous earth.

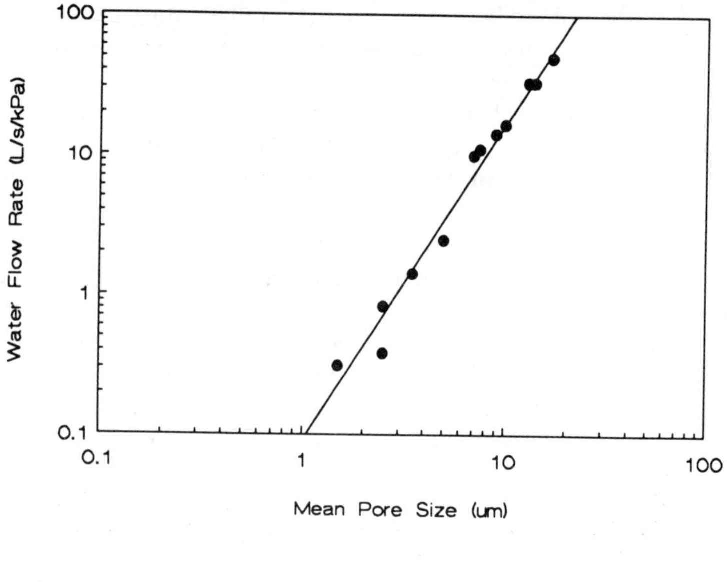

Fig. 7-8. The relationship between mean pore size and the flow rate of several filter aids.

Fig. 7-9. A pressure leaf filter.

mixture to provide a zeta-potential collection mechanism for very fine particles.

c. *Operation*

Once the precoat has been applied, the wine or juice can be introduced into the filter chamber. In order for the cake to remain permeable during the run, new diatomaceous earth, referred to as body feed, is introduced into the filter together with the wine. This is achieved by metering in proportions of the slurry from the slurry tank. The rate of addition of the slurry will be determined by the concentration of suspended solids in the feed stream. The loading rate can vary from 1:1 diatomaceous earth to solids, for crystalline solids to 5:1 or more for compressible solids. Since this may vary throughout the run, it will be necessary for an operator to monitor the progress of the filtration. When the cake has grown so large that it fills the space between the adjacent leaves, the resistance will increase rapidly and the run will have to be terminated. The wine will be drained from the filter housing and the screens cleaned before the precoat cycle begins again.

Some units are built so that the screens can be exposed for cleaning while other designs provide a shaking mechanism or water sprays to free the cake from the screens. Most designs provide a pan for the collection of the dislodged cake.

d. *Manufacturers*

The most common types of pressure leaf filters are those made by Velo, Padovan, Seitz, Schenk, Durco, and Gasquet. The units can vary from small, 2.0-m^2 area, units to larger units with several hundred times this area. Almost all of the units used in the U.S. industry are made of stainless steel for both the screens and the housing. The major producers of diatomaceous earth filter aids are Manville (Celite), Eagle-Picher (Celatom), and Great Lakes Carbon (Dicalite).

2. Pad Filters

A simpler approach to filtration that does not require the use of precoats and body feed is the application of preformed sheets or pads of cellulose and diatomaceous earth. These filtrations are considerably more expensive than pressure leaf filtrations, but the ease of use has made them widespread among small and medium-sized wineries. Many wineries will employ pressure leaf filtrations prior to bottling, but then prefer to have a final pad filtration in conjunction with membrane filtration and bottling.

a. *Sheet or Pad Filtrations*

Filter pads are designed to collect particles in their interior rather than to develop a cake at the surface. They are constructed of cellulose fibers with particles of diatomaceous earth trapped in between. They are usually classified by their capacity for water flow and most manufacturers offer pads with capacities ranging from 1200 $L/m^2/hr$ for nominally sterile filtrations to 240,000 $L/m^2/hr$ for coarse, clarifying filtrations. Although an equivalent (or average) pore size can be estimated from the water flow tests, it should be understood that, like the diatomaceous earth filter cakes, a range of pore sizes actually exists in the pad. Up until the mid 1970s, tight pads containing asbestos fibers were used to remove proteins and other colloids and microorganisms from wines due to the zeta-potential mechanism. This permitted fine negatively charged particles to be captured in the pad when they would normally pass right through, based on porosity considerations. At present a range of cellulose acetate and other polymeric fibers are used in what are referred to as charge-modified or zeta-enhanced filter pads.

b. *Plate-and-Frame Filters*

Plate-and-frame filters can be used in one of two general ways. The first and more common way is for filter pads (or sheets) to be used as the filtration medium, while the second is for a paper and a cake of diatomaceous earth to be the medium.

The name comes from the use of alternating support plates to retain the filter medium and to collect the filtrate interspaced with frames which distribute the incoming fluid across the filter medium. The units are set up with multiple plates and frames (Figure 7-10), and each plate (or frame) is fed by (or feeds) a common manifold which provides access ports to all other plates (or frames). Any one portion of the wine only passes through the filter once and capacity is increased by adding more plate-and-frame pairs.

The plates and frames are generally square in shape and hang from two supporting bars at each side of the filter stack. The liquid seal is made by the compression of the plates and frames between a capstan at one end and the end plate at the other. The number of plates (and frames) that are used determines the filter area and the number may be adjusted for the particular filtration run.

The degree of clarification is determined by the grade of the diatomaceous earth or pad which is used. For rough filtrations, fluxes of 2000 to 4000 $L/hr/m^2$ are typical, while with finer media this can fall to 800 to 2,000 $L/hr/m^2$ at pressure drops of 100 to 200 kPa.

c. *Flow Pattern*

The feed stream enters the end plate and is divided into two streams, an upper channel and a lower channel, which will feed all of the frames from one side. The frames are designed so that on one side the ports are open to allow the feed to enter, while on the other side, the ports allow fluid to pass from one neighboring plate to the other without entering the frame itself. The plates have a similar arrangement so that they can collect filtrate and direct it to the outlet ports (top and bottom) on the opposite side of the filter unit.

The feed stream moves from the end plate into the first frame from the top and bottom corner ports. The majority of the feed continues on along the channel made by the successive ports, passing through the port but not entering each of the plates. The feed will be able to enter each of the frames from this side.

Once in the frame, the flow direction will change, moving through the medium and into the receiving plate. The flow then changes as it is directed to the outlet ports of the plate. The filtrate then passes through the port of

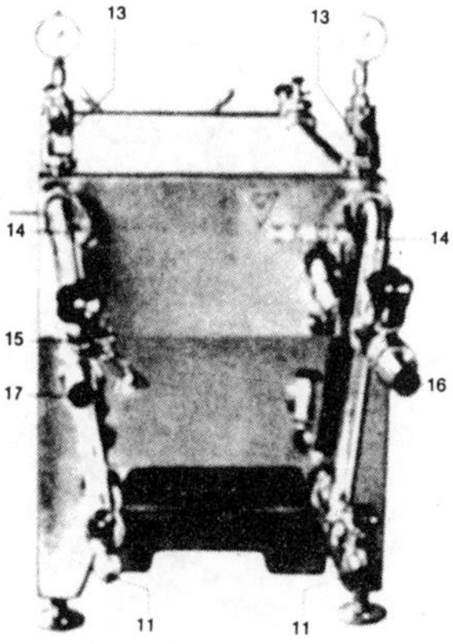

1 Stationary filter cover (fittings cover)
2 Filter plates
3 Movable filter cover
4 Vent valves
5 Vent valve (also steam connection)
6 Vent valve (also pressure gas connection)
7 Support rods
8 Filter crossover
9 Tightening spindle
10 Hand-wheel with two-stage planetary gears
11 Drain valves
12 Plastic collecting tray
13 Sight glasses with vent valve and glycerine filled pressure gauges
14 Feedpipes
15 Sampling valve
16 Infeed (filter inlet)
17 Discharge (filter outlet)

Fig. 7-10. A plate and frame filter.

each frame onto the next plate where it combines with the flow from that plate. At the end plate, the top and bottom filtrate streams are combined, leaving the filter as a single stream. The net effect is that each portion of the wine passes through one small part of the whole stack.

There are usually pressure gauges mounted on the front end plate to indicate the pressure of each stream so that the pressure drop across the filter (which indicates the resistance to flow) can be calculated.

d. Mode of Operation

The application with pads involves the setting up of the filter with only the plates, alternating them so that every second one is a distributing or feed plate while the other is a receiving or collection plate. The pads are placed so that the wavy, rippled surface will face the distributing plate (or incoming wine) and the mesh pattern side will be against the collecting plate. The air is displaced from the fluid manifold by use of the sampling valves, and the filtration continues until the pressure difference across the filter exceeds the recommended value or the filtration is completed.

When diatomaceous earth is used, a slurry of the earth is filtered to develop a thin precoat layer of the earth on the surface of each plate. The earth is retained by a filter paper or a plastic mesh which covers the plate, or a finer grade of filter pad. During the actual filtration a small flow of the diatomaceous earth slurry (referred to as the body feed) is fed to the filter along with the wine. A diatomaceous earth cake builds up on each plate surface, incorporating the suspended solids which are being collected into it. A more detailed description of the proportions of diatomaceous earth and flow conditions to be used for precoating and operation is given in Sections 1.b and 1.c above.

As the filtration progresses, the resistance builds up due to the accumulation of solids and the increase in cake thickness, and the flow will decline in a manner that depends on the type of pump which is being used. The run will be terminated when the frames become filled with the cake, when the flow falls to an unacceptable rate, when the inlet pressure rises to an unacceptable value, or the filtration is complete.

e. *Manufacturers*

The most common types of plate and frame filters in U.S. wineries are made by Seitz and Schenk. The main suppliers of pads and filter sheets to the wine industry are Scott (Seitz), Cellulo, and KLR (Beco).

Fig. 7-11. A typical membrane filter housing.

3. Cartridge and Membrane Filters

Traditional membrane filters are the perpendicular flow membranes used for the sterile filtration of wines just prior to bottling. The filter cartridges (Figure 7-11), are made of a synthetic polymer (such as polycarbonate, polysulfone, or polypropylene) with pore sizes of 0.45, 0.65, 0.80, or 1.2 μm. They are called membrane filters since they collect particles at surface pores rather than within the torturous path in the body of the pad filters. They have a closely controlled range of pore size, unlike diatomaceous earth and pad filters. The membranes are rated based on the size of the largest pore rather than the average or effective pore size that is determined from flow conditions.

The size of the largest pore is crucial for the complete removal of microorganisms by filtration and methods have been developed in which filter cartridges are tested to determine this value. The ability to release a bubble from a pore into a surrounding liquid is determined by the circumference of the pore, the surface tension of the fluid and the differential pressure between the gas behind the bubble and the fluid facing it. The pressure at which the bubble is released is referred to as the bubble point and for a fluid such as wine, it is related to the size of the largest pore. The bubble point testing involves filling the membrane housing with wine and applying regulated gas pressure to the inlet side. The pressure is gradually increased until the first bubbles appear in the outlet side. Nitrogen is the gas of choice and carbon dioxide is not used for reasons of its high solubility. The bubble point procedure and the related forward-flow test for membrane filters are used to ensure that the filter is intact and that the housings have been mounted correctly before each filtration. These tests are discussed in more detail in Chapter 11.

Filters of this type have a very limited holding capacity for solids and the majority of the solids load should have been removed by earlier clarification or prefilters. These filters are not used as filters in the usual sense, but rather as final collectors to ensure absolute removal of the few remaining cells and micron-sized particles which have passed through earlier filters.

a. *Types of Membrane Filters*

The most common arrangement is for the membrane to be made into a cartridge which is installed in a vertical cylindrical housing. The cartridges have a central steel tube with small holes to allow for the collection of the filtrate. The membrane material is then applied and a plastic mesh is placed over the membrane to keep it in place. The flow is from the body of the cartridge housing, radially inward through the membrane surface and down the central tube, discharging at the base. Housings which hold several cartridges are used for larger applications while single-cartridge units are common in small wineries. A common arrangement is the use of two parallel cartridges so that the first is used until exhausted and the flow is redirected to the second without the need to open the line and go through the subsequent sterilization.

The alternative arrangement is for membrane discs to be placed onto disc supports and stacked on top of each other. The stack is then covered by a short cylindrical housing. The flow pattern is from the body of the housing through channels in the circumference of the disc, down and out the bottom of the disc, through the membrane and into the upper section of the disc below, into the central collection port.

b. *Manufacturers*

The companies providing most of the membrane filters for wine applications are Millipore, Sartorius, and Pall. These companies also produce cartridge prefilter units with some depth collection capacity for use upstream of their membranes. The cartridges often have approximate pore sizes of 1.2 to 2.0 μm in diameter. Pore sizes of 0.65 μm are required for yeast removal and 0.45 μm for the removal of bacteria.

4. Cross-Flow Filters

This description of filtration has so far focused on the currently used, traditional, perpendicular flow filters. In this arrangement, all of the filtrate passed through the filter medium on the first pass and the suspended solids content played a major role in the fouling of the filter surface, or the filter cake even with the introduction of diatomaceous earth in order to maintain porous filter cakes as the run progressed.

Cross-flow filters, as the name implies, are set up so that most of the fluid passes rapidly across the filter surface with only a very small fraction of it permeating as the filtrate. In the general terminology of cross-flow filters, the filtrate is referred to as the *permeate* and the fraction which is not filtered is known as the *retentate*. The cross-flowing but unfiltered fluid is recycled and passes across the surface many times during the run. A typical cross-flow filtration system is shown in Figure 7-12. The use of a cross-flow arrangement greatly reduces the role of the suspended solids in slowing the filtration rate as they are continually being swept along and are not accumulating as a cake on the filter surface. The disadvantage with this type of arrangement is that the fluxes are orders of magnitude smaller than with conventional filters, requiring much larger surface areas and much longer filtration times

Fig. 7-12. A cross-flow microfilter installed in a California winery.

for larger batches. The application of cross-flow filters to juice clarification was briefly discussed in Chapter 3.

Microfiltration is generally defined to be filtrations that collect suspended particles in the microbial range 0.1- to 1-μm diameter. By comparison, ultrafiltration and reverse osmosis both involve the removal of solutes from the filtrate based on molecular volume. In this range it is more usual to talk in terms of molecular weight which is more easily measured than molecular size. The nominal cutoff value is an average of a range of weights that are rejected to various extents rather than a sharp cutoff as the names of the filters might indicate. In many systems, the accumulation of solutes will not plug the filter in the usual sense, but it usually reduces the filtrate flux due to concentration gradients near the membrane surface.

The application of cross-flow filters to winemaking will be considered according to the three distinct applications, microfiltration, ultrafiltration, and reverse osmosis.

a. *Microfiltration*

There are several alternative filter designs and materials of this type. The nominal pore size is in the range 0.2 to 0.8 μm and flux rates per unit of pressure difference are of the order of 30 to 50 $L/m^2/hr$ with wine at transmembrane pressures of 50 to 100 kPa.

Four potential applications are in the following areas of winemaking:

1. Sterile Juice—Production of sterile filtered juice in a single filtration step after a preliminary clarification by either a centrifuge or a rough diatomaceous earth filtration. This would enable juice to be stored near ambient temperatures, but without the energy consumption of evaporative concentration, and without the need for the high levels of sulfur dioxide required by the sulfiting process.

2. Recovery of Yeast and Bacteria—Selected yeasts and bacteria are not presently recovered because of the grape solids. If the juice was clarified by a microfilter first, it could be refiltered on the microfilter to recover the inoculum. This might be used for fermentation or as an industrial protein source. Fermentations could be accelerated by larger inocula since the resulting population would be recovered after the fermentation. Two of the major practical considerations of the malolactic fermentation in wines is the propagation of sufficient bacteria to make the desired inoculation and the encouragement of their growth in the wine. The efficient recovery of large bacterial cultures by cross-flow filtration may reduce the need for their growth in wine. This has been done successfully with cultures of lactic acid bacteria in a fermentation medium using a ceramic cross-flow microfilter (Taniguchi et al. 1987).
3. Recovery of Immobilized Enzymes—The use of more selective adsorbents and enzyme treatments, which currently would be unacceptable from a cost point of view, could be justified if these were used in a slurry/particulate form so as to enable their recovery, regeneration, and reuse by a cross-flow microfilter.
4. Microbe-Free Wine—Recovery of the yeast and bacteria as discussed above would simultaneously remove wild organisms and provide sterile wine for storage and aging. A final sterile filtration at bottling would still be needed due to the possibility of contamination during transfers, fining, and aging.

Studies on the application of microfilters in the clarification of juices and wines are numerous (Boulton 1976; Poirier et al. 1984; Gaillard and Berger 1984; Berger 1985; Romat et al. 1986; Cattaruzza et al. 1987; Ludemann 1987; Peri 1987; Peri et al. 1988; Serrano et al. 1988; Schmitt et al. 1989; Descout 1989; Gaillard 1989; Serrano 1992). These studies have shown that the performance is considerably more dependent on the collodial properties of wine and the filter medium being used than for diatomaceous earth and pad filtrations (Wucherpfennig et al. 1984; Castino and Delfini 1984; Cattaruzza et al. 1987; Belleville et al. 1991). The initial rapid decline in flux observed in almost all studies has led to a focus on the nature of the polysaccharide components involved in this. There have been several recent studies of the isolation and fractionation of wine polysaccharides (Brillouet et al. 1990; Zimmer et al. 1992), and their behavior during microfiltration (Brillouet et al. 1989; Wucherpfennig and Dietrich 1989; Belleville et al. 1991). There was a period when the polysaccharides were thought to have an effect on the sensory properties of wines but several studies have shown this to be insignificant in the microfiltration applications (Gaillard and Berger 1984; Will et al. 1991). The modification of the colloidal content is significant with the ultrafiltration applications and can have subsequent effects on physical stability (Brillouet et al. 1991) and there are demonstrated effects on the tartrate stability of wine (Escudier and Moutounet 1987; Escudier et al. 1987) as might be expected.

b. Types of Cross-Flow Filters

Cross-flow can be set up in several ways and various manufacturers have propriety arrangements. The filters can be classified into flat-plate, hollow-fiber or spiral-wound depending on the configuration. The filter medium can also vary from polypropylene and polysulfone polymers to porous stainless steel, ceramic, or zirconium composites. There are several makers of cross-flow filters and these include APV, Ceraflo, DDS, Dorr-Oliver, IMECA, Rhone-Poulenc, SFEC, Membrana, Memcor, Mott, Sartorius, Koch-Romicon, Seitz, and Schenk.

c. Ultrafiltration

One definition of ultrafiltration is the cross-flow separation of large-molecular-weight solutes rather than suspended particles. Ultrafilters are generally classified according to their molecular weight cutoff, or MWCO, that is the average size of the range of molecule that they will effectively retain and this would range between 1,000 and 100,000 daltons. The more common cutoff values for filters being used commercially for the removal of proteins from milk or apple juice are 10,000 and 40,000 daltons. The solutes in the 50,000 to 200,000 range are polysaccharides that have been produced by the grape and the yeast. Those in the 10,000 to 50,000 range are most of the protein fractions of white wines. The main commercial filtration applications with polymeric membranes are from companies such as Millipore, Romicon-Koch, Dorr-Oliver, Patterson Candy (PCI), Sartorius, and DDS. The aggregate composites are produced by Cereflo and SFEC.

I. Protein Stabilization. For wine use, a number of 10,000 MWCO membranes have been tried for the removal of proteins which have a molecular weight range of between 20,000 to 40,000 in an attempt to provide heat or protein stability in the wine. This application, which would be a processing alternative to the application and removal of bentonites, has received considerable research attention (Gaillard and Berger 1984; Poirier et al. 1984; Miller et al. 1985; Cattaruzza et al. 1987; Hsu et al. 1987; Flores et al. 1988) but it is not widely used commercially because of the undesirable removal of phenolic components which are retained by the 20,000 MWCO membranes for reasons other than size (Peri et al. 1988). The removal of haze precursors is not always successful since peptides (MW < 10,000), either alone or in complexes involving phenolics, are often involved in these instabilities (Yokotsuka and Singleton 1987).

There are various flow arrangements (hollow-fiber, spiral, and flat-plate) but most of the differences are due to the nature of the synthetic polymer membranes that are employed. The flux rates (that is the volumetric flow rate per unit area) with wines are of the order of 5 to 20 $L/m^2/hr$.

II. Tannin and Color Removal. Trials have been conducted using 500 to 2000 MWCO membranes for the removal of red pigments and/or astringent tannin from press fractions. The BATF currently considers this to be a significant alteration of the wine composition and it has not therefore been approved as a winemaking practice in the United States.

d. Reverse Osmosis

The most common application of reverse osmosis has been the filtration of inorganic salts from sea water. Since osmosis is the passage of water through a membrane into a salt (or organic solute) solution, the extraction of water from such solutions has led to the term *reverse osmosis*. The molecular exclusion applies to the neutral species, but the membranes have considerable rejection of small ions due to additional charge rejection effects. Pore sizes for this application are now of the order of 10 to 100 MWCO (or atomic/ionic weight), and flux rates are between 10 to 20 $L/m^2/hr$ at transmembrane pressures of 1 and 2 MPa.

The flux rate is dependent on the difference between the osmotic pressure difference across the membrane (the retentate is higher in osmotic pressure) and the fluid transmembrane pressure difference developed by the pump. For this reason once the retentate reaches an osmotic pressure comparable to that of the transmembrane pressure difference, the flux will fall to zero. For juices, this occurs at about 25 Brix for many systems, while for wines there is often precipitation of concentrated organic components before the zero flux condition is approached. The major companies involved with the reverse osmosis applications in beverages are Enka, Millipore, and Patterson Candy (PCI).

I. Low-Ethanol Wine Production. The use of reverse osmosis (RO) membranes with an MWCO of approximately 75 to 100 can provide a filtrate which contains primarily water (MW = 18), a small fraction of other organics (MW = 20 to 60), and ethanol (MW = 46). All other major constituents, amino acids, sugars and major organic acids, phenolics, etc., are essentially retained or rejected due to their charge. In the simplest process, water is added back to the retentate to produce a wine of lower alcohol content, but essentially the same in all other constituents. The filtrate is discarded as a dilute ethanol byproduct. There are several ways of operating such an application from a continuous multistage process to successive batch operations with a single stage and the semicontinuous feed and bleed approach (Light et al. 1986).

In the United States there are legal and reporting requirements pertaining to the change in alcohol content and this usually requires a license similar to that for production and disposal of wine spirits. This technology has been used commercially to produce low-alcohol beers (Niefind and Schmitz 1981; Light et al. 1986) and wines (Cuenat et al. 1989; Bourderioux and Vican 1989) for the past decade and has the advantage of being a selective, low-energy, low-temperature process without the energy consumption required by evaporation.

The alternative evaporative processes for the production of low-ethanol wine are vacuum stripping of volatiles in equipment such as a stripping column, the Centritherm unit, or the Spining Cone approach.

II. Acetic Acid Removal. A recently commercialized process for the removal of acetic acid from wine involves reverse osmosis to yield an acetic acid-rich-permeate which is treated by ion exchange to remove the acid. The acetic acid is mostly un-ionized in wine and passes through the membrane while most other inorganic ions and larger organic ions are retained due to charge exclusion. The treated permeate is then recombined with the retentate to produce the wine with little change other than in the acetic acid concentration.

III. Juice Concentration. Other applications of reverse osmosis that have been suggested are the production of juice (and wine) concentrates without the application of heat, but this is not very suitable for grape products due to the osmotic pressure of the starting material at 20 Brix (3.5 MPa) and a present practical upper limit of a final product that is only 25 Brix (4 MPa).

The limitations due to transmembrane pressure have been overcome in two ways. The first, developed by the Du Pont Corporation involves the application of two different membranes at high pressures to develop concentrates above 60 Brix in a two-stage concentration. The other uses a strong salt (or sugar) solution (of higher osmotic pressure) for the receiving fluid and this permits the water to be drawn from the juice as vapor through a membrane rather than forced from it. The membrane used in this application is made by Hoechst Celanese. The salt solution is then concentrated to remove the transferred water and to return to its initial condition. One application of this approach is the production of juice concentrates at strengths comparable to those produced by evaporative means (60 to 66 Brix) but without the temperature-time conditions associated with that process (Thompson 1991). This approach has been called *osmotic distillation* even though the term *distillation* is generally associated with an evaporative concentration process. The colloid content of juices (and wines) would be expected to provide considerable fouling and rapidly declining filtration rates on these membranes and pretreatment of the juice would be necessary. There is little published production data related to this application.

E. FILTRATION TESTING AND MODELING

The interest in testing and modeling juice and wine filtrations arises from the natural variation in colloidal content of most juice products and the role that this plays in the fouling of filters at the microfiltration level. One reason for adopting a routine testing procedure for wine filtrations would be the detection of filtration problems in advance, while another would be the prediction of actual filter performance prior to operation in order to estimate the time required or pressures developed for a particular wine and filtration setup.

There are several acceptable filter test systems available; however, the more important factor is usually the way in which the data are collected and interpreted. There are essentially three alternative approaches: the calculation of some kind of numerical fouling index, the estimation of the maximum volume that can be filtered, and the analysis of the nature of the fouling by determining the manner in which the resistance develops during the filtration.

If the purpose of the testing is simply to obtain relative values of filterability on the same filter medium, the first is applicable. It is of limited use in that the initial resistance of the filter is combined with that developed during the filtration and therefore cannot be used to compare different grades of filters. Examples of indices of this kind are those proposed by Ribéreau-Gayon and Peynaud (1961), the index of fouling (Geoffroy and Perin 1962; Laurenty 1972 in Descout et al (1976)), modifications of them (Descout et al. 1976), and the Millipore filterability index (Meglioli et al. 1983). The formulas used for these different indices are summarized in Table 7-6.

A more useful interpretation is to estimate the maximum volume that can pass through the filter V_{max} using the formulas developed by Raible and Bantleon (1968) and Esser (1972). These are based on the slope of transformed plots originally proposed by Hermans and Bredee (1936). The maximum volume is a better measure of filter capacity than the indices in that the initial resistance of the filter is separated from the slope determination. This approach has been used in a number of studies of the pad and membrane filterability of wines (Salgues et al. 1982; Gaillard 1984; Serrano et al. 1982, and Piracci 1988) in which the filtrate volume was determined at several times during the test. Unfortunately, the same result can be determined by simply setting up a test condition and simply noting the filtrate volume when the filter has plugged. It remains a relative value which provides little information about the rate at which the resistance develops and it seems to be more suitable for very clear beers and wines. The rate of fouling is usually the more significant factor in the performance of the full-scale filtration than the maximum volume that can be filtered.

The third approach attempts to determine the way in which the resistance of the filter is changing with respect to the volume that has been filtered rather than the time. It uses a rate basis for estimating the resistance rather than the more usual volume and time values of other approaches. It also uses models that take into account the initial resistance of the filter, excluding them from the estimated fouling constants. This approach was originally developed by Sperry for diatomaceous earth (or cake) filtrations (Purchas 1967) and has been extended to two general cases of nonlinear fouling that are more usual in the filtration of wines using pads and membranes (De La Garza and Boulton 1984). It can also be extended to describe the fouling and flux reduction in cross-flow filters as will be discussed

Table 7-6. Formulas of alternative filterability indices.

Author	Name	Formula[a]	Recommendation
Ribéreau-Gayon and Peynaud (1961)	Pouvoir de Colmatage	$PC = (T_{560} - T_{510}) - T_{50}$	
Geoffroy and Perin (1962)	Indice de Colmatage	$IC = T_{100} - 2 * T_{50}$	
Laurenty (in Descout et al. 1976)	Indice de Colmatage	$IC = T_{400} - 2 * T_{200}$	IC < 20
Descout et al. (1976)	Indice de Colmatage Modifie	$ICM = 2 * ([T_{400} - T_{300}] - [T_{300} - T_{200}])$	MIC < 10
Meglioli et al. (1983)	Millipore Filterability Index	$MFI = (T_{600} - T_{200}) - 2 * (T_{400} - T_{200})$	

[a]Where T_{50} is the time taken to filter the first 50 mL and T_{600} is that taken for the first 600 mL.

in a later section. This approach differs from those previously discussed in that it can be incorporated into fluid flow calculations for the full-scale filtration, taking into account the characteristics of the pump, features of the piping, and liquid levels in the feed and receiving tanks. It is presently the only modeling approach capable of doing this and, accordingly, will be described in more detail.

1. Early Filtration Descriptions

The earliest theoretical description of the rate of flow in granular beds was that developed by Darcy (Sperry 1917) in which the rate was related to the resistance developed by the bed:

$$dV/dt = \Delta P * A/R$$

where the dV/dt is the rate of filtration, ΔP is the pressure difference across the filter; A is the filter area; and R is the resistance of the bed. Sperry (1917) expanded this description for the collection of fine granular materials in filter cakes. He proposed that the resistance of the filter began with that of the bed alone and then it increased linearly with the quantity of material collected. The filtration rate would then fall inversely with the volume of filtrate and the nature of the material being collected by the filter. In contemporary terms Sperry's equation can be expressed as:

$$dV/dt = \Delta P * A/[R_m + \alpha * C * V/A]$$

where R_m is the medium resistance, due to the initial filter cake and its support; and α, the specific cake resistance, is a property of the material being collected in the cake. The values of R_m and $\alpha * C$ can be determined from a filtration test in which filtrate volume and time are recorded at several points along the way to plugging. The filter resistance can be estimated over successive intervals by dividing the product of the pressure difference, the filter area, and the time of the interval by the change in volume during the interval. A plot of the filter resistance R against the filtrate volume per unit area V/A, will yield a straight line with an intercept at $V = 0$ of R_m and a slope of $\alpha * C$.

Sperry's equation has been used to successfully describe the fouling of a wide range of diatomaceous earth filtrations. Studies with grape juices using various grades of filter material (Harris 1964) have been analyzed using this approach (Boulton 1980) and one example is presented in Figures 7-13a and 7-13b. This description is also suitable for the interpretation and prediction of wine filtrations through diatomaceous earth filters.

2. Pad and Membrane Filtrations

The filtration of wines with a pad or membranes will generally display a nonlinear resistance curve and cannot be described by Sperry's equation. This is because the collection of material cannot be described by the granular bed analogy in the absence of a filter aid. The filter fouling then displays an accelerating resistance characteristic which can be described by either one or both of the following equations.

The first, referred to as the Exponential model (De La Garza 1982), considers the resistance of the filter to increase in an exponential manner with the volume filtered:

$$dV/dt = \Delta P * A/[R_m * \exp(b \cdot V/A)]$$

with

$$R = R_m * \exp(b * V/A)$$

where b is now a fouling coefficient related to the filter type and the materials being collected from the wine under consideration.

The constants R_m and b can be evaluated by calculating the resistance over each interval as described above and plotting the logarithm of the resistance against the volume per unit area, V/A. The intercept will then be log (R_m) and the slope of the semilog graph, the constant, b. Alternatively, a nonlinear regression program can be used to evaluate these constants in a nontransformed manner. The fil-

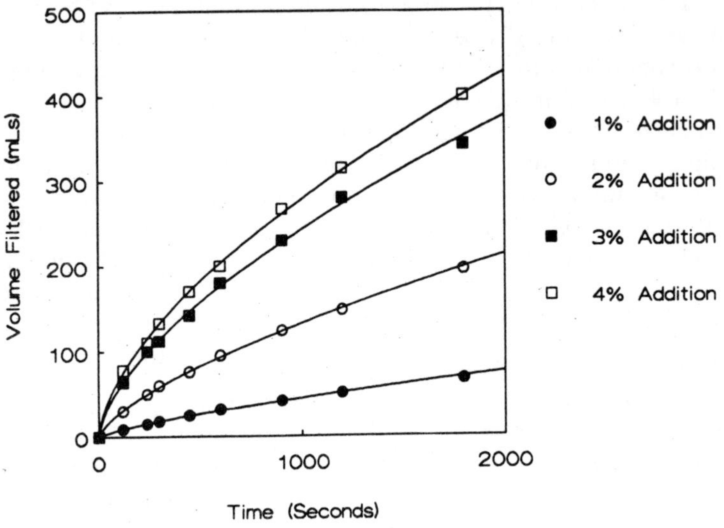

(a)

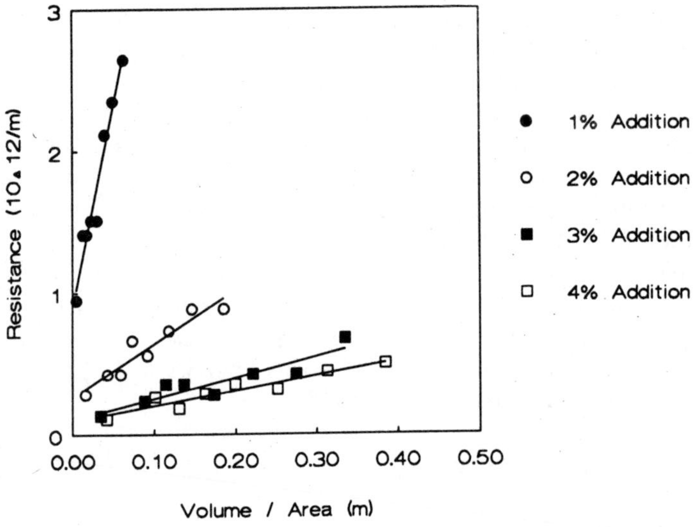

(b)

Fig. 7-13. The effect of dosing rate on the filterability of a grape juice.

tration of a 1981 Sauvignon blanc wine using a Seitz 200 pad filter is shown in Figure 7-14.

The second description, referred to as the Power model, considers the resistance to accumulate in an additive manner like Sperry's equation except that higher-order fouling relationships are permitted:

$$dV/dt = \Delta P * A/\left[R_m + a(V/A)^b\right]$$

with

$$R = R_m + a(V/A)^b$$

where the constants R_m, a and b are estimated from a log-log plot of the term $(R - R_m)$ against the volume per unit area, V/A. The constant R_m, is estimated successively until the best straight line is obtained and the resulting intercept is then log (a) and the slope is the constant b. An example of the Power model to

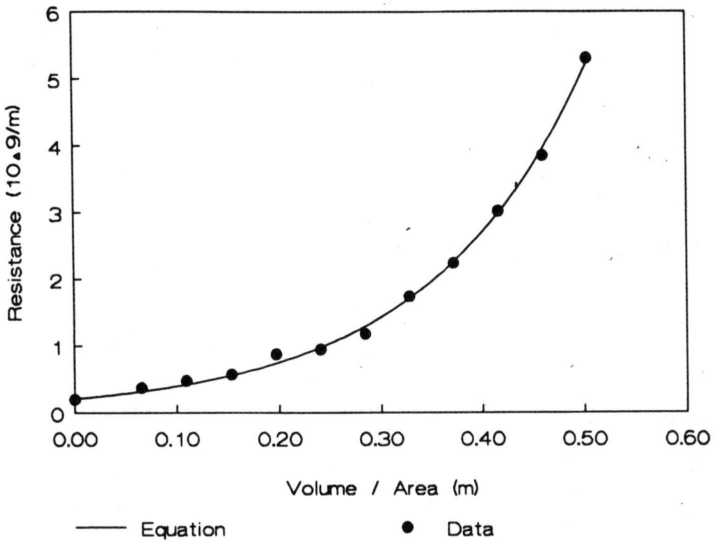

Fig. 7-14. The development of resistance during a wine filtration and its description by the exponential model.

the filtration of the same wine and filter as shown in Figure 7-14, is shown in Figure 7-15.

The Power form is a general description in which no prior assumptions are made as to the kind of fouling law that exists. It can be shown to be the general form of many earlier blocking laws such as the cake, intermediate, standard, and absolute types of Hermans and Bredee (1936) when the index *b* has the values 1, 2, 2.5, and 3. It is also more generally applicable than the different forms used for data plots that are based on these laws (Raible and Bantleon 1968; Esser 1972; Dubourdieu et al. 1976; Eyben and Duthoy 1979; Salgues et al. 1982; Serrano et al. 1982; Piracci 1988). The suitability of these descriptions to the quantitative description of many wine and pad combinations has been presented (De La Garza and Boulton 1984). These have also been applied to the interpretation of apple (Bayindirli et al. 1989) and other juice filtrations and are generally applicable to filtration systems that

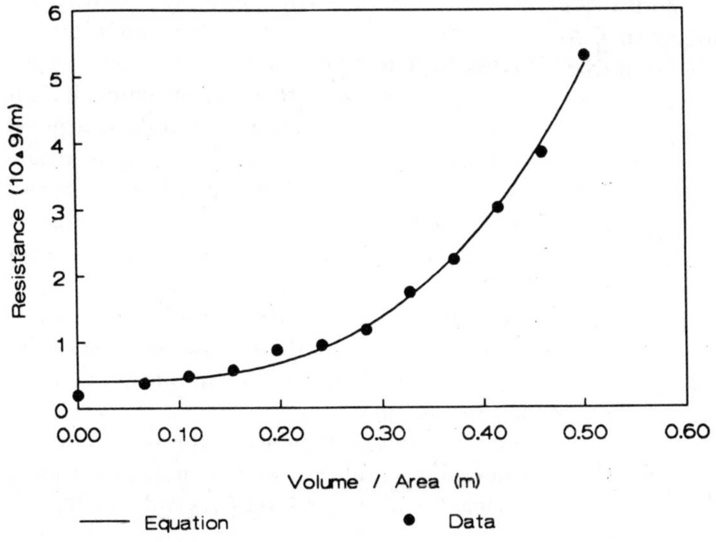

Fig. 7-15. The development of resistance during a wine filtration and its description by the power model.

show the nonlinear fouling characteristics associated with the collection of compressible or gelatinous materials such as fruit pulp, yeast, bacteria, and colloidal components.

Computer programs have been written that perform these calculations (De La Garza 1982) and these have been incorporated into the filter testing procedure of a number of wineries in California.

3. Cross-Flow Filtrations

It is usual in studies of cross-flow filtration to plot the flux rate rather than the filtrate volume, against the filtration time. Examples of such measurements with wines show the rapid initial decline in the flux rate, followed by a very slow fall in rate as the filtration continues (Boulton 1976; Gaillard and Berger 1984; Ludemann 1987). The filtration then continues for quite some time with little, if any, further fouling. This in contrast to the continual and often accelerated fouling of perpendicular flow filters.

The description of the flux rates associated with cross-flow filtrations can also be described by an extension of the model presented above. The major difference is that under cross-flow conditions there is more dramatic initial reduction in the filtration rate, followed by a stage in which progressive fouling of the filter takes place at a much slower rate than it does with the perpendicular flow arrangements. A concentration gradient of suspended material at the filter surface is established during the initial stage and maintained throughout the filtration, providing an essentially constant resistance to the wine or juice as it passes through the filter surface. The gradually increasing concentration of suspended matter as the filtrate volume increases can be described by a volume per unit area term but with a weaker dependency than those of the above cases. The description for the cross-flow filtration situation is then:

$$1/A * dV/dt = \Delta P/R$$

with

$$R = R_m + d*[1 - \exp(-e*V/A)] *[V_o/(V_o - V)]$$

where d and e are the characteristics of the resistance due to the boundary layer; and V_o is the initial volume to be filtered. The actual resistance of this layer develops exponentially with the volume filtered and it also increases due to the progressive concentration of the suspended particles as the filtration progresses.

In this approach, the magnitude of the additional resistance developed under cross-flow operation is estimated from a filter test of the wine and filter combination. The application of this form of the filter model to the data for microfiltration of wine (Ludemann 1987) is shown in Figure 7-16. A more theoretical approach to the estimation of this resistance has been developed (Bennasar and Tarodo de la Fuente 1987) but this requires a number of membrane-specific properties to be known. It is usually more convenient to estimate the characteristic constants from the actual filtration performance in the manner described previously.

4. Filter Testing

Perhaps the most poorly quantified aspect of wine processing is the ability to predict the interaction of a wine with a given filtration medium. There are at least two reasons for wanting to predict this performance in advance of the actual filtration and these are: (1) To decide whether the filtration is appropriate (does it foul too rapidly, or is it even necessary); and (2) to predict the full-scale filtration rates so that the time required to filter a given volume can be estimated.

In order to answer either of these questions it is necessary to conduct a filtration test of the wine with the filter medium in question and to be able to interpret the results. There is far too much variation between the filterability of wines to generalize about their performance, especially with regard to filters with small pore

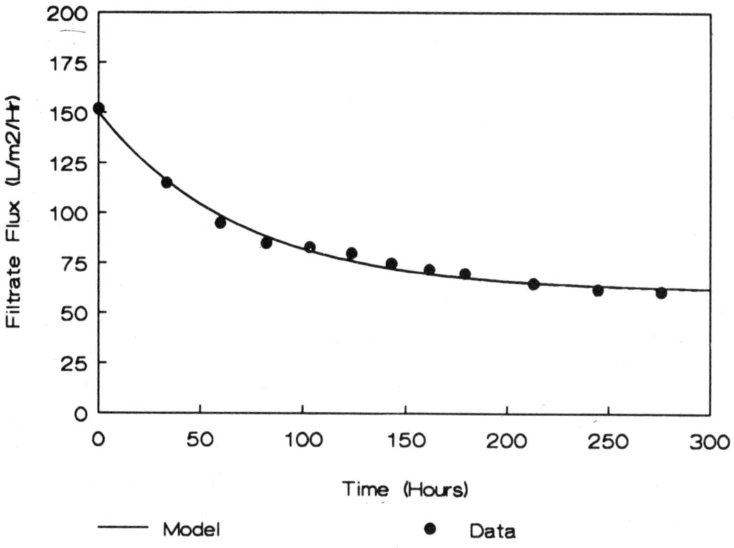

Fig. 7-16. The decay in filter flux during a wine filtration and its description by the crossflow model.

sizes and when the filtration medium is more valuable.

These laboratory tests can be classified into two general groups; one in which overall capacity information is sought and the other in which the rate of fouling is measured with a view to modeling of the fouling for full-scale prediction.

a. *Filter Performance Criteria*

The simplest form of the overall performance test typically attempts to find whether the volume filtered up to the plugging point exceeds a predetermined value of overall capacity (volume per unit area). The next level is to include a time factor to find if this volume can be filtered within a certain time (or the inverse test of how long it takes for a given volume to be filtered). There are several fouling indices which have been proposed (Table 7-6) that use the times to obtain successive filtration fractions.

While both of these tests can be used to generate a numerical scale that can be used to compare wines for the same filter test conditions, they have little application to the full-scale filtrations. The maximum volume estimates (Table 7-7) are of limited use since complete plugging is rarely sought during production conditions. They are also not unique since an infinite number of alternative fouling rates can lead to the same final volume, even if at different times.

b. *Filtration Rate Tests*

Filtration tests can be conducted under either constant pressure or constant flow conditions and several testing units are commercially

Table 7-7. Formulas of alternative filterability measures.

Author	Name	Formula[a]	Comment
Raible and Bantleon (1968)	Filter factor	$FF = (T_2 - V_2/V_1T_1)/(V_2^2[1 - V_1/V_2])$	Derived for Earth Filtrations
	Precoat factor	$PF = (2T_1[V_2/V_1] - T_2)/(V_2[V_2/V_1 - 1])$	Sometimes negative
Esser (1972)	Maximum volume	$V_{max} = (T_2 - T_1)/(T_2/V_2 - T_1/V_1)$	Uses $T_2 = 5$ and $T_1 = 2$ minutes

[a]Where V_1 and V_2 are the filtrate volumes after times T_1 and T_2.

available which are suitable for diatomaceous earth, pad, or membrane filtrations. An example of simple filter test setup is provided by De La Garza and Boulton (1984).

The usual procedure is a constant pressure test in which the volume filtered is measured at several points in time. The volume to be filtered should be such that when divided by the area of the test filter being used, it has the same (or larger) volume to area ratio that is expected in the full-scale filtration. The readings should be closely spaced to provide good estimates of the changing rate and the measurements should continue until the time taken for a volume increment has increased to three or four times that for the first such increment. This means that the filtration rate has fallen to one-third or one-quarter of the initial rate, and the filter resistance has increased to three or four times its initial value. The cleaner the wine, the larger the volume needed for this to occur. If there is little change in the time taken for similar volume increments, the entire test volume should be filtered.

An alternative method is the constant flow rate test which uses a positive displacement pump to control the flow rate and the pressure drop across the filter is measured. The flow rate should be set to approximately that expected in the full-scale filter. The test is halted when the pressure difference exceeds that recommended by the manufacturer and the time or filtrate volume is noted. This provides a more realistic measure of the volume per unit area to be expected at the full-scale filtration. If the pressure at several points throughout the test is noted, the filtration models described previously can be used to develop model constants for the wine and filter combination. This method is not widely used, presumably due to the cost and availability of the test systems.

c. *Test Conditions*

The validity of the test will depend on the extent to which the test conditions approximate those of the full-scale filtration. The wine used in the test should be in the condition that it will be in when it sees the corresponding full-scale filter. This may be prefiltered, fined, or chilled depending on the handling of the wine in question. The test temperature is especially important for small pore earth, pad or membrane filters where the solubility of colloidal matter such as protein-phenol complexes and polysaccharides is quite temperature dependent. At lower temperatures such as 0°C to 5°C, the colloidal materials are far less soluble and they become an important factor in the fouling mechanism and rate, (De La Garza and Boulton 1984). The similarity of flow rate conditions is especially important when a charge-modified filter medium is being used since the flow rate will determine the role that the zeta-potential contribution will play in the collection mechanism and the fouling rate. The tests will generally be performed under pressure rather than by vacuum since there can be significant bubble formation within the filter medium, leading to modified flow and resistance conditions.

5. Full-Scale Prediction

While one application of the above development is to characterize the filter performance of wine on a relative basis, its real value is in its application to the prediction and control of full-scale juice and wine filtrations.

The shortcoming of almost all other filtration test procedures is that they generally attempt to predict filterability by ignoring the interaction that exists between the filter, the pump, and the other components of the filtration setup. The heights of the wine surfaces in the tanks being used and the length and diameter of the transfer lines, as well as the type of fittings in the lines, can and usually do have a significant influence on the actual resistances that the pump experiences in addition to that of the filter.

The filtration equations developed above are descriptions of the fluid resistance that a filter develops due to the passage of wine through it at some particular rate. The resistance associated with the passage of wine through the transfer line can be calculated from a knowledge of the flow configuration and friction relationships.

The relationship between the flow rate generated by a pump and the pressure difference across the pump is referred to as the pump characteristic and is usually available from the pump supplier or it can be determined experimentally. These expressions can be incorporated into a general relationship that defines the flow rate that will result from the use of any particular pump. Such relationships have been programmed and solved using a computer, and the logical extension of any filter testing is then the rapid prediction of the full-scale filtration performance of a particular wine in a given setup before the filtration takes place. This approach has direct benefits in the advanced detection of problem filtrations and the avoidance of inappropriate setup or pump arrangements.

The way in which a pump, filter, and components of the transfer line interact are considered in more detail in Chapter 13.

F. REFERENCES

BACH, H. P., and P. HOFFMAN. 1978. "Der einfluss unterschiedlicher mostbehandlung auf geshmack und zusammensetzung der weine." *Weinwirt.* 41:1259–1265.

BAUER, H., M. HORISBERGER, D. A. BUSH, and E. SIGARLAKI. 1972. "Mannan as a major component of the bud scars of *Saccharomyces cerevisiae*." *Arch. Mikrobiol.* 85:202–208.

BAYINDIRLI, L., M. OEZILGEN, and S. UNGAN. 1989. "Modeling of apple juice filtrations." *J. Food Sci.* 54:1003–1006.

BELLEVILLE, M.-P., J.-M. BRILLOUET, B. TARODO DE LA FUENTE, L. SAULNIER, and M. MOUTOUNET. 1991. "Differential roles of red wine colloids in the fouling of a cross-flow microfiltration alumina membrane." *Vitic. Enol. Sci.* 46:100–107.

BENNASAR, M., and B. TARODO DE LA FUENTE. 1987. "Model of the fouling mechanism and of the working of a mineral membrane in tangential filtration." *Sci. Aliments* 7:647–655.

BERG, L. A., G. GODWIN-AUSTIN, and K. ROBISON. 1986. "Effect of fibers added during pressure leaf filtration on the membrane filterability of white table wines." *Am. J. Enol. Vitic.* 37:174–178.

BERGER, J. L. 1985. "Etude de la microfiltration tangentielle sur des Beaujolais." *Rev. des Oenol.* 36:17–21.

BLADE, H. W., and R. B. BOULTON. 1988. "Adsorption of protein by bentonite in a model wine solution." *Am. J. Enol. Vitic.* 39:193–199.

BOBET, R. A., A. C. NOBLE, and R. B. BOULTON. 1990. "Kinetics of the ethanethiol and diethyl disulfide interconversion in wine-like solutions." *J. Agric. Food Chem.* 38:449–452.

BOULTON, R. 1976. "Crossflow filtration of Juices and Wines." Unpublished Data.

BOULTON, R. 1980. "The quantitative evaluation of juice and wine filtrations." *Proc. U.C. Davis Grape and Wine Cent. Symp.* 16–19.

BOURDERIOUX, M., and C. VICAN. 1989. "La preparation de boissons a faible degre alcoolique a partir du vin par osmose inverse." *Rev. des Oenol.* 51:31–32.

BRILLOUET, J.-M., C. BOSSO, and M. MOUTOUNET. 1990. "Isolation, purification and characterization of an arabinogalactan from a red wine." *Am. J. Enol. Vitic.* 41:29–36.

BRILLOUET, J.-M., M. MOUTOUNET, and J. L. ESCUDIER. 1989. "Fate of yeast and grape pectic polysaccharides of a young red wine in the cross-flow microfiltration process." *Vitis* 28:49–63.

BRILLOUET, J.-M., M.-P. MOUTOUNET, and M. MOUTOUNET. 1991. "Possible protein-polysaccharide complexes in red wines." *Am. J. Enol. Vitic.* 42:150–152.

CAPUTI, A. JR., and R. G. PETERSON. 1965. "The browning problem in wines." *Am. J. Enol. Vitic.* 16:9–13.

CASTINO, M. and C. DELFINI. 1984. "La filtrabilita dei vini in funzione del tenore in colloidi." *Vini d'Italia* 26:45–56.

CATTARUZZA, A., C. PERI, and M. ROSSI. 1987. "Ultrafiltration and deep-bed filtration of a red wine: Comparative experiments." *Am. J. Enol. Vitic.* 38:139–142.

CHIBATA, I., T. TOSA, T. MORI, T. WATANABE, and N. SAKATA. 1986. "Immobilized Tannin." *Enz. Microbiol. Technol.* 8:130–136.

CHIBATA, I., T. TOSA, T. MORI, T. WATANABE, K. YOMASHITA, and N. SAKATA. 1982. "Applications of immobilized tannin for protein and metal absorption." In *Enzyme Engineering VI*, I. Chibata et al. Eds. New York: Plenum Press.

CUENAT, P., D. KOBEL, and E. ZUFFEREY. 1989. "L'osmose inverse et l'oenologie." *Bull. O.I.V.* 62:519–537.

DEAN, J. A. 1987. *Handbook of Organic Chemistry*. New York, NY: McGraw Hill.

DE LA GARZA, F. 1982. "The modeling of wine filtrations." MS thesis, Davis, CA: University of California.

DE LA GARZA, F., and R. BOULTON. 1984. "The modeling of wine filtrations." *Am. J. Enol. Vitic.* 35:189–195.

DESCOUT, J. J. 1989. "Utilisation des metaux frittes dans la filtration des vins." *Rev. d'Oenol.* 51:11–17.

DESCOUT, J. J., J. L. BORDIER, J. LAURENTY, and G. GUIMBERTEAU. 1976. "Contribution a l'etude des phenomenes de colmatage lors de la filtration des vins sur filtre ecran." *Conn. Vigne Vin* 10:93–123.

DUBOURDIEU, D., A. LEFEBRE, and P. RIBÉREAU-GAYON. 1976. "Influence d'un traitement physique d'iltradispersion sur la filtraton des vines." *Conn. Vigne Vin.* 10:73–92

ESCUDIER, J. L., and M. MOUTOUNET. 1987. "Filtration tangentielle et stabilisation tartrique des vins. 2. Apport de la microfiltration tangentielle dans la stabilisation tartrique d'un vin rouge." *Rev. Fr. Oenol.* 109:44–50.

ESCUDIER, J. L., M. MOUTOUNET, and P. BENARD. 1987. "Filtration tangentielle et stabilisation tartrique des vins. 1. Influence de l'ultrafiltration sur la cinetique de cristallisation du bitartrate de potassium des vins." *Rev. Fr. Oenol.* 108:52–57.

ESSER, K. D. 1972. "Zur Messung der Filtrierbarkeit." *Monats. Brauer.* 25:145–151.

EYBEN, D., and J. P. DUTHOY. 1979. "The filterability of wort and beer." *Mast. Brew. Assoc. Amer. Tech. Quart.* 16:135–141.

FEUILLAT, M. 1987. "Stabilisation et clarification des vins: Aspects colloidaux." *Rev. d'Oenol.* 45:7–17.

FEUILLAT, M., C. CHARPENTIER, G. PICCA, and P. BERNARD. 1988. "Production des colloides par levures dans le vin mousseux elabore selon la methode champenoise." *Rev. Fr. Oenol.* 111:36–45.

FLORES, J. H., D. A. HEATHERBELL, J. C. HSU, and B. T. WATSON. 1988. "Ultrafiltration of White Riesling juice: Effect of oxidation and pre-UF juice treatment on flux, composition and stability." *Am. J. Enol. Vitic.* 39:180–187.

FULLER, W. L., and H. W. BERG. 1965. "Treatment of white wine with nylon 66." *Am. J. Enol. Vitic.* 16:212–218.

FUSSNEGGER, B., R. MAURER, and J. DETERING. 1992. "Unlosliche, komplexbildende polymere als potentielle substitutionsprodukte fur kaliumhexacyanoferrat(II) zur schwermetallverminderung in wein." *Die Weinwissen*. 47:8–23.

GAILLARD, M. 1984. "La filtration finale des vins sur membranes." *Vignes Vin* 326:22–41.

GAILLARD, M. 1989. "Essais de microfiltration tangentielle de vins avec le filtre Memcor." *Rev. des Oenol.* 51:65–68.

GAILLARD, M., and J. L. BERGER. 1984. "Ultrafiltration et microfiltration tangentielle. Resultats d'essais sur mout et vin." *Rev. Fr. d'Oenol.* 95:39–62.

GEOFFROY, P., and J. PERIN. 1962. "La filtration." *Vigneron Champenois* 83:33–39.

HARRIS, M. B. 1964. "Grape juice clarification by filtration." *Am. J. Enol. Vitic.* 15:54–62.

HAUROWITZ, F. 1963. *The Chemistry and Function of Proteins*, 2nd ed. New York: Academic Press.

HERMANS, P. H., and H. L. BREDEE. 1936. "Principles of the mathematical treatment of constant-pressure filtration." *J. Soc. Chem. Ind.* 55:1–4.

HSU, J. C., D. A. HEATHERBELL, J. H. FLORES, and B. T. WATSON. 1987. "Heat unstable proteins in grape juice and wine: 2. Characterization and removal by ultrafiltration." *Am. J. Enol. Vitic.* 38:17–22.

JAKOB, L. 1965. "Bedeutung und verhaltensweise der sogenannten natrium- und calcium-Bentonite in der kellerwirtschaft." *Weinblatt.* 59:613–619.

JAKOB, L. 1968. "Eiweissgehalt und Bentonitschonung von Wein." *Wein-Wissen.* 23:255–274.

JENNESS, R. 1970. "Protein composition of milk." In, *Milk Proteins—Chemistry and Molecular Biology*. H. A. McKenzie, Ed. New York: Academic Press.

KERN, K. K., and K. WUCHERPFENNIG. 1991. "Entfernung von Eisen, Kupfer und Zink aus Weinen mit Einenchelatharz— einen Alternative zur Blauschonung." *Die Weinwissen*. 46:69–77.

KERN, K. K., K. WUCHERPFENNIG, H. DIETRICH, and O. SCHMIDT. 1992. "Chelatbildner zur Schwermallentfernung." *Weinwirt.-Technik* 5:45–50.

LAY, H., and W. LEIB. 1988. "Uber das Vorkommen der Metalle Zink, Cadmium, Blei und Kupfer in Most, Wein und in den bei der weinbereitung anfallenden nebenproduckten." *Wein-Wissen* 43:107–115.

LAY, H., and E. LEMPERLE. 1981. "Kupfergehalt auf Weintrauben, in Traubenmost und in Wein nach anwendung Kupferhaltiger Peronospora-fungizide." *Weinwirt.* 117:908–912.

LEMPERLE, E. 1989. "Wirkstoffruckstande nach Fungizidanwendung." *Weinwirt.-Technik* 125 (3):14–26.

LIGHT, W. G., L. A. MOONEY, H. C. CHU, and S. K. WOOD. 1986. "Alcohol removal from beer by reverse osmosis." *Am. Inst. Chem. Engrs. Symp. Series,* Vol 82, (250):1–8.

LLAUBÈRES, R. M. 1990. "Structure of an extracellular β D-glucan from *Pediococcus* sp., a wine lactic bacteria." *Carbohydr. Res.* 203:103–107.

LLAUBÈRES, R. M., D. DUBOURDIEU, and J.-C. VILLETTAZ. 1987. "Exocellular polysaccharide from *Saccharomyces* in wine." *J. Sci. Food Agric.* 41:277–286.

LOUBSER, G. L., and R. D. SANDERSON. 1986. "The removal of copper and iron from wine using a chelating resin." *S. Afric. J. Enol. Vitic.* 7:47–51.

LUDEMANN, A. 1987. "Wine clarification with a crossflow microfiltration system." *Am. J. Enol. Vitic.* 38:228–235.

MEGLIOLI, G., A. BATTEZZATI, and C. MARCHESINI. 1983. "L'indice di filtrabilita: Principi teorici ed applicazioni." *Ind. Bevande* 12:445–450.

MENNETT, R. H., and T. O. M. NAKAYAMA. 1970a. "The adsorption of hydroxybenzoic acids by poly-N-vinyl pyrrolidone." *Am. J. Enol. Vitic.* 21:169–175.

MENNETT, R. H., and T. O. M. NAKAYAMA. 1970b. "Temperature dependency of tannin adsorption by poly-N-vinyl pyrrolidone." *Am. J. Enol. Vitic.* 21:162–167.

MILLER, G. C., J. M. AMON, R. L. GIBSON, and R. F. SIMPSON. 1985. "Loss of wine aroma attributable to protein stabilization with bentonite or ultra filtration." *Aust. Grapegrower & Winemaker* (4):46–50.

MOBIUS, C. H., and S. GÖRTGES. 1976. "Bentonit zur most- und weinbehandlung." Pts 1–3. *Deu. Weinbau* 27:1081–1082, 28:1103–1105, 29:1136–1139.

MORRIS, T. M. 1984. "Particle size analysis of beer solids using a Coulter Counter." *J. Inst. Brew.* 90:162–166.

NIEFIND, H. J., and F.J. SCHMITZ. 1981. "New process for alcohol reduction of beer through dialysis". *Euro. Brew. Conv. Proc.* 18th Congr. Copenhagen. 599–606.

OECHSLE, D., and T. SCHNEIDER. 1992. "Gerbstoffe entfernen mit PVPP." *Weinwirt. Technik* 5:54–58.

OH, H., and J. E. HOFF. 1987. "pH dependence of complex formation between condensed tannins and proteins." *J. Food Sci.* 52:1267–1269.

OH, H., J. E. HOFF, and L. A. HAFF. 1985. "Immobilized condensed tannins and their interaction with proteins." *J. Food Sci.* 50:1652–1654.

OUGH, C. S., and M. A. AMERINE. 1988. *Methods for Analysis of Musts and Wines.* 2nd ed. New York: John Wiley & Sons.

OUGH, C. S., E. A. CROWELL, and J. BENZ. 1982. "Metal content of California wines." *J. Food Sci.* 47:825–828.

PARENT, Y. O., and W. A. WELSH. 1986. "Davison protein removal system development." *Practical Winery* 7(3):80–83.

PERI, C. 1987. "Les techniques de filtration tangentielle des mouts et des vins." *Bull. O.I.V.* 60:789–800.

PERI, C., M. RIVA, and P. DECIO. 1988. "Crossflow membrane filtration of wines: Comparison of performance of ultrafiltration, microfiltration and intermediate cut-off membranes." *Am. J. Enol. Vitic.* 39:162–168.

PIRACCI, A. 1988. "I test di filtrabilita: Alcune perplessita da evidenze sperimentali." *Ind. Bevande.* 17:305–311.

POIRIER, D., F. MARIS, M. BENNASAR, J. GILLOT, D. GARCERA, and B. TORADO DE LA FUENTE. 1984. "Clarification et stabilisation des vins par filtration tangentielle sur membranes minerales." *Ind. Aliment. Agric.* 101:481–490.

POSTEL, W., B. MEIER, and R. MARKERT. 1986a. "Einfluss verschiedener Behandlungsstoffe auf den Gehalt des Weins an Mengen- und Spurenelementen. I. Bentonit." *Mitt. Klost.* 36:20–27.

POSTEL, W., B. MEIER, and R. MARKERT. 1986b. "Einfluss verschiendener Behanlungsstoffe auf den Gehalt des Weins an Mengen- und Spurenelementen. II. Aktivkohle." *Mitt Klost.* 37:219–226.

POSTEL, W., B. MEIER, and R. MARKERT. 1987. "Einfluss verschiendener Behanlungsstoffe auf den Gehalt des Weins an Mengen- und Spurenelementen. III. Kieselguhr und Perlite." *Mitt Klost.* 37:219–226.

POWERS, J. H., C. W. NAGEL, and K. WELLER. 1988. "Protein removal from a wine by immobilized grape proanthocyanidins." *Am. J. Enol. Vitic.* 39:117–120.

PURCHAS, D. B. 1967. *Industrial Filtration of Liquids.* Cleveland, OH, USA, CRC Press.

RAIBLE, K., and H. BANTLEON. 1968. "Uber die Filtrationseigenschaften von Bier." *Monats. Brauer.* 21:277–285.

RANKINE, B. C., and W. W. EMERSON. 1963. "Wine clarification and protein removal by Bentonite." *J. Sci. Food Agric.* 14:687–689.

RIBÉREAU-GAYON, J., and E. PEYNAUD. 1961. *Traite d'Oenologie,* Vol 2, p. 742. Paris: Beranger.

RODRIGUEZ, J. L. P., A. WEISS, and G. LAGALY. 1977. "A natural clay organic complex from Andalusian black earth." *Clay and Clay Minerals* 25:243–251.

ROMAT, H., J.-J. DESCOUT, and G. GUIMBERTEAU. 1986. "Etude de l'utilization des parois metaliques poreuses frittees pour la filtration des vins." *Conn. Vigne Vin* 20:215–231.

ROSSI, J. A., JR., and V. L. SINGLETON. 1966. "Flavor effects and adsorptive properties of purified fractions of grape-seed phenols." *Am. J. Enol. Vitic.* 17:240–246.

SALGUES, M., C. DUMON, and F. MARIS. 1982. "Etude de quelques conditions influencant la filtration des vins sur membrane." *Conn. Vigne Vin* 16:257–269.

SAYWELL, L. G. 1934a. "Clarification of vinegar." *Ind. Eng. Chem.* 26:379–385.

SAYWELL, L. G. 1934b. "Clarification of wine." *Ind. Eng. Chem.* 26:981–982.

SCHMITT, A., H. KOHLER, P. MILTENBERGER, and K. CURSCHMANN. 1989. "Vergleich verschiedener cross-flow filtrationssysteme." *Weinwirt. Technik* 1:7–14.

SERRANO, M., D. DUBOURDIEU, and P. RIBÉREAU-GAYON. 1982. "Mise au point d'un test de filtration sur plaques utilisable en oenologie." *Sci. Aliments* 2:313–328.

SERRANO, M., A. C. VANNIER, and P. RIBÉREAU-GAYON. 1988. "Clarification des vins par filtration en flux tangential (ultrafiltration). Incidence sur la composition chimique et qualites organoleptiques. Evolution des produits au cours du vieillissement." *Conn. Vigne Vin* 22:49–71.

SERRANO, M., B. PONTENS, and P. RIBÉREAU-GAYON. 1992. "Etude de differentes membranes de microfiltration tangentielle. Comparison avec la filtration sur precouche de diatomees." *J. Int. Sci. Vigne Vin* 16:97–116.

SIDDIQUI, M. K. H. 1968. *Bleaching Earths,* Chapter 3. Oxford, England: Pergamon Press.

SINGLETON, V. L. 1964. "Application of charcoal in wine clarification." *Wines & Vines* 45:March: 29–31.

SINGLETON, V. L. 1967. "Adsorption of natural phenols from beer and wine." *Mast. Brew. Assoc. Am. Tech. Quart.* 4:245–253.

SINGLETON, V. L., and A. C. NOBLE. 1976. "Wine flavor and phenolic substances." In *Phenolic, Sulfur, and Nitrogen Compounds in Food Flavors,* G. Charlambous and I. Katz, Eds, Am. Chem. Soc. Symp. Series, Number 26:47–70. Washington, DC: Am. Chem. Soc.

SPERRY, D. R. 1917. "The principles of filtration." *Chem. Met. Eng.* 17:161–166.

SUDRAUD, R., and J. CAYE. 1985. "Observations sur la composition et le controle d'efficacite des bentonites." *Rev. Fr. Oenol.* 97:21–24.

TANIGUCHI, M., N. KOANI, and T. KOBAYASHI. 1987. "High-concentration cultivation of lactic acid bacteria in fermentor with cross-flow filtration." *J. Ferment. Technol.* 65:179–184.

TERCELJ, D. 1965. "Etude des composes azotes du vin." *Ann. Technol. Agric.* 14:307–319.

THOMPSON, D. 1991. "The application of osmotic distillation for the wine industry." *Aust. Grapegrower Winemaker* 328:11–14.

USSEGLIO-TOMASSET, L. 1976. "Les colloides glucidiques soluble des mouts et des vins." *Conn. Vigne Vin* 10:193–226.

VILLETTAZ, J.-C. 1988. "Les colloides du mout et du vin." *Rev. Fr. Oenol.* 111:23–27.

WAGENER, W. W. 1970. "Effects of fining agents on the settling of Riesling and Steen musts of the 1970 vintage." *Die Wynboer* 466:July:18–20.

WATANABE, T., T. MORI, N. SAKATA, K. YAMASHITA, T. TOSA, I. CHIBATA, Y. NUNOKAWA, and S. SHIINOKI. 1979. "Continuous fining of sake with immobilized tannin." *Hakkokogaku* 57:141–147.

WATERS, E. J., W. WALLACE, M. E. TATE, and P. WILLIAMS. 1993. "Isolation and partial characterization of a natural haze protective factor from wine." *J. Agric. Food Chem.* 41:724–730.

WEETALL, H. H., J. T. ZELCO, and L. E. BAILEY. 1984. "A new method for the stabilization of white wine." *Am. J. Enol. Vitic.* 35:212–215.

WELSH, W. A., and Y. O. PARENT. 1985. "New protein removal process." *Practical Winery* 6(1):34–38.

WILL, F., W. PFEIFER, and H. DIETRICH. 1991. "The importance of colloids for wine quality." *Vitic. Enol. Sci.* 46:78–84.

WUCHERPFENNIG, K., R. AQUILLINA, and R. ANKELE. 1975. "Gelatine and Kieselsol for treatment of grape juice and wine." *Proc. 4th Intl. Enology Symposium.* Valencia, Spain, pp. 95–110.

WUCHERPFENNIG, K., and H. DIETRICH. 1989. "The importance of colloids for clarification of musts and wines." *Vitic. Enol. Sci.* 44:1–12.

WUCHERPFENNIG, K., H. DIETRICH, and R. FAUTH. 1984. "Uber den Einfluss von Polysacchariden auf die Klarung und Filterfahigkeit von Weinen unter besonderer Beruck-sichtigung des Botrytisglucans." *Deut. Lebens-Rund.* 80:38–44.

WUCHERPFENNIG, K., and P. POSSMANN. 1972. "Beitrag zur kombinierten Gelatin-Kieslsolschonung." *Fluss. Obst.* 2:48–52.

WÜRDIG, G., and R. WOLLER. 1989. *Chemie des Weines.* Stuttgart, Germany: Ulmer.

YOKOTSUKA, K., K. NOZUKI, and T. KUSHIDA. 1983. "Turbidity formation caused by interaction of must proteins with wine tannins." *J. Ferm. Technol.* 61:413–416.

YOKOTSUKA, K., and V. L. SINGLETON. 1987. "Interactive precipitation between graded peptides from gelatin and specific grape tannin fractions in wine-like model solutions." *Am. J. Enol. Vitic.* 38:199–206.

ZIMMER, E., C.-D. PATZ, and H. DIETRICH. 1992. "Direct determination of molecular weight distribution of high molecular substances in wines and juices." *Vitic. Enol. Sci.* 47:121–129.

CHAPTER 8

The Physical and Chemical Stability of Wine

The major physical instability in bottled wines continues to be the precipitation of the tartaric salts, potassium bitartrate, and calcium tartrate. Prevention of this precipitation in bottled wines is desirable because consumers find it objectionable and an indication of poor quality control. Precipitation of these salts can be due to one or more reasons, such as the incomplete stabilization in the cellar, the use of a nonrepresentative sample for the stability test, the use of an inappropriate stability test, the removal of colloidal materials at the point of final filtration that have previously inhibited the precipitation and natural chemical changes, especially the polymerization of phenolic pigments. The initial instability is caused by supersaturated levels in juices that are augmented by the decrease in solubility due to ethanol and the low temperatures used for wine storage.

With respect to the precipitation of tartrate salts, wines are still treated in a manner that results in incomplete precipitation, even after being held at low temperatures for five or more days. A number of alternative crystallization and contacting methods have been developed and these are reviewed below in Section A.4.

Other common but sporadic physical instabilities include the precipitation of colloids such as the protein, peptide-tannin, and polysaccharide hazes. The pinking of certain white wines, the rapid browning of some white and rosé wines and oxidation of all wines are examples of chemical changes and these are discussed in further detail in Chapter 10.

The addresses of equipment companies mentioned in this chapter can be found in Appendix I.

A. TARTRATE STABILITY

1. Factors Influencing Solubility

Grape juices display a wide variation in potassium and tartaric concentrations, with lesser variation in the calcium content. The levels in any particular juice depend primarily on the season, the level of maturity, and the cultivar, with secondary effects due to the rootstock and soil conditions. The tartaric concentration in a given cultivar is essentially independent of temperature effects during the growing season and seems to be influenced only by synthesis and berry expansion during maturation. The potassium concentration in berries is more dependent on the growing conditions, the rootstock, and the competition for transport into the developing canes and leaves. The growing conditions include potassium availability, soil moisture and composition, and the influence of climate on the rate of maturation and the time on the vine. Unless ion exchanged, the potassium content of the wine reflects that of the must, whereas higher calcium can be due to pickup during calcium carbonate treatment or contact with concrete tanks.

The influence of potassium on the solution equilibria in a wine is complicated by its role in establishing the pH and the ionic strength (and therefore the ion activities and the fraction of tartaric acid that is in the bitartrate form). The solubility of potassium bitartrate in ethanol solutions has been determined by Berg and Keefer (1958) shown in Table 8-1, and shows a 60% decrease as the temperature is decreased from 20°C to 0°C at 12% v/v ethanol. The effect of ethanol is to reduce the solubility by almost 40% for each increase of 10%v/v at 20°C. The solubility of calcium tartrate under similar conditions was determined by Berg and Keefer (1959) and displays almost a 50% decrease from 20°C to 0°C as shown in Table 8-2. The effect of ethanol is to reduce the solubility by almost 30% for each rise of 10% v/v. The influence of pH is to determine the fraction of the tartaric acid that exists in the bitartrate and tartrate ion forms. These fractions are presented in Table 8-3 and are calculated based on the pK values for an ethanol content of 12% v/v rather than the more usual aqueous values. The equations used for such calculations are discussed in more detail in Chapter 15.

The fraction in the bitartrate form rises from 43 to 71% over the range 3.0 to 4.0 with a maximum of 73% at a pH of 3.8. The fraction that is in the tartrate form rises from 1 to 19% over the same range, doubling between the pH values 3.7 and 4.0.

The range in some mineral contents of commercial California wines is presented in Table 8-4 (Ough et al. 1982) and a comprehensive report of potassium and calcium contents is given by Berg et al. (1979).

2. Stability Criteria for Potassium Bitartrate

Although many juices are saturated with potassium bitartrate (and crystals have even been observed in the cells of grape berries), the concern arises from the reduction of solubility due to the formation of ethanol and the potential for precipitation when wines are held at lower temperatures.

In general, the species present in the precipitate are not in stoichiometric proportions, and there is considerable evidence by both crystal shape and composition, of interactions

Table 8-1. Solubility of potassium bitartrate (g / L) in model solutions.

	Ethanol content (%v/v)				
Temperature (°C)	0	10	12	14	20
0	2.25	1.26	1.11	0.98	0.68
5	2.66	1.58	1.49	1.24	0.86
10	3.42	2.02	1.81	1.63	1.10
15	4.17	2.45	2.25	2.03	1.51
20	4.92	3.08	2.77	2.51	1.82

Source of data: Berg and Keefer (1958).

Table 8-2. Solubility of calcium tartrate (g / L) in model solutions.

	Ethanol content (%v/v)				
Temperature (°C)	0	10	12	14	20
0	1.56	0.65	0.54	0.46	0.27
5	1.82	0.76	0.64	0.54	0.32
10	2.13	0.89	0.75	0.63	0.38
15	2.48	1.05	0.88	0.75	0.45
20	2.90	1.24	1.04	0.88	0.53

Source of data: Berg and Keefer (1959).

with other phenolic and colloidal entities (Rodriguez-Clemente and Correa-Gorospe 1988).

Wines have been shown to be capable of holding considerably more of this salt than model solutions of the same ionic strength and ethanol content (Berg and Keefer 1958; Usseglio-Tomasset et al. 1992). Some red wines, at stability, contain almost 40% more of this salt than comparable white wines (DeSoto and Yamada 1963; Berg and Akiyoshi 1971). This enhanced solubility is most likely due to complexing of the bitartrate (and perhaps tartrate) ions with proteins in white wines and possibly more extensively with the pigment-tannin complexes of red wines (Pilone and Berg 1965; Balakian and Berg 1968; Kantz and Singleton 1990). There is little evidence that potassium ions are involved in such complex formation as they show almost no chelation in solution.

There are two basic approaches to establishing the stability values of these salts in wines. The first, developed by Berg and Keefer, was to attempt to describe the solubility of the salts in terms of observable concentration products by allowing for the effects of pH, ethanol content, and temperature and making a general assumption about the ionic strength of all wines. Later, workers developed recommended concentration product values for each wine type, but this assumed that all wines of a given type had the same holding capacity for these salts.

Table 8-3. Fraction of tartaric acid in the ion forms at various pH values.

pH	% Undissociated Acid	% Bitartrate Ion	% Tartrate Ion
2.8	66.6	32.8	0.55
3.0	55.5	43.3	1.15
3.2	43.7	54.0	2.28
3.4	32.4	63.4	4.24
3.6	22.6	70.0	7.43
3.8	14.8	72.9	12.26
4.0	9.19	71.7	19.1
4.2	5.38	66.5	28.1

The alternative approach addresses each wine individually and involves the establishment of ideal conditions for crystals to grow if the wine contains more of the salt than it is capable of holding at that temperature. This approach, referred to as the crystallization rate approach, provides a result that is wine-specific and eliminates the need for generalizing assumptions concerning wines within a given type. The effects due to the ionic strength and phenolics are naturally incorporated into the particular result.

a. *Solubility Products and Concentration Products*

The equilibrium relationship between the activity of ions and their solubility at any temperature is usually referred to as the solubility product (SP), or K_{sp}.

For potassium bitartrate this is:

$$K_{sp} = \alpha_1[K^+] \cdot \alpha_1[HTa^-]$$

where α_1 is the activity coefficient for ions carrying a single charge in the solution, while

Table 8-4. Alkali metal content of some commercial California wines.

Statistic	Potassium (mg/L)	Sodium (mg/L)	Calcium (mg/L)	Magnesium (mg/L)
		White table wine (138 samples)		
Average	803	51	88	106
Standard Deviation	254	38	24	24
		Rosé wine (9 samples)		
Average	980	45	84	98
Stardard Deviation	445	24	18	21
		Red table wine (124 samples)		
Average	1102	53	79	129
Stardard Deviation	325	42	34	26
		Sparkling wine (16 samples)		
Average	808	62	90	86
Stardard Deviation	258	30	18	14

Source: From Ough et al. (1982).

for calcium tartrate it is:

$$K_{sp} = \alpha_2[Ca^{++}] \cdot \alpha_2[Ta^{=}]$$

where α_2 is the activity coefficient of the ions carrying a double charge in the solution.

Berg and Keefer (1958, 1959) and others since have used the simplified forms of the Debye-Huckel equation for the estimation of the activity coefficients. A more detailed description of this equation, its use, and its limitations can be found in Chapter 15.

These authors used this concept to establish a simplified product, K'_{sp} that for potassium bitartrate is:

$$K'_{sp} = [K^+] \cdot [HTa^-] = K_{sp}/(\alpha_1)^2$$

by using generalized values of the activity coefficients, based on an average ionic strength of 38 mM/L. This concentration product, or CP, was determined for model solutions of ethanol and potassium bitartrate at different temperatures. However, when they analyzed wines that had been held at −4°C for an extended period, they found that the observed CP values were much higher than would be expected from the solubility of potassium bitartrate in model solutions. Further, the measured CP values of the wines were a function of wine type, indicating the role of other factors in the tartrate holding capacity of wines (see Table 8-5 for potassium bitartrate CP values and Table 8-6 for the corresponding calcium tartrate values).

Table 8-5. Comparison of measured and predicted potassium content in wines (data of Berg and Keefer 1958).

Wine type	Concentration Product (held at −4°C) × 10^4	Solubility Product (at 20°C) × 10^4	Potassium (mg/L) Actual	Potassium (mg/L) Prediction from K_{sp}
Semillon	1.80	1.51	897	1111
Semillon	1.69	1.54	741	997
Semillon	1.73	1.51	663	854
Grey Riesling	1.59	1.66	936	1443
Pinot blanc	1.64	1.64	819	1209
Rosé	1.67	1.66	741	1088

Table 8-6. Comparison of measured and predicted calcium content in wines (data of Berg and Keefer 1959).

Wine type	Concentration Product (held at −4°C) × 10^6	Solubility Product (at 20°C) × 10^6	Calcium (mg/L) Actual	Calcium (mg/L) Predicted from K_{sp}
Sauterne	2.00	1.07	76	39
Red Chianti	5.00	1.04	92	20
Sherry	1.13	0.356	84	26
Sherry	0.918	0.361	68	21
White Port	1.53	0.366	56	13
Red Port	2.69	0.361	76	10

DeSoto and Yamada (1963) extended the CP concept by determining the final CP values for several types of wines and reported the highest found and their recommended CP values for various wine types (Table 8-7). This work was, however, primarily related to fortified wine styles with only 20 of their 72 samples being table wines, and of those only four were white wines. Their recommended values for table wines have been used extensively in the past as criteria for both the stability of the potassium and calcium salts. The variance of the calcium tartrate values is generally twice those of the corresponding potassium products, and this is probably due to the complexing of calcium ions in addition to the previously mentioned complexing of the tartrates. The distribution of the concentration product values for the white and red table wines are not significantly different from each other, even though different mean values were recommended. For some wine types, the recommended values are 10 to 15% above the sample means, while for others they are similarly below the mean values.

The application of these values to wines made from other cultivars and grown in other regions has led to poor results, as might be expected, because of the variations in chemical and physical composition. This is especially true of the table wine values which are based on a few samples of mixed-cultivar wines. The differences between the mean values of different wine types are presumably due to phenolic interactions with the tartrate pool. The cultivars used in the production of wines in California (and elsewhere) today bear little resemblance to those that were used for the wines at that time.

One example of the large variation in the CP values found in wines from different regions is the study by Pilone and Berg (1965).

Table 8-7. Recommended concentration products values (adapted from DeSoto and Yamada 1963).[1]

Potassium bitartrate CP × 10^4		Calcium tartrate CP × 10^6
	White table wines (4 samples)	
1.64 (μ = 1.69, SD = 0.19)		2.00 (μ = 1.84, SD = 0.38)
	Red table wines (16 samples)	
3.00 (μ = 2.93, SD = 0.33)		4.00 (μ = 3.56, SD = 1.07)
	White Port wine (6 samples)	
1.05 (μ = 0.86, SD = 0.26)		1.55 (μ = 1.54, SD = 0.28)
	Red Port wine (16 samples)	
2.00 (μ = 2.05, SD = 0.28)		2.75 (μ = 3.20, SD = 0.65)
	Sherry (17 samples)	
1.71 (μ = 1.39, SD = 0.23)		1.25 (μ = 1.58, SD = 0.25)

[1] μ-average, SD = standard deviation.

The values reported for 10 red wines held at +1°C for approximately 80 days averaged 2.45 (SD of 0.78) × 10^{-6} while those for 10 white wines averaged 0.83 (SD of 0.20) × 10^{-6}. The red wine values were approximately 83% of the recommended values of DeSoto and Yamada (1963) and the white wine values were almost 50% of their values.

A more comprehensive survey of the CP values of nearly 1000 wines of different cultivars and types and from seven regions of California was reported by Berg and Akiyoshi (1971). They held bentonited samples of the wines for 21 days at +1°C with the addition of 4 g/L of potassium bitartrate seed crystals. They found that the unseeded samples gave CP values for white and red table wines essentially the same as the recommended values of DeSoto and Yamada (1963), but approximately twice those of the corresponding seeded samples. This shows that actual stability is not achieved at the recommended C.P levels. With the white wines there was a 20% variation in the CP value between the cultivars and for the red wines this was closer to 30%. Similar findings were reported by Haushofer and Szemeliker (1973), who found effects due to ultrasonic treatment, seeding, and glass crystal additions on both the rate and extent of the crystallization.

The CP criterion is of limited value for the above reasons and should not be used to determine tartrate stability in wines. It has been presented here only to give a better understanding of the problems related to tartrate stability and to provide a historical perspective.

The relative supersaturation approach, developed by Rhein and Kappes (1979), has the same limitations due to differences in the holding capacity of different wines. They suggested that supersaturation levels of 20% (based on the solubility in ethanol-water solutions) could exist in apparently stable wines and much higher levels were needed before crystals would form. The limitations of the supersaturation criterion are discussed in more detail in Section 3.d.

b. Crystallization Rate Phenomena

The crystallization of potassium bitartrate from wine is generally limited by the low concentration of nuclei and the poor conditions for the formation of others on which the salt can grow. The rate at which new nuclei develop is strongly dependant on the number of existing nuclei, their size, the degree of supersaturation, and level of fluid turbulence. Supersaturation is the condition in which a solution has a concentration above its solubility limit. The rate equation for the growth of nuclei (and the loss of salt from solution) can be written:

$$dC_w/dt = -k_n[C_w - C_s]^a[N]^b[\Omega]^c[D_p]^d$$

where C_w and C_s are the concentrations of potassium bitartrate in the wine and at saturation; Ω is the agitation rate; N and D_p are the concentration and particle diameter of the nuclei; and k_n is the rate constant for nucleation. Values of the nucleation order a have been estimated to be between 4.0 and 6.0 and reported to be 4.49 in a white wine (Nishino and Tanahashi 1987). The strong dependence of the nucleation rate on the level of supersaturation together with the temperature effect on the saturation levels cause the spontaneous formation of nuclei to be favored as the temperature is lowered. While some solutes require a critical level of supersaturation to exist before spontaneous nucleation can occur, this has not been shown to be true for either of the tartrate salts.

Once a significant number of nuclei are present, the slowest step in crystallization becomes the rate at which the crystals can grow. This growth rate may be controlled by either diffusion of the species through a boundary layer adjacent to the crystal surface or by their movement across the crystal surface to the growing edge. The rate of solute depletion when this diffusion is rate limiting can be written:

$$dC_w/dt = -k_d AD[C_w - C_s]/\lambda$$

where k_d is the growth rate constant; A, is the surface area of the crystals; D is the diffusivity of the slower solute (presumably the larger tartrate ions); λ is the boundary layer thickness. Diffusion-controlled regions have been identified during the crystallization of potassium bitartrate from wines (Dunsford and Boulton 1981). The rate of diffusion is first order with respect to the concentration difference between the wine and the crystal surface. During this period the concentration will follow an exponential decrease with respect to time.

In contrast, the migration of species over the crystal surface until they reach the growing interface can become a limiting process. The rate of this surface integration step often follows a higher-order relationship and the surface integration rate can be written:

$$dC_w/dt = -k_s A[C_w - C_s]^n$$

where k_s is the rate constant for surface integration, A is the crystal surface area; and n is the order of the surface reaction. An order of two has been identified for this reaction with potassium bitartrate during the later stages of wine crystallizations (Dunsford and Boulton 1981).

Typical crystallization curves for a Sauvignon blanc wine seeded with 20 g/L of seed crystals at three temperatures are shown in Figure 8-1. The crystallization curves of different wines, (a Sauvignon blanc, a Cabernet Sauvignon, and a Pinot noir wine) seeded with crystals at 20 g/L and held at 0°C are shown in Figure 8-2.

One important feature of all of the rate equations for crystallization is that they reduce to zero when the wine concentration reaches the saturation level. It is this aspect that can be used to determine the saturation levels in individual wines and it has been used to develop a test in which ideal crystallization is encouraged by employing a large concentration of nuclei in a well-mixed condition at the temperature of interest (Boulton 1983; Vialatte 1984). The final equilibrium is then the true saturation condition at the test temperature for the wine being considered. This condition represents the composition which cannot support the growth of any crystals of the salt, even under ideal crystal conditions, taking into account the complexing associated with other components. It is used to establish saturation conditions on a wine-by-wine basis and should not be correlated or used for other wines of the same type.

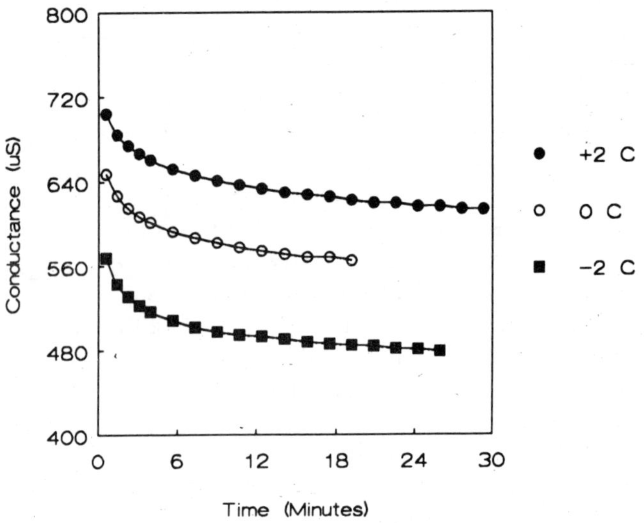

Fig. 8-1. The influence of temperature on the crystallization of potassium bitartrate from a Sauvignon blanc wine.

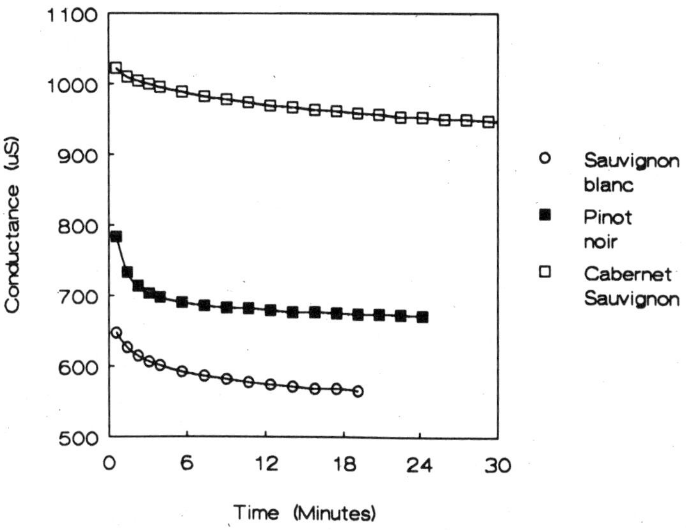

Fig. 8-2. The crystallization of potassium bitartrate from different wines at 0°C.

3. Stability Testing for Potassium Bitartrate

There are three commonly used criteria for potassium bitartrate stability in wines. These are (1) The recommended CP values of DeSoto and Yamada (1963), Berg and Akiyoshi (1971), or similar determinations; (2) the hold-cold or freeze test, in which the sample is chilled to about (or below) its freezing point, held for a period of time, and, after thawing, visually checked for the presence of crystals; and (3) the conductivity test, which looks for the change in the conductivity of a seeded sample at a designated temperature to indicate instability and determine the final composition that provides saturation conditions.

A number of semiempirical alternative tests based on the addition of seeds and the measurement of conductivity have been proposed. The first of these is the method using 5 g/L at 4°C (Muller and Würdig 1978). This was later modified so that the change in conductivity observed due to the dissolving of seed crystals during the test at 20°C was used to estimate the saturation temperature of the wine (Würdig et al. 1980a, 1980b, 1983, 1985). This was then extended to a 30°C test by Maujean et al. (1985). These tests will be discussed in more detail in Section 3.d.

a. *Recommended CP Values*

The concentration products are determined by analyzing the wine for pH, potassium, and tartaric acid concentrations. These are then expressed on a molar basis and the fraction of the tartaric acid that is present as the bitartrate ion is determined from tables or by computation. The molar product of the potassium and bitartrate concentrations is then the CP value.

Concentration product values that have been recommended according to wine type were considered to be those of stable wines. They were obtained by averaging the CP values for each wine type after storage at ambient temperature (21°C to 29°C) for between 16 and 28 months (DeSoto and Yamada 1963). The basis for these values is considered in detail in Section A.2.a of this chapter.

The use of such generalized values for wines today is questionable at best due to the recognized role of phenolic pigments and other components on the potassium bitartrate holding capacity of wine. The general acceptance of significant seasonal variation in almost all aspects of composition, and the widespread practice of making single-cultivar wines from grapes grown under conditions with considerably different cultural practices, make these values of little use.

b. The Cold or Freeze Tests

The hold-cold or freeze test relies on the formation of significant crystals after holding the wine at a reduced temperature for a period of time. The sample may actually be frozen over an 8 to 24 hour holding time (for the freeze version of the test) or held close to freezing temperature for several days or weeks (for the hold-cold test) and the presence of crystals after the ice has melted is taken to mean that the wine is unstable. The absence of crystals is taken to mean that the wine is stable. The less severe cold form of the test is conducted at above freezing temperature but usually allows several days for crystal formation.

Variations of this approach are tests in which the concentration of potassium bitartrate is deliberately increased prior to the samples being held at cold temperatures. One example of such a dosed cold test is that in which between 200- and 600-mg/L additions are made (from a 10- to 13-g/L solution of potassium bitartrate) and the wine held at temperatures between −2°C and 5°C for five days (Schmitt et al. 1980). Another involves the dissolution of 250 to 1250 mg/L in the wine at 35°C and then a stepwise cooling to 10°C and then −5°C. The interpretation of crystal appearance compared to the control is used to determine the saturation temperature of the sample, (Boiret et al. 1991).

This approach does address the compositional uniqueness of each wine rather than comparing it to generalized values, but as noted previously, the cold test values will not be true stability values if potassium bitartrate seeds are not added. They are not usually added since they obscure the visual interpretation of the test.

A serious concern with the freeze test is that as ice formation occurs, all solutes, including the potassium, tartaric acid, and ethanol, are concentrated and the precipitation that then occurs is not related to wine concentration conditions. The use of freezing temperatures has a distorting effect on the coagulation of colloidal components, and these will generally interfere with the natural nucleation and crystal growth.

These tests are actually crude crystallization rate tests rather than stability tests since there is no requirement for stability to have been achieved and the time of the test is predetermined. They are not recommended. The main limitation with these tests is that they can provide false positive results. An unstable wine which is slow to develop crystals due to either low supersaturation or inhibition by other wine components, would be interpreted to be stable, simply because not enough time for crystal growth was allowed by the test and no crystals are observed.

c. The Davis Conductivity Test

Due to the limitations of the concentration product approach for stability, a test was developed based on the rate approach outlined previously. The Davis Conductivity Test (Boulton 1983; Vialatte 1984) aims to determine if a wine has any potential to precipitate at a chosen temperature. It establishes an environment that encourages rapid crystal growth if any supersaturation exists at the test conditions. It was developed during studies of the crystallization kinetics of potassium bitartrate (Dunsford and Boulton 1981) and is a more specific version of earlier tests of this kind (Muller and Würdig 1978). A stirred, seeded sample of wine is brought to the test temperature. The crystallization of potassium bitartrate is monitored by the change in wine conductivity due primarily to the loss of free potassium ions from solution as the crystallization occurs. If the wine is unstable at the test conditions, the conductivity will fall, while if it is stable, the conductivity will rise. The conductivity will remain constant only if the wine is exactly stable at the temperature of the test. The final value of the conductivity is the saturation condition and can be used to monitor the progress of the full-scale treatment of only the wine that was tested.

The change in wine conductivity due to the change in the potassium concentration is pH-dependent. This is because hydrogen ions contribute to the conductivity and the crystallization can cause a change in pH to occur. Hydrogen ions have approximately 10 times the molar conductance of potassium ions and, at typical wine levels, potassium at concentrations ranging between 10 to 50 mM/L (390 to 1950 mg/L). At higher pH values, for example pH = 4.0 ($[H^+]$ = 0.1 mM/L), the contribution of the protons to the conductivity reading is quite small, making the conductivity more sensitive to changes in potassium concentration. At pH = 3.0, ($[H^+]$ = 1 mM/L), the contribution from protons is 10 times higher and similar to that due to the potassium ions. While the wine conductivity has contributions from species other than potassium and bitartrate ions, the change in conductance associated with this test will be directly proportional to the changes in the concentrations of only these ions. There is little value in trying to correlate or average these final conductivity values for other wines, owing to variations in mineral content, pH, and tartrate-binding compounds.

An important feature of this test is that if the wine sample is filtered at the end of the test and analyzed for titratable acidity and pH, these will be the values that the wine will have after the stabilization treatment. If they are not acceptable, acidity adjustments can be made and evaluated at the testing stage, before the full-scale treatment is attempted.

The test requires at least 15 g/L of fresh powdered potassium bitartrate to be added to the sample at the desired temperature. This level is deliberately higher than in other tests in order that any fouling of the seeds by colloidal materials does not influence the final result.

The test temperature will generally be the lowest temperature that the wine is expected to see during shipping, storage, or serving. This might be in the range 0 to 5°C for white wines that are expected to be held at domestic and commercial refrigerator conditions, or at higher temperatures (up to 10°C) for aged red wines held in cellars or on retail shelves.

The test is applicable to other wine types (late-harvest, sparkling, and fortified wines) and it has been applied to the stability of base wines for sparkling wine production by fortifying the base wine to the level of ethanol expected after the secondary fermentation and then conducting the test as described.

I. Equipment for the Test. The test requires a meter capable of reading conductances in the ranges of 100 μS to 1.0 mS and 1.0 to 10 mS with an accuracy of 0.5% of the full-scale value or better. (The unit of conductance is the Siemen, S, and it is equal to the reciprocal of the resistance of the solution in Ohms. The use of the unit mho is not encouraged although some older meters will have scales in these units. The unit of conductivity most commonly used is S/cm, although the corresponding metric unit is S/m). Temperature compensation is a desirable feature but tank samples taken during the stabilization process should be brought to the test temperature before a reading is taken. The temperature compensation function is usually based on that of a potassium chloride solution and the ionic species in wine are sufficiently different so as to use the same temperature for all tests and comparative readings, rather than to rely on the compensation correction. The test is best conducted in a controlled temperature bath using water (or glycol solutions for temperatures below 3°C). Magnetic stir bars can be driven by a submerged air-driven (or water-driven) magnetic turbine. Several of these can be connected in series, to allow multiple samples to be tested at the same time.

II. The Test Procedure. The temperature of the test is chosen from a consideration of the actual conditions that can be expected in the transportation, storage, and retailing of the wine. This might be 0°C to 2°C for white wines that would be expected to be held in retail and domestic refrigerators, to 10 to 15°C for aged red wines that are expected to be held at ambient or wine cellar temperatures.

An alternative approach is to test wines from previous years in order to estimate the temperature at which they are stable.

A 100-mL sample of the wine is brought to temperature in a stirred 250-mL beaker. The conductance cell should be checked so that the electrodes are fully submerged and that no gas bubbles are adhering to them, interfering with the reading. A quantity of 1.5 g of powdered potassium bitartrate is added and the initial conductivity is noted. The conductance after approximately 20 minutes (or when three successive one-minute readings are the same) is then noted for the interpretation.

III. Interpretation of the Test. If the conductivity remained constant during the test, no new crystals have formed and the seed crystals have not dissolved, indicating that the wine is stable at the test temperature. If the conductivity increased during the test, some of the seed crystals have dissolved, indicating that the wine is less than saturated at the test temperature. If the conductivity decreased during the test, some of the potassium bitartrate in the wine has crystallized and the wine is unstable at the test temperature. A true change should be at least twice the accuracy of the meter in the range being used.

The final conductivity corresponds to that of the stable wine at the test temperature. This can be used to determine when stability is reached during the full-scale treatment of the wine. Samples drawn during the full-scale treatment need only be brought to the temperature of the test and the conductivity value compared to that determined by the test. If the final solution is filtered and analyzed for titratable acidity and pH, these will be the values of the stabilized wine. Thus, unacceptably large decreases in titratability can be foreseen and acidity adjustments can then be evaluated prior to full-scale stabilization.

d. Other Seeded and Conductivity Tests

Variations of the seeded conductivity test include a number of similar proposals in which other seeding levels are used, other test conditions maintained, and other interpretations are made.

The quantities of potassium bitartrate seed crystals suggested by most authors have been in the range 0.5 to 10 g/L (Haushofer and Szemeliker 1973), but most have suggested values such as 4 g/L (Rhein 1977; Rhein and Neradt 1979) and 5 g/L (Muller and Würdig 1978; Droux and Vialatte 1983). It is now well established that the final conductivities obtained with these levels are dependent on the levels employed in this range. Our own studies, together with those of Postel and Prasch (1977) and Hagen (1979), have shown that in some wines at least 15 g/L are needed to get a true equilibrium value that is independent of the seeding level. There is considerable evidence of the interference of crystallization both in the test and the full-scale treatment due to colloidal components. This interference is quite wine-specific and is often altered by such treatments as aging, blending, acidity adjustments, the use of charge-modified filter media, and membrane filtration. It is important that these effects be overcome during the stability determination since their levels in finished wines will be different and unpredictable.

There are several alternative interpretations that make use of the apparent saturation temperature and its relationship to actual wine stability. These range from assuming that the stability limit of a wine is at a temperature between 2°C and 6°C below its apparent saturation temperature (Würdig et al. 1983) to as much as 15°C below it (Maujean et al. 1985). Both of these criteria consider that wines can be held at several degrees below their apparent saturation temperature without any risk of nucleation or crystallization. It is important to note that all of the wines considered by these authors were white table wines. A more recent study which included pigmented wines recommends stability temperatures that range from 5°C (white wine) to 10°C (red wine) below the apparent saturation temperature (Vallee et al. 1990). These conclusions were based on the results of holding the wines at −2°C to −4°C for several days and comparing this with the formation of crystals at 10 to 12°C over a period of two years.

In a different approach, introduced by Maujean et al. (1985) the saturation temperature is estimated by determining the temperature at which a two samples of a wine (one seeded and the other natural) provide the same conductivity as the temperature is raised in small increments. The seeded wine has crystals added at the rate of 4 g/L, while the other has 1 g/L of potassium bitartrate dissolved into it at a warm temperature. The basis of this approach is the assumption that wines can support a supersaturation level of 1 g/L before they will undergo spontaneous precipitation. These authors used this criterion to establish the result that the stability temperature of wine was simply 15°C below the saturation temperature, as mentioned previously.

Extending this approach, Gaillard et al. (1988), developed a temperature stepping system to implement the method of Maujean et al. (1985), but favored a seeded test to establish the change in conductivity at 0°C (similar to the Davis method, previously described) for pigmented wines. In a comparison of these methods using 20 white wines and 22 red wines, Gaillard et al. (1990), found that the saturation temperature was not strongly correlated with the fall in conductivity of a seeded test at 0°C for red wines but showed a better correlation between these values with the white wines.

Domeizel et al. (1992) developed a criterion based on two determinations of the saturation temperature, one with increasing temperature and the other by decreasing temperature. The difference between these was considered to be a measure of supersaturation in the wine. These values varied greatly within each wine type and suffer from the same limitations as other saturation tests.

There is little value in attempting to correlate the results of the conductivity test for different wines. This is because there are other ionic species that contribute to the conductivity but not to the stability, as well as un-ionized components that influence the stability but not the conductivity. The saturation temperature is not considered to be a reliable indicator of the ability of a wine to precipitate crystals at lower temperatures. While some solutes have a critical level of supersaturation that must be exceeded before spontaneous crystallization will occur, there is no evidence that this is 1 g/L for potassium bitartrate in either aqueous or wine-like solutions, let alone in a natural product such as wine where spontaneous nucleation would be expected to be influenced by the presence of phenolics and colloidal components. These methods do not permit the determination of the final acidity and pH that will result from the treatment as part of the test.

The effect of temperature on the solubility and stability of polysaccharide, proteinaceous, and phenolic colloids requires that the test be performed in the wine of interest and at the temperature of interest if a reliable result is to be obtained.

4. Crystallization Processes

The principal problems with natural crystallizations are that low levels of supersaturation lead to poor if any spontaneous nucleation resulting in limited and slow crystal growth. If there is poor nucleation, the crystal area available for growth will also be small and the overall rate reduced accordingly. Some wines have levels of natural colloids such as polysaccharides, peptide-tannin complexes, and proteins, which can deposit on new nuclei or growing crystals, leading to a cessation of crystal growth, and hence precipitation, even though some level of supersaturation exists in the wine.

A number of alternative treatments have been proposed in attempts to increase the crystal surface area and to cause more extensive fluid-solid interaction. Most involve significant agitation and crystal seeding, some rely on ice formation (and enhanced natural nucleation), while most attempt to minimize the energy required by interchanging energy between the incoming and the exiting streams.

a. *Treatment Effects*

Oxidation, aging, fining, and thermal treatments will affect the potassium bitartrate holding capacity of wine, especially red wines. The fining with bentonite has been shown to alter the holding capacity of wines (Pilone and Berg 1965; Berg et al. 1968). The changes in the concentration products of dry white and dry red wines was found to be in the range 15 to 20% and 25 to 30% respectively, almost independent of the fining level. These changes are due to either the removal of potassium bitartrate components by bentonite, the removal of materials that are inhibiting the growth of crystals (and, thereby, the extent of precipitation), or by partial esterification of tartaric acid (Edwards et al. 1985).

b. *Jacketed Tanks*

Currently the most common cellar treatment is to cool the wine down to temperatures in the range of −4°C to 0°C and to hold it under these conditions for several days or weeks (see also Chapter 14 for a more complete discussion of the heat exchangers suitable for these operations). This is generally done on a tank-by-tank basis and rarely is any agitation or seeding introduced.

Many wineries use jacketed tanks for this purpose and there are particular problems associated with the development of ice on the inside wall of the tank in the vicinity of the jacket. This will occur whenever the cooling medium produces a wall temperature that is below the freezing point of the wine. This usually occurs at −2°C for table wines at 12% v/v ethanol, and the freezing point at other ethanol and sugar contents is given in Figure 8-3. Once the ice layer is formed, the cooling rate is decreased due to the additional heat transfer resistance imposed by the ice.

The batch treatment is particularly inefficient in terms of both the energy consumed per volume treated and the time required to reach the desired temperature. The use of jackets and the tank-by-tank approach effectively prevent the recovery of the energy by interchange between other warmer wines and the treated wine. By filtering the cold wine from the crystals and allowing it to reach the storage temperature by ambient heat gains, the energy extracted during the initial cooling is lost to the surroundings.

The time taken to cool the wine is also the longest possible due to the heat transfer ar-

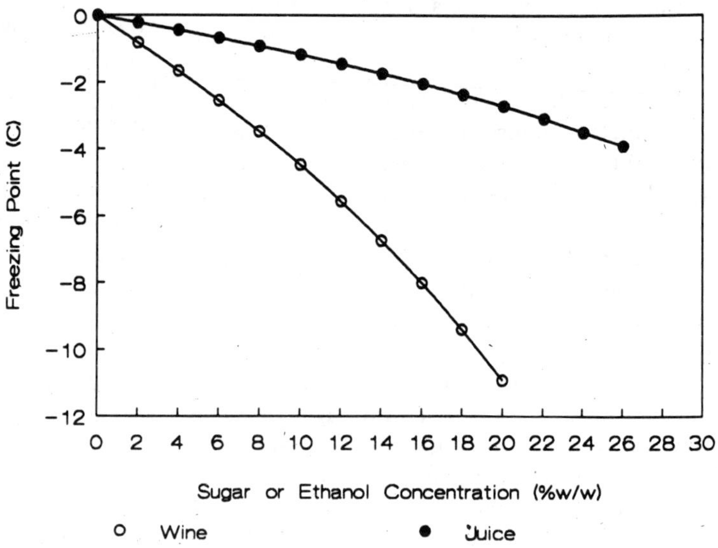

Fig. 8-3. Estimated freezing points of wines and juices.

rangement of batch cooling (see the heat transfer examples in Chapter 14). The rate of cooling in this situation depends on the difference in temperature between the wine at the inner surface of the tank and the coolant temperature. As the wine is cooled this differential is decreased, resulting in a proportional reduction of the heat transfer rate. The wine temperature will then approach that of the coolant exponentially, taking progressively longer for each cooling increment as the wine temperature falls. The reduction in the cooling rate is further exaggerated if the wine adjacent to the tank wall is not disturbed. The absence of tank mixing and the reliance on natural convection currents can result in thermal stratification and radial temperature gradients in which the wall conditions do not represent those of the tank contents. The option of using a colder coolant temperature to increase the temperature driving force is offset by the increased likelihood of forming ice at the inside wall of the tank.

The time required for the cooling of wine can be greatly improved by the use of two external heat exchangers in a two-stage cooling sequence. The first stage performs the cooling down to within approximately 5°C of the treatment temperature. This is conveniently done on a semicontinuous basis as the wine is transferred from one tank to another. Such a system also permits energy conservation by interchanging cold wines that have been stabilized with warmer ones that are about to be stabilized, most conveniently by means of a plate heat exchanger (for a more complete description of these units, refer to Chapter 14). The second stage involves the cooling of the wine down to the stabilization temperature (often −5°C or −6°C). In order to prevent ice formation in the exchanger at these temperatures, a scraped-surface heat exchanger (refer to Chapter 14) is used. This will permit a fraction of the wine to be frozen during the cooling process depending on the operating conditions that are chosen (Riese and Boulton 1980). The formation of ice in this way, commonly 5 to 10% of the wine on a volume basis, helps to concentrate the wine temporarily, thereby providing a higher supersaturation level for spontaneous nucleation and crystal growth. The ice is allowed to melt during the following days so that further cooling is reduced and the general composition of the wine is not altered. The formation of ice can also be used to reduce the volume of wine treated in the second stage. By overcooling (and partially freezing) the fraction that passes through the scraped-surface exchanger, it can be combined with an untreated cold fraction, to provide the desired stabilization temperature. One report of such an application reported a reduction of treatment time from three to four weeks to five to six days (Scraped-surface 1976).

c. *Proprietary Stabilization Processes*

During the past 20 years there have been several proprietary process developments for the faster and more complete stabilization of wine with respect to potassium bitartrate. These include the proprietary systems developed by the Vinipal, Sietz, Gasquet, Alfa-Laval, Westphalia, and Imeca companies.

These processes generally employ an agitated crystallization tank, either a diatomaceous earth filter or a disc centrifuge for final crystal removal, and they transfer energy between the incoming wine and the treated wine for energy conservation, commonly in a plate heat exchanger. The differences between them arise from the temperatures employed, whether or not seed crystals are added, the design of the crystallization vessels, and the use of proprietary heat exchangers and separation equipment. A comparative review of several of these systems with a limited number of wines has been published (Ferenczi et al. 1982). These systems usually have the capability of stabilizing wines within 20 to 30 minutes, but their cost has generally limited their adoption to less than 200 installations worldwide.

One of the most widely used systems, the Vinipal process, was one of the first developed, in the mid 1970s. It incorporates its own refrigeration system, chilling wines to below their freezing point in a two-stage sequence. The wine slurry then flows up from the base of a conical-cylindrical reaction vessel that allows larger crystals to settle out and collect in a bed at the base of the cone. The wine is then filtered in a diatomaceous earth filter and interchanged with the incoming wine in a plate heat exchanger. It is a semicontinuous process being interrupted only by the cleaning of the filter. Evaluations of this system with a limited number of wines are reported by Vialatte (1979) and Serrano and Ribéreau-Gayon (1981).

The Gasquet and Imeca systems are very similar to the Vinipal process except that alternative second-stage exchangers were used and slightly different reactor dimensions were employed (Ferenczi et al. 1982). The Sietz process, commonly referred to as the Spica or contact process, was developed in 1977 and differs in that it used seed addition, recovery, and regrinding and avoided ice formation by operating at close to 0°C. It is a multiple-batch, semicontinuous process. It uses a seeding level of 4 g/L and several agitated cylindrical tanks in a rotation sequence that allows a holding time of up to two hours. The incoming wine was pad filtered to remove suspended fouling components and heat was recovered in a plate heat exchanger. Rhein (1977), Müller-Spath (1979), Rhein and Neradt (1979), and Blouin et al. (1979) provide further details of this process and its performance.

The Crystalflow system was the first truly continuous process that introduced a disc centrifuge in place of the diatomaceous filter used by other systems. Developed by Alfa-Laval, it refined the second-stage cooling with a Contherm exchanger and employed a large, agitated, reaction vessel. Ferenczi et al. (1982) and Blouin and Desenne (1983) provide reports of its performance with some table wines.

A process which embedded seed crystals in the cake of diatomaceous earth filtration was proposed and evaluated by Scott et al. (1981).

The application of a disc centrifuge in combination with a battery of hydrocyclones for the recovery of crystals was introduced into the contact process described above by Bott and Schottler (1985). The hydrocyclones were used to remove the majority of the crystal load. The partially clarified wine and the fine particles were then directed to a centrifuge for separation. These particles were considerably contaminated with colloidal components and are discarded. The underflow stream from the hydrocyclone, containing the larger, relatively clean, bitartrate crystals was recycled after grinding.

A further modification of the Vinipal process in which a modified agitated reactor and settling tank is introduced together with a conductivity probe in the outlet stream, is described by Esteve (1988). This system has an option for the introduction of seed crystals, but the use of a diatomaceous filter for their removal is its practical limitation. It can perform on-line measurements of the outlet conductivity with a dedicated computer and is referred to as the Crystalloprocess.

The alternative approach to seeding and crystal recovery is the application of crystal-bed techniques such as a packed or fluidized bed in a vertical column. The shortcoming of the packed bed and moving bed approaches (Walter 1970) is that rapid crystal growth at the base of the bed can lead to blockage of the flow channels. This can be overcome by the use of a fluidized bed, in which the particles are held in a dense suspension and not in direct contact with each other. Bench-scale trials in our laboratories have shown the suitability of the fluidized bed crystallizer for the stabilization of wines together with energy interchange between the inlet and outlet streams common to earlier processes. The use of larger particles and vertical flow in such a column enables almost all of the crystals to remain in the column, practically eliminating the need for crystal recovery by diatomaceous earth filtration or centrifuging. The two or more columns could be operated in parallel to enable crystal recovery from the bed when needed. The crystals from the column would be an ideal form for the recovery of tartrates, free of diatomaceous earth and other solids.

All of these processes appear to be capable of conferring potassium bitartrate stability to table wines. The choice depends on the balance between crystallization efficiency, treatment capacity, energy minimization and installation ,and operating costs.

5. Stability Criteria for Calcium Tartrate

Calcium tartrate can also precipitate from table wines provided its level exceeds the holding capacity of the wine. Like potassium bitartrate, its holding capacity is greater than that expected from model solutions due to complexing by wine constituents, and there are colloidal effects on the onset of crystal formation (Berg and Keefer 1959; Postel 1983; Curvelo-Garcia 1987). While less common than potassium bitartrate precipitation, it is more of a concern because it is not readily removed by the low-temperature crystallization of potassium bitartrate. It is particularly troublesome in fortified wines, where calcium salts have been used to treat wines (Clark et al. 1988) or where significant calcium pickup has occurred from concrete tanks. At a tartaric acid content of 6 g/L, the recommended calcium content (based on previously recommended CP values) in a white wine would be approximately 5 mg/L at pH 4, and 50 mg/L at pH 3. Many wines are close to instability naturally with concentrations of 80 to 100 mg/L of calcium (Table 8-4).

a. Calcium Tartrate Concentration Products

The concentration product (CP) concept (refer to Section 2.a of this chapter) has also been applied to this instability (Berg and Keefer 1959). Typical values indicating the role of wine components on this type of solubility are indicated in Table 8-6. The highest and recommended values based on the San Joaquin Valley wines (DeSoto and Yamada 1963) are presented in Table 8-7.

While the CP values have the same limitations previously discussed for potassium bitartrate salt, the calcium tartrate values have greater variance, presumably due to complexing of the calcium ions. However they have been used widely for this stability testing in the absence of alternative tests.

b. Crystallization Rate Phenomena

Although the solubility of calcium tartrate decreases with decreasing temperature, the utilization of low temperatures to promote enhanced crystallization has been found to be of little benefit. The reason appears to be an inherent difficulty in the spontaneous nucleation of this salt in wines (Abgueguen and Boulton 1993) even when the supersaturation is increased by lowering the temperature. As a result, crystallization is not enhanced simply by holding the wine at low temperatures for several days or weeks. Those wines which are unstable with respect to this salt are more likely to develop crystals in the presence of potassium bitartrate crystals during cold storage within the winery.

Attempts to speed up the crystallization rate at low temperatures by the addition of seed crystals of racemic calcium tartrate are of limited success in that while calcium contents can be reduced, at 1°C, it takes approximately eight hours with 4 g/L of seeds (Sudraud and Caye 1983). The use of this salt is not presently approved for winemaking.

Unlike the precipitation of the potassium bitartrate, there are few studies of the crystallization kinetics for calcium tartrate from wine. Recent work (Abgueguen and Boulton 1993) has shown that when seed crystals of Ca L(+)tartrate are added, the precipitation from either model solutions or wines is both rapid and second order with respect to concentration over the entire desaturation reaction. The corresponding rate law is then:

$$dC_w/dt = -k_s A[C_w - C_s]^2$$

where k_s is the second-order rate constant; A is the crystal surface area; and C_w and C_s are the concentrations of calcium tartrate in the wine and at saturation.

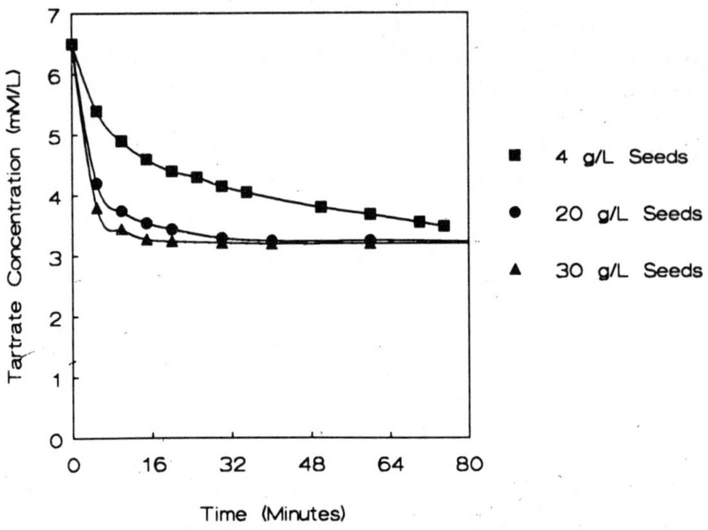

Fig. 8-4. The effect of seeding level on the crystallization of calcium tartrate.

The effect of seed loading has a dramatic effect on the rate of crystallization as shown in Figure 8-4, and the effect of temperature has both a rate and equilibrium effect as shown in Figure 8-5. The crystallization curves of several different wines (Pinot noir, Pinot blanc and Cabernet Sauvignon) are shown in Figure 8-6. The second-order rate constant can be expressed in an Arrhenius form and the activation energies of several single-cultivar wines are presented in Table 8-8.

6. Stability Testing for Calcium Tartrate

A seeded calcium tartrate stability test analogous to that previously developed for the potassium bitartrate salt has been developed (Abgueguen and Boulton 1993). The changes in conductivity due to the calcium tartrate are considered to be too small for the use of the conductivity approach and the more specific approach is to determine the calcium concentration before and after the test. The major

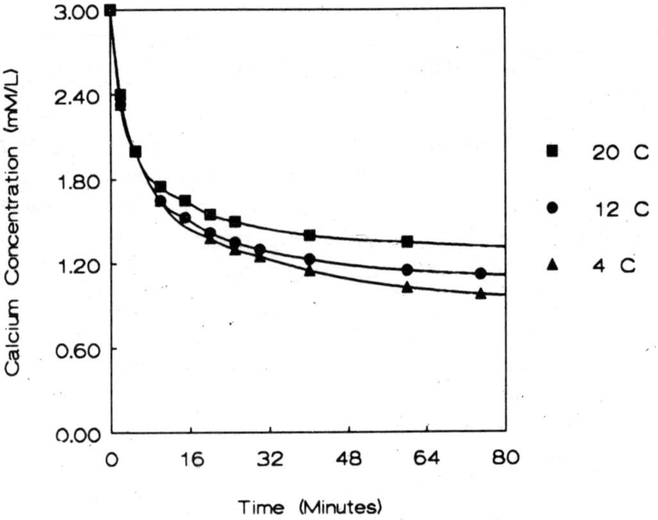

Fig. 8-5. The effect of temperature on the crystallization of calcium tartrate.

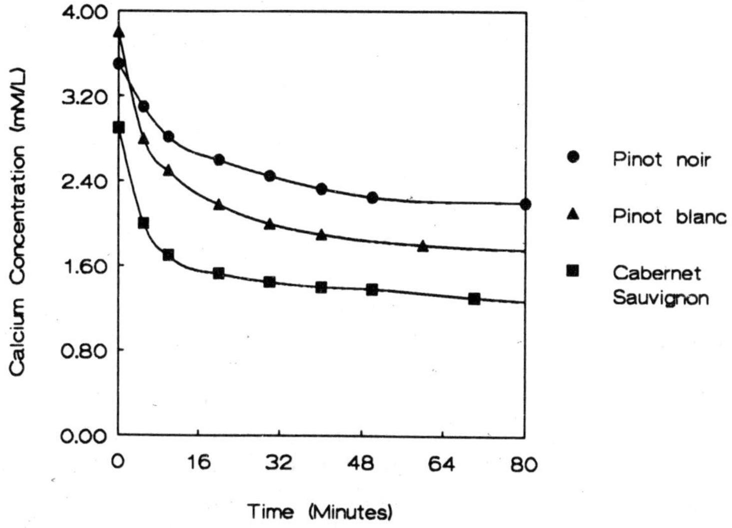

Fig. 8-6. The crystallization of calcium tartrate from different wines.

limitation is the procurement of pure calcium tartrate seed crystals since most commercial samples contain approximately 5% of a basic impurity and this causes significant pH changes when added. The results described were obtained using freshly prepared calcium tartrate seed crystals.

The test conditions are a seeding level of 4 g/L of the crystals at the desired temperature and the membrane filtration of the sample after approximately 100 minutes. The initial and final samples are then analyzed for calcium content by atomic absorption or a comparable method. The changes in calcium content are often too small to be detected by conductivity under these conditions. A similar interpretation is applied to determine whether the wine has precipitated calcium, shown no change, or dissolved calcium under the test conditions.

Corresponding saturation temperature tests have been proposed for calcium tartrate solubility (Görtges and Stocké 1987, Muller et al. 1990), using the changes in conductivity to determine the ability of a wine to dissolve calcium tartrate at temperatures between 10°C and 30°C. These tests have the same limitations as those described previously (Section 3.e) for the potassium bitartrate solubility, with further limitations due the difficulty of spontaneous nucleation and are not recommended.

a. *Action of Calcium Cation Additions*

Calcium sulfate additions have been used to lower the pH of wine without increasing the titratable acidity and are probably limited to wine production in the Sherry region of Spain. The increase in calcium concentration causes precipitation of calcium tartrate and allows further ionization of the existing tartaric acid

Table 8-8. The influence of temperature on the rate of calcium tartrate from wines.

Cultivar	Temperature (°C) 4	12	20	Activation energy (kJ/Mole)
Chardonnay	158.5	78.4	62.1	34.5 ± 7.40
Pinot blanc	123.4	66.5	—	52.8 ± 11.6
Pinot noir	85.4	68.4	57.4	16.6 ± 2.90
Cabernet Sauvignon	151.3	112.7	74.2	30.0 ± 2.00

(and the bitartrate ions). The result is a release of protons and a fall in pH with no change in titratable acidity. The extent of the change is dependent on the amount of calcium tartrate precipitated and the buffer capacity at the wine (i.e., the presence and strength of other acids). There is no change in the titratable acidity because the calcium tartrate contains no ionizable hydrogens, unlike potassium bitartrate. Since supersaturation levels must be reached in order for the precipitation to occur, a subsequent calcium tartrate instability would be expected unless the wine is further treated to remove any excess calcium tartrate. Ideally the crystals from the precipitation might be used as nuclei for the calcium tartrate stabilization if cooling and stirring are employed before removal of the calcium tartrate. This may be acceptable for wine treatments, but is less so for juices due the change in solubility with ethanol content. The treatment is not approved in the United States.

7. Calcium Mucate

An unusual instability that can occur in wines from botrytis-infected grapes is due to the precipitation of mucic acid. The acid is thought to be formed by an enzymatic oxidation of galacturonic acid, which forms the backbone of grape pectin. Much of the pectin content is degraded by botrytis and levels of mucic acid can be as high as 1 to 2 g/L (Würdig 1976). The solubility of the calcium mucate is very low and the precipitate is characterized by small white clumps rather than more usual crystalline shape of other salts. The quantity of the acid in the mucate form approximately doubles between pH 3.0 and 3.25 and again between 3.25 and 3.5. This means that the quantity of calcium at saturation must decrease by one-half and one-quarter over the same range. In a wine containing 10% v/v ethanol, the calcium content at saturation with 100 mg/L mucic acid is approximately 400 mg/L at pH 3.0, 160 mg/L at pH 3.25, or 80 mg/L at pH 3.5 (Würdig 1976). With average calcium contents of approximately 90 mg/L in table wines (Table 8-4), the saturation levels for the salt would be reached with approximately 450 mg/L at pH 3.0, 185 mg/L at pH 3.25, and 90 mg/L at pH 3.50.

8. Metal Stabilities

Transition metals, in particular copper and iron, are involved in a number of solubility and complex ion equilibria as well as altering the solubility and stability of certain protein fractions in wines. The concentration of a number of the transition metals in wines is shown in Table 8-9 (Ough et al. 1982). Levels

Table 8-9. Levels of some transition metals in California wines.

Statistic	Copper (mg/L)	Iron (mg/L)	Zinc (mg/L)	Lead (mg/L)
		White table wine (138 samples)		
Average	0.13	3.0	0.66	0.04
Standard Deviation	0.11	1.8	0.38	0.07
		Rosé wine (9 samples)		
Average	0.16	3.7	0.62	0.03
Standard Deviation	0.11	1.7	0.23	0.01
		Red table wine (124 samples)		
Average	0.17	3.8	0.93	0.04
Stardard Deviation	0.18	1.6	0.74	0.03
		Sparkling wine (16 samples)		
Average	0.07	3.3	0.95	0.03
Stardard Deviation	0.05	1.0	0.72	0.01

Source of Data: Ough et al. (1982).

of copper or iron as low as 1.0 mg/L have been shown to be involved in protein-metal hazes (Kean and Marsh 1957). In these cases, the protein content of the haze is several times the weight of the accompanying copper. Sources of contamination can be copper or brass fittings in storage vessels or the residues of applications of copper sulfate in the vineyard (Lay and Lemperle 1981; Lay and Leib 1988) or any additions made in the winery to remove hydrogen sulfide. Methods for the removal of copper and iron in particular are discussed in more detail in Chapter 7.

B. PROTEIN STABILITY

The slow development of protein hazes in white table wines is perhaps the next most common physical instability after the precipitation of potassium bitartrate. The levels of total protein show only a poor correlation with the incidence of protein hazes (Bayly and Berg 1967), and this is not surprising given the influence of pH on the solubility proteins. Of more importance are the isoelectric properties of the various protein fractions, their solubilities under wine conditions, and their concentrations in wine.

While earlier approaches were concerned with the total protein content and heat denaturation, the more common protein instabilities today are those that occur sometime after bottling and shelf storage and these appear to be primarily due to the solubility of particular fractions rather than thermal denaturation.

1. Factors Influencing Solubility

Proteins become cations at low pH and anions at high pH due to the ionization of their carboxylic acid and amine components. The pH value at which they carry no overall charge is referred to as the isoelectric point (pI), and this is essentially the same as the isoionic point for most proteins.

The importance of the isoelectric point is that it is also the pH value at which the solubility of the protein is at a minimum. For many proteins a change of 0.2 pH units in either direction can lead to a significant increase in solubility, with greater increases in low-strength salt solutions. The role of salt strength up to 20 mM/L is to enhance the solubility of several proteins in aqueous conditions. Since many wines will have salt strengths in the range 40 to 60 mM/L, wine proteins are expected to be made more soluble due to this effect. The reverse is true of the influence of ethanol, but the extent to which it reduces the salt effect at wine conditions has yet to be determined.

Like other colloidal components, there is relatively little known about the factors influencing the rate of nucleation and aggregation of the insoluble form. By analogy with the solubility of organic salts, the proteins appear to be able to remain in a supersaturated state for considerable periods of time before precipitation occurs. This poses some difficulties in the development of suitable stability tests, especially those that address the level of supersaturation rather the protein concentration alone.

2. Wine Proteins

Wine proteins have isoelectric points between 2.5 and 8.7 (Yokotsuka et al. 1977; Anelli 1977) and molecular weights in the range of 20,000 to 40,000 Dalton. They appear to be subunits of cellular proteins from grapes, disrupted by the pH change when berries are crushed. Studies of the changes in total protein content during maturation of the grapes (Tyson et al. 1980, 1981; Murphey et al. 1989) have shown levels between 100 and 800 mg/L depending both on the cultivars and the protein methods employed. Polypeptides (generally defined to be MW < 10,000) released by yeast leakage and autolysis have been shown to be thermally stable in wine (Bayly and Berg 1967) but may be involved in peptide-tannin hazes (to be discussed in Section C.3 of this chapter).

The fractions of wine proteins separated by anion exchange chromatography (Bayly and

Berg 1967) have been shown to have quite different properties in terms of the incidence of heat stability. This study provided strong evidence about the fractional nature of protein properties and behavior. They found that the late eluting peak, the fraction with the lowest pI value, to be the most unstable under the heat test conditions. Similar but more recent results, showing variable response of fractions to the heat test, have been obtained by the differential precipitation with ammonium sulphate (Waters et al. 1991) and by HPLC anion exchange fractions (Fukuda 1992).

The multiplicity of protein fractions in two common cultivars are shown in the HPLC separations in Figures 8-7a and 8-7b (Trousdale and Boulton 1987). This separation method has been used to study the response

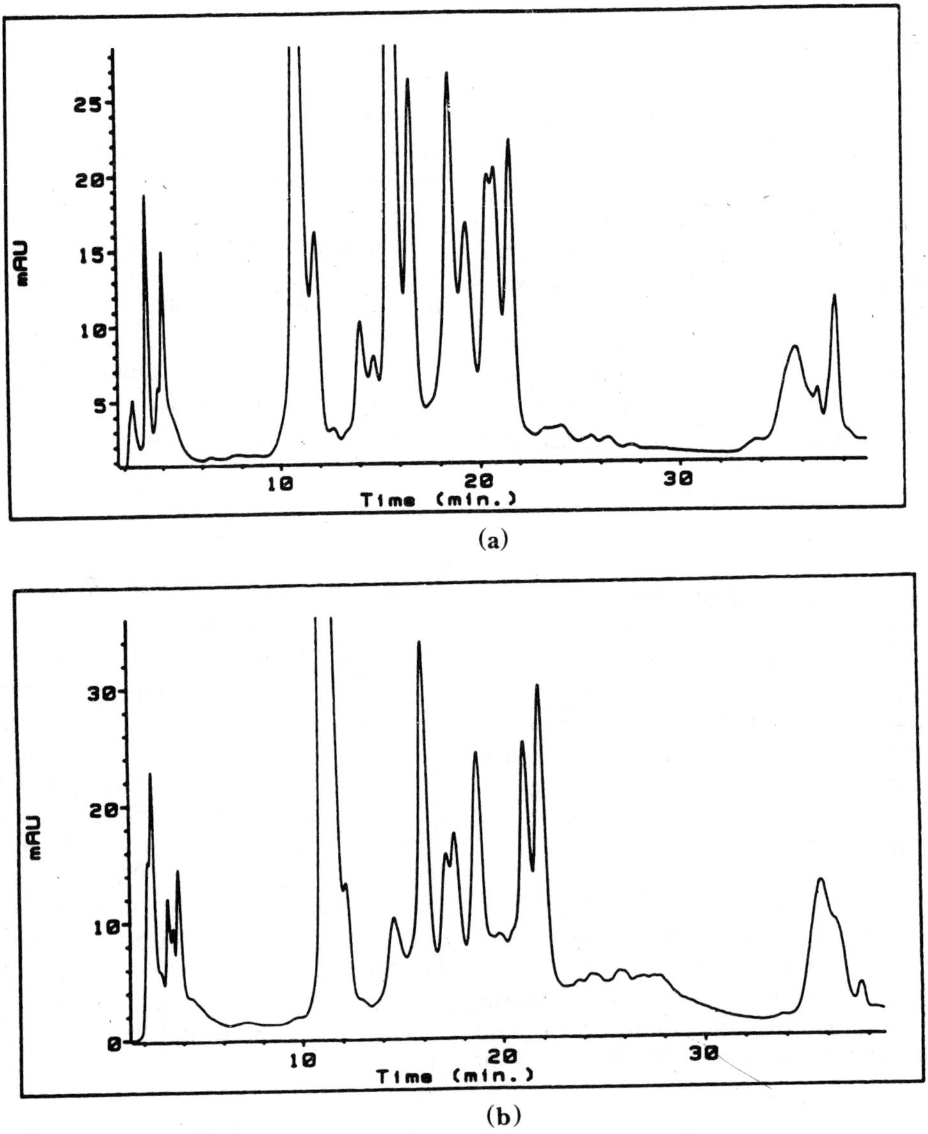

Fig. 8-7. Separation of the protein fractions in (a) Chardonnay; and (b) Sauvignon blanc.

of the different fractions to various stability tests, bentonite fining, and protease treatment (Fukuda 1992). A number of other studies have recently applied alternative separation methods to study juice and wine proteins (Interesse et al. 1987; Correa et al. 1988; Paezold et al. 1990).

Early studies of the effect of pH and protein content effects found that wines with 90 to 125 mg/L were stable at pH values of 2.93 to 3.15, but unstable at pH values above this (Moretti and Berg 1965). There was little effect of pH on the heat stability of three wines that had protein contents above 200 mg/L. No general correlations between total protein content and instability by the heat test could be found. There was a trend in protein instability with increasing wine pH above 3.2.

Protein fractions are selectively removed by bentonite fining, with those carrying the largest positive charge being removed first. Unfortunately, there are combinations of cultivar and pH which can lead to protein fractions being close to neutrality, which are then most likely to be unstable and yet poorly removed by bentonite. Because of the influence of pH on both protein solubility and its charge, wines fined with bentonite at one pH and either adjusted in acidity (with a change in pH) or placed in a blend at a new pH are again susceptible to instability, even with the dilution effects. In most cases, bentonite fining should be performed at the lowest possible pH, in order to be most effective with as many protein fractions as possible in a cationic form.

3. Tests for Protein Stability

Stability tests can be classified into four main groups: (1) Total protein assays (such as the Biuret, Coomassie blue, Pierce protein reagent); (2) chemical denaturation treatments (such as the trichloroacetic acid, TCA, or phosphomolybdic acid, PMA, tests); (3) heat denaturation tests (for conditions ranging from 90°C for one hour to 50°C for 24 hours); and (4) solubility tests (such as ethanol participation). The total protein content is of limited use in quantifying the tendency for precipitation, and the Coomassie blue and the Pierce protein reagents have interferences due to phenols and copper, tannin (Godshal 1983), and glutathione (Fukuda 1992) respectively, when used directly in wines. The Coomassie blue procedure also displays different responses to different proteins (Bradford 1976; Spector 1977; Read and Northcote 1981; Tal et al. 1980), and this is of concern in its use in wines.

The trichloroacetic acid (TCA) test (Berg and Akiyoshi 1961) involves boiling the sample for two to five minutes in the presence of the acid, cooling, and measuring haze formation. The Bentotest approach (Jakob 1968), which used phosphomolybdic acid, is similar but was performed at room temperature. Both of these are gross chemical denaturations of protein structure under very acidic conditions. They are effectively crude protein assays and again show little relationship to the solubility or stability of unstable fractions. They are not recommended.

a. *Heat Tests*

The heat tests provide the conditions for the thermal denaturation of proteins (at temperatures that wines should not be exposed to) and their use is of limited application to the precipitation of protein fractions due to solubility. The thermal denaturation properties of a protein fraction are not related to its pI and the fractions addressed in these tests may be very soluble in the wine at normal conditions.

The conditions for these tests range from one hour at 90°C to two days at 50°C, followed by chilling to enhance the precipitation. The poor correlation between different versions of the test indicates that the accelerated results of this kind are unreliable. Both Jakob (1969) and Pocock and Rankine (1973) found that there were different responses to the temperature used in the test when different wines where tested.

A concern with the longer tests, those using 24 and 48 hours, is the accelerated oxidation and condensation of phenolics (even in the absence of air) under these conditions. This may lead to combined precipitates between peptides and phenolic dimers (as described in Section C.3 of this chapter) which are artifacts of the test.

There is some rationale for the use of the heat-test on the basis that it tests for the heat-unstable components. These might form precipitates after the wine has been exposed to elevated temperatures during poorly controlled shipping or storage conditions. However, the application of treatments to pass these tests implies that the wine must be capable of sustaining such a thermal treatment without any precipitation and still be suitable for sale. This can result in a gross overtreatment of the wine and the problem of poor temperature control during transport and storage should be handled more directly.

Another concern with the application of the heat tests is that the precipitates are generally considered to be proteinaceous and that only bentonite should be used as the agent of treatment. In many wines this results in excessive bentonite applications when other components such as polysaccharides and phenolics may be contributing to haze formation in the test.

The recent isolation of a haze-protecting factor from white wine (Waters et al. 1993) which reduces the haze formation during heat tests adds to the complications in the interpretation of such tests. This factor was shown to be mainly polysaccharide (96%) with a small protein component (4%). The polysaccharide was found to comprise mostly mannose (78%) and glucose (13%). This finding might lead to the development of natural additives that can function in a similar way, perhaps preventing much of the haze formation observed in wines.

b. The Ethanol Test for Colloidal Stability

A more direct approach to the quantification of colloidal solubility is to deliberately force the least soluble components out of solution under defined conditions and to quantify the amount of haze produced. This has led to the application of ethanol as the forcing agent in a general colloidal stability tests for wines. This test aims to cause the precipitation of the least soluble colloidal fractions, at wine pH, with the agent most responsible for limiting their solubility. It involves the addition of 10 mL of absolute ethanol to a 10-mL degassed wine sample and the two are thoroughly mixed. The resulting haze can be measured in a matter of minutes at either room temperature or at lower temperatures. The lower temperatures provide somewhat higher readings but are complicated by the condensation of water vapor on the tube wall. The resulting ethanol content is approximately 56% v/v, which is considerably lower than that used by some groups for the detection of pectins or polysaccharides. Our use of this test uses the response of the haze to treatments, rather than the ethanol content of the mixture, to identify the components involved.

Protein fractions are usually one of the major components of the haze that results from the ethanol test. The extent to which proteins are involved can be determined by the response of the haze to treatments such as bentonite trials and the shifting of pH. The concentration of other colloids such as polysaccharides will not be altered significantly by these treatments.

The results obtained by the successive application of ethanol additions to a heat-unstable Sauvignon blanc wine are shown in Figure 8-8. The influence of pH on the solubility of its haze is clearly demonstrated. This wine would be more stable at either the higher or lower pH values, preferably the lower one in terms of bentonite effectiveness. The removal of unstable protein by bentonite is demonstrated on the same wine in Figure 8-9. The results of a one-hour, 90°C heat test of this wine indicated that bentonite levels in excess of 1.0 g/L would be required while the ethanol test would indicate somewhere between 240 and 600 mg/L would suffice. Such results are not generally found in all white wines. Table 8-10 provides a comparison of the similar tests for 10 white wines. A correlation is shown between the total protein content and the

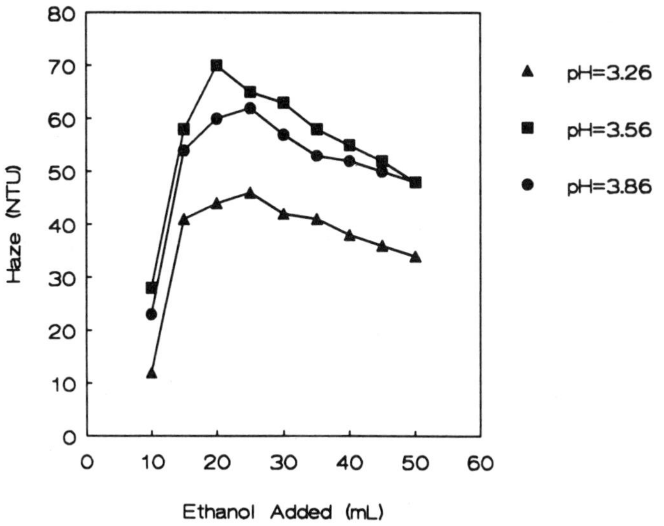

Fig. 8-8. Ethanol titration curves for a Sauvignon blanc wine at 3 pH conditions.

haze produced by the TCA method, but no relationship can be found between the heat test haze and the ethanol precipitation values, as might be expected.

4. Methods of Protein Stabilization

The most widely used agent for the treatment of wine for protein instability is bentonite. The mechanism of its action and the development of alternative treatments is considered in detail in Chapter 7.

The application of ultrafiltration to the removal of proteins from wines is complicated by the presence of the polysaccharide content. The evidence of phenolic retention by the use of certain 10,000 and 20,000 Dalton cutoff filters (Peri et al. 1988) is an additional factor making it less suitable for wine treatment.

The application of high-temperature short-time (HTST) treatments for the denaturation of proteins has found mixed success but limited acceptance, in part due to the poor precipitation of colloidal matter following the treatment. Recent advances in the characterization of the polysaccharide fractions may lead to a better understanding of such conditions

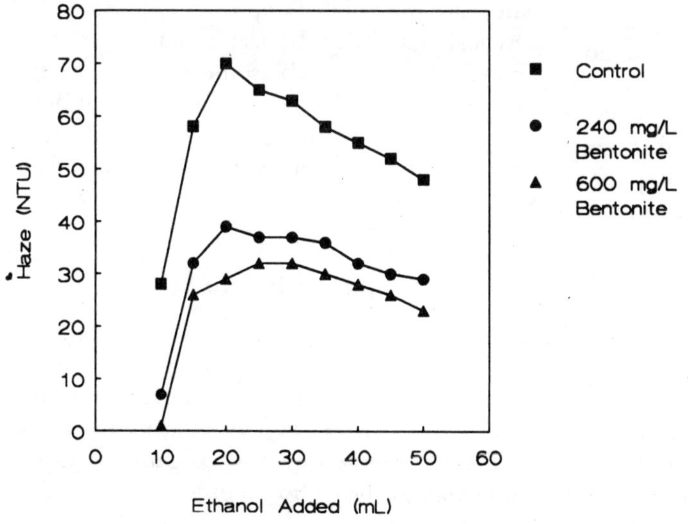

Fig. 8-9. Ethanol titration curves for a Sauvignon blanc wine at two bentonite levels.

Table 8-10. A comparison of alternative stability tests.

Wine	pH	Total protein[1] (mg/L)	TCA haze[2] (NTU)[B]	Heat haze (NTU)	Ethanol haze (NTU)
Chardonnay	3.00	8.3	16	3	24
Chardonnay	3.12	12.6	33	9	40
Riesling	3.11	12.5	88	14	25
Chardonnay	3.50	12.8	68	28	30
Sauvignon blanc	2.85	14.2	90	16	24
Muscat Canelli	3.44	17.9	100	70	40
Riesling	3.42	18.5	117	38	52
Chardonnay	3.41	19.6	184	52	57
Sauvignon blanc	3.18	24.6	162	25	25
Sauvignon blanc	3.56	29.6	242	120	53

[1]Coomassie Blue assay.
[2]Trichloroacetic acid assay.
[3]NTU = Nephelos turbidity unit.

and improvements in the effectiveness of this treatment option.

C. COLLOIDAL STABILITY

Colloids can be defined as partially soluble components whose distribution between its soluble and insoluble phases is dependent on the temperature, dielectric properties, and the polarity of the surrounding solvent. In juices and wines, the colloids can be classified simply into proteins (MW = 10,000 to 60,000 Dalton), polysaccharides (MW = 100,000 to 500,000), and complexes between proteins and phenols and between proteins and polysaccharides. However, there is significant variation between the protein fractions in terms of charge and hydrophobic nature and thinking of them as a single group when discussing their colloidal behavior is an oversimplification. The same can be said of the polysaccharides, where their properties are strongly tied to their carbohydrate composition and origin.

There is relatively little known about the nucleation, development, and redissolving of colloid particles in general let alone in natural products such as wine. However, in terms of general solubility concepts, they can remain in a state of supersaturation for long periods of time before precipitating, and once formed they can produce a suspended phase that is not easily redissolved.

The positively charged character of most wine proteins and the negatively charged character of some of the polysaccharides may lead to additional charge couplings between these partially soluble components. The formation of a colloidal envelope around an oppositely charged ionic component can alter the interaction with the solvent causing changes in solubility. These changes can either increase or decrease the solubility of the aggregate, depending on the nature of the components. Such combinations of colloids are generally referred to as protective colloids. They are especially important in aspects of physical stability and haze formation in wines and can become troublesome when their equilibrium state has been disturbed by treatments such as bentonite fining and filtration through charge-modified filter media. A recent study of such complexes in red wines is that by Brillouet et al. (1991).

1. The Polysaccharides of Wines

Polysaccharides can be found in wines at levels between 300 mg/l and 1000 mg/L (Usseglio-Tomasset 1976). They can be divided into two main groups, those originating from the grape and those released by microorganisms during winemaking (Usseglio-Tomasset and Di Stefano 1977; Villettaz 1988). Recent advances in the rapid quantification of polysaccharide levels has led to significant advances in our knowledge of this pool of wine constituents (Wucherpfennig and Dietrich 1983; Dubourdieu et al. 1986; Dietrich and Zimmer 1989; Zimmer et al. 1992).

The first group includes the pectins, which are polymers of galacturonic acid that are partially esterified with methyl groups. These polysaccharides have molecular weights in the range 10,000 to 50,000 and are made up of galactose, arabinose, galacturonic acid, rhamnose, and glucose. The major fractions are rhamnogalacturans, arabinogalactans, and arabans (Brillouet et al. 1990; Dietrich et al. 1992). They will also include polymers such as the β glucan, with a molecular weight in the range 100,000 to 1,000,000, produced by botrytis infection. This infection also degrades the pectin considerably and can double the level of other polysaccharides in the juice. Heating of musts during thermovinification (70°C, 30 minutes) also increases the pectin and neutral polysaccharide content (Mourges et al. 1982).

The second group includes those released by yeast during and following fermentation and by certain bacteria. The bud scars of Saccharomyces have been shown to contain high levels of a mannan (Bauer et al. 1972; Aspinall 1970) and the release of 150 to 300 mg/L of polysaccharides (mostly mannan) paralleled the yeast population during fermentation (Llauberes et al. 1987; Feuillat et al. 1988; Dietrich et al. 1992). There are differences between the yeast strains, and the effects of nutrient availability would be expected to influence the amount formed by determining the extent of yeast growth. The release of β glucan by a lactic acid bacteria has also been reported (Llauberes 1990). The continued release of polysaccharides during the sur lees contact has also been demonstrated (Parentheon and Feuillat 1978; Llauberes et al. 1987; Feuillat et al. 1988).

A number of the components that have been classified as polysaccharide also have a significant protein component and vice versa. When this is a structural part of the protein they are referred to as glycoproteins. One of the fractions associated with the decline in filtration flux of a 0.2-μm pore, ceramic, cross-flow filter has been identified as being high molecular weight and rich in mannose, arabinose, and protein (Belleville et al. 1991).

The changes in the levels of these polysaccharides after fermentation will be influenced by their ability to remain soluble during aging, storage, and wine treatments and their interaction with fining agents that might be used. There is evidence that some fractions such as the arabinogalactans are not appreciably altered during winemaking (Dietrich et al. 1992). In general, the level of polysaccharides can hamper the clarification by natural settling and filtration (Wucherpfennig et al. 1984). The recent isolation of a polysaccharide fraction (containing primarily mannose and glucose with a small protein component) that interferes with the formation of haze during the heat test for proteins (Waters et al. 1993), raises many questions about the role of polysaccharides in all aspects of the physical stability of wines.

The application of sterile filtration with pads, perpendicular flow membranes (0.65- or 0.45-um pore size) or cross-flow microfiltration (0.2-μm pore size) has an insignificant effect on the level of polysaccharides in wine. However, the application of ultrafiltration with membranes with MWCO values of 20,000 and 50,000 Dalton has been shown to remove the majority of the polysaccharide from wines (Peri et al. 1988; Brillouet et al. 1989; Wucherpfennig and Dietrich 1989). The role of colloidal materials in the inhibition of nucleation of potassium bitartrate has been known for some time but the natural protection offered by them is not easily quantified. Recent studies of potassium bitartrate stability in wines that have been ultrafiltered have shown that they are much more unstable than the untreated wine (Maujean et al. 1986; Escudier et al. 1987; Escudier and Moutounet 1987; Wucherpfennig and Dietrich 1989; Willy et al. 1991). This is not likely to be an issue since there has been little acceptance of ultrafiltration applications and the move is toward the use of cross-flow microfilters.

2. Protein-Tannin Complexes

The addition of protein fining agents for the lowering of tannin concentrations is an example of a mutual adsorption and a change in solubility that can occur between previously soluble components. The extent of adsorption will not generally be the same for all tannins, and the nature of adsorption is such that there will be concentrations of the tannins, the protein, and their complexes remaining in solution following the precipitation. The soluble complex remaining in solution is expected to be low in concentration but to behave like a colloid in terms of delayed precipitation and its response to temperature. In red wines, the concentration of tannins is expected to precipitate essentially all natural proteins and those added at usual levels. In white wines, higher concentration of proteins and the lower concentrations of tannin suggest that these wines are more likely to have both components coexisting and the potential for significant residues of the complex. The effect of pH on the solubility of such complexes is similar to that of the protein involved (Oh and Hoff 1987).

Haze formation between polymeric phenols and grape proteins has been demonstrated at levels of 66 mg/L for the largest-molecular-weight tannin fraction in a wine protein solution (Yokotsuka et al. 1983). Higher amounts were required of smaller-molecular-weight polymeric phenols to produce similar hazes. The nontannin fraction of the phenols was not able to form such hazes with the wine proteins. By comparison, when different molecular weight fractions of gelatin were added to solutions of grape tannin or phenolic dimers, considerable differences were found in haze formation. With the tannin solution there was little effect of the molecular weight on the amount of haze formation, However, with the dimer solution, haze formation occurred between the smaller peptide fractions (2,000 and 5,000 dalton) and the dimer but not with the larger-molecular-weight protein fractions (Yokotsuka and Singleton 1987).

These results indicate that the phenol dimers and small peptide fractions may be significant components in the formation of colloidal instability of white wines. There is a need for further studies of the size and nature of the peptide pool in juices and wines.

D. IMMOBILIZED AGENTS FOR WINE TREATMENT

1. Immobilized Enzymes

There are several reasons for the interest in the application of immobilized enzymes to winemaking. In some cases the activity (in terms of pH and ethanol) may be enhanced or the stability (in terms of pH, ethanol, and temperature) improved over that of the soluble form. The enzyme might be expensive so that its recovery and reuse are of economic interest. The immobilized enzyme could be used in a fixed-bed reactor and its activity enhanced by exposing the wine to a warmer treatment temperature for short periods of time. Such reactors would greatly speed up the reaction rate due to the high concentrations of the enzyme in it. Enzymes that could be considered for such applications are:

- Proteases—For the hydrolysis of wine proteins and peptides, to enhance colloidal and heat stability of white wines, and to replace the use of bentonite. In particular, acid proteases and preparations that might be unstable otherwise in a wine medium (Bakalinsky and Boulton 1985).
- Pectinases—For the hydrolysis of pectins, to enhance colloidal stability and perhaps filterability rather than for free-run juice recovery, which is the more common use.
- Glucanases—For the hydrolysis of ß glucans, to enhance filterability of late-harvest and botrytized wines, as has been demonstrated

by the soluble preparations (Dubourdieu et al. 1981; Villettaz et al. 1984). Possible enhancement of stability and for recovery of an expensive and less commonly used enzyme.

- Ureases—For the hydrolysis of urea, a precursor of ethyl carbamate if the wine is heated in shipment or storage, as has been shown with soluble preparations (Trioli and Ough 1989; Fujinawa et al. 1990). In particular, to speed up the hydrolysis by an immobilized enzyme reactor.
- Glucosidases—For the hydrolysis of terpene glucosides in cultivars (Muscat, Gewürztraminer, Riesling) rich in them in order to enhance their aroma and perhaps to enhance colloidal stability in special cases.

E. REFERENCES

ABGUEGUEN, O., and R. B. BOULTON. 1993. "The crystallization kinetics of calcium tartrate from model solutions and wines." *Am. J. Enol. Vitic.* 44:65–75.

ANELLI, G. 1977. "The proteins of musts." *Am. J. Enol. Vitic.* 28:200–203.

ANON. 1976. "Scraped-surface heat exchanger reduces wine cold stabilization time." *Food Eng.* 48(Nov):155.

ASPINALL, G. O. 1970. *Polysaccharides.* Pergamon Press, New York, pp. 89–92.

BAKALINSKY, A. T., and R. BOULTON. 1985. "The study of an immobilized acid protease for the treatment of wine proteins." *Am. J. Enol. Vitic.* 36:23–29.

BALAKIAN, S., and H. W. BERG. 1968. "The role of polyphenols in the behavior of potassium bitartrate in red wines." *Am. J. Enol. Vitic.* 19:91–100.

BAUER, H., M. HORISBERGER, D. A. BUSH, and E. SIGARLAKI. 1972. "Mannan as a major component of the bud scars of *Saccharomyces cerevisiae.*" *Arch. Mikrobiol.* 85:202–208.

BAYLY, F. C., and H. W. BERG. 1967. "Grape and wine proteins of white wine varietals." *Am. J. Enol. Vitic.* 18:18–32.

BELLEVILLE, M.-P., J.-M. BRILLOUET, B. TARODO DE LA FUENTE, L. SAULNIER, AND M. MOUTOUNET. 1991. "Differential roles of red wine colloids in the fouling of a cross-flow microfiltration alumina membrane." *Vitic. Enol. Sci.* 46:100–107.

BERG, H. W., and M. AKIYOSHI. 1961. "Determination of protein stability in wine." *Am. J. Enol. Vitic.* 12:107–110.

BERG, H. W., and M. AKIYOSHI. 1971. "The utility of potassium bitartrate concentration product values in wine processing." *Am. J. Enol. Vitic.* 22:127–134.

BERG, H. W., M. AKIYOSHI, and M. A. AMERINE. 1979. "Potassium and sodium content of California wines." *Am. J. Enol. Vitic.* 30:55–57.

BERG, H. W., R. DESOTO, and M. AKIYOSHI. 1968. "The effect of refrigeration, bentonite clarification and ion exchange on potassium behavior in wines." *Am. J. Enol. Vitic.* 19:208–212.

BERG, H. W., and R. M. KEEFER. 1958. "Analytical determination of tartrate stability in wine: 1. Potassium bitartrate." *Am. J. Enol.* 9:180–193.

BERG, H. W., and R. M. KEEFER. 1959. "Analytical determination of tartrate stability in wine: 2. Calcium tartrate." *Am. J. Enol. Vitic.* 10:105–109.

BLOUIN, J., and A. DESENNE. 1983. "Essai d'un appareil de traitment des vins par le froid en continu (Systeme Crystal-flow, Alfa-Laval)." *Conn. Vigne Vin* 17:137–150.

BLOUIN, J., G. GUIMBERTEAU, and P. AUDOUIT. 1979. "Prevention des precipitations tartriques dans les vins par le procede par contact." *Conn. Vigne Vin* 13:149–169.

BOIRET, M., A. MARTY, C. FABREGA, A. GUITTARD, A. TIXIER, A. SCHAEFFER, and A. SCHLEWITZ. 1991. "Indice de stabilite tartrique des vins et risque de precipitation." *Rev. Fr. Oenol.* 128:53–58.

BOTT, E. W., and P. SCHOTTLER. 1985. "Optimizing tartrate separation through the use of centrifuges." *Filtration and Separation* 22: 364–365.

BOULTON, R. 1983. "The conductivity method for evaluating the potassium bitartrate stability of wines." Pts 1,2. *Enology Briefs* 2,3 Cooperative Extension, Davis, CA: University of California.

BRADFORD, M. M. 1976. "A rapid and sensitive method for the quantitation of microgram quantities of protein utilizing the principle of protein-dye binding." *Anal. Biochem.* 72:248–254.

BRILLOUET, J.-M., M.-P. BELLEVILLE, and M. MOUTOUNET. 1991. "Possible protein-polysaccharide complexes in red wines." *Am. J. Enol. Vitic.* 42:150–152.

BRILLOUET, J.-M., C. BOSSO, and M. MOUTOUNET. 1990. "Isolation, purification and characterization of an arabinogalactan from a red wine." *Am. J. Enol. Vitic.* 41:29–36.

BRILLOUET, J.-M., M. MOUTOUNET, and J. L. ESCUDIER. 1989. "Fate of yeast and grape pectic polysaccharides of a young red wine in the cross-flow microfiltration process." *Vitis* 28:49–63.

CLARK, J. P., K. C. FUGELSANG, and B. H. GUMP. 1988. "Factors affecting induced calcium tartrate precipitation in wine." *Am. J. Enol. Vitic.* 39:155–161.

CORREA, I., M. C. POLO, L. AMIGO, and M. RAMOS. 1988. "Separation des proteines des mouts de raisin au moyen de techniques electrophoretiques." *Conn. Vigne Vin.* 22:1–9.

CURVELO-GARCIA, A. S. 1987. "O producto de solubilidade do tartarato de calcio em meios hidroalcoolicos em funcão dos sues factores determinantes." *Ciencia Tec. Vitiv.* 6:19–28.

DESOTO, R. T., and H. YAMADA. 1963. "Relationship of solubility products to long range tartrate stability." *Am. J. Enol. Vitic.* 14:43–51.

DIETRICH, H., H. SCHMITT, and K. WUCHERPFENNIG. 1992. "The alteration of the colloids of must and wine during winemaking. II. Change of the charge and molecular weight distribution of the polysaccharides." *Vitic. Enol. Sci.* 47:87–95.

DIETRICH, H., and E. ZIMMER. 1989. "Die Kolloidbestimmung von Weinen: ein Methodenvergleich." *Mitt. Klost.* 44:13–19.

DOMEIZEL, M., J. GALEA, J. REY, S. MARCHANDEAU, and A. GUITTARD. 1992. "Mise au point d'une methode de prevision des precipitations tartriques dans le vin." *Rev. Fr. Oenol.* 139:15–24.

DROUX, F., and C. VIALATTE. 1983. "Utilisation du procedure "mini contact" pour l'etude des precipitations tartriques dans le vins." *Rev. d'Oenol.* 29:13–14.

DUBOURDIEU, D., R.-M. LLAUBERES, and C. OLIVIER. 1986. "Estimation rapide des constituants macromdeculaires des mouts et des ving par chromatographie liquide haute pression de tamisage moleculaire." *Conn. Vigne Vin.* 20:119–123.

DUBOURDIEU, D., J. C. VILLETTAZ, C. DESPLANQUES, and P. RIBÉREAU-GAYON, 1981. "Degradation enzymatique du glucane de Botrytis cinerea." *Conn. Vigne Vin* 15:161–177.

DUNSFORD, P., and R. BOULTON. 1981. "The kinetics of potassium bitartrate crystallization from table wines. Pts. 1 and 2." *Am. J. Enol. Vitic.* 32:100–105 and 106–110.

EDWARDS, T. L., V. L. SINGLETON, and R. BOULTON. 1985. "Formation of ethyl esters of tartaric acid during wine aging: Chemical and sensory changes." *Am. J. Enol. Vitic.* 36:118–124.

ESCUDIER, J. L. and M. MOUTOUNET. 1987. "Filtraton tangentielle et stabilisation tartrique des vins. II. Apport de la microfiltration tangentialle dans la stabilisation tartrique d'un vin rouge." *Rev. Fr. Oenol.* 109:44–50.

ESCUDIER, J. L., M. MOUTOUNET, and P. BENARD. 1987. "Filtration tangentielle et stabilisation tartrique des vins. I. Influence de l'ultrafiltration sur la cinetique de cristallisation du bitartrate de potassium des vins." *Rev. Fr. Oenol.* 108:52–57.

ESTEVE, J. L. 1988. "La stabilisation des vins contre les precipitations tartriques par systeme Crystalloprocess." *Rev. d'Oenol.* 47:25–27.

FERENCZI, S., A. ASVANY, and L. ERCZHEGYI. 1982. "Stabilisation des vins contre les precipitations par le froid." *Bull. O.I.V.* 613:203–220.

FEUILLAT, M., C. CHARPENTIER, G. PICCA, and P. BERNARD. 1988. "Production des colloides par levures dans le vin mousseux elabore selon la methode champenoise." *Rev. Fr. Oenol.* 111:36–45.

FUJINAWA, S., G. BURNS, and P. DE LA TEJA. 1990. "Application of acid urease to reduction of urea in commercial wines." *Am. J. Enol. Vitic.* 41:350–354.

FUKUDA, Y. 1992. The behavior of protein fractions in white wines. M.S. thesis, Davis, CA: University of California.

GAILLARD, M., B. RATSIMBA, and J. L. FAVAREL. 1990. "Stabilite tartrique des vins: Comparison de differents tests, mesure de l'influence des polyphenols." *Rev. Fr. Oenol.* 123:7–13.

GAILLARD, M., B. RATSIMBA, and C. LAGUERIE. 1988. "La stabilisation tartrique: Reserche d'une plus grande securite." *Rev. d'Oenol.* 47:21–23.

GODSHAL, M. A. 1983. "Interference of plant polysaccharides and tannin in the Coomassie Blue G250 test for protein." *J. Food Sci.* 48:1346–1347.

GÖRTGES, S., and R. STOCKÉ. 1987. "Minikontaktverfahren zur Beurteilung der Calciumtartratstabilitat." *Weinwirt. Tech.* 123:19–21.

HAGEN, M. M. 1979. "Les precipitation tartriques." *Rev. Fr. Oenol.* 74:63–69.

HAUSHOFER, H., and L. SZEMELIKER. 1973. "Die Forderung der Weinsteinausscheidung bei Weinen durch Zugabe von Impfkristallen, Kratzen an Glaswanden und Anwendung von Ultraschall." *Mitt. Klost.* 23:259–284.

INTERESSE, F. S., V. ALLOGIO, F. LAMPORELLI, and G. D'AVELLA. 1987. "Proteins in must estimated by size exclusion HPLC." *Food Chem.* 23:65–78.

JAKOB, L. 1968. "Eiweissgehalt und Bentonitschönung von Wein." *Wein-Wissen.* 23:255–274.

JAKOB, L. 1969. "Eiweissgehalt und Eiweiss stabilisier ung von Wein." *Deu. Weinbau.* 24:177–189.

KANTZ, K., and V. L. SINGLETON. 1990. "Isolation and determination of polymeric polyphenols using Sephadex LH-20 and analysis of grape tissue extracts." *Am. J. Enol. Vitic.* 41:223–228.

KEAN, C. E., and G. L. MARSH. 1957. "Investigations of copper complexes causing cloudiness in wines. 1. Chemical composition." *Am. J. Enol.* 8:80–86.

LAY, H., and W. LEIB. 1988. "Über das Vorkommen der Metalle Zink, Cadmium, Blei und Kupfer in Most, Wein und in den bei der Weinbereitung anfallenden Nebenprodukten." *Wein-Wissen.* 43:107–115.

LAY, H., and E. LEMPERLE. 1981. "Kupfergehalt auf Weintrauben, in Traubenmost und in Wein nach Anwendung kupferhaltiger Peronospora-Fungizide." *Weinwirt.* 117:908–912.

LLAUBERES, R. M. 1990. "Structure of an extracellular β D-glucan from *Pediococcus* sp., a wine lactic bacteria." *Carbohydr. Res.* 203:103–107.

LLAUBERES, R. M., D. DUBOURDIEU, and J.-C. VILLETAZ. 1987. "Exocellular polysaccharide from *Saccharomyces* in wine." *J. Sci. Food Agric.* 41:277–286.

MAUJEAN, A., L. SAUSY, and D. VALLEE. 1985. "Determination de la saturation en bitartrate de potassium d'un vin. Quantification des effets colloides protecteurs." *Rev. Fr. Oenol.* 100:39–49.

MAUJEAN, A., D. VALLEE, and L. SAUSY. 1986. "Influence de la granulometrie des cristaux de tartre de contact et des traitements et collages sur la cinetique de cristallisation du bitartrate de potassium dans les vins blancs." *Rev. Fr. Oenol.* 104:34–41.

MORETTI, R. H., and H. W. BERG. 1965. "Variability among wines to protein clouding." *Am. J. Enol. Vitic.* 16:69–78.

MOURGES, J., P. BENARD, A. MATIGNON, T. CONTE, and M. MIKOLAJCZAC. 1982. "Effet du chauffage de la vendage sur la solubilisation des polyosides et sur clarification des mouts, des moutes et des vin." *Sci. Aliments.* 2:83–96.

MULLER, T., and G. WÜRDIG. 1978. "Das Minikontaktverfahren—ein einfacher Test zur Prüfung auf Weinsteinstabilität." *Weinwirt.* 114:857–861.

MULLER, T., G. WÜRDIG, G. SCHOLTEN, and G. FRIEDRICH. 1990. "Bestimmung der Calciumtartrat- Sättigungstemperatur von Weinen durch Leitfähigkeitsmessung." *Mitt. Klost.* 40:158–168.

MÜLLER-SPATH, T. 1979. "La stabilisation du tartre avec le procede a contact." *Rev. Fr. Oenol.* 73:41–47.

MURPHEY, J. M., J. R. POWERS, and S. E. SPAYD. 1989. "Estimation of soluble protein concentration of white wines using Coomassic Brilliant Blue G-250." *Am. J. Enol. Vitic.* 40:189–193.

NISHINO, H., and H. TANAHASHI. 1987. "Properties of nucleation and crystal growth of potassium bitartrate in wine." *Proc. 8th Intnl. Oenol. Symp.*, Cape Town, South Africa, 172–193.

OH, H., and J. E. HOFF. 1987. "pH dependence of complex formation between condensed tannins and proteins." *J. Food Sci.* 52:1267–1269.

OUGH, C. S., E. A. CROWELL, and J. BENZ. 1982. "Metal content of California wines." *J. Food Sci.* 47:825–828.

PAEZOLD, M., L. DULAU, and D. DUBOURDIEU. 1990. "Fractionnement et caracterisation des glycoprotenes dans les mouts de raisins blancs." *J. Int. Sci. Vigne Vin.* 24:13–28.

PARENTHEON, A., and M. FEUILLAT. 1978. "Les colloides solubles du vin de champagne en relation avec le rumage." *Conn. Vigne Vin* 3:177–193.

PERI, C., M. RIVA, and P. DECIO. 1988. "Crossflow membrane filtration of wines: Comparison of performance of ultrafiltration, microfiltration and intermediate cut-off membranes." *Am. J. Enol. Vitic.* 39:162–168.

PILONE, F. B., and H. W. BERG. 1965. "Some factors affecting tartrate stability in wine." *Am. J. Enol. Vitic.* 16:195–211.

POCOCK, K. F., and B. C. RANKINE. 1973. "Heat test for detecting protein instability in wine." *Aust. Wine Brew. Spirit Rev.* 91(5):42–43.

POSTEL, W. 1983. "La solubilité et la cinétique de cristallisation du tartrate de calcium dans le vin." *Bull. O.I.V.* 56(629–630):554–568.

POSTEL, W., and E. PRASCH. 1977. "Das Kontaktverfahren, eine neue Möglichkeit der Weinsteinstabilisierung." *Weinwirt*. 113:866–878.

READ, S. M., and D. H. NORTHCOTE. 1981. "Minimization of variation in the response to different proteins of the Coomassie Blue G dye—Ginding assay for protein." *Anal. Biochem*. 116:53–64.

RHEIN, O. H. 1977. "Weinsteinstabilisierung auf natürlichem Wege." *Weinwirt*. 113:515–519.

RHEIN, O. H., and W. KAPPES. 1979. "Weinstein-Berechnungen." *Weinwirt*. 115:227–236.

RHEIN, O. H., and F. NERADT. 1979. "Tartrate stabilization by the Contact process." *Am. J. Enol. Vitic*. 30:265–271.

RIESE, H., and R. BOULTON. 1980. "Speeding-up cold stabilization." *Wines and Vines* 61:Nov. 68–69.

RODRIGUEZ-CLEMENTE, R., and I. CORREA-GOROSPE. 1988. "Structural, morphological and kinetic aspects of potassium hydrogen tartrate precipitation from wines and ethanolic solutions." *Am. J. Enol. Vitic*. 39:169–179.

SCHMITT, A., R. MILTENBERGER, K. CURSCHMANN, and H. KOHLER. 1980. "Einfacher Test zur Bestimmung der Weinsteinstabilität." *Deu. Weinbau* 35:194–196.

SCOTT, R. S., T. G. ANDERS, and N. HUMS. 1981. Rapid cold stabilization of wine by filtration. *Am. J. Enol. Vitic*. 32:138–143.

" Scraped-surface heat exchanger reduces wine cold stabilization time." *Food Eng*. 48 (Nov):155.

SERRANO, M., and P. RIBÉREAU-GAYON. 1981. "Prevention des precipitations de bitartrate de potassium par le procede Vinipal." *Conn. Vigne Vin* 15:142–145.

SPECTOR, T. 1978. "Refinement of the Coomassie Blue method of protein quantification." *Anal. Biochem*. 86:142–146.

SUDRAUD, R., and J. CAYE. 1983. "Elimination du calcium du vin par le procede par contact utilisant du tartrate neutre de calcium." *Rev. Fr. Oenol*. 91:19–22.

TAL, M., A. SILBERSTEIN, and E. NUSSER. 1980. "Why does Coomassie Brillant Blue R interact differently with different proteins? A partial answer." *J. Biol. Chem*. 260:9976–9980.

TRIOLI, G. and C. S. OUGH. 1989. "Causes for inhibition of an acid urease from *lactobacillus fermentus*." *Am. J. Enol. Vitic*. 40:245–252.

TROUSDALE, E. K., and R. B. BOULTON. 1987. "The fractionation and quantification of wine proteins by three HPLC methods." *Proc. 38th. Ann. Meeting, Am. Soc. Enol. Vitic*, p. 16.

TYSON, P. J., E. S. LUIS, W. R. DAY, and T. H. LEE. 1981. "Estimation of soluble protein in must and wine by high performance liquid chromatography." *Am. J. Enol. Vitic*. 32:241–243.

TYSON, P. J., E. S. LUIS, and T. H. LEE. 1980. "Soluble protein levels in grapes and wine." *Proc. Cent. Symp*., Davis, CA: University of California.

USSEGLIO-TOMASSET, L. 1976. "Les colloides glucidiques soluble des mouts et des vins." *Conn. Vigne Vin* 10:193–226.

USSEGLIO-TOMASSET, L., and R. DI STEFANO. 1977. "Osservazioni sui costituenti azotati dei colloidi dei mosti, dei vini e dei colloidi ceduti dal lievito al substrato fermentativo." *Rev. Vitic. Enol*. 11:1–20.

USSEGLIO-TOMASSET, L., M. UBIGLI, and L. BARBERO. 1992. "The potassium acid tartrate oversaturation in wines." *Bull. O.I.V.* 739–740:703–719.

VALLEE, D., A. BAGARD, C. BLOY, P. BLOY, and L. BOURDE. 1990. "Appreciation de la stabilite tartrique des vins par la temperature de saturation —Influence du facteur temps sur la stabilite (duree de stockage)." *Rev. Fr. Oenol*. 126:51–61.

VIALATTE, C. 1984. "Test de stabilite bitartrate de potassium (Boulton)." *Rev. Oenol*. 34:20.

VIALATTE, G. 1979. "Stabilisation des vins en continu, vis-a-vis, du bitartrate de potassium." *Rev. Fr. Oenol*. 73:67–71.

VILLETTAZ, J.-C. 1988. "Les colloides du mout et du vin." *Rev. Fr. Oenol*. 111:23–27.

VILLETTAZ, J.-C., D. STEINER, and H. TROGUS. 1984. "The use of a beta-glucanase as an enzyme in wine clarification and filtration." *Am. J. Enol. Vitic*. 35:253–256.

WALTER, E. G. 1970. "Stabilization of wine by passage through a column of potassium hydrogen tartrate crystals." U.S. Patent 3,498,795.

WATERS, E. J., W. WALLACE, and P. J. WILLIAMS. 1991. "Heat haze characteristics of fractionated wine proteins." *Am. J. Enol. Vitic*. 42:123–127.

WATERS, E. J., W. WALLACE, M. E. TATE, and P. J. WILLIAMS. 1993. "Isolation and partial characterization of a natural haze protective factor from wine." *J. Agric. Food Chem*. 41:724–730.

WILLY, J., R. WEINARD, and H. DIETRICH. 1991. "Beeinflusst crossflow die weinsteinstabilitat?" *Weinwirt. Tech.* 127:24–29.

WUCHERPFENNIG, K., and H. DIETRICH. 1983. "Bestimmung des Kolloidgehaltes von Weinen." *Lebens.* 15:246–253.

WUCHERPFENNIG, K., and H. DIETRICH. 1989. "The importance of colloids for clarification of musts and wines." *Vitic. Enol. Sci.* 44:1–12.

WUCHERPFENNIG, K., H. DIETRICH, and R. FAUTH. 1984. "Über den Einfluss von Polysacchariden auf die Klärung und Filterfähigkeit von Weinen unter besonderer Berücksichtigung des Botrytisglucans." *Deut. Lebens. Rund.* 80:38–44.

WÜRDIG, G. 1976. "Schleimsäure—ein Inhaltsstoff von Weinen aus botrytisfaulem Lesegut." *Weinwirt.* 112(1–2):16–17.

WÜRDIG, G., T. MULLER, and G. FRIEDRICH. 1980a. "Methode pour caracteriser la stabilite du vin vis-a-vis du tartre par determination de la temperature de saturation." *Bull. O.I.V.* 613:220–228.

WÜRDIG, G., T. MULLER, and G. FRIEDRICH. 1980b. "Untersuchungen zur Weinsteinstabilität. Bestimmung der Sättigungstemperatur von Weinen durch Leitfähigkeitsmessung." *Weinwirt.* 116:720–726.

WÜRDIG, G., T. MULLER, and G. FRIEDRICH. 1983. "Prüfung auf Weinsteinstabilität in Traubensäften durch Bestimmung der Weinsteinsättigungstemperatur." *Flüss. Obst.* 50: 564–568.

WÜRDIG, G., T. MULLER, and G. FRIEDRICH. 1985. "Untersuchungen zur Weinsteinstabilität. 3. Mitteilung: Bestimmung der Weinsteinsättigungstemperatur durch verbesserte Leitfähigkeitmessung." *Weinwirt. Tech.* 121:188–191.

YOKOTSUKA, K., K. NOZUKI, and T. KUSHIDA. 1983. "Turbidity formation caused by interaction of must proteins with wine tannins." *J. Ferm. Technol.* 61:413–416.

YOKOTSUKA, K., and V. L. SINGLETON. 1987. "Interactive precipitation between graded peptides from gelatin and specific grape tannin fractions in wine-like model solutions." *Am. J. Enol. Vitic.* 38:199–206.

YOKOTSUKA, K., M. YOSHII, T. AIHARA, and T. KUSHIDA. 1977. "Isolation and characterization of proteins from juices, musts and wines from Japanese grapes." *J. Ferm. Technol.* 55:510–515.

ZIMMER, E., C.-D. PATZ, and H. DIETRICH. 1992. "Direct determination of molecular weight distribution of high molecular substances in wines and juices." *Vitic. Enol. Sci.* 47:121–129.

CHAPTER 9

MICROBIOLOGICAL SPOILAGE OF WINE AND ITS CONTROL

This chapter includes the descriptions and origins of various kinds of microbiological spoilage organisms—and the prevention of their presence and the control of their growth if present. It is important for the winemaker to know which spoilage has occurred in any given instance and to understand potential spoilage problems, but obviously it is better to forestall spoilage than to diagnose it. The taxonomic identifications of the yeasts are given in Chapter 4, and the lactic acid bacteria in Chapter 6. For the aerobic bacteria, the taxonomies are given at the end of this chapter.

A. DEFINITIONS OF MICROBIOLOGICAL SPOILAGE

Microbiological spoilage organisms can be said to be any of those which are unwanted at a particular place and time. Obviously, this includes those organisms which produce off-flavors, odors, colors, or precipitates, or have the potential to do so, under the conditions of the present and future storage of the wine. However, this definition also includes bona fide desirable wine yeast and bacteria when they are unwanted in a particular wine, for example, Montrachet yeast in semidry bottled wine or *Leuconostoc oenos* ML34 in bottled wine susceptible to malolactic fermentation. To complicate further the definition of microbiologic spoilage, one has to come to a decision on with which flavors, odors, colors, and turbidities are to be considered "off." Sediments may be acceptable in aged red wines; oxidized, aldehydic tones and brown hues are required in sherries; and slightly reduced, sulfurous notes might be found in aged sparkling wines. Another complication is that the distinct scents of wine from certain geographic regions, while being expected in those wines, are unacceptable—spoiled—in others, but have nothing to do with microbial spoilage: for example, foxiness or muscadine flavors in wines made from American grape varieties. Another complication is that sometimes the acceptance of distinct odors and flavors caused by certain microbes is controversial, as those seem to be which are be caused by *Brettanomyces* yeast (Section F.6). And finally, one more complication to add to the list is that winemakers may become so accustomed to their own wines that unusual flavors and odors—unacceptable to other tasters—are unnoticed. Winemakers are admonished habitually to taste the wines of other producers and to have their own wines habitually tasted by sensitive colleagues.

B. ORIGINS OF WINE SPOILAGE MICROORGANISMS

The source of microorganisms, good and bad, in the winery comes mainly from infections in the winery cooperage and winery equipment, especially the equipment used at the grape reception area and used for the transport of must or juice into the winery.

This idea flies in the face of the assumption that most of the natural microorganisms found in wine must arise from the vineyard. However, on sound, healthy, and intact grapes, the berry surface is not much different than that which would be found on any inert surface outdoors. It is true that the wild yeasts, such as *Kloeckera* and *Hansenula*, are exceptional; they *are* found on healthy berries—near the pedicel. Their presence may be related to the expectation that the grape skin surface at this region seems to allow some contact with the nutrients within (Belin 1972; Belin and Henry 1972). These nutrients, having a high content of sugars and a low pH, are selectively attractive to these yeasts. Why the presence of a correspondingly high concentration of wine yeast, that is, strains of *Saccharomyces cerevisiae* (Chapter 4, Section A.2), is also not found is not clear.

Of course not all of the grapes are healthy; breaks in the skin arise from normal conditions such as strong winds brushing berries against each other or against the woody parts of the vine. These breaks in the skin then allow unrestricted growth of all sorts of microorganisms. Other sources of breakage of the skins are bird pecks, hail, or even heavy rainstorms. So it could be expected that even under the best conditions of berry ripening, a substantial portion of the berries would give some exposure of the contents and allow enough growth of all sorts of organisms giving an incipient infection in the juice or must when it arrives inside the winery.

The description given several years ago (van der Walt and van Kerken 1958, 1961) of the origins of *Brettanomyces* spoilage in some wines in South Africa can serve as the scenario for the origins of many kinds of infections, including those of both good and bad wine microbes. In the *Brettanomyces* work it was discovered that during the crushing and destemming operations there was some buildup of the infecting organisms in the pools of juice associated with this equipment. Acceptance of only the most healthy fruit and interruption of the crushing operations and washing of the equipment from time to time would tend to minimize this buildup. However, as mentioned above, even the most healthy fruit is not completely devoid of all unwanted organisms. Furthermore, the washing operations, if not done thoroughly enough, might only aggravate the situation. That is, the dilution of the grape juice brings about a lowered concentration of sugar and an increased pH, and an encouragement of growth of various yeast and bacteria. This is especially true when pools of diluted grape juice are left standing for an extended time, such as overnight. To continue with the scenario, the diluted pools of juice can serve as ideal starter culture media for all sorts of microorganisms. Contamination from them eventually reaches into the winery, into fermenting juice and eventually into stored wine. When this sort of starter culture comes in contact with undiluted juice and wine, then only those that thrive on anaerobic conditions at low pH and probably cooler temperature, that is to say, the wine-related microorganisms, will survive. And if nutrients are available, they will grow. The conclusion of the scenario is that if even a single, viable organism under these conditions finds its way into a demijohn, barrel, or tank of wine, with enough time, this organism can multiply to spoilage concentrations.

This same scenario can apply to all sorts of wine spoilage organisms, and even to desirable wine organisms, including wine strains of *Saccharomyces cerevisiae* and coveted malolactic bacteria.

In the *Brettanomyces* studies, the proper prevention was found to be in very thorough cleaning of the crushing equipment and of the piping or hoses from the reception area into the winery, including judicious use of sulfur dioxide to aid in sanitizing. This means that every several hours, there should be a complete halt to the operations and thorough enough washings of the equipment to leave no diluted pools of juice. The washing operations needed to be especially thorough at the end of the day, and at the beginning of the next. Where continuous crushing is done, very thorough washing operations should be made several times during each 24-hour period. Such washing is not a sterilization procedure, but helps prevent buildup of contaminants.

We have found that the piping or hoses transporting the juice and must into the winery can be very susceptible to accumulation of contaminating microbes. In one winery with an especially difficult situation with *Brettanomyces* infection, the piping was underground and made a right angle from the reception to the winery. Over the years, the bend in the piping had allowed a collection of a large mass of material, which sheltered all sorts of contaminants, some seemingly carrying over from season to season. The contamination problem was solved only by unearthing and replacing the piping, and redirecting it to give only gentle curvatures.

Microbes also enter the winery simply coming in with wine from another facility for storage or possibly to be blended. We know of another example where it was not realized that the incoming wine harbored a moderate concentration of *Brettanomyces*. This wine was used for topping of barrels, and indeed contaminated essentially the entire winery.

Although these examples have to do with *Brettanomyces*, they apply equally to other yeasts and bacteria as well. The resident microbial population, good and bad, in a winery where starter cultures of yeast and bacteria have not been used, arises in these ways. Prevention includes the special cleaning operations we have outlined above plus stringent control measures concerning wine coming into the winery: knowing where it came from and where it is going. This applies equally to equipment and barrels, especially if previously used elsewhere.

C. DIAGNOSIS OF SPOILAGE AS MICROBIOLOGICAL

Before making a diagnosis of the kind of spoilage of a particular wine, which is what this chapter is about, it is important to ascertain that the spoilage is indeed of microbial origin. Besides noting the smell, taste, and appearance of the spoiled wine, it is helpful for the investigator to be familiar with the history of the production of the wine and the various operations involved. Hazes and turbidities are of many types and sources, especially protein, metaloprotein, carbohydrate, organic acids—sometimes crystalline and sometimes amorphous—all discussed in Chapter 7. Off-odors include oxidations, giving aldehydic tones (Chapter 4), and reductions, giving sulfurous notes (Chapter 4), all of which may involve the yeast employed for the primary fermentation, itself, but the spoilage arising from improper winemaking conditions.

The operative step in diagnosis is the use of the microscope. If the spoilage is microbiological, and if it is recent and the wine has been untreated, the spoilage organisms will be obvious by microscopic examination. We recommend for this examination, and for all of the microscopic work described here, the use of a binocular microscope fitted with oil-immersion and phase-contrast optics. It is essentially impossible to distinguish microscopically some wine bacteria from common grape debris without using the highest magnification with phase contrast (Figure 9-1). Viable stains can be employed to distinguish live organisms from

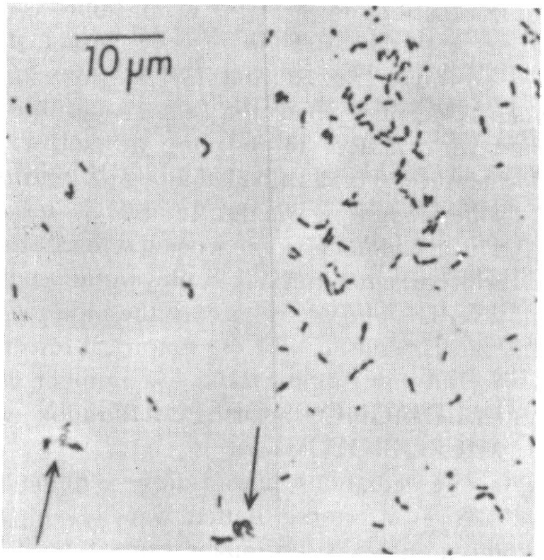

Fig. 9-1. Photomicrographs of *Leuconostoc oenos* ML 34 grown on grape juice medium for use as starter cultures. Arrows indicate nonbacterial debris from grapes. (From Kunkee 1974, used by permission.)

dead ones and from other debris, but in our experience, the convenience of phase-contrast optics outweighs the difficulties and uncertainties in the use of stains. With either viewing method, with staining or without, in order to see bacteria at high magnification, the bacteria need to be at a rather high concentration. About 10^6 bacteria/mL are needed for observing a few cells per viewing field at high magnifications (1000x). Of course, one may scan multiple fields. Some wine microbiologists have suggested that the wine be centrifuged to concentrate the microorganisms; however, we have found this unnecessary if the spoilage is fresh, and never helpful in other cases. If the wine is very turbid but no microorganisms are seen under the microscope, undoubtedly much amorphous or crystalline material will be seen. In this case, the spoilage is probably of physical or chemical origin, and other diagnostic tests should be employed (Chapter 8). Sometimes remnants of cells, ghosts, or other materials appearing to be parts of cell walls, are found. This in itself gives little clue as to the identity of the spoilage agent.

As important as the microscopic detection of the spoilage agents is the appraisal as to whether they are alive or not. Viability is best determined by spreading (plating) a small sample (0.1 or 0.2 mL) of the wine onto a solid nutrient medium in a Petri dish with the aid of a sterile pipette. The spreading is done with a Pasteur pipette, which has been sealed at one end and bent at right angles about 3 cm from that end in the form of a miniature hockey stick; the fashioning of the hockey stick being easily done with the use of a Bunsen burner. The hockey stick is sterilized by being dipped into ethanol, or other alcohol, and then touched momentarily to a flame (but not flamed, itself) to burn off the alcohol. The specific kinds of nutrient media to be used for the plating are given below. When a number of wines are to be examined, several samples can be placed on one plate by use of an inoculating loop, using one-fourth or one-third of the plate for each plating. This puts about 1% of the number of cells on the plate for each sample as compared with the larger sample of 0.1 or 0.2 mL. Some wine microbiologists suggest in order to assure the presence of enough viable cells per sample, that a sterile membrane filter be used. A larger sample of the wine is filtered though the sterile membrane, and the membrane is incubated on the nutrient medium—as is done with quality control of sterile bottling of wine (Chapter 11). Again, we have never had difficulty in obtaining viable cells by the use of the direct plating method, expect with very old wines or wine treated subsequent to spoilage.

With some organisms, for example, some strains of *Lactobacillus fructivorans*, the unadapted cells do not grow well at first as surface colonies. In these cases the initial inoculations can be made in a liquid medium, usually containing ethanol to prevent the growth of extraneous microbes (Appendix F).

Diagnosis of the microbiological causes of old or treated spoiled wines may be impossible using the techniques just outlined. Speculations based on chemical and sensory analyses may be the only alternative, if tenuous, avenues available.

Also difficult is the detection of incipient spoilage, especially if no sensory irregularities are as yet noticed. Again, concentration of the organisms by centrifugation has not proved helpful. The detection of any specific end products, such as those which might be produced by *Brettanomyces* yeast (Section F.6), may be far more sensitive than the microbiological methods, and far more useful in these cases.

A special, but very important, situation has to do with wines which contain very low, but real, concentrations of a spoilage yeast, for example, *Brettanomyces*, and in spite of which a marketing decision has been made to bottle the wine without removal of the spoilage organisms by filtration. Neither plating techniques nor microscopic examinations are going to be practical in predicting the percentage of bottles which will end up with one or more of the spoilage cells. Determination of the concentration of this yeast by the use of filtration of small samples though sterile membranes as described above is not practical since the wine has previously not been filtered and the membrane will silt up immediately. Furthermore, microscopic examination is ineffectual since the concentration of this yeast is far too low to be noticed in the microscopic field, even at moderate magnification, except by chance. A procedure which has probably never been reduced to practice in this situation, since it is labor-intensive and because it utilizes large volumes of wine, is application of the Poisson distribution (Taylor 1962; Meynell and Meynell 1965) to determine the MPN (the most probable number) of cells in a sample. For this, relatively large volumes of the wine to be bottled, say, 100-mL portions, are supplemented with, say, 900-mL of a sterile nutrient medium, incubated, and later assessed for growth, that is, increased turbidity—which will have taken place only in those samples which contained one or more viable cells. Solve the Poisson equation: $p = e^{-m}$ where p is the proportion (the probability) of lots having no viable cells with no increase in turbidity (and $1 - p$ is the proportion of lots having increased turbidity). Solving for m gives the mean concentration of the cells in the undiluted wine. Taylor (1962) and Meynell and Meynell (1965) have provided tables giving the MPN depending upon the number of serial (10-fold) dilutions, and the scoring of numbers of turbid and not turbid samples within each dilution. The alternatives are for the wine producer to be content with the empirical results of the bottling, hoping for a low number of returned bottles; or resorting to filtration of the wine.

Another situation where spoilage is difficult to assess is in stored bottled wine awaiting shipment, in which the quality control results obtained after a supposedly sterile bottling (Chapter 11) show evidence of contamination. As contrasted to the above situation, each of the bottles here is expected to have the same, if small, concentration of contaminating organisms. The most expensive recourse is *dumping*, an enological term for the opening of all of the bottles and emptying all of the contents, making necessary salvaging adjustments and rebottling or selling the product off as bulk wine. Before the dumping order is given, it should be realized that the quality control procedures may detect cells grown in the enriched medium used for this, whereas the organisms in the stored wine may not be vigorous enough to grow in the nutritionally deficient wine. An assessment of the concentration of cells in the stored bottles should be made periodically. If the cell concentration remained steady or decreased, the product could be deemed safe for shipment. However, if the concentration showed a continual increase, dumping would eventually be the only recourse.

D. KINDS OF MICROBIOLOGICAL SPOILAGES OF WINE

Even before the understanding of the biological nature of what we now know as microbiological spoilages of wine, various names had been applied to various kinds. For example, Pasteur (1866) used common descriptors such as *tourné* (turned) and *pousse* (pushed, as in pushing the cork?) for wines having unwanted secondary fermentations without and with gas production, respectively (Vaughn 1955; Kunkee 1967). Pasteur recognized these spoilages as being biological. However, his identifications were more or less restricted to microscopic examinations of the spoilage organisms, and to his excellent hand drawings of these. It was not until later, with the establishment of techniques for cultivation of single strains that a wine spoilage could be identified with the predominate organism involved (Hansen 1896; Kunkee 1984). It is now common practice to name a wine spoilage by the microorganism responsible for it (Kunkee 1967; Amerine et al. 1980); although this information may come not only from identification of the major contaminant, but also from recognition of the symptoms (see below). Some workers have suggested that spoilages are generally associated with a succession of various microorganisms (Lüthi 1957) (Section G.3). There have been experimental demonstrations of this; for example, the induction of a malolactic fermentation by a leuconostoc strain has resulted in an increased pH in the wine to allow a further growth of a less acid-tolerant pediococcal strain (Chapter 6). In fact, in our examinations of some very spoiled wines, sometimes we have found yeast together with aerobic and anaerobic bacteria; but as far as we know, each of these classes represented a single strain of say, *Brettanomyces*, *Lactobacillus*, and *Acetobacter*. More generally, we have found that spoilages can be considered to have originated from a single organism, and from this we can name the spoilage. Although, precise naming of wine-related microorganisms with respect to species is complex, and respect to strains, exceedingly difficult, the classifications of spoilage by the main type of organism, say the genus, is relatively simple. Thus, we may speak of spoilage coming from a deleterious strain of *Lactobacillus*; an infection by *Brettanomyces*; refermentation of semidry bottled wine by a bona fide wine strain of *Saccharomyces*; or vinegary spoilage by *Acetobacter*. If we divide the kinds of spoilage grossly as arising from yeast, anaerobic bacteria, or aerobic bacteria, we can discuss them, below, in this order. However, another helpful description, implied in the above examples, is the distinction between wines spoiled during storage in cellars as compared to those spoiled after they have been bottled, and thus, the classifications by organism will be so subdivided. The significance of presence of large populations of molds associated with the grapes at harvest will also be discussed, even though as strict aerobes they do not grow in properly managed wine.

E. IDENTIFICATION OF WINE SPOILAGE MICROORGANISMS

1. Importance of Identification

Guides for step-by-step identification of types of wine spoilages often rely heavily on a descriptive analysis or gross sensory assessment of the wine: giving expected odors, color, turbidity, gassiness, etc. We indicated above that this is an important first step—and historically, pre-Pasteur, it was the only one. The employment of such guides, along with ascertaining as much as possible about the production of the wine, can give the investigator a head start as to the cause and solution of the problem. However, it must be emphasized that no real understanding of the spoilage is obtained until and unless the nature of the causative agent is found; that is, until the spoilage microorganism has been identified.

Obviously, once the identification is made, the corrective and future preventative measures, taken from the literature or from the winemakers previous experience, can be applied. Some identifications may require a long period, and the spoilage problem may have been corrected by measures empirically derived before the microorganism has been identified. Nevertheless, it is worthwhile to continue the identification procedures to finality. The remedial operations, even if empirical, provide a background of appropriate procedures to be immediately instituted, if the spoilage comes again—and after a quicker, if presumptive, identification of the returned infection is made.

2. Cultivation, Isolation, and Purification of Wine Microbes

Preliminary to the microscopic examination of a spoiled wine, a macroscopic examination of the wine should be recorded. One should note the off-color, turbidity, off-odors, and perhaps off-taste. It is helpful to know if malolactic fermentation has occurred, and to know, or determine, the free SO_2 content, pH, and volatile acidity. Following this, microscopic examination is vital. One should look for yeasts or bacteria, and for amorphous or crystalline materials. If microbes are present, a tentative identification from the morphology should be made, and an estimation of cell numbers (Appendix H). While this tentative identification can be made from the cell morphology, and this may give a head start for the further tests, it must be emphasized that conclusive results cannot be obtained from microscopic examination alone.

However, it is valid for an experienced wine microbiologist to conclude immediately whether the organisms are yeasts or bacteria from the microscopic appearance. The yeast are generally obviously larger than the bacteria; although, some larger *Acetobacter* may approach the size of some of the smallest yeast. The difference in type of cell division is an easy guide for differentiation: all of the wine bacteria divide by fission, and essentially all of the wine yeast divide by budding. *Schizosaccharomyces*, a fission yeast, is the exception, but they are large and are not to be confused with bacteria. However, in spoiled wine the organisms may be in the resting phase, and the determination of cell division morphology may have to wait until the cells have been cultivated.

If the spoilage seems to be of microbiological origin, platings of the wine onto solid media are then made, as described above, not only to determine that the organisms are viable, but also to obtain viable material to use in the identification tests. For yeast, a wort or malt medium is used (Appendix F), with or without added cycloheximide (Acti-dione®). The use of cycloheximide provides a preliminary screening for *Brettanomyces* spp. (Section F.6). For bacteria, a modified de Man, Rogosa and Sharpe (MRS) medium (de Man et al. 1960), containing malic acid, cycloheximide, and fruit juice, for example, apple Rogosa medium (Appendix F) is used. If vinegar bacteria (*Acetobacter*) are suspected, by their mixed, swollen, and curved morphologies (Section H), culturing might also be done on a very acid medium (Appendix F). The special case of *Lactobacillus fructivorans* has been mentioned (Chapter 6). If the presence of this organism is suspected, a 10% inoculum of this wine should be made into liquid apple Rogosa medium containing 6% ethanol (Appendix F).

For identification tests, it is important to have in hand not only the viable culture, but also a pure one. The isolation and purification procedures of the spoilage organisms described here can, of course, be applied as preidentification steps for any wine-related microbes, including the selection of in-house resident yeast or bacteria to be used eventually as starter cultures.

The inoculated plates should be incubated at room temperature or slightly above. Yeast colonies may appear in two days; bacteria may take two weeks. When colonies appear, their macroscopic morphology should be noted. A microscopic reexamination of the wine and of the cells of the colony is suggested to compare their cellular morphologies. The comparisons may not be exact, since the cells were cultured under very different growth conditions.

After colonies have appeared, one colony should be selected for the isolation procedure (restreaking) (see below), to separate this organism from others. In fact, there may be a mixture of organisms on the plate, which is apparent by differences in colony appearance. Of course, similar appearances do not guarantee similar organisms. However, the selection of a colony, or colonies, is not so complicated as it at first might seem. Ecological studies, such as determination of the yeast population on a ripe grape berry, are truly difficult. For that, each colony from each yeast cell needs to be selected and identified. On the contrary, in the study of spoiled wine, it is expected there is a preponderance of the spoilage organism(s), and the colonies formed are going to reflect this narrow diversity. In our experience, spoilages and the resulting colonies formed from them, may represent the action of a mixture of more than one kind of microorganism; but we have been satisfied in the assumption that only one strain of each kind is present. For firmer grounding of this assumption, acid-base color indicators can be added to the medium to give an additional marker to colonies, depending on the acid production, which would otherwise be missed. The Wallerstein Laboratory nutrient medium and differential medium recipes (Appendix F) include the addition of brom-cresol green and they can be used for this. However, see the discussion on *Brettanomyces* (Section F.6) for some other difficulties with these two media.

The restreaking is made by touching the selected colony with a sterile loop, and making a streak or two toward the edge of another fresh Petri dish of nutrient medium. The loop is then sterilized (flamed) and cooled (touched to the agar)—and a second streak is made across the first one (Figure 9-2). This process is repeated, crossing the sterile loop over the last part of the previous streak. This procedure guarantees, no matter how few or how many cells were taken up with the first pass of the loop, that growth will result in at least a few isolated colonies. Following incubation of the isolation plate, the process is repeated using one of the isolated colonies to give a purified culture on the third plate. Finally, one of the purified colonies should be transferred to an agar slant for yeast or aerobic bacteria and a stab culture for lactic acid bacteria. It may be well to make up several of these slants or stabs, in order not only to have copies of the organism for culture collection storage, but also to have abundant culture material for the identification tests to follow. It is also helpful to make up some liquid cultures for some of the tests.

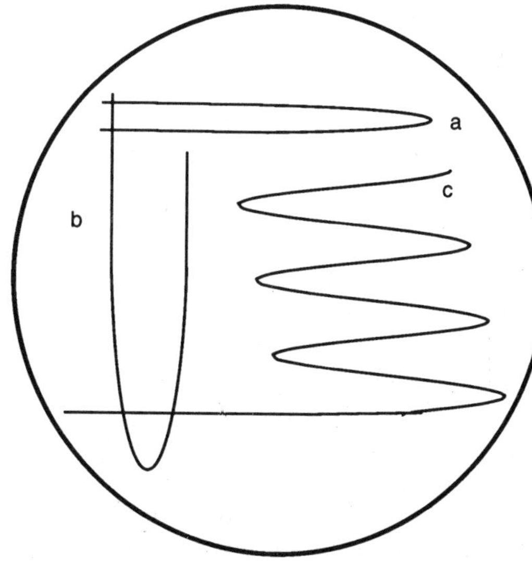

Fig. 9-2. Proper streaking methodology for obtaining isolated colonies.

The purification of the culture should be followed with microscopic examination, bearing in mind there may be morphological diversity even in pure cultures, especially with some yeast and some acetobacter. In stubborn cases of separation of yeast from bacteria, the isolation may be aided by a thorough suspension and mixing of a loopful of the culture in sterile nutrient medium. A loop of this material is then streaked out, as given above. In *very* stubborn cases, antibiotics and fungicides have been used, but we have never had to resort to this.

The isolated and purified cultures are then ready for the identification tests, which follow.

F. SPOILAGE BY MOLDS AND YEASTS

1. Spoilage by Molds

We have discussed many molds that might be found on the grapes in the vineyard (Chapter 4). Nevertheless, spoilage by growth of molds in must or wine in itself does not pose a problem. The low pH of grape juice and the anaerobic conditions of the vinification fermentation renders them harmless, even if they might come into the winery by the scenario described above. However, the attack of grapes by molds before or at the time of harvest can have an important spoilage effect.

The conditions which allow a serious mold infection in the vineyard are variable and include temperature, humidity, wind conditions, grape variety, and viticulture practices such as irrigation regimes, canopy management, and fungicide applications. In addition, except for *Botrytis cinerea,* mold infections require some sort of break in the skin of the berry; not an infrequent happening (see above). *Botrytis cinerea* seems to be able to perforate the berry skin without this extra assistance (Coley-Smith et al. 1980). A substantial infection of the grapes at the time of harvest becomes of great concern to the winemaker. Either while still on the vine, or more likely, during the transport of the grapes from the vineyard to the winery, there is an exposure of the juice of the broken berries to whatever microorganisms are present. This can bring about a premature alcoholic fermentation by wild yeast, and the resulting low concentrations of ethanol can be oxidized to acetic acid by acetic acid bacteria. In extreme situations, the concentration of acetic acid can be high enough to have an important detrimental effect on the metabolic activity of the wine yeast and result in a sluggish or protracted fermentation (Drysdal and Fleet 1989) (Chapter 4). Acetaldehyde is also often found. The damage is exacerbated by high ambient temperature and long transport distances. Whether mechanical or hand harvesting is used also plays a role. Mechanically harvested berries have broken skins and exposed juice; however, precautions are often taken to prevent premature fermentation by keeping the transport distances short (which may include field crushing), by addition of sulfur dioxide at harvest, and by harvesting during the coolest hours. Furthermore, most mechanical harvesting strategies remove and collect only the heavy, intact berries, leaving those light from mold infections behind.

2. Corkiness

Corkiness is a term applied to a moldy smell of some corks, and to the wine into which the unpleasant smell migrated. The defect is generally found only in a few percentage of bottles with cork stoppers. This percentage is high enough to be financially unacceptable to the wineries—although it has not been high enough to allow for a good grasp on the origin of the problem. The microbiological implications in corkiness are not clear (Lefebvre et al. 1983; Davis et al. 1982). The problem, and some solutions, are discussed in detail in Chapter 10, Section G.

3. Spoilage by Wild Yeasts

We do not think of wild yeast, that is, those genera found in rather high concentrations on the grape and which can carry out a limited alcoholic fermentation (*Kloeckera*, *Hansenula*, and *Hanseniaspora*) (Chapter 4), as spoilage organisms. How much influence they have on the alcoholic fermentation depends upon the winemaking conditions, use of sulfur dioxide, and/or starter cultures of wine yeast, but in any case they should become inert after the ethanol concentration reaches 5% or so. It has been reported (Fleet et al. 1988) that species of *Kloeckera* can continue alcoholic fermentation to substantial concentrations of ethanol at low temperatures, but we have not been able to confirm this. Procedures for taxonomical identification of the yeasts discussed in this section are given in Chapter 4.

Other wild yeasts can show up as contaminates in young wine, especially if good attention has not been paid to proper storage conditions: SO_2 addition and the avoidance of oxygen. Species of *Pichia* and *Candida* may appear as white scum on the wine surface, having a cheese-like appearance. The presence of *Candida* seems to be merely a cosmetic problem, but *Pichia* can bring about deleterious concentrations of ethyl acetate. The origin of either of these yeasts would seem to follow the scenario described above (Section B). Correction of these conditions involves first the physical removal, skimming off, of the solid material; addition of sulfur dioxide as necessary, and assuring anaerobic conditions in the headspace. Old remedies included hanging of a *bouquet garni* of a mixture of metabisulfite and potassium bitartrate in the headspace of the storage tank or putting the same mixture of solids on a plate and floating it on the wine! The humidity of the headspace acting on the bitartrate buffer allows a continuous but slow escape of gaseous sulfur dioxide.

Other wild yeasts which might be at low concentrations in new wine, but never seem to create a problem during storage, are species of *Metschnikowia*, *Torulaspora*, and *Debaryomyces*. We will mention the latter two genera again, below.

However, infection of stored wine can come from the much feared *Saccharomycodes ludwigii*, the "winemaker's nightmare" (Thomas 1993). This rather large, bipolar-budding yeast has great resistance to ethanol; it might be classified as a wine yeast (Chapter 4) except that it is also a strong producer of acetaldehyde, up to 200 mg/L (Lafon-Lafourcade 1983). The latter trait probably confers upon it its high resistance to SO_2, and like *Zygosaccharomyces*, it also shows high resistance to sorbate (see below). Spoilage by *Saccharomycodes* (there is only one species) has also been reported in bottled wine, where flocculent masses settle as cohesive chunks. It is also said to impart a sliminess. As far as we know, this horror has never been seen either in wines or wineries of California.

4. Spoilage by Wine Yeasts

We have defined wine yeasts as those which will carry out a complete fermentation of grape juice without producing any atypical sensory effects. These then include several races of *Saccharomyces cerevisiae*, or using the preferred old-new taxonomy (Chapter 4), two species of *Saccharomyces*, *S. cerevisiae* and *S. bayanus*. Other yeast genera which can complete a vinification fermentation and might be expected to be included are *Schizosaccharomyces*, *Zygosaccharomyces*, and *Brettanomyces / Dekkera*. We have never encountered *Schizosaccharomyces* in improperly stabilized wine, and the other genera will be discussed below in the next sections. While we have nothing but great fondness for the wine yeasts, they become spoilage organisms when they are found where they are not wanted—that is, in finished, bottled wine. As little as 1 g/L of fermentable sugar will support the growth of enough yeast to produce a haze. Therefore bottled wine must either be fermented to complete dryness or some measures must be taken to prevent further yeast growth in it. The term *dryness* also implies the lack of perceptible sweetness. The chemical determination of dryness is done by measurement of the concentration of residual reducing sugars, very conveniently done in wines at the end of alcoholic fermentation with the use of Clinitest® tablets (Ough and Amerine 1988). Reducing sugars include any residual fermentable sugars, glucose, and fructose, and about 2 g/L of pentoses, the latter not metabolized by wine yeasts. By the Clinitest,® something less than 2.25 g/L of reducing sugar indicates dryness. More precise measurements can be made of the fermentable sugars themselves by use of enzymatic methods or by use of specific electrodes. Very often only glucose is measured, and 0 g/L is taken as the measure of dryness. This is generally satisfactory, but the winemaker should be aware that essentially all of the wine yeasts are glucophilic, meaning they will utilize glucose faster and in preference to fructose. Thus, the absence of glucose might still mean that the presence of enough fructose has been left to make the wine unstable. Enzyme kits are also available which will measure both glucose and fructose.

a. *Physical Means of Microbiological Stabilization*

The method of choice, and widely used, for stabilizing mellow (nondry or slightly sweet) wine is the removal of all of the yeasts by sterile filtration, followed by sterile bottling. As described in the section on sterile bottling (Chapter 11), depth filters are often used for the primary filtration, since they have the capacity for removal of large amounts of particulate material before showing the effects of fouling or silting. This filtration is generally followed by a membrane filtration; membranes having a defined pore size to give an absolute filtration and the special advantage of providing for integrity testing in place (Chapter 11). Membranes of 1.1-μm porosity will remove wine yeast, but smaller pore-sized membranes are often used. The whole filter assembly and all of the bottling material downstream from the filters must be sterilized by treatment with hot water or steam; chemical sterilants are unsatisfactory for this operation. Methods for microbiological quality control of the product are given in the section on sterile bottling (Chapter 11). When properly performed, sterile filtration has no detectable sensory effect on the product.

Heating of the wine itself can be used to kill the yeast. The HTST (high-temperature short-time) procedure is satisfactory for this, but all of the equipment downstream from the heat exchanger must be sterilized, as is needed for sterile filtration, anyway. Therefore, sterile filtration is preferred to this sort of pasteurization.

Hot bottling, heating the wine during the bottling procedure and allowing the contents to cool slowly in the bottle can also be used for stabilization, but the generally detrimental effect on the sensory quality of the wine makes this procedure extremely rare in the modern winemaking scene. However, we were surprised at the results of some of our recent work (Malletroit et al. 1991), which showed that this procedure can safely be used for stabilization of wine in small bottles (375 mL). With the smaller volume of wine, the exterior portions of the sample do not have to be heated so high or for so long to bring up the temperature of the interior, as with regular-sized bottles (750 mL). This procedure would seem to be a solution to the difficulties in large-scale sterile bottling at high speeds for small bottles of semidry wine.

b. *Chemical Means for Microbiological Stabilization*

Two chemicals are being used to stabilize nondry wines: potassium sorbate (Sorbistat®) and dimethyl dicarbonate (Velcorin®).

Sorbic acid (2,4-hexadienoic acid) has a long history of use in the wine industry and in other foods. Sorbate has some sensory character, especially when esterified with ethanol, although most people would have difficulty detecting the presence of it except under stringent taste panel conditions; however, other individuals can easily detect it and find it offensive. It has an advantage of being persistent, that is, its fungistatic activity is not diminished with time; thus, it can be added at any time during wine storage before the bottling procedure. Besides the sensory effect, another disadvantage is that the chemical is a fungistat, not a fungicide; the yeasts are inactivated but not killed. This means that the microbiological quality control as used with sterile bottling (Chapter 11) cannot be used here. There is a synergistic effect between sorbate's activity and the inhibitory activities of sulfur dioxide and ethanol (Ough and Ingraham 1960). Thus, in wine, in combination with the sulfur dioxide and ethanol, the effective dosage against yeast is about 200 mg/L. Most countries specify a maximum limit for use in wine (Appendix B), and any use in wine in Japan, and perhaps other countries, is illegal. The dosage of 200 mg/L is recommended regardless of the concentration of yeast it is expected to control. That is, the use of sorbate along with sterile filtration, say, for extra assurance, still requires this relatively high concentration.

Although sorbate shows little activity against bacteria—another disadvantage—some lactic acid bacteria can metabolize it to give, in wine, a strong off-odor. The bacteria reduce sorbic acid to sorbyl alcohol, which, in the presence of ethanol and low pH gives a rearrangement to 2-ethoxyhexa-3,5-diene, the latter having a peculiar geranium-like odor (Crowell and Guymon 1975).

Dimethyl dicarbonate (DMDC) (Velcorin), which is toxic to yeast, especially *Saccharomyces*, has only recently been made available for stabilization of semidry wine. It is unstable when added to wine, with a half-life of a few hours, depending upon the temperature. Actually this property can be an advantage, since the material will be dissipated and not present in the bottled wine. The major end products are carbon dioxide and methanol, the amounts of either are inconsequential. The disadvantage is that DMDC must be added *at the time of bottling*. This involves the use of special, and expensive, metering equipment to allow a constant rate of addition of DMDC uniformly to the flow of the wine just before it enters the filler. The chemical, and the metering equipment for it, are somewhat difficult to handle and require the use of specially trained personnel. Another current disadvantage is the relatively high price of the DMDC. The use of DMDC to control bacteria is discussed in Section G.

In the next sections we will discuss two of the most important spoilage yeasts: *Zygosaccharomyces* and *Brettanomyces*.

5. Spoilage by *Zygosaccharomyces* Yeast

Zygosaccharomyces (Chapter 4), like *Saccharomyces*, also may be found in semidry bottled wine. Many of the species of *Zygosaccharomyces* will carry out complete fermentation of grape juice; strains of *Z. fermentati* having vigorous fermentation rates (Romano and Suzzi 1993). Strains of *Z. bailii*, the main spoilage species, are unusual in that they are fructophilic, rather than glucophilic, as are most of the other grape juice fermenters (Peynaud and Domercq 1955). There are several interesting characteristics of the members of this genus with respect to their malic acid utilization and their foaming and flocculation qualities (Romano and Suzzi 1993). From a genetics point of view, all of the members of this genus are special—spending most of their growth cycle as heterothallic haploids (Chapter 4) (Kreger-van Rij 1984).

Zygosaccharomyces is an important spoilage yeast because it is resistant to potassium sorbate. However, as a spoilage organism, its origin in wine is not from a primary fermentation. While this spoilage might arise in stored wine by the scenario we outlined above for other organisms (Section B), it is much more likely to be found in semidry bottled wine. Its origin is predominately from grape juice concentrate, which is sometimes added to wine at the time of bottling to provide sweetness. We are primarily concerned with the species *Z. bailii*; but all of the eight species of the genus are highly sugar tolerant and will grow, some species more vigorously than others, in 50% glucose (Kreger-van Rij 1984). The use of properly stored grape juice concentrate does not seem to bring about the problem with *Zygosaccharomyces* contamination. The problem arises from extended storage of concentrate at room temperature, rather than cellar temperature, and with little attention paid to SO_2 content. Although some strains of *Zygosaccharomyces* may be more sensitive to SO_2, as compared to wine yeast and bacteria, others are more resistant; accordingly larger concentrations of SO_2 should be maintained. Since the concentrate is going to be used as a sweet reserve, its dilution when added to wine overcomes any objections to the presence of excess SO_2. Obviously the risk from storage is more acute when inventories of concentrate are high and refrigeration space is at a premium.

Spoilage by *Zygosaccharomyces* is mainly a cosmetic problem, the odors and flavors of these wines are generally described as being wine-like; however, the yeast deposits itself as a granular material, falling to the bottom of the bottle. The deposit has the appearance and color of beach sand. With time, the sediment gradually becomes more or more colored, reaching yellow and medium brown. Thus, in old bottles of wine the spoilage has been confused with the precipitation of proteins, as might happen in a wine with a noticeable metaloprotein haze.

The problem of contamination of wine at bottling with *Zygosaccharomyces* yeast is best solved, as it is with *Saccharomyces*, with the use of sterile filtration and bottling. What is best is not always done. Over the last few years the use of grape juice concentrate to sweeten wine at bottling has been more widespread in the large-scale production of lower-priced wines, where potassium sorbate (see above) has been used to stabilize the wine. As we have said, *Zygosaccharomyces* is resistant to sorbate. This has caused considerable distress for wineries in this category, but generally the problems have been solved either by paying closer attention to the storage of concentrate, or finally by resorting to installation of sterilizable bottling equipment.

We have given taxonomic procedures for identification of species of *Zygosaccharomyces* (Chapter 4). Presumptive identification of wine spoilage species of *Zygosaccharomyces* can be made by plating the suspected organism on solid medium containing 1% acetic acid (Appendix F); no species of *Saccharomyces* will grow in the presence of this concentration of acetic acid. This is presumptive evidence because some species of *Hansenula*, *Torulaspora*, *Pichia*, and *Debaryomyces* will also grow in the presence of 1% acetic acid. These latter genera are easily distinguished from *Zygosaccharomyces* in that *Hansenula* grows on nitrate as a nitrogen source, *Torulaspora* does not assimilate cadaverine, enological species of *Pichia* (that is, *P. fermentans* and *P. membranaefaciens*) form pellicles, and *Debaryomyces* never strongly ferments glucose. However, if the contamination is found in bottled wine sweetened with grape juice concentrate and stabilized with sorbate, it almost certainly is *Z. bailii*.

Another rather easy identification method is microscopic examination of a culture growing on malt agar without acetic acid. These organisms are heterothallic haploids (Chapter 4) and the cells tend to conjugate readily and show a characteristic dumbbell appearance before sporulating (Figure 4-1e). Another closely related species, *Z. bisporus* fits many of the same descriptions as *Z. bailii*, in fact, only these two species of the genus are acetic acid-tolerant. *Z. bisporus* is somewhat smaller and all strains of it are sucrose negative. In spite of the close similarities, we have never encountered *Z. bisporus*, or any other species of the genus, as a wine spoilage organism.

6. Spoilage by *Brettanomyces* Yeast

Brettanomyces is described as the nonsexual, nonsporulating form of *Dekkera* (Chapter 4). The difference in taxonomy is extreme, but in morphology it is rather subtle. The sporulation conditions, elevated temperature, and increased micronutrient concentration (Ilagan 1979), seem to be more exacting than for other genera and the detection of the spores with the light microscope is rather arduous for the inexperienced worker. Spore stains are available (Bartholomew and Mittwer 1950), but they do not seem to be especially useful because of the sparseness of this sporulation. Indeed it was only in the latest taxonomic treatment (Kreger-van Rij 1984) that the perfect sporulating form was recognized. Both *Brettanomyces* and *Dekkera* have been isolated from wine, but it is not clear yet how important spoilage of wine by *Dekkera* is. However, it is clear that conditions of winemaking and wine storage would work against sporulation of *Dekkera* yeast if they were present. There is some evidence of discreet differences in the sensory characteristics of wine made by *Brettanomyces*, as compared to *Dekkera* (Fugelsang et al. 1993), but these differences may reflect variations in strain rather than in genus. For the discussion here, we group the genera together, asking *Brettanomyces* to stand for both.

As with other wine yeasts, both *Brettanomyces* and *Dekkera* are capable of completing an alcoholic fermentation of grape juice, albeit very slowly. In fact, these wines, when tasted very fresh, have among other flavors, some fruity, rather pleasant notes. Indeed a specialty beer of Belgium, Lambic beer, having a distinct flavor, variously described, but certainly different from regular beers, is brewed by this yeast (Guinard 1990), which adds fuel to a blustery controversy over the role of these yeasts as spoilers of wine (Hock 1990).

There is no controversy that *Brettanomyces* contamination can have an important influence on the odor and flavor of wine—that is, wine fermented by *Saccharomyces*. However, in wine, the odors from *Brettanomyces* contamination have been described as: barnyard-like, horsey, horse blanket, wet dog, tar, tobacco, creosote, leathery, pharmaceutical, and perhaps mousey (see Section G.6 also). The infected wines often have an increased volatile acidity[1]. However, the controversy arises as to whether the odors described in *Brettanomyces*-infected wines, if more than subliminal, are attractive or disgusting. A thoughtful discussion of this point, giving no doubt on which side of the barnyard fence the authors of this text stand, is given in Chapter 16. All we can do here is to indicate how to prevent the *spoilage*, how to detect this *spoilage* if it is not prevented, how to identify the *spoilage* microorganisms involved, and the best means of control of the *spoilage* infection if it already has been established.

a. Prevention of Brettanomyces Spoilage

The scenario given above describing how spoilage microbes can arise as resident populations in a winery is based on actual experiences with *Brettanomyces* infections (van der Walt and van Kerken 1958, 1961; van Zyl 1962). Thus, the first line of defense must be at the reception area during harvest, stopping the crushing and stemming operations often for thorough washing of the equipment, addition of SO_2, if not with every crushing lot at least from time to time; and providing clean, unobstructed lines and hoses into the winery. Also, one should have a thorough knowledge of the microbial history of all wine coming into the winery and a thorough knowledge of where this wine is being used. In depicting the scenario, it was pointed out that if conditions are favorable and with enough time, a viable microbe from any source is a potential focus for contamination—of the wine stored in that vessel. Even with the best attention to the reception area at harvest time, there is eventually some sort of likelihood of contamination from unidentified sources. Thus, it is imperative that in the unspoiled cellar, scrupulous attention be paid to general cleanliness, frequent sanitation of equipment, and to SO_2 concentrations. It is generally accepted that the proverbial 0.8 mg/L molecular SO_2 be maintained for control of *Brettanomyces*, as well as many other spoilage organisms. Another source of alien organisms is the acquisition of used wooden barrels. We know of no sure way to sterilize infected barrels. In any case it is important to have a good idea of the true conditions and history of any used barrels which are brought into the winery.

b. Detection of Brettanomyces Spoilage

The most desirable form of detection of *Brettanomyces* infection would be one which detects the characteristic off-flavors in the incipient stages. Two volatile phenols found in some wines may be responsible for the phenolic, sweaty, horsey, or stable off-odors: 4-ethyl phenol and 4-ethyl guaiacol. These can come from the enzymatic decarboxylation and reduction of hydroxycinnamic acids (p-coumaric acid and ferulic acid)—of the musts or possibly ex-

[1] The pungent aroma notes coming from old cultures of *Brettanomyces* on solid medium, used in taxonomic diagnosis of the genera (Chapter 4), are reminiscent of butyric acid—and other medium-chain-length organic acids.

tracted from new wood (Figure 9-3) (Heresztyn 1986a; Chatonnet et al. 1992). The corresponding enzymes, cinnamate decarboxylase and vinyl-phenol reductase are found in *Saccharomyces* and in *Brettanomyces* and *Dekkera*; however the enzymes in *Saccharomyces*, which seem to be highly dependent upon yeast strain, but are said to be inhibited by tannins (Chatonnet et al. 1989; 1993). It is hoped that analytical tools can be developed which would detect these compounds as an early warning system before the infection is detectable by other means.

In the meantime, the only sure method for detection is microbiological, the plating of the suspected samples on a selection medium, upon which only colonies of *Brettanomyces* will appear (Chapter 4). While the conditions of identification can be made definite (see below) this procedure is labor-intensive. In the unblemished winery, one would expect such plating procedures to give, in effect, a cell count of 0 cells/mL. More realistically, there will be some primary presence of the organisms, and a baseline, say 1 to 10 cells/mL, can be determined. The proper cellar procedures outlined above should keep it at or below that basal concentration. Monitoring showing increased concentrations of 100 to 1000 cells/mL is cause for alarm. However, more information is needed concerning the relationship between the concentration of these yeasts and the formation of the odd flavors and odors since we have prepared wines with concentrations of much greater than 1000 cells of viable *Brettanomyces* per mL with no adverse sensory effects. This discrepancy may be due to strain variation or to substrate materials, which are discussed further below under methods of control.

c. *Identification of Brettanomyces Spoilage*

Presumptive identification of *Brettanomyces* can be obtained from winery samples most easily utilizing their resistance to cycloheximide. Plating on malt or wort plates prepared with 10 mg/L of this fungicide (Appendix F) is often used—noting that about one-half of the activity of this inhibitor is destroyed during the autoclaving process and double the concentration is empirically used. While some other organisms are also resistant to this concentration of cycloheximide, they are unlikely to be found in wine. More definitive identification comes with the use of 100 mg/L cycloheximide in the medium, but the disadvantage of use of this medium is that the growth of the *Brettanomyces* colonies takes from 10 to 14 days. It should be noted that cycloheximide has been indicated as a reproductive toxin in animals (Alleva et al. 1979); its use and its disposal need to be carefully managed. Differential platings, using media without cycloheximide, are often used to determine whether other microorganisms might also be present. Differential media prepared for other laboratory uses are commercially available, for example, Wallerstein nutrient medium and Wallerstein differential medium. However, these are not

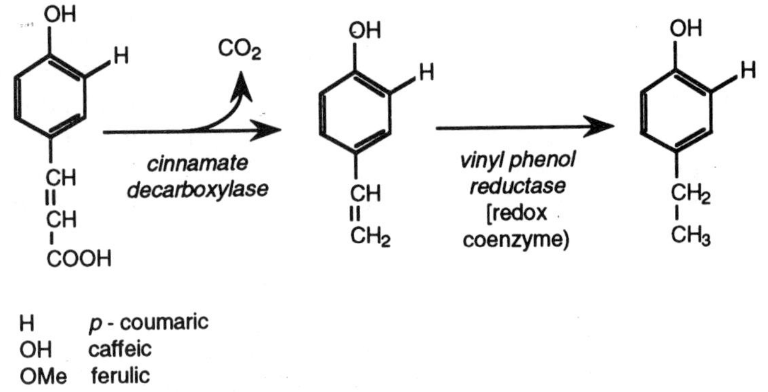

Fig. 9-3. Formation of vinyl and ethyl phenols of decarboxylation of hydroxy cinnamic acids.

satisfactory as differential media for detection of *Brettanomyces*, since the latter contains only 3 mg/L cycloheximide. Furthermore, *Brettanomyces* seems to be more nutritionally fastidious than other wine-related microorganisms; the medium for them should be supplemented with thiamine and other micronutrients, not found in Wallerstein nutrient medium. We generally add 2 g/L of tryptone powder to the malt medium (Appendix F).

Unambiguous identification of *Brettanomyces* and *Dekkera*, comes from use of the taxonomic key given in Charter 4. This methodology is especially important in the testing of nonwine material, where the presumptive methods cannot be employed. Some nonwine species of *Saccharomyces* are resistant to 1000 mg/L cycloheximide (Chapter 4).

d. Control of Brettanomyces Spoilage

Control of *Brettanomyces* in stored wine starts with the prevention schemes mentioned above, but includes rough filtrations to remove the bulk of the offending organism. After being filtered, the wine should be returned to sanitized cooperage, and treated with SO_2. This can well be accomplished with stainless steel tanks, but it is next to impossible with barrels, except, of course, brand new ones. In an already infected cellar, it is not realistic to use full sterilization tactics, but rather to attempt to keep the contamination under control.

There is some evidence that new barrels are more susceptible to growth of *Brettanomyces* yeast, and possibly malolactic bacteria, than are old barrels (Larue et al. 1991). This brings up the point raised above as to what the substrate conditions are which encourage *Brettanomyces* growth, or at least the formation of the off-flavors. On the one hand, one can imagine that some of the phenolic materials being extracted from *new* wood might be substrates for oxidation, or reduction, reactions by *Brettanomyces* to give some creosote, tar, or other odoriferous compounds (Amon et al. 1987). We say oxidation or reduction, since the *Brettanomyces* fermentation is rather unique. They exhibit a kind of negative Pasteur effect called Custer's effect, where oxygen stimulates fermentation (Wijsman et al. 1984; Gaunt et al. 1988; van Urk et al. 1990) rather than inhibiting it (Chapter 4) (Lagunas et al. 1982). The end pathway of glucose fermentation to ethanol in *Brettanomyces* is unexpected. Acetaldehyde coming from pyruvate is oxidized, at the expense of NAD^+, to acetic acid—rather than being reduced to ethanol with simultaneous reoxidation of NADH (Figure 9-4). The oxidation of the aldehyde may not be substrate specific, and it is this reaction that is probably the source of the butyric acid, and other medium-chain organic acids, noticed in the spoiled wines—and in the diagnostic plates—as well as the increased volatile acidity, also often associated with this spoilage (see above). The oxidation of aldehydes to organic acids as end products also means that the energy economy of the cell is even more dependent on the reoxidation of coenzymes (NAD^+) than is the common alcoholic fermentation as found in *Saccharomyces*. Thus, control of the redox potential, and air contact via headspace, of wines infected with *Brettanomyces* is critical. This would explain the opinion of some enologists who believe sampling of wine for detection of this yeast ought to be done near the top the vessel, although others indicate the yeast is more likely to be found near the bottom. On the one hand, one might speculate that oxidation of other aldehydes, extracted from new wood, might also be a source of flavorful end products. On the

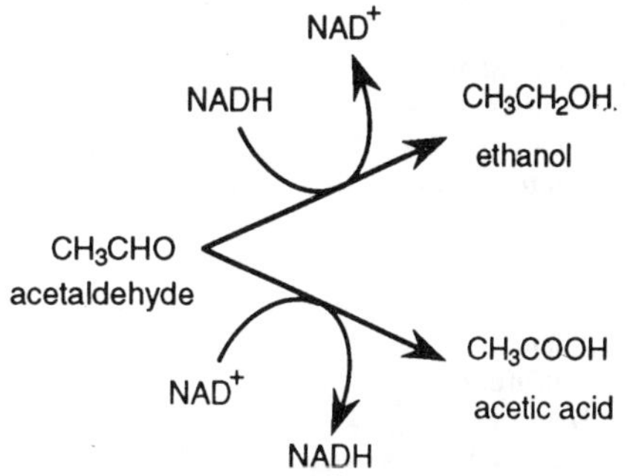

Fig. 9-4. End products of glycolysis by *Brettanomyces* showing the Custer's effect.

other hand, cellulose and hemicellulose fragments are also leached of wood of new barrels (Humphries et al. 1992). Many species of these yeast can assimilate cellobiose, an α-linked disaccharide of glucose, a fragment of cellulose. Table 9-1 shows the relationship of the species of *Brettanomyces* and *Dekkera* having capabilities of assimilating cellobiose with their habitats, the origins of the type species studied (Kreger-van Rij 1984). Only small concentrations of cellulose fragments would need to be leeched out of the wood. Very low concentrations of substrate materials are needed to produce a haze by the growth of yeast up to 10^5 cells/mL, which is more than the concentration of cells often associated with *Brettanomyces* infections. Of course, no strains of *Saccharomyces* can utilize cellulose or its fragments.

The metabolism of glucose itself may be an overriding component in the *Brettanomyces* spoilage puzzle. Some winemakers believe they have found a relationship between residual glucose in the wine, meaning 1 to 2 g/L, and the chance of later spoilage. *Their* advice would be to bottle any suspicious wine only if it is completely free of residual glucose.

For control of *Brettanomyces*-infected wine at time of bottling, the only procedure to assure protection against later spoilage is to remove these yeasts by sterile bottling and sterile filtration. For very fine wines, marketing fashions and labeling practices may prohibit the use of filtration. In this situation, the only guides as to the feasibility of delivery of uncontaminated product are microbial analyses to give the current titer of the yeast and the experience of the producer. If chances of bottle spoilage are low enough, say less than in 1% of the bottles, the winemaker may be content to forego the finishing operations, depending upon the expectations of the clientele.

More information is needed on the protective effect by use of sorbate or DMDC, but wine producers wishing to avoid finishing operations would also probably balk at the use of chemical stabilizing agents.

The problem of cellared wines in which the *Brettanomyces* spoilage is already evident is serious. The wine itself can be stabilized from further deterioration by the tactics outlined above. Sometimes long-term storage will bring about a lessening of the off-flavors. Alternately, the wine might be blended to dilute offending materials to a subthreshold level; perhaps giving a positive increase in complex-

Table 9-1. The relationship between the species of *Brettanomyces* and *Dekkera* and their capacities for assimilating cellobiose. Also given are the origins of the species studied.

Species	Assimilates cellobiose	Origin of strains studied
Brettanomyces		
abstinens	+	ginger ale
anomalus	+	bottled stout beer, cider, beer
bruxellensis	−	Lambic beer, porter beer
claussenii	+	beer, cider, sherry vat
custersianus	−	equipment in sorghum beer breweries
custersii	+	equipment in sorghum beer breweries
intermedius	+	grape must; wines from Arbois, Mâcon, Gironde, Médoc, and South Africa; equipment in sorghum beer breweries
lambicus	−	Lambic beer
naardensis	+	soft drink, carbonated water
Dekkera		
bruxellensis	−	stout beer
intermedia	+	beer, wine, winery equipment, tea beer fungus

Source: Selected from Kreger-van Rij (1984).

ity. The blended wine should be monitored to assure that the contamination does not recommence. At the time of bottling of the blend, it is imperative to user sterilizing procedures (Chapter 11). Stainless steel storage tanks used to hold this wine can be sanitized and reused; however, any wooden cooperage should be discarded.

G. SPOILAGE BY LACTIC ACID BACTERIA

The wine lactic acid bacteria are defined as those producing lactic acid from fermentation of glucose (Chapter 6). *Leuconostoc, Lactobacillus*, and *Pediococcus* are the wine genera involved. Descriptions and identification procedures for these genera, and their species, have been given in the chapter on malolactic fermentation (Chapter 6); although not all of the members of these genera are actually converters of malic acid to lactic acid. They are all catalase negative, but they will grow in the presence of oxygen. Thus we are grouping them here together, actually as microaerophilic bacteria, distinguishing them from the obligate-aerobic, catalase-positive acetic acid bacteria and bacilli, discussed below.

As we have seen, the malolactic fermentation and conversion are respected and frequently desired operations in commercial wine production. However, there are at least two situations where the fermentation must be considered undesirable, that is, spoilage: when it occurs where it is not wanted or needed, and where the dominant strain carrying out the fermentation produces enough off-odors or flavor modification to ruin the product.

1. Misplaced Malolactic Fermentations

With the notable exception of the traditional Vinhos Verdes wines of northern Portugal, a malolactic fermentation occurring in wine after it is bottled is a spoilage analogous to that of growth of *Saccharomyces* in semidry bottled wine (Chapter 6). The prevention is similar. If the wine has not undergone malolactic fermentation, and is susceptible to it, which is largely a question of its pH, then it must be treated to prevent further growth. Under California winemaking conditions, with proper additions of SO_2, a pH of less than 3.3 is empirically taken as safe; but with pHs higher than that, one of the following physical or chemical treatments ought to be made. As with the *Saccharomyces* spoilage, sterile filtration and sterile bottling are the methods of choice (Chapter 11). Since the bacteria are smaller than yeast, the membrane pore size accordingly needs to be smaller: 0.45-μm pore size is recommended. Membranes are available at even tighter porosity, the pharmaceutical industry routinely uses membranes of 0.22-μm pore size. However, the use of the tighter membranes, with the associated decreased flow rate, has been shown to be unnecessary for use in wine. Other physical methods employed for removal or inactivation of *Saccharomyces*, with their liabilities, may also be used (see above).

Chemical methods for stabilization of wine against malolactic fermentation are also available, but the use of potassium sorbate (Section F.4.b) is not one of them, since the bacteria are resistant to this additive at the allowed concentrations, 200 mg/L, even in the presence of ethanol and SO_2 at wine pH. Laboratory results indicate that DMDC can be used to control malolactic bacteria, where the ethanol and the low pH together with added SO_2 are toxic to the bacteria (Ough et al. 1988). We are not aware of its use in practice to control bacteria. However, fumaric acid addition can be used for stabilization. Fumaric acid is completely safe, and if used properly, very effective. Proper conditions are defined as wines with pH less than 4, low concentrations of bacteria, and reasonable amounts of SO_2. All of these conditions can be obtained under good cellar practices, and when used in this way the lactic acid bacteria are not only inhibited but killed. Two disadvantages are that the addition of fumaric acid is not approved in most winemaking regions outside of the United States, and that the acid is rather insoluble in wine. The latter obstacle can be overcome by intermediate stirring of the wine after the addition and again for a few successive days, which, however, is impractical with very large wine lots.

Unplanned and unwanted malolactic fermentations may also occur in the wines during cellar storage; for example, in wines of rather low acidity awaiting bottling. If the fermentation comes about by resident malolactic organisms and no off-flavors are found, the winemaker is advised to wait a few days to assure the cessation of bacterial growth before performing the finishing operations: addition of SO_2 with some aeration and rough filtration (Chapter 6). These operations should also probably include addition of acid. As mentioned before (Chapter 6), the acidulating agent of choice in these cases is tartaric acid, malic acid undoubtedly reinitiates microbial activity.

2. Malolactic Fermentation by Undesirable Bacteria

In Chapter 6 it was pointed out that some strains of malolactic bacteria may produce off-flavors. This might simply be the formation of larger amounts of the fermentation product diacetyl than desired. For example, diacetyl in red wine at less than 5 mg/L is considered to add complexity, but greater than that, to constitute spoilage (Kunkee et al. 1965). With white wines, the spoilage threshold is lower. Thus, various malolactic strains may be spoilage organisms in some cases, but not in others. In addition, fermentation conditions, such as redox potential and presence of citric acid are also important in the production of diacetyl (Chapter 6). Other undesirable strain-specific end products may also be formed. Some of these end products are known, such as hydrogen sulfide, but others are not. Others may be similar to those coming from *Brettanomyces* infections (Section F.6.b).

The best solution to the problem of undesirable malolactic bacteria is prevention, and the tactics for that are the same as used for prevention of *Brettanomyces*; these should be reviewed (Section F.6.b). If the infection has already occurred, the solutions for salvaging the wine are the same as with *Brettanomyces* spoilage. However, the problem with prevention of the growth of the undesired bacteria may have a special solution in the case of malolactic bacteria. Large inoculations of expanded cultures (Chapter 6) of commercially available malolactic bacteria ought to displace any resident populations in the equipment or in cooperage, especially after they have been sanitized.

3. Ropy Wines

Spoilage indicated by a marked, and sometimes disgusting, increase in viscosity in wine, often giving a slimy appearance like that of raw egg white, has been given the descriptive name of ropiness. The awareness of the microbial nature seems to go back to the time of Pasteur, when the malady of *les vins filants* was recognized. Ropiness has long been supposed to come from dextrans, formed by leuconostocs—perhaps from the sucrose in ameliorated wines. However, the first studies to effectively demonstrate the microbiological origin of this spoilage were by Lüthi (1957), who reported that the contamination arose from a mixed culture, or rather a sequential infection, of *Streptococcus mucilaginous* and *Acetobacter rancens*. It is not clear what the current equivalent names for the organisms are, but he gives a convincing, and dramatic, photograph of the effects of this contamination. He is shown drawing out, with the aid of a glass rod, a repulsive long string of ropy wine, for some 5 cm at nearly right angles to the wine sample. The photo shows some sag in the rope, but it remains intact. These kinds of results were the bases of Lüthi's contention that vinification fermentations, good and bad, were a succession of microbial onslaughts (Lüthi 1957).

We have not seen ropiness in American wines, but the infection is apparently still a problem elsewhere. It is not surprising to think that species of *Acetobacter* might be involved with this spoilage. *A. xylinum*, an old species name but now again accepted (Section H.3), is described as producing a "thick, leathery, zoogloeal, and cellulosic" membrane from vinegar (Buchanan and Gibbons 1974), and is a common contaminant in vinegar production (Rose 1961). We have seen this sort of product formed on the top of a beaker of vinegar, and which could be lifted out of the beaker intact. When dried the material had many of the properties of a small piece of paper.

However, the most recent studies of ropiness ascribe the infections not to acetobacter, but to pediococci (Lonvaud-Funel 1986; Lonvaud-Funel et al. 1990), and thus we have included the discussion in this section. Llaubères used the earlier finding as the groundwork for her studies on troublesome polysaccharides produced by pediococci in wine (Llaubères 1988; Canal-Llaubères et al. 1989), which are difficult to remove with current fining and filtration procedures (Chapters 7 and 8).

It may well be that ropiness is caused by a mixture or a succession of microorganisms. *Saccharomyces* yeast have also been shown to produce exocellular polysaccharides (Llaubères et al. 1987). In apple wine, the origins of slime have been ascribed to a heterofermentative lactobacilli, to two different leuconostocs, and to two pediococci (Beech and Carr 1977). The substrates for these fermentations included the various hexoses of apple juice, and also the pentoses. The higher pH of cider would allow the growth of other species of leuconostocs, including dextran formers, and corresponding forms of other wine bacteria. Furthermore, Beech and Carr (1977) pointed out that when the bacteria were grown in the presence of weakly or nonfermenting yeasts, for example, *Candida krusei*, slime production was increased. Slime formation in beer has been attributed to *Pediococcus damnosus*.

4. Ferocious *Lactobacillus* Fermentations

In the last several years, there have been reports of lactic acid bacterial infections occurring early in the alcoholic fermentation, so swift and so abundant that their growth is evident within a few days after the grapes are crushed. Part of the evidence is the rapid formation of high concentrations of acetic acid, so high as to impede the continued growth and fermentation by *Saccharomyces*. Examination of the stuck wines reveals that the bacteria in abundance are not acetic acid bacteria, as expected, but lactobacilli. Although lactic acid bacteria certainly can produce acetic acid, it was unexpected that they could produce so much. In the field, these wild lactobacilli have been named ferocious lactobacilli! The infection seems to be from red grapes, usually Pinot noir, and to be vineyard-specific. In many of these cases the winemakers had been using controversial practices such as no addition of SO_2 at the time of crushing and very often the storage of the fresh must for several days before yeast addition. After examination of many of these wines, it was realized that the infection had not been found in musts with initial pHs of less than 3.5. Even though the infection seems to be vineyard-specific, we were never able to isolate any lactic acid bacteria from the surfaces of the suspected grapes, and only found the infection in juice from the crusher where no SO_2 had been used. This spoilage has apparently been eliminated in the problem wineries by use of the recommended procedure, moderate amounts of SO_2, and immediate addition of yeast starter culture, especially in red grapes with an initial pH of greater than 3.5. This seems to be an illustration of new problems sporadically introduced when tried-and-true practices, such as SO_2 additions, are changed in response to politically correct views.

5. Spoilage of Fortified Wines by *Lactobacillus*

Some species of lactobacilli are exceedingly ethanol-tolerant, and can survive and grow in dessert/appetizer wines fortified to contain 20% (vol/vol) ethanol. The current name for the most famous of these species is *Lactobacillus fructivorans* (Holt 1986); but older winemakers may remember, with apprehension, the species name *L. trichodes* (Fornachon et al. 1949). Trichodes means hair-like, and its microscopic appearance (Figure 6-8) is remarkably like a wad of hair. Its macroscopic appearance also resembles a wad of hair, or cotton, as if a wad were deliberately placed in the wine bottle. Goswell and Kunkee (1977) and Amerine et al. (1980) relate histories of the effects of these bacteria and the devastation they caused even in fortified wines in many wine regions of the world, including South Africa, Australia, and the San Joaquin Valley in California. Devastation is not too strong a word since in at least one case, the winery suffering the infection was financially ruined; and perhaps needlessly, since the organism turns out not to be especially resistant to SO_2. Judicious use of this antiseptic eventually has made this problem a thing of the past —to those who appreciate the past. There are several remarkable characteristics of these bacteria—and probably of its close relative, *L. hilgardii*, which was first isolated from a California wine (Holt 1986). One interesting characteristic is, that in spite of its high tolerance to ethanol, it is relatively sensitive to SO_2. Another is that some strains of *L. fructivorans* have a requirement for ethanol (Radler and Hartel 1984). While these infections have primarily been noticed in fortified wines, table wines are also susceptible. Perhaps because of the special sensitivity of the table wines to bacterial infections, they are given more diligent cellar attention, as compared to those with greater alcohol content, and have been largely spared.

6. Mousey Wines

The odor of mousey wines is reminiscent of the smell of mouse nests or mouse urine; but more genteelly compared with the smell of acetamide, or some impurity usually associated with the latter. However, it is now established that this spoilage arises rather from substituted piperidines/pyridines, coming as oxidation products of lysine (see below). The oxidation involvement seems to explain an old-time procedure of rubbing a small volume of a subject wine between the hands to accentuate any of the spoilage character, which action in this case helps to induce formation of aroma compounds as well as to volatilize them. There seems to be good agreement amongst enologists worldwide as to the sensory character of the spoilage; but there is no good agreement as to what brings it about, except that it certainly must be microbiological. Koch's postulates have been fulfilled in that three species of *Brettanomyces* and two of *Lactobacillus* have been isolated from mousey wines, and reinfection of a model medium with any of them brought about the mousey taint and the formation of the piperidines (Heresztyn 1986b). Furthermore, the offensive compounds were not formed by *Brettanomyces* yeast except when lysine was available; nor by the lactobacilli unless ethanol, or propanol, was present. However, mousiness is not one of the usual or important descriptors applied to *Brettanomyces* spoilage (Section F.6); nevertheless, we have smelled wines which were assuredly infected with at least *Brettanomyces*, and which were just as assuredly mousey. Lactobacilli, and other lactic acid bacteria, and acetic acid bacteria, as well, have strong anecdotal support as being the causative microbial agents.

The first research showing the involvement of substituted piperidines came from work with English cider, which seems to be especially susceptible to mousey spoilage (Beech 1993)—probably because of it higher pH and lower ethanol concentration, as compared to grape wine, and perhaps because it has a more subtle baseline aroma. The discovery of the acetamide impurity (2,4,6-trimethyl-1,3,5-triazine) (Figure 9-5) led Tucknott to suggest that an alkyl-substituted Δ'piperidine (that is, 2-ethyl-3,4,5,6-tetrahydropyridine) (Figure 9-5) might be the smelly component of mousy cider (Tucknott and Williams 1973). Later, this com-

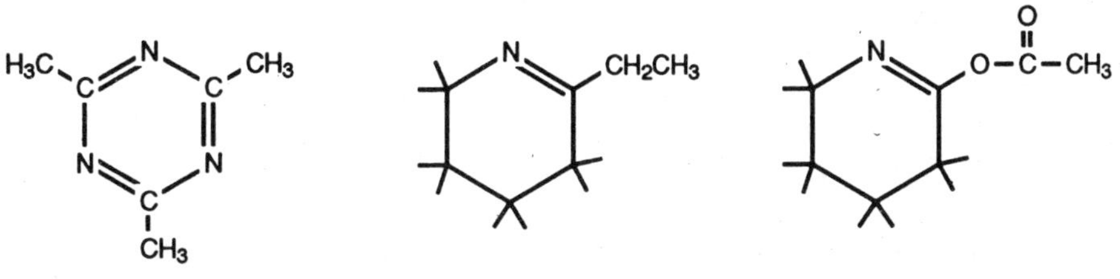

Fig. 9-5. Organic compounds having been implicated in aromatic character of mousey wine.

pound was reported in mousey wine (Craig and Heresztyn 1984), and then corrected to be either of the two carbonyl analogues (2-acetyl-3,4,5,6-tetrahydropyridine or the 1,4,5,6 isomer) (Figure 9-5) (Heresztyn 1986b). These components have not been identified in normal, sound wines (Rapp 1988).

The discovery of the role of oxygen led to important changes in cider production in England to prevent oxidation during fermentation and filtration, especially just prior to the bottling operations.

7. Other Spoilages by Lactic Acid Bacteria

Mannitol spoilage or *mannite* disease, depicted by Pasteur (1866), is caused by certain strains of heterolactic bacteria. These bacteria, at least under particular conditions, are capable of bringing about sliminess and complex flavor changes to wine; the latter has been described as a vinegary-estery taste with a slight sweetness (Sponholz 1994). These flavors are apparently due to formation of mannitol, propanol, butanol, and acetic acid, and perhaps diacetyl. In Chapter 6, one of the procedures given for the identification of lactic acid bacteria was the capacity of the heterolactic bacteria to reduce fructose to mannitol.

Acrolein spoilage in wine is seen as an unacceptable increase in bitterness. Acrolein (CH_2 = CH-CHO) itself is not bitter but seems to react with various phenolic groups of anthocyanin to produce bitterness (Sponholz 1994); the spoilage problem is usually associated with red wines with high phenolic content (Dittrich 1987). This spoilage, described by Pasteur (1866) and called the *amertume* disease at that time, arises from dehydration of glycerol by some lactic acid bacteria, although the dehydratase enzyme has been demonstrated in only a few of them (Sponholz 1994).

Further histories and decriptions of ropiness, mousiness, and the other lactic acid bacterial spoilages, including those which degrade tartaric acid, can be found in Amerine, et al. (1980) and Dittrich (1987). All of these spoilages are prevented by diligent sanitation regimes and by judicious use of SO_2; they are essentially unknown in modern-day wines of California.

H. SPOILAGE BY ACETIC ACID BACTERIA

As a class, acetic acid bacteria are obligate aerobes, mostly catalase positive, producing acetic acid from glucose. The wine-related acetic acid bacteria generally also produce acetic acid from ethanol and are loosely categorized as vinegar bacteria (Asai 1968; Drysdale and Fleet 1988). Taxonomic identification of these bacteria is given at the end of this section.

1. Kinds of Wine-Related Acetic Acid Bacteria

The bacteria discussed in this section are those accepted and described in *Bergey's Manual of Systematic Bacteriology* (Holt 1984) and in accord with the ninth edition of *Bergey's Manual of Determinative Bacteriology* (Holt et al. 1993). Some species of acetic acid bacteria are not tolerant to high (wine) concentrations of ethanol. The latter organisms, such as *Gluconobacter*, *Frateuria*, and *Acetobacter hansenii*, might be found in grape must before the buildup of ethanol or found associated with winery equipment (Drysdale and Fleet 1988). (Actually, *Frateuria* has only been found in fruit juices other than grape juice, but it is included here for completeness.) However, with extremely moldy, bunch-rotted grapes, or ill-treated mechanically harvested grapes, showing premature alcoholic fermentations (Section F.1), the complement of acetic acid bacteria may more closely resemble that found in wine. In wine, the most important species is *Acetobacter aceti*, which is highly ethanol-tolerant, and in fact is the species of choice for use in commercial vinegar production (Ebner 1982). This organism is easily controlled (see below) by maintenance of anaerobic conditions and reasonable amounts of SO_2 (0.8 mg/L molecular SO_2). In recent years another species of acetobacter, *A. pasteurianus*, has been found as a spoilage organism in several wineries. These occurrences may come from the current popular tendency to produce and store wines with lowered ethanol content and maintained with lowered concentrations of SO_2. More research needs to be done on the relative sensitivities of the strains of these two species to SO_2.

2. Prevention and Control of Acetic Acid Bacterial Spoilage

Acetic acid bacteria are ubiquitous and *A. aceti* is undoubtedly found in the indigenous population of all cellars. Naturally, winemakers will avoid the acceptance of moldy grapes, but it is doubtful whether the acceptance or not would have much effect on the resident microflora of the cellar. The importance of keeping these bacteria in control cannot be overemphasized. On the one hand, the methodology is simple: frequent topping of barrels or tight bunging, with the barrels rolled on their sides; use of inert gases for headspaces in tanks; and frequent monitoring of SO_2 concentrations. On the other hand, during the hectic time of harvest, and during heavy bottling schedules, these labor-intensive regimes are easily scrimped. Wines badly spoiled by acetic acid bacteria are difficult to correct, and are usually diverted to vinegar. Refermentation is not a solution since *Saccharomyces* cannot utilize acetic acid. Blending is only a limited solution. A recent procedure involving reverse osmosis and ion exchange to remove acetic acid before returning the permutate and its flavors back to the wine can be useful, but avoidance of production of acetic acid is still preferable. This procedure is ineffective in removing ethyl acetate.

In this regard, it should be pointed out that acetic acid is not the only product of acetobacter metabolism; ethyl acetate is also produced. Ethyl acetate has a much lower sensory threshold. Acetic acid is usually the compound which is measured, mainly because of the ease of its analysis, especially compared to the determination of ethyl acetate. Generally one expects the concentration of acetic acid to reflect the amounts of ethyl acetate present, again owing to the chemical equilibration, and wines smelling strongly of vinegar would also show a high concentration of acetic acid. But that is not always the case. For example, in the wines spoiled by the ferocious lactobacilli (Section G.4), the acetic acid concentrations were exceedingly high, but the wines had little smell of ethyl acetate.

3. Taxonomy of the Wine-Acetic Acid Bacteria

The acetic acid bacteria of concern are *Frateuria aurantius*, *Gluconobacter oxydans*, and the four species of acetobacter: *A. aceti*, *A. hansenii*, *A. liquefaciens*, and *A. pasteurianus*. Other species of the first two genera are mentioned at the end of this section. Preliminary identification of the wine-related acetic acid bacteria as a class can often be made with the light microscope by the experienced observer (Figure 9-6). "Involution forms are frequent ... and may be spherical, elongated, swollen, club-shaped, curved, or filamentous" (Holt et al. 1993), whereas the other wine-related bacteria, especially the lactic acid bacteria, are far more regular in shape—and generally much smaller. A more objective identification begins with a positive result from the catalase test (Appendix G). Some strains of *A. pasteurianus* are catalase negative, therefore all suspected aerobes should be examined in the tests given below. For species identification of the acetic acid bacteria, several kinds of solid media are employed: $CaCO_3$-Ethanol, Glucose-Yeast extract-Calcium carbonate (GYC), Frateur and Modified Carr (Appendix F). All of the acetic acid bacteria should grow on at least one of these (Holt 1984). These media have various concentrations of yeast extract, with either glucose or ethanol as carbon sources and $CaCO_3$. The latter is solubilized by the acetic acid formed from glucose or ethanol by these bacteria. This is evidenced by a dramatic clearing of the solid white background surrounding the bacterial growth. Modified Carr medium is generally not used and may only be needed for identification of some strains of *A. pasteurianus*.

Table 9-2 gives a dichotomous key for the determination of the species of wine-related acetic acid bacteria. The prerequisite for use of this key is that the organism shows obvious growth and/or obvious clearing on at least one of the four media listed above. *Frateuria*, included for completeness, can be distinguished from all of the rest of these bacteria, and eliminated from further consideration by

Table 9-2. A dichotomous taxonomic key for determination of the wine species of acetic acid bacteria*.

(Media formulae given in Appendix F)

1. Obvious growth on $CaCO_3$-Ethanol, Frateur, GYC, or Modified Carr media?	Yes:	go to 2
	No:	not acetic acid bacteria
2. Obvious clearing on $CaCO_3$-Ethanol medium?	Yes:	go to 4
	No:	*Acetobacter hansenii* or *A. pasteurianus*: go to 3
3. Ketogenesis from glycerol medium, giving a positive "Clinitest" assay for reducing sugars? (see text)	Yes:	*A. hansenii* **
	No:	*A. pasteurianus*
4. Forms water-soluble brown pigment on GYC medium (pigment penetrates solid medium)?	Yes:	*A. liquefaciens*
	No:	go to 5
5. Ketogenesis from glycerol medium, giving a positive "Clinitest" assay for reducing sugars? (see text)	Yes:	go to 6
	No:	*A. pasteurianus*
6. Clearing and reclouding (irisation) of Frateur or $CaCO_3$-Ethanol medium (that is, growth on acetate)?	Yes:	*A. aceti*
	No:	Gluconobacter oxydans

*Assumes strains of *Frateuria* are not present (see text).

**Also possibly *A. xylinum* [not accepted in *Bergey's Systematics*, (Holt 1984)], but unlike *A. hansenii*, producing a very characteristic surface membrane (see text).

Acetic acid bacteria species for use as positive and negative controls in the above tests

Test	Positive	Negative
Brown pigment	*A. liquefaciens*	*A. aceti*
Ketogenesis	*A. aceti*	*A. pasteurianus*
Clears $CaCO_3$-Ethanol	*A. aceti*	*A. hansenii*
Reclouds Frateur	*A. aceti*	*Gluconobacter oxydans*

Source: Selected from Asai (1968), Holt (1984), and Holt et al. (1993).

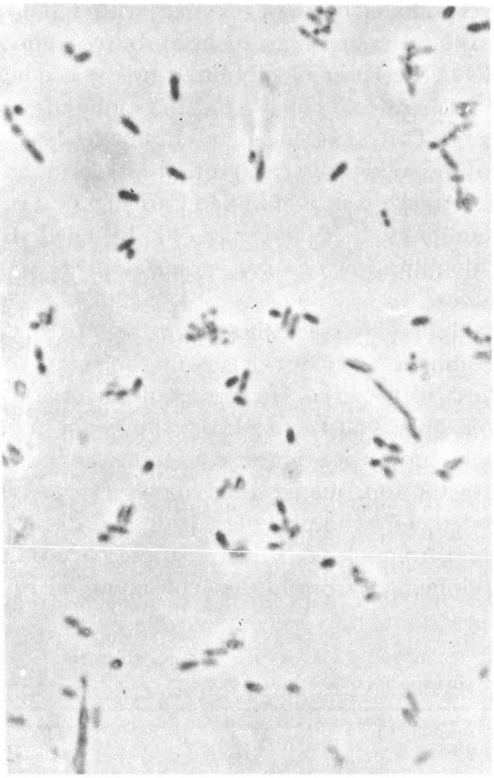

Fig. 9-6. *Acetobacter aceti.*

their ability to grow on 30% D-glucose; but more easily by their formation of yellow colonies on solid mannitol medium (MYP; Appendix F) used for storage of the acetic acid bacteria. In the next step in the key (Table 9-2), organisms which do not show obvious growth on $CaCO_3$- ethanol medium are distinguished as *A. hansenii* or as a strain of *A. pasteurianus*. In spite of no obvious growth on $CaCO_3$-ethanol medium, some strains of *A. hansenii* may still produce enough acetic acid to show some faint clearing. Differentiation of a strain of *A. pasteurianus* from *A. hansenii* as this stage of the key is made by testing for oxidation, ketogenesis, of glycerol in liquid medium. This can be detected by use of Clinitest tablets (Ough and Amerine 1988), when, after good growth on glycerol medium (Appendix F) is evidenced, a positive test (*A. hansenii*) of the liquid is a faint olive drab color, as compared to the bright blue of a negative test (*A. hansenii*). In the next step in the key, organisms forming water-soluble brown pigment on GYC are distinguished as *A. liquefaciens*. With *A. liquefaciens*, the brown pigment is not merely associated with colonial growth, but pervades the solid medium, eventually to the edges (Figure 9-7). Other strains of *A. pasteurianus*, not already designated, are distinguished from the remaining species of the key by showing, again, no ketogenesis of glycerol (a negative Clinitest evaluation). The two remaining species of the key, *A. aceti* and *G. oxydans*, both clear the $CaCO_3$ of Frateur medium. However, on Frateur medium, *A. aceti* will further metabolize, overoxidize, the acetate formed, and the dissolved $CaCO_3$ will reprecipitate. The *Gluconobacter* does not show such subsequent reclouding. The reprecipitated $CaCO_3$ has a silkier appearance as compared to the initial suspended $CaCO_3$. The reprecipitation commences near the colony, and its appearance has sometimes been described as *irisation*, having the appearance of an iris of the eye (Holt 1984) (Figure 9-8).

This key deals with the species accepted in *Bergey's Manual of Systematic Bacteriology* (Holt 1984). The ninth edition of *Bergey's Manual of Determinative Bacteriology* (Holt et al. 1993) gives three additional species of acetobacter: *A. diazotrophicus*, which grows on 30% D-glucose, *A. methanolicus*, which grows on methanol, and *A. xylinum*. *A. xylinum* has been isolated from vinegar and gives the "production of a thick, leathery, zoogloeal, cellulosic" membrane on the surface of liquids (Buchanan and Gibbons 1974). The characteristics of *A. xylinum* are much like *A. aceti*, except the former will not show growth on $CaCO_3$-ethanol medium (see also the discussion on ropy wine in Section G3). The ninth edition of *Bergey's Manual of Determinative Bacteriology* (Holt et al. 1993) also lists two additional species of gluconobacter: *G. frateuril* which will grow on ribitol and *G. asaii* which require nicotinate for growth.

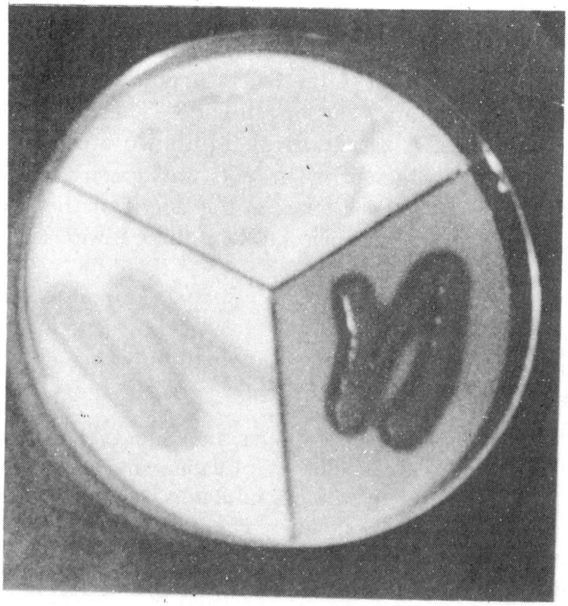

Fig. 9-7. Formation of soluble brown pigments by *Acetobacter liquefaciens*. GYC medium: Top: *A. pasteurianus*; Right: *A. liquefaciens*; Left: *A. aceti*.

I. SPOILAGE BY OTHER AEROBIC BACTERIA

1. Spoilage by *Bacillus*

Spoilages by *Bacillus* spp. have previously been reported in experimental dessert wines (Gini and Vaughn 1962). More serious have been the reports of widespread infections of bacilli in wines from the former Eastern bloc countries (Bisson and Kunkee 1991). We ourselves have isolated bacilli from several wines from the Balkans. The damage seems to be cosmetic; bench tastings of the these wines indi-

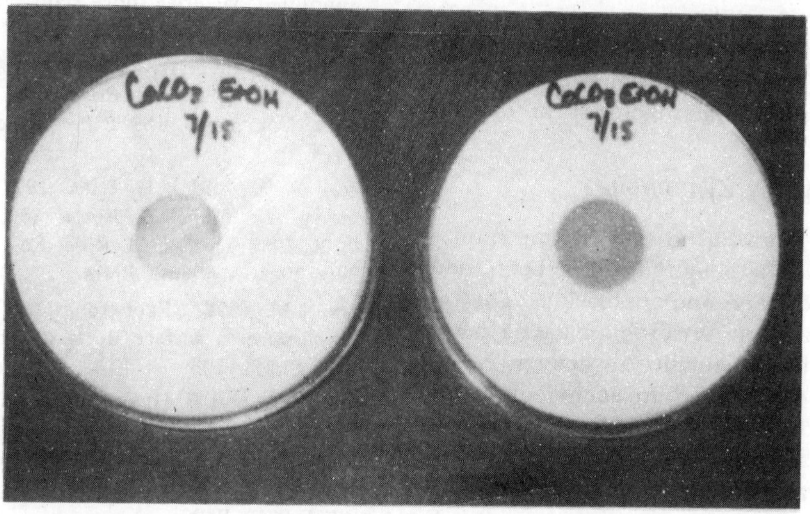

Fig. 9-8. Reclouding of calcium carbonate medium by *Acetobacter aceti*. Left: clearing and subsequent reclouding (irisation) of $CaCO_3$-Ethanol medium by *A. aceti*. Right: clearing of $CaCO_3$-Ethanol medium and no reclouding by *Gluconobacter oxydans*.

cated no off-characters, in fact, they were excellent. The bacteria are obligate aerobes, and the anaerobic conditions of the bottled wine probably limit the spoilage damage. However, in stored wines, in tank or barrels, the chances of increased oxygen tension in the wine is real. We have had reports, clandestine but limited, of this kind of spoilage in some wineries in California. The only preventative and control measures that can currently be given are the same as those given for the acetic acid bacteria, above. However, bacilli are endospore formers, the spores being demonstrably resistant to heat. More research is needed to determine if the spore-forming capability also renders the bacteria more resistant to chemical additives, namely, SO_2.

The species of *Bacillus* are identified as being catalase positive (see above) and show no clearing of $CaCO_3$-ethanol plates, see above. Spores, if present, are heat-resistant, retaining viability after being heated for one minute at 100°C. Spore formation is usually observed in old cultures. Their formation is stimulated in media containing 40 mg/L $MnSO_4$. Suspected organisms should be grown on bacillus-sporulation medium (Appendix F); and after good growth, heated as given above and then plated out for detection of viable cells. The spores are also resistant to 70°C for 10 minutes or to 95% ethanol for 20 minutes. The bacilli are a "diverse assemblage that is a grouping of convenience" (Holt 1986); establishment of genus identification is probably as much as the wine microbiologist can expect.

2. Spoilage by *Zymomonas*

Actually we know of no case of wine spoilage by *Zymomonas*, although they have been found as spoilers of beers and apple wines. They are facultative aerobic/anaerobic bacteria having much of the fermentative capacity of *Saccharomyces* wine yeast, and are included here for completeness. They are catalase positive and easily tolerate 5% ethanol and pHs as low as 3.5. They are distinguished from *Acetobacter* and *Gluconobacter* in that they grow under both aerobic and anaerobic conditions, produce gas from glucose, and quantitatively ferment glucose (and fructose and sucrose) to ethanol and carbon dioxide. There is one species, *Z. mobilis*, divided into two subspecies: *mobilis*, which grows at 36°C; and *pomaci*, which does not. *Zymomonas* is the agent in the fermentation of agave sap to pulque (Swings and DeLey 1977).

J. REFERENCES

ALLEVA, J. J., P. F. BONVENTRE, and C. LAMANNA. 1979. "Inhibition of ovulation in hamsters by the protein synthesis inhibitors diphtheria toxin and cycloheximide." *Proc. Soc. Exp. Biol. Med.* 162:170–174.

AMERINE, M. A., BERG, H. W., KUNKEE, R. E., OUGH, C. S., SINGLETON, V. L. SINGLETON, and WEBB, A. D. 1980. *The Technology of Wine Making*, 4th ed. Westport, CT: Avi Publishing Co.

AMON, J. F., R. F. SIMPSON, and J. M. VANDEPEER. 1987. "A taint in wood-matured wine attributable to microbiological contamination of the oak barrel." *Austral. N. Z. Wine Ind. J.* 2:35–37.

ASAI, T. 1968. *Acetic Acid Bacteria; Classification and Biochemical Activities*. Baltimore: University Park Press.

BARTHOLOMEW, J. E., and T. MITTWER. 1950. "A simplified bacterial spore stain." *Stain Technol.* 25:153–156.

BEECH, F. W. 1993. Yeasts in cider-making. In, *The Yeasts*, 2nd ed., A. H. Rose and J. S. Harrison, Eds., Vol. 5, pp. 169–213, London: Academic Press.

BEECH, F. W., and J. G. CARR. 1977. "Cider and perry." In *Economic Microbiology*, Vol. 1, Alcoholic Beverages, A. H. Rose, Ed., pp. 139–313. New York: Academic Press.

BELIN, J.-M. 1972. "Recherches sur la répartition des levures à surface de la grappe de raisin." *Vitis* 11:135–145.

BELIN, J.-M., and P. HENRY. 1972. "Contribution a l'étude écologique des levures dans le vignoble. Répartition des levures à la surface du pédicelle et de la baie de raisin." *C. R. Acad. Sci.* Paris 274D:2318–2320.

BISSON, L. F., and R. E. KUNKEE. 1991. "Microbial interactions during wine production." In, *Mixed Cultures in Biotechnology*, G. Zeikus and E. A. Johnson, Eds., pp. 37–68. New York: McGraw-Hill, Inc.

BUCHANAN, R. E., and N. E. GIBBONS. 1974. *Bergey's Manual of Determinative Bacteriology*, 8th ed. Baltimore: Williams & Watkins.

CANAL-LLAUBÈRES, R.-M., D. DUBOURDIEU, B. RICHARD, and A. LONVAUD-FUNEL. 1989. "Structure moléculaire ß-D-glucane exocullulaire de *Pediococcus* sp." *Conn. Vigne Vin.* 23:49–52.

CHATONNET, P., D. DUBOURDIEU, J.-N. BOIDRON, and M. PONS. 1992. "The origin of ethylphenols in wines." *J. Sci. Food Agric.* 60:165–178.

CHATONNET, P., D. DUBOURDIEU, J.-N. BOIDRON, and V. LAVIGNE. 1993. "Synthesis of volatile phenols by *Saccharomyces cerevisiae* in wines." *J. Sci. Food Agric.* 62:191–202.

CHATONNET, P., D. DUBOURDIEU, and J.-N. BOIDRON. 1989. "Incidence de certains facteurs sur la décarboxylation des acides phénols par la levure." *Conn. Vigne Vin* 23:59–62.

COLEY-SMITH, J. R. , K. VERHOEFF, and W. R. JARVIS. 1980. *The Biology of Botrytis*. New York: Academic Press.

CRAIG, J. T., and T. HERESZTYN. 1984. "2-Ethyl-3,4,5,6-tetrahydropyridine-An assessment of its possible contribution to the mousy off-flavor of wines." *Am. J. Enol. Vitic.* 35:46–48.

CROWELL, E. A., and J. F. GUYMON. 1975. "Wine constituents arising from sorbic acid addition and identification of 2-ethoxyhexa-3,5-diene as source of geranium-like off-odor." *Am. J. Enol. Vitic.* 26:97–102.

DAVIS, C. R., T. H. LEE, and G. H. FLEET. 1982. "Inactivation of wine cork microflora by a commercial sulfur dioxide treatment." *Am. J. Enol. Vitic.* 33:124–127.

DE MAN, J. C., M. ROGOSA, and M. E. SHARPE. 1960. "A medium for the cultivation of *lactobacilli*." *J. Appl. Bacteriol.* 23:130–135.

DITTRICH, H. H. 1987. *Mikrobiologie des Weines*. 2nd ed. Stuttgart, Germany: Ulmer.

DRYSDALE, G. S., and G.H. FLEET. 1988. "Acetic acid bacteria winemaking: A review." *Am. J. Enol. Vitic.* 39:143–154.

DRYSDALE, G. S., and G. H. FLEET. 1989. "The effect of acetic acid bacteria upon the growth and metabolism of yeasts during the fermentation of grape juice." *J. Appl. Bacteriol.* 67:471.

EBNER, H. 1982. Vinegar. In, *Prescott & Dunn's Industrial Microbiology*, 4th ed., G. Reed, Ed. Westport, Connecticut: AVI Publishing Co.

FLEET, G.H., G. M. HEARD, and C. GAO. 1988. "The effect of temperature on the growth and ethanol tolerance of yeast during fermentation." *Yeast* 5:543–546.

FORNACHON, J. C. M., H. C. DOUGLAS, and R. H. VAUGHN. 1949. "Lactobacillus trichodes nov. spec., a bacterium causing spoilage in appetizer and dessert wines." *Hilgardia* 19:129–132.

FUGELSANG, K. C., M. M. OSBORN, and C. J. MULLER. 1993. *Brettanomyces* and *Dekkera*: Implications in wine making. In *Beer and Wine Production—Analysis, Characterization, and Technological Advances*. ACS Symposium Series 536, B. H. Gump and D. J. Pruett, Eds., pp. 110–131. Washington, DC: American Chemical Society.

GAUNT, D. M., H. DEGN, and D. LLOYD. 1988. "The influence of oxygen and organic hydrogen acceptors on glycolytic carbon dioxide production in *Brettanomyces anomalus*." *Yeast* 4:249–255.

GINI, B., and R. H. VAUGHN. 1962. "Bacilli in wine." *Am. J. Enol. Vitic.* 30:24–27.

GUINARD, J.-X. 1990. *Lambic*. Boulder, CO: Brewers Publications.

GOSWELL, R. W., and R. E. KUNKEE. 1977. "Fortified wines." In *Economic Microbiology*, Vol. 1, Alcoholic Beverages, A. H. Rose, Ed., pp. 478–535. New York: Academic Press.

HANSEN, E. C. 1896. *Practical Studies in Fermentation*, pp. 512. New York: Spon and Chamberlain.

HERESZTYN, T. 1986a. "Formation of substituted tetrahydropyridines by species of *Brettanomyces* and *Lactobacillus* isolated from mousy wines." *Am. J. Enol. Vitic.* 37:127–132.

HERESZTYN, T. 1986b. "Metabolism of volatile phenolic compounds from hydroxycinnamic acid by *Brettanomyces* yeast." *Arch. Microbiol.* 146:96–98.

HOCK, S. 1990. "Coping with *Brettanomyces*." *Pract. Wine Vine*. January/February:26–31.

HOLT, J. G. 1984. *Bergey's Manual of Systematic Bacteriology*, Vol 1. Baltimore: Williams & Wilkins.

HOLT, J. G. 1986. *Bergey's Manual of Systematic Bacteriology*, vol 2. Baltimore: Williams & Wilkins.

HOLT, J. G., N. R. KRIEG, P. H. A. SNEATH, J. T. STALEY, and S. T. WILLIAMS. 1993. *Bergey's Manual of Determinative Bacteriology*, 9th ed. Baltimore: Williams & Wilkins.

HUMPHRIES, J. C., T. M. JANE, and M. A. SEFTON. 1992. "The influence of yeast fermentation on volatile oak extractives." *Austral. Grapegrow. Winemak.* No. 343 July:17–18.

ILAGAN, R. D. 1979. "Studies of the Sporulation of *Dekkera*." M.S. thesis, Davis, CA: University of California.

KOCH, R. 1881. "Zur Züchtung von pathogenen Mikro-organismen." *Kaiserl. Gesundheitsampte* 1, 4–48.

KREGER-VAN RIJ, N. J. W. 1984. *The Yeasts, A Taxonomic Study*. Amsterdam: Elsevier Science Publishers.

KUNKEE, R. E. 1967. "Malolactic fermentation." *Adv. Appl. Microbiol.* 9:235–279.

KUNKEE, R. E. 1974. "Malolactic fermentation and winemaking." In *The Chemistry of Winemaking*, Adv. Chem. Ser. 137, A. D. Webb, Ed., pp. 151–170. Washington, DC: American Chemical Society.

KUNKEE, R. E. 1984. "Selection and modification of yeasts and lactic acid bacteria for wine fermentation." *Food Microbiol.* 1:315–332.

KUNKEE, R. E., G. J. PILONE, and R. E. COMBS. 1965. "The occurrence of malo-lactic fermentation in Southern California wines." *Am. J. Enol. Vitic.* 16:219–223.

LAFON-LAFOURCADE, S. 1983. "Wine and brandy." In *Biotechnology, A Comprehensive Treatise in 8 Volumes*, Eds. H.-J. Rehm and G. Reed, Vol. 5, pp. 81–163. Weinheim: Verlag Chemie.

LAGUNAS, R., C. DOMINGUEZ, A. BUSTURIA, and M. J. SAEZ. 1982. "Mechanisms of appearance of the Pasteur effect in *Saccharomyces cerevisiae*." Inactivation of the sugar transport system. *J. Bacteriol.* 152:19–25.

LARUE, F., N. ROZES, I. FROUDIÈRE, C. COUTY, and G. P. PERREIRA. 1991. "Incidence du développement de *Dekkera / Brettanomyces* dans les moûts et les vins." *J. Int. Sci. Vign Vin* 25:149–165.

LEFEBVRE, A., J.-M. RIBOULET, J.-N. BOIDRON, and P. RIBÉREAU-GAYON. 1983. "Incidence des microorganismes du liège sur les altérations olfactives du vin." *Sci. Ali.* 3:265–278.

LLAUBÈRES, R.-M. 1988. Les polysaccharides sécrétés dans les vins par Saccharomyces cerevisiae et Pediococcus sp. PhD thesis, Talence, France.: University of Bordeaux II.

LLAUBÈRES, R.-M., D. DUBOURDIEU, and J. C. VILLETTAZ. 1987. "Exocellular poly-saccharides from *Saccharomyces* in wine." *J. Sci. Food. Agric.* 41:27.

LONVAUD-FUNEL, A. 1986. Recherches sur les bactéries lactiques du vin. Fonctions métaboliques, croissance, génétique plasmidique. PhD thesis, Talence, France: University of Bordeaux II.

LONVAUD-FUNEL, A., A. JOYEUX, and C. ROULLAND. 1990. "Etude d'altérations des vin par les bactéries lactiques." In, *Actualities OEnologiques 89*, P. Ribéreau-Gayon and A. Lonvaud, Eds., pp. 378–382. Paris: Dunod.

LÜTHI, H. R. 1957. "Symbiotic problems relating to bacterial deterioration of wines." *Am. J. Enol. Vitic.* 8:176–181.

MALLETROIT, V., J.-X. GUINARD, R. E. KUNKEE, and M. J. LEWIS. 1991. "Effect of pasteurization on microbiological and sensory quality of white grape juice and wine." *J. Food Process. Preserv.* 15:19–29.

MEYNELL, G. G., and E. MEYNELL. 1965. *Theory and Practice in Experimental Bacteriology*. Cambridge, U.K.: Cambridge University Press.

OUGH, C. S., and M. A. AMERINE. 1988. *Methods for Analysis of Musts and Wines*. New York: John Wiley and Sons.

OUGH, C. S., and J. L. INGRAHAM. 1960. "Use of sorbic acid and sulfur dioxide in sweet table wines." *Am J. Enol. Vitic.* 11:117–122.

OUGH, C. S., R. E. KUNKEE, M. R. VILAS, E. BORDEU, and M.-C. HUANG. 1988. "The interaction of sulfur dioxide, pH, and dimethyl decarbonate on the growth of *Saccharomyces cerevisiae* Montrachet and *Leuconostoc oenos* MCW." *Am. J. Enol. Vitic.* 38:279–282.

PASTEUR, L. 1866. etudes sur le Vin. Paris: Victor Masson et Fils.

PEYNAUD, E., and S. DOMERCQ. 1955. "Sur les epèces de levures fermentant sélectivement le fructose." *Ann. Inst. Past.* 89:346–351.

RADLER, F., and S. HARTEL. 1984. *Lactobacillus trichodes*, ein Alkoholabhändiges Milchsäurebakterium. *Wein-Wissen.* 39:106–112.

RAPP, A. 1988. "Wine aroma substances form gas chromatographic analyses." In, *Wine Analysis, Modern Methods of Plant Analysis*, H. F. Linskens and J. F. Jackson, Eds., New Series Vol. 6, pp. 29–66. Berlin: Springer-Verlag.

ROMANO, P., and G. SUZZI. 1993. "Potential use for *Zygosaccharomyces* species in Winemaking." *J. Wine Res.* 4:87–94.

ROSE, A. H. 1961. *Industrial Microbiology*. Washington, DC: Butterworths.

SPONHOLZ, W.-R. 1994. "Identification of wine aroma defects caused by yeast and bacteria." *Proceedings of the Twenty-Third Annual New York Wine Industry Workshop*, pp. 78–95. Geneva, New York: New York State Agricultural Experiment Station.

SWINGS, J., and J. DELEY. 1977. "The biology of *Zymomonas*." *Bacteriol. Rev.* 41:1–46.

TAYLOR, J. 1962. "The estimation of numbers of bacteria by tenfold dilution series." *J. Appl. Bacteriol.* 25:54–61.

THOMAS, D. S. 1993. "Yeasts as spoilage organisms in beverages." In, *The Yeasts*, 2nd edition, A. H. Rose and J. S. Harrison, Eds., Vol 5, pp. 517–561. New York: Academic Press.

TUCKNOTT, O. G., and A. A. WILLIAMS. 1973. "Taints in fermented juice products." *Annual Report Long Ashton Research Station for 1972*, p. 159. Dorchester, UK: H. Ling.

VAN DER WALT, J. P., and A. E. VAN KERKEN. 1958. "The wine yeasts of the Cape, Part II." *Ant. Leeuvwen.* 25:449–459.

VAN DER WALT, J. P., and A. E. VAN KERKEN. 1961. "The wine yeasts of the Cape, Part V." *Ant. Leeuvwen.* 27:81–90.

VAN URK, H., W. S. L. VOLL, W. A. SCHEFFERS, and J. P. VAN DIJKEN. 1990. "Transient-state analysis of metabolic fluxes in Crabtree-positive and Crabtree-negative yeasts." *Appl. Environ. Microbiol.* 56:281–287.

VAN ZYL, J. A. 1962. "Turbidity in South African dry wines caused by the development of the *Brettanomyces* yeast." *Dept. Agric. Tech. Ser., Pretoria, Sci. Bull.* No. 381.

VAUGHN, R. H. 1955. "Bacterial spoilage of wines with special reference to California conditions." *Adv. Food Res.* 6:67–108.

WIJSMAN, M. R., J. P. VAN DIJKEN, B. H. VAN KLEEFF, and W. A. SCHEFFERS. 1984. "Inhibition of fermentation and growth in batch cultures of the yeast *Brettanomyces intermedius* upon a shift from aerobic to anaerobic conditions (Custers effect)." *Ant. Leeuwen.* 50:183–192.

CHAPTER 10

The Maturation and Aging of Wines

A. BACKGROUND AND OBJECTIVES

1. Definitions

In total, wine aging can be considered to be all the reactions and changes that occur after the first racking that lead to improvement at some stage rather than spoilage. Aging, like all groups of reactions, takes more or less time depending upon temperature and other conditions. In early times malolactic fermentation, final clarification, and tartrate stabilization come about during the postfermentation period and were part of "aging." As the details of such reactions became understood they were separated from aging and considered in their own right. This process continues today as separate reactions of the overall process are dissected apart. A great deal has been learned by studying various component reactions, conditions, and procedures. By such study, wine aging is easily seen to be not an entity but a family of changes. Wine aging should not be thought of as a single procedure nor even a single result.

Two major stages, bulk and bottle, are useful subcategories of this family of processes. During bulk storage wine may be relatively easily exposed to conditions such as oxidation and to further treatments. During storage in bottle or even in simulations of bottle storage in larger containers, further processing or modification is unproductive. Debottling is obviously costly and wasteful. Disruption of the essentially anaerobic condition in bottles or bottle-like storage defeats part of the intent for such storage.

A useful distinction is to define the bulk storage period as maturation and the bottle or equivalent storage as aging or bottle aging. When properly matured the wine is ripe to bottle. All the affordable processes including blending that bring the wine to the condition optimum for bottling should have been completed when the wine is mature. Aging in bottle then will permit slower reactions to continue and reactions requiring different conditions, particularly freedom from air contact and from escape of highly volatile substances.

To be sure we are understood and to make useful distinctions a few sensory terms need definition. *Aroma* includes the odors derived from the grape such as varietal aromas. *Bouquets* are the odors derived from processing or aging, such as fermentation bouquet or bottle bouquet. To be *odorous* a substance must be volatile and stimulate odor receptors in the nose. *Taste* is restricted to those sensations that require placing the wine in the mouth. *Astringency*, *bitterness*, *tartness*, and *sweetness* are important feelings and tastes in wines. *Flavor* is the overall character including feelings, tastes and odors or a general term when both or either oral and nasal sensations may be involved.

2. Historical and Economic Aspects

There have been many papers on specific aspects of wine aging and we will cite some of them later, but relatively few cover general aspects (Malvezin 1903; Singleton 1962, 1979; Ribéreau-Gayon 1986).

Food preparation and distribution today emphasize freshness and storage without appreciable change. We tend to forget that some dishes taste better the second day or warmed over (even if many do not). To some, canned green beans are better than fresh frozen ones and at least a valuable alternative. It is common that processed products exhibit an initial quality gain as judged by sensory panels a few weeks after processing, followed by first-order degradation (*Open* 1979). There are a number of foods and beverages in addition to wine that are considerably improved by appropriate aging. Sugar-cured and smoked ham, salami, many cheeses, vinegars, whiskey. and other spirituous beverages come to mind. Perfumes and condiments such as mustard preparations and tabasco sauces are others.

The point is that aging for modification, improvement, and to command a higher price is by no means confined to wines. A second point is that the results of wine aging are attractive to the consumer. Unwarned, the person familiar only with young wines may be startled by the differences in aged wines and might be wary of what has happened to them. The aged wine flavors are, however, inherently and immediately attractive and do not require learned appreciation in the way Limburger cheese may.

A third point is that the methods of wine maturation and aging considered traditional today were not deliberately developed, but grew out of simple efforts to extend availability and preservation of wines. The procedures such as protection from excessive air contact, storage in wooden cooperage, use of cork stoppers, etc., grew out of the use of materials at hand. Adaptation and spread of particular usages occurred slowly as the products were seen to be protected or improved by that procedure. It is a tortuous path from the unglazed ceramics and raw, hair-inside goatskins of biblical times to the present wine containers. Now we have the best synthesis of older practices, combined with much clearer understanding of the processes and modern techniques ensuring safety and sanitation. Part of the esteem for good aged wine as it occurred in Roman times must have been from its rarity as well as its charm. Today, properly aged wines are not just lucky escapes from hazards, but regularly are attainable goals which can be adjusted for types and styles of particular wines.

Wine maturation and aging to some degree is inevitable. It takes some time after wines are fermented to prepare them for marketing. Bottled wines do not reach customers immediately and are often consumed months or years later. If wines are to be continuously available in retail shops all over the country, there is obviously need to consider changes and differences that may result. Every change is not automatically an improvement. Loss of fresh grape aroma may be undesirable with some wines and expected with others. This and other examples of flavor losses and gains with storage are of concern whether one wishes to prevent or profit from them.

Economics change so fast that it is not very useful to be specific, but a few general perspectives seem important. A small producer of a premium wine generally would like each wine to be all sold and shipped by the time the next vintage is ready to be released. If it is all gone too soon the risk is run that retailers, restaurants, and customers will forget about that winery before the next release. There will be a temptation to release too soon. Too rapid movement may be slowed by allocation or price increases, but in the long run price must be justified by quality compared to competition. The more common problem of too slow movement can only partly be combated by lowering the price. Obviously, if costs are not recovered the winery cannot remain financially sound. Furthermore, costs are incurred in longer storage, which raises the break-even price.

A cost that is obvious, but sometimes forgotten, is the cost of the capital tied up in the aging wine. Either the cost of the interest on the loan or the lost interest that could have been earned had the wine been sold and the money invested are real considerations. Unless the selling price of the wine can be raised to cover this and other aging costs, the producer who has the option would be advised to sell the young wine and invest the returns elsewhere. Assume annual compounded costs of wine storage to be 14% (a value probably low including costs of capital, insurance, and warehousing and about 3% annual loss by evaporation in bulk storage or extra costs and risks after bottling). If a wine could be sold at a break-even price of $1/L right after vintage, after three years in bulk and two in bottle one would need $1.93/L or nearly double to still break even. This does not even include capital and depreciation costs of barrels and other equipment, labor, and other potential costs and risks. Aging by the winemaker should definitely not be prolonged beyond the point that quality improvement and salability justify a net increase in return. In the long run it cannot be if the winery is to remain economically viable.

Particularly in some old wine areas in other countries this has not always been realized. As production exceeded consumption, stocks accumulated. Well-financed holders visualized their aging stocks of wine as equivalent to gold bars in a vault. In terms of security they might be justified, but wine is more perishable than gold. If such assets do not appreciate as fast as costs plus inflation, their real value drops. Meanwhile, no current return is earned. A number of examples have occurred in our experience where such aged wines at relatively low prices are discovered by wine consumers and bought out over a few years. The producers find that they cannot afford to replace these stocks with equally aged wines. The quality drops, the consumer loses interest, and either the cycle eventually repeats or that particular wine type disappears. Like any other business operation, wine maturation and aging must be scrutinized as to costs, efficiency, benefits, and rewards.

Consider a large winery with a brand name to support. In order to keep stocks on hand in shops over the nation, they may need to bottle and ship their major nonvintage types at frequent intervals, say weekly throughout the year. If they matched production to sales and used first-in first-out inventory management, the last bottling before wines of the new vintage were available would be one year old and the next bottling would be unaged. Even under this scenario the average age upon shipment would be six months, the absolute minimum if wine is to be continuously available. The net effect would be a sudden change as the new vintage came on line. This probably would engender consumer reaction. The more regular and discerning consumers, the most valuable ones, would be the most likely to complain.

A way to counteract such sudden changes resulting from age and vintage differences is to blend a proportion increasing with time of the younger with the older wine. The minimum constant average age possible would be 12 months. The minimum carry over of the previous year's vintage to make this possible is a six months' supply. Therefore, just after vintage the winery following this program would need to have on hand one and one-half times their annual sales. For example, then, the first weekly bottling after the new vintage was finished would have 1/52 of its volume the new vintage and 51/52 the old. Increasing the proportion of the newer wine 1/52 each week it would become the old wine at 12 months age just before the next vintage was available. Of course, by American law such blending cannot exceed 5% of the volume from another calendar year for wines bearing a vintage date. This is an example of the freedom for wine improvement given up by the winemaker in order to comply with regulatory limits on label descriptions deemed prestigious.

One and one-half years total aging is to be expected as the minimum age at consumption for all wines not expressly hurried through the system, allowing 12 months to bottle and six months from bottling to consumption. Therefore, wine maturation and aging are to be considered by all winemakers regardless of the wines they are making and the price category targeted.

The actual inventory of all Californian wine on December 31 and the annual shipments for several calendar years are shown in Table 10-1. Separate consideration of dessert wines in recent years indicates a slightly shorter average age than for table wines. Sparkling wine inventories are only half or less of the annual sales. This suggests six-month aging is typical once the wine is identified as sparkling, but probably the base wines are inventoried as table wines. There are several caveats in using such figures. For example, wine shipped between vintage and December 31 would skew and shorten the apparent age. This would include the nouveau types and some blush wines. Such wines are hurried to market to keep them fresh and fruity, but they would also distort the figures for the other wines. Furthermore, shipments do not directly equate to sales to the public and certainly not to consumption. Nevertheless, the figures do agree with an approximate average age by shipment of the order of 12 months for the average wine.

Table 10-1. Yearly shipments to all markets and December 31 inventories of Californian wines.[1]

Year	Shipments (ML)	Inventory (ML)	S/I[1]
1970	742	1017	1.37
1975	1032	1572	1.52
1980	1281	2175	1.70
1981	1356	2155	1.59
1982	1357	2503	1.84
1983	1376	2322	1.69
1984	1412	2284	1.68
1985	1483	2278	1.66
1986	1603	2203	1.50
1987	1605	2113	1.45
1988	1561	2107	1.46
1989	1500	2116	1.52
1990	1478	2086	1.52
1991	1419	2115	1.49
1992	1448	2035	1.41

[1]Corrected 1983+ by exclusion of nonwine portions of wine coolers.

Wine Industry Statistical Reports (annual), San Francisco, Wine Institute.

The large unanticipated increase in inventory in 1982 (Table 10-1) resulted from an uncommonly big vintage coinciding with additional vineyards coming into bearing. Although the increased proportion of inventory to shipments only increased the stock from about 1.60 to 1.84 year's supply, this was sufficient to create considerable consternation about excess wine supply. Discussion of this excess in the press may have helped prevent continued increase of consumption typical for the period as distributors and consumers anticipated decreased prices. This shows that at least under prevalent economic conditions, building inventory by increasing general aging is not an attractive option for wine producers as a group.

It would appear from these data that only a small proportion of wines receive more than 12 months of aging before shipment. This is not so surprising considering that premium wines are a small but increasing portion of the total wine volume. One would expect red table wines to be matured longer than white and Chardonnay longer than other whites. Among vintage-dated, varietal wines available at retail in October 1991 the age indicated (by subtracting vintage year from current year) and averaging for all the different Californian labels available in a large shop was 1.5 years for Chenin blanc, 1.6 years for Sauvignon blanc, 2.2 years for Chardonnay, 2.6 years for Zinfandel, and 4.5 years for Cabernet Sauvignon. These figures are considered representative.

With wines which benefit considerably from aging, there is a very rough direct correspondence among age, price, and quality. The higher-priced wine should be higher quality and is likely to be aged longer. Competition helps set the price and production costs may not be higher for a wine in demand than for a lower priced one because it is not known. The naive visualize that the quality of the wine only rich people can afford is very great compared to that they can afford. The fact is that the average quality increment per dollar of increased bottle price is greater at the lower end of the price range than at the high-priced end. When scarcity and past reputation sets the price, there is no guarantee of a quality increment with higher price. On the other hand, producers receiving a high price can afford longer aging and meticulous attention to every detail. They have a great incentive and pride in justifying and improving the premium their wines enjoy. Wine is unusual among agricultural products in that there is direct linkage from the farmer to the winemaker to the consumer. Considerations like these keep, and we hope always will keep, wine from being just a commodity. The romantic and sensuous aspects of wine would be shallow if only based on mystique, but they are validated by complexities of science and technology. Greater knowledge has not only caused the average quality of wine to be much better but it has also made the best wines better and more prevalent. Modernizing and controlling of aging has helped greatly and bids to do more in the future in the effort to make superlative wine widely available at equitable prices.

3. Objectives

The general objectives of maturation and aging fall into four groups that may be termed *subtraction*, *addition*, *carry over*, and *multiplication*. The final consideration is integration of these objectives into a whole for each wine. Keep in mind that there is no single reaction that defines the process. Aging is traditionally slow and for flavor to be changed relatively few molecules of key compounds need be changed. The optimum or usual regime and specific objectives differ by wine, by producer, and by consumer group.

a. *Subtraction*

Some characteristics and conditions present at first racking need to be removed or diminished. Among these may be removal of the gassiness of the carbon dioxide of fermentation and of yeast effects on flavor and appearance. Harsh or "green" flavors may be present and need modification. Young wines may be excessively tart or tannic (astringent) and require adjustments.

A good rule here, and everywhere during wine processing, is to limit treatments to the truly necessary minimum. A problem that will correct itself in the course of other treatments can be allowed to do so. For example, CO_2 will ordinarily drop to an acceptable level in the course of further racking, etc. It could be removed quickly by N_2 sparging, but this would be more costly, it is usually unnecessary, and it risks loss of desirable volatile components. On the other hand, some situations demand prompt aggressive action to prevent or subtract a threatened action. For example, if a residual level of fermentable sugar is desired in a sweet table wine, prompt removal of yeast at the correct point is required as is immediate prevention if regrowth threatens during storage.

Certain off-flavors may or may not be present in young wines. It is preferable, of course, to prevent their occurrence rather than subtract them after they do occur. An example is hydrogen sulfide. If not avoided or removed by other means (Chapters 4 and 7), it can be lessened by aeration. It is important to deal with H_2S-related off-flavors in the earliest stages because, during aging, modification reactions can produce skunky and garlicky derivatives worse in flavor and harder to remove.

b. Addition

An important group of effects sought in maturation and aging is the addition of further characteristics. Extraction of flavors from oak, development of color and flavor from oxidation, and development of bottle bouquets are members of this group. As a rule, such additions must be limited and subtle so as to complement rather than overshadow the wine's underlying flavors. Excessive oakiness, for example, has been frequently seen in mismanaged wines. Oxidation that is appropriate in sherries and other maderized wines would be highly excessive and undesirable in white table wines.

c. Carry Over

As much as possible of the attractive grapey-fruitiness and especially the varietal aromas and flavors should be retained and carried forward during maturation and aging. The same is true of the desirable vinous flavors from the wine fermentation. Aging may strengthen some such flavors as, for example, acid hydrolysis of their glycosides can augment the volatile terpenes of Muscat family varieties.

d. Multiplication, Complexity

For the majority of wines whose flavors do not depend primarily upon processing, the character of a young well-made example can be quite attractive and its quality high. Nevertheless, appropriate maturation and aging can contribute breadth, depth, and complexity and increase its value without overthrowing its fundamental nature. The effect can be likened to adding instruments to an orchestra even though the same score is played. Another analogy is adding a pinch of several spices rather than none or too much of one to an elegant food recipe. Complexity and increased interest will result if properly done. The concert, the meal, or the wine will be more intriguing, less rapidly tiring, and less likely to satiate if it is complex and displays many facets to the senses.

As mentioned under addition, the changes must be small and subtle if complexity is to be enhanced. Multiplication of flavors may be illustrated best by an example that is essentially hypothetical. At the end of fermentation there are four alcohols present, say ethanol and three amyl alcohol isomers. If each was partially oxidized to an aldehyde and those in turn to carboxy acids the four compounds would have become 12. If each alcohol esterified with each acid, 16 additional compounds would result for a total of 28. The aldehydes might form hemiacetals and acetals with the alcohols and at least theoretically this could add 16 hemiacetals and 64 acetals to give a maximum of 108 compounds from the original four. Each of these compounds would have slight to great effects on flavor and would certainly add to complexity. If all the alcohols had been completely oxidized to acids, we would be back to just four compounds and less desirable ones at that. Complexity is maximum at the intermediate stage that accommodates the greatest number of flavorful compounds and diminishes before and after this stage. Furthermore in this example, since esters are more odorous and flavorful (have lower flavor thresholds) than alcohols, there would be an increase of overall odor intensity in the intermediate stages.

Although such arguments seem sound, we know of only one experimental effort to prove that increased complexity of flavor gives increased quality. Singleton and Ough (1962) compared 68 individual wines, pairing like with like as to type and variety along with a 50 to 50 blend of the two paired. In seven of the 34 sets the blend was rated by a panel as better than the higher rated wine of the two. There was no significant lowering of the quality rating of the blends compared to the better wines even when the poorer wine was considerably lower in quality rating. All 34 blends were rated as improved, compared to the mean quality score of the two constituent wines. This effect was not due to balancing defects such as a flat wine with a tart one and was considered evidence for the value of complexity.

Almost any process one can think of has been tried as a quick-aging process for wine (Singleton 1962). The typical sequence has been that the first reports for an exotic new process are favorable, subsequent reports are mostly negative, and finally that process is abandoned as unreliable. This sequence can be understood on the basis of complexity. Almost anything, even the production of a new flavor foreign to wine, can add to complexity if very restrained and the treatment sufficiently delicate. Unusual treatments intensive enough to make the new flavor obvious are likely to reveal that it is unattractive, and certainly can reduce complexity. No one is interested in introducing unattractive flavors even if sufficiently diluted they could add to complexity.

e. *Integration of Objectives and Aging Efficiency*

The combination of the above objectives and aging treatments designed to promote them for any one type and style of wine involve compromise. If one wishes to maximize retention of desirable flavors from the young wine over time, protected cold storage is attractive. If one wishes to enhance loss of undesirable flavors or flavor multiplication effects, warm storage is indicated. Overtreatment defeats the desirable increase in complexity. A low level of oxidation may be desirable in some table wines, but bottle bouquet development is opposed in wines exposed to appreciable air.

Judicious blending (see Section 10.F) obviously can have value in achieving complexity as well as in converting wines with deficiencies to improved blends. Overtreatment of a portion of the wine to be added back to the nontreated portion can permit standardization with less risk than treating the whole portion. However, stratification and competitive reaction effects may complicate efforts to make maturation or aging more rapid and efficient. Suppose it is determined that a given wine will be improved by the oxidation provided by a certain amount of air. Adding all that air at once to the headspace of the storage tank may allow *Acetobacter* and other aerobes to grow. Even if microbial growth could be prevented one would expect differences based on whether the wine was stirred or not. In large winery containers at fairly low and constant temperature there is not much roiling. The wine at the top would be expected to become more oxidized with a gradient to little or no oxidation at the bottom unless the tank was stirred. Stirring would be expected to give limited uniform reaction instead of a high to low gradient. The gradient should give more complexity. Overtreatment of a portion and blending with the untreated majority could give both ends of the gradient, but would increase risk of different effects from overtreatment and might not be equivalent to the full range of the gradient.

A treatment that obviates the necessity for an aspect of aging is frequently as good as and cheaper than the aging treatment. For example, a tannic wine may withstand but also require considerable oxidation during maturation to bring the astringency and bitterness within the desired range. Decreased pomace contact during fermentation coupled with exposure to less oxidation may shorten the maturation period considerably. The maturation and aging processes involve so many variables that traditional regimens are not likely to be easily displaced. They work and they are photogenic, but there are no evident blocks to more rapid and efficient procedures based on present knowledge and that expected from further research.

B. TIME-TEMPERATURE RELATIONSHIPS AND TRADITIONAL REGIMES FOR DIFFERENT CLASSES OF WINES

1. Cellar Temperature and Rate Effects

Like all chemical reactions, maturation and aging will be affected by temperature. Things that happen in a given time at a lower temperature almost always happen in a shorter time at a warmer temperature. When a specific reaction's contribution is known and its kinetics have been studied, accurate prediction of its extent and effect under any time-temperature regime can be made. Some useful generalizations for all reactions can be made. A temperature coefficient called the Q_{10} is commonly estimated at about 2 among chemical reactions. This means that the rate of a typical reaction at temperature $T + 10°C$ is about two times the rate at T°C. If the concentration of a reaction product went from 0 to 500 mg/L in a wine kept at 20°C for six months, one would expect about 250 mg/L in three months at 20°C, six months at 10°C, or one and one-half months at 30°C.

A Q_{10} of 2 is fairly typical, but individual reactions may be somewhat lower or several times higher. In spite of some claims to the contrary, enzymic reactions do not seem to be a significant part of traditional wine maturation and aging. One bit of evidence is that the activity of enzymes added to wine falls to undetectable within several weeks or a few months even under cool storage. Their activity is usually inhibited by the low pH and high alcohol content. Enzymes naturally present are apt to have been removed by tannins or by fining agents. Enzymic reaction rates are increased by increased temperature at low levels, up to an optimum temperature. The optimum temperature is fairly low because of the destruction of the enzyme's highly ordered but weakly bonded, catalytically active center as temperatures exceed the optimum. The Q_{10} for enzyme inactivation is in the hundreds, not 2. Pasteurization conditions, say three minutes at 80°C, are enough for complete destruction of all common enzymes and, as a result, microorganisms. Extrapolating back, if Q_{10} were 2, 3.2 hours at 20°C would destroy all enzymes regardless of initial concentration, and that is not true.

Another example of a reaction not displaying a constant Q_{10} of 2 would be one where the concentrations of reactants are affected. Gases like oxygen are more soluble in liquids including wine at lower temperatures and increased gas pressure. Obviously, in such reactions as oxidation by air the rate does not have a simple direct relationship between temperature and time. Nevertheless, the $Q_{10} = 2$ concept and, better yet, greater understanding of reaction kinetics gives valuable perspective and potential control of specific portions of the complex changes during aging.

Maturation and aging involve quite a few reactions and a flux of decrease of some components including desirable ones while others are forming. Suppose two desirable reactions A and B have respective measured temperature coefficients (Q_{10}) of 1.8 and 2.8 in the wine cellar range of temperatures. Reaction B will be relatively enhanced as the temperature is raised. Both will be slowed by lower temperature but A less so than B. If it is important to maintain a balance between the products of the two reactions and the resultant complexity in the wine, the temperature cannot be very warm. If it is important to have a reasonable rate and not prolong storage unreasonably, it cannot be very cold. Such considerations militate for a moderately low temperature for wine maturation and aging. Relatively brief periods of very low temperatures for special purposes such as removal of excess potassium bitartrate are appropriate, but do not accomplish much toward development of the wine. There is some anecdotal opinion that prolonged cold storage of bottled wine modifies flavor and prevents normal development later. Truly high temperatures must be avoided because flavor developments that are overpowering quickly result. Even baked wines like Madeiras and California baked sherries are generally considered better following a longer period of less elevated temperature than shorter periods at high temperatures within the general range of 35°C to 50°C and to about six months. Other wines kept too warm, especially if oxygen is available, quickly become changed in type and style to an unacceptable degree. They begin to resemble Madeiras and are said to be maderized.

Cooke and Berg (1971, 1984) surveying practices in California found cellar temperatures for varietal white wines ranged from 7°C to 24°C averaging 16°C in 1971 and 13°C in 1984 with a range of 7°C to 21°C. Similarly, in 1971, varietal red table wine cellaring temperature averaged 18°C with a 10°C to 24°C range and in 1984 averaged 15°C, with a range of 7°C to 21°C. The trend downward in temperatures from 1971 to 1984 reflects new recommendations and experience gained. Probably no further drop but perhaps a narrowing of the range has occurred since 1984. Some difference in practice is likely in relation to the portion of the cellar contents in wood versus that in stainless steel. In stainless steel tanks one is likely to want to minimize change and may keep them cooler than barrels. Considering the range indicated of about 14°C and assuming normal temperature effects, six months in the warmest cellar might be equivalent to about 17 months in the coolest. Nevertheless taking 13°C for white bulk storage and 15°C for red as typical and about optimum, we can consider aging times as roughly comparable.

Temperature for bottle aging (largely by customers) is generally recommended about 13°C with a range from no lower than 10°C if a reasonable rate of development is desired to perhaps 20°C if you are impatient or getting old yourself. Constant temperature is desirable especially for bottle aging, to avoid pressure change and cork movement, but also in bulk to control headspace variation or possible overflow. If temperature fluctuates appreciably, as already explained, the warm periods will produce so much more effect that the expected timetable will need adjustment. If only the calendar is followed some wine may be overaged or spoiled.

2. Aging Programs Considered Traditional or Typical for Wines of Various Types

The particular program of maturation and aging chosen for a particular wine depends on the type of wine, the style within that type, the price category, and the marketing approach. By marketing approach we mean such factors as making wines with a proprietary name, nonvintage blends, vintage-dated varietal wines, etc. These variables can apply in every type and most styles of wine. By style we mean such things as complex "dinner" wines at one extreme versus more simple fresh "picnic" wines at the other. Stylish differences that distinguish one producer from another may exist within any one type or class of wines whether these categories are traditional or legal classes. As an example, vintage-dated Sauvignon blanc wine could emphasize the grape aroma and fresh fruitiness on the "picnic" extreme and oak-matured complexity on the "dinner" extreme of style. Examples of each extreme and intermediates are available on the market and meet the regulations without necessarily any special descriptions on the label. Of course, for reasons of economy as well as consumer attitudes the least expensive wines tend to have had the least maturation and aging.

Wines made for rapid marketing and consumption not only have had relatively little aging, but also might not respond well to aging in many cases for various reasons. Conversely, some wines made to be matured and aged would not show well if tasted too young.

Since we are considering table wines as the most common and important class, maturation and aging of them will be emphasized and white versus red differences noted. Dessert wines have similar programs to table wines except longer extreme maturation and aging times. Specialty products such as wine coolers, blush and rosé wines, and carbonic maceration wines can be considered as like light dry wines with as little maturation or aging as possible. Vermouths would be generally like unflavored ports or muscatel in aging practices. This leaves the classes of sparkling and sherry-like wines as worth special comments.

Sparkling wines are usually prepared from a blended cuvee of wines nominally like white table wines, although ordinarily from less ripe grapes higher in acidity, lower in pH, and lower in alcohol. This wine may well be from more than one vintage and thus have some maturation. Ordinarily but not invariably, detectable flavor from maturation in small oak is avoided. This semifinished base wine, clarified and stabilized, is then refermented to give sparkling wine. From a maturation and aging viewpoint the period that the refermented wine is left on the yeast lees is considered significant. Cuvee aging and appreciable aging after separating the sparkling wine from the yeast are generally considered unnecessary or even detrimental. Certain producers might not agree and postdisgorging bottle-aged Champagnes were once a fad in England, but generally speaking, time on the yeast is the only stage of special interest during sparkling wine aging. A few months aging after disgorging, dosage and resealing can be necessary to set the shape of the cork, etc.

The characteristic flavor changes are attributed to yeast autolysis. The special flavor of aged-on-yeast sparkling wine can increase through at least five years on the yeast according to a limited number we have tested. Most producers age from six months to a year between starting the refermentation and disgorging the wine. However, there is no specific regulation in the United States requiring such age. In France, Champagnes are aged one-year minimum and vintage ones three years. Other European sparkling wines, including Spanish Cavas, are mostly required to have a minimum of nine months age on the yeast. Producers fermenting sparkling wine in large tanks rather than in bottles do not usually age as long on the yeast, but may use stirring or other treatments to hasten yeast autolysis. Such details tend to be proprietary and more discussion can await specialized treatment elsewhere.

Sherries and related wines are unusual from the maturation and aging viewpoint in that oxidation in one form or another is much more necessary and extensive than in other types of wines. The oxidation may be microbiological as in the flor sherries, chemical reaction with air as in oloroso-type sherries, a combination of the two as in amontillado types, and accelerated air oxidation by heating as in Madeira types including California baked sherries. Bottle aging, particularly for the fino-flor types, is undesirable in that it produces changes reverting the flavors away from oxidation. Also, associated with sherries because of its development in the Sherry districts of Spain is a maturation and fractional blending system we will refer to as the solera system.

Sizable disquisitions have been written on the maturation, aging, and blending of sherry-type wines (e.g., Joslyn and Amerine (1964)). Almost all of the character and differences among types of these wines result from the maturation processes and not from grape aromas or initial fermentation effects. Our discussion must be brief here.

The production of flor sherries by submerged aerobic yeast culture need not involve much time. The principle involves growing yeast throughout an aerated dry wine. The yeast converts some of the ethanol to acetaldehyde and produces additional flavor effects. The process used for traditional fino-type sherries, aerobic surface-film growth of yeast, is fairly slow and a considerable portion of the flavor may come from associated maturation effects. Two of these are flavor extraction from the oak containers and flavor effects from autolytic yeast breakdown. Although the yeast is unquestionably causing oxidation as shown by production of aldehydes from alcohol, the oxidation-reduction potential is low (reduced) and the wine color remains light under an intact, active yeast film.

Manzanilla and other light fino types are the epitome of this style of sherry. Such wines of flor type may be matured under conditions such that the wine slowly gains in alcohol and no longer allows aerobic yeast growth, or alcohol could be added. In the traditional Spanish process, as the wine is passed along through the process for about four years, some of the yeast film falls and can autolyze and affect flavor. These flavor effects do not appear to have anything in common with sparkling wine flavors attributed to autolysis, but gradually contribute to more complex flavors evidently including nutty characteristics (although these also appear in nonflor sherries).

Amontillado-type sherries are fino types aged longer after the film yeasts have largely finished. They can have more yeast autolysate, nuttiness, and darker amber color. They are, to some extent, intermediate in characteristics between fino and oloroso types having some of the character of both. Fino or oloroso sherries are selected for their further processing after the alcoholic fermentation. The sherry material, shermat, for oloroso wines has or is fortified to a higher alcohol level, about 18%, so that the yeast film does not grow. Fino sherries start in a fairly narrow range near 15–16% alcohol. The oloroso-type sherry is usually a darker amber wine. It may be sold sweet, but ordinarily is aged dry and then sweetened with an aged very sweet wine made for the purpose.

All these wines must be in containers kept partly empty so that surface area is available for the aerobic yeast film (finos) and for oxygen absorption from the air (olorosos). Table 10-2, adapted from Martinez De La Ossa et al. (1987) shows typical processing conditions for traditional Spanish wines of these types. Note that total time suggested for the fino types is four years and for oloroso and amontillado 12 years. Although solera systems can be of a various number of stages, capacities, and throughput rates, the ones they studied are representative. Each stage was composed of 500 oak butts holding 600 L each. With the five stages, this totaled 2500 butts per solera system and they studied 20 such systems. If each butt was 80% full, each solera system would contain 1.2 million L of wine with, at equilibrium for the flor type, an annual input of one-fifth that total and a similar draw off for sale, minus evaporative and handling losses. A five-stage system and four years' aging requires fivefold inventory to shipment ratio and more stages or slower throughput would require even more.

The operation of the solera fractional aging and blending system is more subtle and has more effects than might be immediately perceived over and above providing time and conditions for long bulk aging. The solera system or modifications of it have been used for other wines, notably port and older red table wines. If it is used for table wines, efforts such as keeping the containers full are necessary to prevent excessive oxidation as well as aerobic microbial growth including film yeasts.

Note (Table 10-2) that estimated residence time in each stage from the youngest nursery stage (third criadera in these examples) to the final solera stage is equal, i.e., 0.75 years for the fino types and two years for the amontillado and oloroso types. The apparent age that results for the oloroso is 12 years and for

Table 10-2. Average estimated cumulative aging time (in years) for each stage and type of sherry (Martinez De La Ossa et al. 1987).

Stage		Aging			
No.	Name	Fino	Manzanilla	Oloroso	Amontillado
1	Sobretablas	1.00	1.00	—	*
	Añada	—	—	4	—
2	Third criadera	1.75	1.75	6	6
3	Second criadera	2.50	2.50	8	8
4	First criadera	3.25	3.25	10	10
5	Solera	4.00	4.00	12	12

*For the Amontillado, the first four years corresponds to biological aging in a fino system.

amontillado 16 years. There are three key principles in properly operating a solera-type system: (1) Each container in each stage is never completely emptied, maximum removal at any one time is about 25% or less; (2) when wine is withdrawn from the final (solera) stage it is replenished by an equal amount of wine from the next younger stage in that particular solera system, and so on throughout the stages; and (3) when wine is drawn from each container of the next younger stage, some of that wine is placed in proportion in all of the containers of the older stage. In old practice wine drawn from each container was specifically distributed to every one of the next older stage's containers. The same objective can be reached by mixing all the wine drawn from the younger stage and then adding the appropriate volume of this blend to each container of the next older stage. This requires considerable, but less labor and close attention than the old process.

To illustrate briefly, suppose one of the fino soleras previously described (Martinez De La Ossa et al. 1987) was tapped only once per 0.75 years for 100 L/butt (one-fifth of contents). The removed wine would be combined and bottled for sale. The first criadera stage (next youngest) would be drawn down 100 L/butt, the 50,000 L mixed, and the solera stage replenished 100 L/butt to its original level. Similarly the second criadera would replenish the first, the third criadera would replenish the second, and finally the youngest sobretabelas wine would replenish the third criadera. Note that, with the figures given, no wine in the solera could be less than four years old. But, with continued operation and considering the butts are never more than fractionally emptied, some of the wine in each stage except sobretablas would be in fact older than the indicated age. A few drops would be as old as the start of the solera. Obviously vintage dates are not appropriate on such wines, but sometimes the starting date of that particular solera system is noted. Baker et al. (1952) developed the mathematics of the process and showed that after about 15 years or more of operation and 25% annual withdrawal from the final stage a constant average age is reached of about eight years for a four-stage system, 10 years for five stages, 12 years for six stages, and nearly 14 years for seven stages.

The solera system has disadvantages of the large stocks required, costly labor, the risks involved in long storage, and the fact that if one barrel develops a bad microbial contaminant it can be spread to all barrels of subsequent stages. Nevertheless it has great advantages because differences between vintages are smoothed, a relatively constant composition, and a constant average age are achieved. These advantages can be achieved during maturation in stainless steel containers as well as wooden ones.

Coming back to what is being done generally for typical wines in California, the best available surveys are those by Cooke and Berg (1971, 1973, 1984). They show that practices vary greatly by producer, by variety of grape, and by price range and producing area (Tables 10-3, 10-4, 10-5). In view of this variation and considering that successful wineries can have very different aging programs for a given type of wine, it does not seem particularly useful to consider averages. Table 10-6 makes an effort to suggest recommendable ranges under modern economic conditions.

C. BULK MATURATION — VARIABLES, CHEMISTRY AND QUALITY EFFECTS

1. Containers for Maturation in Bulk

A cooper is one who makes or repairs wooden casks or tubs and cooperage is his products or his shop. By extension, all winery tanks, vats, and barrels are called cooperage whether or not made of wood. A wine container ideally would be impervious, inert, durable, strong, easy to clean, easy to maintain, convenient, and cheap. It should impart no flavors or the imparted flavors should be desirable. Obviously, some compromises may need to be

Table 10-3. Nonvarietal (generic) table wine storage practices.

Winery	Capacity (1000 gal.)				Time stored (months)
	Redwood	Stainless stell	Lined steel	Concrete	
A	18				[a]
B		100–600	300–600		1–4
C	50	130			0.3–9
D	5–28	8–340	110–640	40–95	[a]
E		6–1,200	6–1,200		10–18
F	0.5–25	1–30			6–18
G		9–125	125–600	65	0.3–12
H		10–200	300–600		3–24
I	0.5–50	7–140		30–100	10
J		4–195	185		6–12

[a]Shipped as soon as possible.
Source: Adapted from Cooke and Berg (1973).

made. A wooden barrel can impart desirable flavor and is therefore not inert, for example, nor is it easy to clean if contaminated. A new 200-L barrel of European oak may cost more than $400. It may be found to be nearly exhausted of direct flavor contribution by four cycles of use and need replacement. Each of the 800 L of wine so matured must bear its share of the barrel cost at $0.50/L. Hardly cheap, this is nearly half or more of the cost of the premium grapes required to make the wine.

Container materials that have been used for bulk storage of wine include ceramics, concrete, metals, wood, and, in more recent times, plastics. Without going into the engineering aspects, relative general utility and costs, there are a few comments necessary from the viewpoint of container use for maturation. Plastics such as fiberglass polystyrene tanks pass light that can effect wine detrimentally. They may, if not especially freed of them, contribute monomers of the plastic itself or extractable plasticizers. Some plastics transmit oxygen rather readily, polyethylene for example, although it does not need plasticizers and may be useful for brief storage. Concrete can be used if properly coated with wax or other impervious coating, but it can give calcium and other minerals to the acidic wine, which erodes it.

Mild steel tanks and fittings similarly contribute iron to wine. Ferrous or ferric ions catalyze seriously undesirable reactions in wine. Brass and copper contribute undesirable copper ions that will cause ills in wines at even lower levels than iron. This leaves stainless steels and wooden containers as most useful for modern wine storage and maturation.

Table 10-7 (*1988 Wine* 1989) shows 1988 data on storage cooperage in California. There has been a continuing rise in the proportion of stainless steel as well as the total capacity of cooperage over the last two decades. Concrete usage has fallen drastically (32% of total cooperage in 1966) and will continue to do so, as probably will use of coated mild steel. Oak has risen again in recent years, but other woods (nearly all redwood, *Sequoia sempervirens*, in California) have fallen. Oak will probably remain a relatively small but important part of the total cooperage capacity, reserved mostly for Chardonnay and varietal red table wines.

Considering usual practices of keeping the tanks full and/or the headspace blanketed with nitrogen or carbon dioxide to exclude air, storage in stainless steel can be considered inert except for the effects of time and the continuation of reactions already in progress. Large metal tanks are commonly insulated by thick external layers of polyurethane foam. The contents are refrigerated to a proper cel-

Table 10-4. **Aging months of varietal white table wines by variety, container type[a], and winery.[b]**

Variety	A	B	C	D	E	F	G	H	J	K	L	M	P	Q	R	T
	Winery															
Chardonnay	K6S12–18	K5–8[c]	K4–5	KR6[f]	K6S2	K9S3[g]	K3S6[h]	KS10–14[i]	K6S4	K5–8S7–14	KS6[o]	K6–9S3–6	K3	KS6[g]	KS12[g]	K9
Chenin blanc	S6–18	KS6[d]	S5–12	R6	S1–7	K2S6[d]	—	KS6–12[i]	S4	S6–12	S4	S6–9	S3–6	S6	—	K6
Colombard	S6–18	KS6[d]	S5–12	R6	S1–7	—	—	KS3–12[k]	—	K1S6–12	—	—	S3–6	S6	—	—
Grey Riesling	—	KS6[d]	R2–3S1–12	—	—	K2S6[d]	—	KS4–10[l]	—	S6–12	—	—	S3–6	S3	—	—
Gewürztraminer	S6–18	S9	R2–3S1–12	R6	S1–7	S6	—	KS3–12[m]	—	S6–12	S4	—	S3–6	S6	—	—
Sauvignon blanc	K6S12–18	KS12[e]	K4–5	KR6[f]	K2S2	K9S5[e]	K3S6[k]	KS8–16[i]	K5S4	K1–2S6–10	—	K6S6	K3	K3S3	KS7–8[m]	K9
Sémillon	S6–18	KS12[e]	—	R6	S1–7	—	—	KS6–16[i]	—	S6–12	—	—	S3–6	—	—	—
Sylvaner	S6–18	KS6[d]	—	R6	S1–7	K1S9[d]	—	KS3–8[i]	—	S6–12	—	—	S3–6	—	—	—
White Riesling	S6–18	KS8[d]	R2–4S2–12	R6	—	S10	S6	KS4–12[i]	S4	S6–12	S4	—	S3–6	S6	S3	KS6[g]
Rosé	S6–18	S9	—	R6	S1–7	S8	S5	KS4–12[n]	S4	S6–12	—	S6–9	S3–6	S6	—	S6

[a]K = oak barrels or casks; R = redwood tanks; S = stainless steel tanks.
[b]Cellar temperatures ranged from 7°C to 21°C, with a mean of 13°C.
[c]95% in oak.
[d]90% in stainless steel.
[e]80% in oak.
[f]70% redwood.
[g]75% in oak
[h]30-50% in oak, 100% in stainless steel.
[i]50% in oak.
[j]85% in stainless steel.
[k]95% in stainless steel.
[l]75% in stainless steel.
[m]70% in stainless steel.
[n]80% in stainless steel.
[o]30-70% in oak.
Source: Adapted from Cooke and Berg (1984).

Table 10-5. Aging years of varietal red table wines by variety, container type[a], and winery[b].

Variety	Winery													
	A	B	D	E	F	H	J	K	M	N	Q	R	S	T
Barbera	W2–3	—	W3[e]	—	—	—	—	—	—	—	—	—	—	—
Cabernet Sauvignon	W2–3	WS2–3[c]	W2.5[f]	W1–3	WS4[g]	WS2[j]	WS2	WS2–2.5	W1.3–1.6	W1.5	WS3	WS1.5[h]	W1.6–2	W1.6–2
Gamay Beaujolais	W1–2	WS0.25–0.5[d]	W2	W1.5–2.5	—	WS0.3–0.6[i]	—	—	—	—	S0.5	—	—	—
Napa Gamay	—	—	W1.5–2	—	WS3[h]	WS0.5–0.6[i]	—	S1.5	—	—	WS0.5–2	—	—	W1
Pinot noir	W1–2	WS2[c]	W2[f]	WS1–2	WS4[g]	WS0.6–1.5[j]	—	WS2	W0.8–1	W1–1.25	WS3	WS0.6[l]	—	W1.25-2
Petite Sirah	W2–3	WS2[c]	W2.5	WS1–3	—	WS0.5–1.5[j]	—	WS3	—	—	WS3	WS1.5[h]	W1.8–2.2	W1.6–2
Zinfandel	W2–3	WS2[c]	W1–3	WS1–3	WS3[i]	WS0.6–1.5[j]	WS1.5	WS1.5	W0.6–1	W0.8–1.25	WS3	—	W1.5	W1–1.3

[a]W = oak barrels or casks or redwood tanks. S = stainless steel tanks.

[b]Cellar temperatures ranged from 7° to 21°C with a mean of 15°C.

[c]W90%, S10%.

[d]W10%, S90%.

[e]Old American oak barrels.

[f]Start in larger containers until after malolactic fermentation.

[g]90% in wood 42 months, 10% in stainless steel 6 months.

[h]80% in wood, 20% in stainless steel.

[i]75% in wood, 25% in stainless steel.

[j]95% in wood, 5% in stainless steel.

[k]50% in wood.

Source: Adapted from Cooke and Berg (1984).

Table 10-6. Wine types—Estimated typical or recommendable aging regimes.

		Barrel	Bottle
White Table			
Dry	light	0	0?
	robust	0–6 months	4 years
Sweet	light	0	0?
	robust	6 months	4–10 years
Red table			
Dry	light	0–6 months	0–12 months
	robust	3 years	10 years
Sweet		1+ year	5+ years
Port			
Ruby		0–2 years	0–2+ years
Tawny		4+ years	0–2
Vintage		6 months–2 years	10+ years
Muscatel		1–10 years	0+
Sherry			
Flor		1–3+ (used)	0–
Amontillado		3+ (used)	0+
Oloroso		1–3+ years	0+
Madeira	(baked sherry) (35°–50°, 6 months–3 months)	0–3 years	0+
Sparkling wine			
Cuvee		0–12 months	—
Bulk		0–12 months	0
Bottle Fermented		—	1–3+ years, 0?

lar temperature and, even outside in direct summer sunlight without further cooling, temperature rise should be only of the order of 0.5°C/month. Different formulations of stainless steel may be used (see Appendix C), but beware of salvaged tanks from older dairies. They may be Monel metal which, owing to copper content, is injurious to wine. Although both are vulnerable to pitting by SO_2, type 316 stainless steel is more resistant than type 304.

Table 10-7. Winery storage cooperage in California, December 31, 1988

California	Total cooperage (ML)	Stainless steel (%)	Other metal	Oak (%)	Other wood (%)	Concrete (%)	Other (%)
North Coast	496	64.2	1.0	19.8	10.6	1.5	3.0
Sierra Foothills	6	58.3	0.0	26.7	11.4	0.0	3.5
Central Coast	290	68.5	2.2	9.1	19.1	0.8	0.3
Sacramento Valley	14	27.7	0.1	5.8	5.9	59.2	1.4
North San Joaquin Valley	1591	54.1	38.2	1.7	2.3	3.8	0.0
South San Joaquin Valley	1536	51.6	34.4	0.2	2.9	10.8	0.1
Southern California	24	39.9	3.3	3.9	33.8	19.0	0.0
Total	3957	55.3	29.0	4.0	5.0	6.3	0.4

Source: 1988 Wine Industry Statistical Report. San Francisco, Wine Institute.

Chlorine cleaning solutions can cause pitting and eventual leakage.

Properly cared for, stainless steel tanks and others lined with inert materials are excellent containers for wine during maturation storage. They don't contribute directly or indirectly to good or bad changes in the wine, and can last indefinitely. Wooden containers, however, certainly may contribute to flavor changes. They are discussed in detail in Section 10.D. The best internal coatings for wine tanks of mild or carbon steel are epoxy formulations or glass linings. They can be just as satisfactory as stainless steel. However, the coating must be thorough and continuous without skips, dings, cracks, crazing, or other damage. As stainless steel has become available and prices per unit contents have dropped, new and replacement winery cooperage has usually been of this, if metallic. Recent cost for large-sized stainless steel wine tanks has been of the order of $0.30/L of contents. The price increases per liter as the tank size decreases because of fittings being a larger part of the total, greater metal surface per unit volume, and other factors.

2. Additional Variables and Reactions of Maturation

In addition to conditions already cited, (time-temperature, container material, stratification) agitation and evaporation can be significant physical variables. Evaporation will increase the concentration of all nonvolatiles in the remaining wine. Although all volatiles will decrease in amount as they evaporate, their concentration and relative concentration in wine will depend on their volatility relative to each other and to water. Evaporation of water will increase the color and taste intensity of the wine, but aroma is likely to decrease and will change. Agitation can make differences as mentioned earlier regarding stratification as oxidation (or evaporation, etc.) occurs from the top down. Adsorption, precipitation, and reaction can be encouraged as stirring obviates the long diffusion paths of dilute solutions. Agitation appears unlikely to have much effect during bottle aging, with the possible exception of inhibiting agglomeration and precipitation. Evaporation is essentially limited to the bulk maturation period, unless bottle closures fail.

Some chemical reactions are completed during maturation (e.g., volatile aroma ester hydrolysis), some require conditions absent after bottling (e.g., oak extraction, oxidation), and some continue during both phases (e.g., tartaric acid esterification). Several of these reactions are discussed more fully in other sections. The focus will be upon effects, particularly sensory ones, known to be important to wine characteristics.

An illustrative reaction is that of hydrolysis of odorous (volatile) esters. Such esters are present as part of the volatiles of all grapes and young wines from them. If small enough and sufficiently low in polarity to be appreciably volatile they are all odorous and almost all have pleasant, fruity odors. Fermentation of clarified musts at a low temperature gives white or blush wines with a characteristic fermentation bouquet consisting of esters. Since the acids that lead to volatile esters are low in wines as are the alcohols except for ethanol, the equilibria favor hydrolysis (Ramey and Ough 1980). Fermentation bouquet does not survive bulk storage unless the wines are kept cold. Several days or a few weeks at room temperature cause the complete loss of this special and pleasant characteristic bouquet. This is a proven example of wines that are said to not travel well. If a winemaker wishes to market such a product, it probably can only be done at the winery or a few nearby outlets willing to keep the wine continuously cold until actually consumed. In such instances maturation and aging are minimized to as near zero as possible, rather than accentuated.

Conversely, the esterification of tartaric acid to ethyl bitartrate (and similar reactions for malic, lactic, or succinic acids) proceeds slowly with time. Because the ethanol and tartaric acid precursors are high in concentration in wines the reaction proceeds to equilibrium at a significant level of ethyl bitartrate. The reaction rate is enhanced by high tartaric acid, low pH, and high ethanol concentration (Edwards et al. 1985). Because the hydrolysis rate is about as rapid as the esterification rate, it takes a long time for a wine to reach equilibrium (Table 10-8). The ethyl bitartrate has no direct effect on flavor but the 1.5 g/L or so formed decreases the sensory tartness of the wine. This is particularly important because it is best for wines that are to be stored a long time to have a low pH and high acidity. If they did not mellow in this way they would remain too tart.

D. WOODEN COOPERAGE

The nature, use, and effects of wooden cooperage are so complex that they require further amplification. Maturation in wooden containers has three effects not available when stainless steel alone is used: extractives are furnished from the wood to the wine, evaporation occurs through the wood, and because evaporation produces ullage, air contact and oxidation may be encouraged. All of these are surface related and, therefore, the shape and size of the wooden container have roles.

1. Shape

For a given volume, a sphere has the smallest surface of any geometrical shape. A cube has about 124% of the surface of an equal volume sphere, a cylinder twice as tall as its diameter about 120%, and a barrel about 108% calculated as an ellipsoid with cut-off ends or 110% as two frustums base to base. This frustum is a right circular cone with the point sliced off parallel to the base. By either model (and the truncated ellipsoid is usually slightly more precise), a barrel is a near approach to a sphere and quite economical of surface per unit contents. A simple method to estimate the surface of a barrel is to compute the surface for a sphere of the same volume and multiply by 1.08. To hasten maturation more surface per liter would be desired, but for practical engineering reasons the barrel shape was chosen. The double arch gives not only an easily rolled shape but also a very strong one. The hoops can be driven down to squeeze the staves together and tighten them around the heads. A good barrel does not leak even though the staves just butt together without tenons or glue. No other shape accomplishes these things so well. Upright wooden tanks generally have straight staves, but are shaped like a single frustum for similar reasons. A great deal of

Table 10-8. Estimated equilibrium concentration of ethyl acid tartrate in various wines and the necessary aging time to reach it.

Tablewine[a]			18% alcohol model solution[b]		
pH (Temperature 34°C)	Ethylacid tartrate (mg/L)	Time (years)	pH (Temperature 34°C)	Ethylacid tartrate (mg/L)	Time (years)
2.91	1650	2.5	2.92	2700	3.3
3.25	1130	3.0	4.10	400	29.0
3.67	550	3.1			
Temperature (pH 3.2)			Temperature (pH 3.2)		
13.2°C (55.8°F)	1480	13.5	34°C (93.2°F)	2700	7.1
34.0°C (93.2°F)	1490	4.0	48°C (118.4°F)	2240	1.6
48.0°C (118.4°F)	1500	1.7			

[a]Conditions: 12% ethanol, 6 g/L tartaric acid.

[b]Conditions: 6 g/L tartaric acid.

Source: Edwards et al. (1985).

artisan know-how has gone into the development of wooden barrels, casks, and tanks, reaching back to Roman times in essentially the same form we have today.

2. Size of Container

For any given shape and barrels in particular, the larger the container the smaller the container surface per unit of contents. This surface-to-volume ratio is a key factor in all those important maturation effects which depend on surface (Singleton 1974). If the volume of a barrel decreases by a factor of 10, the surface per liter increases about twofold. If the volume increases 1000-fold, the surface per liter decreases to exactly 0.1 as much. This means that if three years in a 200-L barrel is considered optimum for a given wine, one would need one and one-half years but 10 times as many 20-L barrels or 30 years if a 200,000-L cask was used. No doubt results of unrecorded trials in the dim past as well as such matters as convenience of manhandling have led to about 200 L being the best compromise between too many barrels and maximum surface per liter for fastest maturation. Approximately this size has become standard in all areas for red table wine and most aged spirits; slightly larger was often preferred for wines that were soon overoaked or those that were stored for very long times. At 200 L there is about 90 cm^2 of surface per L in a barrel.

Inert containers like stainless steel are less costly per unit of contents the larger they are. Of course, a winemaker needs the number and sizes of cooperage necessary to keep the required wines segregated and unblended during preparation and maturation. Many small stainless steel containers are generally too expensive and historically were unavailable. Barrels at 200 L are convenient for segregation of small lots.

3. Type of Wood, Composition, Sensory Effect

Many different woods have been used for liquid-tight cooperage (Singleton 1974), but for wine barrels only white oak is widely used today. Chestnut is suitable but more porous and not widely available. Most other woods are not as suitable. For large sizes, white oak is still the preferred wood. California redwood, certain eucalyptus, and a few other species have been used for very large wine tanks. Some continue to be used, but extractives from these woods do not have attractive flavors in concentrated form so that favorable results in wine maturation depend on either such large size or such long use that extractives are not appreciable.

White oak heartwood is preferred for barrels because of especially favorable natural wood structure as well as pleasant but not especially distinctive or strong-flavored extractives. Softwoods are not very suitable for tight barrels. They often are poorly bendable, have narrow medullary rays and, except for redwood, generally have low extractives or give resinous flavors. This is not necessarily bad, retsina is pine resin-flavored Greek wine, but tends to overpower other wine flavors. Among hardwoods, oaks have several advantages. They have the widest medullary rays. These rays form a radius of the trunk parallel to the ground and serve as conduction tissue between the inside and outside tissues. Rays make up about 30% of the volume of *Quercus alba* wood, and only 15% in most other hardwoods, 8% in conifers. Oak wood is strong, durable, and bendable to make the bilge of the barrel. Oaks are ring-porous having large pores in the spring wood paralleling the trunk, but in white oaks suitable for cooperage these pores are plugged by tyloses as the sapwood changes to heartwood (Figure 10-1). If this fails to happen, the barrel will leak from the ends of that stave.

All species of oak do not form tyloses and those which do not (those outside the white oak, leucobalanus subgroup) would not be suitable for barrels (Singleton 1974). Also, for barrels, one needs large, straight-grained trees. Scrubby or crooked trees, whether by species or habitat, would not be suitable. For barrels, *Quercus* (oak) species used in North America

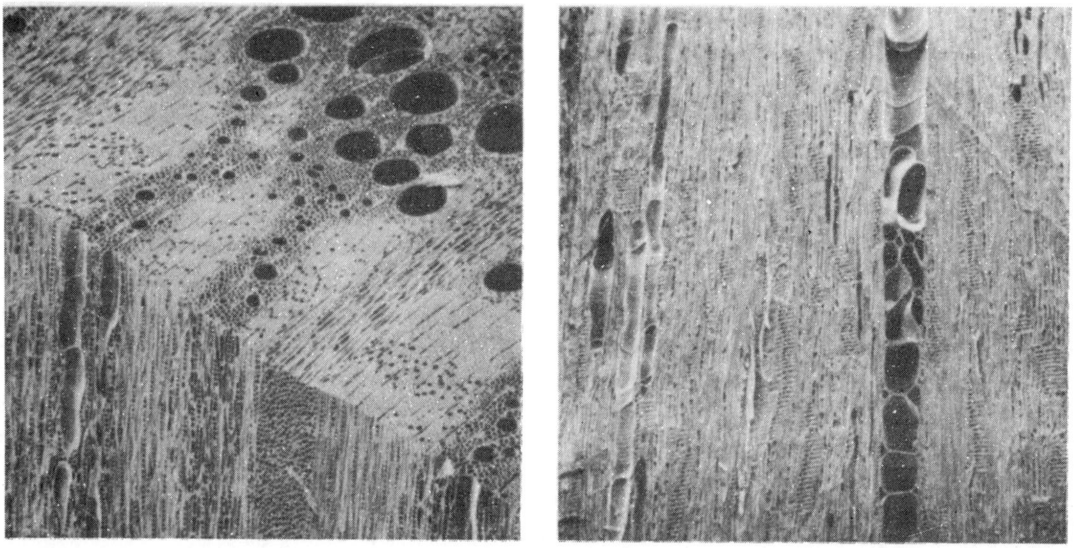

Fig. 10-1. Microscopic views of white oak heartwood showing (left) a section of an annual ring with the ring-porous spring or early wood in the upper right and the much less porous summer wood in the forward part of the horizontal section. A multiserate medullary ray is emphasized in the right front of the vertical portion. A large heartwood pore or vessel is (right) blocked by tyloses. The photomicrographs were graciously supplied by Dr. B. G. Butterfield of the Department of Plant and Microbial Sciences, University of Canterbury, Christchurch, New Zealand.

include *Q. alba* and possibly six others of lesser importance, *prinus*, *bicolor*, *muehlenbergii*, *stellata*, *macrocarpa*, and *lyrata*. In Europe and the Near East coopers oaks are considered *Q. robur* or *pedunculata* and *Q. sessilis*, but several other minor species might be used (Singleton 1974). Each species has preferred growing conditions so that several may or may not be found in the same area. If they do occur in the same vicinity they seem to interbreed readily. A particular tree may not be a textbook example of a single species. Botanists have trouble in firm identification, and loggers more so. In fact, some botanists lump both major European cooperage oaks into a single species *Q. petraea*.

At least by studies so far reported, the different species of oak, even American vs. European, differ in amounts and relative amounts of important extractives rather than by having unique chemical components of significance. The quantitative differences are large, however, between European and North American cooperage oak. Average solids extractable by aqueous alcohol from dry wood was 6.4% for North American and 10.4% for European samples (Singleton 1974). Similarly, each gram of extracted solid averaged 365 mg (GAE) of phenols for the American and 561 mg (GAE) for the European.

European oak barrels can be expected (new and untreated) to contribute nearly double the solids (160%) and more than double (250%) the phenols as compared to American oak barrels of the same size (Singleton 1974). It is fortunate that a 200-L barrel has generally over 30 individual pieces of wood. In the course of barrel production these are certain to represent different parts of a tree and usually several different trees so that each barrel is a fairly random wood sample. This is important for some uniformity among barrels because there is a large difference in composition within the heartwood of any one tree. If tree age, site, and growth rate differ there is further often great tree-to-tree variation. For this reason it is very difficult to obtain the same characteristics for barrels from subsequent years even if the forest area is specified.

The specific plot logged must differ year by year, since it takes on the order of 100 years to mature a cooperage oak tree.

The content of extractables is higher at the base of the tree than at the top and considerably higher in the heartwood nearest the sapwood compared to the center of the tree. Individual stave and heading pieces obviously represent a specific location within a tree and can differ in analysis by a factor of two- to threefold in solids or phenols. Rapidly growing oak trees are better for liquid retention when made into barrels, but slower-growing ones (more annual rings per cm of tree radius) are higher in extractives (Singleton 1974).

Sensory threshold effects on wine differ by stave roughly in proportion to its extractable solids. As a general estimate about 500 mg of typical dry oak wood will produce a flavor threshold detectable difference when extracted into a liter of wine. This can range from about 200 mg/L for light white table wine to about 800 mg/L for heavy port. Interestingly, the amount of new, untreated wood to produce a detectable flavor difference is about the same for American or for European oak. This is attributed to the fact that the European oak contains double the less flavorful carbohydrates and tannins while American oak contains more volatile odorants. European oak also gives more brown color to the wine and is historically more likely to have been toasted.

Measurement of the depth of penetration of wine into the staves from old barrels shows that 6 mm is not unusual. Calculating from an average density of dry oak of 0.85 g/cm^3 this would equal 45.9 g/L ($0.6 \times 90 \times 0.85$) of oak extracted or roughly 100 × threshold in a 200-L barrel. The barrel could be filled and emptied with 20,000 L of wine and, if timing was just right, all this wine flavored to a barely detectable level (Singleton 1974). Analysis of the wine itself has indicated up to the equivalent of 15.5 g of dry oak (31 × threshold) may be extracted in one year in a new European oak barrel. Subsequent refillings of the same barrel decrease the extractives on the order of half, or require twice as long for similar extraction (Singleton 1974; Rous and Alderson 1983). However, as the extraction continues, American and European barrels become more similar and the effect on wine continues to be appreciable if time is long enough even with well-used barrels.

The nonvolatile extract includes hemicellulose fragments and wood sugars like xylose, lignin fragments, and lignans (Dada et al. 1989), and ellagitannins (Quinn and Singleton 1985; Herve du Penhoat et al. 1991). The odorous components include vanillin and related compounds particularly syringaldehyde and sinapaldehyde, oak lactone (*trans*-4-hydroxy-3-methyloctanoic-γ-lactone) (Kepner et al. 1972), furfurals (Nabeta et al. 1986), and isoprenoids (Sefton et al. 1990).

About 90% of the oak phenols are nonflavonoid in nature, ellagitannins are by far the major contributors (Singleton 1974). Since wines not aged in oak are low and fairly constant in nonflavonoid phenols, it is possible to analyze for increases in nonflavonoid phenols and equate that with oak extraction (Singleton et al. 1971). Like other tannins, ellagitannins are astringent and precipitate with proteins. They can augment red wine astringency, add some to white wines, and help remove proteins to stabilize white wines. At 500 mg of dry wood per liter of wine, American oak would be expected to contribute about 30 mg of extracted solids and about 8 mg of gallic acid equivalent (GAE) phenol. Similarly, European oak should yield about 50 mg of extracted solids and 26 mg GAE of total phenol/L.

The nature of the extract changes somewhat with the alcohol content. It is maximum at about 55% ethanol by volume, the traditional barreling proof for spirits (Singleton and Draper 1961). The ratio of substances extracted by high ethanol content is somewhat different from that extracted by water or table wine. Water extracts the more soluble carbohydrates and tannins; alcohol the more hydrophobic lignin fragments. The extraction rate is rapid, being essentially complete, as far as extractants not requiring reaction, by one week at room temperature (Singleton and Draper 1961) when shavings 1 mm or less thick are being extracted. In the barrel, since only one face can be contacted, the extraction rate should be half (i.e., twice as long) for the first mm and progressively slower the deeper into the wood and/or the larger the molecule being extracted. Nevertheless, wine in new barrels should be tested early and frequently to be sure it's removed before extract content becomes excessive. Of course, deliberately high oakiness in one portion of wine can be a very useful blending stock.

4. Coopering, Specifications

Considerable effort has been made to identify areas in Europe, and less in the United States, from whence to draw cooperage wood. While real differences can be identified when given shipments are compared, for reasons discussed above it does not seem worth too much emphasis because shipments in later years will certainly reflect different woodland areas even if the same region is specified. Furthermore, there is no way to be sure such specifications are met except the reliability of and confidence in the cooper supplying the barrels. It is recommended that winemakers regularly needing barrels develop a mutual understanding with their suppliers.

On the other hand, with close inspection of barrels before acceptance and experience with products from a given cooperage a number of potential problems or differences can be understood. The width of a stave or piece of heading must be parallel to a radius of the tree in order to place the medullary rays tangential to the surface of the barrel (Figure 10-2). This accomplishes two things: the rays are opposed to the diffusion of wine through the sides of the barrel and the difference in dimension between dry and wet staves is minimized. The change in length (along the wood grain) between fully expanded by moisture and dry wood is only about 0.2%. Stave width changes more (along the rays, this change is about 4%, but thickness is about 8%). Even 4% is considerable and if a soaked-tight barrel

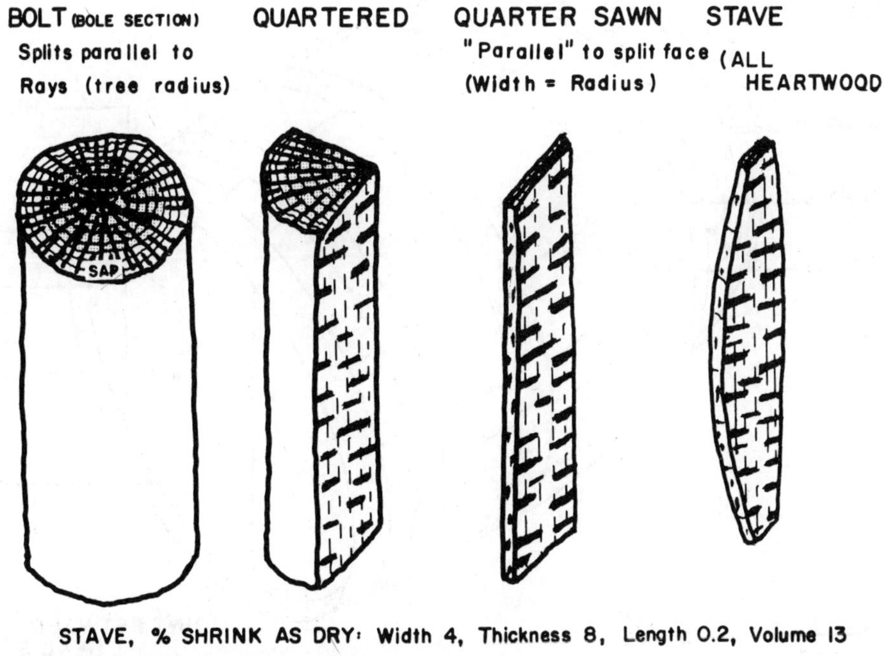

Fig. 10-2. Stave orientation in a properly quartered bolt.

is 250 cm around the bilge there could be a total of 10-cm gap between the staves when it is dried out. The importance of keeping barrels humidified to avoid leaks is obvious, as is the fact that staves not properly quartered will give even greater risks.

Quartering involves the splitting or sawing of the staves from a face of a tree trunk section split into quarters. This places the stave width on a radius of the tree. Quartersawing can be done sloppily whereas splitting can only be done along a radius. If both are done properly there should be little or no difference and sawing is more economical of wood and of labor. One reason only trees 45 cm in diameter or larger should be used is the excessive wastage and difficulty of ray placement on the stave width with smaller trees. Inspection of the stave ends in a barrel will detect whether or not the rays parallel the width of the stave. A minimum of three rays should go from edge to edge of each stave.

Proper quartering places the annual rings at right angles to the width of the stave or heading pieces. The rate of tree growth can be evaluated by annual ring width. Staves (and heading) should be free of sapwood which is low in extractives and lacks tyloses. It may be detected by its lighter color. Look for it at the center edges of the staves.

Stave and heading pieces are ordinarily cut, stacked, and aged to dry slowly. It is generally agreed that the staves should not be used sooner than six months to a year, else excessive warping and green flavors may result. A 100-year-old tree is likely to have 10 to 15 years of living sapwood, but the heartwood is formed and filled with extractables as the xylem dies. Thus, the extractives in the middle of the tree have been reacting and aging for 85 to 90 years.

The staves in the setup barrel are heated either over a fire or by steaming so that they can be windlassed and trussed to the familiar

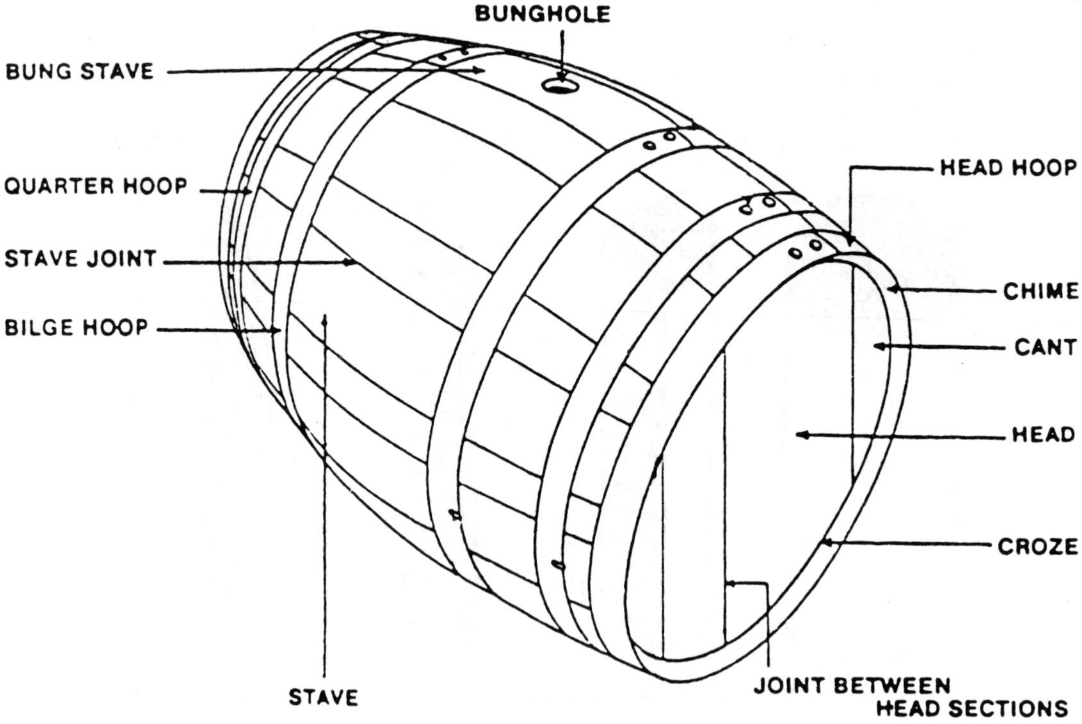

Fig. 10-3. Terminology of barrel parts.

barrel shape, smaller at both ends than in the middle. They are usually heated again after bending to help relieve the strain and minimize cracking at the bilge. If open fire is used, the inside of the barrel may be scorched (toasted) to a variable degree. This toasting modifies the surface extractables and may impart desired complexity or, if overdone, contribute smoky, bacon-like flavors detectable in wine. Different winemakers for different wines may prefer no, light, medium, or heavy toasting. European barrels have traditionally been fired and North American ones steamed, both have given good results depending upon the circumstances. Current practice involves specified levels of toasting for both types.

The hoops are today made of iron and to minimize rusting are often galvanized. The number and arrangement of the hoops are variables that may be significant in maintenance and repair of barrels, but do not have bearing on the maturation effect on the wine. Other details as well, such as how the heads are fitted to the croze or how much chime overhangs the heads (Figure 10-3) can be factors in handling barrels and cellar appearance, but not on the wine as long as the barrels do not leak.

Stave thickness for 200-L white oak barrels is of the order of 25 mm. Much less makes the barrels weaker (barrels are often stacked five or more high). Routing or shaving the inside of barrels exhausted of extractives can rejuvenate them, but they are not found to be fully equivalent to new barrels (Rous and Alderson 1983).

5. Barrel Management, Problems

Barrels are a nuisance to the winemaker in many ways. They have survived only because of their fine maturation effects. They require considerable care and attention. They are difficult to clean and often impossible to sterilize if they have become contaminated with undesirable microorganisms. A very vinegary barrel or one contaminated by other undesirable microorganisms should be removed from the winery. Efforts to reclaim it are likely to lead to more spoiled wine and no good results. Prevent such things rather than attempt to rectify them.

It is important to prevent access of air to wine in barrels, particularly to prevent aerobic microorganism growth. Two ways to accomplish this are to top up or tight bung. If the barrel, cask, or other container of wine is completely full no aerobic growth is possible. If headspace or ullage develops, additional wine of the same type can be used to refill the container. If this procedure is followed, depending on the temperature and humidity of the cellar, topping of barrels will be needed every seven to 18 days. Too long allows too much space to develop. Since the topping wine and the act of adding it will introduce some oxygen, topping will promote slight chemical oxidation compared to tight bunging.

In tight bunging, a silicone, tasteless rubber, or firmly driven wooden bung is applied and the sealed barrel left undisturbed for six months to a year or more. White oak wetted with wine is not permeable to air whereas dry wood is little barrier to oxygen diffusion. Presumably, if left so long that some of the inside surface became too distant to wick up wine and keep it wet, the wine would become aerated and rapidly spoil. This is one reason that pallet storage of barrels head up is more worrisome; more inside wood surface is exposed for a given ullage. Tight-bunged barrels develop a vacuum inside as water and alcohol evaporate through the semipermeable surface of the barrel (Peterson 1976). This evaporation produces the ullage whether or not the barrel is tightly bunged and runs to 2 to 5% of the barrel contents per year or 4 to 10 L from a standard barrel. It can be more if the wine is cooling, leaking, etc., or the cellar temperature warm, humidity low, or external air circulation high. If a tight-bunged barrel has a tiny leak, it can draw air in and still not leak wine (Peterson 1976). It is often said incorrectly that wooden barrels pass air through the staves to the wine. If that were true, vacuum could not develop. It is true that oxygen would be consumed and vacuum could still result, but air is about 80% nitrogen which is slightly smaller (therefore more diffusible) than oxygen, about equally soluble, and inert. A completely sound barrel tightly bunged develops headspace full of wine gases and vapor and not external air. The wine in a tight-bunged barrel is likely to be more protected from air than if topped. Of course, during racking, transfer, processing, blending, etc., wine from both types of storage would contact some air.

Owing to different molecular sizes, water (18) versus ethanol (46), and gradient effects of relative humidity, the ethanol concentration in wine in barrels increases slowly in dry cellars and decreases in moist. The balance point is about 70% relative humidity and is affected by ethanol vapor in the cellar (Blazer 1991). Larger and nonvolatile components, of course, invariably increase slightly.

If wine containers are kept completely full, temperature changes produce either more ullage as the wine cools or overflow if it warms. This is because container surface changes as a function of the square of the linear change due to temperature, whereas the volume is a function of the cube.

If the wine must be stored for a long time in small barrels (an important factor years ago), it can be important to pretreat a new barrel to diminish its contribution of flavorous extractives. This was usually accomplished by a few days' treatment of the new barrel with dilute alkali in the form of about 1.25 g/L sodium or potassium carbonate. Today, barrels are desired for their flavor contribution and commercial wine can be moved to stainless steel cooperage when barrel-mature. Therefore, pretreatment of barrels is avoided except to ensure the new barrel is clean and not leaking.

The best way to handle empty wine barrels is to not have any—refill them as they are emptied. If it is necessary to hold used barrels empty of wine, various regimens have been successfully used. They depend on cleaning the barrel of residual wine and tartar and storing it so that microbes do not grow in it. Molds are a particularly likely surface contaminant on the inside of an empty barrel and they can be prevented by either filling the barrel with an acidic SO_2 solution or by drying the barrel inside so that, with occasional SO_2 gassing, microorganisms do not grow. If the solution is used, both the volume and SO_2 content must be monitored and replenished as needed. If dry storage is used, it needs to be in a humidified room so that staves are maintained near 18% moisture and do not become loose.

E. OXIDATION AND BROWNING

Rather extensive oxidation and associated changes, including browning, are desirable in a few wine types such as Madeiras, Malagas, certain sherries and tawny ports. At the other extreme, many white and most blush and rosé table wines are considered blemished with any evidence of oxidation or browning. Between these extremes, depending in part upon the style of a given winery, more golden color for white and tawny for red wines may be desired or at least tolerated in order to get the flavor desired. There is an optimum for such wines beyond which oxidation is overdone and quality suffers. It is not yet possible to define by rote or formula how much oxygen a given wine has consumed or should be subjected to for optimum quality. However, the fundamental nature of the reactions involved and the important parameters are known (Singleton 1987). Must and juice oxidation are discussed in Chapter 3.

1. Oxygen in Wine

If a typical table wine is saturated in air at a cool room temperature, its oxygen content will reach about 6 mL/L or 8 mg/L. Unless temperature is lowered or oxygen pressure increased, this saturation level cannot be exceeded. In normal winery practice the wine is seldom saturated because contact is insufficient and effort is usually made to minimize oxygen pickup. In pumping over fermenting red wine, for example, the rapid evolution of carbon dioxide sweeps air away. In racking and pumping wine that is free of CO_2, the draw and delivery hoses are arranged so as to incorporate no entrained air. In fact, if saturation with O_2 is desired, considerable splashing or sparging is necessary to mix the wine thoroughly with air and allow time for O_2 dissolution. Thus, unless special efforts are made, wine is seldom fully saturated with air even briefly. On the other hand, with racking, topping, and other operations, wine in bulk is frequently in contact with some air. If free air is allowed above a table wine, growth of *Acetobacter* and conversion to vinegar begins. It is estimated that usual processing and maturation in barrels gives about 20 mL of oxygen per liter of contents in the first year and half or more of that in subsequent years plus any contacted during final bottling operations. This fairly small but continuing contact with oxygen is an important part of bulk maturation and the cumulative amount can be considerable.

Oxygen dissolved in wine is consumed by reaction with wine components and ordinarily falls from saturation to undetectable by about a week at room temperature. This is chemical autoxidation. Reaction in must (enzymic) is much faster and ordinarily oxygen cannot be measured in musts by the time they reach deep tanks away from crusher-stemmers and other sources of air incorporation. Unless resupplied, initial reaction obviously terminates when O_2 is gone but oxidation products may interact so that the effects of oxidation continue for a time. As a bottled wine's oxygen is consumed the oxidation-reduction potential falls to a rest potential and other reactions, even reduction, take over.

Wine maturing in a closed stainless steel tank with no headspace or one filled with inert gas does not contact oxygen until the wine is transferred or processed. Topping of barrels introduces oxygen as will racking or other operations. Although oxidation of barreled wine results from evaporation losses through the wood, oxygen per se is believed not to enter the wine through the wet staves of the body of the barrel, contrary to statements in the literature. The experimental evidence presented by Peterson (1976) is a good argument for this belief. Furthermore, as oxygen diffuses into a stave of a barrel filled with wine it will encounter oxidizable substrates inside the wood including wine that has diffused into the inner wood cells. The oxygen should therefore be consumed within the wood and not reach the wine inside the container. Products of the oxidation tend to be larger molecules (polymers) than the substrates and they should therefore not readily diffuse back from the wood cells into the wine. It is believed that one of the reasons barrels have been historically good wine containers is that they resist excessive oxygen contact with the body of the wine.

2. Substrates for Oxidation in Wines

A number of constituents found in wines can be oxidized, some more readily than others. Ferrous ions, sulfite, ascorbic acid, phenols, and ethanol come readily to mind. For our purposes the natural grape wine phenols, in particular those with a vicinal 1,2-dihydroxyphenyl unit, an *ortho*-hydroquinone, are the most important. One reason we know this is because the capacity of a wine to consume oxygen is roughly proportional to its total phenol content. The correlation is rough because individual phenols, malvidin-3-glucoside for example, may not be readily oxidizable because they cannot be readily oxidized to a quinone. Nevertheless, light white wines have less capacity to consume oxygen than do red wines and heavier red wines have more than do less tannic ones. As wines are oxidized their content of phenols decreases. If wines are treated so as to completely remove phenols, with activated carbon for example, the wine's ability to react with oxygen is lost. Furthermore, the capacity of a wine to consume oxygen is so large that the amount of most other possible substrates is simply too small to account for it.

This is not to say other substances do not participate. Ascorbic acid has a sufficiently low oxidation-reduction potential that it will reduce most quinones back to hydroquinones and become itself oxidized. For this reason ascorbic acid prevents oxidative browning as long as it is present in excess, but, unless added later, it is usually consumed during must preparation and gone from wines. Ethanol is not readily autoxidized alone as evidenced by the stability of aqueous alcohol solutions, but it and other constituents including SO_2 may be oxidized along with phenols. Catechol and pyrogallol derivatives react with O_2 in wines and model solutions to produce hydrogen peroxide (Wildenradt and Singleton 1974; Tulyathan et al. 1989). Since ethanol is relatively high in concentration in wines, the hydrogen peroxide generated as phenols are oxidized nonenzymically produces acetaldehyde from ethanol. Coupled oxidation of this type can produce additional products from any wine constituent oxidizable by hydrogen peroxide whether or not it is oxidizable directly by O_2.

Reaction of a vicinal dihydroxy phenol (caftaric acid, catechins, cyanidin derivatives, and gallic acid are predominant examples from wines) with oxygen to produce its quinone and hydrogen peroxide does not stop the reaction at this point. The quinones are quite electrophilic and spontaneously combine with nucleophiles such as sulfhydryl compounds, phenols (including more of the original one), and certain amines. The dimeric or polymeric product of such reaction rearranges by a process analogous to enolization and the *ortho*-dihydroxyphenyl unit is regenerated ready for another cycle of oxidation. Figure 10-4 shows an example with caftaric acid and glutathione. Phloroglucinol (1,3,5-trihydroxybenzene) does not react directly with oxygen (Figure 10-5). In a mixture with gallic acid it did not enhance oxidation over gallic acid alone, but with caffeic acid it did.

This is a highly significant reaction for un-

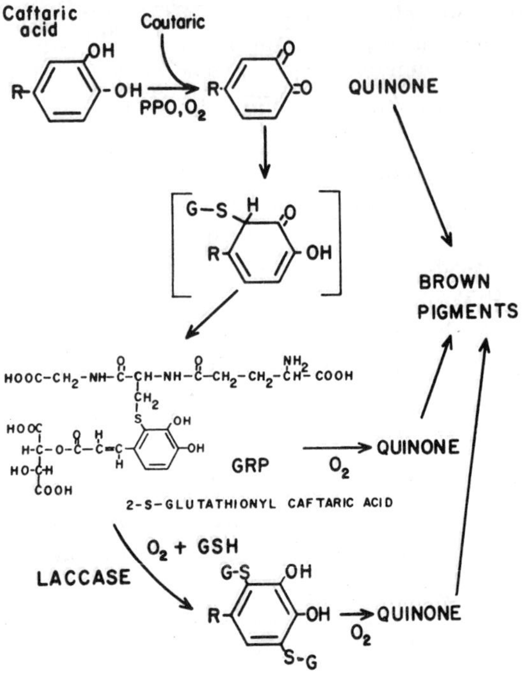

Fig. 10-4. Oxidized caftaric acid couples with glutathione to regenerate an oxidizable hydroquinone: 2-S-glutathionyl caftaric acid.

derstanding wine browning, because the A-ring of flavonoids behaves like phloroglucinol. The regenerated dimeric unit when oxidized produces a more conjugated quinoid, therefore, browner in color. Oxidized caffeic acid is a golden color, but substituted, the oxidation product becomes more brown. Browning in white wine is more a function of their flavonoid content than their content of other phenols (Singleton 1969). Furthermore, the dimeric product has a lower oxidation-reduction potential than the original phenol.

The importance of this is twofold: The product is more readily oxidized further than for more of the original phenol to be oxidized, and, if the original phenol is oxidized to its quinone the dimer hydroquinone can reduce it so that the dimer disappears into new products while the original phenol is preserved. A clear-cut example of such reactions is in the oxidation of caftaric or caffeic acid in the presence of excess glutathione (Figure 10-4). The initial product is 2-S-glutathionyl caftaric acid (GRP) (Cheynier et al. 1986). This product is no longer a substrate for grape phenolase (PPO) as shown by the fact it does not disappear when mixed alone with PPO and O_2 (Singleton et al. 1985). However, adding fresh caftaric acid will cause disappearance of GRP and the appearance of 2,5-S-diglutathionyl caftaric (or caffeic) acid (Salgues et al. 1986; Cilliers and Singleton 1990a; Cheynier, et al. 1990).

Since substitution with glutathione and other nucleophiles regenerates the hydroquinone form, and these first stage products are not then visibly colored, high levels of

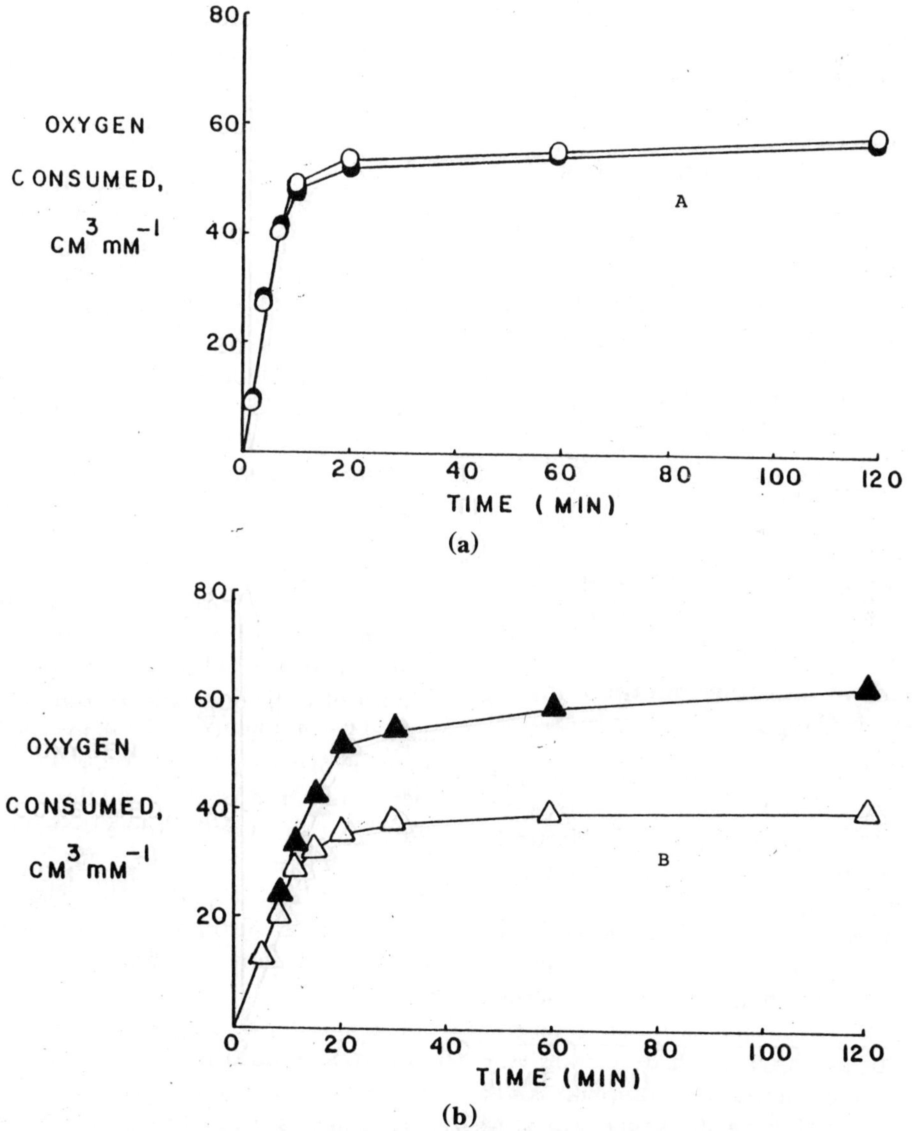

Fig. 10-5. Oxygen uptake under alkaline conditions by (a) gallic acid alone ● and with phloroglucinol ○ and (b) caffeic acid alone △ and with phloroglucinol ▲ at pH 14.

these effective nucleophiles prevent browning. As soon as they become depleted, browning results (Cilliers and Singleton 1990a). If the new substituent furnishes further conjugation to the molecule, as would phloroglucinol or A-ring linked flavonoids, intense browning results from further oxidation of the dimer and larger polymers. Since the reaction can continue and the dimeric or larger polymer is increasingly easily oxidized, still larger polymers form. By steric hindrance of molecular approach for further substitution or reduction in these larger heterogeneous molecules some quinoidal structures are retained and the brown color becomes permanent. It cannot be fully decolorized by ascorbic acid, SO_2, or other means. Quinones are hydrophobic compared to hydroquinones and this fact plus the increasing size make brown polymers from phenol oxidation eventually insoluble. They can precipitate or form a crust on the inside of containers including bottles. Depending upon solubility, size, and particular nature, oxidation products from phenols will be usually less or at least different in astringency and bitterness compared to the original wine's components. Decreased apparent amount from precipitation, complexation, adsorption, etc., will further mellow and smooth the flavor, while the color becomes more tawny.

3. Reaction Conditions and the Capacity of Wines for Oxygen

The capacity of a given wine to take up oxygen ranges from several to many times the saturation level. As a consequence oxygen electrodes or oxidation-reduction measurements are not very useful in measuring this capacity. One can periodically expose the wine to known amounts of air or oxygen and study the effects, being careful to avoid growth of aerobic microbes, or one can measure the actual consumption of oxygen by methods such as Warburg-type respirometry. Oxygen uptake is slow and prolonged if normally acidic wines are studied, but as the pH is raised the reaction accelerates. At pH 9 or so the reaction becomes so fast that oxygen uptake into a shaken small sample is complete by about 30 minutes. There is, of course, concern whether one is measuring the same reaction at pH 9 that would pertain at pH 3.2 in wine. We believe the reaction is essentially the same except for explainable rate effects (Cilliers and Singleton 1989; 1990b). It is well known that high-pH wines (highly ripe grapes from warm vineyards) do not age well, are poor in quality, and deteriorate badly. It is believed that the reason that pH has such a great effect on wine oxidation is that it is the phenolate ions that are being oxidized. A phenolate ion can transfer an electron to an oxygen molecule converting it to a superoxide anion free radical and leaving the phenol in the form of a semiquinone free radical. The oxidation becomes a chain reaction and proceeds rapidly producing quinones and hydrogen peroxide. The pKa of most phenols is about 10, but there is a tiny amount of phenolate even at wine pH and oxidation rate appears proportional to the phenolate concentration.

If wine is made alkaline and exposed to oxygen, the total oxygen consumed at essential termination is from about 50 to several hundred mg O_2/L. If the wine has consumed oxygen under its normal acidic condition, the amount that it will then consume when made alkaline is decreased, but much less than the amount of oxygen actually consumed while it was acidic (Table 10-9) (Singleton 1987). The atoms of oxygen consumed per mole of total phenol under alkaline conditions are fairly constant at about five in white wines and about half that in red wines. This difference is attributed at least in part to the relatively high proportion of the phenols of red wines that are malvidin derivatives and not directly oxidizable.

The amount of oxygen consumed per unit of phenol disappearing at wine pH in comparison to that during alkaline oxidation is about 4–12 times as much for white and twice for red wines. From 1.4 to 18 times as much oxygen was consumed under acidic conditions

Table 10-9. Comparison of oxygen uptake under slow (acidic) conditions followed by fast (alkaline) conditions.

Wine	PhOH mg/L	Oxygen uptake mg/L (acid)	mg/L (alkaline)	At/M.PhOH (alkaline)	At/M.PhOH (acid)*	Acid/alkaline**
Chardonnay	266	0	132	5.3	—	—
Chardonnay	249	105	126	5.4	66	18
White	193	0	89	4.9	—	—
White	162	63	76	5.0	22	5
Rosé	265	0	79	3.2	—	—
Rosé	195	39	51	2.8	6	1.4
Red	676	0	158	2.5	—	—
Red	526	63	130	2.6	4.4	2

*Atoms of oxygen per mole of gallic acid equivalent phenol lost during the reaction with oxygen under the wine's natural acid condition.

**Mg of oxygen absorbed under acidic conditions per mg of oxygen decreased alkaline absorption resulting from acidic exposure.

Source: Adapted from Singleton (1987).

compared to the decrease in the total amount of oxygen required when the system was made alkaline (Table 10-9).

On the basis of 2.5 atoms of oxygen per mole of GAE phenol a very rough young red table wine with 5000 mg GAE/L total phenol would take up about 1.2 grams of oxygen if made alkaline and double or more that amount if kept normally acidic, albeit much more slowly. At about 1.4 g of O_2 per liter of oxygen gas at standard temperature and pressure that wine could consume nearly its own volume of oxygen, more when acidic. Since air is about 20% oxygen, a liter of such a red wine could consume the oxygen from five to 10 or more liters of air! White table wines would be expected to consume about one-tenth of this amount, which is still quite large. Wines not only have a large capacity to consume oxygen, but their phenols have substrate, catalyst, and buffer roles during oxidation. No wonder this family of reactions is so important during wine maturation.

4. Desirable Levels of Oxidation in Wines

Only limited experimentation has so far been reported upon the limits of acceptable and desirable levels of oxidation in wines. Combining available data (Singleton et al. 1979) on white wines with red wine data not yet published (Singleton 1989), the pattern shown in Figure. 10-6 is estimated. It is intended to convey several ideas. On the sensory score scale indicated, 13 is the level for standard wine without obvious defects; 12 and below is increasingly lower quality and above 13 higher quality. The broad bands are intended to suggest a range for different individual wines. With white table wine some wines may improve with the first few saturations, but by 10 saturations white table wines become defective (brown and maderized) from oxidations. Most white table wines which do not have a defect improved by oxidation (H_2S for example) seem best with no oxidation beyond that incident to modern wine processing.

Sherries would reach minimal standard oxidation at about the same level that oxidation becomes a defect in table wine, about 10 saturations. Red table wines display a wide range of responses, but generally improve at least up to about 60 mL O_2/L (10 saturations) and begin to be lowered in quality beyond 150 mL O_2/L or 25 saturations from air. Some red wines appear to be further improved by oxidation in the 70- to 130-mL O_2/L range and others appear to be relatively unchanged in overall quality. Although these observations are based on extensive experimentation it was with few wines and are open to revision in the

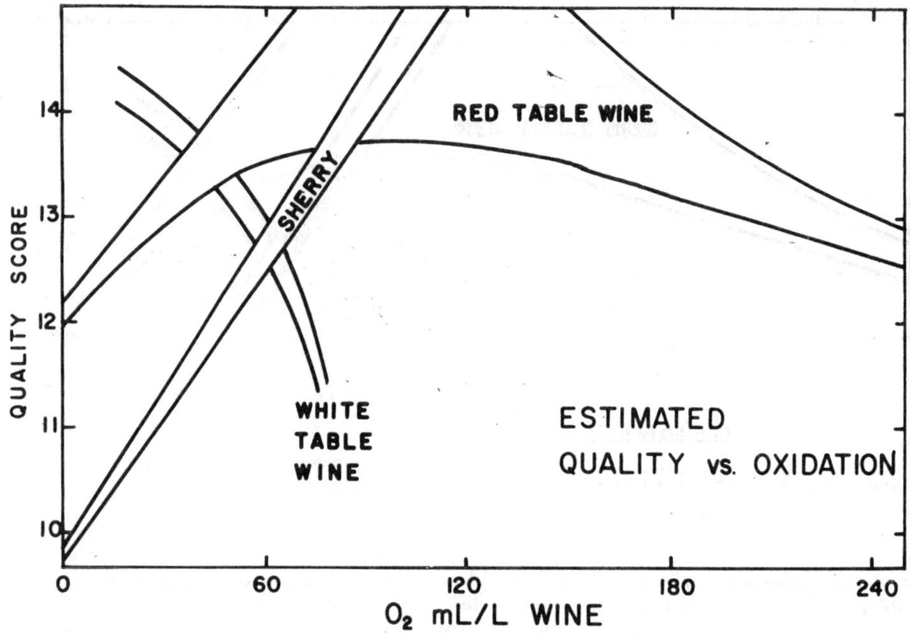

Fig. 10-6. Estimated optimum oxygen consumption by various wine types.

future. They are not at variance with generally recognized good winery practices.

5. Further Chemistry of Wine Oxidation, Gallic, and Caffeic Acid Model Systems

Two major observations need to be explained about oxidation: the very high total oxygen capacity and why that capacity is less with faster (alkaline) oxidation than with normally acidic wine. The nature of some specific oxidation products would also help understanding. Wines are too complex to study usefully at least for the present. Much has, however, been learned by detailed study of model systems, particularly of gallic or caffeic acids. These represent pyrogallol and catechol types of phenols common in wines and other foods. Monophenols and their equivalent *meta*-diphenols and substituted phenols (especially methoxy derivatives) are not readily oxidized directly because they do not produce quinones.

Note again (Figure 10-5) that phloroglucinol alone does not consume O_2 even when made alkaline. It does not augment O_2 consumption by gallic acid but does increase that of caffeic acid. Evidently phloroglucinol regeneratively dimerizes or polymerizes with caffeic quinone but not with gallic acid quinone. Examples of monophenols that would not be expected to participate in oxidation in wines (unless oxidized to vicinal diphenols by PPO or incorporated into reoxidable polymers with previously oxidized vicinal diphenols) are coutaric acid, kaempferol, and engeletin. Examples of methoxylated derivatives that also would not oxidize directly include malvidin-3-glucoside and peonidin-3-glucoside and all their various related forms, vanillin, vanillic acid, and fertaric acid. Examples of wine phenols that would be expected to oxidize readily in the mode of catechol (1,2-dihydroxybenzene) include caffeic and caftaric acids, protocatechuic acid, catechin and epicatechin, catechin tannins, quercetin, cyanidin-3-glucoside, and perhaps petunidin-3-glucoside. Examples of wine phenols that would be expected to oxidize even more readily in similar fashion to pyrogallol (1,2,3-trihydroxybenzene) include gallic acid, myricetin, and delphinidin-3-glucoside.

By detailed study and numerical analysis of the experimental data it has been shown that gallic acid in alkaline solution oxidizes with the uptake of about 4.9 atoms of oxygen and generation of about two moles of hydrogen peroxide per mole of gallic acid completely oxidized (Tulyathan et al. 1989). Ellagic acid (gallic acid dimeric lactone) reacted similarly and gave similar products. The mechanism proposed to explain these data is shown in Figure 10-7. High oxygen consumption and the disappearance of phenol via conversion to aliphatic derivatives is explained. About 97% of the total gallic acid was oxidized in these studies via the dimer equivalent to ellagic acid and only about 3% via either additional polymerization or direct ring opening of the monomeric gallic quinone.

Caffeic acid, on the other hand, oxidizes with very little ring opening, less but still large oxygen uptake and production of several different dimeric and larger polymeric derivatives (Cilliers and Singleton 1989, 1991). The latter polymers have regenerated vicinal diphenolic rings capable of further oxidation, but the mixture of products is relatively constant as long as some caffeic acid remains. Chromatograms (HPLC) during 0 to 168 hours of caffeic acid oxidation at pH 7.0 are shown in Figure 10-8 (Cilliers and Singleton 1989). Structures of identified products are shown in Figure 10-9 (Cilliers and Singleton 1991). Although the sequence and relative amounts of the different oxidation products are affected somewhat by pH, the same products occurred at higher and lower pHs down to pH 4. The reaction was so slow at pH 4 and below that it was very difficult to study. Nevertheless, it is believed the reactions are similar.

That the total oxygen uptake is greater with slow (acidic) conditions than with fast (alkaline) conditions is attributed to more poly-

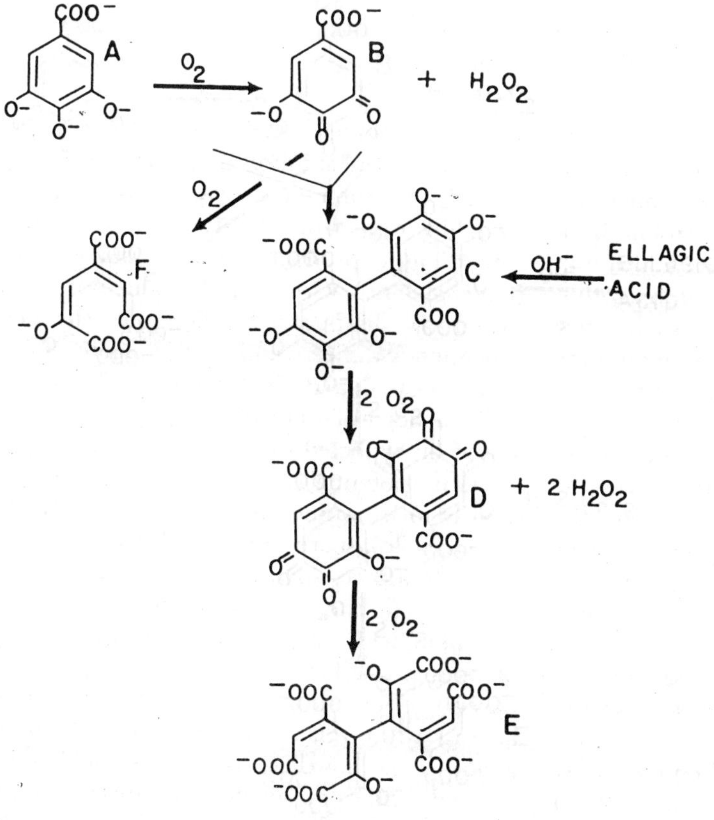

Fig. 10-7. The mechanism of autoxidation of gallic or ellagic acids in aqueous solution at pH 14: A = gallic acid, B = gallic acid quinone, C = gallic dimer, D = quinone of dimer, E = open-ring product of dimer, F = open-ring product of gallic acids. (Tulyathan et al 1989).

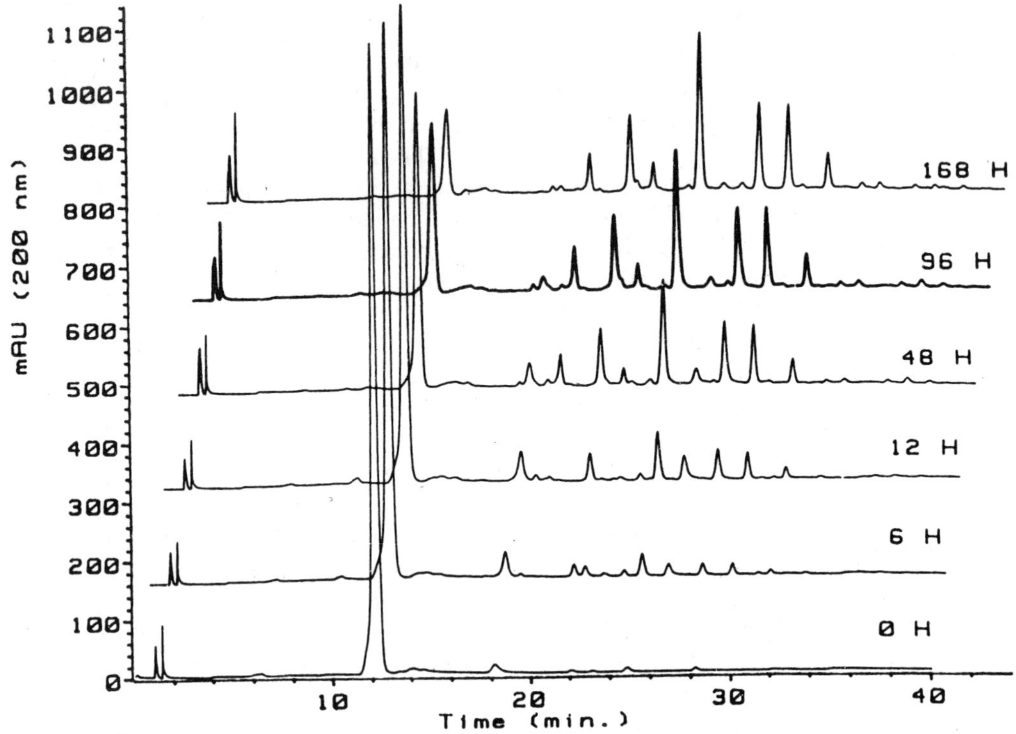

Fig. 10-8. Oxidation of caffeic acid at pH 7 for up to 168 hours.

merization regenerating oxidizable units under the slower conditions. If all the oxidizable phenols are rapidly converted to quinones, the slower polymerization reaction is minimized. There are soon no phenols remaining to link with the quinones and extended oxidation stops. Conversely, if few phenolates exist, few quinones are rapidly formed, but each quinone would have much greater chance to be substituted by another phenolic molecule or other nucleophile regenerating a hydroquinone. Further slow oxidation would maximize the chances that each cycle would extend the polymeric substitution-regeneration reaction while sparing more of the original phenol. Making the wine alkaline at any stage would hasten the oxidative reaction for the remaining phenols, but decrease the ultimate total uptake of oxygen by limiting the hydroquinone regeneration reactions.

Oxidation of caffeic acid in the presence of phloroglucinol or flavonoids with their phloroglucinol-like A-ring would encourage nucleophilic substitution into caffeic quinone of the electron-rich positions between the *meta*-dihydroxy groups of the phloroglucinol. The dimeric product would consume some phloroglucinol, whereas phloroglucinol alone would not disappear. Furthermore, the heterogeneous dimer could oxidize again across both rings to a diphenoquinone. Thus, the introduction of the phloroglucinol moiety would be expected to lower the oxidation reduction potential considerably, contribute heavily to browning (as flavonoids have been shown to do), spare caffeic acid from dimerizing with and consuming itself, and contribute to increasing the total oxygen consumed.

Gallic acid apparently does not readily progress alone beyond the dimer stage. It apparently does not incorporate phloroglucinol at least at the relative levels tested. The pyrogallol ring, however, readily is oxidatively opened. Different phenols obviously behave

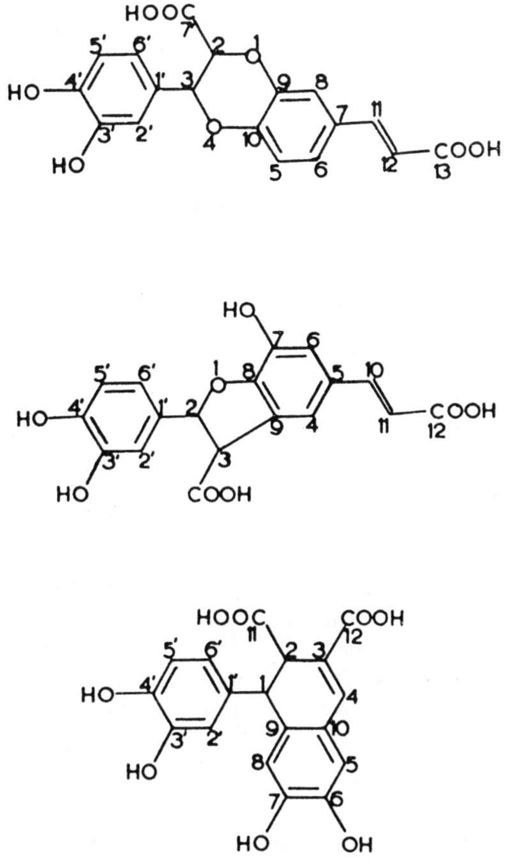

Fig. 10-9. Structures of identified products of caffeic acid oxidation in model solution (Cilliers and Singleton, 1991).

very differently yet contribute to the overall oxidative browning reactions. Although not discussed here to avoid complicating the picture further, amino acids and other compounds can react with quinones and affect browning and oxidation effects.

These explanations clarify what is happening as wines oxidize. The actual situation in maturing wines is obviously extremely complex. Oxidation is very slow and protracted allowing for maximum polymerization. Wines have complex mixtures of phenols and they differ greatly wine by wine. Even a model solution of a single phenol oxidized as fast as possible produces several compounds. Possible interactions in a mixture as complex as a red wine are mind-boggling. Nevertheless, it is possible to understand and control the process in broad practical terms.

F. BLENDING

Blending of beverages is an outwardly simple and easily understood operation. While the mixing of two or more wines is intuitively obvious, the optimum blending is not only far from simple but is often the difference between great winemakers/winemaking and the ordinary. Wine blending is often said (by romantic writers about wine) to be where art replaces science in winemaking. The most skillful wine blender does need to have broad and acute sensory capabilities not teachable per se, but must supplement them with experience, attention, rational approaches, and solid technology to be consistently successful.

There is no single "when" to blend wines; blending may be appropriate at several stages of winemaking and processing. Some wines are blended as they are made, notably fortified wines and ameliorated wines. The former involve addition of wine spirits to arrest fermentation with residual sugar and the latter addition of water and sugar to correct imbalance of acid and sugar in the musts. Nevertheless, the best practice seems to be to make each wine as good as possible, with preliminary blending as needed, and then assemble a final blend fairly late in the bulk processing and aging of the wine, often shortly before bottling. For this reason this discussion of blending has been placed here rather than in sections on earlier processing.

1. General Considerations

Even how to blend is not entirely obvious. The blended wine must be uniform throughout when the blending is complete and before any further operations are attempted. If blending is by mixing portions (batch blending) stirring should be forceful enough to mix the wine in every part of the container. Large paddles or other slow, gentle mixers are preferable to small, high-speed propellers that may produce cavitation and other undesirable effects. Stirring must also be prolonged enough to ensure complete mixing (about five to 30 minutes, depending on container size and the relative differences among the components blended). Depending on the accuracy of the metering and the turbulence at the point of entry, in-line blending (adding the wines together proportionally as a flowing stream) can be a very satisfactory method, particularly for blending small portions into very large ones, but (if conditions permit) a final stirring of the completed blend is reassuring.

Blended proportions should be based on careful preparation and evaluation of small trial blends in advance of the irrevocable production blending. A small group of trusted tasters is often helpful, but the winemaker (master blender, owner) must make the final decision in light of the specific goals of the blending. It is preferable to reevaluate the most promising blends after a period of complete detachment and sensory rest to ensure that fatigue has not skewed the results. Detailed records should be kept of these trial blends and *must* be kept of any production lot blending in case it becomes necessary to prove what was done for government regulators or other interested parties.

The regulations are increasingly restrictive if the final wine is to be labeled with a grape variety, viticultural site name, and vintage date. If all of these are to be used, the remaining leeway for blending approaches zero in a small winery. Subject to the realities of bookkeeping, available tanks, etc., greater opportunities remain for improving the final wines by blending the more different lots are kept separate. Blending in the vineyard or at the crusher is generally to be shunned, since this forecloses options and may saddle the winemaker with wines difficult to optimize.

It does not do much good to segregate a uniform lot of grapes into more than one lot and treat the lots all the same, because the statistical similarity of truly replicate wine lots is high, but vineyard sections, harvest dates, differing inocula (yeasts, malolactic fermenters), etc., can produce wine lots differing enough to be useful in blending even when meeting the stringencies of vintage, vineyard, and varietal regulations. If less restricting labeling is planned, more creative blending is possible. This is one reason that large, well-managed wineries that market inexpensive wines to a large market usually have a high minimum quality in their bottled wines. To use the French term, the *negociant-eleveur* (one who buys and improves wines) traditionally bought wines from many farmer-vintners and improved them not only by improved cellaring, but by blending as well. The best wines are almost invariably blended ones, at least in larger production.

When two essentially finished wines stable alone are blended there may be new instabilities and untoward reactions; therefore, a "marrying" period to allow flavor and other changes and final testing for instabilities is recommended before bottling. Pretesting of the trial blend, including stability tests, helps avoid surprises and can be used to help develop appropriate treatments. Trial blending is recommended to be in at least two stages, tasting trials and then precisely made larger amounts (10 L or more) of the preferred blend for marrying and stability tests as well as to confirm the tasting results. Of course, the production blend should be itself subjected to stabilization trials before treatment. Three weeks is considered minimal for the marrying period for production blends of commercial wines in the typical situation when no appreciable flavor or stability changes continue or remain uncorrected. It is not uncommon for wine to be blended just before bottling, if there has been sufficient experience with the particular situation.

2. Objectives of Blending Wines

Addition or augmentation of characteristics or diminution and dilution are the two alternative objectives for including any one component wine in a blend. Of course, the objective of blending is to make the final wine better. This may be to standardize it, balance it, achieve complexity, achieve a certain style, or optimize it under the specific economic conditions.

Standardization and uniformity are objectives of blending in large production of wines sold regularly in a specific market. Several years ago a visitor from a company that bought wine and distributed it door-to-door daily in a large European city said that their biggest problem was one day's delivery of wine considerably better than usual. The consumers complained the following day! Wineries in the United States wanting to keep a brand on the store shelf with consistent character year-round use appropriate blending to do so. The typical total inventory of Californian wine in December has been about 1.5 times annual sales (Table 10-1), allowing carry over for blending. Of course many factors, in addition to age, are involved in standardization to relatively constant color, acidity, alcohol, sweetness, etc., depending on the wine and the variability of the wines available for blending.

In marketing wines to a bulk buyer or contract bottler's specifications, blending to meet those specifications may be necessary. Such requirements do not necessarily and automatically make the blend a higher quality.

Correcting deficiencies is another reason for blending. If one wine is too acidic and another too flat, the obvious solution is to put them together so that they both become improved. This is a frequent problem for the producer of fortified dessert wines, particularly on a large scale. In this case it is often necessary to balance the cellar by making the next production lot so as to correct imbalances among the previous ones. For example, if the wines on hand for a port-type blend are too alcoholic, too low in sugar, and too weak in color, then one or more new production lots must be *made* more alcoholic, sweeter, and redder in the proper volume to standardize the final blend. This is less often a problem with table wines. Nevertheless, it is important for the winemaker to keep the final objectives in mind throughout the winemaking processes and head off as many potential later problems as possible during vinification and the earlier stages of processing.

A wine that has a serious defect such as mousiness or obvious acetification is *not* a good candidate to be hidden in an acceptable blend and such problems should have been prevented. Frequently, Concord and other nonvinifera grapes need to be diluted with wines from more bland varieties to prevent their flavor from being too strong for a table beverage to accompany food. This is why the minimum legal requirement for varietal labeling of Concord wines is not 75%, but 51%. Even some Muscat, Gewürztraminer, or Sauvignon blanc wines can be more varietally intense than the winemaker/customers desire.

If one desires to hide a poor flavor or dilute a good but too strong flavor, it is well to remember the Weber-Fechner relationship. Named for two of the early researchers, it states that while compositional changes follow a linear relationship, sensory estimates of flavor strength follow a geometric (power function) progression. For example, a 10% change in composition may not seem very different and 50% or more may be required for appreciable sensory change. This works for us if we are trying to extend a good flavor, but against us in disguising a bad one. A strong Sauvignon blanc diluted with 25% of a nondescript, but nondefective white wine may be rated as not much less strong and in fact improved by a tasting panel. A mousy wine may still be detectably mousy when blended with a large amount of good wine, thus spoiling the blend, at least for the sensitive consumer. Of course these observations are affected by the typical sensory sensitivity to the compounds involved.

A potent flavor agent may be noted by the senses, but be very difficult to analyze chemically at the levels that occur. A desirable flavor well above its sensory recognition threshold may make a wine a good blending component. It can add to complexity in the blend, particularly if below the recognition threshold, but above its minimum difference threshold in the blend. For such reasons, it is often useful to deliberately make certain portions of a wine for blending too high in some desirable characteristic as a more efficient and controllable method of reaching a particular and reproducible flavor level. A wine that is too oaky itself may be used to make a blend that is more suitable and reproducible than if the whole lot was oak-aged.

That complexity is a positive wine quality attribute was discussed earlier in this chapter. This is a general finding: subtle, coherent complexity improves perceived quality in esthetic evaluation. The more complex is more interesting and over a longer span than the simple. This holds true for wines as well as music, art or playgrounds. However, wine complexity must be within the desired style of the wine being made. For example, a blend of two or more diverse distinctive varieties (e.g., Cabernet, Grenache) would confuse the consumer and while complex, could become a less distinctive mishmash.

Another objective of blending can be economic. Typically a winery has relatively large amounts of good wine and less superlative wine. Because it is probably from less expensive grapes, lesser reputed vineyards, etc., the good wine is less expensive. It becomes important to use as much of the inexpensive wine as possible in each blend, depending on the price bracket targeted. You may be selling wine in bulk or contract bottled to the buyer's specifications. Meeting those specifications most economically governs profit or loss. A large winery may blend in superlative lots to raise the average quality, but then would have no special lots to tout. A small premium producer may sell his less than superlative lots in bulk or as a second label, reserving those deemed best for the top of the line. Economics become crucial, woe betide the winemaker who misjudges!

3. Blending Mathematics

If the blending is of wines similar in composition and controlled entirely by sensory evaluation, fit-and-try methods are necessary, but in blending to compositional standards more precise methods are needed. It is assumed in the methods to be described that changes are linearly proportional to the amounts of the wines blended. As already stated, this is generally true for chemical composition, but not for sensory characteristics. Wines are ordinarily blended based on volumes rather than weight. This can introduce two kinds of errors when one tries to match a certain composition by blending: those due to density differences and to temperature effects. For table wines under usual circumstances these can probably be ignored, but may result in slight analytical differences between the trial and production blends. Trial blends should be prepared with the wines at the temperature they will be when the production blend is made. Ordinarily this means they should be freshly drawn cellar samples. Tasting, on the other hand, should be after the blend has reached near room temperature for most careful evaluation. Correction of the volume according to the temperature is possible using standard tables in handbooks for dilute aqueous solutions. The volume increase as the temperature rises from 15°C to 28°C is only about 3 mL/L. Proportions of blends would not change as long as all blend components were at the same temperature.

As the sugar of a must is fermented, the volume changes slightly as alcohol is formed. If ethanol is added to wine or water, the volume increases, but slightly less than the sum of the mixed volumes owing to a contracting effect of the water-alcohol solution. While these differences are not large, they can be important in meeting precise regulations of the Bureau of Alcohol, Tobacco, and Firearms in the United States and similar agencies elsewhere. They are primarily relevant only with dessert wines or distilled beverages. Reference should be made to the appropriate regulations, if necessary (see also *Gauging* (1950) and Guymon and Bachmann (1962).

If only two wines are to be blended and one component is of interest, a simple proportion is usable as demonstrated by the Pearson square. The two left corners are given the values of the constituent's concentration in each wine, the center the desired concentration of the blend and the diagonal corners on the right the differences between each wine's content and that desired. Figure 10-10 illustrates the situation if wine A has 11% alcohol, wine B has 14%, and the blend should have 12%. The right-hand values are the ratio for the blend; namely, two volumes of wine A per volume of wine B. It is, of course, possible to compute a summation blend involving several wines by adding up the volumes necessary to achieve the desired content with one of the wines combined with each other wine in turn.

Blending to specific composition can be treated more generally as a series of simultaneous linear equations involving each component. Of course pH is not described by a linear relationship because of its nature and the buffering capacity of different wines. Red color is another value that is not well explained in young red wines by linear blending equations because it is affected by pH and the proportions of the pigments in different forms. Many other components can, however, be satisfactorily calculated according to the amount (concentration times volume) contributed by each wine in a blend. Papers by Costa (1968), Moore and Griffin (1978), and Datta and Nakai (1992) illustrate the mathematics of blending and the application of computers to solving blending problems. Computers are particularly useful if several wines are to be blended to a specific standard for several components, not useful if wines are to be blended for optimum sensory quality, and not needed if only a few wines and few components are considered.

To illustrate the procedure, computerized or not, suppose wines A, B, C, and D with known analyses for alcohol, total acidity, residual sugar, and iron content are to be blended to give a wine with specified concentration of these components. First of all, at least one wine must have less than the desired content of each component if others have more. Even so, depending on the distribution of the other components, it may not be possible to reach the desired composition with this group of wines. One equation is the volume of each wine used in the blend summed equals the desired volume of the blend (A + B + C + D = V). An equation is derived for each of the analytical components, e.g., alcohol: $\mathrm{alc}(A) + \mathrm{alc}(B) + \mathrm{alc}(C) + \mathrm{alc}(D) = \mathrm{alc}(V)$. The final volume ($V$, can be 1 or 100%) and the alcohol contents of each wine and the desired blend are known and are substituted into the equations. It is similar for the equations for the other three components specified in this example. The resultant five simultaneous equations can be solved algebraically for the four unknown volumes of the component wines necessary to produce the desired blend.

Computerization allows iterative solutions, calculation of the limit volume producible

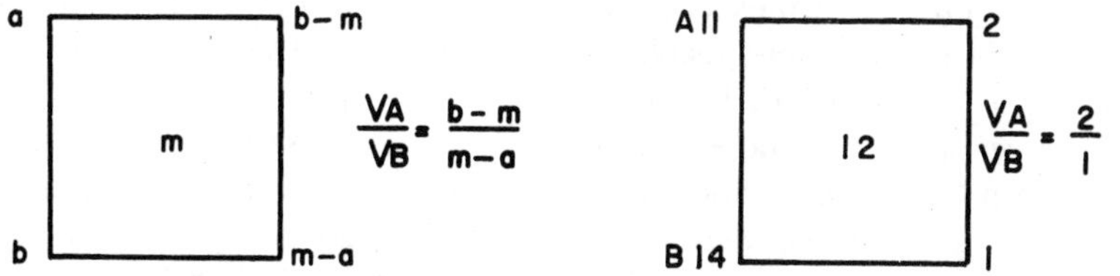

Fig. 10-10. The Pearson square, an example. Wine A has 11% alcohol and B has 14%. The desired blend will have 12% (presuming constant weight/volume relationships). The desired blend will be two parts A for each part of B, or made up of 2/3 A and 1/3 B. By algebra:

$$VA + VB = 1,\ VA = 1 - VB$$
$$11VA + 14VB = 12\,(VA + VB)$$
$$3VB = 1,\ VB = 1/3,\ VA = 2/3$$

when insufficient wine is available to produce the desired blend volume, and other refinements (Moore and Griffin 1978). A graphical method limited to three wines per blend is a useful illustration and easy to apply (Salgues 1975). An equilateral right triangle is used to plot the data with the corners each representing one of the three wines in pure form. The two sides are graduated in fractions of one or 100% of two wines relative to that axis and the third wine's (C) volume by difference. The example given by Salgues (1975) is illustrated in Figure 10-11. Wines A, B, and C had, respectively, alcohol of 12%, 11%, 11.5%; iron of 7 mg/L, 10 mg/L, 15 mg/L; total acidity of 7 g/L, 3 g/L, 4 g/L; and relative costs of 12, 9, 11 (francs/L or $/gal.). The blend is to have alcohol 11.5%, minimum cost, iron of 11 mg/L or less, and acidity of 4.75 g/L or less. The graphical solution is shown in Figure 10-11 where the composition is met by any mixture on the line X-Y and minimum cost by the blend Y of 37% A, 37% B, and 26% C which would analyze 11.5% alcohol, 10.2 mg/L Fe, 4.74 g/L acid, and have a relative cost of 10.63. Graphing is somewhat easier for the third wine using triangular coordinate 0–100% graph paper, but results are the same.

4. Fractional Blending

Fractional blending is more often referred to as the solera system that was developed in Spain for blending sherries (see also Section 10.B.2). It could be used for any wine, but is the most obviously useful for wines aged in many different wooden containers (each of which may produce some difference in flavor) and where differences among vintages are to be masked. Properly executed, solera-type fractional blending can produce a wine of constant average age that varies imperceptibly as new vintages are incorporated. It has disadvantages, foremost being that severalfold amounts of wine must be in the system compared to the annual withdrawal (sales) rate. Especially as originally operated in Spain, it is costly in labor. If one container develops microbial spoilage, it will (unless special care eliminates that container beforehand) spread the spoilage to all subsequent stages. Owing to costs, inventory, risks of undesirable oxidation, etc., this system has not been widely used, except in Spain for sherries. It can, especially in modified forms, be useful for dessert wines in addition to sherries and possibly for red table wines or sparkling wine base wines where more age is desired and vintage dating is not.

G. BOTTLE AGING AND POST-BULK-MATURATION STORAGE

The package of wine to be sold to consumers is intended to retain contents and exclude oxygen. Storage in such containers at least for limited times and conditions should prevent undesirable changes. Prolonged bottle storage can allow continuation of reactions not completed during bulk maturation and new effects that do not occur during bulk maturation. Ethyl bitartrate increase is an example of a slow reaction unlikely to be completed before bottling. Accumulation of highly volatile products such as dimethylsulfide and reductive reactions or others opposed by periodic exposure to air would not occur in bulk but would in bottle. The reason that bottle aging can be desirable on top of bulk maturation is new and additional mellowing and complexing of flavors.

The 750-mL wine bottle sealed with a 5-cm natural cork is considered the standard of comparison for bottle aging. For long-term storage with the intent of improvement by further aging no other container has so far proven as satisfactory or been as well tested. However, in 1987, only about 25% of retailed table wine from California was sold in that size and some of that with screw caps. For short-term storage, say up to six months, screw caps and other containers may be satisfactory and have advantages. A multilayer collapsible bag (often in a semirigid box, therefore termed *bag-in-box* here and *cask* in Australia) has the advantage of collapsing without admitting air

	Wine	Alc.%	Fe mg/L	Acid g/L	Rel. Cost
Given:	A	12	7	7	12
	B	11	10	3	9
	C	11.5	15	4	11
Desired:	Blend	11.5	11 max.	4.75 max	min.

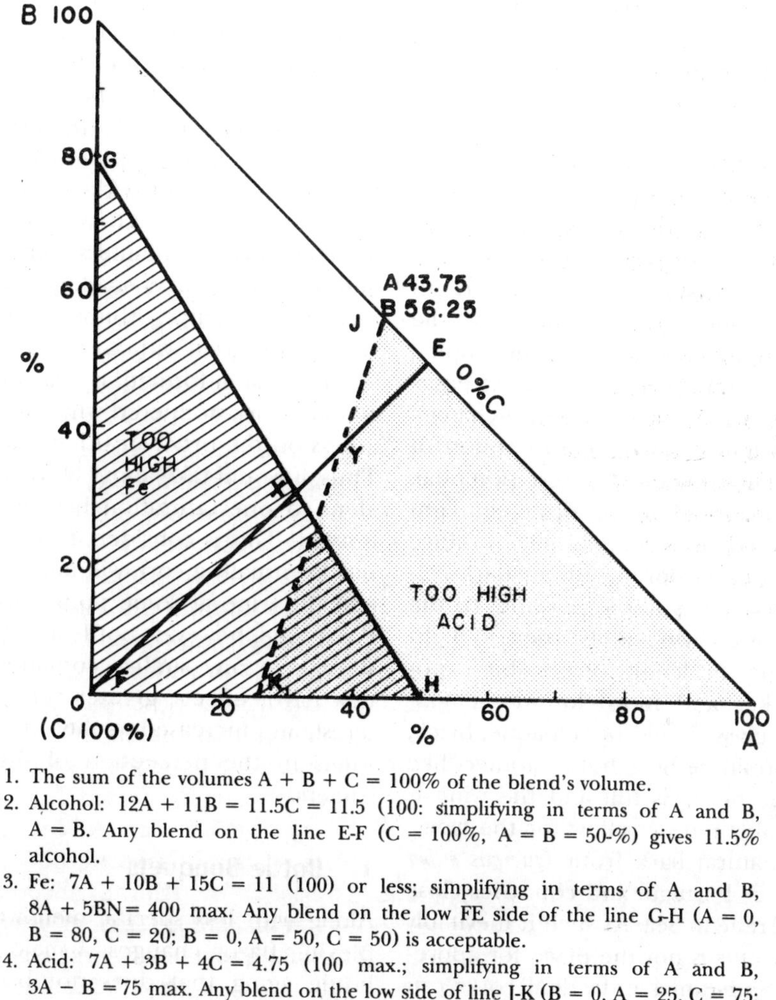

1. The sum of the volumes A + B + C = 100% of the blend's volume.
2. Alcohol: 12A + 11B = 11.5C = 11.5 (100: simplifying in terms of A and B, A = B. Any blend on the line E-F (C = 100%, A = B = 50-%) gives 11.5% alcohol.
3. Fe: 7A + 10B + 15C = 11 (100) or less; simplifying in terms of A and B, 8A + 5BN= 400 max. Any blend on the low FE side of the line G-H (A = 0, B = 80, C = 20; B = 0, A = 50, C = 50) is acceptable.
4. Acid: 7A + 3B + 4C = 4.75 (100 max.; simplifying in terms of A and B, 3A − B = 75 max. Any blend on the low side of line J-K (B = 0, A = 25, C = 75; C= 0, A = 43.75, B = 56.25 by iteration) is acceptable.
5. Minimum price: Any blend along the segment X-Y is compositionally acceptable. Since in these blends A = B and their combined price is 10.50, the lowest C blend has the minimum price. Therefore blend Y has the minimum price.
6. The chosen blend is 37% A, 37% B, and 26% C.

Fig. 10-11. Graphical blending of three wines to be specified composition. (Adapted from Salgues (1975)).

as wine is dispensed. In this regard, it can be preferable to a glass bottle or decanter that is used for more than a short time after removing the original cork. The layers can include, say, polyethylene nearest the wine to avoid off-flavors and thin metal foil to exclude light and oxygen. Considerable know-how has gone into such packaging and other plastic containers and stoppers for wine. They are not intended for long storage, but may be quite satisfactory for the short term. The tests so far reported (e.g., Boidron and Bar 1988; Ough 1987) have generally indicated sensory differences after about six months between the same wine in such containers and in bottles with good natural corks, the difference favoring the traditional package. The remainder of our comments will focus on the traditional corked wine bottle.

The glass of wine bottles is not entirely inert and identifiable but commonly insignificant inorganic extraction may occur depending on the glass and its pretreatment, sodium, and silicates for examples. The color is intended to exclude light, particularly the shorter wavelengths such as ultraviolet, violet, and blue. Short wavelengths are most energetic and can cause the most chemical change. For example, light catalyzes consumption of oxygen and achievement of a rest potential. Even a few minutes of strong direct sunlight on wine in a colorless bottle may produce off-flavors. If wine is stored only in dark cellars, the bottle color is not important. To the degree the bottled wine is exposed to light and considering the length of possible exposure, the darker and more low-wavelength-absorbing the glass should be. Opaque, black, or dark red would be best, but customers like to see that the bottle is full and the wine is clear and suitably red or yellow for the type.

Cork is a natural bark from *Quercus suber* grown mainly in Portugal and countries close to the Mediterranean Sea. As such it inevitably is variable and this is not the place for appreciable detail. Sometimes individual corks can carry moldy and other tastes to the wine they stopper. Such off-flavored bottles, termed *corky*, may cause returns and loss of customers. This is an active area as cork suppliers and wineries work to get the incidence as low as possible in the face of high demand for bottle corks as premium table wines make up a larger fraction of total wines. The most clearly recognized culprit is 2,4,6-trichloroanisole which has a moldy newspaper odor detectable at a few parts per billion. Incidence is one or two bottles out of a hundred as noted at recent wine judgings. Some wineries with some lots of cork have in the past found several times this incidence.

This trichloroanisole odor appears to be the result of a combination of factors thought to include bleaching of corks with chlorine during manufacture and molds occurring on or in the corks. At this point all that one can suggest for practical use by the winemaker is to build a relationship with a cork supplier. Pretest a number of corks before using a new lot by some means such as immersion of them in small closed containers with water or wine and after a few days smelling carefully to detect any incidence. Abnormal lots should be returned unused with an explanation.

The best information available suggests a soundly cork-stoppered wine bottle may allow access on the order of 0.1 mL of O_2/L/year. Thus, it would take about 60 years to be equivalent to one saturation before the wine was bottled! This is considered essentially anaerobic. Eventually a cork will fail. Ullage develops and the wine at some point rapidly declines. For a time, however, bottle aging or anaerobic storage in any similar container contributes new flavor effects, greater complexity and interest, and increased quality, at least in certain wines in the perception of discerning consumers.

1. Bottle Bouquets

Along with less specific mellowing and complexing flavor changes, a major change with bottle aging that does not become evident during bulk aging is the development of bottle bouquets. The bottle bouquet of white wines may be described as a sun-dried linen or boiled artichoke smell. Once a good example has been enjoyed it is much more easily recognized than described. Its exact chemical nature is not certain. It probably consists of more than one significant compound. One of these is dimethylsulfide. This compound occurs in juice, but is very volatile and easily lost from wine in open containers. It does increase with bottle age, especially in Riesling wines (Loubser and DuPlessis 1976). Alone it has a boiled fresh corn smell, however, unlike bottle bouquet but probably contributory. It occurs in other wines and in a series of Cabernet wines varied from 42 to 910 $\mu g/L$ (threshold 60 $\mu g/L$) correlated more with vintage than with bottle age (De Mora et al. 1987).

Another group of compounds that increases with bottle age and are believed contributory to bottle bouquet especially in white wines are derived from isoprenoid-terpene sources. Of course, monoterpenes and norisoterpenes contribute to muscat and certain other varietal aromas, but they can change from glycoside hydrolysis and other reactions during aging. It is our experience, however, that bottle bouquet of the usual white table wine type does not become recognizable in muscat wines. This may be from overshadowing of the delicate bouquet by the more odorous muscat terpenes, but Riesling readily develops bottle bouquet. Vitispirane (Simpson et al. 1977) and 1,1,6-trimethyl-1,2-dihydronaphthalene (TDN) (Simpson 1978) rose with time in bottle along with linalool oxide, nerol oxide, and the carbohydrate breakdown products furfural and ethyl furoate (Simpson 1979). Ethyl *n*-decanoate and other volatile esters tend downward early. The carbohydrate derivatives and vitispirane were below flavor thresholds and the oxides were less flavorful than the parent alcohols, linalool and nerol.

The naphthalene derivative (TDN) is an important contributor to bottle bouquet in a few wines notably Rieslings. However, it has a kerosene smell that is not automatically attractive if strong. Other wines may have different bottle bouquets. That of ports is more plummy-fruity and old dry red wines develop a fruity-varnishy character somewhat different from the sunny linen white wine bottle bouquet. Some red table wines, particularly lighter ones and rosés, often will develop essentially the same bottle bouquet that white wines do. Not all wines of a given class develop nicely with age. Some lose their original attractiveness gaining little in return by long bottle storage (light fino sherries belong in this category). Others may hold rather well but do not develop the extra nuances expected from bottle age. This is partly a varietal and partly a processing result. Riesling, Sémillon, and Chardonnay table wines usually develop well in the bottle. Muscat and Chenin blanc usually have not in our experience. Red wines take longer, as a rule, and become less readily distinguishable by grape variety, but nearly all dry table reds that do not depend too heavily on grape aromas for their charm can develop with bottle age.

2. Time-Temperature Effects

Dry white table wines stored in the same cellar immediately after bottling at a controlled temperature of 12°C were rated blindly on a 10-maximum scale for bottle bouquet (Table 10-10) (Singleton, et al. 1964). The average bottle bouquet rating increased up to four years of storage. The maximum ratings were received after five years and some wines never developed recognizable bottle bouquet of the expected type (notably but not confined to Muscats). If one assumes a Q_{10} of 2, and that bottle bouquet development as estimated sensorially behaves as a typical chemical reaction, two years at 22°C, one year at 32°C, six months at 42°C, and three months at 52°C should give similar bottle bouquet development to four years at 12°C. Maximum temperature to avoid undesirable reactions is about 52°C (Singleton and Kramling 1976).

Table 10-10. Effect of length of storage of white dry table wines in bottles at 12°C on bottle bouquet rating.

Years of storage	Number of wines	Minimum and maximum rating (0–10 scale)	Average rating (0–10 scale)
2	25	0–4	1.36
3	31	0–7	2.71
4	51	1–8	4.10
5	35	1–9	3.94
6	15	1–8	4.13

Source: Adapted from Singletonet al. (1964).

Bottle bouquet was readily developed in bottled wines heated when freed of oxygen with CO_2 or especially with N_2 but not if air or O_2 was present (Singleton et al. 1964). The mean sensory rating for grape aroma decreased rapidly, but bottle bouquet and complexity increased slowly with prolonged heating to 32 days at 53°C. Corks must be tied down or other closures used. The data from these and subsequent tests are consistent with the cellar data in regard to Q_{10} for bottle bouquet development near but perhaps slightly higher than 2 and all that implies. Again, the importance of O_2-free conditions and a low oxidation-reduction potential during bottle bouquet development, with or without heat, is emphasized. Also, grapey-fruity aromas are lost more rapidly with warm storage than with cool. Major parts of the advantage of cool storage for wine aging are that the fruity-varietal aromas are retained longer as bottle bouquet develops and the wine is both improved and preserved over a longer time at cooler temperatures. Of course, too cold, reaction is prevented (see previous discussion).

H. RAPID MATURATION AND AGING

There is a persistent barrier to the adoption of deliberate technological acceleration of maturation and aging of wines related to the dichotomy that premium wine producers want their customers to know they use the time-honored traditional processes. Customers for more inexpensive wines do not understand or want aged characters in their wines because they have not been exposed to them. It may be true that ultimate quality of the best wines matured and aged by the traditional processes is higher than can be achieved, at present, by improved, cheaper and faster technology. It is true, however, that the traditional methods do not convert every wine to ultimate quality by rote application; results are variable and not infrequently disappointing in proportion to their costs.

Traditional processes, especially four years of bottle age, frequently are not economically feasible at the winery. The choice is often little or no maturation and aging versus application of specific, controlled techniques gaining the benefits of traditional processes in faster, less expensive ways. This type of economic pressure is likely to intensify. Pleasant as the simple, fresh, fruity wines are, it would be sad to lose the additional diversity, excitement, fascination, and satisfaction of well-matured and aged wines. The average quality of inexpensive wines can certainly be raised by adopting improved procedures when traditional ones are outmoded or become too expensive.

Methods should be considered such as using oak bits in stainless steel tanks to provide extractives, deliberate but controlled and limited oxidation, and anaerobic warming to provide bouquet. Each winemaker should be aware of possibilities and new developments as they occur and consider them in relation to their situation. It remains important to produce attractive, healthful, diverse wines for the benefit of consumers in general, not just expensive varieties for the rich.

Such procedures do not necessarily produce compromised quality. For example, a better wine might be possible by judicious blending of one wine to retain fruity-varietal character with another contributing barrel-matured quality and a third contributing bottle-aged bouquet than would have been possible from any one of the three alone matured and aged by traditional and expensive methods.

I. REFERENCES

1988 Wine Industry Statistical Report. 1989. San Francisco: Wine Institute.

BAKER, G. A., M. A. AMERINE, and E. B. ROESSLER. 1952. "Theory and application of fractional blending systems." *Hilgardia* 21:383–409.

BLAZER, R. M. 1991. "Wine evaporation from barrels." *Prac. Wine / Vin.* 12:20–23.

BOIDRON, J. N., and M. BAR. 1988. "Influence du matériau sur l'évolution du vin conditionné en contenant de faible volume." *Connais. Vigne Vin* 22:73–83.

CHEYNIER, V., J. RIGAUD, and M. MOUTOUNET. 1990. "Oxidation kinetics of *trans*-caffeoyltartrate and its glutathione derivatives in grape musts." *Phytochemistry* 29:1751–1753.

CHEYNIER, V., E. K. TROUSDALE, V. L. SINGLETON, M. J. SALGUES, and R. WYLDE. 1986. "Characterization of 2-S-glutathionylcaftaric acid and its hydrolysis in relation to grape wines." *J. Agric. Food Chem.* 34:217–221.

CILLIERS, J. J. L., and V. L. SINGLETON. 1989. "Nonenzymic autoxidative phenolic browning reactions in a caffeic acid model system." *J. Agric. Food Chem.* 37:890–896.

CILLIERS, J. J. L., and V. L. SINGLETON. 1990a. "Caffeic acid autoxidation and the effects of thiols." *J. Agric. Food Chem.* 38:1789–1796.

CILLIERS, J. J. L., and V. L. SINGLETON. 1990b. "Nonenzymic autoxidative reactions of caffeic acid in wine." *Am. J. Enol. Vitic.* 41:84–86.

CILLIERS, J. J. L., and V. L. SINGLETON. 1991. "Characterization of the products of nonenzymic autoxidative phenolic reactions in a caffeic acid model system." *J. Agric. Food Chem.* 39:1298–1303.

COOKE, G. M., and H. W. BERG. 1971. "Varietal table wine processing practices in California. II. Clarification, stabilization, bottling, and aging." *Am. J. Enol. Vitic.* 22:178–183.

COOKE, G. M., and H. W. BERG. 1973. "Table wine processing practices in the San Joaquin Valley." *Am. J. Enol. Vitic.* 24:153–158.

COOKE, G. M., and H. W. BERG. 1984. "A reexamination of varietal table wine processing practices in California. II. Clarification, stabilization, aging, and bottling." *Am. J. Enol. Vitic.* 35:137–142.

COSTA, E. N. 1968. "A simple analog computer for blending calculations." *Am. J. Enol. Vitic.* 19:84–90.

DADA, G., A. CORBANI, P. MANITTO, G. SPERANZA, and L. LUNAZZI. 1989. "Lignan glycosides from the heartwood of European oak *Quercus petraea*." *J. Nat. Prod.* 52:1327–1330.

DATTA, S., and S. NAKAI. 1992. "Computer-aided optimization of wine blending." *J. Food Sci.* 57:178–182, 205.

DE MORA, S. J., S. J. KNOWLES, R. ESCHENBRUCH, and W. J. TORREY. 1987. "Dimethyl sulfide in some Australian red wines." *Vitis* 26:79–84.

EDWARDS, T. L., V. L. SINGLETON, and R. B. BOULTON. 1985. "Formation of ethyl esters of tartaric acid during wine aging: Chemical and sensory effects." *Am. J. Enol. Vitic.* 36:118–124.

Gauging Manual. 1950. Washington, DC: Bureau of Internal Revenue, U. S. Treasury Deptartment.

GUYMON, J. F., and J. A. BACHMANN. 1962. "Interconversion tables for percentage of ethyl alcohol in water." *Leaflet* 145:1–11. Berkeley, CA: California Expt. Sta. Extension Service.

HERVE DU PENHOAT, C. L., V. M. F. MICHON, A. OHASSAN, S. PENG, A. SALBERT, and D. GAGE. 1991. "Roburin A, a dimeric ellagitannin from heartwood of *Quercus robur*." *Phytochem.* 30: 329–332.

JOSLYN, M. A., and M. A. AMERINE. 1964. *Dessert, Appetizer and Related Flavored Wines. The Technology of Their Production*. Berkeley CA: University of California, Division of Agricultural Sciences.

KEPNER, R. E., A. D. WEBB, and C. J. MULLER. 1972. "Identification of 4-hydroxy-3-methyloctanoic acid γ-lactone [5-butyl-4-methyldihydro-2(3H)-furanone] as a volatile component of oak-wood-aged wines of *Vitis vinifera* var. Cabernet Sauvignon." *Am. J. Enol. Vitic.* 23:103–105.

LOUBSER, G., and C. S. DUPLESSIS. 1976. "The quantitative determination and some values of dimethyl sulfide in white table wines." *Vitis* 15:248–252.

MALVEZIN, F. 1903. *Viellisement des Vins et Spiritueux. Nouveau Traitement des Vins ou Pasteuroxyfrigorie.* Bordeaux, France: Feret et Fils.

MARTINEZ DE LA OSSA, E., I. CARO, M. BONAT, L. PEREZ, and B. DOMECQ. 1987. "Dry extract in sherry and its evolution in the aging process." *Am. J. Enol. Vitic.* 38:321–325.

MOORE, D. B., and T. G. GRIFFIN. 1978. "Computer blending technology." *Am. J. Enol. Vitic.* 29:50–53.

NABETA, K., J. YONEKUBO, and M. MIYAKE. 1986. "Analysis of volatile constituents of European and Japanese oaks." *Mokuzai Gakkaishi* 32: 921–927.

Open Shelf-Life Dating of Food. 1979. Washington, DC: Office of Technology Assessment.

OUGH, C. S. 1987. "Use of PET bottles for wine." *Am. J. Enol. Vitic.* 38:100–104.

PETERSON, R. G. 1976. "Formation of reduced pressure in barrels during wine aging." *Am. J. Enol. Vitic.* 27:80–81.

QUINN, M. K., and V. L. SINGLETON. 1985. "Isolation and identification of ellagitannins from white oak wood and an estimation of their roles in wine." *Am. J. Enol. Vitic.* 36:148–155.

RAMEY, D. D., and C. S. OUGH. 1980. "Volatile ester hydrolysis or formation during storage of model solutions and wines." *J. Agric. Food Chem.* 28:928–934.

RIBÉREAU-GAYON, P. 1986. "Self-life of wine." In *Handbook of Food and Beverage Stability*. G. Charalambous, Ed., pp. 745–772. New York: Academic Press.

ROUS, C., and B. ALDERSON. 1983. "Phenolic extraction curves for white wine aged in French and American oak barrels." *Am. J. Enol. Vitic.* 34:211–215.

SALGUES, M. 1975. "Determination d'un assemblage par programmation lineare." *Prog. Agric. Vitic.* 175(20):605–609; (23):723–730.

SALGUES, M., V. CHEYNIER, Z. GUNATA, and R. WYLDE. 1986. "Oxidation of grape juice 2-S-glutathionyl caffeoyl tartaric acid by *Botrytis cinerea* laccase and characterization of a new substance: 2,5-di-S-glutathionyl caffeoyl tartaric acid." *J. Food Sci.* 51:1191–1194.

SEFTON, M. A., I. L. FRANCIS, and P. J. WILLIAMS. 1990. "Volatile norisoprenoid compounds as constituents of oak wood used in wine and spirit maturation." *J. Agric. Food Chem.* 38:2045–2049.

SIMPSON, R. F. 1978. "1,1,6-Trimethyl-1,2-dihydronaphthalene: an important contributor to the bottle bouquet of wine." *Chem. Ind.* :37.

SIMPSON, R. F. 1979. "Aroma composition of bottle aged white wine." *Vitis* 18:148–154.

SIMPSON, R. F., C. R. STRAUSS, and P. J. WILLIAMS. 1977. "Vitispirane: A C_{13} spiro-ether in the aroma volatiles of grape juice, wines, and distilled grape spirits." *Chem. Ind.* :663–466.

SINGLETON, V. L. 1962. "Aging of wines and other spiritous products, acceleration by physical treatments." *Hilgardia* 32:319–392.

SINGLETON, V. L. 1969. "Browning of wines." *Die Wynboer* (455):13–14.

SINGLETON, V. L. 1974. "Some aspects of the wooden container as a factor in wine maturation." *Adv. Chem.* 137:254–277.

SINGLETON, V. L. 1979. "Recent developments in wine aging." *Proc. 5th Wine Ind. Tech. Seminar*, November 25 1978, Monterey, California, pp. 31–37.

SINGLETON, V. L. 1987. "Oxygen with phenols and related reactions in musts, wines, and model systems: Observations and practical implications." *Am. J. Enol. Vitic.* 38:69–77.

SINGLETON, V. L. 1989. "Browning and oxidation of musts and wines." *Proc. 4th Ann. Midwest Regional Grape and Wine Conf.* 4:87–93.

SINGLETON, V. L., and D. E. DRAPER. 1961. "Wood chips and wine treatment; the nature of aqueous alcohol extracts." *Am. J. Enol. Vitic.* 12:152–158.

SINGLETON, V. L., and T. E. KRAMLING. 1976. "Browning of white wines and an accelerated test for browning capacity." *Am. J. Enol. Vitic.* 27:157–160.

SINGLETON, V. L., and C. S. OUGH. 1962. "Complexity of flavor and blending of wines." *J. Food Sci.* 27:189–196.

SINGLETON, V. L., C. S. OUGH, and M. A. AMERINE. 1964. "Chemical and sensory effects of heating wines under different gases." *Am. J. Enol. Vitic.* 15:134–145.

SINGLETON, V. L., M. SALGUES, J. ZAYA, and E. TROUSDALE. 1985. "Caftaric acid disappearance and conversion to products of enzymic oxidation in grape must and wine." *Am. J. Enol. Vitic.* 36:50–56.

SINGLETON. V. L., A. R. SULLIVAN, and C. KRAMER. 1971. "An analysis of wine to indicate aging in wood or treatment with wood chips or tannic acid." *Am. J. Enol. Vitic.* 22:161–166.

SINGLETON, V. L., E. TROUSDALE, and J. ZAYA. 1979. "Oxidation of wines. I. Young white wines periodically exposed to air." *Am. J. Enol. Vitic.* 30:49–54.

TULYATHAN, V., R. B. BOULTON, and V. L. SINGLETON. 1989. "Oxygen uptake by gallic acid as a model for similar reactions in wines." *J. Agric. Food Chem.* 37:844–849.

WILDENRADT, H. L., and V. L. SINGLETON. 1974. "The production of aldehydes as a result of oxidation of polyphenolic compounds and its relation to wine aging." *Am. J. Enol. Vitic.* 25:119–126.

CHAPTER 11

The Bottling and Storage of Wines

The bottling of wines is arguably the most important of all winemaking operations since it determines the condition in which the wine is delivered to the market. It is the culmination of the sequence that began long before, starting with grape development, harvesting, fermentation, and aging. Mistakes are costly to rectify and quality control is of primary importance.

The glass bottles used for wine are generally the 750-mL size, of clear or colored glass and in a number of traditional shapes. Other volumes, smaller and larger, are also used depending on the interest in further aging, the setting in which it is likely to be consumed, and the value of the wine. The inertness and protection offered to wines by glass bottles has been verified by many years of usage. The most vulnerable aspect of bottled wine is the nature of the closure or seal that is employed. For many years corks have been unquestioned as the closure of choice due to their compressible, relatively inert nature. However, in recent decades, the elimination of many defects due to improved winemaking technology has made the incidence of defects attributable to corks to be a major problem in some wines (Lee and Simpson 1992).

The preparation of wines for bottling, the steps involved in bottling and the aspects of their behavior under bottle storage conditions are the subjects addressed in this chapter. The addresses of equipment companies mentioned in this chapter can be found in Appendix I.

A. PREPARATION FOR BOTTLING

The preparation of wines for bottling involves any final adjustments of chemical composition, final filtration, and modification of the dissolved oxygen and carbon dioxide levels in the wines. The preparation of blends, fining, stabilization, and adjustments of acidity should not be considered as finishing operations and will generally have been attended to some period before the time of bottling.

1. Final Filtration

The type and style of wine will somewhat influence whether filter pads or a membrane are to be employed as the final filtration. The use of nominally sterile pads is widely practiced, particularly with dry wines, while wines containing residual sugar, or those in which the malolactic fermentation has been prevented, will generally be membrane filtered. The assumption that dry wines that have completed malolactic fermentation will not support additional microbial growth is not always true in practice (Lee et al. 1984). While the incidence of later microbial spoilage is lower in such cases, it is not eliminated entirely. The continuing trend for the use of lower levels of chemical additives and the desire to use minimal concentrations of sulfur dioxide only enhance the recommendation of membrane filtrations as the means to prevent unwanted microbial action in bottled wines.

Concerns about color removal from red wines by membrane filters have no sensory basis since the material collected on such filters has already precipitated from solution and insoluble particles have no taste or flavor associated with them. Such material will usually deposit in the bottle within the first months after being bottled and the collection of it on the filter is simply deferring the onset of such a deposit. The removal of yeast and bacterial cells, which also have no taste contribution in themselves, is for reasons of quality control and the assurance that the wine that is consumed closely resembles that which was put into the bottle. The point is, that only soluble components that can be sensed by taste receptors on the tongue or volatile ones reaching the nasal cavity can have a sensory impact and there is no evidence that soluble components and small volatile molecules are significantly removed by such filtrations.

The need to remove all microbes by filtration is a far more acceptable approach to controlling unwanted microbial activity than the chemical additive approach. The variation in quality due to microbial effects can often be seen in wines that have not been filtered, within the first two years after bottling. Tasting of a series of wines from different vintages made in this style by the same producer will generally show such changes and they are undesirable in vintage-dated varietal wines.

The notion of stripping of wine components by filtration has little scientific basis. While some individuals claim to have shown this to be real, there are no panel tests or published results to support it. It has become fashionable, in some circles, to claim that unfiltered or unfined wines are superior, but this has no basis in fact. There are wines that will not need to be fined and perhaps not need to be filtered, but they are not necessarily any better than those that have been. These arguments are generally driven by public relations efforts that try to distinguish wineries from one another or by wine writers who try to be controversial rather than educational in their comments. Bottle sickness, a temporary lowering of flavor in freshly bottled wines, appears to result from the disturbance of an established vapor-liquid equilibrium and not from filtration.

2. Membrane Filtration of Wines

Membrane filters are made of synthetic polymers such as cellulose acetate, cellulose nitrate, and polysulfone. They have closely controlled pore sizes and are set up so that the flow is perpendicular to and through the membrane (with pore sizes of 0.45, 0.65, 0.8, and 1.2 μm). Membrane filters rely on their pore size to exclude larger particles (microorganisms or crystals) or partially soluble colloids (proteins, polysaccharides, or tannins and complexes involving them). They have far less capability to collect suspended matter internally in the way that filter cakes and pads do, and so generally wine is prefiltered with a depth-collection pad or cartridge or a fine grade of diatomaceous earth before it is contacted with a membrane filter. The membrane should be thought of as the capture surface for the few particles that are not collected by the prefilter. A more detailed discussion of filtration and filter testing can be found in Chapter 7.

a. *Fouling of Membrane Filters*

With the use of more extensive clarification and prefiltration, the fouling, or silting, of membrane filters is commonly due to colloidal rather than suspended components. The performance of membrane filters depends on the colloid content of the wine and the extent to which this has been modified by fermentation, fining or cold storage, or prefiltration. Many wineries do not currently perform filter testing of wines, or attempt to measure the colloid content, to be aware of troublesome filtration conditions.

The principal cause of poor membrane life with certain wines appears to be due to colloidal complexes of proteins, phenols, and other entities and of polysaccharides from grapes and yeasts. Although soluble, they have an adsorption affinity for the surface of the membrane. The practice of using warm wine temperatures (up to 25°C) during such filtrations to enhance the solubility of such colloids is not generally used. The traditional use of cold wine temperatures for the bottling of white wines and especially sweet wines only accentuates the difficulties of filtration with such wines. The fouling of membranes and pads by polysaccharides can usually be distinguished from particulate plugging by successful regeneration with hot water rinsing at neutral or higher pH. The polysaccharides are often soluble under such conditions while other particulates, commonly microorganisms or suspended particles are not.

Some of the earliest indications of the role of colloidal components on the fouling of membranes are due to studies by Berg in 1975. Unpublished reports of his data show the effects of certain colloidal fractions on the membrane throughput and the positive influence of various pretreatments such as low-temperature holding, the use of fining agents and their sequence, as well as the use of prefilters on membrane performance.

3. Preparations for Membrane Filtration

While sterile filtration can often be accomplished by use of depth pads alone, it is more commonly done with a membrane filtration following the pad filtration (Chapter 7). The pad filtration provides for removal of unwanted particulate materials before they reach the membrane, thus allowing for a high-volume throughput of wine before there is significant fouling of the membrane. The use of a membrane as a final filter also allows for integrity testing of the filtration assembly.

a. *Sterilization of the Bottling Equipment*

It must be emphasized that all equipment downstream from, and including, the filtration assembly must be made sterile; and this sterilization *must* be done by heat. Hot water, or steam, is sent through the filters and their holders, through all of the lines leading to the filler, through the filler bowl and all of the filler spouts. The recommendations are that hot water (entering at 82°C and exiting at 72°C) or live steam (with 2 cm of invisible vapor) flows out of the filler spouts for at least 20 minutes. This is not to say that 20 minutes of such heat in direct contact is required for killing microorganisms; the time has been empirically determined to be sufficient for killing all of the unwanted microbes with which the heat does not come in direct contact. In situations where the filters are distant from the filler apparatus, this time period or the entrance water temperature should be made correspondingly greater. Heat sterilization is most effective when all of the surfaces, including threads of connection fittings, are clean and free from organic material. Thus, pretreatments with detergents and sanitizing agents are highly recommended. However, it must be stressed that the sterilization of the equipment for sterile bottling cannot be accomplished by use of chemical sterilizing agents alone.

In case of failure in the quality control tests for sterility in the bottling line samples, direct microbiological investigations have to be made at various control points of the bottling line. These include standard microbiological samplings of airborne microbes in the bottling area and of bottle and cork washings. Also touch plates, or swabbings, of inaccessible areas need to be made of the filter outlet, the filler centering bell and spouts, and of the hopper, chutes, and jaws of the corker. The facilities and procedures used in the quality control tests should also be scrutinized. See Neradt (1982) for more details.

b. Integrity Testing of Membrane Filters

The bubble point and forward-flow tests are used to ensure that the membrane filter is not defective and that it has been installed correctly. These tests are based on equations used in filtration research, and in the quality control of membrane production. Nevertheless, an examination of the equations involved is helpful for a better understanding of the intricacies of membrane filtration. Recent reviews of these procedures have been given by Meier and Hoechlin (1989) and Emory (1989).

The precise relationship between the pore size of the largest pore of the membrane and the minimum pressure required to force a gas bubble through this pore (that is, the bubble point pressure), is defined by the following equation:

$$\Delta P = K4\sigma \cos \Theta / d, \qquad (11.1)$$

where ΔP is the bubble point pressure, K is a correction factor for nonideal surface contact, σ is the surface tension of the liquid being tested, Θ is the angle between the tangent of the bubble and the surface of the membrane (also the angle between the slope of the meniscus at the top of the membrane pore and the side of the pore), and d is the diameter of the pore. This equation tells us two important things about the bubble point. First, since surface tension is involved, it is important that the bubble point test be made with the same wine as to be filtered. The surface tension of ethanolic solutions is lower than that of water, and the bubble point will be correspondingly affected. Second, since the reciprocal of the diameter of the largest pore is involved, any flaw in the membrane or in improper setting of the cartridge, will provide a larger d, and thus a correspondingly lower bubble point. Of course, this is the basis of the test—if the bubble point obtained is lower than specified, something is wrong. Since something might go wrong during the filtration, it is recommended that the bubble point test be carried out again at the end of the filtration—or during break periods in filtrations of long duration.

The bubble point that should be observed for wines can be estimated from the relationship between ethanol content and surface tension. For table wines, this results in bubble points that are approximately 30% lower than the corresponding water values. While the traditional testing procedure involves the use of water for the initial determination to avoid effects of ethanol on the surface tension (and bubble point value). Most manufacturers prefer the use of water values rather than product values, but this then requires that the filters be thoroughly rinsed with water at the end of a filtration in order to perform the postfiltration check. With clean membrane filters the bubble point is directly proportional to the surface tension and the ratio of bubble points will be in the ratio of the surface tension of the product to that of water. For standard table wines with 12% v/v ethanol, the bubble point at 20°C will be 49.5/73.0 times that of water, where 49.5 and 73.0 are the relative values of the surface tensions of the ethanol solution and of water respectively. For other ethanol contents, they can be estimated from the following relationship:

$$\mathrm{BP_{20}\ wine} = \mathrm{BP_{20}\ water}\ \frac{*\exp[2.722 + 57.83/(36.85 + \mathrm{E})]}{73 \cdot 0} \qquad (11.2)$$

where E is the ethanol content in percent by volume, the exponential function is the relationship between the surface tension and ethanol content, and 73.0 is the corresponding surface tension for water.

For membrane installations with large surface areas, the gas diffusion through the membrane during the test can be significant and this leads to false bubble point determinations.

In an alternative test, the bubble point is determined by observing the change in the rate of gas permeation rather than the point of first bubble formation. A plot of the log of Q (the flow rate of gas through the membrane) against the log of ΔP (the gas pressure against the wetted membrane) gives a straight line with a shallow slope (Figure 11-1), until ΔP reached a certain point at which place there is an abrupt increase in the slope. This point of inflection is, of course, taken as the bubble point. The shallow slope at the lower pressures is the indication of gases coming through the membrane by diffusion through the liquid within the pores. With membranes of small surface area, this gas flow is negligible; but with membranes of very large surface areas, especially in cartridges with fluted membranes, the diffusion flow becomes noticeable. The fast-forward test, involving this aspect, is based on a second equation:

$$Q = \frac{\rho \cdot D \cdot \Delta P \cdot R \cdot T \cdot A \cdot \varepsilon}{MW \cdot K_H \cdot L \cdot P_d}, \qquad (11.3)$$

where Q is the volumetric flow rate of the gas (mL/s); ρ the density of the liquid (kg/m^3); K_H is the Henry's Law constant (atm) of the gas, D is its diffusivity (in m^2/s); R is the gas constant (m^3 atm/(mole K)); and T is the absolute temperature of the liquid (K). The membrane area is A (m^2), ε is the porosity (or void fraction) of the membrane; MW is the molecular weight; L is the length (m) of the liquid column through which the gas must pass, that is, the thickness of the membrane, and P_d, the downstream pressure. The porosity is indicated by the relative amount of surface area that is open (the total pore area) to the total surface area. It is to be noted that the size of any individual pore d is not included in this equation; that is, the gas flow can be substantial even before the legitimate bubble point is reached. With the initial production of these kinds of membranes, it was at first thought that the use of the bubble point test for them would become superfluous. However, with experience it was discovered that the size of the bubbles and the amount of diffused gas is usually qualitatively and quantitatively unlike the gas flow found when the pressure reaches that of the bubble point and beyond. Nevertheless, the use of the fast-forward test should be limited to personnel who have had experience with it and with the particular type of membrane to be tested.

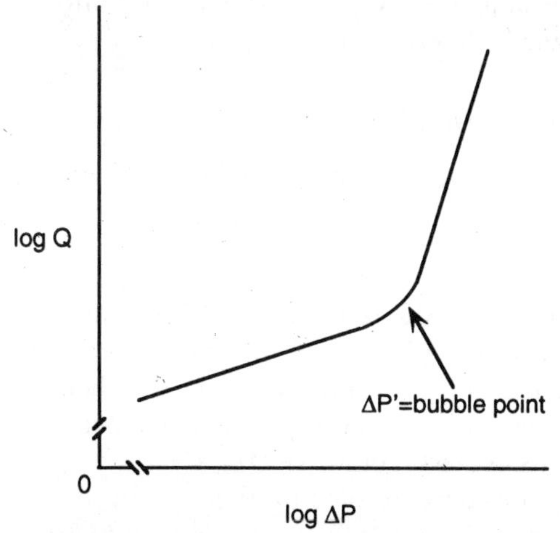

Fig. 11-1. The relationship between gas flow and pressure difference of a membrane filter.

4. Charge-Modified Filter Media

Many of the colloidal components involved in trace haze formation and membrane filter fouling are neutral or slightly negatively charged at wine pH. These are usually much smaller in diameter than the pore size of tight pads or membranes and are not removed from wine during these filtrations. There are, however, several fibrous materials which develop a surface charge under flow conditions, generally referred to as a zeta-potential and very fine negatively charged colloids can be captured and retained by this mechanism. It was the zeta-potential action of asbestos that made it a part of most filter preparation until the mid 1970s. Today, alternative polymeric substitutes, commonly cellulose acetate or cellulosic fibers, are used in many filter pad formulations and as a precoat and body feed component in earth filtrations (Berg et al. 1986). The zeta-potential mechanism provides some advantage in that there is an additional mechanism for the removal of partially soluble material, but it has some disadvantage in that it can contribute to physical instabilities in wines if it is not used correctly. A more complete discussion of this topic can be found in Chapter 7.

The properties of this type of media that are important to final filtrations and bottle stability can be summarized as follows. Firstly, the zeta-potential effect and its collection mechanism are only present when the wine is flowing across the fibers. Secondly, the exhaustion of this capturing effect is not related to the fouling of the filter and when it has been consumed there is no way to determine this either by preliminary testing or during the filtration. Thirdly, the zeta-potential generated is a function of wine velocity through the pad, pH, and temperature. While it is an advantage to be able to rinse the pad with water to recover most of the charge-modified effect, it can lead to problems if an acidic solution is used for rinsing between wines.

The use of a charge-modified filter medium when the wine will continue immediately on to either a bottling line or a membrane filter is not recommended. There will be variations with time in the residual colloidal content during the filtration. Instead, the wine should be filtered as a batch into an intermediate tank and mixed to make it uniform before the filtration through the membrane filter and into the bottles.

A more detailed discussion of the nature of colloidal properties, of complexes between the protein and peptide fractions and phenolic and polysaccharide components is discussed in Chapter 8. However, a special case of wine instability, in which the use of charge-modified filters presents a special concern, is that due to protective colloids. These colloid fractions are usually made up of a central core with an outer coating of a second component. These can be relatively stable in wine but they can be rendered unstable by depletion of the outer coating during charge-modified filtrations. The protection of cations (metallic or proteinaceous) by negatively charged polysaccharide components is the best example of such a situation. The resulting less-protected colloid fractions are then relatively unstable and again this effect often varies throughout a filtration run.

5. Dissolved Gases in Wines

Both nitrogen and oxygen are far less soluble in water (and wine) than carbon dioxide. At 0°C their solubilities in water are 23.5, 48.9, and 1797.0 mL/L, respectively. Nitrogen is the preferred inert gas to be used in tank headspace, for some transfers and sparging and for displacing air from bottles immediately prior to filling. There is some practice of using argon as the inert gas for oxygen displacement due to its low solubility and the fact that it is denser than air. The elimination of oxygen from the headspace of tanks is primarily a volumetric displacement and this is not greatly enhanced by the density of the inert gas. The stripping of dissolved oxygen from wines is not improved by the use of argon since it depends on the partial pressure of oxygen in the inert gas, not the density of that gas. The additional expense of argon is difficult to justify given this understanding.

The level of oxygen dissolved in table wines can be in the range of 6 to 9 mg/L when saturated, depending on the temperature, with higher levels at the lower temperatures. The solubility of oxygen in wine-like ethanol solutions is described by:

$$[O_2]_{diss}(\text{mg/L}) = \exp[-3.606 + 1713/(T + 273.3)], \tag{11.4}$$

where T is the temperature of the wine in °C. The effect of ethanol on oxygen solubility is slight, with an additional 4 to 5% being dissolved at wine strength and cellar temperatures (Kutsche et al. 1984).

The oxygen pickup that might have occurred during final transfers should be lowered prior to bottling in one of several ways depending on the type of wine being produced. This can be done by either gas sparging with nitrogen or carbon dioxide, by hot bottling at temperatures in the range of 30°C to 40°C or the addition of oxygen-consuming components such as ascorbic acid or its isomer, erythorbic acid. Since free SO_2 can only retard the rate of oxidation at acceptable levels (see Chapter 12), the principle control lies in minimizing the level of oxygen in the wine at the end of the bottling operation.

The level of dissolved carbon dioxide is important for reasons of sensory attributes, physical stability of the bottled wine due to its high solubility, and the response of that solubility to temperature. This feature can lead to significant changes in the headspace pressure as the temperature changes and if bottled wines are not packaged with such changes in mind. The solubility of carbon dioxide in wines is described by:

$$[CO_2]_{diss}(g/L) = \exp[-7.288 + 2244/(T + 273.3)] \quad (11.5)$$

where T is the temperature of the wine in °C. Recommended levels of carbon dioxide for bottled wines are in the range 0.2 to 0.5 g/L for aged, red wines and 0.5 to 1.8 g/L for lighter-pigmented and white wines (Müller-Späth 1982).

The levels of CO_2 and of O_2 after various filling procedures is most influenced by wine temperature and gas exposure, with a wine temperature of 15°C leading to oxygen pickup in the 0.5 to 1.5 mg/L range and that for carbon dioxide in the 0.2 to 0.4 g/L range when exposed to air or gas flushing of equipment. The level of CO_2 in wine bottles is also important from both legal and analytical considerations. Table wines made in the United States must contain less than 3.92 g/L or additional tax must be paid. This level is about twice the saturation level under a CO_2 headspace at 20°C and ambient pressure or equal to that obtained under a CO_2 headspace at 1.5 atmospheres pressure at 0°C. The solubility of CO_2 in dry wine under a CO_2 headspace as a function of temperature is presented in Figure 11-2. The level of dissolved carbon dioxide in wines can be controlled by the use of nitrogen-carbon dioxide mixtures in which the levels of 1.0 g/L CO_2 can be obtained at storage temperatures of 0°C, 5°C or 10°C by the use of blends containing 40%, 47%, or 54% CO_2 in the mixture, respectively.

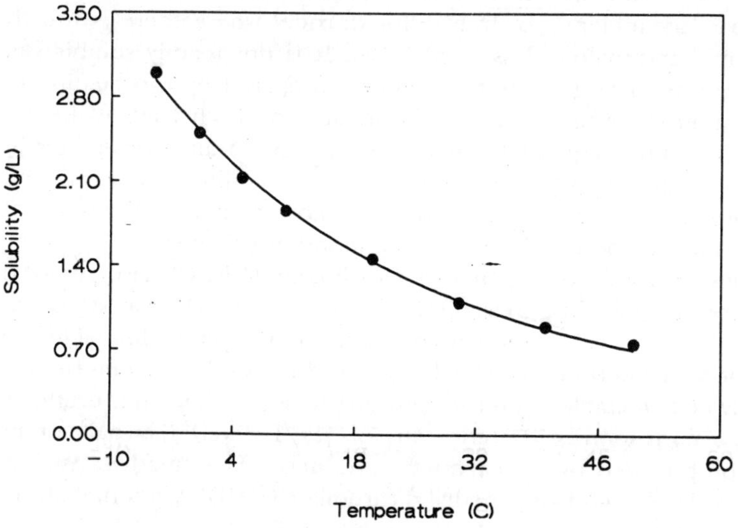

Fig. 11-2. The solubility of carbon dioxide in dry table wine at various temperatures.

An alternative description of CO_2 solubility in wines that includes terms for the effect of ethanol content and sugar level is that proposed by Lonvaud-Funel and Matsumoto (1979):

$$\ln(\alpha_v^T) = (7 \times 10^{-5}E - 0.02905)T - 0.0179E - 0.00111S + 0.51912, \quad (11.6)$$

where α_v^T is the solubility coefficient of carbon dioxide in wine (on a volumetric basis, L/L) at T °C, where the ethanol content E is expressed in % by volume and the sugar content S is in g/L. The solubility expressed as mg/L is obtained by multiplying the α value by 1977, the saturation value at 0°C.

6. Acidity Effects of Dissolved CO_2

The contribution of dissolved CO_2 to the titratable acidity of the wine can be taken to be one proton for every molecule of the CO_2. At pH 8.2 (the titration end point) almost all of the dissolved CO_2 is in the bicarbonate form, while at wine pH it is present as carbonic acid. The saturation level of 1.5 g/L CO_2 at 20°C and ambient pressure corresponds to approximately 2.6 g/L as tartaric acid in the titratable acidity of the wine. While this would be the saturation level found in wines held under a CO_2 headspace at ambient pressure, at the end of the ethanol and malolactic fermentations, the levels are usually significantly greater than the saturation levels. While this is the reason for using a hot-water titration procedure in the determination of the titratable acidity, it still provides a sensory contribution when wine at normal temperature is tasted. The desired levels of dissolved carbon dioxide in table wines are discussed in the previous section.

Even at half of this level, the contribution in titratable acidity will generally be detectable in tasting. In sparkling wines, a correspondingly higher contribution will be provided by the dissolved CO_2. Carbon dioxide also contributes, at relatively high levels, to a cooling and a prickling sensation in wines intended for thirst-quenching refreshments.

7. Chemical Additives

An alternative to the removal of yeasts and bacteria by microfilters is the use of antimicrobial chemicals such as sorbic and fumaric acids in addition to sulfur dioxide to inhibit microbial activity. The trend of the past two decades has been away from such food additives and their future is increasingly questionable. Sorbic acid is generally added as the more soluble potassium or sodium sorbate and is effective in its undissociated form ($pK_a = 4.75$), so that less is required for inhibition of most yeasts at lower pHs. Some yeasts are resistant to it so that it is not a comprehensive solution (see Chapter 9). It is usually at above threshold when used at the levels required for fungicidal action. Its use is illegal in Japan. It will not inhibit or kill bacteria, and bacterial activity, usually malolactic fermentation, in the presence of sorbate will produce the distinctive spoilage of a geranium off-odor (Crowell and Guymon 1975), (see Chapter 9).

Fumaric acid ($pK_a = 3.05$) can prevent bacterial growth, and it is the undissociated form that is the active component. It is far more effective at low pH values, at low concentrations of bacteria and with appropriate amounts of free sulfur dioxide, where there is usually less need for it. It is not readily soluble but solutions can be prepared by the heating of malic acid and this approach leads to higher solubility. It is rarely used and regulations in the United States limit additions to less than 3 g/L in wines. A more complete discussion of its use can be found in Chapter 9.

Diethyl dicarbonate (DEDC), also referred to as diethyl pyrocarbonate (DEPC), was previously used as a short-lived yeast-killing additive in wine (Ough 1983). It was banned more than 20-years ago due to suggestions that urethane (at the tens of μg/L level) was part of its breakdown products. The methyl analog, dimethyl dicarbonate (DMDC), has the advantage of not forming ethyl carbamate and has been approved for use in wines.

DMDC has a desirable feature of undergoing hydrolysis rapidly at wine pH and having no significant residual in the long term. The rate of hydrolysis is first order with respect to DMDC and has a half-time of 25 minutes at 20°C and 60 minutes at 10°C. The commercial product has the trade name Velcorin and special dosing units and handling techniques are required with its use. The dilemma with this additive is that while it is very effective at killing many strains of wine and spoilage yeasts, it is far less effective with the bacteria commonly found in wines. The levels required for various wine organisms (Ough 1983). Since the microbial count in finished wines will be made up of both yeast and bacteria and the final filtration will remove the larger yeasts more readily than the bacteria, the level of any chemical addition should be directed toward that required for the bacteria rather than the yeasts. Like most microbial inhibitors, the actual concentration and effectiveness after an addition is dependent on the number of cells present, with higher cell counts leading to significant adsorption and less than expected effectiveness.

The selection of microfiltration with perpendicular flow membranes remains the most effective and desirable alternative to these chemical additions. The use of temperature for the killing of microorganisms, in particular the application of high-temperature short-time (HTST) treatments can be effective, but there are few studies of flavor changes associated with the treatment. One study has shown that hot bottling (tunnel pasteurization) can be used to stabilize wine in small bottles (375 mL) without detriment (Malletroit et al. 1991).

B. BOTTLING OPERATIONS

Bottling systems are made up of several components and these are usually similar to bottling operations for many other beverages. The main components of such systems generally include the following: dedusting or rinsing units for bottles, filling machines (fillers), cork-inserting machines (corkers or cappers), labeling machines (labelers), and capsulating or foiling machines.

The bottling line can vary from a manual operation in which several people may be handling hundreds of bottles per hour to an automated line with two to three operators handling several hundred bottles per minute. For many small wineries, the use of a mobile bottling unit, even for sterile bottling, in which the entire bottling line is housed within a contractor's trailer, is preferable to maintaining a technically inferior or similar but expensive line for the time that it is used. Not only are the economics favorable for a small winery, but such contractors usually have considerably more experience in the operation of bottling equipment.

Some lines are set up in a straight line, with materials flowing from one end to the other, while it is also common to use a U-shaped layout with the finished bottles being returned to a point close to where they were first dumped from their cartons.

The major bottling components will generally be enclosed in a separate room specially designed for ease of cleaning (tiled floors and tiled or stainless steel paneled walls) and sometimes, a sterile atmosphere (positive-pressure, membrane-filtered air). Other considerations with respect to the bottling line will be the access of pallets and cases for both empty and full bottles and a restriction of nonessential foot traffic.

1. Quality Control

Quality control procedures are instigated to ensure that the sterile bottling has been carried out successfully; that is, that all of the unwanted microorganisms, yeast, or bacteria (Chapter 9), have been removed. It is impossible to be assured of *absolute* success, that all of the bottles are completely free from contamination, without resorting to testing *each* bottle coming off of the line. Compromises are made by testing a reasonably small proportion of the bottles. The extent of compromise is related to the previous experience of the production manager and the experience with the particular bottling line.

Before discussing compromises, we must emphasize the importance of obtaining a positive bubble point test, both at the beginning of the bottling session and at its end. Since the bubble point test is only applicable for filtration with membrane filters, this recommendation in effect says that any filtration with depth pad filters ought to be followed by filtration through a bubble point-able membrane (Chapter 7). A correct bubble point test assures that the membrane is not flawed, there are no pores of diameter greater than specified, and that the membrane has been installed correctly; but it tells nothing about the success of the sterilization treatment of the filter or of any of the equipment downstream.

In a new installation, or with new personnel, it is reasonable to remove bottles from the line for testing very often, certainly at the beginning and end of the run, and after temporary shutdowns and breaks, and several times an hour during the run. Indeed, when sterile bottling was first being introduced in California some 25 years ago, the dread of failure was compensated for by overzealously testing. With the spectacular success of this procedure, the production line managers are now content with much less sampling. One rule of thumb is to sample a dozen bottles of wine from every pallet, the bottles being removed at random. Earlier, the entire contents of the bottles were taken for testing, but nowadays it is more usual for only one or two filter holders (one-half bottle) of wine to be passed through the test membrane.

The bottled wines removed from the line are sometimes tested for contamination immediately or allowed to accumulate for several days and then tested all at one time. For the testing, the contents of the bottles are filtered under sterile conditions through a 47-mm-diameter membrane. For this, the corks are removed partway, with the use of a corkscrew, after the bottle neck (without capsule) has carefully been dipped into alcohol (methanol, isopropanol, or 70% ethanol) and flamed. The process is repeated until the cork is completely removed and the neck of the bottle is then directly flamed. The filter holder and screen can be easily sterilized in a boiling water bath for 15 minutes. The base of the holder is generally surface-sterilized with one of the above alcohols. Membranes usually are purchased as sterile, but they can also be sterilized in boiling water. The membrane is then aseptically removed from the filter holder and placed on a nutrient medium. Agar plates can be used as the nutrient support medium, or hermetically sealable dishes, 47-mm diameter containing a filter pad onto which 1.5 mL of sterile medium is added, are also available. Malt extract or wort media are used for testing for yeast, and apple Rogosa medium for bacteria (Appendix F). For detection of yeast, the plates can be incubated at room temperature or up to perhaps 30°C; but for bacteria, the plates should be incubated no higher than 23°C to 25°C. Colonies from healthy wine yeasts will appear in three days; bacterial colonies, especially lactic acid bacteria, may take as long as 10 days. Colonies from sorbate- or DMDC-treated wines will require five days of incubation. For success, no colonies should appear. It has been demonstrated that if only a few colonies appear, the wine is probably stable, since the chances of growth in the unfavorable environment of wine is much less than that on the nutrient medium used for testing (Neradt 1982). However, in fact, it is routine to find the formation of no colonies. If that is the baseline, then the sudden appearance of a few colonies should be cause for alarm. Common situations giving negative quality control results are: inadequate heating of the filter and equipment, having the bottling equipment too far from the filters, failure to sterilize makeup water used to cool the equipment, an O-ring in a filling spout not receiving sanitization and sterilization treatments, failure to heat continuously (sterilize) the corker jaws, and inadequate sanitation or sterilization of the microbiological laboratory space and equipment.

Procedures for rapid detection, at least for yeast, have been presented (Kunkee and Neradt 1974), but none of them has shown itself suitable as routine procedures under production situations.

2. The Bottling Room

The bottling room should be a dustfree environment, often maintained under a positive pressure of filtered air. This will usually require at least some outside air to be introduced rather than simply recycled air. The growth of organisms on the exposed surfaces of bottling equipment has not been shown to be a major contribution to contamination at the point of bottling but the reduction in the number of airborne organisms would seem to reduce this risk (Neradt 1982), especially if the bottling area is close to the fermentation areas. The room is generally tiled or lined to allow for the ongoing wash down and sanitization on a daily basis. The most critical stage of the bottling operation is the path of the open bottles from the filler to the corker since they are least protected against airborne contamination at this point. Stainless steel canopies are relatively inexpensive and their use to cover the distances between the units is recommended. Another advantage of an isolated bottling room is to control the insensitive foot traffic: production and management personnel and visitors.

3. Dedusting and Rinsing of Bottles

Bottles generally contain some dust and/or cardboard fibers when they are first removed from their cartons. These fibers can be removed by inverting the bottle and directing either an air or a water jet into the bottle neck. This is usually done with the aid of an inverting railing on a continuous line or rinsing by hand as part of a manually operated line. When made, glass bottles are sterile and may retain both cleanliness and sterility if shrink-wrapped and quickly used.

The use of sulfite solutions for the sanitizing of bottles was widely practiced for many years, but is rarely used today, being replaced with peracetate solutions, which generate peroxide, or by ozone-generating systems (Zürn 1982). Sterilization is particularly important with reused bottles (Cooke 1977) or new bottles that have been stored, and with certain water supplies, including make-up water used for cooling after heat sterilization of equipment.

4. Filling Machines

The fillers on continuous lines take the bottles, which are supplied from the moving trays on one side and positioning them underneath the filling head to initiate the filling procedure. The bottle is usually taken in a complete circle from the point where it was picked up. The base plate, on which the bottle stands, is raised (triggering the valve in the spout to open) and filled. Once filled, the bottle is lowered, shutting off the valve in the filling spout, and repositioned on the conveyor and advanced toward the corker. Most fillers can be modified with interchangeable parts to handle a range of bottle shapes, heights, and volumes.

Fillers can be separated into gravity, counterpressure, and vacuum/counterpressure units. As the names imply, they employ different forcing conditions prior to and during the filling operation. The gravity fillers range from small hand-operated units (with six to 10 spouts) to large continuous units (40 to 120 spouts). The filling is driven by the difference in level between the wine in the filler bowl and that in the bottle by a syphoning action.

Some special problems with reinfection have been found with pressure fillers (Neradt 1982), especially with older ones where there is a pressure release into the atmosphere. This air movement and atomizing of wine can lead to contaminated valves. The newer pressure fillers have release channels with central outlets which avoids this misting into the surroundings. Other problems can occur when the wine temperature is much lower than that of the ambient air. Here condensed water can form in the filler bowl, run down the side, and collect at the centering bell rim. In the presence of stray yeast, this will infect the valves and the bottle mouth rims. It is also important that in fillers, where the wine from overfill bottles is returned to the filler bowl, that the return bowl be small to allow a quick washout of any chance contamination from a stray contaminated bottle.

Counterpressure units seal the bottle once it has engaged with the filling spout and the pressurized wine enters the bottle against a restricted gas-venting valve. The vacuum/counterpressure units draw a vacuum to assist in the filling before the application of pressure to slow the final stage of the filling operation.

While the total volume of wine in each bottle must be that indicated on the label, overfilling is wasteful and leads to problems with the control of headspace pressures (the gas volume between the wine level and the closure) after corking. The customer often dislikes bottles showing different fill heights, so it is important to provide stated volumes, uniform fill levels, and normal headspace in each bottle. Too much headspace suggests a short fill or leakage since filling, while too little headspace (< 5 mL in a 750-mL bottle) leads to wider pressure fluctuations with temperature changes and perhaps cork movement or leakage.

5. Corks and Cork-Insertion Machines

Corks, with their highly irregular surfaces, are essentially impossible to sterilize, even those which have had the cavities smoothed. Nevertheless, the current treatment of exposure of damp corks in sealed plastic bags to SO_2-gas seems to inactivate any wine-related microorganisms. However, this treatment has little or no influence on the penchant for individual corks to induce the formation of a corky taint in wine (Chapter 10) Section 6.

The corker takes the filled bottle and positions it beneath the corking plunger. The jaws of the corker then radially compress the cork to a diameter that is smaller than the bottle neck. It then pushes the compressed cork into the bottle neck with a single swift plunging movement, so that the top of the cork is flush with the top lip of the bottle. The corkers differ according to whether they do or do not draw a vacuum in the headspace before the cork is inserted. If a vacuum is not drawn, the cork displacement (typically 14 to 15 mL for a 24-mm long cork) will cause compression of the headspace into approximately half its original volume with a corresponding increase in bottle and headspace pressure of close to two atmospheres. In vacuum corkers, the vacuum is often of the order of 0.3 to 0.6 atm so that the resulting pressure is approximately atmospheric after the cork is in place.

The surfaces of the cork jaws, receiving spilled wine from overfilled bottles, can be one of the most serious sources of recontamination of corks—and thus of infections of sterile wines. To prevent this, corkers are available with corker jaws designed to be heated, to about 80 to 90°C, either by means of hot air blowers, internal electric elements, or gas burners (Neradt 1982). The heated jaws can be an anathema to production line managers since they tend to cause problems with paraffin- or silicon-treated corks. In our experience the most common source of microbial instability in supposedly sterile wine has come from the discontinuation of heating of the cork jaws.

6. Labeling Machines

The traditional labeling operation involves the attachment of a glued front label to the bottle, with options for the attachment of a back label and a neck label as required. The continuous labeling machines remove a bottle from the line and during one cycle of its rotation, pick up a label, apply glue to it, place the label onto the bottle, then brush it around the bottle before returning the bottle to the main line. There is now a general trend toward the use of self-adhesive labels, peeled from a backing paper as they are applied, which eliminate the troublesome gluing operation. More advanced labeling units can also place a back label and/or a neck label on during this operation.

7. Capsulators and Foiling Machines

The final operation is to place a plastic cover (or metal foil) over the corked bottle and to shrink this tight by heat (or to spin tighten it) onto the bottle. The placement is often done by hand even for automated lines while the spinning (or shrinking) is done by the machine. The cap or foil are applied for cosmetic reasons and to cover any wine that may have splashed or mold growth that may appear on the outer face of the cork.

8. Gas Exchange During Bottling Operations

The transfer of wine from the bottling tank through a final filter and into the filler bowl can be accomplished with a minimum of oxygen pickup if steps are taken to control the gas atmosphere which contacts the wine. The concerns relate to the pickup of oxygen from the air during the filling of the bottle and prior to the cork insertion. The wine will most likely dissolve oxygen while it streams down the bottle wall or as it falls to the base in a fine spray. Under these conditions, the transfer area between the wine and the gas in the bottle is many times that experienced at any other time during the bottling operations. The mass transfer is greatly enhanced by the turbulent nature of the wine and gas movements as the wine displaces the gas from the bottle.

The partial pressure of the oxygen in the gas phase in the bottle is a crucial factor in the extent of the oxygen pickup during this operation, as is the temperature of the wine. The rate of absorption will be proportional to its partial pressure. The temperature will influence the oxygen solubility in the wine, with lower temperature having higher solubility. It is rare for a wine to reach the saturation level of 6 mg/L, but between 0.5 and 1.5 mg/L is not uncommon under commercial conditions.

The release of dissolved carbon dioxide by the wine during filling can serve to reduce the partial pressure of oxygen and the gas transfer from the headspace. However, it will generally be more of a problem due to bubble formation and foaming than a benefit. Gas release can be controlled during filling conditions by employing lower wine temperatures, but often there will be significant heating of the wine from the ambient temperature of the bottles, especially for the wine near the wall. The previous handling of the wine will determine if the carbon dioxide is near saturation levels at this point.

The bottle may have been previously flushed with nitrogen or carbon dioxide and the completeness of air volume displacement will determine the partial pressure of oxygen that exists in the headspace during the filling process. The ideal gas-displacement situation is one in which the nitrogen is delivered to the base of the bottle and there is practically no back-mixing of the air with the incoming gas. This would essentially be a piston-like displacement with a minimum of back-mixing leading to a theoretical requirement of one volume of nitrogen per bottle, and the oxygen concentration in the bottled wine would be practically zero. The actual gas-flushing operation attempts to accomplish this ideal situation with fast gas-flushing rates. The turbulent gas flow causes significant mixing of the incoming and exiting streams, reducing the effectiveness of the gas used. The time available for flushing is also a consideration with high-speed lines. Under a completely intermixed situation, the oxygen concentration would only fall to about one-third of its initial value with the first volume of nitrogen. A second volume, if used, would reduce the concentration to about one-ninth of its initial value. The oxygen concentration in air can give rise to approximately 9 mg/L of dissolved oxygen in cold wine if it reaches equilibrium. The single-volume, turbulent gas flush would result in a potential of 3 mg/L dissolved oxygen to remain after filling, while after a second volume of flushing, the potential concentration would be at the 1-mg/L level. A third volume should lead to potential concentrations of 0.3 mg/L after filling.

The actual gas-flushing operation achieves something between the ideal and the mixed situations depending on the type of filler employed, and there is a range of partial saturation conditions experienced in practice.

The impact of oxygen pickup can be seen in the potential for 1 mg/L of oxygen to react with as many as 8 mg/L of total sulfur dioxide over the weeks that follow. The change in the free sulfur dioxide content will depend on the extent to which acetaldehyde has been formed during this period and the proportions of free and bound forms in the wine. Many wines will have the capability to consume the majority of the oxygen present by reactions with the phenolic components (or added ascorbate) in the days that follow bottling. If, however, there has been significant previous oxidation during winemaking, the short-term, oxygen uptake capacity of the wine will be lowered and more of the oxygen consumption will fall to the slow reaction with the available sulfite and a corresponding increase in the amount of total sulfur dioxide lost.

9. Pressure in Filled Bottles

The pressure that exists within filled bottles is influenced by several factors. In table wines, the major factor is the gas compression that occurs when the cork is inserted without an adequate vacuum being drawn in the neck of the bottle. The amount of this compression is determined by the volume from the wine surface to the top of the bottle and the length of the cork. The other contributions are the compression of the headspace gas caused by thermal expansion of the wine, the vapor pressure that results from the ethanol and water components, and the increase in headspace gases associated with any previously dissolved gas that comes out of solution at warm temperatures. (In sparkling wines, bottle pressure is dominated by the dissolved carbon dioxide that has been kept in solution during corking by the use of close-to-freezing temperatures and the avoidance of the filling step.)

a. *Pressure Changes due to Increasing Temperature*

The effect of an increase in wine temperature is to increase the bottle pressure, but these pressure changes have several components to them. The first is that of liquid expansion causing an increase in headspace pressure, a pressure increase for noncondensable gases due to temperature alone, increases in the vapor pressures of ethanol and water due to temperature, and changes in the solubility of carbon dioxide causing further gas pressure. The increase in vapor pressure with temperature due to the water and ethanol components is shown in Figure 11-3.

For example, the thermal expansion of wine is approximately 0.8% between 20°C and 40°C and in a 750-mL bottle, such a rise in wine temperature results in a loss in headspace volume of 6 mL and increasing headspace pressure by 1.67 times, assuming a headspace of 15 mL. The effect of temperature on the noncondensable gas components is 303/293, or a 7% increase from that at 20°C, as predicted from the ideal gas law, while the effect on the vapor pressures of water and ethanol is an exponential function with an approximate change of threefold over this range. The combined effects of these components can be evaluated for particular situations with perhaps the largest variation coming from the extent of the dissolved carbon dioxide concentration.

b. *Pressure Changes due to Decreasing Temperature*

In contrast to the above situation, wine cooling will generally lead to lower bottle pressure as wine contraction and carbon dioxide solubility increase. An exception to this trend occurs when the wine begins to freeze and significant volume expansion and gas release oc-

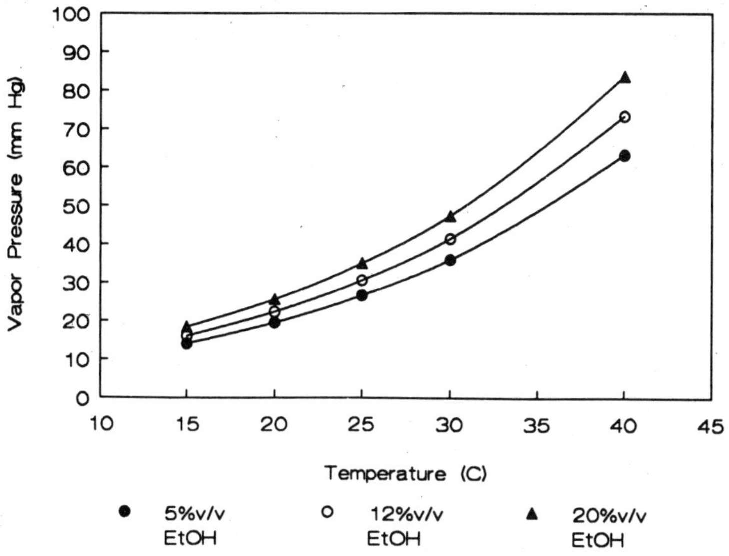

Fig. 11-3. The effect of temperature on the vapor pressure of table wine.

cur due to ice formation. This can result in more than twice the pressure increase that results from warming a bottle from 20°C to 30°C. This is because the ice formed has essentially no gas in it and this gas displacement has a greater effect than the increased gas solubility at lower wine temperatures. For this reason, the precaution to consumers against storing a bottle of sparkling wine, with its wired stopper, at freezing temperatures to avoid an explosion, must be taken seriously.

c. *Pressure Changes due to Freezing*

The analysis of the cooling of bottles (Section C.2 of this chapter) suggests that when exposed to freezing conditions, the narrowest section of the bottle, that is the neck, will be the quickest to cool and the first to form ice if the surroundings are cold enough. If the freezing continues until bottle breakage, the most likely location for bottle fracture is around the base, depending on the uniformity of the bottle wall thickness. The rupture can also occur at the wall, depending on the freezing conditions and the wall thickness.

The expansion of water into ice as it freezes will cause the headspace to be reduced by approximately 60 mL in a 750-mL bottle, but this will rarely happen since the resulting increase in ethanol content will lower the freezing point of the remaining solution. Even at partial freezing, of say 10%, the headspace will be reduced by 6 mL due to ice formation alone. With a headspace of 15 mL this will cause the internal pressure to increase by a factor of at least 1.67, into the range that will cause corks to be displaced.

The headspace gas itself will be slightly reduced in volume due to temperature effects, but this represents only about a 7% reduction in pressure from 20°C to 0°C. The dissolved carbon dioxide will be released from the 10% that forms ice while the pressure rise and lower temperature will cause more to become dissolved. Its solubility increases by approximately 50% over this temperature range. As a result, it is common for the cork to be partially pushed from the bottle, breaking its seal and conformation to the bottle wall and permitting air influx and possible wine leakage when thawing occurs.

10. Other Operations

A number of other operations may be associated with the bottling sequence, but these usually have to do with the logistics of warehousing and shipping rather than bottled wine.

These range from stacking cases in particular ways (bottles placed upright versus bottles inverted), to coding labels, bottles, and cases with bottling dates and times, and to stacking cases in preferred arrangements or providing plastic wraps or bands to retain the cases within the stack during pallet movements.

The practice of stacking cases so that the bottles are in the upright position is widely practiced and it aims to provide time for the cork to recover into its new shape and to allow any excess bottle pressure to be vented. The time required for the cork to fully recover from its compression at the time of insertion is generally thought to be less than 24 hours. The alternative practice of stacking cases so that the bottles are in the inverted position immediately after bottling also has its practitioners, where the belief is that the wine contact with the cork is to keep the cork moist and swollen, without the possibility of drying out. The control of cork moisture content to narrow limits (typically 5 to 8% by weight) prior to use involves storage in atmospheres that are less than saturated (50 to 70% relative humidity). The headspace within an upright bottle would be essentially at 100% relative humidity after corking and the corks would normally be in a swollen state even without wine contact. The other consideration of bottle inversion is the detection of faulty closures due to poor quality or damaged corks or excess bottle pressures caused by malfunctioning filling or corking machines.

C. TRANSPORT AND STORAGE CONSIDERATIONS

The most dramatic effects on bottled wines are those due to the storage temperature and the daily and seasonal variations associated with it. There is a tendency to generalize about the rates of reactions proportional to temperature over small temperature ranges such as those involved in the storage of wines (5° to 30°C). While wine will not deliberately be held at temperatures above 20°C, there will be instances when wines placed in rooms or vehicles during the summer months can experience temperature in excess of 40°C for significant times.

1. Storage Temperature and Temperature Variations

While the rates of the most reactions that can occur in bottled wines increase with increasing temperatures, this effect is nonlinear and increases quickly even at moderate temperatures. The rate of oxygen uptake reactions in a white wine (Ribéreau-Gayon 1933) can been shown to have an apparent activation energy of 137.7 kJ/mole, while those associated with browning reactions in white wines (Berg and Akiyoshi 1956, Ough 1985) have apparent activation energies of 66.4 and 74.6 kJ/mole respectively. The rates of decline in total sulfur dioxide (Ough 1985) display apparent activation energies of 35.7 in red wine and 13.4 kJ/mole in white wine, indicating different rate-controlling steps in the disappearance reactions. Based on these values, and our general knowledge of the exponential nature of the rate increases, the relative rate of these reactions at temperatures other than 10°C can be estimated and these are summarized in Table 11-1. For the browning reaction in white wines, the rates are 2.5 to 3 times faster at 20°C then at 10°C and between 15 and 20 times faster at 40°C. The rates of decline in total sulfur dioxide in the red wine is considerably more sensitive to warmer temperatures than that of the white wine, but both rates are less sensitive to temperature than the browning reactions. Although bottled wines will not usually have significant oxygen in the headspace, the greatly enhanced rate of oxygen uptake at warmer temperatures shows why even short exposures to air can be disastrous during the storage or transfer of wines.

Of additional concern is the cyclic variation in storage temperatures, especially those on a daily basis. The concern is one of variations in bottle pressure caused by the thermal expansion and contraction and secondary effects of

Table 11-1. The relative rates of selected reactions in wines.

Reaction	Relative rate[1] at temperature (°C)						
	5	15	20	25	30	35	40
Oxygen Uptake (Ribéreau-Gayon 1933)	0.35	2.76	7.35	18.9	47.3	114	270
Browning (Berg and Akiyoshi 1956)	0.60	1.63	2.62	4.13	6.42	9.84	14.9
Browning (Ough 1985)	0.57	1.73	2.94	4.91	8.07	13.0	20.7
Total SO_2 decline:							
Red wine (Ough 1985)	0.76	1.30	1.67	2.15	2.72	3.43	4.28
White wine (Ough 1985)	0.90	1.10	1.21	1.33	1.46	1.59	1.73

[1]Relative to the rate at 10°C.

increased vapor pressure and diminished carbon dioxide solubility associated with such cycles. The development of bottle pressures of the order on 0.67 to 1.0 atm over ambient are approaching those which can cause cork movement or headspace venting and the subsequent cooling and contraction and vacuum can then permit air introduction to the bottle.

2. The Cooling and Warming of Bottled Wine

Typical examples of heat transfer to and from bottled wines would be those associated with the chilling of a bottle in a refrigerator (or an ice bucket) or the exposure of bottles to heating or cooling conditions during transportation or storage in a warehouse. The following methods are presented to enable the calculation of the cooling (or warming) times for bottles exposed to sudden changes in the temperature of the surroundings.

There are two calculation procedures that can be used to evaluate these unsteady heat transfer situations. Both assume that the conductive heat transfer within a bottle is essentially that found in an infinite cylinder, that is a cylinder that is several diameters long. The first is the use of a graphical solution known as a Gurney-Lurie chart to estimate the temperature at some radial position, such as at the center of the bottle as a function of time. The second is the use of a series expansion to compute the average temperature of the wine in the bottle as a function of time.

a. *Gurney-Lurie Charts*

These charts were developed by Gurney and Lurie in (1923) to provide a graphical solution of the unsteady heating or cooling of fluids and solids in various geometries and for conditions under which there is significant resistance to heat transfer at the surface. Reproductions of these charts can be found in most heat transfer texts such as Kern (1950) and Foust et al. (1960). These charts plot the dimensionless temperature in terms of the radial location in the cylinder and the ratio of surface resistance to thermal conduction. They are especially useful in estimating the time for which annular sections of a bottle have been at a given temperature.

There are a number of other graphical solutions of the unsteady heat transfer to shapes such as cylinders and spheres, but these usually assume that there is negligible resistance to transfer at the surface. Examples of these are the solutions of Carslaw and Jaeger (1959) (also given in Bird et al. (1960)) from which the temperature distributions within the bottle (the cylinder) could be estimated for the special case of water or liquid immersion. More useful versions of the Gurney-Lurie charts that estimate the centerline temperature and provide better interpolations are the Heisler charts (Hayes 1987). These charts are redrawn versions the original Gurney-Lurie charts but use a linear temperature scale that provides better graphical estimates at short times.

The unsteady cooling of a wine bottle can be approximated to that of a cylinder whose length is several times its diameter. The Gurney-Lurie (and Heisler) charts relate the fractional temperature change (usually expressed as the dimensionless temperature change) at some radial position, to a variable referred to as the dimensionless time. The dimensionless temperature is the temperature change that has occurred at some time divided by the ultimate temperature change at steady state. The dimensionless time is simply the actual time scaled by a group of system properties whose product has the units of time. Two graphical charts, both for estimating the center temperature of bottles, one for water-bottle conditions and the other for air-bottle conditions, are presented in Figure 11-4a.

For a bottle, the dimensionless time is expressed as $4\alpha t/D^2$, where D is the diameter of the bottle and α is the thermal diffusivity $(k/\rho/C_p)$ of the wine. The temperature at any

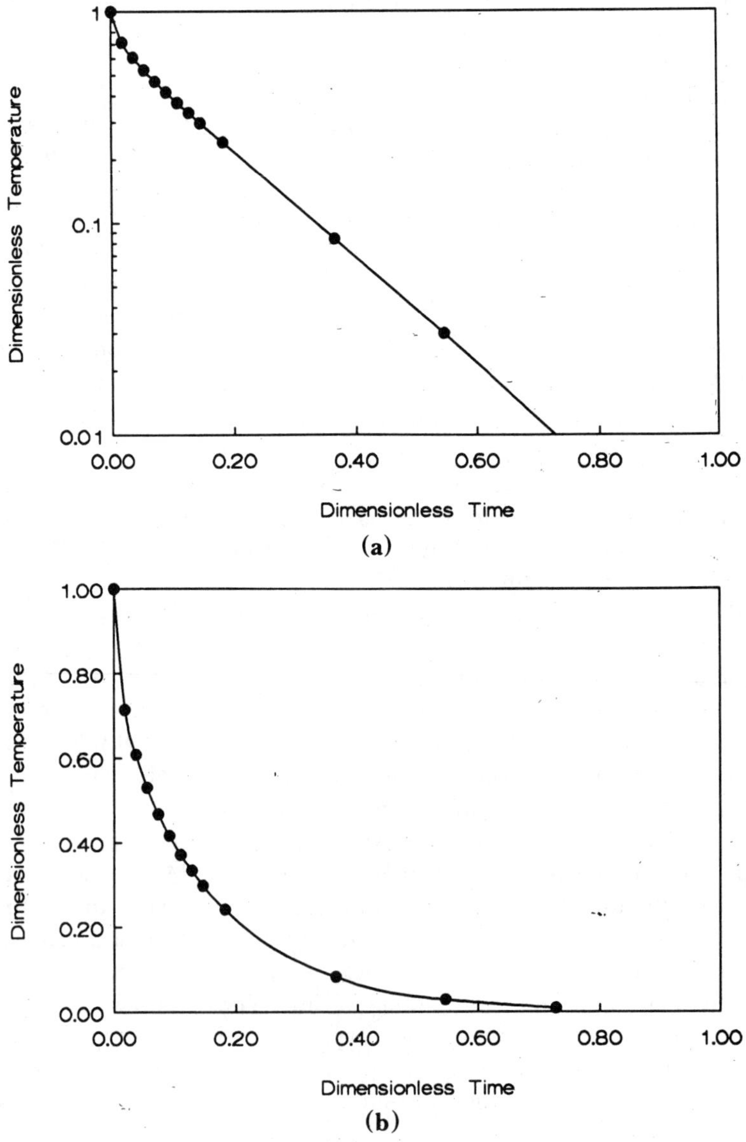

Fig. 11-4. The cooling curves for the average temperature of a wine bottle—Dimensionless form: (a) Logarithmic scale; and (b) Linear scale.

radial position in the bottle can be expressed in terms of the outside water temperature T_w and the initial wine temperature T_i. For the estimation of the temperature at the center of the cylinder T_c, the dimensionless temperature becomes:

$$Y = [T_w - T_c]/[T_w - T_i].$$

Another dimensionless group known as the Nusselt number N_{Nu}, becomes the parameter that determines the way in which the temperatures within the bottle will change with time. The Nusselt number is the product of the heat transfer coefficient at the outer wall h to the thermal conductivity of the wine k scaled by half the diameter:

$$N_{Nu} = hD/(2k),$$

and it represents the ratio of the rate of transfer of energy at the bottle surface to that accumulating within the bottle by conduction.

If the wine is considered to be at the ambient temperature of 15°C and in a standard 750-mL glass bottle, the cooling time will be measured from the time at which it is immersed into the ice bucket, which is assumed to contain a mixture of water and ice that has equilibrated at 0°C. The physical and thermal properties can be found in Table 11-2.

$$N_{Nu} = hD/2k = 81.5$$

for T_c = 10 and 5°C

$$Y = [T_o - T_c]/[T_o - T_s] = 0.674 \text{ and } 0.332$$

from chart, Figure 11-4a

$$[4\alpha t/D^2] = 0.177 \text{ and } 0.329$$

that is 132 and 246 minutes.

By repeating the calculation for other times, the temperature pattern for the center of the bottle can be obtained as shown in Figure 11-4b. It can be seen that under these conditions, the center temperature has fallen to 10°C and 5°C at times of 132 and 246 minutes.

Table 11-2. Properties and Conditions Used In Bottle Cooling Example.

Wine thermal conductivity, k = 0.536 W/mK
Wine heat capacity, C_p = 4.50 kJ/kgK
Wine density, ρ = 990 kg/m^3
Wine thermal diffusivity, $\alpha = k/(C_p\ \rho) = 1.20 \times 10^{-4}$
Bottle diameter, D = 75 mm
Initial wine temperature, T_i = 15°C
Water-ice temperature, T_w = 0°C
Surface heat transfer coefficient, h, = 1100 W/m^{2}K

The corresponding cooling of a bottle placed in a refrigerator, where the air is now the cooling medium and a much poorer transfer coefficient is in effect, indicates that the center temperature will require 280 minutes to fall to 10°C and 640 minutes to reach 5°C. The same kind of calculation can be performed for other radial positions within the bottle by using the appropriate position line on the original charts.

b. Series Expansion Approach

Of more general interest in many situations is the relationship between the average temperature of the wine and time. This can be calculated from the analytical solution for the unsteady heat transfer into a long cylinder (McCabe and Smith 1967). The dimensionless temperature is now written:

$$Y = [T_w - T_{av}]/[T_w - T_i],$$

and its value at any time is calculated from the following series:

$$Y = 0.692 \exp(-5.7 * N_{Fo}) + 0.131 \exp(-30.5 * N_{Fo}) + 0.0534 \exp(-74.9 * N_{Fo}) + \cdots \quad (11.7)$$

where $N_{Fo} = \alpha\ t/R^2$ and is known as the Fourier Number, and T_{av} is the average temperature of the cylinder. The Fourier number represents the ratio between the rate of energy transfer by conduction to that accumulating within the element.

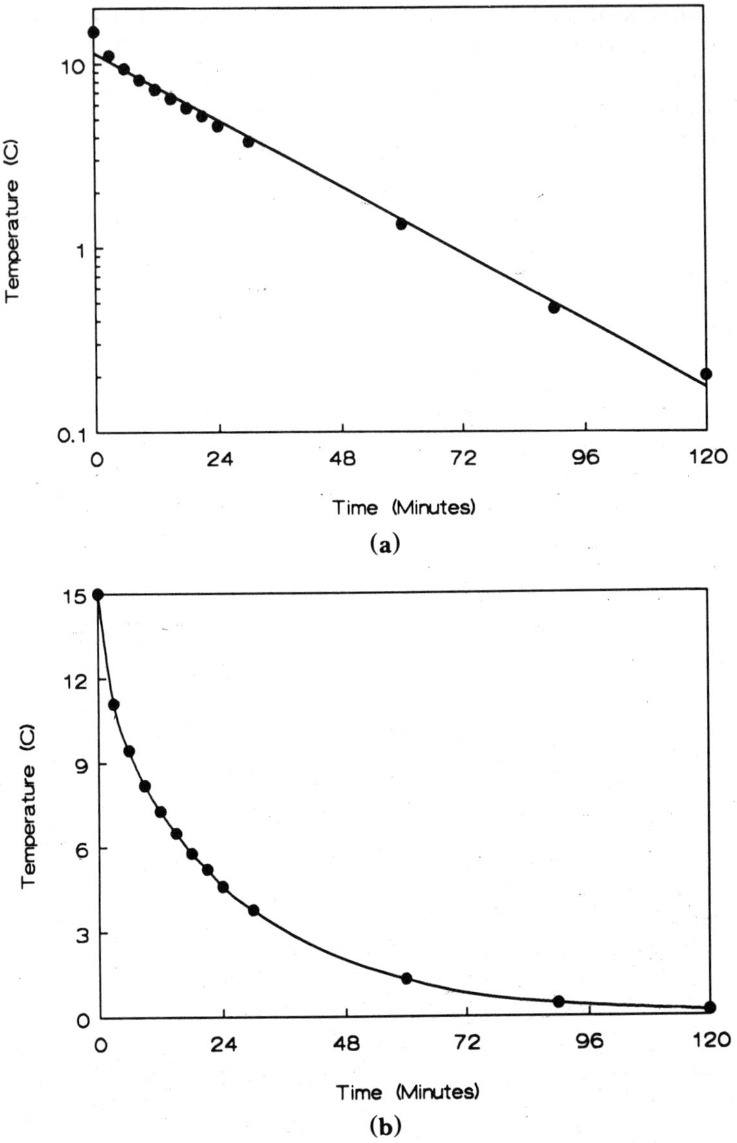

Fig. 11-5. The cooling curve for the average temperature of wine bottle (initially at 15°C into ice water at 0°C). (a) Logarithmic scale; and (b) Linear scale.

The calculated temperature history for the cooling of a bottle, that has been placed in an ice bath, is presented in dimensionless form in Figure 11-5a and as actual temperature in Figure 11-5b. In this example, with an initial temperature of 15°C, the average wine temperature has fallen to approximately 10°C after 18 minutes and to approximately 5°C after 96 minutes. This is considerably faster than the decline in center line temperatures that require 132 and 246 minutes to reach these values. The average temperatures are heavily weighed by the colder temperatures of the regions closer to the wall.

The calculation procedures presented here can be generally applied to analogous heating conditions. Conditions under which the heating or cooling is by air rather than water should only use the graphical approach since there will be significant resistance to heat transfer at the surface. A surface coefficient of approximately 5 W/m^2/K is suggested for this case.

D. REFERENCES

BERG, H. W., and M. AKIYOSHI. 1956. "Some factors involved in browning of white wines." *Am. J. Enol.* 7:1–7.

BERG, L. A., G. GODWIN-AUSTIN, and K. ROBISON. 1986. "Effect of fibers added during pressure leaf filtration on the membrane filterability of white table wines." *Am. J. Enol. Vitic.* 37:174–178.

BIRD, R. B., W. E. STEWART, and E. N. LIGHTFOOT. 1960. *Transport Phenomena*, p. 357. New York: John Wiley & Sons.

CARSLAW, H. S., and J. C. JAEGER. 1959. *Conduction of Heat in Solids*, p. 200. Oxford, UK: Oxford University Press.

COOKE, M. J. 1977. "Encore! and bottle recycling." *Wines & Vines* (4):48.

CROWELL, E. A., AND J. F. GUYMON. 1975. Wine constituents arising from sorbic acid addition and identification of 2-ethoxy-3,5-diene as a source of geranium-like off odor. *Am. J. Enol. Vitic.* 36:97–102.

EMORY, S. F. 1989. "Principles of integrity-testing hydrophilic microporous membrane filters." *Pharm. Technol.* 13(9):68–77 and (10):36–46.

FOUST, A. S., L. A. WENZEL, C. W. CLUMP, L. MAUS, and L. B. ANDERSEN. 1960. *Principle of Unit Operations*, p. 133, New York: John Wiley & Sons.

GURNEY, H. P., and J. LURIE. 1923. "Charts for estimating temperature distributions in heating or cooling solid shapes." *Ind. Eng. Chem.* 15:1170–1172.

HAYES, G. D. 1987. *Food Engineering Data Handbook*, p. 55. New York: John Wiley & Sons.

KERN, D. Q. 1950. *Process Heat Transfer*, p. 653. New York: McGraw-Hill.

KUNKEE, R. E., and F. NERADT. 1974. "A rapid method for detection of viable yeast in bottled wines." *Wines & Vines* (12):37–39.

KUTSCHE, I., G. GILDEHAUS, D. SCHULLER, and A. SCHUMPE. 1984. "Oxygen solubilities in aqueous alcohol solutions." *J. Chem. Eng. Data* 29:286–287.

LEE, T. H., G. H. FLEET, P. R. MARK, D. WIBOWO, C. R. DAVIS, P. J. COSTELLO, and T. HENICK-KLING. 1984. "Options for the management of malolactic fermentation in red and white table wines." *Proc. Int'l. Symp. on Cool Climate Viticulture and Enology*, Corvallis, OR, pp. 496–515.

LEE, T. H., and R. F. SIMPSON. 1992. "Microbiology and chemistry of cork taints in wine." In *Wine Microbiology and Technology*, G. H. Fleet, Ed. Chur, Switzerland: Harwood Academic Publishers.

LONVAUD-FUNEL, A., and N. MATSUMOTO. 1979. "Le coefficient de solubilité du gaz carbonique dans les vins." *Vitis* 18:137–147.

MALLETROIT, V., J.-X. GUINARD, R. E. KUNKEE, and M. J. LEWIS. 1991. "Effect of pasteurization on microbiological and sensory quality of white grape juice and wine." *J. Food Process. Preserv.* 15:19–29.

MCCABE, W. L., and J. C. SMITH. 1967. *Unit Operations of Chemical Engineering*, 2nd ed. p. 291. New York: McGraw-Hill.

MEIER, P. M., and J. HOECHLIN 1989. Microbial stability with membrane cartridge filtration. *Pract. Winery Vineyard* (Nov/Dec): 25–30.

MÜLLER-SPÄTH, H. 1982. "Die Rolle der Kohlensaure beim Stillwein." *Weinwirt.* 118:1031–1037.

NERADT, F. 1982. "Sources of reinfections during cold-sterile bottling of wine." *Am. J. Enol. Vitic.* 33:140–144.

OUGH, C. S. 1983. "Dimethyl dicarbonate and diethyl dicarbonate." In *Antimicrobials in Foods*, A. L. Branen and P.M. Davidson, Eds., pp. 299–325. New York: Marcel Dekker.

OUGH, C. S. 1985. "Some effects of temperature and SO_2 on wine during simulated transport or storage." *Am. J. Enol. Vitic.* 36:18–21.

RIBÉREAU-GAYON, J. 1933. Contribution des oxydations et reductions dans les vins. Application a l'etude du viellisement et des casses. Doc. thesis, Bordeaux, France: University of Bordeaux.

ZÜRN, F. 1982. "Flaschensterilisation mit Ôzon." *Weinwirt.* 118:793–794, 796–797, 800.

CHAPTER 12

The Role of Sulfur Dioxide in Wine

While the use of sulfur dioxide in winemaking dates back to Egyptian and Roman times (Bioletti 1912), the full extent of its role in wines is often not understood because of the multiple activities and reactions in which it is involved. It had been estimated in the early part of this century that the free forms possessed approximately 50 times the antiseptic activity of the bound forms (Bioletti 1912). While most of the sulfur dioxide found in wine is deliberately added to the must, juice, or wine, significant amounts are normally produced by yeast during fermentation (Weeks 1969; Bidan and Collon 1985).

The physical and chemical reactions of interest include the killing and growth inhibition of unwanted bacteria and yeast, the inhibition of phenoloxidase activity, the interaction with wine phenols in the competitive oxidation, the reaction of sulfite with peroxide, the binding of acetaldehyde, pyruvate, keto-glutarate, and the anthocyanin pigments, and the delay of brown pigment development. A knowledge of the rate and extent to which sulfur dioxide is involved in these reactions is crucial to the selection of appropriate timing and level of addition as well as the evaluation of any alternative treatment options that would replace it in winemaking.

This chapter attempts to describe the behavior of sulfur dioxide by developing a comprehensive description of its properties in order to provide a better understanding of its physical, chemical, and microbial activities.

A. PHYSICAL PROPERTIES

1. Solubility

Sulfur dioxide is a gas under normal conditions with a molecular weight of 64.06, a liquid density of 2.93 g/L at 0°C, and a normal boiling point of −10°C. It is very soluble in water with solubilities ranging from 228.3 g/L at 0°C, 162.1 at 10°C, and 112.9 at 20°C to 78.1 at 30°C. Expressed another way, approximately 40 volumes of gas are soluble for each volume of water at 20°C and 55 volumes of gas for each volume of water at 10°C. The solubility at 0°C is 77,918 mL/L compared to those of oxygen, nitrogen, and carbon dioxide which are 48.9, 23.5, and 1797.0 mL/L, respectively.

The influence of temperature on the solubility is considerable and is of practical importance. It can be used to advantage in the rapid preparation of solutions from sulfur dioxide gas at lower temperatures. It is also important to realize that a solution saturated at 10°C, but warmed up to 20°C has the potential to release approximately 50 g/L (or some 15 volumes of gas per volume of solution) of sulfur dioxide gas. When sulfur dioxide solutions are held in a gastight vessel this can cause the internal pressure to rise to several atmospheres and to present a hazard on opening, while in a loosely capped container it will result in considerable leakage of the gas into the surroundings. It is for these reasons that sulfur dioxide solutions should be stored in suitable pressure canisters in a low-temperature environment and in a ventilated situation. Alternatively, solutions can be made up from either gas or crystalline forms as needed, rather than being stored for extended periods of time. The exposure limits for sulfur dioxide in the workplace are given in Appendix E.

2. Ionization

Sulfur dioxide, when dissolved in water, is a moderately strong acid with pK_a values of 1.77 and 7.20 (King et al. 1981), while in juices and wines there are solvent and ion effects. The first dissociation constant in the presence of ethanol and ions has been calculated (Usseglio-Tomasset and Bosia 1984) and shown to be closer to 2.0 under wine-like conditions. A more complete discussion of the solvent and ion effects can be found in Chapter 15. In aqueous solutions, the pH at saturation is approximately 0.8 at 20°C. The dissociation curves are shown in Figure 12-1.

The hydrated SO_2, or the molecular form, is the major form at pH values below 1.86. Previously this undissociated form was called sulfurous acid and written H_2SO_3 which is not correct (Schroeter 1966; Wedzicha 1984). The first ionized form, HSO_3^-, is referred to as the bisulfite or monohydrogen sulfite ion and is the major form at pH values between 1.86 and 7.18 (and consequently in juices and wines). The second ion form, $SO_3^=$, the sulfite ion, is the dominant species at pH values above 7.18. There is spectral evidence of other ion forms such as the metabisulfite ion ($S_2O_5^=$) in aqueous solution (Schroeter 1966) but there is little

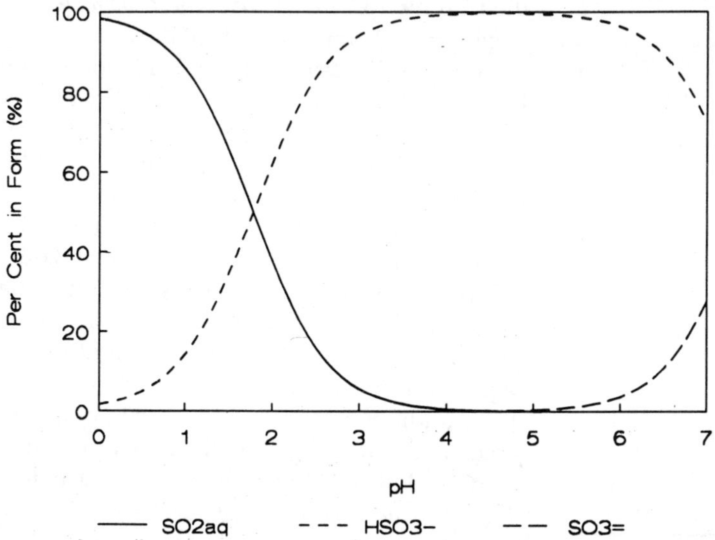

Fig. 12-1. The dissociation diagram for sulfur dioxide in 14%(v/v) ethanol, 80-mM ion strength.

data about the extent of this formation and published ionization constants and other calculated physical properties have been developed considering this to be insignificant.

The percentage of free sulfur dioxide in various ion forms in the range of interest to winemaking is shown in Table 12-1 together with the level of free SO_2 required to maintain a molecular concentration of 0.825 mg/L. The basis for wanting to maintain the molecular concentration at such a level is discussed in Section B.1 below.

a. The Molecular Form

The molecular form is the most important species in winemaking since it is the form responsible for the primary antimicrobial activity which prevents spoilage (Rahn and Conn 1944; Rhem 1964; Macris and Markakis 1974; Beech et al. 1979; King et al. 1981), for the capturing of hydrogen peroxide and for the sensory detection of sulfur dioxide in the headspace vapor above wines that contain it. It is this volatility that is responsible for the evaporative loss of sulfur dioxide from wines (and solutions) either under the natural circumstances of barrel aging or the deliberate conditions established as part of the aeration oxidation method of analysis (Ough and Amerine 1988). Within the pH conditions of wine, there is only a very small fraction of the free sulfur dioxide in this form and this changes by more than an order of magnitude over the range of wine pH, from 6% at pH 3.0 to 0.6% at pH 4.0. As a result, the antimicrobial effectiveness and peroxide trapping capability of a free sulfur dioxide concentration of 6.6 mg/L at a pH of 3.0 is equivalent to that of 20 mg/L at pH 3.5 or 66 mg/L at pH 4.0. The same concept can be applied to the headspace concentration, which is directly related to the molecular concentration rather than the free sulfur dioxide level.

Table 12-1. The percentage of sulfur dioxide forms in solution at various pH values. Solution conditions are 14% v / v ethanol and 80 mM ion strength.

pH	Molecular SO_2	Bisulfite ion	Sulfite ion	Free SO_2 for 0.825 mg/L molecular
2.7	10.5	89.5	0.00283	7.85
2.8	8.54	91.5	0.00364	9.66
2.9	6.90	93.1	0.00467	12.0
3.0	5.56	94.4	0.00596	14.8
3.1	4.47	95.5	0.00759	18.5
3.2	3.58	96.4	0.00964	23.1
3.3	2.87	97.1	0.0122	28.8
3.4	2.29	97.7	0.0155	36.0
3.5	1.83	98.2	0.0196	45.1
3.6	1.46	98.5	0.0248	56.5
3.7	1.16	98.8	0.0312	71.1
3.8	0.924	99.0	0.0394	89.3
3.9	0.736	99.2	0.0497	112.0
4.0	0.585	99.4	0.0627	141.0

b. The Bisulfite Ion Form

It is the bisulfite form that is perhaps the least desirable from the enologist's viewpoint because it is involved in the binding with the carbonyl oxygen atoms of acetaldehyde, the keto acids, glucose, quinones, and with the four position carbons of monomeric anthocyanins of red wines making them colorless. These products are responsible for the bound fraction of the total sulfur dioxide found in wine. These bisulfite addition compounds are generally referred to as hydroxy-sulfonates and their binding properties are discussed in more detail below. At wine pH, that is the range 3.0 to 4.0, the proportion of free sulfur dioxide in the bisulfite form rises from 94 to 99%, with a maximum at approximately pH 4.5.

One positive aspect of the formation of the hydroxy-sulfonates is the binding of acetaldehyde that is formed as a result of oxidative reactions that occur during aging. Acetaldehyde will be bound by any free sulfur dioxide present and will be unable to contribute to the aroma of the wine. By adding sulfur dioxide, oxidized aldehydic white wines can often be made more acceptable. Another advantage is the interference in the development of brown pigments from phenolic compounds, both under conditions of enzymatic oxidations in juices and chemical oxidations in wines. It is thought that it either reduces the first oxidation products (quinones) back to phenols and/or forms quinone addition products that are colorless. In either case, it interferes with and delays the development of the brown melanin polymers. Both of these reactions result in the loss of free sulfur dioxide. The reduction of quinones results in the formation of sulfate and a loss of total sulfur dioxide, while the formation of additional compounds leads to an increase in bound sulfur dioxide (if the compound is hydrolyzable) or a loss in total sulfur dioxide if it is not hydrolyzable.

The hydroxy-sulfonates are generally considered not to be microbially and chemically active forms, yet they account for the majority of the total sulfur dioxide found in wines. They are especially troublesome when it comes to the analysis of the free sulfur dioxide content. This is because some of them display hydrolysis rates that are significant in the time of analysis and this results in an overestimation of the actual free sulfur dioxide pool in wine.

One recent study of the inhibition of the phenoloxidase enzyme (Sayavedra-Soto and Montgomery 1986) concludes that it is the bisulfite form that is responsible for the irreversible inactivation and inhibition of this enzyme. Using labeled sulfite, in the pH range 4 to 7, it could be shown that the sulfite was released from the enzyme complex after the inactivation. This suggests that exposure and contacting alone might be adequate for the inactivation of this enzyme in juices and there may be nonresidue approaches that can be used for this treatment in the future.

c. *The Sulfite Ion Form*

This is the antioxidant form and it is at very low concentrations under wine pH conditions. While the sulfite ion reacts rapidly with oxygen in aqueous systems at higher pH, its ability to consume dissolved oxygen at wine conditions is limited by the very low concentrations of the ion, typically at the 1- to 3-μM level and perhaps a slowing of the rate due to the presence of ethanol. One study of sulfite oxidation under model wine conditions (Poulton 1970) showed that the time required for the consumption of half of one saturation of oxygen was close to 30 days. Unfortunately, this is not comparable to the rate of consumption with natural wine constituents where the half-time has been shown to be approximately two days for a white wine and presumably less for a red wine. As a result, there is essentially no oxygen-consuming capability provided by free sulfur dioxide under wine conditions. The reaction of the molecular form with hydrogen peroxide, however, appears to be much faster than that of the sulfite form with oxygen (Halperin and Taube 1952). It is this reaction that is responsible for the quenching of the peroxide produced during the oxidation of certain phenols and the retardation of acetaldehyde formation and browning in wines. The sulfite is thought to react with quinones to form monosulfonates under wine pH conditions (Lu Valle 1952).

3. Volatility

The vapor phase concentration above solutions containing free sulfur dioxide is the most important feature from the evaporative loss and the sensory point of view. The vapor pressure is proportional to the concentration of molecular form in the solution and not simply the free sulfur dioxide concentration. As a result, the vapor phase concentration at pH = 3.0 is three times that of the same solution at pH 3.5 and 10 times that of the solution at pH = 4.0 (Table 12-1).

The relationship between the concentration of the molecular form in solution and the partial pressure in the vapor is generally expressed by Henry's Law:

$$VP_{SO2} = K_H[SO_2]_m, \qquad (12.1)$$

where VP is the vapor pressure of sulfur dioxide in mm of mercury; K_H is the Henry constant, and $[SO_2]_m$ is the molecular sulfur dioxide concentration in the liquid, expressed as g/L. The Henry constant is a measure of the volatility of a component and is useful in this context for understanding the evaporative loss and odor of sulfur dioxide in juices and wines.

Some references (e.g., Sherwood (1925) and Foust et al. (1960)) note that sulfur dioxide does not obey Henry's Law, but these original measurements have not been corrected for the influence of concentration on the ionization and pH of the resulting solutions. The Henry constants calculated from these measurements are based on total solution concentrations and are not based on the molecular sulfur dioxide concentrations. The data of Sherwood (1925), when corrected for the concentration and ionization effects, provide the calculated values of this constant at several temperatures, as shown in Figure 12-2. Aqueous solutions do obey this equation at concentrations greater than 1 g/L, but there is a need for more complete data at levels below this, which include typical wine levels. Sherwood's data indicated that at 20°C, the Henry constant is approximately 540 for concentrations between 500 mg/L and 100 g/L, but increases to 1100 at 200 mg/L. The actual value at concentrations as low as 25 to 50 mg/L is not presently known, although the pattern would suggest that the Henry constant would be greater than 1000. Data for the solubility of sulfur dioxide in ethanol solutions is also needed.

The influence of temperature on the volatility, K_H, is well described by the following relationship:

$$K_H = 1.759 \times 10^8 \exp\left[\frac{-3587}{T + 273.3}\right], \quad (12.2)$$

where T is the temperature in °C. This relationship indicates that the volatility doubles for a temperature increase of 20°C and can be used in phase separation calculations and design procedures for processes aimed at removing sulfur dioxide from wines and juices.

4. Sensory Thresholds

As noted above, it is the molecular form of the free sulfur dioxide in wine that is in equilibrium with the vapor or headspace above the wine. For this reason, the sensory contribution of a particular free sulfur dioxide content is both temperature- and pH-dependent. Reported thresholds for sulfur dioxide are 10 ppm in air, and 15 to 40 mg/L in wine (Amerine and Roessler 1983), although since the molecular form is involved, this would depend on the pH. There appears to be considerable variation in the detection threshold concentration for sulfur dioxide among individuals, with some people having much less ability to detect or identify it.

The effect of temperature on the vapor pressure of sulfur dioxide is especially impor-

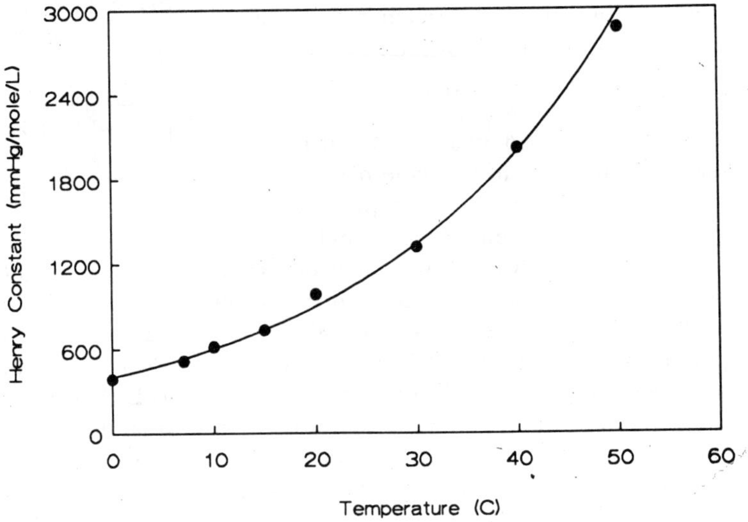

Fig. 12-2. The effect of temperature on the Henry constant for sulfur dioxide.

tant for sensory considerations. It forms a basis for the well-known practice of serving wines that are low in pH and high in free sulfur dioxide at colder temperatures in order to suppress the headspace concentration of this component.

5. Preparations

The most convenient form in which to prepare and add sulfur dioxide is in the form of concentrated aqueous solutions, usually either 5 or 10% by weight. These can be made up from gaseous sulfur dioxide by sparging into chilled water or on a weight basis by the direct addition of liquid SO_2 using a set of scales. It can also be made from the addition of salts, commonly as potassium metabisulfite, since acidic conditions such as those in a juice or wine are needed to release SO_2 from such salts.

The preparation using gaseous sulfur dioxide should be made by bubbling the gas into a partially filled closed container, but vented with a filling tube. The gas is introduced into cold water through a stainless steel porous sparging tube. The vapor from the vessel vent should be trapped in a lime solution because of the personal hazards associated with this gas at these concentrations. A saturated solution at 20°C contains 11.3% SO_2 by weight; this solution is convenient for the preparation of 10% working solutions. The use of colder water will favor the solubility and reduce the vapor phase concentration since the vapor pressure is approximately halved for each 20°C decrease in the temperature.

Preparations made from stored metabisulfite and sulfite salts are unreliable due to the rapid oxidation of sulfite to sulfate if the salt is exposed to the moisture and oxygen of the air. The salts are alkaline in their own solutions and will quickly lose sulfite due to oxidation at these conditions.

a. *Density Determination*

The concentration of sulfur dioxide in the working solution is commonly determined by a density measurement, typically using a hydrometer, and the reference densities are shown in Table 12-2 (Willson et al. 1943), although other data is available (Schopper and Aerny 1985).

This method is subject to errors from the density contribution of existing dissolved salts unless distilled or completely deionized water is used. It also requires a temperature measurement for a correction at temperatures other than 20°C. The sample volume required for such a determination is usually between 100 and 200 mLs. The density at 20°C has been expressed as the apparent Brix, so that the hydrometers generally available to winemakers can be used for these determinations.

The density method cannot be used with the preparation from salts unless additional corrections are made for the density contribution of the cations introduced. For example, with potassium metabisulfite, $K_2S_2O_5$, the extract contributed by the potassium ions will be almost 40% of the density reading.

Table 12-2. The density of sulfur dioxide solutions at 20°C.

Sulfur Dioxide Concentration (% Weight)	Solution density[1]	Apparent degrees Brix
0.5	1.001	0.30
1.0	1.003	0.92
1.5	1.006	1.53
2.0	1.008	2.15
2.5	1.011	2.76
3.0	1.013	3.36
3.5	1.016	3.96
4.0	1.018	4.56
4.5	1.020	5.16
5.0	1.023	5.76
5.5	1.025	6.35
6.0	1.028	6.94
6.5	1.030	7.53
7.0	1.032	8.11
7.5	1.035	8.69
8.0	1.037	9.27
8.5	1.039	9.84
9.0	1.042	10.42
9.5	1.044	10.99
10.0	1.047	11.56

[1] *Source of data:* Willson et al. (1943).

b. Spectrophotometric Determination

An alternative method of establishing the concentration of sulfur dioxide in the working solutions is to measure the absorbance of a sample of the solution with a UV-visible spectrophotometer. The cuvette should be sealed to prevent sulfur dioxide vapors from escaping and causing damage to the instrument.

The absorbance at a wavelength of 295 nm is related to the concentration of the molecular form with insignificant contributions from the bisulfite and sulfite forms. The molar extinction of the molecular form has been determined to be 297.89, while that of the bisulfite ion is 1.13 (Tenscher 1986). The concentration can be determined by diluting a sample into the range of 0 to 1 absorption units (or 0 to 2 or 0 to 5, depending on the spectrophotometer used), referring to Table 12-3 and correcting for the dilution factor. This method is not interfered with by the presence of ions from any salt preparation or those present in the water used, is less sensitive to temperature, and requires a much smaller sample to be drawn for testing, typically 1 to 2 mL.

The relationship between the concentration of dissolved sulfur dioxide and absorbance at 295 nm is based on a prediction of the pH of aqueous sulfur dioxide solutions together with the calculation of the molecular and bisulfite forms from the first ionization equation by ignoring the second dissociation. The absorbance is not linear with the sulfur dioxide concentration due to the more extensive ionization in the more dilute solutions. The calculation also assumes that there are no significant basic salts in the water such as carbonates or phosphates.

The effect of temperature on this estimation procedure is primarily that of the dissociation constants and it is quite small when compared to those involved with the density determination. The need for dilute solutions can be avoided by using thin 1-mm pathlength cells. The absorbance of typical working solutions can then be determined directly and will be far less sensitive to the interferences noted above. Figure 12-3 provides the absorption values at 295 nm for working concentrations of sulfur dioxide solutions based on the calculation procedure outlined above.

Table 12-3. Calculated absorbances of dilute sulfur dioxide solutions at 20°C.

Sulfur Dioxide (g/L)	Solution pH	Absorbance at 295 nm
0.10	2.84	0.041
0.20	2.57	0.140
0.30	2.42	0.278
0.40	2.32	0.444
0.50	2.24	0.633
0.60	2.18	0.840
0.70	2.13	1.061
0.80	2.09	1.296
0.90	2.05	1.541
1.00	2.02	1.796
2.00	1.81	4.680

B. CHEMICAL PROPERTIES

1. Antimicrobial Action

The antimicrobial activity of sulfur dioxide in wines and juices is due primarily to the molecular form, although there is some evidence of weaker secondary effects due to the acetaldehyde-bound sulfur dioxide species. There are a number of studies that have investigated the antimicrobial action of sulfur dioxide and most have used wine organisms. Unfortunately, most of them have been performed in defined media without ethanol, some at pH values of 4 and above, and several have involved short-term exposure but enumerated after two or three days of plate growth.

There are studies that have shown a loss of cell viability while others show an inhibition of growth. In several yeast studies there is an initial delay or enhanced lag phase due to the presence of free sulfur dioxide, but this is usually followed by growth at normal rates once this phase is completed (Schanderl 1959). In many of the studies, the initial conditions of sulfur dioxide levels are established, but not

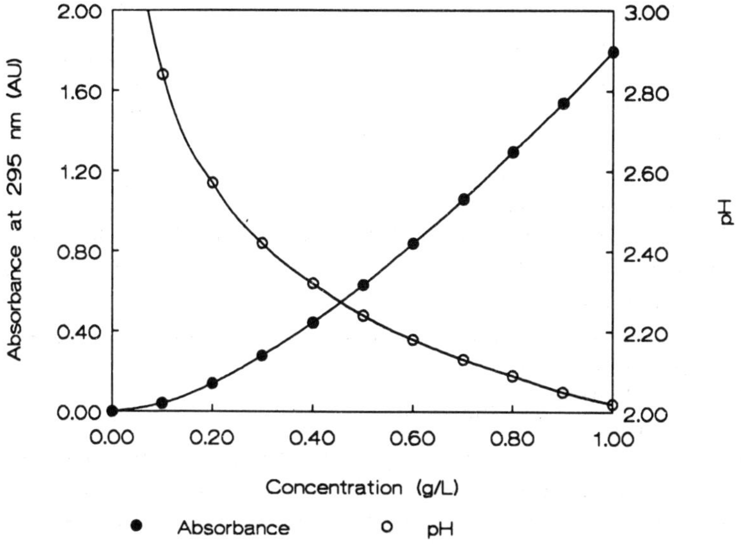

Fig. 12-3. The estimated absorbance and pH of aqueous sulfur dioxide solutions.

monitored throughout the experiments and rarely analyzed at the end. As a result, effects such as bisulfite binding by cell products and evaporative loss have not been taken into account and the effects observed are usually attributed to the initial concentration.

There are age-related effects on the sensitivity of wine yeast strain to sulfur dioxide and it is presumed that this is generally true of wine bacteria and other spoilage organisms. In winemaking, the applications will range from the prevention of growth of existing cells in juices and musts where there is no ethanol to the prevention of growth or the killing of existing populations of spoilage organisms in wines after the malolactic fermentation. Cruess (1912) observed differences in the sensitivity of different yeasts and bacteria to added sulfur dioxide, and in the following sections the studies relating to yeast and bacteria will be considered separately.

a. *Yeast*

The studies involving yeasts have been in better agreement as to the role of the molecular form. The mechanism(s) of the killing action is not clear, although there are several suggestions and several effects have been demonstrated in vitro. As mentioned previously, some studies have shown an increase in the delay before growth and this may be due to the secretion of components such as acetaldehyde or keto acids until the sulfur dioxide is bound and then normal growth begins (Minarik 1978). The age of the culture also has a dramatic effect on the susceptibility with late exponential or transition cultures showing far more resistance than early exponential cultures (Schimz 1980; Katchmer 1990).

The study by Macris and Markakis (1974) used labeled sulfur dioxide to show that its removal from the solution by *Saccharomyces* was rapid (in less than two minutes). The effect of concentration followed a Michaelis-Menton type of curve and they assumed that this was evidence of enzyme-mediated transport and uptake. However, binding of any of the forms to sites on the outer membrane could also show such a time scale and the same response to concentration. They also showed that the amount of binding was proportional to the molecular sulfur dioxide concentration. Schimz and Holzer (1979) proposed that sulfur dioxide was binding to a membrane-bound ATPase causing uncontrolled loss of cellular ATP and, hence, cell viability. Cell membrane binding rather than transport is supported by the studies of Anacleto and Van Uden (1982), who reported the presence of multiple binding sites. Other studies have concluded that it is the molecular form that enters the cell by diffusion (Stratford and Rose 1986), but the temperature responses of the transport rates do not support this. They found the fastest rates of uptake at the lowest concentrations and the temperature dependence was not what would be expected of a diffusion-controlled mechanism.

The toxicity associated with the acidic forms of sulfite solutions was noted in early studies by Müller-Thurgau and Osterwalder (1915) and Perry and Beal (1920), although attributing it to the molecular form appears to be a later realization by Rahn and Conn (1944) and Vas (1949). In studies with *Saccharomyces cerevisiae*, Rhem and Wittmann (1962) concluded that the molecular form was several hundred times more toxic than the bisulfite form. The viability experiments of Macris and Markakis (1974) involved contact times of between five to 30 minutes, followed by washing and plating for three days at 30°C. They demonstrated a relationship between molecular concentration and loss of viability, as have King et al. (1981) and Uzuka and Nomura (1986) with *Saccharomyces cerevisiae* using washing and plating methods.

Of particular interest to winemakers is the level of molecular sulfur dioxide that is necessary for the prevention of growth of typical wine yeast and bacteria. The existence of different survival patterns of log-phase growing cells and stationary-phase cells to sulfite has been noted with yeast (Schimz 1980) and at conditions similar to those in wine (64 mg/L SO_2 and pH of 3.35). The recommended levels are based on estimates of the killing concentration with adjustments for the cell count and medium from which they were derived. Table 12-4 summarizes the level of molecular sulfur dioxide required to eliminate viable yeast. The absence of good mathematical descriptions of the rate of killing prevent the analysis of alternative concentration-time combinations that would lead to the more effective use of sulfur dioxide.

Table 12-4. The molecular sulfur dioxide requirements for control of *Saccharomyces cerevisiae.*

Author(s)	Medium	Molecular SO_2 (mg/L)
Macris and Markakis (1974)	medium	1.3
Minarik (1978)	juice	6.4
Beech, et al. (1979)	model wine	0.825
King et al. (1981)	medium	1.56
Sudraud and Chauvet (1985)	wine	1.5

b. *Bacteria*

The literature concerning the antibacterial properties of sulfur dioxide is more complicated than that for yeast. There are several studies indicating a more significant contribution due to the bound forms (Fornachon 1963; Lafon-Lafourcade and Peynaud 1974; Hood 1983) and some evidence that levels of free sulfur dioxide can inhibit growth without any decline in viability (Hammond and Carr 1976), while at higher levels declines in viability are observed.

It is important to realize that in addition to the effect of either free or bound forms of sulfur dioxide on the survival of many bacterial strains, there is an extra contribution due to pH alone in many of these studies. There are no direct comparisons of the effects of pH on the growth and viability of these organisms so that our comments are limited to the role of the molecular and bound forms. Clearly, any reference to the antimicrobial activity of free sulfur dioxide in wines must include a description of the pH conditions that also exist.

Early suggestions that acetaldehyde-bound sulfur dioxide might be inhibitory to bacteria came from Bioletti (1912), Fornachon (1963), and Rhem, Wallnofer and Wittmann (1965). In a high-pH (4.2) supplemented juice medium Fornachon found inhibition of the growth of *Lactobacillus hilgardii* and *Leuconostoc mesenteroides* when an excess of acetaldehyde was present. These organisms consumed some of the acetaldehyde present, releasing free sulfur dioxide that prevented further growth. However, a strain of *Lactobacillus arabinosus* failed to grow in the presence of 100 mg/L bound sulfur dioxide. Lafon-Lafourcade and Peynaud (1974) found effects on both growth and malolactic fermentation due to both free and bound sulfur dioxide at pH of 4.8. Under wine conditions (pH = 3.5), they found that 10 mg/L of acetaldehyde-bound sulfur dioxide reduced growth significantly, but not completely, while at the 30-mg/L level, loss of viable cells occurred. They found the malate degradation by a *Leuconostoc gracile* (*L. Oenos*) to be more affected by both forms than that of a *Lactobacillus hilgardii* and the bound form to be about half as effective as free sulfur dioxide. Mayer et al. (1975) found Leuconostoc oenos to be especially sensitive to levels of aldehyde-bound sulfur dioxide in the 20 to 60 mg/L range.

The bacteriostatic effect at levels of free sulfur dioxide below 1.5 mg/L molecular was observed over three days with *Lactobacillus plantarum* at pH values of 3.4 and 4.0 (Hammond and Carr 1976). Hood (1983) demonstrated that as little as 6 mg/L of acetaldehyde-bound sulfur dioxide was inhibitory to growth of a *Leuconostoc oenos*, *Lactobacillus brevis* and *Pediococcus pentosaceus* at low pH (3.4). He also showed that the *Leuconostoc oenos* was more susceptible to the presence of acetaldehyde-bound sulfur dioxide, but this could have been due to the release of free sulfur dioxide on the consumption of acetaldehyde or its sensitivity to the bound form.

The most significant studies of the loss of cell viability are those in which short-term viability reductions were measured for a range of wine-related organisms (Beech et al. 1979). They determined the levels of sulfur dioxide required to reduce a nongrowing yeast (or bacterial) population by 10,000 viable cells/mL over a 24-hour period. These experiments were conducted in buffered solutions at 10% v/v ethanol, and the values reported are generally applied to table wines of 12 to 14% v/v ethanol without any correction, due to our limited understanding of the effect of ethanol. The investigation showed that a molecular level of 0.825 mg/L was required for one *Saccharomyces cerevisiae* strain and the levels required by other test organisms are presented in Table 12-4.

The higher levels required for particular strains of *Zygosaccharomyces bailii* and *Lactobacillus plantarum* (Table 12-5) are not used since they are of less importance in wine spoilage owing to the effects of ethanol. The sensitivity of the spoilage yeast *Brettanomyces* to sulfur dioxide is the major feature in the control strategy for this organism in wines today. These aspects are covered in more detail in Chapter 9. Additional information concerning the antimicrobial effects of sulfur dioxide can be found in the reviews by Ough (1983), Beech and Thomas (1985), and Romano and Suzzi (1992).

c. *Short-Term Viability Reduction*

There are apparently no published values of the corresponding killing requirements at other ethanol levels or for a number of the more common wine bacteria. These would be particularly useful for the improved microbial protection of low-ethanol and fortified wines. It would also provide a more quantitative approach to the conditions required to prevent the malolactic fermentation in certain wines as well as the better protection of wines after it.

The results of two other studies of the short-term survival of yeast indicate the above recommendations (0.825 mg/L molecular) to be conservative since typically more than half of the yeast viability was lost within the first 30 minutes at a concentration of 0.80 mg/L

Table 12-5. Examples of the molecular sulfur dioxide requirements for the elimination of cell viability.

Organism	Molecular SO_2 requirement (mg/L)
Saccharomyces cerevisiae	0.825
Brettanomyces	0.825
Zygosaccharomyces bailii	1.50
Lactobacillus plantarum	4.0

Source: Adapted from Beech et al. (1979).

molecular (Uzuka and Nomura 1986). These yeasts were sampled during the exponential growth phase under anaerobic conditions. This very rapid killing is similar to the results of Macris and Markakis (1974), who took growing yeast and found a decade reduction time (the time to reduce the viable population by 90%) of 83 minutes with a molecular concentration of 0.025 mg/L. This corresponds to approximately 30 minutes to reduce the viable population by 50%, in agreement with Uzuka and Nomura (1986). The reduction of viable cells by 10^4 cells per mL in a 24-hour period (Beech et al. 1979) corresponds to an average decade reduction time of six hours at 0.825 mg/L molecular while the data reported by King et al. (1981) indicate decade reduction times of approximately 20 hours. The wide variation in these values points out the need for more investigation of the short-term viability effects under wine conditions.

d. Descriptions of Death Kinetics

The death kinetics of many organisms can be described by a first-order form that applies to the killing by sorbic acid and hypochlorite:

$$dX_v/dt = -k_d X_v \qquad (12.3)$$

where X_v is the viable cell concentration, and k_d is a rate constant for death that depends on environmental conditions such as the concentration of the disinfecting agent, pH, and temperature. This expression is generally referred to as Chick's law (Bailey and Ollis 1977) and when integrated, it leads to the following relationship between the viable fraction and time:

$$X_v = X_t \exp(-k_d t), \qquad (12.4)$$

where X_t is the total cell concentration.

When the logarithm of the viable cell count (expressed as a fraction of the total) is plotted against time, this death relationship provides a linear plot with a slope of minus k_d. The thermal death of wine yeasts at elevated temperatures follows this relationship (Van Uden et al. 1968), but the rates become insignificant at ambient conditions.

The rate of killing of wine yeast does not follow Chick's law, but instead shows a falling sigmoid curve in many situations. This can be interpreted as being due to several subgroups of the population with different survival abilities or different sensitivity due to cell age or the extent of scarring. At short times and high cell viability, the rate of killing is low, but at intermediate times and viabilities it increases rapidly before slowing again at long times and low viabilities. This kind of relationship is found both with the death caused by ethanol as well as that caused by sulfur dioxide.

The most rigorous criterion for levels of sulfur dioxide to be used in winemaking will be that related to the concentration time conditions required for the most tolerant fraction of the population. There is a need to improve our understanding of the death rates of yeast in order to better quantify the temporal effects of such additions, to manipulate the levels of this compound in a more effective manner, and to better consider alternative exposure and contacting options in the future.

One recent study has shown that such curves can be described by an empirical description known as the Gompertz equation:

$$N_v = a \exp[-b \exp(k \cdot t)], \qquad (12.5)$$

where N_v is the viable fraction of yeast at time t, with the following constants: $a = 107.368$, $b = 0.071$, and $k = 0.101$ (Uzuka et al. 1985; Uzuka and Nomura 1986). The decline in viability with time corresponding to these values is shown in Figure 12-4.

The Gompertz description has been used to describe the behavior of a number of traits in populations of several species, especially for death relationships in actuarial studies, and might be useful in future studies of the death rates of wine organisms. The more usual situation of exponential death occurs when the death rate is proportional to the number of viable cells (Equation 12-3). One interpreta-

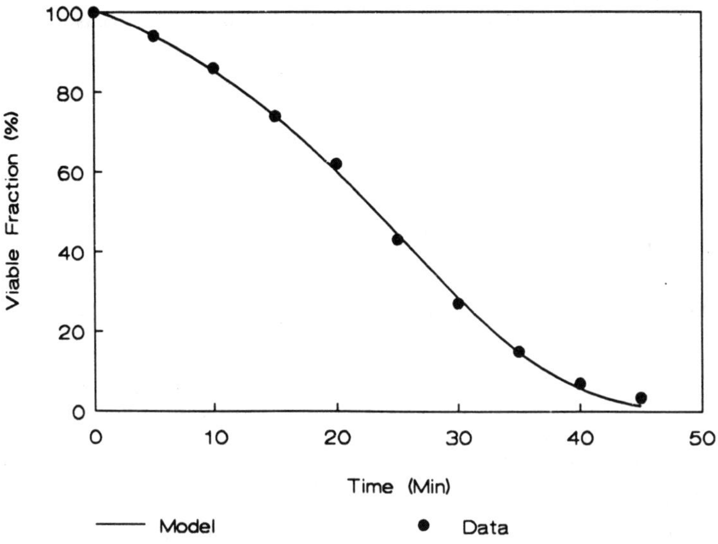

Fig. 12-4. The loss of yeast viability due to SO_2 with time. Data of Uzuka et al. (1985).

tion of the Gompertz function is that the sensitivity of the susceptible cells is changing in an exponential manner as their numbers are decreasing.

There is a need for further studies related to the rate of cell death due to components such as ethanol and sulfur dioxide so that better understanding can be applied to the influence of time on these phenomena.

2. Enzyme Inhibition

While there are a number of studies of sulfite slowing of the polyphenoloxidase activity and browning in various fruit and vegetables, most of these have been at a pH of 5 or above and are of limited relevance to juice conditions. The extent that the enzyme activity is slowed by sulfur dioxide in grape juices has been discussed elsewhere (Chapter 3) and levels of 50 mg/L added are adequate to reduce the activity by more than 90% (Dubernet and Ribéreau-Gayon 1973; Amano et al. 1979).

The nature of the inhibition has received far less attention but it becomes increasingly important if alternatives to sulfites are to be found. Sayavedra-Soto and Montgomery (1986) studied this enzyme from pear, using ^{35}S labeled $SO_3^=$ and gel electrophoresis. They showed that the active form appears to be the HSO_3^- ion and that irreversible structural modification, rather than a binding inhibition, is the mode of action.

There is a second and quite different effect of sulfur dioxide on the browning caused by enzyme-mediated oxidation. This is the binding of quinone products by the bisulfite ion, minimizing the formation of the brown quinoidal polymers. This is discussed further in Section 6.b of this chapter.

3. Carbonyl Binding

One of the secondary features of sulfur dioxide is the ability of the bisulfite ion to form additional products with the carbonyl group of many compounds (Burroughs and Sparks 1973a, 1973b, 1973c). The most common of these in wines is with acetaldehyde to form ethane sulfonic acid, a strongly acidic species in an equilibrium that leaves essentially no free acetaldehyde in the solution. This adduct is the major component of the bound sulfur dioxide in wines and the level in finished wine is determined primarily by the level of the addition of sulfur dioxide to the juice, the yeast strain used, and the thiamin of the juice. Since acetaldehyde is an intermediate in the biochemical production of ethanol, any added sulfur dioxide is bound to the aldehyde released during fermentation.

The other major carbonyl compounds that are important in the binding of sulfur dioxide in wines are the keto acids, pyruvic and glutaric. Elevated levels of these are mainly caused by nutritional deficiencies, especially vitamins due to mold infection of grapes or the ion exchange of juices.

Other carbonyls such as oxidation products of phenols and of ascorbic acid and the furfurals produced from sugars by sustained heating are evidently involved with this aspect of the sulfur dioxide equilibria in wines. While not documented in wine conditions, the binding of bisulfite to yeast, bacteria and certain protein or cellular fragments would be expected to occur, even if only significant in the high grape solids suspended in musts or the high cell concentrations such as those found in yeast lees or certain separation processes.

The relationship between the bound and the free HSO_3^- can be written as a reversible equilibrium:

$$HSO_3^- + C \underset{k_d}{\overset{k_f}{\rightleftarrows}} A, \qquad (12.6)$$

where C is the concentration of the free carbonyl; A is that of the sulfonate adduct; k_f is the formation rate constant; and k_d is the dissociation rate constant. For the most common carbonyl, acetaldehyde, there are no ionizable forms of the carbonyl, but this is not true for components such as pyruvic and α-keto-glutaric acid. The effect of pH on the binding equilibrium generally involves the ionization of both the bisulfite and carbonyl forms. The equilibrium constant for the binding reaction can be expressed:

$$K_{eq} = \frac{[A]}{[HSO_3^-][C]} = k_f/k_d, \qquad (12.7)$$

and these have been evaluated for several components (Burroughs and Sparks 1973a, 1973b, 1973c) and are presented in Table 12-6.

Table 12-6. Dissociation equilibrium constants for some wine components

Compound	*K* dissociation (pH = 3)	*K* dissociation (pH = 4)
Acetaldehyde	1.5×10^{-6}	1.4×10^{-6}
Malvidin 3 glucoside	6.0×10^{-5}	n/a
Pyruvate	1.4×10^{-4}	2.2×10^{-4}
2-Ketoglutarate	4.9×10^{-4}	7.0×10^{-4}
Galacturonate	1.6×10^{-2}	2.1×10^{-2}
Glucose	6.4×10^{-1}	n/a

Source: Burroughs and Sparks (1973a); Beech et al. (1979).

By analogy with other physical adsorption and enzyme binding equilibria, the concentration of bound carbonyl can be written:

$$[A] = \frac{[A]_{max}[HSO_3^-]}{K_b + [HSO_3^-]}, \qquad (12.8)$$

where $[A]_{max}$ is the maximum concentration of adduct that can be formed, and K_b is a measure of the affinity of bisulfite for the carbonyl, similar to the K_m in enzyme binding. The constant K_b is equal to k_f/k_d (or K_{eq}) and it is the concentration of bisulfite at which half of the carbonyl is bound. For acetaldehyde this is 1.5 μM/L, while for pyruvate and α-ketoglutarate it is 140 and 490 μM/L respectively. The value of $[A]_{max}$ is equal to the total concentration of the carbonyl in all forms, or $[C]$ plus $[A]$. Equation (12.8) can be rewritten to give the fraction of the carbonyl that is bound at any free bisulfite concentration:

$$\frac{[A]}{[A] + [C]} = \frac{[HSO_3^-]}{K_b + [HSO_3^-]}, \qquad (12.8a)$$

and the binding curves for acetaldehyde, malvidin-3-glucoside, pyruvic and α-keto-glutaric acids are presented in Figure 12-5. In juices, the binding of glucose is significant, and approximately 50% of the sulfur dioxide added at levels of 50 to 100 mg/L will be bound in this way. In dry wines, the glucose content is essentially zero and the contributions of this to the bound SO_2 pool are insignificant.

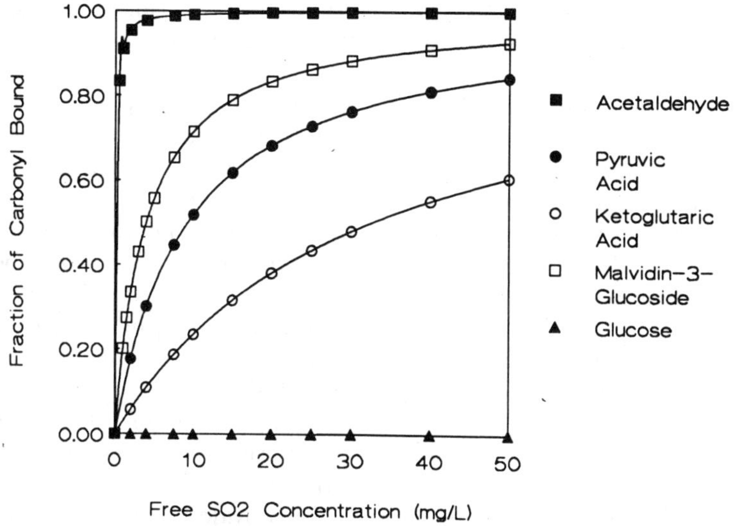

Fig. 12-5. The extent of binding of various components as a function of free sulfur dioxide.

The concept of rest SO_2 was developed and introduced by Kielhofer and Wurdig (1960) during their studies of the variation in bound and free levels in wines made from mold-infected and healthy grapes. The rest SO_2 is that fraction of the bound sulfur dioxide that cannot be accounted for by acetaldehyde and glucose binding. It is, therefore, a measure of the bisulfite bound to keto acids such as the natural levels of pyruvic, α-keto-glutaric, and others which may be produced by mold action on grapes, such as 5-keto-gluconic and 2-keto-galacturonic (Wurdig and Schlotter 1968).

4. The Kinetics of Binding Reactions

The binding of the bisulfite forms with the carbonyl compound mentioned above has important implications when it comes to the antimicrobial action and the analytical determination of the free sulfur dioxide in wines. The combination of carbonyls with bisulfite ions is only one aspect of the binding equilibrium. At equilibrium there is an equal and opposite hydrolysis reaction which returns the addition product to its original components. It is the ratio of the formation and dissociation rate constants that determines the magnitude of the equilibrium constant for the binding reaction.

The rate at which bound form dissociates can be written:

$$d[A]/dt = k_f[C][HSO_3^-] - k_d[A], \quad (12.9)$$

where the terms are as defined in Equation (12.6). Values of the formation and dissociation rate constants for a number of components are presented in Table 12-7. During the analysis of free sulfur dioxide by the titration or aeration oxidation methods, the concentration of bisulfite is reduced to low levels by reagent or gas stripping and the rate of adduct formation decreases accordingly. The change

Table 12-7. Formation and dissociation rate constants of bisulfite addition compounds at 25°C.

	Formation rate constant (1/M/s)	Dissociation rate constant (1/s)
Acetaldehyde (I = 0.85 M)[1]		
HSO_3^-	1.0	1.3×10^{-4}
$SO_3^=$	$3.0 \times 10^{+4}$	3.6×10^{-4}
Pyruvate ion (I = 0.157 M)[1]		
HSO_3^-	$1.03 \times 10^{+1}$	1.4×10^{-3}
$SO_3^=$	unknown	unknown
Glucose[2]	1.39×10^{-3}	2.40×10^{-3}

[1]Tenscher (1986).
[2]Vas (1949).

in adduct concentration will then decrease based on the rate of the dissociation. Adducts for which the dissociation rate is slow will remain in the bound form, and the acetaldehyde adduct is an example of this. In contrast, adducts of the pyruvate ion (and perhaps also the α-keto-glutarate ion) and the anthocyanins have rates of dissociation that are much faster than their addition reaction, and this leads to a much more dynamic interchange of bound form into free sulfur dioxide.

The rate of dissociation of these addition compounds is especially important when the free sulfur dioxide is to be measured. The traditional methods for this determination are the direct titration of acidified samples with iodine (or iodate) in the Ripper method and the sparging and trapping approach of the aeration oxidation method (Ough and Amerine 1988). Under the latter conditions, the rapidly dissociated bound components will break down and their bound bisulfite will be removed as molecular SO_2 in the carrier gas. This will then appear in the free sulfur dioxide determination along with the actual free forms in the wine. The aeration oxidation procedure, while quite reproducible as a method, can result in erroneously high values in wines with significant pyruvate or α-keto-glutarate. By comparison, the poor reproducability of the direct titration is due to the rapid dissociation of pyruvate-like components during the determination and the drifting end point that results from it.

The use of a rapid, direct titration procedure in which the end point is determined using a dual platinum electrode would seem to be the most applicable determination of practical use for the closest determination of the free forms under solution equilibrium. In this amperometric procedure, the potential is measured while a small current (typically 5 microamperes) is passed through the solution from the polarizing electrode connection (often designated the Karl Fischer connection) of most commercial pH meters. Such procedures have been investigated over the past decades (Ingram 1947; Pataky 1958; Brun et al. 1961; Schneyder and Vlcek 1977; Vahl and Converse 1980; Villeton-Pachot et al. 1980; Pontallier et al. 1982), but they are not commonly used in wineries, even today. They offer the fastest and most easily automated method of free sulfur dioxide analysis and most commercial autotitration units can be set up to perform this task. While some hydrolysis is inherent in this approach, it will be always be smaller than other slower methods, and a knowledge of the titration time and the rate of hydrolysis would permit a reasonable correction to be made, if desired.

The recent development of alternative methods for the determination of free sulfur dioxide using capillary electrophoresis (Collins and Boulton 1995) provides a more effective way of removing the hydrolysis component of the free sulfur dioxide from the determination.

5. Thiamin Destruction

Thiamin is an important vitamin for the growth of many microorganisms. Almost all of the culture media used for the propagation of yeast and bacteria contain it at levels in the range 100 to 1000 μg/L. Levels of thiamin in grapes and wine average 100 and 1200 μg/L, respectively (Amerine et al. 1972). The destruction of thiamin by bisulfite has been known for many years, but the rate at which this occurs has not generally been appreciated. For microorganisms which have an absolute requirement for thiamin, for example spoilage yeast such as *Brettanomyces* and certain *Lactobacilli* (Hammond and Carr 1976), one of the antimicrobial effects of the usage of sulfur dioxide in wines may be the destruction of trace levels of thiamin, and, thereby, the prevention of their growth. A similar cleavage reaction with folic acid has been reported (Vanderschmitt et al. 1967) and there are several reports of a sulfur dioxide and NAD reaction (Pfleiderer et al. 1956; Rhem 1964).

The cleavage of thiamin by bisulfite ions yields a pyrimidine (6-amino-2-methyl pyrimid-5-yl) methane-sulfonic acid and a (5-ß-hydroxy-ethyl-4-) methyl thiazole (Leichter and Joslyn 1969). The reaction is thought to be a nucleophilic displacement, similar to the cleavage of disulfides by sulfite (Bobet et al. 1990), but with the bisulfite rather than the sulfite ion. It is important to quantify the rate at which this reaction proceeds in order to understand the effects that occur during the storage of juices and concentrates that contain SO_2.

a. *Kinetics*

The extent of the reaction at various times can be obtained by integration of the rate equation. The kinetics of reaction are second order overall, but first order with respect to both thiamin and bisulfite concentrations. The rate of thiamin cleavage can be expressed:

$$d[Th]/dt = -k[Th][SO_3^{=}], \quad (12.10)$$

where k is the second-order rate constant. Values of k are 0.046 and 0.008 L/mole/hr at pH of 3.0 and 4.0, respectively (Leichter and Joslyn 1969).

b. *Effect of Temperature*

Leichter and Joslyn (1969) found the bimolecular rate constant to double for each increase of 10°C at pH of 5.0 (giving an activation energy of 56.9 kJ/mole) over the range 20°C to 70°C. A corresponding study has also been reported by Jaulmes and Bres (1973).

c. *Effect of pH*

The rate constant k seems to be related to the cation form of thiamin and the bisulfite ion and both of these are functions of pH. The general form of the rate expression for all pH values is:

$$d[Th]/dt = -k[Th]\frac{K_a}{[K_a + [H^+]]} \cdot [HSO^{3-}] \times \frac{[H^+]K_{a1}}{\left[[H^+]^2 + [H^+]K_a + K_{a1}K_{a2}\right]}, \quad (12.11)$$

where the pK_a for thiamin is 4.5 and pK_{a1} and pK_{a2} for sulfur dioxide are 1.86 and 7.18, respectively. By incorporating the activation energy found by Leichter and Joslyn (1969), the Arrhenius form of the second-order rate constant (L/mole/s) is given by:

$$k = 8.22 \times 10^{15} \times \exp\frac{[-56{,}900]}{[R(T + 273.2)]}. \quad (12.12)$$

Leichter and Joslyn (1969) found that the destruction was maximal at a pH of 5.5 to 5.8 and was found to be slower at higher pH values in both studies. This is expected from the ionization of the two reactants since the product of the reactive fractions has a pH maximum at 5.8. At juice and wine pH value the reaction is pseudo first order due to the dominance of the sulfur dioxide compared to that of thiamin. The effect of pH on the rate is determined by the ionization of thiamin since there is little change in the fraction in the bisulfite form under conditions of pH between 3.0 and 4.0. The rate increases more than threefold for each rise in pH of 0.5 units in this range.

The decrease in the rate of thiamin cleavage as a function of pH is shown in Figure 12-6a. The effect of temperature on the rate is shown in Figure 12-6b. The rates are for a free sulfur dioxide concentration of 10 mg/L and at 20°C and correspond to the rates expected in juice and wine. The half-time for the reaction at pH = 3.0 is 219 days, while that for the reaction at pH = 3.5 is 72 days. This is not fast enough for the prevention of thiamin-dependent microbial growth during the first months of aging. The corresponding condition at pH = 4.0 would have a half-time of 27 days. While this might seem to be a contributing factor in preventing the growth of certain organisms, the molecular component of the 10 mg/L free sulfur dioxide would be ineffective against

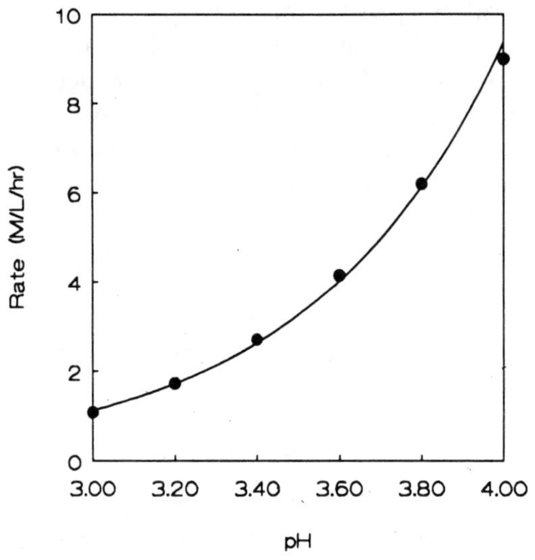

Fig. 12-6a. The effect of pH on the rate of thiamin cleavage by SO_2.

practically all organisms in this condition. The other conditions in which this reaction is significant are stored juices and concentrates with elevated sulfur dioxide levels.

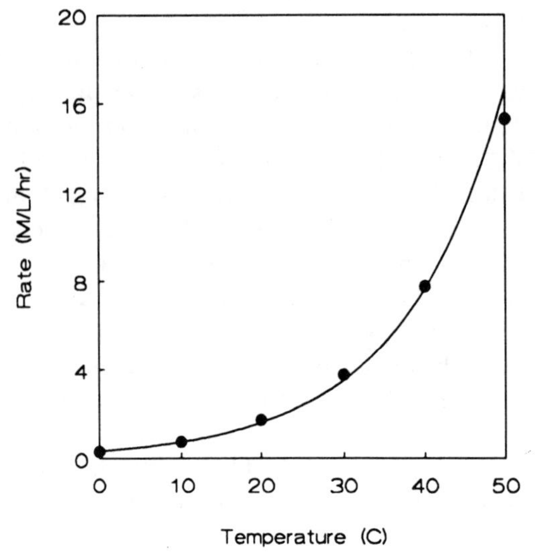

Fig. 12-6b. The effect of temperature on the rate of thiamin cleavage by SO_2.

Table 12-8. The effect of temperature and pH on the second-order rate constant for thiamin cleavage.

Temperature (°C)	pH = 3.0	pH = 3.5	pH = 4.0
0	0.230	0.771	1.90
5	0.361	1.15	2.98
10	0.557	1.72	4.60
15	0.846	2.62	7.00
20	1.27	3.93	10.5
25	1.87	5.79	15.5

The values of the rate constant at other temperatures and pH conditions of interest to winemakers are shown in Table 12-8.

6. Sulfite Oxidation

The development of golden brown tints during aging, the loss of varietal character, the formation of aldehydic compounds, and the ongoing browning of wine in the bottle are all aspects of undesirable chemical changes in white wines. These same reactions occur to a similar degree in red wines, but the results are not as obvious due to the natural pigmentation of these wines and the higher substrate content.

The form of sulfur dioxide that reacts with oxygen is the sulfite ion which is always the least abundant form at wine pH. The fraction in the sulfite form is small even at pH = 4.0, but it is one-tenth as much at pH = 3.0. It undergoes the redox reactions:

$$SO_3^{=} + H_2O \leftarrow\text{---}\rightarrow SO_4^{=} + 2H^+ + 2e^-$$

$$E° = -0.08\ V$$

and

$$1/2\ O_2 + 2H^+ + 2e^- \leftarrow\text{---}\rightarrow H_2O$$

$$E° = 1.229\ V.$$

These reactions suggest that 16 mg of oxygen consumes 64 mg of sulfur dioxide, that is a pattern of 4 mg SO_2 per mg of oxygen. At a total SO_2 of 100 mg/L only 25 mg/L of oxygen could theoretically be consumed by sulfite. Actual oxygen consumption in wine can be much higher.

a. *The Rate of Oxygen Consumption*

There have been very few kinetic studies of the sulfite reaction under wine conditions (pH less than 4.0, 110 g/L ethanol), but the reaction might be expected to be first order with respect to oxygen and sulfite concentrations in most wine situations.

$$d[O_2]/dt = -k_1[O_2][SO^{3=}] = -k_1'[O_2], \quad (12.13)$$

where k_1 is the second-order rate constant; and k_1' is the pseudo first-order rate constant when the sulfite ion concentration is well above that of the oxygen.

The oxygen uptake measurements in a model wine and white wine (Poulton 1970) display a first-order rate law and an exponential decline in the concentration of the reactants:

$$[O_2] = [O_2]_i \exp(-k_1't). \quad (12.14)$$

The pseudo first-order rate constant k_1' for the reaction between the sulfite ion and oxygen (with a free sulfur dioxide concentration of 30 mg/L, pH = 3.6) have been reported to be $2.66 \times 10^{-7} s^{-1}$ corresponding to a half-time of approximately 30 days. By comparison, the corresponding experiment using ascorbate (at a concentration of 100 mg/L) had a rate constant of $3.27 \times 10^{-4} s^{-1}$ or a half-time of approximately 35 minutes. The rates of oxygen consumption for these reactions are shown in Figure 12-7. This clearly demonstrates the almost nonexistent oxygen removal capacity of sulfur dioxide under wine pH and ethanol conditions. The ascorbate-oxygen reaction is almost 1700 times faster than the sulfite-oxygen reaction at this pH.

The more important values are those of the wine itself and Poulton's other measurements were with one white wine and additions of ascorbate to it. He found the oxygen uptake rate in a white wine due to its phenolic and other constituents to have a rate constant of $6.51 \times 10^{-6} s^{-1}$ or a half-time of approximately 1.2 days. These results have been redrawn and are presented in a combined form in Figure 12-8.

The first-order rate law for oxygen consumption could only occur if either the sulfite concentration (or that of the ascorbate or the phenols) was in excess of the oxygen, or the slowest step was the formation of an oxygen-derived intermediate, such as some oxygen-related radical.

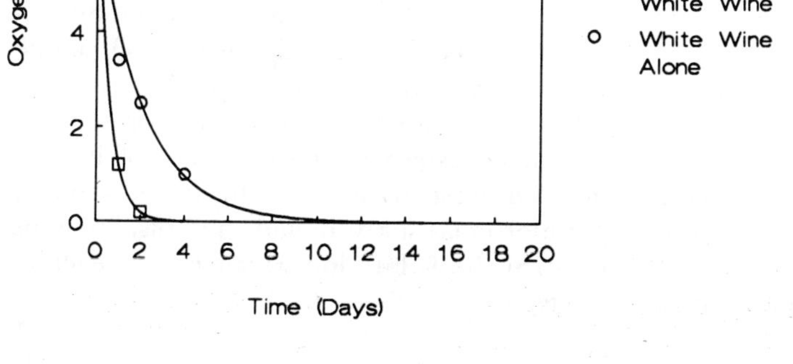

Fig. 12-7. The consumption of dissolved oxygen by sulfite and ascorbate in model solution. Data of Poulton (1970).

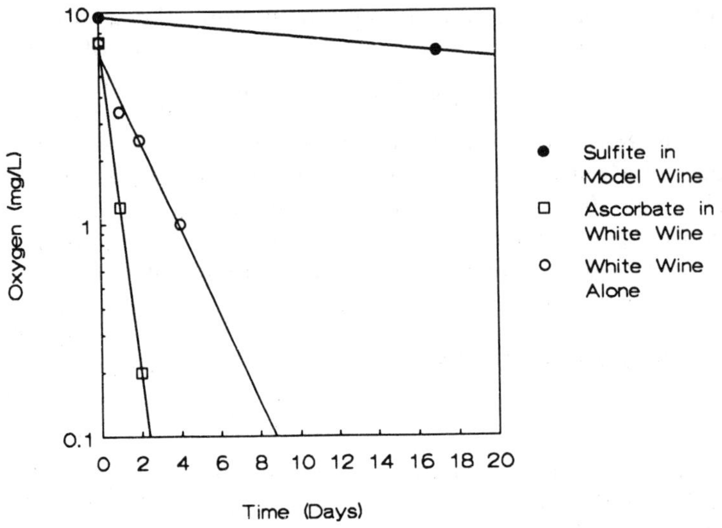

Fig. 12-8. The consumption of dissolved oxygen by a wine and ascorbate in a wine. Data of Poulton (1970).

In Poulton's (1970) study, the sulfite was not far from the stoichiometric levels and could not be considered to be in excess. The formation of a reaction intermediate, which then reacts quickly with sulfite, appears to be closer to the actual situation. While the majority of the literature related to the sulfite oxidation reaction has reported rate laws involving the sulfite concentration (and generally not the oxygen concentration), there are studies that support free radical mechanisms (Fuller and Crist 1941), the formation of a superoxide ion under higher pH conditions (Fridovich and Handler 1961) and others (McCord and Fridovich 1969; Yang 1970, 1973) that show superoxide's dissociation to form oxygen and peroxide has a dramatic effect on rates of the sulfite reaction. The contributions of the superoxide ion and hydrogen peroxide formation to the oxygen reactivity in wines are not well understood at present.

The rate constant k_1', can be expected to vary due to increases in temperature, in an exponential manner, as predicted by the Arrhenius equation. There does not appear to be a value reported for the activation energy of this reaction derived from wine-like conditions, but estimates of it can be made from old studies of this kind (Ribéreau-Gayon 1933). Based on the rates of uptake of oxygen in a wine at temperatures over the range -2°C to 30°C (Figure 12-9), it can be shown to first order with respect to oxygen. The effect of temperature on this rate of oxygen uptake (L/mL/day) can be written:

$$k_1' = 8.41 \times 10^{23} \times \exp\frac{[-137{,}700]}{[R(T + 273.2)]}, \quad (12.15)$$

where k_1' is the pseudo first-order rate constant, the activation energy is 137.7 kJ/mole, and R is the gas constant (8.314×10^3 kg m^2 s^{-2} kgmole^{-1} K). This is shown graphically in Figure 12-10.

Wines are known to have different rates of oxygen consumption and this appears to alter with more oxygen exposure (Rossi and Singleton 1966, Perscheid and Zürn 1977). While the observed rate of the oxidation reaction will depend upon the pH, the constant k_1 should be essentially independent of it. The main effect of pH is on the dissociation of the molecular sulfur dioxide and bisulfite ions to form the sulfite ion which is the reacting entity.

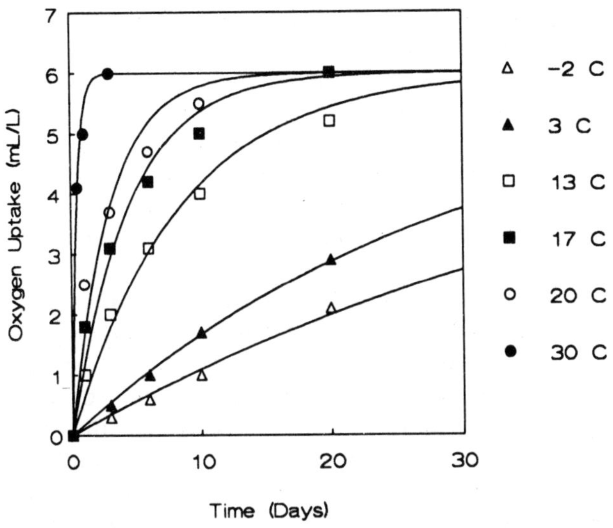

Fig. 12-9. The effect of temperature on oxygen consumption by a wine. Data of Ribéreau-Gayon (1933).

There have been studies of the rate of disappearance of free sulfur dioxide in bottled wine (Ough 1985) and although Arrhenius-type plots are presented, these are not necessarily due to the oxidation reaction described above. The apparent activation energies for the loss in total sulfur dioxide in red and white table wines was 35.7 and 13.4 kJ/mole, respectively. The formation of brown color in white wines has displayed apparent activation energies of 66.4 (Berg and Akiyoshi 1956) and 74.5 (Ough 1985) kJ/mole, compared to those for the oxygen consumption, 137.6 kJ/mole, noted previously.

Sulfate formation has been proposed as an alternative indicator of the extent of the oxidation reaction rather than the loss in total SO_2, but not all of the lost sulfite appears as sulfate and the analysis by methods other than ion chromatography is tedious. The evaporative loss of sulfur dioxide from barrels and the interaction with quinones to form monsul-

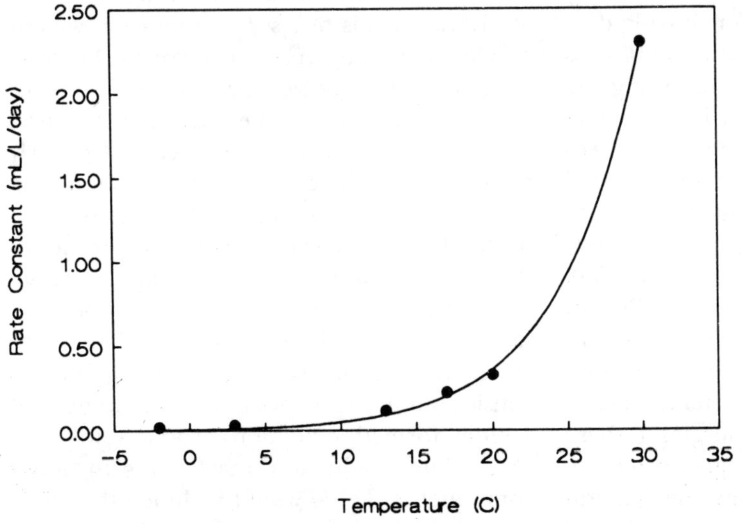

Fig. 12-10. The effect of temperature on the rate of consumption of oxygen by a wine.

fonates (Lu Valle 1952) can lead to incorrect assessments of the extent of oxidation when the total sulfur dioxide method is used.

The differences in redox potential might be thought to indicate that sulfite should be as extensively oxidized as ascorbate, yet less extensively than phenols, based on the corresponding redox potentials:

$$\text{Ascorbate} \leftarrow \text{---}\rightarrow \text{Dehydro-ascorbate} + 2H^+ + 2e^- \quad E^\circ = -0.06$$

$$\text{Catechol} \leftarrow \text{---}\rightarrow \text{1,2 Benzoquinone} + 2H^+ + 2e^- \quad E^\circ = -0.792,$$

however, the extent of these reactions in the short term turns out to be controlled by their rates of reaction rather than the redox equilibria. The rate of sulfite oxidation is known to be much slower in ethanol solutions than in water (Bioletti 1912) and the studies of Poulton (1970) and Wedzicha and Lamikanra (1987) confirm this.

b. Loss of Total Sulfur Dioxide after Bottling

The loss of sulfur dioxide in the days and weeks following bottling has several causes. One study has shown that for two white wines in corked bottles, the total sulfur dioxide had fallen by between 20 to 30% after a five-year period at 12°C (Müller-Späth 1982). One study of the changes in the free sulfur dioxide during an accelerated storage condition (10 days at 50°C) in beer showed a decline during the first six days without any changes in the sulfate content (Kuriowa and Hashimoto 1970). Another, showing the changes in color and total sulfur dioxide in red and white table wines during 21 days at temperatures between 28°C and 49°C, is especially interesting (Ough 1985). While the rates of the changes in color (loss in absorbance at 520 nm for the red wine, gain in absorbance at 420 nm for the white wine) were different, the response to temperature, as indicated by the activation energies of these reactions were the same. This suggests that the same kind of reaction, perhaps the general condensation of phenols, was rate-limiting in both situations. The rate of loss of the total sulfur dioxide was between two and three times faster in the red wine than the white wine. The activation energies of these losses, however, were quite different, indicating that the rate-limiting reaction in the loss of total sulfur dioxide in the red wine was different from that in the white wine.

The reactions involved in the loss of total sulfur dioxide are (1) The loss as vapor past the cork; (2) the oxidation of sulfite by oxygen within the bottle; (3) the formation of strongly bound bisulfite addition compounds that are not hydrolyzed as part of the analysis; and (4) the slow oxidation of sulfite by previously oxidized phenols.

The first is not significant under normal storage temperatures and the second would require 4 mg/L of SO_2 for each mg/L of oxygen, but this reaction has been shown to be very slow. The reactions of the third kind may be involved due to the possible formation of addition compounds with quinones (Embs and Markakis 1965), and a number of unsaturated carbonyl compounds have been shown to form irreversibly bound sulfonates (Burton et al. 1963). There appears to be little study of the ability of the aromatic quinones and carbonyls found in wines to bind with the bisulfite ion. This reaction was also noted to interfere with the carbonyl/amine browning in certain foods, but this is of less importance in wines.

The remaining reaction involves the rearrangement of oxidized and reduced components in the wine, especially those favored kinetically rather than energetically. The early pattern of products from the oxidation of a phenolic mixture such as wine will be controlled by the relative rates of reaction rather than the strength of their redox reaction. However, in the long term, there can be rearrangements of these reactions that more closely follows that expected from equilibrium considerations. It is thought that a number of rapidly formed oxidation products will undergo later reduction reactions with other components. These would include other phenols and sulfite that do not exhibit rapid oxidation rates. Under long-term storage conditions, in which further oxidation has been essentially eliminated, these rearrangements are expected to occur. The oxidation of sulfite by oxidized phenols would lead to the formation of sulfate and the loss of total sulfur dioxide. This would also delay the condensation of the quinoidal phenols and defer the formation of brown pigments, as observed in white wines. Quinones produced by polyphenol oxidase activity have been converted back to diphenols by sulfite (Walker (1975), but this has not been shown to occur under wine conditions. A recent kinetic study of the inhibition of polyphenol oxidase by metabisulfite (Valero et al. 1992) has been able to show that in order to explain the delay in and rate of brown formation, the reaction between bisulfite and quinones has to be accounted for. This is indirect evidence of such a reaction for enzyme oxidation products and further work is needed to establish the presence of a similar reaction for quinones formed during the chemical oxidation of wines.

The same thinking can be applied to the more rapid decline of free (and presumably total) sulfur dioxide in the presence of ascorbic acid additions. Ascorbate is known to react at similar rates to many of the other phenols in wine (Poulton 1970), but based on its redox potential, there are a number of other phenols that should be more easily oxidized. The regeneration of phenols from their quinones by ascorbic acid in the absence of oxygen is generally accepted. However, the faster-than-usual depletion of free sulfur dioxide in the presence of ascorbate, noted by Müller-Späth, suggests that ascorbate is involved in enhancing these sulfite reactions.

7. Sulfur Dioxide-Peroxide Reactions

Among the oxidation substrates of wine is a class of phenols whose nonenzymic reaction with oxygen results in the formation of almost stoichiometric levels of hydrogen peroxide (Wildenradt and Singleton 1974). This group is the vicinal-dihydroxy phenols, the most important of which is caffeic (or caftaric) acid in white and significant in all wines. It is of particular concern that ascorbate reaction with oxygen follows the same pattern.

The formation of peroxide in wines can lead to a corresponding increase in the level of acetaldehyde (from the oxidation reaction with ethanol) in the absence of available sulfite ions, and both caffeic acid and ascorbate have been shown to be able to produce one mole of aldehyde for each mole of substrate under accelerated test conditions (Wildenradt and Singleton 1974).

Unlike the reaction of oxygen with sulfite, the reaction of hydrogen peroxide at low pH involves the molecular form (Halperin and Taube 1952) rather than the sulfite ion form (Mader 1958). The fraction of the free sulfur dioxide that is in the molecular form is very low at pH conditions that are high for wines but is more significant in low pH wines.

The rate is expected to follow a second-order rate law, first order with respect to peroxide and molecular concentrations, and is thought to have a maximum rate at a pH of 1.9 (Sawyer 1991). Wildenradt and Singleton (1974) have demonstrated the effect of this reaction in limiting the acetaldehyde formation when pyrogallol or ascorbic acids are oxidized in the presence of free sulfur dioxide under wine-like conditions. They found that the acetaldehyde produced at elevated temperatures could be lowered to approximately 20%, but in the presence 180 mg/L of free sulfur. This indicates that the rate of the peroxide-ethanol reaction is several times that for the peroxide-sulfur dioxide reaction. Under wine conditions and normal storage temperatures the extent of the reaction may be quite different. There do not appear to be any kinetic studies of the peroxide-sulfur dioxide reaction, let alone any under wine conditions.

The only significant contribution of the sulfur dioxide as an antioxidant in wine appears to be in this reaction with hydrogen peroxide, generated from the oxidation of the vicinal, dihydroxy phenols. While some slowing of the sulfite-oxygen reaction in the presence of ethanol has been noted (Bioletti 1912; Wedzicha and Lamikanra 1987), a corresponding effect on the peroxide-sulfur dioxide reaction might not be expected. It is thought that the peroxide-sulfur dioxide reaction continues to be many times faster than the oxygen-sulfite reaction under wine conditions. This is supported by the general observation that the maintenance of free sulfur dioxide levels in the range 5 to 25 mg/L in wines will prevent the development of acetaldehyde. If this was simply due to the binding of any acetaldehyde formed, the bound level would increase while the total remained the same and this is not observed. Sulfur dioxide is therefore a moderate antioxidant for the peroxide reaction under wine conditions even though it is of limited value in the oxygen reaction.

C. REFERENCES

AMANO, Y., M. KUBOTA, and M. KAGAMI. 1979. "Oxygen uptake of Koshu grape must and its control." *Hokkokogaku Kaishi* 57:92–101.

AMERINE, M. A., H. W. BERG, and W. V. CRUESS. 1972. *The Technology of Wine Making,* p. 110. Westport, CT: Avi Publishing.

AMERINE, M. A., and E. B. ROESSLER. 1983. *Wines—Their Sensory Evaluation,* 2nd ed., p. 37. New York: Freeman Company.

ANACLETO, J., and N. VAN UDEN. 1982. "Kinetics and activation energetics of death in *Saccharomyces cerevisiae* induced by sulfur dioxide." *Biotechnol. Bioeng.* 24:2477–2486.

BAILEY J. E., and D. F. OLLIS. 1977. *Biochemical Engineering Fundamentals,* p. 407. New York: McGraw-Hill.

BEECH, F. W., L. F. BURROUGHS, C. F. TIMBERLAKE, and G. C. WHITING. 1979. "Progres recents sur l'aspect chimique et antimicrobienne de l'anhydride sulfureux." *Bull. O.I.V.* 52(586):1001–1022.

BEECH, F. W., and S. THOMAS. 1985. "Action antimicrobienne de l'anhydride sulfureux." *Bull. O.I.V.* 58(652–653):564–581.

BERG, H. W., and M. AKIYOSHI. 1956. "Some factors involved in the browning of white wines." *Am. J. Enol.* 7:1–7.

BIDAN, P., and Y. COLLON. 1985. "Metabolisme du soufre chez la levure." *Bull. O.I.V.* 58(652–653):544–563.

BIOLETTI, F. T. 1912. "Sulfurous acid in winemaking." *8th Int. Cong. Appl. Chem.* 14:31–59.

BOBET, R. A., A. C. NOBLE, and R. B. BOULTON. 1990. "Kinetics of ethanethiol and diethyl disulfide interconversion in wine-like solutions." *J. Agric. Food Chem.* 38:229–452.

BRUN, P., C. GASQUET, S. DE STOUTZ, and A. NICOLI. 1961. "Application de l'amperometrie a la determination de l'anhydride sulfureux dans les vins." *Ann. Fals. Exp. Chim.* 54:412–420.

BURROUGHS, L. F., and A. H. SPARKS. 1973a. "Sulphite-binding power of wines and ciders. I. Equilibrium constants for the dissociation of carbonyl bisulphite compounds." *J. Sci. Food Agric.* 24:187–198.

BURROUGHS, L. F., and A. H. SPARKS. 1973b. "Sulphite-binding power of wines and ciders. II. Theoretical consideration and calculation of the sulphite-binding equilibria." *J. Sci. Food Agric.* 24:199–206.

BURROUGHS, L. F., and A. H. SPARKS. 1973c. "Sulphite-binding power of wines and ciders. III. Determination of carbonyl compounds in a wine and calculation of its sulphite-binding power." *J. Sci. Food Agric.* 24:207–217.

BURTON, H. S., D. J. MCWEENY, and D. O. BILTCLIFFE. 1963. "Non-enzymic browning: The role of unsaturated carbonyl compounds as intermediates and of SO_2 as an inhibitor of browning." *J. Sci. Food Agric.* 14:911–920.

COLLINS, T. S., and R. B. BOULTON. 1995. "A rapid method for the detection of free sulfur dioxide in wine using capillary electrophoresis." *Am. J. Enol. Vitic.* (In press).

CRUESS, W. V. 1912. "The effect of sulfurous acid on fermentation organisms." *Ind. Eng. Chem.* 4:581–585.

DUBERNET, M., and P. RIBÉREAU-GAYON. 1973. "Presence et significance dans le mouts et vins de la tyrosinase du raisin." *Conn. Vigne Vin* 7:283–302.

EMBS, R. J., and P. MARKAKIS. 1965. "The mechanism of sulfite inhibition of browning caused by polyphenol oxidase." *J. Food Sci.* 30:753–758.

FORNACHON, J. C. M. 1963. "Inhibition of certain lactic acid bacteria by free and bound sulphur dioxide." *J. Sci. Food Agric.* 14:857–862.

FOUST, A. S., L. A. WENZEL, C. W. CLUMP, L. MAUS, and L. B. ANDERSEN. 1960. *Principles of Unit Operations*. New York: John Wiley & Sons.

FRIDOVICH. I., and P. HANDLER. 1961. "Detection of free radicals generated during enzymic oxidations by the initiation of sulfite oxidation." *J. Biol. Chem.* 236:1836–1840.

FULLER, E. C., and R. H. CRIST. 1941. "The rate of oxidation of sulfite ions by oxygen." *J. Am. Chem. Soc.* 63:1644–1650.

HALPERIN, J., and H. TAUBE. 1952. "The transfer of oxygen atoms in oxidation-reduction reactions. IV. The reaction of hydrogen peroxide with sulfite and thiosulfate, and of oxygen, manganese dioxide and permanganate with sulfite." *J. Am. Chem. Soc.* 74:380–382.

HAMMOND, S. M., and J. G. CARR. 1976. "The antimicrobial activity of SO_2—With particular reference to fermented and non-fermented fruit juices." In *Inhibition and Inactivation of Vegetative Microbes*, F. A. Skinner and W. B. Hugo, Eds. London: Academic Press.

HOOD, A. 1983. "Inhibition of growth of wine lactic-acid bacteria by acetaldehyde-bound sulphur dioxide." *Aust. Grapegrower & Winemaker* 232:34–43.

INGRAM, M. 1947. "An electrometric indicator to replace starch in iodine titrations of sulphurous acid in fruit juices." *J. Soc. Chem. Ind.* 66:50–55.

JAULMES, P., and J. BRES. 1973. "Cinetique de l'action de l'anhydride sulfureux sur la thiamine et la cocarboxylase." *Bull. O.I.V.* 46(508):507–515.

KATCHMER, J. 1990. Effects of sulfur dioxide and bisulfite-binding compounds on short term yeast viability in a model wine solution. M.S. thesis, Davis, CA: University of California.

KIELHOFER, E., and G. WÜRDIG. 1960. "Die an unbekannte Weinbestandteile gebundene schweflige Saure (Rest SO_2) und ihre Beduetung fur den Wein (I)." *Weinberg Keller* 7:313–328.

KING, A. D. JR., J. D. PONTING, D. W. SANSHUCK, R. JACKSON, and K. MIHARA. 1981. "Factors affecting death of yeast by sulfur dioxide." *J. Food Prot.* 44:92–97.

KURIOWA, Y., and N. HASHIMOTO. 1970. "Sulfur compounds responsible for beer flavor." *Brewer's Digest* 45(5):44–54.

LAFON-LAFOURCADE, S., and E. PEYNAUD. 1974. "Sur l'action antibacterienne de l'anhydride sulfureux sous forme libre et sous forme combinée." *Conn. Vigne Vin* 8:187–203.

LEICHTER, J., and M. A. JOSLYN. 1969. "Kinetics of thiamin cleavage by sulphite." *Biochem. J.* 113:611–615.

LU VALLE, J. E. 1952. "The reaction of quinone and sulfite. I. Intermediates." *J. Am. Chem. Soc.* 74:2970–2977.

MACRIS, B. J., and P. MARKAKIS. 1974. "Transport and toxicity of sulfur dioxide in *Saccharomyces cerevisiae* var ellipsoideus." *J. Sci. Food Agric.* 25:21–29.

MADER, P. M. 1958. "Kinetics of the hydrogen peroxide-sulfite reaction in alkaline solution." *J. Am. Chem. Soc.* 80:2634–2638.

MAYER, K., U. VETSCH, and G. PAUSE. 1975. "Hemmung des biologischen Saurabbaus durch gebundene schweflige Saure." *Schw. Z. Obst-Wein.* 23:590–596.

MCCORD, J. M., and I. FRIDOVICH. 1969. "The utility of superoxide dismutase in studying free radical reactions." *J. Biol. Chem.* 244:6056–6063.

MINARIK, E. 1978. "Progres recents dans la connaissance des phenomenes microbiologiques en vinification." *Bull. O.I.V.* 51(567):352–367.

MÜLLER-SPÄTH, H. 1982. "Die Rolle der Kohlensaure beim Stillwein." *Weinwirt.* 118:1031–1037.

MÜLLER-THURGAU, H., and A. OSTERWALDER. 1915. "Prevention by sulfur dioxide of alcoholic fermentation in fruit and grape juice." *Landwirt. Jahrb. Schweiz.* 29:421–432.

OUGH, C. S. 1983. "Sulfur dioxide and sulfites." In: *Antimicrobials in Foods*. A. L. Branen and P. M. Davidson, Eds., pp. 177–203. New York: Marcel Dekker.

OUGH, C. S. 1985. "Some effects of temperature and SO_2 on wine during simulated transport or storage." *Am. J. Enol. Vitic.* 36:18–22.

OUGH, C. S., and M. A. AMERINE. 1988. *Methods for Analysis of Musts and Wines,* 2nd Ed. New York: Wiley Interscience.

PATAKY, B. 1958. "Die jodometrische Bestimmung von Schwefeldioxyd in Wien—Die elektrometrische Endpunktbestimmung." *Mitt. Rebe u. Wein, Klostern.* 8:199–204.

PERRY, M. C., and G. D. BEAL. 1920. "The quantities of preservatives necessary to inhibit and prevent alcoholic fermentation and the growth of molds." *Ind. Eng. Chem.* 12:253–255.

PERSCHEID, M., and F. ZÜRN. 1977. "Der Einfluss von Oxydationsvorgangen auf die Weinqualitat." *Weinwirt*. 113:10–12.

PFLEIDERER, G., D. JEKEL, and T. WEILAND. 1956. "Uber der Einwirkung von Sulfit auf einige DPN hydrierende Enzyme." *Biochem. Z.* 328:187–194.

PONTALLIER, P., J. P. CALLEDE, and P. RIBÉREAU-GAYON. 1982. "Dosage de SO_2 libre dans les vins rouges par titrage potentiometrique automatique. Mise en evidence d'un comportment specifique dans les vins jeunes." *Sciences Aliments* 2:329–339.

POULTON, J. R. S. 1970. "Chemical protection of wine against oxidation." *Die Wynboer* 466:July:22–23.

RAHN, O., and J. E. CONN. 1944. "Effect of increase in acidity on antiseptic efficiency." *Ind. Eng. Chem*. 36:185–187.

RHEM, H. J. 1964. "The antimicrobial action of sulphurous acid." In *Microbial Inhibitors in Food*, Ed. Molin, N. Stockholm, Sweden: Almquist, and Wiksells.

RHEM, H. J., P. WALLNOFER, and H. WITTMANN. 1965. "Beitrag zur Kenntnis der antimickrobeillen Wirkung der schwefligen Saure. IV. Dissoziation und antimikrobeille Wirkung einiger Sulfonate." *Z. Lebens. Forsch*. 127:72–85.

RHEM, H. J., and H. WITTMANN. 1962. "Beitrag zur Kenntnis der antimickrobeillen Wirkung der schwefligen Saure. I. Ubersicht uber einflussnehmende Faktoren auf die antimikrobeillen Wirkung der schwefligen Saure." *Z. Lebens. Forsch*. 118:413–425.

RIBÉREAU-GAYON, J. 1933. Contribution des oxydations et reductions dans les vins. Application a l'etude du vieillissement et des casses. Doc. thesis, Bordeaux, France: University of Bordeaux.

ROMANO, P., and G. SUZZI. 1992. "Sulfur dioxide and wine microorganisms." In *Wine—Microbiology and Biotechnology*. G. H. Fleet, Ed. pp. 373–393. Chur, Switzerland: Harwood Academic Publishers.

ROSSI, J. A., and V. L. SINGLETON. 1966. "Contributions of grape phenols to oxygen absorption and browning of wines." *Am. J. Enol. Vitic.* 17:231–239.

SAWYER, D. T. 1991. *Oxygen Chemistry*, p. 112. New York: Oxford University Press.

SAYAVEDRA-SOTO, L. A., and M. W. MONTGOMERY. 1986. "Inhibition of polyphenoloxidase by sulfite." *J. Food. Sci*. 51:1531–1536.

SCHANDERL, H. 1959. *Die Mikrobiologie des Mostes und Weines*. 2nd Ed. Stuttgart, Germany: Eugen Ulmer.

SCHIMZ, K.-L. 1980. "The effect of sulfite on the yeast *Saccharomyces cerevisiae*." *Arch. Microbiol.* 125:89–95.

SCHIMZ, K.-L., and H. HOLZER. 1979. "Rapid decrease of ATP content in intact cells of *Saccharomyces cerevisiae* after incubation with low concentrations of sulfite." *Arch. Microbiol.* 121: 225–229.

SCHNEYDER, J., and G. VLCEK. 1977. "Massanalytische Bestimmung der freien Schwefligen Saure in Wein mit Jodsaure." *Mitt. Klost. Rebe Wein Obstbau Frucht*. 27:87–88.

SCHOPPER, J.-F., and J. AERNY. 1985. "Le role de l'anhydride sulfureux en vinification." *Bull. O.I.V.* 58(652–653):515–542.

SCHROETER, L. C. 1966. *Sulfur Dioxide. Applications in Foods, Beverages and Pharmaceuticals*. Oxford, UK: Pergamon Press.

SHERWOOD, T. K. 1925. "Solubilities of sulfur dioxide and ammonia in water." *Ind. Eng. Chem.* 17:745–747.

STRATFORD, M., and A. H. ROSE. 1986. "Transport of sulphur dioxide by *Saccharomyces cerevisiae*." *J. Gen. Microbiol.* 132:1–6.

SUDRAUD, P., and S. CHAUVET. 1985. "Activite antilevure de l'anhydride sulfureux moleculaire." *Conn. Vigne Vin* 19:31–40.

TENSCHER, A. C. 1986. The kinetics of sulfite- hydrogen-sulfite-binding with acetaldehyde and pyruvic acid. M.S. thesis, Davis, CA: University of California.

USSEGLIO-TOMASSET, L., and P. D. BOSIA. 1984. "La prima constante di dissociazione dell'acido solforoso." *Vini d'Italia* 26:7–14.

UZUKA, Y., and T. NOMURA. 1986. "Determination of sulfite resistance in wine yeasts." *Proc. 6th Aust. Wine Ind. Tech. Conf.*, T. H. Lee, Ed., p. 141–145.

UZUKA, Y., R. TANAKA, T. NOMURA, and K. TANAKA. 1985. "Method for the determination of sulfite resistance in wine yeasts." *J. Ferm. Technol.* 63:107–114.

VAHL, J. M., and J. E. CONVERSE. 1980. "Ripper procedure for determining sulfur dioxide in wine." *J. Assoc. Off. Anal. Chem.* 63:194–199.

VALERO, E., R. VARON, and F. GARCIA-CARMONA. 1992. "Kinetic study of the metabisulfite on polyphenol oxidase." *J. Agric. Food Chem.* 40:904–908.

VAN UDEN, N., P. ABRANCHES, and C. CABECA-SILVA. 1968. "Temperature functions of thermal death in yeasts and their relation to the maximum temperature for growth." *Arch. Mikrobiol.* 61:381–393.

VANDERSCHMITT, D. J., K. S. VITOS, F. M. HUENEKENS, and K. G. SCRIMGEOUR. 1967. "Addition of sulfite to folate and dihydrofolate." *Arch. Biochem. Biophys.* 122:448–493.

VAS, K. 1949. "The equilibrium between glucose and sulfurous acid." *J. Soc. Chem. Ind.* 68: 340–343.

VILLETON-PACHOT, J. P., M. PERSIN, and J. Y. GAL. 1980. "Titrage coulometrique du dioxyde de soufre dans les vins avec detection electrochimique du point equivalent." *Analysis* 8(9): 422–427.

WALKER, J. R. L. 1975. "Enzymic browning in foods: A review." *Enz. Technol. Dig.* 4:89–100.

WEDZICHA, B. L. 1984. *Chemistry of Sulphur Dioxide in Foods*. London: Elsevier Applied Science Publishers.

WEDZICHA, B. L., and O. LAMIKANRA. 1987. "Kinetics of autoxidation of sulphur (IV) oxospecies in aqueous ethanol." *Food Chem.* 23:193–205.

WEEKS, C. 1969. "Production of sulfur dioxide-binding compounds and of sulfur dioxide by two *Saccharomyces* yeasts." *Am. J. Enol. Vitic.* 20:31–39.

WILDENRADT H. L., and V. L. SINGLETON. 1974. "The production of aldehydes as a result of oxidation of polyphenolic compounds and its relation to wine aging." *Am. J. Enol. Vitic.* 25:119–126.

WILLSON, K. S., W. O. WALKER, C. V. MARS, and W. R. RINELLI. 1943. "Liquid sulfur dioxide in the fruit industries." *Fruit Prod. J.* 23:72–82.

WURDIG, G., and H. A. SCHLOTTER. 1968. "SO_2 bildung durch sulfatreduktion wahrend der garung. I. Versuche und beobachtungen in der praxis." *Weinwissen*. 23:356–371.

YANG. S. F. 1970. "Sulfoxide formation from methionine or its sulfide analogs during aerobic oxidation of sulfite." *Biochemistry* 9:5008–5014.

YANG. S. F. 1973. "Destruction of tryptophan during the aerobic oxidation of sulfite ions." *Environ. Res.* 6:395–402.

CHAPTER 13

Must, Juice, and Wine Transfer Methods

INTRODUCTION

This chapter deals with the transfer of musts, juices, and wines by the energy imparted by mechanical pumps and by pressure differences. The various pumps that can be used are described, as well as the manner in which they are used. The calculation procedures for the sizing of pumps and of estimating flow rates are presented, together with typical examples.

The transfer of juices and wines should be made with clean lines and well-maintained pumps so that there is no leakage of material, introduction of air, or contamination by foreign matter. The transfer of musts should be performed so as to minimize the generation of additional solids.

The addresses of equipment companies mentioned in this chapter can be found in Appendix I.

A. TYPES OF PUMPS

Pumps are used to provide more rapid and convenient transfer of must (juice and skins), juice, wine, and even pomace from one location to another. In general, the pumps that are used for juice transfers can also be used for wine, while those that are suitable for must have special requirements, and the pumps that are designed for pomace transfer are a particular case. There is an array of manufacturers for some pump types such as the centrifugal pumps and a number of somewhat proprietary designs for others.

A desirable feature for the selection of pumps for juice and wine applications is the adoption of standards such as the 3-A Standard for dairy and other food applications as defined by the U.S. Public Health Service. This standard requires that all of the wetted surfaces of the pump must be made of a 300-type stainless steel or an equivalent material in terms of corrosion resistance. It also requires smooth surfaces that are free of crevices and minimum curvature of wetted surfaces. The pump designs should avoid the use of internal threads and permit easy dismantling for cleaning and inspection.

One classification of the pumps used in winemaking is shown in Figure 13-1. They can

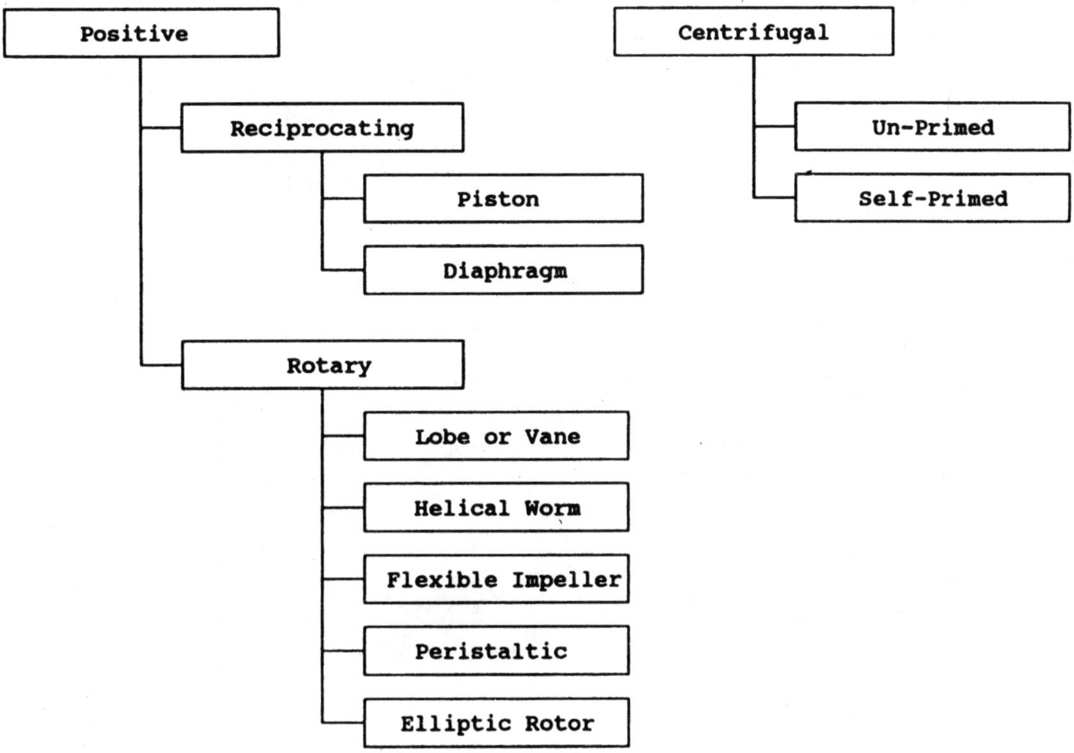

Fig. 13-1. A classification of types of pumps used in winemaking.

be sorted based on whether the flow rate is essentially proportional to the motor speed and other features that will be discussed in the following sections. There are also differences due to the nature of the pump drive, the presence or absence of speed control, and other considerations such as cart-mounted or fixed options and cleaning-in-place (CIP) installations.

The following discussion will be by pump type rather than its use in winemaking, and consideration will be given to the pumps shown in Figure 13-1. Three common types are shown in Figure 13-2.

1. Positive Displacement Pumps

As the name implies, these pumps have designs which can cause positive displacement of the fluid in the pump cavity, be it liquid or gas. They do not require priming as they can displace gas and will draw liquid in. They are more important because they have a throughput which is in proportion to their speed and they can be used as metering pumps for the in-line addition of materials such as SO_2 and pectic enzyme solutions and bentonite slurries.

In general, these pumps will continue to develop pressure at their discharge when a restriction or resistance develops downstream of the outlet. This can cause problems such as the separation of hoses from fittings or even hose rupture in some situations, if no exit is provided. The advantage of a predictable throughput is usually more important in general transfer and metering applications. The more expensive pumps of this type often have variable speed drives so that the flow rate can be varied as needed.

a. Reciprocating Piston Pumps

The piston pumps have a reciprocating piston within a cylindrical cavity. The fluid is usually drawn in during the reverse stroke and dis-

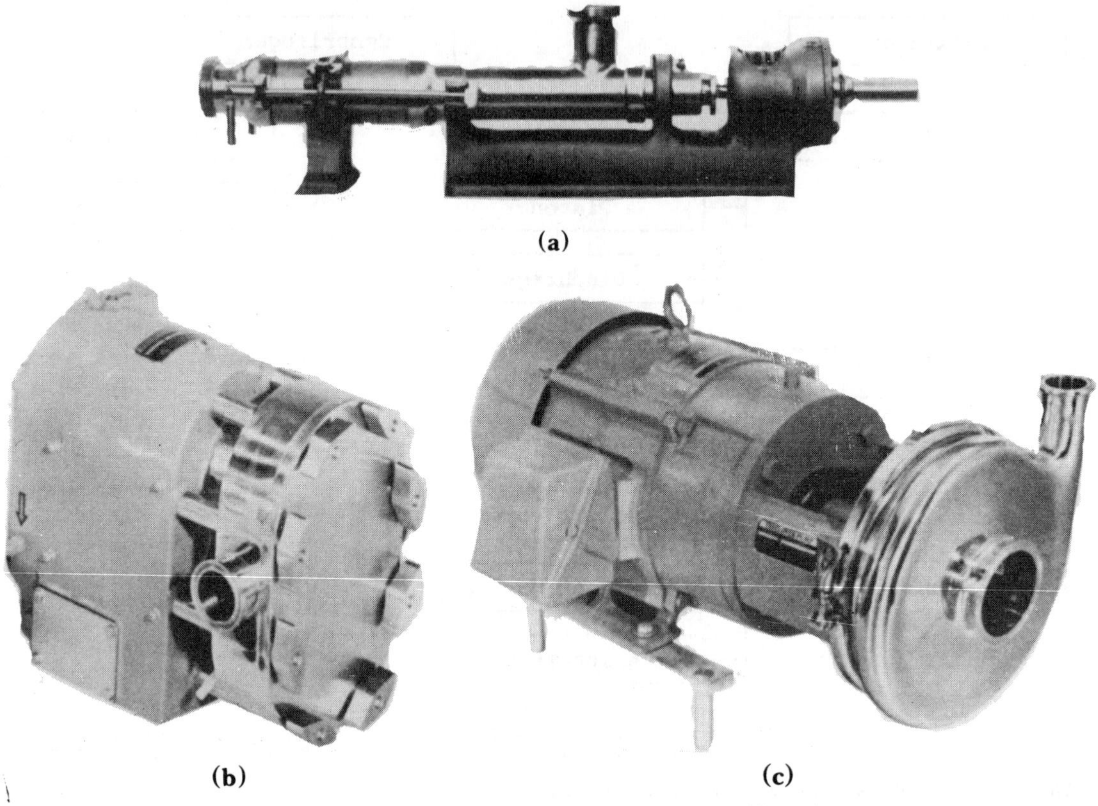

Fig. 13-2. Pumps used for juice and wine transfers; (a) Progressive cavity pump; (b) rotary vane pump; and (c) centrifugal pump.

placed during the forward stroke. Some models are double-acting in that displacement can be occurring on one side of the piston while intake is occurring on the other. There are usually two adjacent cylinders with opposite strokes and these usually share the intake and discharge manifolds.

These pumps are most commonly used for must pumps and are generally fixed in place next to the crusher. They can have capacities of 10 to 50 Tm/hr and the main manufacturers include Healdsburg, Demoisy, Manzini, Ragazini, and Vaslin. Portable units with similar capacities which are sometimes used for wine transfers include the Manzini and Enopompe units.

b. Progressive Cavity Pumps

The progressive cavity (or helical worm) pumps have a stainless steel helical rotor which turns within a larger helical cavity within a surrounding casing. The rotor is in close proximity to the casing, a similar position of each thread, generating a helical annulus of space that is tapered at each end. This helical cavity is displaced forward as the rotor turns, and a gentle pumping action results. The handling of must makes use of an auger section of the impeller that feeds the skins into the first pump cavity.

This is especially desirable for the minimization of the generation of fine suspended solids during the transfer of musts, juices, and wines. These pumps are commonly used for the transfer of shear-sensitive food and vegetable slurries.

The close spacing between the rotor and the cavity housing can lead to abrasion by granular solids (sand or bentonite) and the pump should not be used with such slurries, and in general, not unless there is fluid within the cavity.

The pumps can have capacities of up to 30 to 60 Tm/hr and the main manufacturers include Mono, Neztsch, and Vaslin. They are often fitted with variable speed motors to permit a wider range of operation.

c. *Rotary Vane Pumps*

There are many kinds of rotary vane pumps with the major differences being in the shape of the vane or lobe. There are two-, three- and four-segment stars and these vary in shape according to the model. The rotary vanes are mounted on parallel axles and the vanes are geared to rotate at the same speed in opposite directions. They are mounted so that as the lobes of one rotor move into the spaces of the other during a rotation, the fluid is displaced and swept out through the outlet. A more complete review is given by Little (1985).

Rotary vane pumps can be used for must pumps, juice, and wine transfers. They too should not be used when granular materials are present. They are available in capacities from 7,200 L/hr to 30,000 L/hr and the more common brands are Waukesha, Triclover, and APV-Crepaco.

d. *Flexible Impeller Pumps*

The flexible impeller pumps have a Buna rubber star wheel which is mounted in a deformed cylindrical housing. The axle allows the star fingers to be extended for the majority of the rotation, but the deformed shape causes these to compress as the finger approaches the two o'clock position. The rotation is generally in a counterclockwise direction with the inlet section being near the ten-o'clock to eleven-o'clock points and the outlet at the one-o'clock to two-o'clock points. These pumps have limited outlet pressure conditions and are more suited to wine transfers over short distances. The units should not be run without liquid as the friction rapidly causes the impeller to become scorched.

These pumps are suitable for juice and wine transfers only. The pumps are often referred to as Jabsco after one of the widely marketed designs, although other brands are available. They range in capacity from 6,000 L/hr to 12,000 L/hr.

e. *Diaphragm Pumps*

The air-operated diaphragm pumps are reciprocating units in which two adjacent cylindrical diaphragms are connected to an oscillating shaft. The shaft movement is controlled by compressed air, with the direction reversing at the end of each stroke. The speed can be controlled by the regulation of air supply and these pumps are particularly suitable for dedicated applications such as fixed-in-place pump-over arrangements, damp and wet environments where electrical insulation and grounding is difficult, and sump pumps. The inlet manifold is capable of feeding both chambers, filling one while the other is emptying in an oscillating action (Rupp 1985). The two main manufacturers of this type of pump are the Wilden and the Rupp Companies, whose models carry the Sandpiper name. The flow rates of these pumps range from 3,000 to 60,000 L/hr for air flows of 10 to 40 L/s. The air operating the pump does not contact the fluid, being on the other side of the diaphragm. There are now sanitary models of these pumps which are preferred for juice and wine applications.

2. Centrifugal Pumps

Centrifugal pumps provide rotational momentum to the liquid from a rotating disc or impeller, rather than relying on the actual displacement of a fluid volume as discussed previously. They are not usually self-priming, meaning that the pump cavity must be filled with liquid and a continuous liquid connection exists with the inlet, in order for the pump to function properly when started. The impeller has a considerable space between its outside edge and the housing so that a positive displacement of fluid does not occur. The liquid intake is at the center of the impeller housing and the discharge is at the wall in a tangential outlet. The flow can be restricted at the outlet without development of excessively large pressures, and this approach is generally used to control the flow rate. Restriction of the inlet flow by long, small-diameter lines, an inlet valve, or a reduced inlet pipe size can lead to cavitation and considerable foaming with wines due to the rapid removal of dissolved carbon dioxide.

There are many makers of sanitary centrifugal pumps (Triclover, Fristam, and APV-Crepaco) and pumps of this kind typically have capacities ranging from 12,000 to 60,000 L/hr.

3. Pomace Pumps

There is a limited number of pumps designed for the transfer of red skins from fermentors to the press. While this transfer can be performed by a specially designed pump, the operation generally results in significant tearing of the skins and seeds with a subsequent increase in the tannin pickup during pressing.

One kind is the elliptic rotor pumps that operate at relatively low rotational speeds (30 to 60 rpm) and displace the pomace cake with a sweeping motion of a star-shaped or an ovoid-shaped rotor and a scraping blade. They are not suitable for fluid transfer, but are included in the present discussion due to their pumping action. They are fed from an attached hopper by conveying screws and have a large-diameter outlet tube. The Egretier and Diemme units are the more common pumps of this kind and they can have capacities of 5 to 50 Tm (dry pomace)/hr. Another type is a four-bladed gear pump with an eccentric rotor that displaces the pomace as the clearance between the rotor and the outer wall reduces as it approaches the outlet port. The manufacturers of this design include Ragazini and Mori.

B. PUMP CHARACTERISTICS

The relationship between the pressure rise developed at the discharge (or outlet) by a pump and the flow rate which corresponds to this is known as the pump characteristic. For positive displacement pumps this is generally a linear relationship with a very steep negative slope, as shown in Figure 13-3. This shows that the developed pressure rises rapidly as the flow is reduced due to either back-pressure or a flow restriction. By comparison, the centrifugal pumps have a less steep, more parabolic curve, as shown in Figure 13-4, rising from the maximum flow when no resistance is encountered to the maximum pressure that can be developed when no flow exists.

The pump characteristic curve is similarly shaped for a given design but can be altered by the choice of different motor sizes or impeller diameters and speeds, as can be seen in Figures 13-3 and 13-4. The efficiency of the pump and the suction head developed will also vary at different points along the characteristic. The selection of a pump will usually be based on the region of the characteristic which has the highest efficiency. Kittredge (1985) provides a recent review of pump selection methods.

The characteristic is especially important for the selection of the appropriate pump, taking into account the flow rate and resistance in pipe arrangements and filters that will be used. The pump characteristic can usually be obtained from the manufacturer or it can be determined experimentally by measuring the flow rate and outlet pressure at various outlet resistance conditions. This is done by placing a butterfly or ball valve and a pressure gauge in the outlet line and measuring the flow rate and developed pressure at several valve closures. This measured characteristic will also show if the pump is performing at below the design values due to worn parts.

C. THE CALCULATION OF FRICTIONAL LOSSES

The selection and operation of pumps requires some understanding of the flow condi-

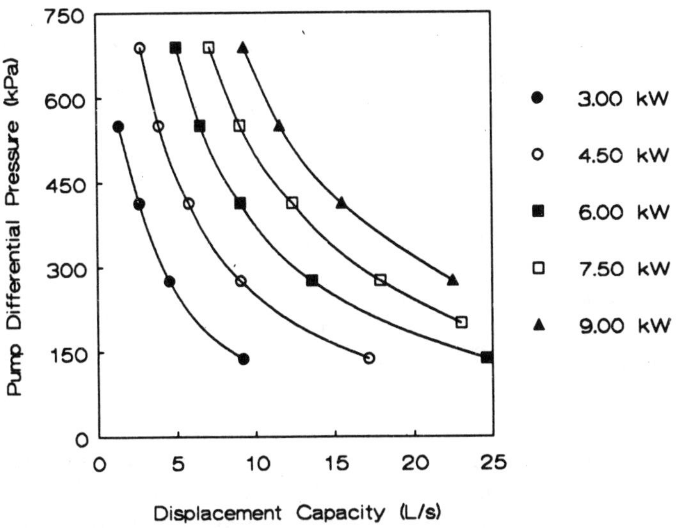

Fig. 13-3. Pump characteristic for a rotary vane pump.

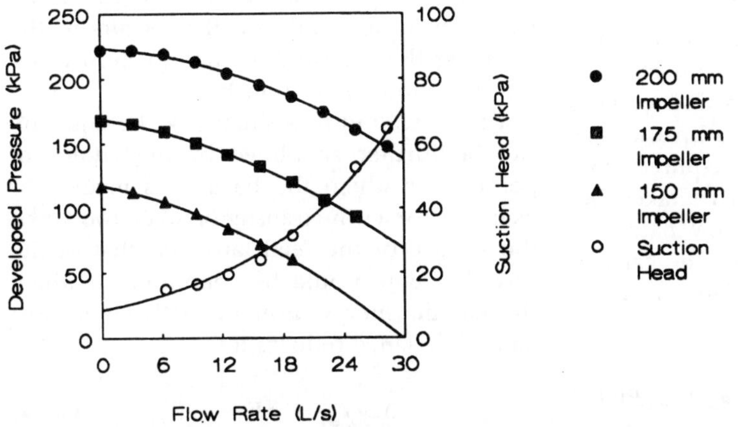

(a)

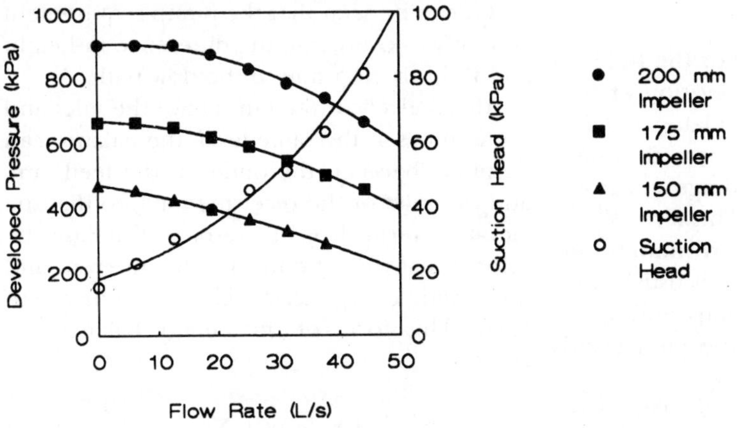

(b)

Fig. 13-4. The characteristic curves of a centrifugal pump: a) 1750 rpm b) 3500 rpm.

tions which the fluid will encounter in a given operation. The desired flow rate, the frictional losses and the changes in liquid level will need to be known before an appropriate selection can be made.

The following section provides the relationships that can be used in the evaluation of a number of pumping and wine transfer situations. It provides the methods that can be employed to estimate the frictional loss associated with the dimensions and fittings of the transfer lines and the way in which it is related to differences in surface elevation and energy input of the pumping system. The relationship is generally applicable to gravity-induced and gas-displacement flow situations as well as those resulting from the action of pumps.

1. The Energy Balance and Fluid Friction

The energy balance of a fluid describes the changes in the various energy forms between the final and initial conditions and equates this to the friction that results from the flow and the external energy that is required from the pump. The differences can be taken between any two points in the flow path and these can be selected to simplify the calculations. In its general form the balance is (Foust et al. 1960):

$$\Delta E + \Delta\left[v^2/(2g_c\alpha)\right] + \Delta zg/g_c + \Delta[PV] = Q - W_f - \Sigma F, \qquad (13.1)$$

where E is the internal energy of the fluid; v is the fluid velocity; z is the elevation of the fluid surface above a reference plane; and PV is the work term for gases. The heat absorbed by the fluid (from the surroundings and from friction) is represented by Q. The term W_f is the energy transferred to the surroundings in the course of the movement (this is usually the energy input required of the pump) and ΣF is the total fluid friction due to the piping and its fittings.

For most piping and pump calculations of interest in winemaking, the fluids will be liquids and the transfers will have a negligible energy increase. The result is that the heat absorbed, the change in internal energy, and the expansion work can be set to zero:

$$Q, \Delta E \text{ and } \Delta[PV] = 0,$$

so that a simpler form of the energy balance becomes:

$$\Delta\left[v^2/(2g_c\alpha)\right] + \Delta zg/g_c + \Sigma F = -W_f \qquad (13.2)$$

(One important situation in which this simplification cannot be made is when the fluid is recirculated and the accumulated heat Q (due to friction) is not negligible and the temperature of the liquid will rise. Such a case would be the heat accumulation that occurs in the recycling flow of the retentate in most cross-flow filtration applications).

For most fluid flow situations, the equation can be further simplified by the choice of points over which the balance is made. For example, for a wine transfer between two tanks, the surface of the feed tank and that of the receiving tank would be conditions in which the kinetic energy term would become zero and the balance reduces to:

$$\Delta zg/g_c + \Sigma F = -W_f, \qquad (13.3)$$

and it can be seen that the pump requirement is simply to overcome the difference in height and fluid friction due to the flow path.

Alternatively, if the tanks have the inlet and outlet pipes at the same level, the balance can be made between the outlet of the feed tank and the inlet of the receiving tank, so that the elevation term drops to zero. In this case the velocities at these points may be different and the kinetic energy term will need to be calculated. This form of the energy balance becomes:

$$\Delta\left[v^2/(2g_c\alpha)\right] + \Sigma F = -W_f. \qquad (13.4)$$

This second case requires considerably more calculation and it is the form shown in Equation (13.3) which is generally used for pumping calculations.

The energy balance calculation is usually performed on a unit mass basis so that the pump energy requirement W_f, would be expressed as energy per mass of fluid. The fluid power requirement of the pump (and its mechanical or electrical equivalent) is given by:

$$\text{Fluid Power} = W_f w = W_f v \rho A, \quad (13.5)$$

where w is the mass flow rate; ρ is the fluid density; and A the cross-sectional area of the pipe where the linear velocity v exists. This power requirement is that required for the fluid movement only and is also called the liquid or water power in some industries.

For a centrifugal pump, the fluid power requirement (Equation 13.5) can be written:

$$\text{Fluid Power (kW)} = 9797 vAH \text{ (s.g.)},$$

where H is referred to as the pump head, in meters; v is the velocity, in meters per second; A the cross-sectional area, in square meters; and s.g. is the specific gravity of the fluid.

For the rotary vane pumps, the fluid power requirement (Equation 13.5) can be written:

$$\text{Fluid Power (kW)} = \frac{vA\Delta P}{3.67 \times 10^5},$$

where ΔP is the differential pressure generated by the pump, in Pascals.

When an electrical motor is used on the pump, as is commonly the case, the energy efficiency of the motor and coupling must also be taken into account. The actual power required, generally referred to as the brake power (or in older units, brake horsepower) is related to the fluid power by the pump efficiency:

$$\text{Brake Power} = \frac{\text{Fluid Power}}{\eta}, \quad (13.6)$$

where η is the fraction of the applied power that is transferred into fluid power.

2. The Estimation of Fluid Friction in Pipes

The friction that a fluid experiences as it moves through pipes or tubes can be expressed as a combination of two terms, the first is due to the surface of the pipe wall, while the second is due to shape effects which cause the fluid to change its flow direction. The first can be thought of as that caused by a length of straight pipe or tubing and the second is due to fittings, bends, expansions, and contractions in the flow path. The general procedure for evaluating the total friction term ΣF is to use available equations for the friction factor of a straight pipe or tube and to express the various fittings and expansions as their equivalent length of straight pipe.

The friction factor (f) is a measure of the energy lost by the fluid to friction and is numerically equal to (ΣF) scaled by the kinetic energy of the fluid as it flows ($v^2/2g_c$), where v is a characteristic fluid velocity in the pipe. Where different pipe diameters exist, the term is evaluated in each section and the individual values totaled.

There are general correlations of the friction factor for pipe flows in terms of the Reynolds number N_{Re}, and the pipe roughness, ε/D. The solution procedure requires a trial-and-error calculation of the resulting fluid velocity.

$$\text{Friction Factor } f = \frac{\Sigma FD}{v^2/2g_c \Sigma L} = f[N_{Re}, \varepsilon/D], \quad (13.7)$$

where $N_{\text{Re}} = Dv\rho/\mu$; and ε/D is the relative roughness of the pipe wall.

The general relationships between the friction factor and the Reynolds number for flow in tubes is usually presented in the form of charts and these are generally available in most engineering texts and handbooks (Foust et al. 1960; Bird et al. 1960). The friction factor chart shows that all flows in the laminar region (that is with a Reynolds number less than 64) behave similarly. In the turbulent region of higher Reynolds numbers, the friction factor becomes a function of the relative roughness ε/D also.

a. *Juice, Must, and Wine Viscosity*

The viscosity (measured in Pascal-seconds, Pa · s) of most fluids is temperature-dependent and the temperatures of interest for winemaking application usually range between 0°C and 30°C. The viscosity of most liquids can be described by a general exponential form in terms of the inverse absolute temperature (Bird et al. 1960).

The viscosity of wine (based on a 12% by volume ethanol solution) can be expressed over the temperature range 0°C to 50°C by the following equation, (R = 8.134 J/mole/K):

$$\mu = 1.287 \times 10^{-7} \exp\left[\frac{22{,}460}{R(T + 273.2)}\right] \text{Pa} \cdot \text{s}, \tag{13.8a}$$

and the corresponding relationship for a juice (based on a 22 Brix sugar solution) is:

$$\mu = 2.778 \times 10^{-8} \exp\left[\frac{26{,}900}{R(T + 273.2)}\right] \text{Pa} \cdot \text{s}. \tag{13.8b}$$

The apparent viscosity of musts is generally assumed to be five to 10 times that of juice at the same temperature. It varies depending on the extent to which juice and skins have separated and the presence of stems.

For calculations involving water flows, the viscosity is described by the following relationship:

$$\mu = 8.132 \times 10^{-5} \exp\left[\frac{6{,}890}{R(T + 273.2)}\right] \text{Pa} \cdot \text{s}. \tag{13.8c}$$

b. *Estimation of Pipe Roughness*

The pipe roughness ε influences the relationship between flow rate and frictional resistance and must be taken into account. The pipe roughness is a measure of the finish on the flow surface and has an estimated value of 2.0×10^{-5} for stainless steel pipe, 5.0×10^{-4} for plastic hose, and $1.5 \times$ x10^{-4} for rubber hose. This is then scaled by the pipe diameter to produce the relative roughness ε/D used in the friction factor charts.

For smooth tubing typical of stainless steel and plastic tubing, and the use of typical pipe diameters used in wine transfers, the relative roughness can be taken to be 0.00002 and the friction factor in the turbulent region is described by:

$$\log_{10}(f) = \frac{4.513}{\log_{10}(N_{\text{Re}})} - 2.640. \tag{13.9}$$

This form can be conveniently incorporated into computer calculations for the frictional loss.

3. Friction in Pipe Fittings

While the first component of the fluid friction is that due to pipe walls, the second is associated with changes in flow velocity caused by bends and fittings in the line. The magnitude of these losses will depend on both the pipe diameter and the nature of the fittings. These losses can be estimated either in terms of their equivalent length in pipe diameters from nomograms, equations, or tables or by the use of the K factor approach. The K factor is the ratio of the energy loss (due to the fitting) to the kinetic energy of the flowing fluid ($v^2/2g_c$) (McCabe and Smith 1967). It is similar to the friction factor for straight pipes and the loss can then be expressed as an equivalent length of pipe. It is particularly useful in estimating the effect of discharge into and out of tanks, or changes in pipe or hose sizes, both situations which are of importance in wine transfers.

a. *Bends and Tees*

The resistance of many common fittings have been determined and are resented in most texts dealing with piping networks and flows

Table 13-1. The flow resistance of some pipe fittings (Foust et al. 1960).

Type of fitting	Equivalent length (pipe diameters)
90° standard elbow	30
45° standard elbow	16
90° long radius elbow	20
Square corner elbow	57
Standard tee	
flow through branch	60
flow through straight	20
Sharp return bend	75

(Foust et al. 1960; Messina 1985). The resistance of fittings commonly used in wineries is presented in Table 13-1.

A standard 90° elbow causes a loss equal to that of a pipe that is 30 pipe diameters in length. A long radius 90° elbow is equivalent to only 20 pipe diameters, while a square corner elbow is equivalent to 57 pipe diameters. A close pattern return (or U) bend is equivalent to 75 pipe diameters of loss while a 45° bend provides only 16. Flow through the straight run of a T fitting causes a loss equivalent to a length of 20 pipe diameters and flow through the branch of the tee results in a loss of 60.

4. Friction in Valves

The flow resistance of valves is quite different between types of valves and depends also on the degree to which the flow is restricted. Valves can be a major component in the friction loss due to the fittings as evidenced by their use to adjust and control the flow rate. Their contribution to the total frictional loss will be especially important in short pipe lines and rises rapidly as the closure increases.

a. *Ball Valves*

These valves are especially desirable for applications in which there are grape skins and pulp present. They comprise a solid sphere with a large hole through its center that is encased by a metal block. The diameter of the sphere (i.e., the ball) is usually about 1.5 times that of the pipe and that of the hole is equal to that of the pipe. When in the open position, there is no obstruction and the pipe wall appears to be continuous. They can be used in conjunction with tank mixers that require the center of the pipe to be clear. When turned through 90°, the ball completely blocks off the pipe diameter. They provide relatively little resistance when fully open but will contribute a resistance of 50 pipe diameters in equivalent length at 50% closure. The valve opening is designed to provide a good sanitary liquid seal and the sharp edges will provide a further 150 pipe diameters in resistance between the 50% and 60% closure positions. The resistance (expressed as the equivalent length in pipe diameters) is described by the following equation:

$$\text{Resistance} = 0.122 \exp(0.124\,[\%\ \text{closure}]), \tag{13.10a}$$

and this is shown in Figure 13-5.

b. *Butterfly Valves*

These valves are the most commonly used alternative to the ball valves and provide insignificant resistance when fully open. The valve element is a circular disc that is mounted vertically in the center of the pipe so that when fully closed, the disc blocks the pipe completely. When fully open, the disc presents only the disc thickness to the fluid. These valves cannot be used with tank mixers that require the center of the pipe to be clear. There exists a chance that solids, such as skins or stems, can become lodged between the disc edge and the pipe wall and this leads to an incomplete seal and leakage. They can give rise to a resistance of 30 pipe diameters in equivalent length at 50% closure. Like the ball valves, they display an increase of 90 pipe diameters in resistance as the closure increases from 50 to 60%. The resistance is described by

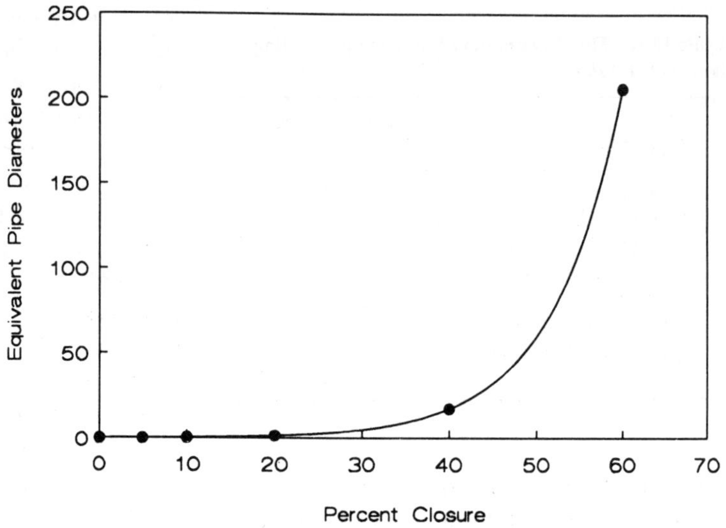

Fig. 13-5. The flow resistance of a ball valve.

the following equation:

$$\text{Resistance} = 0.0934\exp(0.119\,[\%\ \text{closure}]), \quad (13.10b)$$

and this is shown in Figure 13-6.

c. *Diaphragm Valves*

The diaphragm valves are more common in nonwine applications due to the difficulty in cleaning them. They are made up of a smooth, raised hump in the floor of the pipe that occupies about 30% of the flow area. From the roof of the pipe there is a deformable rubber element that is moved down until it reaches the raised floor surface, sealing the pipe. They require several revolutions of the valve stem to accomplish this movement. They are often used as part of flow control systems in water and utility piping and are included with those applications in mind. They provide relatively little flow resistance due to the smooth surface of the diaphragm and the valve housing. They provide only three pipe diame-

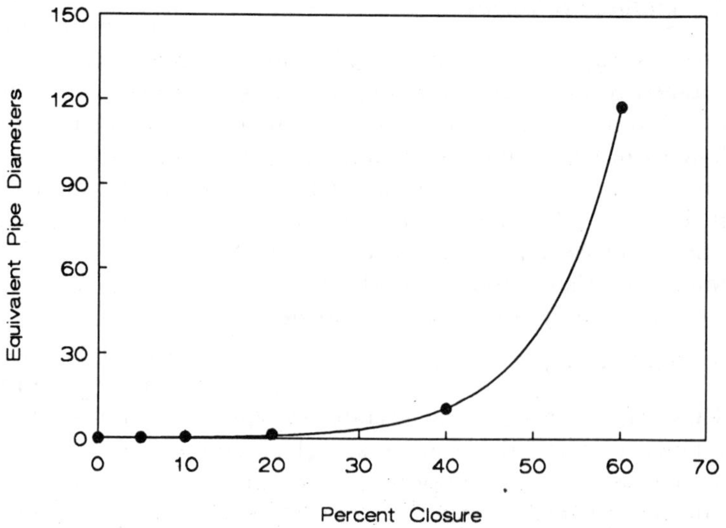

Fig. 13-6. The flow resistance of a butterfly valve.

ters in equivalent length at 50% closure and although the resistance increases with further closure, it is only 20 pipe diameters at 75% closure. The resistance is described by the following equation:

$$\text{Resistance} = 2.30 + 0.0235\exp(0.0891\,[\%\ \text{closure}]), \qquad (13.10c)$$

and this is shown in Figure 13-7.

5. Expansions and Contractions in Pipe Diameter

In most transfer situations there will be some contractions and enlargements of the flow area associated with the flow. These will usually be at the tank to pipe connections but can also occur if there are changes in pipe diameter within the lines. The estimation of the equivalent pipe diameters for changes in the pipe diameter due to a sudden expansion or contraction can be made with the aid of the relationship between the ratio of the upstream and downstream pipe diameters. These have been determined experimentally (Foust et al. 1960) and can be described by the following functions:

$$K \text{ factor (expansion)} = 1.0\left(1.0 - [D_1/D_2]^2\right)^{2.00} \qquad (13.11a)$$

and

$$K \text{ factor (contraction)} = 0.5\left(1.0 - [D_1/D_2]^2\right)^{1.35}, \qquad (13.11b)$$

where D_1 is always the smaller and D_2 the larger of the two diameters. These relationships are shown in Figure 13-8 and Figure 13-9 respectively. The relationship is also suitable for changes in pipe size when different hoses are connected, as sometimes occurs in practices.

The relationship between the K factor and the equivalent length of pipe depends on the pipe diameter. For nominal pipe diameters of 25, 50, and 75 mm and for K factors up to 5.0, the relationship is of the general form:

$$\text{Equivalent length (pipe diameters)} = B\ (K \text{ factor}),$$

where B has the values 54, 56, and 60 for the 25-, 50-, and 75-mm diameters respectively.

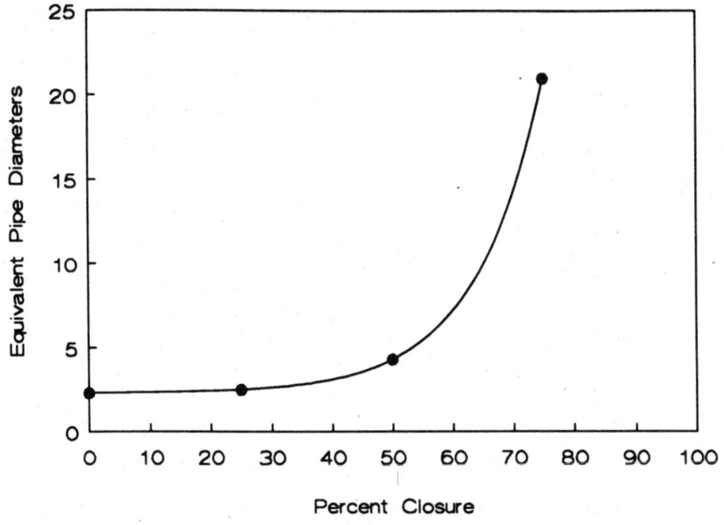

Fig. 13-7. The flow resistance of a diaphragm valve.

There are a number of other pipe entrance configurations that are less common in winery applications, and the resistance of these can be found in most text dealing with pipe flow calculations (e.g., Foust et al. 1960).

6. Examples of Fluid Transfer

The following examples illustrate the application of these formulas to the estimation of flows in typical wine transfer situations. The calculations can be used to calculate the expected flow for a given arrangement of liquid levels, piping and pump size, or to calculate the required pump size or (applied pressure) in order to achieve a specified flow rate. The situation to be analyzed involves the transfer of wine from a tank in which the level is 10 m above the base, to an adjacent tank, initially empty, of similar dimensions. The flow rate that results for a 100-m pipeline, 50 mm in diameter, with 10-kW pump operating at 80% efficiency will be calculated. This transfer line includes two 90° bends, a ball valve that is 20% closed, and a butterfly valve that is 50% closed.

The ΣL term in Equation 13.7 will be the equivalent length of the transfer hose and its fittings, including the outlet of the first tank and the inlet of the second tank. Reference to Figure 13-8 shows that the resistance of these valves is 1.5 and 36 pipe diameters respectively, while that of the two 90° bends (Table 13-1) adds another 30 pipe diameters each. The inlet contraction and outlet expansion contribute another 27 and 54 pipe diameters in effective length. The effective length of the line is then the 100 m of actual length and an additional equivalent length of 9 m due to the fittings and flow changes.

In this example, it is convenient to choose the liquid levels in each tank as the reference points at which to apply the energy balance. The choice of the surface also eliminates the kinetic energy term since the fluid velocity at the surface will be zero.

Equation (13.3) is the form of the balance to be applied and since the unknown fluid velocity appears in both the fluid power and the friction terms, a trial-and-error calculation is required.

Three points within the transfer will be considered; the start (when the first tank is full and the second tank is empty), the midway point (at which the levels are the same), and the end (when the transfer is almost completed).

At the start, the height of the wine adds to the work done by the pump. An initial esti-

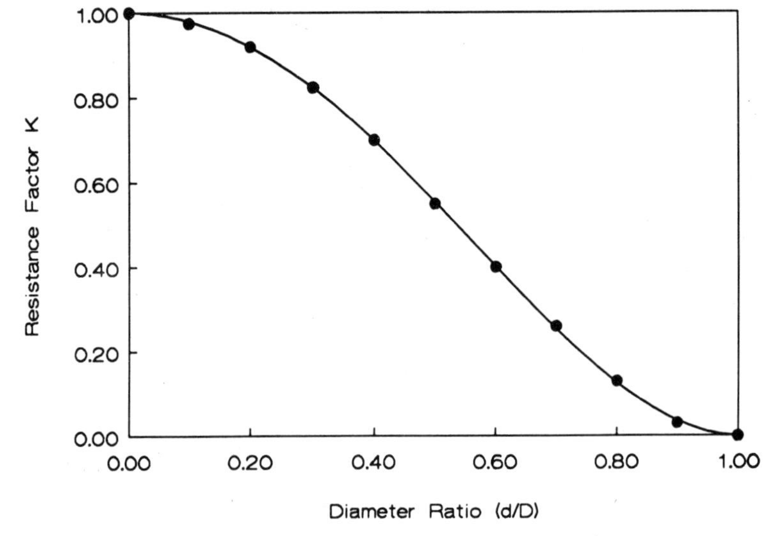

Fig. 13-8. The flow resistance due to sudden expansions in pipe diameter.

mate of the velocity can be made and the Reynolds number. This permits the evaluation of the friction factor by Equation (13.9) and the calculation of the ΣF term by Equation (13.7).

The balance can then be written (Equation (13.3)):

$$\Delta zg/g_c + \Sigma F = -W_f$$

$$-10 + \Sigma F = -W_f.$$

The right-hand side of the equation is calculated from Equations (13.5) and (13.6) and will include the estimated fluid velocity. Depending on the relative magnitude of the two sides, a second estimate of the fluid velocity is made and the procedure repeated until both sides are essentially equal. The flow rate at the beginning of the transfer is 5.68 m/s, corresponding to a volumetric flow rate of 9.66 L/s.

At the midway point the levels will be the same in similar tanks and the elevation term is reduced to zero. The calculation procedure remains the same, but with a modified energy balance (Equation (13.3)):

$$\Delta zg/g_c + \Sigma F = -W_f$$

$$0 + \Sigma F = -W_f.$$

The flow rate at the midpoint of the transfer is 5.23 m/s, corresponding to a volumetric flow rate of 9.03 L/s.

At the end of the transfer the elevation term is acting against the pump and the energy balance becomes (Equation 13.3):

$$\Delta zg/g_c + \Sigma F = -W_f$$

$$+10 + \Sigma F = -W_f. \qquad (13.3)$$

The flow rate at the end of the transfer is 4.95 m/s, corresponding to a volumetric flow rate of 8.40 L/s.

If a smaller pump (5 kW) had been used, the corresponding flow rates would have been 7.78, 7.10 and 6.37 L/s at the same three points within the transfer. If a 75-mm-diameter line had been used, the corresponding flow rates would have been 21.1, 18.76, and 16.2 L/s. While the effect of liquid level is significant, it only alters the flow rates by approximately 20% in this example.

7. Graphical Solutions

The alternative to performing these calculations is the use of a generalized graphical solution procedure such as that developed by the Waukesha pump company. This pipe flow nomogram provides a means of solving the equations graphically and is considerably faster

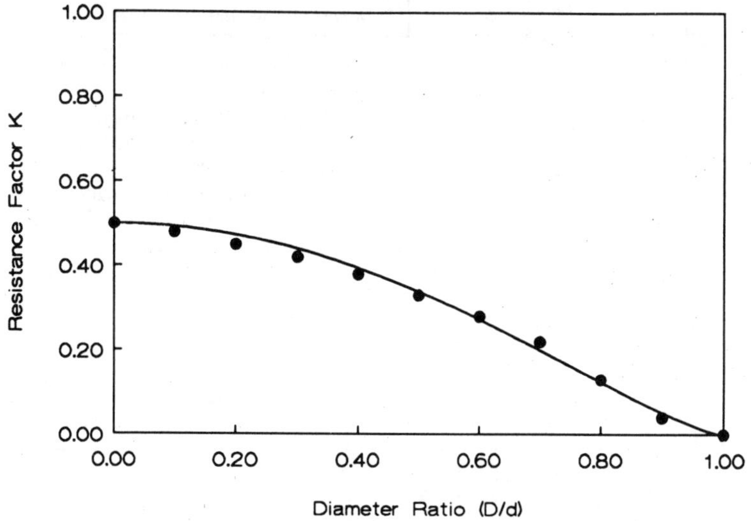

Fig. 13-9. The flow resistance due to sudden contractions in pipe diameter.

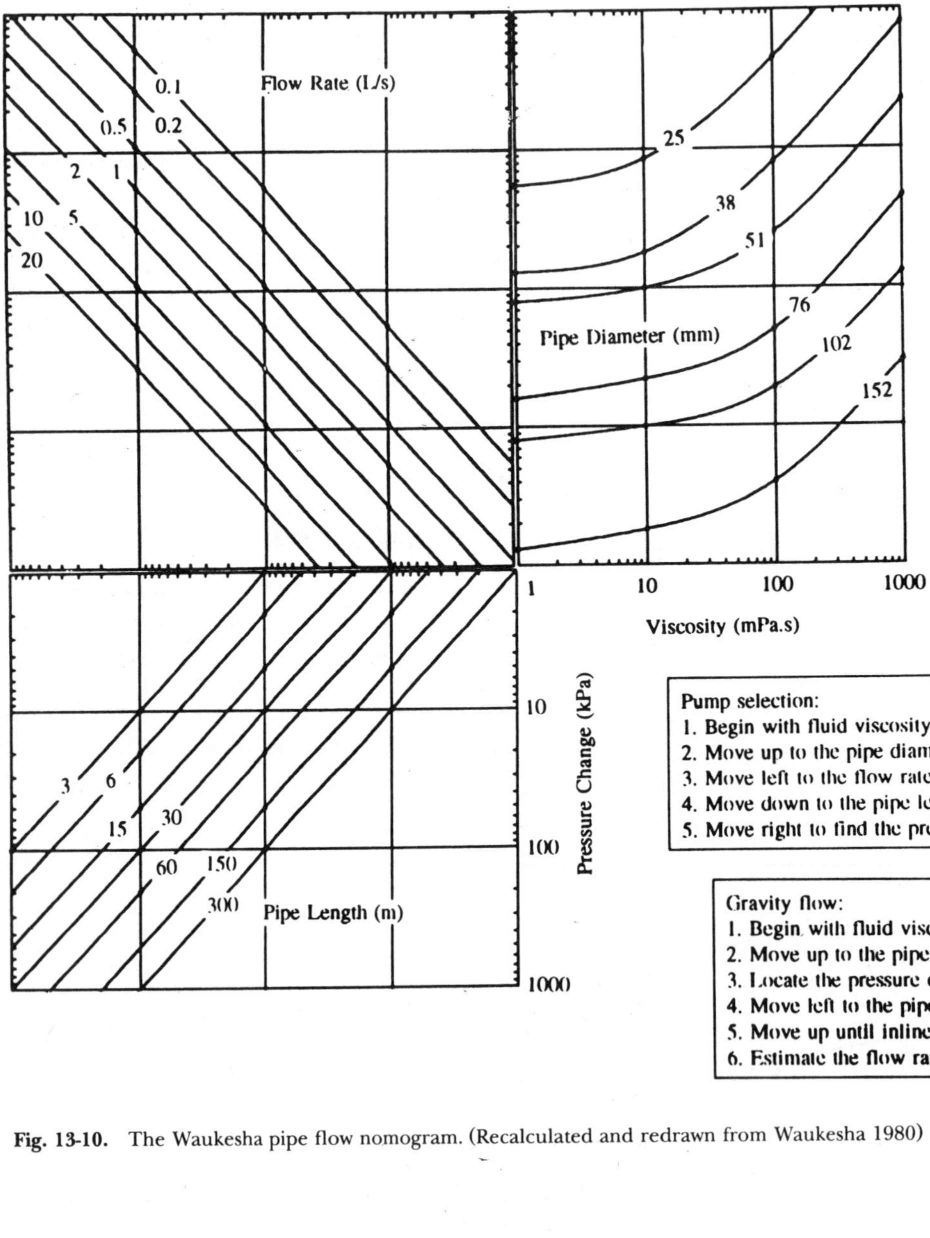

Pump selection:
1. Begin with fluid viscosity.
2. Move up to the pipe diameter.
3. Move left to the flow rate.
4. Move down to the pipe length.
5. Move right to find the pressure change.

Gravity flow:
1. Begin with fluid viscosity.
2. Move up to the pipe diameter.
3. Locate the pressure change.
4. Move left to the pipe length.
5. Move up until inline with 2.
6. Estimate the flow rate.

Fig. 13-10. The Waukesha pipe flow nomogram. (Recalculated and redrawn from Waukesha 1980)

than hand calculation, but is less accurate. In many cases the graphical solution will be sufficiently accurate for many transfer situations. The nomogram is best suited to flow problems that do not involve pumps, and the aim is to estimate the frictional loss expected for a specified flow rate in a given pipeline. The knowledge of the flow rate and the expected frictional loss will then permit the pump to be selected. For other situations such as gravity flows or pressurized transfers, the nomogram can be used to estimate the expected flow rate. The metric version of this nomogram has been drawn and is presented in Figure 13-10.

The use of the nomogram can be illustrated with two practical examples that do not involve pumps. The first estimates the length of line required to provide a specified flow rate under the action of gravity over a particular elevation. The second estimates the pressure required to transfer wine at a specified flow rate over a given length of line and up to a specified elevation. These will be considered in more detail in the following section.

D. ALTERNATIVE TRANSFER METHODS

1. Gravity Transfers

Not all juice and wine transfers require mechanical pumping in order for the fluid to be transferred. Wineries and cellars that are located on hillsides, or winery designs where different aspects of the production are at different levels, can usually take advantage of gravity for downward flows, by syphoning. Gas pressure may be used to return the wine to higher elevations. The rates of such transfers are generally smaller than with mechanical pumps, but in the case of the filling and emptying of barrels this is often not a disadvantage but actually desirable. It is important to ensure that the feed tank is vented, since even with gravity flows, the vacuum generated is sufficient to buckle the tank.

The energy balance approach presented above can be used to analyze these situations but with the pump energy term W_f set to zero. Alternatively, the graphical solution using the nomograph can easily be applied to analyze these situations. The important condition is that now the difference in surface elevations is the driving force for the gravity flows (as is the applied gas pressure for the pressurized return flows).

An example of gravity flow involves the transfer of wines from a tank at one level to a barrel at another, some 20 m below. If a nominal 25-mm diameter line is used, what length of line is required so that a flow rate of 75 L/minute is achieved?

The pressure difference to overcome the friction is related to the elevation and the wine density. Using the nomogram (Figure 13-10), the pipe diameter (mm) is located at a viscosity of 2×10^{-3} (Pa · s) and drawn across until it intersects the flow rate line (L/s). A vertical line is then drawn down to the pressure loss of 19 kPa corresponding to the elevation. The length of the line required is read by interpolation to be approximately 61 m.

2. Gas-Aided Transfers

As mentioned previously, return of liquid to a higher elevation using inert gas pressure is a very real alternative to mechanical pumping in smaller wineries. The lateral transfer between barrels and tanks is merely a special case of transfer in which the elevation is less important. The added convenience of the gas transfer approach is that the barrel operations are generally intermittent, requiring repetitive stopping and starting of the flow. This is not the best condition under which to use a mechanical pump with an electrical motor, even if a remote on-off switch lead is used. The alternative use of a manual shutoff in the gas line provides a more direct control of the wine flow but also has a pressure carry over. A double-action solenoid that shuts off both wine flow and the gas line simultaneously is the ideal arrangement for fast shutoff without the carry over.

An example of a gas-aided transfer involves the transfer between barrels in which one is at ground level while the other is 3 m above the ground and the 25-mm-diameter transfer line is 30 m long. The desired flow rate is 20 L per minute and the wine will be transferred by gas pressure. What pressure should be set on the regulator in order to get the desired flow rate?

By reference to the nomogram (Figure 13-10), the pipe diameter is located at a viscosity of 2×10^{-3} (Pa · s) and a line is drawn across to the flow rate (L/s) and then down to the line representing the line length (m). The pressure for this flow rate can be read off the pressure axis (2.6 kPa). This represents the pressure to overcome the friction in the pipe due to the flow rate and to this is added the pressure required to overcome the elevation, giving a value of 5.3 kPa total pressure. The supply vessel must be gastight and able to withstand the necessary pressure. As a general rule, the tank should be capable of withstanding twice the operating pressure. Since the gas is in contact with the wine in such situations, compressed inert gases should be used rather than air.

E. IN-LINE ADDITIONS AND TREATMENTS

The consideration of pumping and liquid transfers would not be complete without some consideration of the measurement of flow rates for reasons of introducing and mixing reagents with juices or wines and the blending together of several juices or wines in particular proportions.

1. Measurement of Flow Rate and Volume Transferred

Liquid flows can be measured in a number of ways, but the two most important commercially are those that introduce some kind of flow restriction and measure the corresponding pressure loss and those which are based on volumetric displacement. The first group includes orifice plates and the Venturi tubes, while the second includes several commercial instruments that employ a range of displacement paddle wheels, turbines, or propellers whose rotational speed is measured. Other alternatives include various types of mass flowmeters.

In winemaking, there are additional considerations related to the presence of suspended solids, the ease of cleaning, and sanitizing. Combination meters which indicate the instantaneous flow rate as well as the accumulated volume are especially recommended since they are often the only convenient indication of the progress of a wine or juice transfer, the use of a heat exchanger for the recovery of energy between two wines, or process filtration.

Other reasons for employing a flow rate indicator (and/or accumulator) is the desire to accurately proportion a slurry into a wine such as the addition of a fining agent by a metering pump. The use of such flow measurements allows the use of in-line additions to be made during tank-to-tank transfers, often permitting the removal of the agent by a filter or a centrifugal separator prior to its introduction into the second tank. The addition of a slurry in this way ensures thorough mixing immediately after the addition in the turbulent flow of the transfer line rather than the generally inefficient mixing of a large tank volume. Such separations or clarifications are far easier to operate because the solids level remains essentially constant throughout the transfer, the time taken is then just that of the transfer and the solids may be kept out of the second tank.

Similarly, the interchange of energy from a cold-stabilized wine to a second, yet-to-be cooled wine will require good indications of the flow rate in order to achieve the optimal exchange conditions.

2. Solution and Suspension Metering

The metering of sulfur dioxide, ascorbic acid, and/or pectic enzyme preparations to musts and juices, the introduction of nutrient mixtures and yeast or bacteria inocula, and the addition of bentonite or protein slurries are some of the applications that can be greatly improved by the in-line approach.

The high viscosity of enzyme preparations or the abrasive nature of bentonite slurries make the use of conventional pumps impractical. A more suitable delivery system is to employ a small dispensing diaphragm pump and preferably one in which both the stroke and speed can be altered to suit the required delivery rate. Precise, proportional, and continual metering, as well as good downstream mixing, are important when small proportions of another solution (such as an SO_2 or bentonite mixture) are being introduced.

3. Mixing and Sparging

There are a number of occasions in which two wines or a wine and a secondary solution are to be mixed. One approach is to transfer the wines into a tank and to proceed with the mixing of the tank. A more suitable alternative is often the use of in-line mixing devices such as an in-place turbine, a short section of wire grids or screens, or one of several proprietary designs of packings that are mounted within a section of pipe. These mixing sections can be added into transfer lines when needed so that the mixing is more extensive between the streams when they first come together, rather than attempting to develop a good mixing pattern within a much larger vessel.

The same approach can be used for in-line gas spargers where the extent of contact between the two phases is greatly favored by an in-line mixing device. The use of short lengths of pipe fitted with porous stainless steel tubing makes an easily added unit that is easily taken apart and cleaned. While the use of in-line sparging has been widespread for many years, these operations are often inefficient due to the formation of large bubbles and inadequate mixing after the point of gas injection.

F. REFERENCES

BIRD, R. B., W. E. STEWART, and E. N. LIGHTFOOT. 1960. *Transport Phenomena*. New York: John Wiley & Sons.

FOUST, A. S., L. A. WENZEL, C. W. CLUMP, L. MAUS, and L. B. ANDERSEN. 1960. *Principle of Unit Operations*. New York: John Wiley & Sons.

KITTREDGE, C. P. 1985. "Centrifugal pumps: General performance characteristics." In *Pump Handbook*, 2nd ed., I. J. Karassik, W. C. Krutzsch, W. H. Fraser, and J. P. Messina, Eds. New York: McGraw-Hill.

LITTLE, JR., C. W. 1985. "Rotary pumps." In *Pump Handbook*, 2nd ed., I. J. Karassik, W. C. Krutzsch, W. H. Fraser, and J. P. Messina, Eds. New York: McGraw-Hill.

MCCABE, W. L., and J. C. SMITH. 1967. *Unit Operations of Chemical Engineering*, 2nd ed. New York: McGraw-Hill.

MESSINA, J. P. 1985. "General characteristics of pumping systems and system-head curves." In *Pump Handbook*, 2nd ed., I. J. Karassik, W. C. Krutzsch, W. H. Fraser, and J. P. Messina, Eds. New York: McGraw-Hill.

RUPP, W. E. 1985. "Diaphram pumps." In *Pump Handbook*, 2nd ed., I. J. Karassik, W. C. Krutzsch, W. H. Fraser, and J. P. Messina, Eds. New York: McGraw-Hill.

Waukesha Pump Engineering Manual. 3rd ed. 1980. Waukesha, WI: Waukesha Foundry Division, Abex Corporation.

CHAPTER 14

Heating and Cooling Applications

Process heat transfer is used at several points during winemaking to control or retard unwanted enzyme, microbial, and chemical reactions. These will generally include:

1. Must cooling in association with juice draining or skin contact prior to fermentation
2. Juice cooling prior to fermentation
3. Both the heating and cooling requirements of high-temperature short-time (HTST) denaturation of enzymes or to kill microorganisms
4. Heat removal for temperature control during fermentations
5. Cooling of wines for control of temperature during storage
6. Cooling of wines to enhance potassium bitartrate crystallization
7. Energy recovery by interchanging heat between warm and cold wines
8. Heating of juice for thermovinification
9. Cooling and air conditioning of the winery or aging cellars.

The type of heat exchanger that is best suited to perform a particular heat transfer function will generally depend on the particular conditions of the juice or wine, such as the presence of suspended skins and seeds or the possibility of ice formation.

While many wineries use their process refrigeration for the air conditioning of the winery, the temperature requirements for this application are much warmer than most wine cooling applications. The use of cold refrigerant temperatures for ambient temperature applications is not an efficient use of a refrigeration system and is a relatively expensive solution for the temperature control of a building. It will not be considered further.

In general, the use of a coolant stream that is more than 15°C below the warm fluid temperature is not a very energy-efficient situation. On the other hand, designs will usually require at least a 5°C temperature difference for acceptable transfer rates during the transfer operation. A poor and energy-expensive solution arises when the selection of an inefficient heat transfer arrangement is compensated for by the use of low coolant temperatures in order to get acceptable transfer rates.

A more conservative energy strategy is to use the warmest coolant temperature that is practical and to have this coupled with heat exchangers that have high coefficients of heat transfer.

The addresses of equipment companies mentioned in this chapter can be found in Appendix I.

A. HEATING AND COOLING APPLICATIONS

A general summary of the alternative types of heat exchangers that can be used for the various heat transfer applications in winemaking can be found in Figure 14-1. The alternative types are shown when more than one type is suitable for the application, with the recommended type listed first.

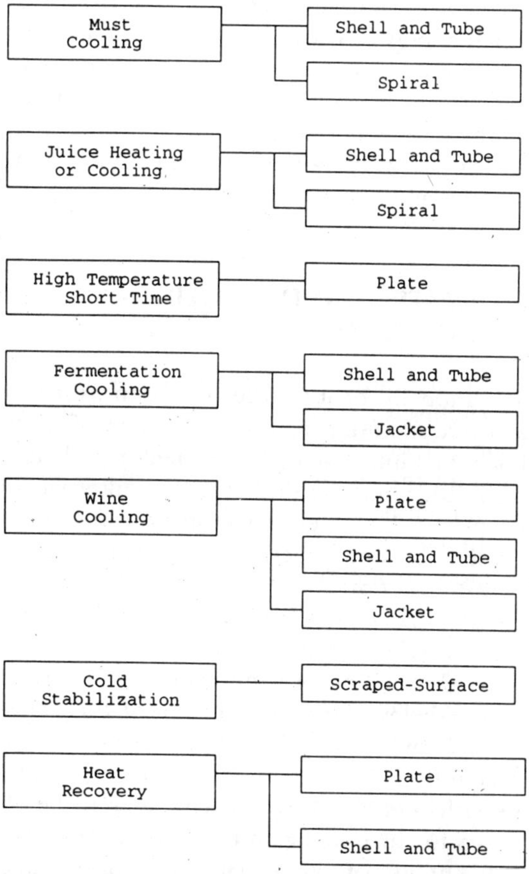

Fig. 14-1. A classification of heat transfer applications and suitable heat exchangers.

1. Must and Juice Cooling

The cooling of musts will generally require the use of a shell and tube heat exchanger, with large-diameter (75 mm or larger) tubing to minimize plugging by skins and stem fragments. These units usually have large radius return bends that are mounted externally to assist in the release of possible blockages and for ease of cleaning. An alternative would be the use of a spiral heat exchanger with its wide flow channels. For juice cooling, both of these units are acceptable for turbid juices but clarification by settling or mechanical means or the removal of seeds and stem fragments by screens would permit the use of a plate heat exchanger.

2. High-Temperature Short-Time Treatments

The application of high-temperature for short-time treatments for the inactivation of oxidative enzymes will usually involve rapid heating of the juice to 90°C to 95°C and holding it at this temperature for between 5 and 60 seconds before rapidly cooling it back to cellar temperature. The heat exchanger that can perform this task most effectively is a plate heat exchanger, in which the juice is distributed through each alternate plate while the heating medium (usually steam) is flowing countercurrent through the plates in between. The holding time can be controlled using a length of pipe with the desired residence time and the juice is then cooled in a second section of the plate exchanger in which the steam is replaced with refrigerated glycol. The plate exchanger provides a thin film of juice that can be heated (or cooled) from both sides, very rapidly, usually within a second or two. This arrangement also provides overall heat transfer coefficients that are between five to seven times those found in the shell and tube exchangers and provides the most control over temperatures and holding times.

3. Fermentation Cooling and Temperature Control During Storage

The removal of heat during fermentation can be achieved by the use of external cooling jackets on the fermentor, internal plates placed within the fermentor, or by an external shell and tube heat exchanger. The heat exchange is often scheduled to coincide with the pump-over operations in medium and large fermentors. The jacket or internal plate has coolant running through it but there is slow-moving juice at best on the warm side. This results in a low heat transfer coefficient on the juice side and a poor overall heat transfer coefficient for the arrangement. The use of the shell and tube exchanger provides flowing juice on the warm side and the coefficients are usually an order of magnitude higher. The same is true when using jackets or plates for the control of temperature in storage tanks. In storage situations there is even poorer circulation than in the fermentor, and this can result in temperature stratification. The denser, colder wine descends toward the base of the tank, in a natural convection current. The existence of such a current often leaves the warmest wine at the top unmixed and unable to be cooled since it is above the cooling jacket. A secondary concern with internal plates is the possibility of a refrigerant leak into the wine and the hindrance or need to be removed during cleaning.

4. Cooling for Cold Stabilization

The cooling of wines for stabilization is a special case since the coolant is generally going to be below the freezing point of the wine and ice formation is to be expected. The scraped-surface heat exchanger is designed to remove the ice as it forms, allowing only a thin ice layer to remain. Exchangers of this type can be used to deliberately form ice at levels such as 5 to 10% by volume. The ice slurry formed in this way can be mixed with the cool but icefree wine to cool it further as it melts the ice. It can also be used to temporarily concentrate the wine constituents and to favor the onset and rate of crystallization. The ice is usually allowed to melt back into the wine so that there is no net change in ethanol content or wine volume.

5. Heat Recovery Options

The heating and cooling medium will also vary with the application, from direct evaporation of a refrigerant to chilled glycol solutions, wine-to-wine energy transfers to steam heating. The kind of heat exchanger that is best suited for the application will also depend on the presence or absence of suspended solids and the extent to which energy is to be recovered. The preferred alternatives would be the plate heat exchanger in the absence of solids (due to its high coefficient) and the shell and tube exchanger in their presence. The extent to which energy is recovered is also influenced by the scheduling of heat transfer operations and the greatest improvements would appear to be in the sequential stabilization of wines with energy recovery rather than the more common parallel approach, without it.

B. HEATING AND COOLING CALCULATIONS

Traditionally, heat transfer has been primarily a batch operation in which the tank of must, juice, or wine is heated or cooled in isolation, with little attention to the possible alternatives for more efficient energy transfer. Many of the present cooling practices use relatively poor heat transfer arrangements and these require colder than necessary refrigerant temperatures to compensate.

In the cooling of wines to temperatures of 0°C or below, for the induction of the potassium bitartrate crystallization, it is common practice for several tanks to be cooled simultaneously and then several days later to be allowed to warm up again by heat gain from the ambient air of the cellar. The control and planning of the timing of these stabilization treatments so that wines are treated successively can reduce the energy consumption by as much as 70%. This can be achieved by interchanging the wine to be warmed up with the next wine to be cooled down to within 5°C of the stabilization temperatures with countercurrent wine flows in a plate heat exchanger. The refrigeration system would then be used to provide only the remaining temperature reduction, rather than the entire cooling load. Such an arrangement allows the interchange to take place in the time that it takes for a tank transfer to be completed rather than the more usual cooling period of a day or so. It also provides very efficient energy transfer, by allowing the higher coefficient of such an arrangement to provide the exchange at the warmest possible coolant temperature. This scheme would be optimized with two heat exchangers (one plate, the other scraped-surface) and similar-sized treatment volumes of wine.

The present, widely practiced alternative of employing a much colder refrigerant (often below the freezing temperature of the wine) and jacket cooling is perhaps the least energy-efficient arrangement. The operation is more wasteful due to the higher electrical energy requirement to generate the colder refrigerant, the poorer transfer rate of the jacket, the higher heat gain from the ambient air, and the problems of ice formation on the inside wall of the tank in the vicinity of the jacket. Ice formation on the outside of the jacket is an indication of significant energy loss during formation, although it acts as a thermal insulator once formed. The use of the jacket (or internal plate) also suffers from an ever-decreasing cooling rate that is characteristic of batch coding. This is due to the declining temperature difference as the wine approaches the coolant temperature. This arranagement requires the longest time to reach the desired temperature since the rate is continually decreasing, and with larger energy losses, due to the time taken. With jackets, there is no means of recovering energy unless a second external exchanger is used.

The practice of trickling water over the side of fermentors and storage tanks to provide some evaporative cooling effect is still used in some areas of the world. The advantages are a low energy consumption option for fermentation cooling, but there are several limitations of this approach. The coolest water temperature that can be attained is the wet bulb temperature of the surrounding air and this will be site specific and depend on the time of day. The evaporative conditions are favored in dry, low-humidity climates and this is not likely in coastal regions. Even with cool water on the outside wall, the heat transfer is limited by the coefficient at the inside surface, and the overall coefficient is poor. In areas where water hardness is a factor it can lead to appreciable scale deposits on the outside of the tanks and in some dry regions the water is too valuable to be used for this purpose.

Enologists need to be able to analyze and compute the time required for the cooling loads expected for various situations. The following summary of design equations attempts to cover the various applications that might arise during winemaking and to provide a basis for the selection of suitable exchangers. The equations are simply presented and the terms defined since they are based on the theoretical development of others and are generally available in standard heat transfer texts (Kern 1950; McCabe and Smith 1967).

The symbols used follow the definition of T for the temperature of the warmer fluid and t for that of the cooler fluid. The subscript 1 is used to refer to the entering stream and 2 for the leaving stream. A summary of the properties used throughout this chapter is presented in Table 14-1.The range of batch heat transfer arrangements is covered first followed by the continuous transfer cases.

1. Batch Heating or Cooling with Mixing

The following series of calculations can be used to estimate the time required (and heat loads) for the batch cooling of a tank of juice or wine. The assumption in this first series of

Table 14-1. The density, viscosity, heat capacity, and thermal conductivity of wine-related materials at 20°C.

	DENSITY kg/m^3		
Juice	= 1090	Wine	= 990
Water	= 1000	40% ethanol	= 940
Ethanol	= 789		
	VISCOSITY $mPa \cdot s$		
Juice	= 2.55	Wine	= 1.55
Water	= 1.00	40% ethanol	= 3.00
Ethanol	= 1.20	Ethylene glycol	= 24.0
Freon 12	= 0.28	Ammonia	= 0.12
	HEAT CAPACITY $kJ/kg/°C$		
Juice	= 3.80	Wine	= 4.50
Water	= 4.19	Ethanol	= 2.34
Ethylene glycol	= 1.00		
	THERMAL CONDUCTIVITY $W/m^2/(°C/m)$		
Juice	= 0.60	Wine	= 0.536
Water	= 0.610	Ethanol	= 0.156
Ethylene glycol	= 0.265		
Concrete	= 0.076	Copper	= 384
Cork	= 0.043	Glass	= 1.09
Ice	= 2.22	Kapok	= 0.035
Mild steel	= 45.0	Stainless steel	= 16.3
Urethane	= 0.031	Wood	= 0.21

calculations is that the tank is well mixed so as to provide a uniform juice temperature. There are several possible cases: heating with condensing steam, heating with hot water, cooling with evaporating ammonia (or freon), and cooling with glycol or cold water. The differences between these cases is whether the temperature is constant or changing within the exchanger.

The rate at which heat is removed is related to the volume V, heat capacity C, and temperature change $dT/d\theta$ of the juice or wine. It can also be related to the overall heat transfer coefficient U, the heat transfer area A, and the logarithmic mean temperature driving force, $[T - t]_{LMTD}$.

$$dH/d\theta = \rho VCdT/d\theta = F_T UA[T - t]_{LMTD}, \tag{14.1}$$

where T and t are the warm and cool fluid temperatures, respectively; θ is time, and F_T is the extent to which true countercurrent flow is in effect.

The logarithmic mean of the temperature differences is used because of the exponential rather than linear changes in temperature as the fluids flow through the exchanger. It provides a better measure of the effective temperature difference that exists within the exchanger. In its complete form, the log mean difference is written:

$$[T - t]_{LMTD} = \frac{(T_1 - t_2) - (T_2 - t_1)}{\ln (T_1 - t_2)/(T_2 - t_1)}, \tag{14.2}$$

where $(T_1 - t_2)$ is the temperature difference between the hot fluid entering and the cold fluid leaving at one end of the exchanger; and $(T_2 - t_1)$ is that at the other end.

The F_T term is a correction factor for the temperature difference that accounts for the extent to which cross-flow and cocurrent flows exist within the exchanger. For true counter-current flow the F_T factor is unity, but with certain flow arrangements, such as multiple passes of one of the fluids, then it will be something less than one. A discussion of this factor as it relates to particular exchangers is given in section c-2 of this chapter.

a. *Jacketed Heating*

The widespread use of jackets makes them an important case to consider even though the heating case is not common and the efficiency of their transfer is poor. The general form of the heat transfer equation becomes:

$$dH/d\theta = \rho VcdT/d\theta = F_T UA[T - t]_{LMTD}$$
$$= WC[T_1 - T_2] = W'\lambda, \qquad (14.3a)$$

where W is the mass flow rate of the heating fluid; C is its heat capacity; W' is the condensation rate; and λ is the latent heat of the condensing fluid. There are two situations and these are:

1. If the heating medium is condensing and has a constant temperature, the entering and leaving streams have the same temperatures ($T_1 = T_2$) and an example of this case is the heating of a juice with condensing steam.

   Integration of the rate equation leads to:

   $$\ln[T - t_0]/[T - t] = F_T UA/[\rho Vc]\theta, \quad (14.3b)$$

   and the fractional temperature change is given by:

   $$[T - t_0]/[T - t] = \exp(\theta/\tau), \quad (14.3c)$$

   where $1/\tau = F_T UA/(\rho Vc)$, and τ is the time constant of the temperature response. Larger values of τ will mean slower responses in temperature. The time constant is dependent on the volume and heat capacity of the juice (or wine), the heat transfer area A, and the overall heat transfer coefficient U. This is true only in the case in which there is an excess of heat supplied in the form of steam so that the condensing temperature of the steam is constant.

   The time constant is the time required for 63.3% of the overall temperature change to occur. After two time constants, 86.5% of the overall change will have occurred and after three, 95.0% will have occurred. The time constant can also be applied to the temperature change that is remaining after a particular time. It is 1.44 times the half-time, or the time required for half of the change to be accomplished.

2. In the absence of a phase change, the heating medium cools down as it heats the cooler stream. The temperature of the heating fluid is not constant, T_1 is greater than T_2 and an example of this case is the heating of a juice with hot water. The fractional temperature change is given by:

   $$[T_1 - t_1]/[T_1 - t_2] = \exp(\theta/\tau), \quad (14.3d)$$

   where $1/\tau = WC/(\rho Vc)[K_1 - 1]/K_1$ and $K_1 = \exp(F_T UA/WC)$.

   The time constant τ is now also dependant on the K_1, which involves the flow rate and heat capacity of the heating fluid as well as the properties of the exchanger.

b. *Jacketed Cooling*

The widespread use of jackets for the cooling of juices in smaller tanks and fermentors makes this case especially important. The general form for the jacket cooling equation is:

$$dH/d\theta = \rho VcdT/d\theta = F_T UA[T - t]_{LMTD}$$
$$= wc[t_1 - t_2] = w'\lambda, \qquad (14.4a)$$

where w is the mass flow rate; c is the heat capacity of the cooling fluid; and w' is the evaporation rate; and λ is the latent heat of the evaporating fluid. There are two situations and these are:

1. If the cooling medium is evaporating and has constant temperature, the entering and leaving streams are the same, $T_1 = T_2$ and this is the case of cooling a juice with an evaporating refrigerant such as ammonia.

   Integration of the rate equation leads to:

   $$\ln[t_0 - T]/[t - T] = F_T UA/[\rho Vc]\theta, \quad (14.4b)$$

and the fractional temperature change is given by:

$$[t_0 - T]/[t - T] = \exp(\theta/\tau), \quad (14.4c)$$

where $1/\tau = F_T UA/(\rho Vc)$.

The effect of the coolant temperature on the rate of juice cooling is shown in Figure 14-2. A 5-kL volume of juice that is well mixed is being cooled by an evaporating ammonia in a jacket with a heat transfer area of $8 m^2$. The juice, initially at 30°C, is cooled to only 24°C after 10 hours with the 15°C ammonia, but even with a coolant at 0°C, the temperature has only fallen to 16°C after the same period. The poor overall coefficient of this arrangement is the reason for the slow cooling rate.

2. In the absence of a phase change, the cooling medium heats up as it cools the warmer fluid, the temperature of the cooling fluid is not constant, t_1 is less than t_2 and an example of this case is the cooling of the juice with glycol or cold water. The fractional temperature change is given by:

$$[T_1 - t_1]/[T_2 - t_1] = \exp(\theta/\tau), \quad (14.4d)$$

where $1/\tau = wc/(\rho Vc)[K_2 - 1]/K_2$ and $K_2 = \exp(F_T UA/wc)$.

Like the heating case above, the time constant τ is now also dependant on K_2, which involves the flow rate and heat capacity of the cooling fluid as well as the properties of the exchanger.

Higher values of the overall heat transfer coefficient U (by mixing or more turbulent flow across the heat transfer surface) or A (larger heat transfer area) lead to smaller time constants and faster response; higher values of V lead to larger time constants and slower temperature response. In wine and juice applications, there is little variation in the juice properties density ρ and heat capacity C.

The alternative to the use of jacketed tanks is the use of an external exchanger and this is generally chosen for larger tanks and for more efficient heat transfer that results from higher overall coefficients. The exchanger most commonly used for this is a shell and tube unit.

c. Heating with an External Exchanger

Like the jacket example there are two important cases, one involving condensation of the heating fluid, and the other involving cooling of the heating fluid.

1. The heating medium has constant temperature, the entering and leaving streams have the same temperatures ($T_1 = T_2$); this is the case of using condensing steam to heat a juice (wine).

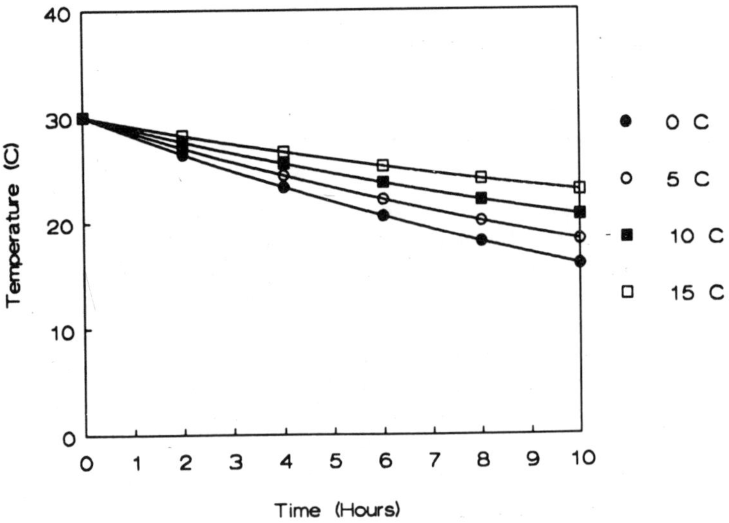

Fig. 14-2. The effect of coolant temperature on the rate of juice cooling by a jacket in a mixed tank.

The fractional temperature change is then:

$$[T_1 - t_1]/[T_1 - t_2] = \exp(\theta/\tau), \quad (14.5a)$$

where $1/\tau = wc/(\rho Vc)[K_2 - 1]/K_2$ and the variables are the same as defined previously.

2. The heating medium cools down as it heats the cooler stream, the temperature of the heating fluid is not constant, $T_1 > T_2$; this is the case of heating juice with hot water.

   The fractional temperature change is then:

$$[T_1 - t_1]/[T_1 - t_2] = \exp(\theta/\tau), \quad (14.5b)$$

where $1/\tau = (K_3 - 1)/(\rho Vc)wWC/(K_3WC - wc)$ and $K_3 = \exp(F_T UA[1/wc - 1/WC])$.

Note that now the time constant is also a function of the flow rates of the two fluids w and W, and their heat capacities c and C.

d. Cooling with an External Exchanger

1. The cooling medium has constant temperature, the entering and leaving streams have the same temperature $T_1 = T_2$; this is the case of an evaporating refrigerant cooling the juice.

   The fractional temperature change is then:

$$[T_1 - t_1]/[T_2 - t_1] = \exp(\theta/\tau), \quad (14.6a)$$

where $1/\tau = WC/(\rho VC)[K_1 - 1]/K_1$ and the variables are the same as defined previously.

The effect of the coolant temperature on the rate of juice cooling for this case is shown in Figure 14-3. A 5-kL volume of juice that is well mixed is being cooled by evaporating ammonia in an external shell and tube exchanger with a heat transfer area of 8m^2. The juice, initially at 30°C, is cooled to the coolant temperature after 10 hours. The arrangement shows a half-time of approximately two hours. The higher overall coefficient of this arrangement is the reason for the faster cooling rate than the previous example (Fig. 14-2).

2. The cooling medium heats up as it cools the warmer fluid, the temperature of the cooling fluid is not constant, $t_1 < t_2$; this is the case of glycol (or cold water) cooling the juice.

   The fractional temperature change is then:

$$[T_1 - t_1]/[T_2 - t_1] = \exp(\theta/\tau), \quad (14.6b)$$

where $1/\tau = (K_4 - 1)/(\rho Vc)Wwc/(K_4wc - WC)$ and $K_4 = \exp(F_T UA[1/WC - 1/wc])$.

Note that now the time constant is also a function of the flow rates of the two fluids w and W, and their heat capacities c and C.

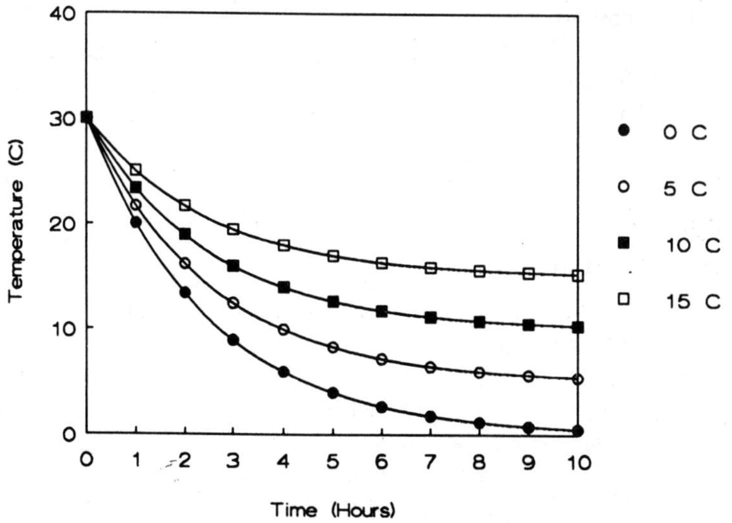

Fig. 14-3. The effect of coolant temperature on the rate of juice cooling by a shell and tube exchanger in a mixed tank.

2. External Heating or Cooling Without Mixing

The interest in having the contents of the tank mixed in the above analysis goes beyond the simplified mathematics of the results. The heat transfer using jackets is generally limited by the resistance to transfer at the inside tank wall. Swirling or mixing of the wine will often double the coefficient and it can be seen from the above equations that an increase in the transfer coefficient U, whether using a jacketed tank or an external heat exchanger, will reduce the time required to heat or cool the batch. However, a second feature of having the tank uniformly mixed is that the mean driving force is continually decreasing and this causes the exponential approach to the final temperature that is characteristic of these solutions.

The alternative case, which is the more common situation in most wineries, is for the contents of the tank not to be agitated. It can be shown by example that the shortest time for heating or cooling is actually obtained if the fluid is taken from the bottom of the tank and returned to the top without any mixing of the two layers. The actual winery tank will be somewhat more mixed when the fluid is returned to the tank, but it will approximate this case. It will be favored by tall, small-diameter tanks and return fittings that will favor the layering of the warmer fluid rather than its mixing.

In the following simplified analysis, the heating and cooling fluids are considered to be isothermal and the external exchanger is operating in true countercurrent mode.

a. *Condensing Heating Medium*

The heating temperature T_1 is constant and the initial juice temperature is t_1. The rate equation for the heat gain by the juice in terms of the logarithmic mean temperature difference is:

$$wc(t_1 - t) = F_T UA(t_1 - t)/\ln([T_1 - t]/[T_1 - t_1]). \quad (14.7a)$$

The temperature of the juice as it leaves the exchanger during the first circulation (and that of the juice in the tank after the first circulation) is given by:

$$t(1) = T_1 - (T_1 - t)/K_2, \quad (14.7b)$$

where K_2 has been previously defined.

The temperature at the end of N heating circulations is given by:

$$t(N) = T_1 - (T_1 - t)/K_2^N. \quad (14.7c)$$

The time taken for a circulation is $\rho V/w$, that is the mass of the juice divided by the recirculation rate and the time required for N circulations is then:

$$\theta = N\rho V/w. \quad (14.7d)$$

b. *Evaporating Cooling Medium*

The cooling temperature t_1 is constant and the initial juice temperature is T_1. The rate equation for the heat gain by the juice in terms of the logarithmic mean temperature difference is:

$$WC(T_1 - T) = F_T UA(T_1 - T)/\ln([T - t_1]/[T_1 - t_1]). \quad (14.8a)$$

The temperature of the juice as it leaves the exchanger during the first circulation (and that of the juice in the tank after the first circulation) is given by:

$$T(1) = t_1 - (t_1 - T)/K_1, \quad (14.8b)$$

where K_1 has been previously defined. The temperature at the end of N heating circulations is:

$$T(N) = t_1 - (t_1 - T)/K_1^N. \quad (14.8c)$$

The time taken for a circulation is $\rho V/w$, that is the mass of the juice divided by the recirculation rate and the time required for N circulations is:

$$\theta = N\rho V/W. \quad (14.8d)$$

An example of this approach to juice cooling is shown in Figure 14-4. The conditions are the same as those used in the two previous examples (Figures 14-2 and 14-3), except that the juice in the tank is not mixed. In this example the circulation time is approximately 1.5 hours and the temperatures at 1.5, 3.0, 4.5, and 6.0 hours correspond to those after one, two, three, and four circulations. It can be seen that the coolant temperature is essentially reached after four circulations (in six hours), even with the same coolant temperature and exchanger used in the example presented in Figure 14-3 that took 10 hours to obtain the same juice temperatures.

For the case of nonisothermal heating and cooling fluids, the temperatures of both fluids leaving the exchanger is unknown. This is not as simple as those above but the temperature relations after each circulation are given by as follows.

I. Heating Without a Phase Change. The temperature of the juice as it leaves the exchanger during the first circulation (and that of the juice in the tank after the first circulation) is given by:

$$t_1 = t + S(T_1 - t), \quad (14.9a)$$

where $S = [K_9 - 1]/[K_9R - 1]K_9 = \exp[F_TUA/wc(R - 1)$ and $R = wc/WC$.

For the second circulation, the juice temperature is given by:

$$t_2 = t + S(T_1 - t_1), \quad (14.9b)$$

leading to:

$$t_N = t_{N-1} + S(T_1 - t_N), \quad (14.9c)$$

for N circulations.

II. Cooling Without a Phase Change. The temperature of the juice as it leaves the exchanger during the first circulation (and that of the juice in the tank after the first circulation) is given by:

$$T_1 = T - S(T - t_1), \quad (14.10a)$$

where $S = [K_9 - 1]/[K_9R - 1]K_9 = \exp[F_TUA/WC(R - 1)$ and $R = wc/WC$.

For the second circulation, the juice temperature is given by:

$$T_2 = T_1 - S(T_1 - t_1), \quad (14.10b)$$

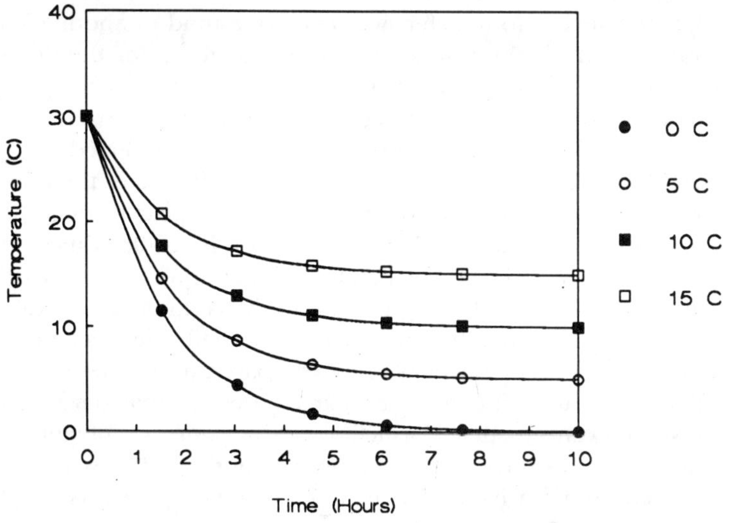

Fig. 14-4. The effect of coolant temperature on the rate of juice cooling by a shell and tube exchanger in an unmixed tank.

leading to:

$$T_N = T_{N-1} - S(T_{N-1} - t_1), \quad (14.10c)$$

for N circulations.

These formulas will permit the analysis of practically all of the batch cooling situations which are likely to occur in winemaking.

3. Continuous Interchange for Heating and Cooling

The transfer of energy between a cold wine and a warm wine can be accomplished during the cold stabilization of wines or in the warming of wines prior to bottling. Although the more common approach is to allow wines to warm up by heat gain from the surroundings, this is particularly slow and inefficient in terms of energy usage. The ability to interchange and recover energy between wines, especially during the cold handling and storage of wines can be accomplished by either a plate or shell and tube exchanger.

The exchange between the streams can also be shown to be:

$$dH/dt = WC(T_1 - T_2) = wc(t_1 - t_2), \quad (14.11a)$$

where W and w are the mass flow rates; and C and c are the heat capacities of the two fluids. With wine (or juice) on both sides, the heat capacity terms cancel and the ratio of the temperature changes experienced is inversely related to the ratio of the mass flows W/w:

$$W/w = (t_1 - t_2)/(T_1 - T_2), \quad (14.11b)$$

provided that T_2, the cooler temperature of the warmer wine is always higher than t_2, the warmer temperature of the cooler wine with true countercurrent flows.

The need for a minimum temperature difference of approximately 5°C will mean that not all of the excess energy in one stream can be captured by the other, but in most applications between 70 and 80% can be recovered. If the transfer arrangement is a shell and tube exchanger with more than one pass, a correction factor F_T will need to be applied to account for some parallel flow within the exchanger. This factor is generally in the range 0.75 to 1.0 and is further described in most heat exchange texts (Kern 1950). With true countercurrent arrangements such as the plate exchangers the factor becomes unity.

C. GENERAL HEAT EXCHANGER DESIGN CONSIDERATIONS

The design and selection of heat exchangers begins with the selection of a suitable exchanger type based on physical requirements such as the presence of solids, the possibility of ice formation, or a need for rapid heating and cooling. The design involves the specification of desired flow rates and temperatures and evaluating the overall heat transfer coefficient U for the type of exchanger and flow arrangement. This will lead to the calculation of the appropriate area A that is needed to provide the desired transfer rate under the conditions. While the conditions for certain applications may be similar for most wineries, the flow rates will usually be quite specific to the winery, based on typical treatment volumes and the choice of treatment time.

It can be shown that the most efficient way to transfer heat from one fluid to another, in the absence of phase changes, is for the fluids to flow on different sides of a surface, in opposite directions, in what is referred to as countercurrent flow. This is preferred since the average temperature difference, the driving force for the transfer, is larger throughout the exchanger and the outlet colder fluid can even be heated to a temperature above that of the leaving hot fluid. The countercurrent case has been extensively studied and exchanger designs are often compared to it. There are a number of exchanger designs that have flow patterns which contains some cocurrent or cross-flow components and so the extent to which true countercurrent flow exists is of interest in the design and selection of exchangers.

1. Extent of Countercurrent Flow

The rate of transfer $dH/d\theta$, is related to the overall heat transfer coefficient, the heat transfer area, and the effective temperature difference (Equations 14.3 and 14.4):

$$dH/d\theta = wc(t_2 - t_1) = WC(T_1 - T_2)$$
$$= F_T UA[T - t]_{LMTD},$$

where F_T is the thermal correction factor; and *LMTD* is the log mean terminal temperature difference. For true countercurrent flow, such as that exhibited by a double-pipe heat exchanger, the F_T factor is unity and this has become a reference condition when other flow arrangements are discussed. The need to make exchangers more compact and requiring less material has led to alternative designs in which fluid patterns are often less than ideal in terms of countercurrent flow, and their performance is usually expressed in terms of the true countercurrent case.

2. The F_T Factor

The temperature correction factor F_T, is a measure of thermal efficiency and its value will determine the extent to which the outlet temperature of the colder fluid can approach or exceed that of the leaving warmer fluid. For shell and tube heat exchangers, the F_T factor can be calculated from established formulas (Kern 1950). For the case of a 1-2 shell and tube exchanger, the formula takes the form:

$$F_T = \frac{\sqrt{(R^2+1)}\ln(1-S)/(1-RS)}{(R+1)\ln\dfrac{(2 - S[R + 1 - \sqrt{(R^2+1)}])}{(2 - S[R + 1 + \sqrt{(R^2+1)}])}}, \tag{14.12a}$$

and the two parameters R and S are the heat capacity ratio:

$$R = [T_1 - T_2]/[t_2 - t_1] = wc/WC, \tag{14.12b}$$

and the thermal effectiveness:

$$S = [t_2 - t_1]/[T_1 - t_1]. \tag{14.12c}$$

Standard texts provide more complete formulas for other exchanger arrangements, but typically the results are presented in graphical form for the more common flow configurations (Kern 1950; Saunders 1988). The corresponding F_T factor charts for plate heat exchangers have recently been published (Anon 1986; Raju and Chand 1980; Saunders 1988). The thermal effectiveness S has been used by some authors as a measure of efficiency since it relates to the temperature change obtained within one fluid $[t_2 - t_1]$ to the maximum possible between the two fluids $[T_1 - t_1]$. However, it would take an infinitely long exchanger for the maximum temperature rise to be attained. Instead, it is more practical to use the ratio of the heat transfer obtained to that of the corresponding countercurrent unit, that is the F_T factor, as the efficiency measure. The correction factor approach is straightforward when the flow rates and terminal temperatures are known, as is usual in the design situation.

3. Heat Transfer Units

An alternative design approach involves the concept of *transfer units*, in which the number of heat transfer units (NHTU) can be used to determine S and R without calculating F_T. This approach was developed by Ten Broeck (1938) for the evaluation of existing exchangers for other applications in which all of the terminal temperatures were often not known. The ratio can be defined for either fluid:

$$NHTU_c = UA/wc \quad \text{or} \quad NHTU_h = UA/WC, \tag{14.13}$$

and Ten Broeck (1938) and Saunders (1988) provide charts of NHTU curves (with R and S as the parameters) for shell and tube exchangers; Raju and Chand (1980) provide those for plate exchangers. This provides a more rapid calculation procedure but the designer is less aware of the extent of non-countercurrent flow. Some manufacturers use the term *thermal length* or *theta value* instead of heat transfer units, but this is a confusing term since it does not have the units of length. The number of transfer units can be used to classify exchangers with shell and tube units typically providing 0.5 HTU/pass while plate heat exchangers can provide between 2 and 4 HTU/pass, typically with only a single pass.

4. Specific Pressure Loss

The transfer unit concept is also useful in evaluating the compromise between the pressure loss expended in establishing fluid velocity within the exchanger and the corresponding transfer efficiency. The specific pressure loss, sometimes referred to as the Jensen number, is defined:

$$Je = \Delta P/NHTU, \qquad (14.14)$$

and should be in the range 20 to 100 kPa/HTU (3 to 15 psi/HTU) for optimal exchanger designs (Walker 1990).

5. The Estimation of Heat Transfer Coefficients

The overall coefficient in an exchanger can be related to the coefficient at the inside surface h_i, the thermal conductivity k_w and thickness x, of tube or plate wall and the coefficient at the outside surface h_0:

$$1/U = 1/h_i + \Delta x/k_w + 1/h_0. \qquad (14.15)$$

The inside and outside coefficients depend on the physical and thermal properties of the fluids involved and the fluid velocity at the surface. Correlations for the heat transfer coefficients take the general form:

$$Nu = aRe^x Pr^y (\mu/\mu_w)^z \qquad (14.16)$$

where Nu is the Nusselt number (hD/k); Re is the Reynolds number (DG/μ); and Pr is the Prandtl number $(C\mu/k)$. The last term is a viscosity correction factor that incorporates the viscosity at the wall temperature. The a, x, y, and z are empirical constants, determined for the particular type of exchanger. The fluid properties, thermal conductivity k, viscosity μ, and heat capacity C are evaluated at the average temperature of the fluid and the geometry of the flow arrangement will determine the values of the diameter (or its equivalent) D and the mass flow rate, G. From the type of flow channel, the flow rate, and fluid properties, the heat transfer coefficient can be estimated.

There are correlations that can be used for the inside and outside coefficients, and for shell and tube exchangers these have quite different constants, while for plate exchangers they are the same for a given plate type. Typical values of these constants are given in Table 14-2 for turbulent flows that would be expected in wine applications. Although the exponent of the Reynolds number is less than 1.0, it can be seen that increasing the mass velocity G will increase the heat transfer coefficient h. The exchanger type and channel geometry influence the effective diameter D, and the mass velocity is usually a compromise of energy expended in the form of frictional loss and improved transfer coefficient.

When the fluid involved is either evaporating or condensing, different correlations are used and the coefficients are typically an order of magnitude larger and provide an insignificant contribution to the overall resistance. The material used for the construction of the exchanger will determine the thickness, and the use of stainless steel rather than more conductive metals is for reasons of cleaning and sanitation rather than for optimal heat transfer.

The deposition of matter onto the surface during extended operation is generally re-

Table 14-2. Summary of correlations for heat transfer coefficients.

Exchanger type	Author(s)	Constants in Equations (14.16) and (14.18)						
		a	*x*	*y*	*z*	*b*	*c*	*d*
Shell and tube								
tube side: Sieder and Tate (Kern 1950)		0.027	0.8	0.333	0.14	—	—	—
shell side: Kern (1950)		0.36	0.55	0.333	0.14	—	—	—
Plate:								
Buonopane et al. (1963)		0.2563	0.65	0.4	0.0	—	—	—
Marriott (1971)		0.374	0.668	0.333	0.15	—	—	—
Cooper (1974)		0.28	0.65	0.4	0.0	—	—	—
Saunders (1988)	30° Chevron	0.348	0.663	0.33	n/a	—	—	—
	60° Chevron	0.306	0.529	0.33	n/a	—	—	—
Spiral:								
Overall: Finlay and Bourzutschky (1987)		n/a	0.8	n/a	n/a	—	—	—
Scraped-Surface								
jacket: Anton (1977)		0.0225	0.8	0.4	0.0	—	—	—
inside: Skelland et al. (1962)		0.039	1.0	0.70	0.0	0.62	0.55	0.53
van Boxtel and de Fielliettaz Goethart (1983)		0.0158	0.8	0.4	0.0	0.5	N/A	N/A

[1]Constants in Equation (14.16) $Nu = aRe^xPr^y(\mu/\mu_w)^z$ and in Equation (14.18) $Nu = aRe^xPr^y(D_cN/v)^b(D_s/D_c)^c n_B^d$.

ferred to as fouling and its thermal resistance is usually included in the design as a fouling factor R_f. In some cases fouling may be confined to one side of the exchanger, in others, different factors might be applied to the two sides. The extent to which fouling becomes important is influenced by the frequency and nature of the cleaning cycles, and the batch use followed by cleaning, typical of winery applications should keep this to a minimum. The inclusion of a fouling factor ensures that the desired heat transfer performance can be obtained even when some fouling exists. In such cases the overall coefficient is written:

$$1/U = 1/h_i + \Delta x/k_w + 1/h_0 + R_{fi} + R_{fo} \tag{14.17}$$

and the values of the combined fouling factors might be in the range of 0.001 to 0.003 for shell and tube exchangers. In juice applications, more fouling due to protein denaturation and polysaccharides would be expected in the HTST applications. In heat recovery operations, the fouling of plate heat exchangers will be considerably less than that of the shell and tube equivalent. The deposition of tartrate salts on the exchanger wall during cooling is an example of fouling, but the use of the scraped-surface exchangers and frequent cleaning make this less of a concern.

D. TYPES OF HEAT EXCHANGERS

The most commonly used exchangers in wineries are of the shell and tube kind, since there has been limited concern about thermal efficiency or energy recovery when cooling juices and wines. The use of plate exchangers is more suited to energy recovery applications associated with more efficient potassium bitartrate treatments and the introduction of wine to wine heat exchange. The spiral exchangers are only rarely used in wineries today although they are perhaps more suited to must cooling than the shell and tube units commonly used for this application. The scraped-surface exchanger is ideally suited to cooling wines to temperatures close to their freezing point and their adoption will enable more efficient refrigerant temperatures to be employed.

1. Shell and Tube Heat Exchangers

Tube-in-tube heat exchangers are the simplest form of a shell and tube exchanger. A small-diameter tube (usually 25 to 50 mm) carrying the fluid to be cooled (or heated) is mounted within a larger-diameter tube. The cooling (or heating) medium moves in a counter direction in the outer annular region. An example of such an exchanger is shown in Figure 14-5.

Shell and tube units used for juice and wine applications often have as many as ten tubes within the shell and these may be connected in a number of ways so that the fluid being cooled has one or more passes by the cool surface. The simplest situation involves the juice entering the tubes from one end and leaving at the other, flowing countercurrent to the coolant in what is referred to as a 1,1 or single-pass arrangement. The next alternative is for the juice to pass along five of the tubes to one end before it passes through a return bend and moves back to the inlet end by way of the other five tubes. This kind would be referred to as a 1,2 or double-pass exchanger. Other arrangements involving directional changes of the coolant as well would be a 2,4 exchanger, in which the coolant makes two passes while the juice makes three changes in direction. The motivation for such arrangements is the more effective transfer that results from the temperature gradients in such flow situations. The analysis of such exchangers can be related to the logarithmic temperature difference by a design factor that depends on the particular flow pattern employed. Further details of the evaluation of such exchangers can be found in standard heat transfer texts such as Kern (1950), McCabe and Smith (1967), Foust et al. (1960) or Bell (1986b).

The coolant in the shell can be either a glycol solution or an evaporating refrigerant.

Fig. 14-5. A shell and tube heat exchanger.

These units have overall heat transfer coefficients (OHTC) of 600 to 900 W/m^2/°C. Shell and tube units with 75-mm-diameter tubes are used for must cooling and those with tubes > 50 mm in diameter are suitable for juice and wine cooling. They can also be used for cooling fermentations by being placed in the line that is used for the pump-over operation.

2. Spiral Heat Exchangers

Spiral heat exchangers are made of two adjacent flat jackets which have been rolled up into a coil. In a typical arrangement, there are two ports at the top of the unit and two other ports at either side at the center. The fluids flow in opposite directions, the fluid being cooled would enter at the base and move through several revolutions of the spiral path before it exits at one of the central ports. The coolant would enter at the opposite side at the center and pass through the alternate spiral path until it exits at the top of the unit. An example of such an exchanger is shown in Figure 14-6.

Spiral exchangers have fluid paths which are between 5 and 25 mm wide and they are most suitable for must cooling applications. Overall heat transfer coefficients are in the range 1800 to 2500 W/m^2/°C for water flows (*Heat Exchanger* 1987). Values in the range 1600 to 4000 W/m^2/°C have been reported with sugar cane juice (Finlay and Bourzutschky 1987) and are calculated to be between 760 and 1060 W/m^2/°C with musts (data of Ellis 1977). There are very few of these units in use in the United States although they are in more common use in other countries for must cooling applications. Spiral exchangers made by Alfa-Laval, APV Crepaco, Mueller, and Schmidt are available in the United States.

In the design of spiral exchangers, it is usual to evaluate effectiveness factors which are the transfer units, as previously discussed. These values, like the F_t factor, are a function of the channel spacing and particular exchanger arrangement and standard heat transfer handbooks provide design formulas for the temperature changes that can occur in these cases.

3. Plate Heat Exchangers

The plates are thin and rectangular, usually two to three times as long as wide. The inlet and outlet ports are at the corners, similar to those of the plates of a plate filter. The plates are suspended from an overhead bar and held together by end plates. Each plate is fitted with a polymer gasket that acts both as a seal and distributor for the flow. The thin film of fluid that passes down the plate is between 5 and 10 mm in thickness. An example of such an exchanger is shown in Figure 14-7.

The plates generally have a wavy surface to promote turbulence in the film for a better heat transfer coefficient and generally come in two forms. The first, called a high theta plate, has low-angle chevron ridges and the second, called low theta plates, have more pointed chevrons. By alternative combinations of these two basic plate types, three distinct channel shapes can be made with different flow and heat transfer performance. This has been extended with the introduction of asymmetric plates that can permit even more subtle optimization of the plate combinations to be made (Lines 1987).

The fluid flow pattern can be set up in one of two ways, either in a parallel arrangement or in a series arrangement. In the parallel case, sometimes called the single-pass setup, the fluid to be heated passes into every second plate while the heating medium (usually steam) passes in the opposite direction in the alternate plates. In the series case, sometimes called the three-pass setup, all of the fluid passes through the first plate before passing through the third and the fifth (three passes), while the heating medium enters from the other end so that countercurrent flow paths exist. The series case is more suited for nonisothermal heating and cooling media, while the parallel arrangement is preferred for isothermal heating and cooling media. The available heat transfer area A is $(N - 2)$ times the area per

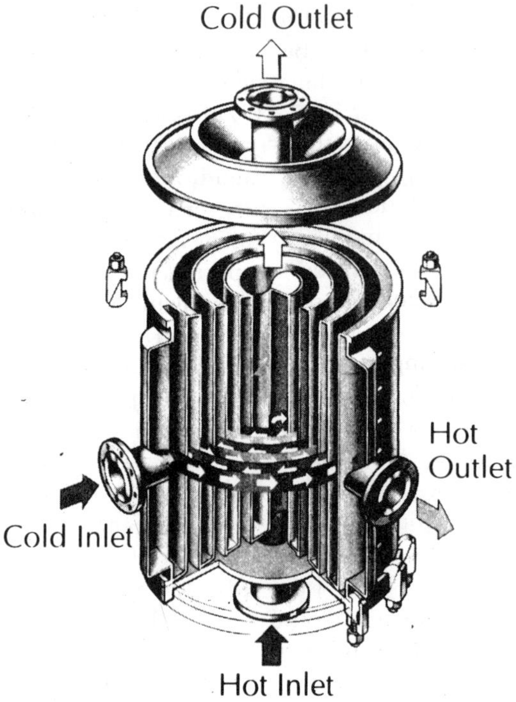

(a)

(b)

Fig. 14-6. A spiral heat exchanger: a) Cutaway and b) Winery installation.

plate since the first and last plates have only fluid on one side or half of the usual area (Raju and Chand 1980; Bond 1981).

For the high-temperature short-time (HTST) applications the stack is divided into two sections, the first for heating and the second for cooling. Steam is generally used for the heating medium while glycol solutions are generally used for the cooling medium in juice and wine applications. Extra plates can be added to increase the surface area (and hence the capacity of the unit).

In the design of plate heat exchangers, it is usual to use an effectiveness factor, θ, which is the same as the number of heat transfer units (NHTU) previously defined. The θ value, like the F_T factor, is a function of the design of the plate selected and the plate configuration. There are a number of plate designs in which the angle of the ridges within the plate is varied. Those with more acute angles, while providing larger pressure losses per pass, have the higher θ values (or more HTUs per plate) and are more efficient but more costly alternatives.

Typical heat transfer coefficients for plate heat exchangers are in the range 3500 to 5500 $W/m^2/°C$ for water applications (*Heat Exchanger* 1987) compared with corresponding values of 1200 to 1800 $W/m^2/°C$ for shell and tube heat exchangers (Raju and Chand 1980). Values of between 2400 to 3600 $W/m^2/°C$ are expected in juice and wine applications. Correlations for heat transfer coefficients and design procedures can be found in several articles (Bond 1981; Bell 1986a; Raju and Chand 1986a, 1986b).

The manufacturers of plate heat exchangers include the Alfa-Laval, APV-Crepaco, Cherry-Burrel, Schmidt and Graham companies.

4. Scraped-Surface Heat Exchangers

The particular application of chilling wines down to 0°C or −2°C for the promotion of

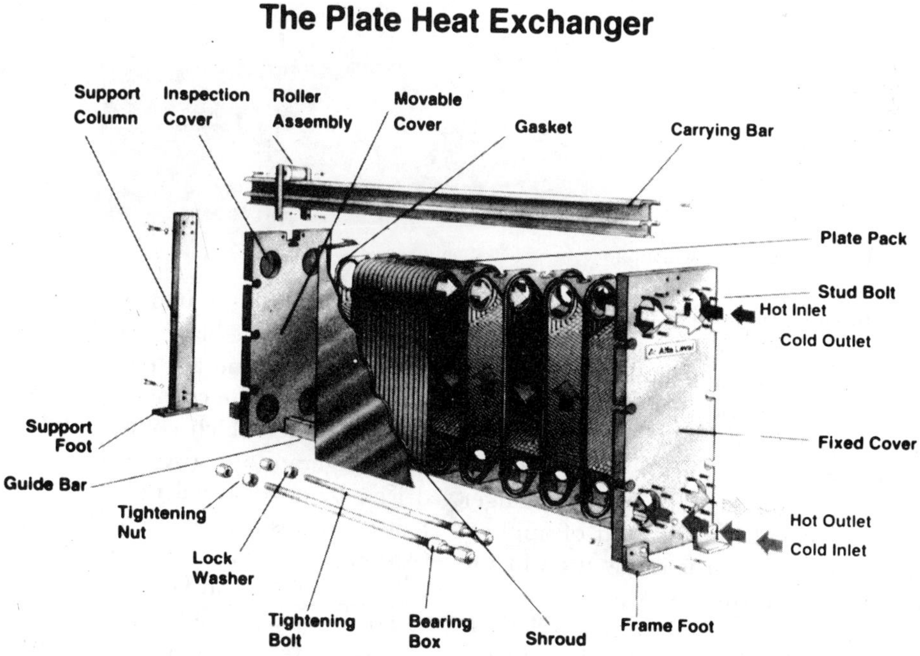

Fig. 14-7. A plate heat exchanger: a) Exploded view.

Fig. 14-7. b) Winery installation.

the crystallization of potassium bitartrate requires that the wine not be allowed to freeze at the exchanger wall and build up to block the flow. With shell and tube units, use of a glycol temperature of −2°C or lower, will freeze the wine and quickly plug the exchanger. The scraped-surface heat exchanger is specially designed for this kind of application but unfortunately it is rarely used in the cold stabilization of wines.

The scraped-surface unit has a relatively short cylinder (0.75 m long, 0.15 m in diameter) usually with two (but sometimes four) scraping blades mounted on the extremities of the diameter. The blades run the entire length of the cylinder and are mounted on a central spinning axle. The cylinder is chilled from an annular jacket which contains either expanding refrigerant or a glycol solution. The axle is driven by an external pulley and motor and typical speeds are between 300 and 500 rpm (Anton 1977). An example of such an exchanger is shown in Figure 14-8.

For wine applications, the flow is set to generate a predetermined percentage of ice in the exit stream, typically 5 to 10%. Generally

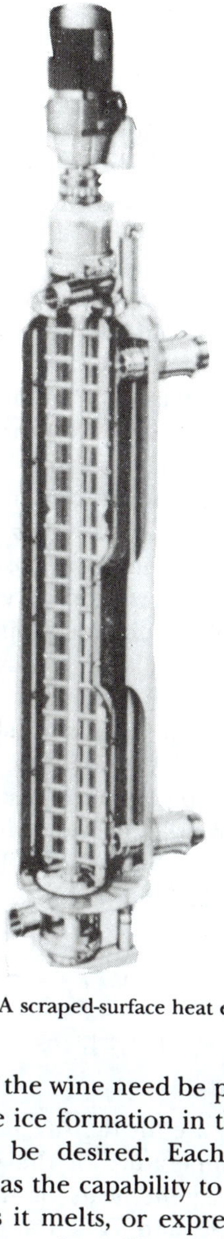

Fig. 14-8. A scraped-surface heat exchanger.

not all of the wine need be passed through the unit since ice formation in the stabilizing tank may not be desired. Each kilogram of ice formed has the capability to cool 73 L of wine by 1°C as it melts, or expressed another way, 5% ice formation will cool the associated wine by the equivalent of 3.8°C as it melts.

The inside coefficient can be estimated from correlations of the form:

$$Nu = aRe^{x}Pr^{y}(D_cN/v)^{b}(D_s/D_c)^{c}n_B^{d}, \quad (14.18)$$

where N is the rotational speed (rpm); n_B is the number of blades; v is the vertical fluid velocity; and D_c and D_s are the diameters of the cylinder and the shaft, respectively.

The overall heat transfer coefficients for these exchangers are in the range between 600 and 2,000 $W/m^2/K$ with water and aqueous extracts (Cuevas and Cheryan 1982), 500 and 1700 with water and dilute flour solutions (Yamamoto et al. 1987) and 400 and 700 with viscous sauces (van Boxtel and de Fielliettaz Goethart 1983). The product-side coefficient was two to three times higher and found to vary with the square root of the rotational speed. The coefficients of these exchangers are several times those of the standard shell and tube exchanger even though the available data has been developed in the absence of ice. The most common commercial forms of these exchangers are the Contherm unit by Alfa-Laval and models by APV-Crepaco. Some manufacturers offer swept-surface units which generally have a larger clearance, a thicker ice film, and, therefore, a lower heat transfer coefficient. These require a lower coolant temperature to obtain the same cooling rate.

5. Tank Jackets

The widespread use of jackets for the cooling of small to medium-sized fermentors and storage tanks is primarily one of convenience. As noted previously these units have very poor heat transfer coefficients due to the stationary fluid at the inside surface of the tank. The effectiveness of the jacket is quickly reduced as the size of the tank is increased since the jacket area per volume decreases inversely with the tank diameter. In many wineries the poor coefficient and the reduced effectiveness usually require that a very cold refrigerant temperature is employed to provide adequate cooling capability.

There do not appear to be any report of measurements of heat transfer coefficients for jackets but our estimates from cooling curves suggest that overall coefficients are in the range of 12 to 60 $W/m^2/°C$, depending on the extent of fluid movement within the tank.

If the diameter is increased twofold, the wall area is increased fourfold, the volume is increased eightfold, but the area per unit volume is halved. Small glass fermentors, 10 to 20 L in volume, will have large values of area per volume and can easily provide isothermal fermentations due to easy dissipation of heat to the surroundings. The same fermentation conducted on a commercial scale of 100,000 L, with 50% of the wall area jacketed will require a coolant temperature of 5°C in order to control the fermentation at 25°C (Boulton 1979).

E. COOLING BY DIRECT HEAT TRANSFER

Direct heat transfer occurs when the two materials are in contact with each other and heat transfer takes place. Common examples include the use of ice cubes to cool drinks and the addition of injected steam to heat milk for coffee. In such cases the added material transfers the latent heat associated with the melting (or condensation) and remains in the mixture. The application of liquified inert gases to the cooling of grapes, musts, and juices has certain advantages over mechanical refrigeration and heat exchangers. These include the ability to cool whole grapes before they are crushed, the lack of residue from the resulting gas, the ease of developing occasional large cooling loads, the development of an inert headspace, the potential for ice formation under controlled conditions, and an easily transported cooling medium without a need for power. The cost usually dictates that only carbon dioxide is practical and there are certain safety factors that need to be considered in enclosed spaces. Carbon dioxide is ideally suited for direct heat transfer because it sublimes under atmospheric conditions (BP = −78.4°C), that is it goes directly from a solid to a gas, and removes the combined latent heats for fusion and evaporation from the surroundings.

1. Solid Carbon Dioxide

In a number of winery situations it is useful to consider solid carbon dioxide (or dry ice) as a cooling medium. When added directly to a juice or wine, this evaporation has the capability of drawing the temperature down to freezing conditions and to even produce ice, depending on the proportions of juice and carbon dioxide used. The gas formed from the sublimation bubbles off, forming a dense layer above the liquid surface. It leaves no liquid or solid residue in the juice or wine and provides oxygen stripping and an inert headspace as well.

Solid CO_2 can be used to cool juices or wines in tanks that are not fitted with normal refrigeration or in gondolas which are transporting either whole grapes or must, and it has a special application to the freeze concentration of small lots of juice. It has approximately twice the refrigeration effect of an equivalent mass of melting ice without the dilution effects that would be associated with water. Commercially, tanker delivery of liquid CO_2 is usually the most feasible option for the treatments requiring large volumes, although solid blocks and a snow form can also be used.

The amount of solid carbon dioxide M required to cool a volume of juice V is given by the following balance:

$$\Delta H = m\lambda_{SLW} + \rho Vc(T_1 - T_2) = M[\lambda_{SL} + \lambda_{LV}], \qquad (14.19a)$$

where ρ, c, and T_1 are the density, heat capacity, and initial temperature of the juice; λ_{SL} and λ_{LV} are the latent heats of fusion and evaporation of CO_2; and T_2 is the final juice temperature. The mass of ice formed in the juice m will be zero for the cooling applications. For whole grape applications, the mass of grapes can be used instead of the product ρV. The heat capacity of the carbon dioxide has been neglected since its contribution is small when compared to the latent heat terms.

The latent heat of sublimation for CO_2 is 25.2 kJ/mol (or 573 kJ/kg). That for the evaporation of liquid CO_2 is 17.3 kJ/mol (or 393 kJ/kg).

a. Cooling of Juice

In the absence of ice formation, the quantity of solid carbon dioxide M required to cool juice is given by a modified form of Equation (14.19a):

$$\rho Vc(T_1 - T_2) = M[\lambda_{SL} + \lambda_{LV}]. \quad (14.19b)$$

When using solid CO_2 for the cooling of juices it will take 44.2 kg/kL to lower the temperature by 5°C, and at a unit cost of $0.75/kg this corresponds to $6.6/kL/°C.

b. Ice Formation in Juice

The latent heat of freezing for water is 0.108 kJ/kg and once the juice, temperature has been brought down to the freezing point of the juice (typically −3°C), ice will begin to form. This will require significant mixing to avoid localized freezing from the outset. Once the juice is at its freezing point, 0.58 kg of CO_2 will be required for each kilogram of ice produced. The appropriate form of the heat balance (Equation 14.19a), which includes the mass of ice formed in juice, is:

$$(m\lambda_{SLW} + \rho Vc[T_1 - T_2]) = M[\lambda_{SL} + \lambda_{LV}], \quad (14.19c)$$

where m is the mass if ice formed; λ_{SLW} is the latent heat of water; and T_2 is now the freezing temperature of the juice. The other terms are as defined in Equation (14.19).

There are harvest conditions in which the concentration of juice by 5 to 10% would be desirable and this is a convenient method for small juice volumes. At the level of 10% ice formation, approximately 52.2 kg of solid CO_2/kL of wine would be required. At commercial rates for solid CO_2 of $0.75/kg, this corresponds to a cost of approximately $39.2/kL.

2. Liquid Carbon Dioxide

The use of liquid carbon dioxide in a direct cooling arrangement is similar to that of solid carbon dioxide, except that the cooling effect (the latent heat of evaporation and a small heat capacity effect) is approximately 40% lower. This is often compensated for by the ability to produce the snow form, the ease of transport to remote locations, the ease of handling, and a lower unit price ($0.25/kg versus $0.75/kg).

a. Cooling of Juice

In the juice cooling application, the quantity of liquid carbon dioxide, M, can be estimated from a modified form of Equation (14.19a):

$$\rho Vc(T_1 - T_2) = M\lambda_{LV}, \quad (14.19d)$$

where the latent heat of fusion has been deleted. Using the above assumptions, the corresponding quantity of liquid CO_2 required is 64.5 kg/1000 L for a 5°C cooling effect and this corresponds to a cost of $3.2/kL/°C.

b. Ice Formation in Juice

Like the application of solid carbon dioxide, the liquid form can also be used to form ice in juices. This requires controlled flows and extensive mixing to ensure that the freezing temperature of the juice is reached and localized freezing does not occur. If an excess of the liquid CO_2 is added, the temperature will fall to the freezing point of the juice leading to complete freezing of the juice rather than the selective removal of water as ice. The partial removal of water from low-sugar juices by the generation of 5 to 10% ice formation can be used to concentrate juices by 1 to 2 Brix in certain years, subject to legal considerations.

The quantity of liquid carbon dioxide required, M, can be estimated from the following form of Equation (14.19a):

$$(m\lambda_{SLW} + \rho Vc[T_1 - T_2]) = M\lambda_{LV}. \quad (14.19e)$$

Once the juice is brought to its freezing point, 0.85 kg of liquid CO_2 is required for each kg ice produced. For the formation of 10% ice in juice, the corresponding mass of liquid CO_2 is

76.5 kg CO_2/kL and at $0.25/kg, this corresponds to a cost of $19.1/kL.

F. REFRIGERATION SYSTEMS

Mechanical refrigeration is used in a number of applications throughout the sequence of winemaking operations. These range from the cooling of must, juice, wine, or air (in cellars and barrel rooms) to maintaining temperature by heat removal during fermentation and storage.

In certain locations, ambient conditions can be used to contribute to cooling applications either as evaporative water in films or cooling towers and as air cooling for cellars at night during the summer. The more reliable and common cooling situation will be the use of one or more mechanical refrigeration systems.

1. The Refrigeration Cycle

The principle of the refrigeration cycle is to allow a liquid to evaporate under reduced pressure, drawing the latent heat for the phase change from the surroundings and thereby cooling them. The vapor is then brought to higher pressure in a compressor and then condensed to form a liquid at this pressure. This liquid is then allowed to expand as it flows to a lower pressure through an expansion valve and to evaporate again. It is the latent heat that is drawn from the surroundings that produces the refrigeration effect and the cost of doing this is the energy required to operate the compressor.

The fluid which evaporates and is recompressed is called the refrigerant, and the compressor, condenser, expansion valve, and evaporator are the major equipment components in the refrigeration system. The choice of the fluid and pressure to which the vapor is compressed determines the temperature at which it condenses. The pressure condition in the evaporator (that is, the suction pressure of the compressor) determines the temperature at which the evaporation takes place, and, hence the coldest temperature of the refrigerant.

The expansion of the refrigerant can take place in a heat exchanger and provide the desired cooling effect directly, such systems are referred to as direct or direct expansion refrigeration systems. Alternatively, it can be set up to cool an intermediate fluid (such as water or a glycol solution) which then provides the cooling effect to the warm fluid in what is referred to as an indirect refrigeration system.

2. Refrigerants

The desirable features of a refrigerant are that it should have high latent heat, (so that less of it is required and so systems can be more compact) and evaporating and condensing temperatures that are practical at moderate pressures. The most common refrigerants used for industrial systems today are ammonia (R 717) and freon 12 (R 12, CFC-12). Ammonia is poisonous and can be detected by most people at concentrations of a few parts per million in the vapor phase. It is especially dangerous in that sustained exposure can lead to a loss of detection by the nose, leading to a false sense of security during extended exposure. It is compatible with most steels including stainless steels but it is not compatible with many copper-based alloys such as brass and bronze or galvanized fittings. Freon 12 is odorless and colorless, but it is one of a family of the chlorohydrocarbons that are now being phased out of refrigeration applications, based on their chlorine content. At present the alternatives refrigerants HFC-134a, HCFC-123, HFC-125, and HFC-152a are being phased in for industrial refrigeration systems.

3. Refrigeration Units

Most refrigeration systems will be rated in the units "tons of refrigeration" (T_R). This is another way of saying a heat transfer rate of 3.52 kW. The term originated from the cooling rate required to melt a ton of ice (2000 lb) in 24 hours. Since water has a latent heat of freezing of 334.2 kJ/kg, melting 908 kg of ice

in 24 hours would be 12,644 kJ/hr or 3.52 kW (kJ/s). Typical systems can range from 1 to 2 tons
for small wineries to 100s of tons at larger wineries.

The efficiency of the refrigeration system will be expressed as the refrigeration effect obtained in proportion to the power required for compression, i.e., kW consumed per ton of refrigeration. For an ideal vapor ($\beta = 5.74$), the efficiency would be:

$$kW/T_R = 3.52kW/\beta = 0.613,$$

while for ammonia ($\beta = 4.85$) the efficiency would be 0.725 kW/T_R and for freon 12 ($\beta = 5.00$) the value is 0.703 kW/T_R. The actual power requirement will be slightly higher than these theoretical values.

While there are ongoing efforts to find acceptable replacements for the freon refrigerants, in the short term many new refrigeration installations will probably return to ammonia as the refrigerant of choice with a renewed awareness of its safety requirements.

4. Control of Refrigerant Temperature

The temperature that the refrigeration system will provide during the evaporation is determined by the pressure in the evaporator, or correspondingly, the suction pressure of the compressor. The pressure to which the refrigerant is compressed will determine the condensing temperature and this is chosen (often 38°C) so that either ambient air or water can be used for this purpose.

During harvest, the temperature of the cooling fluid (either the refrigerant directly or a glycol solution) will need to be at least 5°C below the coolest juice or wine temperature when efficient heat transfer arrangements are chosen, often 13°C to 10°C. In some cases, separate systems running at temperatures more suited for white and red wine fermentation temperatures are used. At other times, for example during cold stabilization, wine temperatures of −2°C can be desired, requiring coolant temperatures of −7°C. To achieve this, the suction pressure at the compressor can be changed (decreased) to make the evaporation occur at a lower temperature. In poor heat transfer arrangements, it is a common yet inefficient practice to compensate by using much colder coolant temperatures and at a considerable operating expense.

5. Temperature Requirements

The temperatures to which juices and wines need to be cooled will depend on the style and type of wine. At the juice stage, the need for cooling of musts will depend on the temperature at delivery and this can range from extremes of 40°C at midafternoon on hot days to 15°C or so during night harvesting. The extent of cooling will depend on the desired fermentation temperature and whether fermentation is to be delayed by deliberately holding the must or juice cold. Typical desired temperatures before fermentation will be 15°C to 20°C for white juices and 25 to 35°C for red musts. The specific heat of juice (and must) is 3.8 kJ/kg/°C and the density is 1090 kg/m^3, hence the volumetric heat capacity of juice is 4142 kJ/kL/°C. This means that each kiloliter will require 4142 kJ to change the temperature by 1°C. Expressed in other forms this becomes 4.142 kJ/L/°C or approximately 2485 kJ/Tm/°C as juice and 3727 kJ/Tm/°C as must.

The desirable fermentation temperatures will vary from 10 to 20°C for white wines, depending on the style, and between 25°C and 35°C for red wines. The quantity of heat released by the fermentation is independent of the temperature, although the rate of release is obviously temperature-dependent. The heat of fermentation is approximately 100 kJ/mole (Williams 1982) and with a juice or must at 22 Brix, this corresponds to 133 kJ/L of juice. There will be approximately 10% of this heat lost in the form of water and ethanol vapor that leaves the fermentation with the 56 L of carbon dioxide released by each liter of juice, and there will also be some ambient losses to the surroundings, depending on the size of the fermentor and the cellar conditions. The value of 120 kJ/L is recommended for cooling calculations and this corresponds to 72 MJ/Tm as juice or 108 MJ/Tm as must.

During storage and aging the wines will be held at temperatures ranging from 5°C to 15°C, depending on the aging strategy and wine style. The cooling requirements during this time will be initially to cool the wines to the desired temperature and then to make up for the losses to the surroundings. Wine has a specific heat of 4.5 kJ/kg/°C and with a density of 990 kg/m^3 it has a volumetric heat capacity of 4455 kJ/kL/°C or 4.455 kJ/L/°C of wine.

The temperatures employed for the cold stabilization range from −4°C to 0°C for white wines and from 0°C to 5°C for red wines, depending of the wine style. This application will require the coldest refrigerant temperatures, but the load is usually distributed over several months. The common practice of cooling a tank to the desired temperature and holding it for several weeks is quite energy-intensive since this is often attempted by the use of jackets in small to medium-sized wineries. The energy losses can also be considerable and it is not usual for the wine to be removed from the crystals and allowed to warm up by heat from the surroundings. The cooling requirement is 4.455 kJ/L/°C and all of this will be lost unless heat interchange with other wines is practiced. The energy losses while at the low temperatures are related to ambient temperature, tank insulation, tank size, and wine temperature. These variables are very site-specific.

6. Load Requirements

The power consumption and the refrigeration capacity are related to the rate of energy transfer rather than the quantity transferred. The time in which the cooling of juices or wines must take place will determine these rates and the heat transfer system will control whether or not it can be achieved. For juice cooling, the 4.142 kJ/L/°C will translate into a cooling load of 4.142 kJ/L/hr if a 10°C temperature reduction is required in 10 hours but only half this rate if it is to be accomplished in 20 hours. For a 20-kL volume of juice, to be cooled by 10°C in 10 hours, the load would be 4142 kJ/hr or 1.15 kW and this is equivalent to 0.33 tons of refrigeration.

The rate of heat release during fermentation displays a bell-shaped curve, building slowly at first, then faster to a maximum at approximately the middle of fermentation and then falling away toward the end of fermentation. For white wines fermenting at a rate of 2 Brix/day, the rate of heat release is approximately 0.46 kJ/L/hr, while for red wines the rate might be as high as 6 Brix/day, releasing 1.36 kJ/L/hr. For a 20-kL fermentation volume this corresponds to 0.72 and 2.15 tons of refrigeration for the white and red fermentations respectively (Boulton 1982).

The rates of cooling required during the storage of wines in tanks is dependent on several factors as noted previously. There are additional effects due to wine speed and solar radiation for outside storage tanks and secondary load effects due to ambient air temperature and air intake rates when the process refrigeration is used for air conditioning within the building. The actual rates have to be estimated on a case-by-case basis.

7. Direct Expansion vs Intermediate Fluid

Two of the key decisions in the design of a refrigeration system are the choice of the refrigerant temperature and the use of direct expansion or an intermediate fluid. In a direct expansion system the liquid refrigerant is distributed to the point of application and permitted to vapor as it draws in heat. The entire system is pressurized and the volume of refrigerant is considerable. The alternative is to use an intermediate fluid with a low freezing point, such as an ethylene glycol solution, as the distributed liquid. In such systems there is no phase change at the application point and the heat transferred results in a temperature in the intermediate fluid. The volume of the glycol solution is then considerable and one exchanger, a glycol chiller, transfers heat from the glycol and vaporizes the refrigerant.

The need for a colder refrigerant temperature in the intermediate system requires a larger compressor capacity and results in higher operating expenses in terms of compression power and coolant pumping. This option also suffers from poorer heat transfer rates as the glycol temperature rises, and this can be overcome by using larger glycol flow rates in the exchangers and jackets, but at additional expense. There are also distribution considerations regarding liquid refrigerants versus intermediate fluid and the choice often becomes site-specific.

The energy requirement per ton of refrigeration is essentially doubled as the suction pressure is modified to lower the refrigerant temperature from 8.3°C to −12.2°C (Figure 14-9). This is a compounding rate of approximately +10% in energy for every 2.5°C drop in coolant temperature. For a given installation, this translates into halving the nominal refrigeration capacity of the system as the suction pressure is lowered to produce refrigerant at −12°C rather than at 8°C. The effect of generating a refrigerant that is 5°C colder for the case of an intermediate fluid system would result in a loss of 20% in refrigeration capacity for the compression system indicated.

G. ENERGY REQUIREMENTS AND CONSERVATION

While there are several stages in winemaking that consume electricity, the largest portion of the process electricity (sometimes as much as 75%) is consumed by the refrigeration system. The quantity of electrical energy used will depend on several factors such as the proportion of white to red wine produced, the extent of cooling, stabilizing, and conservation practices, and effects due to equipment and winery size. The cooling and fermentation loads might be expected to be similar in a given region, irrespective of winery size, but the energy losses will be related to surface area per volume, the extent of insulation, the choice of coolant temperature, and the use of heat recovery practices. The specific electricity consumption for 26 wineries in California in the late 1970s is shown in Figure 14-10. The specific consumption ranges from 40 kWh/Tm to 120 kWh/Tm, displaying a threefold increase over

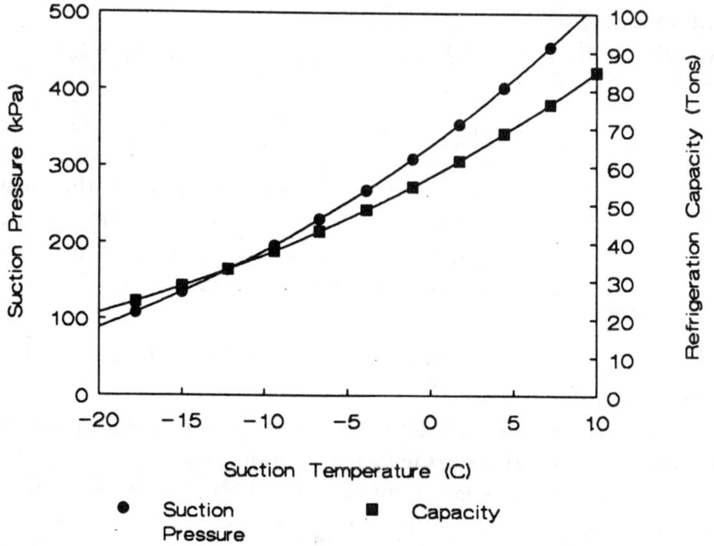

Fig. 14-9. The performance characteristics of a typical ammonia refrigeration system.

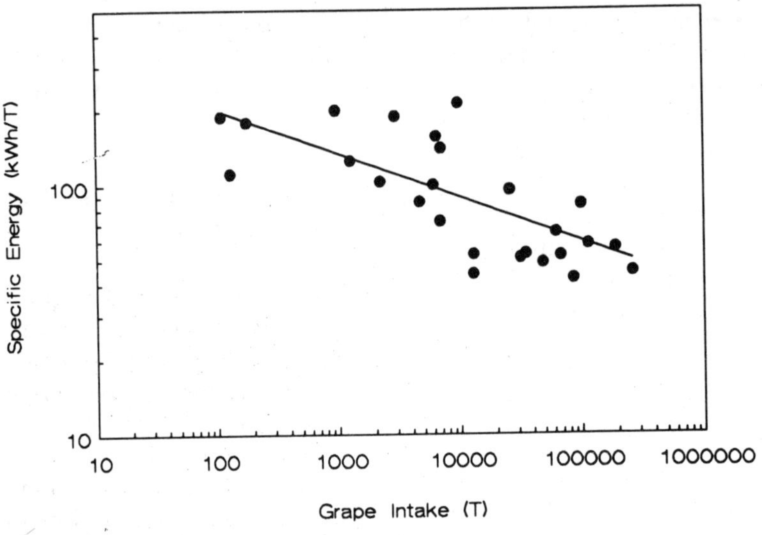

Fig. 14-10. The influence of winery size on the annual energy consumption.

a thousandfold change in grape intake. There is some tendency for a scale effect with the lower consumptions at the larger facilities, but there exists a threefold range even at the 10,000-Tm grape intake level. These values are annual figures and they do not show the variation in electrical usage throughout the year. The highest consumption is during the harvest months when juice cooling, fermentation, and air conditioning are responsible for most of the usage. The control of cellar and tank temperatures during aging and the extent and timing of cold stabilization, as well as the methods used will affect the electrical usage during the rest of the year.

The recovery of thermal energy from cold wines by exchanging them with warmer wines which are to be chilled is not widely practiced in the United States. This practice reduces the refrigeration demand for the cold stabilization of wines provided the wines are cooled and stabilized in succession rather than all at once.

By the use of a plate heat exchanger, a tube-in-tube (1,1) exchanger or shell and tube (1,2 or 2,4) exchangers which are dedicated for this application (or thoroughly cleaned prior to use), the cold wine can be passed through the shell while the warmer wine is passed through the tubes. Typically, a wine at 0°C can be warmed up to 10°C, while an equivalent volume at 15°C is cooled down to 5°C without the need for any refrigeration. The wine to be stabilized would then be further chilled using a scraped-surface exchanger, but the energy used would only be one-third of that when no heat recovery is practiced.

The exchange between the streams can also be shown to be (Equation 14.11):

$$dH/dt = WC(T_1 - T_2) = wc(t_1 - t_2),$$

where W and w are the mass flow rates; and C and c are the heat capacities of the two fluids. With wine (or juice) on both sides, the heat capacity terms cancel and the ratio of the temperature changes experienced is inversely related to the ratio of the mass flows, W/w:

$$W/w = (t_1 - t_2)/(T_1 - T_2), \quad (14.11b)$$

provided that T_2, the cooler temperature of the warmer wine is always higher than t_2, the warmer temperature of the cooler wine with true countercurrent flows.

H. OFF-PEAK GENERATION OF COOLING CAPACITY

In a number of locations throughout the world, the cost of electricity is determined by the time of the day at which it is used. In parts of California for example, the unit cost of energy used at midday during the summer months is twice that used at midnight.

The major refrigeration loads during the harvest will be for the cooling of white juices prior to fermentation, and there are two strategies to reduce the cost of this cooling requirement. The first is the adoption of night harvesting, primarily by machines, to bring in cooler fruit that will require less cooling at the winery. The second is the use of off-peak electricity for the generation of this cooling capacity, rather than on an as-needed basis during the day. The first approach is presently employed by a number of wineries, but the second will hopefully become more widespread in the future.

An off-peak system involves the use of a larger-than-usual insulated reservoir of a cooling medium from which energy is extracted slowly during the low-cost period. This may be simply water, in either a chilled form or as ice, to an expanded glycol reservoir, many times the usual volume employed in indirect systems. The cooling reservoir can be either a storage tank located underground or in a well-insulated tank above the ground. While the initial expense to install such an arrangement is considerable, the future savings in energy costs will often repay the investment in a short time.

Additional advantages of such cold storage systems are that they can continue to provide cooling for a time in the event of power failure, when the usual refrigeration systems would not be functional. They can also provide a more uniform cooling demand that allows the refrigeration compressors to run continually for periods of time rather than with the intermittent starting and stopping that accompanies the widely used on-demand generation systems.

I. REFERENCES

ANTON, J. D. 1977. "The Contherm scraped surface heat exchanger." *Inst. Fd. Sci. Technol. Proc.* 10:137–142.

BELL, K. J. 1986a. "Plate heat exchangers." In *Heat Exchanger Sourcebook*, J. W. Palen, Ed., pp. 537–547, Washington, DC: Hemisphere Publishing.

BELL, K. J. 1986b. "Preliminary design of shell and tube heat exchangers." In *Heat Exchanger Sourcebook*, J. W. Palen, Ed., pp. 107–127, Washington, DC: Hemisphere Publishing.

BOND, M. P. 1981. "Plate heat exchangers for effective heat transfer." *The Chem. Engr.* 367: 162–169.

BOULTON, R. 1979. "Heat transfer characteristics of wine fermentors." *Am. J. Enol. Vitic.* 30:152–156.

BOULTON, R. B. 1982. "Winemaking." In *ASHRAE Handbook, 1982 Applications*, pp. 38.7–38.9. Atlanta, GA: American Society of Heating Refrigeration, and Air-Conditioning Engineers.

BUONOPANE, R. A., R. A. TROUPE, and J. C. COOPER. 1963. "Heat transfer design method for plate heat exchangers." *Chem. Eng. Prog.* 59(7):57–61.

COOPER, A. 1974. "Recover more heat with plate heat exchangers." *The Chem. Engr.* 285:275–279.

CUEVAS, R., and M. CHERYAN. 1982. "Heat transfer in a vertical, liquid-full scraped-surface heat exchanger. Application of the penetration theory and Wilson plot models." *J. Fd. Proc. Engng.* 5:1–21.

ELLIS, J. 1977. "The use and performance of the spiral heat exchanger." *Proc. 3rd. Wine Ind. Tech. Conf.*, Albury, Australia. Australian Wine Research Institute pp. 79–81.

FINLAY, E., and H. BOURZUTSCHKY. 1987. "Spiral heat exchangers for the cane sugar industry—Test results." *Zuckerind.* 112:892–895.

FOUST, A. S., L. A. WENZEL, C. W. CLUMP, L. MAUS, and L. B. ANDERSEN. 1960. *Principles of Unit Operations*. New York: John Wiley.

Heat Exchanger Guide, 4th ed. 1987. Tumba, Sweden: Alfa-Laval AB.

Heat Transfer Handbook, 1986. New York: APV.

KERN, D. Q. 1950. *Process Heat Transfer*. New York: McGraw-Hill.

LINES, J. R. 1987. "Asymmetric plate heat exchangers." *Chem. Eng. Prog.* 83(7):27–30.

MARRIOTT, J. 1971. "Where and how to use plate heat exchangers." *Chem. Eng.* 78(8):127–134.

MCCABE, W. L., and J. C. SMITH. 1967. *Unit Operations of Chemical Engineering,* 2nd ed. New York: McGraw-Hill.

RAJU, K. S. N., and J. CHAND. 1980. "Consider the plate heat exchanger." *Chem. Eng.* 86:133–144.

RAJU, K. S. N., and J. CHAND. 1986a. "Design of plate heat exchangers." In *Heat Exchanger Sourcebook*, J. W. Palen, Ed., pp. 563–582, Washington, DC: Hemisphere Publishing.

RAJU, K. S. N., and J. CHAND. 1986b. "Plate heat exchanger and their performance." In *Heat Exchanger Sourcebook*, J. W. Palen, Ed., pp. 549–562, Washington, DC: Hemisphere Publishing.

SAUNDERS, E. A. D. 1988. *Heat Exchangers. Selection, Design and Construction*. Longman Scientific & Technical. (New York: John Wiley & Sons).

SKELLAND, A. H. P., D. R. OLIVER, and S. TOOKE. 1962. "Heat transfer in a water-cooled scraped-surface heat exchanger." *Br. Chem. Eng.* 7:346–353.

TEN BROECK, H. 1938. "Multipass exchanger calculations." *Ind. Eng. Chem.* 30:1041–1042.

VAN BOXTEL, L. B. J., and R. L. DE FIELLIETTAZ GOETHART. 1983. "Heat transfer to water and some highly viscous food systems in a water cooled scraped surface heat exchanger." *J. Fd. Proc. Engng.* 7:17–35.

WALKER, G. 1990. *Industrial Heat Exchangers. A Basic Guide,* 2nd. ed., New York: Hemisphere Publishing Corp.

WILLIAMS, L. A. 1982. "Heat release in alcoholic fermentation. A critical reappraisal." *Am. J. Enol. Vitic.* 33:149–153.

YAMAMOTO, H., K. ITOH, S. TANEYA, and Y. SOGO. 1987. "Heat transfer in a scraped surface heat exchanger." *J. Japan. Soc. Fd. Sci. Technol.* 34:559–565.

CHAPTER 15

JUICE AND WINE ACIDITY

The acidity of a juice or wine, in particular the pH, plays an important role in many aspects of winemaking and wine stability (see also Chapters 3, 8, and 12). The ability of most bacteria to grow, the solubility of the tartrate salts, the effectiveness of sulfur dioxide, ascorbic acid, and enzyme additions, the solubility of proteins and effectiveness of bentonite, the polymerization of the color pigments, as well as oxidative and browning reactions are all influenced by the juice or wine pH. The titratable acidity is an important parameter in the sensory evaluation of finished wines. It and the pH are also important in aging reactions.

In certain situations, the conditions of grape development and maturation or microbial and physical changes during winemaking can cause imbalance in the acidity of wines and corrections are required to ensure the desired values. It is for these reasons that a comprehensive consideration of both juice and wine acidity is presented.

The acidity has four main features, the acids themselves, the extent of their dissociation, the resultant titratable acidity, and pH. Although the titratable acidity and pH are easily measured quantities these values tell little about the nature of the underlying acid mixture. They are resultant or dependent measures and it is the acids themselves and their concentrations that actually determine the structure of the juice acidity. It is important to realize that the values of pH and titratable acidity are also not unique, there are various combinations of the different acids and neutralization that can give the same pH and titratable acidity values.

The final aspect of the acidity relates to the extent to which the equilibrium is altered as the concentrations of the acids change. This is referred to as the buffering or buffer capacity of the mixture. It will determine the change in pH accompanying carbonate deacidifications, the malolactic fermentation, or the addition or precipitation of tartaric acid during winemaking.

A. ACID CONCENTRATIONS

1. Tartaric Acid

Tartaric acid is present in grapes at levels of between 5 to 10 g/L and is usually the major acid in juices and wines. It is characteristic of grapes and is not found in other common fruits. Its concentration is primarily determined by synthesis, which is cultivar-dependent, and the final berry volume at harvest. The isomer found in grapes is the L(+) form and appears to be synthesized from glucose via galacturonic, glucuronic, and ascorbic acids (Saito and Kasai 1978). Tartaric acid is partially converted to gluconic and other acids by *Botrytis cinerea* and is degraded at a pH above 4 by a few bacterial strains. It is not modified by microorganisms at wine pH levels. Its partially soluble salts of potassium bitartrate and calcium tartrate are involved in the physical stability of wines (refer to Chapter 8 for a more complete discussion of this). Slowly with time in wine a portion is esterified with ethanol to ethyl bitartrate (Edwards et al. 1985).

2. Malic Acid

Malic acid, the most widespread fruit acid, is present in grapes at concentrations in the range 2 to 4 g/L generally. It can be as high as 6 g/L in small berries in cool growing conditions and nearly absent in overripe grapes from hot growing regions. The levels vary considerably with cultivar and respiration due to temperature conditions during maturation. Its final concentration is also influenced by berry volume. The malic acid isomer found in grapes is the L(+) form and it is synthesized from glucose via pyruvic acid.

Malic acid is converted almost completely into lactic acid by the malolactic fermentation. It has limited solubility as the calcium salt and can be partially removed during calcium carbonate treatment and by yeast fermentation.

3. Amino Acids

The amino acids of grape juice are generally in the range of 1 to 3 g/L depending on cultivar, the availability of nitrogen during maturation, the growing conditions, and the berry volume. The major acid is usually arginine at levels of 200 to 800 mg/L and most cultivars are also high in proline at the 750- to 1500-mg/L level. Nitrogen-rich acids such as glutamine, asparagine, glutamic, and aspartic acids are usually high when nitrogen is readily available during the growing season. The nitrogen content usually assimilated by yeast includes all of the amino acids other than proline, weighted according to the number of available amine groups per molecule, together with the ammonia content. It is the most relevant of several aggregate nitrogen measures for correlating yeast growth rates and fermentation rates. Most of the amino acids will be taken up and incorporated into yeast cell mass during fermentation and thus do not contribute significantly to the buffer capacity of wines.

4. Inorganic Acids

The basic inorganic species that are transported into the berries during maturation are involved to a lesser degree in the pH and buffer capacity of juices and wines. Components such as phosphate can be found at natural levels of 300 mg/L in wine depending on the cultivar and berry volume. The average natural sulfate content of wine is 775 mg/L (Ough and Amerine 1988), also depending on cultivar and berry volume. There are also known effects on the inorganic anion content due to the rootstock, but the form of the ions actually taken up (i.e., dihydrogen or monohydrogen phosphate, or hydrogen sulfate or sulfate) is not well resolved. There will be slight effects on the acidity and buffer capacity of juices due to large additions of diammonium phosphate and these will change due to their utilization during fermentation.

5. Lactic and Succinic Acids

The lactic acid in wines is primarily derived from malic acid during the malolactic fermentation. The concentrations in wines can range from 0 to 2.5 g/L and the form produced from malic acid is the L(+) isomer. The lactic acid salts are quite soluble under wine conditions, and once formed this acid undergoes little change in concentration.

Succinic acid is formed during fermentation and the levels are influenced by the malic and amino acid concentrations and the yeast strain involved. It can be found at levels in the range 0.5 to 1.5 g/L. Its salts are quite soluble at the levels found in wines.

6. Other Acids

The levels of several other organic acids (acetic, galacturonic, pyruvic, α-keto-glutaric, etc.) are generally found in sound wines at the tens to hundreds of mg/L levels and contribute little to the titratable acidity or pH of either the juice or the wine. The exceptions are the presence of acids such as gluconic and other sugar acids in juices from botrytis-infected berries.

B. ACIDITY MEASURES

The two most commonly measured aspects of juice and wine acidity are the titratable acidity and the pH. The titratable acidity has no known effect on chemical or enzyme reactions or microbial activity and is of primary importance only to the sensory perception of finished wines.

One interpretation of why the titratable acidity is sensorially important is because at least a partial titration of the acidity occurs in the mouth by the saliva (slightly basic, containing mostly bicarbonate ions). The sensation of the presence of the wine causes a saliva flow somewhat in proportion to the quantity of neutralization required and this is generally correlated with the titratable acidity. While this is true for an individual judge, there is considerable variation in the saliva flow rate between individuals.

By comparison, the pH value is merely an indication of the extent to which the acid mixture has been neutralized during grape maturation and acidity adjustments. It is not correlated with the amount of acids present but is more influenced by their ability to dissociate or their strength. Its only sensory contribution appears as a sensation on the tongue that is only detected in wines with very low pH (3.0 and below).

1. Titratable Acidity

The titratable acidity is determined by titrating the juice or wine to an end point with a strong base and expressing the number of protons recovered as an equivalent concentration of some chosen acid. In the United States the end point chosen is pH = 8.2 and the acid for reference is tartaric acid. Values range between 6 to 12 g/L and are primarily influenced by cultivar and berry volume. In some other countries, France for example, the end point is pH = 7.0 and the reference acid is sulfuric.

The titratable acidity of grape juice, like most fruit juices, is always less than expected from the organic acid concentrations. The number of hydrogen ions recovered from a juice is typically only 70 to 80% of those expected from the analytical tartaric and malic acid concentrations (Boulton 1980d). This is because of a particular exchange mechanism involving protons from the grape acids and the potassium (and to a lesser extent, sodium) ions, as is described in more detail below.

While the lower than expected titratable acidity has long been recognized from total cation and anion balances (Peynaud and Maurie 1956), the special relationship involving only the monovalent cations has only recently been demonstrated (Boulton 1980a, 1980c).

2. pH

The pH value is an equilibrium measure of hydrogen ion concentration or activity and is affected by the degree to which the acids in a solution are neutralized. It is easily measured using a pH meter and an electrode, but the factors that determine its value are more complicated and less obvious. It is particularly important since the extent of ionization of several chemical components, the rate of a number of chemical reactions, and physical properties and microbial stability of juices and wines are all functions of it.

The pH value of a juice is dependent on many factors including the degree of maturity at harvest, the cultivar, the crop level, the season, the soil moisture content during maturation, and the mineral composition available to the vine. Values can range from 2.8 to 3.0 in early-maturity fruit to be harvested for sparkling wine or base wine for distillation, to a desirable range of 3.0 to 3.3 for table wines. Fruit in which the exchange reactions have been more extensive can have pH values between 3.5 and 4.0 and even higher pH values are sometimes observed in extreme conditions, particularly overripe grapes or in regions with an extended growing season due to cool conditions and an absence of early rainfall.

The pH of juice can undergo further changes during fermentation due to several effects. These include a shift in the dissociation constants due to the ethanol concentration, the precipitation of some potassium bitartrate, the utilization of some of the malic acid, the production of succinic acid, and the consumption of most amino acids (other than proline) by the yeast and the possibility and extent of a concurrent malolactic fermentation. Similarly, the pH of newly fermented wines can undergo similar changes during aging, the most important factors being malolactic fermentation and some potassium bitartrate precipitation, and partial esterification of tartaric acid. The direction and extent of these changes will be described in more detail in later sections.

3. The Physiological Exchange Reaction of Protons for Mineral Cations

In grape cells, and most if not all plant cells, the organic acids are synthesized biochemically from sugars as the neutral acid anion and its corresponding protons. As the berry matures it transports some of the protons obtained from these acids across its membranes in exchange for certain monovalent metal cations, such as potassium (Boulton 1980b). This exchange process is quite selective and involves only the monovalent cations, primarily potassium, less so sodium, (and to a far lesser extent rubidium and lithium), and possibly ammonium. There appears to be no effect on this transport mechanism due to multivalent cations such as calcium, magnesium, or others. The relationship can then be written:

$$[K^+]+[Na^+]+[H^+] = [H^+]\text{equivalent of the organic acid anions,} \qquad (15.1)$$

and plots of data from juices (Figures 15-1a and 15-1b) and wines (Figures 15-2a and 15-2b) confirm it.

The loss of protons by this mechanism accounts for the neutralization that occurs during ripening. The fraction of the hydrogen ions from the acid pool that are lost in this way can be expressed as the extent of exchange:

$$\text{Extent of Exchange} = \frac{[K^+] + [Na^+]}{[H^+]\text{equivalent of organic acids anions}}$$

With no exchange, the pH would be that of the acid mixture, about 2.2 for wines, while complete exchange would lead to complete neutralization and a pH of approximately 7.5. The pH range of 3.0 to 4.0 represents a partially neutralized acid mixture in which the extent of exchange is between 20 and 40%. The pH is more precisely a function of the extent of exchange and the ratio of the major acids in the buffer:

$$\text{pH} = f([\text{extent of exchange}] \text{ and } [\text{tartaric/malic}]),$$

since tartaric to malic acids have different acid strengths and this will affect the pH at a given extent of exchange.

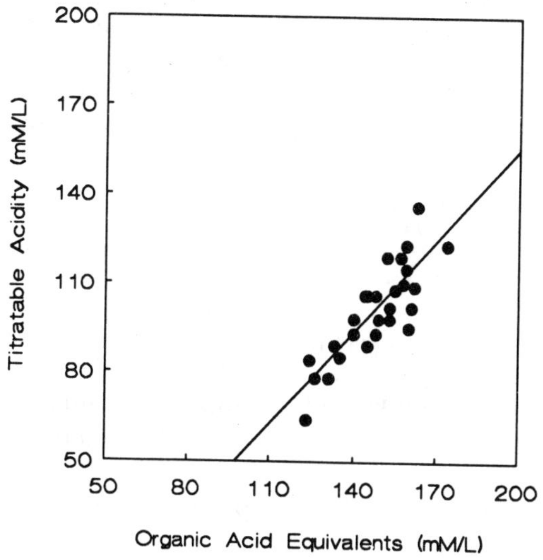

Fig. 15-1a. Relationship between titratable acidity and organic acid concentration in juices.

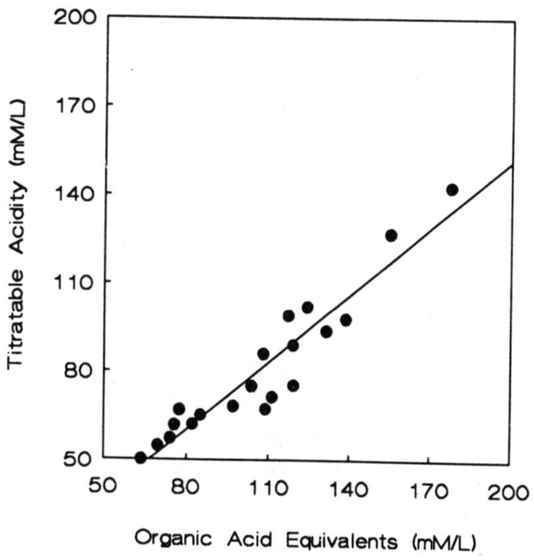

Fig. 15-2a. Relationship between titratable acidity and organic acid concentration in wines.

This selective exchange is thought to be carried out by a membrane-bound enzyme known as an adenosine triphosphatase (commonly referred to as an ATPase), which exchanges three protons for three monovalent cations as it hydrolyzes ATP to ADP in order to get the energy needed for the exchange. The actual energy substrate is a magnesium-ATP complex. This enzyme is commonly distributed throughout plants and the most preferred ion is potassium which generally accounts for some 90% of the uptake of this group (Leonard and Hodges 1973; Boulton 1980b). While these ions in themselves have a

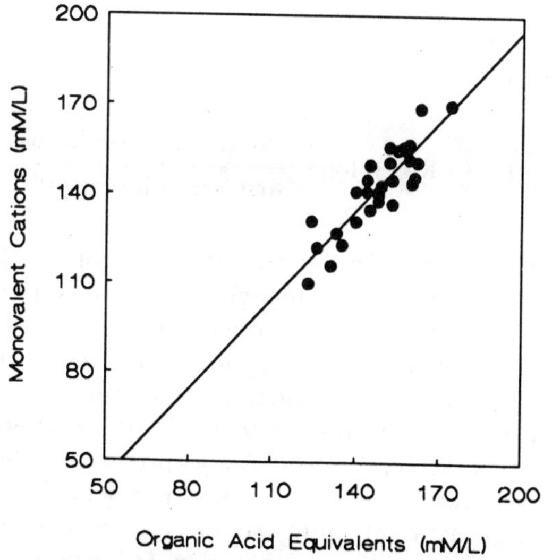

Fig. 15-1b. Relationship between monovalent cations (K^+,Na^+,H^+) and organic acid concentration in juices.

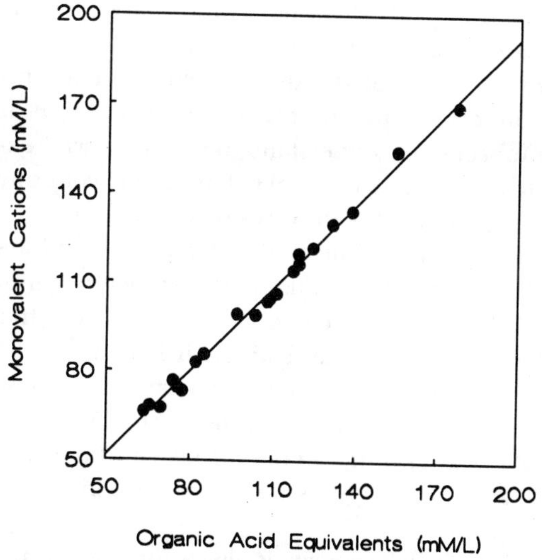

Fig. 15-2b. Relationship between monovalent cations (K^+,Na^+,H^+) and organic acid concentration in wines.

negligible effect on pH, the protons that are exchanged for them are lost from the acid equilibrium, providing a more neutralized solution, a lower titratable acidity, and a higher pH than would be expected from the organic acid composition (Boulton 1980c).

There are many aspects of vine cultivation that influence potassium uptake and these can affect the pH and titratable acidity of its grapes (see Chapter 2). The availability of potassium in the soil, the soil moisture content, the size and age of the root system, the number of clusters on the vine, and the number of days that the grapes are able to take up potassium all contribute to the potassium content at harvest. There are additional effects due to the canopy, leaf area, and water status of the vine, since these influence the production of sugar, the nonberry tissue, and the length of the maturation period.

4. Buffer Capacity

The property of a juice or wine that resists changes in pH during acid or base changes is referred to as the buffer capacity or buffer index. It is defined as the number of protons per liter that are needed to shift the pH by one unit, and it can be defined in either the acidic or basic direction. Numerically it is the inverse slope of the titration curve in the region of the pH of the juice or wine. It is important to understand because it will explain the changes in pH that result from any change in acidity in musts or wines.

The units of the buffer capacity are moles H^+ ions (or OH^- ions) per liter per pH unit (M/L/pH) but because of the values of buffer capacity in juices and wines, it is common to express them in millimolar terms and these are generally in the range of 35 to 50 mM/L/pH unit, although they can be as low as 25 and as high as 60 under certain conditions.

The buffer capacity is also a function of pH and is related to the proximity of the mixture pH to the pK_as of the component acids as well as their concentrations. It has two components at pH below 7.0, one due to water and the other due to the acids. The equation for predicting the buffer capacity, β, of a monoprotic acid in solution is (Butler 1964):

$$\beta = \frac{[H^+]}{K_w} + 2.303\frac{[H^+]K_aC}{([H^+] + K_a)}, \quad (15.2)$$

where K_a is the dissociation constant of the acid; C is the concentration of the acid in all forms; and K_w is the ionization constant of water (10^{-14}). It can be seen that the buffer capacity of the acid is greatest when $[H^+]$ equals K_a (or when the pH is equal to the pK_a of the acid). This relationship can be used for mixtures of monoprotic acids and many diprotic acids (by considering them to be made up of two monoprotic acids). Unfortunately, this is not true for most of the diprotic acids found in grapes and wines because the second dissociation is not completely independent of the first.

The commonly used Henderson-Hasselbach equation (Segal 1976):

$$pH = pK_{a1} + \log\frac{[\text{first ionization form}]}{[\text{undissociated acid}]}$$

and

$$pH = pK_{a2} + \log\frac{[\text{second ionization form}]}{[\text{first ionization form}]}$$

is not valid when the pK_as of the diprotic acids are less than approximately two pH units apart and there is interaction between the first and second dissociated acid forms. This results in an equilibrium in which the intermediate ion form begins to dissociate at pH values where the undissociated acid is also present. Under these conditions, there is no intermediate pH range at which only two species are present and alternative expressions must be used to determine the buffer capacity and acid ionization. Such an expression for the buffer capacity is given by (Butler 1964):

$$\beta = \frac{[H^+]}{K_w} + 2.303CK_{a1}[H^+] \times \frac{\left([H^+]^2 + 4K_{a2}[H^+] + K_{a1}K_{a2}\right)}{\left([H^+]^2 + K_{a1}[H^+] + K_{a1}K_{a2}\right)^2} \quad (15.3)$$

where K_{a2} is the second ionization constant and the other terms are as defined in Equation (15.2). It can be seen that the buffer capacity is strongly pH-dependent. The expression for a mixture of two monoprotic acids reduces to this form only when the K_{a2} is less than 5% of the K_{a1}, or expressed another way, when the pK_as differ by more than 1.98.

The dissociation and buffer capacity of the important diprotic acids in juice and wine, that is tartaric and malic (and also succinic and aspartic acids) need to be calculated in this manner. The dissociation curves for tartaric and malic acids are shown in Figures 15-3 and 15-4. Sulfur dioxide, however, does obey the Henderson-Hasselbach equations, since its pK_as are more than 5 units apart.

a. *Buffer Capacity Curves*

The buffer capacity terms of different acids in a mixture are additive and the buffer capacity of juices and wines can be estimated from the acid concentrations and the pH. Typical buffer capacity curves for a juice and a wine are shown in Figures 15-5a and 15-5b. The values below pH of 2.5 are due to water alone and (the two peaks are due to higher buffer capacity in the region of the 3.0 to 3.4 are due to the first ionization of tartaric and malic acids). The buffer capacity is highest in this range, falling off as the pH moves away in either direction.

Based simply on the reported concentrations of tartaric and malic acids, the buffer capacities of several juices have been estimated and are presented in Table 15-1. These estimates do not include the contributions of the amino acids, bisulfate, or dihydrogen phosphate ions and have not been corrected for activity since ion strengths of the juices are unknown. The buffer capacities can be seen to vary due to the season, location, and cultivar. Of particular importance is the relatively uniform buffer capacity values of the Cabernet Sauvignon juices reported for one vineyard during several years in Bordeaux (Peynaud and Maurie 1956), compared to the wide variation between cultivars at one location in Washington (Johnson and Nagel 1976) and the effects of the growing conditions on the

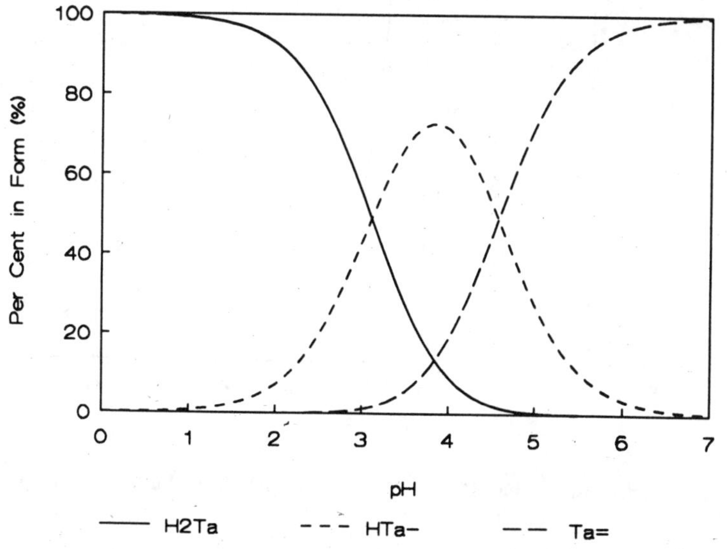

Fig. 15-3. The dissociation diagram for tartaric acid in wine.

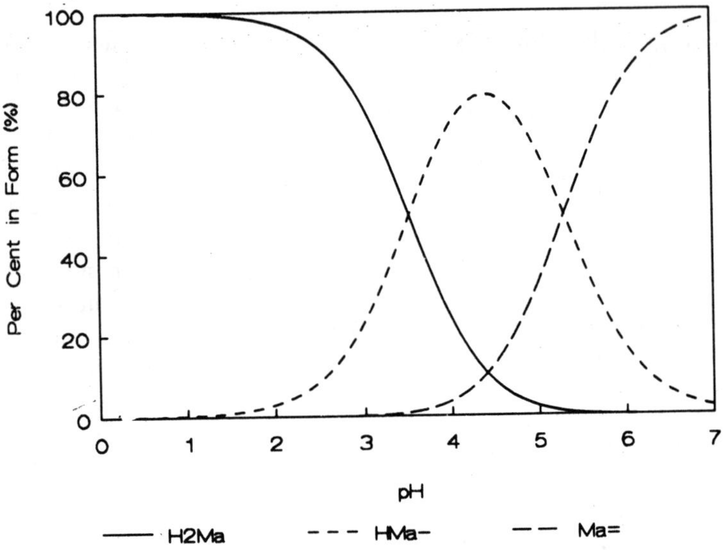

Fig. 15-4. The dissociation diagram for malic acid in wine.

variation within a cultivar (Steele and Kunkee 1978, 1979).

In practice, the determination of acid concentrations and the computation of the buffer capacity are usually not justified since its analytical determination is more easily performed. A juice or wine sample can simply be titrated in either direction for one-half or a full pH unit and the volume of titrant noted. This can be done directly to the sample without concern about dissolved carbon dioxide interference.

The buffer capacity at typical juice or wine is unaffected by any acid or base whose pK_a is more then 2 units above or below the pH value. This is true for dissolved carbon dioxide and the phosphate, sulfate, chloride, and nitrate ions.

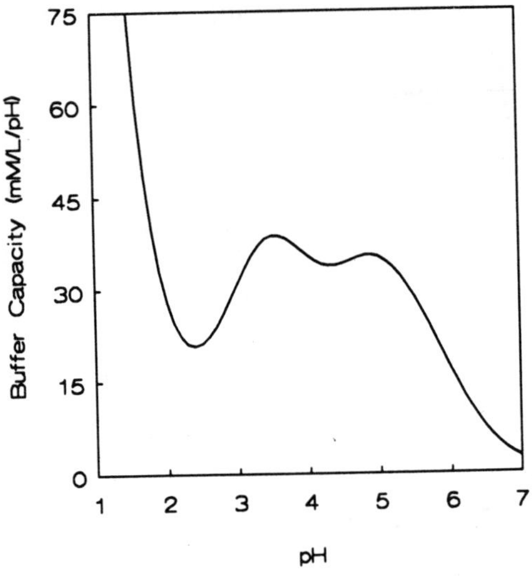

Fig. 15-5a. The effect of pH on the buffer capacity in juice.

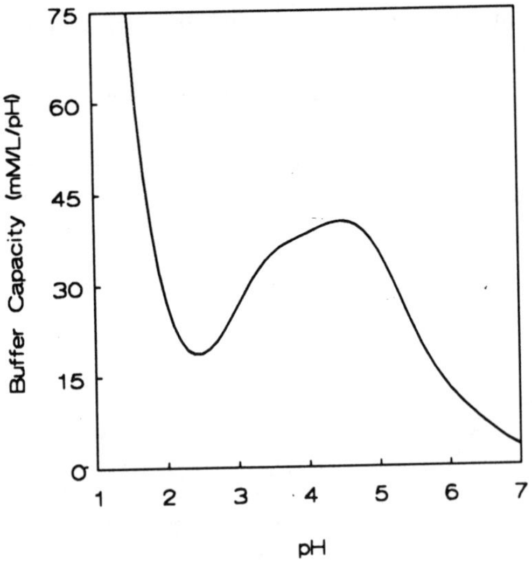

Fig. 15-5b. The effect of pH on the buffer capacity in wine.

Table 15-1. Juice acidity measures of various cultivars and locations.

Year and cultivar	pH	Titratable Acidity g/L	Malic acid g/L	Tartaric acid g/L	Estimated buffer capacity mM/L/pH
		France, Medoc (Peynaud and Maurie 1956)			
1952 Cabernet Sauvignon	3.38	8.40	2.95	8.10	50.4
1953 Cabernet Sauvignon	3.22	7.73	3.35	8.40	25.3
1954 Cabernet Sauvignon	3.10	8.40	2.08	9.45	50.6
1955 Cabernet Sauvignon	3.20	6.60	2.41	9.00	51.2
1952 Merlot	3.52	5.55	2.08	7.13	41.8
1953 Merlot	3.30	5.93	1.01	8.00	42.4
1954 Merlot	3.15	8.10	1.21	10.6	53.3
1955 Merlot	3.40	5.85	1.61	8.93	48.2
		Australia, Barossa and Renmark (Rankine et al. 1971)			
1959 Syrah	3.44	6.5	3.0	5.7	39.8
1960 Syrah	3.43	6.7	2.7	6.5	43.0
1961 Syrah	3.59	5.9	2.8	6.0	39.9
1962 Syrah	3.58	6.1	2.3	6.5	39.8
1959 Riesling	3.12	8.8	2.4	8.4	47.4
1960 Riesling	3.12	8.7	2.1	8.8	48.1
1961 Riesling	3.28	8.2	2.7	7.9	48.0
1962 Riesling	3.21	8.2	1.7	9.0	48.5
		Germany, Wein (Wejnar 1971)			
1963 Müller-Thurgau	3.22	8.0	2.80	7.52	46.2
1964 Müller-Thurgau	3.36	6.0	2.08	5.92	36.7
1965 Müller-Thurgau	3.48	7.2	3.91	4.79	39.9
1966 Müller-Thurgau	3.25	9.1	7.77	5.05	55.2
1963 Riesling	2.94	9.8	3.80	8.39	47.6
1964 Riesling	3.11	10.0	3.38	9.62	56.1
1965 Riesling	2.88	14.2	9.07	6.76	53.0
1966 Riesling	2.82	17.1	10.3	9.95	65.0
		South Africa, Stellenbosch (Du Plessis 1968)			
1964 Cabernet Sauvignon	3.3	8.5	3.5	8.0	51.9
1964 Pinotage	3.2	9.4	4.1	7.7	51.8
1964 Pinot noir	3.1	12.0	6.3	9.0	36.2
1964 Syrah	3.5	8.0	1.9	9.0	49.4
1964 Zinfandel	3.5	8.2	2.0	9.2	50.8
1964 St. Emilion	3.4	7.8	5.2	4.4	43.6
		United States, Washington (Johnson and Nagel 1976)			
1973 Foch	4.04	9.2	6.73	9.66	69.8
1973 Limberger	3.44	8.3	4.20	9.06	60.2
1973 Chardonnay	3.60	8.8	6.80	9.50	73.6
1973 Müller-Thurgau	3.58	7.8	2.90	6.53	42.7
		United States, California (Steele and Kunkee 1978, 1979)			
1976 Cabernet Sauvignon	3.47	6.4	2.8	6.8	43.8
1976 Cabernet Sauvignon	3.85	4.3	1.9	6.6	37.2
1976 Merlot	3.63	5.4	3.3	6.0	42.0
1976 Merlot	3.82	4.3	2.4	6.2	37.7
1976 Pinot noir	3.58	7.7	5.4	6.2	52.8
1976 Pinot noir	4.02	6.4	5.1	6.3	48.6
1976 Zinfandel	3.20	8.5	5.2	5.8	47.5
1976 Zinfandel	3.46	6.4	3.9	6.7	48.3

Table 15-1. (*Continued*)

Year and cultivar	pH	Titratable Acidity g/L	Malic acid g/L	Tartaric acid g/L	Estimated buffer capacity mM/L/pH
	United States, California (Steele and Kunkee 1978, 1979)				
1976 Chardonnay	3.52	6.0	4.1	7.0	50.5
1976 Chardonnay	3.96	5.4	3.1	6.5	41.5
1976 Gewürztraminer	4.04	6.1	4.1	7.3	48.8
1976 Gewürztraminer	4.28	6.0	3.9	7.0	46.1
1976 Riesling	3.23	7.3	2.6	8.1	48.2
1976 Riesling	3.77	4.8	2.5	7.0	41.9
1976 Sauvignon blanc	3.63	6.0	3.2	6.0	41.5
1976 Sauvignon blanc	3.77	5.4	2.6	6.0	38.0

C. PREDICTING PH AND TITRATABLE ACIDITY VALUES

1. Ionization Equations

In order to quantify the behavior of acidity in juices and wines it is necessary to predict acid ionization and pH for these mixtures. The aqueous ionization constants for the major acids found in wine are presented in Table 15-2. These are the values which have been used in the acidity and ionization calculations throughout this book.

2. Estimated pK_as in Juice and Wine

The presence of significant sugar and ethanol concentrations in juices and wines lead to changes in the effective dissociation constants of the organic acids. These changes are due to changes in the dielectric properties of the solvent and its effect on the strength of bonds within the carboxylate groups. The influence of the solvent properties on the dissociation of the inorganic acids is less apparent and generally such changes in the constants are not attempted.

There are two approaches to determining these effects on dissociation constants. The first is the experimental determination of the effects of ethanol concentration of the pK_as as has been done for the major organic acids (Usseglio-Tomasset and Bosia 1978), and the other is the application of general relationships that have been developed for predicting

Table 15-2. The aqueous dissociation constants for some wine constituents.

Acid	pK_{a1}	pK_{a2}	pK_{a3}
Tartaric	2.98[1],3.07[4]	4.34[1],4.39[4]	
Malic	3.48[4]	5.10[4]	
Lactic	3.86[3],3.89[4]		
Succinic	4.19[3],4.21[4]	5.57[3],5.64[4]	
Sulfurous	1.8[2]	7.2[2],7.7[5]	
Citric	3.06[3]	4.74[3]	5.40[3]
Oxalic	1.19[3]	4.21[3]	
Glutaric	2.47[6]	4.68[6]	
Galacturonic	3.50[4]		
Gluconic	3.81[4]		
Glucuronic	3.26[4]		
Pyruvic	2.94[2], 2.71[4]		
Ascorbic	4.1[3]	11.79[3]	
Arginine	2.17[3]	9.04[3]	
Proline	1.99[3]	10.60[3]	
Aspartic	2.09[3]	3.86[3]	9.82[3]
Glutamic	2.19[3]	4.25[3]	9.67[3]
Ammonia	9.2[2]		
Carbonic	6.4[2]	10.3[2]	
Acetic	4.8[2], 4.78[4]		
Sorbic	4.76[3]		
Phosphoric	2.1[2]	7.2[2]	12.4[2]
Sulfuric	−9.0[7]	2.0[2]	
Nitric	−1.4[2]		
Gallic	4.41[3]		
Cinnamic	4.44[1]		
Hydrogen Sulfide	7.0[2]	12.9[2]	

[1] Weast (1977). [2] Aylward and Findlay (1966). [3] Segal (1976). [4] Usseglio-Tomasset and Bosia (1978). [5] King et al. (1981). [6] Dawson et al. (1969). [7] Stranks et al. (1965).

Table 15-3. The acid dissociation constants in ethanol solutions. (Data of Usseglio-Tomasset and Bosia 1978).

	12% ethanol		14% ethanol	
Acid	pK_{a1}	pK_{a2}	pK_{a1}	pK_{a2}
Tartaric	3.23	4.59	3.27	4.63
Malic	3.64	5.32	3.67	5.36
Citric	3.32	4.91	3.35	4.95
Succinic	4.38	5.84	4.41	5.90
Lactic	4.06		4.09	
Acetic	4.89		4.91	
Pyruvic	2.82		2.86	
Gluconic	3.99		4.03	
Galacturonic	3.68		3.71	
Glucuronic	3.44		3.48	

the effect of solvent properties on the dissociation constants (Sen et al. 1979).

Usseglio-Tomasset and Bosia (1978) determined the dissociation constants for tartaric, malic, citric, succinic and lactic, acetic, pyruvic, galacturonic, gluconic, and glucuronic acids in solutions up to 20% ethanol. Their values for these acids are summarized for 12% and 14% ethanol in Table 15-3. The effect of ethanol in wine is to make the effective pK_as 0.15 to 0.2 units higher than their aqueous values and this leads to less dissociation of the acids than that observed in water solutions. The similar effect of ethanol on the pK_{a1} of sulfur dioxide has also been shown (Usseglio-Tomasset and Bosia 1984).

The effects of ethanol on the dielectric properties of the solution (and acid dissociation) are similar to those caused by the presence of the sugars, glucose and fructose. There do not appear to be any corresponding calculations for juice conditions and so the following approach is useful for both juice and wine conditions.

3. The Influence of Solvent on pK_a Values

The relationship between the dissociation constants and the dielectric constant of an aqueous organic solvent for a number of organic acids has been shown (Sen et al. 1979) to be of the form:

$$pK_a^* = pK_a + b\left[\frac{1}{\varepsilon_1} - \frac{1}{\varepsilon_2}\right] \qquad (15.4)$$

where pK_a^* is the dissociation constant in the solvent mixture and ε_1 and ε_2 are functions of the dielectric properties of the solvents involved. The constant b can be thought of as the sensitivity of the acid ionization to the dielectric constant of the solution.

The ε_1 term is given by:

$$\varepsilon_1 = \varepsilon^* + (\varepsilon_{water} - \varepsilon_{organic}), \qquad (15.4a)$$

where ε_{water} and $\varepsilon_{organic}$ are the dielectric constants for water and the organic component; and ε^* is that of the mixture. The ε_2 term is related to the constants for water and the organic component:

$$\varepsilon_2 = 2\varepsilon_{water} - \varepsilon_{organic} \qquad (15.4b)$$

where the definitions are the same as those in Equation (15.4a).

Based on the results for malonic, formic, acetic, lactic, and succinic acids, whose pK_as range from 2.75 to 4.76 (Sen et al. 1979), a correlation for the constant b in terms of the acid pK_as has been determined for organic acids to be:

$$b = 268.9 + 55.2\, pK_a, \qquad (15.4c)$$

and this is shown in Figure 15-6.

The use of this set of equations (15.4), allows the pK_a values of similar organic acids, such as tartaric and malic acids, to be estimated in sugar and ethanol solutions. The effect of the change in dielectric properties on the dissociation of the inorganic acids, such as sulfurous, is assumed to be similar.

4. Sugar and Ethanol Solutions

The dielectric constant for sugar and ethanol solutions can be found in the International Critical Tables or other handbooks and these have been correlated to be for glucose at

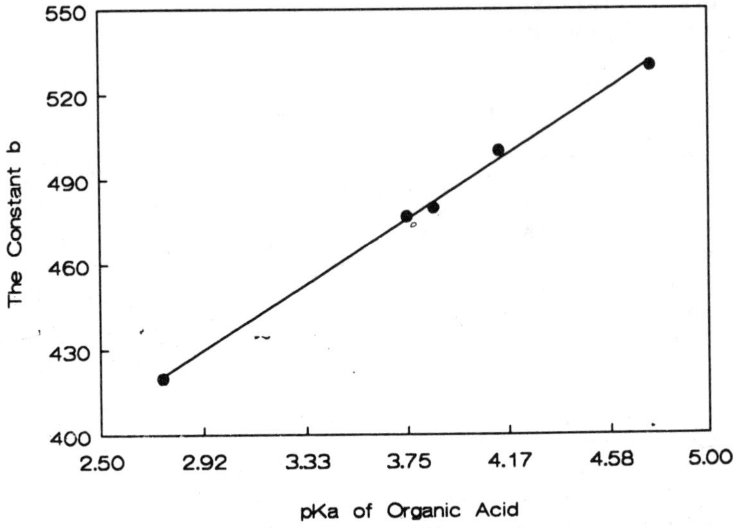

Fig. 15-6. The relationship between pKa and the constant *b* (Equation (15.4c)).

25°C:

$$\varepsilon^* = 78.5 - 0.270\,[G], \qquad (15.5a)$$

where $[G]$ is the weight percent of glucose, and for ethanol at 25°C:

$$\varepsilon^* = 78.5 - 0.587\,[E], \qquad (15.5b)$$

where $[E]$ is the weight percent of ethanol.

The effect of fructose is very similar to that of glucose and these relationships have been incorporated into the calculation procedures for estimating the pH and buffer capacity of juices and wines.

5. Activity Coefficients

The calculation of most solution equilibria involve the use of activity coefficients to correct for nonideal behavior of the ions. The departure from ideal behavior is more pronounced for ions with a double charge than those with a single charge. This becomes especially important in the estimation of the second dissociation forms of tartaric and malic acids. The main factor in these corrections is the effect of all of the other ions in solution, and this is generally referred to as the ionic strength or salt strength.

a. *The Debye-Hückle Equations*

One of the earliest means of estimating the activity coefficients in the presence of other ions was developed by Debye and Hückle (Butler 1964), and their first suggestion has become known as the Limiting Law. The activity coefficient γ, is given by the following relationship:

$$\log(\gamma) = -A|z^+z^-|\sqrt{(I)}, \qquad (15.6)$$

where I is the ionic strength of the solution; $|z^+z^-|$ is the modulus of the ion charge product; and the constant A has a value of 0.509 for water solutions at 25°C.

The value of the ionic strength is calculated as one-half of the sum of the weighted contributions of all of the ions in solution:

$$I = 0.5\Sigma\left[C_i z_i^2\right], \qquad (15.7)$$

where C_i is the molar concentration of the ion; and z_i is the charge of the ion.

This early form was soon found to be inadequate in describing the actual ion behavior at even moderate ionic strengths, and the Extended Law (Butler 1964) was proposed instead:

$$\log(\gamma) = -0.509|z^+z^-|\frac{\sqrt{(I)}}{1 + Ba\sqrt{(I)}}, \qquad (15.8)$$

where the constant "B" has the value 0.328 in water at 25°C, and the constant a was related to the size of the ion. Values of a have been tabulated for many ions (Butler 1964) and range from 3 for ions such as potassium to 4 for bisulfite and acetate to 5 for carbonate and 6 for calcium.

The values of a are not available for many of the anions such as bitartrate and bimalate that are of interest in wines and it is not easy to predict them from our present knowledge, making the use of Equation (15.8) of limited value even though it provides better estimates in many solutions.

The concentration product calculations of Berg and Keefer (1958, 1959) used the Extended Law with a value of unity for the product B times a. Others have used the original limiting law form in more recent solubility calculations (Curvelo-Garcia 1987). Neither of these equations provides a very good estimate of the activity coefficients in salt solutions at the 50- to 100-mM level typical of juices and wines.

b. The Davies Equation

A more general approach that has been adopted is the equation developed by Davies (Butler 1964). It assumed the product B times a in the extended law to be unity and, based on several salts, introduced an empirical loading for the ionic strength in a correction term:

$$\log(\gamma) = -0.509|z^+z^-| \times\left[\frac{\sqrt{(I)}}{(1+\sqrt{(I)})} + 0.20\,I\right] \quad (15.8)$$

This equation is perhaps the most suitable for calculations of the acidity, chemical reaction, and solubility relationships involving ionic species in juices and wines and it is recommended for such. It has been used in the calculation of buffer capacity and pH changes presented in this chapter.

6. Ionic Strength

The estimation of activity coefficients will require an estimate of the ionic strength of a juice or wine. This is obtained by determining the concentrations of all of the ionic species in solution or using ranges such as those reported by Ough and Amerine (1988). The most widely used value of the ionic strength of wines is the 38-mM value used by Berg and Keefer (1958, 1959) in their tartrate stability studies. Recent estimates (Abgueguen and Boulton 1993), based on more species, suggest that the value is in the range of 75 to 85 mM.

7. Influence of Activity on The pK_a Values

The dissociation constants published in most handbooks are not corrected for the effects of ion strength on the activity coefficients, and many texts that describe acidity calculations do not take them into account. The simplest form of this correction is:

$$pKa^* = pK_a - \log\frac{(\gamma)[\text{base}]}{(\gamma)\,[\text{acid}]}, \quad (15.9)$$

where pK_a is the value in the absence of ion strength effects; and pK_a^* is the value in their presence. This form is based on the unit activity for the hydrogen ions. If the activity coefficients are estimated from the Davies equation, described previously, the correction equation becomes:

$$pK_a^* = pK_a - n\left(0.509\left[\frac{\sqrt{(I)}}{(1+\sqrt{(I)})} + 0.20\,I\right]\right), \quad (15.10)$$

where n is a constant related to the ionization involved. The coefficient n is equal to twice the charge on the dissociating species minus one:

$$n = (2z_d - 1), \quad (15.10a)$$

where z_d is 0 for the undissociated acid ($n = -1$), -1 for the first acid anion ($n = -3$), and -2 for the second acid anion ($n = -5$) (Daniels and Alberty 1975).

The ion strength effect on ionization is especially pronounced for the second pK_a of the acids, and this leads to much higher pH values for the maximum bitartrate ion concentration, often referred to as 3.6 or 3.7 based on aqueous pK_as, but more like 4.1 when salt strength and ethanol effects are taken into account.

The pK_a values corrected for the effects of ethanol (Equation (15.4)) and ion strength using the Davies equation (Equation (15.8)) have been used in the calculations presented and are recommended.

D. ESTIMATING CHANGES IN PH AND TITRATABLE ACIDITY

1. Deacidification

One reason for wanting to be able to predict the pH and buffer capacity of juices and wines is to be able to estimate the effects of various changes in the acidity (see Chapter 3). These include the effect of malolactic fermentation in high-malate juices and the effect of extensive precipitation of potassium bitartrate in high-potassium wines. It also applies to the changes that might be expected during acidification and deacidification treatments.

a. *Carbonate Deacidification*

In the deacidification of juices with calcium carbonate in the double-salt procedure, there are two major reactions that will affect the final acidity. The first is the extensive neutralization of the acid mixture in the volume being treated. The second is the precipitation of calcium tartrate and, to a lesser degree, calcium malate. The first causes predictable changes in the titratable acidity and pH of the treated juice; however, the second has contributions that will depend on the extent of the salt precipitations.

The calcium salt precipitations do not lead to loss of titratable acidity since there are no titratable hydrogen ions in them. They do have an impact by limiting the rise in pH during the treatment due to the additional dissociation of their bitartrate and bimalate forms that follow the precipitation. This reduction in the concentrations of the tartrate and malate also decreases the buffer capacity of the juice following treatment. This can be on the order of 20 to 30% and is significant in determining the pH after treatment. The extent of precipitation is influenced by the initial concentrations of tartrate and malate, the level of seed crystals, the degree of agitation, the proportions of juice and carbonate, and the treatment temperature. It is the uncertainty in the precipitation that limits the accuracy of the estimation the acidity changes under these conditions.

b. *Malolactic Deacidification*

Malolactic fermentation (see Chapter 6) is an example in which the changes in titratable acidity and pH are predictable. The conversion of malic to lactic acid causes one titratable hydrogen to be lost and the exchange of a weaker acid for a stronger one in the buffer. The changes in the buffer capacity are of secondary importance to the loss of titratable acidity. Each gram per liter of malic acid converted into lactic acid will give rise to a loss of 7.46 mM/L of titratable hydrogens (or 1.12 g/L as tartaric). The expected changes in the pH are presented in Table 15-4 for different initial levels of malic acid and wine buffer capacity. The variation in the buffer capacity with pH is shown in Figure 15-5b for a typical wine.

2. Acidification

The acidification of juices or wines with tartaric acid can have variable results depending

Table 15-4. Predicted effect of the malolactic fermentation on the increase of wine pH.

Buffer Capacity (mM/L)	Initial malic acid concentration 1 g/L	2 g/L	3 g/L
35	0.21	0.42	0.64
50	0.15	0.30	0.45
65	0.11	0.22	0.34

on the initial pH. The addition in itself will lead to a predictable increase in titratable acidity, but the change in pH will depend on both the pH and the buffer capacity of the juice or wine. This is because the pH determines the extent of ionization of the added acid and it is only the ionized hydrogen ions that contribute to the pH decrease. The buffer capacity will determine the effect that these released ions have on the pH.

Each tartrate ion formed will yield two protons, while only one will come from each bitartrate ion. For a wine at a pH of 4.0, the added acid will ionize to give a proton yield of 46%, while at a pH of 3.5 it is 32% and at pH = 3.0 it is 16%. The proton yield and pH shift caused by an addition of 1 g/L of tartaric acid to a typical juice are shown over this pH range in Table 15-5. The corresponding values for the addition to a typical wine are given in Table 15-6.

If the addition results in the precipitation of potassium bitartrate then there are additional effects that can cause the pH to either rise or fall depending on the pH conditions. This will be discussed further in the following section.

3. Precipitation of Tartaric Acid Salts

The precipitation of potassium and calcium salts of tartaric acid provide quite different effects on the pH of the resulting wine. The extent of the precipitation is often difficult to predict, but it can best be determined at the laboratory scale as part of the stability tests discussed in Chapter 8. The precipitation of potassium bitartrate will result in the loss of 1 g/L of titratable acidity for each 2.51 g/L of the salt formed, while that of calcium tartrate will have no loss at all.

When these salts precipitate, there will be a rearrangement of the acid equilibria that can cause some of the undissociated acid to ionize and for some of the dianion to recombine with available protons. It is the net effect of these two reactions that will determine whether additional protons are released into the buffer or some are consumed from it, thereby lowering or raising the pH, respectively. For tartaric acid, the point at which these opposing reactions nullify each other is the pH of the maximum bitartrate concentration. For a water solution containing only tartaric acid, this would be at approximately 3.6 based on the pub-

Table 15-5. The buffer capacity, proton yield, and pH changes for the addition of tartaric acid and the pH changes for the precipitation of the potassium and calcium salts in a typical juice[a].

pH	Buffer capacity (mM/L/pH)	Proton yield (%)	Δ pH 1 g/L KHTa added	Δ pH 1.25 g/L KHTa precipitated	Δ pH 1.25 g/L CaTa precipitated
2.7	25.2	10.05	−0.05	−0.21	−0.48
2.8	27.4	12.06	−0.06	−0.18	−0.43
2.9	29.8	14.35	−0.06	−0.16	−0.38
3.0	32.2	16.90	−0.07	−0.14	−0.34
3.1	34.4	19.69	−0.08	−0.12	−0.31
3.2	36.3	22.66	−0.08	−0.10	−0.28
3.3	37.7	25.78	−0.09	−0.09	−0.26
3.4	38.5	28.98	−0.10	−0.07	−0.25
3.5	38.7	32.19	−0.11	−0.06	−0.23
3.6	38.4	35.36	−0.12	−0.05	−0.22
3.7	37.6	38.46	−0.14	−0.04	−0.22
3.8	36.7	41.48	−0.15	−0.03	−0.21
3.9	35.7	44.40	−0.17	−0.02	−0.21
4.0	34.8	47.26	−0.18	−0.01	−0.20

[a]Juice contains 6 g/L tartaric acid, 3 g/L malic acid, and is 20 Brix.

Table 15-6. The buffer capacity, proton yield, and pH changes for the addition of tartaric acid and the pH changes for the precipitation of the potassium and calcium salts in a typical wine[a].

pH	Buffer capacity (mM/L/pH)	Proton yield (%)	Δ pH 1 g/L KHTa added	Δ pH 1.25 g/L KHTa precipitated	Δ pH 1.25 g/L CaTa precipitated
2.7	22.9	9.22	−0.05	−0.24	−0.53
2.8	24.8	11.11	−0.06	−0.21	−0.48
2.9	27.1	13.28	−0.07	−0.18	−0.43
3.0	29.4	15.71	−0.07	−0.16	−0.38
3.1	31.7	18.39	−0.08	−0.13	−0.34
3.2	33.8	21.29	−0.08	−0.11	−0.31
3.3	35.5	24.34	−0.09	−0.10	−0.28
3.4	36.8	27.51	−0.10	−0.08	−0.26
3.5	37.7	30.71	−0.11	−0.07	−0.24
3.6	38.2	33.90	−0.12	−0.06	−0.23
3.7	38.5	37.02	−0.13	−0.04	−0.22
3.8	38.5	40.07	−0.14	−0.03	−0.21
3.9	38.5	43.01	−0.15	−0.02	−0.20
4.0	38.5	45.88	−0.16	−0.01	−0.19

[a]The model wine contains 6 g/L of tartaric acid, 2 g/L of lactic acid, 1 g/L of succinic acid, and 12% ethanol by volume.

lished aqueous pK_a values, but in the presence of ethanol and ion content of wine it is more like 4.1. At pH values below this, the precipitation of potassium bitartrate results in a net release in protons and a reduction in pH while at pH values above it there will be a net consumption of protons and the pH will rise. In actual wines these changes will be lessened by the presence of other buffer components (primarily malic or lactic acid), but the general trend is followed.

a. *Potassium Bitartrate*

The precipitation of potassium bitartrate from wine usually occurs to some degree during fermentation and aging periods. It can be used to further lower the pH of a juice or wine after an addition of tartaric acid by the induction of the crystallization at lower temperatures. This will usually occur naturally in wines that are held at lower temperatures but will require the addition of seed crystals and some agitation to encourage the crystallization in some wines (see Chapter 8).

The change in pH caused by the precipitation of 1.25 g/L of potassium bitartrate in these conditions is also given in Tables 15-5 for a typical juice and 15-6 for a typical wine. This precipitation is equivalent to a loss in titratable acidity of 0.5 g/L. Note that while significant reductions in pH occur at low pH, these diminish with increasing pH until at pH 4.0, where the pH reduction due to the precipitation is practically zero.

b. *Calcium Tartrate*

The precipitation of calcium tartrate is rare at wine conditions but it is significant during the deacidification with calcium carbonate (see Chapter 3) or when a neutral salt of calcium, such as calcium sulfate, is added directly to wine, as is sometimes practiced.

The advantage of this form of precipitation is that there is no loss of titratable acidity and the dissociation caused is maximal, giving a larger pH shift per mole of tartrate precipitated than with the potassium salt. The change in pH associated with the precipitation of 1.25 g/L of calcium tartrate is shown for a typical juice and wine in Tables 15-5 and 15-6, respectively. The effect of the calcium salt precipitation is almost twice that of the potassium salt at low pH, but it is far more effective in the range 3.5 to 4.0.

The disadvantages of such a treatment are a wine that will be saturated with the calcium salt after the treatment and the possible sensory effects of elevated sulfate levels. Potassium sulfate is known to be salty tasting. Recent advances in the understanding of nucleation in the calcium tartrate crystallization (Abgueguen and Boulton 1993) provide a practical means of quantifying and enhancing the treatment for this instability. There appear to be no reports of the sensory effects of the treatment in table wines.

The effect of removing the tartrate anion can be seen to have a dramatic effect on the pH of the wine without altering the titratable acidity. It is this effect which also occurs during the use of anion (combined with cation exchange) for the adjustment of pH. The removal of tartrate ions during such an exchange parallels that of the calcium precipitation without making the corresponding wine saturated with respect to this salt.

E. REFERENCES

ABGUEGUEN, O., AND R. B. BOULTON. 1993. "The crystallization kinetics of calcium tartrate from model solutions and wines." *Am. J. Enol. Vitic.* 44:65–75.

AYLWARD, G. H., AND T. J. V. FINDLAY. 1966. *Chemical Data Book*. 2nd ed., Sydney, Australia: John Wiley & Sons.

BERG, H. W., AND R. M. KEEFER. 1958. "Analytical determination of tartrate stability in wine: 1. Potassium bitartrate." *Am. J. Enol.* 9:180–193.

BERG, H. W., AND R. M. KEEFER. 1959. "Analytical determination of tartrate stability in wine: 2. Calcium tartrate." *Am. J. Enol.* 10:105–109.

BOULTON, R. 1980a. "The general relationship between potassium, sodium and pH in grape juices and wines." *Am. J. Enol. Vitic.* 31:182–186.

BOULTON, R. 1980b. "A hypothesis for the presence, activity and role of potassium/hydrogen, adenosine triphosphatases in grapevines." *Am. J. Enol. Vitic.* 31:283–287.

BOULTON, R. 1980c. "The relationships between total acidity, titratable acidity and pH in grape tissue." *Vitis* 19:113–120.

BOULTON, R. 1980d. "The relationships between total acidity, titratable acidity and pH in wine." *Am. J. Enol. Vitic.* 31:76–80.

BUTLER, J. N. 1964. *Ionic Equilibrium*. Reading, MA: Addison-Wesley.

CURVELO-GARCIA A. S. 1987. "O producto de solubilidade do tartarato de calcio em meios hidroalcoolicos em funcão dos seus factores determinantes." *Ciena Tec. Vitic.* 6:19–28.

DANIELS, F., AND R. A. ALBERTY. 1975. *Physical Chemistry*, 4th ed. New York: John Wiley & Sons.

DAWSON, R. M. C., D. C ELLIOTT, W. H. ELLIOTT, AND K. M. JONES. 1969. *Data for Biochemical Research*. Oxford, UK: Clarendon Press.

DU PLESSIS, C. S. 1968. "Changes in major organic acids of ripening grapes." *S. Afric. J. Agric. Sci.* 11:237–248.

EDWARDS, T. L., V. L. SINGLETON, AND R. B. BOULTON. 1985. "Formation of ethyl esters of tartaric acid during wine aging: Chemical and sensory effects." *Am. J. Enol. Vitic.* 36:118–124.

JOHNSON, T. L., AND C. W. NAGEL. 1976. "Composition of central Washington grapes during maturation." *Am. J. Enol. Vitic.* 27:15–20.

KING, JR., A. D., J. D. PONTING, D. W. SANSHUCK, R. JACKSON, AND K. MIHARA. 1981. "Factors affecting death of yeast by sulfur dioxide." *J. Fd. Protect.* 44:92–97.

LEONARD, R. T., AND T. K. HODGES. 1973. "Characterization of plasma membrane-associated adenosine triphosphatase activity in oat roots." *Plant Physiol.* 52:6–12.

OUGH C. S., AND M. A. AMERINE. 1988. *Methods for Analysis of Musts and Wines*, 2nd ed. New York: John Wiley & Sons.

PEYNAUD, E., AND A. MAURIE. 1956. "Nouvelles recherches sur la maturation du raisin dans le Bordelais, annees 1952, 1953 et 1954." *Ann. Technol. Agric.* 5:111–139.

RANKINE, B. C., J. C. M. FORNACHON, E. W. BOEHM, AND K. M. CELLIER. 1971. "The influence of grape variety, climate and soil on grape composition and the composition and quality of table wines." *Vitis* 10:33–50.

SAITO, K. AND Z. KASAI. 1978. "Conversion of labelled substrates to sugars, cellwall polysaccharides, and tartaric acid in grape berries." *Plant Physiol.* 62:215–219.

SEGAL, I. 1976. *Biochemical Calculations*. 2nd ed., New York: John Wiley & Sons.

SEN B., R. N. ROY, J. J. GIBBONS, D. A. JOHNSON, AND L. H. ADCOCK. 1979. "Computational techniques of ionic processes in water-organic mixed solvents." In *Thermodynamic Behavior of Electrolytes in Mixed Solvents*, W. F. Furter, Ed., pp. 215–248. *Adv. Chem. Ser.* 177, Washington, DC: American Chemical Society.

STEELE, J. T., AND R. E. KUNKEE. 1978. "Deacidification of musts from the western United States by the calcium double-salt precipitation process." *Am. J. Enol. Vitic.* 29:153–160.

STEELE, J. T., AND R. E. KUNKEE. 1979. "Deacidification of high acid California wines by calcium double-salt precipitation." *Am. J. Enol. Vitic.* 30:227–231.

STRANKS, D. R., M. L. HEFFERNAN, K. C. LEE DOW, P. T. MCTIGUE, AND G. R. A. WITHERS. 1965. *Chemistry—A Structural View*. London: Melbourne University Press.

USSEGLIO-TOMASSET, L., AND P. D. BOSIA. 1978. "Determinazione delle constanti di dissociazione dei principali acidi del vino in soluzioni idroalcoliche di interesse enologico." *Rivista Vitic. Enol.* 31:380–403.

USSEGLIO-TOMASSET, L., AND P. D. BOSIA. 1984. "La Prima costante di dissociazione dell'acido solforoso." *Vini d'Italia* 26(5):7–14.

WEAST, R. C. 1977. *CRC Handbook of Chemistry and Physics*, 58th ed. Cleveland, OH: CRC Press.

WEJNAR, R. 1971. "Etude l'influence de l'acide tartrique et l'acide malique sur le pH du vin." *Conn. Vigne Vin* 5:535–562.

CHAPTER 16

Preparation, Analysis, and Evaluation of Experimental Wines

There are many instances when a winemaker wishes to modify or consider modification of the usual winemaking practices. In fact, from vintage to vintage every wine is made somewhat differently depending upon circumstances. If the wines have been highly satisfactory, replicating previous practices as closely as possible may be the objective. If small improvements are sought in the commercial-sized lots, small incremental changes intended to correct the deficiencies may be made in the practices employed. In this chapter, we are thinking primarily of proposed changes of larger magnitude that may make notable and possibly detrimental changes in the wines produced. How should the winemaker proceed? How should the new wines be evaluated? How is the decision made to capitalize on the results of the experimentation?

These are not trivial or uncommon questions. Almost all wineries make some experimental wines every year; large wineries may have a special staff doing nothing else. Wasteful and misleading results can be very costly and it is important to make and evaluate such wines so as to avoid as many pitfalls as possible. Furthermore, appreciation of proper controls, replication, analysis, and statistical treatment during experimental winemaking is essential to making use of research results published by other experimenters. Five concepts are important in beginning such experimentation. The objective must be well understood and usually limited to changing one operation or parameter at a time. Adequate controls and replicates must be used. Complete and detailed records must be kept. The results must be carefully evaluated to place conclusions on a sound basis. Care must be taken that the findings are meaningful when adapted to commercial operations.

A sixth concept is useful if new products or drastic changes are contemplated. Bold modifications that include some that are likely to be excessive are informative, particularly in early experimentation. For example, if time is the factor being investigated and only four experimental conditions can be considered, a geometrical progression of one, two, four, and eight days is likely to be more informative than a linear one of one, two, three, and four days. Until you are sure that eight days is excessive for some reason, even larger factors may be better, e.g., one, three, nine, 27 days. The larger the steps in the experimental parameter, the more likely it is that follow-up experiments will be needed to home in on the optimum condition, but two or more sets of experiments will be more efficient and more certainly correct than creeping up on the target in small steps. An applicable tenet of visually adjusting artillery fire is to get an "over" and a "short" and then, and only then, try to hit the target by progressively splitting each following interval.

A. SIZE OF EXPERIMENTAL LOTS, CONTAINERS

If commercial-sized lots are used, experimental wines that turn out poorer than acceptable represent a serious loss. For this reason, and also because wineries seldom have many similar tanks available, experimental treatments and replications will be limited if experimental volumes are large. Furthermore, with large tanks it is more difficult to keep them all the same with identical conditions and identical starting musts or wines in all of them.

Smaller containers can more easily be replicated, handled identically, and filled with the same must or wine. However, special care is often necessary to produce experimental findings with them that are directly applicable in large-scale commercial practice. For example, a small leak of air into a large experiment may have little effect, but the same leak with a small container may be catastrophic. Sedimentation is faster and stratification less severe in smaller containers. Extraneous temperature variation and its control may or may not be greater problems with larger containers.

The material of the containers affects experimental conditions and practicality. Glass is impractical for large containers. It has the advantage that the experiment can be observed, but if light is a factor, the results can be different from those found in stainless steel. Wooden containers themselves inherently differ so that extra replication to evaluate this effect is often necessary if they are used. Plastic containers for small experiments can have special problems such as leaching of components of the plastic or transmission of oxygen. For example, polyethylene generally lacks plasticizers and flavorful leachables, but is rather permeable to oxygen. Recycled polyethylene, often found in garbage receptacles, will have unknown materials present and is not suitable for food containers. The time involved in the experiments is a factor. Virgin polyethylene is generally suitable for brief fermentation experiments, but not for storage.

The minimum size of an experimental lot, assuming that such factors as oxygen access are controlled, is determined by the amount of wine needed to perform the desired processing and to end up with the necessary final volume for analysis, sensory panel evaluation, and other planned tests. Even if laboratory-sized filters, etc., are available, we do not recommend less than about 10-L batches for most experimental musts or wines.

The containers must be fitted with suitable fermentation bungs or other means to allow carbon dioxide to escape (unless sparkling wines are being tested), but to prevent entry of air. If containers are small and temperature differences minor, control of the ambient air temperature around the group of experimental samples may be adequate. If heat transfer rates are too small, better control may be needed, such as by immersing the containers in a controlled temperature water bath. Any other condition, such as humidity or light must be identical for all samples and preferably controlled unless you are certain it has no influence on the parameters of the test. This does not mean an educated guess that it has no effect, it means knowing or proving it does not. The container affects such conditions and may obviate certain effects. For example, opaque, impervious containers should eliminate any role for external humidity or light.

Creative solutions to problems in experimental winemaking can be helpful, but may introduce other considerations and need to be included in the descriptions of the procedures employed. For example, a case came to our attention of white table wine experimentation by a group that lacked a crusher-destemmer. They made the wines by fermentation in plastic bags arranged to allow carbon dioxide to escape when pressure exceeded that necessary to pass a rubber band constriction around the neck. The grape clusters were trodden in the closed bag instead of a crusher. The products were compared as white table wines without further description, but differed in at least two important ways from standard commercial practice. The crushed grapes were fermented not only in the presence of berry solids, but also with stems. Since air was largely excluded when the grapes and inocula were placed in the bags, the resultant must was essentially unexposed to air. Either of these facts might have been useful subjects for experimentation, but made the direct comparison of results with any other research or commercial sample very uncertain.

B. REPRESENTATIVE SAMPLES

There are two related problems here: an analytical sample must represent all of the particular experimental batch of grapes, must, or wine; an experimental lot must be essentially identical with the other lots being compared in all respects except that being tested. While always important, these objectives are sometimes easily achieved and sometimes not. If the samples and sublots are taken from a master lot of clear and well-mixed wine or white juice must, the problem solves itself as long as appreciable differences of aeration or such are not introduced by the transfer. With inhomogeneous materials such as whole musts, grapes, etc., the problem is much more important. Representative sampling of grapes in the vineyard to decide when to pick them has already been discussed (Chapter 2) and it would be useful to review that section.

Suppose the experimental objective is to convert a large lot of grapes into a commercial batch and several smaller experimental batches of wine. Suppose further that it is necessary to obtain one or more analytical samples of the grapes for baseline analyses. Assume that the load or loads of grapes for the large commercial lot are received at the winery and are to be crushed, destemmed, and processed as a unit. This large lot will become homogenous and representative of the average composition of the grapes as it is processed, but how can one ensure the smaller lots are also? One way is to crush and destem the whole mass, mix it well, and then subsample it. Even then it may, depending upon the experiment, be necessary to take a separate representative sample of the grapes and determine such parameters as percentage of the weight due to stems, average berry weight, and weight and volume of must obtained from a given weight of berries or clusters. In order to get a truly representative sample of grapes at the winery, it is necessary to sample throughout the load, since different portions of any load will come from different vines in different parts of the vineyard and even different vineyards may be involved. This is particularly necessary if chemical compositional data from the grapes are needed, and is more important the greater the natural variation in the particular components of interest.

One approach we have found generally quite successful has been to select one cluster per 20 (or some other sizable proportion) throughout the load(s) in question. A similar approach could select 1 kg from each 20 kg of grapes, one second per 20 seconds of auger flow, etc. If the resultant first sample is unmanageably large, it can be reduced by randomly selecting subunits such as 10 berries per cluster, alternate top, middle, or bottom thirds from each cluster, etc. If a fruit sample per se is not required by the nature of the experiment, whole musts are seldom satisfactory for experimentation unless special efforts are employed to ensure randomized uniformity. It is generally satisfactory to collect all the crushed must in one container and, while mixing it, subsample for the experimental batches by, for example, dipping sequentially a small portion into each of the separate lots.

To illustrate, 1 Tm of grapes is to be converted to five 20-L experimental lots and a remainder larger lot for red table wine. To be certain of 20 L of wine allow a bit more must volume. We have usually estimated 2 kg grapes per liter of final experimental wine. Thus, $2 \times 5 \times 20 = 200$ kg of grapes will go to the experiment and 800 kg to the large lot. From the crushed, mixed (presumably SO_2-added) whole must, the most certain procedure would be to dip sequentially 1 L (i.e., 1/20 of the final volume) into each of the five experimental lots followed by four dips into another tank for the remainder lot. Continue until the original receiving tank is empty. It is important that the source container be kept stirred enough to remain homogenous during the dipping. It is also important that the five experimental lots receive exactly the same number and volume of dips.

Any and all treatments of the lots which are not part of the experimental differences must remain identical and the experimental differences, of course, must be as precise and well-controlled as possible. Inocula must be the same, cap management identical, etc.

C. CONTROLS AND REPLICATION

The control experimental sample(s) must be identical to the other experimental samples except they are the ones without the new experimental differences under study. Ordinarily they are the ones with the standard practice. A commercial lot made from the same grapes or the remainder lot as just described may be a useful comparison as well, but it should be in addition to, not instead of, the proper experimental control sample. Since the experimental control is often needed in greater amount than the other experimental samples, particularly for taste testing, it may be necessary either to make additional lots of the control or to make excess volume of the other experimental samples to match the size of the control.

In all biological materials including grapes and wine there are considerable variations. In order to estimate whether or not a result obtained from experimentation is likely to be real and not a happenstance, analysis of variance or other statistical examination is required. To apply statistics, it is necessary to have sufficient replication (repeated samples or experiments) so that the inherent variation can be estimated. Replication, of course, is costly of effort and materials, so it should not be excessive or applied where unnecessary. The usual error, however, is too little rather than too much replication. If wines are to be made to study a viticultural situation, replicates are usually necessary in the vineyard. Depending upon the goal of the experiments, it may be necessary to keep harvests from these vineyard replicates (plots, etc.) separate and make wines from each. However, it is not usually necessary to make duplicate or truly repeat wines from the same lot of grapes if proper technique is followed. Two portions of the same must separated as indicated so as to be truly representative, inoculated and fermented identically give essentially identical wines.

However, to be sure that the findings are applicable in general it is usually important to replicate the whole experimental procedure several times with new grapes. For example, it is much more certain that the results of an experiment apply to, say, red wines in general or even Cabernet Sauvignon in particular, if several lots of red grapes from several varieties or Cabernet Sauvignon grapes from diverse sources have been investigated. Seasonal variation is likely to be high and replication over several vintages is necessary to determine whether or not the results are the norm or only applicable in certain seasons. Remember that, at the usually chosen confidence level, significant results are to be expected by accident once in 20 trials. Of course, winery owners are not scientists and may press hard for financially useful results at low cost. Since today winemaking is based on good standards of practice, an erroneous result is likely to prove more costly in the long run than carefully done, proper research.

Often wine research centers around assessment of yeast strain or on altering the microbial dynamics of winemaking. Examples include testing the impact on quality by wild yeasts or of particular malolactic bacteria. In these types of studies, it is critical to include as part of the procedure reisolation of the organism utilized. If no effect is noted after addition of a novel microbe, this might be because it does not, in fact, produce the effect, but it could be that it was not successful against the competition and failed to grow or metabolize at all. Many wineries have resident microflora that are well adapted to the growth conditions of the winery.

Microbial growth and metabolic activities are strongly impacted by nutrient composition as well as by physical parameters of temperature and pH. Overcooling or superheating of one trial lot will dramatically affect the experimental results. Such lots should be deleted from further analysis. How the inoculum is prepared is an important variable, particularly for studies of the malolactic bacteria. Inoculum regime can affect preadaptation and viability and may introduce carry over of nutrients or end products to the wine lots. Unless special yeasts or bacteria are to be tested, it is probably best to use commercial preparations: active dry yeast or freeze-dried bacteria individually reconstituted for each experiment according to the manufacturer's instructions.

Sample handling is also critical. If a sample is simply removed from the tank and stored in the refrigerator, there could be further microbial growth and metabolism making this sample no longer representative of the condition from which it was taken. Such samples could be filter sterilized to remove microbes and prevent further activity. Storage at or below -20°C would also stop microbial and most chemical activity; however, such a low temperature causes tartrates and other compounds to precipitate, affecting the chemical parameters of the sample. Possible variable growth or chemical reaction such as oxidation during thawing of frozen samples is another problem.

Many studies of nutrient addition undertaken commercially suffer from the problem of a compound simply being added with no knowledge of the starting concentration of that compound. Very little, if anything, can be learned from these kinds of trials. Similar problems arise from addition of other non-nutrient reactants in chemical as well as in microbiological experiments.

Depending upon the magnitude of the experimental differences found in relation to the variation among the different control samples, more or less replication is required for a given level of confidence.

Consultation with a biometric statistician or at least application of statistical methods described in good current texts are recommended, but are beyond the scope of this presentation. Modern computer programs have made statistical analysis relatively easy, but should be applied appropriately. A bit more about statistics will be mentioned in connection with chemical and sensory analysis of experimental wines.

D. CHEMICAL AND PHYSICAL ANALYSES OF EXPERIMENTAL WINES

All wines should be subjected to appropriate analyses during their production and storage to meet the requirements of regulatory agencies and to give the winemaker information to monitor the operations properly. Experimental wines often require additional analyses to obtain more complete information and study the specific effects of the experimental conditions. There is no sense in doing the experiments unless analytical methods are available to evaluate the results. Planning for these analyses and the labor and timing for them should precede initiation of the experiments. Some analyses can be done more or less at leisure on the finished wine, others must be done at specific moments or the experiment is spoiled. Sometimes interim samples can be quickly frozen and held for later analyses as a group. Other cases arise where this is not possible for experimental or logistic reasons.

Since analyses for experimental wines often involve new or seldom-applied analyses, familiarity with current research and/or a literature search through Chemical Abstracts is very helpful. Much good fundamental and most applied research can be done, however, applying standard wine and must analyses such as described by Ough and Amerine (1988). Even if new and unusual analyses are also applied, sufficient standard analyses are needed to characterize and validate the wines. Since analyses vary as do subsamples, it is usually wise to run analyses at least in duplicate and to retest so as to discard erratic results when the duplicates do not agree. Statistical methods are useful to validate application of new analytical procedures. It is important to not confuse replicating an analysis of the same sample or even of duplicate subsamples with replicating an experiment for statistical analysis of the findings.

E. SENSORY EVALUATION

Even the most sophisticated chemical analysis cannot now, and probably never will, define the subtle flavors that make one wine greater than another in the opinion of observant consumers. That is as it should be. As a consequence, it is almost always necessary to compare wines by sensory analysis in addition to chemical and physical methods. This is true of commercial wines, but often especially so with experimental wines. More details of panel selection, testing procedures, statistical analysis, and other aspects of sensory evaluation of wines than can be covered here are given by Amerine and Roessler (1983).

In spite of opinion to the contrary by wine writers and some winemakers, one person's opinion is hardly definitive on any wine's sensory character and quality. That is not to say that one taster may not be better than another in natural ability, concentrated effort, amount of experience, and/or comparative memory. Furthermore, there is considerable agreement among expert tasters after simultaneous but independent evaluation of a group of wines. Most prestigious wine show judgings have every wine evaluated individually by at least four judges and usually the winning wines twice or more after recoding and re-presentation blind. In evaluation of the sensory qualities of one or more wines a panel of tasters is necessary. This panel should be as sensitive and experienced as possible, but each individual is erratic, biased, or unobservant on some occasions, hence the need for panels and statistical evaluation of the tasting results.

The size of the panel is affected by the availability of competent and willing participants. They must be steadfast during repeated tastings of samples not identified to them and not discussed with their colleagues during the duration of the trials. In general, the panel should be as large as possible, but in practical terms about 10 is usual. Statistical evaluation almost always shows significant differences in ratings for the same wines among judges and a judges x treatment rating interaction unless the panel is highly selected and intensively trained, i.e., judges differ in assessment of wines and treatment effects. Too few judges risks excessive effects from unusual palates; a large panel is more costly.

The question of whether it is better to have a highly selected panel acutely sensitive to particular wine features under study or a large panel that more closely resembles the whole consuming public can never satisfactorily be given a single answer. If a trained panel cannot find a significant difference between two wines, one can safely conclude the public would not care about any small differences that might be found after more exhaustive study by a larger panel. One cannot conclude, however, that the public would detect, care about, or unanimously prefer a small flavor difference between two wines as found by a small expert panel.

Unanimity of preference is a rare occurrence; we have all known individuals who liked foods we could not abide. For this reason it is usual to distinguish between difference and hedonic taste testing. It is somewhat an article of faith that if a difference is easily detected there will be one level inherently better than another. This is only certain if the higher level of the flavor involved is either detested or desired by everyone. Even then a low level of an unattractive flavor can add to complexity and be seen as favorable. The public is susceptible to being sold a flavor seen in other contexts as bad and indicating lower quality. An example will serve to clarify this idea. *Brettanomyces* infection of wine can lead to a rather strong, easily recognized, barnyardy or horsey flavor. Such infection arising in a winery's wine previously free of it leads to consternation and strenuous efforts to eliminate it. However, in certain nameless foreign areas of the world such infection has been so common that, even after blending with the available healthy wines, the horseyness is detectable.

We have no objection if a winery or wine appellation group attempts to make a virtue of an ordinarily objectionable situation. However, faculty and graduates of the University of California at Davis have been criticized for wanting wines to be too sanitary (!) and supposedly therefore uninteresting. This debate actually centers around the issue of the definition of an appellation. Does appellation refer to varietal and viticultural character unique to a specific region or should it also be applied to the character of a regional wine arising solely as a consequence of winemaking style, a style that could be practiced anywhere? Our bias is clearly for the first definition, but we recognize the fact that many European appellations fall into the second definition or are a combination of the two. To again use *Brettanomyces* as the example, the *Brettanomyces* barnyard character is distinctive and independent of any soil or climatic factors. This yeast is resident in wineries, particularly prevalent in poorly sanitized barrels and wooden tanks. It can be found anywhere in the world. The same *Brettanomyces* characters will be imparted to all varieties in all climates. *Brettanomyces* metabolites are dominant and mask other flavors. In wines possessing a poor varietal profile, *Brettanomyces* might add nuances important to an otherwise bland wine devoid of significant character of its own. Exceptional varietal character is masked, not improved, by *Brettanomyces* infection. In our considerable experience with consumer groups, most do not like the *Brettanomyces* character even without knowing the origin of the off-flavors and aromas. Nevertheless, customers who have learned to expect the *Brettanomyces* character are discomfited if it is called a defect and downgraded.

The flavors and effects of the grape, the climate, the vintage, the terroir, the fermentation, and the processing after fermentation can only come through as the winemaker plans, if the wine is clean and not subject to some unforeseen and experimentally uncontrolled variable. If these intentions are clouded by unknown or uncontrolled microbiology or other conditions, the wines will not be reproducible. This might be considered romantic by some, but it certainly has no place in good experimentation and is a disservice to producers and consumers alike, wine writers to the contrary notwithstanding.

1. Difference Testing

As the name implies, difference testing procedures are intended to answer whether or not there is a detectable difference between two wines, and by extension, among wines. The simplest is a paired test: two glasses identified only by codes are presented and the panelist asked to identify the wine highest in some characteristic. The characteristic should be named specifically such as acidity, oakiness, bitterness, etc. It becomes a hedonic test to ask which is higher in *quality*, a term requiring opinion as well as detection. "Do they differ" is almost invariably answered "yes" and is uninformative. The need for a specific and perhaps revealing question is a weakness of paired testing for differences, but it is often the procedure most sensitive to small differences.

Chances of a correct guess are 50%, and the detection threshold is the minimum concentration of the named characteristic found by the panelists at 50% above chance frequency. Difference is called a one-tailed test, because only the high end of the frequency distribution is involved. Various levels of significance may be used, but the most common is a probability of 0.05, i.e., only once out of 20 trials could such a result be an accident. Tables (Amerine and Roessler 1983) give the minimum number of agreeing or correct judgments to establish such statistical significance following different numbers of trials (panelists × replicate sample pairs). For 10 trials, nine must be correct or agree for significance, and similarly 15 out of 20 or 26 out of 40 trials are significant in paired testing.

Another procedure used for difference testing is the triangular test where three glasses are presented and the panelist told that two contain the same wine and one is different. The task is to match the two that are alike (or identify the different). Clearly there is a correct answer, no leading question need be asked, and the probability of guessing correctly is one out of three. Significance ($p = 0.05$) requires 7/10, 11/20, or 20/40 correct trials (Amerine and Roessler 1983).

2. Sample Presentation, Biases

Human beings have many subtle biases of which they are unaware. To ensure that the tasting results are not skewed by these biases or faults of presentation, the samples, codes, order, etc., must be randomized. Randomization should be accomplished by means such as casting dice, drawing from an equal number (and returning, mixing after each draw) of colored marbles, or, best of all, using a table of random numbers. Do not simply choose a series that seems to be without order. Codes to be used to designate wine glasses such as A and B are biased and usually A is chosen over B. It has been found generally preferable to use three-digit numbers randomly chosen as serving glass markers. Which sample is served first, second, etc., in a series or on the left in pairs should also be randomized. When unable to tell differences, right-handers tend to choose the right-hand sample, left-handers choose the left. Aberrant significance might be obtained if one treatment was always on one side and the panel was all right-handed.

Wine color often biases flavor opinion. If flavor differences are sought, mask color differences by opaque sample glasses, special lighting, and perhaps even screened spittoons. If possible, arrange things so the panelists are prevented from biasing the results, but are unaware of restrictions. For example, it was found that some panelists could do better if mild unsalted crackers were available to "clear the palate" between wines, but if forced to take a bit of cracker each time, they did poorer. A panel manager should take every care to ensure that the panelists are comfortable, not distracted, and kept interested and happy. It is desirable to limit the samples judged at one sitting to a small number, perhaps 10, depending upon the panelists and the fatiguing nature of the samples. Of course, it is important to see that the panelists are expectorating the wines. About 30 mL is the minimum sample to get reliable results.

3. Hedonic, Preference, or Quality Comparisons

All the concerns and cautions with regard to sample coding, randomization, etc., mentioned above are probably even more important during quality testing because the decisions are more difficult, more a matter of personal opinion, and more wines are probably being presented together. In many cases difference testing will precede hedonic testing. At least some preliminary testing should be done. If no difference can be detected, why look for quality differences? However, a difference may be detectable, but too small or too controversial to produce a significant preference. If half of a panel liked it considerably and half did not, significant preference would never be achieved, but two derived products might improve the total market.

If paired testing is used and the question is which do you prefer, it is called a two-tailed test because both extremes of the distribution curve are important. At the same significance level, $p = 0.05$, preference will be more difficult to obtain, but the required degree of agreement is nearly the same, nine of 10 trials, 15 of 20, and 27 of 40 trials (Amerine and Roessler 1983). Other test procedures can be used, of course, including three-sample difference tests, if followed by a preference or quality rating in those instances where the difference was correctly detected. Ranking is difficult to apply, because the relative difference among the samples may be confusing. Five samples may be ranked in a certain order, but four may be relatively similar and the fifth much different. Hedonic scale ratings may be useful and graphic, computerized, or based on statements such as "like extremely," "like moderately," "like slightly," on down to "dislike extremely." For statistical analysis, these ratings are converted to numbers (not including zero), or numbered ratings can be made directly by the panelists. Various scales can be used, often 10, 20, or 100 points, and each has its advocates. In fact, studies have suggested that humans cannot usefully rate unspoiled, commercially acceptable foods or wines beyond about eight sensorily hedonic levels owing to time-to-time variation by the same person much less variation among people. For this reason a scorecard approach which rates acceptable commercial wines from a low of 13 to a high of 20 (eight levels) has had considerable use both in teaching prospective wine judges to consider a wine in the proper order (visual, odor, flavor, and integrated quality) and for rating experimental wines. In the latter case, it is often more useful to analyze clarity or color by spectrophotometry and mask improper levels with dark serving glasses so as to devote the full range of ratings to odor and flavor characteristics.

Descriptive analysis is useful in selecting sensory terms to characterize the differences sought, training the panelists to use these terms similarly, and to exclude individuals from the final evaluations who are erratic, otherwise unreliable, or outliers.

Statistical analysis of variance and sometimes additional mathematical procedures such as principal component analysis can be used to determine whether or not a group of wines differs or relates in rated qualities. Coupling sensory with chemical analysis may show or at least suggest why the differences occur. If the tested treatments have been found significantly effective over replicate experiments in improving wine quality or keeping the same quality more effectively or at lower cost, commercial application is warranted. Obviously, it is safest to verify the commercial applicability by further testing at the commercial-sized level. Scale-up is not always automatically equally satisfactory.

Experimental winemaking followed by careful commercial introduction of the improvements discovered has been crucial in advancing California and other newer areas to the forefront among wines. Older areas have more and more accepted research results and rejuvenated their own research. These trends are certain to continue and, owing to the solution of the easier problems, wine and grape research must continue to improve and become more sophisticated.

F. REFERENCES

AMERINE, M. A., and E. B. ROESSLER. 1983. *Wines, Their Sensory Evaluation*, Revised ed., New York: W. H. Freeman and Co.

OUGH, C. S., and M. A. AMERINE. 1988. *Methods for Analysis of Musts and Wines*, 2d ed. New York: John Wiley & Sons.

APPENDIX A

METRIC UNIT CONVERSION CHART — SI, U.S. AND COMMON

(Read across)

Length

Inches	Feet	Millimeters	Meters
1	8.333×10^{-2}	25.4	2.54×10^{-2}
12.00	1	304.8	0.3048
3.937×10^{-2}	3.281×10^{-3}	1	1.000×10^{-3}
39.37	3.281	1000	1

Area

Square feet	Square meters
1	0.0929
10.76	1

Volume

Cubic feet	Gallon (U.S.)	1000 Gallons	Liters	Cubic meter
1	7.481	7.481×10^{-3}	28.32	2.832×10^{-2}
0.1337	1	1.000×10^{-3}	3.786	3.786×10^{-3}
133.7	1000	1	3786	3.786
3.531×10^{-2}	0.2642	2.642×10^{-4}	1	1.000×10^{-3}
35.31	264.2	0.2642	1000	1

Mass

Pounds	Tons (U.S.)	Grams	Kilograms	Tons (Metric) (T_m)
1	4.46×10^{-4}	453.6	0.4536	4.536×10^{-4}
2240	1	$1.016 \times 10^{+6}$	1016	1.016
2.205×10^{-3}	9.843×10^{-7}	1	1.000×10^{-3}	1.000×10^{-6}
2.205	9.843×10^{-4}	1000	1	1.000×10^{-3}
2205	0.9843	$1.000 \times 10^{+6}$	1000	1

Volumetric flow rate

ft^3/s	1000 gal./hr	gal./min	L/s	m^3/s
1	29.10	485.0	28.32	2.832×10^{-2}
3.447×10^{-2}	1	15.48	0.9737	9.737×10^{-4}
2.205×10^{-3}	6.460×10^{-2}	1	6.309×10^{-2}	6.309×10^{-5}
3.531×10^{-2}	1.027	15.85	1	1.000×10^{-3}
35.31	1027	1.585×10^{4}	1000	1

Density

lb/ft^3	g/cm^3	kg/m^3
1	1.602×10^{-2}	16.02
62.4	1	1000
6.240×10^{-2}	1.000×10^{-3}	1

Viscosity

lb/ft/hr	Centipoise	Pascal.second
1	0.4134	4.134×10^{-2}
2.419	1	1.000×10^{-3}
2419	1000	1

Thermal conductivity

$Btu/hr/ft^2/(°F/ft)$	$W/m^2/(°C/m)$
1	1.731
0.5778	1

Diffusivity

ft^2/hr	m^2/s
3.875×10^{4}	1
1	2.581×10^{-5}

Heat capacity

Btu/lb/°F	J/kg/°C
1	4.187
0.239	1

Heat transfer coefficient

$Btu/hr/ft^2/°F$	$W/m^2/°C$
1	5.68
0.1761	1

Mass transfer coefficient

lb-mole/hr/ft^2/mole fraction	kg-mole/s/m^2/mole fraction
1	1.356×10^{-3}
737.5	1

Force

lb$_f$	Newton
1	4.444
0.2250	1

Pressure

mm Hg	psi	Atmosphere	Bar	kPascal
1	1.934×10^{-2}	1.316×10^{-3}	1.333×10^{-3}	0.1333×10^{2}
51.71	1	6.805×10^{-2}	$.895 \times 10^{-2}$	6.895×10^{3}
760.0	14.70	1	1.013	101.3×10^{5}
750.1	14.50	0.9869	1	1000×10^{5}
75.01×10^{-3}	1.450×10^{-4}	9.870×10^{-6}	1.000×10^{-5}	1

Heat, energy, or work

BTU	kWhr	ftlb$_f$	Calorie	Joule
1	2.930×10^{-4}	778.2	252.0	1055
3413	1	$2.655 \times 10^{+6}$	$8.604 \times 10^{+5}$	$3.600 \times 10^{+6}$
1.285×10^{-3}	3.766×10^{-7}	1	0.3241	1.356
3.966×10^{-3}	1.162×10^{-6}	3.086	1	4.184
9.484×10^{-4}	2.772×10^{-7}	0.7376	0.2390	1

Power

Horsepower	Kilowatt	Ftlb$_f$/s	BTU/s	Watt/s
1	0.7457	550.0	0.7068	745.7
1.341	1	737.56	0.9478	1000
1.818×10^{-3}	1.356×10^{-3}	1	1.285×10^{-3}	1.356
1.415	1.055	778.16	1	1055
1.341×10^{-3}	1.00×10^{-3}	0.7376	9.478×10^{-4}	1

Volumetric Flux

gal./ft^2/hr	m^3/m^2/s	L/m^2/s
1	9.767×10^{-5}	9.767×10^{-2}
10,239	1	1000
10.24	1.000×10^{-3}	1

Energy flux

Btu/ft^2/hr	W/m^2
1	3.155
0.3170	1

Gas constant, R

8.314 kPa m^3/kg-mole K (J/gm-mole K)

Common unit abbreviations and prefixes

meter = m	Newton = N
Pascal = Pa	Watt = W
gram = g	liter = L
Joule = J	second = s

μ = micro 10^{-6} m = milli 10^{-3} k = kilo 10^{+3} M = mega 10^{+6}

APPENDIX B

BATF Regulations

1. Approved Wine Treatments and Additives

The U.S. winemaking regulations are established by the publication of a proposed rule which is followed by a comment period in which winemakers, members of wine companies, trade organizations, and the public can submit opinions. These are then considered by the ATF staff and a decision is made and published in the *Federal Register*. The major philosophies are that permitted treatments should be "good commercial winemaking" practices, juices or wines should not undergo major changes in composition, and healthfulness must not be compromised.

The most recent version of these is listed in *Federal Register*, Volume 55, Number 118, June 19, 1990, pages 25019 to 25021 with amendments listed in *Federal Register*, Volume 58, Number 193, October 7, 1993, pages 52222 to 52232. The list covers the materials and treatments that have been approved for winemaking and these are summarized in Table B-1 with related comments. It should be understood that these are individually and generally permitted, but no single wine would have more than a few additions or treatments. Several are alternatives to achieve the same result, many involve treatments that leave no residue and some are aimed at special but rare circumstances. A treatment or additive not specifically allowed by the regulations is prohibited until a Conditional Use Permit is granted or new regulations or interpretations are forthcoming.

Regulations in other countries are not the same. The U.S. practice has been to allow importation of wines as long as they are legally made in their home country and honestly labeled. The reverse frequently has not been the case. The Office International Vigne et Vin (OIV) is the international organization that attempts to set uniform regulations worldwide, but tends to view the European practices as sacrosanct.

Labeling is controlled by additional regulations governing what must be stated on the label, e.g., alcohol content, what may be stated, and the tolerances of concentrations.

Table B-1. Approved materials and the limits of their use in winemaking (BATF 1990, 1993).

Materials	Use	Reference or limitation
Acacia (gum arabic)	To clarify and stabilize wine	The amount used shall not exceed 2 lb/1000 gal. (0.24 g/L) of wine (GRAS)[1].
Activated carbon	To assist precipitation during fermentation, to clarify and to purify wine	The amount used to clarify and purify wine shall be included in the total amount of activated carbon used to remove excessive color in wine (GRAS).
	To remove color in wine and/or juice from which the wine as produced	The amount used to treat the wine, including the juice from which the wine was produced, shall not exceed 25 lb/1000 gal. (3.0 g/L). If the amount necessary exceeds this limit, a notice is required (GRAS).
Albumen (egg white)	Fining agent for wine	May be prepared in a light brine 1 oz (28.35 grams) potassium chloride, 2 lb (907.2 grams) egg white, 1 gal. (3.785 L) of water. Usage not to exceed 1.5 gal of solution/1,000 gal. of wine (GRAS).
Aluminosilicates (hydrated) e.g., bentonite (Wyoming clay) and kaolin	To clarify and to stabilize wine or juice	(GRAS)
Ammonium carbonate	Yeast nutrient to facilitate fermentation to wine	The natural fixed acids shall not be reduced beow 5 g/L. The amount used shall not exceed 2 lb/1000 gal. (0.24 g/L) (GRAS).
Ammonium phosphate (*mono-* and *dibasic*)	Yeast nutrient in wine production and to start secondary fermentation in the production of sparkling wines	The amount used shall not exceed 8 lb/1000 gal. (0.96 g/L) of wine (GRAS).
Ascorbic acid, *iso*-ascorbic acid (erythorbic acid)	To prevent oxidation of color and flavor components of juice and wine.	May be added to fruit, grapes, berries, and other primary winemaking materials, or to the juice of such materials, or to the wine, within limitations which do not alter the class or type of the wine (GRAS).
Calcium carbonate (with or without calcium salts or tartaric and malic acids)	To reduce the excess natural acids in high acid wine, and in juice prior to or during fermentation	The natural or fixed acids shall not be reduced below 6 g/L (GRAS).
	A fining agent for cold stabilization	The amount used shall not exceed 30 lb/1000 gal. (3.60 g/L) of wine.
Calcium sulfate (gypsum)	To lower pH in sherry wine	The sulfate content of the finished wine shall not exceed 2.0 g/L, expressed as potassium sulfate (GRAS).
Carbon dioxide (including food grade dry ice)	To stabilize[2] and to preserve wine	(GRAS)
Casein, potassium salt of casein	To clarify wine	GRAS)
Citric acid	To correct natural acid deficiencies in wine	(GRAS)
	To stabilize wine other than citrus wine	The amount of citric acid shall not exceed 5.8 lb/1000 gal. (0.7 g/l) (GRAS).

Table B-1. (Continued)

Materials	Use	Reference or limitation
Copper sulfate	To remove hydrogel sulfide and/or mercaptans from wine	The quantity of copper sulfate added (calculated as copper) shall not exceed 0.5 parts copper per million parts of wine (0.5 mg/L) with the residual level of copper not to be in excess of 0.5 parts per million (0.5 mg/L) (GRAS).
Defoaming agents: (polyoxyethylene 40 monostearate, silicon dioxide, dimethylpolysiloxane, sorbitan monostearate, glyceryl monooleate, and glyceryl dioleate).	To control foaming, fermentation adjunct	Defoaming agents which are 100% active may be used in amounts not exceeding 0.15 lb/1000 gal. (0.018 g/L) of wine, defoaming agents which are 30% active may be used in amounts not exceeding 0.5 lb/1000 gal. (0.05 g/L) of wine. Silicon dioxide shall be completely removed by filtration. The amount of silicon remaining in the wine shall not exceed 10 parts per million.
Dimethyl dicarbonate	To sterilize and to stabilize wine, dealcoholized wine, and low alcohol wine	DMDC may be added to wne, dealcoholized wine, and low-alcohol wine in a cumulative amount not to exceed 200 parts per million (200 mg/L).
Enzymatic activity		The enzyme preparation used shall be prepared from nontoxic and nonpathogenic microorganisms in accordance with good manufacturing practice and be approved for use in food by either FDA regulation of by FDA advisory opinion.
Carbohydrase (*alpha*-amylase)	To convert starchs to fermentable carbohydrates	The amylase enzyme activity shall be derived from *Aspergillus niger, Aspergillus oryzae, Bacillus subtilis*, or barley malt from *Rhizopus oryzae* from *Bacillus licheniformis*.
Carbohydrase (*beta*-amylase)	To convert starches to fermantable carbohydrates	The amylase enzyme activity shall be derived from barely malt.
Carbohydrase (glycoamylase, amyloglucosidase)	To convert starches to fermantable carbohydrates	The amylase enzyme activity shall be derived from *Aspergillus niger* or *Aspergillus oryzae* or from *Rhizopus oryzae* or from *Rhizopus niveus*.
Catalase	To clarify and to stabilize wine	The enzume activity used shall be derived from *Aspergillus niger* or bovine liver (GRAS).
Cellulase	To clarify and to stabilize wine and to facilitate separation of the juice from the fuit	To enzyme activity used shall be derived from *Aspergillus niger* (GRAS).
Glucose oxidase	To clarify and to stabilize wine	The enzyme activity used shall be derived from *Aspergillus niger* (GRAS).
Pectinase	To clarify and to stabilize wine and to facilitate separation of juice from the fruit	The enzyme activity used shall be derived from *Aspergillus niger* (GRAS)
Protease (general)	To reduce or to remove heat labile proteins	The enzyme activity used shall be derived from *Aspergillus niger* or *Bacillus subtilis* or from *Bacillus licheniformis* (GRAS).

Table B-1. (Continued)

Materials	Use	Reference or limitation
Protease (bromelin)	To reduce or to remove heat labile proteins	The enzyme activity used shall be derived from *Ananus comosus* or *Ananus bracteatus*(L) (GRAS).
Protease (ficin)	To reduce or to remove heat labile proteins	The enzyme activity used shall be derived from *Ficus spp*. (GRAS).
Protease (papain)	To reduce or to remove heat labile proteins	The enzyme activity used shall be derived from *Carica papaya* (L) (GRAS).
Protease (pepsin)	To reduce or to remove heat labile proteins	The enzyme activity used shall be derived from porcine or bovine stomachs (GRAS)
Protease (trypsin)	To reduce or to remove heat labile proteins	The enzyme activity used shall be derived from porcine or bovine pancreas (BRAS).
Ethyl maltol	To stabilize wine	Use authorized at a maximum level of 100 mg/L in all standard wines except natural wine produced from *Vitis vinifera* grapes.
Ferrocyanide compounds (sequestered complexes)	To remove trace metal from wine	No insoluble or soluble residue in excess of 1 part per million shall remain in the finished wine and the basic character of the wine shall not be changed by such treatment (GRAS)
Ferrous sultate	To clarify and to stabilize wine	The amount used shall not exceed 3 oz/1000 gal. (0.022 g/L) of wine (GRAS).
Fumaric acid	To correct natural acid deficiencies in grape wine, to stabilize wine	The fumaric acid content of the finished wine shall not exceed 2.4 g/L.
Gelatin (food grade)	To clarify juice or wine	(GRAS)
Granular cork	To smooth wine	The amount used shall not exceed 10 lb/1000 gal. of wine (1.2 g/L) (GRAS).
Hydrogen peroxide	To remove color from the juice of red and black grapes	The amount used shall not exceed 500 parts per million. The use of hydrogen peroxide is limited to oxidizing color pigment in the juice of red and black grapes (GRAS).
Ion exchange	To adjust acidity and/or pH	Treatment does not reduce the pH of the juice or wine to less than pH 2.8 nor increase the pH to more than pH 4.5.
Isinglass	To clarify wine	(GRAS)
Lactic acid	To correct natural acid deficiencies in grape wine	(GRAS)
Malic acid	To correct natural acid deficiencies in juice or wine	(GRAS)
Malolactic bacteria	To stabilize grape wine	Malolactic bacteria of the type *Leuconostoc oenos* may be used in treating wine (GRAS).
Maltol	To stabilize wine	Use authorized at a maximum level of 250 mg/L in all standard wine except natural wine produced from *Vitis vinifera* grapes (GRAS).

Table B-1. (Continued)

Materials	Use	Reference or limitation
Milk (pasteurized whole or skim)	Fining agent for white grape wine or sherry	The amount used shall not exceed 2.0 L of pasteurized milk per 1000 L of white grape wine or sherry (0.2% v/v).
Nitrogen gas	To maintain pressure during filtering and bottling or canning of wine and to prevent oxidation of wine	(GRAS)
Oak chips or particles, uncharred and untreated	To smooth wine	
Oxygen and compressed air	May be used in juice and wine	None.
Polyvinylpolypyrrolidone (PVPP)	To clarify and to stabilize wine and to remove color from red or black wine or juice	The amount used to treat the wine, including the juice from the wine was produced, shall not exceed 60 lb/1000 gal. (7.9 g/L) and shall be removed during filtration. PVPP may be used in a continuous or batch process. The finished wine shall retain vinous character and shall have color of not less than 0.6 Lovibond in a one-half inch cell.
Potassium bitartrate	To stabilize grape wine	The amount used shall not exceed 35 lb/1000 gal. (4.19 g/L) of grape wine (GRAS).
Potassium carbonate and/or potassiumbicarbonate	To reduce excess natural acidity in wine and in juice prior to or during fermentation	The natural or fixed acids shall not be reduced below 5 parts per thousand (5 g/L) (GRAS).
Potassium citrate	pH control agent and sequestrant in treatment of citrus wines	The amount of potassium citrate shall not exceed 25 lb/1000 gal. (3.0 g/L) of finished wine (GRAS).
Potassium metabisulfite	To sterilize and to preserve wine	The sulfur dioxide content of the finished wine shall not exceed the limitations (GRAS).
Silica gel (colloidal silicon dioxide)	To clarify wine	Use shall not exceed the equivalent of 20 lb colloidal silicon dioxide at a 30% concentration per 1000 gal. of wine (2.4 g/L). Silicon dioxide shall be completely removed by filtration (GRAS).
Sorbic acid and potassium salt of sorbic acid	To sterilize and to preserve wine; to inhibit mold growth and secondary fermentation	The finished wine shall contain not more than 300 milligrams of sorbic acid per liter of wine (GRAS).
Soy flour (defatted)	Yeast nutrient to facilitate fermentation of wine	The amount used shall not exceed 2 lb/1000 gal. (0.24 g/L) of wine (GRAS).
Sulfur dioxide	To sterilize and to preserve wine	The sulfur dioxide content of the finished wine shall not exceed the limitations (GRAS).

Table B-1. (Continued)

Materials	Use	Reference or limitation
Tannin	To adjust tannin content in apple juice or in apple wine	The residual amount of tannin shall not exceed 3.0 g/L calculated as gallic acid equivalents (GAE). Total tannin shall not be increased by more than 150 mh/L by the addition of tannic acid (polygalloylglucose).
	To clarify or to adjust tannin content of juice or wine (other than apple)	The residual amount of tanning, calculated in gallic acid equivalents, shall not exceed 0.8 g/L in white wine and 3.0 g/L in red wine. Only tannin which does not impact color may be used in the cellar treatment of juice or wine. Total tannin shall not be increased by more than 150 mg/L by the addition of tannic acid.
Tartaric acid	To correct natural acid deficiencies in grape juice/wine and to reduce the pH of grape juice-wine where ameliorating material is used in the production of grape wine	(GRAS)
Thermal gradient processing	To separate wine into low-alcohol and high-alcohol wine fractions	The fractions derived from such processing shall retain vinous character. Such treatment shall not increase the lacohol content of the high-alcohol fraction to more than 24% by volume. The addition of water other than that originally present in the wine prior to processing will render standard wine "other than standard."
	To separate juice into low Brix and high Brix juice fractions	The low Brix fraction derived from such processing may be used in wine production. The high Brix fraction derived from such processing shall not be diluted with water for use in wine production.
Thiamine hydrochloride	Yeast nutrient to facilitate fermentation wine	The amount used shall not exceed 0.005 lb/1000 gal. (0.6 mg/L) of wine or juice (GRAS).
Yeast, autolyzed	Yeast nutrient to facilitate fermentation in the production of grape or fruit wine	GRAS)
Yeast, cell wall/membranes of autoluzed yeast	To facilitate fermentation of juice/wine	The amount used shall not exceed 3 lb/1000 gal. (0.36 g/L) of the wine or juice (GRAS).

[1]GRAS—an acronym for "generally recognized as safe." The term means that the treating material has an FDA listing in title 21, Code of Federal Regulations, part 182 or part 184, or is considered to be generally recognized as safe by advisory opinion issued by the U.S. Food and Drug Administration.
[2]To stabilize—to prevent or to retard unwanted alteration of chemical and/or physical properties.

APPENDIX C

STAINLESS STEELS AND THEIR CLEANING

Stainless steels are widely used in the wine and food industries due to their freedom from staining and discoloration, their inertness to oxidation and corrosion, and the ease with which their surfaces can be cleaned. The inertness of stainless steels is due to the presence of at least 18% chromium in the alloy and a thin oxide film that adheres to the surface. Nickel (and in some cases also molybdenum) is generally added to further enhance the corrosion resistance. The presence of up to 8% carbon and the 18% chromium has led to the term 18-8 steels. These are also described as *austenitic* and they are nonmagnetic.

1. Types of Stainless Steels

The two main types of stainless steels that are used in wine and juice applications are 304 and 316. The 304 steels can contain between 16 and 25% chromium and 7 and 12% nickel and are highly ductile. This form is widely used in wineries throughout the United States although they are susceptible to pitting by dilute sulfur dioxide solutions and attack by concentrated sulfuric and hydrochloric acids. The 316 steels have chromium contents in the 16 to 18% range, nickel between 10 and 14%, and molybdenum added at the 2 to 3% level and are more resistant to sulfur dioxide and inorganic anions such as sulfuric, phosphoric, and hydrochloric acids. Both series are vulnerable to chloride ions, but 316 is less so. In other countries other designations are often used for these steel types (Table C-1).

2. Passivation of Stainless Steel

The protective oxide film can be destroyed by improper cleaning and maintenance procedures and the metal which is exposed is then susceptible to oxidation and corrosion. The use of chlorine solutions with concentrations above 200 mg/L and scraping of the surface by steel wool, tools, or other metal objects and welding without adequate cleaning and passivation are common reasons for corrosion of stainless surfaces.

Passivation of the stainless steel is a process in which the surface is cleaned and the oxide

Table C-1. Cross reference of stainless steel types (Troost 1980).

England	EN	58 E	~ 58 H	58 B, 58 C
France	Afnor	Z 6 CN 18—10	Z 3 CND	Z 10 CNT
Germany	DIN	X 5 CrNi	X 5 CrNiMo	X 10 CrNiTi
	17006 (7)	18/9	18/10	18/9
		1.4301	1.4401	1.4541
Italy	UNI	X 6 CN	X 8 CND	X 8 CNT
		1911	1712	1808
				X 8 CNT
				1810
Sweden	SIS	2333	—	2237
United States	AISI	304	316	321

film is encouraged to develop. If corrosion exists, passivation is one approach to preventing further deterioration. While the oxide film will form naturally on clean exposed surfaces, the formation is aided by the use of strong acid mixtures and oxidizing agents. The washing of the surface with such a solution also dissolves any free iron present on the surface of the stainless steel and passivation can be used to remove rust spots from these surfaces.

The 300 series of stainless steels can be passivated by using a 50% by volume solution made from concentrated nitric acid and water. A solution temperature of 55°C is recommended for fastest results, although ambient temperature is acceptable for larger applications. The person performing the treatment should be wearing protective clothing, and for internal surface treatments or applications in confined spaces, the vessel or area should be well ventilated. The solution should be applied to the entire surface and this should be covered repeatedly. The surface being treated should be kept wet for approximately one hour before rinsing. The rinsing solution should be clean warm water and thorough rinsing is required to remove all traces of the acid. The surface should be wiped dry with a clean cloth and this should show no signs of discoloration when the treatment has been successful. The vessel is then ready for use. For applications using a solution-recirculating or CIP (clean-in-place) system, all fittings that are made of materials that would be attacked by the acid solution should be removed in order to prevent attack and possible plating of the stainless surface, notably with copper.

3. Types of Corrosion

There are several different kinds of corrosion. The two most important for winemaking applications are pitting and stress-corrosion cracking. The understanding of these in regard to the operating conditions will help to prevent future problems and assist in the specification of equipment materials.

Pitting can occur in steels that are apparently immune to certain solutions. It usually occurs as small deep pits that are confined to localized spots rather than across the general surface. The site can be a scratch, indent, or surface deposit that can lead to the breaking of the oxide film. Once the pit is formed the corrosion becomes accelerated due to local electrolytic action. In wine tanks that are made of 304 stainless steel, this can easily occur in headspace above a wine when the tank is partially full. The condensation of water droplets on the walls of the tank dissolves sulfur dioxide from the headspace and a local low-pH corrosion site develops. The corrosion is not always obvious at first and once started it can continue even after the tank is emptied. This is less of a concern with 316 steels, but it is a good practice to avoid partially filled tanks wherever possible.

Stress-corrosion cracking occurs when there is a combination of corrosion and applied stress in the metal. One particularly troublesome agent for the austenitic steels is the long-term exposure to chloride ions. Under winemaking conditions this can occur from dried deposits from the use of rinse waters that are high in chloride or inadequate rinsing following the use of hypochlorite solutions. It can also occur in equipment which is under periodic stress, such as pump impellers and housings, and equipment that is periodically heated and cooled during use, such as heat exchangers that use steam as a heating medium.

TROOST, G. 1980. *Technologie des Weines*, 2nd ed. p. 769. Stuttgart, Germany, Eugen Ulmer.

APPENDIX D

WATER UTILIZATION

1. Water Usage

Water is used in wineries for several purposes, but the greatest demand is for washing and sanitizing tanks, fermentors, barrels, and other process equipment during the harvest. The volumes used during the six- to eight-week harvest period are often between one-fifth and one-half those used during the entire year. Typical water usage figures for a number of wineries in California are presented in Figures D-1 and D-2 and the values are expressed on a specific basis. The volume used depends on the size of the winery (and, indirectly, that of its fermentors), the extent of barrel usage for fermentation and aging, the ease of cleaning of the winery equipment and floors, and the approach that is adopted toward rinsing.

Water requirements for the cleaning of tanks will usually be proportional to tank surface area. The surface area of a cylindrical tank is proportional to the tank volume raised to the power 2/3 or 0.667 and the water required per volume of wine would then be proportional to tank volume raised to the power -1/3 or -0.33. With barrels, the same relationship would be expected for the cleaning of the inner surface area but the volume used may be closer to the volume of the barrel, especially so for soaking and rinsing treatments. The other components will be related to the rinsing of pipe lines, floor areas, and process equipment and these will not generally follow any particular geometric scaling law.

The observed values (Figures D-1 and D-2) are well correlated by the following relationships:

Harvest:

$$\text{Water consumption } (\text{L}/\text{T}_\text{m} \text{ crushed}) = 10{,}168\, [\text{T}_\text{m}]^{-0.292}$$

Annual:

$$\text{Water consumption } (\text{L}/\text{T}_\text{m} \text{ crushed}) = 50{,}920\, [\text{T}_\text{m}]^{-0.326}$$

where the exponents -0.292 (harvest) and -0.326 (annual) are like those expected from the surface area function but with significant water usage for other purposes, especially during the harvest.

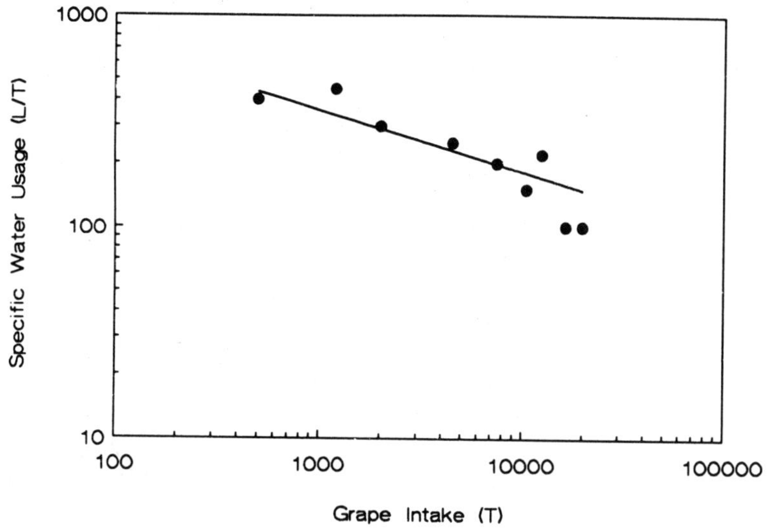

Fig. D-1. The seasonal water usage of California wineries.

2. Wastewater Characteristics

The importance of the water consumption is that it generally becomes the wastewater volume that needs to be treated and discharged. The seasonal nature of the water usage in wineries will require special design considerations, and the batch and cyclical use associated with equipment rinsing during the days of harvest will also need special flow dampening components in order that efficient performance be obtained by any treatment system.

The components of winery wastewater that are important to a biological treatment system are the biological oxygen demand or BOD, the pH, the suspended solids content, and the presence or absence of microbial inhibitors and nutrients for the microorganisms. The level of the suspended solids will usually deter-

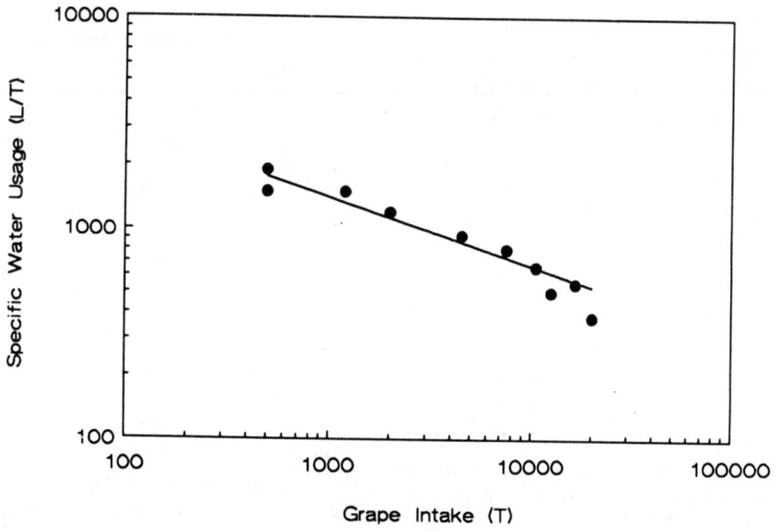

Fig. D-2. The annual water usage of California wineries.

mine the frequency of sludge removal, and the pH will determine the spectrum of organisms that can grow successfully in the pond or digester. The biological oxygen demand is a measure of the microbially degradable solutes present in the water and will be related to the rate at which oxygen must be transported into the water for effective microbial growth and metabolism in aerobic systems.

In winery wastewater, the major BOD components will be the sugars, glucose and fructose from juices and from wine it will be ethanol, glycerol, and tartaric and malic acids. There will be a significant chemical oxygen demand (COD) from wines due to the phenols and sulfite. All of these will be diluted out with general rinse water and some pickup will occur from grape solids and yeasts that are washed away. There may be a major BOD contribution due to citrate that has been used in acidic rinse waters. The contribution from sugars will disappear after the fermenting season and the water characteristics will approach those associated with wine residues from rinsing and the sanitizers, detergents, and softeners associated with equipment cleaning.

The rinse water can also contain significant chemical sanitizers such as hypochlorite. These will be especially destructive to the microflora of a treatment pond, especially at a pH of 6.0 to 8.0. Sulfur dioxide solutions that are dumped have the potential to be particularly damaging, but if the pH is raised to 7.0, the antimicrobial activity will be lost and the sulfite becomes a component of the chemical oxygen demand.

The organic acid content of juices and wines and the presence of citrate will cause significant swings in the buffer capacities in winery rinse water streams and this will require a more sophisticated pH adjustment system than those commonly used in other applications.

While many winemakers are aware of the importance of trace nutrition for microorganisms on successful growth rates and byproduct formation, the same is not generally true when the activity of wastewater treatment culture is concerned. The corresponding practice of inoculating wastewater with active cultures and providing sufficient vitamin, nitrogen, and phosphorus is still in its infancy with a general tendency to use standard supplements of ammonia and phosphorus, based on the nutritional requirements of other wastes.

There are only a few published reports of the compositional characteristics of winery wastewater. Ranges for the major design characteristics are given in Table D-1, based on the reports by Rice (1978) and Crites (1987).

The usable nitrogen and phosphorus contents are especially low and the pH is close to neutral when large volumes of water are used. The data of Rice (1978) indicate a water consumption of almost four volumes of water per volume of wine and come from a time when water usage was less of a concern. The values reported by Rice also show variations of almost twofold, both above and below the means in BOD and COD during the season. The seasonal pH variation ranged from 3.7 to 11.7 and the suspended solids content ranged from 40 to 2250 mg/L. The specific BOD load for this winery was 9.2 kg/T_m of grapes.

The current limit for BOD in one coastal region of California is 50 mg/L with a oneday maximum of 90 mg/L. Other limits are shown in Table D-2.

Table D-1. Reported waste water characteristics for wineries.

Characteristic[1]	Harvest period	Nonharvest	General
BOD (mg/L)	2550	2840	950
COD (mg/L)	3530	4050	n/a
SS (mg/L)	250	400	286
NH_3 (mg N/L)	4.3	4.2	10
TN (mg N/L)	19.3	27.2	33
TP (mg P/L)	4.2	5.9	n/a
pH	7.5	7.0	6.5

[1]BOD is the biological oxygen demand.
COD is the chemical oxygen demand.
SS is the suspended solids content.
NH_3 is the nitrogen concentration in the form of ammonia.
TN is the total nitrogen concentration.
TP is the total phosphorus concentration.

Table D-2. Typical discharge limits for one water control region in California.

Characteristic	Daily maximum	30-day average
BOD (five day, mg/L)	80	50
Suspended solids (mg/L)	80	50
Settleable solids (mL/L)	0.2	0.1
pH	6.5 to 8.5	6.5 to 8.5

BOD is the biological oxygen demand.

3. Efficient Use Strategies

The more efficient use of winery water will require a closer examination of the purpose for each use. There are some situations in which the development of separate rinsing, sanitizing, and acidifying streams could be used several times before discharge provided that the stream is filtered to remove suspended matter. The ability to incorporate separate streams with recycling depends on the ease with which any cleaning stream can be captured and recovered. The development of separate tanks for such streams together with appropriate filtration and/or sterilization components has the potential to reduce water usage to a fraction of present levels. The containment of such streams would also permit more specific treatment of them prior to discharge so as to minimize disturbances to the treatment system.

CRITES, R. W. 1987. "Winery wastewater land applications." *Proc. Am. Soc. Civil Eng. Irrigation and Drainage Division*, Special Conf., Portland, Oregon, July 28–30.

RICE, A. 1978. "Long-term activated sludge treatment of winery waste waters." *Am. J. Enol. Vitic.* 29:177–180.

APPENDIX E

Safety Limits of Some Wine-Related Compounds

There are a number of federal and state codes that apply to conditions of worker exposure and working environments, fire protection, buildings, and the transport of flammable and hazardous materials by road and air.

1. Exposure Limits

The exposure limits that are generally used are the time-weighted average (TWA) values for a normal eight-hour workday (or 40-hour work week), to which nearly all workers can be exposed, day after day, without adverse effects. Excursions above the limit are allowed if compensated by for excursions below the limit (Crowl and Louvar 1990). The rotation of personnel and the seasonal and periodic nature of many winery operations can sometimes provide variances to these requirements.

2. Flammability Limits of Vapors

The flammability limits of a vapor are the limits of the range of vapor compositions for which it is flammable. There is no combustion of the vapor below the lower flammability limit (LFL) or above the upper flammability limit (UFL). Alternative terms for these limits that are used by some agencies are the lower and upper explosive limits (LEL and UEL, respectively).

Table E-1. Time weighted average exposure limits

Compound	Threshold limit values (ppm vapor)	Threshold limit values (mg/m^3 25°C)
Acetaldehyde	10	180
Acetic acid	10	25
Ammonia	25	18
Carbon dioxide	5000	9000
Ethyl acetate	400	1400
Ethyl alcohol	1000	1900
Ethyl mercaptan	0.5	1
Gasoline	300	900
Hydrogen sulfide	10	14
Isoamyl acetate	100	525
Isoamyl alcohol	100	360
Methyl mercaptan	0.5	1
Sulfur dioxide	2	5

Table E-2. Flammability limits, density and sensory threshold of selected vapors

Compound	Flammability limits* (% v/v) Lower	Upper	Relative vapor density (air = 1.0)	Sensory Threshold (ppm vapor)
Ammonia	15.5	27.0	0.59	100
Sulfur Dioxide	nonflammable		2.2	10
Ethanol	3.28	18.95	1.59	n/a
Benzene	1.3	7.9	2.70	n/a
Toluene	1.2	7.1	3.19	n/a

* In air (Crowl and Louvar 1990).

Table E-3. Flash points of ethanol solutions and selected solvents.

Liquid wine (% vol/vol EtOH)	Flash point °C (F) Literature[a]	Predicted[b]
(10%)	45.6 (114.0)	49.0 (120.2)
(12%)	43.8 (110.8)	46.1 (115.0)
(14%)	41.8 (107.2)	43.7 (110.7)
(20%)	36.0 (96.8)	38.1 (100.6)
(40%)	n/a	26.6 (79.9)
Ethanol	12.8 (55.0)[c]	
Benzene	-11.1 (12.0)[c]	
Toluene	5.0 (40.0)[c]	

[a]Interpolated from data of Wine Institute 1979.
[b]Boulton (1991).
[c]Crowl and Louvar (1990).

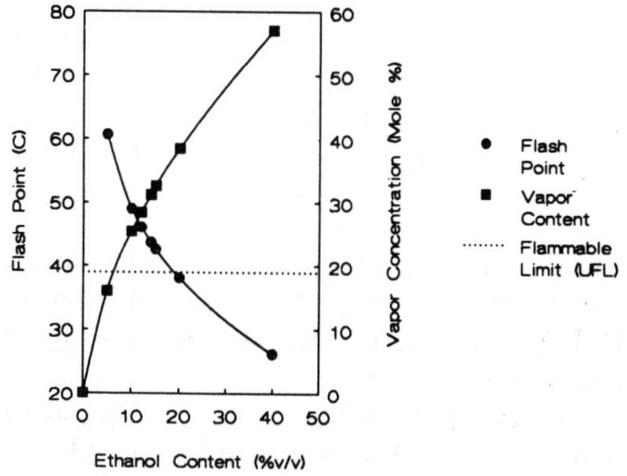

Fig. E-1. The flash point and vapor concentration of ethanol solutions.

3. Flash Points of Liquids

The flash point, often abbreviated simply as FP, is the lowest temperature at which a liquid gives off an ignitable mixture in air. At the flash point, the vapor will burn, but only briefly since insufficient vapor is produced to maintain combustion. A somewhat arbitrary choice of 100°F (37.8°C) has been chosen by a number of agencies as the reference temperature for determining the flammability classifications for many liquids. Based on this criterion, table wines are not flammable in that their flash points are above 37.8°C, while fortified wines and spirits are. A more complete relationship for the flash point as a function of ethanol content is shown in Figure E-1.

BOULTON, R. B. 1991. Unpublished calculations.

CROWL, D. A., AND J. F. LOUVAR 1990. *Chemical Process Safety: Fundamentals with Applications*. Englewood Cliffs, NJ: Prentice Hall.

APPENDIX F

MEDIA

Unless otherwise indicated, pH adjustments are made either with solutions of KOH or H_3PO_4. See main text for specific applications and literature references.

Acetate agar: 9.8% potassium acetate, 2.5% yeast extract, 1.0% glucose, adjust to pH 8.4 with NaOH, 15% agar.

Acid Plates (for some acetic acid bacteria): 0.5% yeast extract, 2% glucose, 0.5% KH_2P0_4, 2% agar. Acidify autoclaved, cooled molten medium with 0.1 mL concentrated HC1 per 100 mL (to give a final pH of about 4).

AR (apple Rogosa broth): 2% tryptone, 0.5% yeast extract, 0.5% peptone, 0.5% glucose, 0.005% Tween 80 (added as a 5% solution) made up in 20% apple juice, adjust to pH 5.5.

ARA agar (apple Rogosa with Acti-dione): AR broth with 1 mg/100 mL Acti-dione®[1] (cycloheximide), 2% agar.

Arginine broth: AR containing 2% glucose (rather than 0.5%) plus 0.6% L-arginine.

Bacillus sporulation broth: 8% nutrient broth (Difco Laboratories 0003-01), 5 mg% $MnSO_4 . H_2O$.

$CaCO_3$-Ethanol Agar: 0.5% yeast extract, 2% agar, and 2% Precipitated $CaCO_3$ (3% ethanol added to autoclaved, cooled molten medium[2]).

$CaCO_3$-wort agar: To W agar add 2% Precipitated $CaCO_3$.

$CaCO_3$—YM agar: To YM agar add 2% Precipitated $CaCO_3$.

Cornmeal agar: 1.7% cornmeal agar (Difco Laboratories 0386-02).

Frateur agar: 1% yeast extract (adjust to pH 6–7), 2% agar, and 2% Precipitated $CaCO_3$ (20 mL of 95% ethanol added to autoclaved, molten agar$_2$).

Fructose broth: AR broth with 2% fructose.

Glycerol broth: 2% glycerol and 0.5% yeast extract.

Gorodkowa agar: 0.1% glucose, 1.0% peptone, 0.5% NaCL, 2% agar.

---

[1]Acti-dione® (cycloheximide) Sigma Chemical Company (C-6255). Amounts added are twice those given above, since approximately one-half of its activity is lost during autoclaving.

[2]Solid media with $CaCO_3$ need to be vigorously swirled in the cooled molten state immediately before being poured in order to resuspend the precipitate.

GYC agar: 5% glucose, 1% yeast extract (adjust to pH 4.5), 3% Precipitated $CaCO_3$, and 3.0% $agar_2$.

HOAC agar: 10% glucose, 1% tryptone, 2% yeast extract, 2% agar (add 1% glacial acetic acid to autoclaved, cooled molten medium).

Mannitol agar: 5% yeast extract, 2.5% mannitol, 3% peptone, 2.5% agar.

Methylene Blue Reagent: 0.4% methylene blue, 10% ethanol (95%), 0.4 M KH_2PO_4.

V-8 agar: 350 mL V-8 juice, 5 g Baker's yeast cake, 350 mL H_2O, 14 g agar.

Wagar (wort): 10% wort (e.g., Fleischmann's Diamalt, often clarified by being heated to boiling and roughly filtered), 0.3% yeast extract, 0.5% peptone, 2% agar.

W^+ agar (wort with Acti-dione): W Agar plus 1 mg/100 mL Acti-dione® (cycloheximide)[1].

WLD (W L differential agar): Difco Laboratories (0425-17) and BBL (11816); same as WLN with Acti-dione[1] (2 mg/L).

WLN (W L nutrient agar): Difco Laboratories (0424-01) and BBL (11818); already contains agar and a pH indicator.

YM agar: 0.3% yeast extract, 0.3% malt extract, 0.5% peptone, 1.0% glucose, 2% agar.

YM^+ agar: YM Agar plus 1 mg/100 mL Acti-dione (cycloheximide)[1].

APPENDIX G

CATALASE TEST

AEROBIC VS ANAEROBIC BACTERIA

The catalase test is used to determine whether the bacteria in question are in the broad sense "aerobes" or "anaerobes:" aerobes are catalase-positive, and anaerobes are catalase-negative. For wine-related bacteria, the catalase-positive organisms are bacilli and acetic acid bacteria (Chapter 9). These are considered to be *obligate* aerobes requiring the presence of molecular oxygen for abundant growth. However, limited growth may also occur under conditions of low oxygen concentration, perhaps depending upon the redox potential. For example, *bacillus* spoilage has been found in bottled wines (Chapter 9). The wine-related catalase-negative bacteria include only lactic acid bacteria (Chapter 6). They are facultative anaerobes, not inhibited by atmospheric molecular oxygen, and generally growing as well as surface colonies as in submerged cultures. The lactic acid bacteria are microaerophic (Chapter 6) and growth in "stab cultures" often is stronger in the stab a few mm below the surface—although a small mass of growth in characteristically also seen at the surface.

SIGNIFICANCE

Molecular oxygen is toxic to all bacteria, if the concentration is high enough, because of formation from it of hydrogen peroxide (H_2O_2), which is toxic, and of small quantities of the free radical, superoxide (O_2^-), which is even more toxic. The obligate aerobic bacteria utilize O_2, but are protected from its toxicity by containing the enzyme *superoxide dismutase*. The latter prevents accumulation of superoxide by catalyzing the reaction of it with protons to produce O_2 and H_2O_2:

$$2O_2^- + 2H^+ \xrightarrow[\text{superoxide dismutase}]{} O_2 + H_2O_2$$

All aerobic organisms contain this enzyme. Most of the aerobic bacteria also produce *catalase*, which decomposes H_2O_2 to O_2 and water:

$$2H_2O_2 \xrightarrow[\text{catalase}]{} 2H_2O + O_2$$

The lactic acid bacteria contain *superoxide dismutase,* but are catalase-negative. They protect themselves from the toxic effects of H_2O_2 coming from O_2 by the use of their *peroxidase* enzymes. These enzymes reduce H_2O_2 to water, in the course of oxidation of organic compounds.

The obligate anaerobes, clostridia, for example (not found in wine), do not have superoxide dismutase.

PROCEDURE

Apply a loop of pure and freshly grown bacterial culture to a drop of 3% H_2O_2 (a fresh ten-fold dilution of a commercial 30% solution) onto a microscope slide. Within a few seconds organisms which are catalase-positive will show bubbling or foaming. Yeast can be used as a positive control. The use of a hand-lens may be of assistance in the evaluation in some cases, or the use of either a very dark or a very light surface as background. The H_2O_2 can be added directly to a colony on solid nutrient medium, but of course all bacteria coming in contact with the H_2O_2 will be killed. It should be noted that a hot loop in H_2O_2 will also give some bubbling. For catalase-negative organisms, not only will there be no bubble formation, but the form of the mass of bacterial material will remain entire, more-or-less intact, and not become visibly frayed—as happens, along with the foaming, with catalase-positive organisms.

EXCEPTIONS

Some strains of *Acetobacter pasteurianus* are catalase-negative. Confirmation of these catalase-negative bacteria as (aerobic) acetic acid bacteria can be obtained by growth on, and clearing of, various calcium carbonate media (Chapter 9). Lactic acid bacteria are sometimes found to be catalase-negative when cultivated on nutritionally deficient media. The procedures for identification of lactic acid bacteria given in Chapter 6 obviate this possibility.

APPENDIX H

MICROSCOPIC CELL COUNTING

A very useful skill for the winemaker is proficiency with the microscope for quick determination of the presence or population of yeast or bacteria in liquid suspensions. This technique is especially helpful in preparation of yeast starter cultures for sparkling wine fermentation and of bacteria starter cultures for malolactic fermentation. In these cases, unlike the preparation of yeast starter cultures for regular vinification fermentations, there are few macroscopic clues—such as obvious turbidity and foaming—to indicate the maturity of the culture. Microscopic cell counting is also useful as a preliminary step for making colony counts—where the sample is spread on a nutrient agar plant and incubated (Chapter 9); the microscopic examination indicates the number of aseptic, serial dilutions required to give the proper number of cells per plate. Furthermore, cell counting skill is also useful in the evaluation of incipient microbiological spoilage of stored wines. Cell counts obtained over various times showing static or decreasing cell concentrations probably indicate a harmless situation. However, the opposite condition, of increasing cell counts with time, indicates that special attention and further treatment should be applied promptly to the stored wine. The microscopic cell counting technique has its limitations, especially in the spoilage situations just mentioned, in that low concentrations ($< 10^4$ cell/mL) cannot be evaluated with precision. In these instances, the winemaker must rely on viable counts, either as spread plates (Chapter 9), or as used in the quality control procedure for sterile bottling (Chapter 11). These methods require several days' incubation before results are obtained.

Two kinds of counting chambers are used for the microscopic procedure. Both of the chambers have the same cell counting grid of a "large" square, measuring 1.0 mm per side, divided into 25 "medium" squares, and each of the latter further subdivided into 16 "tiny" squares (Figure H-1). The grids have raised borders, on which a cover glass is placed, and which sets the height of the chamber, that is, the volume of liquid defined by the grid. The main difference between the two chambers is that the height for Levy-Hausser is 0.1 mm, while that for the Petroff-Hausser is 0.02 mm.

Thus, the decision on which chamber to use is partly determined by the concentration of the cells: the Levy chamber generally used for lower suspensions, and the Petroff for higher suspensions. Nominally, this limits the Levy chamber to the counting of yeast and the Petroff chamber to the counting of bacteria. The factor used for calculation of cell concentration of the suspension being measured is 10^4 times the number of cells found in the "large" square for the Levy-Hausser, and $2x10^7$ times the number of cells found in a "tiny" square of the Petroff-Hausser. Generally the "hi-dry" microscopic objective lens (40x) is used with the Levy-Hausser, and the oil-immersion objective (100x) for the Petroff. Another feature of the Petroff-Hausser is that the chamber itself is thin enough to allow for microscopic viewing with oil-immersion and phase-contrast optics. This is an important feature for the counting of lactic acid bacteria. Some Levy-Hausser chambers are also manufactured for use with phase-contrast optics.

Concerning the coverslips used for the chambers, at the dimensions employed the surface tension of the water, or wine, is not inconsequential. There will be a natural bowing of a thin slip, which decreases the volume of the fluid in the chamber. To overcome this, special thick coverslips can be used for the Levy-Hausser, although attention must be paid to the objective lens being used to assure that its depth of focus is great enough to penetrate below the lower surface of this thicker cover slip. For the Petroff-Hausser, regular, thin coverslips are available, onto which are mounted rigid plastic frames, strong enough to overcome the surface tension. (In supply catalogs,

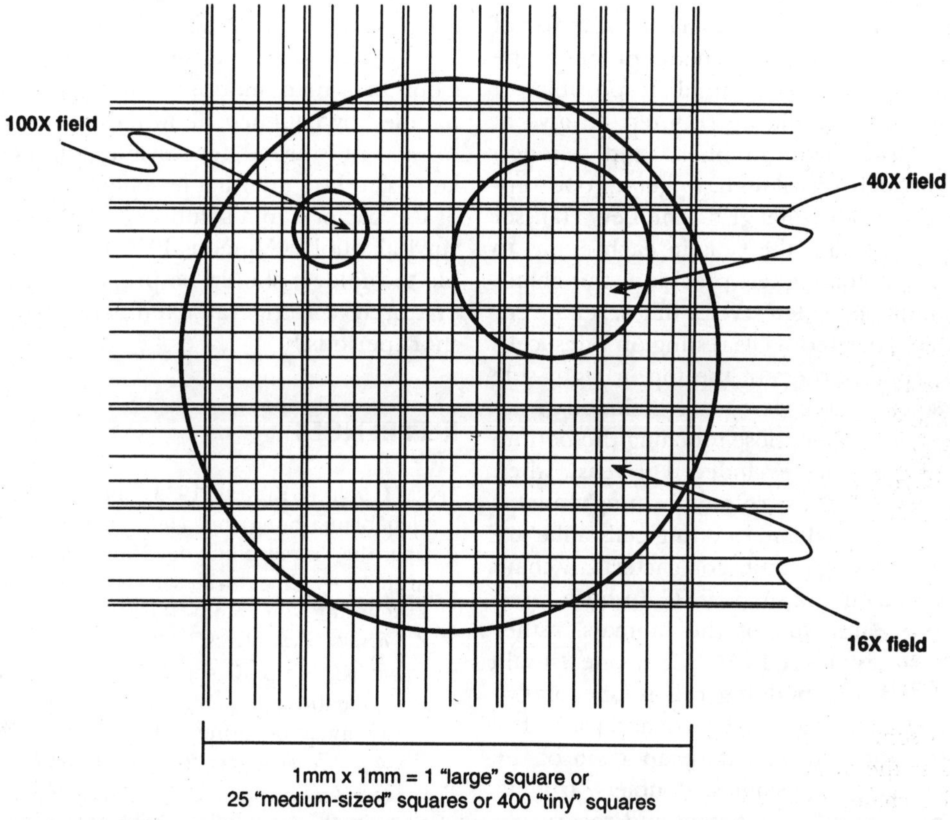

Fig. H-1. Grid dimensions of Hausser counting chambers.

the special coverslips and the chambers are often listed under "hemocytometer," which is the main use of the Levy-Hausser chambers.)

In operation, the coverslip is placed over the grid and a drop of the cell suspension (thoroughly mixed) is added by means of a pasteur pipette to one edge of the coverslip. Capillary action will pull the liquid into and fill the chamber. If the coverslip is bumped or otherwise disturbed such that too much liquid enters the chamber, it is advised to start over. The weight of the coverslip is insufficient to displace excess liquid from the grid. It is helpful as a preliminary step to use the low-power objective to locate the grid of a dry, unloaded chamber and to note the microscope stage setting in order to return the chamber to the same position after the sample is loaded. The "medium" squares are double-lined (sometimes triple-lined), which aids in their location (Figure H-1).

The number of squares, and the number of cells to be counted is dependent upon the concentration of the sample. If possible, at least 100 cells should be counted, to give at least a three-digit number, and enough squares, widely distributed, to get a good representation of the total grid. The Levy-Hausser has two grids, and the cells in each ought to be counted. For highest precision, the chambers should be loaded several times. A convention is employed for cells resting on lines: cells touching the borders of the top or right side of the square being viewed are included in the enumeration, while those touching the bottom or left borders are excluded. For yeast, when the number of cfu's (colony forming units) is desired, individual and budding cells alike are counted as a single unit. For bacteria, a chain of cells is taken as a single CFU. In both cases, where an estimation of the biomass, rather than CFUs, is desired, for yeast, one should assess whether a budding cell is one or two units, or something in between; and for bacteria, assess the approximate proportion of the bacterial chains as singles, doublets, triplets, etc. One should be consistent and record observations and assumptions carefully.

For yeast a rough indication of the viability of the culture can also be obtained microscopically. For this, a mixture is made of approximately 1:1 of the culture and a solution of methylene blue stain (Appendix F) (Fink and Kühles 1933; Townsend and Lindgren 1953; Painting and Kirsop 1990). The mixing can be done directly on a microscope slide. The viable cells will take up the stain and reduce it to its colorless form, giving an unstained cell, whereas the dead cells will take up the stain without reduction, giving a blue cell. The terminology here is somewhat uncertain. Viability in this case is dependent of a cell's capacity to ferment, to carry out some portion of glycolysis. The term may not exactly coincide with capability of a cell to reproduce and form a colony when placed on nutrient medium. Also, this test must be done on fresh cells, not on samples that have been stored.

Difficulties in obtaining precise cell counts often come from streaming of the cells across the field of view, and, especially for bacteria, from Brownian motion. The former is best handled by patience, allowing the microscope to sit undisturbed for several minutes. The latter can be somewhat lessened by suspension of the bacteria in a solution of 4% PVA (polyvinyl alcohol). (Aqueous PVA is very susceptible to mold. It should be prepared as needed or stored at refrigerator temperature for only short periods.)

REFERENCES

FINK, H., AND R. KÜHLES. 1933. "Beiträge zur Methyleneblaufärbung der Hefezellen und Studien über die Permeabilität der Hefezellmembran. II. Mitteilung. Eine verbessert Färbeflüssigkeit zur Erkennung von toten Hefezellen." *Hoppe-Seyler Z. Physiol. Chem.* 218:65–66.

PAINTING, K., AND B. KIRSOP. 1990. "A quick method for estimating the percentage of viable cells in a yeast population, using methylene blue staining." *World J. Microbiol. Biotechnol.* 6:346–247.

TOWNSEND, G. F., AND C. C. LINDGREN. 1953. "Structures in the yeast cell revealed in wet mounts." *Cytologia* 18:183.201.

APPENDIX I

ADDRESSES OF MANUFACTURERS OF WINERY EQUIPMENT[1]

Abcor (*see* Koch Membranes Systems)

Alfa-Laval, P.O. Box 500, S-147 00 Tumba, Sweden

Amos Maschinenfabrik GmbH, Postfach 1160, D-74081 Heilbronn, Germany

APV-Crepaco, 395 Fillmore Avenue, Tonawonda, NY 14150, USA

Bird Machine Co., Rucaduc Road, South Walpole, MA 02071, USA

Blachere & Cie.,[2] 4 rue Levat, 34 Montpellier, France

Bucher (*see* Bucher-CMMC)

Bucher-CMMC, F-49290 Chalonnes sur Loire, France

Ceraflo (*see* Norton Co.)

Cherry-Burrel, P.O. Box 35600, Louisville, KY 40232, USA

Contherm (*see* Tetra Laval Food)

Coq[2] (*see* Bucher-CMMC)

Cellulo Co., 124 M Street, Fresno, CA 93721, USA

Celite Corp., P.O. Box 519, Lompoc, CA 93438-0519, USA

Cuno Inc., 400 Research Parkway, Meriden, CT 06450, USA

DDS (De Danske Sukkerfabrikker), P.O. Box 149, DK-4900 Nakskov, Denmark

Demoisy, B.P. 135, F-21204 Beaune, France

Diemme Costruzioni Enolmeccaniche SPA, Lugo, Italy

Dorr-Oliver Inc., 77 Havemeyer Lane, Stamford, CT 06904, USA

E. I. Du Pont Nemours & Co., 1007 Market Street, Wilmington, DE 19898, USA

Durco (Duriron Co.), 9542 Hardpan Road, Angola, NY 14006, USA

Eagle Picher Industries, 580 Walnut Street, Cincinnati, OH 45202, USA

Egretier, D.F 301, Narbonne, France

Enopompe snc, Via 25 Aprile, 42015 Correggio-RE, Italy

Fristam Pumps Inc., P.O. Box 620065, Middle-

---

[1] This list is limited to the principal offices of manufacturers of widely distributed products for winemaking that have been mentioned in this book. It does not include manufacturers of bottling and packaging equipment due to the limited coverage of these topics. This is not a complete list and does not attempt to provide names of local agents or representatives. In the United States there are compilations of such in the annual directories of several industry magazines such as Practical Winery, Vineyard & Winery Management and Wines & Vines. There is no attempt to endorse or otherwise indicate preference for these products.

[2] Of historical interest, limited involvement at present or no longer in business.

ton, WI 53562-0065, USA

Gasquet Soc., 80 rue Reully, F-7500 Paris, France

Graham Manufacturing Co., 20 Florence Avenue, Batavia, NY 14020, USA

Great Lakes Corp., 2500 Irving Park Road, Chicago, IL 60618, USA

Guth KG., Postfach 1309, D-76829 Landau, Germany

Healdsburg Machine Company, 452 Healdsburg Avenue, Healdsburg, CA 95448, USA

Hoechst Celanese, 13800 South Lakes Drive, Charlotte, NC 28273, USA

Howard Rotavator Co.,[2] P.O. Box 100, Harvard, IL 60033, USA

IMECA, Zone industrielle, B.P. 94, F-34800 Clermont-l'Herault, France

ITT Fluid Technology Corp., P.O. Box 2158, Costa Mesa, CA 92628-2158, USA

Jabsco (*see* ITT Fluid Technology Corp.)

Johnston Bar Screen (*see* Wheelabrator Eng. Systems)

KLR, 350 Morris Street, Suite E, Sebastapol, CA 95472, USA

Koch Membrane Systems (Romicon), 850 Main Street, Wilmington, MA 01887-3388, USA

Luigi Mori snc, Via B. Naldini, 23, 50028 Tavarnelle val di Pesa, Italy

Mabille[2]

MacKenzie[2]

Manville (*see* Celite Corp)

Manzini (*see* Teodoro Manzini)

Marzola[2]

Membrana (Ghia), 7070 Commerce Circle, Pleasanton, CA 94566, USA

Memcor (Memtec), Oakes Road, Old Toongabbie, NSW 2146, Australia

Millipore Corp., 80 Ashby Rd, Bedford, MA 01730, USA

Moyno (*see* Robbins Myers)

Mori (*see* Luigi Mori)

Mott Metallugical Corp., Farmington Industrial Park, Farmington, CT 06032, USA

Neztsch Inc, 119 Pickering Way, Exton, PA 19341-1393, USA

Norton Co., 1 New Bond Street, Worcester, MA 01601, USA

Novo Ferment Ltd., Vogesenstrasse 132, CH-4056 Basle, Switzerland

Padovan spa, 31015 Conegliano, Veneto, Italy

Pall Corp., Rte 281, Cortland, NY 13045, USA

PCI (Patterson Candy Intl.), Laverstoke Mill, Whitchurch, Hampshire RG 287NR, U.K.

Paul Mueller Co., P.O. Box 828, Springfield, MO 65801, USA

Pera SA,[2] F-34510 Florensac Herault, France

Ragazini Off. Mecc. srl, Via Volta, 8, 48018 Faenza-RA, Italy

Rhone Poulenc Chemie, 21 rue Jean Goujan, F-25360 Paris, France

Robbins Myers, P.O. Box 960, Springfiled, OH 45501, USA

Rupp (*see* Warren Rupp)

Santa Rosa Stainless Steel, P.O. Box 518, Santa Rosa, CA 95402, USA

Sartorius Corp., 140 Wilbur Place, Bohemia, NY 11716, USA

Scott Laboratories, P.O.Box 4559, Petaluma, CA 94955-4559, USA

SFEC (Soc. Fabr. d'Elements Catalytiques), B.P. F-33-84599 Bollene, France

Seitz Werke GmbH, Postfach 889, D-55543 Bad Kreuznach, Germany

Schenk Filterbau GmbH, Bettringer Strasse 42, D-7355 Waldstetten, Germany

Teodoro Manzini srl, Via Enrico Fermi, 8, 42015 Correggio-RE, Italy

Tri-Clover Inc., 9201 Wilmont Road, Kenosha, WI 53140, USA

Valley Foundry Machine Works,[2] 2510 So. East Avenue, Fresno, CA 93717, USA

Vaslin (*see* Bucher-CMMC)

Velo spa, Via Piave, 55 Fraz. Caselle, 31030 Altivole-TV, Italy

Vinipal, Rua Oliva Teles 251, Praia da Granja, 4405, Portugal

Warren Rupp, P.O. Box 1568, Mansfield, OH 44901, USA

Waukesha Foundry, 1300 Lincoln Avenue, Waukehsa, WI 53186, USA

Wedge Wire Co., P.O. Box 157, Wellington OH 44090, USA

Westec Winery Equipment, P.O. Box 338, Healdsburg, CA 95448

Westphalia Separator AG, D-59302 Oelde, Germany

Wheelabrator Eng. Systems, P.O. Box 64118, St. Paul, MI 55164, USA

Wilden Pumps, 22069 Van Buren Street, Colton, CA 92324, USA

Willmes Maschinenbau KG, Postfach 143, D-64625 Bensheim, Germany

Winery Systems Corp.[2]

York Machine Works, 1401 Charter Oak Avenue, St. Helena, CA 94574, USA

GLOSSARY

Definitions given are usually specific wine-related meanings. General dictionaries should be consulted as well.

Acetification: The oxidative conversion of wine to vinegar, ethanol to acetic acid. An aerobic fermentation by *Acetobacter*.

Acidity: Titrable or titratable acidity is that determined by quantitative titration with alkali. Usually it is expressed in grams of tartaric acid per liter in wines. Older French literature used g/L as H_2SO_4 and % tartaric or g/100mL has been common. Total acidity has been used as the same value to include fixed and volatile acidity. This can be misleading in that a portion of the tartaric acid (and others) is present as neutralized anions and therefore not directly titrable. Volatile acidity, as acetic acid, is very low in wines unless activity of vinegar bacteria has been appreciable. (*See also* **pH.**)

Aging: The general time-related improvement of wines specifically after bottling, but sometimes applied to the whole period of wine storage after fermentation. (*See also* **Maturation.**)

Alternative products: Products that, when produced, remove an equivalent portion of wine, e.g., vinegar or juice concentrate.

Amelioration: A specific meaning in winemaking applies especially to must betterment, particularly from fruits other than wine grapes. It involves lowering of excessive acid, usually by dilution with water, and increasing the sugar content so that palatable and stable wines result.

American Society for Enology and Viticulture (ASEV): Headquartered in Davis, California, this organization is more international than the name implies having sizable groups of members in Japan and elsewhere. In addition to activities including an annual meeting, they publish the *American Journal of Enology and Viticulture* (AJEV), undoubtedly the most important reviewed scientific and technical journal of the field in English and arguably in the world regardless of language.

Aroma: The odors in wines related to the grape from which they were made as distinguished from process and aging odors. (*See also* **Bouquet.**)

Azeotrope: A combination of two or more substances that boil at a constant and usually lower temperature than the components. Ethanol and water form an azeotrope which, depending on atmospheric pressure, boils at 25.6°C rather than 26.8°C for pure ethanol. The azeotrope is 95.5% by weight ethanol (4.5% water) and purer ethanol cannot be made by simple distillation.

Bacteriophage: A virus that affects bacteria.

Barrel: Sometimes used too generally, a barrel is an oaken liquid container with a double-arched truncated ellipsoid shape made liquidtight by appropriate taper of side units (staves) and ends (heads) wedged together by driven metal hoops. The usual sizes for wine, regardless of region, have been in the range of 190 to 230 L, more or less. Historically, other sizes had special names (firkin, keg, hogshead, tun, etc.) and other shapes also (oval, upright, etc.). The use of the equivalent French term *barrique* is an affectation. Barrels for other commodities had other standard sizes: beer, 31 gallons and bourbon whiskey, 50 gallons, for example.

BATF (Bureau of Alcohol, Tobacco, and Firearms): The U.S. federal agency which has been responsible for regulating and controlling all aspects of production, labeling, and marketing of wine and other alcoholic beverages. A part of the Treasury Department.

Body: The mouth-filling characteristic of wines related to viscosity ranging from thin and watery to full and high-bodied.

Bordeaux mixture: A fungicidal spray prepared from copper sulfate and calcium hydroxide (slaked lime) in water.

Bottle: A standard wine bottle contains 750 mL of wine. Formerly, U.S. wine bottles were called fifths because they held 1/5 gal. or 757 mL.

Bottle aging: Storage of wine in bottle or similar essentially anaerobic container and the effects (usually desirable) eventually produced.

Bouquet: The odors in wines resulting from processing and aging as distinguished from the raw material's odors, e.g., fermentation or bottle bouquets. (*See also* **Aroma**.)

Brandy: A high-content alcoholic beverage product or component distilled from grape wine.

Brix: Solution property equivalent to that of reference aqueous solutions of sucrose in grams per 100 grams of solution at 20°C. Usually measured by hydrometry (density) or in juices by refractometry. Balling first prepared tables, but Brix improved them and the term *Balling* is obsolete. Brix is nearly universal in the food industry, but Baume and Oechsle are convertible units used in other countries. The Brix in the past has tended to be termed degrees Brix, but this unnecessary and is not followed in other food industry practice.

Byproduct: A product produced incidentally to winemaking not made from or diminishing the yield of wine. Cream of tartar or grape seed oil are examples. (*See also* **Alternative** and **Specialty products**.)

°C: Temperature in Celsius (or Centigrade) degrees. Water freezes at 0°C and boils at 100°C.

Case: A standard wine case contains 12 bottles, 750 mL each, and therefore a total of 9 liters.

Champagnes: Either sparkling (high-CO_2) wines from the Champagne district in France or (clearly designated) similar wines from elsewhere including the United States. The French argue for only the first definition and as a result terms such as Sekt in Germany and Cava in Spain have been substituted.

Chaptalization: Term for the addition of sugar to musts before fermentation in order to obtain adequate alcohol in the wine. Regulated by laws in most countries, prohibited in California, similar results may be permitted by adding grape concentrate or reserved sweet juice. Named for the Frenchman popularizing it, Chaptal.

Charmat process: Secondary fermentation of sparkling wine in large (bulk) tanks rather than individual bottles. Named for the French originator.

Climate: The typical weather for a given place, usually large-scale areas. **Climatic Regions I–V**: A system of characterizing and comparing vineyard regions and subregions based upon average heat summation. **Mesoclimate**: Local variations within a vineyard or among nearby vineyards which affect typical weather seen by grapevines, e.g., a sun-facing slope versus a relatively shaded one.

Microclimate: The weather as modified by very local conditions in and about a specific vine.

Clone: A new vine or a group of vines produced from a cutting of one parent vine and therefore genetically identical. By extrapolation and with increasing chance for slight variation depending upon the number of transfers, the term may be used (misused) for propagants from a group of vines representing a uniform varietal vineyard.

Cold Duck: A nearly vanished recent faddish type of sparkling wine blended from red (often Concord in the United States) and white base wines and produced by the Charmat process.

Concentrate: Concentrated grape juice, white unless otherwise stated, prepared by vacuum and low temperature for use in sweetening other food products including musts and wines. Rectified concentrate is a term being introduced from Europe with legalistic limitations involving further processing to eliminate most characteristics other than sugar.

Coolers: A blended beverage commonly about half wine and half dilute acidic solution or fruit juices and other flavorings ostensibly for hot-weather and lower-alcohol (6% or so) situations. Dwindling in importance.

Cooperage: Winery containers generally. Derived from barrels and other wooden containers made by coopers.

Cream of tartar: Potassium bitartrate, the predominant crystalline deposit forming in wine. Purified from wine tartar (argols), it is a byproduct useful in cooking.

Crusher destemmer: Usually a single machine, but possibly two separate units, to remove the grape berries from their rachises and break them open for fermentation or juice removal. The objective is ordinarily complete removal of the cluster stems and 100% opening of the berries with minimal grinding or solids dispersal into the fluid.

Cuvee: The term (derived from French) for the particular blend of base wines to be used to make a sparkling wine.

Decanting: Transfer of relatively clear wine (usually bottled wine) by pouring off leaving undisturbed sediments and crusts behind. (*See also* **Racking**.)

Delle concept: Noting that high content of either sugar or alcohol prevented yeast growth and a combination of the two gave more microbial stability than the same content of either alone, Delle (a Russian) devised a scheme of units to predict stability of sweet wines. The units are not very reliable, but the concept is important in explaining why table wines at relatively low alcohol content (Sauternes, for example) are stable if their sugar is high enough. The phenomenon appears to result from stress on the yeast by either or both components.

DMDC (Dimethyl dicarbonate): Supersedes DEPC (diethyl pyrocarbonate). Kills yeasts to sterilize wines. Decomposes spontaneously in aqueous solution to carbon dioxide and small amounts of methanol.

Dry: The descriptor for a wine without fermentable sugar and/or no detectable taste of sweetness from sugar. Commonly, less than 2 g/L of reducing sugars.

Dyer: Preferred English term for the French *tienturier* (same meaning) used here for a red grape that has red pulp and juice and not just red berry skin, as is usual. Such varieties are useful to make a very red wine for blending with wines undesirably weak in red color.

Enology: The science and technology (and residual artful know-how) of making and processing wine in all of its complexity. The original spelling was oenology.

Estate bottling: Various wordings and legal nuances are involved, but the intent is to indicate that the grapes were produced by or at minimum under the specific control of the ownership of the bottling winery. Progressively less direct control is indicated by such terms as "produced and bottled by," "cellared and bottled by," or "bottled by."

Ester: A type of chemical compound formed from an acid and an alcohol by the elimination of water or hydrolyzed back to its constituent acid and alcohol by addition of the elements of water. The smallest major ester of interest in wines is the four-carbon ethyl acetate formed from acetic acid and ethyl alcohol. Organic esters of this type, especially those with about eight carbons, are attractively fruity in smell.

Exp: The exponent of the natural logarithm base *e* (exp(2) is e^2).

Extract: Extract in wines is defined as the nonvolatile dissolved solids of the wine and ordinarily is expressed in Brix (see Brix). It is important to recognize that residual sugar contributes to extract and to pay attention to whether the values given are total extract or sugarfree extract. A high-extract dry wine is one that has had considerable pomace contact and also may have high glycerol from fermentation.

°F: Fahrenheit temperature, water freezes at 32°F and boils at 212°F. Replace with °C. (*See also* **°C**.)

FAN (Free Amino Nitrogen): Amino acid nitrogen exclusive of proline (an imino acid), usable by yeasts, ammonia is not included.

Fermenter: The agent for fermentation; one who or that which causes or conducts fermentation. For examples "he is a fermenter of Cabernets" or "that yeast is a galactose fermenter."

Fermentor: An apparatus for fermentation. "The wine was fermented in a stainless steel fermentor."

Fining: Clarification of wines or possibly musts by addition of agents, usually insoluble or colloidal ones such as bentonite or gelatin, which combine with incipient haze formers and precipitate them and themselves from solution.

Flavonoid: Natural C_{15} phenols formed with two benzene rings connected by a three-carbon bridge including anthocyanins, catechins (flavan-3-ols), flavonols, and condensed tannins in grapes and wines. They are responsible for the red colors, much of the brown colors, the astringency, and the known bitterness of wines. (*See also* **Phenols**.)

Flavor: The overall sensory character including odors, tastes, and feelings such as astringency, body, or perhaps "texture."

Flavored wines: Vermouths and Special Natural Wines are those that incorporate flavors from other sources (natural) besides grapes.

Fortification: (*See* **WSA**).

Fractional blending: (*See* **Solera System**).

Fusel oil: A distillation fraction from wine or its constituents in wines, primarily higher (more than two-, usually five-carbon) alcohols.

GAE (Gallic Acid Equivalent): Based upon phenol assay (usually by Folin-Ciocalteu reagent) with gallic acid as comparison standard usually in mg/L for wines or mg/kg for grapes.

GRAS (Generally Recognized As Safe): A term introduced into food regulations to cover substances considered to have such long and widespread usage that further specific testing is superfluous and wasteful, sucrose for example.

Grafting: The operation of splicing a scion cutting to a rootstock to produce a single combined vine.

Grape seed oil: Oil expressed or extracted from grape seeds. A good food, it resembles olive oil in composition. It can be a useful byproduct of winemaking, but has been seldom economic.

Hard: The less desirable flavor impression of a red wine both bitter and tart and often tannic. The antonym of soft—a wine without excess in these features. It may or may not disappear with appropriate maturation and aging, but it should improve. Softer wines can, of course, also improve with age.

Headspace: The gas volume, usually deliberate, above the wine in a container including bottles, for example, "That wine was bottled with a headspace of 5 mL, but with 10 years of aging an ullage (see Ullage) of 50 mL developed."

Hectare: An are is 10 × 10 m or 100 square m. A hectare is therefore 100 × 100m = 10,000 m^2 or 2.47 acres.

Hectoliter: One hundred liters. A common unit for wine processing tabulations in Europe equal to 26.4 U.S. gallons. We prefer kiloliters (10 hectoliters) for two major reasons: more directly related to metric tons and easier to visualize in relation to old practices in the U.S. wine industry (lbs/1000 gal.). (*See also* **Kiloliter.**)

HPLC (High Performance Liquid Chromatography): A modern instrumental technique to separate and quantitate compounds present in complex solutions such as wines. GLC, gas-liquid chromatography, is a separate but analogous procedure limited to volatile compounds.

HTST (High-Temperature Short-Time): Pasteurization treatments.

Higher alcohols: Isoamyl alcohol and relatives with more than two carbons produced by fermentation and contributing to heavy, fusely tastes, especially in WSA wines and brandies (not always undesirable flavors at low levels). (*See also* **Fusel oil.**)

Kiloliter: One thousand liters or one m^3 (a stere). Although hectoliters (1/10 kL) are most commonly used in Europe, kL is preferred in America and one m^3 is the SI unit of volume. It is easier to visualize (1 m^3) and is more mentally compatible with the obsolete usage of lb/1000 gal. One U.S. gallon = 3.785 L; 1 kL = 264.2 gal.; 1 lb/1000 gal. = 120 g/L; 100g/kL = 0.83 lb/1000 gal.

Laccase: Phenol-oxidizing enzymes not present unless produced in grapes by mold infection, but important in browning and related reactions of moldy grapes. Different and usually wider substrate specificity than grape PPO (*See also* **PPO.**)

Lactic acid bacteria: Those bacteria capable of producing lactic acid (not present from grapes or yeasts) in wines, usually by malolactic fermentation. (*See also* **Malolactic Fermentation.**)

Lees: Sediments (yeast, tartrates, seeds, fining agents, etc.) settled to the bottom of wine containers.

Maceration: Steeping crushed grapes before drawing off juice or young wines. Alternative expressions include skin contact, pomace fermentation, etc.

Maceration, carbonic: Holding whole grape clusters in a closed container in an atmosphere of carbon dioxide (possibly self-generated by respiration) so that they metabolize some of their sugar anaerobically. This is properly done at fairly warm temperature and for sufficient time, at least several days, so that a special flavor and light tannin plus vivid color and fruity flavor result in the wine made from the pressed juice. The wines so produced are termed *nouveau* style by analogy to *Beaujolais nouveau*.

Maderization: A rather confusing term probably better dropped in favor of oxidation or/and heated. It derives from the chemical and sensory characters of Madeira-type wines that are both oxidized and baked. It is not related to wood-extract flavors as Spanish speakers might assume.

Malolactic fermentation: The conversion by specific bacteria of malic acid into lactic acid with associated reduction in total acidity and other flavor changes.

Marc: See Pomace.

Maturation: The time-related improvement of wines before bottling, especially bulk maturation in oak containers. After maturation appropriate to the type and style, a wine is considered mature, ready, and ripe to bottle.

Mildews: Filamentous fungi (molds) including downy mildew and powdery mildew that cause disease on grape vines or others that may cause unsightly growths on winery walls, etc. Obligate aerobes, they can not grow in properly stored wine.

MOG (Material Other than Grapes): Contaminants such as leaves in harvested grapes.

Must: The grape material ready to be fermented. Whole must is usually crushed but destemmed grapes and must pumps are designed to handle this mash without appreciable grinding. When the pomace has been removed, the resultant juice, whether further clarified or not, can be called must if it is to be fermented or further fermented, but the general term *must* usually implies whole must, and *juice* or *young wine* are the terms preferred for certain clarity, if they are meant.

Muté: Pronounced "mutay," this is grape juice prevented from fermentation, often by high additions of SO_2 or other means, intended for later use in making wines. An adopted French term.

Noble rot: The term for desired infection of wine grapes by *Botrytis cinerea* under circumstances of weather and season such that a shriveled berry results with high sugar content suitable for making sweet table wines such as Sauternes or Trockenbeerenauslesen.

OIV (The Office International de la Vigne et du Vin): Based in Paris, performs many useful functions in gathering worldwide grape and wine statistics, codifying regulations and analytical procedures, etc. It publishes their *Bulletin* (BOIV), which also includes useful briefs on other publications.

Overcropped: The condition of a vine carrying so much crop load that it is unable to produce enough photosynthesis to properly mature the fruit. Ordinarily indicated by inadequate sugar development and failure to ripen properly.

Pectin: Complex polysaccharides involving galacturonic acid, its methyl ester, and other sugar derivatives. They contribute to viscosity and sometimes hazes of musts and wines. Shortened and solubilized by pectinase enzymes.

Pedicel: The small cap stem attaching each grape berry to the rachis.

Peptides: Short polymers of amino acids, pieces (polypeptides longer) of proteins. (*See also* **Proteins.**)

pH: An acidity scale. The negative of the logarithm of the molar hydrogen ion concentration in a solution such as wine or must. At pH 7.0 the solution is neutral, below it is increasingly acidic and tart to a minimum of zero, and above increasingly alkaline to a maximum of 14. For wine grape juices and wines, 3.2–3.8 is generally to be expected, with lower than that relatively underripe and sour or above overripe and flat-tasting. Since pH is an exponential (base 10) function, relatively small numerical differences in pH correlate with large reactivity and flavor differences.

Phage: (*see* Bacteriophage)

Phenols: Chemical compounds consisting of a benzene ring with at least one hydroxyl group. Those naturally occurring in plants are termed *polyphenols* and usually have at least two hydroxyl groups, usually vicinal (side by side). The group includes phenolic acids, cinnamates, flavonoids, and tannins in grapes and wines.

Phylloxera: A serious grape insect pest native to Eastern North America which, when introduced to European grape vines, causes vineyard decline and death. *Dactylasphaera vitifoliae* (formerly called *Phylloxera vitifoliae* or *P. vastatrix*) has a complicated life cycle, including a flying form causing leaf galls on resistant grape species in humid climates and the universal and more devastating small yellow root louse forms. *Vitis* species native to the endemic areas for this pest are resistant and can be used as rootstocks or breeding stock for resistance. Other species of phylloxera specifically attack other plants, oak, for example.

Pomace: The solids (grape skins and seeds especially) left after wine or juice is drained and pressed from the whole must or young wine. Marc and press cake are essentially the same. Pronounced "pumice," pomace may be sweet (unfermented) or dry (fermented) and may be the source of recoverable alcohol or other byproducts as well as a waste disposal problem.

ppm (Parts per million): For wine, usually milligrams per liter, but any value, preferably in the same units, such as lb/million lb. A confusing term which should be replaced by more specific SI units. Particularly confusing in comparing liquid and gaseous concentrations. (See Chapter 1).

PPO (Polyphenol Oxidase): The natural browning enzyme of grapes and most other plant products. Present in juices to varying degrees.

Proof: A measure of alcohol content usually limited to distilled beverages. One % by volume of ethanol equals 2 U.S. proof measured at 60°F. British proof is slightly different. Proof spirit is 100 proof (50% vol/vol ethanol).

Proof gallon: One U.S. gallon (3.785 L) of 100 proof (50% vol/vol) ethanol or the equivalent amount of ethanol.

Proteins: Relatively large chains of amide-linked amino acids. Twenty amino acids are commonly involved and may also be linked to other subunits such as carbohydrates (glycoproteins). Enzymes are proteins and the most common haze producers in white wines are proteins.

Pump over: The operation of transferring fluid, especially fermenting red wine, from low in the container back over the surface, particularly the cap of floating grape skins. The term may be applied to similar procedures such as mixing tanks of wine to distribute or keep distributed fining agents, etc. *Punching down* is an alternative procedure of submerging the cap during macerations such as red wine fermentations.

Quality: The summation of intrinsic factors such as color, odor, and flavor that cause knowledgeable and discriminating customers to say that that one wine is better and worth more than another one. Obviously varying from wine type to wine type, subjective, and prone to frequent disagreement even among enologists, high quality is, nevertheless, an all-important goal with wine.

Rachis: The stem of the grape cluster.

Racking: The process almost invariably followed during transfer of bulk wine by pumping or siphoning the relatively clear top portion away without or prior to disturbing the sediment (lees). Like decanting, except applied to bulk wine handling and not to simple pouring of wine from one container to another or individual bottles.

Racking arm: A gooseneck tube and valve arrangement through the lower end of a tank rotatable so as to enable removal of clear fluid down to near the lees.

Raisin: The French word for grape which, in English, has become restricted to *raisins sec* or dried grapes, ordinarily sun-dried with the characteristic flavor, high sugar, brown color, etc.

Rosé: The French word for pink (pronounced rozay) applied to light red wines, especially pink table wines.

Saccharomyces: Literally "sugar fungus" from Latin; the generic (genus) scientific name for yeasts of the type used in wine fermentations.

Scion: The portion of a vine that carries the aboveground grape variety when grafted to a rootstock.

Skin contact: The operation (and conditions, especially time and temperature) of macerating the solids (pomace, skins, seeds) of grapes with the fluid juice or fermenting wine. Necessary in the typical conversion of red grapes into red wine, but sometimes used in other contexts, such as making heavier white wines.

Sluggish fermentation: A fermentation that proceeds more slowly than it should. (*See* Stuck)

Solera system: A fractional blending system developed for Spanish sherry.

Sparkling wines: Champagnes and other wines fermented a second time in a closed system (Charmat tank or individual bottle) so that the carbon dioxide generated remains in the wine. Distinguished from carbonated wines which are charged with separately collected carbon dioxide in the same way as soda pop.

Specialty product: Wine or wine-containing product not usually or traditionally made, e.g., wine coolers, dealcoholized wine. (*See also* **Alternative products and Byproducts**)

Spoilage yeast: Those yeasts, in the context of this book, which may or may not be able to complete a fermentation of grape juice, but produce off odors, off flavors, or turbidity where not wanted. Species of all the 19 or so wine-related yeast genera can be included. (*See also* **Yeast**).

Statistics: (1) Collected data, usually numerical, characterizing wine production, e.g., L or T_m by variety, vintage, area, etc.; and (2) the branch of mathematics and the procedures employed to estimate the typicality and believability of experimental or variable results.

Stemmy: A characteristic flavor imparted by not or incompletely removing the cluster stems (rachises) during winemaking. It is reminiscent of herbaceous, peppery, bitter components.

Stuck: A fermentation that has halted before the expected completion owing to excessively high temperature, unanticipated nutrient shortage, etc.

Style: The characteristics within a wine type that are intended to distinguish one wine from another. For example, in the category of young varietal Zinfandel red table wines, we would emphasize a raspberry-fruity style, others might emphasize more vinous, tannic character.

Sulfur dioxide: The gas (SO_2) formed by burning sulfur in air. Quite soluble in water and easily compressed to a liquid, it is unpleasant to work around, but useful for hundreds of years as a constituent or additive in juices and wines to prevent undesirable chemical and microbial deterioration. It may be liberated under appropriate conditions (especially acidity) from its salts such as potassium metabisulfite (pyrobisulfite, $K_2S_2O_5$) or other bisulfites and sulfites.

Sur lies: A French term meaning "on lees" used to designate a rather specific type of maceration on the yeast lees, usually with periodic stirring and especially with barrel-fermented Chardonnay wine. A complex flavor can result from the yeast leakage over time.

Table wines: Here the term means all those grape wines that are made by a single, complete fermentation. They are therefore limited to about 12% alcohol (under 14% by U.S. tax category) unless made from botrytized musts or dried grapes. They are intended as a beverage to accompany a meal. In other languages, table wine can be a slightly denigrating term signifying ordinary quality, but that is not implied here. Table wines include the finest wines of the types and styles as well as the everyday ones.

Tannin, tannic: Large, astringent, protein-precipitating natural phenols and their flavor effect in wines. Grapes contain, especially in the seeds, condensed tannins (flavonoid polymers), whereas oak barrel extract and tannic acid used in fining are hydrolyzable into gallic and/or ellagic acid. They have similar flavor and hide-to-leather tanning effects, but different chemistry.

Taste: Strictly, the mouth sensations sensed by the taste buds including bitter, salty, tart (acidic), and sweet. Commonly, the other oral sensations of astringency, body, and hotness or pungency are also included. (*See also* **Flavor**).

Tawny: The brick-red color which develops as red wine ages usually with some oxidation, as opposed to bright red or blue-red. A defect in wines intended to be fresh and fruity like most rosés, but expected and often a mark of quality in mature red wines. It indicates a special style in ports, and, if produced by heating the wine, is not necessarily viewed as a quality improvement.

TCA: A perfect example of why we detest jargon. This term has been used for the tricarboxylic acid cycle (Kreb's or citric acid cycle) of aerobic metabolism, trichloroacetic acid (a protein precipitant), and 2,4,6-trichloroanisole (an active corky odorant).

Terpene: A class of compounds biochemically derived from mevalonic acid and made up of five-carbon isoprene units. Ten-carbon monoterpenes are important odorants of the highly aromatic muscat grapes and wines from them and relatives.

Tm: See Ton, metric.

Ton, metric: Sometimes written tonne and essentially equivalent to a long ton in the obsolete English system, it is 1000 kg. One T_M equals 2204.6 lb or 1.1 U.S. English tons. A quintal (q) is 0.1 T_M, 100 kg, or 220.5 lb. The equivalent term *megagram*, Mg, is seldom used, probably from potential confusion with milligram, mg.

Ullage: The amount that a container lacks of being full, especially if occasioned by loss from an originally full condition. (Pronounced uh-lage) (*See* **Headspace**).

VA (Volatile Acidity): The portion of the total acidity that is volatile (distillable away from the fixed acidity) representing acetic acid and relatives. It is considered indicative of microbiological (acetobacter) spoilage, if appreciable. Red table wines with more than 1.4 g/L as acetic and other grape wines with more than 1.2 g/L are by U.S. regulations too high to be marketed as unspoiled wines. Wines high in acetic acid are or become also high in ethyl acetate and the latter is more odorous.

Varietal: A wine named for the variety of grapes from which it was made. By U.S. regulations it must be from a minimum of 75% of the named grape, with additional rules if more than one variety is named.

Vector: Transporting agent for disease, e.g., nematodes can be vectors for grapevine viruses.

Veraison: The French word for ripening now adopted specifically for the onset of ripening of grapes. The transition stage marking the beginning of sugar accumulation, berry softening, chlorophyll loss, and anthocyanin formation.

Vinegar: Wine and other (designated) alcoholic beverages aerobically converted by *Acetobacter* into condiments rich in acetic acid and ethyl acetate for salad dressing and similar usage. Formerly, now seldom, a spoiled wine. An alternate product for wineries.

Vinification: The process of making wines from grapes.

Vinous: The flavor that denotes wine without specific varietal aromas or special bouquets.

Vintage: A specific harvest season for grapes and the resultant wine. By U.S. regulations designation on a wine label of the year of harvest requires that 95% of the wine was made from grapes harvested during that year.

Vintner: Properly, a seller of wines.

Viticulture: The science and technology of grape growing.

Vitis: The botanical genus of grapes. Species include most importantly *vinifera* (the classic wine grapes), *labrusca* or *labruscana* (Concord and relatives), and several other species less known for fruit, but useful for other purposes. Hybrids are genetic crosses involving more than one species of grape.

Wild yeasts: Yeasts which can initiate a fermentation of grape juice, but are not tolerant enough to ethanol to complete the fermentation. They are usually associated with the grape berry. Species are included from the genera: *Hansenula, Kloeckera, Hanseniaspora*, and *Metschnikowia*. (*See also* **Yeast**)

Winemaking: The part of enology specifically related to selecting and converting grapes to wine ready to be consumed. The single word is preferred, unless special meaning is to be expressed. Winemaking and that of beer are interesting to contrast. Preferable usage could be "making of wine and beer are interesting to contrast."

Wine spirits: Alcohol and associated components of the distillate prepared from grape wine. By laws in the United States and many other (but not all) countries, other fermentation sources can not be used in wines or brandies, much less ethanol from petroleum.

Wine yeast: Yeasts that can ferment wine grape juice to completion (dry) and produce a wine free of off-flavors and off-odors. Rather limited to species of the genus *Saccharomyces* and perhaps *Schizosaccharomyces*. They can also be spoilage yeasts, if present in an unwanted situation, e.g., semisweet bottled table wine. (*See also* **Yeasts**)

WSA (Wine Spirits Addition): Fortification, the addition of distilled alcohol during winemaking. The technique used to make stable sweet wines by arresting the fermentation before completion by adding brandy of high proof. Traditional ports, sherries, muscatels, etc., are made this way, and commonly are 18% alcohol.

Yeast: By brief scientific definition, a single-celled fungus. Wine-related yeasts are those found associated with grapes, vineyards, winery equipment, wine storage containers, or in wine. Here they are subdivided into three groups: wine yeasts, wild yeasts, and spoilage yeasts.

Yeast hulls: Empty (autolyzed) yeast cell walls. Sometimes called yeast ghosts.

INDEX

B

C

D

E

F

G

H

M

P

Q

R

S

Z